PRACTITIONER TAX LIBRARY

# The Taxation of Private Pension Schemes and their Beneficiaries

Practitioner Tax Library

# THE TAXATION OF PRIVATE PENSION SCHEMES AND THEIR BENEFICIARIES

7th Edition

MATTHEW HARRISON

Sweet & Maxwell

First Edition 2018
Second Edition 2019
Third Edition 2020
Fourth Edition 2021
Fifth Edition 2022
Sixth Edition 2023
Seventh Edition 2024

Published in 2024 by Thomson Reuters, trading as Sweet & Maxwell.
Thomson Reuters is registered in England & Wales, Company No. 1679046.
Registered office and address for service:
5 Canada Square, Canary Wharf, London E14 5AQ.

For further information on our products and services, visit *http://www.sweetandmaxwell.co.uk*.

Computerset by Sweet & Maxwell.
Printed in Great Britain by Hobbs the Printers Ltd, Totton, Hampshire, SO40 3WX.
A CIP catalogue record of this book is available from the British Library.

ISBN (print): 978-0-414-12085-3

ISBN (e-book): 978-0-414-12088-4

ISBN (print and e-book): 978-0-414-12087-7

Crown copyright material is reproduced with the permission of the Controller of HMSO and the King's Printer for Scotland.

All rights reserved. No part of this publication may be reproduced or transmitted in any form or by any means, or stored in any retrieval system of any nature, without prior written permission, except for permitted fair dealing under the Copyright, Designs and Patents Act 1988, or in accordance with the terms of a licence issued by the Copyright Licensing Agency in respect of photocopying and/or reprographic reproduction. Application for permission for other use of copyright material, including permission to reproduce extracts in other published works, should be made to the publishers. Full acknowledgement of author, publisher and source must be given.

Thomson Reuters, the Thomson Reuters Logo and Sweet & Maxwell ® are trademarks of Thomson Reuters.

© 2024 Thomson Reuters

# Preface

The subject matter of this book is the taxation of private pension schemes and the beneficiaries of such schemes. The book is split into two parts, dealing respectively with registered and unregistered pension schemes. All private pension schemes are covered: occupational and non-occupational, large and small, money purchase and defined benefit. It does not cover public sector schemes or the state pension.

The purpose of this work is to assist practitioners to understand the law. My general approach has been to consider, and where possible explain, the underlying principles on which the legislation is based. Since the introduction of the general anti-abuse rule in July 2013, all tax advice must take into account the underlying principles. If a particular tax analysis is inconsistent with the principles on which the relevant tax provisions are based, the adviser may soon find himself in difficulty.

It is generally helpful to approach the law in this area with no preconceived ideas about what is and is not permissible. The changes brought about by the Taxation of Pensions Act 2014, for example, created for money purchase schemes a regime of unprecedented flexibility. In many cases, the benefits provided under a registered pension scheme need not resemble a "pension" as that term has been traditionally understood. Such changes inevitably affect the interpretation of tax law relating to unregistered pension schemes (especially in relation to the application of anti-avoidance provisions).

The importance of pension legislation and other non-tax law cannot be overstated. A large body of pension legislation and case law has developed over the last 30 years, and any tax advice will be incomplete (at best) if it fails to take this into account. I have referred to the relevant non-tax law where appropriate, but a detailed analysis of such provisions is outside the scope of this book.

HMRC's *Pensions Tax Manual* (PTM) contains extensive guidance on the *practical* application of the tax rules as they apply to registered pension schemes and relevant non-UK schemes. To this extent, it is an excellent resource, and it is not the purpose of this book to duplicate such guidance. To the extent that the PTM represents HMRC's interpretation of the *technical* aspects of the law, it is more open to scrutiny. When compared to other areas of tax, there seems to be a greater tendency amongst those advising on the taxation of pension schemes to treat HMRC guidance as a definitive statement of the law. As is evident from *HMRC v Sippchoice Ltd* [2020] UKUT 149 (TCC), any adviser approaching the PTM in this way is likely to be doing his client a disservice.

The views expressed in this book are put forward for consideration only. Neither the publisher nor the author accept any responsibility for any loss to any person arising as a result of any act or omission in reliance of this work.

With a view to improving future editions of this work, comments from readers are encouraged.

The law is intended to be up to date to 6 April 2024.

*Matthew Harrison*

July 2024

# Abbreviations

| AVC | additional voluntary contribution |
|---|---|
| BCE | benefit crystallisation event |
| BIM | Business Income Manual |
| CAA 2001 | Capital Allowances Act 2001 |
| CA 2006 | Companies Act 2006 |
| CGT | capital gains tax |
| CH | Compliance Handbook |
| CPA | Civil Partnership Act |
| CPI | Consumer Prices Index |
| CTA 2009 | Corporation Tax Act 2009 |
| CTA 2010 | Corporation Tax Act 2010 |
| DWP | Department for Work and Pensions |
| EEA | European Economic Area |
| EFRBS | employer-financed retirement benefits scheme |
| EGLP | excepted group life policies |
| EGLS | excepted group life scheme |
| EU | European Union |
| FA | Finance Act |
| FP | fixed protection |
| FRS | Financial Reporting Standard |
| FSMA | Financial Services and Markets Act |
| FTT | First-tier Tribunal (Tax Chamber) |
| FURBS | funded unapproved retirement benefits scheme |
| HMRC | the Commissioners for, or officers of, His Majesty's Revenue & Customs (as the context requires) |
| ICTA 1988 | Income and Corporation Taxes Act 1988 |
| IHTA 1984 | Inheritance Tax Act 1984 |
| IHTM | Inheritance Tax Manual |
| IPTM | Insurance Policyholder Taxation Manual |
| IR12 (2001) | the Inland Revenue's Occupational Pension Schemes Practice Notes on the Approval of Occupational Pension Schemes (2001 version) |
| IR76 (2000) | the Inland Revenue's Personal Pension Scheme Guidance Notes (2000 version) |
| IRPS | investment-regulated pension scheme |
| ITA 2007 | Income Tax Act 2007 |
| ITEPA 2003 | Income Tax (Earnings and Pensions) Act 2003 |

| | |
|---|---|
| ITTOIA 2005 | Income Tax (Trading and Other Income) Act 2005 |
| LLP | limited liability partnership |
| LAEF | lifetime allowance enhancement factor |
| LS | lump sum |
| LS allowance | lump sum allowance |
| LSDB | lump sum death benefit |
| LS&DB allowance | lump sum and death benefit allowance |
| MPAA | money purchase annual allowance |
| NICs | national insurance contributions |
| NIM | National Insurance Manual |
| OECD | Organisation for Economic Co-operation and Development |
| PA | Pensions Act |
| PCELS | pension commencement excess lump sum |
| PCLS | pension commencement lump sum |
| PSA | Pension Schemes Act |
| PSO | pension sharing order |
| PTM | Pensions Tax Manual |
| QNUPS | qualifying non-UK pension scheme |
| QROPS | qualifying recognised overseas pension scheme |
| Relevant BCE | relevant benefit crystallisation event |
| RNUKS | relevant non-UK scheme |
| ROPS | recognised overseas pension scheme |
| RPI | Retail Prices Index |
| SDLT | stamp duty land tax |
| SDLTM | Stamp Duty Land Tax Manual |
| SLA | standard lifetime allowance |
| SSCBA 1992 | Social Security Contributions and Benefits Act 1992 |
| STSM | Stamp Taxes on Shares Manual |
| TCGA 1992 | Taxation of Chargeable Gains Act 1992 |
| TFEU | Treaty on the Functioning of the European Union |
| TIOPA 2010 | Taxation (International and Other Provisions) Act 2010 |
| TMA 1970 | Taxes Management Act 1970 |
| TPA 2014 | Taxation of Pensions Act 2014 |
| UFPLS | uncrystallised funds pension lump sum |
| UK | United Kingdom of Great Britain and Northern Ireland |
| UT | Upper Tribunal (Tax and Chancery Chamber) |
| UURBS | unfunded unapproved retirement benefits scheme |

| VATA 1994 | Value Added Tax Act 1994 |
| WRPA 1999 | Welfare Reform and Pensions Act 1999 |

# TABLE OF CONTENTS

| | |
|---|---|
| *Preface* | v |
| *Abbreviations* | vii |
| *Table of Cases* | xix |
| *Table of Statutes* | xxxix |
| *Table of Statutory Instruments* | lxiii |

### PART ONE: REGISTERED PENSION SCHEMES

1   FA 2004: Overview, Background, Development

| | |
|---|---|
| Introduction | 1-001 |
| FA 2004 Pt 4 | 1-002 |
| Overview of Recent Developments | 1-025 |
| Overview of Current Issues | 1-026 |

2   Important Concepts

| | |
|---|---|
| Introduction | 2-001 |
| "Registered Pension Scheme" | 2-002 |
| "Pension Scheme" | 2-005 |
| "Member" | 2-027 |
| "Arrangement" | 2-036 |
| "Payment" | 2-053 |
| "Loan" | 2-081 |
| "Connected Persons" | 2-098 |
| Valuation | 2-116 |

3   A Day Transitional Provisions

| | |
|---|---|
| Introduction | 3-001 |
| Pre-commencement pension schemes | 3-021 |
| The lifetime allowance | 3-024 |
| Protection for pre-commencement pension rights | 3-088 |
| Miscellaneous provisions | 3-097 |

4   Registration and De-Registration

| | |
|---|---|
| Introduction | 4-001 |
| Registration | 4-004 |
| De-registration | 4-023 |

5   The Scheme Administrator

| | |
|---|---|
| Introduction | 5-001 |
| Identifying the scheme administrator | 5-003 |
| Duties and liabilities of the scheme administrator | 5-020 |
| The scheme sanction charge | 5-025 |
| Authorising a practitioner | 5-061 |

6   Contributions

| | |
|---|---|
| Introduction | 6-001 |

## CONTENTS

Contributions by or on behalf of a member .................................... 6-004
Employer contributions ........................................................ 6-036
Salary sacrifice .............................................................. 6-139
Member and employer contributions ............................................. 6-144
Tax on pre-owned Assets ....................................................... 6-155

### 7  THE ANNUAL ALLOWANCE

Overview ...................................................................... 7-001
Step One: pension input amounts ............................................... 7-005
Step Two: determining the individual's annual allowance ....................... 7-022
Step Three: default chargeable amount ......................................... 7-031
Step Four: member has flexibly accessed pension rights ........................ 7-032
The annual allowance charge ................................................... 7-050
Reporting obligations ......................................................... 7-057

### 8  SCHEME INVESTMENTS (AND SCHEME BORROWING)

Introduction and Overview ..................................................... 8-001
Income of the Scheme .......................................................... 8-014
Capital Gains ................................................................. 8-048
Unauthorised Borrowing ........................................................ 8-051

### 9  TAXABLE PROPERTY

Introduction .................................................................. 9-001
The provisions ................................................................ 9-003
Deemed unauthorised payment (s.174A) .......................................... 9-085
Scheme chargeable payment under s.185A ........................................ 9-134
Scheme chargeable payment under s.185F ........................................ 9-148

### 10  THE LIFETIME ALLOWANCE (PRE-6 APRIL 2024)

Introduction .................................................................. 10-001
BCES and amounts crystallised ................................................. 10-005
Amount of available lifetime allowance ........................................ 10-020
Availability of lifetime allowance on a BCE ................................... 10-049
The lifetime allowance charge ................................................. 10-053
Reporting obligations ......................................................... 10-065

### 11  AUTHORISED MEMBER PAYMENTS

Introduction .................................................................. 11-001
Scheme administration member payments ......................................... 11-002

### 12  PENSION TRANSFERS

Introduction .................................................................. 12-001
Recognised transfers .......................................................... 12-004
The overseas transfer charge .................................................. 12-018

### 13  AUTHORISED PENSIONS

Authorised pensions ........................................................... 13-001

## CONTENTS

Scheme pension ................................................................. 13-014
Lifetime annuity ................................................................ 13-023
Drawdown pension ........................................................... 13-031
Pensions paid in error ...................................................... 13-042
Reporting obligations ...................................................... 13-049

### 14 AUTHORISED LUMP SUMS

Authorised lump sums ..................................................... 14-001
Pension commencement lump sum .................................. 14-018
Pension commencement excess lump sum ...................... 14-023
Uncrystallised funds pension lump sum .......................... 14-025
Serious ill-health lump sum ............................................. 14-027
Short service refund lump sum ........................................ 14-030
Refund of excess contributions lump sum ....................... 14-032
Trivial commutation lump sum ........................................ 14-034
Winding-up lump sum ..................................................... 14-037
Lifetime allowance excess lump sum (pre-6 April 2024) ... 14-039
Other authorised lump sums ............................................ 14-041
Enhanced Allowances ...................................................... 14-056
Reporting obligations ...................................................... 14-072

### 15 AUTHORISED DEATH BENEFITS

Introduction and overview ............................................... 15-001
Authorised pension death benefits ................................... 15-015
Authorised lump sum death benefits ............................... 15-044
Trusts of death benefits ................................................... 15-077

### 16 PENSIONS ON DIVORCE

Introduction ..................................................................... 16-001
FA 2004 and pension sharing orders ............................... 16-003

### 17 AUTHORISED EMPLOYER PAYMENTS

Introduction ..................................................................... 17-001
Authorised Surplus Payments ......................................... 17-002
Compensation Payments ................................................. 17-007
Authorised Employer Loans ............................................ 17-008
Scheme Administration Employer Payments .................. 17-033

### 18 UNAUTHORISED PAYMENTS

Overview .......................................................................... 18-001
Unauthorised payments ................................................... 18-009
Actual unauthorised payments ........................................ 18-014
Deemed unauthorised member payments ........................ 18-059
Deemed unauthorised employer payments ...................... 18-153
Taxation of unauthorised payments ................................. 18-159
Genuine errors ................................................................. 18-192
Reporting obligations ...................................................... 18-195

## 19 COMPLIANCE

Introduction and overview .................................................................. 19-001
Requirement to preserve documentation .......................................... 19-003
Requirement to provide information and documentation ................ 19-008
Penalties ............................................................................................ 19-022
Assessments ...................................................................................... 19-026
Appeals ............................................................................................. 19-043

## 20 INTERNATIONAL ASPECTS

Introduction ...................................................................................... 20-001
Non-UK registered schemes ............................................................. 20-003
Contributions .................................................................................... 20-010
The annual allowance ....................................................................... 20-013
Scheme investments ......................................................................... 20-015
The LS&DB allowance .................................................................... 20-016
Benefits ............................................................................................. 20-039

## 21 INHERITANCE TAX

Introduction ...................................................................................... 21-001
Contributions .................................................................................... 21-014
Disposals of scheme interests .......................................................... 21-059
Devaluing interests ........................................................................... 21-061
Relevant property ............................................................................. 21-070
Omitting to exercise rights ............................................................... 21-084
Death of a beneficiary ...................................................................... 21-086
Form IHT409 ................................................................................... 21-112

## 22 MISCELLANEOUS TOPICS

Introduction ...................................................................................... 22-001
VAT and pension schemes ............................................................... 22-002
Anti-avoidance provisions ............................................................... 22-017
The chargeable event regime ........................................................... 22-028
Compensation payments for loss of pension rights ......................... 22-029

## PART TWO: UNREGISTERED PENSION SCHEMES

## 23 INTRODUCTION AND OVERVIEW

Overview of part two ....................................................................... 23-001
Provisions with general application ................................................. 23-003
Categories of pension scheme ......................................................... 23-008
Overview of current issues .............................................................. 23-018

## PART A: PROVISIONS WITH GENERAL APPLICATION

## 24 CONTRIBUTIONS

Introduction ...................................................................................... 24-001
Relief in respect of relevant migrant members ............................... 24-006

| | | |
|---|---|---|
| | Transitional corresponding relief | 24-026 |
| | Relief under double tax treaties | 24-037 |
| | Non-tax advantaged arrangements | 24-038 |
| | National insurance contributions | 24-058 |
| | Salary sacrifice | 24-061 |
| | Annual payments | 24-071 |
| | In specie contributions | 24-072 |
| | Tax on pre-owned assets | 24-073 |
| 25 | SCHEME INVESTMENTS | |
| | Introduction | 25-001 |
| | UK schemes | 25-002 |
| | Non-UK schemes | 25-009 |
| | The income tax settlements provisions | 25-017 |
| | The transfer of assets abroad provisions | 25-050 |
| | The CGT settlements provisions | 25-089 |
| 26 | BENEFITS | |
| | Overview | 26-001 |
| | Income tax | 26-003 |
| | Foreign pensions | 26-007 |
| | UK pensions | 26-039 |
| | Employment-related annuities | 26-041 |
| | Voluntary annual payments | 26-051 |
| | Exempt pensions | 26-053 |
| | Other provisions which could apply to lump sums | 26-059 |
| | Tax treaties | 26-068 |
| | Unilateral relief for foreign tax paid | 26-069 |
| | National insurance contributions | 26-070 |
| 27 | DISGUISED REMUNERATION | |
| | Overview | 27-001 |
| | Pt 7A Ch.1: the general provisions | 27-008 |
| | Relevant steps | 27-019 |
| | Exceptions | 27-040 |
| | Part 7A Ch.2: the charge to tax | 27-079 |
| | Part 7A Ch.3 | 27-118 |
| | Interaction with other legislation | 27-133 |
| | National insurance contributions | 27-139 |
| 28 | INHERITANCE TAX | |
| | Overview | 28-001 |
| | Contributions | 28-021 |
| | Disposals of scheme interests | 28-034 |
| | Relevant property | 28-035 |
| | Omitting to exercise rights | 28-067 |
| | Death of a beneficiary | 28-071 |
| 29 | DOUBLE TAX TREATIES | |
| | Introduction | 29-001 |

## CONTENTS

Application to Retirement Benefit Schemes ..................... 29-014
Cross Border Contributions ............................................ 29-017
Cross Border Investment Income/gains ........................... 29-031
Pension Transfers ........................................................... 29-032
Cross Border Pension Benefits ........................................ 29-034

### PART B: CATEGORIES OF PENSION SCHEME

30 RELEVANT NON-UK SCHEMES

Overview ........................................................................ 30-001
What is a relevant non-UK scheme? ................................ 30-004
Taxation of RNUKS ........................................................ 30-017
The member payment charges ......................................... 30-029
The taxable property provisions ...................................... 30-079
The annual allowance provisions ..................................... 30-100
The overseas transfer charge ........................................... 30-114
The lifetime allowance (pre-6 April 2024) ....................... 30-120

31 OVERSEAS PENSION SCHEMES

Introduction and overview .............................................. 31-001
What is an overseas pension scheme? .............................. 31-007
Taxation ......................................................................... 31-039

32 RECOGNISED OVERSEAS PENSION SCHEMES

Introduction and overview .............................................. 32-001
What is a ROPS? ............................................................ 32-005
Taxation ......................................................................... 32-020

33 QUALIFYING RECOGNISED OVERSEAS PENSION SCHEMES

Introduction and overview .............................................. 33-001
Taxation ......................................................................... 33-022
The overseas transfer charge ........................................... 33-023
Information requirements ............................................... 33-043

34 QUALIFYING NON-UK PENSION SCHEMES

Introduction and overview .............................................. 34-001
What is a QNUPS? ......................................................... 34-009
Taxation ......................................................................... 34-041

35 EMPLOYER-FINANCED RETIREMENT BENEFITS SCHEMES

Introduction ................................................................... 35-001
What is an EFRBS? ........................................................ 35-009
Relevant benefits ............................................................ 35-019
Taxation ......................................................................... 35-058
Reporting obligations ..................................................... 35-103

36 EXCEPTED GROUP LIFE SCHEMES

Introduction ................................................................... 36-001

|    | Relevant life policies ........................................................... 36-007 |
|    | Taxation ............................................................................. 36-017 |

## 37 SECTION 615 FUNDS

|    | Overview ............................................................................ 37-001 |
|    | What is a section 615 fund? ............................................... 37-004 |
|    | Taxation ............................................................................. 37-013 |

## 38 FUNDED UNAPPROVED RETIREMENT BENEFITS SCHEMES

|    | Introduction ...................................................................... 38-001 |
|    | What is a FURBS? ............................................................ 38-006 |
|    | Taxation ............................................................................. 38-009 |

## 39 CORRESPONDING SCHEMES

|    | Overview ............................................................................ 39-001 |
|    | What is a corresponding scheme? ..................................... 39-004 |
|    | Taxation ............................................................................. 39-011 |

*Index* ............................................................................................ 837

# TABLE OF CASES

A Pension Plan, Re [2020] 5 WLUK 646; 24 I.T.E.L.R. 201 Royal Ct (Gue) .............. 2-080
Abbott v Philbin (Inspector of Taxes), sub nom. Philbin (Inspector of Taxes) v Abbott
  [1961] A.C. 352; [1960] 3 W.L.R. 255; [1960] 2 All E.R. 763; [1960] 6 WLUK 67; 53 R.
  & I.T. 487; 39 T.C. 82; (1960) 39 A.T.C. 221; [1960] T.R. 171; (1960) 104 S.J. 563 HL .... 24-053
ACT Construction Co Ltd v Customs and Excise Commissioners [1981] 1 W.L.R. 1542;
  [1982] 1 All E.R. 84; [1982] S.T.C. 25; [1981] 12 WLUK 55; (1981) 125 S.J. 864; *Times*,
  December 4, 1981 HL ................................................................... 11-004
Addy v Inland Revenue Commissioners [1975] S.T.C. 601; [1975] 1 WLUK 629 DC ...... 36-010
Agassi v Robinson (Inspector of Taxes), sub nom. Agassi v Robertson (Inspector of Taxes);
  Set v Robinson (Inspector of Taxes) [2006] UKHL 23; [2006] 1 W.L.R. 1380; [2006] 3
  All E.R. 97; [2006] S.T.C. 1056; [2006] 5 WLUK 430; 77 T.C. 686; [2006] B.T.C. 372; 8
  I.T.L. Rep. 1106; [2006] S.T.I. 1542; (2006) 103(22) L.S.G. 27; (2006) 156 N.L.J. 880;
  (2006) 150 S.J.L.B. 671; *Times*, May 18, 2006 HL .................... 20-002, 20-042, 35-074
AGCO Ltd v Massey Ferguson Works Pension Trust Ltd [2003] EWCA Civ 1044; [2003] 7
  WLUK 504; [2004] I.C.R. 15; [2003] I.R.L.R. 783; [2003] O.P.L.R. 199; [2003] Pens.
  L.R. 241; (2003) 100(35) L.S.G. 37; (2003) 147 S.J.L.B. 1085; *Times*, July 24, 2003 CA
  (Civ Div) ............................................................................... 35-024
Aim (Perth) Ltd v Revenue and Customs Commissioners [2017] UKFTT 533 (TC); [2017]
  6 WLUK 581 FTT (Tax) .................................................. 5-021, 5-042, 18-184, 18-193
Air Jamaica Ltd v Charlton; joined case(s) Air Jamaica Ltd v Clarke; Air Jamaica Ltd v
  Goodall; Air Jamaica Ltd v Philpotts [1999] 1 W.L.R. 1399; [1999] 4 WLUK 280; [1999]
  O.P.L.R. 11; [1999] Pens. L.R. 247; (1999-2000) 2 I.T.E.L.R. 244 PC (Jam) ...... 25-013, 28-038
Airedale NHS Trust v Bland [1993] A.C. 789; [1993] 2 W.L.R. 316; [1993] 1 All E.R. 821;
  [1993] 2 WLUK 69; [1993] 1 F.L.R. 1026; [1994] 1 F.C.R. 485; [1993] 4 Med. L.R. 39;
  (1993) 12 B.M.L.R. 64; [1993] Fam. Law 473; (1993) 143 N.L.J. 199; *Times*, February
  5, 1993; *Independent*, February 5, 1993; *Guardian*, February 5, 1993 HL ............... 21-089
Airtours Holiday Transport Ltd (formerly My Travel Group) v Revenue and Customs
  Commissioners, sub nom. Airtours Holidays Transport Ltd v Revenue and Customs
  Commissioners; Revenue and Customs Commissioners v Airtours Holiday Transport
  Ltd [2016] UKSC 21; [2016] 4 W.L.R. 87; [2016] 4 All E.R. 1; [2016] S.T.C. 1509;
  [2016] 5 WLUK 192; [2016] B.V.C. 17; [2016] S.T.I. 1529 SC .................. 22-006, 22-007
Alands Vindkraft AB v Energimyndigheten (C-573/12) EU:C:2014:2037; [2014] 7 WLUK
  9; [2015] 1 C.M.L.R. 10; [2015] Env. L.R. 7 ECJ (Grand Chamber) .................. 33-015
Albon (t/a NA Carriage Co) v Naza Motor Trading Sdn Bhd [2007] EWHC 9 (Ch); [2007]
  1 W.L.R. 2489; [2007] 2 All E.R. 719; [2007] 1 All E.R. (Comm) 795; [2007] 1 Lloyd's
  Rep. 297; [2007] 1 WLUK 436; [2007] Bus. L.R. D87 Ch D ........................... 18-046
Alexander M'Kinlay v Archibald Wilson (1885) 13 R. 210; [1885] 11 WLUK 66 IH (1
  Div) ...................................................................................... 37-026
Allan v Revenue and Customs Commissioners [2015] UKUT 16 (TCC); [2015] S.T.C.
  890; [2015] 1 WLUK 496; [2015] B.T.C. 502 UT (Tax) .............................. 38-015
Alloway v Phillips (Inspector of Taxes) [1980] 1 W.L.R. 888; [1980] 3 All E.R. 138; [1980]
  S.T.C. 490; [1980] 3 WLUK 161; [1980] T.R. 111; (1980) 124 S.J. 346 CA (Civ Div) ..... 35-075
Allum v Marsh (Inspector of Taxes) [2004] 11 WLUK 675; [2005] S.T.C. (S.C.D.) 191;
  [2005] S.T.I. 97 Sp Comm ............................................. 6-008, 35-015, 35-016, 35-018, 35-075
Alway Sheet Metal Ltd v Revenue and Customs Commissioners [2017] UKFTT 198 (TC);
  [2017] 2 WLUK 649; [2017] S.F.T.D. 719; [2017] S.T.I. 1200 FTT (Tax) ............... 24-043
Aspect Capital Ltd v Revenue and Customs Commissioners [2014] UKUT 81 (TCC);
  [2014] S.T.C. 1360; [2014] 2 WLUK 628; [2014] B.T.C. 508; [2014] S.T.I. 873 UT
  (Tax) ..................................................................................... 2-091
Associated Provincial Picture Houses Ltd v Wednesbury Corp [1948] 1 K.B. 223; [1947] 2
  All E.R. 680; (1947) 63 T.L.R. 623; [1947] 11 WLUK 26; (1948) 112 J.P. 55; 45 L.G.R.
  635; [1948] L.J.R. 190; (1947) 177 L.T. 641; (1948) 92 S.J. 26 CA ..................... 4-023
ATP PensionService A/S v Skatteministeriet (C-464/12), sub nom. ATP Pension Service
  A/S v Skatteministeriet (C-464/12) EU:C:2014:139; [2014] S.T.C. 2145; [2014] 3
  WLUK 376; [2014] Pens. L.R. 223; [2014] B.V.C. 17; [2014] S.T.I. 1566 ECJ (5th
  Chamber) .............................................................................. 22-015, 22-016
Att-Gen (I) v Jameson [1905] 2 Ir. R. 201 ................................................ 21-005
B (A Beneficiary) v Inland Revenue Commissioners [1999] 4 WLUK 201; [1999] S.T.C.

## TABLE OF CASES

(S.C.D.) 134; 1 I.T.L. Rep. 705 Sp Comm ................................. 25-075, 25-076
Baird v Baird [1990] 2 A.C. 548; [1990] 2 W.L.R. 1412; [1990] 2 All E.R. 300; [1990] 4
   WLUK 208; [1990] I.C.R. 525; [1990] Pens. L.R. 87; [1991] Fam. Law 96; (1990) 134
   S.J. 725; *Times*, May 3, 1990 PC (Trin) ........................................... 21-087
Baker (Inspector of Taxes) v Archer Shee, sub nom. Archer Shee v Baker (Inspector of
   Taxes) [1927] A.C. 844; [1927] 7 WLUK 70 HL .................................... 25-004
Ballard v Revenue and Customs Commissioners [2013] UKFTT 87 (TC); [2013] 1 WLUK
   678 FTT (Tax) .......................................................... 35-027, 35-030, 35-042
Bambridge v Inland Revenue Commissioners [1955] 1 W.L.R. 1329; [1955] 3 All E.R.
   812; [1955] 12 WLUK 22; 48 R. & I.T. 814; 36 T.C. 313; (1955) 34 A.T.C. 181; [1955]
   T.R. 295; (1955) 99 S.J. 910 HL ................................................... 25-056
Barclays Bank Plc v Holmes; joined case(s) Barclays Bank Plc v Barclays Pension Funds
   Trustees Ltd [2000] 11 WLUK 646; [2001] O.P.L.R. 37; [2000] Pens. L.R. 339 Ch D ...... 2-009,
                                                                                            31-019
Barclays Bank Plc v Revenue and Customs Commissioners, sub nom. Revenue and
   Customs Commissioners v Barclays Bank Plc [2007] EWCA Civ 442; [2008] S.T.C.
   476; [2007] 5 WLUK 271; 79 T.C. 18; [2007] B.T.C. 338; [2007] S.T.I. 1436; (2007)
   151 S.J.L.B. 675; *Times*, June 5, 2007 CA (Civ Div) ...... 6-008, 12-005, 18-030, 18-031, 27-015,
                                                                         35-017, 35-031, 35-036, 35-041
Barclays Wealth Trustees (Jersey) Ltd v Revenue and Customs Commissioners [2017]
   EWCA Civ 1512; [2018] 1 W.L.R. 2312; [2017] S.T.C. 2465; [2017] 10 WLUK 331;
   [2017] B.T.C. 27; [2017] W.T.L.R. 917 CA (Civ Div) ............................... 28-038
Barker v Baxendale Walker Solicitors [2017] EWCA Civ 2056; [2018] 1 W.L.R. 1905;
   [2018] S.T.C. 310; [2017] 12 WLUK 203; [2018] P.N.L.R. 16; [2018] B.T.C. 6 CA (Civ
   Div) ................................................................................. 28-031
Barlow Clowes International Ltd (In Liquidation) v Vaughan, sub nom. Vaughan v Barlow
   Clowes International Ltd [1992] 4 All E.R. 22; [1991] 7 WLUK 225; [1992] B.C.L.C.
   910; *Times*, March 6, 1992 CA (Civ Div) ........................................... 37-026
Barnes v Revenue and Customs Commissioners [2014] EWCA Civ 31; [2014] 1 WLUK
   731; [2014] B.T.C. 5 CA (Civ Div) ................................................. 35-053
Barry v Cordy, sub nom. Smith Barry v Cordy [1946] 2 All E.R. 396; 62 T.L.R. 614;
   [1946] 7 WLUK 51; 28 T.C. 250; [1946] W.N. 170; 176 L.T. 111; (1946) 90 S.J. 528 CA .... 8-019
BAV-TMW-Globaler-Immobilien Spezialfonds v Revenue and Customs Commissioners
   [2019] UKFTT 129 (TC); [2019] 2 WLUK 494; [2019] S.F.T.D. 631 FTT (Tax) ... 20-002, 20-003
Bayfine UK Products v Revenue and Customs Commissioners [2011] EWCA Civ 304;
   [2012] 1 W.L.R. 1630; [2012] Bus. L.R. 796; [2011] S.T.C. 717; [2011] 3 WLUK 726;
   [2011] B.T.C. 242; 13 I.T.L. Rep. 747; [2011] S.T.I. 1208 CA (Civ Div) ............... 29-004
Bayonet Ventures LLP v Revenue and Customs Commissioners [2018] UKFTT 262 (TC);
   [2018] 5 WLUK 212 FTT (Tax) ......................... 5-004, 5-031, 17-008, 19-026
Baytrust Holdings Ltd v Inland Revenue Commissioners; joined case(s) Thos Firth & John
   Brown (Investments) Ltd v Inland Revenue Commissi [1971] 1 W.L.R. 1333; [1971] 3
   All E.R. 76; [1971] 3 WLUK 99; [2008] B.T.C. 7044; (1971) 50 A.T.C. 136; [1971] T.R.
   111; (1971) 115 S.J. 624 Ch D ............................................... 28-063, 37-007
Beauty Consultants Ltd v Inspector of Taxes [2002] 4 WLUK 83; [2002] S.T.C. (S.C.D.)
   352; [2002] S.T.I. 1095 Sp Comm ................................. 6-050, 6-053, 6-062
Bentleys Stokes & Lowless v Beeson (Inspector of Taxes) [1952] 2 All E.R. 82; [1952] 1
   T.L.R. 1529; [1952] 5 WLUK 71; 45 R. & I.T. 461; 33 T.C. 491; (1952) 31 A.T.C. 229;
   [1952] T.R. 239; [1952] W.N. 280; (1952) 96 S.J. 345 CA ............................ 6-044
Blain, Ex p., sub nom. Sawers, Re (1879) 12 Ch. D. 522; [1879] 8 WLUK 3 CA ........ 20-042
Boake Allen Ltd v Revenue and Customs Commissioners, sub nom. NEC Semi Conductors
   Ltd v Revenue and Customs Commissioners [2007] UKHL 25; [2007] 1 W.L.R. 1386;
   [2007] 3 All E.R. 605; [2007] S.T.C. 1265; [2007] 5 WLUK 579; [2007] 3 C.M.L.R. 6;
   [2007] Eu. L.R. 701; [2007] B.T.C. 414; 9 I.T.L. Rep. 995; [2007] S.T.I. 1585; (2007)
   104(23) L.S.G. 30; (2007) 151 S.J.L.B. 707; *Times*, May 24, 2007 HL ................. 29-009
Boardman v Revenue and Customs Commissioners [2022] UKFTT 238 (TC); [2022] 8
   WLUK 29 FTT (Tax) ............................................................... 11-011
BOC International v Customs and Excise Commissioners [1982] 1 WLUK 7; [1982]
   V.A.T.T.R. 84 VAT Tr ............................................................... 22-008
Boyle v Revenue and Customs Commissioners [2013] UKFTT 723 (TC); [2013] 11 WLUK
   857 FTT (Tax) ....................................................................... 25-053
Bray (Inspector of Taxes) v Best [1989] 1 W.L.R. 167; [1989] 1 All E.R. 969; [1989] S.T.C.
   159; [1989] 2 WLUK 304; 62 T.C. 705; (1989) 86(17) L.S.G. 43; (1989) 139 N.L.J. 753;
   (1989) 133 S.J. 323 HL ............................................................. 27-085

## TABLE OF CASES

Bridge Trustees Ltd v Yates, sub nom. Bridge Trustees Ltd v Houldsworth; Houldsworth v Bridge Trustees Ltd [2011] UKSC 42; [2011] 1 W.L.R. 1912; [2012] 1 All E.R. 659; [2011] 7 WLUK 797; [2011] I.C.R. 1069; [2011] Pens. L.R. 313; *Times*, August 9, 2011 SC ............................................................................ 2-041
British Insulated & Helsby Cables Ltd v Atherton (Inspector of Taxes), sub nom. Atherton (Inspector of Taxes) v British Insulated & Helsby Cables Ltd [1926] A.C. 205; [1925] 12 WLUK 65; 10 T.C. 155 HL........................................................ 6-071, 22-029
Brodie's Trustees v Inland Revenue Commissioners [1947] 1 WLUK 101; 17 T.C. 432 ..... 6-150, 13-024, 26-060, 29-060
Brooks v National Westminster Bank 8 November 1983 CA ......................... 35-024
Browne v Revenue and Customs Commissioners [2017] UKFTT 867 (TC) FTT (Tax) ..... 18-181
Brown's Executors v Inland Revenue Commissioners [1996] 5 WLUK 431; [1996] S.T.C. (S.C.D.) 277 Sp Comm.................................................... 28-033
Burns v Revenue and Customs Commissioners [2009] 1 WLUK 99; [2009] S.T.C. (S.C.D.) 165; [2009] S.T.I. 262 Sp Comm ............................................. 25-079
Camas Plc v Atkinson (Inspector of Taxes), sub nom. Atkinson (Inspector of Taxes) v Camas Plc [2004] EWCA Civ 541; [2004] 1 W.L.R. 2392; [2004] S.T.C. 860; [2004] 5 WLUK 55; 76 T.C. 641; [2004] B.T.C. 190; [2004] S.T.I. 1163; (2004) 101(22) L.S.G. 33; (2004) 148 S.J.L.B. 571; *Times*, May 27, 2004 CA (Civ Div)........................ 6-065
Cameron v M&W Mack (ESOP) Trustee Ltd [2001] 11 WLUK 239; [2002] W.T.L.R. 647 Ch D................................................................. 27-023
Campbell (Trustees of Davies Education Trust) v Inland Revenue Commissioners, sub nom. Davies Educational Trust (Campbell) v Inland Revenue Commissioners [1970] A.C. 77; [1968] 3 W.L.R. 1025; [1968] 3 All E.R. 588; [1968] 10 WLUK 59; 45 T.C. 427; [1968] T.R. 327; (1968) 112 S.J. 864 HL ............................... 26-060, 29-060
Carvill v Inland Revenue Commissioners (Transfer Purpose) [2000] 3 WLUK 558; [2000] S.T.C. (S.C.D.) 143; [2000] S.T.I. 584 Sp Comm ............. 25-057, 25-061, 25-075, 25-076
Century Life Plc v Pensions Ombudsman; joined case(s) Britannia Life Ltd v Pensions Ombudsman [1995] 5 WLUK 177; [1995] C.L.C. 1276; [1995] O.P.L.R. 351; [1995] Pens. L.R. 135; [1996] C.O.D. 317; *Times*, May 23, 1995 QBD ................ 9-010, 11-004
Chalcot Training Ltd v Ralph, sub nom. Chalcot Training Ltd v Stoneman [2021] EWCA Civ 795; [2021] 5 WLUK 389 CA (Civ Div)..................................... 6-058
Chamberlain v IRC (1943) 25 T.C. 317 ........................................ 25-031
Champagne Perrier-Jouet SA v HH Finch Ltd [1982] 1 W.L.R. 1359; [1982] 3 All E.R. 713; [1982] 4 WLUK 151; (1983) 80 L.S.G. 93; (1982) 126 S.J. 689 Ch D .............. 2-093
Chappie v Inland Revenue Commissioners, sub nom. Inland Revenue Commissioners v Chappie [1953] 1 WLUK 63; 46 R. & I.T. 418; 34 T.C. 509; (1953) 32 A.T.C. 45; [1953] T.R. 69 CA......................................................... 18-121, 25-067, 28-032
Chen v Wong [2006] T.L.I. 262 ............................................... 21-087
Chinn v Hochstrasser (Inspector of Taxes), sub nom. Chinn v Collins (Inspector of Taxes) [1981] A.C. 533; [1981] 2 W.L.R. 14; [1981] 1 All E.R. 189; [1981] S.T.C. 1; [1980] 12 WLUK 102; 54 T.C. 311; [1980] T.R. 467; (1981) 125 S.J. 49 HL ............... 2-088, 25-025
Chow Yoong Hong v Choong Fah Rubber Manufactory [1962] A.C. 209; [1962] 2 W.L.R. 43; [1961] 3 All E.R. 1163; [1961] 12 WLUK 8; (1961) 105 S.J. 1082 PC (FMS) .... 2-085, 2-093
CIR v Anglo Brewing Co Ltd [1925] 12 T.C. 803 ................................ 6-059
CIR v Leiner (1964) 41 T.C. 589 .............................................. 35-034
CIR v Tai Hing Cotton Mill [2008] 2 HKLRD 40; (2007) 10 HKCFAR 704 ............. 36-010
Clark v Revenue and Customs Commissioners [2020] EWCA Civ 204; [2020] 1 W.L.R. 3354; [2020] 4 All E.R. 652; [2020] S.T.C. 589; [2020] 2 WLUK 255; [2020] Pens. L.R. 18; [2020] B.T.C. 4; [2020] S.T.I. 402 CA (Civ Div) .. 2-010, 2-074, 2-075, 2-079, 18-055, 18-062, 18-162
Clark (Inspector of Taxes) v Oceanic Contractors Inc [1983] 2 A.C. 130; [1983] 2 W.L.R. 94; [1983] 1 All E.R. 133; [1983] S.T.C. 35; [1982] 12 WLUK 161; 56 T.C. 183; (1982) 13 A.T.R. 901; (1983) 133 N.L.J. 62; (1983) 127 S.J. 54 HL ............ 20-002, 20-042, 20-046
Clarke (Inspector of Taxes) v BT Pension Scheme Trustees, sub nom. British Telecom Pension Scheme Trustees v Clarke (Inspector of Taxes); Clark (Inspector of Taxes) v British Telecom Pension Scheme Trustees; Clark (Inspector of Taxes) v Trustees of the British Telecom Pension Scheme; Clarke (Inspector of Taxes) v Trustees of BT Pension Scheme; Trustees of BT Pension Scheme v Clark (Inspector of Taxes) [2000] S.T.C. 222; [2000] 2 WLUK 863; [2000] O.P.L.R. 53; [2000] Pens. L.R. 157; 72 T.C. 472; [2000] B.T.C. 64; [2000] S.T.I. 217; (2000) 97(10) L.S.G. 37; (2000) 144 S.J.L.B. 119; *Times*, March 7, 2000 CA (Civ Div) .................................................... 8-040, 8-041
Clixby v Pountney [1968] Ch. 719; [1968] 2 W.L.R. 865; [1968] 1 All E.R. 802; [1967] 12

# TABLE OF CASES

WLUK 34; 44 T.C. 575; (1967) 46 A.T.C. 398; [1967] T.R. 383; 117 N.L.J. 1343; (1968) 112 S.J. 16 Ch D.................................................................. 6-018, 9-005, 26-007

Collins v Addies (Inspector of Taxes); joined case(s) Greenfield v Bains (Inspector of Taxes) [1992] S.T.C. 746; [1992] 7 WLUK 469; *Times*, August 25, 1992; *Independent*, August 24, 1992 CA (Civ Div)............................................................. 27-032

Colquhoun v Brooks (1889) 14 App. Cas. 493; [1889] 8 WLUK 24; 2 T.C. 490 HL ....... 20-042, 25-010, 29-001, 35-074, 38-021, 39-015

Colquhoun v Revenue and Customs Commissioners [2010] UKUT 431 (TCC); [2011] S.T.C. 394; [2010] 12 WLUK 154; [2011] B.T.C. 1511; [2011] S.T.I. 131 UT (Tax)....... 24-047

Commission of the European Communities v Denmark (C-150/04), sub nom. Taxation of Pension Contributions, Re (C-150/04) EU:C:2007:69; [2007] S.T.C. 1392; [2007] E.C.R. I-1163; [2007] 1 WLUK 637; [2007] 2 C.M.L.R. 16; [2007] S.T.I. 254 ECJ ............. 24-004

Commission of the European Communities v Spain (C-71/92) EU:C:1993:890; [1993] E.C.R. I-5923; [1993] 11 WLUK 206 ECJ........................................................ 33-015

Cooper v Billingham (Inspector of Taxes), sub nom. Billingham (Inspector of Taxes) v Cooper; Edwards (Inspector of Taxes) v Fisher; joined case(s) Fisher v Edwards (Inspector of Taxes) [2001] EWCA Civ 1041; [2001] S.T.C. 1177; [2001] 7 WLUK 136; 74 T.C. 139; [2001] B.T.C. 282; [2001] S.T.I. 1017; (2001) 98(31) L.S.G. 37; *Times*, July 16, 2001; *Independent*, July 13, 2001 CA (Civ Div) ................................................. 25-067

Cooper v Reilly 57 E.R. 897; (1829) 2 Sim. 560; [1829] 3 WLUK 71 Ct of Chancery ...... 26-034

Cooper (Inspector of Taxes) v C&J Clark Ltd [1982] S.T.C. 335; [1982] 1 WLUK 62; 54 T.C. 670; [1982] B.T.C. 130 Ch D .................................................................. 8-023

Copeman (Inspector of Taxes) v Coleman, sub nom. Copeman (Inspector of Taxes) v Coleman Minors [1939] 2 K.B. 484; [1939] 3 All E.R. 224; [1939] 5 WLUK 67 KBD......... 25-024

Copeman (Inspector of Taxes) v William Flood & Sons [1941] 1 K.B. 202; [1940] 10 WLUK 31 KBD .................................................................. 6-046, 6-051, 6-062, 6-065

Corbett's Executrices v IRC 25 T.C. 305 ............................................................. 25-057

Cory Bros & Co Ltd v Owners of the Turkish Steamship Mecca [1897] A.C. 286; [1897] 4 WLUK 33 HL.................................................................. 37-026

Countess Fitzwilliam v Inland Revenue Commissioners [1993] 1 W.L.R. 1189; [1993] 3 All E.R. 184; [1993] S.T.C. 502; [1993] 7 WLUK 16; 67 T.C. 614; [1993] S.T.I. 1038; (1993) 90(45) L.S.G. 46; (1993) 137 S.J.L.B. 184; *Times*, July 9, 1993 HL .............. 25-027

Courage Group's Pension Schemes, Re; joined case(s) Ryan v Imperial Brewing & Leisure [1987] 1 W.L.R. 495; [1987] 1 All E.R. 528; [1986] 12 WLUK 119; [1987] 1 F.T.L.R. 210; (1987) 84 L.S.G. 1573; (1987) 131 S.J. 507; *Times*, December 22, 1986; *Financial Times*, December 16, 1986 Ch D ............................................................. 8-053

Coventry & Solihull Waste Disposal Co Ltd v Russell (Valuation Officer) [1999] 1 W.L.R. 2093; [2000] 1 All E.R. 97; [1999] 11 WLUK 844; [2000] R.A. 1; [1999] E.G. 141 (C.S.); (1999) 96(47) L.S.G. 32; (2000) 144 S.J.L.B. 10; [1999] N.P.C. 146; *Times*, November 30, 1999 HL .................................................................. 35-032

Cowan v Scargill, sub nom. Mineworkers Pension Scheme Trusts, Re [1985] Ch. 270; [1984] 3 W.L.R. 501; [1984] 2 All E.R. 750; [1984] 4 WLUK 137; [1984] I.C.R. 646; [1984] I.R.L.R. 260; [1990] Pens. L.R. 169; (1984) 81 L.S.G. 2463; (1984) 128 S.J. 550 Ch D .................................................................. 8-002

Craddock Bros Ltd v Hunt [1923] 2 Ch. 136; [1923] 3 WLUK 121 CA ................... 2-080

Crossfield v Revenue and Customs Commissioners [2018] UKFTT 390 (TC); [2018] 6 WLUK 387 FTT (Tax) .................................................................. 5-028

Crossland (Inspector of Taxes) v Hawkins [1961] Ch. 537; [1961] 3 W.L.R. 202; [1961] 2 All E.R. 812; [1961] 5 WLUK 18; 39 T.C. 493; (1961) 40 A.T.C. 126; [1961] T.R. 113; (1961) 105 S.J. 424 CA.................................................................. 25-023

Cunard's Trustees v IRC (1945) 27 T.C. 122 ............................................................. 15-078

Curtis v Revenue and Customs Commissioners [2022] UKFTT 172 (TC); [2022] 6 WLUK 74; [2022] Pens. L.R. 10; [2022] S.F.T.D. 1150; [2022] S.T.I. 921 FTT (Tax) ............ 18-187

Customs and Excise Commissioners v British Railways Board, sub nom. British Railways Board v Customs and Excise Commissioners [1976] 1 W.L.R. 1036; [1976] 3 All E.R. 100; [1976] S.T.C. 359; [1976] 5 WLUK 39; [1977] I.C.R. 100; (1976) 120 S.J. 472 CA (Civ Div).................................................................. 22-008

Customs and Excise Commissioners v Redrow Group Plc [1999] 1 W.L.R. 408; [1999] 2 All E.R. 1; [1999] S.T.C. 161; [1999] 2 WLUK 219; [1999] B.T.C. 5062; [1999] B.V.C. 96; [1999] E.G. 20 (C.S.); (1999) 96(9) L.S.G. 32; (1999) 143 S.J.L.B. 58; [1999] N.P.C. 18; *Times*, February 18, 1999; *Independent*, February 18, 1999 HL ................... 22-007

Dale v Inland Revenue Commissioners [1954] A.C. 11; [1953] 3 W.L.R. 448; [1953] 2 All E.R. 671; [1953] 7 WLUK 94; 46 R. & I.T. 513; 34 T.C. 468; (1953) 32 A.T.C. 294;

# TABLE OF CASES

[1953] T.R. 269; (1953) 97 S.J. 538 HL..................................................2-018
Dalriada Trustees Ltd v Faulds [2011] EWHC 3391 (Ch); [2012] 2 All E.R. 734; [2011] 12
  WLUK 530; [2012] I.C.R. 1106; [2012] Pens. L.R. 15; (2012) 162 N.L.J. 93 Ch D .. 2-019, 8-018,
                                                                18-052, 18-137, 18-140, 18-141
Dalriada Trustees Ltd v Revenue and Customs Commissioners [2023] UKFTT 314 (TC);
  [2023] 3 WLUK 434 FTT (Tax)................. 2-079, 5-038, 18-054, 18-063, 18-141, 18-186
Dalriada Trustees Ltd v Woodward [2012] EWHC 21626 (Ch); [2012] 6 WLUK 323;
  [2012] W.T.L.R. 1489 Ch D ................................................................ 25-013
Danish Bacon Co Ltd Staff Pension Fund Trusts, Re, sub nom. Christensen v Arnett [1971]
  1 W.L.R. 248; [1971] 1 All E.R. 486; [1970] 10 WLUK 34 Ch D....................... 21-087
Danner v Finland (C-136/00) EU:C:2002:558; [2002] S.T.C. 1283; [2002] E.C.R. I-8147;
  [2002] 10 WLUK 80; [2002] 3 C.M.L.R. 29; [2003] C.E.C. 156; [2003] O.P.L.R. 293;
  [2002] Pens. L.R. 469; 5 I.T.L. Rep. 119; [2002] S.T.I. 1343 ECJ (5th Chamber) ......... 24-004
Danvers v Revenue and Customs Commissioners [2016] UKUT 569 (TCC); [2017] S.T.C.
  555; [2017] 1 WLUK 42; [2017] Pens. L.R. 6; [2017] B.T.C. 502; [2017] S.T.I. 138 UT
  (Tax).......................................... 5-043, 18-003, 18-030, 18-037, 18-038, 18-041
Davenport (Inspector of Taxes) v Chilver [1983] Ch. 293; [1983] 3 W.L.R. 481; [1983]
  S.T.C. 426; [1983] 4 WLUK 37; (1983) 127 S.J. 462 Ch D ............... 8-033, 8-034, 36-020
Davies v Revenue and Customs Commissioners [2020] UKUT 67 (TCC); [2020] S.T.C.
  649; [2020] 3 WLUK 133; [2020] B.T.C. 542; 22 I.T.L. Rep. 537; [2020] S.T.I. 843 UT
  (Tax) ...................................................................................... 29-011
Davis v Powell [1977] 1 W.L.R. 258; [1977] 1 All E.R. 471; [1977] S.T.C. 32; [1976] 12
  WLUK 1; (1976) 242 E.G. 380; 51 T.C. 492; [1976] T.R. 307; (1977) 121 S.J. 15; *Times*,
  December 2, 1976 Ch D ................................................................... 8-034
Davis v The Duke of Marlborough 36 E.R. 303; (1818) 1 Swans. 74; [1818] 3 WLUK 7 Ct
  of Chancery................................................................................ 26-034
Davy's of London (Wine Merchants) Ltd v City of London Corp; joined case(s) Davy's of
  London (Wine Merchants) Ltd v Saxon Land BV [2004] EWHC 2224 (Ch); [2004] 10
  WLUK 107; [2004] 3 E.G.L.R. 39; [2004] 49 E.G. 136; [2004] 42 E.G. 161 (C.S.);
  [2004] N.P.C. 144; [2005] 1 P. & C.R. DG8 Ch D...................................... 5-040
Dennis v Revenue and Customs Commissioners [2018] UKFTT 735 (TC); [2018] 12
  WLUK 495; [2019] S.F.T.D. 593; [2019] S.T.I. 707 FTT (Tax)......................... 2-083
Devaynes v Noble, sub nom. Baring's Case; Brice's Case; Clayton's Case; Houlton's
  Case; Johne's Case; Palmer's Case; Sleech's Case; Warde's Case 35 E.R. 767; (1816) 1
  Mer. 529; [1816] 7 WLUK 44 Ct of Chancery .............................. 26-019, 37-026
Devon and Somerset Fire and Rescue Authority v Howell [2023] EWHC 257 (Ch); [2023]
  2 WLUK 193; [2023] I.C.R. 686; [2023] Pens. L.R. 8 Ch D........................... 13-003
Dewar v Inland Revenue Commissioners [1935] 2 K.B. 351; [1935] 7 WLUK 4 CA ...... 26-032,
                                                                                       26-034
Dextra Accessories Ltd v MacDonald (Inspector of Taxes), sub nom. MacDonald (Inspec-
  tor of Taxes) v Dextra Accessories Ltd [2005] UKHL 47; [2005] 4 All E.R. 107; [2005]
  S.T.C. 1111; [2005] 7 WLUK 201; [2005] Pens. L.R. 395; 77 T.C. 146; [2005] B.T.C.
  355; [2005] S.T.I. 1235; (2005) 102(29) L.S.G. 33; *Times*, July 11, 2005 HL ..... 24-024, 24-043,
                                                                   24-057, 27-024, 30-013
Dollar (t/a IJ Dollar) v Lyon (Inspector of Taxes) [1981] S.T.C. 333; [1981] 1 WLUK 105;
  54 T.C. 459 Ch D ......................................................................... 6-056
Dominica Social Security Board v Nature Island Investment Co Ltd [2008] UKPC 19;
  [2008] 4 WLUK 47 PC (Dom) .............................................. 8-018, 18-033
Dorrell v May & Baker Ltd [1990] 5 WLUK 138; [1991] Pens. L.R. 31 Ch D ............ 35-024
Dougall v Lornie (1899) 1 F. 1187; [1899] 7 WLUK 81 IH (1 Div) .................... 37-026
Drummond (Inspector of Taxes) v Austin Brown [1985] Ch. 52; [1984] 3 W.L.R. 381;
  [1984] 2 All E.R. 699; [1984] S.T.C. 321; [1984] 4 WLUK 52; 58 T.C. 67; (1984) 81
  L.S.G. 1844; (1984) 128 S.J. 532 CA (Civ Div)......................................... 8-034
Duke of Buccleuch v Inland Revenue Commissioners, sub nom. Duke of Devonshire's
  Trustees v Inland Revenue Commissioners [1967] 1 A.C. 506; [1967] 2 W.L.R. 207;
  [1967] 1 All E.R. 129; [1966] 12 WLUK 85; [1967] R.V.R. 25; [1967] R.V.R. 42; (1966)
  45 A.T.C. 472; (1966) T.R. 393; (1967) 111 S.J. 18 HL................................. 21-005
Duke of Roxburghe's Executors v Inland Revenue Commissioners 1936 S.C. 863; 1936
  S.L.T. 538; [1936] 7 WLUK 46 IH (1 Div)........................................ 18-193, 18-194
Dunn Trust v Williams [1950] 1 WLUK 105; 43 R. & I.T. 924; 31 T.C. 477; [1950] T.R.
  271........................................................................................ 8-027
Dunne v Revenue and Customs Commissioners [2007] 12 WLUK 242; [2008] S.T.C.
  (S.C.D.) 422; [2008] S.T.I. 141 Sp Comm............................................... 2-019

# TABLE OF CASES

Earl Howe v Inland Revenue Commissioners [1919] 2 K.B. 336; [1919] 4 WLUK 46; 7 T.C. 289 CA .................................................. 6-150, 13-024, 26-060, 29-060
Earl of Carnarvon's Chesterfield Settled Estates, Re; joined case(s) Earl of Carnarvon's Highclere Settled Estates, Re [1927] 1 Ch. 138; [1926] 6 WLUK 87 Ch D ............. 2-029
Earlspring Properties Ltd v Guest (Inspector of Taxes) [1995] S.T.C. 479; [1995] 3 WLUK 94; 67 T.C. 275; [1995] S.T.I. 433; *Times*, March 17, 1995; *Independent*, May 1, 1995 CA (Civ Div) ............................................................................. 6-056, 6-062
Ede (Inspector of Taxes) v Wilson & Cornwall [1945] 1 All E.R. 367 KBD ............ 35-089
Eden Consulting Services (Richmond) Ltd v Revenue and Customs Commissioners [2017] UKFTT 596 (TC); [2017] 8 WLUK 6 FTT (Tax) ........................... 17-008, 18-193
Edwards v Roberts 19 T.C. 618 CA .................................................. 24-055
Edwards (Inspector of Taxes) v Bairstow; joined case(s) Edwards (Inspector of Taxes) v Harrison [1956] A.C. 14; [1955] 3 W.L.R. 410; [1955] 3 All E.R. 48; [1955] 7 WLUK 81; 48 R. & I.T. 534; 36 T.C. 207; (1955) 34 A.T.C. 198; [1955] T.R. 209; (1955) 99 S.J. 558 HL ................................................................................. 8-021
Edwards (Inspector of Taxes) v Clinch [1982] A.C. 845; [1981] 3 W.L.R. 707; [1981] 3 All E.R. 543; [1981] S.T.C. 617; [1981] 10 WLUK 235; 56 T.C. 367; [1981] T.R. 393; (1981) 125 S.J. 762; *Times*, October 23, 1981 HL ........................................... 2-018
Emery v Inland Revenue Commissioners [1981] S.T.C. 150; [1980] 1 WLUK 98; 54 T.C. 607; [1980] T.R. 447 Ch D ............................................................ 18-031
E.ON UK Plc v Revenue and Customs Commissioners [2023] EWCA Civ 1383; [2024] S.T.C. 59; [2023] 11 WLUK 581; [2024] Pens. L.R. 5; [2023] B.T.C. 31; [2023] S.T.I. 1665 CA (Civ Div) ..................................................................... 22-029
Equity Trust (Singapore) Ltd v Revenue and Customs Commissioners, sub nom. TMF Trustees Singapore Ltd v Revenue and Customs Commissioners [2012] EWCA Civ 192; [2012] S.T.C. 998; [2012] 3 WLUK 108; [2012] S.T.I. 545 CA (Civ Div) . 31-005, 31-016, 31-022, 33-015, 34-014, 34-016
European Commission v Spain (C-151/12) EU:C:2013:690; [2013] 10 WLUK 752 ECJ ... 33-015
European Parliament v Council of the European Union (C-48/14) EU:C:2015:91; [2015] 2 WLUK 391 ECJ ....................................................................... 33-015
Executors of Clark v Revenue and Customs Commissioners [2019] UKFTT 473 (TC); [2019] 6 WLUK 733 FTT (Tax) ........................................................ 35-037
Fernance v Wreckair Pty Ltd [1992] 9 WLUK 88; [1993] Pens. L.R. 191 District Ct (NSW) ...... 13-005
Finanzamt Koln-Nord v Becker (C-104/12) EU:C:2013:99; [2013] 2 WLUK 578 ECJ ..... 22-008
Fisher v Revenue and Customs Commissioners [2021] EWCA Civ 1438; [2022] 1 W.L.R. 651; [2021] S.T.C. 2072; [2021] 10 WLUK 27; [2021] B.T.C. 29; [2021] S.T.I. 2283 CA (Civ Div) ..................................................................... 25-061, 25-076
Flavel's Will Trusts, Re, sub nom. Coleman v Flavel [1969] 1 W.L.R. 444; [1969] 2 All E.R. 232; [1969] 2 WLUK 64; (1969) 113 S.J. 189 Ch D ............................ 37-007
Foley v Fletcher 157 E.R. 678; (1858) 3 Hurl. & N. 769; [1858] 11 WLUK 77; (1858) 28 L.J. Ex. 100 Ex Ct .................................................................. 13-024, 29-060
Forde & McHugh Ltd v Revenue and Customs Commissioners, sub nom. Revenue and Customs Commissioners v Forde & McHugh Ltd [2014] UKSC 14; [2014] 1 W.L.R. 810; [2014] 2 All E.R. 356; [2014] S.T.C. 724; [2014] 2 WLUK 840; [2014] I.C.R. 403; [2014] Pens. L.R. 203; 82 T.C. 165; [2014] B.T.C. 8; [2014] S.T.I. 739 SC .. 6-138, 6-139, 24-055, 24-056, 24-058, 26-070, 27-141, 35-038, 35-092, 36-018, 38-004, 38-009
Forsakringsaktiebolaget Skandia v Riksskatteverket (C-422/01), sub nom. Ramstedt v Riksskatteverket (C-422/01) EU:C:2003:380; [2003] S.T.C. 1361; [2003] E.C.R. I-6817; [2003] 6 WLUK 670; [2004] 1 C.M.L.R. 4; [2003] All E.R. (EC) 831; [2003] C.E.C. 484; [2004] O.P.L.R. 253; [2003] Pens. L.R. 189; [2003] B.T.C. 435; 5 I.T.L. Rep. 1042; [2003] S.T.I. 1874 ECJ (5th Chamber) ....................................... 24-004
Forsyth v Revenue and Customs Commissioners [2014] UKFTT 915 (TC); [2014] 9 WLUK 526; [2014] S.T.I. 3430 FTT (Tax) ........................................ 35-036
Foskett v McKeown [2001] 1 A.C. 102; [2000] 2 W.L.R. 1299; [2000] 3 All E.R. 97; [2000] 5 WLUK 521; [2000] Lloyd's Rep. I.R. 627; [2000] W.T.L.R. 667; (1999-2000) 2 I.T.E.L.R. 711; (2000) 97(23) L.S.G. 44; *Times*, May 24, 2000; *Independent*, July 3, 2000 HL ....................................................................... 18-043, 18-069
Fothergill v Monarch Airlines Ltd [1981] A.C. 251; [1980] 3 W.L.R. 209; [1980] 2 All E.R. 696; [1980] 2 Lloyd's Rep. 295; [1980] 7 WLUK 141; (1980) 124 S.J. 512 HL ......... 29-004
Fowler v Revenue and Customs Commissioners [2020] UKSC 22; [2020] 1 W.L.R. 2227; [2021] 1 All E.R. 97; [2020] S.T.C. 1476; [2020] 5 WLUK 264; [2020] B.T.C. 15; 22 I.T.L. Rep. 679; [2020] S.T.I. 1315; *Times*, June 2, 2020 SC ...... 29-005, 29-007, 29-008, 29-039

# TABLE OF CASES

Fox v Stirk, sub nom. Ricketts v City of Cambridge Electoral Registration Officer; Ricketts v Registration Officer for the City of Cambridge [1970] 2 Q.B. 463; [1970] 3 W.L.R. 147; [1970] 3 All E.R. 7; [1970] 5 WLUK 37; 68 L.G.R. 644; (1970) 114 S.J. 397 CA (Civ Div) .................................................................... 24-010
Fryer v Revenue and Customs Commissioners [2010] UKFTT 87 (TC); [2010] 2 WLUK 497; [2010] S.F.T.D. 632; [2010] W.T.L.R. 815 FTT (Tax) .......................... 28-069
Garforth (Inspector of Taxes) v Newsmith Stainless Ltd [1979] 1 W.L.R. 409; [1979] 2 All E.R. 73; [1979] S.T.C. 129; [1978] 11 WLUK 148; 52 T.C. 522; [1978] T.R. 477; (1978) 122 S.J. 828 Ch D .................................................... 2-055, 2-059
Gartside v Inland Revenue Commissioners, sub nom. Gartside's Will Trusts, Re [1968] A.C. 553; [1968] 2 W.L.R. 277; [1968] 1 All E.R. 121; [1967] 12 WLUK 56; (1967) 46 A.T.C. 323; [1967] T.R. 309; (1967) 111 S.J. 982; *Times*, December 14, 1967 HL ........ 28-003
Gaspet Ltd (formerly Saga Petroleum (UK)) v Elliss (Inspector of Taxes) [1987] 1 W.L.R. 769; [1987] S.T.C. 362; [1987] 3 WLUK 15; (1987) 84 L.S.G. 1241 CA (Civ Div) ... 6-018, 9-005, 26-007
Gasque v Inland Revenue Commissioners [1940] 2 K.B. 80; [1940] 4 WLUK 50 KBD .... 35-101
Goodwin v Curtis (Inspector of Taxes) [1998] S.T.C. 475; [1998] 2 WLUK 346; 70 T.C. 478; [1998] B.T.C. 176; (1998) 95(12) L.S.G. 27; (1998) 142 S.J.L.B. 91; *Times*, March 2, 1998; *Independent*, March 2, 1998 CA (Civ Div) ............................... 24-010
Gough v Revenue and Customs Commissioners [2021] UKFTT 273 (TC); [2021] 7 WLUK 596 FTT (Tax) .................................................................. 10-038, 10-039
Goyal v Goyal [2016] EWCA Civ 792; [2016] 4 W.L.R. 140; [2016] 7 WLUK 869; [2017] 2 F.L.R. 223; [2017] 1 F.C.R. 174; [2016] Fam. Law 1220 CA (Civ Div) ............... 25-074
Granada Group Ltd v Law Debenture Pension Trust Corp Plc [2016] EWCA Civ 1289; [2017] Bus. L.R. 870; [2016] 12 WLUK 443; [2017] B.C.C. 57; [2017] 2 B.C.L.C. 1; [2017] Pens. L.R. 5 CA (Civ Div) .................................................. 38-001
Grant v Watton (Inspector of Taxes), sub nom. Andrew Grant Services Ltd v Watton (Inspector of Taxes) [1999] S.T.C. 330; [1999] 2 WLUK 182; 71 T.C. 333; [1999] B.T.C. 85; *Times*, March 31, 1999; *Independent*, March 1, 1999 Ch D ........................ 2-091
Gratton v Revenue and Customs Commissioners, sub nom. Revenue and Customs Commissioners v Gretton [2012] UKUT 261 (TCC); [2012] S.T.C. 2061; [2012] 7 WLUK 674; [2012] B.T.C. 1656; [2012] S.T.I. 2463 UT (Tax) ............................... 33-004
Gray v Inland Revenue Commissioners, sub nom. Executors of Lady Fox v Inland Revenue Commissioners; Lady Fox's Executors v Inland Revenue Commissioners [1994] S.T.C. 360; [1994] 2 WLUK 137; [1994] 2 E.G.L.R. 185; [1994] 38 E.G. 156; [1994] R.V.R. 129; [1994] S.T.I. 208; [1994] E.G. 32 (C.S.); [1994] N.P.C. 15; *Times*, February 24, 1994 CA (Civ Div) ................................................................. 11-011
Green v Revenue and Customs Commissioners [2014] UKFTT 396 (TC); [2014] 4 WLUK 734; [2014] S.T.I. 2235 FTT (Tax) ................................................ 11-011
Grenfell v The Dean and Canons of Windsor and Others 48 E.R. 1292; (1840) 2 Beav. 544; [1840] 6 WLUK 104 Ct of Chancery ............................................. 26-034
Griffin (Inspector of Taxes) v Citibank Investments Ltd, sub nom. Citibank Investments Ltd v Griffin (Inspector of Taxes) [2000] S.T.C. 1010; [2000] 11 WLUK 23; 73 T.C. 352; [2000] B.T.C. 324; [2000] S.T.I. 1546; (2000) 97(45) L.S.G. 42; (2000) 144 S.J.L.B. 266; *Times*, November 14, 2000 Ch D ............................................... 2-092
Hallett's Estate, Re, sub nom. Knatchbull v Hallett (1880) 13 Ch. D. 696; [1880] 2 WLUK 20 CA ............................................................................ 37-026
Hanbury, Re, sub nom. Comiskey v Hanbury [1962] 1 WLUK 269; 38 T.C. 588 CA ....... 6-150, 13-024, 26-060, 29-060
Hancock (Surveyor of Taxes) v General Reversionary and Investment Co Ltd [1919] 1 K.B. 25; [1918] 10 WLUK 2 KBD ................................................... 22-029
Hargreaves v Revenue and Customs Commissioners [2022] UKUT 34 (TCC); [2022] S.T.C. 455; [2022] 2 WLUK 220; [2022] B.T.C. 504; [2022] S.F.T.D. 258; [2022] S.T.I. 309 UT (Tax) ...................................................................... 6-016
Hargreaves Lansdown Asset Management Ltd v Revenue and Customs Commissioners [2019] UKUT 246 (TCC); [2019] S.T.C. 1745; [2019] 8 WLUK 36; [2019] B.T.C. 522; [2019] S.T.I. 1483 UT (Tax) ....................................................... 26-060, 29-060
Harmony & Montague Tin and Copper Mining Co, Re, sub nom. Spargo's Case (1872-73) L.R. 8 Ch. App. 407; [1861-73] All E.R. Rep. 261; [1873] 6 WLUK 120 CA in Chancery ... 2-061
Harris v Lord Shuttleworth [1993] 11 WLUK 313; [1994] I.C.R. 991; [1994] I.R.L.R. 547; [1994] Pens. L.R. 47; *Independent*, November 26, 1993 CA (Civ Div) .... 13-005, 15-019, 35-024, 35-027
Harris v Revenue and Customs Commissioners [2010] UKFTT 385 (TC); [2010] 8 WLUK

## TABLE OF CASES

216; [2010] S.F.T.D. 1159; [2011] W.T.L.R. 55 FTT (Tax) ............................ 18-100
Hartland v Diggines (Inspector of Taxes) [1926] A.C. 289; (1926) 24 Ll. L. Rep. 94; [1926]
    1 WLUK 89 HL ........................................................................ 24-055
Haseldine v Revenue and Customs Commissioners [2012] UKFTT 480 (TC); [2012] 7
    WLUK 950; [2012] S.T.I. 3166 FTT (Tax) ........................... 29-025, 29-026, 34-043
Hay & Co v Torbet 1908 S.C. 781; (1907) 15 S.L.T. 627; [1907] 12 WLUK 63 IH (2 Div) .. 37-026
Heaton (Inspector of Taxes) v Bell [1970] A.C. 728; [1969] 2 W.L.R. 735; [1969] 2 All
    E.R. 70; [1969] 3 WLUK 43; (1969) 48 A.T.C. 73; [1969] T.R. 77; (1969) 113 S.J. 245
    HL. ........................................................... 6-139, 24-055, 24-062
Henwood v Barlow Clowes International Ltd (In Liquidation) [2008] EWCA Civ 577;
    [2008] 5 WLUK 584; [2008] B.P.I.R. 778; [2008] N.P.C. 61; *Times*, June 18, 2008 CA
    (Civ Div). ............................................................................ 39-005
Hills v Revenue and Customs Commissioners [2016] UKUT 189 (TCC); [2016] 4 WLUK
    523; [2016] B.V.C. 513 UT (Tax). ..................................................... 6-150
Hillsdown Holdings Plc v Inland Revenue Commissioners; joined case(s) R. v Inland
    Revenue Commissioners Ex p. Hillsdown Holdings Plc [1999] S.T.C. 561; [1999] 3
    WLUK 177; [1999] O.P.L.R. 79; [1999] Pens. L.R. 173; 71 T.C. 356; [1999] B.T.C. 194;
    *Times*, May 13, 1999; *Independent*, March 22, 1999 Ch D ..... 2-053, 2-055, 2-065, 2-066, 2-067,
                                                                        2-072, 2-076, 2-079
Hirst v Revenue and Customs Commissioners [2014] UKFTT 924 (TC); [2014] 9 WLUK
    630; [2015] S.T.I. 135 FTT (Tax). .................................................... 2-017
HMRC v Gresh & RBC Trust Company (Guernsey) Ltd (2009-10) G.L.R. 239 .......... 39-016
HMRC v Knowledgepoint 360 Group Ltd [2013] UKUT 007 ........................ 35-021
Hochstrasser (Inspector of Taxes) v Mayes; joined case(s) Jennings v Kinder (Inspector of
    Taxes) [1960] A.C. 376; [1960] 2 W.L.R. 63; [1959] 3 All E.R. 817; [1959] 11 WLUK
    120; 53 R. & I.T. 12; 38 T.C. 673; (1959) 38 A.T.C. 360; [1959] T.R. 355 HL ..... 24-055, 35-075
Hoey v Revenue and Customs Commissioners [2022] EWCA Civ 656; [2022] S.T.C. 902;
    [2022] 5 WLUK 150; [2022] B.T.C. 15; [2022] S.T.I. 820 CA (Civ Div)... 19-026, 27-112, 35-070
Holland v Hodgson (1871-72) L.R. 7 C.P. 328; [1872] 5 WLUK 58 Ex Chamber .......... 9-016
Hoover Ltd v Hetherington [2002] EWHC 1052 (Ch); [2002] 5 WLUK 748; [2002]
    O.P.L.R. 267; [2002] Pens. L.R. 297 Ch D ........................... 35-024, 35-028, 35-029
HSBC Life (UK) Ltd v Stubbs (Inspector of Taxes); joined case(s) Abbey Life Assurance
    Co Ltd v Colclough (Inspector of Taxes); Lloyds TSB Life Assurance Co Ltd v
    Colclough (Inspector of Taxes); Nationwide Life Ltd v Crisp (Inspector of Taxes); TSB
    Life Ltd v Colclough (Inspector of Taxes) [2001] 11 WLUK 148; [2002] S.T.C. (S.C.D.)
    9; [2001] S.T.I. 1667 Sp Comm ....................................................... 2-086
Hudson v Gribble 4 T.C. 522 .......................................................... 24-055
Hydrodan (Corby) Ltd (In Liquidation), Re, sub nom. Hydrodam (Corby) Ltd (In Liquida-
    tion), Re [1993] 12 WLUK 265; [1994] B.C.C. 161; [1994] 2 B.C.L.C. 180; *Times*,
    February 19, 1994 Ch D .............................................................. 2-018
Hymanson v Revenue and Customs Commissioners [2018] UKFTT 667 (TC); [2018] 11
    WLUK 293 FTT (Tax). ........................................ 10-033, 10-035, 10-036, 10-037, 18-194
Iliffe News & Media Ltd v Revenue and Customs Commissioners [2012] UKFTT 696
    (TC); [2012] 11 WLUK 30; [2014] F.S.R. 6; [2013] S.F.T.D. 309; [2013] S.T.I. 388 FTT
    (Tax) ............................................................................... 36-010
Inco Europe Ltd v First Choice Distribution [2000] 1 W.L.R. 586; [2000] 2 All E.R. 109;
    [2000] 1 All E.R. (Comm) 674; [2000] 1 Lloyd's Rep. 467; [2000] 3 WLUK 267; [2000]
    C.L.C. 1015; [2000] B.L.R. 259; (2000) 2 T.C.L.R. 487; 74 Con. L.R. 55; (2000) 97(12)
    L.S.G. 39; (2000) 144 S.J.L.B. 134; [2000] N.P.C. 22; *Times*, March 10, 2000; *Independ-
    ent*, March 15, 2000 HL. ....................................................... 6-016, 31-032
Ingram v Inland Revenue Commissioners [2000] 1 A.C. 293; [1999] 2 W.L.R. 90; [1999] 1
    All E.R. 297; [1999] S.T.C. 37; [1998] 12 WLUK 241; [1999] L. & T.R. 85; [1998]
    B.T.C. 8047; [1998] E.G. 181 (C.S.); (1999) 96(3) L.S.G. 33; (1999) 143 S.J.L.B. 52;
    [1998] N.P.C. 160; *Times*, December 16, 1998; *Independent*, December 15, 1998 HL ..... 21-053,
                                                                                              21-054
Inland Revenue Commissioner v Cosmotron Manufacturing Co Ltd [1997] 1 W.L.R. 1288;
    [1997] S.T.C. 1134; [1997] 7 WLUK 574; 70 T.C. 292; [1997] B.T.C. 465; (1997) 141
    S.J.L.B. 215 PC (HK). ................................................................ 6-059
Inland Revenue Commissioners v Botnar [1999] S.T.C. 711; [1999] 6 WLUK 318; 72 T.C.
    205; [1999] B.T.C. 267; *Times*, July 6, 1999 CA (Civ Div) ........................... 25-067
Inland Revenue Commissioners v Brackett, sub nom. Brackett v Chater (Inspector of
    Taxes); Charter v Brackett [1986] S.T.C. 521; [1986] 1 WLUK 694; [1987] 1 F.T.L.R. 8;
    60 T.C. 134 Ch D .................................................................... 25-053

## TABLE OF CASES

Inland Revenue Commissioners v Brebner [1967] 2 A.C. 18; [1967] 2 W.L.R. 1001; [1967] 1 All E.R. 779; 1967 S.C. (H.L.) 31; 1967 S.L.T. 113; [1967] 2 WLUK 88; 43 T.C. 705; (1967) 46 A.T.C. 17; [1967] T.R. 21; (1967) 111 S.J. 216 HL (SC). 25-076, 25-077, 36-010, 36-011
Inland Revenue Commissioners v Church Commissioners for England [1977] A.C. 329; [1976] 3 W.L.R. 214; [1976] 2 All E.R. 1037; [1976] S.T.C. 339; [1976] 7 WLUK 39; 50 T.C. 516; [1976] T.R. 187; (1976) 120 S.J. 505 HL ................................. 2-094
Inland Revenue Commissioners v Commerzbank AG; joined case(s) Inland Revenue Commissioners v Banco do Brasil SA [1990] S.T.C. 285; [1990] 2 WLUK 138; (1990) 87(13) L.S.G. 44; *Times*, February 22, 1990; *Independent*, February 26, 1990 Ch D ............. 29-004
Inland Revenue Commissioners v Crossman, sub nom. Crossman, Re; Paulin, Re; joined case(s) Inland Revenue Commissioners v Mann [1937] A.C. 26; [1936] 1 All E.R. 762; [1936] 3 WLUK 52 HL........................................................................ 21-005
Inland Revenue Commissioners v Dean Property Co 1939 S.C. 545; 1939 S.L.T. 411; [1939] 6 WLUK 12 IH (1 Div)................................................................ 8-025
Inland Revenue Commissioners v Desoutter Bros Ltd [1946] 1 All E.R. 58; [1945] 11 WLUK 38 CA..................................................................................... 8-018
Inland Revenue Commissioners v Herdman [1969] 1 W.L.R. 323; [1969] 1 All E.R. 495; [1968] 1 WLUK 657; (1969) 48 A.T.C. 1; [1969] T.R. 1; (1969) 113 S.J. 127 HL .. 25-057, 25-073
Inland Revenue Commissioners v Leiner [1964] 1 WLUK 288; 41 T.C. 589; (1964) 43 A.T.C. 56; [1964] T.R. 63............................................... 25-024, 25-093, 35-021
Inland Revenue Commissioners v Levy [1982] S.T.C. 442; [1982] 1 WLUK 190; 56 T.C. 68; [1982] B.T.C. 235; (1982) 79 L.S.G. 988; (1982) 126 S.J. 413 DC .... 18-121, 25-025, 25-031, 25-067, 28-032
Inland Revenue Commissioners v Lysaght, sub nom. Lysaght v Inland Revenue Commissioners [1928] A.C. 234; [1928] All E.R. Rep. 575; [1928] 3 WLUK 25; 13 T.C. 511 HL ............................................................................................. 24-010
Inland Revenue Commissioners v Macpherson [1989] A.C. 159; [1988] 2 W.L.R. 1261; [1988] 2 All E.R. 753; [1988] S.T.C. 362; [1988] 5 WLUK 181; [1988] 2 F.T.L.R. 199; [1988] B.T.C. 8065; (1988) 132 S.J. 821 HL ............................... 21-036, 25-057
Inland Revenue Commissioners v Montgomery [1975] Ch. 266; [1975] 2 W.L.R. 326; [1975] 1 All E.R. 664; [1975] S.T.C. 182; [1974] 12 WLUK 43; 49 T.C. 679; [1974] T.R. 377; (1975) 119 S.J. 152 Ch D ............................................................ 8-033
Inland Revenue Commissioners v Parker, sub nom. Tomlinson v Inland Revenue Commissioners [1966] A.C. 141; [1966] 2 W.L.R. 486; [1966] 1 All E.R. 399; [1966] 1 WLUK 1053; 43 T.C. 396; (1966) 45 A.T.C. 1; [1966] T.R. 1; (1966) 110 S.J. 91 HL...... 36-010
Inland Revenue Commissioners v Plummer [1980] A.C. 896; [1979] 3 W.L.R. 689; [1979] 3 All E.R. 775; [1979] S.T.C. 793; [1979] 11 WLUK 2; 54 T.C. 1; [1979] T.R. 339; (1979) 123 S.J. 769 HL .................................................. 25-024, 35-021, 35-034
Inland Revenue Commissioners v Port of London Authority, sub nom. Port of London Authority v Inland Revenue Commissioners [1923] A.C. 507; (1923) 15 Ll. L. Rep. 139; [1923] 5 WLUK 18 HL.................................................................... 2-093
Inland Revenue Commissioners v Pratt [1982] S.T.C. 756; [1982] 1 WLUK 191; 57 T.C. 1; (1982) 79 L.S.G. 1444 .............................................................. 25-061
Inland Revenue Commissioners v Reinhold 1953 S.C. 49; 1953 S.L.T. 94; [1953] 1 WLUK 486; 46 R. & I.T. 108; 34 T.C. 389; (1953) 32 A.T.C. 10; [1953] T.R. 11 IH (1 Div) .. 8-020, 8-025
Inland Revenue Commissioners v Wachtel [1971] Ch. 573; [1970] 3 W.L.R. 857; [1971] 1 All E.R. 271; [1970] 7 WLUK 101; 46 T.C. 543; [1970] T.R. 195; (1970) 114 S.J. 705 Ch D ..................................................................................... 25-035
Inland Revenue Commissioners v Willoughby [1997] 1 W.L.R. 1071; [1997] 4 All E.R. 65; [1997] S.T.C. 995; [1997] 7 WLUK 218; 70 T.C. 57; [1997] B.T.C. 393; (1997) 94(29) L.S.G. 28; (1997) 147 N.L.J. 1062; (1997) 141 S.J.L.B. 176; *Times*, July 16, 1997 HL .... 25-053, 25-073, 25-074, 25-076, 25-077
Inland Revenue Commissioners v Zorab 11 T.C. 289 ............................. 24-010
International Power v Healey [2001] P.L.R. 121 ................................ 17-006
Irby v Revenue and Customs Commissioners [2012] UKFTT 291 (TC); [2012] 4 WLUK 416; [2012] S.T.I. 2246 FTT (Tax)................................................. 3-025
IRC v Doncaster (1924) 8 T.C. 623 .............................................. 2-060
IRC v Hogarth (1940) 23 T.C. 491; 1941 S.C. 1 ................................ 13-032
Irving v Revenue and Customs Commissioners [2008] EWCA Civ 6; [2008] S.T.C. 597; [2008] 1 WLUK 429; [2008] Pens. L.R. 197; 79 T.C. 836; [2008] B.T.C. 36; [2008] S.T.I. 186 CA (Civ Div) ..... 2-054, 6-010, 6-012, 6-128, 6-130, 35-021, 35-080, 38-015, 38-016, 38-018
ITC v Sutherland [1952] A.C. 469; [1952] 6 WLUK 17; (1952) 31 A.T.C. 419 ........... 24-062

# TABLE OF CASES

J and A Young (Leicester) Ltd v Revenue and Customs Commissioners [2015] UKFTT 638 (TC); [2015] 12 WLUK 197 FTT (Tax).............................. 9-014, 9-015, 18-032

J Bibby & Sons Ltd (Pension Trust Deed), Re, sub nom. Davies v Inland Revenue Commissioners [1952] 2 All E.R. 483; [1952] 2 T.L.R. 297; [1952] 7 WLUK 29; 45 R. & I.T. 722; (1952) 31 A.T.C. 355; [1952] T.R. 321; [1952] W.N. 402; (1952) 96 S.J. 580 Ch D ..................................................................... 21-088

Jackson v Revenue and Customs Commissioners [2017] UKFTT 341 (TC); [2017] 4 WLUK 405 FTT (Tax)..................................................... 3-025

James Buchanan & Co Ltd v Babco Forwarding & Shipping (UK) Ltd [1978] A.C. 141; [1977] 3 W.L.R. 907; [1977] 3 All E.R. 1048; [1978] 1 Lloyd's Rep. 119; [1977] 11 WLUK 64; [1978] R.T.R. 59; [1978] 1 C.M.L.R. 156; (1977) 121 S.J. 811 HL........... 29-004

Jenkins v IRC 26 T.C. 265 ............................................................ 25-035

Jenkinson (Inspector of Taxes) v Freedland [1961] 7 WLUK 9; 39 T.C. 636; (1961) 40 A.T.C. 190; [1961] T.R. 181; (1961) 105 S.J. 609 CA.............................. 8-025

John Mander Pension Scheme Trustees Ltd v Revenue and Customs Commissioners [2015] UKSC 56; [2015] 1 W.L.R. 3857; [2015] 4 All E.R. 896; [2015] S.T.C. 2231; [2015] 7 WLUK 877; [2015] B.T.C. 25; [2015] S.T.I. 2530; Times, August 11, 2015 SC........... 19-026

Johnson v Holleran (Inspector of Taxes) [1989] S.T.C. 1; [1989] 1 WLUK 500; 62 T.C. 428; Times, December 3, 1988 ........................................... 13-017, 29-041

Johnson v Johnson [1952] P. 47; [1952] 1 All E.R. 250; [1952] 1 T.L.R. 309; [1951] 12 WLUK 67; (1952) 96 S.J. 131 CA............................................... 18-031

Jones v Garnett (Inspector of Taxes) [2007] UKHL 35; [2007] 1 W.L.R. 2030; [2007] 4 All E.R. 857; [2008] Bus. L.R. 425; [2007] S.T.C. 1536; [2007] 7 WLUK 722; [2007] I.C.R. 1259; [2007] 3 F.C.R. 487; 78 T.C. 597; [2007] B.T.C. 476; [2007] W.T.L.R. 1229; [2007] S.T.I. 1899; (2007) 157 N.L.J. 1118; (2007) 151 S.J.L.B. 1024; Times, August 9, 2007 HL .......................... 22-018, 25-019, 25-023, 25-025, 25-031, 25-037, 28-032

JP Whitter (Waterwell Engineers) Ltd v Revenue and Customs Commissioners, sub nom. JP Whitter (Water Well Engineers) Ltd v Revenue and Customs Commissioners [2018] UKSC 31; [2018] 1 W.L.R. 3117; [2018] 4 All E.R. 95; [2018] S.T.C. 1394; [2018] 6 WLUK 227; [2018] B.T.C. 24; [2018] S.T.I. 1110; Times, June 20, 2018 SC .............. 4-025

JTC Employer Ser Trustees Ltd v Khadem [2021] EWHC 2929 (Ch); [2021] 11 WLUK 34; [2022] W.T.L.R. 203 Ch D ........................................................... 29-012

Kempe v Inland Revenue Commissioners [2004] 7 WLUK 625; [2004] S.T.C. (S.C.D.) 467; [2004] W.T.L.R. 955; [2004] S.T.I. 1941 Sp Comm............................. 28-076

Kensington Income Tax General Commissioners v Aramayo, sub nom. R. v Kensington Income Tax Commissioners Ex p. Aramayo [1916] 1 A.C. 215; [1915] 7 WLUK 76 HL.... 35-053

Kent v Revenue and Customs Commissioners [2009] UKFTT 358 (TC); [2009] 12 WLUK 341; [2010] S.T.I. 685 FTT (Tax)........................................................ 2-019

Kerr v British Leyland (Staff) Trustees Ltd [1986] 3 WLUK 306; [2001] W.T.L.R. 1071 CA (Civ Div)......................................................................... 21-088

Kerrison v Revenue and Customs Commissioners [2019] UKUT 8 (TCC); [2019] 4 W.L.R. 8; [2019] S.T.C. 614; [2019] 1 WLUK 254; [2019] B.T.C. 502; [2019] S.T.I. 625 UT (Tax) ............................................................................... 2-117

Khoo Tek Keong v Ch'ng Joo Tuan Neoh [1934] A.C. 529; [1934] 7 WLUK 38 PC (Shanghai) .................................................................... 8-018, 18-033

Killik and Co LLP v Revenue and Customs Commissioners [2023] UKFTT 653 (TC); [2023] 7 WLUK 553; [2023] S.F.T.D. 1101 FTT (Tax).................................. 6-016

Kuehne & Nagel Drinks Logistics Ltd v Revenue and Customs Commissioners [2012] EWCA Civ 34; [2012] S.T.C. 840; [2012] 1 WLUK 580; [2012] B.T.C. 58; [2012] S.T.I. 221 CA (Civ Div)................................................................... 22-029

Lady Lloyd-Webber v Revenue and Customs Commissioners, sub nom. Lord Lloyd-Webber v Revenue and Customs Commissioners [2019] UKFTT 717 (TC); [2019] 12 WLUK 165; [2020] S.F.T.D. 346 FTT (Tax) ............................................ 22-029

Landau (A Bankrupt), Re, sub nom. L (A Bankrupt), Re; Pointer v Landau [1998] Ch. 223; [1997] 3 W.L.R. 225; [1997] 3 All E.R. 322; [1996] 12 WLUK 328; [1997] 2 B.C.L.C. 515; [1997] 2 F.L.R. 660; [1997] B.P.I.R. 229; [1996] O.P.L.R. 371; [1997] Pens. L.R. 25; [1998] Fam. Law 68; (1997) 94(4) L.S.G. 25; (1997) 141 S.J.L.B. 28; Times, January 1, 1997 Ch D .............................................................. 18-066, 21-054

Landid Property Ltd v Revenue and Customs Commissioners [2017] UKFTT 692 (TC); [2017] 9 WLUK 171; [2017] S.T.I. 2631 FTT (Tax) .................................. 24-043

Law v Coburn, sub nom. Bonar Law v Coburn (Inspector of taxes) [1972] 1 W.L.R. 1238; [1972] 3 All E.R. 1115; [1972] 6 WLUK 37; [1972] T.R. 133; (1972) 116 S.J. 666 Ch D ... 18-056

Learoyd v Whiteley, sub nom. Whiteley v Learoyd; Whiteley, Re (1887) 12 App. Cas. 727;

## TABLE OF CASES

| | |
|---|---|
| [1887] 8 WLUK 4 HL. | 8-002 |
| Lee v IRC 24 T.C. 207 | 2-093 |
| Lee v Lee's Air Farming Ltd [1961] A.C. 12; [1960] 3 W.L.R. 758; [1960] 3 All E.R. 420; [1960] 10 WLUK 37; (1960) 104 S.J. 869 PC (NZ). | 2-018 |
| Lee-Verhulst (Investments) Ltd v Harwood Trust [1973] Q.B. 204; [1972] 3 W.L.R. 772; [1972] 3 All E.R. 619; [1972] 7 WLUK 99; (1972) 24 P. & C.R. 346; (1972) 116 S.J. 801 CA (Civ Div). | 9-024 |
| Levene v Inland Revenue Commissioners [1928] A.C. 217; [1928] All E.R. Rep. 746; [1928] 3 WLUK 26; 13 T.C. 486 HL | 24-010 |
| Lewis Emanuel & Son Ltd v White 42 T.C. 369 | 8-023 |
| LG Berry Investments Ltd v Attwooll (Inspector of Taxes) [1964] 1 W.L.R. 693; [1964] 2 All E.R. 126; [1964] 3 WLUK 52; 41 T.C. 547; (1964) 43 A.T.C. 61; [1964] T.R. 67; (1964) 108 S.J. 318 Ch D. | 6-056, 6-064, 6-065 |
| Linotype and Machinery Ltd v C&E Comrs (1978) V.A.T.T.R. 123 | 22-008 |
| Lion Co v Revenue and Customs Commissioners [2009] UKFTT 357 (TC); [2009] 12 WLUK 282; [2010] S.F.T.D. 454; [2010] S.T.I. 683 FTT (Tax) | 6-127 |
| Lloyds & Scottish Finance v Cyril Lord Carpet Sales [1979] 3 WLUK 256; [1992] B.C.L.C. 609; (1979) 129 N.L.J. 366 HL. | 2-086 |
| Lobler v Revenue and Customs Commissioners [2015] UKUT 152 (TCC); [2015] S.T.C. 1893; [2015] 3 WLUK 811; [2015] B.T.C. 515; [2015] S.T.I. 1398 UT (Tax) | 10-034 |
| Lord Vestey's Executors v Inland Revenue Commissioners; joined case(s) Lord Vestey's Executors v Colquhoun (Inspector of Taxes) [1949] 1 All E.R. 1108; [1949] 5 WLUK 16; (1949) 42 R. & I.T. 325; (1949) 42 R. & I.T. 314; 31 T.C. 1; [1949] T.R. 149; [1949] W.N. 233 HL. | 18-121, 25-035, 25-067, 28-032 |
| Lott v Revenue and Customs Commissioners [2014] UKFTT 947 (TC); [2014] 10 WLUK 198 FTT (Tax). | 7-002 |
| Lowe v Walker, sub nom. Lowe v Peters 20 T.C. 25 CA (Civ Div) | 6-129 |
| LPA Umbrella Trust, Re, sub nom. Pensions Regulator v A Admin Ltd [2014] EWHC 1378 (Ch); [2014] 5 WLUK 261; [2014] Pens. L.R. 319 Ch D. | 18-089 |
| Lynall v Inland Revenue Commissioners, sub nom. Lynall (Deceased), Re [1972] A.C. 680; [1971] 3 W.L.R. 759; [1971] 3 All E.R. 914; [1971] 10 WLUK 88; 47 T.C. 375; [1971] T.R. 309; (1971) 115 S.J. 872 HL. | 11-011, 21-005, 21-090 |
| Mackay v Revenue and Customs Commissioners [2018] UKUT 378 (TCC); [2019] S.T.C. 83; [2018] 11 WLUK 391; [2018] B.T.C. 529 UT (Tax). | 27-086, 38-001 |
| Macklin v Revenue and Customs Commissioners [2015] UKUT 39 (TCC); [2015] S.T.C. 1102; [2015] 2 WLUK 96; [2015] B.T.C. 503; 17 I.T.L. Rep. 780 UT (Tax) | 12-027, 12-029, 29-016, 29-021, 31-008, 34-010 |
| MacNiven (Inspector of Taxes) v Westmoreland Investments Ltd, sub nom. Westmoreland Investments Ltd v MacNiven (Inspector of Taxes) [2001] UKHL 6; [2003] 1 A.C. 311; [2001] 2 W.L.R. 377; [2001] 1 All E.R. 865; [2001] S.T.C. 237; [2001] 2 WLUK 213; 73 T.C. 1; [2001] B.T.C. 44; 3 I.T.L. Rep. 342; [2001] S.T.I. 168; (2001) 98(11) L.S.G. 44; (2001) 151 N.L.J. 223; (2001) 145 S.J.L.B. 55; Times, February 14, 2001; Independent, March 19, 2001 HL. | 6-010, 6-013 |
| Magraw v Lewis 18 T.C. 222 | 26-032 |
| Mairs (Inspector of Taxes) v Haughey [1994] 1 A.C. 303; [1993] 3 W.L.R. 393; [1993] 3 All E.R. 801; [1993] S.T.C. 569; [1993] 7 WLUK 266; [1993] I.R.L.R. 551; 66 T.C. 273; [1993] B.T.C. 339; Times, July 23, 1993; Independent, August 16, 1993 HL (NI) | 18-121, 22-029, 25-067, 28-032 |
| Mallalieu v Drummond (Inspector of Taxes) [1983] 2 A.C. 861; [1983] 3 W.L.R. 409; [1983] 2 All E.R. 1095; [1983] S.T.C. 665; [1983] 7 WLUK 286; 57 T.C. 330; (1983) 80 L.S.G. 2368; (1983) 133 N.L.J. 869; (1983) 127 S.J. 538 HL. | 6-045 |
| Manchester Ship Canal Co v Customs and Excise Commissioners [1982] S.T.C. 351; [1982] 1 WLUK 259 QBD. | 22-008 |
| Marks v Sherred (Inspector of Taxes) [2004] 6 WLUK 492; [2004] S.T.C. (S.C.D.) 362; [2004] W.T.L.R. 1251; [2004] S.T.I. 1729 Sp Comm. | 11-011 |
| Marley v Rawlings [2014] UKSC 2; [2015] A.C. 129; [2014] 2 W.L.R. 213; [2014] 1 All E.R. 807; [2014] 1 WLUK 446; [2014] 2 F.L.R. 555; [2015] 1 F.C.R. 187; [2014] W.T.L.R. 299; 16 I.T.E.L.R. 642; [2014] Fam. Law 466; (2014) 158(4) S.J.L.B. 49; Times, January 28, 2014 SC | 2-080 |
| Marren (Inspector of Taxes) v Ingles [1980] 1 W.L.R. 983; [1980] 3 All E.R. 95; [1980] S.T.C. 500; [1980] 7 WLUK 293; 54 T.C. 76; [1980] T.R. 335; (1980) 124 S.J. 562 HL | 2-097 |
| Marson (Inspector of Taxes) v Morton [1986] 1 W.L.R. 1343; [1986] S.T.C. 463; [1986] 7 | |

# TABLE OF CASES

WLUK 321; 59 T.C. 381; (1986) 83 L.S.G. 3161; (1986) 130 S.J. 731 Ch D .. 8-018, 8-020, 8-022, 18-033

Mattioli Woods Plc v Revenue and Customs Commissioners [2022] UKFTT 179 (TC); [2022] 6 WLUK 163 FTT (Tax) .............................................. 6-015

McCall v Revenue and Customs Commissioners [2009] NICA 12; [2009] S.T.C. 990; [2009] N.I. 245; [2009] 2 WLUK 671; 79 T.C. 758; [2009] B.T.C. 8059; [2011] W.T.L.R. 1823; [2009] S.T.I. 1124 CA (NI) ......................................... 8-018, 8-033

McCarthy v McCarthy & Stone Plc [2007] EWCA Civ 664; [2008] 1 All E.R. 221; [2007] 7 WLUK 71 CA (Civ Div). .......................................... 27-115, 35-070

McKelvey v Revenue and Customs Commissioners, sub nom. McKelvey (Deceased), Re [2008] 6 WLUK 461; [2008] S.T.C. (S.C.D.) 944; [2008] W.T.L.R. 1407; [2008] S.T.I. 1752 Sp Comm ....................................................... 21-042

McMann (Inspector of Taxes) v Shaw [1972] 1 W.L.R. 1578; [1972] 3 All E.R. 732; [1972] 3 WLUK 61; 71 L.G.R. 185; 48 T.C. 330; [1972] T.R. 47; (1972) 116 S.J. 903 Ch D ...... 13-017, 29-041

McWhinnie v Revenue and Customs Commissioners [2013] UKFTT 588 (TC); [2013] 10 WLUK 590; [2014] Pens. L.R. 1 FTT (Tax) ................................. 38-012

Medical Defence Union Ltd v Department of Trade [1980] Ch. 82; [1979] 2 W.L.R. 686; [1979] 2 All E.R. 421; [1979] 1 Lloyd's Rep. 499; [1978] 12 WLUK 176; [1979] E.C.C. 101; (1979) 123 S.J. 338 Ch D ........................................... 18-121

Meredith-Hardy v McLellan [1995] S.T.C. (SC D) 270 ................... 13-011, 26-034

Michael O'Sullivan v Canada Life Assurance (Ireland) Ltd [2014] IEHC 217 ........... 29-032

Mihlenstedt v Barclays Bank International Ltd [1989] 7 WLUK 394; [1989] I.R.L.R. 522; [1989] Pens. L.R. 91; *Times*, August 18, 1989; *Independent*, August 25, 1989 CA (Civ Div). ............................................................. 21-088

Moffat v Revenue and Customs Commissioners [2006] 4 WLUK 260; [2006] S.T.C. (S.C.D.) 380; [2006] S.T.I. 1519 Sp Comm ............................. 35-018, 35-039

Morgan Lloyd Trustees Ltd v Revenue and Customs Commissioners [2017] UKFTT 131 (TC); [2017] 2 WLUK 21 FTT (Tax) .... 5-027, 5-028, 5-046, 5-048, 5-049, 9-017, 9-018, 18-002, 18-183

Mortimore v The Commissioners of Inland Revenue 159 E.R. 347; (1864) 2 Hurl. & C. 838; [1864] 1 WLUK 252 Ex Ct. ........................................... 2-097

Moss Empires Ltd v Inland Revenue Commissioners [1937] A.C. 785; [1937] 3 All E.R. 381; 1937 S.C. (H.L.) 35; 1937 S.L.T. 433; [1937] 6 WLUK 34 HL (SC)... 6-150, 13-024, 26-060, 29-060

Muir v Inland Revenue Commissioners [1966] 1 W.L.R. 1269; [1966] 3 All E.R. 38; [1966] 5 WLUK 88; 43 T.C. 367; (1966) 45 A.T.C. 185; [1966] T.R. 165; (1966) 110 S.J. 448 CA ............................................................ 25-035, 25-099

N v Inspecteur van de Belastingdienst Oost/Kantoor Almelo (C-470/04) EU:C:2006:525; [2008] S.T.C. 436; [2006] E.C.R. I-7409; [2006] 9 WLUK 72; [2006] 3 C.M.L.R. 49; [2007] C.E.C. 98; [2006] S.T.I. 2180 ECJ (2nd Chamber). ......................... 33-014

Nanaimo Community Hotel Ltd, Re [1944] 4 D.L.R. 638 ........................ 18-031

National Grid Co Plc v Mayes, sub nom. National Grid Co Plc v Laws; joined case(s) International Power Plc (formerly National Power Plc) v Healy; Jefferies v Mayes; Laws v National Grid Co Plc; National Grid Co Plc v Lewis; National Power Plc v Feldon [2001] UKHL 20; [2001] 1 W.L.R. 864; [2001] 2 All E.R. 417; [2001] 4 WLUK 71; [2001] I.C.R. 544; [2001] I.R.L.R. 394; [2001] O.P.L.R. 15; [2001] Pens. L.R. 121; (2001) 98(23) L.S.G. 38; (2001) 151 N.L.J. 572; (2001) 145 S.J.L.B. 98; *Times*, April 10, 2001; *Independent*, April 11, 2001 HL ........................................ 2-063

National Provincial & Union Bank of England v Charnley [1924] 1 K.B. 431; [1923] 11 WLUK 54 CA. ....................................................... 27-129

NBC (Administration Services) Ltd v Revenue and Customs Commissioners [2024] UKFTT 120 (TC); [2024] 2 WLUK 152; [2024] Pens. L.R. 8 FTT (Tax) ...... 4-014, 4-023, 4-025, 4-029, 5-011

NCL Investments Ltd v Revenue and Customs Commissioners [2022] UKSC 9; [2022] 1 W.L.R. 1829; [2022] S.T.C. 599; [2022] 3 WLUK 313; [2022] B.T.C. 8; [2022] S.T.I. 584 SC. ............................................................ 24-044

Nelson Dance Family Settlement Trustees v Revenue and Customs Commissioners, sub nom. Revenue and Customs Commissioners v Nelson Dance Family Settlement Trustees [2009] EWHC 71 (Ch); [2009] S.T.C. 802; [2009] 1 WLUK 361; 79 T.C. 605; [2009] B.T.C. 8003; [2009] W.T.L.R. 401; [2009] S.T.I. 260; [2009] N.P.C. 11 Ch D ............ 28-033

Nichols v Gibson (Inspector of Taxes) [1996] S.T.C. 1008; [1996] 6 WLUK 159; 68 T.C.

## TABLE OF CASES

611; (1996) 140 S.J.L.B. 155; *Times*, July 9, 1996; *Independent*, July 29, 1996 CA (Civ Div) .................................................................................. 35-074, 35-076
Nichols (Deceased), Re, sub nom. Nichols v Inland Revenue Commissioners [1975] 1 W.L.R. 534; [1975] 2 All E.R. 120; [1975] S.T.C. 278; [1974] 12 WLUK 115; [1974] T.R. 411; (1974) 119 S.J. 257 CA (Civ Div)................................................. 21-054
Nicholson v Revenue and Customs Commissioners [2018] UKFTT 14 (TC); [2018] 1 WLUK 28 FTT (Tax) ........................................................................... 6-056
Nicoll v Austin [1947] 1 WLUK 429; 19 T.C. 531 ............................. 24-062, 35-089
Nilebond Ltd v Revenue and Customs Commissioners [2023] UKFTT 14 (TC); [2022] 12 WLUK 487 FTT (Tax) ........................................................................... 17-008
O'Brien (Inspector of Taxes) v Benson's Hosiery (Holdings) Ltd [1980] A.C. 562; [1979] 3 W.L.R. 572; [1979] 3 All E.R. 652; [1979] S.T.C. 735; [1979] 10 WLUK 207; 53 T.C. 241; [1979] T.R. 335; (1979) 123 S.J. 752 HL............................................ 22-029
OCO Ltd v Revenue and Customs Commissioners [2017] UKFTT 589 (TC); [2017] 7 WLUK 1; [2018] S.F.T.D. 123 FTT (Tax)............... 2-057, 24-024, 24-043, 24-057, 30-013
O'Driscoll v Manchester Insurance Committee [1915] 3 K.B. 499; [1915] 6 WLUK 89 CA .. 2-097
Olds Discount Co Ltd v John Playfair Ltd [1938] 3 All E.R. 275; [1938] 6 WLUK 30 KBD .. 2-093
O'Leary v McKinlay (Inspector of Taxes) [1991] S.T.C. 42; [1990] 12 WLUK 98; 63 T.C. 729; [1991] B.T.C. 37; *Times*, December 13, 1990; *Independent*, December 24, 1990 Ch D ...................................................................................... 8-052, 37-010
Omar v Revenue and Customs Commissioners [2011] UKFTT 722 (TC); [2011] 11 WLUK 224 FTT (Tax) ................................................................................. 38-015
O'Mara v Revenue and Customs Commissioners [2017] UKFTT 91 (TC); [2017] 1 WLUK 293 FTT (Tax) ...................................................................... 5-028, 18-182, 18-185
Orchard Parks v Pogson [1964] 1 WLUK 422; 42 T.C. 442; (1964) 43 A.T.C. 344; [1964] T.R. 369................................................................................... 8-025
O'Shea Ex p. Lancaster, Re [1911] 2 K.B. 981; [1911] 7 WLUK 36 CA ............... 18-054
Owen, Re, sub nom. Owen v Inland Revenue Commissioners [1949] 1 All E.R. 901; [1949] 3 WLUK 115; [1949] T.R. 189; [1949] W.N. 201; [1949] L.J.R. 1128; (1949) 93 S.J. 287 Ch D ...................................................................................... 6-033
Padmore v Inland Revenue Commissioners [2001] S.T.C. 280; [2001] 1 WLUK 424; 73 T.C. 470; [2001] B.T.C. 36; 3 I.T.L. Rep. 315; [2001] S.T.I. 99; (2001) 98(6) L.S.G. 46; (2001) 145 S.J.L.B. 27; *Times*, February 21, 2001 Ch D............................ 29-010
Parry v Cleaver [1970] A.C. 1; [1969] 2 W.L.R. 821; [1969] 1 All E.R. 555; [1969] 1 Lloyd's Rep. 183; [1969] 2 WLUK 15; 6 K.I.R. 265; (1969) 113 S.J. 147 HL........... 28-037
Parry v Revenue and Customs Commissioners, sub nom. Revenue and Customs Commissioners v Parry [2020] UKSC 35; [2020] 1 W.L.R. 3692; [2021] 1 All E.R. 365; [2020] S.T.C. 1836; [2020] 8 WLUK 134; [2021] Pens. L.R. 4; [2020] B.T.C. 24; [2020] W.T.L.R. 1151; *Times*, September 18, 2020 SC................................................ 21-037
Parsons v Equitable Investment Co [1916] 2 Ch. 527; [1916] 7 WLUK 25 CA ........... 18-056
PDC Copyright (South) v George [1997] S.T.C. (S.C.D.) 326 ......................... 6-061
Pearson v Inland Revenue Commissioners, sub nom. Pilkington Trustees v Inland Revenue Commissioners [1981] A.C. 753; [1980] 2 W.L.R. 872; [1980] 2 All E.R. 479; [1980] S.T.C. 318; [1980] 5 WLUK 1; [1980] T.R. 177; (1980) 124 S.J. 377 HL......... 21-008, 28-003
Peczenik's Settlement Trusts, Re, sub nom. Cole v Ingram [1964] 1 W.L.R. 720; [1964] 2 All E.R. 339; [1964] 4 WLUK 39; (1964) 108 S.J. 462 Ch D ..................... 8-018, 18-033
Pegler v Abell [1973] 1 W.L.R. 155; [1973] 1 All E.R. 53; [1973] S.T.C. 23; [1972] 11 WLUK 62; 48 T.C. 564; [1972] T.R. 261; (1972) 116 S.J. 921 Ch D ................... 6-022
Pensioneer Trustees (London) Ltd v Revenue and Customs Commissioners [2016] UKFTT 346 (TC); [2016] 5 WLUK 396 FTT (Tax) ............................................. 9-013
Perrin v Dickson (Inspector of Taxes) [1930] 1 K.B. 107; [1929] 7 WLUK 67 CA .. 13-024, 29-060
Perrin v Revenue and Customs Commissioners [2014] UKFTT 488 (TC); [2014] 5 WLUK 732 FTT (Tax)............................................................................. 3-025
Philippi v Inland Revenue Commissioners [1971] 1 W.L.R. 1272; [1971] 3 All E.R. 61; [1971] 5 WLUK 62; 47 T.C. 75; (1971) 50 A.T.C. 16; [1971] T.R. 167; (1971) 115 S.J. 427 CA (Civ Div) ....................................................................... 25-076
Philpott v Revenue and Customs Commissioners [2014] UKFTT 853 (TC); [2014] 8 WLUK 418; [2014] S.T.I. 3299 FTT (Tax).......................................... 35-007, 38-012
PI Consulting (Trustee Services) Ltd v Pensions Regulator, sub nom. Dalriada Trustees Ltd v Nidd Vale Trustees Ltd [2013] EWHC 3181 (Ch); [2013] 10 WLUK 635; [2013] Pens. L.R. 433 Ch D............................................. 2-009, 4-016, 27-046, 31-019
Pirelli Cable Holding NV v Inland Revenue Commissioners; joined case(s) Pirelli General Plc v Inland Revenue Commissioners; Pirelli Plc v Inland Revenue Commissioners;

## TABLE OF CASES

Pirelli SpA v Inland Revenue Commissioners; Pirelli Tyre Holding NV v Inland Revenue Commissioners [2006] UKHL 4; [2006] 1 W.L.R. 400; [2006] 2 All E.R. 81; [2006] S.T.C. 548; [2006] 2 WLUK 188; [2006] Eu. L.R. 827; 77 T.C. 409; [2006] B.T.C. 181; 8 I.T.L. Rep. 872; [2006] S.T.I. 381; (2006) 103(9) L.S.G. 32; (2006) 150 S.J.L.B. 226; *Times*, February 13, 2006 HL .................................................................... 29-006
Pitt v Holt; joined case(s) Futter v Futter; Futter v Revenue and Customs Commissioners; Pitt v Revenue and Customs Commissioners [2013] UKSC 26; [2013] 2 A.C. 108; [2013] 2 W.L.R. 1200; [2013] 3 All E.R. 429; [2013] S.T.C. 1148; [2013] 5 WLUK 232; [2013] Pens. L.R. 195; 81 T.C. 912; [2013] B.T.C. 126; [2013] W.T.L.R. 977; 15 I.T.E.L.R. 976; [2013] S.T.I. 1805; [2013] 2 P. & C.R. DG14; *Times*, June 10, 2013 SC .......... 10-032, 10-034
Pitts v Jones [2007] EWCA Civ 1301; [2008] Q.B. 706; [2008] 2 W.L.R. 1289; [2008] 1 All E.R. 941; [2008] 1 All E.R. (Comm) 548; [2008] Bus. L.R. 1279; [2007] 12 WLUK 97; [2008] 1 B.C.L.C. 613; [2007] 2 C.L.C. 947; (2007) 151 S.J.L.B. 1594; *Times*, December 19, 2007 CA (Civ Div) ................................................ 2-083
Platt v Revenue and Customs Commissioners [2011] UKFTT 606 (TC); [2011] 9 WLUK 343 FTT (Tax).................................................................................. 3-025
Postlethwaite's Executors v Revenue and Customs Commissioners, sub nom. Aspinall v Revenue and Customs Commissioners [2006] 11 WLUK 509; [2007] S.T.C. (S.C.D.) 83; [2007] W.T.L.R. 353; [2007] S.T.I. 346 Sp Comm ...... 21-007, 21-031, 21-035, 28-024, 28-026, 28-028, 28-064, 36-022
Potts Executors v Inland Revenue Commissioners [1951] A.C. 443; [1951] 1 All E.R. 76; [1951] 1 T.L.R. 152; [1950] 12 WLUK 67; 44 R. & I.T. 136; 32 T.C. 211; [1950] T.R. 379 HL ......................................................................................... 2-085
Powell v Osbourne [1992] 11 WLUK 214; [1993] 1 F.L.R. 1001; [1993] 1 F.C.R. 797; [1993] Fam. Law 287; *Times*, December 3, 1992 CA (Civ Div) ........................ 21-089
Powell v Owners of the Proceeds of Sale of the Halcyon Skies (No.1) [1977] Q.B. 14; [1976] 2 W.L.R. 514; [1976] 1 All E.R. 856; [1976] 1 Lloyd's Rep. 461; [1975] 12 WLUK 1; (1975) 120 S.J. 27; *Times*, December 2, 1975 QBD (Admlty) ................ 28-037
Power's Will Trusts, Re, sub nom. Public Trustee v Hastings [1947] Ch. 572; [1947] 2 All E.R. 282; [1947] 6 WLUK 51; (1947) 111 J.P. 245; 177 L.T. 245; (1947) 91 S.J. 409 Ch D ............................................................................................ 18-033
Prudential Assurance Co Ltd v Bibby (Inspector of Taxes) [1999] S.T.C. 952; [1999] 7 WLUK 9; 73 T.C. 142; [1999] B.T.C. 323; *Times*, July 24, 1999 Ch D.................... 35-053
Punter Southall Governance Services Ltd v Benge [2022] EWHC 193 (Ch); [2022] 2 WLUK 5 Ch D ................................................................................... 21-087
R. v Department of Social Security Ex p. Overdrive Credit Card Ltd [1991] 1 W.L.R. 635; [1991] S.T.C. 129; [1991] 2 WLUK 102; [1991] C.O.D. 334; *Times*, February 27, 1991; *Daily Telegraph*, March 8, 1991 DC......................................................... 24-059
R. v Inland Revenue Commissioners Ex p. Roux Waterside Inn Ltd [1997] S.T.C. 781; [1997] 4 WLUK 59; [1999] O.P.L.R. 239; [1997] Pens. L.R. 123; 70 T.C. 545; [1997] B.T.C. 270; (1997) 94(16) L.S.G. 29; *Times*, April 23, 1997 QBD ...................... 4-023
R. v Quillan (Gary); joined case(s) R. v Edmonson (Andrew); R. v Garrett (Gregory); R. v Garrett (Peter); R. v Hoole (Christopher); R. v Thomson (Neal) [2015] EWCA Crim 538; [2015] 1 W.L.R. 4673; [2016] 2 All E.R. 653; [2015] 3 WLUK 740; [2015] 2 Cr. App. R. 3; [2015] Lloyd's Rep. F.C. 321; [2015] B.T.C. 16; [2015] Crim. L.R. 618 CA (Crim Div)............................................................................. 2-037, 6-145
R. v Secretary of State for the Environment Ex p. McClorry 3 September 1998 QBD ...... 13-005
R. (on the application of Britannic Asset Management Ltd) v Pensions Ombudsman, sub nom. Britannic Asset Management Ltd v Pensions Ombudsman; R. (on the application of Brittannic Asset Management Ltd) v Pensions Ombudsman [2002] EWCA Civ 1405; [2002] 4 All E.R. 860; [2002] 10 WLUK 310; [2003] I.C.R. 99; [2003] O.P.L.R. 93; [2002] Pens. L.R. 527; (2002) 99(44) L.S.G. 33; *Times*, October 22, 2002 CA (Civ Div).... 9-010, 11-004, 12-027, 12-029, 29-020, 31-008, 34-010
R. (on the application of Cherwell DC) v First Secretary of State [2004] EWCA Civ 1420; [2005] 1 W.L.R. 1128; [2004] 10 WLUK 736; [2005] 1 P. & C.R. 22; [2005] 1 P.L.R. 11; [2005] J.P.L. 768; [2004] 45 E.G. 125 (C.S.); (2004) 101(45) L.S.G. 32; (2004) 148 S.J.L.B. 1284; [2004] N.P.C. 159; *Times*, November 4, 2004 CA (Civ Div) ......... 6-018, 9-005
R. (on the application of Mander) v Inland Revenue Commissioners [2001] EWHC Admin 358; [2002] S.T.C. 631; [2001] 4 WLUK 329; 73 T.C. 506; [2002] S.T.I. 677 QBD (Admin)........................................................................................... 4-023
R. (on the application of N) v Lewisham LBC, sub nom. R. (on the application of CN) v Lewisham LBC; R. (on the application of ZH) v Newham LBC; joined case(s) R. (on the application of H (A Child)) v Newham LBC [2014] UKSC 62; [2015] A.C. 1259; [2014]

# TABLE OF CASES xxxiii

3 W.L.R. 1548; [2015] 1 All E.R. 783; [2014] 11 WLUK 331; [2015] H.L.R. 6; [2014] B.L.G.R. 842; [2015] 1 P. & C.R. 13; (2014) 158(45) S.J.L.B. 37; *Times*, December 1, 2014 SC. .................................................................... 9-012
R. (on the application of S) v Social Security Commissioner [2009] EWHC 2221 (Admin); [2010] P.T.S.R. 1785; [2009] 9 WLUK 27; (2009) 12 C.C.L. Rep. 654; (2009) 153(34) S.J.L.B. 29 QBD (Admin) .......................................... 6-018, 9-005, 26-007
Radley v Revenue and Customs Commissioners [2016] UKFTT 688 (TC); [2016] 10 WLUK 339 FTT (Tax) ................................................................ 3-025
Ramsden v Inland Revenue Commissioners [1957] 1 WLUK 390; 50 R. & I.T. 662; 37 T.C. 619; (1957) 36 A.T.C. 325; [1957] T.R. 247. ...................................... 2-093
Ransom v Higg [1974] 1 WLUK 741; 50 T.C. 1 ................................... 8-030
Ransom (Inspector of Taxes) v Higgs, sub nom. Dickinson v Kilmorie (Aldridge) Downes; joined case(s) Dickinson (Inspector of Taxes) v Downes; Grant (Inspector of Taxes) v Downes Settlement Trustees; Kilmorie (Aldridge) Ltd v Dickinson (Inspector of Taxes); Motley (Inspector of Taxes) v Higgs Settlement Trustees; Motley v Higgs Trustees; Restorick v Godber, Parry [1974] 1 W.L.R. 1594; [1974] 3 All E.R. 949; [1974] S.T.C. 539; [1974] 11 WLUK 66; [1974] T.R. 281; (1974) 118 S.J. 849 HL ............ 28-063, 37-007
RCC v Colquhoun [2010] UKUT 431 ............................................ 35-030
Ready Mixed Concrete (South East) Ltd v Minister of Pensions and National Insurance; joined case(s) Minister for Social Security v Greenham Ready Mixed Concrete Ltd; Minister for Social Security v Ready Mixed Concrete (South East) Ltd [1968] 2 Q.B. 497; [1968] 2 W.L.R. 775; [1968] 1 All E.R. 433; [1967] 12 WLUK 33; 4 K.I.R. 132; [2010] B.T.C. 49; (1967) 112 S.J. 14; *Times*, December 11, 1967 QBD ................ 2-017
Reed Employment Plc v Revenue and Customs Commissioners [2015] EWCA Civ 805; [2015] S.T.C. 2518; [2015] 7 WLUK 840; [2015] B.T.C. 24; [2015] S.T.I. 2531 CA (Civ Div) ................................................................... 6-139, 24-061
Reichhold Ltd v Wong [2000] 3 WLUK 31; [2000] Pens. L.R. 277 CJ (Gen Div) (Ont) ..... 2-009, 31-019
Resolute Management Services Ltd v Revenue and Customs Commissioners; joined case(s) Haderlein v Revenue and Customs Commissioners [2008] 8 WLUK 271; [2008] S.T.C. (S.C.D.) 1202; [2008] S.T.I. 2124 Sp Comm. ....................... 29-039, 29-040, 35-021
Revenue and Customs Commissioners v Aimia Coalition Loyalty UK Ltd (formerly Loyalty Management UK Ltd) [2013] UKSC 42; [2013] 4 All E.R. 94; [2013] S.T.C. 1476; [2013] 6 WLUK 538; [2013] B.V.C. 282; [2013] S.T.I. 2215 SC ................ 22-007
Revenue and Customs Commissioners v Bella Figura Ltd [2020] UKUT 120 (TCC); [2020] S.T.C. 922; [2020] 4 WLUK 167; [2021] Pens. L.R. 1; [2020] B.T.C. 544; [2020] S.T.I. 1095 UT (Tax). ........................................ 1-003, 18-008, 18-185, 19-041
Revenue and Customs Commissioners v Coal Staff Superannuation Scheme Trustees Ltd, sub nom. Coal Staff Superannuation Scheme Trustees Ltd v Revenue and Customs Commissioners [2022] UKSC 10; [2022] 1 W.L.R. 2359; [2022] 3 All E.R. 335; [2022] S.T.C. 776; [2022] 4 WLUK 205; [2022] B.T.C. 14 SC. .............................. 8-015
Revenue and Customs Commissioners v Dhanak [2014] UKUT 68 (TCC); [2014] S.T.C. 1525; [2014] 2 WLUK 304; [2014] B.T.C. 506; [2014] S.T.I. 745 UT (Tax) ............. 38-018
Revenue and Customs Commissioners v E.ON UK Plc, sub nom. E.ON UK Plc v Revenue and Customs Commissioners [2023] EWCA Civ 1383; [2024] S.T.C. 59; [2023] 11 WLUK 581; [2024] Pens. L.R. 5; [2023] B.T.C. 31; [2023] S.T.I. 1665 CA (Civ Div). ..... 22-029
Revenue and Customs Commissioners v Fowler, sub nom. Fowler v Revenue and Customs Commissioners [2020] UKSC 22; [2020] 1 W.L.R. 2227; [2021] 1 All E.R. 97; [2020] S.T.C. 1476; [2020] 5 WLUK 264; [2020] B.T.C. 15; 22 I.T.L. Rep. 679; [2020] S.T.I. 1315; *Times*, June 2, 2020 SC. .................................................. 29-007
Revenue and Customs Commissioners v Holland, sub nom. Holland v Revenue and Customs Commissioners; Paycheck Services 3 Ltd, Re [2010] UKSC 51; [2010] 1 W.L.R. 2793; [2011] 1 All E.R. 430; [2011] Bus. L.R. 111; [2011] S.T.C. 269; [2010] 11 WLUK 650; [2011] B.C.C. 1; [2011] 1 B.C.L.C. 141; [2011] B.P.I.R. 96; [2010] S.T.I. 3074; *Times*, November 30, 2010 SC. ........................................... 2-018
Revenue and Customs Commissioners v Newey (t/a Ocean Finance) (C-653/11), sub nom. Newey v Revenue and Customs Commissioners (C-653/11) EU:C:2013:409; [2013] S.T.C. 2432; [2013] 6 WLUK 585; [2013] B.V.C. 259; [2013] S.T.I. 2304 ECJ (3rd Chamber). .................................................................. 22-006
Revenue and Customs Commissioners v Parry, sub nom. Parry v Revenue and Customs Commissioners [2020] UKSC 35; [2020] 1 W.L.R. 3692; [2021] 1 All E.R. 365; [2020] S.T.C. 1836; [2020] 8 WLUK 134; [2021] Pens. L.R. 4; [2020] B.T.C. 24; [2020] W.T.L.R. 1151; *Times*, September 18, 2020 SC . . 21-034, 21-036, 21-037, 21-063, 21-066, 21-068,

## TABLE OF CASES

21-085, 21-105, 28-069, 28-070
Revenue and Customs Commissioners v Sippchoice Ltd, sub nom. Sippchoice Ltd v Revenue and Customs Commissioners [2020] UKUT 149 (TCC); [2020] 4 W.L.R. 80; [2020] 5 WLUK 116 UT (Tax) ..., 2-054, 5-040, 5-043, 5-044, 5-045, 6-013, 6-014, 6-015, 6-127, 6-131, 20-003
RFC 2012 Plc (In Liquidation) (formerly Rangers Football Club Plc) v Advocate General for Scotland, sub nom. Advocate General for Scotland v Murray Group Holdings Ltd; RFC 2012 Plc (In Liquidation) (formerly Rangers Football Club Plc) v Advocate General for Scotland; Revenue and Customs Commissioners v Murray Group Holdings Ltd [2017] UKSC 45; [2017] 1 W.L.R. 2767; [2017] 4 All E.R. 654; [2017] S.T.C. 1556; 2018 S.C. (U.K.S.C.) 15; 2017 S.L.T. 799; 2017 S.C.L.R. 517; [2017] 7 WLUK 77; [2017] B.T.C. 22; [2017] W.T.L.R. 1093; [2017] S.T.I. 1610; 2017 G.W.D. 21-357; *Times*, July 17, 2017 SC (SC) ................................ 6-138, 24-055, 24-056, 35-060
Rialas v Revenue and Customs Commissioners [2020] UKUT 367 (TCC); [2021] S.T.C. 186; [2020] 12 WLUK 437; [2021] B.T.C. 3; [2021] S.T.I. 553 UT (Tax) ............... 25-075
Ridge Securities Ltd v Inland Revenue Commissioners [1964] 1 W.L.R. 479; [1964] 1 All E.R. 275; [1963] 12 WLUK 47; 44 T.C. 373; (1963) 42 A.T.C. 487; [1963] T.R. 449; (1964) 108 S.J. 377 Ch D ................................................. 6-150, 13-024, 26-060, 29-060
RKW Ltd v Revenue and Customs Commissioners [2014] UKFTT 151 (TC); [2014] 1 WLUK 757; [2014] S.T.I. 1633 FTT (Tax) ........................................... 2-097
Robinson v Robinson (1851) 42 E.R. 547; (1851) 1 De G.M. & G. 247; [1851] 12 WLUK 108 QB .................................................................................. 8-002
Rochdale BC v Dixon [2011] EWCA Civ 1173; [2012] P.T.S.R. 1336; [2011] 10 WLUK 578; [2012] H.L.R. 6; [2012] B.L.G.R. 251; [2011] 43 E.G. 105 (C.S.) CA (Civ Div) . 6-018, 9-005
Root 2 Tax Ltd v HMRC [2019] UKFTT 744 ................................................ 35-033
RP Medplant Ltd v Pensions Regulator [2017] UKUT 385 (TCC); [2017] 10 WLUK 106; [2018] Pens. L.R. 3 UT (Tax) ............................................................. 31-020
Russell-Cooke Trust Co v Prentis (No.1) [2002] EWHC 2227 (Ch); [2003] 2 All E.R. 478; [2002] 11 WLUK 34; [2003] W.T.L.R. 81; (2002-03) 5 I.T.E.L.R. 532; (2002) 152 N.L.J. 1719 Ch D ................................................................................. 37-026
Rutter (Inspector of Taxes) v Charles Sharpe & Co Ltd [1979] 1 W.L.R. 1429; [1979] S.T.C. 711; [1979] 7 WLUK 51; 53 T.C. 163; [1979] T.R. 225; (1979) 123 S.J. 522 Ch D ... 6-072
Rysaffe Trustee Co (CI) Ltd v Inland Revenue Commissioners, sub nom. Customs and Excise Commissioners v Rysaffe Trustee Co (CI) Ltd; Rysaffe Trustee Co (CI) Ltd v Customs and Excise Commissioners [2003] EWCA Civ 356; [2003] S.T.C. 536; [2003] 3 WLUK 609; [2003] B.T.C. 8021; [2003] W.T.L.R. 481; (2002-03) 5 I.T.E.L.R. 706; [2003] S.T.I. 452; (2003) 100(22) L.S.G. 31; (2003) 147 S.J.L.B. 388; [2003] N.P.C. 39; *Times*, April 29, 2003 CA (Civ Div) .................................................. 28-038
Safir v Skattemyndigheten i Dalarnas Lan (formerly Skattemyndigheten i Kopparbergs Lan) (C-118/96) EU:C:1998:170; [1999] Q.B. 451; [1999] 2 W.L.R. 66; [1998] S.T.C. 1043; [1998] E.C.R. I-1897; [1998] 4 WLUK 413; [1998] 3 C.M.L.R. 739; [1998] Pens. L.R. 161; [1998] B.T.C. 8028; *Times*, May 1, 1998 ECJ .............................. 24-004
Salt v Chamberlain [1979] S.T.C. 750; [1979] 1 WLUK 392; 53 T.C. 143; [1979] T.R. 203; (1979) 123 S.J. 490 ........................................................................ 8-023
Samuel Dracup & Sons v Dakin [1957] 1 WLUK 418; 50 R. & I.T. 594; 37 T.C. 377; (1957) 36 A.T.C. 250; [1957] T.R. 169 ................................... 6-050, 6-052, 6-062
Saunders v Vautier 41 E.R. 482; (1841) Cr. & Ph. 240; [1841] 6 WLUK 43 Ct of Chancery .. 2-070
Schmidt v Rosewood Trust Ltd, sub nom. Angora Trust, Re; Everest Trust, Re; Rosewood Trust Ltd v Schmidt [2003] UKPC 26; [2003] 2 A.C. 709; [2003] 2 W.L.R. 1442; [2003] 3 All E.R. 76; [2003] 3 WLUK 807; [2003] Pens. L.R. 145; [2003] W.T.L.R. 565; (2002-03) 5 I.T.E.L.R. 715; (2003) 100(22) L.S.G. 31; *Times*, March 29, 2003 PC (IoM) ........ 21-004
Scientific Investment Pension Plan (No.3), Re, sub nom. Kemble v Hicks (No.2) [1999] 6 WLUK 228; [1999] O.P.L.R. 1; [1999] Pens. L.R. 287 Ch D .................. 2-009, 31-019
Scottish and Universal Newspapers Ltd v Fisher (Inspector of Taxes) [1996] 6 WLUK 311; [1996] S.T.C. (S.C.D.) 311 Sp Comm ......................................................... 35-016
Scotts Atlantic Management Ltd (In Liquidation) v Revenue and Customs Commissioners [2015] UKUT 66 (TCC); [2015] S.T.C. 1321; [2015] 2 WLUK 494; [2015] B.T.C. 504 UT (Tax) ................................................................ 6-045, 6-057, 6-062, 6-127, 24-043
Scurfield v Revenue and Customs Commissioners [2011] UKFTT 532 (TC); [2011] 8 WLUK 62 FTT (Tax) ......................................................................... 3-025
Secretary of State in Council of India v Scoble, sub nom. Scoble v Secretary of State in Council for India [1903] A.C. 299; [1903] 6 WLUK 49 HL ................... 13-024, 29-060
Sempra Metals Ltd v Revenue and Customs Commissioners [2008] 7 WLUK 193; [2008]

# TABLE OF CASES

S.T.C. (S.C.D.) 1062; [2008] S.T.I. 1923 Sp Comm . . . . . . . . . . . . . . . . . . . . . 6-069, 24-043, 27-011
Shadford (Inspector of Taxes) v H Fairweather & Co Ltd [1966] 1 WLUK 815; 43 T.C. 291; (1966) 45 A.T.C. 78; [1966] T.R. 75; 116 N.L.J. 667. . . . . . . . . . . . . . . . . . . . . . . . . . . . 8-025
Sharkey (Inspector of Taxes) v Wernher, sub nom. Wernher v Sharkey (Inspector of Taxes) [1956] A.C. 58; [1955] 3 W.L.R. 671; [1955] 3 All E.R. 493; [1955] 11 WLUK 20; 48 R. & I.T. 739; 36 T.C. 275; (1955) 34 A.T.C. 263; [1955] T.R. 277; (1955) 99 S.J. 793 HL . . . . . 8-026
Shilton v Wilmshurst (Inspector of Taxes) [1991] 1 A.C. 684; [1991] 2 W.L.R. 530; [1991] 3 All E.R. 148; [1991] S.T.C. 88; [1991] 2 WLUK 77; 64 T.C. 78; (1991) 135 S.J. 250; *Times*, February 13, 1991; *Independent*, February 20, 1991; *Financial Times*, February 12, 1991; *Guardian*, February 12, 1991 HL. . . . . . . . . . . . . . . . . . . . . . . . . . . . . . . . . . . . . . 35-075
Simmons (Liquidator of Lionel Simmons Properties) v Inland Revenue Commissioners [1980] 1 W.L.R. 1196; [1980] 2 All E.R. 798; [1980] S.T.C. 350; [1980] 6 WLUK 198; 53 T.C. 461; (1980) 124 S.J. 630 HL . . . . . . . . . . . . . . . . . . . . . . . . . . . . . . . . . . . . . . . . . . . 8-026
Simpson v Maurice's Executor; joined case(s) Simpson v Kay's Executor [1947] 1 WLUK 565; 14 T.C. 580 . . . . . . . . . . . . . . . . . . . . . . . . . . . . . . . . . . . . . . . . . . . . . . . . . . . . . . . . . . . 18-044
Sinnamon v Revenue and Customs Commissioners [2016] UKFTT 168 (TC); [2016] 3 WLUK 256 FTT (Tax) . . . . . . . . . . . . . . . . . . . . . . . . . . . . . . . . . . . . . . . . . . . . . . . . . . . . . . 26-009
Smallwood v Revenue and Customs Commissioners, sub nom. Revenue and Customs Commissioners v Smallwood; Trevor Smallwood Trust, Re [2010] EWCA Civ 778; [2010] S.T.C. 2045; [2010] 7 WLUK 257; 80 T.C. 536; [2010] B.T.C. 637; 12 I.T.L. Rep. 1002; [2010] W.T.L.R. 1771; [2010] S.T.I. 2174; (2010) 154(27) S.J.L.B. 30 CA (Civ Div). . . . . . . . . . . . . . . . . . . . . . . . . . . . . . . . . . . . . . . . . . . . . . . . . . . . . . . . . . . . . . . . 29-004
Smith v Smith [1923] P. 191; [1923] 7 WLUK 5 CA . . . . . . . . . . . . . . . . . . . . . . . 26-060, 29-060
Smithton Ltd (formerly Hobart Capital Markets Ltd) v Naggar [2014] EWCA Civ 939; [2015] 1 W.L.R. 189; [2014] 7 WLUK 419; [2014] B.C.C. 482; [2015] 2 B.C.L.C. 22; (2014) 158(29) S.J.L.B. 37; *Times*, August 19, 2014 CA (Civ Div). . . . . . . . . . . . . . . . . . . . 2-018
Smyth v Stretton (1904) 5 T.C. 36 . . . . . . . . . . . . . . . . . . . . . . . . . . . . . . 6-139, 24-055, 24-061
Snell v Revenue and Customs Commissioners [2006] EWHC 3350 (Ch); [2007] S.T.C. 1279; [2006] 12 WLUK 575; 78 T.C. 294; [2007] B.T.C. 62; [2007] S.T.I. 115; (2007) 104(3) L.S.G. 30 Ch D . . . . . . . . . . . . . . . . . . . . . . . . . . . . . . . . . . . . . . . . . . . . . . . . . . . . . 2-007
Sothern-Smith v Clancy (Inspector of Taxes) [1941] 1 K.B. 276; [1941] 1 All E.R. 111; [1940] 12 WLUK 14 CA . . . . . . . . . . . . . . . . . . . . . . . . . . . . . . . . . . . . . . . . 2-094, 13-024, 29-060
Spooner v British Telecommunications Plc [1999] 10 WLUK 362; [2000] O.P.L.R. 189; [2000] Pens. L.R. 65 Ch D . . . . . . . . . . . . . . . . . . . . . . . . . . . . . . . . . . . . . . . . . . . . . . . . . . 35-024
Stafford v Fiddon 53 E.R. 151; (1857) 23 Beav. 386; [1857] 2 WLUK 29 Ct of Chancery . . . 8-002
Stanley v Inland Revenue Commissioners [1944] K.B. 255; [1944] 1 All E.R. 230; [1944] 1 WLUK 50 CA . . . . . . . . . . . . . . . . . . . . . . . . . . . . . . . . . . . . . . . . . . . . . . . . . . . . . . . . . . 15-078
Stannard v Fisons Pension Trust Ltd [1991] 11 WLUK 72; [1992] I.R.L.R. 27; [1991] Pens. L.R. 225; *Times*, November 19, 1991 CA (Civ Div) . . . . . . . . . . . . . . . . . . . . . . . . . . . . . . . 21-088
Stanton Ltd v Drayton Commercial Investment Co Ltd [1983] 1 A.C. 501; [1982] 3 W.L.R. 214; [1982] 2 All E.R. 942; [1982] S.T.C. 585; [1982] 7 WLUK 98; [1982] Com. L.R. 198; 55 T.C. 286; (1982) 79 L.S.G. 1176 HL. . . . . . . . . . . . . . . . . . . . . . . . . . . . . . . . . . . . 2-117
Stedeford (Inspector of Taxes) v Beloe [1932] A.C. 388; [1932] 3 WLUK 35 HL . . . 6-150, 24-040, 26-008, 26-039, 26-051, 35-075
Steele (Inspector of Taxes) v EVC International NV (formerly European Vinyls Corp (Holdings) BV), sub nom. Steele (Inspector of Taxes) v European Vinyls Corp (Holdings) BV; Steeple v European Vinyls Corp (Holdings) BV [1996] S.T.C. 785; [1996] 5 WLUK 113; 69 T.C. 88; [1996] B.T.C. 425 CA (Civ Div) . . . . . . . . . . . . . . . . . . . . . . . . . . . . . . . . 25-095
Stevenson (Inspector of Taxes) v Wishart [1987] 1 W.L.R. 1204; [1987] 2 All E.R. 428; [1987] S.T.C. 266; [1987] 4 WLUK 154; [1987] 1 F.T.L.R. 69; 59 T.C. 740; (1987) 84 L.S.G. 1575; (1987) 131 S.J. 744 CA (Civ Div). . . . . . . . . . . . . . . . . . . . . . . . . . . . 15-078, 26-061
Street v Mountford [1985] A.C. 809; [1985] 2 W.L.R. 877; [1985] 2 All E.R. 289; [1985] 5 WLUK 8; (1985) 17 H.L.R. 402; (1985) 50 P. & C.R. 258; [1985] 1 E.G.L.R. 128; (1985) 274 E.G. 821; [2008] B.T.C. 7094; (1985) 82 L.S.G. 2087; (1985) 135 N.L.J. 460; (1985) 129 S.J. 348 HL . . . . . . . . . . . . . . . . . . . . . . . . . . . . . . . . . . . . . . . . . . . . . . . . . . . . . . . . . . . 2-091
Suenson-Taylor's Settlement Trusts, Re, sub nom. Moores v Moores [1974] 1 W.L.R. 1280; [1974] 3 All E.R. 397; [1974] 6 WLUK 16; (1974) 118 S.J. 757 Ch D. . . . . . . . . . . . . . 8-053
Sun Life Assurance Society v Davidson (Inspector of Taxes); joined case(s) Phoenix Assurance Co Ltd v Logan (Inspector of Taxes) [1958] A.C. 184; [1957] 3 W.L.R. 362; [1957] 2 All E.R. 760; [1957] 7 WLUK 9; 50 R. & I.T. 530; 37 T.C. 330; (1957) 36 A.T.C. 152; [1957] T.R. 171; (1957) 101 S.J. 590 HL. . . . . . . . . . . . . . . . . . . . . . . . . . . . . . . . . . . . . . . . 6-064
Swinburne, Re, sub nom. Sutton v Featherley [1926] Ch. 38; [1925] 10 WLUK 6; 44 A.L.R. 619 CA . . . . . . . . . . . . . . . . . . . . . . . . . . . . . . . . . . . . . . . . . . . . . . . . . . . . . . . . . . . . . . . . . 6-033

… 8-027

Taylor v Good (Inspector of Taxes) [1974] 1 W.L.R. 556; [1974] 1 All E.R. 1137; [1974] S.T.C. 148; [1974] 2 WLUK 92; 49 T.C. 277; [1974] T.R. 15; (1974) 118 S.J. 422 CA (Civ Div)................................................................. 8-027
Telent Plc v Revenue and Customs Commissioners [2007] 8 WLUK 259; [2008] S.T.C. (S.C.D.) 202; [2007] S.T.I. 2234 Sp Comm ........................................ 38-004
Temple Finance Ltd v Revenue and Customs Commissioners, sub nom. Revenue and Customs Commissioners v Temple Finance Ltd [2017] UKUT 315 (TCC); [2017] S.T.C. 1781; [2017] 8 WLUK 70; [2017] B.V.C. 524; [2017] S.T.I. 1862 UT (Tax) ............. 11-010
Templeton (Inspector of Taxes) v Jacobs [1996] 1 W.L.R. 1433; [1996] S.T.C. 991; [1996] 5 WLUK 344; 68 T.C. 735; (1996) 140 S.J.L.B. 150; *Times*, June 6, 1996; *Independent*, July 8, 1996 Ch D ..................... 6-136, 18-122, 24-024, 24-057, 30-012, 30-013, 35-060
Tennant v Smith (Surveyor of Taxes) [1892] A.C. 150; (1892) 19 R. (H.L.) 1; [1892] 3 WLUK 49 HL (SC)....................................................... 24-053
The Queen v John Cruikshank (1977) 77 DTC 5226 ................................. 29-051
Thorpe v Revenue and Customs Commissioners [2010] EWCA Civ 339; [2010] S.T.C. 964; [2010] 3 WLUK 418; [2010] B.T.C. 425; (2010) 12 I.T.E.L.R. 929; [2010] S.T.I. 1439 CA (Civ Div).......................................... 2-070, 2-071, 2-074
Tilley v Wales (Inspector of Taxes), sub nom. Wales (Inspector of Taxes) v Tilley [1943] A.C. 386; [1943] 1 All E.R. 280; [1943] 2 WLUK 21 HL ........ 20-042, 22-029, 24-059, 35-075
Tipping v Revenue and Customs Commissioners [2017] UKFTT 485 (TC); [2017] 6 WLUK 169 FTT (Tax) ................................................... 3-025
Tolsma v Inspecteur der Omzetbelasting, Leeuwarden (C-16/93) EU:C:1994:80; [1994] S.T.C. 509; [1994] E.C.R. I-743; [1994] 3 WLUK 59; [1994] 2 C.M.L.R. 908; [1994] B.V.C. 117; [1994] S.T.I. 424; *Times*, March 29, 1994 ECJ (6th Chamber)................ 22-006
Toone v Ross, sub nom. Implement Consulting Ltd (In Liquidation), Re [2019] EWHC 2855 (Ch); [2020] S.T.C. 382; [2019] 10 WLUK 457; [2020] 2 B.C.L.C. 537; [2020] B.T.C. 5 Ch D............................................................. 6-058
Townley v Revenue and Customs Commissioners [2018] UKFTT 624 (TC); [2018] 10 WLUK 513 FTT (Tax) .................................................... 3-043
Travel Document Service v Revenue and Customs Commissioners [2018] EWCA Civ 549; [2018] 3 All E.R. 60; [2018] S.T.C. 723; [2018] 3 WLUK 457; [2018] B.T.C. 13; [2018] S.T.I. 649 CA (Civ Div) ........................................................ 36-010
Trustees Executors and Agency Co v Reilly [1941] V.L.R. 110 ....................... 18-046
Trustees of Barclays Bank Pension Fund v HMRC [2005] UKSPC SPC00520 .... 35-014, 35-015, 35-016
Twaite v Revenue and Customs Commissioners [2017] UKFTT 591 (TC); [2017] 7 WLUK 782 FTT (Tax)........................................................... 3-025
Underwood v Revenue and Customs Commissioners [2008] EWCA Civ 1423; [2009] S.T.C. 239; [2008] 12 WLUK 410; 79 T.C. 631; [2009] B.T.C. 26; [2009] S.T.I. 256; [2009] 1 E.G. 76 (C.S.); [2008] N.P.C. 139 CA (Civ Div).............................. 22-029
Uratemp Ventures Ltd v Collins; joined case(s) Uratemp Ventures Ltd v Carrell [2001] UKHL 43; [2002] 1 A.C. 301; [2001] 3 W.L.R. 806; [2002] 1 All E.R. 46; [2001] 10 WLUK 341; (2001) 33 H.L.R. 85; [2002] L. & T.R. 15; [2001] 3 E.G.L.R. 93; [2002] R.V.R. 162; 2001 Hous. L.R. 133; [2001] 43 E.G. 186 (C.S.); (2001) 98(41) L.S.G. 35; [2001] N.P.C. 145; [2002] 1 P. & C.R. DG15; *Times*, October 18, 2001; *Independent*, December 3, 2001; *Daily Telegraph*, October 16, 2001 HL (SC) ....................... 9-012
Venables v Hornby (Inspector of Taxes), sub nom. Trustees of the Fussell Pension Scheme v Hornby (Inspector of Taxes) [2003] UKHL 65; [2003] 1 W.L.R. 3022; [2004] 1 All E.R. 627; [2004] S.T.C. 84; [2003] 12 WLUK 88; [2004] I.C.R. 42; [2004] O.P.L.R. 19; [2004] Pens. L.R. 75; 75 T.C. 553; [2003] B.T.C. 559; [2003] S.T.I. 2275; (2003) 147 S.J.L.B. 1431; *Times*, December 5, 2003 HL .... 2-066, 2-067, 2-068, 2-071, 2-072, 2-073, 2-074, 2-076, 2-078, 2-079, 35-024, 35-027
Vestey v Inland Revenue Commissioners; joined case(s) Baddeley v Inland Revenue Commissioners; Payne v Inland Revenue Commissioners [1980] A.C. 1148; [1979] 3 W.L.R. 915; [1979] 3 All E.R. 976; [1980] S.T.C. 10; [1979] 11 WLUK 190; 54 T.C. 503; [1979] T.R. 381; (1979) 123 S.J. 826; *Times*, November 24, 1979 HL . 25-012, 25-054, 25-061
Vodafone Cellular Ltd v Shaw (Inspector of Taxes) [1997] S.T.C. 734; [1997] 3 WLUK 472; 69 T.C. 376; [1997] B.T.C. 247; (1997) 141 S.J.L.B. 93; *Times*, March 31, 1997 CA (Civ Div) ................................................................. 6-045, 22-029
Walker v Southall (1887) 56 LT 882 ............................................... 8-053
Walsh v Lonsdale (1882) 21 Ch. D. 9; [1882] 3 WLUK 102 CA .................... 18-066
Webb v Stenton (1883) 11 Q.B.D. 518; [1883] 6 WLUK 25 CA ...................... 2-097
Weight v Salmon [1935] UKHL T.C. 19 174 ........................................ 35-089

# TABLE OF CASES

Weiser v Revenue and Customs Commissioners [2012] UKFTT 501 (TC); [2012] 8 WLUK 129; [2012] S.F.T.D. 1381; 15 I.T.L. Rep. 157; [2012] S.T.I. 3238 FTT (Tax) ............ 29-054

Welsh Development Agency v Export Finance Co Ltd [1991] 11 WLUK 227; [1992] B.C.C. 270; [1992] B.C.L.C. 148; *Times*, November 28, 1991; *Financial Times*, November 27, 1991 CA (Civ Div) .................................................................. 2-089

West (Inspector of Taxes) v Trennery, sub nom. Tee v Inspector of Taxes; Trennery v West (Inspector of Taxes) [2005] UKHL 5; [2005] 1 All E.R. 827; [2005] S.T.C. 214; [2005] 1 WLUK 444; 76 T.C. 713; [2005] B.T.C. 69; [2005] W.T.L.R. 205; [2005] S.T.I. 157; (2005) 149 S.J.L.B. 147; [2005] N.P.C. 10; *Times*, February 1, 2005 HL... 25-013, 25-034, 25-098

Westdeutsche Landesbank Girozentrale v Islington LBC, sub nom. Islington LBC v Westdeutsche Landesbank Girozentrale; joined case(s) Kleinwort Benson Ltd v Sandwell BC [1996] A.C. 669; [1996] 2 W.L.R. 802; [1996] 2 All E.R. 961; [1996] 5 WLUK 343; [1996] 5 Bank. L.R. 341; [1996] C.L.C. 990; 95 L.G.R. 1; (1996) 160 J.P. Rep. 1130; (1996) 146 N.L.J. 877; (1996) 140 S.J.L.B. 136; *Times*, May 30, 1996 HL ............... 2-057

Westminster City Council v Haywood (No.1) [1998] Ch. 377; [1997] 3 W.L.R. 641; [1997] 2 All E.R. 84; [1997] 1 WLUK 394; [1998] I.C.R. 920; (1997) 9 Admin. L.R. 489; [1997] O.P.L.R. 61; [1997] Pens. L.R. 39; *Times*, February 12, 1997; *Independent*, February 12, 1997 CA (Civ Div) ........................................................ 2-009, 13-017, 29-051, 31-019

WHA Ltd v Revenue and Customs Commissioners [2013] UKSC 24; [2013] 2 All E.R. 907; [2013] S.T.C. 943; [2013] 4 WLUK 744; [2013] B.V.C. 155; [2013] S.T.I. 1769 SC... 22-006

Wheels Common Investment Fund Trustees Ltd v Revenue and Customs Commissioners (C-424/11) EU:C:2013:144; [2014] S.T.C. 495; [2013] 3 WLUK 192; [2013] Pens. L.R. 149; [2013] S.T.I. 589 ECJ (1st Chamber) ........................................ 22-015

White v Revenue and Customs Commissioners [2016] UKFTT 802 (TC); [2016] 11 WLUK 788 FTT (Tax) ................................................................ 5-043, 18-038, 18-039

Whitney v CIR (1924) 10 T.C. 88 ............................................ 20-042, 35-074

Whitney v Inland Revenue Commissioners [1926] A.C. 37; [1925] 11 WLUK 28 HL ..... 19-026, 29-001, 35-053

Whitworth Park Coal Co v Inland Revenue Commissioners, sub nom. Inland Revenue Commissioners v Whitworth Park Coal Co; joined case(s) Brancepath Coal Co v Inland Revenue Commissioners; Ramshaw Coal Co v Inland Revenue Commissioners [1961] A.C. 31; [1959] 3 W.L.R. 842; [1959] 3 All E.R. 703; [1959] 11 WLUK 14; 52 R. & I.T. 789; 38 T.C. 531; (1959) 38 A.T.C. 295; [1959] T.R. 293; (1959) 103 S.J. 938 HL .. 6-150, 13-024, 26-060, 29-060

Wielockx v Inspecteur der Directe Belastingen (C-80/94) EU:C:1995:271; [1996] 1 W.L.R. 84; [1995] S.T.C. 876; [1995] E.C.R. I-2493; [1995] 8 WLUK 74; [1995] 3 C.M.L.R. 85; [1995] All E.R. (E.C.) 769; [1995] Pens. L.R. 203; *Times*, October 3, 1995 ECJ ....... 24-004

Wild v Pensions Ombudsman, sub nom. Wild v Smith [1996] 4 WLUK 38; [1996] 2 F.L.R. 680; [1997] 1 F.C.R. 248; [1996] O.P.L.R. 129; [1996] Pens. L.R. 275; [1996] C.O.D. 412; [1996] Fam. Law 667; (1996) 140 S.J.L.B. 108; *Times*, April 17, 1996 QBD ......... 15-019

Wilkins v Rogerson [1961] Ch. 133; [1961] 2 W.L.R. 102; [1961] 1 All E.R. 358; [1960] 12 WLUK 52; 39 T.C. 344; (1960) 39 A.T.C. 425; [1960] T.R. 379; (1961) 105 S.J. 62 CA .... 35-089

Willey v Revenue and Customs Commissioners [2013] UKFTT 328 (TC); [2013] 6 WLUK 4; [2013] Pens. L.R. 229 FTT (Tax) ....................... 5-027, 5-041, 5-042, 5-047, 18-003

Williams v Atlantic Assurance Co Ltd [1933] 1 K.B. 81; (1932) 43 Ll. L. Rep. 177; [1932] 5 WLUK 21 CA ................................................................. 18-069

Williams v Singer; joined case(s) Pool v Royal Exchange Assurance [1921] 1 A.C. 65; [1920] 5 WLUK 98 HL........................................................... 25-004

Wragg, Re, sub nom. Wragg v Palmer [1919] 2 Ch. 58; [1919] 4 WLUK 20 Ch D ......... 8-018

X v Riksskatteverket (C436/00) EU:C:2002:704; [2004] S.T.C. 1271; [2002] E.C.R. I-10829; [2002] 11 WLUK 612; [2003] 3 C.M.L.R. 13; 5 I.T.L. Rep. 433; [2002] S.T.I. 1539 ECJ (5th Chamber) ........................................................ 33-014

Yablon v Revenue and Customs Commissioners [2016] UKFTT 814 (TC); [2016] 12 WLUK 190 FTT (Tax) ............................................................. 3-025

Young v Associated Newspapers [1971] 1 WLUK 453; (1971) 11 K.I.R. 413 ............ 35-024

Young (Inspector of Taxes) v Pearce; joined case(s) Young (Inspector of Taxes) v Scrutton [1996] S.T.C. 743; [1996] 3 WLUK 304; 70 T.C. 331 Ch D ........................... 25-037

Zim Properties Ltd v Procter (Inspector of Taxes), sub nom. Procter (Inspector of Taxes) v Zim Properties [1985] S.T.C. 90; [1984] 1 WLUK 935; 58 T.C. 371; (1985) 82 L.S.G. 124; (1985) 129 S.J. 68; (1985) 129 S.J. 323 Ch D ................................... 8-034

# TABLE OF STATUTES

1890 Partnership Act (c.39)
    s.1(1) . . . . . . . . . . . . . . 8-012, 21-015
1891 Stamp Act (c.39)
    Pt II s.57 . . . . . . . . . . . . . . . . . . . 6-154
1918 Income Tax Act (c.40)
    Pt III s.33 . . . . . . . . . . . . . . . . . . . 6-064
1921 Finance Act (c.32) . . . . . . . . . . . . 37-005
    Pt III s.32 . . . . . . . . . . . . . . . . . . . 6-129
1925 Law of Property Act (c.20)
    Pt II s.53(1)(c) . . . . . . . . . . . . . . 21-087
    Pt IV s.136 . . . . . . . . . . . . . . . . . 18-069
1927 Superannuation and other Trust Funds (Validation) Act (c.41) . . . . . . . . 37-007
1939 Pensions (Navy, Army, Air Force and Mercantile Marine) Act (c.83)
    s.3 . . . . . . . . . . . . . . . . . . . . . . . . 7-006
    s.4 . . . . . . . . . . . . . . . . . . . . . . . . 7-006
    s.5 . . . . . . . . . . . . . . . . . . . . . . . . 7-006
1955 Pensions (India, Pakistan and Burma) Act (c.22) . . . . . . . . 13-009, 15-022, 26-006
1958 Overseas Service Act (c.14) . . . . . 13-009, 15-022, 26-006
1960 Finance Act (c.44)
    Pt II s.37 . . . . . . . . . . . . . . . . . . 35-076
    s.38 . . . . . . . . . . . . . . . . . . . . . . 35-076
1968 International Organisations Act (c.48)
    s.1 . . . . . . . . . . . . . . . . . 31-010, 34-012
        (1) . . . . . . . . . . . . . . . . . . . . . 12-031
1970 Taxes Management Act (c.9)
    Pt I s.2 . . . . . . . . . . . . . . . . . . . . 19-003
    Pt II s.7 . . . . . . . . . . . . . . . . . . . 19-032
        ss.7–9 . . . . . . . . . . . . . . . . . . . 27-113
    s.8 . . . . . . . . . . . . . . . . 6-016, 19-032
    s.8A . . . . . . . . . . . . . . . . . . . . . . 6-016
    s.9(1) . . . . . . . . . . . . . . . . . . . . . 19-032
        (a) . . . . . . . . . . . . . . . . . . . . . 19-032
        (1A) . . . . . . . . . . . . . . . . . . . 35-104
    s.9A . . . . . . . . . . . . . . . . . . . . . . 19-034
        (2)(a) . . . . . . . . . . . . . . . . . . . 19-034
    s.9B . . . . . . . . . . . . . . . . . . . . . . 19-036
    s.9C . . . . . . . . . . . . . . . . . . . . . . 19-036
    Pt IV s.28A . . . . . . . . . . . . . . . . . 19-037
    s.28C . . . . . . . . . . . . . . . . . . . . . 19-033
    s.29 . . . . . . . . . . . . . . . . . . . . . . 19-039
        (1) . . . . . . . . . . . . . . . . . . . . . 19-039
        (2) . . . . . . . . . . . . . . . . . . . . . . 6-016
    s.34(1) . . . . . . . . . . . . . . . . . . . . 19-042
    s.36 . . . . . . . . . . . . . . . . . . . . . . 10-062
        (1) . . . . . . . . . . . . . . . . . . . . . 19-042
        (1A) . . . . . . . . . . . . . . . . . . . 19-042
    s.42 . . . . . . . . . . . . . . . . . . . . . . . 5-054
    s.43 . . . . . . . . . . . . . . . . . . . . . . . 5-054
    Pt V s.50(6) . . . . . . . . . . . . . . . . 18-193
    Pt VII s.71 . . . . . . . . . . . . . . . . . 25-004
    Pt IX s.86 . . . . 12-042, 19-019, 19-031, 33-041
    Pt X s.98 . . . . . . . . . . . . 5-019, 19-023
        (1)(b) . . . . . . . . . . . . . . . . . . . 19-015
        (2) . . . . . . . . . . . . . . . . . . . . . 19-015
    Sch.1A . . . . . . . . . . . . . . . . . . . . . 5-054
        para.5 . . . . . . . . . . . . . . . . . . . 19-034
1970 Income and Corporation Taxes Act (c.10)
    Pt IX Ch.I s.208 . . . . . . . . . . . . . 3-021
    s.218 . . . . . . . . . . . . . . . . . . . . . 37-004
    Ch.II s.222 . . . . . . . . . . . . . . . . . 35-081
1970 Finance Act (c.24)
    Pt II Ch.II . . . . . . . . . . . . . . . . . . 35-081
1972 European Communities Act (c.68)
    Pt I s.1 . 5-004, 12-029, 31-012, 34-039
    Sch.1 . . . . . . . . 12-029, 31-012, 34-039
1973 Matrimonial Causes Act (c.18) . . . 16-003, 25-074
    Pt II ss.25B–25D . . . . . . . . . . . . 16-001
    s.28 . . . . . . . . . . . . . . . . . . . . . . 16-001
1973 Overseas Pensions Act (c.21) . . . . 13-009, 15-022, 25-039, 26-006
1975 Inheritance (Provision for Family and Dependants) Act (c.63)
    Pt 2 s.9(1) . . . . . . . . . . . . . . . . . 21-089
1976 Divorce (Scotland) Act (c.39) . . . . 16-003
1978 Interpretation Act (c.30) . . . . 8-043, 9-034
    Sch.1 . . . 5-004, 6-071, 12-029, 19-043, 31-012, 34-039
1983 Medical Act (c.54) . . . . . . 14-027, 34-033
1984 Matrimonial and Family Proceedings Act (c.42)
    Pt III . . . . . . . . . . . . . . . . . . . . . 16-003
    Pt IV . . . . . . . . . . . . . . . . . . . . . 16-003
1984 Inheritance Tax Act (c.51) . . . . . . 21-093, 21-106, 24-074, 28-001, 28-003, 28-022, 28-031, 28-035, 28-038, 28-058, 28-066, 28-077, 34-002, 34-041
    Pt I s.2(1) . . . . 21-002, 21-015, **21-025, 21-029, 21-101, 28-029, 28-061**
        (2) . . . . . . **21-025, 21-091, 21-101, 28-029**
        (a) . . . . . . . . . . . **21-040, 21-057**
        (b) . . . . . . . . . . . **21-040, 21-057**
        (3) . . . . . . . . . . . . . . . . . . . **28-061**
    s.3(1) . . . . . 21-002, 21-007, 21-015, 24-069, 28-011
        (2) . . . . . . . . . . . . . . . . . . . . . 28-011
        (3) . . . . . . 18-007, 21-003, 21-011, 21-066, 21-068, 21-084, 24-069, 28-001, 28-012, 28-013, 28-067, 28-068, 28-069, 28-070
        (4) . . . . . . . . . . . . . . . . . . . . **28-029**
    s.3A(1A)(c)(i) . . . . . . . . . . . . . 21-057
        (2) . . . . . . . . . . . . . . . . . . . . . 21-057
        (b) . . . . . . . . . . . . . . . . . . . . 21-058
    s.4(1) . . . . . 21-089, 21-105, 28-006, 28-011, 28-076
    s.5(1) . . . . . 21-004, 21-048, 21-060, 21-098, 28-006, 28-008, 28-076
        (a)(ii) . . . . . . . . . . . . . . . . . 28-071

1984 Inheritance Tax Act—*cont.*
    (b) . . . . . . . . . . . 28-011, 28-072
    (2) . . . . . . 21-004, 21-066, 21-105,
        21-107, 28-013, 28-076, 28-077
  s.6(1) . . . . . . . . . . . . . . . . . . . . 28-010
  s.7(2) . . . . . . 21-002, 28-042, 28-049
  s.10 . . . 6-035, 6-132, 6-152, 21-012,
      21-015, 21-018, 21-022, 21-024,
      21-029, 21-030, 21-032, 21-033,
      21-034, 21-035, 21-036, 21-039,
      21-040, 21-049, 21-053, 21-056,
      21-066, 21-067, 21-068, 21-085,
      21-105, 21-110, 24-069, 25-026,
      28-001, 28-022, 28-025, 28-027,
      28-028, 28-032, 28-046, 28-070,
               36-022, 36-023
    (1) . . . . . . 21-029, 21-038, 21-050,
                          28-070
      (a) . . . . . . . . . . . . . . . . . 21-038
      (b) . . . . . . . . . . . . . . . . . 21-039
    (3) . . . . . . . . . . . . . . . . . . . 28-070
  ss.10–17 . . . . . . . . . . 21-062, 21-084
  s.11 . . . . . . . 21-040, 21-042, 21-056
    (1) . . . . . . . . . . . . 21-040, 21-041
  s.12 . 6-152, 21-015, 21-018, 21-093,
                  22-022, 36-023
    (1) . . . . . . . 6-132, 21-011, 21-015,
      21-016, 21-017, 21-018, 21-025,
      21-026, 28-001, 28-022, 28-023,
                          28-024
    (2) . . 6-008, 6-068, 6-132, 21-011,
      21-015, 21-016, 21-017, 21-025,
      21-027, 21-028, 28-001, 28-022,
                          34-027
    (2ZA) . . . 21-011, 21-068, 21-084,
              28-001, 28-067, 34-027
  s.12A(1) . . . . . . . . . 21-011, 21-084
  s.13 . 6-152, 21-015, 28-001, 28-022,
                28-029, 28-032, 28-064
    (2) . . . . . . 28-030, 28-031, 28-032
      (d) . . . . . . . . . . . . . . . . . 28-031
    (3) . . . . . . . . . . . . . . . . . . . 28-030
    (4) . . . . . . . . . . . . . . . . . . . 28-030
    (5) . . . . . . . . . . . . 28-029, 28-030
  Pt II Ch.I . . . . . . . . . . . . 21-062, 21-084
  s.18 . . . . . 21-032, 21-044, 21-056,
                          21-064
  s.19 . . . . . . . . . . . . . . . . . . . . 21-056
  s.21 . . . . . 21-018, 21-045, 21-056,
                          24-069
    (1) . . . . . . . . . . . . . . . . . . . 21-046
  s.28 . . . . . . . . . . . . . . . . . . . . 21-047
    (4) . . . . . . . . . . . . . . . . . . . 28-031
  Pt III Ch.I s.43(1) . . . . . . . . . . . 21-004
    (2) . . . . . . . . . . . . . . . . . . . 21-004
      (a) . . . . . . . . 21-071, 34-028
      (c) . . 21-071, 28-004, 34-028
  s.44 . . . . . . . . . . . . . . . . . . . . 21-079
    (1) . . . . . . . . . . . 21-078, 28-037
    (2) . . . . . . . . . . . . . . . . . . . 28-038
  s.47 . . . . . . . . . . . . . . . . . . . . 28-072
  s.47A . . . . 21-004, 21-048, 28-076
  s.48 . . . . . . . . . . . . . . . . . . . . 28-072
    (3) . . . . 28-035, 34-028, 35-101
      (a) . . . . . . . . . . . . . . . 28-010
    (3B) . . . . . . . . . . . . . . . . . . 28-010
    (3E) . . . . . . . . . . . . . . . . . . 28-010
  Ch.II s.49 . . . . . . . . . . . . . . . . 21-097
    (1) . . . . 28-006, 28-008, 28-071
    (1A) . . . . . . . . . . . . . . . . . . 28-008
  ss.49–53 . 21-060, 21-069, 21-097,
                  28-001, 28-003
  s.49A . . . . . . . . . . . . . . . . . . 28-005
  s.49D . . . . . . . . . . . . . . . . . . 28-005
  s.50 . . . . . . . . . . . . . . . . . . . . 28-006
    (2) . . . . . . . . . . . . . . . . . . . 28-009
    (3) . . . . . . . . . . . . . . . . . . . 28-009
  s.51 . . . . . . . . . . . . . 28-006, 28-071
  s.52 . . . . . . . . . . . . . 28-006, 28-071
    (1) . . . . . . . . . . . . . . . . . . . 28-011
    (2A) . . . . . . . . . . . . . . . . . . 28-011
  s.53(1) . . . . . . . . . . . . . . . . . 28-011
  s.55 . . . . . . . . . . . . . . . . . . . . 28-066
  s.55A . . . . . . . . . . . . . . . . . . 21-050
  Ch.III s.58(1) . . . . . . 28-007, 28-035,
                    34-028, 35-101
      (b) . . . . . . . . . . . . . . . . . 28-061
      (d) . . 21-011, 21-072, 21-073,
             21-076, 21-077, 21-078,
             25-077, 28-001, 28-012,
             28-018, 28-035, 28-057,
             34-027, 34-028, 34-041,
             34-042, 35-101, 38-031,
                          39-020
      (f) . . 28-011, 28-035, 34-028,
                          35-101
    (1A) . . . . . . . . . . . . . . . . . . 28-061
    (2) . . . . 21-075, 21-076, 21-077
    (2A) . . . . . . . . . . . . . . . . . . 21-074
      (a) . . 21-073, 21-074, 28-001,
                     34-041, 34-042
      (b) . . 28-001, 34-041, 34-042
  s.59(1) . . . . . . . . . . . . . . . . . 28-005
  s.60 . . . . . . . . . . . . . . . . . . . . 28-052
  s.62 . . . . . . . . . . . . . . . . . . . . 28-050
    (1) . . . . . . . . . . . . . . . . . . . 28-040
  s.62A . . . . . . . . . . . 28-040, 28-054
  s.63 . . . . . . . . . . . . . . . . . . . . 28-047
  s.64 . . . . . . . . . . . . . 28-066, 34-028
    (1) . . . . . . . . . . . . . . . . . . . 28-039
  s.65 . . . . . . . . . . . . . 21-082, 28-066
    (1) . . . . 28-045, 28-046, 28-047
    (4) . . . . . . . . . . . . . . . . . . . 28-047
    (6) . . . . . . . . . . . . . . . . . . . 28-046
    (6)–(8) . . . . . . . . . . . . . . . . 28-047
    (7) . . . . . . . . . . . . . . . . . . . 28-011
    (9) . . . . . . . . . . . . . . . . . . . 28-046
  s.66(1) . . . . . . . . . 28-039, 28-042
    (2) . . . . . . . . . . . . . . . . . . . 28-043
    (3) . . . . . . . . . . . . . . . . . . . 28-039
      (b) . . . . . . . . . . . . . . . . . 28-041
      (c) . . . . . . . . . . . . . . . . . 28-042
    (4) . . . . . . . . . . . . . . . . . . . 28-040
    (5) . . . . . . . . . . . . . . . . . . . 28-041
  s.67(1) . . . . . . . . . 28-041, 28-050
    (3)(b) . . . . . . . . . . . . . . . . 28-041

1984 Inheritance Tax Act—cont.
    s.68(1) ................ 28-049
        (2) ................ 28-052
        (3) .......... 28-052, 28-055
        (4)(c) .............. 28-049
    s.69(1) ................ 28-053
        (4) ................ 28-055
    s.70(3)–(10) ............ 28-066
        (5) ................ 28-066
        (10) ............... 28-066
    s.72 ............ 28-066, 34-028
        (2) ................ 28-066
        (3) ................ 28-066
        (5) ................ 28-066
    s.81 ..... 21-078, 21-080, 36-024
        (1) ................ 21-078
    Ch.IV s.86 .. 6-152, 21-015, 21-047,
        28-001, 28-017, 28-035, 28-061,
        28-064, 28-065, 28-066, 34-028,
        35-007, 35-101, 36-024, 37-008,
        38-005
        (1) ..... 6-152, 28-030, 29-048
            (a) ............. 28-063
        (2) ................ 28-062
        (3) ................ 28-064
        (4) ................ 28-066
    s.89B ................. 28-005
    Pt IV s.94 ................ 21-015
        (1) ................ 21-015
    s.98 .................. 21-101
    s.102(1) .... 21-015, 28-029, 28-030
    Pt V Ch.I s.103(1) ........... 28-048
    Ch.II s.115(1) ............. 28-048
    Ch.V s.151 . 21-093, 25-077, 28-012,
        28-018, 28-073, 38-031, 39-020
        (2) .... 21-011, 21-090, 21-091,
            21-092, 21-094, 21-095,
            21-096, 28-001, 28-071,
            34-027
            (a) .. 21-092, 21-093, 21-097
            (b) .. 21-092, 21-094, 21-097
        (3) .... 21-011, 21-060, 21-069,
            21-092, 21-097, 21-098,
            28-001, 28-003, 28-034,
            28-071, 34-027
        (4) ........... 21-105, 28-077
        (5) ................ 21-079
    s.153 ................. 28-070
    Pt VI Ch.I s.160 ..... 21-005, 21-089,
        21-090
    Ch.II s.171 . 21-086, 21-101, 21-102
        (2) ................ 21-090
    Pt VII s.201(4) .............. 28-038
    s.210 .................. 21-105
    Pt IX s.267A ............... 21-015
        (d) ................ 21-015
    s.268 .................. 21-036
        (1) ................ 28-070
    s.270 ............ 21-038, 28-031
    s.271A .......... 34-002, 34-009
        (1) ................ 34-009
    s.272 ...... 21-003, 21-004, 21-011,
        21-048, 28-076

    Sch.A1 ............ 28-010, 34-006
1985 Family Law (Scotland) Act (c.37)
    ...................... 16-003
1986 Finance Act (c.41) ............ 17-006
    Pt V s.102 ................ 21-051
        (3) .................. 21-051
    ss.102A–102C ........... 21-054
1986 Insolvency Act (c.45)
    Pt VII s.249 ................. 8-005
    Pt XVIII s.435 ............... 8-005
1986 Social Security Act (c.50)
    Pt I s.7 ................ 14-031
1988 Income and Corporation Taxes Act (c.1)
    ..................... 3-011, 37-010
    Pt I (1) ............. **28-014, 38-006**
        (2) .................. **38-006**
    s.11(1) ................ 39-011
    Pt IV Ch.VIII s.129B .... 8-015, 8-042
    Pt V Ch.II s.165 ............ 37-001
    Pt VII Ch.I s.273 ........... 26-043
    Pt IX s.369 ................. 35-090
    Pt XIV Ch.I .......... 3-021, 22-019
    s.590 ...... 3-080, 3-085, 27-047
        (2) ................. 3-005
            (a) .......... 4-014, 27-046
            (b) ............. 37-009
            (c) .............. 4-004
            (e) .............. 4-004
        (3) .................. 3-005
    ss.590–612 ............... 3-004
    s.591(1) .......... 3-005, 38-003
    s.591B ........... 3-010, 26-046
    s.591C .................. 3-010
    s.592 ................... 3-005
        (1)(a) .......... 3-006, 4-004
        (2) .................. 3-008
        (4) ............. 3-007, 6-043
        (6) .................. 3-007
        (7) .................. 3-007
        (8) .................. 3-007
    s.595 .... 38-011, 38-023, 38-028
        (1) ..... 6-128, 27-061, 38-015
    s.596A ...... 2-070, 2-071, 2-072,
        35-074, 35-076
    s.596B .......... 35-074, 35-076
    s.598(2) ................. 3-009
    s.600 . 2-066, 2-067, 2-071, 2-072,
        18-048
    s.601 . 2-063, 2-065, 2-067, 2-072,
        3-011
        (6)(a) ................ 2-065
    ss.601–603 .............. 3-011
    s.611 .................. 19-013
        (1) ........... 3-004, 38-006
        (2) .......... 35-015, 38-006
    s.611AA ................. 3-022
    s.611A .................. 3-021
    s.612 .... 35-025, 35-055, 38-007,
        38-008, 38-022
        (1) ........... 3-004, 35-034
    Ch.II s.613(4)(b)–(d) ........ 3-021
    s.614 .................. 25-039
        (5) ................. 37-018

# TABLE OF STATUTES

1988 Income and Corporation Taxes Act—*cont.*
    s.615 .... 21-011, 21-027, 25-039,
        28-019, 34-041, 37-001, 37-002,
        37-003, 37-004, 37-005, 37-010,
        37-011, 37-012, 37-013, 37-014,
        37-015, 37-016, 37-018, 37-019,
        37-020, 37-021, 37-022, 37-023,
        37-024, 37-025, 37-026, 37-027,
        37-028, 38-001
      (3) ........... 21-027, 37-022
      (6) ........... 37-001, 37-004
        (b) ................ 37-008
        (c) ................ 37-009
      (6A)(b) .............. 37-010
        (c) ................ 37-010
        (d) ................ 37-010
      (6D) ................. 37-010
      (7) .................. 37-010
      (11) ................. 37-012
      (12) ................. 37-012
      (13) ........... 28-019, 37-011
      (14) ................. 37-011
    Ch.III s.620 ......... 3-021, 3-022
    s.621 ............... 3-021, 3-022
    s.622(3) ................ 3-021
    s.624 ............ 38-031, 39-020
      (1) .... 26-067, 28-014, 28-018,
        28-020, 37-004, 38-032
      (2) ........... 28-015, 38-032
    Ch.IV .................... 3-021
    s.630 ............ 3-014, 27-047
      (1) ............ 3-015, 6-137
    s.634A ............ 3-058, 3-059
      (4) ........... 3-059, 14-036
    s.638(1) ................ 3-022
    s.640(1) ................ 3-015
      (2) .................. 3-015
    s.641A .................. 3-015
    s.643(2) ................ 3-015
    Pt XV Ch.IA s.660A(7) ....... 22-019
    Ch.IV s.686(2)(c) ... 38-004, 38-019
    Sch.22 .................. 3-011
1989 Finance Act (c.26)
    Pt II Ch.I s.43 ........ 24-041, 27-024
    s.76(1) ................ 38-009
      (3) .................. 38-009
    Pt III s.178 ... 12-042, 19-019, 19-031,
        33-041
    Sch.6 Pt I para.9 ....... 35-074, 35-076
1992 Social Security Contributions and Benefits
    Act (c.4) .................... 37-025
    Pt I ....................... 26-043
    s.1(6) .................... 24-047
      (a) .................... 37-027
    s.2 ....................... 37-027
    s.6 ............... 24-047, 27-141
      (1) ........... 22-029, 24-058
    s.10 ............. 24-047, 35-047
    s.10A ..................... 24-047
1992 Taxation of Chargeable Gains Act (c.12)
    .... 2-118, 9-149, 9-151, 9-152, 9-160,
        22-029
    Pt I Ch.1 s.1(3) ...... 25-092, 25-101,

      25-103, 25-105, 25-106,
      25-107
    s.1A .................... 25-008
      (3) ................... 38-021
    s.1H .................... 25-008
    s.1I ..................... 38-020
    Ch.2 s.2(1) ........ 38-021, 39-015
    Ch.3 s.3 ................ 38-024
    s.5 ..................... 38-020
    s.10 ....... 25-015, 38-021, 39-015
    s.12 .................... 25-110
    s.13 .................... 25-100
    s.14B ................... 25-015
    s.14D(1) ................ 39-015
    Pt II Ch.I s.17 .............. 2-117
    s.18(1) .................. 9-155
      (6)–(8) ................ 2-123
    Ch.II s.21(2) ............. 9-152
    s.22 ...... 8-033, 22-029, 36-020
      (1) ................... 9-152
      (c) ................... 22-029
    s.24(1) .................. 9-152
    s.25A .................... 9-152
    s.26(3) .................. 2-123
    s.28 ..................... 9-154
    ss.29–34 ................. 9-152
    s.30 ..................... 2-117
    Ch.III s.37 ............... 9-149
    s.38(1) .................. 9-155
      (a) ........... 2-117, 9-158
      (b) .................... 9-158
    s.39 ..................... 9-149
    s.42 ............... 9-157, 9-158
    s.44 ...... 9-162, 18-125, 18-189
    s.45(1) .................. 9-162
    Pt III Ch.II .............. 25-007
    s.68 ....... 6-152, 25-007, 25-093
    s.68A .................... 25-007
    s.68B .................... 25-007
    s.69 ..................... 25-007
    s.71(1) .................. 9-152
    s.86 ..... 23-004, 25-001, 25-089,
      25-090, 25-091, 25-092, 25-093,
      25-094, 25-101, 25-102, 25-104,
      25-106, 25-107, 32-021
      (1) ........... 25-092, 25-100
      (e) ................... 25-098
    s.87 ..... 23-004, 25-001, 25-090,
      25-091, 25-101, 25-102, 25-103,
      25-104, 25-106, 25-107, 25-110,
      25-111, 26-027, 26-066, 32-021
    ss.87–97 ................ 25-089
    s.87B(2) ................ 25-110
    s.87D ................... 25-108
    s.87G ................... 25-109
    s.87I ................... 25-109
    s.91 .................... 25-111
    s.97(1) ................. 25-105
      (4) ................... 25-105
      (7) ................... 25-104
      (7A) .................. 25-104
    Pt IV Ch.II s.127 ............. 9-153
    s.137 .................... 2-007

# TABLE OF STATUTES

1992 Taxation of Chargeable Gains Act—*cont.*
    Ch.III s.144(1) ............. 9-152
    Pt V Ch.I s.161 .............. 9-152
    Ch.II s.165 ................. 6-152
        s.169B ................. 6-152
    Pt VI Ch.I s.171 ............ 9-160
    Ch.III s.210 ................ 36-020
    Pt VII s.225 ................ 9-163
        s.237 ............ 22-029, 26-067
            (a) ............ 22-029, 35-038
        s.239 ............. 6-152, 21-047
        s.239A ................. 4-030
        s.260 .................. 6-152
        s.262 .................. 9-166
        s.263 .................. 9-167
        s.263B ................. 8-015
        s.271 ............. 8-049, 8-050
            (1)(c)(ii) . 23-004, 25-001, 37-019
            (g) .................. 3-008
            (1A) ..... 8-048, 12-003, 23-004,
                25-001, 25-016, 25-091, 31-001,
                31-039, 33-011, 34-043, 38-021,
                39-015
            (12) ..... 25-016, 25-091, 31-039,
                34-043, 38-021, 39-015
    Pt VIII s.272 ..... 2-118, 8-071, 9-020,
        9-100, 9-120, 14-021, 17-008
            (5) .................. 2-120
    ss.272–274 ................ 2-118
        s.273 .................. 2-118
        s.286 ............ 21-038, 28-031
    Sch.1C para.5 .............. 38-020
        (2) ................... 25-008
    Sch.4ZA ................... 25-013
        para.1 ............ 2-101, 8-012
    Sch.5 ..................... 25-089
        para.1 ................ 25-100
            (3) ................. 25-100
        para.2(1) ............. 25-096
            (3) ................. 25-097
            (4) ................. 25-096
        para.5A ............... 25-092
        para.5B ............... 25-092
        para.6 ................ 25-101
        para.7 ................ 25-093
        para.8(1) ............. 25-093
            (3) ................. 25-093
            (4) ................. 25-094
            (6) ................. 25-093
    Sch.7 Pt I para.2 ............ 6-152
1993 Pension Schemes Act (c.48) ..... 12-030
    Pt I s.1 .. 2-011, 4-016, 35-011, 37-018
        (1) ...... 12-030, 25-074, 35-014,
              37-008
        (2)(a) ................ 2-045
    Pt III Ch.I s.8 .......... 7-011, 7-018
            (3) ................. 14-031
        s.15 .................. 10-025
        s.16 .................. 10-025
    Ch.II s.42A(3) ............. 14-031
    Pt IV ..................... 14-030
        Ch.I .................. 12-006
            s.71 ............... 14-030

        Ch.II .................. 10-025
        Ch.III ................. 10-025
        Ch.IV s.93A .............. 7-019
        Ch.V s.101AA(1) .......... 14-030
            s.101AB(1) ........... 14-030
    Pt IVZA Ch.I .............. 12-001
    Pt X s.146 ................. 11-004
        (4) ...... 11-004, 29-020, 31-008,
              34-010
    Pt XI s.159 .......... 7-055, 18-077
    Pt XII s.181 .......... 2-017, 2-041
        (1) .................. 14-030
1994 Value Added Tax Act (c.23)
    Pt I s.3(1) ................. 22-003
        s.4(1) ................ 22-003
            (2) ................. 22-003
        s.19(5) ............... 11-010
        s.24(1) ............... 22-005
            (2) ................. 22-004
    Pt II s.31(1) ............... 22-003
    Sch.3 para.1 ............... 22-003
    Sch.9 ............... 22-003, 22-015
1995 Pensions Act (c.26) ..... 12-030, 25-074,
            37-018, 38-005
    Pt I s.3 .................... 8-005
        s.7 .................... 5-054
        s.10 ................... 8-005
        ss.33–36 ............... 8-003
        s.34 ................... 8-004
        s.35 ................... 8-004
        s.36A .................. 8-052
        s.37 ............ 17-002, 17-003
        s.38 ................... 14-037
        s.40 ... 2-084, 8-005, 9-066, 17-008,
            17-035, 37-018
            (5) .................. 8-005
        s.47 ............. 8-006, 22-013
        s.67A(6) ............... 18-189
        s.75 ................... 6-122
        s.76 ............ 17-002, 17-004
        s.91 . 7-010, 18-077, 18-094, 21-005,
            21-059, 24-055, 28-013, 35-038
            (1) ............ 13-021, 18-094
                (a) ............... 22-030
            (5) ............ 18-077, 18-094
                (b)(ii) .............. 13-021
        s.92(2) ............... 13-015
            (4) ................. 13-015
            (5) ................. 13-015
        s.93 .................. 13-015
        s.123 .................. 8-005
    Pt IV s.176 .......... 25-074, 37-018
1996 Finance Act (c.8)
    Sch.9 para.13(4) ........... 36-010
1998 Finance Act (c.36)
    Sch.18 Pt IV para.24 ......... 19-034
        Pt V para.36 ............. 19-033
1998 Human Rights Act (c.42)
    s.3 ...................... 38-015
1999 Welfare Reform and Pensions Act (c.30)
    ............. 3-061, 16-003, 22-018
    Pt II s.11(2)(h) ...... 25-038, 25-039
    Pt IV Ch.I s.28(1) ..... 16-003, 35-043

# TABLE OF STATUTES

1999 Welfare Reform and Pensions Act—*cont.*
    s.29 .................. 10-043
        (1) ..... 3-066, 16-003, 16-009,
                16-010
    s.46(1) ................ 16-003
2000 Financial Services and Markets Act (c.8)
    .... 2-004, 4-004, 4-022, 8-006, 22-019
    Pt II s.22 ................. 8-006
    Pt XVII Ch.I s.235 ...... 8-031, 9-060
    s.237 .................... 8-031
        (1) .................... 9-061
    Sch.1 Pt III para.18 .......... 9-061
    Sch.15A Pt 4 .............. 2-003
2000 Trustee Act (c.29) ............. 8-002
    Pt V s.31 .................. 2-121
        (1) .................... 5-024
    Pt VI s.36 ................. 8-002
2001 Capital Allowances Act (c.2) ..... 35-069
2003 Income Tax (Earnings and Pensions) Act
    (c.1) ... 2-016, 6-140, 14-004, 18-121,
          19-024, 23-018, 24-047, 24-053,
          24-063, 26-018, 30-015, 30-030,
          30-074, 30-075, 35-003, 35-094,
                35-105
    Pt 1 s.1(1) .... **27-008, 27-021, 27-029,**
        **27-036, 27-059, 27-087, 30-008**
        (a) .... 24-053, **27-017, 38-010,**
                    **38-016**
        (b) .... **27-017, 38-010, 38-016**
        (c) .................. **38-016**
        (2) ...... **27-038, 27-059, 27-087,**
                    **30-008**
        (3) ............ **27-059, 27-087**
    Pt 2 ................. 22-029, 35-002
    Ch.1 s.4 .......... 2-016, 27-010
    s.5 ................ 2-016, 27-010
        (3) .................... 2-018
    Ch.2 ..................... 35-069
    s.6(1)(a) ................ 24-053
        (3) .................... 35-091
    s.7(2)(c) ................ 28-047
        (3) .................... 24-053
        (4) .... 27-080, 27-107, 27-110,
                35-069, 35-091
        (6) .................... 28-047
        (c) .................. 35-091
    s.8 ............. 30-102, 30-104
    Ch.3 ..................... 35-069
    s.9 ...................... 22-029
        (2) .................... 24-053
        (4) .......... 27-080, 35-069
    s.10(2) ... 30-102, 30-104, 30-105
        (3) .......... 27-110, 35-070
        (3)–(5) .......... 30-102, 30-104
    s.12(1) .......... 27-080, 35-069
    s.13 .................... 36-022
        (3) .......... 27-107, 35-070
    Ch.4 ..................... 35-069
    s.15 .................... 35-084
        (1A) ................ 37-015
        (2) .................... 29-039
    s.16 .................... **27-084**
        (1)–(4) ........ 27-083, 27-084

        (2) ................ 27-085
    s.17 .......... 27-087, 27-088
        (1)–(3) .............. 27-083
    s.18 .................... 24-039
    s.19 .................... 24-039
    Ch.5 ss.20–41ZA .......... 27-100
    s.24A .......... 27-102, 27-103
    s.26A ... 27-100, 27-101, 27-102,
                    27-103
    s.27 ..... 24-006, 24-013, 35-075
    s.39B .................. **35-019**
    Ch.5A ........... 20-003, 35-075
    Ch.8 s.50 ................ 27-092
    Pts 2–7 .................. 24-040
    Pt 3 Ch.1 s.62 . 24-040, 27-092, 35-021,
                    35-089
        (2) ................ 24-053
        (3) ................ 24-053
    Ch.2 s.63(4) .............. 18-129
    s.67 .................... 18-130
    s.68 .................... 18-129
    s.69A ..... 6-141, 24-064, 36-018
    s.69B .......... 6-142, 24-065
    Chs 2–7 .................. 18-121
    Ch.3 ............ 26-039, 26-040
    Ch.5 s.99 ................ 9-015
    s.105(2)(a) .............. 35-089
        (b) .................. 35-089
    s.106 .................... 35-089
        (2) .................... 35-089
    Ch.6 s.164 ................ 14-025
        (2) .................... 14-025
    s.166(a) ................ 35-094
        (b) .................. 35-094
    Ch.7 s.188 ........ 18-141, 27-032
    s.191 .................... 18-141
        (1) .................... 18-141
        (2) .................... 18-141
    Ch.10 ..... 18-135, 24-057, 30-011,
          30-012, 30-013, 30-014, 35-066
    s.201 ..... 6-136, 24-057, 30-011
    s.202 .................... 30-011
    s.203(1) ................ 24-067
        (2) .................... 18-135
    s.203A .................. 24-067
        (2) ............ 6-140, 24-063
    s.204 .................... 18-158
    s.205(3) ................ 18-135
        (4) .................... 18-135
    s.207 .................... 18-135
    s.208 .................... 14-004
    s.209 .................... 14-004
    Ch.11 s.216 .............. 18-129
    Ch.12 s.222 ...... 27-115, 35-070
    Pt 4 ... 27-040, 27-048, 27-049, 30-102
    Ch.1 s.227(3) ............ 27-048
    s.228A .......... 6-143, 24-066
    Ch.2 s.231(1) ............ 30-103
    s.232 .................... 35-069
    s.233(1)(a) .............. 30-104
        (b) .................. 30-104
    s.235 .................... 30-103
    Ch.5 s.262 .............. 35-069

# TABLE OF STATUTES

2003 Income Tax (Earnings and Pensions) Act—*cont.*
  Ch.9 .................... 27-049
    s.307 . 1-025, 3-007, 3-015, 6-136,
      6-139, 6-143, 24-024, 24-057,
      24-066, 27-049, 27-126, 30-004,
      30-008, 30-010, 30-011, 30-014,
      30-015, 30-022, 30-036, 30-077,
      30-102, 30-104, 30-105, 30-112,
      31-042, 33-024, 35-060, 36-018,
      37-015
      (1) ........... 35-066, 36-018
      (1A) ......... 30-014, 36-018
    s.308 . 1-025, 3-007, 3-015, 6-133,
      6-135, 6-138, 6-139, 6-143,
      24-053, 24-055, 27-049, 29-018,
      29-029, 31-026, 36-018, 37-015
    s.308A ... 6-143, 24-024, 24-034,
      24-053, 24-066, 25-039, 27-049,
      30-004, 36-018, 37-015, 39-014
    s.308B .... 6-143, 27-049, 27-050
      (4) .................. 6-143
    s.308C ................. 6-143
  Ch.11 s.316 ............. 18-134
  Pt 5 Ch.1 s.327(3) ........... 35-069
    (4) ................. 35-069
  Ch.2 ............. 7-024, 39-006
    s.333(1)(a) ............. 39-006
    (3)(b) ............... 39-006
    s.355 .... 24-021, 24-027, 39-004,
      39-005, 39-008, 39-011, 39-012
  Ch.6 ................... 35-084
  Pt 6 .................... 35-047
  Ch.1 ................... 35-001
    s.386 .... 24-056, 38-011, 38-012,
      38-013, 38-014, 38-015, 39-007
      (1) ..... 3-005, 27-061, 28-016,
      35-027, 38-009, 38-010,
      38-012, 38-013, 38-015,
      38-016, 38-021, 38-023,
      38-028, 38-032, 39-007,
      39-011
      (6) ........... 38-011, 38-018
    s.387(2)(a) ............. 39-007
      (b) ............... 39-007
      (c) ............... 39-007
    s.388 .... 38-011, 38-012, 38-014
    s.390 .... 24-034, 27-072, 27-073,
      27-075, 39-004, 39-006, 39-007,
      39-008, 39-011
    s.392 .......... 38-018, 38-028
      (1) .... 38-016, 38-017, 38-018
      (c) ............... 38-018
      (6) ............... 38-018
  Ch.2 ...... 23-013, 24-047, 27-106,
      35-001, 35-059
    s.393(1) .. 35-017, 35-068, 35-075
      (2) ................. 38-008
    s.393A(1) ....... 35-009, 35-013
      (2)(b) ............... 37-020
      (2)(a) ............... 35-053
      (4) ........... 35-014, 35-015
    s.393B .. 22-029, 24-060, 26-074,
      27-056, 27-124, 35-019, 35-021,
      35-024, 35-027, 35-030, 35-034,
      35-051, 35-055, 35-082, 37-004,
      38-008
      (1) ........... 35-026, 35-031
      (a) ............... 35-026
      (b) ............... 35-026
      (c) .. 35-026, 35-027, 35-031,
      35-056
      (d) ................ 35-041
      (2) .... 26-074, 35-044, 35-048,
      35-050
      (a) .. 24-060, 26-025, 27-052,
      27-056, 35-021, 35-046,
      35-052, 38-022, 38-030,
      39-017
      (b) .. 30-077, 35-052, 35-053,
      39-018
      (c) ................ 36-019
      (3) .... 24-047, 27-045, 35-054,
      35-056, 35-059, 36-004
      (a) ............... 36-007
      (b) ............... 36-007
      (c) ............... 36-019
      (b) ............... 39-019
      (d) ............... 36-007
      (4) ................ 36-007
      (a) ............... 36-019
      (5) ................ 35-043
    s.394 .... 2-070, 24-040, 26-025,
      26-059, 26-063, 27-068, 27-136,
      30-002, 30-077, 33-022, 35-002,
      35-004, 35-030, 35-036, 35-047,
      35-048, 35-050, 35-051, 35-053,
      35-059, 35-067, 35-068, 35-074,
      35-075, 35-076, 35-077, 35-081,
      35-083, 35-086, 35-090, 35-091,
      36-003, 37-020, 37-027, 38-021,
      38-022, 38-023, 38-024, 38-025,
      38-027, 38-029, 38-030, 39-017,
      39-018, 39-019
      (1) .... 29-039, 35-036, 35-069,
      35-070, 35-075, 35-077,
      35-078, 35-104
      (1A) ................ 35-078
      (2) ........... 35-069, 35-104
      (4) .......... 27-108, 35-071
      (4A)–(4C) ........... 35-004
      (4B) ............... 27-136
      (4C) ............... 35-002
      (5) ................ 35-003
    s.394A .. 35-070, 35-077, 35-078,
      38-022, 39-017
      (3)(d) ............... 35-077
    s.395 .... 23-018, 35-080, 35-086,
      38-022, 38-030, 39-017
    s.395A ................. 35-081
    s.395B .. 35-074, 35-076, 35-082,
      35-085, 35-086
      (1)(e) ............... 35-086
    s.395C ......... 26-016, 35-084
    s.396 ................. 38-021
    s.397 ................. 38-021

2003 Income Tax (Earnings and Pensions) Act—*cont.*
   s.398 ................. 35-089
     (1) ................. 35-036
   s.399 ................. 35-090
   s.399A ......... 35-072, 35-103
   Ch.3 ..................... 6-137
    s.401 .... 24-047, 29-039, 35-027,
      35-030, 35-055, 35-067, 35-074,
      37-016
     (3) ................. 35-067
    s.402(4) ........ 35-067, 37-016
    s.403 ........... 35-036, 37-020
    s.406 ................. 35-055
    s.408 ........... 6-137, 35-067
    s.414A ................. 37-020
   Pt 7 ..................... 30-105
   Ch.1 s.420 ............ 27-029
   Ch.4 s.465(4) ............ 27-031
   Ch.6 s.488 ............... 6-026
   Ch.7 s.516 ............... 6-026
   Pt 7A . 13-010, 15-022, 15-081, 22-020,
      22-021, 22-022, 22-027, 22-029,
      23-006, 24-048, 26-004, 27-001,
      27-033, 27-042, 27-066, 27-070,
      27-107, 27-110, 27-123, 27-134,
      27-136, 27-138, 27-141, 27-142,
      29-039, 35-002, 38-030
    Ch.1 ...... 27-003, 27-118, 27-119,
      27-120
     s.554A ... 27-006, 27-007, 27-008
      (1) ................. 27-015
       (a) ................. 27-011
       (b) ................. 27-011
       (c) ................. 27-013
        (ii) ............. 27-011
      (2) ................. 27-019
      (4) ................. 27-032
      (5A)–(5C) ............ 27-007
      (7) .... 22-029, 27-016, 27-031
       (a)–(c) ............ 27-121
       (b) ................. 27-118
      (11) ... 15-081, 22-027, 27-002,
       27-017, 27-018
     s.554AA ............... 27-007
      (1)(a) ............... 24-045
      (b) ................. 24-045
      (c) ................. 24-045
     ss.554AA–554AF ....... 27-007
     s.554AD ............... 27-010
     s.554B .. 24-050, 27-019, 27-020,
      27-021, 27-022, 27-023, 27-025,
      27-026, 27-027, 27-042, 27-043,
      27-044, 27-055, 27-056, 27-063,
      27-064, 27-073, 27-074, 27-085,
      27-108, 27-117, 27-118, 27-120,
      27-123, 27-141, 37-017
      (1) ................. 36-018
       (a) ................ 27-022
       (b) ................ 27-022
      (2) ................. 27-024
     s.554C .. 27-019, 27-022, 27-026,
      27-029, 27-034, 27-055, 27-056,

      27-067, 27-070, 27-073, 27-074,
      27-085, 27-093, 27-108, 27-141,
      35-038, 39-022
      (1) ................. 27-032
       (a)–(c) ............ 27-094
       (aa) ........ 27-005, 27-032
       (ab) . 27-005, 27-020, 27-032
       (b) ................ 27-096
       (c) ................ 27-096
       (d) ................ 27-058
       (e) ................ 27-096
      (3A) ................ 27-032
      (3B) ................ 27-032
      (3C) ................ 27-032
     s.554D .. 27-019, 27-022, 27-026,
      27-035, 27-055, 27-056, 27-096,
      27-108, 27-141
      (1) ................. 27-036
      (2) ................. 27-038
     s.554E ................ 36-003
      (1)(d) . 27-040, 27-045, 27-046,
       35-045, 36-018, 36-019
      (g) .. 22-021, 22-022, 22-027,
       27-040
      (h) .. 22-023, 22-024, 22-025,
       27-040
     s.554F ................ 27-041
     s.554G ................ 27-041
     s.554H ................ 27-041
     s.554OA ............... 27-005
     s.554P ......... 27-040, 27-049
     s.554Q ......... 27-042, 27-128
     s.554R ......... 27-043, 27-128
      (4) ................. 27-043
     s.554RA ........ 27-005, 27-044
     s.554S .. 27-018, 27-022, 27-040,
      27-051, 27-052, 27-053, 27-055,
      27-125, 27-137, 37-021, 37-023,
      37-027, 39-017
     s.554T ......... 27-040, 39-017
      (1) .......... 27-056, 27-057
     s.554U .. 27-040, 28-013, 35-002,
      35-050, 38-022, 38-029
      (1)–(3) ............. 27-059
     s.554V .. 26-014, 27-040, 27-063,
      27-066, 27-069, 39-017
     s.554W .. 26-014, 27-040, 27-067,
      27-070, 35-002, 35-050, 37-021,
      37-022, 37-023, 37-024, 38-029,
      38-030, 39-017, 39-019
     s.554X .. 27-034, 27-040, 27-072,
      27-073, 39-022
     s.554XA ............... 27-005
     s.554Z(3) ............. 27-009
      (7) .... 18-162, 27-032, 27-081
      (13)–(16) ........... 27-098
     s.554Z1 ........ 24-045, 27-012
    Ch.2 ...... 22-021, 22-023, 22-026,
      24-048, 26-005, 26-010, 27-003,
      27-006, 27-018, 27-020, 27-022,
      27-025, 27-026, 27-042, 27-043,
      27-044, 27-045, 27-049, 27-053,
      27-055, 27-056, 27-061, 27-063,

# TABLE OF STATUTES

2003 Income Tax (Earnings and Pensions) Act—*cont.*
    27-064, 27-067, 27-073, 27-076, 27-079, 27-080, 27-107, 27-116, 27-117, 27-118, 27-120, 27-125, 27-133, 27-136, 27-137, 27-138, 27-139, 27-140, 27-141, 30-078, 35-004, 35-050, 35-067, 37-023, 39-017
    s.554Z2 . 18-162, 27-101, 35-002, 38-030
      (1) .... 27-079, 27-083, 27-107
      (2) ................ 27-134
    s.554Z2A .............. 27-007
    s.554Z3 . 18-162, 27-081, 27-082, 27-095, 27-097
    s.554Z4 . 27-082, 27-083, 27-088, 27-092, 27-095, 27-097, 37-017, 37-023, 37-027
      (4) ................ 35-002
      (a) .. 27-085, 27-088, 37-021, 37-022, 37-023, 37-024
      (7) .......... 27-089, 35-002
    ss.554Z4–554Z6 .. 27-095, 27-097
    s.554Z4A ....... 27-110, 35-002, 38-022, 38-030, 39-017
    s.554Z5 . 23-018, 27-005, 27-081, 27-082, 27-090, 27-092, 35-004
    s.554Z6 .. 27-082, 27-092, 27-133
    s.554Z7 ............... 27-082
    s.554Z8 . 27-063, 27-082, 27-093, 27-099, 35-038
      (2) .......... 27-094, 27-095
      (3)(b) ............. 35-038
      (6) .......... 27-096, 27-097
    s.554Z9 ......... 27-102, 27-106
    ss.554Z9–554Z11A ...... 27-100
    s.554Z10 ........ 27-101, 27-106
    s.554Z11A ...... 27-106, 35-002, 38-022, 38-030, 39-017
    s.554Z11B .............. 27-005
    ss.554Z11B–554Z11G .... 27-105
    s.554Z11C .............. 27-005
    s.554Z12 ........ 27-108, 27-142
      (7) ................ 27-108
      (8) ................ 27-109
    s.554Z13 ........ 27-116, 27-142
    s.554Z14 . 27-117, 27-132, 27-142
    Ch.3 ...... 22-029, 27-003, 27-016, 27-118, 27-119, 27-121, 27-122, 27-123
    s.554Z16 .............. 22-029
    s.554Z17 .............. 27-120
    s.554Z18 ....... 27-120, 27-125, 27-127, 27-132, 27-141
    s.554Z19 ....... 27-120, 27-125, 27-129, 27-131, 27-132, 27-141
    s.554Z20(3) ............. 27-130
      (6) ................ 27-131
    s.554Z21 ........ 27-132, 27-142
    Pt 9 ...... 1-003, 1-006, 1-018, 3-009, 3-015, 13-008, 13-011, 13-012, 14-001, 14-004, 14-015, 14-017, 14-033, 15-024, 15-030, 15-031, 15-078, 18-001, 18-160, 19-024, 20-045, 22-029, 23-002, 23-005, 23-011, 24-047, 24-056, 24-060, 26-003, 26-014, 26-020, 26-021, 26-022, 26-023, 26-024, 26-025, 26-027, 26-031, 26-035, 26-038, 26-050, 26-074, 26-075, 27-040, 27-052, 27-056, 27-116, 27-124, 27-137, 27-138, 28-047, 30-001, 30-026, 30-030, 30-035, 30-074, 31-041, 33-003, 34-043, 35-002, 35-044, 35-046, 35-047, 35-049, 35-050, 35-059, 35-075, 35-103, 36-019, 37-023, 38-008, 38-021, 38-022, 39-017
    Ch.1 s.565 .............. 35-046
    Ch.2 ........... 13-009, 15-022
    s.566(1) ........ 13-009, 35-046
      (3) ................ 27-054
      (4) ................ 26-003
    s.567 ................. 26-004
      (1) ................ 35-046
      (2) .... 13-010, 15-022, 35-046
      (3) ................ 35-046
      (4) ................ 35-046
      (5) ................ 23-018
    s.567A ... 13-010, 15-022, 26-004, 26-005, 27-138, 30-024
    Ch.3 ...... 22-029, 26-003, 26-039, 37-021
    s.569 ................. 26-039
      (1) ................ 27-052
    s.572A ......... 26-040, 27-052
    Chs 3–15A .............. 26-006
    Ch.4 ...... 20-041, 20-043, 25-077, 26-003, 26-007, 26-008, 26-011, 26-025, 26-032, 26-034, 26-059, 27-052, 27-053, 28-013, 30-023, 30-024, 30-026, 30-030, 30-031, 30-074, 33-022, 34-043, 35-046, 35-048, 35-091, 37-023, 38-030, 39-017, 39-018
    s.573 ........... 26-011, 30-024
      (1) ........... 26-007, 27-052
      (2) .... 20-041, 26-007, 30-031, 30-035
      (2A) .. 26-029, 27-056, 35-044, 35-048
      (2A)–(2D) ............ 30-024
      (2B) .. 26-030, 27-056, 35-044, 35-048
      (2D) ............... 26-029
      (4) ................ 30-026
    s.574(1) ............... 26-008
      (aa) ............... 36-019
    s.574A ... 23-018, 36-019, 37-027
      (1) ................ 26-010
      (b) .. 27-053, 37-023, 39-017
      (2) .......... 26-010, 30-023
      (3) .... 26-014, 26-025, 27-056, 31-001, 35-010, 35-044, 35-050

2003 Income Tax (Earnings and Pensions) Act—*cont.*
 s.575 . . . . . . . . . . . 26-029, 26-035
  (1) . . . . . . . . . . . 26-032, 35-046
  (3) . . . . . . . . . . . 26-033, 35-091
 s.576 . . . . . . . . . . . . . . . . . 26-034
 s.576A . . . 26-035, 26-036, 30-075
  (4) . . . . . . . . . . . . . . . . . 26-037
  (5) . . . . . . . . . . . . . . . . . 26-038
 Ch.5 . . . . . . . . . . . . . . . . . . . 38-030
 s.577 . . . . . . . . . . . . . . . . . . 23-018
 Chs 5–14 . . . . . . . . . 26-007, 26-039
 Ch.5A . . . . . 13-009, 13-012, 14-004,
  20-039, 20-040, 20-041, 20-042,
  20-043, 22-029, 26-007, 26-023,
  26-039, 26-045, 30-031, 30-074,
        30-075
 s.579A . . . 7-024, 13-009, 14-003,
  15-022, 15-046, 19-024, 26-021,
    30-030, 30-035, 30-073
  (2) . . . . . . . . . . . . . . . . . 26-022
 s.579B . . 13-006, 13-010, 13-043,
     20-044, 26-032
 s.579C . . . . 3-034, 13-011, 30-073
 s.579CZA(1) . . . . . . . . . . . . 15-022
  (2) . . . . . . . . . . . . . . . . . 15-022
  (3)–(6) . . . . . . . . . . . . . . . 15-022
  (6) . . . . . . . . . . . . . . . . . 15-022
 s.579CA . . . . . . . . . . . . . . . 20-045
 s.579D . . . . . . . . . 13-009, 14-001
 Ch.8 s.597 . . . . . . . . . . . . . . 13-043
 Ch.10 . . . . . . 26-003, 26-007, 26-041
 s.609 . . . . . . . . . . . 26-041, 26-043
 s.610 . . . . . . . . . . . 26-041, 26-044
 s.611 . . . . 26-041, 26-045, 35-016
  (1) . . . . . . . . . . . . . . . . . 35-016
  (2) . . . . . . . . . . . 35-015, 35-016
 s.611A(1) . . . . . . . . . . . . . . 26-046
 s.612 . . . . . . . . . . . . . . . . . . 26-047
 s.613 . . . . . . . . . . . . . . . . . . 26-048
 s.614 . . . . . . . . . . . . . . . . . . 26-050
 Ch.11 s.615 . . . . . . . 23-002, 23-004,
  23-007, 23-008, 23-015, 24-042,
  24-051, 25-001, 26-019, 26-070,
  27-040, 27-067, 27-106, 35-005,
        35-010
 Ch.14 s.629 . . . . . . . . . . . . . 25-039
 s.630 . . . . . . . . . . . . . . . . . . 25-039
 Ch.15 . . . . . . 26-003, 26-051, 26-052
 s.633 . . . . . . . . . . . . . . . . . . 26-051
 s.634 . . . . . . . . . . . . . . . . . . 26-052
 s.635 . . . . . . . . . . . . . . . . . . 26-052
 s.636 . . . . . . . . . . . . . . . . . . 15-076
 Ch.15A . . . . 10-021, 13-009, 13-012,
  14-004, 14-007, 14-013, 14-056,
  14-059, 14-063, 14-065, 14-066,
  14-067, 14-068, 14-069, 22-029,
    26-006, 30-026, 30-033
 s.636A . . . . . . . . . . . . . . . . 26-062
  (1) . . . . . . . . . . . . . . . . . 26-021
   (a) . . . . . . . . . . . . . . . 26-021
   (b) . . . . . . . . . . . . . . . 26-021
  (1A) . . . . . . . . . . . . . . . . 26-021
  (3) . . . . . . . . . . . . . . . . . 26-021
  (4) . . . . . . . . . . . 26-021, 26-022
  (5) . . . . . . . . . . . 26-020, 26-022
 s.636C . . . . . . . . . . . . . . . . 20-044
 s.637A . . . . . . . . . . . . . . . . 14-003
 ss.637A–637N . . . . . . . . . . 30-035
 s.637B . . . . . . . . . . . . . . . . 14-003
 s.637C . . . . . . . . 14-063, 30-030
  (1) . . . . . . . . . . . . . . . . . 14-003
  (2) . . . . . . . . . . . . . . . . . 14-003
 s.637D . . . . . . . . . . . . . . . . 14-063
  (1) . . . . . . . . . . . . . . . . . 14-003
 s.637E . . . . . . . . . . . . . . . . 14-003
 s.637F . . . . . . . . . . . . . . . . 14-003
 s.637G . . . . . . . . . . . . . . . . 14-003
  (2) . . . . . . . . . . . . . . . . . 26-014
 s.637H . . . . . . . . 14-063, 15-046
  (5) . . . . . . . . . . . . . . . . . 15-046
  (6) . . . . . . . . . . . . . . . . . 15-046
 s.637I . . . . . . . . . . . . . . . . . 14-063
  (3) . . . . . . . . . . . . . . . . . 15-046
  (4) . . . . . . . . . . . . . . . . . 15-046
 (3) . . . . . . . . . . . . . . . . . . . 26-014
 s.637J . . . . . . . . . 14-063, 15-046
  (5) . . . . . . . . . . . . . . . . . 15-046
  (6) . . . . . . . . . . . . . . . . . 15-046
 s.637K . . . . . . . . . 14-063, 15-046
  (3) . . . . . . . . . . . . . . . . . 15-046
  (4) . . . . . . . . . . . . . . . . . 15-046
 s.637L . . . . . . . . . 14-063, 15-046
  (5) . . . . . . . . . . . . . . . . . 15-046
  (6) . . . . . . . . . . . . . . . . . 15-046
 s.637M . . . . . . . . 14-063, 15-046
  (5) . . . . . . . . . . . . . . . . . 15-046
  (6) . . . . . . . . . . . . . . . . . 15-046
 s.637N . . . . . . . . . . . . . . . . 15-046
 s.637P . . . . . . . . . . . . . . . . 14-005
 s.637Q . . 14-007, 14-014, 30-061,
        30-063
 s.637R . . . . . . . . . . . . . . . . 14-011
 s.637S . . 14-013, 14-015, 20-018,
  20-033, 24-008, 30-061, 30-063
  (6) . . . . . . . . . . . . . . . . . 14-063
 Ch.16 s.637 . . . . . . . . . . . . . 15-046
 Chs 16–18 . . . . . . . . . . . . . . 27-054
 Ch.17 . . . . . 13-009, 15-022, 26-003,
     26-006, 26-014
 s.641(1) . . . . . . . . . . . . . . . . 7-006
 s.643 . . . . . . . . . . . . . . . . . . 25-039
 s.644 . . . . . . . . . . . . . . . . . . 26-053
 s.644A . . . . . . . . . . . . . . . . 26-055
 s.646B . . . . . . . . . 15-022, 26-031
  (4) . . . . 13-009, 15-024, 15-030,
        15-031
 s.646C . . . . . . . . . 15-022, 26-031
  (1) . . . . . . . . . . . . . . . . . 15-022
 s.646D . . 26-031, 27-056, 35-044,
        35-049
 s.646E . . 26-031, 27-056, 35-044,
        35-049
 Ch.18 . . . . . . 13-009, 15-022, 26-006
 Pt 10 . . . . . . . . . . . . . . . . . . . 18-121
 Pt 11 . . . . . . . . . . . . . 18-121, 20-044

# TABLE OF STATUTES

2003 Income Tax (Earnings and Pensions) Act—*cont.*
    Ch.1 s.683(1)(b) .......... 20-044
        (2)(b) ....... 27-110, 35-070
        (3) ................ 20-044
        (3ZA) ........ 27-110, 35-070
        (3B) ............... 20-045
    Ch.2 s.684(7A)(b) ......... 27-112
    Ch.3 s.687 ............... 35-070
       s.687A ................ 27-110
       s.689 .......... 27-111, 27-112
    Ch.4 s.695A .............. 27-110
    Pt 12 ........ 13-010, 15-022, 26-004
    Pt 13 s.721 .......... 18-130, 39-005
        (1) ................... 27-102
    Sch.3 Pt 2 para.5 ............ 35-086
2003 Finance Act (c.14) .. 9-103, 9-111, 9-142, 36-005
    Pt 4 s.48 ....... 9-029, 9-102, 9-106
       (1) ..................... 9-110
       s.51 .......... 6-153, 9-103, 9-111
       s.52 .......... 6-153, 9-103, 9-111
       s.53 ..................... 6-153
       s.54(2) .................. 6-153
       s.116(3)(b) ............... 9-013
       s.118 .................... 2-118
    Sch.4 para.1(1) ............. 6-153
       paras 2–8 .......... 9-103, 9-111
       para.3 ................... 6-153
       para.8 ............ 6-153, 12-003
         (1) ................... 9-107
       paras 9–16 ............... 9-111
       paras 9–19 ............... 9-103
    Sch.5 para.2(4)(a) ....... 9-109, 9-142
       para.3 .. 9-101, 9-109, 9-115, 9-117, 9-120, 9-142
       para.8(1) ............ 9-109, 9-142
    Sch.15 Pt 3 para.10 ........... 8-012
       para.12 .................. 8-012
       para.18 .................. 8-012
       para.20 .................. 8-012
       para.39 .................. 8-012
    Sch.17A para.2 ............... 9-111
       para.3(1) ................. 9-111
         (2) ................... 9-111
       para.4(1) ................. 9-111
         (2) ................... 9-111
       paras 5–7A ............... 9-111
       para.8(1) ................. 9-111
         (2) ................... 9-111
       para.9 ................... 9-111
       para.15 .................. 9-113
       para.16 .................. 9-111
    Sch.24 ............. 24-043, 39-011
       para.1(2)(a) .............. 2-057
       para.8(b) ................ 39-011
2004 Gender Recognition Act (c.7)
    Sch.5 Pt 3 para.14(3) ......... 13-015
       para.15(3) ............... 13-015
2004 Finance Act (c.12) .. 1-018, 1-025, 2-062, 2-063, 2-065, 2-069, 2-076, 2-077, 4-007, 4-009, 4-017, 5-001, 5-002, 5-007, 5-008, 5-011, 5-041, 5-061, 6-003, 6-071, 6-073, 6-077, 6-130, 6-148, 7-032, 8-009, 8-013, 10-003, 10-049, 11-014, 12-005, 15-009, 17-008, 17-011, 18-001, 18-029, 18-043, 18-047, 18-048, 18-056, 18-057, 18-121, 18-189, 20-002, 21-084, 24-055, 29-028, 29-061, 30-071, 30-075, 31-035, 35-012, 35-051, 36-002, 37-010
    Pt 1 ...................... 3-001
       (1) ... **2-006, 6-066, 11-002, 17-033**
       (2) ... **2-082, 6-066, 11-002, 17-033**
       (3) ... **2-082, 6-066, 11-002, 17-033, 18-024, 27-060**
       (4) .. **2-082, 11-002, 17-033, 18-024**
       (5) ............... **2-082, 17-033**
       (6) ..................... **6-066**
       (a) ..... **2-015, 6-124, 9-028, 9-041, 18-010, 18-012, 18-147**
       (b) ..... **2-015, 6-124, 9-028, 9-041, 18-010, 18-012, 18-147**
       (c) ......... **6-124, 9-028, 18-147**
       (d) .................... **18-147**
       s.12(2) .................. 21-027
    Pt 2 ...................... 3-001
    Pt 3 ...................... 3-001
    Ch.2 s.32 .................. 2-003
       s.37(3) ................. 17-003
       s.53 .................... 6-071
    Ch.3 s.58 ................. 21-077
    Ch.4 s.86 ................. 28-057
       (1) .................... 8-029
    Pt 4 ...... 1-001, 1-002, 1-003, 1-006, 1-007, 1-015, 1-016, 1-017, 1-018, 1-019, 2-001, 2-011, 2-012, 2-022, 2-026, 2-027, 2-036, 2-053, 2-054, 2-055, 2-058, 2-062, 2-074, 2-076, 2-081, 2-083, 2-098, 2-099, 2-117, 2-121, 3-001, 3-020, 3-035, 4-023, 5-002, 5-004, 5-005, 5-008, 5-021, 5-025, 5-026, 5-031, 5-053, 5-054, 5-055, 6-068, 6-071, 6-084, 6-087, 6-091, 6-127, 6-130, 6-131, 6-145, 7-027, 8-007, 8-052, 8-059, 8-061, 10-042, 10-045, 10-058, 12-001, 12-006, 12-018, 12-041, 13-008, 13-017, 13-024, 14-001, 14-015, 14-017, 15-006, 15-007, 15-008, 16-002, 16-003, 16-004, 17-008, 18-001, 18-007, 18-020, 18-028, 18-033, 18-035, 18-050, 18-056, 18-064, 18-142, 18-162, 18-164, 19-016, 19-024, 19-032, 19-041, 19-043, 20-001, 20-002, 20-003, 21-011, 21-077, 22-025, 23-011, 24-002, 26-022, 26-028, 30-001, 30-030, 30-031, 30-033, 30-034, 30-058, 30-059, 30-074, 30-113, 30-128, 31-035, 33-003, 33-022, 34-045, 35-006, 35-012, 37-002, 37-010, 39-018
    Ch.1 .................... 1-002
       s.150(1) .... 2-006, 2-008, 2-009,

## TABLE OF STATUTES

2004 Finance Act—*cont.*
    2-011, 2-012, 2-014, 4-004,
    6-024, 6-068, 8-035, 12-001,
    18-017, 21-077, 26-010,
    27-063, 30-004, 31-007,
    33-015, 34-009, 35-011
  (a) ................ 2-014
  (a)–(e) . 2-008, 2-009, 2-010,
    2-013
  (b) ................ 2-014
  (c) ................ 2-014
  (d) ................ 2-014
  (e) ................ 2-014
  (2) ................ 33-015
  (5) ....... 2-015, 2-023, 4-004,
    26-044, 31-011, 33-015,
    34-036
  (5A) ............... 2-026
  (6) ........... 2-021, 2-023
  (7) .... 26-009, 27-072, 31-002,
    31-007
  (8) ..... 6-075, 18-097, 32-001,
    32-005
s.151 .......... 24-009, 26-010
  (1) ............ 2-027, 2-028
  (2) ............ 2-030, 6-020
  (3) ................ 2-027
  (4) ............ 2-027, 2-042
  (5) ........... 2-027, 16-003
s.152 ........... 2-039, 8-059
  (1) . 2-036, 3-035, 6-087, 7-027,
    8-059
  (3) ................ 2-043
  (5) ................ 2-043
Ch.2 ............... 1-002, 4-001
s.153 . 2-004, 2-011, 2-014, 4-004,
    20-002, 25-039
  (2) ................ 4-005
  (b) .......... 4-009, 4-022
  (3) ....... 4-007, 4-017, 4-022
  (5) ................ 4-013
    (a)–(c) ............ 4-022
    (d) ............... 4-022
    (e) ............... 4-022
    (f) ..... 1-016, 4-014, 4-016,
      4-022
    (g) ............... 4-022
  (7) ................ 4-004
  (8) . 2-003, 3-093, 4-004, 5-016,
    5-032, 10-024, 12-006,
    18-027
  (8A) ................ 2-003
s.153A ..... 4-010, 4-013, 4-020,
    4-022, 5-011, 5-015
  (3) ....... 4-011, 4-013, 4-020
s.153B ..... 4-010, 4-013, 4-020,
    4-022, 5-015
ss.153C–153F ............ 4-020
s.154 ....... 2-004, 4-004, 4-022
  (1)(b) ............... 2-026
s.156 .......... 4-019, 19-043
s.156A .......... 4-019, 19-043
s.157 . 4-023, 4-024, 4-025, 4-028

s.158 ................ 4-023
  (2)–(4) ............. 2-116
  (7)–(10) ............ 4-023
s.159 ........... 4-029, 19-043
s.159A .......... 5-011, 5-015
s.159B .......... 4-023, 5-015
Ch.3 ..................... 1-002
s.160(1) .. 1-020, 11-001, 22-023,
    22-025
  (2) ........... 2-074, 18-010
    (a) .. 18-011, 18-017, 18-062
    (b) ......... 11-014, 18-011
  (4) ................ 18-012
    (a) ........ 18-013, 18-062
    (b) ............... 18-013
  (4A) ........ 18-165, 18-178
  (4B) ............... 18-165
  (5) ................ 18-009
s.161(1) ............... 2-054
  (2) .......... 11-002, 22-023
  (3) . 3-093, 5-032, 8-036, 8-054,
    9-051, 11-008, 12-005,
    13-023, 18-019, 18-020,
    18-024, 18-025, 18-026,
    18-027, 18-028, 18-029,
    18-030, 18-033, 18-034,
    18-035, 18-036, 18-037,
    18-038, 18-040, 18-041,
    18-051, 18-053, 18-054,
    18-055, 18-058, 18-063,
    18-138, 18-140, 22-024,
    35-012
  (4) ...... 3-093, 8-036, 13-023,
    13-035, 18-017, 18-020,
    18-024, 18-026, 18-028,
    18-033, 18-034, 18-041,
    22-023, 22-024, 27-040
  (5) .... 11-002, 11-004, 17-008,
    18-045, 18-049
  (5)–(7) ........ 2-098, 18-064
  (6) .... 18-124, 18-146, 18-155
  (7) .... 18-025, 18-124, 18-146,
    18-155, 18-158
s.162 . 2-082, 2-083, 2-084, 6-110,
    9-051
  (3) ................ 2-083
  (4) ...... 2-084, 2-095, 8-054,
    11-013, 11-014, 17-011
s.163 ................ 8-054
  (2) ................ 8-056
  (3) ..... 8-054, 18-149, 18-157
  (4) ............ 8-058, 8-059
s.164 ...... 1-020, 2-062, 30-034
  (1) ...... 1-020, 2-056, 11-001,
    13-002, 14-001, 15-015,
    15-044, 18-014, 18-015,
    18-061
    (a) ..... 4-007, 4-013, 4-014,
      4-022, 4-023, 13-002
    (b) ..... 4-007, 4-013, 4-014,
      4-022, 4-023, 14-001,
      15-044
    (c) ......... 12-004, 18-050

## TABLE OF STATUTES

2004 Finance Act—*cont.*
    (c)–(f) ............. 4-014
    (e) ............... 16-004
    (f) .. 10-005, 10-019, 14-041, 14-042
  s.165 ..... 2-029, 13-046, 26-076, 30-058, 31-005, 32-004, 32-015, 34-032, 34-034, 35-094
    (1) ........... 13-002, 19-013
    (2) .... 13-002, 13-017, 14-001
    (3) .... 10-005, 12-007, 13-003, 13-023, 15-030
      (a) ......... 14-018, 14-021
      (b) .... 2-027, 7-019, 10-005, 13-032, 14-018
    (3A) ................ 26-037
  s.166(1) ........ 1-022, 14-002
    (2) .......... 10-051, 14-025
      (a) .... 7-010, 7-017, 10-005, 14-018
      (aa) ............... 10-005
      (b) ............... 10-005
  s.167 .......... 15-015, 30-058
    (1) ..... 3-038, 15-025, 18-045, 18-088
    (2) ................ 15-016
    (2A) ................ 26-037
  s.168 ................ 15-044
    (1) ..... 3-038, 18-045, 18-088, 21-074, 34-041
    (2) .......... 15-045, 21-074
  s.169 ..... 2-033, 12-005, 12-045, 32-001
    (1) ...... 2-028, 7-017, 12-005, 12-006, 13-007, 23-011, 32-019, 33-022
      (b) .............. 33-002
    (1A) .......... 3-038, 12-007
    (1B) ............... 12-007
    (1C) ......... 12-005, 12-007
    (1D) ... 12-005, 12-011, 13-038
    (2) ................ 33-016
    (2)–(8) .............. 33-001
    (3) ................ 33-016
    (4) ................ 33-016
    (5) .... 33-016, 33-017, 33-020, 33-046
    (7) ................ 33-018
  s.170(2) .............. 33-019
  s.171 ...... 2-058, 9-055, 18-043, 18-048, 18-053, 18-057, 18-080
    (1)–(4) ............. 11-002
    (3)(a) .............. 18-050
    (4) ................ 11-012
  s.172 ...... 2-078, 5-036, 16-004, 18-059, 18-065, 18-074, 18-076, 18-077, 18-085, 18-086, 18-087, 18-088, 18-093, 18-098, 18-104, 21-059
    (1) ................ 18-070
    (2) .......... 16-004, 18-070
    (3) ................ 18-072
    (4) ................ 18-072

  ss.172–174A ..... 1-020, 18-029, 33-044
  s.172A ..... 2-078, 5-036, 8-058, 12-005, 13-021, 16-004, 17-005, 18-059, 18-078, 18-079, 18-080, 18-081, 18-082, 18-085, 18-086, 18-090, 18-092, 18-094, 18-098
    (2) ................ 18-079
    (5) ................ 21-064
      (a) ............... 16-004
      (c) .. 13-021, 14-029, 18-082
    (9) ................ 18-078
    (10A) ............... 18-091
  s.172B .... 2-078, 5-036, 13-021, 18-059, 18-095, 18-097, 18-102, 18-103, 18-104
    (1) ................ 18-101
    (2) ................ 18-097
  s.172C ..... 2-078, 3-035, 5-036, 7-014, 18-059, 18-105, 18-106, 18-107, 18-108, 18-111, 18-114
    (1)(a) ......... 6-018, 6-069
    (5) ................ 18-109
  s.172D .... 2-078, 5-036, 18-059, 18-108, 18-114, 18-118
    (2) ................ 18-115
  s.173 . 2-057, 2-078, 2-079, 8-011, 9-002, 18-029, 18-059, 18-063, 18-071, 18-119, 18-122, 18-123, 18-125, 18-126, 18-127, 18-128, 18-132, 18-134, 18-138, 18-140, 18-141, 18-158, 18-163, 18-189, 18-195, 19-021
    (1) .... 18-120, 18-129, 18-130, 18-131
    (4) ................ 18-120
    (5) ................ 18-131
    (7A) ......... 9-002, 30-079
    (8)(b) .. 18-132, 18-134, 18-141
    (9) ................ 18-141
    (10) ................ 18-134
  s.174 . 2-057, 2-062, 2-064, 2-078, 2-117, 8-011, 8-054, 18-059, 18-062, 18-071, 18-153
    (1) ................ 18-144
    (3) ................ 18-147
  s.174A ..... 2-038, 2-078, 9-003, 9-085, 9-086, 9-091, 9-093, 9-118, 9-119, 9-122, 9-139, 18-059, 18-150, 18-151, 18-152, 30-055, 30-079, 30-090, 30-091, 30-095, 30-097, 30-098
    (1) ....... 9-088, 9-113, 9-123
      (a) ................ 9-087
    (2) ................ 9-123
    (3) ........... 9-088, 9-124
  s.175 ...... 1-023, 2-056, 17-001, 18-014, 18-015, 18-141
  s.177 ................ 17-002
  s.178 .... 17-003, 17-007, 18-189
  s.179 ..... 9-054, 17-003, 17-008, 18-184
    (1)(a) ............... 2-116

## TABLE OF STATUTES

2004 Finance Act—*cont.*
    (2) . . . . . . . . . . . 17-028, 17-029
    (3) . . . . . . . . . . . . . . . . . 17-020
    (7) . . . . . . . . . . . . . . . . . 17-008
  s.180 . . . . . . . 2-058, 6-110, 9-055,
        17-035, 18-043, 18-048, 18-057
    (1)–(4) . . . . . . . . . . . . . . . 17-034
    (1)–(5) . . . . . . . . . . . . . . . 17-033
    (3)(a) . . . . . . . . . . . . . . . 18-050
    (5) . . . . . . . . . . . . 2-116, 17-035
  s.181 . 1-023, 2-064, 2-117, 8-054,
            9-055, 18-029, 18-153
  s.181A(3) . . . . . . . . . . . . . . . 5-025
  s.182 . . . . . . . . . . . . . 8-059, 8-061
    (3) . . . . . . . . . . . . . . . . . . 2-116
  ss.182–185 . . . . . . . . . . . . . . 8-051
  s.183 . . . . . . . . . . . . . . . . . 8-059
    (2) . . . . . . . . . . . . . . . . . 8-051
  s.184 . . . . . . . . . . . . . 8-059, 8-066
    (3) . . . . . . . . . . . . . . . . . . 2-116
  s.185 . . . . . . . . . . . . . . . . . 8-059
    (2) . . . . . . . . . . . . . . . . . 8-051
  s.185A . . . . . 5-033, 5-060, 8-045,
        9-003, 9-033, 9-108, 9-134,
        9-149, 19-013, 30-084
  ss.185A–185I . . . 18-150, 30-079,
               30-084, 30-085
  s.185F . . . . . 5-033, 5-034, 5-060,
        8-050, 9-003, 9-108, 9-148,
        9-151, 9-162, 19-013
  s.185G . . . . . . . . . . 9-170, 9-171
    (7) . . . . . . . . . . . . . . . . . . 9-171
  s.185H . . . . . . . . . . 9-157, 9-171
  s.185I . . . . . . . . . . . . . . . . 30-084
  s.185J . . . . . . . . . . . . . . . . 14-018
  Ch.4 . . . . . . . . . . . . . . 1-002, 6-003
  s.186 . 6-149, 8-035, 8-036, 8-037,
            8-047, 8-049, 9-012
    (1) . 8-017, 8-029, 8-037, 8-045,
                8-052
    (a) . . . . . 8-014, 8-015, 8-018,
                   18-021
    (b) . . . . . . . . . . 8-039, 8-041
    (2) . . . . . . . . . . . . . . . . . 8-042
    (2A) . . . . . . . . . . . . . . . . 8-045
    (3) . . . . . . . . . . . . 8-016, 18-033
    (4) . . . . . . . . . . . . 8-016, 18-033
  s.188 . . . . . . 6-007, 9-100, 18-111,
      21-026, 24-013, 24-021, 27-058
    (1) . 2-034, 6-005, 6-007, 6-008,
        6-009, 6-010, 6-011, 6-012,
        6-013, 6-019, 6-024, 6-025,
        6-027, 6-028, 6-033, 6-034,
        6-131, 6-152, 7-013, 12-001,
        16-004, 24-019, 29-018
    (2) . . . . . . . 3-026, 6-007, 6-018,
                24-014
    (3) . . . . . . 3-026, 6-007, 24-014
    (b) . . . . . . . . . . . . . . . . 6-007
    (3A) . . . . . 3-026, 6-007, 24-014
    (3A)–(3C) . . . . . . . . . . . 6-007
    (4) . . . . . . . . . . . . 6-025, 16-004
    (5) . . . . . . . 6-003, 6-024, 6-152,

            12-001, 20-014, 28-019
  ss.188–195A . . . . . . . . . . . . 6-010
  s.189(1) . . . . . . . . . . . . . . . 6-021
    (c) . . . . . . . . . . . . . . . . 20-016
    (2)(ba) . . . . . . . . . . . . . . 31-031
    (2)–(7) . . . . . . . 6-022, 24-015
  s.190 . . . . . . . . . . . . . . . . 14-032
    (1) . . . . . . . . . . . 6-027, 24-019
    (2) . . . . . . . . . . . 6-027, 24-019
    (3) . . . . . . . . . . . . . . . . . 6-027
    (4) . . . . . . . . . . . . . . . . . 6-027
  s.191 . . . . . . . . . . . . . . . . . 6-028
    (2) . . . . . . . . . . . . . . . . . 6-029
    (3) . . . . . . . . . . . . . . . . . 6-030
    (7) . . . . . . . . . . . . . . . . . 6-027
  s.192 . 5-020, 6-019, 6-029, 7-025
    (10) . . . . . . . . . . . 6-006, 6-019
  s.193(4) . . . . . . . . . . . . . . . 7-024
    (8) . . . . . . . . . . . . . . . . . 6-006
  s.194 . . . . . . . . . . . . . . . . 24-020
    (1) . . . . . . . . . . . . . . . . . 7-024
  s.195 . 6-010, 6-013, 6-026, 6-130,
              6-131, 24-017
    (1) . . . . . . . . . . . 6-009, 6-026
  s.195A . . . . . . . . . . 6-007, 24-014
  s.196 . 6-018, 6-063, 6-066, 6-067,
      6-125, 6-127, 6-131, 9-100,
           24-022, 24-035
    (1) . 6-037, 6-061, 6-067, 6-068,
        6-069, 6-070, 6-071, 6-073,
        6-127, 24-023, 24-035
    (2) . . . . . . . . . . . . . . . . . 6-067
    (a) . . . . . . . . . . 6-071, 22-029
    (b) . . . . . 6-070, 6-072, 6-073,
                6-125
    (2)–(5) . . . . . . . 24-022, 24-033
    (3) . . . . . . . . . . . . . . . . . 6-067
    (b) . . . . . . . . . . . . . . . . 6-070
  ss.196–200 . . . . . . 6-037, 29-018,
                29-028
  ss.196–202 . . . . . . . . . . . . 24-022
  s.196A . . 6-074, 24-022, 32-020,
              35-065
  s.196B . . . . . . 6-080, 6-106, 6-110
    (1) . . . . . . . . . . . . . . . . . 6-085
    (2)(a)(iii) . . 6-093, 6-094, 6-095
  ss.196B–196L . . . . 6-079, 24-022
  s.196C . . . . . . . . . . . . . . . . 6-089
  s.196D . . . . . . . . . . . 6-080, 6-110
  s.196E . . . . . . . . . . . . . . . . 6-101
  s.196F . . . . . . . . . . . 6-080, 6-110
  s.196G . . . . . . . . . . . . . . . . 6-103
  s.196I . . . . . . 6-104, 6-105, 6-106,
         6-107, 6-108, 6-109
  s.196K . . . . . . . . . . . 6-110, 6-111
  s.196L(4) . . . . . . . . . . . . . . 6-087
  s.197 . 6-112, 6-118, 6-119, 6-120,
              24-022
    (7)(a) . . . . . . . . . . . . . . . 2-030
  s.198 . . . . . 6-117, 6-120, 24-022
  s.199 . . . . . . . . . . . 6-122, 24-022
  s.199A . . . . . 6-118, 6-119, 24-022
  s.200 . 6-124, 6-125, 6-126, 6-127,

# TABLE OF STATUTES

liii

2004 Finance Act—*cont.*
  6-131, 24-022, 24-033
  Ch.5 .................... 1-002
  s.204(1) ........ 13-012, 14-004
  s.205 ..... 1-018, 14-003, 18-001,
    30-030
  s.205A .......... 1-007, 30-030
  s.206 ..... 1-018, 15-046, 15-047,
    18-001, 26-022, 30-026, 30-030
    (8) .... 15-079, 15-080, 27-018
    (9) ................ 15-049
    (b) ............... 15-077
  s.207 .... 17-005, 17-006, 18-001
  s.208 .... 13-012, 14-004, 18-159,
    18-161, 19-041, 30-028, 30-030
    (2) .... 18-049, 18-052, 18-064,
      19-027, 30-073
    (3) ................ 18-049
    (8) ..... 1-018, 18-001, 18-160,
      26-022
  s.209 .... 13-012, 14-004, 18-159,
    18-169, 19-041, 30-030
    (3) .... 18-052, 19-027, 30-073
    (5) ................ 18-179
  s.210 ................. 18-170
  s.211 ................. 18-173
  s.212 ...... 3-025, 3-053, 10-041,
    14-003, 14-036, 18-174
    (1) ........... 14-025, 14-027
    (2) ........... 14-025, 14-027
  s.213 ................. 18-176
  s.214 ........... 10-054, 26-020
  ss.214–226 ...... 10-004, 26-022
  s.215 ................. 10-054
    (9) ................ 10-056
  s.216 .... 10-005, 14-016, 33-022
  s.217 .......... 10-059, 30-128
    (2) ..... 3-034, 19-027, 19-032,
      19-041
  s.218(2C) ................ 1-025
    (2D) ................. 1-025
    (6) .................. 3-091
  s.219 ........... 3-073, 10-049
  s.220 .... 16-004, 16-008, 16-009
  ss.221–226 ............... 2-034
  s.224 .................. 12-043
  ss.224–226 .............. 12-001
  s.227(1) ........ 7-050, 13-015
    (4) .................. 7-050
    (4A) ................. 7-050
    (5) ...... 1-008, 7-050, 11-005,
      30-113
  ss.227–238A ............. 7-001
  s.227B(3) ............... 7-048
  s.227C ................. 7-037
  s.227D .......... 7-038, 7-048
    (4) .................. 7-040
  s.227F ................. 7-042
  s.227G .......... 7-033, 30-106
  s.228(1) ................ 7-022
  s.228ZA(4) .............. 7-024
    (5) .................. 7-025
  s.228ZB ................. 7-027

  s.228A .... 7-029, 30-108, 30-109
  s.229(1) ................ 7-005
    (3) .................. 7-006
    (4) .................. 7-006
  s.230 .................. 7-008
    (1) ................. 30-102
    (5B) .......... 2-030, 7-012
    (5BC) ................ 2-033
  ss.230–232 .............. 18-116
  s.231 .................. 7-009
  s.232 .................. 7-010
    (2) ................. 16-004
    (3) ................. 16-004
    (8A)(d) .............. 7-010
  s.233 ....... 6-013, 6-152, 7-046
    (1) ............ 7-013, 7-014
    (3) . 3-035, 6-018, 6-069, 7-014,
      18-107, 37-010
    (4) .................. 7-013
  s.234(1) ........ 7-015, 30-102
    (5B) .......... 2-030, 7-020
    (5BD) ................ 2-033
  ss.234–236A ............. 18-116
  s.235 .................. 7-016
  s.236 .................. 7-017
    (2) ................. 16-004
  s.236A ................. 7-019
  s.237 ........... 18-116, 30-107
    (1) .................. 7-021
  s.237A ......... 7-050, 30-113
  s.237B .......... 7-051, 19-017
    (3)(a) ............... 7-051
    (5)(c) .............. 19-017
  s.237BA ................ 7-051
  s.237C ................. 7-055
  s.237D ..... 7-052, 7-056, 19-043
  s.237E ................. 7-053
    (1) ................. 13-015
  s.238ZB ................ 7-004
  s.239 ...... 5-025, 5-034, 9-171,
    18-159, 18-189, 30-021
    (3) ................. 19-027
  s.240(1) ........ 5-030, 18-191
  s.241(1) ............... 5-025
    (2) ........... 18-125, 18-189
    (3) ................. 18-125
  s.242 ........... 4-030, 30-021
  Ch.5A ................. 20-003
  s.242A ................ 20-003
  s.242B ......... 20-004, 20-009
  s.242C ................ 20-003
    (1) ................ 20-003
    (a) ............... 20-003
  s.242D ................ 20-007
  s.242E ................ 20-008
  Ch.6 ................... 1-002
  s.244A .. 18-001, 30-028, 30-114,
    33-023
    (4) ................. 33-027
  s.244AA ........ 12-022, 30-118
  s.244AB(1) ............ 30-115
  s.244AC . 12-034, 12-035, 12-039,
    12-043, 30-114, 33-023, 33-029,

2004 Finance Act—*cont.*
   33-030, 33-034, 33-035, 33-038,
           33-042
 s.244B ... 12-026, 30-072, 33-049
 s.244C ... 12-029, 30-072, 33-049
 s.244D ............... 12-030
 s.244E ............... 12-031
 s.244F ............... 12-032
 s.244G ............... 33-049
  (1) ............... 12-022
  (2) ............... 33-042
  (3) ............... 33-029
 s.244I ................ 12-025
 s.244IA .. 12-033, 12-039, 30-119,
   33-033, 33-036, 33-038, 33-042
  (1) ............... 33-038
 s.244IB .. 12-033, 30-119, 33-033
 s.244IC ......... 12-036, 33-036
 s.244J(1) ............. 12-040
 s.244JA ......... 12-039, 33-038
  (1) ............... 33-038
 s.244K ................ 2-117
  (5) ............... 33-037
  (6) .......... 12-038, 33-037
  (9) ............... 12-038
 s.244M .. 12-035, 12-043, 12-044,
        33-035, 33-044
 s.244N ......... 12-048, 19-043
 s.246 ..... 6-008, 22-022, 35-060,
        35-061, 35-062
  (3) ............... 35-063
 s.246A ............... 35-064
 Ch.7 ................... 1-002
 s.250 ..... 5-020, 19-008, 19-011,
          19-012
 s.251 .... 12-045, 19-008, 35-103
  (1)(b) ........ 5-020, 19-004
 s.254 ............ 19-008, 19-027
  (1) ............... 19-016
  (8) ............... 19-016
 s.255 ............ 19-027, 35-104
 s.257(1) .............. 19-012
  (2) ............... 19-012
  (4) ............... 19-012
 s.258 ................. 19-015
  (2) ............... 19-007
 s.260 ................. 6-152
 s.263 ................. 3-043
 s.264(1) .............. 19-024
  (2) ............... 19-025
 s.265 ................. 14-003
 s.266 ................. 12-013
 s.266A ... 5-052, 18-168, 18-188,
          33-009
  (2) ................ 6-007
 s.266B .......... 5-050, 5-052
 s.267 .......... 10-061, 33-009
  (2) ............... 19-043
  (5) ............... 19-043
 s.268 ..... 5-049, 18-180, 19-043,
          33-009
  (3) ............... 18-182
  (5) ................ 5-036

  (7) ........... 5-041, 18-182
  (a) ............... 18-182
 s.269 ..... 5-049, 10-062, 12-048,
        18-180, 33-009
  (1)(a) .... 5-037, 7-056, 19-043
  (b) ............... 19-043
  (2) ............... 10-062
 s.270 ....... 5-004, 5-016, 5-063,
          33-016
  (1) ............ 5-006, 5-010
  (2) ....... 5-006, 5-010, 5-017
  (a) ... 4-004, 20-001, 33-012
  (c) ........... 5-009, 5-013
  (3) ............ 5-007, 5-017
  (4) ................ 5-004
 s.271 ............. 5-054, 19-043
  (4) ................ 5-054
  (5) ................ 5-054
 ss.271–273A ............ 5-053
 s.272 . 4-030, 5-016, 5-038, 5-055,
   5-058, 9-030, 19-027, 19-032
  (4) ............ 5-056, 19-027
 s.272A(2) .............. 5-054
 ss.272A–272C ........... 5-054
 s.272C ..... 5-054, 5-057, 19-027
  (3) ............... 19-027
  (4) ............... 19-027
  (7) ............... 19-027
 s.273 ..... 5-058, 19-027, 19-032
  (2) ............... 19-027
 s.273ZA ... 5-033, 5-034, 30-079
 s.273A ............... 15-047
 s.273B ......... 1-016, 30-034
 s.274(1) ............... 5-053
  (2) ................ 5-053
 Ch.8 ................... 1-002
 s.274B ................ 2-026
 s.275 ..... 2-003, 26-031, 30-059
  (1) ... 13-015, 13-025, 13-032
  (a) ............... 27-063
  (b) ............... 27-063
 s.276 ...... 3-053, 8-061, 10-009,
   10-041, 14-021, 14-036, 18-173,
       18-174, 20-036
  (2) ............... 30-126
 s.277 . 3-053, 3-055, 7-009, 7-016,
   8-062, 10-023, 10-041, 14-036,
   18-174, 20-020, 20-026, 20-034,
          37-010
  (a) ............... 10-017
 s.278 ........... 14-021, 17-008
  (1) ............ 2-118, 8-071
  (2) ............ 2-081, 11-014
  (3A) ...... 9-020, 9-099, 9-120
  (3B) ............... 9-030
 s.278A ......... 14-025, 16-004
 s.278B ... 14-021, 15-030, 30-053
 s.279 .... 13-004, 14-018, 34-032
  (1) ..... 2-016, 10-018, 16-003,
          32-015
  (1B) ................ 4-013
  (1D) ................ 4-013
  (1F) ............... 14-018

# TABLE OF STATUTES

2004 Finance Act—cont.
    (1G) ................ 14-018
    (2) ..... 5-025, 17-006, 18-017,
                        18-021, 18-028
    (4) .................... 3-090
    s.282(3) ............... 18-064
    s.284(1) ............... 1-003
  Pt 5 ....................... 6-036
  Pt 7 s.307 ................. 30-100
  Pt 9 ....................... 35-103
  Sch.3 Pt 3 para.16 .......... 9-044
  Sch.15 . 6-155, 24-073, 24-082, 24-083
    para.3(2)(a) ............ 24-077
          (b) ............ 24-077
          (3) ............... 24-078
    para.6(2) ............... 24-080
          (3) ............... 24-081
    para.8 .................. 24-082
    para.11(1) .............. 24-074
  Sch.26 para.14(3) .......... 9-036
  Sch.28 ............. 15-025, 30-059
    Pt 1 (1)para.1 ...... 13-005, 14-046,
                   14-048, 34-033
       para.2 . 13-015, 18-086, 21-064
          (4) ............... 13-015
          (d) ............. 16-004
          (6) ............... 13-015
       para.2A ...... 13-015, 13-018,
               13-019, 18-060, 21-064,
                   30-057, 33-044
          (6) ............... 13-019
    (2)para.3 ............... 18-083
          (1) ............... 13-027
          (d) ............. 26-037
          (1A) .............. 13-025
          (2) ............... 13-025
          (2A) .............. 16-004
          (2B) ....... 13-028, 18-088
       para.4 .................. 13-031
       para.6 .................. 18-060
          (1) ............... 13-033
          (1ZA) ............. 13-032
          (1A) .............. 16-004
          (1B) .............. 13-034
          (1E) .............. 12-012
       para.7 ........ 13-035, 15-063
       para.8 . 13-035, 13-040, 15-061
          (1A)(b) ........... 13-038
       para.8A ...... 13-036, 13-038,
                      15-065
       para.8B ................. 13-036
       para.8C ................. 13-036
       para.8D ................. 13-036
       para.9 .................. 13-041
       paras 9–10B ............. 13-041
       para.10(4) .............. 16-004
       para.10B ................ 13-041
       para.14 ........ 13-041, 15-043
    Pt 2 (3)para.15 ............ 15-018
          (2) ............... 15-018
       para.16 ................. 18-060
       paras 16A–16C ......... 15-026
       para.16AA ............ 15-026

       para.16B ............ 15-027
       para.16C(4) ........... 2-035
    (4)para.17 ....... 15-030, 15-031,
                        18-083
          (1)(c) ............. 26-037
          (1ZA) ...... 15-030, 15-031
          (2) ............... 16-004
          (3) ............... 18-088
       para.18 ................. 15-032
       para.20 ................. 18-060
          (1ZA) ............. 15-033
          (1A) .............. 16-004
       para.21 ........ 15-034, 15-063
       para.22 ........ 15-034, 15-061
          (3) ............... 15-042
       para.22A ............... 15-065
       paras 22A–22D ......... 15-035
       para.23 ................. 15-043
       paras 23–24B ......... 15-043
       para.24(4) ............ 16-004
       para.27A ...... 15-009, 15-020
          (1) ............... 21-108
       para.27AA .... 15-030, 15-031,
                   18-060, 18-083
       para.27B ................ 15-032
       para.27C ....... 15-033, 18-060
       para.27D ............... 15-034
       para.27E ............... 15-065
          (1) ............... 15-036
          (3) ............... 15-036
          (4) ........ 10-016, 15-036
          (5) ........ 10-016, 15-036
       para.27F ............... 15-021
       para.27FA .... 15-031, 18-060,
                      18-083
       para.27G ............... 15-032
       para.27H ....... 15-033, 18-060
       para.27J ............... 15-034
       para.27K ...... 15-038, 15-065
  Schs 28–30 ............... 1-002
  Sch.29 .................... 3-094
    Pt 1 para.1(1) ...... 14-018, 14-023
          (2) .... 14-018, 14-023, 35-096
          (3) ................ 14-018
          (4) ................ 14-018
       paras 1–3 .............. 35-096
       para.1A ............... 14-018
       para.1B ............... 14-018
          (2)(a)–(g) ........... 5-036
       para.2 ................. 14-020
       paras 2A–2D ............ 14-021
       para.2C ................ 14-021
       para.2D ................ 14-021
       para.3 ................. 2-122
          (10) ............... 18-060
       para.3A ... 6-145, 6-146, 14-022,
                   18-060, 33-044
       para.3B ............... 14-022
       para.3C ............... 30-062
       para.4 ... 14-027, 31-035, 35-100
          (2A) ............... 14-027
       para.4A ............... 14-025
          (1)(f)(i) ........... 14-025

2004 Finance Act—*cont.*
- para.5 .................. 14-030
- (2) .................. 14-030
- para.6 .................. 14-032
- para.7 .................. 14-034
- para.8 .................. 14-036
- para.9 .................. 14-036
- para.10 .................. 14-037
- (3)(c) .................. 14-037
- para.11 .. 14-039, 26-022, 30-065
- para.11A ......... 1-022, 14-002
- para.12(2)–(4) ... 14-018, 14-034
- (6) .................. 14-001
- Pt 2 para.13 ............. 15-052
- para.14 .................. 15-056
- (3) .................. 15-056
- para.15 .................. 15-053
- (2) .... 15-053, 15-068, 30-050
- (2A) .................. 15-054
- para.16 .................. 15-058
- para.17 .................. 15-060
- para.17A .................. 15-064
- para.18(1) .............. 15-068
- (1A) .................. 15-069
- para.20 .................. 15-072
- (1) .................. 15-046
- para.21A .............. 15-075
- para.22(3) ............. 15-045
- Sch.29A .. 9-004, 9-005, **9-044**, 30-079
- Pt 1 .................... 9-005
- para.1(2) .............. 9-006
- para.2(2) .............. 9-006
- para.4 .................. 9-005
- para.5 ........... 9-086, 18-152
- Pt 2 .................... 18-151
- para.6 .................. 9-011
- para.7 .................. 9-012
- para.8 .................. 9-013
- para.10 .................. 9-014
- (2) .................. 9-088
- Pt 3 para.12 ............. 9-087
- para.13(1) .............. 9-053
- para.14 .................. 9-027
- (1) . 2-117, 9-027, 9-028, 9-030, 9-032, 9-034
- (a) .......... 9-029, 9-107
- (b) .............. 9-107
- (c) .......... 9-029, 9-030
- (2) .................. 9-037
- (a) ......... 9-046, 9-056
- (3) . 9-027, 9-032, 9-033, 9-034, 9-035, 9-036, 9-039, 9-040, 9-046, 9-067, 9-079
- para.15 .... 9-035, 9-039, 30-084
- (4) .................. 9-079
- (5) .................. 9-040
- para.16 ..... 2-081, 9-047, 9-052, 9-066, 9-067, 11-014
- (1) . 9-041, 9-045, 9-046, 9-069
- (a) .................. 9-043
- (b) .................. 9-043
- (2)(a) ......... 9-045, 9-046
- (b) ..... 9-046, 9-048, 9-049,
  9-050, 9-051, 9-054, 9-055,
  9-056, 9-059, 9-132
- (3) . 9-024, 9-054, 9-055, 9-056
- (4) .................. 9-053
- (5) .................. 9-061
- para.17 ..... 9-056, 9-057, 9-061
- (1)(c) .............. 9-066
- paras 17–19 .. 9-045, 9-061, 9-066
- para.18 ........... 9-060, 9-061
- para.19 .................. 9-061
- (1) .................. 9-064
- (7) . 9-052, 9-061, 9-062, 9-065, 9-066
- para.21 ..... 9-068, 9-070, 9-071
- para.22 ..... 9-068, 9-072, 9-074
- para.23 ..... 9-068, 9-073, 9-074
- para.24 ..... 9-072, 9-073, 9-074, 9-075, 9-078
- para.25 ......... 9-075, 9-078
- para.26 ..... 9-068, 9-079, 9-081
- para.27 .... 9-088, 9-116, 30-086
- para.28 ..... 9-089, 9-092, 9-116, 9-128, 30-086
- para.29 ........... 9-078, 9-081
- para.30 .................. 9-082
- Pt 4 .................... 9-091
- para.31(2) .............. 9-092
- para.32(2) .............. 9-095
- (3) ............. 9-097, 9-107
- (4) .................. 9-098
- (5) .................. 9-128
- paras 32–35 ............. 9-095
- paras 32–36 ............. 9-119
- para.33 ..... 9-097, 9-098, 9-102, 9-103, 9-104, 9-105, 9-106, 9-107, 9-109, 9-110, 9-111, 9-112
- (1)(a) .............. 9-105
- (b) .............. 9-105
- (3)(a) .............. 9-107
- (4) .................. 9-106
- para.34 ..... 9-097, 9-098, 9-101, 9-102, 9-106, 9-109, 9-112, 9-115, 9-117, 9-120, 9-141, 9-142
- (2) .................. 30-086
- para.35 .................. 9-097
- para.37 .................. 30-079
- para.38(2) .............. 9-118
- (3) .................. 9-118
- para.39(2) .............. 9-124
- (3) .................. 9-124
- para.40 .................. 9-122
- para.41 ......... 9-125, 9-126
- paras 41–43 . 9-077, 9-144, 9-159, 9-169, 9-171
- para.42 .................. 9-129
- para.43 .... 2-081, 9-130, 11-014
- para.45 .................. 9-133
- Sch.30 .................. 18-162
- para.1 .................. 17-008
- para.4 .......... 17-008, 17-016
- para.5 .................. 17-010

2004 Finance Act—*cont.*
    para.6 .................... 17-025
    para.7 .................... 17-026
    para.8 .................... 17-028
    para.9 .................... 17-029
    para.10 ................... 17-032
    para.11 ................... 17-010
    para.12 ................... 17-012
    para.13 ................... 17-014
    para.15 ................... 17-018
    para.16 ................... 17-022
  Sch.31 ......... 1-002, 13-012, 14-004
  Sch.32 ................. 1-002, 10-004
    para.A2 ............ 7-010, 7-017
      (3) ........................ 7-017
      (5) ........................ 7-017
    para.1 .................... 10-007
    para.2 ............ 10-014, 15-058
    para.3 .................... 10-015
    para.4 .................... 10-015
    para.5 .................... 10-005
    para.6 .................... 10-009
    para.7 .................... 10-005
      (5) ....................... 10-005
    para.8 .................... 10-005
    para.9 .................... 10-005
      (2) ....................... 10-056
    para.9A ................... 10-018
    paras 9A–13 .............. 30-125
    para.10 ................... 10-018
    para.10A .................. 10-018
    para.11(2) ................ 10-018
      (4) ....................... 10-010
    para.12 .................... 3-082
    para.13 ................... 10-005
      (2) ....................... 10-015
      (4) ....................... 10-056
    para.14(1) ................ 10-005
      (2) .............. 10-005, 10-056
    para.14A .................. 10-017
    para.14C ... 10-005, 10-007, 10-016
    para.15 ...... 7-010, 7-017, 10-005
    para.15A .................. 10-005
    para.16 ................... 10-005
    para.17 ................... 10-015
  Sch.33 . 1-002, 24-006, 24-026, 24-030,
      27-058, 27-126, 30-004, 30-112,
            33-024, 39-002
    para.1(1) ................. 24-013
      (2) ....................... 24-019
      (3) ....................... 24-020
      (4) ....................... 24-017
      (5) ....................... 24-021
    para.2 ..... 24-031, 24-033, 24-035,
            30-004, 39-013, 39-014
      (1) ....................... 24-022
    para.3 .................... 30-004
    para.4 .................... 24-008
      (1)(a) .................... 12-027
    para.5 .................... 24-007
      (3) ....................... 24-007
      (4) ....................... 24-007
    para.6 ........... 19-043, 24-007

  Sch.34 . 1-002, 23-003, 23-009, 24-003,
      24-026, 26-019, 27-077, 30-001,
      30-003, 30-004, 30-017, 30-020,
      30-022, 30-028, 30-077, 35-002,
      35-044, 35-051, 35-052, 37-026,
                  38-030
    para.1 ..... 12-040, 18-029, 32-014,
                  33-039
      (1) ....................... 30-033
      (4)(a) .................... 30-087
      (5) .............. 30-004, 30-117
        (a) .................... 30-115
        (d) ............. 30-071, 33-011
      (6) .............. 30-016, 33-024
      (6A) ...................... 33-029
      (6B) ..... 27-077, 30-044, 33-029
      (6C) .............. 30-070, 33-044
      (6D) ............. 30-046, 33-029
      (7) .............. 30-004, 30-036
    paras 1–7 ................ 30-017
    para.2 ..... 30-066, 30-087, 33-044,
              33-045, 34-043
    para.3 .................... 33-024
      (2) .............. 27-077, 30-037
      (3) .............. 27-058, 27-074
      (4) ....................... 27-074
    para.4 .................... 32-014
      (2) .............. 27-077, 30-039
    para.5 .................... 30-073
    para.5ZA .................. 30-035
    para.5A ................... 30-075
    para.6 .................... 30-076
    para.7A .... 30-017, 30-079, 30-080
    para.8 .................... 30-100
      (3) ....................... 30-100
      (4) ....................... 30-100
    paras 8–12 ........ 30-017, 30-108
    paras 9–12 ............... 30-101
    para.9ZA .......... 30-106, 33-044
      (1) ........................ 7-034
    para.9ZB ......... 30-106, 33-044
      (1) ........................ 7-034
    para.9A ................... 30-108
    para.9B ........... 7-029, 30-109
    para.10 ........... 30-102, 30-108
    para.11 ........... 30-104, 30-108
    para.12A .................. 30-112
    para.13(1) ........ 30-120, 30-123
    paras 13–19 .............. 30-017
    para.14(2) ................ 30-121
      (3) ....................... 30-121
    paras 14–19 .............. 30-120
    para.15 ................... 30-122
    para.16 ................... 30-123
    para.17 ................... 30-128
    para.18 ................... 30-124
  Sch.35 .............. 1-002, 7-002
  Sch.36 .... 1-002, 1-024, 3-001, 3-090,
          3-091, 23-018, 30-112
    Pt 1 ................ 2-002, 3-021
    para.1 .................... 4-004
      (1) ....... 3-052, 3-061, 3-063
        (a)–(d) ............. 3-055

2004 Finance Act—*cont.*
    (a)–(e) ............. 3-096
    (a)–(g) ............ 26-046
    (3) ................... 3-021
  para.2 ................... 4-004
  para.3 .................. 18-189
  para.4 ........... 3-022, 5-003
  Pt 2 para.6A ............. 14-056
  para.7 ................... 3-048
    (2) .................. 14-059
    (3) ............ 3-049, 14-060
    (5) ................... 3-051
  para.8 ........... 3-025, 3-053
    (1) ................... 3-052
  para.9 ................... 3-055
    (4) ............ 3-025, 3-055
    (5) ............ 3-025, 3-055
    (6) ................... 3-028
  para.10 ................. 14-036
    (1) ................... 3-058
    (2) ............ 3-058, 10-041
  para.11 .......... 3-061, 16-004
  para.11A ................. 3-062
  para.11B ................. 3-063
  para.11C ................. 3-064
  para.11D ................. 3-064
  para.12 .......... 3-025, 14-063
    (1) ................... 3-025
    (2) ................... 3-025
    (2A) .................. 3-041
    (2B) .................. 3-041
    (2C) .................. 3-041
    (5) ................... 3-025
    (6) ................... 3-025
    (7) .................. 10-030
  para.13(b) ............... 3-028
  para.14(1) ............... 3-026
    (3)–(3D) .............. 3-027
    (4) ................... 3-027
  para.15 .................. 3-029
    (4) ................... 3-030
  para.15A ................. 3-034
  para.16 .................. 3-033
  para.17 .................. 3-033
  para.17A ................. 3-035
    (1) .................. 16-004
  para.18 ... 3-066, 16-004, 16-008, 16-010
  para.19 ........... 3-069, 3-088
    (5) ................... 3-073
    (6) ................... 3-073
  para.20 .... 3-068, 3-074, 14-010, 14-016
    (4) .................. 10-044
  para.20A ................ 16-009
  para.20B ................ 20-016
  para.20C(3) ............. 20-019
    (6) .................. 20-024
  para.20D(2) ............. 20-026
    (5) .................. 20-027
  para.20E ........ 20-029, 20-033
  para.20F(3) ............. 20-034
    (6) .................. 20-035

  para.20G(3) ............. 20-036
    (5) .................. 20-037
  Pt 3 paras 21–23 .... 3-088, 32-015, 34-032
  para.22 ................. 12-001
    (5) ..... 3-088, 32-015, 34-032
    (6) ........... 24-011, 24-029
  para.23(5) . 3-088, 32-015, 34-032
  para.23ZA . 3-088, 32-015, 34-032
  para.24(2) .............. 14-061
    (3) .................. 14-061
  paras 24–30 ...... 3-092, 19-013
  para.25 ................. 14-061
  para.26 ................. 14-061
  para.27 ................. 14-063
  para.30 ................. 18-189
  paras 31–34 ....... 3-092, 3-094
  para.32 .................. 3-096
  para.33 .................. 3-096
  para.34 .................. 1-026
  Pt 4 paras 37A–37I ... 3-097, 30-079
  para.45A ................ 26-046
  para.47 ................. 17-005
  para.49 .................. 3-025
  para.51 .. 25-039, 27-126, 39-005, 39-012
    (1) .................. 24-027
    (2) ............ 7-024, 24-027
    (3) .... 24-026, 30-004, 33-024
    (4) .................. 24-027
    (5) .................. 24-029
  para.52 ................. 38-028
  para.53 .......... 23-018, 28-013
    (3) .................. 27-060
  paras 53–55 ............. 38-023
  para.55 .......... 23-018, 38-027
  para.56 ... 6-008, 22-022, 28-019, 28-057, 38-031
  para.57 .......... 28-057, 38-031
  para.58 .......... 28-013, 28-073
2004 Armed Forces (Pensions and Compensation) Act (c.32)
  s.1(2) ................... 7-006
2004 Civil Partnership Act (c.33)
  Sch.5 ................... 16-003
    Pt 6 para.24 .......... 16-001
  Sch.7 ................... 16-003
  Sch.11 .................. 16-003
  Sch.15 .................. 16-003
  Sch.17 .................. 16-003
2004 Pensions Act (c.35) ...... 5-050, 18-168, 24-014
  Pt 1 s.16(1) ..... 5-050, 6-007, 18-168
  s.19(4) . 2-003, 5-050, 6-007, 18-168
  s.21(2)(a) ..... 2-003, 5-050, 6-007, 18-168
  Pt 2 Ch.3 s.132 ............ 7-055
  s.138(2) ................ 13-015
  s.159 .................... 7-055
  Pt 5 s.246 ................ 8-052
  s.252 . 2-008, 4-004, 21-071, 35-014
  s.253 ................... 20-012
  s.255 ... 2-014, 3-038, 3-065, 4-017,

# TABLE OF STATUTES

2004 Pensions Act—*cont.*
    10-030, 15-001, 18-091
2005 Income Tax (Trading and Other Income)
    Act (c.5) ............. 6-036, 24-003
    Pt 2 ..... 6-022, 6-036, 6-112, 24-003,
        24-015
        Ch.2 s.6(2) ............... 39-011
        s.8 .................... 13-011
        Ch.3 s.25(1) ............... 6-037
        Ch.4 s.33 ........... 6-037, 6-071
        s.34(1) ........... 6-037, 6-044
        s.38 .................... 24-043
        (4)(c) .................. 24-023
        Ch.5 s.79 ............... 6-059
    Pt 3 .......... 6-022, 24-015, 31-031
        Ch.3 s.271 ............... 13-011
        s.272 .................. 6-061
    Pt 4 Ch.2 s.369 ............. 14-033
        s.371 ........... 13-011, 25-004
        Ch.3 .................... 27-135
        s.385 ........... 13-011, 25-004
        s.399(2) ............... 25-014
        Ch.9 ............. 22-028, 36-005
        s.461(1) ............... 36-005
        s.473(1)(a) ............. 36-005
        (3) .................... 36-005
        s.479 .... 22-028, 36-005, 36-012
        s.480 .... 36-005, 36-007, 36-019
        (2) .................... 36-008
        (3) .................... 36-009
        ss.480–482 .............. 36-005
        s.481 .................. 36-009
        s.482 .... 36-009, 36-011, 36-018
        s.484(1)(b) ............. 36-005
        s.485(2) ............... 36-005
        s.492(1)(b) ............. 36-005
        s.493(7) ............... 36-005
    Pt 5 ................ 8-014, 22-018
        Ch.2 .................... 24-003
        Ch.5 ........... 21-012, 25-017
        s.620 .................. 2-102
        (1) ........... 25-022, 25-027
        (2) .................... 25-027
        (3) ........... 25-024, 25-027
        s.624 .... 24-073, 24-082, 25-047,
            25-048
        (1) .... 22-018, 22-019, 25-019,
            25-032, 25-036, 25-038,
            25-040, 25-042
        s.625(1) ............... 25-034
        (2) .................... 25-034
        (3) .................... 25-034
        (5) .................... 25-034
        s.626 .................. 25-036
        s.627(2)(c) ...... 22-018, 25-019,
            25-038, 25-039
        (4) .................... 25-041
        (b) .................. 24-068
        s.628A ................. 25-020
        (8) .................... 25-020
        s.628B ................. 25-020
        s.629 .................. 25-047
        (1) .................... 25-043

        s.630A ................. 25-020
        s.631 .................. 25-044
        s.633 .... 25-045, 25-047, 25-048
        s.634(1) ............... 25-046
        s.635 ........... 25-020, 25-047
        s.641(1) ............... 25-045
        ss.643A–643N .......... 25-021
        s.644(3) ............... 25-028
        s.645 .................. 25-028
        (2) .................... 25-041
        s.646 .................. 25-049
        s.648 .................. 25-030
        (1) .................... 25-029
        Ch.7 ........ 6-149, 24-071, 26-055
        s.683 ........... 15-078, 26-060
        s.685 .................. 13-011
        Ch.8 .......... 6-149, 8-039, 8-041
        Pt 6 Ch.8 s.735 ....... 26-055, 26-056
        s.736 .................. 26-056
        s.737 .................. 26-056
        s.738 .................. 26-056
        s.739 .................. 26-056
        s.740 .................. 26-056
        s.742 .................. 26-057
    Pt 8 Ch.1 s.830(1) ........... 8-039
        (2) .................... 8-039
        (4)(c) .................. 35-091
        Ch.2 ....... 26-033, 26-049, 26-052
        s.832 .... 25-069, 37-023, 38-022,
            38-030, 39-017
        Ch.3 ............. 26-033, 26-048
        s.839 ........... 26-048, 26-052
    Pt 9 ............. 15-049, 26-052
        s.848 .................. 8-032
    Pt 10 Ch.2 s.866(5)(c) ....... 24-023
2005 Finance Act (c.7) ............... 6-077
2005 Finance (No. 2) Act (c.22) ...... 18-061,
    18-075, 18-079, 18-081, 18-090,
    18-105, 18-110
2006 Finance Act (c.25) ............. 9-001
    Pt 9 s.173 ................. 32-017
2006 Companies Act (c.46)
    Pt 15 Ch.2 s.386 ............. 4-013
    (3) .................... 4-013
    Pt 25 Ch.A1 s.859A .......... 17-008
    Pt 30 s.994 ................ 25-037
    Pt 38 s.1159(2) ............. 27-119
    s.1169 .................. 4-013
2007 Income Tax Act (c.3)
    Pt 1 s.1(2)(c) .... 5-004, 6-071, 19-043
    Pt 2 Ch.2 s.8 ............... 38-019
    (1) .................... 25-014
    s.9 ....... 25-005, 25-011, 38-019
    (1) .................... 8-047
    s.11 .................... 25-014
    (1) .................... 25-004
    s.12 .................... 25-003
    s.14 ............ 25-004, 25-014
    Ch.3 s.23 ........... 6-032, 7-024
    s.24 ............. 7-024, 25-003
    Pt 3 Ch.4 s.56 ........ 20-011, 20-040
    Pt 8 Ch.6 s.459 ............. 26-043
    s.460(3)(a)–(f) .......... 26-043

2007 Income Tax Act—cont.
 Pt 9 ....................... 25-003
  Ch.2 s.466 ........ 25-013, 27-033
   (2) .................. 25-003
   (4) ................... 2-102
  s.467 .................. 25-003
  s.471 .................. 25-003
  s.474 .................. 27-033
   (1) .................. 25-003
  s.475 .................. 25-003
   (3) .................. 25-053
  s.476 .................. 25-003
  s.477 .................. 25-013
  s.478(b) ............... 25-013
  Ch.3 s.479 .. 8-031, 25-005, 25-011,
       25-013, 38-019
  s.480 .................. 25-005
   (4) .................. 37-018
  Ch.6 s.491 ........ 25-005, 38-019
 Pt 9A s.517B(4) ............... 8-028
  s.517C(1) ................ 8-028
 Pt 13 Ch.1 s.685 .............. 25-077
  Ch.2 ................... 25-050
   s.714(2) .............. 25-051
   s.716(1) .............. 25-052
   (2) .................. 25-053
   s.717 ........... 25-053, 25-055
   s.718 ................. 25-053
   s.719 ................. 25-055
   s.720 .... 25-058, 25-060, 25-063,
     25-066, 25-068, 25-079, 26-064,
          26-065
   ss.720–726 .............. 25-050
   s.721(2) ............... 25-059
   (3C) ................. 25-049
   s.721A(3)(e) ........... 25-068
   s.721B ................. 25-068
   s.722 .................. 25-059
   (3) .................. 25-060
   (4) .................. 25-060
   s.723 .................. 25-059
   s.726 .................. 25-069
   s.727 .... 25-063, 25-065, 25-066,
        25-068, 26-064
   ss.727–730 .............. 25-050
   s.728 .................. 26-064
   (2A) ................. 25-049
   s.729 .................. 26-064
   (3) .................. 25-064
   (4) .................. 25-064
   s.730 .................. 25-069
   s.731 .... 25-066, 25-067, 25-070
   ss.731–735 .............. 25-050
   s.732 .... 25-066, 25-067, 26-065
   s.733(1) ............... 25-067
   s.735 .................. 25-069
   s.737 ............. 25-079, 25-080
   (3) ............. 25-071, 25-072
   (4) ............. 25-071, 25-081
   (6) .................. 25-073
   (7) .................. 25-073
   s.738 .................. 25-082
   s.739 ............ 25-072, 25-081

   s.742A ................. 25-071
  Ch.5B ............. 6-081, 6-091
  Ch.7 .................... 4-015
   s.809ZG ................. 4-015
 Pt 14 Ch.A1 ......... 26-038, 27-101
  s.809B ......... 27-100, 35-084
  s.809D ................. 27-100
  s.809E ................. 27-100
  s.809F(3) .............. 35-091
  Ch.1 s.811 .............. 25-011
  s.812 .................. 25-013
   (1) .................. 25-011
   (2) .................. 25-012
  s.813 .................. 25-011
  s.815 .................. 25-014
  s.816 .................. 25-014
  Ch.2A s.835BA .... 24-027, 25-020,
          25-066
 Pt 15 Ch.3 s.874 ............. 25-014
  Ch.6 ................... 37-022
  Ch.18 ss.971–972 ......... 25-014
 Pt 16 Ch.1 s.989 . 8-019, 8-031, 19-043
  s.993 ...... 2-099, 9-005, 18-045,
         27-012
  s.994(1) .......... 2-100, 2-107
  s.1004 .................. 8-043
  s.1007 .................. 8-031
2007 Finance Act (c.11)
 Sch.18 paras 4–7 ............. 6-007
 Sch.24 Pt 1 para.1 ........... 19-020
  Pt 2 para.4 ................ 19-020
2007 Tribunals, Courts and Enforcement Act
 (c.15)
 Pt 1 Ch.2 s.22 ............... 19-043
2008 Finance Act (c.9) ........ 3-042, 4-007
 Sch.29 para.18(6) ........... 34-002
 Sch.36 . 4-011, 19-008, 19-010, 19-035,
      33-043, 33-047, 35-105
  Pt 1 ..................... 4-023
   para.1 .......... 19-009, 19-035
   para.2 .................. 19-009
   para.3(1) ............... 19-010
   para.4(1) ............... 19-010
   para.5 .................. 19-009
   (3) .................. 19-010
   (4) .................. 19-010
  Pt 2 ..................... 4-023
  Pt 5 para.30(1) ............ 19-010
   para.31 ................ 19-010
   para.32 ................. 4-012
  Pt 6 para.34B ............. 19-010
  Pt 7 ..................... 33-048
   para.39 ................ 19-009
   (2) .................. 4-021
   para.40 ................ 19-009
   (2) .................. 4-021
   para.40A ......... 4-021, 19-009
   para.42 ........... 4-013, 4-020
   para.43 ........... 4-013, 4-020
   paras 44–49 ............. 4-021
   paras 46–49 ............. 4-021
 Sch.41 .................... 19-032

## TABLE OF STATUTES

2008 Housing and Regeneration Act (c.17) ................ 27-012
2009 Corporation Tax Act (c.4) .. 6-071, 6-073
    Pt 1 s.1 ............... 5-004, 6-071
    Pt 2 Ch.1 s.5(2) ............. 39-011
    Ch.3 s.14(1) ............... 5-004
    Pt 3 .......... 6-036, 6-112, 24-003
    Ch.3 s.46(1) . 6-037, 22-029, 24-003, 24-038
    Ch.4 s.53 ..... 6-037, 6-071, 6-073, 22-029, 24-038
        (1) .................. 6-071
        (2) .................. 6-071
    s.54 ............. 6-037, 24-038
        (1)(a) ......... 6-044, 22-029
        (2) .................. 6-046
    Ch.5 s.79 .................. 6-059
    Pt 4 Ch.3 s.210 .............. 6-061
    Pt 6 Ch.6 s.519(2) ............ 2-114
    Pt 8 ...................... 35-063
    Ch.14 s.868 .. 6-037, 6-073, 35-063
    Pt 16 ................ 6-036, 24-003
    Ch.1 s.1218B(1) ............ 6-063
    Ch.2 ...................... 6-112
    s.1219 .................. 6-064
        (1) .................. 6-063
        (3)(a) ................ 6-063
    s.1221(1)(h) .............. 6-063
    Ch.4 s.1249 ............... 24-039
    Pt 20 Ch.1 s.1288 ..... 24-038, 24-039
    s.1290 ... 23-003, 24-003, 24-005, 24-023, 24-035, 24-038, 24-043, 24-046, 28-024, 28-027, 29-018, 29-028, 35-059, 35-060, 35-061, 35-062, 37-013, 39-011
        (1A) ................ 24-049
        (2) ................. 39-014
        (2A) ................ 24-049
        (2B) ................ 24-049
        (3A)–(3H) ........... 24-049
        (4) ................. 24-051
          (a) .............. 36-017
          (b) .............. 37-013
          (c) ......... 24-023, 39-014
    s.1291 ................... 24-047
        (1) ................. 24-044
        (2) ................. 24-045
        (4)(a)(ii) ............. 24-045
    s.1292(1) ................ 35-059
        (5) ............ 6-068, 35-059
          (a) .............. 35-061
        (6A) ................ 24-050
    s.1296(1) . 24-045, 24-046, 24-051
    s.1305(1) ................. 6-058
2009 Finance Act (c.10)
    Sch.55 ................... 19-032
        para.1 ................ 19-020
        para.3 ................ 19-020
        para.4 ................ 19-020
        para.5 ................ 19-020
        para.6 ................ 19-020
    Sch.56 para.1 ............. 19-020

        para.3 .................... 19-020
2010 Corporation Tax Act (c.4)
    Pt 5 ................ 3-038, 10-030
    Pt 10 Ch.2 s.439 ............ 21-015
    s.448 ..................... 2-111
    s.450 ....... 2-107, 9-057, 9-070, 25-095
    s.451 ....... 2-107, 9-057, 9-070, 25-095
    s.452 .................... 15-049
        (2)(b) .......... 5-058, 9-070
    s.453 ..................... 2-112
    s.454 ..... 2-114, 25-095, 28-030
    Pt 16 Ch.2 ....... 6-081, 6-084, 6-091
    s.760(2) ........... 6-081, 6-091
    s.775 .................... 6-087
    Pt 23 Ch.2 s.1000(2) .......... 2-114
    Pt 24 Ch.1 s.1119 ............ 36-010
    s.1122 ............. 2-099, 8-012
        (6) .................. 8-012
        (c) .................. 8-012
        (e) .................. 8-012
        (f) .................. 8-012
        (g) .................. 8-012
        (7) .................. 8-012
    s.1123(1) .................. 2-107
    s.1139 ................... 36-010
    Ch.2 s.1141 ............... 25-086
    s.1142(1) ................. 25-086
    s.1143 ................... 25-086
2010 Taxation (International and Other Provisions) Act (c.8)
    Pt 2 ..................... 29-071
    Ch.1 s.2 .................. 32-017
        (1) ........... 26-040, 29-009
    s.3(1) ................... 29-009
        (2) ................. 29-009
    s.6 ...... 26-040, 27-106, 35-078
        (1) ................. 29-009
        (2) ................. 29-009
          (a) .............. 29-011
        (3) ................. 29-009
          (a) .............. 29-011
        (6) ................. 29-011
    s.9 ...................... 26-069
        (1) ................. 26-069
    s.11 ..................... 26-069
    Ch.2 s.103 ................ 29-070
    Ch.3 s.112 ................ 26-069
    s.113 .................... 26-069
    s.130A ................... 29-071
    Pt 10 Ch.4 s.394 ...... 35-079, 35-080
2010 Equality Act (c.15)
    Pt 5 ................ 3-064, 3-065
    Ch.3 s.67 ................. 10-025
2011 Finance Act (c.11) ....... 1-025, 35-059
    Sch.2 paras 52–59 ........... 27-001
        para.56 ................ 27-042
    Sch.18 Pt 2 para.14 ... 10-021, 14-065
        (9) ................. 10-030

## TABLE OF STATUTES

2011 Pensions Act (c.19)
    Pt 4 s.29 .................... 2-041
2012 Scotland Act (c.11) ............ 9-106
2012 Finance Act (c.14) ....... 1-025, 6-079
    Pt 2 Ch.3 s.76 ................ 6-112
2013 Finance Act (c.29) ....... 1-025, 35-077
    Pt 5 .......... 4-015, 6-019, 26-022
    s.207 ..................... 4-015
    s.212 ..................... 29-010
    Sch.22 .................... 10-021
        Pt 1 para.1 ............... 14-066
    Sch.45 Pt 1 para.1(4) ......... 24-010
        para.2(1) .............. 24-010
            (5) ................ 24-010
        Pt 4 ............... 27-106, 35-078
        para.110 ................ 5-033
2014 Finance Act (c.26) .. 1-025, 4-002, 4-023,
                              5-011
    Pt 1 Ch.4 s.42(2) ............ 14-036
    Sch.6 Pt 1 para.1 ..... 10-041, 14-068
        para.2 .................. 10-041
        para.3 .................. 10-041
        para.4 .................. 10-041
        para.5 .................. 10-041
2014 Wales Act (c.29)
    Pt 2 s.16(2) ................. 9-106
2014 Taxation of Pensions Act (c.30)
    ................... 1-025, 31-006
    Sch.1 Pt 1 para.32(1)(b) ...... 13-039
            (d) ................ 15-039
2015 Finance Act (c.11) .............. 1-025
2015 Finance (No. 2) Act (c.33) ........ 1-025
2016 Finance Act (c.24) ... 1-007, 1-025, 8-028
    Sch.4 Pt 1 .................. 10-021
        para.1 .................. 14-067
        Pt 2 para.9 ........ 10-044, 14-069
        para.10(3) .............. 10-044
            (4) ................ 10-044
        para.11 ................. 10-044
        Pt 3 .................... 10-021
        para.14(7)–(9) .......... 10-045
        para.19 ................ 10-021
    Pt 4 ...................... 10-021
2017 Finance Act (c.10) . 1-025, 6-140, 12-018,
        20-003, 23-002, 24-063, 27-005,
                    27-090, 37-010
    Sch.6 para.2 ................ 27-019
2017 Pension Schemes Act (c.17)
    Pt 1 ...................... 4-013
        s.1 ......... 2-026, 4-013, 19-013
        s.2 ..................... 4-013
2017 Finance (No. 2) Act (c.32) . 1-025, 24-027
    Pt 1 s.37 ................... 24-049
    Sch.11 .................... 27-006
        Pt 3 .................... 27-006
2018 Finance Act (c.3) ... 1-025, 4-003, 4-023,
                            27-007
    Sch.3 para.2(1) ......... 4-013, 4-023
    Sch.10 Pt 1 ................. 25-108
2021 Pension Schemes Act (c.1) ....... 2-044
    Pt 1 s.36(7)(b) .............. 14-018
    Pt 2 s.87(7)(b) .............. 14-018
2021 Finance Act (c.26)
    Pt 1 s.28 ................... 10-020
2022 Finance Act (c.3) ............... 1-025
2023 Finance (No. 2) Act (c.30) . 1-025, 3-025,
                      7-057, 10-022
2024 Finance Act (c.3) .. 1-025, 14-002, 14-018
    Sch.9 Pt 4 para.90(4) ......... 14-065
        para.91(3) .............. 14-066
        para.92(3) .............. 14-068
        para.93(3) .............. 14-067
            (4) ................ 14-069
    Pt 6 para.125 ............... 14-008
        para.126 ................ 14-014
            (4)(a) .............. 14-014
        para.127 ................ 14-017
        para.128 ................ 14-073
        para.130 ................ 14-074
        para.131 ................ 14-012

# TABLE OF STATUTORY INSTRUMENTS

1968 Double Taxation Relief (Taxes on Income) (France) Order (SI 1968/1869)
.................... 26-077, 29-030
Sch.1 ..................... 26-077
1970 Double Taxation Relief (Taxes on Income) (General) Regulations (SI 1970/488)
........................ 29-012
1976 Double Taxation Relief (Taxes on Income) (Republic of Ireland) Order (SI 1976/2151) ... 25-039, 26-077, 29-030
art.1 .............. 26-077, 29-030
art.17A ............ 26-077, 29-030
1978 Matrimonial Causes (Northern Ireland) Order (SI 1978/1045) ........ 16-003
1980 Double Taxation Relief (Taxes on Income) (Canada) Order (SI 1980/709)
.................... 26-077, 29-030
Sch.1 ..................... 26-077
1980 Double Taxation Relief (Taxes on Income) (Denmark) Order (SI 1980/1960)
.................... 26-077, 29-030
1987 Pension Scheme Surpluses (Valuation) Regulations (SI 1987/412) ...... 3-011
1989 Matrimonial and Family Proceedings (Northern Ireland) Order (SI 1989/677)
Pt IV .................... 16-003
1989 Taxes (Interest Rate) Regulations (SI 1989/1297)
reg.3(2) ............. 12-042, 33-041
1991 Occupational Pension Schemes (Preservation of Benefit) Regulations (SI 1991/167) ............... 14-030
1991 Retirement Benefits Schemes (Restriction on Discretion to Approve) (Small Self-administered Schemes) Regulations (SI 1991/1614) ...... 3-080, 3-085, 3-097
reg.4(1)(c) ................. 8-054
1995 Double Taxation Relief (Taxes on Income) (Republic of Ireland) Order (SI 1995/764) ........... 26-077, 29-030
Sch.1 .............. 26-077, 29-030
1995 Taxation of Income from Land (Non-residents) Regulations (SI 1995/2902)
......................... 25-014
1995 Manufactured Payments and Transfer of Securities (Tax Relief) Regulations (SI 1995/3036)
reg.3(1) ................... 8-017
reg.4(1) ................... 8-017
1996 Occupational Pension Schemes (Scheme Administration) Regulations (SI 1996/1715)
Pt II reg.3(3) ................ 8-006
1996 Occupational Pension Schemes (Transfer Values) Regulations (SI 1996/1847)
......................... 12-001
1997 Occupational Pension Schemes (Assignment, Forfeiture, Bankruptcy etc.) Regulations (SI 1997/785)
......................... 13-015
2000 Pension Sharing (Valuation) Regulations (SI 2000/1052) .............. 16-002
2001 Personal Pension Schemes (Restriction on Discretion to Approve) (Permitted Investments) Regulations (SI 2001/117)
reg.6(4) ................... 8-054
2001 Financial Services and Markets Act 2000 (Regulated Activities) Order (SI 2001/544)
Sch.1 Pt II ............ 2-003, 30-084
2001 Social Security (Contributions) Regulations (SI 2001/1004) ... 26-073
Pt 2 reg.22B ......... 27-140, 27-141
Pt 3 reg.40(2)(a) ...... 14-004, 37-014
Sch.3 Pt VI ................ 26-070
para.2 ..... 6-138, 6-139, 13-012, 15-023
(b) ................ 14-004
para.3(a) ........ 39-011, 39-014
(1)(a) ........ 24-025, 26-073
(b) .. 24-036, 39-018, 39-019
(d) ......... 39-017, 39-019
(e) ............... 30-028
para.4 .................. 38-022
para.5 .................. 38-022
para.7 ......... 26-077, 29-030
para.8(a) ................ 35-092
(b) .... 35-093, 38-022, 38-030
para.9 ......... 24-060, 26-075
(1)(a) ............... 35-047
(b) ................ 35-047
(2) .................. 35-021
para.10 .. 26-075, 35-093, 38-022, 38-030
(6)(a)–(c) ............ 35-096
(d) ................ 35-100
para.11 ......... 37-014, 37-025
Pt X para.1 ................ 27-140
para.2A ......... 27-140, 27-142
2001 Financial Services and Markets Act 2000 (Carrying on Regulated Activities by Way of Business) Order (SI 2001/1177)
......................... 8-006
2002 Income Tax (Exemption of Minor Benefits) Regulations (SI 2002/205)
reg.5 ...................... 6-143
2002 Occupational and Personal Pension Schemes (Bankruptcy) (No. 2) Regulations (SI 2002/836)
Pt II reg.2 ................. 25-039
2002 Double Taxation Relief (Taxes on Income) (The United States of America) Order (SI 2002/2848) ....... 26-077, 29-030
Sch.1 ..................... 26-077

2002 Double Taxation Relief (Taxes on Income) (South Africa) Order (SI 2002/3138) .................. 26-077, 29-030
  Sch.1 ..................... 26-077
2003 Income Tax (Pay As You Earn) Regulations (SI 2003/2682)
  Pt 3 (3)reg.57 ........ 20-045, 37-022
  Pt 4 (1)reg.72 .............. 27-112
    reg.80 ................. 27-112
    reg.81 ................. 27-112
2003 Double Taxation Relief (Taxes on Income)(Chile) Order (SI 2003/3200) .................. 26-077, 29-030
2005 Armed Forces and Reserve Forces (Compensation Scheme) Order (SI 2005/439) ................ 35-056
2005 Occupational Pension Schemes (Investment) Regulations (SI 2005/3378) ...... 2-084, 8-003, 9-066, 17-008, 37-018
  reg.1(2) .............. 8-005, 17-035
  reg.2 ...................... 8-004
  reg.3 ...................... 8-004
  reg.4 ...................... 8-004
    (5) ..................... 8-004
    (6) ..................... 8-004
    (7) ..................... 8-004
  reg.5 .......... 8-004, 8-052, 37-010
  reg.7 ...................... 8-052
    (1) ..................... 8-004
    (2) ..................... 8-004
  reg.12 ........ 8-005, 17-008, 17-035
2005 Registered Pension Schemes (Relief at Source) Regulations (SI 2005/3448) ...................... 6-029
  reg.4 ...................... 6-029
  reg.5 ...................... 6-029
  reg.9 ...................... 6-029
  reg.14 ..................... 6-016
  reg.15 ..................... 6-029
    (2) ..................... 4-030
2005 Registered Pension Schemes (Prescribed Interest Rates for Authorised Employer Loans) Regulations (SI 2005/3449) .................. 17-008, 17-016
2005 Registered Pension Schemes (Prescribed Schemes and Occupations) Regulations (SI 2005/3451)
  reg.3 ...................... 3-089
  Sch.1 ..................... 3-069
2005 Registered Pension Schemes (Discharge of Liabilities under Sections 267 and 268 of the Finance Act 2004) Regulations (SI 2005/3452) .... 5-036, 10-061, 10-064, 18-180, 33-009
2005 Employer-Financed Retirement Benefits Schemes (Provision of Information) Regulations (SI 2005/3453)
  reg.4 ..................... 35-103
  reg.5 ..................... 35-103
    (2) .................... 35-103
2005 Registered Pension Schemes (Accounting and Assessment) Regulations (SI 2005/3454) ................ 19-008
  reg.3 ...................... 19-018
  reg.4 ....... 19-027, 19-041, 35-104
  reg.5 ......... 5-035, 19-019, 19-031
  reg.6 ...................... 19-019
  reg.7(2) ............. 19-019, 19-031
  reg.9 ...................... 19-041
2005 Registered Pension Schemes (Restriction of Employers' Relief) Regulations (SI 2005/3458) ........... 6-074, 32-020
  reg.2 ...................... 32-020
  regs 5–8 ................... 6-076
  reg.10 ..................... 6-076
2006 Registered Pension Schemes (Relevant Annuities) Regulations (SI 2006/129) .................. 13-041, 15-043
2006 Registered Pension Schemes (Uprating Percentages for Defined Benefits Arrangements and Enhanced Protection Limits) Regulations (SI 2006/130) ...................... 3-030
2006 Registered Pension Schemes (Enhanced Lifetime Allowance) Regulations (SI 2006/131) ................ 20-022
  reg.4 ...................... 3-025
  reg.4A ..................... 3-034
  reg.5 ................ 3-067, 16-011
  reg.12 ................ 3-025, 3-048
2006 Armed Forces and Reserve Forces (Compensation Scheme) (Excluded Benefits for Tax Purposes) Regulations (SI 2006/132) ................ 35-056
2006 Registered Pension Schemes (Co-ownership of Living Accommodation) Regulations (SI 2006/133) .... 18-136
2006 Pension Benefits (Insurance Company Liable as Scheme Administrator) Regulations (SI 2006/136) .... 15-047
2006 Pension Schemes (Reduction in Pension Rates) Regulations (SI 2006/138)
  reg.2 ..................... 13-015
  reg.3 ..................... 13-015
2006 Pension Schemes (Categories of Country and Requirements for Overseas Pension Schemes and Recognised Overseas Pension Schemes) Regulations (SI 2006/206) .... 31-002, 31-009, 31-035, 32-001, 32-014, 32-019, 33-001, 34-018, 34-021, 34-035, 34-036, 34-037, 34-038, 34-040
  reg.2(1) ................... 31-009
    (a) ............ **32-008, 32-012**
    (b) ............ **32-008, 32-012**
    (2) . 31-009, 31-011, 31-012, 34-040
    (b) .................... 31-012
    (d) .................... 31-012
    (2A) .................... 31-009
    (3) . 31-009, 31-014, 31-036, 34-013, 34-014, 34-016, 34-019, 34-021
  reg.3 ...................... 32-005
    (1) .................... 32-006
    (1A) ............ 32-006, 32-007

## TABLE OF STATUTORY INSTRUMENTS

2006 Pension Schemes (Categories of Country and Requirements for Overseas Pension Schemes and Recognised Overseas Pension Schemes) Regulations—*cont.*
   (1B) .................... 31-009
   (2) ............. 32-006, 32-017
   (4) ....... 32-006, 32-018, 32-019
   (6) . 31-033, 32-006, 32-008, 32-010, 32-011, 32-019
   (6A) ...... 32-006, 32-012, 32-014, 34-034
   (7) ...................... 32-009
   (8) ...................... 32-009
  reg.6 ..................... **34-038**
  Sch.1 .............. 31-021, 34-015

2006 Pensions Schemes (Application of UK Provisions to Relevant Non-UK Schemes) Regulations (SI 2006/207)
.................... 30-003, 30-017
  Pt 2 reg.2 .................. 30-037
  reg.3 ..................... 30-040
  reg.3A ............ 30-017, 30-081
  reg.3B ............ 27-077, 30-044
  reg.3C .................... 30-081
  reg.4(2) ................... 30-049
    (3) .................... 30-089
  reg.4ZA(2) ................. 30-050
    (3)(a) ................. 30-050
      (b) .................. 30-053
  reg.4ZB .......... 30-050, 30-053
  reg.4ZC ................... 30-054
  reg.4ZD ................... 30-057
  reg.4ZE ................... 30-056
  reg.4ZF ................... 30-052
    (6) .................... 30-057
  reg.4A ........... 30-017, 30-079
  reg.4B .................... 30-017
    (2) .................... 30-085
    (3) .................... 30-085
  reg.4C ........... 30-017, 30-084
  reg.4D ........... 30-017, 30-086
  Pt 3 ...................... 30-058
  reg.6 ..................... 30-058
  reg.7 ..................... 30-058
  reg.9 ..................... 30-103
  reg.10 .................... 30-103
  reg.11 .................... 30-059
  reg.12 .................... 30-126
  reg.13 .................... 32-020
  reg.14 ............ 30-060, 34-033
    (6) .................... 30-059
  reg.15(1A) ................. 30-062
    (1B) ................... 30-064
    (1C) ................... 30-061
    (4) ............ 30-060, 34-033
    (8) ............ 26-022, 30-065
  reg.16 .................... 30-125
  reg.17 .................... 30-020
  Pt 4 reg.18 ................ 30-063

2006 Pension Schemes (Information Requirements - Qualifying Overseas Pension Schemes, Qualifying Recognised Overseas Pensions Schemes and Corresponding Relief) Regulations (SI 2006/208) .... 33-043, 33-047
  reg.2 . 24-007, 24-027, 29-019, 39-012, 39-013
  reg.3 ..................... 34-010
    (1) .................... 33-044
    (g) .................... 33-044
    (1A)–(1D) .............. 33-044
    (2) .................... 33-044
    (2B) ................... 33-044
    (2C) ................... 33-044
    (3) .................... 33-044
    (3A) ................... 33-044
  reg.3A ............. 12-025, 33-044
  reg.3AA ........... 33-044, 33-049
  reg.3AB ................... 33-049
  reg.3AC ................... 33-044
  reg.3AD ................... 33-044
  reg.3AE ................... 33-049
  reg.3AF ................... 33-049
  reg.3AG(1) ................. 33-044
    (2) .................... 33-044
    (4) .................... 33-044
  reg.3AH ............ 12-042, 33-041
  reg.3AJ ............ 12-042, 33-041
  reg.3AL ................... 12-043
  reg.3B .................... 33-044
  reg.3C .................... 33-045
  reg.4 ..................... 24-007
  reg.5 ..................... 33-048

2006 Employer-Financed Retirement Benefits (Excluded Benefits for Tax Purposes) Regulations (SI 2006/210)
  reg.2 ..................... 35-057

2006 Registered Pension Schemes (Surrender of Relevant Excess) Regulations (SI 2006/211) ............ 3-025, 18-088

2006 Pension Schemes (Relevant Migrant Members) Regulations (SI 2006/212)
  reg.2 ..................... 24-008

2006 Child Benefit (General) Regulations (SI 2006/223) ................. 27-012

2006 Registered Pension Schemes (Modification of the Rules of Existing Schemes) Regulations (SI 2006/364)
  reg.3(1) .................. 18-189

2006 Registered Pension Schemes (Unauthorised Payments by Existing Schemes) Regulations (SI 2006/365)
  reg.2(1) .................. 18-189

2006 Registered Pension Schemes (Block Transfers) (Permitted Membership Period) Regulations (SI 2006/498)
  reg.2 ............. 24-011, 24-029

2006 Registered Pension Schemes (Transfer of Sums and Assets) Regulations (SI 2006/499) ................ 12-007
  reg.3 ..................... 12-007

2006 Registered Pension Schemes (Transfer of Sums and Assets) Regulations—*cont.*
  (2) . . . . . . . . . . . . . . . . . . . . . . 12-007
  reg.4 . . . . . . . . . . . . . . . . . . . . . . 12-007
  reg.5 . . . . . . . . . . . . . . . . . . . . . . 13-015
  reg.6 . . 12-009, 13-028, 18-060, 18-083
  reg.7(1) . . . . . . . . . . . . . 13-034, 18-060
  reg.8 . . . . . . . . . . . . . . . . . . . . . . 12-007
  reg.9 . . . . . . . . . . . . . . . . . . . . . . 18-060
  reg.10 . . . . . . . . . . . . . . 18-060, 18-083
  reg.11 . . . . . . . . . . . . . . . . . . . . . 18-060
  reg.12 . . . . . . . . . . . . . . . . . . . . . 12-011
    (1) . . . . . . . . . . . . . . . . . . . . . . 12-011
    (2) . . . . . . . . . . . . . . . . . . . . . . 12-011
  reg.13 . . . . . . . . . . . . . . . . . . . . . 12-009
  reg.17 . . . . . . . . . . . . . . . . . . . . . 18-060
  reg.18 . . . . . . . . . . . . . . . . . . . . . 18-060
  reg.19 . . . . . . . . . . . . . . . . . . . . . 18-060
    (1) . . . . . . . . . . . . . . . . . . . . . . 18-083
  reg.20 . . . . . . . . . . . . . . . . . . . . . 18-060
    (1) . . . . . . . . . . . . . . . . . . . . . . 18-083
2006 Registered Pension Schemes (Provision of Information) Regulations (SI 2006/567)
  . 5-020, 7-057, 14-073, 19-008, 19-021, 19-023
  reg.3 . . . . . 5-035, 5-036, 7-057, 9-005, 9-134, 9-148, 10-065, 12-001, 18-195, 19-008, 19-013, 19-021, 29-022, 31-008
    (6) . . . . . . . . . . . . . . . . . . . . . . 19-014
    (7) . . . . . . . . . . . . . . . . . . . . . . 19-014
    (8) . . . . . . . . . . . . . . . . . . . . . . 19-014
  reg.4(3) . . . . . . . . . . . . . . . . . . . . 19-014
  reg.5 . . . . . . . . . . . . . . . . . . . . . . 18-195
  reg.5A . . . . . . . . . . . . . . . . . . . . . 5-035
  reg.6 . . . . . . . . . . . . . . . . . . . . . . . 5-019
  reg.8 . . . . . . . . . . . . . . . . . . . . . . 10-065
  reg.10 . . . . . . . . . . . . . . . . . . . . . 10-066
  reg.10A . . . . . . . . . . . . . . . . . . . . 15-079
  reg.10B . . . . . . . . . . . . . . . . . . . . 15-079
  reg.11A . . . . . . . . . . . . . . . . . . . . . 6-146
  reg.11BA . . . . . . . . . . . 12-001, 12-025
  reg.11BB . . . . . . . . . . . . . . . . . . 12-001
  reg.12 . . . . . . . . . . . . . . . . . . . . . 10-065
  reg.12A . . . . . . . . . . . . . . . . . . . 12-001
  reg.13 . . . . . . . . . . . . . . 18-126, 18-195
  reg.14 . . . . . . . . . . . . . . . . . . . . . 10-065
    (1) . . . . . . . . . . . . . . . . . . . . . . 14-074
  reg.14ZA . . . . . . . . . . . . . . . . . . 19-021
    (1) . . . . . . . . . . . . . . . . . . . . . . . 7-058
  reg.14ZB(1) . . . . . . . . . . . . . . . . . 7-058
    (7) . . . . . . . . . . . . . . . . . . . . . . 20-006
    (8) . . . . . . . . . . . . . . . . . . . . . . 20-005
  reg.14ZC . . . . . . . . . . . . . . . . . . 12-001
    (1) . . . . . . . . . . . . . . . . . . . . . . . 7-058
  reg.14ZCA . . . . . . . . . . . . . . . . . 12-001
  reg.14ZD(1) . . . . . . . . . . . . . . . . . 7-058
  reg.14ZE(1) . . . . . . . . . . . . . . . . . 7-058
  reg.14A(1) . . . . . . . . . . 7-057, 19-013
    (2) . . . . . . . . . . . . . . . . 7-057, 19-013
    (10) . . . . . . . . . . . . . . . 7-057, 19-013
  reg.14B(1) . . . . . . . . . . . . . . . . . . 7-057

  reg.15 . . . . . . . . . . . . . . . . . . . . . 10-065
  reg.15A(1) . . . . . . . . . . . . . . . . . . 7-057
  regs 16–17C . . . . . . . . . . . . . . . . 19-021
  reg.18 . . . . . . . . . . . . . . 5-020, 19-004
2006 Registered Pension Schemes (Prescribed Manner of Determining Amount of Annuities) Regulations (SI 2006/568)
  . . . . . . . . . . . . . . . . . . . . . . . . . . 12-012
  reg.2 . . . . . . . . . . . . . . . . . . . . . . 13-027
  reg.3 . . . . . . . . . . . . . . . 15-030, 15-031
  reg.4 . . . . . . . . . . . . . . . 13-033, 15-033
2006 Registered Pension Schemes (Splitting of Schemes) Regulations (SI 2006/569)
  . . . . . . . . . . . . . 15-047, 18-179, 19-032
2006 Registered Pension Schemes and Overseas Pension Schemes (Electronic Communication of Returns and Information) Regulations (SI 2006/570)
  Pt 2 reg.4 . . . . . . . . . . . . . 4-005, 5-019
  Pt 4 reg.6 . . . . . . . . . . . . . . . . . . . 4-005
  Sch.1 . . . . . . . . . . . . . . . . . . . . . . . 4-005
2006 Taxation of Pension Schemes (Transitional Provisions) Order (SI 2006/572)
  . . . . . . . . . 1-024, 1-026, 3-001, 13-021
  art.2 . . . . . . . . . . . . . . . . 3-093, 18-026
    (3) . . . . . . . . . . . . . . . . . . . . . . 26-046
  art.6 . . . . . . . . . . . . . . . . . . . . . . 15-075
  art.7 . . . . . . . . . . . . . . . . . . . . . . 15-076
  art.8 . . . . . . . . . . . . . . . . . . . . . . 15-075
  arts 9–11 . . . . . . . . . . . . . . . . . . . 3-060
  art.15 . 24-031, 24-035, 27-126, 39-013
    (2) . . . . . . . . . . . . . . . . 30-004, 33-024
  art.16 . . . . . . . . . . . . . . . . . . . . . 24-035
  art.17 . . . . . . . . . . . . . . . . . . . . . 24-034
    (4) . . . . . . . . . . . . . . . . . . . . . . 39-014
  art.25B(3) . . . . . . . . . . . . . . . . . 19-013
    (4) . . . . . . . . . . . . . . . . . . . . . . 19-013
  art.29 . . . . . . . . . . . 3-080, 3-085, 3-087
  art.33 . . . . . . . . . . . . . . . 15-056, 15-058
  art.34 . . . . . . . . . . . . . . . . . . . . . 15-018
  art.34A . . . . . . . . . . . . . . . . . . . . 15-018
  art.35 . . . . . . . . . . . . . . . . . . . . . . 3-038
  art.36 . . . . . . . . . . . . . . . . . . . . . . 3-029
2006 Registered Pension Schemes (Authorised Surplus Payments) Regulations (SI 2006/574)
  reg.2 . . . . . . . . . . . . . . . . . . . . . . 17-002
  reg.3 . . . . . . . . . . . . . . . . . . . . . . 17-002
2006 Registered Pension Schemes (Authorised Payments - Arrears of Pension) Regulations (SI 2006/614)
  reg.2 . . . . . . . . . . . . . . . . . . . . . . 13-043
2006 Occupational Pension Schemes (Payments to Employer) Regulations (SI 2006/802)
  Pt 4 reg.15 . . . . . . . . . . . . . . . . . 17-004
  reg.16 . . . . . . . . . . . . . . . . . . . . . 17-004
  reg.17 . . . . . . . . . . . . . . . . . . . . . 17-004
2006 Employment Equality (Age) Regulations (SI 2006/1031) . . . . . . . . . . . . . . 18-088
2006 Registered Pension Schemes (Authorised Reductions) Regulations (SI 2006/1465)
  reg.2 . . . . . . . . . . . . . . . . . . . . . . 13-015

## TABLE OF STATUTORY INSTRUMENTS

2006 Registered Pension Schemes (Extension of Migrant Member Relief) Regulations (SI 2006/1957)
 reg.2 ..................... 24-011
2006 Pensions Schemes (Taxable Property Provisions) Regulations (SI 2006/1958)
 .......................... 9-091
 reg.3 ...................... 9-106
 regs 3–9 ................... 9-095
 reg.5 ...................... 9-104
 reg.6 ...................... 9-110
 reg.7 ...................... 9-111
 reg.8 ...................... 9-111
 reg.9 ...................... 9-113
 reg.10 ........ 5-033, 5-034, 19-027
2006 Investment-regulated Pension Schemes (Exception of Tangible Moveable Property) Order (SI 2006/1959)
 .......................... 9-055
 art.2 ...................... 9-020
2007 Employer-Financed Retirement Benefits (Excluded Benefits for Tax Purposes) Regulations (SI 2007/3537) ... 35-056
2008 Occupational Pension Schemes (Non-European Schemes Exemption) Regulations (SI 2008/624)
 reg.2 ..................... 20-012
2008 Tribunal Procedure (Upper Tribunal) Rules (SI 2008/2698) ........ 19-043
2009 Tribunal Procedure (First-tier Tribunal) (Tax Chamber) Rules (SI 2009/273)
 .......................... 19-043
 Pt 2 r.10(1)(c) ............. 19-045
 Pt 3 (1)r.20 ................ 19-044
  (2) ................. 19-044
  r.23 ................ 19-045
  (2)r.28 ............. 19-045
2009 Registered Pension Schemes (Authorised Payments) Regulations (SI 2009/1171)
 ............. 10-019, 11-006, 14-041
 Pt 1 reg.3 .... 14-042, 14-045, 14-046, 14-048
 regs 3–5B ................ 10-019
 Pt 2 reg.6 ................ 14-042
 reg.7 ..................... 14-043
 reg.8 ..................... 14-045
 reg.10 ............. 14-046, 14-048
 reg.11 ............. 14-046, 30-050
 reg.11A .... 14-048, 14-049, 30-050
 reg.12 ............. 14-046, 30-050
 Pt 3 reg.13 .......... 13-044, 14-051
 reg.14 .................... 13-045
 reg.15 ............. 13-006, 13-046
 reg.16 ............. 10-019, 13-047
 Pt 4 reg.17 .... 10-019, 14-019, 14-051
 reg.18 ..... 10-019, 14-019, 14-053
 reg.19 ..... 10-019, 14-019, 14-055
 Pt 5 reg.20 ................. 14-030
2010 Inheritance Tax (Qualifying Non-UK Pension Schemes) Regulations (SI 2010/51) ..... 34-002, 34-009, 34-011, 34-013, 34-040
 reg.2 ..................... 34-027
 reg.4 ..................... 34-011
 reg.5 ............. 34-011, 34-013
 reg.6 ............. 34-011, 34-040
  (2) ................. 34-040
  (3) ................. 34-040
  (4) ................. 34-040
 reg.7 ............. 34-011, 34-012
2010 Occupational and Personal Pension Schemes (Automatic Enrolment) Regulations (SI 2010/772) ..... 3-042
2011 Registered Pension Schemes (Notice of Joint Liability for the Annual Allowance Charge) Regulations (SI 2011/1793)
 .......................... 7-051
2011 Employment Income Provided Through Third Parties (Excluded Relevant Steps) Regulations (SI 2011/2696) .... 27-051
 reg.3 .............. 27-040, 39-018
  (1) .............. 27-076, 30-078
  (3)–(4) ............... 27-077
 reg.4 ..................... 22-026
2012 Registered Pension Schemes and Overseas Pension Schemes (Miscellaneous Amendments) Regulations (SI 2012/884)
 reg.3(2)(d) ................ 31-036
 reg.4(d) ................... 31-033
2012 Pension Schemes (Categories of Country and Requirements for Overseas Pension Schemes and Recognised Overseas Pension Schemes) (Amendment) Regulations (SI 2012/1221) ... 33-010
2013 Registered Pension Schemes and Overseas Pension Schemes (Miscellaneous Amendments) Regulations (SI 2013/2259)
 reg.4 ..................... 33-047
 reg.5 .............. 33-045, 33-047
2013 Unauthorised Unit Trusts (Tax) Regulations (SI 2013/2819)
 Pt 2 (1)reg.3 ............... 8-031
 (4)reg.12(1) ............... 8-031
 (3)(d) .................. 8-031
 (6)reg.18(2) ............... 8-031
2014 Enactment of Extra-Statutory Concessions Order (SI 2014/211) ... 35-082, 35-086
2014 Registered Pension Schemes and Relieved Non-UK Pension Schemes (Lifetime Allowance Transitional Protection) (Individual Protection 2014 Notification) Regulations (SI 2014/1842) ................ 10-041
2014 Registered Pension Schemes (Provision of Information) (Amendment) Regulations (SI 2014/1843).............. 10-041
2015 National Health Service Pension Scheme Regulations (SI 2015/94) ..... 27-012
2015 Market Value of Shares, Securities and Strips Regulations (SI 2015/616)
 .......................... 2-119

# TABLE OF STATUTORY INSTRUMENTS

2016 Registered Pension Schemes (Bridging Pensions) and Appointed Day Regulations (SI 2016/1005)
    reg.3 ..................... 13-015
    reg.4 ..................... 13-015

2019 Taxes (Amendments) (EU Exit) Regulations (SI 2019/689)
    Pt 2 reg.12(2) .............. 33-032

2020 Finance Act 2004 (Standard Lifetime Allowance) Regulations (SI 2020/342)
    reg.2 ............... 1-010, 10-020

2022 Finance Act 2021, Schedule 5 (Pension Schemes: Collective Money Purchase Benefits) (Appointed Day) Regulations (SI 2022/874)
    reg.2 ...................... 1-025

2023 Public Service Pension Schemes (Rectification of Unlawful Discrimination) (Tax) Regulations (SI 2023/113) .................. 1-026

2024 Authorised Surplus Payments Charge (Variation of Rate) Order (SI 2024/335) ....................... 17-005

# PART ONE: REGISTERED PENSION SCHEMES

# CHAPTER 1

# FA 2004: Overview, Background, Development

## TABLE OF CONTENTS

| | |
|---|---|
| Introduction | 1-001 |
| FA 2004 Pt 4 | 1-002 |
| The legislation | 1-002 |
| Overview | 1-003 |
| Tax reliefs and exemptions | 1-005 |
| Tax charges | 1-007 |
| Annual and lifetime allowances | 1-009 |
| The unauthorised payments charge and surcharge | 1-011 |
| The scheme sanction charge | 1-012 |
| The de-registration charge | 1-013 |
| Four charges on authorised payments | 1-014 |
| Authorised and unauthorised payments | 1-016 |
| Payments to or in respect of members | 1-020 |
| Authorised pensions | 1-021 |
| Authorised lump sums | 1-022 |
| Payments to or in respect of employers | 1-023 |
| Transitional provisions | 1-024 |
| Overview of Recent Developments | 1-025 |
| Overview of Current Issues | 1-026 |

## INTRODUCTION

This chapter provides an introduction to, and overview of, FA 2004 Pt 4 and Part One of this book generally. **1-001**

## FA 2004 PT 4

### The legislation

FA 2004 Pt 4 comprises eight chapters: **1-002**

(a) Chapter 1 provides an overview and the main concepts.
(b) Chapter 2 sets out the procedure for registering a pension scheme, and HMRC's powers to de-register a registered pension scheme.
(c) Chapter 3 prescribes which payments are authorised and which are unauthorised (and incorporates Schs 28–30).

(d) Chapter 4 provides the tax reliefs and exemptions applicable to registered pension schemes.
(e) Chapter 5 imposes a number of tax charges (and incorporates Sch.31 and Sch.32).
(f) Chapter 6 relates to certain non-UK unregistered schemes (namely, qualifying overseas pension schemes and RNUKS (including QROPS)), where UK tax relief has been obtained (and incorporates Sch.33 and Sch.34).
(g) Chapter 7 contains provisions relating to compliance, penalties, and the scheme administrator.
(h) Chapter 8 contains a number of definitions and other supplementary provisions (and incorporates Sch.35 and Sch.36, the latter of which contains the main transitional provisions appliable to pension schemes established before 6 April 2006).

**Overview**

**1-003**  With effect from 6 April 2006, FA 2004 Pt 4 creates a regime for registered pension schemes.[1] Under that regime, a number of tax reliefs and exemptions are provided in respect of registered pension schemes, and tax charges are imposed in two broad situations:

(a) the value of a member's pension rights exceed annual and/or lifetime limits (although the lifetime allowance charge has been removed with effect from 6 April 2023); and
(b) unauthorised payments are made (or deemed to be made) to or in respect of a member or sponsoring employer of the pension scheme.

As is noted below, most authorised pensions and lump sums are also subject to income tax at the recipient's marginal rate (albeit under ITEPA 2003 Pt 9 rather than FA 2004 Pt 4).

**1-004**  In order to provide HMRC with effective oversight, the regime imposes obligations on members, employers, trustees, scheme administrators, insurance companies and personal representatives to provide information and documentation to each other, to HMRC, and to other persons. Penalties are imposed for non-compliance.[2]

**Tax reliefs and exemptions**

**1-005**  The following tax reliefs and exemptions apply in relation to registered pension schemes:[3]

(a) Scheme members generally obtain tax relief in respect of contributions. Employer contributions usually obtain a tax deduction for the employer,[4] and are not taxable on the employee.
(b) The scheme's investment income and gains are not subject to tax.
(c) Certain categories of distribution are wholly or partly tax-free (to the extent that they do not exceed the member's lifetime allowance):

---

[1] FA 2004 s.284(1). The essence of the regime is summarised in *HMRC v Bella Figura Ltd* [2020] UKUT 120 (TCC) at [72]–[74].
[2] For the compliance requirements, see Ch.19. Also see PTM160000.
[3] The reliefs and exemptions are examined where appropriate in Ch.6 (contributions), Ch.8 (scheme investments), Ch.13 (authorised pensions), Ch.14 (authorised lump sums), Ch.15 (authorised death benefits) and Ch.21 (inheritance tax).
[4] In contrast to the pre-A Day position, a tax deduction is not automatic: it must be made wholly and exclusively for the purpose of the employer's trade. See Ch.6.

(i) A pension commencement lump sum (PCLS), broadly equivalent to 25% of the member's rights, is tax-free.
(ii) 25% of an uncrystallised funds pension lump sum (UFPLS) is tax-free (with the remaining 75% taxable at the member's marginal rate of income tax).
(iii) A serious ill-health lump sum paid prior to the member's 75th birthday is tax-free.
(iv) All death benefits paid in respect of a member who died before his 75th birthday are tax-free, except for dependants' scheme pension.[5]
(d) Neither contributions nor benefits are subject to NIC.
(e) In the normal course of events, inheritance tax will not have any application to the fund of a registered pension scheme, and the rights of members are generally disregarded for inheritance tax purposes.

Authorised pension benefits are not usually taxable under FA 2004 Pt 4; they are instead taxable under ITEPA 2003 Pt 9 at the recipient's marginal rate of income tax. If, when the taxpayer retires, his marginal rate of income tax is lower than it was when he obtained tax relief in respect of contributions, there is a clear tax-efficiency. The same tax-efficiency arises if he retires outside of the UK to a jurisdiction with a lower rate of tax. The PCLS and the tax-free element of an UFPLS always represent a clear tax saving. The ability to invest pre-tax money and benefit from gross roll up is also a significant tax advantage.[6]

**1-006**

**Tax charges**

FA 2004 Pt 4 creates 10 charges to income tax:

**1-007**

(a) the annual allowance charge;
(b) the lifetime allowance charge (removed with effect from 6 April 2023);
(c) the unauthorised payments charge;
(d) the unauthorised payments surcharge;
(e) the scheme sanction charge;
(f) the de-registration charge;
(g) four charges on authorised payments:[7]
 (i) the short service refund lump sum charge;
 (ii) the special lump sum death benefits charge;
 (iii) the authorised surplus payments charge; and
 (iv) the overseas transfer charge.

In each case, the legislation expressly provides that the person liable for the charge remains liable irrespective of whether that person (or any other person, such as the scheme administrator or the recipient of the payment) is resident or domiciled in the UK.

**1-008**

Despite being charges to income tax, the events giving rise to these charges are expressly not treated as income for any purpose of the Tax Acts.[8] For this reason: (a) it is not possible to reduce these charges by the use of personal allowances, losses, or reliefs which would otherwise apply to reduce an individual's taxable

---

[5] Dependants' scheme pension is taxed at the dependant's marginal rate even if the member died before reaching age 75. The reason for this apparent anomaly may be that the payment of a dependants' scheme pension is not tested against the member's lifetime allowance.
[6] See M. Grundy, *Essays in International Taxation* (Oxford: Key Haven Publications Plc, 2001), pp.43-45.
[7] There was also a serious ill-health lump sum charge (under FA 2004 s.205A) until FA 2016.
[8] See, e.g. s.227(5) in relation to the annual allowance charge.

income; (b) these charges may not be within the scope of any double tax treaties;[9] and (c) where the member is jointly and severally liable with the scheme administrator, the payment of these charges by the scheme administrator does not give rise to a taxable benefit for the member (because the member does not receive any income).

*Annual and lifetime allowances*

**1-009** If in any tax year the value of an individual's rights under one or more registered pension schemes[10] increases in excess of his "annual allowance", the excess may be subject to the annual allowance charge.[11]

Prior to 6 April 2023, a lifetime allowance charge arose to the extent that the value of the member's benefits "crystallised" by a benefit crystallisation event (BCE) exceeded the member's available lifetime allowance.[12] Certain categories of authorised lump sum could be paid only if the member had some lifetime allowance available at that time. There were two main categories of BCE: (a) those that occurred when some or all of an uncrystallised fund was applied to provide benefits to the member (or *in respect of* the member, following his death), for example by purchasing an annuity for him or creating a flexi-access drawdown fund, and (b) those that occurred on the member's 75th birthday. A BCE also occurred when a fund was transferred from a registered pension scheme to a QROPS.

The lifetime allowance charge was removed with effect from 6 April 2023, and the lifetime allowance was abolished altogether with effect from 6 April 2024. The lifetime allowance has been replaced by two new allowances. First, a lump sum allowance (£268,275), and a lump sum and death benefit allowance (£1,073,100).

The purpose of these charges is to restrict the tax advantages that any single individual can obtain under the registered pension scheme regime. The member is usually liable for these charges,[13] but the scheme administrator is jointly and severally liable for the lifetime allowance charge, and the member may by notice make the scheme administrator so liable for the annual charge. In certain circumstances an individual may have an annual or lifetime allowance which is greater or lesser than the standard allowances.

**1-010** The standard annual and lifetime allowances have been significantly reduced in recent years:

| Tax year | Lifetime Allowance | Annual allowance |
|---|---|---|
| 2024/25 | Removed | £60,000 |

---

[9] This is understood to be HMRC's position. For example, in relation to the lifetime allowance charge, PTM113410 states "The lifetime allowance charge will not be within the scope of, and will not be exempted or overridden by, any of the UK's double taxation agreements […] because it is not a charge on income and so does not come within any of the articles in the treaties." However, in a meeting of the Joint Expatriate Forum Pensions Subgroup on 20 May 2016, HMRC accepted that the unauthorised payments charge may be within the scope of a treaty, e.g., where it arises on the payment of a pension.

[10] Similar provisions apply to "currently-relieved non-UK pension schemes". See Ch.30.

[11] The annual allowance, and the annual allowance charge, are explained in Ch.7. The annual allowance provisions have undergone very substantial changes since 2006.

[12] The lifetime allowance, and the lifetime allowance charge, are explained in Ch.10. In contrast to the annual allowance provisions, the lifetime allowance provisions remained relatively static prior to 6 April 2023 (other than changes to the amount of the standard lifetime allowance and provisions introduced in order to protect members from being prejudiced by such changes).

[13] Where a lifetime allowance charge applies in respect of a deceased member it is usually the death beneficiary that is liable.

| Tax year | Lifetime Allowance | Annual allowance |
| --- | --- | --- |
| 2023/24 | £1,073,100[14] | £60,000 |
| 2020/21 to 2022/23 | £1,073,100 | £40,000 |
| 2019/20 | £1,055,000 | £40,000 |
| 2018/19 | £1,030,000 | £40,000 |
| 2016/17 and 2017/18 | £1,000,000 | £40,000 |
| 2014/15 and 2015/16 | £1,250,000 | £40,000 |
| 2012/13 and 2013/14 | £1,500,000 | £50,000 |
| 2011/12 | £1,800,000 | £50,000 |
| 2010/11 | £1,800,000 | £255,000 |
| 2009/10 | £1,750,000 | £245,000 |
| 2008/09 | £1,650,000 | £235,000 |
| 2007/08 | £1,600,000 | £225,000 |
| 2006/07 | £1,500,000 | £215,000 |

*The unauthorised payments charge and surcharge*

An unauthorised payment is subject to a 40% unauthorised payments charge.[15] If the amount of the unauthorised payment is "significant" (meaning 25% of the member's rights under the scheme, or 25% of the entire scheme in the case of an employer payment, within any 12-month period) the payment is also subject to a 15% unauthorised payments surcharge. The member or the employer is liable for these charges (depending on whether the payment is an unauthorised member payment or an unauthorised employer payment).

**1-011**

*The scheme sanction charge*

The scheme sanction charge, as its name suggests, is a penalty. Most unauthorised payments give rise to a scheme sanction charge, as do unauthorised borrowing and income and gains relating to taxable property.[16] The charge is 40% of the scheme chargeable payment, but this is reduced to 15% if the unauthorised payments charge is paid in full, where applicable. The scheme administrator is solely liable for the scheme sanction charge.

Consequently, an unauthorised payment may give rise to total tax charges equal to 70% of the payment.

**1-012**

*The de-registration charge*

HMRC have the power in certain circumstances to de-register a registered pension scheme.[17] The main consequence of de-registration is that the scheme administrator will be liable for a de-registration charge of 40% of the value of the

**1-013**

---

[14] The Finance Act 2004 (Standard Lifetime Allowance) Regulations 2020 (SI 2020/342) reg.2 and FA 2021 s.28.
[15] For unauthorised payments, see Ch.17.
[16] Scheme chargeable payments, and the scheme sanction charge, are explained in Ch.5.
[17] The circumstances in which HMRC may de-register a scheme and the consequences of de-registration are explained in Ch.4.

scheme property immediately before the scheme ceased to be a registered pension scheme.

*Four charges on authorised payments*

1-014 The short service refund lump sum charge and the authorised surplus payments charge are explicable on the basis that such payments may otherwise escape tax altogether; there is no attempt to penalise these payments. The special lump sum death benefits charge applies to lump sum death benefits paid to a non-individual if the member died on or after his 75th birthday, and also to certain lump sum death benefits paid to non-individuals if the member died before that day and the lump sum is not paid within a two-year period.[18]

1-015 The overseas transfer charge[19] is the most recent tax charge created under FA 2004 Pt 4. It applies where there is a transfer of a fund from a registered pension scheme to a QROPS or where there is a transfer of a fund from one QROPS to another during the relevant period for the original transfer. Exclusions apply where: (a) the member and receiving scheme are both in the same country; (b) the member and the receiving scheme are both in EEA states; (c) the receiving scheme is an occupational pension scheme; (d) the receiving scheme set up by international organisation; and (e) the receiving scheme is an overseas public service scheme. The amount of the charge is equal to 25% of the amount transferred. The purpose of the charge is to regulate the circumstances in which QROPS are utilised.

**Authorised and unauthorised payments**

1-016 One of the chief concerns of FA 2004 Pt 4 is to regulate transactions between the pension scheme and its members and (if the scheme is an occupational pension scheme) its sponsoring employer(s), and persons connected with its members and sponsoring employer(s). There are detailed rules concerning payments "to" or "in respect of" members and sponsoring employers. Such payments are categorised as either authorised payments or unauthorised payments. A registered pension scheme must be established and maintained wholly or mainly for the purpose of making authorised pension and lump sum payments,[20] but there is no requirement that a registered pension scheme must permit all of those payments, and many registered pension schemes do not offer the full range.[21]

1-017 FA 2004 Pt 4 does not generally seek to regulate dealings between the scheme and unconnected third parties, subject to two exceptions: (a) the provisions relating to scheme borrowing; and (b) the provisions relating to investment in taxable property. The purpose of these provisions is to regulate the type of transactions that schemes enter into generally (with anyone), and the policy of doing so is thus quite different.

1-018 The classification of payments into *authorised* and *unauthorised* is primarily of importance in analysing the tax consequences of a payment. All unauthorised payments are charged to tax under FA 2004 Pt 4, but they are not otherwise

---

[18] There is a table summarising the taxation of lump sum benefits in Ch.14 and death benefits in Ch.15.
[19] The overseas transfer charge is explained in Ch.12.
[20] FA 2004 s.153(5)(f). See Ch.4.
[21] FA 2004 s.273B confers on the trustees of a money purchase arrangement the power to make various payments despite any provisions of the scheme rules to the contrary. It was introduced as a permissive override of scheme rules in connection with the April 2015 flexibilities. Section 273B does not give the member a right to any such payments.

chargeable.[22] All authorised pensions and lump sums are chargeable under ITEPA 2003 Pt 9, but not usually under FA 2004[23] or elsewhere.

**1-019** The fact that a payment may be an unauthorised payment for the purposes of FA 2004 Pt 4 does not necessarily mean that the trustees do not have the authority or power to make it (that will depend on other factors such as the scheme rules), or that there would be anything improper about making it. HMRC accept that it is not improper to make an unauthorised payment.[24] In contrast to the regime applicable prior to 6 April 2006, FA 2004 Pt 4 is permissive: it prescribes the tax consequences of a given transaction (which in some cases may be penal), but it contains no prohibitions or restrictions as such.

*Payments to or in respect of members*

**1-020** A payment made to or in respect of a member or former member of a registered pension scheme is an authorised member payment if it is listed in FA 2004 s.164.[25] The following payments are authorised member payments:[26] (a) pensions permitted by the pension rules or pension death benefits rules to be paid to or in respect of a member; (b) lump sums permitted by the lump sum rule or lump sum death benefits rules to be paid to or in respect of a member; (c) recognised transfers; (d) scheme administration member payments; (e) payments pursuant to a pension sharing order or provision; and (f) certain other payments prescribed by regulations. This is an exhaustive list; any other payment to or in respect of a member is an unauthorised member payment. In addition, FA 2004 ss.172–174A contain provisions relating to transactions which are *deemed* to be unauthorised member payments (the deeming is required because they do not involve the making of a payment by the scheme).

*Authorised pensions*

**1-021** There are three categories of authorised pension:[27] (a) scheme pension; (b) lifetime annuity; and (c) drawdown pension, which comprises: (i) short-term annuity and (ii) income withdrawal.[28] Authorised pensions are subject to income tax at the recipient's marginal rate, and disregarded for NIC purposes.[29]

---

[22] FA 2004 s.208(8) provides that an unauthorised payment does not constitute income for tax purposes.
[23] There are two types of authorised lump sums that are subject to tax under FA 2004: short service refund lump sums (s.205) and special lump sum death benefits (s.206).
[24] e.g. PTM063230 states that a scheme can pay a member a lump sum in excess of the PCLS permitted maxim "if they so wish".
[25] FA 2004 s.160(1).
[26] FA 2004 s.164(1).
[27] In addition, certain pensions paid in error are treated as if they were authorised payments.
[28] Drawdown pension replaced "unsecured pension" from 6 April 2011. Unsecured pension operated in a way similar to capped drawdown (see Ch.13), paying between 0% and 120% of an equivalent annuity, but was only available until age 75. If a scheme pension or annuity was not secured at age 75, unsecured pension became alternatively secured pension, which again operated in a way similar to capped drawdown, but paying between 55% and 90% of the equivalent annuity rates. Alternatively secured pension was subject to up to 82% tax on death and so this was considered by many to effectively require members to annuitise at age 75.
[29] See Ch.13.

*Authorised lump sums*

**1-022** There are eight types of authorised lump sum:[30] (a) pension commencement lump sums; (b) uncrystallised funds pension lump sums; (c) serious ill-health lump sums; (d) short service refund lump sums; (e) refund of excess contributions lump sums; (f) trivial commutation lump sums; (g) winding-up lump sums; and (h) lifetime allowance excess lump sums (prior to 6 April 2024). PCLS and UFPLS (and perhaps also trivial commutation lump sums) are the lump sums that members generally consider to be desirable and expect to receive when they reach pension age (assuming that such lump sums are permitted under the scheme rules). A serious ill-health lump sum is a benefit provided in exceptional and unexpected circumstances (namely where the member is expected to live for less than one year). The other authorised lump sums serve an essentially administrative function, in the sense that when a member joins a scheme, he or she does not usually consider such lump sums to be especially desirable.

*Payments to or in respect of employers*

**1-023** A payment to or in respect of a sponsoring employer, or former sponsoring employer, of the pension scheme is an authorised employer payment if it is listed in FA 2004 s.175.[31] The following payments are authorised employer payments:[32] (a) public service scheme payments; (b) authorised surplus payments; (c) compensation payments; (d) authorised employer loans; and (e) scheme administration employer payments. Again, this is an exhaustive list. Any other payment to or in respect of a sponsoring employer is an unauthorised employer payment. In addition, FA 2004 s.181 contains provisions relating to value shifting, which is *deemed* to involve an unauthorised employer payment.

**Transitional provisions**

**1-024** Transitional provisions are dealt with primarily in FA 2004 Sch.36 and SI 2006/572.[33]

---

[30] FA 2004 s.166(1). Certain small payments and lump sums paid in error are also treated as if they are authorised lump sums (see Ch.14). Prior to 6 April 2015 it was also possible to pay an additional authorised lump sum called a transitional 2013/14 lump sum (see FA 2004 Sch.29 para.11A). This was payable where a scheme paid a PCLS before 27 March 2014, but because of the increased trivial commutation lump sum limit with effect from that date, the scheme was subsequently able to commute the entirety of the member's pension.
[31] FA 2004 s.175(1).
[32] FA 2004 s.175(1).
[33] The Taxation of Pension Schemes (Transitional Provisions) Order 2006 (SI 2006/572).

## OVERVIEW OF RECENT DEVELOPMENTS

The following table summarises the main developments since FA 2011:  **1-025**

| Provision | Development |
|---|---|
| FA 2011 | • Reduction in annual allowance from £255,000 to £50,000; introduction of carry forward provisions.<br>• Reduction in standard lifetime allowance from £1.8 million to £1.5 million for 2012/13 tax year; introduction of FP 2012.<br>• Requirement to secure a pension or annuity at age 75 largely removed; introduction of "drawdown pension" (comprising capped and flexible drawdown) for money purchase arrangements. |
| FA 2012 | Introduction of employer asset-backed pension contributions provisions. |
| FA 2013 | • Annual allowance reduced from £50,000 to £40,000.<br>• Lifetime allowance reduced from £1.5 million to £1.25 million for 2014/15 tax year; introduction of FP 2014.<br>• ITEPA 2003 s.308 amended in relation to employer contributions for the benefit of an employee's family member.<br>• Annual withdrawal limit for individuals in capped drawdown increased from 100% to 120% of the value of a comparable annuity. |
| FA 2014 | • Introduction of a number of temporary measures in anticipation of the new flexibilities under TPA 2014.<br>• Maximum trivial commutation lump sum increased from £18,000 to £30,000; commutation limit for small lump sum increased from £2,000 to £10,000.<br>• HMRC given greater powers to counter pension liberation, including additional grounds on which registration can be refused and schemes may be de-registered.<br>• Introduction of IP 2014 in connection with FA 2013 reduction in lifetime allowance. |

| Provision | Development |
|---|---|
| TPA 2014[34] | In outline:<br><br>• Introduction of flexi-access drawdown funds.<br>• Change to definition of lifetime annuity to permit annuities that can pay an income varying in amount from one year to another.<br>• Introduction of uncrystallised funds pension lump sums, a new type of authorised lump sum, 25% of which is tax-free with the balance taxable at the recipient's marginal rate.<br>• Introduction of new "money purchase annual allowance" applicable to individuals who have flexibly accessed their pension rights.<br>• Introduction of "permissive override", creating a power for trustees or managers to make payments to individuals in accordance with the new flexibilities, even where not permitted by scheme rules.<br>• Introduction of the death beneficiary concepts of "nominee" and "successor".<br>• Changed the taxation of death benefits, so that if the member (or other beneficiary) dies before reaching age 75 all lump sum death benefits are tax-free. If the member (or other beneficiary) dies after reaching age 75, pension death benefits are taxable at the recipient's marginal rate and lump sum death benefits are subject to the special lump sum death benefits charge. |
| FA 2015 | Introduction of provisions relating to annuities for nominees and successors. |
| F(No.2)A 2015 | •Further changes to the taxation of lump sum death benefits.<br>•2015/16 tax year split into two "mini" tax years for annual allowance purposes; pension input periods aligned with the tax year; introduction of tapered annual allowance for high-income individuals. |

---

[34] TPA 2014 represented "the most far-reaching reform to the taxation of pensions since the regime was introduced in 1921" (Chancellor George Osborne's Budget 2014 speech, 19 March 2014). It has fundamentally changed many of the underlying principles on which the registered pension scheme regime is based.

# OVERVIEW OF RECENT DEVELOPMENTS

| Provision | Development |
|---|---|
| FA 2016 | • Reduction in standard lifetime allowance from £1.25 million to £1 million for the 2016/17 and 2017/18 tax years; introduction of FP 2016 and IP 2016. Lifetime allowance to rise in line with annual increase in the CPI from 2018/19 onwards.<br>• Serious ill-health lump sums paid after the member reaches age 75 taxed at the recipient's marginal rate (rather than subject to a fixed 45% charge).<br>• Definition of "dependant" modified so that dependants' drawdown pensions can continue to be paid to after a dependant's 23rd birthday.<br>• Introduced exceptions from the annual test that must otherwise be carried out in respect of annual increases to dependants' scheme pensions where the member died after reaching age 75. |
| FA 2017 | • Introduction of overseas transfer charge.<br>• Introduction of provisions relating to non-UK registered schemes.<br>• Introduction of provisions relating to optional remuneration arrangements. |
| F(No.2)A 2017 | • Reduction in money purchase annual allowance from £10,000 to £4,000.<br>• Replaced existing £150 income tax and NIC exemption for employer-funded pensions advice with a new £500 exemption that also covers advice on general financial and tax issues relating to pensions. |
| FA 2018 | HMRC permitted to refuse to register any pension scheme that is an unauthorised master trust, or an occupational pension scheme the sponsoring employer of which is dormant, and to de-register any such schemes that have been registered. |
| FA 2019 | Amendment of ITEPA 2003 s.307 so that beneficiaries need not be limited to the family and household of the employee. |
| FA 2020 | In relation to the tapered annual allowance, the "adjusted income" is increased from £150,000 to £240,000; minimum tapered annual allowance reduced from £10,000 to £4,000. |
| FA 2021 | • FA 2004 s.218(2C) and (2D) (which provide that the standard lifetime allowance will increase in line with the CPI) do not apply for the tax years 2021/22 to 2025/26. The amount of the standard lifetime allowance for each of those tax years remain at the amount for the tax year 2020/21, namely £1,073,100.<br>• Contains provisions relating to "collective money purchase benefits", which did not take effect until 1 August 2022.[35] |

---

[35] See SI 2022/874 reg.2.

| Provision | Development |
|---|---|
| FA 2022 | • Normal minimum pension age will increase to age 57 from 6 April 2028, subject to transitional provisions. Certain "uniformed services pension schemes" (such as the firefighters', police and armed forces pension schemes) are excepted.<br>• The usual deadlines for a member to exercise the annual allowance "scheme pays" option, and for the scheme to report and pay the tax to HMRC, is extended where a change of information given by the employer affects the member's annual allowance for any of the previous six tax years. |
| F(No.2)A 2023 | • Lifetime allowance charge is abolished. Lump sums previously subject to the 55% charge are instead taxed at the recipient's marginal rate. Where the 25% charge previously applied, no charge rises.<br>• Enhanced and fixed protection will usually continue to apply even where further contributions (etc.) are made.<br>• Standard annual allowance increased to £60,000; money-purchase annual allowance increased to £10,000.<br>• In relation to the tapered annual allowance, the "adjusted income" is increased from £240,000 to £260,000; minimum tapered annual allowance increased from £4,000 to £10,000. |
| FA 2024 | • Lifetime allowance is replaced with two new allowances: a lump sum allowance and a lump sum and death benefit allowance.<br>• Taking pension income is not subject to any allowance. |

## OVERVIEW OF CURRENT ISSUES

**1-026** In February 2023, the Chartered Institute of Taxation (CIOT) made the following suggestions in respect of the registered pension scheme regime:[36]

(a) Improving pension scheme administration by fixing problems with scheme block transfers. The rules for block transfers require the transfer of all of a member's benefits so transfers of defined contribution rights without defined benefits rights or vice versa will lose protection because they are classified as partial transfers rather than block transfers and only ring-fenced protection on the individual transfer basis would apply. Block transfers need to be able to carry over protected minimum pension ages, and scheme-specific lump sums. Furthermore, under a block transfer of just DC rights, the scheme-specific lump sum formula applying to the original scheme is reduced by ¼ of the partial transfer, which can lead to a net loss of scheme-specific lump sums across the two schemes. Additionally, at present, a

---

[36] *Employment Taxes and Pensions Tax Regime: Spring Budget 2023 representations by the Chartered Institute of Taxation* (1 February 2023).

member of the transferring scheme cannot be a pre-existing member of the receiving scheme for more than 12 months. Hence, the CIOT believes the existing restrictive block transfer provisions are practical barriers to consolidation and at odds with the government's broader policy goals. To address this, the CIOT suggested that where a "hybrid-type" scheme with both defined benefit and defined contribution entitlements wants to "block transfer" rights to another scheme then: (i) treat a transfer of either all a member's DB or all a member's DC benefits as a block transfer. This will, for example, allow DB and DC benefits to be transferred to separate schemes/insurers when a scheme consolidates or winds-up etc; (ii) allow protected minimum pension ages to pass over the protected minimum pension age to the new scheme, at least in regard to the transferred benefits; (iii) remove the restriction that a block transfer member cannot have been in the receiving scheme for more than 12 months; (iv) remove the "-TV/4" calculation from the post-partial-transfer-out line of the tax-free cash formula,[37] such that any reduction in the scheme-specific lump sum in the first scheme is offset by the PCLS in the receiving scheme.

(b) Improving pension scheme administration by fixing problems with Guaranteed Minimum Pension (GMP) sex equality equalisation conversions. Pension schemes are required to equalise benefits paid to men and women where the scheme provided for different types of benefits to each. This type of benefit rectification project is common in the private sector and the CIOT suggests that consideration is given to replicating the easements provided for in the "McCloud remedy",[38] where other pension schemes carry out similar projects. For example, the easements around pre-crystallisation increases in benefits resulting from "new scheme benefits elections", could be applied in the private sector undertaking similar exercises. The CIOT therefore recommends that the government review the GMP conversion legislation to ensure that it is workable, and amend it if required, and confirm that where a pension scheme equalises their members entitlements under the GMP conversion legislation that no taxable event arises under the pension tax regime (or amend the legislation to provide for this). The CIOT believes that action is urgently needed on this matter so that pension schemes can pay their members the benefits to which they are entitled.

(c) On the basis that the annual allowance and lifetime allowance were reportedly causing workers in certain high demand sectors either to reduce their hours of work or stop working earlier than they might otherwise do (which is detrimental to businesses productivity and, for public bodies like the NHS, affects services to the public), the CIOT suggested that the annual allowance and lifetime allowance limits are increased.

---

[37] Modification of para.34 Sch.36 FA 2004 by paras 2–23 Taxation of Pension Schemes (Transitional Provisions) Order 2006 (SI 2006/572).

[38] The Public Service Pension Schemes (Rectification of Unlawful Discrimination) (Tax) Draft Regulations 2023.

# CHAPTER 2

# Important Concepts

## TABLE OF CONTENTS

| | |
|---|---|
| Introduction | 2-001 |
| "Registered Pension Scheme" | 2-002 |
|     6 April 2006 transitional provisions | 2-002 |
|     Certain annuity contracts | 2-003 |
|     Pension schemes registered with HMRC | 2-004 |
| "Pension Scheme" | 2-005 |
|     "A scheme or other arrangements..." | 2-007 |
|     "Capable of having effect" | 2-010 |
|     "Benefits" | 2-011 |
|     "Persons" | 2-012 |
|     The events in s.150(a)–(e) | 2-013 |
|     "Occupational pension scheme" | 2-015 |
|         "Sponsoring employer" | 2-020 |
|     Non-occupational pension schemes | 2-026 |
| "Member" | 2-027 |
|     "Active member" | 2-030 |
|     The position of death beneficiaries | 2-035 |
| "Arrangement" | 2-036 |
|     The different types of arrangement | 2-039 |
|         "Money purchase arrangement" | 2-042 |
|         "Defined benefits arrangement" | 2-050 |
|         "Hybrid arrangement" | 2-052 |
| "Payment" | 2-053 |
|     Payments on commercial terms | 2-058 |
|     Crediting an account | 2-059 |
|     The release of a debt | 2-063 |
|     Payments in breach of trust (or which otherwise transfer bare legal title only) | 2-065 |
|         Clark v HMRC | 2-074 |
|         Application to deemed unauthorised payments | 2-078 |
|     Effect of rectification | 2-080 |
| "Loan" | 2-081 |
|     The usual meaning of "loan" | 2-085 |
|     Transactions which are not loans | 2-092 |
|     The meaning of "debt" | 2-095 |
| "Connected Persons" | 2-098 |
|     The meaning of "connected" | 2-099 |
|         Individuals | 2-100 |
|         Trustees | 2-101 |
|         Partners | 2-103 |

18                    IMPORTANT CONCEPTS

                Companies .................................. 2-104
                "Control" .................................... 2-106
                  Attribution of rights ...................... 2-109
                "Associate" ................................ 2-111
                "Loan creditor" ............................ 2-112
                "Participator" .............................. 2-114
           Valuation ...................................... 2-116
                Market value .............................. 2-118
                  Quoted shares .......................... 2-119
                  Unit trusts .............................. 2-120
                The effect of scheme borrowing ................ 2-121

# INTRODUCTION

2-001    This chapter explains the meaning of a number of important concepts which are used throughout FA 2004 Pt 4.

# "REGISTERED PENSION SCHEME"

### 6 April 2006 transitional provisions

2-002    Certain categories of pension schemes established before 6 April 2006 automatically became registered pension schemes on 6 April 2006 unless they opted out.[1]

### Certain annuity contracts

2-003    In two circumstances, an annuity contract is deemed to be a registered pension scheme:

(a) an annuity contract made with an insurance company[2] (i) by means of which benefits under a registered pension scheme have been secured, but (ii) which does not provide for the immediate payment of benefits, is treated as having become a registered pension scheme on the day on which it is made.[3] This applies to all deferred annuity contracts, including buyout policies (sometimes referred to as "section 32" policies), which are commonly purchased when a pension scheme is wound up; and

(b) where, under PA 2004 ss.19(4) or 21(2)(a), a court or the Pensions Regulator orders that property or money is transferred, or a sum is paid, towards an annuity contract made with an insurance company, the annuity contract is treated as having become a registered pension scheme on the day on which it is made.[4]

---

[1] FA 2004 Sch.36 Pt 1. See Ch.3 and following.
[2] Insurance company is defined in FA 2004 s.275 as "a person who has permission under Part 4 of FISMA 2000 to effect or carry out contracts of long-term insurance" (being contracts which fall within Pt 2 of Sch.1 to the Financial Services and Markets Act 2000 (Regulated Activities) Order 2001 (SI 2001/544)).
[3] FA 2004 s.153(8).
[4] FA 2004 s.153(8A).

### Pension schemes registered with HMRC

A "pension scheme" established on or after 6 April 2006 is a registered pension scheme if it has been registered with HMRC under FA 2004 s.153.[5] Unless a pension scheme is an "occupational pension scheme", it can be registered under FA 2004 s.153 only if it is established by a person who is authorised to do so under FSMA 2000.[6]

2-004

## "PENSION SCHEME"

Traditionally, a pension scheme is an arrangement under which a member of the scheme is entitled receive pension income in specified circumstances, the amount of which is calculated by reference to: (a) a specified formula (if it is a defined benefits arrangement), or (b) an account which represents contributions relating to the member, and any investment return, which is used to purchase a source of income for the member (if it is a money purchase arrangement).

2-005

FA 2004 s.150(1) provides:

2-006

> "(1) In this Part "pension scheme" means a scheme or other arrangements, comprised in one or more instruments or agreements, having or capable of having effect so as to provide benefits to or in respect of persons—
> (a) on retirement,
> (b) on death,
> (c) on having reached a particular age,
> (d) on the onset of serious ill-health or incapacity, or
> (e) in similar circumstances."

### "A scheme or other arrangements..."

The ordinary meaning of "scheme" is a plan of action devised in order to attain some end, and an "arrangement" is a structure or combination of things for a purpose.[7]

2-007

It is apparent from the definition in s.150(1) that the pension scheme is not merely the arrangements comprised in the instrument(s) specifying the benefit structure (typically a trust deed and rules). The "pension scheme" consists of all of the arrangements comprised in agreements or instruments which may have the effect of providing benefits in any of the circumstances specified in s.150(1)(a)–(e). In the context of an occupational scheme, the "pension scheme" will include any resolutions of the sponsoring employer relating to the provision of benefits, and any undertakings to make contributions to the scheme (usually found in employment contracts or in side letters). A verbal promise by an employer to provide benefits in one or more of the circumstances in s.150(1)(a)–(e) will constitute a pension scheme if the promise amounts to an agreement. Section 150(1) does not impose

2-008

---

[5] The process for registering a pension scheme is explained in Ch.4.
[6] FA 2004 s.154.
[7] See *Snell v HMRC* [2006] EWHC 3350 at [28], in which the Chancellor of the High Court considered the meaning of "scheme or arrangement" in TCGA 1992 s.137, and took both meanings from the Shorter Oxford English Dictionary.

any restrictions regarding the nature of the instruments or agreements which comprise the pension scheme.[8]

**2-009** It can therefore be difficult in practice to determine what does and does not form part of the pension scheme. If an arrangement is capable of providing benefits in one or more of the circumstances specified in s.150(1)(a)–(e), and also in other circumstances, the arrangement may be found to constitute more than one "scheme", and only that part of the scheme which can provide benefits in the circumstances specified in (a)–(e) is a pension scheme for the purposes of s.150(1).[9] Sectionalised pension schemes can be particularly susceptible to this sort of analysis. And two or more arrangements, which appear at first glance to be quite separate, may be found upon investigation to form a single pension scheme.[10]

### "Capable of having effect"

**2-010** The words "capable of having effect" are unlikely to mean capable *in any circumstances* of providing benefits in the specified circumstances. They are intended to make it clear that contingent rights are included. An arrangement is a pension scheme if it is capable, according to its terms (as specified in the instrument(s) or agreement(s) comprising the scheme) of having effect so as to provide benefits in any of the circumstances in s.150(1)(a)–(e).

A scheme which is intended to be established under trusts will not satisfy this requirement if the trusts are void for uncertainty.[11]

### "Benefits"

**2-011** The term "benefits" is plainly broader than pensions, annuities and lump sums. An arrangement that is *capable* of providing benefits other than pensions, annuities and lump sums (even if they are unauthorised payments) can be a pension scheme for the purposes of s.150(1). A scheme which is capable of providing only death benefits is a pension scheme (and may be registered under s.153).[12]

### "Persons"

**2-012** The scheme must be capable of providing benefits to or in respect of "persons" rather than "individuals", which suggests that trustees, companies and other entities may receive benefit under the scheme. It is relatively common for non-individuals to receive lump sum death benefits,[13] but such benefits are paid "in

---

[8] Thus PTM031200 states that a pension scheme may be established as a trust, contract, board resolution or deed poll. However, a funded occupational scheme must be established under irrevocable trusts if it has its main administration in the UK (PA 2004 s.252).

[9] See e.g. *PI Consulting (Trustee Services) Ltd v Pensions Regulator* [2013] EWHC 3181 at [46]; *Barclays Bank v Holmes* [2000] EWHC Ch 457; [2000] P.L.R. 339; *Kemble v Hicks (No.2)* [1999] EWHC 301 (Ch); [1999] O.P.L.R. 1; *Reichhold v Wong* [2000] P.L.R. 277 Superior Court of Justice, Ontario.

[10] See e.g. *Westminster City Council v Haywood (No.1)* [1996] 3 W.L.R. 563; [1996] 2 All E.R. 467 at 477.

[11] See e.g. *Clark v HMRC* [2016] UKFTT 630 (TC) at [83]–[85]. This aspect of the decision was not appealed.

[12] Such a scheme may be an occupational pension scheme for the purposes of FA 2004 Pt 4, but it cannot (since 22 September 2005) be an occupational pension scheme for the purposes of PSA 1993 s.1.

[13] See Ch.15. However, only an individual can be a dependant, nominee or successor (and therefore receive *pension* death benefits).

## "PENSION SCHEME"

respect of" the deceased member. For the purposes of FA 2004 Pt 4, death benefits are not paid "to" or "in respect of" the death beneficiary, so the reference to "persons" in s.150(1) seems to be a reference to the scheme members rather than death beneficiaries.

**The events in s.150(a)–(e)**

For a benefit to be provided "on" one of the events in s.150(1)(a)–(e), there must be a material connection between the occurrence of the event and the provision of the benefit. If benefits will be provided solely as a result of the occurrence of one of the specified events, such benefits are clearly provided "on" the occurrence of that event. Where the member is provided with an option to receive benefits at any time following the occurrence of one of the events, the requirement is satisfied notwithstanding that the immediate cause of the benefit is the exercise of the option. Where the trustees have discretion to provide a benefit in one or more of the specified circumstances, the requirement is satisfied notwithstanding that the immediate cause of the benefit is the exercise of the trustees' discretion. Given that the scheme needs only to be "capable" of providing benefits in one or more of the specified circumstances, it is unlikely that this requirement will cause any difficulties in practice.

2-013

Assuming that "retirement" in s.150(1)(a) means ceasing work altogether (as opposed to merely ceasing to work for a particular employer),[14] the common thread running through the circumstances in s.150(1)(a), (b) and (d) is that the member's ability to earn income is significantly reduced or eradicated. On the face of it, s.150(1)(c) ("having reached a particular age") could apply at any age, but in order to be consistent with the other circumstances, the "particular age" must mean an *advanced* age. If that is correct, it follows that circumstances are likely to be "similar" for the purposes of s.150(1)(e) if they are such that the member's ability to earn income is significantly reduced or eradicated.

2-014

Would an arrangement for the provision of benefits on redundancy or disablement, for example, fall within s.150(1)(e)? If the circumstances must be such that the member's ability to earn income is significantly reduced or eradicated, it seems unlikely that a scheme which provides benefits only on redundancy (but not complete retirement) or disablement (but not serious ill-health or incapacity) will be a "pension scheme" for the purposes of s.150(1).[15] An express restriction on the provision of benefits before minimum pension age (as is usually found in the instrument(s) constituting a registered pension scheme) would not by itself mean that such a scheme is a pension scheme, because there would be no material connection between reaching that minimum age and the provision of the benefits.

**"Occupational pension scheme"**

FA 2004 s.150(5) provides:

2-015

"In this Part "occupational pension scheme" means a pension scheme established by an employer or employers and having or capable of having effect so as to provide benefits to or in respect of any or all of the employees of—

---

[14] For the meaning of "retirement", see Ch.35.
[15] Also see PA 2004 s.255, which requires the trustees or managers of occupational schemes with their main administration in the UK to secure that the activities of the scheme are limited to "retirement benefit activities". The precise scope of this requirement is uncertain.

(a) that employer or those employers, or
(b) any other employer,
(whether or not it also has or is capable of having effect so as to provide benefits to or in respect of other persons)."

**2-016** "Employee" and "employer" have the same meanings as in the employment income parts of ITEPA 2003 and also include *former* employees/employers (and "employment" is construed accordingly).[16] Any person employed under a contract of service or a contract of apprenticeship is an employee, as is any office-holder.[17]

**2-017** A contract of service exists where: (a) an individual agrees that in consideration of some remuneration[18] he will provide his skill in the performance of some service for his master; (b) he agrees, expressly or impliedly, that in the performance of that service he will be subject to the other's control in a sufficient degree to make that other master; and (c) the other provisions of the contract are consistent with its being a contract of service.[19]

**2-018** "Office" includes in particular any position which has an existence independent of the person who holds it and may be filled by successive holders.[20] Company secretaries and company directors (which includes not only directors de jure but also directors de facto[21] and shadow directors[22]) are office-holders.[23]

**2-019** The establisher of the pension scheme must be an employer (i.e. must employ at least one person), and the scheme must be capable of providing benefits to the employee(s) of that employer, or to the employees of any other employer. The scheme may also be capable of providing benefits to persons who are not employees. This is not merely a reference to the provision of death benefits; it is a reference to non-employee members.[24] It is therefore quite possible to establish an occupational scheme which has very little connection with any employment.[25]

---

[16] FA 2004 s.279(1).
[17] ITEPA 2003 ss.4 and 5.
[18] In *Hirst v HMRC* [2014] UKFTT 924 (TC), this requirement was satisfied by a right to receive commission, even though none was in fact paid. It is unclear if such a person would be an "earner" for the purposes of PSA 1993 s.181.
[19] *Ready Mixed Concrete (South East) Ltd v Minister of Pensions* [1968] 1 All E.R. 433.
[20] ITEPA 2003 s.5(3); *Edwards (Inspector of Taxes) v Clinch* [1982] A.C. 845; [1981] 3 W.L.R. 707 at 861 (HL) (Lord Wilberforce).
[21] "The question is whether he was part of the corporate governance system of the company and whether he assumed the status and function of a director so as to make himself responsible as if he were a director" (per Arden LJ in *Smithton Ltd & Naggar v Townsley* [2014] EWCA Civ 939).
[22] Generally, a person is a shadow director if the directors of the company are accustomed to act in accordance with his directions or instructions. He "does not claim or purport to act as director. On the contrary, he claims not to be a director. He lurks in the shadows, sheltering behind others who, he claims, are the only directors of the company to the exclusion of himself. He is not held out as a director by the company" (per Millett J in *Re Hydrodan (Corby) Ltd* [1994] 2 B.C.L.C. 180, cited with approval in *HMRC v Holland* [2010] UKSC 51).
[23] *Lee v Lee's Air Farming Ltd* [1961] A.C. 12. Trustees are also office holders (*Dale v Inland Revenue Commissioners* [1954] A.C. 11; 34 T.C. 468 (HL)). A partner is not an office holder.
[24] This is made clear by the reference to such benefits being provided "to or in respect of" those other persons (i.e. non-employees). Death benefits are provided "in respect of" the member.
[25] That was the case in *Dalriada Trustees Ltd v Faulds* [2011] EWHC 3391 (Ch); [2012] 2 All E.R. 734, in which Bean J observed (at [8]) that "... although pension schemes of the type under consideration are classified as 'occupational pension schemes' and the principal sponsor is traditionally referred to as the 'employer', those terms have in cases such as the present one no more than a vestigial meaning. It is sufficient to qualify a scheme for registration if it has a single employee; others, not employed by the sponsor, can then join in large numbers". This was not the case prior to 6 April 2006 (hence the cases of sham employments: *Dunne v HMRC* [2007] UKSPC SPC00654; *Kent v HMRC* [2009] UKFTT 358 (TC); [2010] S.T.I. 685).

## "Sponsoring employer"

**2-020** It may be important to determine if an employer is a sponsoring employer of an occupational pension scheme, for two reasons:

(a) A payment from the pension scheme to or in respect of a sponsoring employer (including by way of investment on arm's length terms) may constitute an unauthorised payment, in respect of which the sponsoring employer will be liable for any unauthorised payments charge and surcharge.[26]
(b) A sponsoring employer can be liable for certain tax charges for which the scheme administrator would otherwise be liable.[27]

**2-021** FA 2004 s.150(6) provides:

"In this Part "sponsoring employer", in relation to an occupational pension scheme, means the employer, or any of the employers, to or in respect of any or all of whose employees the pension scheme has, or is capable of having, effect so as to provide benefits."

**2-022** It is implicit that this requires the persons to whom benefits may be provided to be beneficiaries *in their capacity as employees of that employer*. The fact that a pension scheme is capable of providing benefits to a person who happens to be employed cannot by itself cause his employer to become a sponsoring employer of that pension scheme. Thus, if an individual becomes employed by a new employer, but continues to be a member of his former employer's occupational scheme, it is plainly *not* intended that his new employer will become a sponsoring employer of his former employer's pension scheme merely by virtue of employing a member of that scheme.[28] A contribution by that new employer to the former employer's pension scheme should not by itself cause the new employer to become a sponsoring employer of that pension scheme (or the member's arrangement under the scheme), provided that the scheme is not capable of providing benefits to that employee in his capacity as employee or former employee of his new employer.[29]

**2-023** HMRC suggest that an employer will not be a sponsoring employer unless the employer either establishes or participates in an occupational pension scheme, and the identity of the sponsoring employer(s) should be clear from the scheme documentation.[30] However, the definition of "sponsoring employer" is not expressly limited to employers who establish or participate in (i.e. formally join, and usually contribute to) a pension scheme. It is more likely that one simply asks: whose employees (in their capacity as such) are intended to benefit under this scheme?

---

[26] For unauthorised employer payments, see Ch.18.
[27] See Ch.5.
[28] If that were not correct, it would have the effect of causing most otherwise non-occupational pension schemes to be occupational schemes, because the person establishing the non-occupational scheme (usually an insurance company) will be an employer, and there will usually be nothing preventing its employees from joining the scheme.
[29] Whether or not this is the case must be determined on the facts of the case; the scheme documentation is not determinative. Where there is a connection between the new employer and former employer, it is perhaps quite likely that a tribunal would find that benefits are capable of being provided under the scheme to the member in his capacity as employee of his new employer. One of the reasons that FA 2004 Pt 4 contains special provisions relating to payments to or in respect of sponsoring employers seems to be because sponsoring employers may be able to improperly influence the payments that are made by a registered pension scheme. If the circumstances are such that the new employer is able to influence the trustees (e.g. as a result of its relationship with the former employer) in the same way as if it formally joined the scheme, it would perhaps be difficult to find any reason that the new employer should not be a sponsoring employer.
[30] PTM022000.

This is particularly clear when one reads ss.150(5) and 150(6) together: s.150(5) provides a two-part definition of occupational pension scheme (namely a pension scheme which is (a) established by an employer and (b) capable of benefitting the employees of that employer) and s.150(6) follows on from the second part only.

2-024 An employer can be a sponsoring employer without making any contributions to a pension scheme. If it is correct that a sponsoring employer need not even agree to be associated with the scheme (by formally joining it), it follows that it may be possible for a sponsoring employer to have no knowledge of the pension scheme.[31] This is a concern, given that a sponsoring employer may be liable for certain tax liabilities relating to the scheme.[32]

2-025 There are no restrictions regarding the nature of the business carried on by a sponsoring employer[33] or regarding the number of registered pension schemes that may be established by a sponsoring employer.[34] An occupational pension scheme may have more than one sponsoring employer, which is why the legislation refers to "a" sponsoring employer rather than "the" sponsoring employer of a pension scheme.

**Non-occupational pension schemes**

2-026 In addition to occupational pension schemes, FA 2004 Pt 4 refers to public service pension schemes, personal pension schemes, and stakeholder pension schemes.[35] "Personal pension scheme" and "stakeholder pension scheme" are not defined. For the purposes of FA 2004 Pt 4, the only material distinction is between occupational pension schemes and non-occupational schemes.

FA 2004 Pt 4 applies to the National Employment Savings Trust and Master Trust schemes[36] that are not occupational pension schemes as if they were occupational pension schemes.[37]

# "MEMBER"

2-027 A "member", in relation to a registered pension scheme, means one of the following:[38]

(a) An "active member" of the pension scheme. This is explained below.
(b) A "pensioner member" of the pension scheme. A person is a pensioner member if he is entitled to the present payment of benefits under the pension scheme and is not an active member.[39] A person becomes "entitled" to a pension: (a) in the case of income withdrawal, whenever sums or assets

---

[31] This is highlighted as an area of concern in *Pension scams: consultation response* (August 2017), at para.4.6.
[32] See Ch.5.
[33] Indeed, prior to 6 April 2018 the employer could be dormant. Since that date HMRC can refuse to register (or de-register) an occupational pension scheme if the employer is dormant (see Ch.4).
[34] Cf. the pre-6 April 2006 position, under which an investment company could not establish an approved pension scheme, and an employer could not establish more than one approved pension scheme.
[35] FA 2004 s.154(1)(b).
[36] Master Trust scheme is defined in the draft legislation in the same way as under PSA 2017 s.1 (FA 2004 s.274B).
[37] FA 2004 s.150(5A), with effect from 15 March 2018.
[38] FA 2004 s.151(1). The terms "active member", "pensioner member, "deferred member" and "pension credit member" are also used in pension legislation, where they mean slightly different things.
[39] FA 2004 s.151(3).

## "MEMBER"

held for the purposes of an arrangement under the pension scheme are designated as available for the payment of drawdown pension; and (b) in any other case, when he first acquires an actual (rather than a prospective) right to receive the pension;[40]

(c) A "deferred member" of the pension scheme. A person is a deferred member if he has accrued rights under the pension scheme and is neither an active member nor a pensioner member.[41]

(d) A "pension credit member" of the pension scheme. A person is a pension credit member if he has rights under the pension scheme which are attributable (directly or indirectly) to pension credits.[42] If a person dies having become entitled to pension credits but without having rights attributable to them, the person is treated as having acquired, immediately before death, the rights by virtue of which the liability in respect of the pension credits is subsequently discharged.[43]

Each category relates to a specific arrangement under the scheme, so an individual with more than one arrangement may fall into more than one of the above categories. It can be very important to know whether or not an individual is a member of a registered pension scheme,[44] but it rarely matters into which of the above categories he falls.

2-028

There is no statutory restriction relating to who may become a member of a registered pension scheme. There is no express requirement that a member must be an individual, but this is perhaps implicit from the pension rules in FA 2004 s.165.[45] There is no minimum or maximum age at which an individual may become a member, and there is no requirement that a member must have any connection with the UK. As noted above, there is no requirement for a member to be employed by, or to have any connection at all with, a sponsoring employer of an occupational pension scheme.

2-029

### "Active member"

A person is an active member of a pension scheme if there are presently arrangements made under the scheme for the accrual of benefits to or in respect of the person.[46] "Accrual" is not defined. It is generally understood to mean *increase*. This terminology is more suited to defined benefits arrangements, where the member's benefits usually increase whilst he is in pensionable service. However, it is implicit that where benefits under a defined benefits or cash balance arrangement increase at a specified annual rate (for example, 5% p/a or in line with the CPI), such an increase does not involve an accrual of benefits such that the member is an active

2-030

---

[40] FA 2004 s.165(3)(b).
[41] FA 2004 s.151(4).
[42] See Ch.16.
[43] FA 2004 s.151(5). The term "pension credit member" is not used elsewhere in FA 2004 Pt 4.
[44] See e.g. FA 2004 s.169(1). If there is a transfer from one pension scheme to another and the individual is not a member (as defined in s.151(1)) of the recipient scheme then it cannot be a recognised transfer within FA 2004 s.169(1) and will, accordingly, be an unauthorised payment.
[45] See Ch.13. The references to normal minimum pension age, ill-health and death suggest that only individuals can be members. However, it may be arguable that these references do not exclude non-individual members; they are merely inapplicable to non-individuals (see e.g. *Earl of Carnavon's Chesterfield Settled Estates, Re* [1927] 1 Ch. 138, in which the argument that the words "of full age" excluded companies was rejected).
[46] FA 2004 s.151(2).

member.[47] There are also some suggestions in the legislation that increases in benefits to reflect increases in the cost of living may not constitute arrangements for the accrual of benefits.[48] Such increases are typical, and if they were to involve an accrual of benefits then members of such schemes would never become deferred members, which cannot have been intended.

**2-031** In relation to an "other" money purchase arrangement (the meaning of which is explained below), the precise meaning of "arrangement for the accrual of benefits" is slightly less clear. If a person undertakes to make contributions to the scheme for or on behalf of the member, such an undertaking constitutes an arrangement for the accrual of benefits to or in respect of the member. This is the case even though, in a money purchase context, there is no absolute connection between contributions and the amount of benefits ultimately provided, because investment losses and expenses (if they are debited from the value of the member's arrangement under the scheme) will reduce the amount of the benefits that may be provided. Determining the precise time at which a person becomes an active member of a money purchase scheme is not straightforward unless there is a commitment to make contributions. If contributions to a money purchase arrangement are made on an ad hoc basis, but further contributions in respect of the member are reasonably expected, it is suggested that the member is an active member. Merely joining a scheme (in the sense of completing the necessary paperwork and being accepted by the trustees or manager) does not by itself make such a person a "member".

**2-032** In the case of a money purchase arrangement, it is implicit that the investment of a member's scheme fund does not constitute an arrangement for the accrual of benefits. If investment return involved an accrual of benefits for these purposes, this would give rise to arbitrary results (i.e. it would depend on whether or not the investments are overall positive, which may change from one month to the next), which may be difficult to determine at any given time. It would also mean that many members of money purchase arrangements may never become pensioner members or deferred members. Again, it is most unlikely that this would have been intended.

**2-033** It is likely that a request for a transfer of funds from one pension scheme to another relating to an individual *will* constitute an arrangement for the accrual of benefits under the recipient scheme.[49] This is important because such a transfer will be a recognised transfer (and therefore an authorised payment) only if it is in con-

---

[47] A member of a cash balance or defined benefits arrangements can be a deferred member notwithstanding his rights increasing in line with a rate specified in the rules (see FA 2004 ss.230(5B) and 234(5B)).

[48] e.g. s.197(7)(a) provides that the spreading rules do not apply to contributions if they are paid with a view to funding an increase in the amount of pensions paid to pensioner members of the pension scheme to reflect increases in the cost of living. If the effect of making such a contribution had the effect of converting pensioner members into active members, then the exclusion would not apply to such members, which is plainly not intended. Also see ss.230(5B) and 234(5B), which provide that if the rights of a deferred member of a cash balance or defined benefits arrangement increase by no more than the RPI or CPI, then the increase is ignored for annual allowance purposes. These provisions expressly apply only to deferred members, and so if such increases had the effect of converting a deferred member into an active member, then the provisions could never apply.

[49] See inter alia, the Pensions Ombudsman's determination relating to complaint by *Stobie* (PO-3105) at para.78 and fn.1. This is supported by FA 2004 ss.230(5BC) and 234(5BD) which both provide that, in determining whether a person is a deferred member, arrangements made under the pension scheme for benefits to accrue as a consequence of (and immediately after) a transfer in to the scheme relating to the individual are disregarded in certain circumstances. These provisions would be otiose if a transfer would not otherwise cause a deferred member to become an active member.

nection with a member of the receiving scheme.[50] As can be seen from the definition of pensioner and deferred member below, such an individual may not otherwise be a member of the receiving scheme were it not for the fact that the request for the transfer itself will make him an active member.

A person must be an active member to obtain tax relief in respect of contributions.[51] It is likely that making a contribution will itself constitute an "arrangement for the accrual of benefits", thereby making the person an active member (assuming that he has joined the scheme, and so he will have rights to benefits after the contribution).

2-034

**The position of death beneficiaries**

Following the death of a member, a death beneficiary appears, on the face of it, to meet the definition of pensioner member (or, possibly, deferred member, depending on how the death benefits are to be provided). The legislation does not provide much indication of whether or not this is the correct interpretation. FA 2004 Sch.28 para.16C(4) appears to have been drafted on the basis that the recipient of a dependants' scheme pension will be a pensioner member. The taxable property provisions also suggest that, following the death of the member, a death beneficiary will become a member.[52] In the context of pension death benefits, the death beneficiary must be a dependant, nominee or successor of the member, and it is in his capacity as such that he is entitled to the death benefits;[53] however, these are not mutually exclusive concepts, so that in itself does not mean that a death beneficiary does not become a pensioner member by virtue of his rights to death benefits.[54]

2-035

# "ARRANGEMENT"

Each member of a registered pension scheme has one or more "arrangements" under the scheme. The "arrangement" concept is of fundamental importance for the purposes of FA 2004 Pt 4. In a rather circular definition, s.152(1) provides:

2-036

> "In this Part "arrangement", in relation to a member of a pension scheme, means an arrangement relating to the member under the pension scheme."

The concept is best understood as being an *agreement* under the scheme as to how to calculate the benefits which will be paid to or in respect of the member.[55] In a money purchase context, the scheme rules usually provide that each member has an *account* (or *fund*) under the scheme, and an amount equal to the value of that

2-037

---

[50] See FA 2004 s.169, explained in Ch.12.
[51] FA 2004 s.188(1).
[52] This is because the taxable property provisions only apply where a member or "related" person can influence the investments, and a death beneficiary will not be "related" to the deceased member once he has died. Therefore, if a death beneficiary did not become member, it would be straightforward to avoid the application of the taxable property provisions, notwithstanding the beneficiaries directing the investment.
[53] For example, death benefits cannot be paid "to" a member (in his capacity as member); they can only be paid "in respect of" a member, and so if a death beneficiary becomes a member then that does not alter the fact that the death benefits are paid in respect of the deceased member.
[54] This does not appear to have any real significance in a tax context, but it clearly could be significant if such a death beneficiary became a member as a matter of pension legislation. For example, in order to be a SSAS all members must be trustees and there can be no more than 11 members, and so it may be important to determine whether death beneficiaries are included.
[55] The concept is briefly considered in *R. v Quillan* [2015] EWCA Crim 538 at [80].

account will be available for the provision of benefits. The provisions setting out how the value of that account is to be calculated represent the member's arrangement under the scheme. In a defined benefits context, the member does not have an account; he simply has the right to receive benefits, which may be calculated by reference to his final salary or some other factor.

**2-038** An arrangement under a pension scheme is to be contrasted with the scheme itself, which provides benefits to a class of persons (i.e. the members and death beneficiaries). It is also to be contrasted, in a money purchase context, with an arrangement under the scheme that does not relate to any particular member, such as a general (or reserve) fund. A general fund forms part of the scheme but is not an arrangement relating to any member because benefits are not provided directly from the general fund. Incorporating such a fund into an occupational scheme can be helpful from an administrative perspective, and can also provide additional flexibility because certain unauthorised payments and scheme chargeable payments apply only where a payment or deemed payment is in respect of an arrangement relating to a member under the scheme.[56] Any sums or assets allocated to a general fund are not taken into account for the purposes of any member's annual allowance or lump sum allowances (or, formerly, his lifetime allowance).

### The different types of arrangement

**2-039** There are five different types of arrangement:[57]

(a) money purchase arrangements, which are sub-categorised into:
   (i) cash balance arrangements;
   (ii) collective money purchase benefits; and
   (iii) other money purchase arrangements;
(b) defined benefits arrangements; and
(c) hybrid arrangements.

**2-040** It is not uncommon for a member to have more than one arrangement under a scheme. For example, in an occupational scheme, the retirement benefits may be money purchase benefits, and death benefits may be defined benefits (e.g. a multiple of salary). Whether an arrangement is of one type or another is primarily of significance for the purposes of the annual allowance and lifetime allowance.[58] It is quite possible for amendments to the scheme documentation to cause an arrangement to change from one type to another.

**2-041** Once a member's benefits have crystallised (i.e. a scheme pension comes into payment, a lifetime annuity is purchased or funds are designated as available for the payment of drawdown pension), the benefits are paid "in respect of" the arrangement. The process of crystallising benefits does not involve the creation of a new arrangement. For example, if a member of a money purchase arrangement becomes entitled to a scheme pension, the right to receive the pension is itself a defined benefit,[59] but this does not affect the classification of the arrangement: the scheme pension is paid in respect of the money purchase arrangement. The purpose

---

[56] e.g. FA 2004 s.174A (taxable property) only applies if the interest is held by the pension scheme for the purposes of an arrangement *relating to a member*.

[57] FA 2004 s.152. "Collective money purchase arrangement" was introduced with effect from 1 August 2022. Note that the terms "money purchase" and "defined benefit" are also important for the purposes of pension legislation, where they have a slightly different meaning.

[58] The method for valuing the member's rights (either annually or on a BCE) is different for each type of arrangement.

[59] Cf. *Houldsworth v Bridge Trustees Ltd* [2011] UKSC 42, in which the Supreme Court held that

of the arrangement is to determine the amount of benefits payable and so, once the benefits have crystallised, the arrangement concept ceases to have much significance.

*"Money purchase arrangement"*

2-042 An arrangement is a "money purchase arrangement" if all the benefits that may be provided to or in respect of the member under the arrangement are cash balance benefits, collective money purchase benefits, or other money purchase benefits. Money purchase benefits are:[60]

"benefits the rate or amount of which is calculated by reference to an amount available for the provision of benefits to or in respect of the member (whether the amount so available is calculated by reference to payments made under the pension scheme by the member or any other person in respect of the member or any other factor)."

2-043 A money purchase arrangement is a "cash balance arrangement" if all the benefits that may be provided to or in respect of the member under the arrangement are cash balance benefits. Cash balance benefits are:[61]

"benefits the rate or amount of which is calculated by reference to an amount available for the provision of benefits to or in respect of the member calculated otherwise than wholly by reference to payments made under the arrangement by the member or by any other person in respect of the member (or transfers or other credits)."

2-044 A money purchase arrangement is a "collective money purchase arrangement" at any time if, at that time, all the benefits that may be provided to or in respect of the member under the arrangement are collective money purchase benefits as defined in PSA 2021. Accordingly, a benefit provided under a pension scheme is a collective money purchase benefit if: (a) the benefit is a "qualifying benefit"; and (b) the scheme is a "qualifying scheme".

2-045 A benefit is a "qualifying benefit" if: (a) it is provided out of the scheme's available assets (meaning, in broad terms, the assets deriving from members' contributions which are available to provide members' benefits collectively); (b) under the scheme rules, the rate or amount of the benefit is subject to periodic adjustments designed to achieve a balance between the value of the available assets and the amount expected to be required (applying appropriate actuarial assumptions) to provide members' benefits collectively); and (c) it is not of a description prescribed in regulations.

A scheme is a "qualifying scheme" if: (a) it is an occupational pension scheme established under an irrevocable trust by a person or persons to whom s.1(2)(a) PSA 1993 applied when the scheme was established; (b) it is used (or intended to be used) only by a single employer or two or more employers that are connected with each other; (c) it is not a relevant public-sector pension scheme; (d) the qualifying benefits provided under the scheme comprise or include the payment of a pension; (e) if the scheme provides both qualifying benefits and other benefits, there is appropriate separation of the qualifying benefits. Appropriate separation is deemed to arise if certain conditions are met, including that the scheme is sectionalised and that none of the sections under which qualifying benefits are provided provides

---

"internal annuities" (i.e. scheme pensions) were not incompatible with money purchase benefits for the purposes of PSA 1993 s.181 (prior to its amendment by PA 2011 s.29).

[60] FA 2004 s.151(4).
[61] FA 2004 s.152(3) and (5).

other types of benefit; and (f) if the scheme provides a combination of qualifying benefits with different characteristics that is described in regulations, there must be appropriate separation of those qualifying benefits. Appropriate separation is deemed to arise if certain conditions are met, including that the scheme is sectionalised and each of the different types of qualifying benefit is provided under a different section.

**2-046** It follows that all money purchase benefits are "benefits the rate or amount of which is calculated by reference to an amount available for the provision of benefits to or in respect of the member". Money purchase benefits focus on the amount available for the payment of benefits, rather than the amount of the benefits that the member will receive. The distinction is meaningless where a lump sum is to be provided (as the amount available to pay the lump sum is the same as the amount that will be received), but in the context of a pension it is the difference between: (a) having £X available to purchase a pension; and (b) providing a pension of £Y per annum. The former is a money purchase benefit, the latter is a defined benefit.

**2-047** The difference between cash balance and other money purchase benefits is that cash balance benefits are "calculated otherwise than *wholly* by reference to payments made under the arrangement by the member or by any other person in respect of the member (or transfers or other credits)". It follows that other money purchase benefits must be calculated "wholly" by reference to such payments (or transfers or other credits).

**2-048** Typically, under a cash balance arrangement, the member has his own fund or account, and there is, in addition, a promise (usually from the employer) relating to the value of that fund. For example, the promise may be that on the member's retirement the value of the fund will not be less than £X. The member does not know what the value of the fund will be at retirement, but he knows that it will not be less than £X. The person giving the promise carries the risk, and that person will be obliged to make further contributions to the scheme if necessary. If the fund is more than £X, the member is entitled to the excess. Alternatively, there may be a promise that the member's fund under the scheme will grow at not less than £X or Y% per annum. So, under a cash balance arrangement there is no promise as to the precise amount of the benefits that will be provided, but there is a promise regarding the minimum size or growth of the fund.

**2-049** Typically, an "other money purchase arrangement" provides that the member has an account which is increased by contributions for his benefit, transfers in, investment return, and is decreased by costs, investment losses and benefits provided to or in respect of the member. If it is an occupational scheme, the employer will usually promise to contribute, but there is no promise or guarantee regarding the size or growth of the fund, or regarding the amount of benefits which may be provided from the fund.

*"Defined benefits arrangement"*

**2-050** An arrangement is a defined benefits arrangement if all the benefits that may be provided to or in respect of the member under the arrangement are defined benefits. Defined benefits:

> "in relation to a member of a pension scheme, means benefits which are not money purchase benefits (but which are calculated by reference to earnings or service of the member or any other factor other than an amount available for their provision)."

**2-051** So, under a defined benefits arrangement, the member has a right to *receive* a certain amount. The focus is on what will be paid to the member. For example, a right to receive a pension of 80% of the member's salary in his final year of employment is a defined benefit. It also seems clear that a right to receive a pension of a specified amount (e.g. £15,000 per annum for life) is a defined benefit. Such a pension would not of course need to be "calculated" at all, so the words in parenthesis (in the definition above) are not relevant, but such a pension is clearly not a money purchase benefit.[62]

*"Hybrid arrangement"*

2-052
An arrangement is a "hybrid arrangement" if all of the benefits that may be provided to or in respect of the member under the arrangement are, depending on the circumstances, to be of one of any two or three of the above types of benefit (i.e. cash balance benefits, other money purchase benefits, or defined benefits). If more than one type of benefit may be provided under an arrangement to or in respect of the member, the arrangement is deemed to be two or three separate arrangements, with one arrangement relating to each of the categories of benefits that may be so provided. For example, if a member has a right to other money purchase benefits on retirement or salary-related death in service benefits (but not both), this is a hybrid arrangement which will become either a money purchase arrangement or a defined benefits arrangement depending upon whether or not the member dies in service.

# "PAYMENT"

2-053
The precise meaning of "payment" is of fundamental importance to the registered pension scheme regime, especially the provisions relating to authorised and unauthorised payments. The term is used throughout FA 2004 Pt 4 and there is no express statement that it is intended to mean different things in different places. One is therefore entitled to start from the position that the term is used consistently.[63]

2-054
FA 2004 s.161(1) provides that a payment includes a transfer of assets and any other transfer of money's worth. This tells us very little. The draftsman presumably considered it desirable to expressly include transfers of assets on the basis that "payment" may otherwise suggest a payment of a sum of money ("transfer" being a more appropriate term in relation to assets).[64] Nowhere else in FA 2004 Pt 4 is the term "payment" expressly defined or described.

2-055
"Payment" is a familiar concept in tax legislation, and the term has been considered in a number of tax cases. Two points emerge clearly from the decisions. First, the courts are reluctant to provide an exhaustive definition of the term.[65] Second, the term has no one settled meaning; it takes its colour very much from the

---

[62] HMRC appear to agree that such a right would be a defined benefit. PTM023300 provides examples of rights which are "likely" to constitute defined benefits arrangements, including "the purchase of added pension of £10,000 per year by a member contribution …".

[63] Per Arden J in *Hillsdown Holdings Plc v IRC* [1999] S.T.C. 561 at [36]. Also see D. Bailey and L. Norbury, *Bennion on Statutory Interpretation*, 7th edn (London: LexisNexis, 2019) at [21.3].

[64] "Payment" is normally interpreted as including a transfer of assets in any event: see *Irving v RCC* [2008] EWCA Civ 6; [2008] B.T.C. 36; *HMRC v Sippchoice Ltd* [2020] UKUT 149 (TCC) at [27].

[65] In *Garforth v Newsmith Stainless Ltd* [1979] 1 W.L.R. 409, Walton J suggested that it may not be possible to give an exhaustive definition of the word. Also see Arden J in *Hillsdown Holdings Plc v IRC* [1999] S.T.C 561 at [37].

**2-056** context in which it is found.[66] The interpretation therefore needs to start with the provisions in FA 2004 Pt 4.

FA 2004 ss.164(1) and 175 list the authorised member payments and authorised employer payments. Each must necessarily involve a payment. They include authorised pensions and lump sums, recognised transfers, authorised employer loans and scheme administration member/employer payments. Such transactions involve an unfettered transfer of the beneficial interest in property (including money), and as such provide the clearest examples of what is meant by "payment". In other cases, the position is less clear.

**2-057** Some guidance can be gleaned from FA 2004 ss.173 and 174.[67] These two provisions relate to deemed unauthorised payments, and they are instructive because they involve, by necessary implication, transactions which do not involve actual payments. Allowing a member to enjoy scheme property on beneficial terms does not involve a payment (otherwise s.173 would be otiose), which strongly suggests that a payment must involve a transfer of ownership is required. Section 174 creates a deemed payment where any act or omission by the trustees or managers causes scheme property to devalue and property owned by a member to increase in value (except on arm's length terms), which suggests that a transaction which *creates* rights (without *transferring* any rights), such as a declaration of trust or the grant of an option, may not involve a payment.[68]

**Payments on commercial terms**

**2-058** A transaction will be a payment for the purposes of FA 2004 Pt 4 even if it does not confer any sort of benefit on the recipient. A payment of money to purchase an asset on arm's length terms is a payment for these purposes. If that were not the case, ss.171 and 180 would be otiose.[69] It is also implicit from these provisions that a loan on arm's length terms involves a payment to the borrower.

**Crediting an account**

**2-059** In *Garforth v Newsmith Stainless Ltd*,[70] Walton J held that the crediting of a sum to a director's loan account with his company, in circumstances such that the funds were placed unreservedly at the disposal of the director (in the sense that the company was legally obliged to pay them if the director had demanded payment; there was no fetter whatsoever), was equivalent to a *payment* to him for the purposes of the income tax PAYE provisions. Walton J considered that there was no real difference between crediting the director's loan account with the company and crediting the director's current account with a bank. He went on to explain:

---

[66] *Garforth v Newsmith Stainless Ltd* [1979] 1 W.L.R. 409.
[67] FA 2004 s.173 applies where an asset held for the purposes of a registered pension scheme is used to provide a benefit (other than a payment) to a member or to his or her family or household. FA 2004 s.174 applies broadly where there is a value shift out of a registered pension scheme. Both provisions are explained in Ch.18.
[68] *Westdeutsche Landesbank Girozentrale v Islington LBC* [1996] A.C. 669 at 706 (Lord Browne-Wilkinson) is authority for the proposition that a declaration of trust *creates* an equitable interest which did not previously exist; nothing is *transferred*. However, in *OCO Ltd v HMRC* [2017] UKFTT 589 (TC) at [389] the FTT rejected the taxpayer's argument that a declaration of trust did not constitute a *payment* or *transfer* for the purposes of FA 2003 Sch.24 para.1(2)(a).
[69] These provisions relate respectively to scheme administration member payments (see Ch.11) and scheme administration employer payments (see Ch.17). They provide that payments to or in respect of a member or sponsoring employer (other than loans) on arm's length terms are a category of authorised payment.
[70] *Garforth v Newsmith Stainless Ltd* [1979] 1 W.L.R. 409.

"Where a director chooses to leave his money seems to me to be a matter entirely of his own choice. If, of course, it is not a matter entirely of his own choice—if, for some reason, the money was not placed unreservedly at his disposal—then I think that very different considerations would arise. After all, if the taxpayer company were to put money into the account with a note on it saying that it is to be paid out only as and when the board of directors decide, or as and when the taxpayer company in general meeting passes a resolution to that effect, or some qualification of that nature, then the money would not be unreservedly at the disposal of the director, he could not do with it what he liked, and we would be a long way away from payment."

In *IRC v Doncaster*,[71] a company passed a resolution to pay a distribution to its ordinary shareholders and did so by crediting the loan account of each shareholder/director. Rowlatt J held that this involved a payment (for the purposes of the super-tax provisions applicable at the time) when the account was credited. He said: 2-060

"I can conceive nothing more complete in the way of payment. It was simply putting it to the credit of what is equivalent to a banking account. Those loans were money in the hands of the company belonging to the shareholder as an individual."

Similarly, in *Re Harmony and Montague Tin and Copper Mining Co, Spargo's Case*[72] the court found that the effect of netting off mutual liabilities between two parties amounted to actual payment. 2-061

For the purposes of FA 2004 Pt 4, it is likely that a "payment" does require property to leave the pension scheme (such that it is no longer held for the purposes of the pension scheme).[73] Placing property unreservedly at the member's disposal should not be a payment unless the trustee expressly declares that the property is held as bare trustee or nominee for the member. Consider, for example, the position of a flexi-access drawdown fund. The designation of sums or assets as available for drawdown pension may well place sums or assets unreservedly at the member's disposal, in the sense that the trustee would be legally obliged to pay the sums or assets to the member on demand. But such designation is not itself on the list of authorised member payments in FA 2004 s.164. It is, therefore, highly unlikely that the designation of funds as available for drawdown pension constitutes a payment to or in respect of the member for the purposes of FA 2004. Conceptually, one would not expect it to be possible to pay the same sums or assets more than once, so if the creation of a flexi-access drawdown fund involved a payment to the member then it would be difficult to see how a subsequent loan to the member (for example) from money held for the purposes of such a fund could also involve a payment of the same money to him. 2-062

**The release of a debt**

The release of a debt owed by a member to the pension scheme may not amount to a payment for the purposes of FA 2004. In *International Power v Healy*,[74] the House of Lords considered whether the release of a debt was a payment for the purposes of a particular provision in the scheme rules. Lord Hoffmann (with whom the other Lords agreed) found that the provision was drafted to reflect ICTA 1988 s.601 and it was therefore highly relevant to determine whether the release was a payment for the purposes of s.601. Section 601 imposed a tax charge when money 2-063

---

[71] *IRC v Doncaster* (1924) 8 T.C. 623.
[72] *Re Harmony and Montague Tin and Copper Mining Co, Spargo's Case* (1872-73) L.R. 8 Ch. App. 407.
[73] Again, the value shifting provisions in s.174 support this analysis.
[74] *International Power v Healy* [2001] UKHL 20; [2001] 1 W.L.R. 864.

was paid to the employer, and the purpose of the tax charge was to recapture the tax deduction that the employer would have obtained when money was contributed to the scheme. As money owed to the scheme but not yet paid would not have obtained a tax deduction, their Lordships found that this was not the sort of transaction at which s.601 was aimed. It followed that the release of the debt did not constitute a payment for the purposes of the scheme rules.

2-064    The release of a debt *would* however be a deemed unauthorised payment under the value shifting provisions in FA 2004 ss.174 or 181.[75] These provisions arguably acknowledge that the release of a debt would not otherwise be a payment. The value shifting provisions do not however apply to a release on arm's length terms.

### Payments in breach of trust (or which otherwise transfer bare legal title only)

2-065    In *Hillsdown Holdings Plc v IRC*,[76] an exempt approved scheme was in surplus and so the trustee agreed (with the approval of the Inland Revenue) to make two payments to the sponsoring employer. At the time, ICTA 1988 s.601 imposed a 40% tax charge where, subject to limited exceptions, "... a payment is made to an employer out of funds which are or have been held for the purposes of ..." an exempt approved scheme. This tax was duly paid. The payments to the employer were subsequently found to have been made in breach of trust and so the employer was directed (by the court) to pay them back to the pension scheme, on the basis that the employer had received trust property with sufficient knowledge to make it liable as a constructive trustee. As the employer had acted in good faith it was not required by the court to repay to the trustee money which had been paid to the Inland Revenue, except to the extent that it recovered such sums from the Inland Revenue. The employer duly requested a repayment of the tax paid but the Inland Revenue refused on the basis that the tax was still due even though the payment was invalid and had been reversed. So the principal question in the action was whether, on a true construction of s.601, there had been a *payment* to the employer.[77] Arden J found that the payments made to the employer in breach of trust were without substance: no beneficial interest passed and they had to be returned to the trustee, and in those circumstances they were not really payments at all.[78]

2-066    The question of whether a payment made in breach of trust is a payment for the purposes of the relevant tax provisions was next considered in *Venables v Hornby*.[79] In that case, payments were paid from an approved pension scheme to a member on the basis that he had retired, notwithstanding his continued employment by the employer in a different capacity. At the time, ICTA 1988 s.600 imposed a charge to tax where an approved scheme made a payment to a member that was not authorised by the rules of the scheme. The Revenue considered that Mr Venables had not retired, and therefore the payments were not authorised by the rules of the scheme and so were taxable under s.600. Lawrence Collins J found that if Mr Venables had not retired then the payments were made in breach of trust and so the money would not have been received free from the trusts of the scheme. Following the decision of Arden J in *Hillsdown* the money would have been recoverable

---

[75] See Ch.18.
[76] *Hillsdown Holdings Plc v IRC* [1999] S.T.C. 561.
[77] Pursuant to ICTA 1988 s.601(6)(a), for the purposes of s.601 "... reference to any payment include references to any transfer of assets or other transfer of money's worth ...". This is therefore very similar to the FA 2004 provisions.
[78] *Hillsdown Holdings Plc v IRC* [1999] S.T.C 561 at [38].
[79] *Venables v Hornby* [2001] S.T.C. 1221.

by the trustees, and if they had been recovered there would have been no effective payment to the taxpayer. It followed that he received nothing and there was therefore no payment to him giving rise to a tax charge.

2-067
The case went to the Court of Appeal, where Chadwick LJ, giving the lead judgment, described the analysis by Lawrence Collins J of the consequences of making the payments in breach of trust as "plainly untenable" and defeating "the obvious purpose of the taxing provision".[80] He distinguished the decision of Arden J in *Hillsdown* on the basis that ss.601 and 600 operate on a different basis. The object of s.601 was in a "rough and ready way" to reverse the tax advantage which an employer would otherwise obtain if there were repaid to it, free of tax, monies derived from contributions which it had made into an exempt approved scheme. By contrast, the charge under s.600 only arises where the payment is unauthorised and in breach of trust. Therefore, if an unauthorised payment is to be treated as no payment at all, the section is self-defeating and that cannot have been Parliament's intention.

2-068
The case went to the House of Lords, who found (by a majority) that the payments were not made in breach of trust, and so it was not necessary to consider this secondary issue.[81] Lord Walker, giving the dissenting judgment, approved the judgment of the Court of Appeal on the secondary issue. The only member of the majority to comment on the secondary issue was Lord Millett, who said:

> "This makes it unnecessary to express a concluded view on the second question, whether the payments were 'made out of' the trust funds if they were paid in breach of trust to a trustee of the scheme in circumstances in which he came under an obligation enforceable in equity to repay them. It depends on whether it is sufficient that the payments were made to the recipient for his own use and benefit and were valid to pass the legal title to the money, or whether they must have been received free from any legal or equitable obligation on the part of the recipient to make restitution. In short it may depend on whether the determining factor is the payment or the receipt."

2-069
The point that Lord Millet seems to be making in the final sentence above (which is of course obiter) is that if the tax charge is intended to apply when a person *receives* something, it is unlikely that Parliament intended to tax a payment made to such a person in circumstances where it needs to be returned. However, if the tax charge is intended to apply when a *payment* is made, it should not be relevant to ask whether the recipient received anything of any value. Given that the FA 2004 unauthorised payment provisions generally focus on the payment rather than the receipt, Lord Millet's comments suggest that an actual unauthorised payment which is made in breach of trust and must be repaid is still a payment.[82]

2-070
The next case in which this issue was considered was *Thorpe v HMRC*.[83] There, the sole member and sole trustee[84] of an occupational pension scheme transferred the entire fund to himself in his capacity as member on the basis that he was the only beneficiary and so the rule in *Saunders v Vautier* allowed him to do this.[85] In fact there were contingent beneficiaries under the pension scheme, meaning that Mr Thorpe did not have the full beneficial entitlement and so the rule in *Saunders v Vautier* did not apply. Consequently, the money was transferred to him in breach

---

[80] *Venables v Hornby* [2002] EWCA Civ 1277 at [27].
[81] *Venables v Hornby* [2003] UKHL 65; [2003] 1 W.L.R. 3022.
[82] The position may be different in relation to some of the deemed unauthorised payments (see Ch.18).
[83] *Thorpe v HMRC* [2009] EWHC 611 (Ch).
[84] In fact it emerged that he had not been properly appointed as trustee, but nothing turns on that for present purposes.
[85] *Saunders v Vautier* 41 E.R. 482; (1841) Cr. & Ph. 240.

of trust. He retained the money in a separate interest-bearing account and paid tax on the interest received. HMRC withdrew approval of the pension scheme and sought to tax him on the payment under ICTA 1988 s.596A, which imposed a charge to tax on most benefits received from non-approved retirement benefit schemes.[86]

2-071 In the High Court, Sir Edward Evans-Lombe considered that Lord Millet in *Venables* was saying that the question (which Lord Millet does not answer) is decided upon whether there has been a *payment* in the sense that legal title to the money has passed to the recipient or whether there has been a receipt of the money by him in circumstances where there is an equitable obligation on the part of the recipient to make restitution. Sir Edward Evans-Lombe could not materially distinguish s.600 (the charging provision in *Venables*) from s.596A (the charging provision in *Thorpe*) so *Thorpe* should follow *Venables*. However, he evidently found the reasoning of the Court of Appeal in *Venables* unattractive and preferred the reasoning of the High Court. He considered that he was not bound by the decision of the Court of Appeal in *Venables* because the "breach of trust" point was reversed by the majority of the House of Lords, who went on expressly to say that it was unnecessary for them to deal with the point under s.600 (because it did not in those circumstances arise). He therefore concluded that he did not need to follow the judgment of Chadwick LJ and instead followed Lawrence Collins J in *Venables* and held that there was no payment to Mr Thorpe.

2-072 However, on the analysis of Chadwick LJ, ss.600 and 596A are easily distinguished: s.600 is concerned with unauthorised payments and s.596A is concerned with essentially authorised benefits from non-approved schemes. One must make a distinction between provisions, such as s.596A, that are intended to reverse previous tax advantages (so that they are broadly neutral from a tax perspective), and those such as s.600 that are intended to discourage certain transactions by imposing a penalty. The latter type of tax charge would be self-defeating if it did not apply to a payment in breach of trust whereas the former would not. This is simply a case of looking at what Parliament must have intended. It is therefore not at all clear why Sir Edward Evans-Lombe felt he had to depart from the reasoning of Chadwick LJ in order to find that such a payment made in breach of trust was not taxable. As an authorised payment, s.596A is similar to s.601 (and therefore more like the relevant provision in *Hillsdown* rather than *Venables*). Furthermore, ss.600 and 596A are easily distinguished on the above reading of Lord Millet: s.600 is concerned with payments whereas s.596A is concerned with receipts, and here there was no receipt.

2-073 The case went on to the Court of Appeal but HMRC did not appeal this point, which is surprising given that the decision of the High Court to depart from the reasoning of the Court of Appeal in *Venables* was clearly open to criticism.

*Clark v HMRC*

2-074 The most recent decision in this line of cases was also the first to consider FA 2004 Pt 4 rather than the previous legislation. *Clark v HMRC*[87] concerned a payment from a pension scheme to an arrangement which was intended to be a pension scheme but was found to be void for uncertainty. As a result, the payment gave rise to a resulting trust in favour of the transferor scheme, and so it was ineffective

---

[86] It was the predecessor to ITEPA 2003 s.394, which imposes a charge to tax on relevant benefits received under EFRBS (see Ch.35).
[87] *Clark v HMRC* [2020] EWCA Civ 204.

to transfer the beneficial interest. Henderson LJ (with whom Nicola Davies and Bean LJJ agreed) expressly preferred the judgment of Chadwick LJ in *Venables* to the subsequent judgment of Sir Edward Evans-Lombe in *Thorpe* in holding that an unauthorised payment paid in breach of trust is still a payment. Henderson LJ in *Clark* described as "deeply unrealistic" the suggestion that the pension transfer was not a payment for the purposes of s.160(2) merely because it failed to transfer the beneficial interest:

> "The money was intended to pass from the control and supervision of one registered pension scheme to another, the Suffolk Life SIPP was thereby left apparently defunct, and legal title (at least) to the money had passed from Suffolk Life to the LML Pension. From a practical and common-sense perspective, why should it make any difference to this analysis if it later transpired that, unknown to everybody at the time, the transfer was in fact defective and gave rise to a resulting trust?"[88]

Henderson LJ concluded:

2-075

> "The question whether a 'payment' is made for these purposes should be answered by looking at the practical, business reality of the transaction, including any composite transaction of which the payment forms part. If the intended purpose and effect of the transactions is that money leaves the scheme and is placed at the free disposal of the member, the mere fact that the money may be subject to an equitable obligation to restore it to the scheme will not prevent it from being a 'payment' in the ordinary sense of that word. To conclude otherwise would deprive the charge to tax of effect in many of the most egregious cases where it is most needed."[89]

However, Henderson LJ went on to acknowledge that different considerations may arguably arise in cases where an unauthorised payment is inadvertently or carelessly made, and the member concerned takes prompt and effective steps to restore it to the fund before any assessment is made by HMRC.

Chadwick LJ was plainly correct in *Venables* to distinguish legislation that neutralises previous tax advantages from legislation that seeks to discourage and penalise certain transactions. The tax charges that apply to actual unauthorised payments under FA 2004 Pt 4 are to discourage rather than neutralise, and so an actual unauthorised payment made in breach of trust should still constitute a payment. Certain *authorised* payments are also, exceptionally, taxable under FA 2004 (including authorised surplus payments—the transaction which gave rise to the dispute in *Hillsdown*) and so such authorised payments made in breach of trust and returned to the scheme should not constitute payments at all.

2-076

It follows from the above analysis that a transfer of bare legal title to property, or a payment of money to or in respect of a member or employer as nominee or bare trustee for the scheme trustees will involve a payment for the purposes of FA 2004. Such a payment may well be an authorised payment by virtue of FA 2004 ss.171 or 180[90] (for example), but in other circumstances it may be an unauthorised payment.

2-077

*Application to deemed unauthorised payments*

How should the above analysis be applied to the various *deemed* unauthorised payments? FA 2004 ss.172 (assignments) and 172A (surrenders) apply to steps

2-078

---

[88] *Clark v HMRC* [2020] EWCA Civ 204 at [40].
[89] *Clark v HMRC* [2020] EWCA Civ 204 at [82].
[90] i.e. a scheme administration member payment or a scheme administration employer payment, if it is on arm's length terms.

taken by the member and so will not involve a breach of trust. Lord Millet's comment in *Venables* that it may be relevant to consider whether the legislation focuses on the payment or the receipt, suggests that the deemed unauthorised payments under ss.172B (increase in rights of connected person on death), 172D (limits on increase in benefits), 173 (benefits) and 174 (value shifting) may not apply if they are made in breach of trust and subsequently set aside. Those provisions appear to focus on what is received. Section 172C appears however to focus on the allocation, so it may apply to an allocation made in breach of trust even if it is subsequently undone. It seems that the policy of the taxable property provisions is to prevent pension schemes from holding property from which members (or their families) *might* be able to obtain a personal benefit (see Ch.9). Given that no actual benefit is necessary, it may be the case that s.174A applies on the acquisition of taxable property even where the acquisition is made in breach of trust and is subsequently set aside.

**2-079** However, the decision of the FTT in *Dalriada Trustees Ltd v HMRC*,[91] casts some doubt on the above analysis in relation to deemed unauthorised payments. The decision (which is considered in more detail in Ch.18) concerned loans made by a pension scheme to members of a different pension scheme in circumstances that conferred a benefit on members of the lending scheme. The loans were found to have been made in breach of trust, so they were void in equity. The taxpayers apparently assumed that s.173 could apply in these circumstances. The FTT acknowledged (despite the lack of any argument to this effect by the taxpayers) that it might be said that no "benefit" arises in these circumstances, but it decided that, on balance, s.173 applied in that case. It gave four reasons for reaching this conclusion: (a) the loans were void primarily because they conferred a benefit on a member of the lending scheme, so it would be circular to conclude that s.173 could not apply because, by virtue of s.173 applying, no benefit arose to the member of the lending scheme; (b) the conclusion that the loans were void did not necessarily mean that the money would be returned; (c) the borrower obtained the benefit of the loan on the day that that loan was advanced, and he has had the unfettered use of that money since that date without so far having had to repay it, which, when viewed from the perspective of a practical person of business and not an equity lawyer versed in trust law, can fairly be described as a "benefit"; and (d) the question of whether a benefit has been conferred should be determined by reference to the facts as they stand at present (at which time the loans had not been repaid), and not by reference to future steps which might be taken to restore the loan to the lending scheme.[92] For those reasons, the FTT was "inclined to agree with the parties that the fact that the [loans] in this case were void in equity does not mean that the borrower under each [loan] did not obtain a 'benefit' for the purposes of [s.173]. However, we think that the impact of the decision in [*Clark*] in that particular context is not as straightforward and obvious as the parties have assumed". The decision appears to be entirely inconsistent with Arden J's analysis in *Hillsdown* and Lord Millett's obiter comments in *Venables* (both of which were binding on the FTT) so it is regrettable that the point was not argued.

---

[91] *Dalriada Trustees Ltd v HMRC* [2023] UKFTT 314 (TC).
[92] *Dalriada Trustees Ltd v HMRC* [2023] UKFTT 314 (TC) at [276].

### Effect of rectification

In a case heard by the Royal Court of Guernsey,[93] pension transfers were made by a number of registered pension schemes to a pension plan which was intended to be a QROPS, but failed to satisfy the necessary requirements due to a drafting error. The transfers were therefore unauthorised payments, and the trustee successfully applied for rectification of the trust deed and rules of the receiving plan. Rectification operates retrospectively, so the instrument takes effect in its rectified form as if that is what the instrument had always said.[94] HMRC were invited to participate and presumably accepted that, once rectified with retrospective effect, the transfers should be viewed as recognised transfers.

2-080

## "LOAN"

Loans are given special prominence in FA 2004 Pt 4:

2-081

(a) A loan to or in respect of a member cannot be a scheme administration member payment, so such a loan will always be an unauthorised payment.[95]
(b) A loan to or in respect of a sponsoring employer cannot be a scheme administration employer payment, and so it will be an unauthorised payment unless it is an authorised employer loan.[96]
(c) If a payment is not a "loan" then it cannot be an authorised employer loan.[97]
(d) Special rules apply to the valuation of any right or interest in respect of money *lent* to any relevant associated person.[98]
(e) Certain parts of the taxable property provisions apply where lending is involved.[99]

Insofar as is material, s.162 provides as follows:

2-082

"(2) "Loan" does not include the purchase of or subscription to debentures, debenture stock, loan stock, bonds, certificates of deposit or other instruments creating or acknowledging indebtedness which are—
    (a) listed or dealt in on a recognised stock exchange (within the meaning of s.1005 of ITA 2007, or
    (b) offered to the public.
(3) A guarantee of a loan made to or in respect of a person who is or has been a member or sponsoring employer of a registered pension scheme, or to or in respect of a person who is connected with a person who is or has been a member or sponsoring employer of a registered pension scheme but is not such a person, is to be treated as a loan to or in respect of the person who is or has been a member or sponsoring employer of an amount equal to the amount guaranteed.
(4) If a person who is or has been a member or sponsoring employer of a registered pension scheme or a person who is connected with a person who is or has been a member or sponsoring employer of a registered pension scheme but is not such a person member or sponsoring employer of a registered pension scheme—

---

[93] In the matter of *A Pension Plan* [2020] GRC019.
[94] *Craddock Brothers v Hunt* [1923] 2 Ch. 136, 151 and 160; *Marley v Rawlings* [2014] UKSC 2 at [66].
[95] For scheme administration member payments, see Ch.11.
[96] For scheme administration member payments, see Ch.17.
[97] For authorised employer loans, see Ch.17.
[98] See FA 2004 s.278(2).
[99] FA 2004 Sch.29A paras 16 and 43.

(a) is liable to pay a debt, the right to payment of which constitutes an asset held for the purposes of the pension scheme, but
(b) is not required to pay it by the relevant date,
the debt is to be treated as a loan made by the pension scheme to the person who is or has been a member or sponsoring employer on that date.

(5) The relevant date is the date by which a person at arm's length from the pension scheme might be expected to be required to pay the debt."

**2-083** Notwithstanding the heading to s.162 ("meaning of 'loan'"), it does not define the term "loan" for the purposes of FA 2004 Pt 4. It provides merely that certain specified transactions are not loans, and other specified transactions are deemed to be loans (thus suggesting that such transactions would otherwise be—or not be—loans for the purposes of s.162).

In relation to s.162(3), there is a distinction between a guarantee and an indemnity, but it is not an absolute one.[100] A guarantee is a type of indemnity,[101] but not all indemnities are guarantees.

**2-084** Section 162 draws a distinction between a loan and a transaction creating a debt. Only those debts that fall within s.162(4) are deemed to be loans. The policy appears to be that (other than authorised employer loans) loans to members or sponsoring employers, even on entirely arm's length terms, are never acceptable,[102] whereas there are circumstances in which a member or employer may become indebted to the pension scheme which may be acceptable. For example, where a member or employer is contractually obliged to contribute money, any delay in doing so will create a debt. It is suggested that loans are treated differently to otherwise becoming indebted to the pension scheme because a loan involves the payment of money from the pension scheme to the member or employer, and that increases the risk for misappropriation.

**The usual meaning of "loan"**

**2-085** A "loan" is commonly regarded as an agreement by which one party (the lender) agrees to pay money to another party (the borrower), or to a third party at the borrower's request, on terms that the borrower will repay the money together with any agreed interest, where the payment is made with a view to giving the borrower financial accommodation.[103] In general, the term need not be limited to a loan of money. It may include the transfer of an interest in non-fungible property subject to an obligation to return that property in the future (i.e. a temporary grant of the right to use an item of property).[104] Conceivably, it could include an outright transfer of fungible property subject to an obligation to return the same sort of property (e.g. stock lending), but in these circumstances the legal characterisation of the transaction will be important. In *Chow Yoong Hong v Choong Fah Rubber Manufactory*,[105] Lord Devlin observed:

---

[100] See *Dennis v HMRC* [2018] UKFTT 735 at [31].
[101] *Anthony Pitts v Andrew Jones* [2007] EWCA Civ 1301 at [21] (Smith LJ).
[102] The same policy appears under the employer-related loan provisions in PA 1995 s.40 and The Occupational Pension Schemes (Investment) Regulations 2005 (SI 2005/3378).
[103] See *Halsbury's Laws* Vol.21 (London: LexisNexis, 2016) at 57, citing *Potts' Executors v IRC* [1951] A.C. 443; [1951] 1 All E.R. 76.
[104] Thus e.g. one person may lend an item of clothing to another person. It is difficult to think of any circumstances in which a pension scheme would make such a loan, which necessarily involves a degree of informality. The grant of a lease of property, or a licence to use property, does not involve a loan of the property.
[105] [1962] A.C. 209; [1962] 2 W.L.R. 43.

"... there are many ways of raising cash besides borrowing. One is by selling book debts and another by selling unmatured bills, in each case for less than their face value. Another might be to buy goods on credit or against a post-dated cheque and immediately sell them in the market for cash... The task of the court in such cases is clear. It must first look at the nature of the transaction which the parties have agreed. If in form it is not a loan, it is not to the point to say that its object was to raise money for one of them or that the parties could have produced the same result more conveniently by borrowing and lending money."

So the mere economic equivalence of a transaction to a loan does not mean that it should be characterised as a loan. And, as was noted by the Special Commissioner in *HSBC Life (UK) Ltd v Stubbs*,[106] the fact that the parties deliberately structure a transaction so that it does not constitute a loan (but is economically equivalent to a loan) is beside the point. In *Lloyds & Scottish Finance Ltd v Cyril Lord Carpets Sales Ltd*,[107] Lord Wilberforce said:

2-086

"... block discounting is essentially a method of providing finance. Commercially and in its economic result, it may not differ from lending money at interest: the 'discounting charge', which represents the finance house's profit, is stated in terms of so much per cent per annum, which percentage is no doubt based upon current interest rates. Legally, however, there is no doubt that discounting is not treated as the lending of money and that the asset discounted is not the subject of a charge."

And he went on to say (at 617):

2-087

"... the fact that the transaction consisted essentially in the provision of finance, and the similarity in result between a loan and a sale, to all of which I have drawn attention, gives to the appellants' arguments an undoubted force. It is only possible, in fact, to decide whether they are correct by paying close regard to what the precise contractual arrangements between them and the respondents were. Given that the trading agreement was a real contract, intended to govern the individual transactions which followed and (as is accepted) that it was not rescinded or varied, the ultimate question must be whether what was done can be fitted into the contractual framework which that agreement set up with such reasonable adaptations as should be needed in commercial practice and as should not transfigure the nature of the contract."

Although a court is required to look at the arrangement as a whole, it is not entitled to disregard the legal form and nature of the transactions carried out.[108]

2-088

In *Welsh Development Agency v Export Finance Co Ltd*,[109] the wording of an agreement indicated that a transaction was a sale of goods, but the court found that it was a loan secured by a charge on the goods. This was because the agreement contained a right of redemption, and this was considered to be wholly inconsistent with a sale. Straughton LJ said:

2-089

"... one can start from the position that statute law in this country, when it enacts rules to be applied to particular transactions, is in general referring to the legal nature of a transaction and not to its economic effect ... There are ... two routes by which this principle can be overcome. The first, which I will call the external route, is to show that the written document does not represent the agreement of the parties. It may, if one wishes, then be called a sham, a cloak, or a device. The second is the internal route, when one looks only

---

[106] *HSBC Life (UK) Ltd v Stubbs* [2002] S.T.C. (S.C.D.) 9 at [73].
[107] *Lloyds & Scottish Finance Ltd v Cyril Lord Carpets Sales Ltd* [1992] B.C.L.C. 609 at 615.
[108] *Chinn v Collins* [1981] S.T.C. 1 at 6; [1981] A.C. 533 at 547 (Lord Wilberforce).
[109] *Welsh Development Agency v Export Finance Co Ltd* [1992] B.C.C. 270; [1992] B.C.L.C. 148.

at the written agreement, in order to ascertain form its terms whether it amounts to a transaction of the legal nature of which the parties ascribe to it."

**2-090** Dillon LJ commented (at 162):

"... the similarity between a loan and a sale ... would make it virtually impossible to decide which the transaction was if it was not permissible to have regard to the words the parties had used in their agreement in describing that transaction on which they had agreed."

**2-091** So, where an agreement is capable of different interpretations, the terms used by the parties may be important. However, where there is no doubt or ambiguity, the words used by the parties cannot affect the legal categorisation of what they have agreed.[110] A payment of money which may in certain circumstances need to be repaid is a loan.[111] The fact that the date of repayment or the amount that must be repaid is not certain does not mean that the payment is not a loan.[112]

## Transactions which are not loans

**2-092** In *Griffin v Citibank Investment Ltd*,[113] the taxpayer purchased a capped call option and a floored put option which between them gave a predetermined sum consisting of a repayment of the purchase price and an additional sum. HMRC argued that the two options should be characterised as a loan, and so taxed under the loan relationship provisions. Patten J found (at [52]) that to recharacterise the two options as a loan would be to disregard the legal form and nature of the transactions in favour of some supposed underlying substance. The Special Commissioners noted that in the event of default, the market value of the option was required to be paid and not the repayment of the purchase price with interest, and they considered this to be a fundamental distinction between an option and a loan.

**2-093** A sale for deferred consideration does not involve a loan by the vendor.[114] The question is whether the vendor has supplied the goods on credit, or supplied credit to buy the goods: it is the legal nature of the transaction that matters. A sale in exchange for the issue of promissory/loan notes does not involve a loan by the purchaser.[115] A purchase of bills[116] or book debts[117] at a discount does not involve a loan. A repurchase arrangement is also not a loan. If a sponsoring employer sells an asset to a pension scheme for £X subject to a call option to repurchase it for £X plus 5% p/a, exercisable at any time in the following five years, that should not involve a loan to the employer, and it should not create a debt unless and until the

---

[110] *Street v Mountford* [1985] A.C. 809 at 826H–827B.
[111] *Aspect Capital Ltd v HMRC* [2014] UKUT 81 (TCC) at [55].
[112] *Grant v Watton (Inspector of Taxes)* [1999] S.T.C. 330; *Aspect Capital v HMRC* [2014] UKUT 81 (TCC) at [56].
[113] *Griffin v Citibank Investment Ltd* [2000] S.T.C. 1010; 73 T.C. 352.
[114] *IRC v Port of London Authority* [1923] A.C. 507; *Champagne Perrier-Jouet SA v HH Finch Ltd* [1982] 1 W.L.R. 1359; [1982] 3 All E.R. 713; *Harman J Ramsden v IRC* 37 T.C. 619; see H.G. Beale (ed.), *Chitty on Contracts*, 3rd edn (London: Sweet & Maxwell, 2018), Vol.2 para.39-261. PTM123100 states "...a registered pension scheme may sell an asset to a scheme member or a person who is connected with a scheme member, but that member may not pay for the asset straight away. There has been no lending of money by the scheme but a debt has been created between the scheme and the member".
[115] *Lee v IRC* 24 T.C. 207.
[116] *Chow Yoong Hong v Choong Fah Rubber Manufactory* [1962] A.C. 209; [1962] 2 W.L.R. 43.
[117] *Olds Discount Co Ltd v John Playfair Ltd* [1938] 3 All E.R. 275.

option is exercised. The analysis would be the same if the scheme had a put option to sell the asset back to the employer.

An annuity does not create a relationship of creditor and debtor, and therefore cannot constitute a loan or a debt. In *IRC v Church Commissioners*,[118] Stamp LJ said:

2-094

> "... if a principal sum be paid as the price of the purchase of a terminable annuity, the whole of each payment is to be regarded as income and liable to income tax. As Greene MR pointed out in *Southern-Smith v Clancy*,[119] in such a case the legal nature of such a contract is beyond question. The property in the principal sum passes absolutely to the recipient of that sum. No relationship of debtor and creditor with regard to that sum is every constituted. The sum as a sum ceases to exists once it is paid. Its place is taken by the promise to pay the annuity and the annuitant's only right is to demand payment of the annuity as it accrues due. The financial results of the transaction will, however, be that the recipient of the annual payments will receive by the end of the period of years a sum equal to the amount which had been paid together with a sum in respect of interest."

**The meaning of "debt"**

A debt owed to a pension scheme is deemed to be a loan made by the scheme in the circumstances specified in s.162(4), namely:

2-095

(a) the debtor is a member or sponsoring employer of the pension scheme, or is connected with such a member or sponsoring employer;
(b) the right to payment of the debt is an asset held for the purposes of the pension scheme; and
(c) the debtor is not required to pay the debt by the date by which a person at arm's length from the pension scheme might be expected to be required to pay the debt (the "relevant date").

Such a deemed loan is treated as made by the pension scheme to the member or sponsoring employer on the relevant date.

This provision requires careful consideration wherever a sponsoring employer enters into ongoing commercial arrangements with the pension scheme (such as a joint venture).

2-096

A "debt" is a sum of money which is now payable or will become payable in the future by reason of a present obligation.[120] In its ordinary meaning the essential precondition for the existence of a debt is the existence of an obligation to pay.[121] It will usually be an obligation relating to money due, but need not be. The meaning of the word depends very much on its context,[122] but the following points may be material:

2-097

(a) A contingent debt which may never become payable is capable of being a debt.[123]
(b) A debt may be incurred even if the date and amount of repayment are not ascertainable until some later time.[124]

---

[118] *IRC v Church Commissioners* [1975] S.T.C. 546 CA at 551.
[119] *Sothern-Smith v Clancy* [1941] 1 K.B. 276; [1941] 1 All E.R. 111.
[120] *Webb v Stenton* (1883) 11 Q.B.D. 518, CA, Per Lindley LJ.
[121] See *RKW Ltd v HMRC* [2014] UKFTT 151 (TC) at [129].
[122] Per Lord Fraser in *Marren v Ingles* [1980] 1 W.L.R. 983; (1980) 54 T.C. 76.
[123] *Mortimore v IRC* 2 Hurl. & C. 838.
[124] *O'Driscoll v Manchester Insurance Committee* [1915] 3 K.B. 499 per Swinfen Eady LJ at 511–513.

(c) A contingent right to receive an unascertainable amount of money at an unknown date is not a debt.[125]
(d) The fact that a debt may not need to be repaid in certain circumstances (e.g. because the lender may release it) cannot be material, because otherwise there would never be a debt.
(e) If there is a transaction under which one party is obliged to pay money to another party in certain circumstances (e.g. a wager), there is no debt until the wager is complete. This is the case even if the circumstances are such that it becomes clear which party will win the wager.

## "CONNECTED PERSONS"

**2-098** For the purposes of FA 2004 Pt 4, it is often necessary to determine whether a person (company or individual) is "connected" with a member or a sponsoring employer.[126]

### The meaning of "connected"

**2-099** For the purposes of FA 2004 Pt 4, whether or not a person is connected with another person is usually determined in accordance with ITA 2007 s.993.[127] For the purposes of these provisions, where a person ("A") is connected with another person ("B"), it follows that B is connected with A.

*Individuals*

**2-100** An individual ("A") is connected with another individual ("B") in any of the following circumstances:
(a) A is B's spouse or civil partner.
(b) A is a relative of B. "Relative" means brother, sister, ancestor or lineal descendant.[128]
(c) A is the spouse or civil partner of a relative of B.
(d) A is a relative of B's spouse or civil partner.
(e) A is the spouse or civil partner of a relative of B's spouse or civil partner.

*Trustees*

**2-101** A person, in the capacity as trustee of a settlement, is connected with:
(a) any individual who is a settlor in relation to the settlement;
(b) any person connected with such an individual;

---

[125] *Marren v Ingles* [1980] 1 W.L.R. 983; (1980) 54 T.C. 76.
[126] See e.g. s.161(5) to (7): payments to persons connected with members or sponsoring employers are generally deemed to be made to the member or sponsoring employer, assets held by a person connected with a member or sponsoring employer are deemed to be held for the benefit of the member or sponsoring employer, and any increase in the value of an asset held by, or reduction in the liability of, a person connected with a member or sponsoring employer is deemed to be an increase or reduction for the benefit of the member or sponsoring employer. Connected persons also feature heavily in the deemed unauthorised payment provisions.
[127] In some cases, it is determined in accordance with the materially identical corporation tax provisions in CTA 2010 s.1122: see e.g. the employer asset-backed contributions rules, and some (but not all) of the provisions relating to taxable property.
[128] ITA 2007 s.994(1).

## "CONNECTED PERSONS"

(c) any close company whose participators include the trustees of the settlement;
(d) any non-UK resident company which, if it were UK resident, would be a close company whose participators include the trustees of the settlement;
(e) any body corporate ("company A") controlled by a company within paragraph (c) or (d) above. For these purposes, "control" means the power of a person ("P") to secure (i) by means of the holding of shares or the possession of voting power in relation to that or any other body corporate, or (ii) as a result of any powers conferred by the articles of association or other document regulating that or any other body corporate, that the affairs of company A are conducted in accordance with P's wishes;
(f) if the settlement is the principal settlement in relation to one or more sub-fund settlements, a person in the capacity as trustee of such a sub-fund settlement; or
(g) if the settlement is a sub-fund settlement in relation to a principal settlement, a person in the capacity as trustee of any other sub-fund settlements in relation to the principal settlement.[129]

"Settlement" has the same meaning as in ITTOIA 2005 s.620, so most registered pension schemes will not be settlements.[130] A "trustee", in the case of a settlement which is not a trust, means any person in whom the property comprised in the settlement is for the time being vested, or in whom the management of that property is for the time being vested.[131]

**2-102**

*Partners*

A person who is a partner in a partnership is connected with:

**2-103**

(a) any partner in the partnership;
(b) the spouse or civil partner of any individual who is a partner in the partnership; or
(c) a relative of any individual who is a partner in the partnership.

But this does not apply in relation to acquisitions or disposals of assets of the partnership pursuant to genuine commercial arrangements.

*Companies*

A company[132] is connected with another company if:

**2-104**

(a) the same person has control of both companies;
(b) a person ("A") has control of one company and persons connected with A have control of the other company;
(c) A has control of one company and A together with persons connected with A have control of the other company; or
(d) a group of two or more persons has control of both companies and the

---

[129] "Sub-fund settlement" and "principal settlement" have the meanings given by TCGA 1992 Sch.4ZA para.1.
[130] For s.620 ITTOIA 2005 (the income tax settlements provisions), see Ch.22.
[131] ITA 2004 s.466(4) (which provides "references, however expressed, to property comprised in a settlement are references to settled property") is disapplied for these purposes.
[132] "Company" includes any body corporate or unincorporated association, but does not include a partnership. A unit trust scheme is treated as if it were a company, and the rights of the unit holders are treated as if they were shares in the company.

groups either consist of the same persons or could be so regarded if (in one or more cases) a member of either group were replaced by a person with whom the member is connected.

**2-105** A company is connected with another person ("A") if A has control of the company, or A together with persons connected with A have control of the company. Any two or more persons acting together to secure or exercise control of a company are connected with (a) one another, and (b) any person acting on the directions of any of them to secure or exercise control of the company.

**"Control"**

**2-106** The commentary above refers to companies "controlled" by trustees or another company. For these purposes, a person is treated as having control of a company if the person (a) exercises, (b) is able to exercise, or (c) is entitled to acquire, direct or indirect control over the company's affairs.

**2-107** In particular, a person is treated as having control of a company if the person possesses or is entitled to acquire:[133]

 (a) the greater part of the share capital or issued share capital of the company;
 (b) the greater part of the voting power in the company;
 (c) so much of the issued share capital of the company as would, on the assumption that the whole of the income of the company were distributed among the participators, entitle the person to receive the greater part of the amount so distributed. Any rights that the person or any other person has as a loan creditor are disregarded for the purposes of this assumption; or
 (d) such rights as would entitle the person, in the event of the winding up of the company or in any other circumstances, to receive the greater part of the assets of the company which would then be available for distribution among the participators.

**2-108** If two or more persons together satisfy any of the above conditions, they are treated as having control of the company.

*Attribution of rights*

**2-109** A person is treated as entitled to acquire anything which the person is entitled to acquire at a future date, or will at a future date be entitled to acquire. If a person possesses any rights or powers on behalf of another person (A), or may be required to exercise any rights or powers on A's direction or behalf, those rights or powers are to be attributed to A.

**2-110** There may also be attributed to a person the following rights and powers, including those attributed to a company or associate under the above paragraph, but not including those attributed to an associate under the following. Such attributions are to be made as will result in a company being treated as under the control of five or fewer participators if it can be so treated. The rights and powers:

 (a) of any company of which the person has, or the person and associates of the person have, control;
 (b) of any two or more companies within (a) above;
 (c) of any associate of the person; or

---

[133] CTA 2010 ss.450 and 451, applied by ITA 2007 s.994(1) and CTA 2010 s.1123(1).

(d) of any two or more associates of the person.

**"Associate"**

The above provisions (attributing rights to a person) refer to an associate of the person. "Associate", in relation to a person, means any of the following:[134]  **2-111**

(a) any relative or partner of the person. "Relative" means a spouse or civil partner, a parent or remoter forebear, a child or remoter issue, or a brother or sister;
(b) the trustees of any settlement in relation to which the person is a settlor;
(c) the trustees of any settlement in relation to which any relative of the person (living or dead) is or was a settlor;
(d) if the person has an interest in any shares or obligations of a company which are subject to any trust, the trustees of any settlement concerned;
(e) if the person is a company, and has an interest in any shares or obligations of a company which are subject to any trust, any other company which has an interest in those shares or obligations;
(f) if the person has an interest in any shares or obligations of a company which are part of the estate of a deceased person, the personal representatives of the deceased; or
(g) if the person is a company, and has an interest in any shares or obligations of a company which are part of the estate of a deceased person, any other company which has an interest in those shares or obligations.

**"Loan creditor"**

The above provisions (relating to the circumstances in which a person controls a company) refer to a loan creditor. "Loan creditor", in relation to a company, means a creditor:[135] **2-112**

(a) in respect of any debt incurred by the company (i) for any money borrowed or capital assets acquired by the company, (ii) for any right to receive income created in favour of the company, or (iii) for consideration the value of which to the company was (at the time when the debt was incurred) substantially less than the amount of the debt (including any premium on the debt). A person who is not the creditor in respect of any such debt or loan capital, but has a beneficial interest in that debt or loan capital, is, to the extent of that interest, treated for the purposes of this Part as a loan creditor in respect of that debt or loan capital; or
(b) in respect of any redeemable loan capital issued by the company.

However, a person carrying on a business of banking is not treated as a loan creditor in respect of any debt or loan capital incurred or issued by the company for money lent by the person to the company in the ordinary course of that business. **2-113**

---

[134] CTA 2010 s.448.
[135] CTA 2010 s.453.

**"Participator"**

2-114 "Participator", in relation to a company, means a person having a share or interest in the capital or income of the company, including in particular:[136]

    (a) a person who possesses, or is entitled to acquire, share capital or voting rights in the company. A person is treated as entitled to do anything which the person is entitled to do at a future date, or will at a future date be entitled to do;

    (b) a loan creditor of the company;

    (c) a person who possesses a right to receive or participate in distributions of the company or any amounts payable by the company (in cash or in kind) to loan creditors by way of premium on redemption. "Distribution" is construed without regard to CTA 2010 s.1000(2) (extended definition of distribution for close companies);

    (d) a person who is entitled to acquire such a right as is mentioned in paragraph (c) above; or

    (e) a person who is entitled to secure that income or assets (whether present or future) of the company will be applied directly or indirectly for the person's benefit.[137]

2-115 This does not affect any provision requiring a participator in one company to be treated as being also a participator in another company.

## VALUATION

2-116 It is frequently important to determine the value of assets held for the purposes of a registered pension scheme:

    (a) One of the grounds for de-registration is that the scheme chargeable payments percentage is 25% or more, and this is determined partly by reference to the market value of the assets.[138]

    (b) Payments to acquire shares in a sponsoring employer are not scheme administration employer payments if the market value of the shares is more than 5% of the total amount of the sums and the market value of the assets held by the scheme.[139]

    (c) Various provisions relating to the lifetime allowance refer to market value. For example, the amount crystallised under BCE 1 is the amount of the sums designated as available for the payment of drawdown pension plus the market value of the assets so designated.

    (d) In relation to the unauthorised borrowing provisions, the 50% restriction relates in part to the market value of the scheme assets.[140]

    (e) In relation to the authorised employer loan provisions, the 50% restriction relates in part to the market value of the scheme assets.[141]

2-117 In almost all cases, where valuation is relevant, FA 2004 Pt 4 refers to the total

---

[136] CTA 2010 s.454.
[137] See also s.519(2) CTA 2009 (investment bond arrangements to be ignored in the application of subsection (2)(e)).
[138] FA 2004 s.158(2)–(4).
[139] FA 2004 s.180(5).
[140] FA 2004 ss.182(3) and 184(3).
[141] FA 2004 s.179(1)(a).

of the "amount of the sums" (i.e. the amount of money) and the "market value" of the assets held for the purposes of the scheme. There are some exceptions: e.g. ss.174 and 181 (value shifting), s.244K (amount of the overseas transfer charge), and Sch.29A para.14(1) (taxable property) refer to the "value" of an asset. In such cases, Parliament presumably intended "value" to mean something other than market value.[142] But what? In most cases it seems very likely that a tribunal will find that market value is in fact the most appropriate method of valuation,[143] but there is clearly scope for argument on the facts.

**Market value**

The market value of an asset must be determined in accordance with TCGA 1992 s.272.[144] No other provision in TCGA 1992 relating to market value (such as s.273, relating to unquoted shares and securities) is incorporated.[145] Section 272 provides that "market value", in relation to any assets, means the price which those assets might reasonably be expected to fetch on a sale in the open market. In estimating the market value of any assets no reduction shall be made in the estimate on account of the estimate being made on the assumption that the whole of the assets is to be placed on the market at one and the same time. However, s.272 goes on to provide that this general rule does not apply to quoted shares and unit trusts.

2-118

*Quoted shares*

The market value of quoted shares is determined in accordance with the Market Value of Shares, Securities and Strips Regulations 2015.[146]

2-119

*Unit trusts*

In relation to any rights of unit holders in any unit trust scheme the buying and selling prices of which are published regularly by the managers of the scheme, market value means an amount equal to the buying price (that is the lower price) so published on the relevant date, or if none were published on that date, on the latest date before.[147]

2-120

---

[142] See *Bennion, Bailey and Norbury on Statutory Interpretation*, 8th edn (LexisNexis, 2020) section 21.3 (same words, same meaning; different words, different meaning): "It is generally presumed that the drafter did not indulge in elegant variation, but kept to a particular term when wishing to convey a particular meaning." In *Stanton v Drayton Commercial Investment Co Ltd* [1982] S.T.C. 585, the House of Lords held that "value" in what is now TCGA 1992 s.38(1)(a), does not mean market value (there is "no need to read in the word 'market' before 'value' where Parliament has not seen fit to use it"). But s.38(1)(a) applies only to transactions between unconnected persons on arm's length terms (otherwise s.17 would apply the market value rule), so in those circumstances a value (namely the price agreed between the parties) is readily available. But that is not the case with the provisions in FA 2004 Pt 4.

[143] See e.g. *Kerrison v HMRC* [2019] UKUT 8 (TCC) at [32]: "We agree that the use of 'value' [in TCGA 1992 s.30] instead of the defined term 'market value' provides at least some indication that Parliament intended a meaning other than that of the defined term. That is not to say that this indicates that it *cannot*, depending on the circumstances, mean market value, but that it provides support for the conclusion that it is not confined to market value".

[144] FA 2004 s.278(1).

[145] cf., for example, FA 2003 s.118, (relating to SDLT), which uses the market value rule in TCGA 1992 by expressly incorporating TCGA 1992 ss.272–274.

[146] Market Value of Shares, Securities and Strips Regulations 2015 (SI 2015/616).

[147] TCGA 1992 s.272(5).

### The effect of scheme borrowing

**2-121** FA 2004 Pt 4 draws a clear distinction between sums (money) and assets. By borrowing £X, the amount of money held for the purposes of the scheme increases by £X. Does the obligation to repay £X decrease the market value of the scheme's assets? If the scheme is established under trusts, the trustee's right of indemnity[148] will usually give the trustee a first charge or lien on the trust fund, conferring an equitable interest in the trust fund in respect of the debt of £X.[149] This does, in a sense, reduce by £X the value of the scheme (or the relevant member's arrangement under the scheme), however, it is most unlikely that this charge or lien could be said to reduce the market value of any of the *assets*, because any purchaser of the assets would take them free of the charge or lien.[150] Plainly, if there is at least £X cash held for the purposes of the scheme, the debt cannot be said to have reduced the value of any of the scheme's assets: the debt can be discharged at any time with the cash. It follows that an unsecured debt will usually not affect the market value of scheme assets.[151]

**2-122** It is for this reason that, for the purposes of the unauthorised borrowing provisions, borrowing money (at least on an unsecured basis) has the rather curious effect of permitting the scheme to borrow more money.[152] That is a peculiar, although perhaps rather benign, effect of unsecured borrowing. In other circumstances, if this analysis is correct, HMRC may consider the effect to be more objectionable. For example, by borrowing money on unsecured terms, a pension scheme can avoid the application of the de-registration threshold.[153] Could a scheme borrow money in order to increase the amount of the sums designated as available for the payment of drawdown pension, and thereby increase the amount of an associated PCLS which may be paid? If the intention is that the debt will be discharged with the money so designated, HMRC would no doubt challenge this on the basis that such sums are not in reality "available" for the payment of drawdown pension, and so should not be taken into account for the purposes of calculating the maximum PCLS.[154] The extent to which that is reasonably arguable by HMRC is likely to depend on the facts of the case.

**2-123** Does it make any difference if the debt is secured against any of the assets? This issue does not arise in a CGT context, because, for CGT purposes, assets are deemed to be acquired and disposed of free of any interest or right by way of security subsisting at the time of any acquisition of it.[155] But given that market value is concerned with the price that persons might be expected to pay for property, and no one would pay the full value for property subject to a charge in favour of a third

---

[148] Under Trustee Act 2000 s.31 and/or the trust instrument.

[149] See L. Tucker, N. Le Poidevin, QC and J. Brightwell, *Lewin on Trusts*, 20th edn (London: Sweet & Maxwell, 2020), para.19-044.

[150] To reiterate the point made above, where valuation is relevant, FA 2004 Pt 4 usually refers to the aggregate of the "amount of the sums" (i.e. the amount of money) and the market value of the assets held for the purposes of the scheme; it does not refer to more general concepts such as the value of the member's arrangement or the value of the scheme.

[151] It may be inevitable that unsecured debts are generally disregarded for valuation purposes, because the scheme's obligation to pay pension benefits to its members could well be characterised as unsecured debts.

[152] See Ch.8.

[153] The scheme rules may restrict the circumstances in which the trustees can borrow money. But in general borrowing in these circumstances would plainly be in the interest of the members.

[154] i.e. the "applicable amount" in FA 2004 Sch.29 para.3. Failing that, HMRC may well argue that the general anti-abuse rule applies.

[155] TCGA 1992 s.26(3). In addition, TCGA 1992 s.18(6)–(8) contains special rules relating to the market value of assets which are subject to restrictions when there is a disposal to a connected person.

party, it is very likely that a secured debt *will* decrease the market value of the asset against which it is secured. However, if this is correct, the effect may be equally objectionable (from HMRC's perspective). For example, in the context of the lifetime allowance, the designation of sums and assets as available for the payment of drawdown pension is BCE 1, and the amount crystallised is the aggregate of the amount of the sums and the market value of the assets designated. If an individual with available lifetime allowance of £500,000 is considering designating an asset with a market value of £1 million as available for the payment of drawdown pension, the scheme could borrow £500,000 and secure it against the asset, thereby reducing the market value of the asset to £500,000. The asset, subject to the security, could then be so designated. The borrowed £500,000 cash could remain in the member's uncrystallised fund and could at some later stage be used to repay the lender, thereby increasing the value of the designated asset without the occurrence of a further BCE. HMRC would no doubt wish to challenge this analysis, but it is not easy to see on what basis they could reasonably do so, except perhaps for the general anti-abuse rule in appropriate circumstances.

# CHAPTER 3

# A Day Transitional Provisions

## TABLE OF CONTENTS

| | |
|---|---|
| Introduction | 3-001 |
|     The position prior to A Day | 3-003 |
|         Occupational pension schemes | 3-004 |
|             Taxation | 3-007 |
|             Surpluses | 3-011 |
|             Limits on benefits | 3-012 |
|         Personal pension schemes | 3-014 |
|             Taxation | 3-015 |
|         The different regimes | 3-016 |
|             Proposals for reform | 3-017 |
| Pre-commencement pension schemes | 3-021 |
|     Deemed registration of existing schemes | 3-021 |
|     Identifying the scheme administrator | 3-022 |
| The lifetime allowance | 3-024 |
|     Enhanced protection | 3-025 |
|         Relevant benefit accrual | 3-026 |
|             Other money purchase arrangements | 3-026 |
|             Cash balance and defined benefits arrangements | 3-028 |
|             Lump sum death benefits | 3-034 |
|         Impermissible transfers | 3-035 |
|             Other money purchase arrangements | 3-035 |
|             Cash balance and defined benefits arrangements | 3-037 |
|         Transfers that are not permitted transfers | 3-038 |
|         Arrangements made otherwise than in permitted circumstances | 3-041 |
|             Auto-enrolment | 3-042 |
|         Consequences of cessation | 3-043 |
|     Lifetime allowance enhancement factors | 3-044 |
|     Primary protection | 3-048 |
|         The primary protection factor | 3-049 |
|         Relevant pre-commencement pension rights | 3-051 |
|         Valuing uncrystallised pension rights | 3-052 |
|         Valuing crystallised pension rights | 3-058 |
|         Increasing the primary protection factor | 3-060 |
|         Reducing the primary protection factor | 3-061 |
|         Protection for lump sum death benefits | 3-062 |
|     Pension credits | 3-066 |
|     Reduced lifetime allowance | 3-068 |
|         Pre-A Day pensions | 3-068 |
|         Protected pension age | 3-069 |

| | |
|---|---|
| Multiple BCEs | 3-073 |
| Availability of lifetime allowance on a BCE | 3-074 |
| Pre-A Day pensions | 3-074 |
| "ARP" where relevant existing pension is drawdown | 3-075 |
| Illustration | 3-078 |
| BCE 2 | 3-080 |
| Scheme pension provided from pre-A Day drawdown pension fund | 3-080 |
| BCE 3 | 3-082 |
| Pre-6 April 2006 entitlement | 3-082 |
| BCE 4 | 3-085 |
| Annuity purchased from pre-A Day drawdown pension fund | 3-085 |
| BCE 8 | 3-087 |
| Drawdown pension funds representing pre-A Day unsecured pension | 3-087 |
| Protection for pre-commencement pension rights | 3-088 |
| Protected pension ages | 3-088 |
| Scheme rights existing before 6 April 2006 | 3-088 |
| Scheme rights existing before 4 November 2021 | 3-090 |
| Pre-6 April 2006 lump sum rights exceeding £375,000 | 3-092 |
| Pre-A Day lifetime annuities | 3-093 |
| Lump sum rights exceeding 25% of uncrystallised rights | 3-094 |
| The pension condition | 3-095 |
| Protected pension schemes | 3-096 |
| Miscellaneous provisions | 3-097 |
| Taxable property | 3-097 |

# INTRODUCTION

**3-001**  FA 2004 Pt 4 includes extensive transitional provisions relating to rights acquired by scheme members under schemes approved prior to A Day. These transitional provisions are found primarily in FA 2004 Sch.36 and the Taxation of Pension Schemes (Transitional Provisions) Order 2006 (SI 2006/572). In outline, Sch.36 deals with the following:[1]

(a) Part 1 prescribes which categories of pre-A Day approved pension schemes automatically became registered pension schemes (unless they opted out), and who is the scheme administrator of such schemes.

(b) Part 2 relates to the lifetime allowance (before 6 April 2024) and the LS allowance and LS&DB allowance (since 6 April 2024). It provides protection for pre-commencement rights (in the form of primary protection, enhanced protection, and pre-commencement pension credits), and reduces an individual's allowance where his pension commences before normal minimum pension age, or where his pension commenced prior to A Day.

(c) Part 3 protects certain pre-commencement benefit rights: (i) rights to take

---

[1] FA 2004 Sch.36 also includes various other provisions which have ceased to have any application.

benefit before normal minimum pension age; (ii) lump sum rights exceeding £375,000; and (iii) entitlement to lump sums exceeding 25% of uncrystallised rights.
(d) Part 4 contains miscellaneous provisions: (i) pre-commencement ill-health insurance contracts; (ii) pre-commencement holdings and acquisitions of taxable property; (iii) pre-commencement loans to sponsoring employers; and (iv) the taxation of certain annuities for dependants purchased pre-commencement.

In order to understand the above provisions, it is helpful to have in mind the regime in place immediately prior to 6 April 2006, which is now summarised.[2]

3-002

**The position prior to A Day**

Prior to 6 April 2006, the regime applicable to pension schemes was one of tax-approval rather than registration.[3] Two separate categories of private pension scheme were capable of approval: (a) occupational pension schemes and (b) personal pension schemes.

3-003

*Occupational pension schemes*

Occupational pension schemes were approved in accordance with ICTA 1988 ss.590–612. There was no definition of "occupational pension scheme" as such. They were "retirement benefits schemes": schemes for the provision of benefits consisting of or including "relevant benefits".[4] Relevant benefits were "any pension, lump sum, gratuity or other like benefit given or to be given on retirement or on death, or by virtue of a pension sharing order or provision, or in anticipation of retirement, or, in connection with past service, after retirement or death, or to be given on or in anticipation of or in connection with any change in the nature of the service of the employee in question, except that it does not include any benefit which is to be afforded solely by reason of the disablement by accident of a person occurring during his service or of his death by accident so occurring and for no other reason".[5]

3-004

"Approval" merely exempted the scheme members from the charge to income tax under ITEPA 2003 s.386(1) on employer contributions to unapproved schemes.[6] In order to qualify for tax relief in respect of contributions (including a statutory right to a tax deduction in respect of employer contributions) and investment income etc.,[7] it was necessary for the scheme to be "exempt approved". There were two routes to exempt approved status: mandatory (or automatic) approval, or discretionary approval. To obtain mandatory approval the scheme was required to satisfy the requirements in ICTA 1988 s.590(2) and (3). If the scheme did not satisfy those requirements, HMRC had discretion under s.591(1) to grant exempt ap-

3-005

---

[2] For further information regarding the historical position, see S. Woodhouse, S. Eden and S. Lippiatt, *Taxation of Pension Schemes* (London: Sweet & Maxwell, 1996); Eden, BTR [1996] 46; Eden, BTR [2003] 185. For a discussion of the various policy issues see A.W. Dilnot and P. Johnson, *The Taxation of Private Pensions* (The Institute for Fiscal Studies, 1993). Also see HMRC's Pension Schemes Office Manual and Pensions Updates.

[3] Pension schemes were approved by the Pension Schemes Office of the Inland Revenue until 1 April 2001, and after that by IR Savings, Pension, Share Schemes. The Inland Revenue merged with Customs and Excise to form HMRC in April 2005.

[4] ICTA 1988 s.611(1).

[5] ICTA 1988 s.612(1).

[6] For the charge under ITEPA 2003 s.386(1), see Ch.38.

[7] Under ICTA 1988 s.592.

proved status to a retirement benefits scheme "having regard to the to the facts of a particular case, and subject to such conditions, if any, as they think proper to attach to the approval". In practice, HMRC would exercise their discretion if the scheme satisfied the requirements set out in the Occupational Pension Schemes Practice Notes on the Approval of Occupational Pension Schemes (usually referred to as "IR12").

**3-006** To obtain mandatory approval it was necessary to significantly limit the range of benefits that may be provided under the scheme (for example, the scheme could not provide a tax-free lump sum, or death in service benefits, or early retirement benefits), and so almost all occupational exempt approved schemes had discretionary approval. The requirements for discretionary approval, as set out in IR12, included the following, some of which are still occasionally referenced in scheme rules:

(a) Other than in exceptional circumstances, the scheme needed to be established under "irrevocable trusts".[8] This required the scheme assets to be set aside to provide relevant benefits for employees (unfunded schemes could not obtain discretionary approval), and to be held on trusts that did not permit the employer to access those assets except in relation to any surplus or in circumstances where reimbursement was considered to be appropriate.[9]

(b) A scheme set up under trust which was both self-administered and provided benefits on a money purchase basis was required to protect the trust from being extinguished by the action of one or more members. IR12 suggested that this should be achieved by expressing the individual member's rights to benefit as being against the funds of the trust as a whole, even though they may be calculated by reference to specific trust assets.[10]

(c) There must at all times have been a person or persons resident in the UK who was responsible for the discharge of all the duties of the administrator, and who was identifiable from the scheme documentation.[11]

(d) The scheme had to be bona fide established, and maintained, for the sole purpose of providing relevant benefits. HMRC considered that the sole purpose test may be breached if the scheme invests in property from which a member was able to derive a benefit, because such a benefit would not be a relevant benefit.[12]

(e) Benefits were generally required to come into payment immediately on leaving service after reaching normal retirement date (being age 50 to 75), and must commence by age 75, even if the member remained in service. The only benefits that could commence after age 75 were an immediate annuity (often referred to as a Hancock annuity). Benefits could be provided before age 55 only in cases of incapacity or where HMRC specifically agreed that the member's profession is such that earlier retirement is normal (for example professional athletes and certain hazardous occupations). Benefits could not commence prior to retirement, so those wishing to draw benefits whilst continuing to work would typically cease employment temporarily.

(f) Membership was limited to employees and former employees of participat-

---

[8] ICTA 1988 s.592(1)(a).
[9] IR12 (2001) para.2.3.
[10] IR12 (2001) para.2.9.
[11] IR12 (2001) paras 2.6 and 2.7.
[12] IR76 (2000) paras 11.8 and 11.9.

# INTRODUCTION

ing employers. There were restrictions on retaining membership whilst temporarily absent from employment or seconded to another employer.
(g) Controlling directors of investment companies were not permitted to be scheme members.
(h) Employers were required to contribute to the scheme. Such contributions had to be at least 10% of the total contributions for each employee, and in any event had to be more than "token contributions of insignificant amounts".[13]
(i) The scheme rules had to preclude contributions by members which did not qualify for tax relief.[14]
(j) Lump sum death benefits were generally only permitted on death in service and were limited to four times the member's final remuneration less retained benefits.

**Taxation** Employer contributions to exempt approved schemes were expressly not taxable as earnings of the employee or as a benefit in kind.[15] The employer would obtain a tax deduction in respect of ordinary annual contributions in the accounting period in which they were paid.[16] HMRC had discretion to require a tax deduction in respect of special contributions (i.e. contributions which were not ordinary annual contributions) to be spread over up to four accounting periods.[17] Tax relief in respect of employee contributions was available but limited to 15% of the employee's remuneration (as limited by the earnings cap, where applicable) in the year.[18] Employer contributions were not subject to the 15% cap, so this encouraged salary sacrifice arrangements.

3-007

Investment income and capital gains of the scheme were generally exempt from income tax and CGT.[19]

3-008

Pension benefits were subject to tax under ITEPA 2003 Pt 9. Part of the member's pension entitlement could be commuted to a tax-free lump sum. Benefits in respect of a member's additional voluntary contributions were generally required to be taken as pension income (without commutation) except in exceptional circumstances such as serious illness. It was generally permissible to refund a member's contributions where he left pensionable service after less than two years, subject to 20% tax.[20] Where a member's total benefits exceeded HMRC's limits any additional voluntary contributions would be refunded subject to income tax at 32% (for basic rate taxpayers).

3-009

HMRC had discretion to withdraw tax approval from a scheme. Doing so gave rise to a tax charge equal to 40% of the market value of scheme assets.[21]

3-010

**Surpluses** Restrictions were imposed on the extent to which the value of a

3-011

---

[13] IR12 (2001) para.5.1.
[14] IR12 (2001) para.4.4.
[15] ITEPA 2003 ss.307 and 308.
[16] ICTA 1988 s.592(4). In contrast to the post-A Day position, such contributions did not need to be made wholly and exclusively for the purposes of the employer's trade. Special rules applied to fully insured schemes (see Appendix VIII to IR12(2001)).
[17] ICTA 1988 s.592(6).
[18] ICTA 1988 s.592(7) and (8).
[19] ICTA 1988 s.592(2) and TCGA 1992 s.271(1)(g). The exemption did not apply to investment returns in respect of scheme assets exceeding 105% of the scheme's liabilities unless suitable proposals were being implemented to reduce the surplus.
[20] See ICTA 1988 s.598(2).
[21] ICTA 1988 ss.591B and 591C.

scheme's assets could exceed the value of its liabilities.[22] If a scheme's assets exceeded 105% of its liabilities the administrator was required to submit proposals to HMRC for reducing the surplus. The actuarial methods to be used for valuation purposes were prescribed and generally considered to be conservative, meaning that a surplus may well exceed 105% using normal funding assumptions. Subject to the scheme rules, a surplus could be reduced by: (a) augmenting benefits (or providing new benefits) under the scheme; (b) suspending or reducing contributions for a period of up to five years; and/or (c) making payments to the employer.[23] Payments of surplus to the employer were subject to 35% tax which could not be off-set against tax losses.[24]

3-012 **Limits on benefits** Although discretionary approval was less restrictive than mandatory approval, there were still limits imposed on the level of benefits that could be paid from exempt approved schemes. The limits were set by reference to the member's "normal retirement date" and his "final remuneration" (as those terms are defined in IR12). For members joining a scheme on or after 17 March 1987, final remuneration was subject to a cap, usually referred to as the "earnings cap" (but referred to in IR12 as the "permitted maximum"). The earnings cap was initially set at £60,000 when it was introduced, and increased in line with the retail prices index. Some schemes still provide benefits calculated by reference to final remuneration as limited by the earnings cap, so the administrators of such schemes will need to continue to calculate the earnings cap.[25]

3-013 These limits were revised in 1989, but only so as to affect new members joining the scheme after the date of revision. This led to the creation of three slightly different regimes applicable to occupational schemes.[26] For a member joining a scheme immediately before 6 April 2006, the maximum pension that could be paid to him at normal retirement date was generally 1/60th of final remuneration (capped by the earnings cap, if applicable) for each year of service up to a maximum of 40 years. The maximum lump sum was generally 3/80th of final remuneration (again capped by the earnings cap, if applicable) for each year of service up to a maximum of 40 years. Different limits applied where the benefits were taken earlier (whether as a result of incapacity or otherwise) or later than normal retirement date. Separate limits applied to death benefits.

*Personal pension schemes*

3-014 A "personal pension scheme" was a pension scheme the sole purpose of which was the provision of annuities and lump sums under arrangements made by individuals in accordance with the rules of the scheme.[27] The provisions relating to personal pension schemes were contained in ICTA 1988 Pt XIV Ch.IV ss.630–655.

3-015 **Taxation** Employer contributions to an employee's personal pension scheme were

---

[22] See ICTA 1988 ss.601–603 and Sch.22 and The Pension Scheme Surpluses (Valuation) Regulations 1987 (SI 1987/412).
[23] ICTA 1988 para.3(3).
[24] ICTA 1988 s.601.
[25] HMRC published a notional earnings cap each year until 2010/11 to assist such schemes. As the earnings cap only applied to exempt approved schemes, FURBS became popular as a secondary means of providing retirement benefits for high earners. FURBS are explained in Ch.38.
[26] Relating to membership commencing: (a) between 1970 and 16 March 1987; (b) between 17 March 1987 and 31 May 1989; and (c) after 31 May 1989.
[27] ICTA 1988 s.630.

# INTRODUCTION

expressly not taxable on the employee as earnings or as a benefit in kind.[28] Tax relief was available in respect of member contributions not exceeding £3,600 or (if higher) a specified percentage of his net relevant earnings.[29] It was possible for contributions to be carried back to the previous tax year in limited circumstances.[30] Investment income and capital gains of the scheme were exempt from income tax and CGT.[31] Benefits were typically provided via the purchase of an annuity, the income from which was taxable under ITEPA 2003 Pt 9. Tax-free lump sums were possible within limits.

*The different regimes*

In addition to the three regimes applicable to occupational schemes, and the regime applicable to personal pensions, there was a grandfathered regime applicable to retirement annuity contracts (established before 30 June 1988), and to certain "Old Code" (pre-1970) schemes, and also provisions relating to unapproved schemes (both funded and unfunded). Thus, prior to 6 April 2006, there were eight different tax regimes applicable to private pension schemes. The complexity created by the existence of the different regimes discouraged people from saving for retirement, added to the cost of administration and financial advice, and acted as a "serious obstacle to entry into the pensions business, thereby damaging competition that could help drive down prices and improve choice".[32]

3-016

**Proposals for reform** On 17 December 2002, three documents containing proposals for reform were released:

3-017

(a) a consultation document "*Simplifying the taxation of pensions: increasing choice and flexibility for all*" published by HM Treasury and the Inland Revenue;[33]
(b) a Green Paper "*Simplicity, security and choice: working and saving for retirement*" (Cm.5677) published by the DWP; and
(c) a document examining the detail of the Green Paper "*Simplicity, security and choice: technical paper*" published by the DWP.

The consultation document referred to the complexity of the eight different regimes and proposed "radical simplification of pensions taxation". The main proposals were summarised as follows:

3-018

"1.6    Unlike previous changes to the taxation of pensions, this reform proposes a clean break. Pension rights built up before the reform is implemented will be respected. All pension saving after implementation will follow a single set of rules which will apply to saving in all kinds of pension schemes. And there will be a single set of simple rules about how pension savings are turned into benefits.

1.7    In the new system the current limits on annual pension contributions and benefits will be replaced by a single lifetime limit on the amount of pension saving that can attract favourable tax treatment. So people will be able to choose when and how much to save in order to achieve the retirement income they want. The

---

[28] ITEPA 2003 ss.307 and 308.
[29] ICTA 1988 ss.630(1) and 640(1) and (2). The specified percentage increased with the age of the member.
[30] ICTA 1988 s.641A.
[31] ICTA 1988 s.643(2).
[32] *Simplifying the taxation of pensions: increasing choice and flexibility for all* (HM Treasury and Inland Revenue, December 2002) para.2.7.
[33] Also see the subsequent consultation document, *Simplifying the taxation of pensions: the Government's proposals* (10 December 2003).

Government intends to set this limit at £1.4 million per person for introduction in 2004 and indexed thereafter. Tax relief at the contributor's marginal rate will continue to be available.

1.8 This lifetime limit will be complemented by a light touch compliance regime with an annual limit on inflows of value to an individual's pension fund—both contributions and growth in pension rights in occupational schemes. The proposed level for introduction in 2004 is £200,000, which will also be indexed thereafter.

1.9 There will also be a single, consistent set of rules about delivery of pension benefits, whether they come from a scheme sponsored by an employer or a private scheme. The maximum tax-free lump sum will be set at 25 per cent of the value of matured pension savings—appreciably more generous than now for many.

1.10 The proposals also drop the outmoded rule preventing people in occupational schemes from mixing work and retirement. Where scheme rules allow it, people will be able to begin to draw benefits from their pension while continuing to work, perhaps with reduced hours or responsibilities. Flexible retirement in this sense is intended to encourage those who can to work longer—allowing the economy to benefit from the skills and experience of older workers and encouraging them to save more to boost their retirement income."

**3-019** The intended advantages of simplification were described thus:

"1.13 The proposed new tax rules for pensions will impose little real constraint on pension savers and pension schemes. For the vast majority of people, the tax system will simply cease to be a consideration when planning for retirement. Instead they will be free to concentrate on the real issues—deciding when and how much to save. This approach will afford scope for substantial innovation in design of pension schemes. Radical simplification should also generate significant savings in administration costs, feeding through to better value for pension savers with real opportunities for financial services firms to streamline their operations.

(i) These proposals for radical simplification will transform the tax rules for pensions. By cutting administration costs and stripping out unnecessary controls, they will give everyone using pensions choice and flexibility."

**3-020** These proposals were ultimately implemented in FA 2004 Pt 4, with effect from 6 April 2006 (commonly referred to as "A Day": an abbreviation of the Appointed Day).

## PRE-COMMENCEMENT PENSION SCHEMES

### Deemed registration of existing schemes

**3-021** The following categories of pension schemes automatically became registered pension schemes on 6 April 2006 (unless they opted out):[34]

(a) Retirement benefit schemes approved under ICTA 1988 Pt 14 Ch.1 (i.e. occupational schemes, including free-standing AVC schemes).

(b) Former approved superannuation funds (usually referred to as "old code" schemes).[35]

---

[34] See FA 2004 Sch.36 Pt 1.
[35] Any fund which immediately before 6 April 1980 was an approved superannuation fund for the purposes of ICTA 1970 s.208 is a former approved superannuation fund unless since 5 April 1980 the fund has been approved for the purposes of ICTA 1988 Pt 14 Ch.1, or any sum has been paid under the fund by way of contribution: FA 2004 Sch.36 para.1(3).

(c) "Relevant statutory schemes"[36] (i.e. public sector schemes) or a pension scheme treated by the Inland Revenue on 6 April 2006 as if it were such a scheme.
(d) Deferred annuity contracts by means of which benefits provided under a pension scheme within paras (a), (b) or (c) have been secured.
(e) Parliamentary pension schemes or funds within ICTA 1988 s.613(4)(b)–(d).
(f) Retirement annuity contracts or trust schemes approved under ICTA 1988 ss.620 or 621, or a substituted contract within the meaning of ICTA 1988 s.622(3). Prior to the introduction of personal pension schemes from 1 July 1988, such contracts or schemes were the only type of approved scheme open to self-employed persons.
(g) Personal pension schemes approved under ICTA 1988 Pt 14 Ch.4 (which includes most stakeholder pension schemes and group personal pension schemes).

**Identifying the scheme administrator**

The first scheme administrator of a scheme that automatically became a registered pension scheme on 6 April 2006 is determined in accordance with FA 2004 Sch.36 para.4:

3-022

| Type of scheme | Scheme administrator on 6 April 2006 |
| --- | --- |
| Approved retirement benefits schemes, former approved superannuation funds, and relevant statutory schemes | The administrator(s) of the scheme under ICTA 1988 s.611AA |
| Parliamentary pension scheme or fund | The trustees |
| Approved personal pension schemes | The administrator of the scheme under ICTA 1988 s.638(1) |
| Deferred annuity contracts, or annuity contract/trust schemes approved under ICTA 1988 ss.620 or 621 (or substituted contracts) | The trustees or insurance company that is a party to the annuity contract |

Such schemes can appoint a new scheme administrator after 6 April 2006 in the same way that any other registered pension scheme can do.

3-023

# THE LIFETIME ALLOWANCE

Protection against the lifetime allowance charge (in the form of primary protection and enhanced protection) was introduced so that members with high value funds were not prejudiced. The lifetime allowance has been removed with effect from 6 April 2024, but the amount that can be paid as one of the tax-efficient lump sums (e.g. PCLS and UFPLS) is impacted where the member has primary and enhanced protection, so these provisions continue to be relevant.[37]

3-024

---

[36] As defined in ICTA 1988 s.611A.
[37] See Ch.14.

**Enhanced protection**

3-025   If an individual is entitled to enhanced protection he could not become liable to the lifetime allowance charge.[38] An individual is entitled to enhanced protection if all of the following apply:[39]

(a) He was a member of a pre-A Day tax approved pension scheme.
(b) He notified HMRC, prior to 6 April 2009,[40] of his intention to rely on Sch.36 para.12. If the total value of his uncrystallised rights on 5 April 2006 was "excessive", he was unable to give such notice unless the excess was surrendered.[41]
(c) If notice to HMRC is given on or after 15 March 2023,[42] any of the following "protection-cessation events" occur on or after 6 April 2006:[43]
  (i) relevant benefit accrual occurs under an arrangement;
  (ii) there is an impermissible transfer into an arrangement;
  (iii) a transfer of sums or assets held for the purposes of an arrangement is made that is not a permitted transfer; or
  (iv) an arrangement relating to the individual is made under a registered pension scheme otherwise than in permitted circumstances.

---

[38] Prior to 6 April 2011 the annual allowance provisions did not apply to individuals with enhanced protection (FA 2004 Sch.36 para.49).

[39] FA 2004 Sch.36 para.12(1) and (2).

[40] The Registered Pension Schemes (Enhanced Allowances) Regulations 2006 (SI 2006/131) reg.4. Late notifications must be considered by HMRC if the individual had a reasonable excuse for not giving the notification before 6 April 2009 and gives the notification without unreasonable delay after the reasonable excuse ceased (SI 2006/131 reg.12). If HMRC refuse to allow the notification, the individual may appeal to the FTT. The question to be answered is: was it reasonable for a responsible person with the same experience and other attributes of the taxpayer and placed in the same situation as the taxpayer to have made a late notification (*Perrin v HMRC* [2014] UKFTT 488 (TC) at [99] and [100], approved in *Twaite v HMRC* [2017] UKFTT 591 at [26] and [27] and *Radley and Gibbs v HMRC* [2016] UKFTT 688 at [51]). Each case will turn on its facts. A number of decisions relating to late notifications for enhanced and primary protection (which has the same *reasonable excuse* threshold) have been released by the FTT. Ignorance of the law may be a reasonable excuse but the FTT has found that, having regard to the information available to the member at the time, ignorance was not reasonable in the circumstances (*Scurfield v HMRC* [2011] UKFTT 532; *Platt v RCC* [2011] UKFTT 606). Relying on a financial adviser to notify HMRC in time has been found to be a reasonable excuse (*Irby v HMRC* [2012] UKFTT 291; *Jackson v HMRC* [2017] UKFTT 341; *Tipping v HMRC* [2017] UKFTT 485; cf. *Yablon v HMRC* [2016] UKFTT 814 and *Radley and Gibbs v HMRC* [2016] UKFTT 688).

[41] The total value of his uncrystallised rights on 5 April 2006 was excessive if it exceeded the maximum permitted pension (see FA 2004 Sch.36 para.9(4) and (5)) for the relevant employment multiplied by 20 (FA 2004 Sch.36 para.12(6)). Uncrystallised rights were valued in accordance with FA 2004 s.212, as modified by Sch.36 para.8 (which provides a different method of valuation for cash balance, other money purchase, defined benefits and hybrid arrangements). The excess must have been surrendered in accordance with The Registered Pension Schemes (Surrender of Relevant Excess) Regulations 2006 (SI 2006/211) (FA 2004 Sch.36 para.12(5)).

[42] The 15 March 2023 restriction was added by F(No.2)A 2023. As a result, the protection-cessation events will rarely have any application to enhanced protection. HMRC's pensions schemes newsletter 148 (March 2023) confirms that: "Members who hold a valid enhanced protection or any valid fixed protections, where this protection was applied for before 15 March 2023, and a certificate or reference number subsequently issued, from 6 April 2023 will be able to accrue new pension benefits, join new arrangements or transfer without losing this protection. They will also keep their entitlement to a higher PCLS."

[43] FA 2004 Sch.36 para.12(2). It is also possible to renounce enhanced protection by notifying HMRC in writing.

# THE LIFETIME ALLOWANCE 63

*Relevant benefit accrual*

**Other money purchase arrangements** Relevant benefit accrual occurs under another money purchase arrangement if a "relevant contribution" is paid under the arrangement.[44] This is the case if:[45]  3-026

(a) A "relievable pension contribution" is paid by or on behalf of the individual under the arrangement. A relievable pension contribution is a contribution by or on behalf of an individual under the pension scheme other than: (i) any contributions paid after the individual has reached the age of 75; (ii) any contributions which are life assurance premium contributions; (iii) any contributions paid by an employer of the individual; and (iv) any contributions made pursuant to an order under certain provisions in PA 2004.[46]

(b) A contribution is paid in respect of the individual under the arrangement by an employer of the individual.

(c) A contribution paid otherwise than by or on behalf of the individual or by an employer of the individual in respect of the individual subsequently becomes held under the arrangement for the purposes of the provision of benefits to or in respect of the individual. A contribution by the individual's employer that is initially unallocated (or allocated to a general fund) and subsequently becomes allocated for the individual does not appear to be a relevant contribution, but the allocation may involve an impermissible transfer into the arrangement.

Contributions are not relevant contributions if they are contributions under a registered pension scheme that must be applied to pay premiums under pre-6 April 2006 life policies,[47] or contributions paid by a sponsoring employer under a relevant hybrid arrangement[48] solely in respect of the provision of lump sum death benefits which are defined benefits or cash balance benefits.[49]  3-027

**Cash balance and defined benefits arrangements** Relevant benefit accrual occurs under a cash balance or defined benefits arrangements if both:[50]  3-028

(a) A "relevant event" occurs in relation to the individual and the arrangement, or any "related" cash balance arrangement or defined benefits arrangement. An arrangement is "related" to another arrangement if they both relate to the same individual and the same employment. An arrangement relates to an employment if the earnings by reference to which benefits under the arrangement are calculated are earnings from the employment, or the person who is the employer in relation to the employment pays contributions under the arrangement in respect of the individual.[51] A relevant event occurs on the occurrence of: (i) the individual becoming entitled to any pen-

---

[44] A relevant contribution under a hybrid arrangement that may provide other money purchase benefits is not relevant benefit accrual, but relevant benefit accrual will occur immediately the arrangement becomes another money purchase arrangement.

[45] FA 2004 Sch.36 para.14(1).

[46] See FA 2004 ss.188(2), (3) and (3A).

[47] Subject to satisfaction of the requirements in FA 2004 Sch.36 para.14(3)–(3D).

[48] A relevant hybrid arrangement is a hybrid arrangement under an occupational pension scheme which subsequently becomes another money purchase arrangement and under which lump sum death benefits would have been payable in respect of the individual if the individual had died on 5 April 2006.

[49] FA 2004 Sch.36 para.14(4).

[50] FA 2004 Sch.36 para.13(b).

[51] FA 2004 Sch.36 para.9(6).

sion or lump sum; or (ii) a permitted transfer to another money purchase arrangement.[52]

(b) The "relevant crystallised amount" exceeds the "appropriate limit".

**3-029** The "relevant crystallised amount" is determined as follows:[53]

(a) If the relevant event is the individual becoming entitled to a pension or lump sum under the arrangement (or any "related" cash balance arrangement or defined benefits arrangement), the relevant crystallised amount is the amount crystallised by that event.[54] If the event is not the first relevant event, the relevant crystallised amount is the total amount crystallised by the relevant event and all previous relevant events occurring in relation to the individual and to the arrangement (or any related cash balance arrangement or defined benefits arrangement). There is no uprating in line with any increase in the standard lifetime allowance to take account of the earlier event(s).

(b) If the relevant event is a permitted transfer occurring in relation to the individual and to the arrangement (or any related cash balance arrangement or defined benefits arrangement), the relevant crystallised amount is the amount of the sums and the market value of the assets transferred. If it is not the first relevant event, the relevant crystallised amount is the total of the amount crystallised by the relevant event and all previous relevant events occurring in relation to the individual and to the arrangement (or any related cash balance arrangement or defined benefits arrangement). Again, there is no uprating in line with any increase in the standard lifetime allowance to take account of the earlier transfer(s). However if the relevant event is a recognised transfer of sums or assets representing crystallised rights under a scheme pension made in connection with the winding-up of the pension scheme, the relevant crystallised amount is nil.[55]

**3-030** The appropriate limit, in relation to a relevant event, is the greater of: (a) the "indexed amount"; and (b) the "earnings recalculation amount".[56] To find the "indexed amount", one starts by finding the total value of the individual's rights on 5 April 2006 under the arrangement (and any related cash balance arrangements or defined benefits arrangements) in the same way that one values the individual's uncrystallised rights for the purposes of primary protection (see below). The indexed amount is that value, increased by the greatest of:

(a) an annualised increase of 5% from 5 April 2006 until the date of the relevant event;

(b) the percentage by which an amount would be increased if it were increased for that period at an annual percentage rate referred to in The Registered Pension Schemes (Uprating Percentages for Defined Benefits Arrangements and Enhanced Protection Limits) Regulations 2006 (SI 2006/130); and

---

[52] i.e. a transfer of funds so as to become held for the purposes of another money purchase arrangement under a registered pension scheme or ROPS, and the value of the funds is equivalent before and after the transfer. A transfer to a QROPS (which is BCE 8) would constitute both types of relevant event.

[53] FA 2004 Sch.36 para.15.

[54] See Ch.10.

[55] SI 2006/572 art.36.

[56] FA 2004 Sch.36 para.15(4).

(c) the percentage by which the RPI for the month in which the relevant event occurs is higher than that for April 2006.

3-031  To find the "earnings recalculation amount", one values the individual's rights on 5 April 2006 under the arrangement (and any related cash balance arrangements or defined benefits arrangements) in the same way one values the individual's uncrystallised rights for the purposes of primary protection (see below), but making the following assumptions:

(a) the individual's age on 5 April 2006 was what it is at the time of the first relevant event; and
(b) the amount of the earnings which would have been taken into account under the arrangement when calculating the amount of benefits payable to or in respect of the individual (if the individual became entitled to the present payment of benefits in respect of the rights under the arrangement on that date) were the lesser of:
  (i) the current amount of the "relevant pensionable earnings" immediately before the first relevant event; and
  (ii) the post-commencement earnings limit.

3-032  The "relevant pensionable earnings" means the description of earnings (or the portion of the description of earnings) of the individual by reference to which the amount of benefits payable to or in respect of the individual would have been calculated if the individual had become entitled to the present payment of benefits on 5 April 2006. The "current amount" of the relevant pensionable earnings immediately before the first relevant event is the amount of the relevant pensionable earnings which, at that time, would have been taken into account in calculating the amount of benefits payable to or in respect of the individual if he had become entitled to the present payment of benefits at that time. If at that time the individual was absent from work in connection with pregnancy, maternity, paternity or adoption, the current amount of the relevant pensionable earnings at that time includes what would be likely to be included in that amount if the individual were not so absent.

3-033  The "post-commencement earnings limit" is determined in accordance with paras 16 and 17 of Sch.36. This involves revaluing pension rights using pensionable earnings at the time of the first relevant event, but putting restrictions on salary growth. Paragraph 16 applies where the individual was subject to the earnings cap before 6 April 2006 and para.17 applies where the member was not subject to the earnings cap. Under para.16, pensionable earnings must be restricted to the highest 12 months earnings in the three years before taking benefits or 7.5% of the lifetime allowance, if lower. Under para.17, pensionable salary must be restricted to the best 12 months' earnings in the three years before first taking benefits if that is less than 7.5% of the lifetime allowance, or his average salary over the three years before he first takes benefits if this is more than 7.5% of the lifetime allowance.

3-034  **Lump sum death benefits** If, on the death of an individual who has enhanced protection, a defined benefits LSDB or an uncrystallised funds LSDB is paid, and the lump sum exceeds the "appropriate limit" (calculated as per the above provisions) then the appropriate limit can be increased under Sch.36 para.15A. In these circumstances, the appropriate limit is increased to the greater of: (a) the value of the individual's pre-commencement rights to death benefits as increased by the relevant indexation percentage; or (b) what would be the value of the individual's pre-commencement rights to death benefits. The value of the individual's pre-commencement rights to death benefits is the aggregate of the maximum amounts that could have been paid in respect of the individual as uncrystallised rights lump sum death benefits under the arrangement or any other related cash balance arrangement or defined benefits arrangement, if the individual had died on 5 April 2006. If para.15A applies, the recipient of the lump sum must also notify HMRC under The Registered Pension Schemes (Enhanced Allowances) Regulations 2006 (SI 2006/131) reg.4A before the later of: (a) five years after the 31 January following the tax year in which the lump sum was paid; and (b) 5 April in the tax year following the tax year in which an assessment is made under ITEPA 2003 s.579C on the recipient.

*Impermissible transfers*

3-035 **Other money purchase arrangements** There is an impermissible transfer into another money purchase arrangement if:[57] (a) sums or assets held for the purposes of an arrangement relating otherwise than to the individual are transferred so as to become held for the purposes of the arrangement relating to the individual (except where the transfer is pursuant to a pension sharing order); or (b) sums or assets which are neither held for the purposes of, nor represent rights under, a pension scheme are so transferred. In each case the sums or assets must be "transferred", which strongly suggests that a reallocation of funds within a pension scheme does not involve an impermissible transfer.[58] The reference in (a) above to an arrangement "relating otherwise than to the individual" suggests that the other arrangement must relate to a different member, because the term "arrangement" in FA 2004 Pt 4 generally means an arrangement relating to a member under a pension scheme.[59] Here there is no reference to the other arrangement "relating to a member" so it may be that "arrangement" is being used in a more general sense. However, it cannot be the case that *every* transfer of sums or assets that become held for the purposes of an arrangement relating to the individual is an impermissible transfer because that would, on the face of it, include investment income received by the scheme relating to the arrangement.

3-036 If the arrangement has been a hybrid arrangement, the above applies as if the references to sums or assets being transferred were to transfer or payment at any time after 5 April 2006.

3-037 **Cash balance and defined benefits arrangements** If the arrangement is a cash balance arrangement or a defined benefits arrangement, there is an impermissible transfer into the arrangement if the arrangement becomes another money purchase arrangement.

*Transfers that are not permitted transfers*

3-038 A transfer of sums or assets held for the purposes of an arrangement is a permitted transfer if they are transferred in one of the following circumstances and the total value of the sums and assets is equivalent before and after the transfer:

(a) they are transferred so as to become held for the purposes of another money purchase arrangement under a registered pension scheme or ROPS;
(b) if the arrangement is a cash balance arrangement or a defined benefits arrangement, the sums and assets are transferred so as to become held for the

---

[57] FA 2004 Sch.36 para.17A.
[58] cf. FA 2004 ss.172C and 233(3), neither of which uses the word "transfer".
[59] See FA 2004 s.152(1).

purposes of a cash balance arrangement or defined benefits arrangement under a registered pension scheme or ROPS:
- (i) in connection with the winding up of the pension scheme[60] and the transferring and receiving arrangements relate to the same employment;
- (ii) in connection with a relevant business transfer;[61]
- (iii) as part of a retirement-benefit activities compliance exercise[62] and the transferring and receiving arrangements relate to the same employment;

(c) there is a transfer of funds which have been applied towards the provision of a scheme pension to an insurance company in connection with the winding up of the transferring pension scheme.[63]

Accordingly, the following are not permitted transfers:  3-039

(a) a transfer from another money purchase arrangement to a defined benefits arrangement or cash balance arrangement;
(b) a transfer from a cash balance arrangement or defined benefits arrangement to a cash balance arrangement or defined benefits arrangements where the transfer is not made in connection with one of the winding up of the transferring scheme, a relevant business transfer or a retirement-benefit activities compliance exercise; and
(c) a transfer from a cash balance arrangement or defined benefits arrangement to a cash balance arrangement or defined benefits arrangement relating to a different employment to the transferring arrangement (except where there has been a relevant business transfer).

If there is a permitted transfer, enhanced protection continues to apply to the receiving arrangement.  3-040

*Arrangements made otherwise than in permitted circumstances*

An arrangement relating to the individual is made in permitted circumstances if it is made:[64] (a) for the purposes of a permitted transfer (see above); or (b) as part of a retirement-benefit activities compliance exercise;[65] or (c) as part of an age-equality compliance exercise.[66] The provisions do not explain precisely when an arrangement is "made", but it seems likely that it is the time at which an arrangement relating to the individual comes into existence. An arrangement is essentially an agreement under the scheme as to how the benefits which will ultimately be paid  3-041

---

[60] See PTM092420 for the circumstances in which HMRC will accept that this requirement is met.
[61] A relevant business transfer is a transfer of an undertaking or a business (or part of an undertaking or a business) from one person to another: (a) which involves the transfer of at least 20 employees; and (b) in the case of which, if the transferor and the transferee are bodies corporate, they would not be treated as members of the same group for the purposes of CTA 2010 Pt 5.
[62] Sums or assets are transferred as part of a retirement-benefit activities compliance exercise if there is a prospective entitlement to authorised death benefits (i.e. pension death benefits within s.167(1) or lump sum death benefits within s.168(1) (or both)) under both the old arrangement and the new arrangement, and the transfer constitutes or forms part of a transaction the purpose of which is to secure that the activities of the pension scheme under which the old arrangement was made are limited to retirement-benefit activities within the meaning of PA 2004 s.255.
[63] SI 2006/572 art.35. Such a transfer is a recognised transfer pursuant to FA 2004 s.169(1A).
[64] FA 2004 Sch.36 para.12(2A).
[65] See FA 2004 Sch.36 para.12(2B).
[66] See FA 2004 Sch.36 para.12(2C).

to or in respect of the member are to be calculated.[67] It seems likely that an arrangement is "made" when the individual joins the scheme, even though he may not become a member until later.[68] If the individual is already a member of the scheme then making a new arrangement must involve a new agreement relating to the calculation of benefits under the scheme to or in respect of that member. HMRC accept[69] that a scheme may increase the rate of benefits provided or even offer new and additional benefits under an arrangement without having to provide it by means of a new arrangement. HMRC also accept[70] that a "reshaping" of existing arrangements either by way of merging multiple arrangements or internal "transfers" of funds between multiple arrangements in the same scheme will not involve the setting up of a new arrangement.

3-042 **Auto-enrolment** HMRC accept that if an employee is automatically enrolled[71] and opts out within the first month period then enhanced protection will not cease because the law treats them as if they were never a member of the pension scheme.[72]

*Consequences of cessation*

3-043 The individual must notify HMRC within 90 days of a cessation event. Where the cessation event is relevant benefit accrual, failure to do so may result in a penalty of £3,000.[73] The loss of enhanced protection will only affect payments occurring after that date, however the amount crystallised prior to cessation will reduce the individual's available LS allowance and LS&DB allowance after that date.

**Lifetime allowance enhancement factors**

3-044 Prior to 6 April 2024, a lifetime allowance enhancement factor applied in the following circumstances. Since that date, the following are LS&DB enhancement factors:[74]

(a) the member is entitled to primary protection (see below);
(b) the member acquires a pension credit on or after 6 April 2006 in relation to rights under another registered pension scheme which consisted of or included rights to a pension already in payment and which came into payment on or after 6 April 2006;
(c) a pension credit was acquired before 6 April 2006 (see below);
(d) certain benefits accrue under a registered pension scheme during a period in which the member is a relevant overseas individual; or

---

[67] For the meaning of "arrangement", see Ch.2.
[68] For the circumstances in which an individual becomes a member, see Ch.2.
[69] PTM092420.
[70] PTM063700.
[71] With effect from 1 April 2015, The Occupational and Personal Pension Schemes (Automatic Enrolment) Regulations 2010 (SI 2010/772) apply so that an employer with reasonable grounds to believe that a jobholder has enhanced protection, FP 2012 or FP 2014, is not required to automatically enrol or re-enrol that jobholder.
[72] HMRC accept (at PTM092420) that the same applies where an employer automatically enrols an employee and this is not under the PA 2008 provisions. Such employees will not lose protection if the scheme has a legally binding rule that treats an individual who opts out of scheme membership as never having been a member of the scheme, or if the individual has cancelled the pension contract under the FCA cancellation rules with the result that the contract is treated as void from the start.
[73] FA 2004 s.263. For a case in which a taxpayer claimed to have notified to HMRC of his intention to rely on FP 2012, but not in the prescribed form, see *Townley v HMRC* [2018] UKFTT 624 (TC).
[74] See Ch.14

# THE LIFETIME ALLOWANCE

(e) benefits accrue in a ROPS and are subsequently transferred to a registered pension scheme.

In each case, the member must claim the lifetime allowance (now LS&DB) enhancement factor by notifying HMRC, and HMRC will provide the individual with a certificate confirming his entitlement. **3-045**

Where a lifetime allowance enhancement factor operated (prior to 6 April 2024) in relation to a BCE the individual's lifetime allowance at the time of the BCE was equal to "SLA + (SLA x LAEF)" where: **3-046**

- *SLA* was the standard lifetime allowance at the time of the BCE (except in the case of the primary protection lifetime allowance enhancement factor, where SLA was £1.8 million if that was greater than the standard lifetime allowance at the time of the BCE); and
- *LAEF* was the lifetime allowance enhancement factor which operated with respect to the BCE and the individual or (where more than one so operated) the aggregate of them. The lifetime allowance enhancement factor was determined in accordance with the provisions described below.

Other than in relation to primary protection, if the BCE occurred before 6 April 2012, SLA was £1.8 million if that was greater than the standard lifetime allowance at the time. If the event occurred between 6 April 2012 and 5 April 2014, SLA was £1.5 million if that was greater than the standard lifetime allowance at the time. If the event occurred between 5 April 2014 and 6 April 2016, SLA was £1.25 million if that was greater than the standard lifetime allowance at the time. **3-047**

## Primary protection

If the value of an individual's pension rights (whether crystallised or uncrystallised) exceeded £1.5 million on 6 April 2006 the primary protection factor operates in relation to all BCEs occurring in relation to that individual provided that notice was given to HMRC prior to 6 April 2009.[75] In contrast to enhanced protection and fixed protection, the accrual of benefits on and after 6 April 2006 does not prejudice primary protection. **3-048**

### *The primary protection factor*

The primary protection factor is "(RR-£1.5 million)/£1.5 million" where *RR* is the value of the relevant pre-commencement pension rights of the individual.[76] **3-049**

For example, if the member had rights valued at £2 million on 6 April 2006, his primary protection factor is (£2 million − £1.5 million)/£1.5 million = 0.33. His lifetime allowance is therefore a third higher than £1.5 million (or a third higher than the standard lifetime allowance if that becomes greater than £1.5 million). In relation to BCEs that occur after 6 April 2012 (when the standard lifetime allowance was reduced from £1.8 million to £1.5 million), SLA is deemed to be £1.8 million if that is greater than the standard lifetime allowance at the time of the event.[77] **3-050**

---

[75] FA 2004 Sch.36 para.7. Late notifications must be considered by HMRC if the individual had a reasonable excuse for not giving the notification before 6 April 2009 and gives the notification without unreasonable delay after the reasonable excuse ceased (SI 2006/131 reg.12). If HMRC refuse to allow the notification, the individual may appeal to the FTT (the circumstances are the same as for enhanced protection: see fn.4).

[76] FA 2004 Sch.36 para.7(3).

[77] FA 2004 s.218(5B).

Therefore, since 6 April 2012, the individual's lifetime allowance is £1.8 million + (£1.8 million x 0.33) = £2,394,000.

*Relevant pre-commencement pension rights*

3-051  The amount of the relevant pre-commencement pension rights of the individual is the aggregate of:[78]

(a) the value of the individual relevant uncrystallised pension rights on 5 April 2006; and
(b) the value of the individual relevant crystallised pension rights on that date.

*Valuing uncrystallised pension rights*

3-052  The individual's rights are uncrystallised if he had not, on 5 April 2006, become entitled to the present payment of benefits in respect of the rights. The value of the individual's relevant uncrystallised pension rights on 5 April 2006 is the total value of his uncrystallised rights on that date under each relevant pension arrangement relating to the individual.[79] A relevant pension arrangement means an arrangement under a pension scheme which automatically became a registered pension scheme on 6 April 2006.[80]

3-053  The method of valuing such uncrystallised rights depends on the type of arrangement.[81] The value of the member's uncrystallised rights under a cash balance arrangement on 5 April 2006 is the amount which would, on the valuation assumptions,[82] be available for the provision of benefits in respect of those rights if the member became entitled the present payment of benefits in respect of the rights on that date. The value of the member's uncrystallised rights under another money purchase arrangement on 5 April 2006 is the total value of the cash and assets held for the purposes of the arrangement on that date as represent those rights. The value of the member's uncrystallised rights under a defined benefits arrangement on 5 April 2006 is equal to "($20^{83}$ x ARP) + LS" where:

- *ARP* is the annual rate of pension to which the member would, on the valuation assumptions, be entitled under the arrangement on 5 April 2006 if, on that date, the member acquired an actual (rather than a prospective) right to receive a pension in respect of the rights; and
- *LS* is the amount of any lump sum to which the member would, on the valuation assumptions, be entitled under the arrangement on 5 April 2006 (otherwise than by way of commutation of pension) if, on that date, the member acquired an actual (rather than a prospective) right to payment of a lump sum in respect of the rights.

3-054  If the arrangement is a hybrid arrangement, the value of the member's uncrystallised rights under the arrangement on the date is the greater of whichever of the above may be applicable.

---

[78] FA 2004 Sch.36 para.7(5).
[79] FA 2004 Sch.36 para.8(1).
[80] These are listed in FA 2004 Sch.36 para.1(1).
[81] See FA 2004 Sch.36 para.8, applying and modifying FA 2004 s.212.
[82] The valuation assumptions require one to value the individual's rights on the assumption that the individual is at the age at which no reduction would apply to the payment of an immediate benefit (e.g. as a result of early retirement), and the individual is in good physical and mental health and so the benefits are not increased as a result of being paid on grounds of ill-health (FA 2004 s.277).
[83] Or such higher valuation factor agreed between HMRC and the scheme administrator under FA 2004 s.276.

THE LIFETIME ALLOWANCE

However, the value of the individual's uncrystallised rights on 5 April 2006 under one of the schemes referred to in FA 2004 Sch.36 para.1(1)(a)–(d)[84] is determined as follows, but only if this produces a lower valuation than the above provisions.[85] The value of the individual's uncrystallised rights on 5 April 2006 that relate to a particular employment[86] is equal to "20 x MPP" where *MPP* is the *maximum permitted pension*, increased as specified below (if applicable). The maximum permitted pension means:[87]

3-055

(a) in the case of an arrangement under a pension scheme which immediately before 6 April 2006 was a relevant statutory scheme, the maximum annual pension that could be paid to the individual under the pension scheme on 5 April 2006. For this purpose, the valuation assumptions are applied;[88] and

(b) in any other case, the maximum annual pension that could be paid to the individual on 5 April 2006 under the arrangement(s) if it was made under a tax-approved retirement benefits scheme without giving HMRC grounds for withdrawing approval of the pension scheme. If the individual had not reached the lowest age at which a pension may be paid under a tax-approved retirement benefits scheme to a person in good health without giving HMRC grounds for withdrawing the approval of the pension scheme, it is assumed that that fact would not give HMRC such grounds.

In either case, it is assumed that if the individual was in the employment to which the arrangement(s) relate on 5 April 2006, the individual left the employment on that date.

3-056

Where, in the case of an arrangement under a relevant statutory scheme, a lump sum could be paid to the individual on 5 April 2006 under the pension scheme otherwise than by commutation of pension, and that lump sum could not be exchanged (in whole or in part) for an increased pension, the maximum permitted pension is the total of what it otherwise would be and so much of the amount of the lump sum as could not be so exchanged.

3-057

*Valuing crystallised pension rights*

The value of the individual's relevant crystallised pension rights on 5 April 2006 is "25 x ARP"[89] where ARP is the total annual rate at which all relevant existing pensions are payable to the individual on 5 April 2006.[90] *Relevant existing pension* means a pension under a pension scheme which automatically became a

3-058

---

[84] The types of scheme are: (a) a tax-approved retirement benefits scheme; (b) a former approved superannuation fund; (c) a relevant statutory scheme (including a pension scheme treated by the Inland Revenue on that date as if it were such a scheme); or (d) an annuity contract by means of which benefits provided under a pension scheme within (a), (b) or (c) have been secured but which does not provide for the immediate payment of benefits.

[85] FA 2004 Sch.36 para.9.

[86] An arrangement relates to an employment if the earnings by reference to which benefits under the arrangement are calculated are earnings from the employment, or the person who is the employer in relation to the employment pays contributions under the arrangement in respect of the individual.

[87] FA 2004 Sch.36 para.9(4) and (5).

[88] The valuation assumptions require one to value the individual's rights on the assumption that the individual is at the age at which no reduction would apply to the payment of an immediate benefit, and the individual is in good physical and mental health at the time so the benefits would not be discounted under the scheme rules as a result of being paid as a result of ill-health (FA 2004 s.277).

[89] Crystallised rights are valued at 25 x ARP (instead of 20 x ARP for uncrystallised rights) to take account of the fact that when the rights crystallised it is likely that a lump sum will have been paid.

[90] FA 2004 Sch.36 para.10(1).

registered pension scheme on 6 April 2006.[91] However, a pension, annuity or right is not a relevant existing pension if entitlement to it is attributable to the death of any person.

**3-059** In the case of income drawdown, the annual rate at which the pension is payable on 5 April 2006 is the amount which, on that date, is the maximum annual amount that could have been drawn down by the individual as income in accordance with the pension scheme or contract concerned. In the case of a right to make income withdrawals under ICTA 1988 s.634A, the annual rate at which the pension is payable on 5 April 2006 is the maximum amount of income withdrawals that could have been made by the individual in the period of 12 months referred to in ICTA 1988 s.634A(4) during which 5 April 2006 falls.

*Increasing the primary protection factor*

**3-060** The primary protection factor of another money purchase arrangement (or hybrid arrangement that may pay other money purchase benefits) can be increased if the arrangement receives compensation in the period between 6 April 2006 and 5 April 2009 in respect of the poor performance of an investment owned before 6 April 2006.[92]

*Reducing the primary protection factor*

**3-061** If an individual has primary protection and after 5 April 2006 his rights under a relevant pension arrangement[93] are reduced by becoming subject to a pension debit, the primary protection factor is recalculated.[94] The recalculation involves reducing "RR" (see above) by the amount by which the individual's rights are reduced. This revised primary protection factor operates in relation to any BCE occurring after the pension debit.[95] A member must notify HMRC if he becomes subject to a pension debit and HMRC will issue a new certificate (unless primary protection ceases to apply altogether). Primary protection will cease to apply if RR becomes less than £1.5 million as a result of the debit.

*Protection for lump sum death benefits*

**3-062** If an individual with primary protection dies before reaching age 75, and a defined benefits LSDB or an uncrystallised funds LSDB is paid in respect of the deceased individual, the payment of the lump sum is BCE 7. If the amount of the lump sum exceeds the deceased member's available primary protection, the recipient of the lump sum can require the value of the primary protection to be increased if the value of the individual's pre-commencement rights to death benefits exceeds

---

[91] See Sch.36 para.10(2). It also includes: (a) an annuity by means of which benefits under such a scheme have been secured; and (b) a right to make income withdrawals under ICTA 1988 s.634A.

[92] See SI 2006/572 arts 9–11. The enhancement factor is increased by increasing the amount of the value of rights under the other money purchase or hybrid arrangement on 5 April 2006 by the amount of compensation.

[93] A relevant pension arrangement means an arrangement under a pension scheme which automatically became a registered pension scheme on 6 April 2006 (see FA 2004 Sch.36 para.1(1)).

[94] FA 2004 Sch.36 para.11.

[95] The reduction due to the pension debit occurs on the effective date of the pension sharing order, which is the transfer date (see WRPA 1999). This will not necessarily be the same as the date that the individual's rights in the arrangement(s) under the scheme are actually split.

# THE LIFETIME ALLOWANCE

RR.[96] In these circumstances, the primary protection factor is recalculated, as if "RR" was the value of the individual's pre-commencement rights to death benefits. The revised primary protection factor operates in relation to the BCE consisting of the payment of the lump sum death benefit, and any other BCE consisting of the payment of a lump sum death benefit in respect of the individual.

**3-063** The value of the individual's pre-commencement rights to death benefits is the total amount that could have been paid if the individual had died on 5 April 2006: (a) in respect of the individual as lump sum death benefits that are attributable to rights in respect of which the individual had not, on 5 April 2006, become entitled to the present payment of benefits; and (b) under relevant pension arrangements[97] relating to the individual.[98]

**3-064** The following amounts are disregarded:[99]

(a) in the case of any lump sum death benefit which could have been paid under a pension scheme in the case of which approval could have been withdrawn, so much of the maximum amount of any lump sum death benefit as could not have been paid without having given grounds for withdrawing approval;

(b) in the case of any lump sum death benefit which could have been paid under an arrangement in the case of which rights to such a benefit are commuted into prospective rights to receive dependants' pensions, any dependants' pension proportion amount. A dependants' pension proportion amount is so much of the maximum amount of any lump sum death benefit which could have been paid under the arrangement as is the dependants' pension proportion of the lump sum death benefit. The dependants' pension proportion is "(UTA − TA)/UTA" where:

- *UTA* is what TA would be if no prospective rights to the payment of any of those lump sum death benefits had been commuted into prospective rights to receive dependants' pensions.
- *TA* is the amount which, at the time when a defined benefits LSDB or uncrystallised funds LSDB is first paid in respect of the individual, is the aggregate of the maximum amounts of any defined benefits lump sum death benefits or uncrystallised funds lump sum death benefits which could be paid under the arrangement in respect of the individual; and

(c) the amount of any lump sum death benefit payable under a policy of life assurance on 5 April 2006 by any scheme (other than an occupational pension scheme with at least 20 members on 5 April 2006) where: (i) the policy does not pay out a lump sum after 5 April 2006; or (ii) the terms of the policy are varied significantly between 5 April 2006 and the date of the individual's death.[100] Any exercise of rights conferred by the policy is regarded for this purpose as a variation;[101] and

(d) the amount of any lump sum death benefit payable from an occupational pension scheme on 5 April 2006 where: (i) the individual was not continuously employed in the period from 5 April 2006 to the date of their death

---

[96] FA 2004 Sch.36 para.11A.
[97] A relevant pension arrangement is an arrangement under a pension scheme which automatically became a registered pension scheme on 6 April 2006. These are listed in FA 2004 Sch.36 para.1(1).
[98] FA 2004 Sch.36 para.11B.
[99] FA 2004 Sch.36 para.11C.
[100] FA 2004 Sch.36 para.11D.
[101] A variation of the terms of a policy of life insurance made in order to comply with the Equality Act 2010 Pt 5, so far as relating to age, is ignored for these purposes.

by either the same employer as they had been on 5 April 2006 or by a person connected with that employer; and (ii) the individual was already entitled to the present payment of benefits under the occupational pension scheme before his death.

**3-065** Where a policy of life insurance held on 5 April 2006 for the purposes of an occupational pension scheme is surrendered and a new one is taken out as part of a retirement-benefit activities compliance exercise;[102] or to comply with the Equality Act 2010 Pt 5, so far as relating to age, the new policy is treated as if it were the same as the old.

**Pension credits**

**3-066** A different lifetime allowance enhancement factor (called the "pre-commencement pension credit factor") applies where the ex-spouse or former civil partner acquired a pension credit[103] before 6 April 2006.[104] It operates in relation to all BCEs occurring in relation to an individual where before 6 April 2006 the individual has acquired rights under a pension scheme which automatically became a registered pension scheme on 6 April 2006 by virtue of having become entitled to a pension credit. The lifetime allowance enhancement factor is the pre-commencement pension credit factor, which is "IAPC/£1.5 million" where *IAPC* is the amount of the pension credit awarded for the purposes of s.29(1) WRPA 1999 as increased by the percentage by which the RPI for April 2006 is greater than that for the month in which the rights were acquired.

**3-067** If the individual has primary protection, he cannot also have this enhancement factor (because the value of the pension credit will have been included in the primary protection factor). The individual must have given notice to HMRC prior to 5 April 2009 and HMRC will have issued a certificate showing the enhancement factor.[105]

**Reduced lifetime allowance**

*Pre-A Day pensions*

**3-068** If a pension commenced prior to 6 April 2006 the individual's available lifetime allowance is reduced in respect of any BCE that occurs on or after 6 April 2006.[106] This is explained in more detail below.

*Protected pension age*

**3-069** If an individual has a protected pension age[107] of less than 50 and a BCE occurs before he reaches normal minimum pension age, his lifetime allowance is reduced[108] by the relevant percentage. This is 2.5 multiplied by the number of complete years

---

[102] This will be the case if the surrender of the old policy and taking out of the new policy constitute or form part of a transaction the purpose of which is to secure that the activities of the pension scheme are limited to retirement-benefit activities within the meaning of PA 2004 s.255, and the rights under the old policy and the new policy are not significantly different.
[103] For pension credits and pension debits, see Ch.16.
[104] See FA 2004 Sch.36 para.18.
[105] SI 2006/131 reg.5.
[106] FA 2004 Sch.36 para.20.
[107] For the meaning of protected pension age, see below.
[108] This does not apply to the schemes listed in SI 2005/3451 Sch.1 (armed forces, firefighters, police etc.).

# THE LIFETIME ALLOWANCE

between the date on which the BCE occurs and the date on which the individual will reach normal minimum pension age.[109]

3-070 For example, if a member's lifetime allowance would normally be £1 million but he has a protected pension age of 40 and he crystallises benefits on his 44th birthday, his lifetime allowance is reduced by 25% (10 x 2.5) to £750,000. If he crystallises £500,000 this will use up 66.67% of his lifetime allowance. If he then crystallises a further £300,000 after his 55th birthday this will not give rise to a lifetime allowance charge (assuming the standard lifetime allowance is £1 million at that time) because his reduced allowance no longer applies. His available allowance before the second BCE is 33.33% of £1 million.

3-071 If the member is entitled to a lifetime allowance which is greater than the standard lifetime allowance then the reduction is applied to the enhanced level of lifetime allowance, rather than the standard lifetime allowance.

3-072 The purpose of this reduction is to reflect the fact that the capital value of a scheme pension that pays say £20,000 per annum (and therefore has a capitalised value of £400,000 for lifetime allowance purposes) is much higher if the member is aged 40 than if he is aged 55 (because it is likely to continue for longer). Whilst such a reduction makes sense in relation to any BCE 2 which occurs before normal minimum pension age, it makes less sense where BCE 4 or BCE 1 occurs.

### *Multiple BCEs*

3-073 If the amount crystallising on a BCE exceeds the available amount of the individual's reduced lifetime allowance, s.219 (which applies to determine the availability of individual's lifetime allowance on the occurrence of a BCE) applies on any future BCE as if the amount previously crystallised were equal to the available amount of the individual's lifetime allowance at that time.[110]

## Availability of lifetime allowance on a BCE

### *Pre-A Day pensions*

3-074 Where a person had an actual (and not merely a prospective) right to a pension on 5 April 2006, the amount of his available lifetime allowance is reduced if a BCE occurs after that date.[111] On the occurrence of such a BCE, one reduces the amount of the individual's available lifetime allowance by the value of his "pre-commencement pension rights" immediately before the BCE. The value of the individual's pre-commencement pension rights is "25 x ARP" where ARP is an amount equal to the total annual rate at which all relevant existing pensions are payable to the individual on the date of the first BCE. "Relevant existing pension" has the same meaning as for primary protection (see above) and broadly means a pension under a scheme which was tax-approved before 6 April 2006 and automatically became a registered pension scheme on that date. The annual rate at which a relevant existing pension is payable at any time is determined in the same way that one values crystallised rights for primary protection purposes (treating the references there to 5 April 2006 as to that time).[112]

---

[109] FA 2004 Sch.36 para.19.
[110] FA 2004 Sch.36 para.19(5) and (6).
[111] FA 2004 Sch.36 para.20.
[112] See Ch.3.

*"ARP" where relevant existing pension is drawdown*

**3-075** Where the pre-commencement pension at the time of the BCE is capped drawdown, ARP is 80% of the maximum annual amount of capped drawdown pension payable (in accordance with pension rule 5) in the drawdown pension year in which the first BCE occurs. This will be determined at the most recent valuation or review of the member's fund.

**3-076** Where the pre-commencement pension was flexible drawdown at any time before 6 April 2015, ARP is 80% of the maximum annual amount of capped drawdown pension that would have been payable in the drawdown pension year in which the flexible drawdown declaration was accepted by the scheme administrator, had the flexible drawdown declaration not been made.

**3-077** Where the pre-commencement pension was capped drawdown immediately before 6 April 2015 and has since converted to a flexi-access drawdown pension, ARP is 80% of the maximum annual drawdown amount that could have been paid under the capped drawdown rules in the drawdown pension year in which the fund converted to flexi-access drawdown pension.

*Illustration*

**3-078** If a member was in receipt of a pension of £20,000 p/a on 5 April 2006 this in itself cannot give rise to a BCE as it commenced before 6 April 2006. If a BCE subsequently crystallises £700,000 and the member has a lifetime allowance of £1.25 million, the capital value of the pre-commencement pension (25 x £20,000 = £500,000) uses up 40% of the member's lifetime allowance (£500,000/£1.25 million x 100 = 40%). 60% of his £1.25 million lifetime allowance is therefore available (i.e. £750,000) so the BCE does not give rise to a chargeable amount.

**3-079** If the value of the pre-commencement pension exceeds the member's lifetime allowance then the member will have no available lifetime allowance on a subsequent BCE. For example, if a member with a pre-commencement pension valued at £2 million has a £1.8 million lifetime allowance (so he has no available lifetime allowance) and he then crystallises £500,000, the chargeable amount will be £500,000 (not the full £700,000).

**BCE 2**

*Scheme pension provided from pre-A Day drawdown pension fund*

**3-080** In the following circumstances, BCE 2 does not occur in respect of so much of the scheme pension that represents the conversion of a drawdown pension to a scheme pension. The circumstances are that on 6 April 2006 the individual was under the age of 75 and he was a member of a scheme which automatically became a registered pension scheme, and he was, on 5 April 2006 entitled to a pension under a money purchase arrangement which:[113]

(a) took the form of income drawdown under an approved retirement benefits scheme or personal pension scheme; or
(b) was paid from the resources of a small self-administered scheme.[114]

---

[113] SI 2006/572 art.29.
[114] As defined in The Retirements Benefits Schemes (Restriction on Discretion to Approve) (Small Self-administered Schemes) Regulations 1991 (SI 1991/1614), or one that was approved under ICTA

# THE LIFETIME ALLOWANCE

BCE 2 will also not occur to the extent that funds derived from any of the above (such as investment returns) are applied to provide a scheme pension.

3-081

## BCE 3

*Pre-6 April 2006 entitlement*

If the individual became entitled to the pension before 6 April 2006, the permitted margin is the greater of:[115]

3-082

(a) what would be the permitted margin calculated as per the post-6 April 2006 entitlement provisions above, applied with effect from the date that the individual became entitled to the pension; and

(b) the amount by which the annual rate of the pension on the day on which the individual became entitled to it would be greater if it had been increased in accordance with the rules of the pension scheme as they stood immediately before 6 April 2006.

The effect of (b) above is that if the scheme rules permit increases in excess of 5% per annum and the RPI, then the increase specified in the scheme rules is the permitted margin. The pre-6 April 2006 cap on increases in pensions in payment was usually the greater of 3% per annum or the RPI.

3-083

The annual increase specified in the scheme rules need not be expressed in the scheme rules as an annual percentage increase. HMRC confirm[116] that increases to reflect revaluation of contracted-out rights (i.e. to a guaranteed minimum pension) or which relate to an element of a pension (such as a contracted-out element) or which are made at the discretion of the trustee will be acceptable provided that they are referred to in the scheme rules on 5 April 2006.

3-084

## BCE 4

*Annuity purchased from pre-A Day drawdown pension fund*

In the following circumstances BCE 4 does not occur in respect of so much of a lifetime annuity that was funded by the surrender of funds representing a drawdown pension. The circumstances are that on 6 April 2006 the individual was below the age of 75 and he was a member of a scheme which automatically became a registered pension scheme, and was, on 5 April 2006 entitled to a pension under a money purchase arrangement which:[117]

3-085

(a) took the form of income drawdown under an approved retirement benefits scheme or personal pension scheme; or

(b) was paid from the resources of a small self-administered scheme.[118]

The above also applies where a lifetime annuity is purchased by the surrender of funds which were transferred from one of the above arrangements (including any subsequent investment growth).

3-086

---

1988 s.590, and the rules of the scheme on 5 April 2006 did not require the purchase of an annuity in respect of the individual.

[115] FA 2004 Sch.32 para.12.
[116] PTM088630.
[117] SI 2006/572 art.29.
[118] As defined in SI 1991/1614, or one that was approved under ICTA 1988 s.590 and the rules of the scheme on 5 April 2006 did not require the purchase of an annuity in respect of the individual.

**BCE 8**

*Drawdown pension funds representing pre-A Day unsecured pension*

3-087    A transfer from a drawdown pension fund that represents unsecured pension in payment on 5 April 2006 expressly does not constitute BCE 8.[119]

# PROTECTION FOR PRE-COMMENCEMENT PENSION RIGHTS

**Protected pension ages**

*Scheme rights existing before 6 April 2006*

3-088    An authorised pension may be provided prior to normal minimum pension age to a member with a protected pension age. The requirements which must be satisfied depend on whether or not the scheme (or any transferee scheme[120]) was, prior to 6 April 2006, an occupational scheme.[121] Where the pension scheme was, prior to 6 April 2006, an approved retirement benefits schemes, a member of that scheme (or any transferee scheme) has a protected pension age in the following circumstances:

(a) on 5 April 2006 the member had an actual or prospective right (i.e. an unqualified right, such that consent of a third party is not required) under the scheme to take any benefit at an age of less than 55;

(b) the scheme rules included provisions conferring such a right on some or all of the members on 10 December 2003;

(c) such a right either was then conferred on the member or would have been had the member been a member of the scheme on that date;

(d) the member becomes entitled to all of his benefits under the scheme on the same date. Alternatively, if he is entitled to more than one of: (i) a scheme pension under a money purchase arrangement; (ii) a scheme pension under a defined benefits arrangement, or (iii) a lifetime annuity, this requirement is satisfied if he becomes entitled to all of his benefits under the scheme within a six-month period;

(e) his becoming entitled to the benefits is not part of an arrangement to avoid tax or NIC;

(f) if the member's protected pension age is less than 50, he does not become employed by a sponsoring employer by whom he is connected after becoming entitled to the benefits; and

(g) if the member's protected pension age is 50 to 54 he does not (subject to the following exceptions) become employed by a person that was a sponsoring employer at any time during the six months before his retirement and

---

[119] SI 2006/572 art.29.

[120] Prior to 6 April 2015, protection was scheme specific and so would not apply to a transferee scheme unless the transfer formed part of a block transfer (see FA 2004 Sch.36 paras 22(5) and 23(5)). Since 6 April 2015 the protected pension age will apply to the member under a transferee scheme provided that the transfer was a recognised transfer (FA 2004 Sch.36 para.23ZA).

[121] See FA 2004 Sch.36 paras 21-23. A member's lifetime allowance is reduced under Sch.36 para.19 if he does have a protected pension age and benefits are provided to him prior to normal minimum pension age, subject to certain exceptions. See PTM062210–PTM062240.

for whom the member worked during the previous six months, or any person connected with such an employer, or a sponsoring employer with whom the member is connected. The exceptions apply where the member is employed by any such employer after a break of at least six months following retirement, or after a break of at least one month if his employment is materially different in nature from his employment before retirement.[122]

Where the pension scheme was, prior to 6 April 2006, an approved personal pension scheme or retirement annuity contract, a member of that scheme (or any transferee scheme) has a protected pension age if all of the following apply:

3-089

(a) on 5 April 2006, he had an actual or prospective right (i.e. an unqualified right, such that consent of a third party is not required) to a pension before age 50;
(b) the member's occupation was one of those referred to in The Registered Pension Schemes (Prescribed Schemes and Occupations) Regulations 2005 (SI 2005/3451) reg.3;[123] and
(c) the member becomes entitled to all of his benefits under the scheme on the same date. Alternatively, if he is entitled to more than one of: (i) a scheme pension under a money purchase arrangement; (ii) a scheme pension under a defined benefits arrangement; or (iii) a lifetime annuity, he becomes entitled to all of his benefits under the scheme within a six-month period.

*Scheme rights existing before 4 November 2021*

FA 2004 Sch.36 para.23ZB applies in relation to a relevant registered pension scheme[124] and a member of the pension scheme if: (a) neither para.22 nor 23 applies in relation to them; and (b) the entitlement condition or the block transfer condition is met in relation to the scheme and the member. The entitlement condition is met if: (a) immediately before 4 November 2021, the member had an actual or prospective right under the pension scheme to any benefit from an age of less than 57; (b) the rules of the pension scheme on 11 February 2021 included provision conferring such a right on some or all of the persons who were then members of the pension scheme; and (c) the member either had such a right under the scheme on 11 February 2021 or would have had such a right had the member been a member of the scheme on 11 February 2021. Where a recognised transfer is made on or after 4 November 2021 in execution of a request made before that date, and that transfer would, if executed before that date, have resulted in the member having an actual or prospective right under a pension scheme to any benefit from the age of less than 57 immediately before that date, the member is treated as having that right under that scheme at that time.

3-090

The block transfer condition is met if the member is a member of the pension scheme (the "transferee pension scheme") as a result of: (a) a block transfer to the transferee pension scheme on or after 4 November 2021 from a pension scheme (the "original pension scheme") where the entitlement condition is met in relation to the original scheme and the member; (b) a block transfer to the transferee pension

---

[122] HMRC's position is that a simple change in hours will not be a materially different employment. They consider that in order to be a materially different employment, the duties and/or the level of responsibility in the new employment must be different from those in the old employment: PTM062230.
[123] The occupations listed include athletes, divers, footballers, models etc.
[124] A registered pension scheme is "relevant" if it is not a uniformed services pension scheme (as defined in s.279(4)).

scheme from a pension scheme (the "original pension scheme") on or before 3 November 2021 where: (i) immediately before the transfer the member had an actual or prospective right under the original pension scheme to any benefit from an age of less than 57; (ii) the rules of the original pension scheme met para.(b) of the entitlement condition; and (iii) para.(c) of that condition is met in relation to the original pension scheme and the member; or (c) a block transfer to the transferee pension scheme from a pension scheme (the "transferor pension scheme") that was a transferee pension scheme in relation to an original pension scheme or another transferor pension scheme by virtue of the previous application of para.(a) or (b) or the previous application (on one or more occasions) of this paragraph. A transfer is a "block transfer", if it involves the transfer, in a single transaction, of all of the sums and assets held for the purposes of, or representing accrued rights under, the arrangements under a pension scheme which relate to the member and at least one other member of the scheme.

The member's protected pension age is the higher of 55 and the age from which the member had an actual or prospective right to any benefit immediately before 4 November 2021 under: (a) in a case where the entitlement condition is met in relation to the member and the scheme, that scheme; or (b) in a case where the block transfer condition is met in relation to the member and the scheme and the entitlement condition is not so met, whichever of that scheme, the original scheme or the transferor scheme that the member was a member of at that time.

But para.23ZB does not have effect so as to give the member a protected pension age of more than 55 at any time before 6 April 2028.

**3-091** FA 2004 Sch.36 para.23ZC applies in relation to sums or assets of a relevant registered pension scheme and the member of the scheme to which those sums and assets relate if: (a) none of paras 22, 23 or 23ZB apply in relation to the scheme and the member; and (b) those sums or assets were subject to a relevant transfer to the scheme. Sums or assets relate to a member of a pension scheme if they are held by that scheme for the purposes of, or represent accrued rights under, an arrangement relating to the member under the pension scheme. Sums or assets were subject to a relevant transfer to a relevant registered pension scheme if they were transferred to that scheme from another relevant registered pension scheme ("the transferor scheme") as a result of a recognised transfer and, immediately before the transfer: (a) they were sums or assets held by the transferor scheme for the purposes of, or representing accrued rights under, an arrangement relating to a member of the transferor scheme; and (b) para.23ZB applied in relation to the transferor scheme and that member or this paragraph applied to those sums or assets and that member as a result of a relevant transfer to the transferor scheme.

If para.23ZC applies in relation to sums or assets ("transferred sums or assets") and a member of a relevant registered pension scheme, FA 2004 Pt 4 (except for s.218(6) and para.19) applies in relation to: (a) the transferred sums or assets while held for the purposes of, or representing accrued rights under, an arrangement under the scheme; and (b) any sums or assets held for the purposes of, or representing accrued rights under, such an arrangement that arise, or (directly or indirectly) derive, from: (i) any of the transferred sums or assets; or (ii) sums or assets which so arise or derive, as if references to normal minimum pension age were to the member's protected pension age under the first relevant registered pension scheme from which there was a relevant transfer of the sums or assets (see para.23ZB(7)).

**Pre-6 April 2006 lump sum rights exceeding £375,000**

**3-092** The lifetime allowance was £1,500,000 on 6 April 2006, which meant that the maximum PCLS payable was £375,000 (being 25% of £1,500,000). Any member

# PROTECTION FOR PRE-COMMENCEMENT PENSION RIGHTS 81

entitled to primary protection or enhanced protection with pre-6 April 2006 rights to a tax-free lump sum in excess of £375,000 was able to protect the entitlement to the lump sum by notifying HMRC of that entitlement.[125] Protection is also available for entitlement to tax-free lump sums over 25% of fund value (although less than £375,000).[126]

**Pre-A Day lifetime annuities**

A lifetime annuity contract purchased before 6 April 2006 is not treated as a registered pension scheme (e.g. under FA 2004 s.153(8)), and any payments or benefits are not within s.161(3) or (4)[127] unless certain conditions are breached.[128] In particular, these conditions will be breached if the terms of the annuity contract are amended on or after 6 April 2006 to allow a payment that would be an unauthorised payment if it had been made by a registered pension scheme.

3-093

**Lump sum rights exceeding 25% of uncrystallised rights**

If an individual did not have protection for lump sum rights exceeding £375,000, he could protect his pre-A Day entitlement to tax-free lump sum exceeding 25% of uncrystallised rights.[129] This protection was available where the "pension condition" was met in relation to the individual and a "protected pension scheme". Where obtained, the PCLS provisions in FA 2004 Sch.29 apply in relation to the individual and the pension scheme with the modifications described below.

3-094

*The pension condition*

The pension condition is that the individual becomes entitled to all the pensions payable to the individual under arrangements under the pension scheme (to which the individual did not have an actual entitlement on or before 5 April 2006) on the same date.

3-095

*Protected pension schemes*

A registered pension scheme is a "protected pension scheme" if it was within any of Sch.36 para.1(1)(a)–(e), and on 5 April 2006 the lump sum percentage of the individual's uncrystallised rights under the pension scheme exceeded 25%. The lump sum percentage of an individual's uncrystallised pension rights under a pension scheme on 5 April 2006 is "VULSR/VUR x 100" where VULSR is the value of the individual's uncrystallised lump sum rights under the pension scheme on 5 April 2006 (calculated in accordance with Sch.36 para.32), and VUR is the value of the individual's uncrystallised rights under the pension scheme on 5 April 2006 (calculated in accordance with Sch.36 para.33). A pension scheme is also a protected pension scheme if the individual is a member of the pension scheme ("a transferee pension scheme") as a result of a block transfer from a protected pension scheme. Any transferee pension scheme is treated as being the same pension scheme as the original pension scheme.

3-096

---

[125] See FA 2004 Sch.36 paras 24–30 and PTM063110 (primary protection) and PTM063120 (enhanced protection).
[126] See FA 2004 Sch.36 paras 31–34 and PTM063130–PTM063150.
[127] FA 2004 s.161(3) and (4) are explained in Ch.17.
[128] See SI 2006/572 art.2.
[129] See FA 2004 Sch.36 paras 31–34 and PTM063130–PTM063150.

## MISCELLANEOUS PROVISIONS

**Taxable property**

**3-097**  FA 2004 Sch.36 paras 37A–37I relate to pre-A Day holdings of taxable property. Broadly speaking, any taxable property acquired before 6 April 2006 (and not improved since that date), and which was permitted under the rules in force at the time,[130] is not subject to the taxable property provisions.

---

[130] e.g. The Retirement Benefits Schemes (Restriction on Discretion to Approve) (Small Self-administered Schemes) Regulations 1991 (SI 1991/1614).

# CHAPTER 4

# Registration and De-Registration

## TABLE OF CONTENTS

| | |
|---|---|
| Introduction | 4-001 |
| Development | 4-002 |
| Registration | 4-004 |
| Provision of information and declarations | 4-005 |
| Information reasonably required by HMRC | 4-006 |
| Declarations | 4-007 |
| Power to obtain information or documentation and to inspect premises | 4-010 |
| HMRC's obligation to register the scheme | 4-013 |
| The "wholly or mainly" purpose test | 4-014 |
| HMRC's decision and the appeal process | 4-018 |
| Appealing against decision not to register or failure to decide | 4-019 |
| Penalties in connection with registration | 4-020 |
| Summary | 4-022 |
| De-registration | 4-023 |
| "May withdraw" | 4-024 |
| The "de-registration threshold" | 4-026 |
| The de-registration process | 4-028 |
| Appealing HMRC's decision to de-register a pension scheme | 4-029 |
| Consequences of de-registration | 4-030 |

## INTRODUCTION

This chapter explains the requirements that a pension scheme must satisfy in order to be a "registered pension scheme", the circumstances in which HMRC can refuse to register a pension scheme despite it satisfying those requirements, or de-register a pension scheme that has been registered, and the consequences of de-registration. The relevant provisions are in FA 2004 Pt 4 Ch.2 (ss.153–159D). **4-001**

### Development

Between 6 April 2006 (when the provisions were first introduced) and 21 October 2013, the requirements that a pension scheme must satisfy, and the process for registering a pension scheme, remained largely unchanged. On the submission of an online application the pension scheme was registered with immediate effect. Where appropriate, HMRC could subsequently request information and documentation to verify the contents of the application. On 21 October 2013, HMRC an- **4-002** nounced they would, as part of their continuing strategy to combat pension liberation, carry out detailed risk assessment activity *before* deciding whether or not to register a pension scheme. A number of supplementary legislative measures were subsequently introduced in FA 2014, with effect from 20 March 2014.

4-003    Changes introduced by FA 2018 permit HMRC to refuse to register an occupational pension scheme the sponsoring employer of which is dormant, and to de-register any such schemes that have been registered in the past.

## REGISTRATION

4-004    On 6 April 2006, all existing tax-approved pension schemes automatically became registered pension schemes unless they opted out.[1] A "pension scheme"[2] established on or after 6 April 2006 is a "registered pension scheme" if HMRC decide to register it following receipt of an application from the scheme administrator.[3] An application cannot be made before the pension scheme comes into existence,[4] and registration cannot be backdated.[5] An application to register a pension scheme may be made only if the pension scheme is an occupational pension scheme or has been established by a person with permission under FSMA 2000 to establish in the UK a personal pension scheme or a stakeholder pension scheme.[6] In contrast to the pre-A Day position, a registered pension scheme need not have any specific connection with the UK,[7] and need not be established under trusts.[8] In addition, deferred annuity contracts issued by insurance companies, by means of which benefits under a registered pension scheme have been secured, are deemed to be registered pension schemes.[9]

---

[1]  FA 2004 Sch.36 paras 1 and 2. See PTM031300 and Ch.3.
[2]  Pension scheme is defined in FA 2004 s.150(1). See Ch.2.
[3]  FA 2004 s.153.
[4]  "Pension scheme" is defined very broadly, but it must comprise one or more "instruments" or "agreements". Although a trust cannot exist until it is properly constituted (i.e. there must be some property which is subject to the trusts of the scheme), it seems clear that a scheme established under trusts *does* exist once its terms are binding, even if the trust is not yet properly constituted (e.g. because no contributions have yet been made).
[5]  See PTM031100. It is implicit from s.153(7) that a scheme cannot be a registered pension scheme before HMRC decide to register it. Prior to A Day it was common for exempt approved status to be backdated.
[6]  FA 2004 s.154. "Occupational pension scheme" is defined in s.150(5): see Ch.2 and following.
[7]  Prior to A Day, it was necessary for the administrator to be resident in the UK (ICTA 1988 s.590(2)(c) and IR-12 (2001) para.2.7) and for the scheme to be established in connection with some trade or undertaking carried on in the UK by a person resident in the UK (ICTA 1988 s.590(2)(e)). The scheme administrator of a registered pension scheme must however be resident in the UK or the EEA (FA 2004 s.270(2)(a)).
[8]  Prior to A Day, an exempt approved scheme was required to be established under irrevocable trusts (ICTA 1988 s.592(1)(a)). Note however that, as a matter of pensions law, a funded occupational scheme must be established under irrevocable trusts if it has its main administration in the UK (PA 2004 s.252). In practice, many private sector registered pension schemes (both occupational and non-occupational) are established under trusts, and this is generally considered to be the most appropriate structure for funded pension schemes (*Pension Law Reform: Pension Law Review Committee Report 1993* (Cm.2342), Vol.1 para.4.1.14; also see, e.g. R. Walker in A.J. Oakley (ed.), *Trends in Contemporary Trust Law* (Oxford: Oxford University Press, 1996), Ch.5).
[9]  FA 2004 s.153(8).

# REGISTRATION

## Provision of information and declarations

The application must be made using HMRC's online service,[10] and must: **4-005**

(a) contain any information reasonably required by HMRC in any form specified by HMRC;[11] and
(b) be accompanied by a declaration that the application is made by the scheme administrator and any other declarations by the scheme administrator which are reasonably required by HMRC.[12]

*Information reasonably required by HMRC*

The legislation does not specify precisely what information must be provided to HMRC when applying to register a pension scheme. HMRC's online application currently requires the scheme administrator to specify the name of the scheme, its structure (e.g. single trust), its country of establishment,[13] the number of current and expected members, whether it is an investment-regulated pension scheme, whether it is an occupational pension scheme, the type of benefits provided (e.g. money purchase or defined benefits), details of any contracts of insurance or annuities by which benefits are secured, details of any scheme bank account, and whether any of the scheme establishers have been dormant in the last 12 months. It is also necessary to provide details of the establisher(s) and the trustee(s).[14] **4-006**

*Declarations*

The legislation does not specify precisely what declarations must accompany an application for the registration of a pension scheme (although s.153(3) does provide that the declaration may include a declaration that the "instruments or agreements by which it is constituted do not entitle any person to unauthorised payments"). HMRC's online application currently requires the scheme administrator to declare that: **4-007**

(a) (In relation to an occupational scheme) to the best of the scheme administrator's knowledge and belief, the sponsoring employer(s) in relation to the scheme have not been dormant in the last 12 months.
(b) The scheme meets all the criteria to be registered as a pension scheme under FA 2004 and in particular, is established and will be maintained wholly or mainly for the purpose of making authorised payments of pensions and lumps sums (i.e. payments falling within FA 2004 s.164(1)(a) or (b)).
(c) The instruments or agreements by which the pension scheme is constituted do not directly or indirectly entitle any person to unauthorised payments, and the way in which the pension scheme is to be administered will not knowingly entitle any person to unauthorised payments.

---

[10] The Registered Pension Schemes and Overseas Pension Schemes (Electronic Communication of Returns and Information) Regulations 2006 (SI 2006/570) regs 4, 6 and Sch.1.
[11] FA 2004 s.153(2).
[12] These declarations are separate to the declarations that must be given by a person in order to become a scheme administrator (which generally relate to the competency and intentions of the scheme administrator: see Ch.5).
[13] Normally, a scheme will be established in the country or territory in which the main decisions relating to the scheme are made. See Ch.31 (relating to overseas pension schemes).
[14] Although it is clearly helpful for HMRC to be provided with this information, it is not immediately apparent why much of it is "reasonably" required by HMRC in order to register the pension scheme. Nevertheless, this is unlikely to be objectionable in most cases.

(d) The scheme administrator understands that he is responsible for discharging the functions conferred or imposed on the scheme administrator of the pension scheme by FA 2004, and he intends to discharge those functions at all times, whether resident in the UK or an EU member state or non-member EEA State.

(e) The scheme administrator will comply with all information notices issued to the scheme administrator under FA 2004 or FA 2008, and understands that he may be liable to a penalty and the pension scheme may be de-registered if he fails to properly discharge those functions.

(f) The scheme administrator understands that he may be liable to a penalty and the pension scheme may be de-registered if a false statement is made on the application, or in any information he provides in connection with the application, and that false statements may also lead to prosecution.

(g) To the best of the scheme administrator's knowledge and belief, the information given in the application to register the pension scheme for the purposes of tax relief is correct and complete. The scheme administrator understands that he is responsible for providing any further information and declarations reasonably required by HMRC in order to consider the application.

**4-008** HMRC consider that these declarations apply only "to matters relating to members who are or have been relevant UK individuals whilst being active members of the scheme".[15] However, neither the legislation nor the application expressly refer to any such limitation.

**4-009** Some of the above declarations are arguably ultra vires the power in s.153(2)(b), which provides that the declarations must be "reasonably required" by HMRC, which must mean reasonably required in order to check that the pension scheme meets the requirements of a registered pension scheme as specified in FA 2004.

**Power to obtain information or documentation and to inspect premises**

**4-010** Once an application is made, HMRC may issue an information notice requiring any person to provide any information or documentation reasonably required by HMRC in connection with the application (including any declaration accompanying the application).[16] HMRC may also enter the business premises of the scheme administrator or any other person and inspect documents that are on the premises, if doing so is reasonably required in connection with the application.[17]

**4-011** Many of the provisions in FA 2008 Sch.36 (concerning HMRC's general information and inspection powers) are expressly applied.[18] These provisions contain a number of important restrictions on HMRC's powers, including: (a) an information notice may require a person to produce a document only if it is in his possession or power; (b) an information notice cannot require a person to produce a document which originates more than six years before the date of the notice, except with the agreement of an authorised officer; and (c) an information notice cannot require a person to provide privileged information. Restrictions also apply to the information that HMRC can require auditors and tax advisers to provide.

**4-012** Any person, other than the scheme administrator, who is given an information

---

[15] See PTM114000.
[16] FA 2004 s.153A.
[17] FA 2004 s.153B.
[18] FA 2004 s.153A(3).

notice may appeal against the notice or any requirement in the notice.[19] No penalties can be imposed where the scheme administrator fails to comply with an information notice; HMRC will simply not register the scheme. As is explained below, penalties may be imposed where any person other than the scheme administrator fails to comply with an information notice, or where the scheme administrator carelessly or deliberately provides materially inaccurate information or a false declaration.

**HMRC's obligation to register the scheme**

Following receipt of an application, HMRC *must* register the pension scheme unless it appears that any of the following are not satisfied:[20]

4-013

(a) Any information contained in the application, or otherwise provided to HMRC by the scheme administrator in connection with the application (including any declaration accompanying it) is inaccurate in a material respect.

(b) Any document produced to HMRC by the scheme administrator in connection with the application (including any declaration accompanying it) contains a material inaccuracy.

(c) Any declaration accompanying the application is false.

(d) The scheme administrator has failed to comply with an information notice under s.153A given in connection with the application (including any declaration accompanying it). This expressly includes a case where the scheme administrator has concealed, destroyed or otherwise disposed of, or has arranged for the concealment, destruction or disposal of, a document.[21]

(e) The scheme administrator has deliberately obstructed HMRC in the course of an inspection under s.153B carried out in connection with the application (including any declaration accompanying it), where the inspection has been approved by the FTT.

(f) The pension scheme has not been established, or is not being maintained, wholly or mainly for the purpose of making payments falling within s.164(1)(a) or (b). This requirement is considered in detail below.

(g) The person who is, or any of the persons who are, the scheme administrator is not a fit and proper person to be a scheme administrator. See Ch.5 for an explanation of this requirement.

(h) The pension scheme is an occupational pension scheme, and a sponsoring employer in relation to the scheme is a body corporate that has been dormant during a continuous period of one month that falls within the period of one year ending with the day on which HMRC's decision is made. "Dormant company" has the same meaning as in CA 2006 s.1169, which provides that a company is dormant during any period in which it has no transactions that are required by CA 2006 s.386 to be entered in the company's accounting records.[22]

---

[19] Following the procedure in FA 2008 Sch.36 para.32.

[20] FA 2004 s.153(5). HMRC are not prohibited from registering a pension scheme if it appears to them that any of these requirements are not satisfied, so they may do so at their discretion.

[21] In breach of FA 2008 Sch.36 paras 42 or 43 as applied by s.153A(3).

[22] Certain minor transactions, such as issuing shares to a subscriber to the memorandum and the payment of certain fees and penalties are expressly disregarded. For the purposes of CA 2006 s.386, accounting records must, in particular, contain entries from day to day of all sums of money received

(i) The pension scheme is an unauthorised master trust scheme.[23] This provision is yet to take effect.[24]

*The "wholly or mainly" purpose test*

**4-014** HMRC may refuse to register a pension scheme if it appears that it has not been established, or is not being maintained,[25] wholly or mainly for the purpose of making payments within s.164(1)(a) or (b) (i.e. authorised pensions or lump sums, including death benefits). The other authorised member payments (such as recognised transfers[26]) are in s.164(1)(c)–(f), so s.153(5)(f) elevates the importance of paying pensions and lump sums above the other types of authorised payments.[27] If the main purpose of a pension scheme is to make one or more of the other authorised payments then HMRC may refuse to register the scheme.[28]

**4-015** Purpose tests such as this are not uncommon in tax and pension legislation, and are usually interpreted as posing a subjective rather than an objective test.[29] This involves an inquiry into the state of mind of the person establishing the scheme (i.e. the employer or insurance company) and also the person "maintaining" the scheme (which will usually be the trustee, manager and/or administrator). In such cases, it may be necessary to distinguish a person's purpose from the consequences of his actions, and a main purpose may need to be distinguished from a subsidiary purpose.

**4-016** In *Pi Consulting (Trustee Services) Ltd v Pensions Regulator*,[30] however, the judge accepted that the purpose test in PSA 1993 s.1[31] should be interpreted objectively. He found that the relevant *purpose* in PSA 1993 s.1 is the purpose of the scheme and not the purpose of the parties to the documents that established the scheme. He considered that it is an objective matter, which turns on the meaning and effect of the scheme, and not on subjective matters such as the motives, inten-

---

and expended by the company and the matters in respect of which the receipt and expenditure takes place, and a record of the assets and liabilities of the company. CA 2006 s.386(3).

[23] A "master trust scheme" means a master trust scheme within the meaning of PSA 2017 ss.1 and 2 whose operation would be unlawful under PSA 2017 Pt 1 were the scheme not authorised under that Part (FA 2004 s.279(1B)). A master trust scheme is "unauthorised" if it is not authorised under PSA 2017 Pt 1 and its operation would be unlawful without such authorisation (FA 2004 s.279(1D)).

[24] See FA 2018 Sch.3 para.2(1).

[25] The words "or is not being maintained" will be relevant only if the scheme has become operational prior to it being registered, which will rarely be the case. These words are more significant in the context of de-registration (see below).

[26] See e.g., *NBC (Administration Services) Ltd v HMRC* [2024] UKFTT 120 (TC); [2024] Pens. L.R. 8, which concerned registered pension schemes established to facilitate transfers from Irish pension schemes to pension schemes outside of the EU.

[27] This is therefore similar to (but less restrictive than) ICTA 1988 s.590(2)(a) and IR12 para.1.4, which required an approved scheme to be established for the *sole purpose* of providing relevant benefits.

[28] HMRC's Pension newsletter 152 (July 2023) states: "Where a scheme does not allow the payment of benefits or has terms and conditions that suggest the scheme will not pay out benefits on normal retirement (for example if a customer wants to take a pension then they have to transfer their funds to another registered pension scheme first), it is unlikely to be satisfying the wholly or mainly test."

[29] By contrast, purpose tests such as the one found in the general anti-abuse rule in FA 2013 Pt 5 impose an objective purpose test: one is required to determine whether it would be reasonable to conclude that the obtaining of a tax advantage was the main purpose, or one of the main purposes, of the arrangements (FA 2013 s.207). Another example of an objective purpose test is in ITA 2007 Pt 13 Ch.7, which requires one to determine if the main benefit that might be expected to accrue from the transaction is the obtaining of a reduction in tax liability (see ITA 2007 s.809ZG).

[30] *Pi Consulting (Trustee Services) Ltd v Pensions Regulator* [2013] EWHC 3181 (Ch).

[31] Which provides that an occupational pension scheme must be established for the purpose of providing benefits to, or in respect of, people with service in employments of a description or for that purpose and also for the purpose of providing benefits to, or in respect of, other people.

tions or beliefs of the parties to the scheme documentation. This was primarily because it is important for everyone involved with a pension scheme (including successors in title, new members, HMRC, regulators and those administering other pension schemes when asked to transfer funds to the relevant scheme), possibly over a long period of time, to know whether a scheme meets this purpose test, and it follows that the subjective reasons of the parties that establish the schemes is not a relevant factor. It is difficult to materially distinguish the purpose test in PSA 1993 s.1 and the one in FA 2004 s.153(5)(f), so the decision in *Pi Consulting* suggests that the test in FA 2004 s.153(5)(f) may be objective. However, this aspect of the decision has been criticised[32] and the better view is that s.153(5)(f) poses a subjective test.

Whether it is subjective or objective, the requirement is plainly not intended to prevent a registered pension scheme from being *capable* of providing other types of authorised payments, or even unauthorised payments. There is a separate requirement that no person can be *entitled* to an unauthorised payment from a registered pension scheme,[33] but it is not uncommon for the trustees or managers of a registered pension scheme to have an express power to make unauthorised payments where they consider it appropriate to do so.[34]

4-017

**HMRC's decision and the appeal process**

Prior to 21 October 2013, registration was automatic and immediate upon the submission of a completed application. Since that date, HMRC carry out risk assessment activity before deciding whether or not to register a pension scheme. If HMRC decide to register a pension scheme, they will notify the scheme administrator of the date from which it is registered and provide the scheme administrator with a pension scheme tax reference.[35] Such a decision does not constitute acceptance by HMRC that the pension scheme meets the requirements of a registered pension scheme; it merely means that, based on the information available to HMRC, they were not aware of any reason not to register the scheme. If HMRC decide not to register a scheme, they will notify the scheme administrator and provide reasons for their decision. There is no specified period of time in which HMRC are required to make a decision, but if they have not made a decision within six months the scheme administrator can appeal to the FTT as if HMRC had decided not to register the scheme.

4-018

*Appealing against decision not to register or failure to decide*

If HMRC decide not to register the pension scheme, or if they fail to make a decision within six months, the scheme administrator may appeal to the FTT.[36] The appeal must be made within 30 days of the day on which the scheme administrator was notified of the decision, or the end of the six-month period. If the FTT decides that the pension scheme ought to have been registered by HMRC, the pension

4-019

---

[32] D. Pollard, "Application of the Proper Purpose Test to Pension Schemes" (2016) 30 Tru. L.I. 159, 165.
[33] See FA 2004 s.153(3).
[34] In addition to the FA 2004 provisions, pension legislation requires the trustees or managers of occupational schemes with their main administration in the UK to secure that the activities of the scheme are limited to "retirement benefit activities" (PA 2004 s.255).
[35] For any scheme where the application for registration was submitted on or after 21 October 2013, the notification of registration letter will be the only evidence that the scheme is registered (see PTM032300).
[36] FA 2004 ss.156 and 156A.

**Penalties in connection with registration**

**4-020** HMRC may impose penalties if:[37]

(a) a person other than the scheme administrator fails to comply with an information notice under s.153A,[38] or deliberately obstructs HMRC in the course of an inspection under s.153B which has been approved by the tribunal;

(b) an application for registration contains information which is materially inaccurate and the inaccuracy is careless or deliberate;

(c) in complying with an information notice under s.153A, a person provides inaccurate information or produces a document that contains a material inaccuracy; or

(d) a declaration accompanying an application for registration is false and the falsehood is careless or deliberate.

**4-021** The penalty for failing to comply with an information notice or deliberately obstructing HMRC in the course of an inspection is £300 followed by penalties of up to £60 for each day that the failure or obstruction continues.[39] In all other cases the maximum penalty is £3,000.[40] Where the information or declaration contains more than one material inaccuracy or falsehood, a penalty is payable for each inaccuracy or falsehood. The person liable to pay the penalty is the scheme administrator, or in the case of a false declaration by another person, that other person.[41]

**Summary**

**4-022** In summary, for a pension scheme to be registered:

(a) the scheme must have a scheme administrator,[42] who is a fit and proper person to be a scheme administrator[43];

(b) the application to register the scheme, and any documentation and declarations accompanying the application, must not contain any inaccuracies or falsehoods[44];

(c) the scheme administrator must not have failed to comply with an information notice under s.153A or deliberately obstructed HMRC in the course of an inspection under s.153B[45];

(d) the scheme must be either: (i) an occupational pension scheme established by a sponsoring employer which is not dormant; or (ii) established by a

---

[37] Under FA 2004 ss.153C–153F.
[38] This expressly includes a person who conceals, destroys or otherwise disposes of, or arranges for the concealment, destruction or disposal of, a document in breach of the FA 2008 Sch.36 paras 42 or 43 as applied by s.153A(3).
[39] See FA 2008 Sch.36 paras 39(2) and 40(2). FA 2008 Sch.36 paras 44–49 concerning HMRC's general powers to impose penalties are expressly incorporated.
[40] See FA 2008 Sch.36 para.40A.
[41] FA 2008 Sch.36 paras 46–49 concerning HMRC's general powers to impose penalties are expressly incorporated.
[42] FA 2004 s.153(2)(b).
[43] FA 2004 s.153(5)(g).
[44] FA 2004 s.153(5)(a)–(c).
[45] FA 2004 s.153(5)(d) and (e).

# DE-REGISTRATION

person with permission under FSMA 2000 to establish in the UK a personal pension scheme or a stakeholder pension scheme[46];

(e) the scheme must be established and maintained wholly or mainly for the purpose of making authorised payments of pensions and lumps sums as falling within FA 2004 s.164(1)(a) or (b)[47]; and

(f) the instruments or agreements by which the scheme is constituted must not directly or indirectly entitle any person to unauthorised payments[48] and the way in which the scheme is to be administered must not knowingly entitle any person to unauthorised payments.[49]

## DE-REGISTRATION

HMRC may withdraw the registration of a pension scheme only if it appears to HMRC[50] that one of the following applies:[51]

4-023

(a) The pension scheme has not been established, or is not being maintained, wholly or mainly for the purpose of making payments falling within s.164(1)(a) or (b) (i.e. authorised pensions and lump sums).[52]

(b) One of the scheme administrators is not a fit and proper person to act as scheme administrator.

(c) The amount of the scheme chargeable payments made by the pension scheme during any period of 12 months exceeds the "de-registration threshold". This is considered below.

(d) The scheme administrator fails to pay a substantial amount of tax (or interest on tax) due from the scheme administrator.

(e) The scheme administrator fails to provide information required to be provided to HMRC under FA 2004 Pt 4 or FA 2008 Sch.36 Pt 1 and the failure is "significant", meaning that the amount of information which the scheme administrator fails to provide is substantial, or the failure to provide the information is likely to result in serious prejudice to the assessment or collection of tax.

---

[46] FA 2004 s.154.

[47] FA 2004 s.153(5)(f).

[48] FA 2004 s.153(3).

[49] The requirement that the way in which the scheme is to be administered will not knowingly entitle any person to unauthorised payments is not found in any legislation but it is currently a required declaration.

[50] In *NBC (Administration Services) Ltd v HMRC* [2024] UKFTT 120 (TC) at [21]–[23], the FTT made three observations in respect of the words "it appears to HMRC". First, the test is clearly not that a ground actually is present. All that is required is that there is an "appearance" that a ground is present. Second, it is a subjective test. If an objective test had been intended, s.157(1) might have said: "it is reasonable to suppose that…". Third, the test is not that HMRC suspect that a ground *might be* present. HMRC must believe it to be so; if they harbour real doubts as to whether it is the case, then it will not appear to them that a ground *is* (as opposed to *might be*) met.

[51] FA 2004 ss.157 and 158. Many of these provisions were added by FA 2014 (but have effect in relation to schemes whenever registered). Prior to 1 June 2014, the provisions in (c)–(f), (i) and (k) only applied.

[52] See Ch.4 for the meaning of this purpose test. Two cases involving the pre-A Day legislation demonstrate how broadly these provisions could be applied in cases where the scheme itself does nothing improper but there is a controlling mind with an overall intention of pension liberation: *R. v IRC Ex p. Roux Waterside Inn Ltd* [1997] S.T.C. 781; [1999] O.P.L.R. 239; *R. (on the application of Mander) v IRC* [2001] EWHC Admin 358; [2002] S.T.C. 631.

(f) Any information contained in the application to register the pension scheme or otherwise provided to HMRC is inaccurate in a material particular.
(g) The scheme administrator fails to produce any document required to be produced to HMRC under FA 2004 Pt 4 or FA 2008 Sch.36 Pt 1.
(h) Any document produced to HMRC by the scheme administrator contains a material inaccuracy in relation to which at least one of three conditions is met:
  (i) the inaccuracy is deliberate or careless (i.e. due to a failure by the scheme administrator to take reasonable care);
  (ii) the scheme administrator knows of the inaccuracy at the time the document is produced to HMRC but does not inform HMRC at that time; or
  (iii) the scheme administrator discovers the inaccuracy some time later and fails to take reasonable steps to inform HMRC.[53]
(i) Any declaration accompanying the application to register the pension scheme, or otherwise made to HMRC in connection with the pension scheme, is false in a material particular.
(j) The scheme administrator has deliberately obstructed an officer of HMRC in the course of an inspection under FA 2004 s.159B or FA 2008 Sch.36 Pt 2 which has been approved by the tribunal.
(k) There is no scheme administrator.
(l) The pension scheme is an occupational pension scheme, and a sponsoring employer in relation to the scheme is a body corporate that has been dormant during a continuous period of one month that falls within the period of one year ending with the day on which the decision to withdraw registration is made.[54] This provision was added by FA 2018 with effect from 6 April 2018. The meaning of "dormant" is explained above in the context of registration. Whilst it is perhaps understandable that a dormant company should not be able to *register* a scheme, it is less clear why it should be objectionable for an employer that has established a scheme in the past to become dormant.[55] It is unclear if a company which has been dissolved can be properly described as "dormant". Similarly, where the provisions of an occupational scheme are amended so that it ceases to have a sponsoring employer,[56] it is difficult to see how it could be said to have a dormant sponsoring employer.[57]

---

[53] FA 2004 s.158(7)–(10).
[54] In *NBC (Administration Services) Ltd v HMRC* [2024] UKFTT 120 (TC) at [19], in response to a question about an occupational pension scheme with significant assets and members, counsel for HMRC said that HMRC would not exercise its deregistration power merely because the original sponsoring employer had ceased trading and was dormant.
[55] In the context of a sponsoring employer managed by a husband and wife (to take a common example), one would expect the employer to become dormant once they both retire. If HMRC are then entitled to de-register the scheme, presumably the scheme members would be compelled to transfer out of the scheme to a non-occupational scheme, at precisely the time that the scheme has been designed to provide benefits.
[56] It is not uncommon to come across small occupational schemes where this has happened in connection with a sale of the sponsoring employer. All powers of the sponsoring employer are typically vested in the trustees. For the meaning of "sponsoring employer", see Ch.2.
[57] It may be objected that that interpretation is too literal, but a purposive interpretation is difficult where the purpose of the provision is so obscure. It is not at all clear why it should be objectionable for an employer that has established a pension scheme in the past to become dormant. Whatever the objection to dormant companies may be, it is difficult to see how it could be less objectionable to have *no* sponsoring employer. HMRC's views on this point are unknown.

# DE-REGISTRATION

The pension scheme is an unauthorised master trust scheme. This is yet to take effect.[58]

(m) It will be apparent that most of the above grounds are materially identical to the grounds on which HMRC may refuse to register a pension scheme.

It should be noted that there is no mechanism by which HMRC may de-register individual arrangements under a registered pension scheme. Only an entire scheme can be de-registered, potentially unfairly penalising members who were unconnected with the activity that caused the scheme to be de-registered.[59]

## "May withdraw"

**4-024** The words "may withdraw" make it clear that s.157(1) confers on HMRC a discretion to withdraw the registration of a pension scheme. They are not required to do so.[60]

**4-025** In NBC (Administration Services) Ltd v HMRC,[61] HMRC asserted that the nature of this discretion is different depending on whether the failure is a breach of: (a) a ground which is not a registration requirement (which HMRC referred to as "abuse"); or (b) a ground which is a registration requirement. In the case of abuse, the abuse must be serious, but if it is a failure to comply with the registration requirements, there is no requirement for the failure to be serious. The FTT held that this distinction was not justified. The approach should be the same.

The FFT considered *JP Whitter (Waterwell Engineers) Ltd v HMRC*[62] and concluded that, as was the case in Whitter, the discretion in s.157 is "desirable ... to allow for cases where the failure is limited and temporary (even if not within the prescribed classes) and poses no practical threat to the objectives of the scheme". Before HMRC can exercise their discretion, therefore, they need to decide whether the ground justifies de-registration or whether it can be addressed in some other, less drastic way without threatening the objectives of the regime. For example, if the sole director of a corporate scheme administrator fails the fit and proper person test due to insufficient experience in the pensions industry, HMRC should explore with the administrator whether this could be addressed by the administrator hiring new staff, or by replacing the scheme administrator. It would be unreasonable to remedy those shortcomings by de-registering a pension scheme without first exploring those options. Similarly, it would be unreasonable to deregister a pension scheme merely

---

[58] See FA 2018 Sch.3 para.2(1). The meaning of "unauthorised master trust scheme" is explained above in the context of registration.

[59] HMRC refer to this at PTM033100, and the page then states that some content has been withheld because of exemptions in the Freedom of Information Act 2000. The restricted text may well indicate that HMRC will be very unlikely to de-register a scheme where doing so would be to the significant detriment of innocent members. In *R. (on the application of Mander) v IRC* [2002] S.T.C. 631, a case involving the pre-6 April 2006 legislation, Mr Mander entered into a tax avoidance scheme which resulted in the Revenue withdrawing approval for his pension scheme. This negatively affected Mrs Mander, who was also a member of the scheme (Mr and Mrs Mander were the only members) and had not entered into the tax avoidance scheme. Sullivan J found that the Revenue had considered Mrs Mander's position and their decision was not *Wednesbury* perverse (see *Associated Provincial Picture House Ltd v Wednesbury Corp* [1948] 1 K.B. 223) because there was no evidence that she was not aware of what her husband was doing, and indeed it was likely that she was aware, and therefore the court would not intervene on that basis.

[60] See PTM033100: "Where a registered pension scheme has given HMRC grounds to de-register the scheme, for example where there is no scheme administrator, deregistration is not automatic. HMRC will consider the facts and circumstances of each case and decide whether or not to de-register the scheme."

[61] *NBC (Administration Services) Ltd v HMRC* [2024] UKFTT 120 (TC) at [16].

[62] *JP Whitter (Waterwell Engineers) Ltd v HMRC* [2018] UKSC 31; [2018] 1 W.L.R. 3117.

because the sponsoring employer was dormant without further enquiry as to the implications of this for the scheme. The focus in all cases should be on the way the pension fund tax regime is designed to operate and preserving the integrity of that regime; as in Whitter, other extraneous factors must be ignored. The FTT then said that "the key feature of the pension fund regime is that it is designed to help and encourage people to make long-term savings for their retirement with certain tax reliefs/benefits. Deregistration, and the tax charge it triggers, runs counter to that objective. That is a very relevant consideration, but, self-evidently, it will not always prevail; if it did, s.157 would be functus officio". The consequences for a pension scheme and its members of being deregistered are so serious that deregistration should be an act of last resort.

The FTT concluded that:

(a) The overall process which led to the de-registration decisions was flawed, because: (i) (despite NBC asking for this) no explanation was given by HMRC of why it proposed to deregister the Schemes or of the evidence on which it had based its assertions; and (ii) NBC was not given an opportunity to draw to HMRC's attention, before the decision was taken, factual or other matters which they may have overlooked or mis-appreciated in their assessment of the grounds for de-registration.
(b) There was material which would justify HMRC concluding that certain of the gating conditions had been met.
(c) However, HMRC did not evaluate the gating conditions which had been met and decide what weight to give them when deciding whether they justified the Schemes being deregistered.
(d) HMRC either did not consider the exercise of their discretion, or, if they did, they reached their conclusions without taking all relevant considerations into account and arrived at a position which, acting reasonably, they could not adopt.

**The "de-registration threshold"**

4-026     Paragraph (c) in the above list applies if the total amount of scheme chargeable payments[63] made by the pension scheme during any period of 12 months exceeds the de-registration threshold. This is the case if the "scheme chargeable payments percentage" is 25% or more. The scheme chargeable payments percentage is the percentage of the pension fund used up on the occasion of that scheme chargeable payment. If there has been more than one scheme chargeable payment during the period of 12 months, it is the total of the percentages of the pension fund used up on the occasion of each of scheme chargeable payment in the previous 12 months. Each time a scheme chargeable payment is made it is valued as a percentage of the pension fund. The percentage of the pension fund used up on the occasion of a scheme chargeable payment is found by dividing the amount of the scheme chargeable payment by the value of the scheme funds, and multiplying the result by 100.

4-027     HMRC provide the following example at PTM033200:

"Two scheme chargeable payments have been made within a 12-month period. The payments were of £14,000 and £10,000. The fund value at the time of the first payment comprised assets with a market value of £80,000 and cash of £20,000 giving a total value of £100,000.

---

[63] For scheme chargeable payments, see Ch.5.

The percentage of the scheme fund used up at the time of the first scheme chargeable payment is:

(£14,000 / £100,000) x (100/1) = 14%

The fund was valued at £88,000 at the time of the second payment, which was of £10,000:

(£10,000 / £88,000) x (100/1) = 11%

Add together 14% and 11% and the aggregate is 25%. The de-registration threshold is exceeded. This means there are grounds for HMRC to de-register the scheme."

## The de-registration process

If HMRC decide to de-register a pension scheme they must notify the scheme administrator.[64] The notification must state the date from which the pension scheme will not be a registered pension scheme. If there is no scheme administrator (which is itself a ground for de-registration), HMRC must instead notify any person who has responsibility for the discharge of any obligation relating to the pension scheme if it is reasonably practicable for HMRC to identify such a person.[65] De-registration cannot occur until such notice is given, and the notice cannot be backdated.

4-028

## Appealing HMRC's decision to de-register a pension scheme

The scheme administrator (or other notified person) may appeal to the FTT within 30 days of notification.[66] The FTT must consider whether the registration of the pension scheme "ought to have been withdrawn". In *NBC (Administration Services) Ltd v HMRC*,[67] the FTT held that:

4-029

(a) This does not require or entitle the FTT to decide whether the FTT would have reached the same decision.
(b) The FTT must decide whether HMRC: (i) properly considered that a ground was present, and (ii) then properly exercised their discretion to withdraw the scheme's registration.
(c) The latter is a discretionary power, so it must be exercised properly and in a way which addresses the reason why Parliament gave HMRC the discretion.
(d) In deciding whether HMRC exercised their discretion properly, the FTT must consider matters such as whether HMRC acted in a way in which no reasonable panel of Commissioners could have acted (which would include not considering the exercise of their discretion) or whether they had considered some irrelevant matter or had disregarded something to which they should have given weight. The FTT may also have to consider whether HMRC erred on a point of law. Process may also be important.
(e) In that case, the process which led to the deregistration of certain pension schemes was flawed because HMRC failed to engage with the scheme administrator (despite the administrator's reply to the "minded to deregister" letter asking for details of HMRC's assertions and underlying evidence) meant that NBC were unable to address HMRC's concerns. They did not know why HMRC thought they were not a fit and proper person and so could not produce evidence which might disprove HMRC's assertions or suggest other ways (less drastic than deregistration) of addressing any residual concerns. Whether NBC

---

[64] FA 2004 s.157.
[65] For the circumstances in which a person other than a scheme administrator may be so responsible, see Ch.5.
[66] FA 2004 s.159.
[67] *NBC (Administration Services) Ltd v HMRC* [2024] UKFTT 120 (TC).

could have addressed HMRC's assertions is neither here nor there; the point is that, despite asking, they were given no opportunity to do this.

The burden of proof lies with HMRC to show that they have correctly decided to withdraw registration.[68] If the FTT decides that the pension scheme ought not to have been de-registered, the pension scheme is treated as having remained a registered pension scheme (subject to any further appeal by HMRC).

**Consequences of de-registration**

**4-030** If a pension scheme is de-registered:

(a) It will henceforth cease to be: (i) entitled to the various tax reliefs and exemptions that apply to registered pension schemes; and (ii) subject to the tax charges that apply specifically to registered pension schemes.

(b) A de-registration charge will arise.[69] The rate of the tax charge is 40% in respect of the amount of the money and the market value of the assets held for the purposes of the pension scheme immediately before it ceased to be a registered pension scheme. The person(s) who were the scheme administrator(s) immediately before de-registration are liable for the charge. If there is no scheme administrator, liability passes to other persons in accordance with FA 2004 s.272.[70] It is reported and paid using the Accounting for Tax return.

(c) If the scheme has operated relief at source, the scheme administrator must provide specified information to HMRC.[71]

(d) For CGT purposes, the trustees or managers of the pension scheme are deemed to acquire the scheme property immediately before the pension scheme is de-registered for a consideration equal to the amount on which the de-registration charge applies (i.e. the market value of the scheme assets).[72] As the trustees or managers are deemed to acquire the scheme property for its current value, on any future disposal the base cost of the scheme property will be calculated by reference to its value immediately before de-registration.

---

[68] *NBC (Administration Services) Ltd v HMRC* [2024] UKFTT 120 (TC) at [11]: "There was some debate […] about where the burden of proof lies in an appeal under s.159, as this is not a case where statute puts the burden on a particular party. We have not needed to decide this case on the burden of proof, but we agree with [counsel for the taxpayer] that, as HMRC are asserting the positive in the terms of the statutory test (that the registration of the scheme ought to have been withdrawn) and also that it appeared to them that one or more gating conditions was present and that they had correctly decided to withdraw the scheme's registration, the burden rests on them."

[69] FA 2004 s.242.

[70] See Ch.5.

[71] The information is specified in The Registered Pension Schemes (Relief at Source) Regulations 2005 (SI 2005/3448) reg.15(2). For relief at source, see Ch.6.

[72] TCGA 1992 s.239A.

# CHAPTER 5

# The Scheme Administrator

## TABLE OF CONTENTS

| | |
|---|---|
| Introduction | 5-001 |
| Identifying the scheme administrator | 5-003 |
|     Appointed in accordance with the scheme rules | 5-005 |
|     The required declaration | 5-007 |
|     Other declarations reasonably required by HMRC | 5-008 |
|     The fit and proper person requirement | 5-011 |
|     Application to deferred annuities | 5-016 |
|     Appointing a new scheme administrator | 5-017 |
|     Ceasing to be a scheme administrator | 5-019 |
| Duties and liabilities of the scheme administrator | 5-020 |
| The scheme sanction charge | 5-025 |
|     The purpose of the scheme sanction charge | 5-027 |
|     De-registration | 5-029 |
|     The amount of the charge | 5-030 |
|     Liability | 5-031 |
|         Payments within s.161(3) | 5-032 |
|         Income and gains where pension scheme is non-resident | 5-033 |
|     Reporting obligations | 5-035 |
|     Discharge of liability | 5-036 |
|         The "just and reasonable" requirement | 5-039 |
|         The "reasonable belief" requirement | 5-040 |
|         Case law | 5-041 |
|         The European Convention on Human Rights | 5-047 |
|     Relief from the scheme sanction charge | 5-050 |
|     Liability of other persons | 5-053 |
|         Former scheme administrators | 5-054 |
|         Trustees, managers, establishers, sponsoring employers | 5-055 |
|         Members: scheme sanction charge and de-registration charge | 5-058 |
|         Taxable property charge where pension scheme is non-resident | 5-060 |
| Authorising a practitioner | 5-061 |

## INTRODUCTION

The office of scheme administrator is of central importance to the registered pension scheme regime. Every registered pension scheme must have a scheme

**5-001**

administrator at the time that it is registered, and HMRC may de-register a pension scheme if it subsequently ceases to have a scheme administrator, or if the scheme administrator fails to discharge its functions properly.[1] A number of duties are imposed upon the scheme administrator under FA 2004, and HMRC's processes and systems relating to the administration of registered pension schemes (which must, in practice, be adhered to[2]) have the effect of imposing further obligations. This chapter describes those obligations, and the circumstances in which other persons (such as the trustees or members) may become responsible for discharging such duties.

**5-002** A registered pension scheme can have only one scheme administrator at any time. The scheme administrator may be comprised of different persons (e.g. where different persons are responsible for different functions conferred or imposed on the scheme administrator under FA 2004).[3] Where more than one person comprises the scheme administrator, each is jointly and severally liable for any tax liabilities and penalties.

## IDENTIFYING THE SCHEME ADMINISTRATOR

**5-003** The first scheme administrator of a scheme that automatically became a registered pension scheme on 6 April 2006 is determined in accordance with FA 2004 Sch.36 para.4.[4]

**5-004** The scheme administrator of a registered pension scheme established on or after 6 April 2006 is the person(s):[5]

(a) appointed in accordance with the rules of the scheme to be responsible for the discharge of the functions conferred or imposed on the scheme administrator under FA 2004 Pt 4, provided that he

(b) is resident[6] in the UK or a Member State of the EU[7] or a non-Member EEA State;[8]

---

[1] The consequences of de-registration are explained in Ch.4.

[2] These processes and systems have no express statutory footing so little can be usefully added to HMRC's guidance, for which see PTM150000-PTM159000 and HMRC's *Online service for scheme administrators and practitioners*.

[3] FA 2004 Pt 4 consistently refers to "the person who is, or one of the persons who are, the scheme administrator".

[4] See Ch.3.

[5] FA 2004 s.270. There is no other way for a person to become a scheme administrator. HMRC have no statutory power or authority to appoint a person as the scheme administrator, or to treat him as if he were the scheme administrator (for a case in which HMRC attempted to do so, see *Bayonet Ventures LLP v HMRC* [2018] UKFTT 262).

[6] The legislation does not specify how to determine the place of residence for these purposes. In relation to an individual, it is likely to involve an application of the common law test of residence (the statutory residence test cannot determine where an individual is resident—it can only determine whether or not he is resident in the UK). In relation to a company, it is likely to be the place where a company's central management and control is exercised. The rule in CTA 2009 s.14(1) (that a company incorporated in the UK is UK resident) applies only for the purposes of the "Corporation Tax Acts", and FA 2004 Pt 4 is an Income Tax Act rather than a Corporation Tax Act (ITA 2007 s.1(2)(c); Interpretation Act 1978 Sch.1; CTA 2009 s.1).

[7] "Member State" means a member of the EU (see European Communities Act 1972 s.1 and Sch.1, applied by Interpretation Act 1978 Sch.1).

[8] "Non-member EEA State" means a State which is a contracting party to the Agreement on the European Economic Area but which is not a Member State (FA 2004 s.270(4)). This currently means Norway, Iceland and Liechtenstein.

# IDENTIFYING THE SCHEME ADMINISTRATOR

(c) has made the required declaration to HMRC; and
(d) has made any other declarations which are reasonably required by HMRC.

## Appointed in accordance with the scheme rules

The "rules" of the pension scheme are presumably the provisions governing the operation of the pension scheme (usually, but by no means necessarily, comprising a trust deed and scheme rules). If the scheme provisions do not expressly appoint a person to be responsible for discharging the functions of the scheme administrator under FA 2004 Pt 4, the trustee or manager of the scheme will, by implication, be the scheme administrator appointed in accordance with the rules, at least until such time as third-party scheme administrator is appointed.

5-005

At first glance, all of the requirements in s.270(1) and (2) will continue to be met in respect of a person who has been a scheme administrator of a scheme, even after he retires or otherwise ceases to act. The requirement in s.270(1) should therefore be read as requiring that the person has been appointed in accordance with the rules *and continues to be so appointed*. He will cease to be a scheme administrator once he ceases to be appointed in accordance with the rules.

5-006

## The required declaration

The "required declaration" is a declaration that the person understands that he is responsible for discharging the functions conferred or imposed on the scheme administrator of the scheme under FA 2004, and intends to discharge those functions at all times.[9] The declaration is required to be given at the time that an application is made to register the pension scheme, and also whenever a new scheme administrator is recorded on HMRC's online system. The "required declaration" is not a general declaration; it relates specifically to the pension scheme in question.

5-007

## Other declarations reasonably required by HMRC

HMRC may determine what are the "other declarations reasonably required by HMRC", and may do so on a case-by-case basis. A number of declarations are required to be given when a person registers with HMRC to become a scheme administrator. Only a person who has registered with HMRC as a scheme administrator can be appointed as the scheme administrator of a registered pension scheme under HMRC's online system. To register with HMRC, a person is required to provide certain basic information and make certain declarations to HMRC, including that he:

5-008

(a) accepts that he is responsible for discharging the functions of a scheme administrator under FA 2004 and understands the implications of failing to do so;
(b) accepts that as a scheme administrator he must make returns of information to HMRC, when they are reasonably required; provide information to members to enable them to meet their tax obligations and pay any tax charges due to be paid by the scheme administrator under FA 2004 Pt 4;
(c) understands that where HMRC believes that a scheme administrator, or one of the persons that make up the scheme administrator of the pension scheme, is not a fit and proper person to be a scheme administrator, HMRC may refuse to register a scheme or, if the scheme is already registered, HMRC may de-register a scheme; and

---

[9] FA 2004 s.270(3).

(d) is a fit and proper person to be a scheme administrator and he has not: (i) been involved in tax fraud, abuse of tax repayment systems or other fraudulent behaviour including misrepresentation and/or identity theft; (ii) had a criminal conviction relating to finance, corporate bodies or dishonesty; (iii) been the subject of adverse civil proceedings relating to finance, corporate bodies or dishonesty/misconduct; (iv) participated in or been connected with designing and/or marketing tax avoidance or pensions liberation schemes; (v) been disqualified from acting as a company director or are bankrupt; (vi) been disqualified from acting as a pension scheme trustee.

**5-009** HMRC have no power to require any person other than the scheme administrator to give the declarations referred to in s.270(2)(c), so where the scheme administrator is a company, the declarations must relate to the company rather than the individual completing the application on behalf of the company. However, in relation to the first part of the fit and proper test in (d) above (i.e. not including items (i)–(vi) above), it is right for HMRC to consider whether the directors (or other persons controlling management of the company) are fit and proper persons.[10] If none of the directors of a company are fit and proper persons, it is extremely difficult to see how the company itself could be a fit and proper person.

**5-010** The person who is the scheme administrator when the pension scheme is registered will continue to be the recorded scheme administrator until such time as a replacement scheme administrator is appointed. Accordingly, there will at all times be a person who is recorded as the scheme administrator on HMRC's online system. But it is important to appreciate that such a person will not in fact be the scheme administrator if he is not appointed in accordance with the rules of the scheme (including where he has ceased to be so appointed), or if he is not (including where he ceases to be) resident in the EEA. If the original scheme administrator (X) is replaced with another person (Y) but X is still shown as the scheme administrator on HMRC's online system, X will not meet the requirement in s.270(1) because he is not currently appointed as such under the rules, and Y will not meet the requirement in s.270(2) because he will not have given the required declaration in relation to that scheme.[11] In such circumstances, there would appear to be no scheme administrator (which is a ground for re-registration).

### The fit and proper person requirement

**5-011** FA 2004 does not specify what it means to be a fit a proper person.[12] HMRC say that they will assume that all persons appointed as scheme administrators are fit and proper unless HMRC holds or obtains information which causes HMRC to question that assumption.[13] If HMRC obtains such information, they say they will normally raise their concerns with the scheme administrator initially, and, where appropriate use its powers to request information and documentation to determine whether the test is failed.[14] In *NBC (Administration Services) Ltd v HMRC*,[15] the sole director of a corporate scheme administrator admitted to HMRC that she had

---

[10] PTM153000.
[11] Unless, exceptionally, he has been the scheme administrator of that scheme in the past and therefore gave the required declaration at that time.
[12] The fit and proper person requirement was introduced in FA 2014 along with a number of other measures designed to counter pension liberation.
[13] PTM153000. Also see *Guidance on the fit and proper person criteria for pension scheme administrators* (1 September 2014).
[14] HMRC's powers are in FA 2004 s.153A where the scheme is not yet registered, and in s.159A where the scheme has already been registered. These powers are explained below.

no experience in the pension industry, and the FTT accepted that this was sufficient for HMRC to conclude that the scheme administrator was not a fit and proper person. Merely taking advice from external experts was not sufficient.

HMRC guidance explains that the scheme administrator is likely to be considered a fit and proper person if the scheme administrator is "familiar with, and capable of competently performing, the scheme administrator's responsibilities and there is nothing in their past behaviour to suggest that they should not be responsible for the financial management of the pension scheme". HMRC consider that relevant factors include (but are not limited to) where it appears to HMRC that the scheme administrator:[16]

5-012

(a) Does not have sufficient working knowledge of the pensions and pensions tax legislation to be fully aware and capable of assuming the significant duties and liabilities of the scheme administrator, or does not employ an adviser with this knowledge.[17]
(b) Has previously been involved in pension liberation.
(c) Has previously been the scheme administrator of, or otherwise involved with, a pension scheme which has been de-registered by HMRC.
(d) Has been involved in tax fraud, abuse of tax repayment systems or other fraudulent behaviour including misrepresentation and/or identity theft.
(e) Has a criminal conviction relating to finance, corporate bodies or dishonesty.
(f) Has been the subject of adverse civil proceedings relating to finance, corporate bodies or dishonesty/misconduct.
(g) Has participated in or been connected with designing and/or marketing tax avoidance schemes.
(h) Employs as an adviser a person who has been involved in pension liberation or tax avoidance.
(i) Has been removed from acting as a trustee of a pension scheme by the Pensions Regulator or a Court, or has otherwise seriously contravened the pensions regulatory system, or the regulatory system of any other professional/governmental regulatory body.
(j) Has been disqualified from acting as a company director or are bankrupt.

It is difficult to see how some of these factors could be reasonably regarded as material.[18] However much one may disapprove of tax avoidance, the suggestion that one may fail the test merely by employing an adviser who has previously been "involved" in tax avoidance seems particularly difficult to justify, given that most large law firms and accountancy practices have at some time been involved in the design of tax schemes.[19] A decision by HMRC to refuse to register a pension scheme, or de-register a scheme that has been registered, on the basis that the

5-013

---

[15] *NBC (Administration Services) Ltd v HMRC* [2024] UKFTT 120 (TC); [2024] Pens. L.R. 8.
[16] Not all of these factors mentioned in HMRC's guidance currently appear in the declarations required to be given by person when he registers with HMRC to become a scheme administrator (as set out above).
[17] It is not necessary for this adviser to be an authorised practitioner (see below) but that is one way to satisfy this requirement.
[18] This may be an important point in the event of a dispute with HMRC, because these declarations appear to relate to the requirement in s.270(2)(c) for a scheme administrator to make any declarations as are "reasonably required" by HMRC. It cannot be reasonable for HMRC to require declarations that are irrelevant.
[19] HMRC appear to acknowledge that the connection between tax avoidance and managing a pension scheme may be tenuous (not to mention self-serving), and suggest that the listed factors are merely indicative, rather than conclusive. However, it is not possible to register as a scheme administrator without giving the declarations listed above. HMRC's online application does not permit any

scheme administrator is not a fit a proper person, can be appealed to the FTT on the basis that HMRC have taken into account irrelevant considerations.

**5-014** Persons who were scheme administrators before the fit and proper person test was introduced are not required to inform HMRC if they think that they may fail the test, but given that failing the test is a ground for de-registration, all scheme administrators should consider their position.

**5-015** In order to satisfy themselves that the scheme administrator meets the fit and proper test, HMRC may issue an information notice requiring information and documentation that is reasonably required for the purpose of considering if the test is met, or enter business premises to inspect documents for this purpose.[20]

**Application to deferred annuities**

**5-016** A deferred annuity contract is deemed to be a registered pension scheme if it is made with an insurance company by means of which benefits under a registered pension scheme have been secured.[21] It seems that s.270 applies to deferred annuities in the same way as to registered pension schemes.[22] Given that a deferred annuity is not in fact registered with HMRC, it is quite possible that the insurance company will not have made the "required declaration" in respect of a deferred annuity contract. Where that is the case, the annuity contract will not have a scheme administrator and so HMRC de-register the annuity contract. HMRC have no statutory power or authority to appoint a person as the scheme administrator, or to treat him as if he were the scheme administrator, however, in most cases, the insurance company, as the person "who controls the management of the pension scheme", will be responsible for the discharge of the scheme administrator's obligations, and liable for any tax (and any interest on tax) due from the scheme administrator.[23]

**Appointing a new scheme administrator**

**5-017** In order for a person to become a scheme administrator of an existing registered pension scheme, he will need to satisfy the requirements in s.270(2) and (3). As a matter of HMRC practice, he will be able to give the "required declaration" in respect of that scheme only if the current registered scheme administrator "associates" the new or additional scheme administrator to the scheme. Again, this has no statutory footing; it is merely a matter of HMRC practice. "Associating" a new or additional scheme administrator is a straightforward process using HMRC's online system. If the current scheme administrator will not do this (or there is no scheme administrator), the prospective scheme administrator will need to contact Pension Scheme Services so that they can perform the necessary "association".

**5-018** Once a new scheme administrator has been associated with a scheme, the new scheme administrator and any incumbent scheme administrator(s) will between them comprise the scheme administrator. The new administrator will therefore become jointly and severally liable for any outstanding liabilities of the scheme administrator, except in relation to any penalties.

---

exceptions: it is simply not possible to progress without ticking the box. The current system is unsatisfactory in this respect.
[20] See FA 2004 ss.153A and 153B if the scheme is not yet registered, and ss.159A and 159B if the scheme has already been registered. These powers are considered in more detail in Ch.4.
[21] FA 2004 s.153(8).
[22] HMRC agree: PTM031300.
[23] FA 2004 s.272, considered below.

### Ceasing to be a scheme administrator

**5-019** A scheme administrator ceasing to act must notify HMRC within 30 days via HMRC's online service.[24] Penalties may be imposed under TMA 1970 s.98 for failing to make the notification on time or providing incorrect information.

## DUTIES AND LIABILITIES OF THE SCHEME ADMINISTRATOR

**5-020** The scheme administrator is responsible for discharging the following functions:

(a) Operating tax relief under the relief at source system.[25]
(b) Preserving certain documents in its possession or under its control.[26]
(c) Providing certain information to HMRC, members, and to others.[27] The three key returns or reports that must be provided to HMRC are: (i) event reports, (ii) the accounting for tax return, and (iii) the pension scheme return. These obligations are considered in detail in Ch.19.

**5-021** In *AIM (Perth) Ltd v HMRC*[28] the FTT suggested that a scheme administrator has a duty to safeguard funds and must take appropriate action to inform itself in order to do so. It also suggested that in order for a scheme administrator to properly discharge its function with an appropriate standard of care, systems and training are required. This was in the context of an application by the scheme administrator to be relieved from the scheme sanction charge and so the comments of the FTT should be viewed as what is *reasonable* rather than what is *required* of the scheme administrator under FA 2004 Pt 4.

**5-022** The scheme administrator is liable for the following tax charges:[29]

(a) The short service refund lump sum charge.
(b) The serious ill-health lump sum charge.[30]
(c) The special lump sum death benefits charge.
(d) The authorised surplus payments charge.
(e) The lifetime allowance charge (except in relation to certain death benefits). Liability is joint and several with the member.
(f) The annual allowance charge, if the member exercises the "scheme pays" option. Liability is joint and several with the member.
(g) The scheme sanction charge.
(h) The de-registration charge.

---

[24] The Registered Pension Schemes (Provision of Information) Regulations 2006 (SI 2006/567) reg.6 and The Registered Pension Schemes and Overseas Pension Schemes (Electronic Communication of Returns and Information) Regulations 2006 (SI 2006/570) reg.4.
[25] The scheme administrator must operate tax relief under the relief at source system (FA 2004 s.192). The relief at source system is explained in Ch.6.
[26] Any person who is or has been the scheme administrator of a registered pension scheme is required to preserve certain documents in their possession or under their control in relation to a registered pension scheme (FA 2004 s.251(1)(b) and SI 2006/567 reg.18). This obligation is considered in detail in Ch.19.
[27] See FA 2004 s.250 and SI 2006/567.
[28] *AIM (Perth) Ltd v HMRC* [2017] UKFTT 533 at [81].
[29] For the reporting and assessment provisions relating to these taxes, see Ch.19.
[30] This charge can only apply to payments made before 16 September 2016.

(i) The overseas transfer charge. Liability is joint and several with the member.

**5-023** If the scheme administrator is the payor of benefits under the scheme (and has a UK presence), he is also required to apply the usual PAYE rules.

**5-024** If the scheme administrator is not a trustee (or an agent of the trustee), he will be indemnified in respect of such tax charges out of the trust property only if such an indemnity is expressly provided.[31]

## THE SCHEME SANCTION CHARGE

**5-025** The scheme administrator is exclusively liable for the scheme sanction charge, and the scope of the charge (and in particular the circumstances in which a scheme administrator may be discharged from liability for the charge) shows what is expected (if not expressly required) of a scheme administrator. The charge arises where a registered pension scheme makes a scheme chargeable payment.[32] The following are scheme chargeable payments:[33]

(a) all unauthorised payments, except for a small number of exempt payments;[34]
(b) unauthorised borrowing by the scheme;
(c) the receipt by an investment-regulated pension scheme of income (including deemed income) relating to taxable property; and
(d) the realisation by an investment-regulated pension scheme of gains (including deemed gains) relating to taxable property.

**5-026** In the case of an unauthorised payment, the scheme sanction charge applies in addition to the unauthorised payments charge and surcharge. In the case of the scheme chargeable payments in (b)–(d) above, the scheme sanction charge is the only charge imposed under FA 2004 Pt 4.

### The purpose of the scheme sanction charge

**5-027** In *Willey v HMRC*,[35] the FTT tentatively suggested that the rationale for the scheme sanction charge, as with the unauthorised payments charge[36] (which together produce an overall tax charge of 55%) may be to recover the tax relief provided in respect of contributions to the scheme and investment growth. However, that suggestion was described as "entirely speculative" in *Morgan Lloyd Trustees Ltd v HMRC*.[37] In that case, the FTT considered that the purpose of the scheme sanction charge is to deter and punish, and it should therefore be properly categorised as a penalty.[38] The FTT reached this conclusion on the basis that, in contrast to the unauthorised payments charge, there is no obvious connection between the scheme

---

[31] A trustee (and an agent of the trustee) will usually be indemnified under Trustee Act 2000 s.31(1), provided that the charges are properly incurred.
[32] FA 2004 s.239. FA 2004 Pt 4 refers to payments being made "by" a pension scheme (rather than by the trustees or managers of the scheme). This is a reference to payments made from sums or assets held for the purposes of the scheme (see s.279(2)).
[33] FA 2004 s.241(1). Prior to 6 April 2011, the failure to pay the minimum required amount of alternatively secured pension was also treated as being a scheme chargeable payment (FA 2004 s.181A(3)).
[34] See Ch.17.
[35] *Willey v HMRC* [2013] UKFTT 328 (TC) at [56].
[36] The case was not one in which the unauthorised payments *surcharge* applied.
[37] *Morgan Lloyd Trustees Ltd v HMRC* [2017] UKFTT 131 (TC) at [109].
[38] The distinction between a charge and a penalty is material to the application of art.1 of Protocol 1 of the European Convention on Human Rights.

sanction charge and the various tax reliefs that apply to registered pension schemes, and so it cannot be seen as a method of clawing back the tax advantages obtained.

Whereas the unauthorised payments charge and surcharge can be seen as regulating transactions between the pension scheme and its members/employers, it is more difficult to discern any meaningful connection between the different scheme chargeable payments.[39] But it is significant that the scheme administrator is exclusively liable for the charge.[40] Taking into account the circumstances in which in unauthorised payment is "exempt" (and therefore not a scheme chargeable payment), and the circumstances in which a scheme administrator may be discharged from liability, it is suggested that the charge is intended to apply where the administration of the scheme can be criticised in some way. The scheme administrator is expected (although not expressly required) to supervise the activities of the scheme. The intention is that the scheme administrator should: (a) understand whether a given transaction involves a scheme chargeable payment; and (b) ensure that processes are in place such that no scheme chargeable payments can be made without his acquiescence, so that he can effectually supervise the activities of the scheme. The scheme sanction charge is a penalty imposed on the scheme administrator where he fails to ensure that a scheme chargeable payment does not occur. For that reason, the scheme administrator may be discharged from the scheme sanction charge if (broadly) the scheme chargeable payment occurs notwithstanding his reasonable efforts.[41]

5-028

**De-registration**

One of the grounds for de-registration is that the amount of scheme chargeable payments made by the pension scheme during any period of 12 months exceeds the de-registration threshold.

5-029

**The amount of the charge**

The rate of the scheme sanction charge is 40% "in respect of" the scheme chargeable payment,[42] which presumably means 40% of the *amount* of the scheme chargeable payment. If the scheme chargeable payment is also an unauthorised payment and some or all of the unauthorised payments charge has been paid, the scheme

5-030

---

[39] Why were the provisions relating to unauthorised borrowing and income/gains from taxable property not dealt with in the unauthorised payments regime? One reason may be to avoid the necessity of determining which member should suffer the charge. Where, e.g. an investment-regulated pension scheme acquires taxable property, an unauthorised payment is only deemed to occur if the property is (directly or indirectly) held for the purposes of a member's arrangement under the scheme. By contrast, the scheme sanction charge in respect of income/gains from taxable property applies whether or not the income/gains can be attributed to any particular member's arrangement. Alternatively the reason may be that, where a scheme chargeable payment is not an unauthorised payment, these are not transactions that result in any value being passed to a member and so it would perhaps be unfair (or just difficult) to attempt to tax the member.

[40] Although the scheme administrator will usually be indemnified in respect of the charge, any such indemnity will typically be subject to restrictions (e.g. in relation to liabilities caused by the scheme administrator's wilful neglect).

[41] In *Crossfield v HMRC* [2018] UKFTT 390 (TC) at [63], HMRC are recorded as asserting that the purpose of the scheme sanction charge is identified in *O'Mara v HMRC* [2017] UKFTT 91 (TC) at [166], namely to recoup the tax relief that was given on the contribution of funds to the scheme rather than to punish the unauthorised payment. However, *O'Mara* is a decision relating to the unauthorised payments surcharge rather than the scheme sanction charge. It appears that *Morgan Lloyd Trustees* was not cited to the FTT, so the fact that the FTT accepted HMRC's assertion (at [76]) should not be taken as meaningful.

[42] FA 2004 s.240(1).

sanction charge is reduced by the lesser of: (a) 25% of the amount of the scheme chargeable payment(s) if the whole or any part of the unauthorised payments charge in relation to it has been paid; and (b) the amount of the unauthorised payments charge which has been paid in relation to the scheme chargeable payment. The interaction between (a) and (b) ensures that the scheme sanction charge cannot be less than 15% of the scheme chargeable payment. A scheme sanction charge occasioned by the unauthorised borrowing provisions, or the provisions relating to income or gains from taxable property, cannot be reduced under these provisions, because these are not unauthorised payments.

**Liability**

5-031   The scheme administrator is exclusively liable for the scheme sanction charge.[43] As with the other charges imposed under FA 2004 Pt 4, liability is not affected by residency or domicile status. Where there is no scheme administrator, liability passes to other persons in accordance with the provision described below. If the payment of the charge depletes a member's scheme funds it will be a payment "in respect of" that member[44] but it will be a scheme administration member payment and therefore an authorised payment.[45] If the payment does not deplete a member's scheme funds (e.g. it is paid from a general fund), it is not a payment "in respect of" a member, so it is neither an authorised nor an unauthorised payment.[46]

*Payments within s.161(3)*

5-032   If FA 2004 s.161(3) applies to a payment or benefit and the pension scheme has been wound up, the person liable for the scheme sanction charge is the scheme administrator immediately before the pension scheme was wound up.[47] Section 161(3) appears to be aimed primarily at situations where a pension scheme has bought an annuity or scheme pension for a member (i.e. in the member's name) from an insurance company. The intention is to ensure that any scheme chargeable payments by the insurance company are within the scope of the scheme sanction charge.[48]

*Income and gains where pension scheme is non-resident*

5-033   Where an investment-regulated pension scheme is established in a jurisdiction outside the UK, and it holds an interest in taxable property which is located outside the UK, liability to pay the scheme sanction charge under s.185A (income from taxable property[49]) or under s.185F (gains from taxable property) does *not* fall on the

---

[43] For a case in which HMRC attempted to assess a person other than the scheme administrator, see *Bayonet Ventures LLP v HMRC* [2018] UKFTT 262. In that case, the scheme administrator was an LLP and HMRC claimed to have "set up" a designated member of the LLP as the scheme administrator "in order to raise this charge".
[44] See Ch.17.
[45] See Ch.11.
[46] See Ch.17.
[47] FA 2004 s.161(3) applies to a payment or benefit provided in connection with investments acquired with scheme funds. It is considered in detail in Ch.17
[48] Pursuant to FA 2004 s.153(8), a deferred annuity is deemed to be a registered pension scheme (with a scheme administrator) and so the scheme sanction charge would apply to it for that reason. However an immediate annuity is not deemed to be a registered pension scheme (and so will not have a scheme administrator) and this provision is intended to fill the gap.
[49] See Ch.9.

scheme administrator.[50] Instead, it is apportioned on a just and reasonable basis between the members of the arrangements to which the interest in taxable property relates. After it has been so apportioned, any UK resident member of the pension scheme, for the purposes of whose arrangement the interest in taxable property is held, is liable to pay the scheme sanction charge. Where a member is temporarily non-resident[51] at a time when a scheme chargeable payment is made under s.185F, that member is liable to the scheme sanction charge as if that scheme chargeable payment were made in the period of return.

If the investment-regulated pension scheme is established outside the UK and it holds taxable property within the UK, the scheme administrator remains liable in the usual way. As noted above, the charge under s.185F applies even if the interest in taxable property is not held for the purposes of an arrangement relating to any member under the pension scheme. It follows that the scheme administrator of a non-UK scheme with exclusively non-UK members will still be liable for the scheme sanction charge if the taxable property is not held for the purposes of an arrangement relating to any particular member. However, if the taxable property were held for the purposes of one or more arrangements, neither the scheme administrator nor any member will be liable for the scheme sanction charge.[52]

**Reporting obligations**

The scheme administrator must provide an event report to HMRC where an unauthorised payment is made,[53] and must provide specified information to HMRC where unauthorised borrowing occurs.[54] Notification must be provided by no later than 31 January following the tax year in which the event occurs. HMRC will then issue an assessment on the scheme administrator for the amount of scheme sanction charge due. If the tax is paid late, interest is due from the 31 January following the tax year in which the charge arose.[55] If HMRC have not issued an assessment by that date, the scheme administrator can pay the tax to HMRC on account in order to avoid the accrual of interest.[56]

**Discharge of liability**

The scheme administrator may apply to HMRC to be discharged from liability for the scheme sanction charge where either:[57]

(a) the scheme chargeable payment is a deemed unauthorised payment under

---

[50] FA 2004 s.273ZA and The Pension Schemes (Taxable Property Provisions) Regulations 2006 (SI 2006/1958) reg.10.
[51] Broadly, if a person ceases to be UK resident but subsequently becomes UK resident again within five tax years, he is temporarily non-resident during that period of non-residence (FA 2013 Sch.45 para.110).
[52] This conclusion is implicit from FA 2004 s.273ZA and SI 2006/1958 reg.10, which provide that there is no liability under s.239 for the scheme sanction charge arising to a non-UK scheme holding non-UK taxable property. The liability (if any) is determined under the regulations and they do not impose any liability in the circumstances envisaged here.
[53] See SI 2006/567 reg.3 and Ch.19.
[54] SI 2006/567 reg.5A. See Ch.19. See PTM124000 for the method of notification.
[55] The Registered Pension Schemes (Accounting and Assessment) Regulations 2005 (SI 2005/3454) reg.5.
[56] See PTM135300.
[57] FA 2004 s.268(5) and The Registered Pension Schemes (Discharge of Liabilities under Sections 267 and 268 of the Finance Act 2004) Regulations 2005 (SI 2005/3452). The application must be made within the time limits referred to in reg.3.

one of FA 2004 ss.172, 172A, 172B, 172C, or 172D[58] and in all the circumstances of the case it would not be just and reasonable for the scheme administrator to be liable to the scheme sanction charge; or
(b) the scheme administrator:
  (i) reasonably believed that the unauthorised payment was not a scheme chargeable payment;[59] and
  (ii) in all the circumstances it would not be just and reasonable for the scheme administrator to be liable to the scheme sanction charge in respect of the payment.

**5-037** It will be apparent that the scheme administrator can apply to be discharged only where the scheme chargeable payment is an unauthorised payment. No such application can be made in respect of a scheme chargeable payment arising under the unauthorised borrowing provisions or the provisions relating to income/gains in respect of taxable property. If HMRC refuse to discharge the scheme administrator from liability he can appeal to the FTT.[60]

**5-038** It will also be apparent that only the scheme administrator can apply to be discharged. Where there is no scheme administrator, and so liability for the scheme sanction charge passes to others in accordance with s.272 (see below), those other persons cannot be discharged.[61]

*The "just and reasonable" requirement*

**5-039** The "just and reasonable" requirement in (a) and (b)(ii) above is the same as the test applicable for the purposes of the unauthorised payments surcharge, so the commentary in Ch.17 is equally applicable here.

*The "reasonable belief" requirement*

**5-040** The "reasonable belief" requirement in (b)(i) above does not require the scheme administrator to have known (or believed) that the scheme chargeable payment was an unauthorised payment.[62] The reasonableness of the scheme administrator's belief is a value judgment, and the FTT, as the fact-finding tribunal, is best placed to make such a judgment.[63]

---

[58] These are all transactions that do not involve a payment by the pension scheme (e.g. an assignment or surrender of pension benefits by the member) so the scheme administrator may well have no knowledge of them (although lack of knowledge is not a requirement). For these deemed unauthorised payments, see Ch.17.

[59] If the scheme chargeable payment is a payment of a lump sum where the conditions in FA 2004 Sch.29 para.1B(2)(a)–(g) are met, it is not necessary for the scheme administrator to have reasonably believed that the unauthorised payment was not a scheme chargeable payment.

[60] FA 2004 s.269(1)(a).

[61] Confirmed in *Dalriada Trustees Ltd v HMRC* [2023] UKFTT 314 (TC) at [394].

[62] This point was expressly confirmed in *Sippchoice Ltd v HMRC* [2017] UKUT 87 (TCC) at [37].

[63] As Lewison J (as he then was) said in *Davy's of London (Wine Merchants) Ltd v City of London Corp* [2004] EWHC 2224 (Ch) at [34]: "What is reasonable in the circumstances of a particular case is a value judgment on which reasonable people may differ. Since judges are people, their views may differ, but some degree of diversity is an acceptable price to pay for the flexibility enshrined in the statute …". A higher tribunal or court will not interfere with such a judgment unless the FTT makes a legal error, for example by reaching a perverse finding or failing to make a relevant finding or misconstruing the statutory test. It follows that a higher tribunal or court will not consider if it would have come to the same conclusion as the FTT, but whether the determination of the FTT contains an error of law (see *Sippchoice Ltd v HMRC* [2017] UKUT 87 at [39]–[42]).

*Case law*

In *Willey v HMRC*,[64] a registered pension scheme made a loan to a sponsoring employer which was not an authorised employer loan. The scheme administrator was assessed to a scheme sanction charge and he contended that his liability should be discharged under FA 2004 s.268(7) on the ground that he reasonably believed that the payment was not a scheme chargeable payment and it was not just and reasonable for him to be liable to the charge. The scheme's bank account was operated solely by the trustees without reference to the scheme administrator and the loan was made without the knowledge of the scheme administrator. The FTT found that the scheme administrator should have systems in place so that he is aware of what payments are going to be made by the trustees. Only then will the scheme administrator be in a position to advise as to the consequences of such payments and effectively protect his own position. In the absence of having any such system in place, there could be no reasonable belief. Such systems will also put the scheme administrator in a position to fulfil his reporting requirements. The FTT found that s.268(7) is generally aimed at relieving a scheme administrator where he has been misled or otherwise misinformed as to the nature of a payment to be made by the pension scheme. The FTT also concluded that it was just and reasonable for the scheme administrator to be liable to the scheme sanction charge. The unauthorised payment was made because the scheme administrator failed to have a system in place to identify the nature of payments before they were made.[65]

5-041

The facts in *AIM (Perth) Ltd v HMRC*[66] were similar to those in *Willey* except that the scheme administrator had full knowledge of the loan but was apparently unaware of its implications. As in *Willey*, there were no systems in place and so the FTT found that there could be no reasonable belief. The FTT added that ignorance of the law is no excuse and so in order for a scheme administrator to properly discharge its functions with an appropriate standard of care, systems and training are required. If the scheme administrator does not have sufficient knowledge then professional advice must be sought. Without such systems, training or (where appropriate) advice, it is not reasonable to believe that a payment is not a scheme chargeable payment.

5-042

In *Sippchoice Ltd v HMRC*,[67] a pension scheme purchased shares in company A, which lent money to company B, which subscribed for shares in company C. Company C then made a loan to the member of the pension scheme whose funds had been used to purchase the shares in company A. It was assumed, for the purposes of the appeal, that this gave rise to an unauthorised payment.[68] The pension scheme bought shares in company A on behalf of approximately 100 members

5-043

---

[64] *Willey v HMRC* [2013] UKFTT 328.
[65] The decision in *Willey* is an example of how unfair the FA 2004 regime can be in relation to loans. The unauthorised payment was a loan of £100,000 to the sponsoring employer, which was in due course repaid. The unauthorised payment charge was £40,000: the same as if the pension scheme had made an outright payment rather than a loan. An employer that was ignorant of the law could repeatedly borrow and repay what is effectively the same money over a short period of time, and doing so would create tax charges far in excess of the scheme funds. In that sense a loan may be taxed much more severely than an outright payment (which could of course only be taxed once).
[66] *AIM (Perth) Ltd v HMRC* [2017] UKFTT 533.
[67] *Sippchoice Ltd v HMRC* [2017] UKUT 87.
[68] Which it almost certainly did: see *Danvers v HMRC* [2016] UKUT 569 and *White v HMRC* [2016] UKFTT 0802 which involved very similar arrangements.

between August 2010 and August 2011.[69] The administrator's knowledge of the transactions changed over time, and HMRC accepted (following an internal review) that the administrator initially met the requirements to be discharged from liability. However, information disclosed by a scheme member in December 2010 caused a manager of the scheme administrator to suspect that the funds were possibly being paid to members, and HMRC argued that from that date the requirements to be discharged from liability were not met. The administrator raised its concerns with company A and received assurances from company A and company B that loans were not being made to members, but it learnt on 7 July 2011 that "loans may be being made by an unconnected party".[70] On 4 August 2011, the administrator received an email from a member stating in clear terms that loans were being provided by a third party in connection with the investment in company A, and the administrator did not permit any investment in company A after that date.

**5-044** In relation to the "reasonable belief" requirement, it was accepted that the scheme administrator believed that no unauthorised payments were being made, and the FTT found that that belief was reasonable in respect of all transactions until 4 August 2011. In particular, it was reasonable for the scheme administrator to have been satisfied with the responses given by company A in respect of the administrator's proportionate enquiries (which focussed on loans to member from either company A or company B), which reasonably appeared to them to be genuine and reassuring. The scheme administrator also acted reasonably in not doing more (and, in particular, by not consulting the members individually).[71] The decision does appear to be fairly generous towards the scheme administrator. It was clear that from August 2010 the administrator felt uneasy about investment in company A. The management accounts to 31 October 2010 showed that the company was not profitable, but investment in the shares received very significant interest from members. The administrator was assured that neither company A nor company B would make loans to members, and that they had no common directors, but a more "sophisticated" series of transactions does not appear to have been considered. On 7 July 2011, they were clearly put on notice that loans were being made but continued to allow the investments.[72] Before the UT, HMRC argued that that no reasonable tribunal could have decided that reasonable belief continued beyond 7 July 2011, but this was rejected.

**5-045** The test to be applied is clearly very fact-sensitive. It is highly likely that it would *not* now be reasonable for a scheme administrator to permit the type of investment allowed in *Sippchoice* without undertaking much more in-depth due diligence. In that case the number of members wanting to invest in company A must have seemed inexplicable, but the level of due diligence undertaken by the scheme administrator seems weak by current standards because the industry now has a much better understanding of pension liberation.

**5-046** In *Morgan Lloyd Trustees Ltd v HMRC*,[73] an investment-regulated pension scheme acquired taxable property shortly after 6 April 2006 that would have been

---

[69] Indeed, it seems that the scheme administrator's willingness to purchase such shares was the reason that members were introduced to the scheme in the first place.
[70] This was a false assurance, as company C was connected with company B.
[71] *Sippchoice Ltd v HMRC* [2017] UKUT 87 at [53].
[72] It appears to have thought that such loans were permissible. In an email to company A in December 2010, the scheme administrator raised concerns about loans to members from company B and added that "Technically this type of transaction doesn't contravene HMRC rules but it is definitely not in the spirit of the rules and I would decline further business if this was the case" (*Sippchoice Ltd v HMRC* [2017] UKUT 87 at [41]).
[73] *Morgan Lloyd Trustees Ltd v HMRC* [2017] UKFTT 131 at [144].

permissible prior to that date. The FTT found that either: (a) the scheme administrator had some suspicions about the legislative changes and their possible application to the proposed transactions but failed to follow up those suspicions by taking expert advice or approaching HMRC, or (b) if it actually believed the transactions did not involve scheme chargeable payments, it was not reasonable in the circumstances for it to hold that belief; in either case, it could not fairly be said that it "reasonably believed that the unauthorised payment was not a scheme chargeable payment". The FTT also found that the taxpayers could not fairly say that it would not be just and reasonable for them to be liable to the scheme sanction charge in respect of the deemed payments.

*The European Convention on Human Rights*

**5-047** In *Willey v HMRC*[74] (discussed above) the scheme administrator argued that the scheme sanction charge assessed on the scheme administrator was a penalty which in all the circumstances was wholly unjust and unreasonable and ought to be set aside on the basis that it:

(a) is an unlawful interference with his right to the peaceful enjoyment of his possessions pursuant to art.1 Protocol 1 of the European Convention on Human Rights (and so may be set aside by the tribunal as being unreasonable and unjust); and/or

(b) is a penalty which engages his rights under art.6 of the Convention.

**5-048** In relation to art.1, the FTT recognised that a penalty must not be disproportionate having regard to the aim of the policy it is seeking to implement, but the FTT tentatively suggested that the scheme sanction charge was a charge rather than a penalty on the basis that both parties had accepted that an overall 55% liability was intended broadly to recover tax relief on contributions and investment tax-free growth.[75] However, the FTT did not determine whether or not it was a penalty because it found that it was in any event not disproportionate or devoid of reasonable foundation and outside the wide margin of appreciation enjoyed by Parliament. In relation to art.6, the FTT simply stated that there was nothing in the material before the FTT to suggest an infringement.

**5-049** Similar arguments were made in *Morgan Lloyd Trustees Ltd v HMRC*[76] in the context of an acquisition of taxable property. The taxpayer observed that not only was it not necessary for the member to receive a payment of benefits, but he may not even be aware of the decision to do so, and argued that this was a breach of the European Convention on Human Rights arts 1 and 6. The FTT found that the surcharge and scheme sanction charge (but not the unauthorised payments charge) did engage arts 1 and 6 but the ability to seek relief under FA 2004 s.268 and appeal under s.269 meant that the articles were not breached.

**Relief from the scheme sanction charge**

**5-050** Pursuant to certain provisions in PA 2004, a court may make an order for sums or assets to be restored to a pension scheme.[77] Where such an order is made following a transaction under which the scheme administrator has become liable to the

---

[74] *Willey v HMRC* [2013] UKFTT 328 (TC).
[75] This was criticised as being "entirely speculative" in *Morgan Lloyd Trustees Ltd v HMRC* [2017] UKFTT 131 at [109].
[76] *Morgan Lloyd Trustees Ltd v HMRC* [2017] UKFTT 131 at [62].
[77] See PA 2004 ss.16(1), 19(4) or 21(2)(a).

scheme sanction charge in respect of an unauthorised member payment, and as a result of the order sums or assets are transferred to a registered pension scheme, the scheme administrator may claim relief from a proportion of the scheme sanction charge.[78] The relevant proportion of the scheme sanction charge is equal to "ASO/UMP", where *ASO* is the amount subject to the relevant order, that is the aggregate of the market value of any property and the amount of any money transferred, or the amount of the sum paid, towards a registered pension scheme pursuant to the relevant order in respect of the unauthorised member payment, and *UMP* is the amount of the unauthorised member payment.

5-051 But if ASO is greater than UMP, the relevant proportion of the scheme sanction charge is the whole of it.

5-052 The relief available to the scheme administrator here (under s.266B) is less restrictive than the equivalent relief that the member may claim under s.266A in respect of the unauthorised payments charge and surcharge.

**Liability of other persons**

5-053 In certain circumstances a person who is not a scheme administrator will become responsible for some or all of the duties imposed on the scheme administrator under FA 2004 Pt 4.[79] Where more than one person is so liable, liability is joint and several.[80]

*Former scheme administrators*

5-054 In general, any liability of a scheme administrator ceases on that person ceasing to be a scheme administrator, and a person becoming a scheme administrator assumes liability for any existing liabilities of the scheme administrator. This is subject to the following three exceptions:

(a) Where a scheme administrator is liable to pay a penalty, he remains liable for that penalty even if he subsequently ceases to be a scheme administrator. A new scheme administrator is not liable for any penalties imposed on the scheme administrator prior to his appointment.

(b) Where a person ceases to be a scheme administrator in circumstances that there is no remaining scheme administrator, he continues to be liable as if he were the scheme administrator (unless he is dead or has otherwise ceased to exist[81]) until another person becomes the scheme administrator.[82] This continuing liability relates only to liabilities imposed on him when he was scheme administrator: he is not liable for any liabilities which arise after he has ceased to be the scheme administrator.[83] Although such a person has continuing liability, he is not a scheme administrator and so he has none of the rights of the scheme administrator (for example, to apply for a discharge from any of the charges). However, a former scheme administrator may ap-

---

[78] FA 2004 s.266B.
[79] See FA 2004 ss.271–273A.
[80] FA 2004 s.274(1) and (2).
[81] In which case, see Heads One to Five below.
[82] FA 2004 s.271(4).
[83] FA 2004 s.271(4) is not entirely clear on this point, however the reference to liability "as scheme administrator" and the use of the word "remain" make it reasonably clear that new liabilities are not included.

ply to HMRC to be released from these continuing liabilities under FA 2004 s.271(5).[84]

(c) A scheme administrator that is an independent trustee,[85] or is appointed by an independent trustee, does not assume responsibility for any tax charges other than the annual allowance charge and the overseas transfer charge.[86] The previous scheme administrator remains liable for these tax charges arising before the date that the independent trustee is appointed. If the former scheme administrator is dead or has otherwise ceased to exist, or cannot be traced or is in serious default[87] the liability passes as per Heads One to Five below. If, after the independent trustee's appointment has ceased, another scheme administrator is appointed, the new scheme administrator becomes liable for the existing liabilities of the scheme administrator (other than any liability to pay a penalty) in the usual way.[88]

*Trustees, managers, establishers, sponsoring employers*

If there is no scheme administrator or former scheme administrator who continues to be liable (or there is but he cannot be traced), or the scheme administrator is in serious default,[89] other persons are responsible for the discharge of all the obligations imposed on the scheme administrator under FA 2004 Pt 4, and liable for any tax (and any interest on tax) due from the scheme administrator.[90] This does not, however, apply to any liability to pay a penalty. 5-055

Responsibility and liability passes in the following order. If a person is liable under one head and he can be traced and has not failed to discharge any of his obligations, no-one assumes liability by virtue of being specified under a later head:[91] 5-056

(a) *Head One*: any trustees of the pension scheme who are resident in the UK.
(b) *Head Two*: any persons who control the management of the pension scheme.[92]
(c) *Head Three*: if alive or still in existence, the person, or any of the persons, who established the pension scheme and any person by whom that person, or any of those persons, has been directly or indirectly succeeded in relation to the provision of benefits under the pension scheme.[93]
(d) *Head Four*: any sponsoring employer (if the scheme is an occupational pension scheme).

---

[84] If HMRC refuse, the person can appeal to the FTT within 30 days of the notification of HMRC's refusal (FA 2004 s.271 and TMA 1970 ss.42 and 43 and Sch.1A).
[85] An independent trustee is a trustee appointed on or after 1 September 2014 by or in pursuance of an order made by the Pensions Regulator under PA 1995 s.7, or by a court on an application made by the Pensions Regulator, and not a trustee of the pension scheme at any time before any such appointment (FA 2004 s.272A(2)).
[86] See FA 2004 ss.272A–272C.
[87] Meaning that he has failed to discharge any obligation imposed on him under FA 2004 Pt 4 and HMRC considers the failure to be of a serious nature. *Serious nature* is not defined.
[88] FA 2004 s.272C.
[89] Meaning that he has failed to discharge any obligation imposed on him under FA 2004 Pt 4 and HMRC considers the failure to be of a serious nature. *Serious nature* is not defined.
[90] FA 2004 s.272.
[91] FA 2004 s.272(4).
[92] It is implicit that this does not apply to a scheme established under trusts. This is particularly significant in the context of a scheme with non-UK resident trustees. It is likely that such trustees will only be liable at Head Five.
[93] This appears to relate to non-occupational schemes, where the person who established the pension scheme will usually be an insurance company.

(e) *Head Five*: any trustees of the pension scheme who are not resident in the UK.

**5-057** However an independent trustee, or a scheme administrator appointed by an independent trustee, does not assume responsibility for any pre-existing liabilities under these rules by virtue of being a trustee or someone who controls the management of the scheme.[94]

*Members: scheme sanction charge and de-registration charge*

**5-058** Where, under the above provisions, a person other than the scheme administrator (or a former scheme administrator) becomes liable to pay either a scheme sanction charge or a de-registration charge but fails to do so, liability may pass to the scheme members under FA 2004 s.273. This will be the case only where the person(s) liable under s.272 have died or ceased to exist, or where HMRC considers the person's failure to satisfy the liability to be of a serious nature. In these circumstances, each person who was a member of the scheme at any time in the three years before the liability arose is liable to pay an "appropriate share" of the unpaid amount, provided that at least one of the following conditions is met:

(a) The pension scheme was not an occupational pension scheme.
(b) At any time in the three years before the liability arose the pension scheme received a transfer of funds from any other pension scheme in which there were represented contributions under a non-occupational pension scheme (whether or not the pension scheme from which the transfer was received) by or in respect of the member.
(c) The pension scheme was an occupational pension scheme and at any time in the three years before the liability to pay the tax arose the member was a controlling director of a sponsoring employer.
(d) At any time in the three years before the liability to pay the tax arose the pension scheme received a transfer of funds from any other pension scheme in which there were represented relevant controlling director contributions made by or in respect of the member. "Relevant controlling director contributions" are contributions under an occupational pension scheme (whether or not the pension scheme from which the transfer was received) made by reference to service (or remuneration in respect of service) as a controlling director[95] of a sponsoring employer.

**5-059** To find the "appropriate share" of the unpaid amount, divide the total value of scheme property at the time when the liability arose by the value of scheme property held for the purposes of such of the arrangements under the scheme as relate to the member or a person connected with the member. The result is then multiplied by so much of the tax (and any interest on it) as remains unpaid.[96]

**5-060** **Taxable property charge where pension scheme is non-resident** Where an investment-regulated pension scheme established outside the UK holds an interest in taxable property which is located outside of the UK, liability to pay the scheme

---

[94] FA 2004 s.272C.
[95] A controlling director is a director who is within CTA 2010 s.452(2)(b) (director able to control 20% of ordinary share capital) in relation to the company.
[96] e.g. suppose that liability arose at a time when the total value of scheme property is £1 million, of which £250,000 is held for the purposes of the member's arrangement, and the unpaid tax is £300,000. In these circumstances the appropriate share of the unpaid amount is £75,000 (being £250,000/£1,000,000 x £300,000).

sanction charge under ss.185A or 185F (income or gains from taxable property) does not fall on the scheme administrator. Instead it is apportioned on a just and reasonable basis between the members of the arrangements to which the interest in taxable property relates. After it has been so apportioned: (a) any member of the pension scheme resident in the UK, for the purposes of whose arrangement the interest in taxable property is held, is liable to pay the scheme sanction charge; (b) where a member is temporarily non-resident at a time when a scheme chargeable payment is made under s.185F (gains realised on the disposal of taxable property), that member is liable to the scheme sanction charge as if that scheme chargeable payment were made in the period of return. If the investment-regulated pension scheme is established outside of the UK and it holds taxable property within the UK, the scheme administrator remains liable in the usual way.

## AUTHORISING A PRACTITIONER

A scheme administrator may appoint an authorised practitioner to act on the scheme administrator's behalf in relation to certain of the scheme administrator's duties, and authorise HMRC to deal with that practitioner. This is not expressly recognised in FA 2004; it is simply a matter of HMRC practice (for which, see PTM157000). As with scheme administrators, a practitioner must register with HMRC before he can be authorised. This involves providing contact details to HMRC and they will provide a practitioner ID and activation token that allow the practitioner to obtain a username and password on HMRC's online system. A practitioner is not required to give any declarations. **5-061**

If a practitioner is authorised by the scheme administrator then the practitioner will be able to view all of the information relating to the scheme that the scheme administrator can see (other than details of other authorised practitioners) and HMRC will correspond with him in the first instance rather than the scheme administrator. An authorised practitioner can carry out any, or any combination, of the following activities on HMRC's online system: **5-062**

(a) file or amend an event report;
(b) file or amend a pension scheme return;
(c) file or amend an accounting for tax return;
(d) amend scheme details;
(e) register to operate relief at source; and
(f) amend the relief at source details.

The following functions can be carried out only by the scheme administrator (and so may not be delegated): **5-063**

(a) submitting an application to register a pension scheme;
(b) making a scheme administrator declaration required in accordance with FA 2004 s.270;
(c) amending scheme administrator personal details;
(d) reporting the cessation as scheme administrator;
(e) authorising a practitioner;
(f) adding a scheme administrator;
(g) associating a new scheme administrator to a pension scheme; and
(h) registering (including pre-registration) a scheme administrator.

**5-064** An authorised practitioner will cease to have authority to act for a scheme if the person who appointed the practitioner ceases to be a scheme administrator. To continue to be an authorised practitioner for the scheme, the practitioner must be appointed by another person who is a scheme administrator of the scheme.

## CHAPTER 6

# Contributions

### TABLE OF CONTENTS

| | |
|---|---|
| Introduction | 6-001 |
|     What is a contribution? | 6-003 |
| Contributions by or on behalf of a member | 6-004 |
|     Obtaining income tax relief | 6-005 |
|         "Relievable pension contributions" paid during the tax year | 6-007 |
|             "Under" the pension scheme | 6-008 |
|             Contributions "paid" | 6-009 |
|             "By" or "on behalf of" | 6-017 |
|         "Active member" | 6-020 |
|         "Relevant UK individuals" | 6-021 |
|         Pension transfers | 6-024 |
|         Pension credits | 6-025 |
|         Eligible shares | 6-026 |
|         Annual limit for relief | 6-027 |
|         Methods of giving relief | 6-028 |
|             Relief at source | 6-029 |
|             Net pay arrangements | 6-030 |
|             Relief on making a claim | 6-032 |
|             When is a contribution "paid"? | 6-033 |
|     National insurance contributions | 6-034 |
|     Inheritance tax | 6-035 |
| Employer contributions | 6-036 |
|     Determining the profits of a trade | 6-037 |
|         Accounting standards | 6-038 |
|             Intermediate payment arrangements | 6-039 |
|             Defined benefit plans | 6-040 |
|             Measurement of the expense | 6-041 |
|         The wholly and exclusively test | 6-043 |
|             General principles | 6-044 |
|             Application to pension contributions | 6-047 |
|             Contributions for controlling company directors | 6-051 |
|             Disguised distributions | 6-058 |
|             Cessation of trade | 6-059 |
|             Property businesses | 6-061 |
|             Summary | 6-062 |
|     Investment businesses: expenses of management | 6-063 |
|     FA 2004 ss.196–200 | 6-066 |
|         Contributions "under" a pension scheme | 6-068 |
|         "In respect of any individual" | 6-069 |

When is a contribution "paid"? ............. 6-070
Rules relating to capital expenditure ............ 6-071
Rules relating to delayed payment of pension
    contributions ............................. 6-073
Contributions in connection with EFRBS ........ 6-074
Employer asset-backed contributions ........... 6-079
    Simple ABC arrangements .................. 6-082
    Condition A ............................. 6-086
    Condition B ............................. 6-089
    Condition C ............................. 6-096
    Complex ABC arrangements involving a new
        partnership .......................... 6-100
    Complex ABC arrangements using an existing
        partnership .......................... 6-102
    Change in lender's position under acceptable
        structured finance arrangement ........... 6-104
    Interaction with scheme administration employer
        payment provisions ..................... 6-110
Spreading of relief .......................... 6-112
    Cessation of business ..................... 6-117
    Indirect contributions .................... 6-118
Deemed contributions ....................... 6-122
No other relief for employers in connection with
    contributions ............................. 6-124
In specie contributions ....................... 6-127
Inheritance tax ............................. 6-132
Taxation of the employee ..................... 6-133
    The earnings charge ...................... 6-133
    The benefits code ........................ 6-136
    Termination payments .................... 6-137
National insurance contributions ................ 6-138
Salary sacrifice .................................. 6-139
    Optional remuneration arrangements .............. 6-140
        The amount forgone ......................... 6-142
        Exemptions ................................ 6-143
Member and employer contributions ................... 6-144
    The annual allowance charge .................... 6-144
    "Recycling" lump sums ........................ 6-145
        The amount of the unauthorised payment ........ 6-147
        Exceptions ................................ 6-148
    Annual payments ............................. 6-149
    In specie contributions ........................ 6-151
        Chargeable gains .......................... 6-152
        Stamp duty land tax ........................ 6-153
        Stamp duty ............................... 6-154
Tax on pre-owned Assets ........................... 6-155

# INTRODUCTION

**6-001** The contribution provisions of a pension scheme differ between money purchase schemes and defined benefits schemes.[1] In relation to money purchase occupational schemes, the employer and members usually each undertake to contribute a specified amount to the scheme (with each member's contributions deducted from his salary and paid by the employer to the trustees). The employer gives this undertaking to the trustees and also to each employee: from the employee's perspective the contributions by his employer are merely a different form of remuneration. In a money purchase occupational scheme established for the owner managers of a small business, contributions will often be made on an ad hoc basis, depending upon the profitability of the business as determined at the year-end. In a non-occupational money purchase scheme, contributions may be fixed and/or ad hoc.

**6-002** Members of defined benefits schemes usually contribute a specified amount (although in some schemes members are not obliged to contribute at all), and the employer undertakes to meet the balance of cost. The precise circumstances in which the employer is required to contribute, and the method for determining the amount the employer is required to contribute, differ from scheme to scheme. The employee does not consider the contributions to be a form of remuneration; instead the accrual of pension rights is his remuneration. In practice, employer contributions are usually set by agreement between the employer and the trustees, after consultation with the scheme actuary.

**What is a contribution?**

**6-003** The term "contribution" is used extensively in FA 2004 Pt 4 Ch.4, but it is not defined. Typically it will involve the outright transfer of money and/or assets such that they become held for the purposes of the pension scheme. It is suggested that the defining characteristic of a "contribution" is that it involves a transfer of value to the pension scheme.[2] If that is correct, the sale of an asset to a pension scheme for less than its market value involves a contribution to the extent of the undervalue. A payment to a third party to discharge a debt of a pension scheme is likely to involve a contribution to the scheme, because it has the effect of transferring value to the scheme. A transfer of money or assets from one pension scheme to another is expressly not a contribution for the purposes of FA 2004,[3] but it would otherwise involve a contribution to the transferee scheme.[4]

---

[1] Or, where a pension scheme provides both types of benefits, between the money purchase and defined benefits arrangements under the scheme.
[2] In the context of a money purchase arrangement it may be more accurate to say that the value is transferred to the member rather than the pension scheme because a contribution increases the value of the member's rights under the scheme. The important point is that any value is transferred to the member via the scheme and so constitutes a contribution to the scheme.
[3] See FA 2004 s.188(5).
[4] By contrast, if a person lent money to a pension scheme interest-free and repayable on demand, it is difficult to see how the interest foregone could be described as a contribution: such a loan would not in itself transfer value to the pension scheme.

# CONTRIBUTIONS BY OR ON BEHALF OF A MEMBER

**6-004** There is no limit to the amount or value of contributions that a member can make to a registered pension scheme. There are, however, limits on the amount of tax relief that he may obtain in respect of such contributions. In addition, there are limits on how much he (or anyone else, including his employer) may contribute without giving rise to an annual allowance charge.

### Obtaining income tax relief

**6-005** An individual is entitled to income tax relief in respect of a contribution if all of the following apply[5]:

(a) The contribution is a "relievable pension contribution" paid during a tax year.
(b) The member is an "active member" of a registered pension scheme.
(c) He is a "relevant UK individual" for that year.

**6-006** Where relief is given to an individual, no tax relief will be available in respect of the contribution under any other provision of the Income Tax Acts, or (in the case of a contribution under an annuity contract) in respect of any other premium or consideration for an annuity under the same contract.[6]

*"Relievable pension contributions" paid during the tax year*

**6-007** A "relievable pension contribution" is a contribution by or on behalf of an individual under the pension scheme, other than[7]:

(a) Any contribution paid after the individual has reached the age of 75.
(b) Any contribution which is a "life assurance premium contribution".[8] A contribution is a life assurance premium contribution if: (i) it constitutes the payment of premium under a "non-group life policy" which is (or later becomes) held for the purposes of the pension scheme; or (ii) the payor intends the contribution (or an amount equivalent to it) to be applied towards paying the premium under such a policy. A "non-group life policy" is a policy of insurance under which the only benefits which may become payable are benefits payable in consequence, or in anticipation, of the death of: (i) the individual; or (ii) one of a group of individuals which includes the individual; or (iii) the deaths of more than one of a group of individuals, which includes the individual, and the other members of the group are connected[9] with the individual. Grandfathering provisions apply to certain "protected" policies.[10] Certain other contributions are deemed to be life assurance premium contributions. Where, for example, the premium under such a policy in a tax year is £10, and the individual contributes £15 to the

---

[5] FA 2004 s.188(1).
[6] FA 2004 ss.192(10) (relief at source) and 193(8) (net pay arrangements).
[7] FA 2004 s.188(2), (3) and (3A).
[8] FA 2004 s.195A.
[9] For these purposes, A is connected with B if: (a) A is B's spouse or civil partner; (b) A is a relative of B; (c) A is the spouse or civil partner of a relative of B; (d) A is a relative of B's spouse or civil partner; or (e) A is the spouse or civil partner of a relative of B's spouse or civil partner. "Relative" means brother, sister, ancestor or lineal descendant.
[10] See FA 2007 Sch.18 paras 4–7.

## CONTRIBUTIONS BY OR ON BEHALF OF A MEMBER

pension scheme, of which £8 is a life assurance premium contribution (and so £7 is not), an additional £2 (being the difference between the £10 and the £8) is deemed to be a life assurance premium contribution. But where the benefits under the policy relate to the death of one or more of a group of individuals, and contributions are also paid under the pension scheme in the tax year by or on behalf of other member(s) of the group, the deemed life assurance premium contribution is limited to what is just and reasonable having regard to the operation of s.188 in relation to the contributions paid by or on behalf of another member or other members of the group.

(c) Any contribution paid by an employer of the individual. This is intended to ensure that both the employer and the member do not obtain tax relief (or a tax deduction) in respect of the same contribution. This only relates to funds that are beneficially owned by the employer immediately prior to the contribution. Such contributions may be contrasted with contributions of the member's earnings that the employee requests or directs his employer to pay to the scheme. The fact that such contributions are, in a literal sense, paid by his employer to the scheme does not prevent s.188(1) from applying, because such a contribution is not, for the purposes of s.188(3)(b), paid "by" the employer; it is paid "by or on behalf of" the member. This analysis applies wherever the member is beneficially entitled to the money paid by his employer, and should also apply wherever the employer is holding money that have been subject to tax as earnings of the member (even if the employee is not strictly beneficially entitled to them).

(d) Any contribution made pursuant to PA 2004 ss.16(1), 19(4), or 21(2)(a). These provisions allow a court, following an application from the Pensions Regulator, to order that a person transfers money or other property to a pension scheme from which property has been misappropriated. If the misappropriation gave rise to an unauthorised member payment, it may be possible to claim relief from the unauthorised payments charge (and surcharge, if applicable) following the transfer back to the registered pension scheme.[11] In these circumstances (i.e. a court order followed by a claim for relief), the transfer to the registered pension scheme is not a relievable pension contribution, except to the extent that it exceeds the amount of the unauthorised payment.[12]

**"Under" the pension scheme**  A relievable pension contribution is a contribution "under" the pension scheme. In this context, the word "under" appears to signify a contribution made *pursuant to the terms of* a pension scheme.[13] The "pension scheme" includes the fund and also any arrangements under which contributions are to be made to the fund,[14] so it is more appropriate to refer to a contribution "under" the scheme rather than "to" the scheme.[15] There seems to be no reason in principle that s.188(1) could not apply to a contribution paid to a "vehicle" (such

**6-008**

---

[11] The relief is claimed under FA 2004 s.266A(2). See Ch.17.
[12] FA 2004 s.188(3A)–(3C).
[13] See *Trustees of Barclays Bank Pension Fund v HMRC* [2005] UKSPC SPC00520 at [72]–[79]; *Allum v Marsh* [2005] S.T.C. (S.C.D.) 191 at [76].
[14] See Ch.2.
[15] e.g. IHTA 1984 s.12(2) refers to a contribution "under" a registered pension scheme. FA 2004 s.246 and Sch.36 para.56 both refer to contributions made "under" a scheme, and it is clear that this is a reference to contributions "pursuant to" the scheme.

as a company or insurance policy) owned by a registered pension scheme. Such a payment would have the effect of transferring value to the scheme.[16]

**6-009** **Contributions "paid"** The individual is entitled to tax relief in respect of relievable pension contributions "paid" during a tax year. HMRC consider that the word "paid" restricts the relief in s.188(1) to cash contributions,[17] except insofar as a transfer of assets is expressly permitted under s.195(1), which provides that:

> "For the purposes of sections 188 to 194 (relief for contributions) references to contributions paid by an individual include contributions made in the form of the transfer by the individual of eligible shares in a company within the permitted period."

**6-010** In general, one would expect the word "paid" to include a payment in kind,[18] but it is a word which takes its meaning from the context in which it is used.[19] Here the context is provided by FA 2004 ss.188–195A, and these provisions do suggest that Parliament had money contributions in mind.[20] Section 195 makes express provision for *in specie* contributions of shares acquired by an individual pursuant to an approved share scheme. The existence of s.195 suggests that such contributions would not otherwise constitute contributions "paid". It is therefore likely that tax relief is available under s.188(1) only for payments of cash or eligible shares.

**6-011** HMRC's longstanding position is that in order to obtain tax relief under s.188(1), a contribution need not be a payment of money but it must be "a monetary amount".[21] HMRC accept that a contribution will be a monetary amount if the member agrees to pay a monetary contribution and then gives effect to the cash contribution by way of a transfer of an asset or assets. Prior to its "clarification" in December 2020, PTM042100 said:

> "For example, if a member wishes to pay a contribution he cannot do this by merely saying 'take this asset and whatever it is worth that is my contribution'.
> There must be:
>
> - a clear obligation on the member to pay a contribution of a specified monetary sum, say, £10,000. This needs to create a recoverable debt obligation.
> - a separate agreement between the scheme trustees and the member to pass an asset to the scheme for consideration.
>
> If the scheme agrees, the cash contribution debt may be paid by offset against the consideration payable for the asset. This is the scheme effectively agreeing to acquire the asset for its market value.
>
> If the asset market value is lower than the contribution debt the balance will be paid in cash. If the cash contribution debt is not created, then the transaction is the acquisition of an asset by the scheme not a contribution."

**6-012** HMRC do not suggest that this is a concession; it is their interpretation of the word "paid" in this context. If s.188(1) did not apply to such contributions, it would be necessary for the member to sell the asset and contribute the sale proceeds so that the scheme can purchase the same asset, and it is most unlikely that this is what

---

[16] Indeed, such a vehicle may in certain circumstances form part of the pension scheme: see Ch.2.
[17] See PTM042100.
[18] See e.g. *Irving v RCC* [2008] EWCA Civ 6 at [21]; *MacNiven v Westmoreland Investments Ltd* [2001] UKHL 6 at [68].
[19] For the meaning of the term payment, see Ch.2.
[20] As will be seen below, the position regarding employer contributions is arguably quite different.
[21] See PTM042100.

Parliament intended.[22] Given HMRC's endorsement of this method of making *in specie* contributions, it became common practice.

However, in April 2017, HMRC warned that the steps described in the guidance are an example and not an exercise to be followed such that tax relief will automatically follow, and suggested that they will scrutinise contributions where the nature of the asset is such that it is may not be capable of being used to meet the pre-existing obligation to make the cash contribution, or where there is insufficient evidence that there was a pre-existing obligation to make a cash contribution.[23] In *Sippchoice Ltd v HMRC*,[24] HMRC denied tax relief in respect of *in specie* contributions of shares on the basis that: (a) the taxpayer failed to create a legally binding debt obligation; and (b) relief is not available under s.188(1) if the taxpayer never intended to make a cash contribution. The FTT accepted that a mere promise to pay (unless executed as a deed) cannot create a legally binding obligation but found that the elements of a contract (offer, acceptance and consideration) were present. It followed that the taxpayer had created a legally binding debt obligation.[25] The FTT went on to consider the ordinary meaning of "contributions paid" and concluded that the transfer of assets in satisfaction of a debt is a "payment".[26] A contribution must have a monetary value to enable the machinery for granting relief to be implemented, but the fact the taxpayer always intended to settle the debt obligation by transferring shares is not material.[27] However, on appeal the UT found in favour of HMRC.[28] It held that s.188(1), interpreted in the light of s.195 in particular, gives relief only for payments of money and not for transfers of assets, and it could see no reason to treat any differently transfers of assets made in satisfaction of a money debt.[29]

**6-013**

As a result of the decision of the UT in *Sippchoice*, in December 2020 HMRC "clarified"[30] its guidance at PTM042000, which now suggests that HMRC will accept that the transfer of an asset is a contribution "paid" where there is contemporaneous documentary evidence of:

**6-014**

(a) a clear obligation on the member to pay a contribution of a specified monetary sum (e.g. £10,000), which creates a recoverable debt obligation;
(b) a separate agreement between the scheme trustees and the member to sell an asset to the scheme for market value consideration; and
(c) a separate agreement whereby the scheme trustees and the member agree

---

[22] See *Irving v RCC* [2008] EWCA Civ 6; [2008] B.T.C. 36 at [32].
[23] Pension Schemes Newsletter 86.
[24] [2018] UKFTT 122.
[25] One practical point that emerges from this is that if one intends to create a debt, the promise should either be executed as a deed or there should be a clear acceptance of the member's offer.
[26] Citing *MacNiven v Westmoreland Investments Ltd* [2001] UKHL 6 at [67]–[69] (Lord Hoffmann).
[27] It was not necessary for the FTT to decide whether a straightforward transfer of assets (otherwise than in satisfaction of a debt) is a contribution "paid", and it expressly made no finding in this regard. However, there are indications in the latter part of the decision ([40]–[47]) that tax relief may be available in respect of such contributions. This is of interest because a straightforward transfer of shares or land to a pension scheme by way of contribution should not give rise to any stamp duty or SDLT, whereas the transfer of shares or land in satisfaction of a debt is subject to stamp duty or SDLT (see below).
[28] *HMRC v Sippchoice Ltd* [2020] UKUT 149 (TCC) (Roth J).
[29] It is suggested that "paid" in FA 2004 s.233 should have a corresponding meaning, so where tax relief is not available under FA 2004 s.188(1) for an *in specie* contribution, it should follow that the annual allowance provisions will not apply to that contribution.
[30] See HMRC's pension schemes Newsletter 126.

that the cash contribution debt may be offset against the consideration payable for the asset.

HMRC added the requirement in (b) above in December 2020, but it is far from clear that this is consistent with the decision in *Sippchoice*.

**6-015** In *Mattioli Woods Plc v HMRC*,[31] the taxpayers made contributions to a SIPP in circumstances similar to those considered in *Sippchoice*. The taxpayers argued that the member's undertaking to make a cash contribution (referred to as an "IOU") was itself a transfer of money (and therefore a "contribution paid") because it was not materially different to a bank transfer. This was rejected by the FTT on the basis that an IOU is a negotiable instrument (it is a promissory note), which is materially different to the usual methods of paying cash contributions, namely direct debits or BACs transfers (both of which involve payments of cash), or cheques (which are bills of exchange).

**6-016** In the most recent case involving such contributions, *Killik and Co LLP v HMRC*,[32] the taxpayers raised a novel argument, namely that the claims for relief were made on the basis of the "practice generally prevailing" at the time they were made. This practice was encouraged by HMRC's published guidance that a transfer of an asset would be a "contribution paid" under the legislation where it followed an agreement to pay a monetary amount. Accordingly:

(a) TMA 1970 s.29(2) (as incorporated by the Registered Pension Scheme (Relief at Source) Regulations 2005 reg.14), applied to the claims for relief; and
(b) as a result, HMRC were prevented from issuing an assessment on a basis contrary to that practice generally prevailing.

The FTT disagreed with (a) above: TMA 1970 s.29(2) applies only where a taxpayer has made and delivered a return under TMA 1970 ss.8 or 8A, and a claim for relief under the Regulations does not involve any such return.

The FTT also rejected the taxpayer's alternative argument that the legislation contains a clear drafting error which the FTT was required to correct when construing the legislation.[33] The FTT also held that, even if s.29(2) did apply, the contributions in this case were not made in accordance with HMRC's guidance as it stood at the time of the contributions (and therefore it was not a practice generally prevailing[34]), because no debt had in fact been created.

**6-017** **"By" or "on behalf of"** A relievable pension contribution must be paid "by" or "on behalf of" a member. In either case, the member is entitled to the tax relief. Clearly, a contribution is paid "by" a member if he is beneficially entitled to the cash or eligible shares prior to the transfer to the pension scheme. Where the member has committed to make specified contributions to the scheme, there can be little doubt that a contribution by a third party (such as the member's parent or grandparent) is made "on behalf of" the member if it relieves the member of his obligation.

**6-018** The words "on behalf of" ordinarily suggest a relationship of agency,[35] but where the context requires they have been interpreted more widely as meaning "in the

---

[31] *Mattioli Woods Plc v HMRC* [2022] UKFTT 179.
[32] *Killik and Co LLP v HMRC* [2023] UKFTT 653 (TC); [2023] S.F.T.D. 1101.
[33] Per *Inco Europe Limited v First Choice Distribution* [2000] 1 W.L.R. 586; [2000] 1 Lloyd's Rep. 467.
[34] Per *Hargreaves v HMRC* [2022] UKUT 34 (TCC); [2022] S.T.C. 455.
[35] See *Gaspet Ltd v Elliss (Inspector of Taxes)* [1985] 1 W.L.R. 1214 at 1220 (Peter Gibson J); *Clixby v Pountney (Inspector of Taxes)* [1968] Ch. 719 at 728–729 (Cross J).

place of", or "for the benefit of" or "in the interests of".³⁶ Employer contributions relating to a particular individual are said to be made "in respect of" that individual,³⁷ and it is suggested that this means "for the benefit of" that individual.³⁸ It is reasonable to assume that "on behalf of" is intended to have a different (and probably more restricted) meaning. However, the better view seems to be that ad hoc contributions by third parties *for the benefit of* the member are made "on behalf of" the member for the purposes of s.188(2). There is no reason, as a matter of policy, why such contributions should not benefit from tax relief, and it would be very surprising if the words "on behalf of" were found to have a more restricted meaning. However, in cases where HMRC are more likely to dispute the availability of tax relief it may assist the member if he can demonstrate that the contribution in some sense relieved him of a prior obligation, or (at the very least) he was aware of the contribution and that he authorised or consented to it.

**6-019** The "by or on behalf of" requirement appears to focus solely on the identity of the person making the contribution and the circumstances in which it is paid. There is no express requirement that the contribution is *for* the member in the sense that it must be allocated to the member's fund under the pension scheme (although this may be implied in most circumstances). If a married couple (A and B) are both members of a pension scheme, and A makes a contribution on behalf of B, it seems that both A and B will meet the requirements of s.188(1). In these circumstances there appears to be a choice regarding by whom the tax relief may be claimed.³⁹

*"Active member"*

**6-020** "Active member" is defined in FA 2004 s.151(2) (see Ch.2). The requirement is that there are presently arrangements made under the pension scheme for the accrual of benefits to or in respect of the member. If a contribution is made to a money purchase arrangement there will, by definition, be arrangements in place for the accrual of benefits. Provided that the individual is a member of the scheme, the act of paying a contribution will itself make him an active member. In relation to a defined benefits arrangement, this will typically require the member to be in pensionable service.

*"Relevant UK individuals"*

**6-021** An individual is a "relevant UK individual" for a tax year if one or more of the following applies⁴⁰:

(a) he has "relevant UK earnings" chargeable to income tax for that year;
(b) he is resident in the UK at some time during that year;

---

[36] See *R. (Cherwell DC) v First Secretary of State* [2004] EWCA Civ 1420; [2005] 1 W.L.R. 1128 at [56]; *R. (S) v Social Security Commissioner* [2009] EWHC 2221 (Admin); [2010] P.T.S.R. 1785 at [27]–[28]; *Rochdale MBC v Dixon* [2011] EWCA Civ 1173; [2012] P.T.S.R. 1336 at [49]–[50].
[37] e.g. FA 2004 s.196.
[38] As opposed to unallocated contributions, which are described as being made "otherwise than in respect of any individual" in FA 2004 ss.172C(1)(a) and 233(3).
[39] Indeed, a literal reading suggests that both A and B may claim tax relief (under the relief at source method) in respect of the same contribution in these circumstances. Section 192(10) would not prevent this because both amounts of tax relief would be available under s.192 (and not "any other provision of the Income Tax Acts"). HMRC would no doubt resist any such claim for double relief and it is likely that they would be successful. If all else failed, it is likely that the general anti-abuse rule in FA 2013 Pt 5 would prevent s.188(1) from having the effect of allowing tax relief for both A and B in these circumstances.
[40] FA 2004 s.189(1).

(c) he was resident in the UK both at some time during the five tax years immediately before that year and when the individual became a member of the pension scheme; or
(d) he, or his spouse or civil partner, has for the tax year general earnings from overseas Crown employment subject to UK tax.

**6-022** "Relevant UK earnings" means any of the following[41]:

(a) Employment income.
(b) Trading income which is chargeable under ITTOIA 2005 Pt 2 and is immediately derived from the carrying on or exercise of a trade, profession or vocation (whether individually or as a partner acting personally in a partnership). One might expect that a share of profits paid to a sleeping partner or an annuity paid to a retired partner is not "immediately derived" from the trade etc.[42] However, HMRC's views on the meaning of very similar terminology in the provisions relating to class 4 NIC suggests that they may accept that such income is immediately derived from the trade etc.[43]
(c) Property income which is chargeable under ITTOIA 2005 Pt 3 and is immediately derived from the carrying on of a UK furnished holiday lettings business or an EEA furnished holiday lettings business (whether individually or as a partner acting personally in a partnership).
(d) Patent income, but only if the individual, alone or jointly, devised the invention for which the patent in question was granted.

**6-023** Relevant UK earnings are treated as not being chargeable to income tax if, in accordance with an applicable tax treaty, they are not taxable in the UK.[44]

*Pension transfers*

**6-024** A transfer to a registered pension scheme from another pension scheme[45] is expressly not a contribution.[46] Note that this is not limited to transfers from pension schemes holding UK tax-relieved funds such as registered pension schemes and QROPS. A transfer from an EFRBS (for example) will not be a contribution for the purposes of s.188(1). A transfer from an arrangement that is not a "pension scheme" (such as an employee benefits trust, for example) may be a contribution, with tax relief available to the member.[47]

---

[41] FA 2004 s.189(2)–(7).
[42] See *Pegler v Abell* [1973] 1 W.L.R. 155 at 161 (Goff J). If the partner was previously active and the income arises from that past activity, such income may derive from the activity but it is unlikely to immediately derive from the activity.
[43] See NIM24523, reflecting a change of view announced in April 2013. The reference to "acting personally" in (b) above (but not in the NIC provisions) does not appear to be a material distinction because the same terminology appears in (c) above (relating to furnished holiday lettings businesses) where partners will frequently be inactive.
[44] Where a UK resident individual performs some or all of his duties outside of the UK, a tax treaty between the UK and that other country will frequently provide that earnings relating to those services are taxable in the country in which the services are performed, and not in the UK (where he is resident for tax purposes).
[45] "Pension scheme" is defined in FA 2004 s.150(1) (see Ch.2).
[46] FA 2004 s.188(5).
[47] Such a transfer may be subject to income tax and NIC under the disguised remuneration provisions.

CONTRIBUTIONS BY OR ON BEHALF OF A MEMBER 127

*Pension credits*

A pension credit which increases the rights of the individual under the pension scheme is treated as a contribution on behalf of the individual unless it derives from another registered pension scheme.[48] So a transfer from an EFRBS *will* be a contribution under s.188(1) if it is a pension credit.[49] This ensures that tax relief is available in respect of pension credits, but does not permit double tax relief. On this basis, it seems likely that a pension credit "derives" from a registered pension scheme if it was contributed to a registered pension scheme, even if it is subsequently transferred to a different scheme such as a QROPS.

6-025

*Eligible shares*

A transfer by an individual of "eligible shares" constitutes a contribution paid by the individual.[50] Shares are "eligible" if:

6-026

(a) the individual exercised a right to acquire them under a SAYE option scheme[51]; or
(b) they were appropriated to the individual under a share incentive plan.[52]

The shares must be transferred within 90 days of the exercise of the right under the SAYE option scheme, or 90 days of the date the individual directed the trustees of the share incentive plan to transfer the ownership of the shares to him. The amount of the contribution is the market value of the shares at the date of the transfer.[53]

*Annual limit for relief*

The maximum amount of relief to which an individual is entitled under s.188(1) for a tax year is the greater of:

6-027

(a) the amount of the individual's "relevant UK earnings" which are chargeable to income tax for the tax year; or
(b) the basic amount.[54]

The basic amount is currently £3,600.[55] If an individual claims relief for an amount which is greater than the amount of his relevant UK earnings which are chargeable to income tax for the tax year, the relief must be claimed under the relief at source method rather than under net pay arrangements.[56]

*Methods of giving relief*

There are two methods of obtaining tax relief under s.188(1): relief at source and net pay arrangements.[57] All non-occupational schemes must use the relief at source method. In practice, most occupational schemes use the net pay method.

6-028

---

[48] FA 2004 s.188(4).
[49] HMRC agree at PTM093800: "... if the pension credit is received from a non-registered pension scheme it is tax relievable".
[50] FA 2004 s.195(1).
[51] See ITEPA 2003 s.516.
[52] See ITEPA 2003 s.488.
[53] FA 2004 s.195.
[54] FA 2004 s.190(1) and (2).
[55] Or such greater amount as the Treasury may by order specify (FA 2004 s.190(4)).
[56] FA 2004 ss.190(3) and 191(7).
[57] FA 2004 s.191.

**6-029** **Relief at source**  The default position is that income tax relief is given under the relief at source method.[58] This method must be used where the member is claiming relief for more than his relevant UK earnings.

Under the relief at source method, when a contribution is paid to the scheme, the scheme administrator may claim from HMRC an amount equal to basic rate (20%) tax on the contribution paid.[59] So, for example, if a member wants to make a total contribution of £100, he will pay £80 to the scheme and the scheme administrator will claim £20 from HMRC and add it to the member's fund. The total contribution is £100. If the member is a higher rate (40%) taxpayer he will be able to claim additional relief of £20 from HMRC through self-assessment after the end of the year (which will show a total contribution of £100).[60] If he is an additional rate (45%) taxpayer he can claim £25. No relief is available in respect of the NIC that the member and his employer will have paid in respect of the earnings contributed (see below).

**6-030** **Net pay arrangements**  Relief may be given under net pay arrangements if[61]:

(a) the pension scheme is an occupational pension scheme;
(b) the member is an employee of a sponsoring employer; and
(c) relief in respect of contributions made under the pension scheme by all of the other members of the pension scheme who are employees of the sponsoring employer is given under net pay arrangements.

**6-031**  If an individual is entitled to tax relief under a net pay arrangement, the member's employer deducts the member's contributions from his or her gross earnings and pays them to the scheme administrator. For example, if a member wishes to make a contribution of £100, his employer will deduct £100 from his gross earnings and pay £100 to the scheme. As the amount paid to the scheme is not taxed as earnings for income tax purposes, the scheme administrator does not need to reclaim any tax from HMRC. Tax relief at the member's marginal rate is therefore effectively received upfront. Such contributions do not reduce the employee's earnings for NIC purposes (see below). If for some reason the employer is not able to deduct the whole amount of the contribution from the individual's employment income, the member may make a claim for excess relief in his self-assessment tax return.

**6-032** **Relief on making a claim**  Where an individual is entitled to relief under net pay arrangements, on the making of a claim the amount of the contribution may be deducted in calculating the net income of the individual for the tax year in which the payment is made.[62]

**6-033** **When is a contribution "paid"?**  Where a contribution is made close to the end of a tax year, it may be important to know which year the tax relief is for. FA 2004 s.188(1) provides that the tax relief is for the tax year in which the contribution is "paid". This may be different to the period in which the contribution is received by the pension scheme. If a member gives a cheque to the administrators of his SIPP

---

[58] FA 2004 s.191(2). In relation to relief at source generally, see The Registered Pension Schemes (Relief at Source) Regulations 2005 (SI 2005/3448). The member must provide information and declarations to the scheme administrator and HMRC (regs 4–6 and 15), and the scheme administrator must provide information and make records available to HMRC (regs 15–16).
[59] FA 2004 s.192 and SI 2005/3448 regs 9–12.
[60] SI 2005/3448 reg.5.
[61] FA 2004 s.191(3).
[62] See Step 2 of the calculation in ITA 2007 s.23.

on last day of the tax year (5 April), and it clears on say 7 April (and is therefore shown in the member's bank account at the end of 5 April), in which tax year is the contribution paid? The property does not pass until the cheque clears,[63] but HMRC accept that the contribution is paid when the cheque is received by the administrators.[64] A cheque is a reasonable method of payment, and once it is provided there is nothing more the payor can do; the fact that the payee may not cash it immediately should not affect the timing of the tax relief.

Is the position any different where relief is given under net pay arrangements? PTM044230 states: "If the employer is operating the net pay arrangement then pension contributions will be by means of payroll deduction. The member's employers will deduct the contribution from the 'gross pay' in the tax year the contribution is made. The employer is able to operate 'PAYE' on the net amount giving full relief at the marginal tax rate". This suggests that, in HMRC's view, the contribution is *paid* when it is deducted from the member's salary.

**National insurance contributions**

Earnings received by an individual are usually subject to income tax and NICs. If the individual contributes some or all of those earnings to a registered pension scheme (or directs his employer to do so on his behalf) he may obtain income tax relief under s.188(1) but there is no equivalent relief for the NICs that he and his employer have suffered. It is for this reason that employer contributions (which are not made "on behalf of" the member) may be more attractive than contributions by or on behalf of a member. This is a key attraction of salary sacrifice arrangements (see below).

**6-034**

**Inheritance tax**

A contribution by a member for his own benefit will not be a transfer of value provided that he has no intention to confer gratuitous benefit on any other person.[65] A contribution by a third party (such as a relative) will be a transfer of value, but will frequently be an exempt transfer.[66]

**6-035**

# EMPLOYER CONTRIBUTIONS

The employer of a scheme member will usually view a pension contribution as a form of remuneration, and as such, will expect it to be recognised as an expense which has the effect of reducing its taxable profits. The statutory provisions relating to the calculation of trading profits are in CTA 2009 Pt 3 (for companies) and ITTOIA 2005 Pt 2 (for unincorporated traders, including partnerships). The statutory provisions relating to the calculation of investment profits are in CTA 2009 Pt 16 (for companies) and the relevant part of ITTOIA 2005 (for example, Pt 3 relates to property income and Ch.2 of Pt 5 relates to intellectual property).

**6-036**

---

[63] *Re Swinburne* [1926] Ch. 38; 44 A.L.R. 619; *Owen v CIR* [1949] 1 All E.R. 901; [1949] T.R. 189.
[64] PTM041000: the deemed date of payment of a contribution by way of cheque is "the date the cheque is given to, or if posted received by, the scheme administrator". And at PTM093800: "... if the contribution is made by cheque then it is paid when the cheque is received by the scheme administrator, as long as the cheque does not bounce".
[65] IHTA 1984 s.10.
[66] The inheritance tax provisions are explained in detail in Ch.21.

## Determining the profits of a trade

**6-037** The profits of a trade must be calculated in accordance with generally accepted accounting practice, subject to any adjustment required or authorised by law in calculating profits for tax purposes.[67] The starting point is to determine the accounting treatment, and then consider if any adjustments are required or authorised by law. In the context of contributions to a registered pension scheme, the following provisions may require or authorise adjustments:

(a) If the employer carries on a trade, the "wholly and exclusively" rule.[68]
(b) If the employer carries on an investment business, the rules relating to expenses of management.
(c) FA 2004 ss.196–200.
(d) If FA 2004 s.196(1) does not apply to a contribution, the rules relating to capital expenditure[69] and the rules relating to delayed pension contributions.[70]

*Accounting standards*

**6-038** Pursuant to Financial Reporting Standard 105, if a contribution is one to which the employee has become entitled as a result of service rendered to the employer during the reporting period then the general position[71] is that the employer recognises the contribution payable[72] for the period as an expense. If the amount paid exceeds the obligation arising from services rendered during the reporting period, the employer recognises that excess as an asset to the extent that the prepayment will lead to a reduction in future payments or a cash refund.

**6-039 Intermediate payment arrangements** If an employer makes a contribution to which its employees are *not* entitled as a result of service rendered to the employer during the reporting period, the pension scheme may constitute an "intermediate payment arrangement". If so, any such contributions are accounted for in accordance with s.7 of FRS 105. To the extent that a contribution is an intermediate payment arrangement there is a rebuttable presumption that the employer has exchanged one asset for another, so the payment itself does not represent an immediate expense. To rebut this presumption at the time the contribution is paid, the employer must be able to demonstrate that either: (a) it will not obtain future economic benefit from the amounts transferred; or (b) it does not have control of the right or other access to the future economic benefit it is expected to receive. One way to rebut this presumption may be to allocate the funds within the arrangement for particular employees, as would be usual under a money purchase pension scheme.[73] Alternatively, if it is clear that a contribution can be allocated only for current employees, in respect of their past services, it is arguable that the employer does not obtain future economic benefits from the contribution. Where that is the case, the contributions are recognised immediately as an expense to profit and loss.

**6-040 Defined benefit plans** If the employer participates in a defined benefit plan and

---

[67] CTA 2009 s.46(1); ITTOIA 2005 s.25(1).
[68] CTA 2009 s.54; ITTOIA 2005 s.34(1).
[69] CTA 2009 s.53; ITTOIA 2005 s.33.
[70] CTA 2009 s.868.
[71] Under FRS 105 s.23.
[72] Note the reference to contributions payable rather than paid: this is an accruals basis.
[73] It may be that the employee's families could also benefit.

has entered into an agreement with the plan that determines how the employer will fund a deficit (such as a Schedule of contributions), the employer recognises a liability for the contributions payable that arise from the agreement (to the extent that they relate to the deficit).

**Measurement of the expense** The expense recognised in profit or loss is equal to the contributions payable for the reporting period. Where contributions are not paid during the reporting period a liability is recognised. If the time value of money is material the liability is discounted to the present value of the contributions payable.[74] The unwinding of the discount is recognised as a finance cost in profit or loss in the period in which it arises.

The provisions under FRS 102 are the same as FRS 105 except insofar as they relate to defined benefits schemes.[75] The provisions relating to defined benefit scheme are complex. Essentially an employer recognises: (a) a liability for its obligations under defined benefit plans net of plan assets; and (b) the net change in that liability during the period as the cost of its defined benefit plans during the period.

6-041

6-042

*The wholly and exclusively test*

Prior to 6 April 2006, an employer contribution to an exempt approved scheme in respect of any individual was automatically allowed as a deduction under ICTA 1988 s.592(4), and so the "wholly and exclusively" issue did not arise. Since that date it has been necessary to determine whether a contribution to a registered pension scheme is made wholly and exclusively for the purposes of the employer's trade.

6-043

**General principles** The ability to deduct expenses in calculating taxable profit is inferred from the fact that it is the *profit* of a trade which is taxed, not the *receipts*. In calculating the profits of a trade, no deduction is allowed for expenses not incurred wholly and exclusively for the purposes of the trade.[76] There are two components to this: the expenditure must be incurred "for the purposes of the trade", and it must also be "wholly and exclusively" so incurred. In *Bentleys Stokes and Lowless v Beeson*,[77] Romer LJ suggested that "wholly" referred to the *quantum* of the money expended and "exclusively" referred to the *motive or object* in the mind of the person incurring the expenditure, however it seems likely that the word "wholly" does not in fact add anything to the word "exclusively".[78]

6-044

The word "exclusively" means that if the expense was also incurred for some other non-trading purpose, it is not deductible. The wholly and exclusively issue is to be determined by the object of the taxpayer in incurring the expense. This is a question of fact but in making that factual assessment a tribunal or court should have regard to a number of principles. In *Vodafone Cellular v Shaw*,[79] Millet LJ derived four propositions from the case law:

6-045

(a) First, the words "for the purposes of the trade" mean "to serve the purposes of the trade". They do not mean "for the purposes of the taxpayer" but for

---

[74] Using the methodology for selecting a discount rate specified in FRS 105 para.23.11.
[75] FRS 102 s.28 is concerned with employee benefits.
[76] CTA 2009 s.54(1)(a); ITTOIA 2005 s.34(1).
[77] *Bentleys Stokes and Lowless v Beeson* [1952] 2 All E.R. 82; (1952) 33 T.C. 491.
[78] See Kerridge, "Deductibility of expenses for Schedule D income tax—the 'all or nothing rule'" [1986] B.T.R. 36; Ward, " 'All or nothing': more than nothing at all" [1987] B.T.R. 141.
[79] *Vodafone Cellular Ltd v Shaw (Inspector of Taxes)* [1997] S.T.C. 734 (at 742 f–j).

"the purposes of the trade", which is a different concept. A fortiori they do not mean "for the benefit of the taxpayer".

(b) Secondly, to ascertain whether the payment was made for the purposes of the taxpayer's trade it is necessary to discover his object in making the payment. Save in obvious cases which speak for themselves, ascertaining the taxpayer's object in making a payment involves an inquiry into the taxpayer's subjective intentions at the time of the payment. In the context of a corporate taxpayer, its mind is the minds of its directors.

(c) Thirdly, the object of the taxpayer in making the payment must be distinguished from the effect of the payment. A payment may be made exclusively for the purposes of the trade even though it also secures a private benefit. This will be the case if the securing of the private benefit was not the object of the payment but merely a consequential and incidental effect of the payment. In *Scotts Atlantic Management Ltd v HMRC*,[80] the UT commented that:

> "another way of phrasing this is that a merely incidental effect of expenditure is not necessarily an object of a taxpayer in making it. However, as Lord Brightman's well-known example in *Mallalieu* (see [1983] S.T.C. 665 at 669; [1983] 2 A.C. 861 at 870) of the medical consultant going to the South of France to treat a friend shows, it may be the case that in fact what would be an incidental effect in some circumstances could be an independent object in others. What the FTT must not do is to conclude that merely because there was an effect, that effect was an object."

(d) Fourthly, although the taxpayer's subjective intentions are determinative, these are not limited to the conscious motives which were in his mind at the time of the payment. Some consequences are so inevitably and inextricably involved in the payment that, unless merely incidental, they must be taken to be a purpose for which the payment was made. As the UT said in *Scotts Atlantic* (at [53]), another way of putting that is that the tribunal must take "a robust approach to ascertaining the purposes of the taxpayer".

**6-046** Where there is a duality of purpose (i.e. expenditure is incurred partly for the purposes of the trade and partly for some other purpose) the wholly and exclusively requirement is not satisfied. However, this does not prohibit a deduction for any identifiable part or identifiable proportion of the expense which is incurred wholly and exclusively for the purposes of the trade.[81] Where there is a duality of purpose in respect of a payment of remuneration, it is possible to dissect the payment.[82] In these circumstances, it is necessary for the FTT, to determine as a fact how much of the payment (if any) was for the purposes of the trade and how much was not.

**6-047** **Application to pension contributions** Except in very exceptional circumstances, a business that does not adequately reward its employees is unlikely to be successful. It follows that rewarding employees is generally a trading purpose. In principle, it makes no difference whether an employee is an ordinary employee or an owner manager: owner managers need to be rewarded; it's just that they may be more flexible about precisely how and when they are rewarded. In this regard, a pension contribution is no different in principle to a payment of cash earnings directly to the employee, or the provision of any other benefit in kind.

---

[80] *Scotts Atlantic Management Ltd v HMRC* [2015] UKUT 66 (TCC); [2015] S.T.C. 1321 at [52].
[81] CTA 2009 s.54(2).
[82] *Copeman v William Flood & Son* [1941] 1 K.B. 202; [1940] 24 T.C. 53.

Typically, an employer will undertake to make contributions as part of the employee's contractual remuneration package, and in such cases, the connection between the provision of services by the employee and the reward by the employer is clear: the employee is motivated on a day-to-day basis by the knowledge that, for as long as he remain employed, contributions will be made. Where a contribution by an employer is made as part of a discretionary bonus arrangement, the connection may be slightly less clear. If the employer has an established policy of providing discretionary bonuses (as is customary in some areas), then the employee's knowledge that discretionary bonuses will be considered is likely to incentivise him: indeed, in appropriate circumstances the variable nature of such benefits may provide an additional incentive for the employee to please his employer, especially where he knows that bonuses may be high. Where the employees are not aware that they will be considered for discretionary bonuses, then the employer's motivation may well be scrutinised by HMRC. Rewarding past behaviour is only likely to have a trading purpose to the extent that it influences future behaviour (i.e. by creating an expectation that it will be rewarded in the future). If the employees are informed that a discretionary bonus is a one-off then a tribunal may well infer that the bonus was not made for a trading purpose.

6-048

The position regarding rewards for owner managers is in a sense more straightforward: as they control the company, they know that they will benefit one way or another if the business is successful. It may take many years until the business is successful, and in such circumstances, it is perfectly in order for them to be rewarded in later years for services provided many years earlier. Assuming that the company's reason for the payment is to reward the director for his services then there is no reason on these facts that a tribunal should infer a non-trading purpose.

6-049

However, in all cases, the wholly and exclusively requirement will be satisfied only if the reason the company makes the contribution is to reward an employee for his services. If an employer decides to make a contribution for the benefit of a director purely because it is tax-efficient for the director, without any thought for whether it is in the interest of the business to make the contribution, that is not made for the purposes of the trade.[83]

6-050

**Contributions for controlling company directors** In *Copeman v William Flood & Son*[84] the employer was a family company that paid a generous level of remuneration to a son and daughter (who were both directors and shareholders) who provided relatively minor services. The General Commissioners appear to have thought that remuneration was necessarily wholly and exclusively laid out for the purposes of the trade. The Revenue appealed and Lawrence J allowed the appeal. The decision is authority for two points: first, that remuneration may or may not be paid wholly and exclusively for the purposes of the trade.[85] Secondly, if sums are not wholly and exclusively for the purposes of the trade then the fact-finding tribunal (usually the FTT) should find out how much of those sums were so expended.

6-051

In *Samuel Dracup v Dakin*[86] the General Commissioners found that pension contributions made for two directors were not wholly and exclusively for the

6-052

---

[83] In *Samuel Dracup v Dakin* [1957] 37 T.C. 377; [1957] T.R. 169 and *Beauty Consultants Ltd v Inspector of Taxes* [2002] S.T.C. (S.C.D.) 352; [2002] S.T.I. 1095 there appears to have been no evidence that the position of the company was ever considered.

[84] *Copeman v William Flood & Son* [1941] 1 K.B. 202; [1940] 24 T.C. 53.

[85] There was no evaluation of the case in hand; instead it was remitted to the General Commissioners for them to find as a fact whether the sums in question were wholly and exclusively laid out or expended for the purposes of the company's trade.

[86] *Samuel Dracup v Dakin* [1957] 37 T.C. 377; [1957] T.R. 169.

purposes of the company's trade, and the High Court held that this conclusion was not unreasonable on the facts, and so it was not overturned. Harman J said:

> "it occurred to [the directors] that if they could have the insurance policies on their own behalf which did not cost them anything, it would be very nice for them; I dare say it would; money paid out by the company which they controlled. Under those circumstances it passes my comprehension that business men who have to review those activities [i.e. the General Commissioners] are not entitled to say this is not a proper business expense; in other words: you were laying out this money for your own advantage and not for that of the Company, or, at any rate, your own advantage came into it. If the Commissioners took that view, it seems that they were amply entitled to do so and, even if I did not agree with it, which I do, I should be quite powerless to review it here."

**6-053** The key part is the words "you were laying out this money for your own advantage *and not for that of the Company*, or, at any rate, your own advantage came into it". In the past, it seems that HMRC have tried to place more reliance on the decision than they do now.[87] It does not appear to have been argued on behalf of the company that the directors were being *rewarded* by the provision of the insurance policies.[88] The decision may have been different if the insurance policies were considered by the company to constitute part of the directors' remuneration package.

**6-054** Immediately before the extract cited above, the judge said:

> "there is no suggestion anywhere in the Case Stated, or in the evidence which was given to the Commissioners, that the reason for taking, out these policies, was because otherwise the directors would resign and leave the business of the Company in the lurch. There is not any suggestion that either of them threatened to leave."

**6-055** The judge is not here saying that a payment will only be for the purposes of the trade if the director would otherwise leave the company; he is simply making the point that there was no evidence to support the argument that the expenses were for the purposes of the trade. His comments appear to relate to a contention made on behalf of the company that the premiums paid in respect of the pension scheme were expended in order to retain the services of the directors. In the context of an owner-managed business, it would be contrived in the extreme for the owner manager to threaten to leave.

**6-056** In *Earlspring Properties Ltd v Guest*[89] a company paid remuneration (including pension contributions) to its sole director and shareholder, by reference to the company's profits for the year. The General Commissioners found that this was not incurred wholly and exclusively for the company's business, and the High Court accepted that they were entitled to reach this conclusion. However, the facts of this case were unusual, as it involved "a diversion of income" from a firm controlled by a husband to a company controlled by his wife (and the remuneration under consideration was paid by the wife's company) and this was done "to achieve a fiscal purpose". The wife's duties were "social" and as the profits were in reality generated by the efforts of the husband (via his firm), it was not appropriate to pay

---

[87] HMRC's current position, at BIM46035, is that the case "confirms that, where there is a non-trade purpose for the payment, then the payment is disallowable, but you should not read more into it than that".
[88] For a similar decision on similar facts see *Beauty Consultants Ltd v Inspector of Taxes* [2002] S.T.C. (S.C.D.) 352; [2002] S.T.I. 1095.
[89] *Earlspring Properties Ltd v Guest* [1993] S.T.C. 473; 67 T.C. 259.

remuneration to the wife by reference to the profits of her company for the year.[90] The Commissioners disallowed all but 5% of the remuneration paid to the wife.[91]

An "earnings distribution model" in which all of the profits of a company are distributed to its directors is sometimes described as a "quasi-partnership". In *Scotts Atlantic Management Ltd v HMRC*[92] the FTT accepted that where the entire profits of a business are attributable to the skills, knowledge or contacts possessed by the directors, it is perfectly in order for the company to pay out the bulk or the entirety of the profits to the directors, and that one would ordinarily expect a corporation tax deduction for such payments if there was a clear expectation during the period that the business model was such that bonuses would be paid. In addition, the FTT confirmed (at [108]) that the fact that the quasi-partners were also the shareholders, to whom dividends could have been distributed on a 50/50 basis had no bearing on the deductibility of the bonuses if the business model was to distribute bonuses. The FTT did however observe that the position may be different if the profits of companies employing considerable capital (such as successful manufacturing companies) were paid out to the directors and the bonuses exceeded the value of the contributions actually made by the directors.

6-057

**Disguised distributions** A contribution in respect of a director who is also a shareholder may be found on proper analysis to be a disguised distribution of profits rather than a reward for services.[93] Where that is the case, a tax deduction will not be available.[94]

6-058

**Cessation of trade** Where there is an imminent or actual cessation of trade, ex gratia contributions cannot be for the purposes of the trade because the business will not obtain any benefit from such contributions. This is likely to be the case even where the employer has an established practice of making ex gratia contributions in respect of employees on their retirement.[95] Where an employer is contractually obliged to make the contributions then one must look at the position at the time that the obligation arose[96] and ask whether the employer's promise to make the contribution(s) was for the purposes of its trade.[97]

6-059

The position is likely to be different with voluntary contributions for controlling directors. Such directors may have worked hard in the past in the expectation of receiving a reward in the future, and whether their entitlement is contractual or not is irrelevant because they control the company.

6-060

---

[90] These facts therefore resemble those in *LG Berry Investments Ltd v Attwooll* [1964] 1 W.L.R. 693; [1964] 2 All E.R. 126, and the result is essentially the same.

[91] Also see *Nicholson v HMRC* [2018] UKFTT 014 and *Dollar v Lyon* [1981] S.T.C. 333; 54 T.C. 459: two decisions involving the provision of benefits to children.

[92] *Scotts Atlantic Management Ltd (In Liquidation) v HMRC* [2013] UKFTT 299 at [105]–[108] in particular.

[93] See *Toone v Ross* [2019] EWHC 2855 (Ch); [2020] S.T.C. 382; *Chalcot Training Ltd v Ralph* [2020] EWHC 1054 (Ch) at [124]–[224]. In the context of a solvent company, it is most unlikely that a contribution purporting to be a reward will be found to be a disguised distribution.

[94] CTA 2009 s.1305(1).

[95] See e.g. *CIR v Anglo Brewing Co Ltd* [1925] 12 T.C. 803, in which Rowlatt J held that payments of pension (commuted to lump sums) in these circumstances were not made for the purpose of the employer's trade (i.e. for the purpose of keeping the trade going, and of making it pay). The purpose of the payments was to wind up the trade and so a deduction was not permitted.

[96] *CIR v Cosmotron Manufacturing Ltd* [1997] 70 T.C. 292.

[97] However there are statutory provisions that expressly allow a tax deduction where an employer permanently ceases to carry on its trade and it makes a payment to an employee in addition to a redundancy payment (limited to three times the amount of the redundancy payment): ITTOIA 2005 s.79 and CTA 2009 s.79.

**6-061** **Property businesses** The profits of a property business are calculated in the same way as a trade (as set out above), subject to certain modifications.[98] In relation to an unincorporated property business, the distinction between remuneration and an appropriation of profits must be considered. Drawings and salaries paid to partners of a partnership are an appropriation of profit[99] and it follows that no deduction will be allowed for a contribution in respect of a partner of a partnership (even if the partnership is an employer and so FA 2004 s.196(1) applies).

**6-062** **Summary** In summary:

(a) Rewarding employees is fundamentally a trading purpose.
(b) However, a tribunal is unlikely to assume, in the absence of any evidence, that a contribution to a pension scheme is a reward.[100]
(c) Where the entire profits of a business are attributable to the skills, knowledge or contacts possessed by the directors, a policy to distribute all of the profits to the persons that generate the profits as remuneration is not inconsistent with the remuneration having a trading purpose.[101] A tribunal may infer that some or all of the remuneration paid to persons who do not generate profits (such as the children and spouses of the persons that do generate the profits) is not in fact a reward.[102]
(d) In the context of an investment business, or a trade that employs considerable capital (for example, a manufacturing business), where the efforts of the individuals involved do not generate the profits (or only have a limited impact), a tribunal may infer that remuneration paid in excess of a market rate was paid because it benefitted the owners rather than because it benefitted the trade.

*Investment businesses: expenses of management*

**6-063** A company with investment business means a company whose business consists wholly or partly of making investments.[103] In calculating the corporation tax to which a company with investment business is liable for an accounting period, expenses of management of the company's investment business which are referable to that period are allowed as a deduction from the company's total profits.[104] "Expenses of management" are expenses of management of a company's investment business so far as they are in respect of so much of the company's investment business as consists of making investments. In general, no deduction is allowed for expenses of a capital nature,[105] however this is not the case if FA 2004 s.196 applies.[106] Section 196 is considered below.

---

[98] CTA 2009 s.210; ITTOIA 2005 s.272.
[99] *PDC Copyright (South) v George* [1997] S.T.C. (S.C.D.) 326.
[100] See *Samuel Dracup v Dakin* [1957] 37 T.C. 377; [1957] T.R. 169 *Beauty Consultants Ltd v Inspector of Taxes* [2002] S.T.C. (S.C.D.) 352; [2002] S.T.I. 1095.
[101] See *Scotts Atlantic Management Ltd (In Liquidation) v HMRC* [2015] UKUT 66 (TCC); [2015] S.T.C. 1321.
[102] See *Copeman v William Flood & Sons* [1941] 1 K.B. 202; [1940] 24 T.C. 53; *Earlspring Properties Ltd v Guest* [1993] S.T.C. 473; 67 T.C. 259.
[103] CTA 2009 s.1218B(1).
[104] CTA 2009 s.1219(1).
[105] CTA 2009 s.1219(3)(a).
[106] CTA 2009 s.1221(1)(h).

## EMPLOYER CONTRIBUTIONS

The term "expenses of management" is not defined but it is clear from case law that it is to be given a wide construction.[107] This will usually include remuneration paid to employees and directors[108] and it follows that a contribution to a registered pension scheme will usually be an expense of management.

**6-064**

There is no express "wholly and exclusively" requirement, so an expense may be an expense of management even if it has more than one purpose or effect.[109] In *LG Berry Investments Ltd v Attwooll*[110] an investment company maintained a policy of paying all surplus profits as directors' fees. In the year in question, the profits were £1,800 and so £600 was paid to each of the three directors. The Special Commissioners found that neither the company nor its directors and shareholders ever consciously determined that the directors should be remunerated for their services as directors by paying them £600 each; all concerned were simply minded to cause the company to dispose of substantially the whole of its profits by paying directors' fees. They considered *Copeman v William Flood & Sons Ltd* and applied it by analogy, allowing a deduction for some but not all of the remuneration paid to the directors. The amount allowed was the amount that the Commissioners considered "reasonably related to the duties performed by the directors". On appeal, the judge observed that the duties of the directors were not very arduous and considered that where the profits are largely determined by the size of the investments (in that case, secured loans) rather than the efforts of the directors, determining directors' fees by reference to the surplus is not consistent with such fees being expenses of management. The judge therefore held that the Special Commissioners took a correct view of the law, and thereby impliedly endorsed the "reasonableness" requirement applied by the Commissioners.

**6-065**

*FA 2004 ss.196–200*

Insofar as is material, s.196 provides as follows:

**6-066**

"(1) This section makes provision about an employer's entitlement to relief in respect of contributions paid by the employer under a registered pension scheme in respect of any individual.

(2) For the purposes of Part 2 of ITTOIA 2005 or Part 3 of CTA 2009 (trading income)—
   (a) the contributions are to be treated as not being payments of a capital nature to the extent that they otherwise would be, and
   (b) if they are allowed to be deducted in computing the amount of the profits of the employer, they are deductible in computing the amount of the profits for the period of account in which they are paid.

(3) For the purposes of Chapter 2 of Part 16 of CTA 2009 (expenses of management: companies with investment business), the contributions—
   (a) are to be treated as being expenses of management to the extent that they otherwise would not be, and
   (b) are referable to the accounting period in which they are paid.

(6) This section is subject to sections 197 and 198 (spreading of relief) (and to transitional provision contained in Part 4 of Schedule 36)."

If s.196(1) applies, the effect of s.196(2) and (3) is to modify the normal rules

**6-067**

---

[107] *Sun Life Assurance Society v Davidson* [1958] A.C. 184; [1957] 3 W.L.R. 362 (per Lord Somervell), which was concerned with an early predecessor to CTA 2009 s.1219: s.33 of the Income Tax Act 1918.
[108] See *LG Berry Investments Ltd v Attwooll* [1964] 1 W.L.R. 693; [1964] 2 All E.R. 126.
[109] *Camas Plc v Atkinson (Inspector of Taxes)* [2004] EWCA Civ 541; 76 T.C. 641 at [26] and [33] (Carnwath LJ).
[110] *LG Berry Investments Ltd v Attwooll* [1964] 1 W.L.R. 693; [1964] 2 All E.R. 126.

for tax deductions in two ways: first, pension contributions will not be treated as payments of a capital nature if they otherwise would be. Secondly, if they are deductible, they can only be deducted for the period of account in which the contribution is paid. It is important to appreciate the limited scope of s.196: it does not provide that a contribution by an employer must be within s.196 in order to obtain a tax deduction.[111]

**6-068** **Contributions "under" a pension scheme**  Section 196(1), and indeed FA 2004 Pt 4 generally, refers to contributions paid "under" a pension scheme.[112] It would perhaps seem more natural to refer to contributions paid "to" a pension scheme (with the benefits provided "under" the scheme), but this terminology reflects the very broad definition of "pension scheme" in s.150(1), which includes an agreement or undertaking to contribute.[113] A contribution pursuant to such an agreement or undertaking is therefore paid "under" the pension scheme because it is made pursuant to the terms of the pension scheme. But it is suggested that *any* payment (whether or not made pursuant to a prior contractual obligation) will suffice provided that it is recognised as a contribution under the scheme rules. Normally the scheme rules specify that contributions must be agreed by (or at least notified to) trustees before they are paid, but that need not be the case. Provided it is clear that a payment is a contribution (and not, for example, a payment of trustee fees), it is suggested that it is paid under the pension scheme. However, in cases where HMRC are more likely to dispute the availability of a tax deduction, it may assist the employer if it can demonstrate that there was a prior agreement to make the contribution (even if the agreement was made very shortly before the contribution was paid).

**6-069** **"In respect of any individual"**  Although s.196(1) can apply only to a contribution by an employer, it is quite clear that it need not be in respect of an employee. The provision refers to a contribution in respect of "any individual". Contributions in respect of individuals connected with employees, for example, may be within s.196(1).[114] Employer contributions which are not allocated under the scheme for any particular member are not "in respect of any individual"[115] and so s.196(1) will not apply to such contributions.[116] Typically, this would be the case where contributions are made to a general fund under the scheme.[117]

---

[111] Section 196 is not a relieving provision. Its title is "relief for employers in respect of contributions paid" because it is about relief, not because it provides relief.

[112] Also see IHTA 1984 s.12(2), which refers to a contribution under a registered pension scheme and CTA 2009 s.1292(5), which refers to a payment or transfer under an EFRBS. It is quite clear that these are references to payments to the scheme.

[113] See Ch.2.

[114] A contribution in respect of a spouse or child or an employee may of course constitute a reward of the employee: see e.g. the "family benefit trust" arrangement in *Sempra Metals v RCC* (2008) S.T.C. (S.C.D.) 1062; [2008] S.T.I. 1923.

[115] Such contributions are described as being "otherwise than in respect of any individual" in FA 2004 s.172C(1)(a) and s.233(3).

[116] FA 2004 s.233(3) suggests that such contributions may be deemed to be contributions made at the time that they are subsequently allocated for a member, however it is reasonably clear that s.233(3) is only relevant for the purposes of the annual allowance provisions and not for determining the timing of the employer's tax deduction.

[117] The provisions relating to intermediate payment arrangements in FRS 102 and FRS 105 should be noted in this regard.

# EMPLOYER CONTRIBUTIONS

**When is a contribution "paid"?** If s.196(1) applies to a contribution, the tax deduction is for the period in which the contribution is "paid".[118] As is explained above in relation to member contributions, this may be different to the period in which the contribution is *received* by the pension scheme.

6-070

*Rules relating to capital expenditure*

If s.196(1) applies to a contribution, it is unnecessary to consider if the contribution is of a capital nature.[119] If s.196(1) does not apply to a contribution (for example, because it is a contribution to a general fund and therefore not "in respect of any individual"), one must consider if the contribution is a capital expense. In calculating the profits of a trade, no deduction is allowed for items of a capital nature.[120] HMRC may argue[121] that the cost of establishing a pension scheme (i.e. the initial settled property and any expenditure incidental to bringing the trust into existence, such as legal or other professional fees) is capital expenditure because the pension scheme is an asset or advantage of an enduring nature for the employer.[122] If this is a concern then it may be prudent to have a small initial contribution to establish the pension scheme.[123] HMRC accept that contributions other than the initial amount are revenue rather than capital.[124]

6-071

Contributions paid by an employer would be capital expenditure if the employer could benefit from such contributions, because each payment would give rise to a corresponding asset of a durable nature.[125] It may therefore be prudent, where s.196(2)(b) will not apply to a contribution, to expressly exclude the employer from benefitting under the scheme (for example, in relation to any surplus which may arise).

6-072

*Rules relating to delayed payment of pension contributions*

If FA 2004 s.196(1) applies to a contribution then a deduction will only be allowed in the period in which it is paid as a result of s.196(2)(b).[126] If s.196(1) does not apply then it seems that CTA 2009 s.868 will apply, and has essentially the same effect.

6-073

---

[118] FA 2004 s.196(2)(b) and (3)(b).

[119] As a result of FA 2004 s.196(2)(a). CTA 2009 s.53(1) is subject to any contrary provision in the "Corporation Tax Acts" (CTA 2009 s.53(2)). The "Corporation Tax Acts" are the enactments relating to the taxation of the income and chargeable gains of companies and of company distributions (including provisions relating to income tax) (Interpretation Act 1978 Sch.1). FA 2004 Pt 4 is generally an Income Tax Act rather than a Corporation Tax Act (ITA 2007 s.1(2)(c); Interpretation Act 1978 Sch.1; CTA 2009 s.1), but it seems reasonably clear that the restriction in s.53 is subject to the FA 2004 provisions.

[120] CTA 2009 s.53; ITTOIA 2005 s.33.

[121] Citing *British Insulated and Helsby Cables v Atherton* (1929) 10 T.C.

[122] See BIM44505, in the context of employee benefit trusts.

[123] Although it is common to refer to a pension scheme being established when the scheme documentation is executed and dated, a trust does not come into existence until there is some property subject to the trust.

[124] See BIM44505: "The capital costs of setting up an EBT include: [a] the initial amount (usually a small amount such as £100) settled by the person setting up the trust [...] to bring a valid trust or settlement into existence [...]; [b] any expenditure incidental to bringing the trust into existence, such as legal or other professional fees".

[125] See *Rutter v Charles Sharpe & Co Ltd* [1979] 53 T.C. 163.

[126] The restriction in CTA 2009 s.53 is subject to the FA 2004 provisions (see fn.115).

## Contributions in connection with EFRBS

**6-074** A tax deduction for contributions in respect of an individual is restricted in two circumstances involving EFRBS.[127] The first is where any of the benefits which may be payable to or in respect of the individual under the registered pension scheme will be payable only if relevant benefits expected to be paid under an EFRBS are not so paid. The second is where, because relevant benefits may be payable to or in respect of the individual under an EFRBS, the total value of any funds held for the purposes of the registered pension scheme which may be transferred by way of a recognised transfer in respect of the individual will or may be less than it otherwise would be. Both therefore envisage a contribution to a registered pension scheme in circumstances where benefits will not be provided under that scheme if benefits are provided under an EFRBS.

**6-075** The restriction will not however apply where the EFRBS is a ROPS[128] and the individual[129]:

(a) was not resident in the UK when he first became a member of the pension scheme;
(b) was a member of the pension scheme at the beginning of his period of residence in the UK (which includes the time when the contributions are paid); and
(c) either: (i) was, immediately before the beginning of that period of residence, entitled to tax relief in respect of contributions paid under the pension scheme under the law of the country or territory in which the individual was then resident; or (ii) was at any time in the ten years before the beginning of that period of residence entitled to tax relief in respect of contributions paid under the pension scheme under the law of the country or territory in which the individual was then resident.

**6-076** If the restriction applies then one is required to determine the individual's pension input amount in accordance with a modified version of the annual allowance provisions,[130] and an amount equal to the total pension input amount in respect of that individual for the period in question is not deductible.[131]

**6-077** HMRC's Explanatory Memorandum to the regulations explains:

"FA 2004 restricts relief on employer contributions to a pension scheme so that a deduction is allowed at the time of the contribution only where the contribution is to a registered pension scheme. For unregistered schemes the deduction is deferred until the benefit is paid out to the employee. The FA 2005 introduced a measure to prevent this rule being circumvented by routing the funding for an unregistered scheme through a registered scheme."

**6-078** It is not easy to envisage circumstances in which a registered pension scheme could fund an EFRBS without making an unauthorised payment (except perhaps by way of a loan). One example may perhaps be where an employer funds a registered pension scheme and also makes an unfunded promise to the member (assuming that the promise amounts to an EFRBS), and any benefits provided under

---

[127] FA 2004 s.196A and The Registered Pension Schemes (Restriction of Employers' Relief) Regulations 2005 (SI 2005/3458).
[128] Within the meaning in FA 2004 s.150(8): see Ch.32.
[129] The requirements in (a)–(c) are essentially the same as the relevant migrant member requirements: see Ch.24.
[130] As set out in SI 2005/3458 regs 5–8.
[131] SI 2005/3458 reg.10.

the EFRBS reduce the benefits available under the registered scheme. This would be objectionable because the employer has effectively obtained an immediate tax deduction in respect of benefits to be provided under the EFRBS.

*Employer asset-backed contributions*

FA 2012 inserted ss.196B–196L into FA 2004, relating to employer asset-backed contributions (ABCs) to registered pension schemes.[132] The provisions are detailed and complex. The essential characteristics of the arrangements being targeted are arrangements where an employer contributes property to a pension scheme and the property is itself a right to receive income from the employer (typically, but by no means necessarily, in the form of lease payments) in the future. Such arrangements are considered to be objectionable because the employer may be able to obtain a tax deduction for the contribution of the property (the value of which is essentially the net present value of the income stream) *and* for each lease payment in the future.

6-079

The legislation contains provisions relating to three slightly different types of arrangement[133]:

6-080

(a) simple ABC arrangements (s.196B);
(b) complex ABC arrangements whereby property is transferred to a partnership as part of the arrangement (s.196D); and
(c) complex ABC arrangements involving a partnership that already holds property (s.196F).

In each case, the provisions will *not* apply if the ABC arrangement is an "acceptable structured finance arrangement". An acceptable structured finance arrangement will, by definition, be a type 1, 2, or 3 finance arrangement for the purposes of ITA 2007 Pt 13 Ch.5B or CTA 2010 Pt 16 Ch.2. The purpose of those provisions is to counter schemes which are intended to enable taxpayers (companies and individuals) to borrow money and obtain effective tax relief for both interest and repayment of principal. The effect of the arrangement being an acceptable structured finance arrangement is that the future lease payments from the employer to the pension scheme are deemed to constitute income of the employer (so any tax deduction would be matched with an equal amount of income).[134] So, if the arrangement is an acceptable structured finance arrangement then the tax result is unobjectionable, and so the ABC provisions do not apply.

6-081

**Simple ABC arrangements**  Before going into the detail of the ABC provisions, it may be helpful to have in mind a simple example. Suppose an employer contributes £1 million to a registered pension scheme and there is an understanding that the scheme will use that £1 million to enter into a purchase and leaseback transaction with the employer. Under the purchase and leaseback, the scheme buys some property from the employer for £1 million and leases it back to the employer for an annual rent of £100,000, and the employer has an option to purchase the property back from the scheme at the end of 15 years for £1,000.

6-082

---

[132] This followed an announcement in the Budget speech delivered on 23 March 2011 and a consultation document published by HMRC and HM Treasury on 24 May 2011 titled *Employer Asset-backed Pension Contributions*.

[133] The legislation was not all introduced at the same time, so the provisions apply differently depending on whether the contribution was made between 29 November 2011 and 21 February 2012 or on or after 22 February 2012. The provisions described here are those applicable to contributions on or after 22 February 2012.

[134] CTA 2010 s.760(2).

**6-083** The sale and leaseback may be on entirely commercial terms, but HMRC considers this to be objectionable because "In effect, the pension scheme has immediately lent back to the employer the value of the pension contribution it received and this 'loan' will be repaid by the income stream payments over the term of the arrangement".[135] The characteristic that makes these transactions objectionable, as HMRC identifies at PTM043310, is that the capital value of the lease (£1 million in this example) is equal to the net present value of the income stream (£100,000 per annum for 15 years equating to £1 million net present value): the property is itself an income stream and so it is objectionable to allow two lots of tax deductions. If the ABC provisions apply, the deduction for the £1 million contribution is denied, but the deductions for the payments of £100,000 per annum are not affected.

**6-084** There are a number of difficulties with the ABC provisions. The first difficulty to overcome is that the draftsman has imported the provisions in CTA 2010 Pt 16 Ch.2, relating to "finance arrangements" without making any real attempt to modify them for the purposes of FA 2004 Pt 4. Not only will these other provisions be unfamiliar to most pension advisers, but they also use terminology which is often counter-intuitive.

**6-085** Turning now to the provisions, s.196B(1) provides that:

"An employer ('E') is not to be given relief in respect of a contribution ('E's contribution') paid by E under a registered pension scheme if conditions A, B and C are met."

**6-086** **Condition A** Condition A is that:

"(a) under an arrangement ('the asset-backed arrangement')—
 (i) a person ('the borrower') receives money or another asset ('the advance') from another person ('the lender'),
 (ii) the borrower, or a person connected with the borrower, makes a disposal of an asset ('the security') to or for the benefit of the lender or a person connected with the lender, and
 (iii) the lender, or a person connected with the lender, is entitled to payments in respect of the security,
(b) the borrower is E or a person connected with E, and
(c) the advance is (wholly or partly) paid or provided by the lender out of E's contribution (directly or indirectly),
 ..."

**6-087** For these purposes, "arrangement" includes an agreement or understanding, whether or not legally enforceable.[136] So, if there is an understanding between the employer and the scheme that the transactions in (a)(i)-(iii) above will take place, there is an asset-backed arrangement. If a contribution is made and then, quite separately, the employer and scheme enter into a purchase and leaseback then there should be no "arrangement" for these purposes.[137]

**6-088** Returning to the above example, the employer is the borrower and the pension scheme is the lender. The "advance" is the £1 million paid from the scheme to the employer to purchase the property. The "security" is the property sold to the pen-

---

[135] PTM043310.

[136] CTA 2010 s.775, as applied by FA 2004 s.196L(4). This is of course different to the usual meaning of *arrangement* in FA 2004 Pt 4 when it is used in relation to a member of the pension scheme (see FA 2004 s.152(1)).

[137] HMRC agree at PTM043320: "It is not intended that outright disposals of property should generally be caught by these rules. e.g. in the scenario above, if the pension scheme has acquired the freehold of the property and happens to lease it back to the employer this might not fall within Condition A. However, if the terms of the lease were pre-agreed such that the value of the interest did seem to rely on a time-limited income stream then Conditions A and C could apply".

sion scheme, subject to the leaseback which entitles the pension scheme to receive payments in respect of the security. The advance is paid by the pension scheme *out of* the employer's initial contribution to the pension scheme. Therefore, Condition A will be met.

**Condition B** Condition B is that the asset-backed arrangement is not an "acceptable structured finance arrangement". The arrangement will be an acceptable structured finance arrangement if conditions M to Q are met.[138] So, if the conditions in M to Q are met then the ABC provisions will not apply to deny the deduction for the contribution. 6-089

Condition M is that in accordance with generally accepted accounting practice, the employer's accounts[139] for the period in which the advance is received record a financial liability in respect of the advance, and the payments reduce the amount of the financial liability. Returning to the example, the advance is the £1 million paid by the pension scheme for the property, and one would expect that in most circumstances this would be recorded as a financial liability of the employer. 6-090

The effect of Condition A and Condition M applying is that the arrangement will be a type 1 finance arrangement for the purposes of ITA 2007 Pt 13 Ch.5B or CTA 2010 Pt 16 Ch.2. As a result, the £100,000 p/a payments from the employer to the pension scheme will be deemed to constitute taxable income of the employer.[140] Such arrangements are therefore considered to be unobjectionable (as far as FA 2004 Pt 4 is concerned) because the £100,000 rental payments will be matched with the £100,000 deemed income. 6-091

Condition N is that: (a) the lender is the trustee or manager of the registered pension scheme (in their capacity as such); (b) the advance is money which is paid by the lender directly to the borrower wholly and directly out of E's contribution; and (c) the advance and the recorded financial liability (as originally recorded) are both of an amount equal to the amount of E's contribution. 6-092

Condition O is that, as at the time the advance is paid, the position of the lender (having regard to any arrangements connected to the asset-backed arrangement) is as follows: 6-093

(a) it is the lender (and not any person connected with the lender) who is entitled to the payments mentioned in s.196B(2)(a)(iii) (i.e. the £100,000 p/a rent in the example);
(b) those payments are to arise at times which have been fixed and fall at intervals of no more than one year (but allowing for payments otherwise due to arise on a non-working day to arise on the next working day). The first payment must arise no later than one year after the day on which the advance is paid;
(c) the lender is to receive each payment no later than three months after the day on which the payment arises (but allowing for payments otherwise due to be received on a non-working day to be received on the next working day);
(d) on receipt by the lender, each payment is directly to become part of the sums held for the purposes of the registered pension scheme;

---

[138] FA 2004 s.196C.
[139] If the borrower is a partnership the reference to the borrower's accounts includes a reference to the accounts of any member of the partnership.
[140] CTA 2010 s.760(2).

(e) the payments are all to be of the same amount[141];
(f) the total amount of the payments is not less than the amount of E's contribution; and
(g) all the payments are to be received by the lender within a period ("the payment period") ending no later than the end of the period of 25 years beginning with the day on which E's contribution is paid.

**6-094** Condition P is that, as at the time the advance is paid, in accordance with generally accepted accounting practice the recorded financial liability is to be reduced to nil by the end of the payment period by (and only by) the payments mentioned in s.196B(2)(a)(iii) (i.e. the £100,000 p/a rent in the example). In the example, the recorded financial liability (if there is one) is only reduced to nil if and when the employer exercises the option and pays the £1,000 so this requirement would not be met.

**6-095** Condition Q is that, as at the time the advance is paid, no commitment (whether or not legally enforceable and whether or not subject to any conditions) has been given (directly or indirectly) to a relevant person[142] to secure that a person receives money or another asset, which is in some way linked to the receipt by the lender of a payment mentioned in s.196B(2)(a)(iii) (i.e. the £100,000 p/a rent in the example).

**6-096** **Condition C**  Condition C is:

"that it is reasonable to suppose that the amount of one or more of the payments mentioned in subsection (2)(a)(iii) has been, or is to be, determined (wholly or partly) on the basis that, in essence, the whole or a part of the advance represents a loan which is (wholly or partly) to be repaid by way of one or more of those payments."

**6-097** Returning to the example, the £1 million paid to the employer will be calculated by reference to the rent payable under the lease. It is reasonable to suppose that the £1 million purchase price is essentially the net present value of £100,000 p/a for the next 15 years, and so Condition C would appear to be met. Although Condition C refers to a loan rather than net present value, one would expect the value of a loan to be determined in this way, and so it seems to follow that net present value is material.

**6-098** Condition C therefore seems to require that the property transferred to the scheme has only a limited lifespan. An income producing asset with a limited life span will always resemble, and may be valued in a similar way to, a loan (at least where the income is predictable).

**6-099** In the example, the £1 million value will also include the value of the right to receive the £1,000 to exercise the option, but that will not make any difference because Condition C is that the £1 million represents a loan which wholly *or partly* is to be repaid by those payments.

**6-100** **Complex ABC arrangements involving a new partnership**  This type of arrangement is similar to the simple version except that Condition A is that the

---

[141] Disregarding negligible differences and increase in line with the CPI or RPI, or an increase not exceeding 5% p/a.
[142] The following are relevant persons: E; a person connected with E; a person acting (directly or indirectly) at the direction or request, or with the agreement, of E or a person connected with E; a person chosen (directly or indirectly) by E or a person connected with E; a person within a class of person chosen (directly or indirectly) by E or a person connected with E; a partnership. However, the trustees or managers of the registered pension scheme (in their capacity as such) are not relevant persons.

employer disposes of the property to a partnership (in which the employer is a partner) instead of to the pension scheme. The pension scheme then joins the partnership (or, if it is already a partner then there is a change in the pension scheme's share of the partnership profits) and uses the employer's contribution to make a capital contribution to the partnership (this is the "advance") in exchange for a share of the partnership income and the scheme's share of the partnership income is determined by reference (wholly or partly) to payments in respect of the property transferred to the partnership by the employer as part of the asset-backed arrangement.

Condition B is that the asset-backed arrangement is not an acceptable structured finance arrangement (meaning that conditions M to Q are not satisfied).[143] Conditions M to Q are essentially the same as those considered above, modified so as to fit the partnership model (so, for example, instead of referring to a borrower, they refer to the partnership).

**Complex ABC arrangements using an existing partnership** This type of arrangement is similar to the partnership model above except that Condition A is that the partnership already holds the property before the asset-backed arrangement is made. The pension scheme then joins the partnership (or, if it is already a partner then there is a change in the pension scheme's share in the partnership profits) and uses the employer's contribution to make a capital contribution to the partnership (this is the "advance") in exchange for a share of the partnership income and the scheme share of the partnership income is determined by reference (wholly or partly) to payments in respect of the property transferred to the partnership by the employer as part of the asset-backed arrangement.

Condition B is that the asset-backed arrangement is not an acceptable structured finance arrangement (meaning, once again, that conditions M to Q are not satisfied).[144] Conditions M to Q are identical to those in the partnership model above.

**Change in lender's position under acceptable structured finance arrangement** Where a tax deduction is not denied under these provisions (on the basis that it is an acceptable structured finance arrangement), this is on the basis that the arrangement will operate over its term in the way described at the outset. If there is a subsequent deviation from those terms[145] then an amount may be brought into charge on the employer under s.196I.

Section 196I applies if the ABC provisions do not apply to a contribution by an employer because it is an acceptable structured finance arrangement (but conditions A and C in the simple version, or condition A in the complex versions are met), and at any time after the advance is paid (i.e. the £1 million paid by the scheme in the example):

(a) the lender's position changes from the lender's original position in any respect (whether as a result of a term of the asset-backed arrangement or another arrangement or otherwise);

(b) an event occurs or does not occur and the occurrence or non-occurrence of the event does not accord with the lender's original position in any respect;

(c) in accordance with generally accepted accounting practice, the recorded

---

[143] FA 2004 s.196E.
[144] FA 2004 s.196G.
[145] e.g. a change made to the amounts of the payments, or a reduction in the recorded financial liability (other than by reason other than the making of a payment under Condition A).

financial liability is reduced to nil other than by the payments of £100,000 p/a (in the example);
(d) a commitment as described in Condition Q is given; or
(e) the employer ceases to be within the charge to corporation tax or income tax (as the case may be) or ceases to exist or enters administration or starts to be wound up.

**6-106** Section 196I also applies if the ABC provisions do not apply to a contribution by an employer because it is an acceptable structured finance arrangement (but conditions A and C in s.196B, or condition A in the complex versions are met), and at any time after the advance is paid (i.e. the £1 million paid by the scheme in the example), in accordance with generally accepted accounting practice, the recorded financial liability is reduced in part other than as a result of the £100,000 p/a payments (in the example).

**6-107** Where a mere administrative error causes s.196I to apply, it is ignored so long as the consequences of the error are remedied promptly. Also ignored are mere changes in the persons who are the trustees of the registered pension scheme or in the persons who control the management of the registered pension scheme.

**6-108** If s.196I applies then the "relevant amount" is treated as taxable profits/income of the employer. The "relevant amount" means either the outstanding amount of the recorded financial liability immediately before the relevant time determined in accordance with generally accepted accounting practice, or the amount of the reduction of the recorded financial liability. However, the amount treated as profit or income, together with any amounts so treated on any previous applications of s.196I in relation to the asset-backed arrangement, cannot exceed the total amount of relief given in respect of E's contribution.

**6-109** If s.196I applies then the structured finance arrangement legislation will cease to apply in relation to the asset-backed arrangement. Where the event was a partial reduction in the recorded financial liability, the structured finance arrangement legislation ceasing to apply could put the employer in a better overall position, and so the legislation provides for *just and reasonable* assessments to tax to be made to ensure that there is no such advantage is to be gained.

**6-110** **Interaction with scheme administration employer payment provisions** If an employer pays a contribution under a registered pension scheme and[146]:
(a) condition A in s.196B, 196D or 196F is met;
(b) the asset-backed arrangement is an acceptable structured finance arrangement for the purposes of s.196B, 196D or 196F (as the case may be) and, accordingly, condition B in that section is not met; and
(c) the advance gives rise to a loan (within the meaning of s.162)

then s.180(4) (which provides that a loan to or in respect of a sponsoring employer is not a scheme administration employer payment) does not prevent the advance from being a scheme administration employer payment (if it would otherwise do so).

**6-111** So the purpose of s.196K is to ensure that a deemed advance is not treated as a loan for the purposes of the scheme administration employer payment provisions. Section 196K should not be taken as meaning that if (a)–(c) do not apply then the advance will be a loan for the purposes of the scheme administration employer payment provisions. Such transactions will usually not constitute a loan for the reason

---

[146] FA 2004 s.196K.

## EMPLOYER CONTRIBUTIONS

given in Ch.11. Similarly, such a transaction will not usually constitute a loan for the purposes of the authorised employer loan provisions.

*Spreading of relief*

If an employer makes contributions in one year that are significantly greater than contributions made in the previous year, FA 2004 s.197 may operate to spread the tax deduction over a number of years. Section 197 applies where: **6-112**

(a) contributions are paid by an employer under a registered pension scheme in two consecutive periods[147];
(b) the amount of the contributions paid in the second chargeable period (ignoring contributions paid for an excepted purpose[148]) exceeds 210% of the amount of the contributions paid in the previous chargeable period; and
(c) the difference between 110% of the previous year contributions and the actual second year contributions ("the relevant excess") is equal to or greater than £500,000.

For example, if an employer contributes £1 million in one chargeable period and then £2.5 million in the next chargeable period, the provisions will apply because £2.5 million exceeds 210% of £1 million (i.e. £2.1 million) and the difference between 110% of £1 million (i.e. £1.1 million) and £2.5 million is more than £500,000. The relevant excess is £1.4 million. **6-113**

It is clear that these provisions cannot apply to the very first contribution to a pension scheme. Indeed, an employer can avoid the application of these provisions simply by making contributions every other year. The provisions apply per pension scheme; employer contributions to more than one scheme are not aggregated. **6-114**

The effect of the provisions applying is that the relevant excess is treated (for tax deduction purposes) as if it were spread as follows: **6-115**

| Amount of relevant excess | Fraction and chargeable period(s) |
| --- | --- |
| £500,000 or more but less than £1,000,000 | One-half of the whole of the amount of the relevant excess is to be treated as paid in the chargeable period immediately after the current chargeable period. |
| £1,000,000 or more but less than £2,000,000 | One-third of the whole of the amount of the relevant excess is to be treated as paid in each of the two chargeable periods immediately after the current chargeable period. |
| £2,000,000 or more | One-quarter of the whole of the amount of the relevant excess is to be treated as paid in each of the three chargeable periods immediately after the current chargeable period. |

Where the previous chargeable period and the current chargeable period are not **6-116**

---

[147] *Chargeable period* means a period of account (where the contributions are deducted in computing profits to be charged under ITTOIA 2005 Pt 2 or CTA 2009 Pt 3), or an accounting period (where relief in respect of the contributions is given under FA 2012 s.76 or CTA 2009 Pt 16 Ch.2).

[148] Contributions are paid for an excepted purpose if they are paid with a view to funding: (a) an increase in the amount of pensions paid to pensioner members of the pension scheme to reflect increases in the cost of living; or (b) benefits which may accrue under the pension scheme to or in respect of individuals who become members of the pension scheme in the current chargeable period as a result of future service as employees of the employer.

of equal length, the previous year contributions must be adjusted by being multiplied by "DCCP/DPCP",
where:

- *DCCP* is the number of days in the current chargeable period; and
- *DPCP* is the number of days in the previous chargeable period.

6-117 **Cessation of business** If the spreading rules apply and then the employer ceases to carry on business before obtaining a tax deduction for the full relevant excess, the "unrelieved" amount is treated as paid in the chargeable period in which the employer ceases to carry on business.[149] Alternatively (at the option of the employer) the amount determined by reference to the following formula can be treated as paid on each day in the period beginning with the current chargeable period, and ending with the day on which the employer ceases to carry on business, ("the relevant period"): "UP/DRP",
where:

- *UP* is the amount of the unrelieved portion; and
- *DRP* is the number of days in the relevant period.

6-118 **Indirect contributions** Section 199A contains provisions which are intended to prevent an employer from sidestepping the spreading rules in s.197 by making a payment that is intended to facilitate the making of a contribution to the pension scheme by another person.

6-119 Section 199A applies if the following four requirements are met:

(a) an employer pays contributions under a registered pension scheme ("the original scheme") in a chargeable period;
(b) the employer makes a payment ("the relevant payment") that is intended to facilitate the payment of pension contributions under the original scheme or a substitute scheme by a person other than the employer and the employer would otherwise be entitled in the next chargeable period to an amount of relief ("the relevant relief") in respect of the relevant payment;
(c) s.197 would apply if, in the chargeable period mentioned in (b), the employer paid pension contributions under the original scheme of the amount of the relevant relief; and
(d) the purpose, or one of the purposes, of facilitating the payment of pension contributions by a person other than the employer is to enable pension contributions to be paid without that section applying.

6-120 For the purposes of ss.197 and 198, the amount of the relevant relief is treated as the amount of a pension contribution paid by the employer under the original scheme in the chargeable period mentioned in (b) above.

6-121 For these purposes, a "substitute scheme" is any registered pension scheme to which there is a relevant transfer in the period of two years ending with the day on which the relevant payment is made, or to which it is envisaged that a relevant transfer will or may be made after that day. A "relevant transfer" is a recognised transfer from the original scheme of more than 30% of the aggregate of: (a) the amount of the sums and the market value of the assets held for the purposes of, or representing accrued rights under, the original scheme immediately before the transfer (where the transfer is made in the of two years before the relevant payment); and (b) the amount of those sums and the market value of those assets on

---

[149] FA 2004 s.198.

the day on which the payment is made (where it is it is envisaged that a relevant transfer will or may be made after the relevant payment). If there is a transfer from a substitute scheme to another registered pension scheme which would have been a relevant transfer had it been a transfer from the original scheme at the time the relevant transfer was made, that other scheme is also a substitute scheme.

*Deemed contributions*

Where a sum is paid to the trustees or managers of a registered pension scheme by an employer towards the discharge of any liability of the employer under PA 1995 s.75,[150] the making of the payment is deemed to a contribution by the employer under the pension scheme.[151]  **6-122**

If the employer's business is discontinued before the payment is made, a tax deduction is available to the same extent as it would have been but for the discontinuance, as if it had been made on the last day on which the business was carried on.  **6-123**

*No other relief for employers in connection with contributions*

FA 2004 s.200 provides as follows:  **6-124**

"No sums other than contributions paid by an employer under a registered pension scheme—
  (a) are deductible in computing the amount of the profits of the employer for the purposes of Part 2 of ITTOIA 2005 or Part 3 of CTA 2009 (trading income),
  (b) are expenses of management for the purposes of Chapter 2 of Part 16 of CTA 2009 (expenses of management: companies with investment business), or
  (c) ...
in connection with the cost of providing benefits under the pension scheme."

The precise scope of s.200 is uncertain. Its effect seems to be to deny a tax deduction in two main circumstances:  **6-125**

  (a) first, where accrued costs are charged in the employer's accounts under generally accepted accounting principles but not actually paid (e.g. in relation to defined benefits arrangements and unfunded arrangements). Until a contribution is "paid", no deduction is allowed[152]; and
  (b) secondly, where services relating to the pension scheme (such as trustee, actuarial, financial or legal services) are provided to the employer and paid for by the employer. If such services are provided to the scheme, but the invoice is settled by the employer, such a payment could well be a "contribution paid", as it relieves the scheme of that cost. But where the services are provided to the employer (which sometimes happens for VAT reasons[153]), it is quite possible that s.200 will prevent a tax deduction.

Notwithstanding the references to "sums" and "paid", s.200 does not appear to be aimed at *in specie* contributions. It clearly does not provide that a contribution must be a "sum" before a tax deduction will be allowed: it provides that "no sums  **6-126**

---

[150] Deficiencies in the assets of a pension scheme.
[151] FA 2004 s.199.
[152] It may be countered that that is what s.196(2)(b) is aimed at, however s.196 only applies to contributions paid "in respect of any individual", so it does not apply to contributions which are in respect of the employer's employees generally (which will often be the case with contributions to defined benefits schemes).
[153] See Ch.22.

other than contributions paid" are deductible, which means that in order for a tax deduction to be denied under s.200 it must first be a "sum". Anything other than a sum (for example, an asset, if that is a material distinction) cannot be affected by s.200 unless "sum" includes assets. The question of whether the words "sum" or "paid" preclude *in specie* contributions is considered below.

*In specie contributions*

6-127   Under general tax principles, it makes no difference whether a contribution is in cash or *in specie*.[154] HMRC suggest that a tax deduction is available only in respect of contributions "paid", and they suggest this requirement can be found in s.196(1).[155] Although s.196(1) does refer to "contributions paid", it is quite clear that a contribution need not satisfy s.196(1) in order to obtain a tax deduction. If there is any provision in FA 2004 Pt 4 that denies a tax deduction for *in specie* contributions, it seems likely that it is s.200 rather than s.196. Although the precise meaning of s.200 is unclear (see above), it is at least clear that (in contrast to s.196) its purpose is to deny a tax deduction in certain circumstances. However, even if the correct interpretation of s.200 is that a tax deduction is denied unless a contribution is "paid", it does not follow that a tax deduction will be denied for an *in specie* contribution.

6-128   In *Irving v HMRC*,[156] the Court of Appeal considered an *in specie* contribution of shares to a FURBS. The question was whether such a contribution was within ICTA 1988 s.595(1), which imposed a charge to tax where an employer "pays a sum" into a FURBS. The Court of Appeal held that although the more natural meaning of the phrase "pays a sum" is "pays a sum of money", it can include the transfer of non-cash assets if the context suggests that it should be given a broader meaning (as it did in that case).[157]

6-129   In *Lowe v Peter Walker (Warrington) and Robert Cain & Sons Ltd*[158] it was not disputed that the transfer of shares to trustees of an approved superannuation fund constituted "any sum paid by an employer ... by way of contribution towards a superannuation fund" for the purposes of FA 1921 s.32 resulting in an allowable deduction for the employer.

6-130   The same reasoning appears to apply in the context of FA 2004 Pt 4.[159] The only possible objection to *in specie* contributions must relate to problems surrounding the valuation of the asset. In other words, there may be concerns that: (a) calculating market value in an objectively correct way may give rise to difficulties; and/or (b) market value may be artificially exploited in some way. It seems likely that, for these reasons, the FA 2004—which itself creates the ability for member tax relief—has simply not provided for *in specie* member contributions except as allowed under s.195. It is not that the FA 2004 expressly disallows them; there is simply nothing

---

[154] See *Lion Co v HMRC* [2009] UKFTT 357, in which a house was transferred to a director as remuneration and a tax deduction was obtained. This was expressly approved in *Scotts Atlantic Management Ltd (In Liquidation) v HMRC* [2013] UKFTT 299 at [133].
[155] See PTM042100, which was "clarified" in December 2020, following the decision in *HMRC v Sippchoice Ltd* [2020] UKUT 149, and extended to employer contributions.
[156] *Irving v HMRC* [2008] EWCA Civ 6; [2008] B.T.C. 36.
[157] In that case it was the word "sum" rather than the word "paid" which the taxpayer argued suggested cash.
[158] *Lowe v Peter Walker (Warrington) and Robert Cain & Sons Ltd* (1935) 20 T.C. 25.
[159] The Special Commissioners in *Irving v RCC* [2008] EWCA Civ 6; [2008] B.T.C. 36 considered the FA 2004 provisions in some detail and considered that a tax deduction would be available for *in specie* employer contributions: see [42]–[44]. Also see the cogent arguments raised by counsel at [10] and [11].

allowing them. On the other hand, a tax deduction for employer contributions is dealt with outside of the FA 2004. So the fact that the FA 2004 is silent on the availability of a tax deduction for employer *in specie* contributions does not have the same effect as being silent on member *in specie* contributions.

Therefore, in contrast to the position relating to member contributions, there appears to be nothing in the FA 2004 Pt 4 that denies a tax deduction in respect of *in specie* contributions by employers (whether or not a prior debt is created). However, the decision in *Sippchoice* is extremely unhelpful in this regard. Although the decision is strictly limited to the meaning of "paid" in s.188(1) (and was strongly influenced by the existence of s.195—a provision which has no application to employer contributions), it is perhaps unlikely that a tribunal would find that "paid" has a different meaning in s.200 (or s.196, if that is relevant). For that reason it may be desirable to comply with the steps described in PTM042100: see above.

6-131

**Inheritance tax**

If the employer is a close company, a contribution may have inheritance tax consequences for its participators. A contribution by an employer in respect of an employee will not be a transfer of value.[160] A contribution by an employer in respect of other persons (such as self-employed consultants or relatives of an employee) will not constitute a transfer of value provided that the employer obtains a tax deduction or if there is no intention to confer gratuitous benefit.[161]

6-132

**Taxation of the employee**

*The earnings charge*

ITEPA 2003 s.308 provides that:

6-133

"No liability to income tax arises in respect of earnings where an employee's employer makes contributions under a registered pension scheme in respect of the employee."

This therefore provides a very clear exemption from the earnings charge where an employer makes a contribution in respect of an employee. The final five words ("in respect of the employee") were added from 6 April 2013. The purpose of the additional words, as explained in HMRC's Explanatory Note, is to counter the use of so called "family pension plans". Paragraph 8 of the Explanatory Notes explains that:

6-134

"Under these arrangements, an employer pays pension contributions into a registered pension scheme of an employee's family member as part of the employee's flexible remuneration package. The effect is that the employee is still exempt from income tax and NICs on the employer contributions into the family member's pension scheme. Furthermore, these contributions do not count towards the £50,000 limit for the employee, avoiding the income tax that would otherwise be due on the employee for contributions in excess of the limit."

So the intention is that on or after 6 April 2013, a contribution by an employer for the benefit of an employee's family member, will (without the protection of ITEPA 2003 s.308) give rise to an earnings charge for the employee. However, it is quite clear that a contribution to a pension scheme will not normally give rise to

6-135

---

[160] IHTA 1984 s.12(2).
[161] Respectively, IHTA 1984 s.12(1) and s.10. These provisions are considered in detail in Ch.20.

an earnings charge under general principles.[162] In those cases, an employer contribution in respect of a person who is not an employee (such as the spouse of an employee) should not give rise to an earnings charge even without the protection of s.308.

*The benefits code*

6-136    The benefits code should not apply to a contribution because those provisions do not apply to a benefit which is itself the right to receive a benefit in the future.[163] Notwithstanding this, ITEPA 2003 s.307 provides that no liability to income tax arises under ITEPA 2003 s.201 (which is the residual head of charge under the benefits code) in respect of provision made by an employee's employer (under a registered pension scheme or otherwise) for a retirement or death benefit. The precise scope of the words *provision made* is not entirely clear but it will clearly include a contribution (and HMRC accept this).[164]

*Termination payments*

6-137    ITEPA 2003 Pt 6 Ch.3 does not apply to a contribution to a registered pension scheme if the contribution is made: (a) as part of an arrangement relating to the termination of a person's employment; and (b) in order to provide benefits for the person in accordance with the terms of the scheme or "approved personal pension arrangements".[165]

**National insurance contributions**

6-138    If an individual receives salary and then contributes it to a registered pension scheme (or directs his employer to do so), he may obtain income tax relief but there is no equivalent relief for the NIC suffered on the salary. It is for this reason that salary sacrifice arrangements are attractive. Sums paid by an employer, other than out of an employee's salary, to provide contingent benefits to an employee under a retirement benefits scheme, are not "earnings" for the purposes of class 1 NIC.[166]

# SALARY SACRIFICE

6-139    A salary sacrifice arrangement is an arrangement under which the employee and employer agree that, henceforth, the employee will receive a reduced salary, but with some other additional benefit.[167] It is therefore more accurate to describe the arrangement as a *variation* of the rights of the employee, rather than a sacrifice.

---

[162] This is explained in more detail in the context of unregistered pension schemes (to which ITEPA 2003 s.308 has no application): see Ch.24.
[163] *Templeton v Jacobs* [1996] 1 W.L.R. 1433; [1996] B.T.C. 416.
[164] ITEPA 2003 s.307 is considered in detail in Ch.30.
[165] ITEPA 2003 s.408. The same exception applies to EFRBS. The term *approved personal pension arrangements* is not defined anywhere. Prior to 6 April 2006 it usually had the meaning given in ICTA 1988 s.630(1). Since 6 April 2006 these words can be disregarded.
[166] *HMRC v Forde and McHugh Ltd* [2014] UKSC 14 at [16] (Lord Hodge); *RFC 2012 Plc v Advocate General for Scotland* [2017] UKSC 45 at [48] (Lord Hodge). There is in any event an express exemption where ITEPA 2003 s.308 applies (The Social Security (Contributions) Regulations 2001 (SI 2001/1004) Sch.3 Pt VI para.2).
[167] The reduction in salary and the value of the other benefit need not be equal, but some benefit must be received by the employee. In *Reed Employment Plc v HMRC* [2012] UKFTT 28 (TC) at [225]

Such an arrangement can be effective for tax purposes only in relation to salary which has not been earned at the time of the variation; otherwise the employee is merely directing the employer to pay his earnings to a third party.[168] If the other benefit does not give rise to a charge to income tax (as earnings or a benefit in kind) and/or NIC, it will be more tax-efficient for the employee to do this, when compared to receiving taxable earnings and then purchasing the other benefit himself. As far as the employer is concerned, there is a saving of 13.8% employer's NIC. In a pensions context, the other benefit is usually a contribution by the employer to a pension scheme for the employee's benefit. Employer contributions to registered pension schemes are not taxed as earnings[169] or a benefit in kind[170] and are not subject to NIC.[171] Given that the contributions are employer contributions, they cannot be refunded to the member as a short service refund lump sum.[172]

**Optional remuneration arrangements**

6-140 FA 2017 introduced provisions relating to "optional remuneration arrangements" into the benefits code in ITEPA 2003. These provisions can apply only where the benefit does not otherwise give rise to a charge to earnings under general principles. If they apply, the employee is deemed for income tax and NIC purposes to receive earnings equal to the "amount forgone" (unless the cash equivalent of the benefit under the benefits code is greater, in which case the benefits code will continue to apply).[173]

6-141 A benefit provided for an employee is provided under "optional remuneration arrangements" to the extent that it is provided under: (a) arrangements under which, in return for the benefit, the employee gives up the right (or a future right) to receive an amount of taxable earnings ("type A arrangements"); or (b) arrangements (other than type A arrangements) under which the employee agrees to be provided with the benefit rather than an amount of taxable earnings ("Type B arrangements").[174] As the name suggests, both types of arrangement require that the remuneration arrangement is "optional" in the sense that the employee has some sort of choice.

*The amount forgone*

6-142 The "amount foregone" means the amount of earnings given up (under type A arrangements) or the amount of earnings that the employee would have received if he did not agree to receive the benefit (under type B arrangements). In relation to a benefit provided for an employee partly under type A arrangements and partly

---

the Tribunal stated that: "In our view a salary sacrifice implies reciprocity: the employee gives up a portion of his or her earnings, even if the portion is variable, in exchange for an identified benefit provided by the employer. Reed, however, did not provide any benefit at all ...". This will not normally create any difficulties.

[168] *Heaton v Bell* [1970] A.C. 728; [1969] UKHL TC 46 211; *Smyth v Stretton* (1904) 5 T.C. 36.
[169] Contributions will frequently not constitute earnings on general principles (see Ch.24). There is also a statutory exemption in ITEPA 2003 s.308.
[170] Contributions will frequently not be taxable benefits in kind on general principles (see Ch.24). There is also a statutory exemption in ITEPA 2003 s.307.
[171] *HMRC v Forde and McHugh Ltd* [2014] UKSC 14; [2014] 1 W.L.R. 810. There is also a statutory exemption in SI 2001/1004 Sch.3 Pt VI para.2.
[172] For short service refund lump sums, see Ch.14. The member's reduced salary may also negatively affect his ability to obtain a mortgage.
[173] See e.g. ITEPA 2003 s.203A(2).
[174] ITEPA 2003 s.69A.

under type B arrangements, the amount foregone is the amounts foregone under the arrangements of each type.[175]

*Exemptions*

6-143 The only exemptions from the benefits code that apply to exempt benefits provided under optional remuneration arrangements are those which are "special case" exemptions and "excluded" exemptions.[176] In a pensions context, the only relevant special case exemption is ITEPA 2003 s.308B (relating to independent advice in respect of conversions and transfers of pension scheme benefits). The following are excluded exemptions: (a) ITEPA 2003, s.307 insofar as it relates to provision made for retirement benefits (but *not* death benefits); (b) ITEPA 2003 s.308 (exemption of contribution to registered pension scheme); (c) ITEPA 2003 s.308A (exemption of contributions to overseas pension scheme); and (d) ITEPA 2003 s.308C (provision of pensions advice). The significance of the two different types of exemption is that special case exemptions already have specific salary sacrifice rules that will continue to apply[177] rather than the rules relating to optional remuneration arrangements, whereas excluded exemptions do not. As a result of the above exemptions, the optional remuneration arrangement provisions will have no application to contributions to registered pension schemes.

## MEMBER AND EMPLOYER CONTRIBUTIONS

### The annual allowance charge

6-144 In relation to other money purchase arrangements, the annual allowance provisions relate solely to the amount of contributions.[178]

### "Recycling" lump sums

6-145 FA 2004 Pt 4 is not generally concerned with where the money come from in order to make a contribution to a pension scheme (so, for instance, there is nothing to prevent a member or employer from borrowing from a third party in order to make a contribution and claiming tax relief or a tax deduction in respect of the contribution[179]). However, FA 2004 Sch.29 para.3A provides an exception to this general rule. Were it not for para.3A, a member who has reached normal pension age may consider it attractive to take a (tax-free) PCLS and then contribute some or all of it to a second registered pension scheme and claim tax relief. He could then perhaps take a PCLS from that second scheme and contribute it to a third registered pension scheme, and so on. HMRC refer to this as "recycling" the PCLS and consider that it allows members "to generate artificially high amounts of tax

---

[175] ITEPA 2003 s.69B.
[176] ITEPA 2003 s.228A.
[177] So, if an employer pays for (or reimburses an employee for) the cost of the provision of independent advice (up to £150) in respect of conversions and transfers of pension schemes to its employees, that is not taxable under the benefits code (per ITEPA 2003 s.308B and The Income Tax (Exemption of Minor Benefits) Regulations 2002 (SI 2002/205) reg.5) but only if the benefits is not provided under a salary sacrifice arrangement (s.308B(4)).
[178] See Ch.7.
[179] "... everybody agrees that an individual active member of a registered pension scheme may fund his relievable pension contributions (up to the yearly ceiling laid down in the legislation) by borrowing for the purpose." (*R. v Quillan* [2015] EWCA Crim 538 at [84]).

relief".[180] The provisions apply in the same way whether it is the member or his employer that makes the contribution.

If para.3A applies in relation to a PCLS paid to the member, the pension scheme is deemed to make an unauthorised payment to the member.[181] It applies if: **6-146**

(a) because of the PCLS, the contributions paid by or on behalf of, or in respect of, the member to the pension scheme (or any other registered pension scheme) are significantly greater than they otherwise would be; and

(b) the member envisaged at the relevant time that that would be so.

The "relevant time" is usually the time when PCLS is paid. However, if the requirement in (a) above is satisfied before the PCLS is paid (for example, because the member has borrowed funds from a third party to finance the contribution, and intends to use the PCLS to discharge the loan), the relevant time is the time when the requirement in (a) above is first satisfied.

*The amount of the unauthorised payment*

The amount of the unauthorised payment is equal to the amount of the lump sum. **6-147**

*Exceptions*

The recycling lump sum provisions do not apply where: **6-148**

(a) the amount of the PCLS, together with any other PCLS paid to the member in the previous 12 months, does not exceed £7,500; or

(b) the increased contributions do not exceed 30% of the amount of the PCLS; or

(c) the member has reached age 75 when the increased contributions are paid, and the contributions are not paid by his employer.[182]

**Annual payments**

If a sponsoring employer or member has a contractual obligation to contribute to a registered pension scheme (as will frequently be the case), the contributions could conceivably be taxable as income of the trustees or managers under ITTOIA 2005 Pt 5 Ch.7 (annual payments) or Ch.8 (income not otherwise charged). HMRC are not known to have taken this point, and it would be surprising if they did, since there are no special rules for registered pension schemes. If these provisions applied to contributions to pension schemes then the tax charge would effectively cancel out the tax relief.[183] **6-149**

A payment is an "annual payment" if the following four tests are met[184]: **6-150**

(a) the payment is income of the recipient, and not a payment of capital by instalments[185];

---

[180] See PTM133810.
[181] The member must notify the scheme administrator of the date on which the unauthorised payment is deemed to have been made, and the amount of the payment, within 30 days (The Registered Pension Schemes (Provision of Information) Regulations 2006 (SI 2006/567) reg.11A).
[182] Paragraph 3A(3)–(6).
[183] It seems unlikely that such contributions could be described as income from investments, so FA 2004 s.186 could not apply to exempt the income tax charge.
[184] "Annual payment" is construed ejusdem generis with "annuity".
[185] *Brodie's Will Trustees v IRC* (1933) 17 T.C. 432.

(b) it is "pure income profit"[186];
(c) there is a legal obligation to pay the sum[187]; and
(d) if not recurring, it is at least capable of recurrence.[188]

The fact that such payments may be contingent and variable in character does not prevent them from being annual payments.[189] It is strongly arguable that a contribution to a money purchase scheme does not constitute "pure income profit" of the trustee, because the trustee is obliged to use the contribution to provide benefits to the member(s). In most cases, a contribution can be viewed as the purchase of benefits under the pension scheme.[190] In relation to a defined benefits scheme, the connection between contributions and the payment of benefits is less direct, although it may still be arguable that the contributions do not constitute pure income profit. Alternatively, if there is a contractual obligation to make the contributions but the trustees are not a party to that agreement (the obligation may arise, for example, in the employment contract between the employee and the employer) then it may be arguable that the contributions received by the trustees are not taxable income because they have no source. In these circumstances, the trustees just receive a series of one-off voluntary payments.[191]

**In specie contributions**

6-151 *In specie* contributions have been considered above in the context of tax relief or a tax deduction. It is also necessary to consider whether such contributions have CGT, SDLT or stamp duty implications.

*Chargeable gains*

6-152 A contribution may have CGT or corporation tax consequences if the contributed asset is standing at a gain. In relation to member contributions, there is no reason in principle that business asset disposal relief could not apply on a disposal of qualifying assets. Gift relief under TCGA 1992 s.165 (gifts of business assets) or TCGA 1992 s.260 (gifts on which inheritance tax is chargeable) will not usually be available in respect of a member contribution,[192] but relief under s.165 may well be available in respect of a contribution of "business assets" by a third party on behalf of the member (for example, by a parent in respect of an adult child) provided that

---

[186] *Re Hanbury* (1939) 38 T.C. 588. So, e.g. agreeing to pay a garage £500 p/a for five years for the hire and upkeep of a car does not constitute annual payments: *Howe v IRC* [1919] 2 K.B. 336; 7 T.C. 289.
[187] See *Ridge Securities Ltd v IRC* (1964) 44 T.C. 373.
[188] See *IRC v Whitworth Park Coal Ltd* [1961] A.C. 31; [1959] 3 W.L.R. 842; 38 T.C. 531.
[189] *Moss Empires Ltd v IRC* 21 T.C. 264.
[190] Alternatively, it might be arguable that a contribution is more in the nature of a payment which must be repaid, with investment return, in the future (akin to a bare trust arrangement, or even a loan). But a purchase of benefits seems more realistic. In *Hills v HMRC* [2014] UKFTT 646 (a VAT case), the FTT rejected the taxpayer's assertion that a SIPP is a bare trust. The drafting of the scheme rules may be relevant.
[191] In this sense, the position of the trustees is no different to the retired schoolmaster in *Stedeford v Beloe* [1932] A.C. 388. In that case, the House of Lords held that a voluntary pension paid from the college to the retired schoolmaster was not chargeable to income tax because he had no right to the pension.
[192] Either because the contribution is not a gift, or because the scheme is a settlor-interested settlement (TCGA 1992 s.169B). For CGT purposes, "settled property" means property held in trust (other than nominee and bare trust arrangements) and "settlement" is construed accordingly (TCGA 1992 s.68).

the donor (as settlor) is excluded from receiving any death benefits.[193] Relief in respect of an employer contribution (and also, conceivably, a contribution by an individual) may be available under TCGA 1992 s.239.[194]

*Stamp duty land tax*

Where a person makes an *in specie* contribution of UK land to a pension scheme, it is necessary to consider if this gives rise to a charge to SDLT. In general, SDLT arises where there is an acquisition of a "chargeable interest" (such as an interest in land), by reference to the "chargeable consideration" given by the person acquiring the chargeable interest. The satisfaction of a debt constitutes chargeable consideration for SDLT purposes,[195] so if (as HMRC suggest) a debt is created and then satisfied by the transfer of land, a charge to SDLT will arise. The same analysis would apply whenever land is transferred in satisfaction of an obligation to make a contribution. Similarly, an assumption of debt constitutes chargeable consideration, and so a contribution of land where the trustees assume responsibility for a mortgage will usually give rise to a charge to SDLT. If a person contributes land to the trustees of a pension scheme in circumstances where there is no satisfaction or assumption of debt, does this give rise to a charge to SDLT? There is clearly an acquisition of a chargeable interest, but it is less clear if any chargeable consideration is given by the trustees for the interest.[196] If there is any chargeable consideration given, it must relate to the trustees' obligation to provide pension benefits.[197] Chargeable consideration generally means any consideration in money or money's worth given by the trustees directly or indirectly for the land.[198] In the context of a defined benefits scheme, it is unlikely that there will be any connection between the

6-153

---

[193] Tax relief under FA 2004 s.188(1) is not available in respect of *in specie* contributions (because they are not "paid"), but for the same reason the annual allowance provisions should not apply (see s.233). It most cases, relief under s.260 will not be available. A contribution to a contract-based pension scheme will not satisfy s.260 because it applies only where the asset is acquired by an individual or by trustees. In most cases, a contribution to a trust-based pension scheme will be a potentially exempt transfer rather than a chargeable transfer (see Ch.21), so will not satisfy s.260 for that reason. However, a contribution to a general fund under a pension scheme should be capable of satisfying s.260 in appropriate circumstances. Where business assets (such as shares in unlisted trading companies) are held by a FURBS or EFRBS, relief under s.165 may be available in respect of a transfer to a registered pension scheme (see TCGA 1992 Sch.7 para.2). Such a transfer is not a contribution (s.188(5)), so cannot be a "relievable pension contribution", meaning that: (a) tax relief is not available under s.188(1); and (b) the annual allowance provisions should have no application. The disguised remuneration provisions will require consideration, however.

[194] Where the employer is a close company, the contribution must be a disposition which "by virtue of" IHTA 1984 s.13 is not a transfer of value for inheritance tax purposes. This is unlikely to mean that IHTA 1984 s.13 must be the *sole* reason that the disposition is not a transfer of value for inheritance tax purposes. The fact that ss.10 or 12 may also apply can hardly be objectionable. For s.13 to apply, the property must be held on trusts of the description specified in IHTA 1984 s.86(1). Sections 13 and 86 are explained in detail in Ch.28.

[195] FA 2003 Sch.4 para.8.

[196] In the context of a contribution transferred to a corporate trustee, it is sometimes suggested that, if the scheme is a settlement (which will not usually be the case), the fact that the transferor may be connected with the trustee will cause the market value consideration provision in FA 2003 s.53 to apply. This however ignores FA 2003 s.54(2), which provides an exception for transfers to professional trustees. The same analysis applies for transfers between schemes.

[197] Although it is not at all clear that this is materially different to a gift to a family discretionary settlement (which is generally accepted as not involving chargeable consideration). In each case, the trustees are obliged to provide benefits at *some* stage. Of course, in the case of a family discretionary settlement the obligation may not arise until the end of the trust period, but for SDLT purposes the value of any chargeable consideration is not discounted on the basis that it is deferred (FA 2003 Sch.4 para.3).

[198] FA 2003 Sch.4 para.1(1). It is not relevant to look at what (if anything) is received by the member.

contribution and any obligation to provide benefits, so it is difficult to see how any chargeable consideration could arise. The position is less clear in relation to contributions to money purchase arrangements, however the better view seems to be that no chargeable consideration will be provided in most cases. Indeed, one would expect the analysis relating to contributions to be the same as the analysis relating to the transfer of land between pension schemes, and HMRC's position is that such transfers do not involve any chargeable consideration.[199]

*Stamp duty*

**6-154**   An *in specie* contribution of shares to a pension scheme should not be subject to stamp duty, unless the contribution discharges a debt.[200]

## TAX ON PRE-OWNED ASSETS

**6-155**   The provisions in FA 2004 Sch.15 are considered in Ch.24. HMRC consider that a charge under those provisions will not arise in relation to a registered pension scheme.[201]

---

FA 2003 s.52 may be a concern where the contribution is made to a deferred annuity contract. It is irrelevant that the annuity may be contingent (FA 2003 s.51 expressly applies). Where s.52 applies, the chargeable consideration is equal to the 12 highest annual payments.

[199] SDLTM31800 provides that "In our view the assumption by the transferee fund or by the trustees of the transferee fund, of obligations to provide benefits is not chargeable consideration". If the *assumption* of such obligations does not constitute chargeable consideration then it is difficult to see why the *creation* of such obligations should constitute chargeable consideration.

[200] Stamp Act 1891 s.57; see STSM082060.

[201] IHTM44114 makes the following, apparently unqualified, statement: "A charge under FA04/Sch15 will not arise in relation to pension arrangements under registered pension schemes ...".

# CHAPTER 7

# The Annual Allowance

## TABLE OF CONTENTS

| | |
|---|---|
| Overview | 7-001 |
| Development | 7-002 |
| Steps involved | 7-003 |
| Pension input periods | 7-004 |
| Step One: pension input amounts | 7-005 |
| Exception: year of death or severe ill health | 7-006 |
| Calculating the pension input amount | 7-008 |
| Cash balance arrangements | 7-008 |
| Other money purchase arrangements | 7-013 |
| Defined benefits arrangements | 7-015 |
| Hybrid arrangements | 7-021 |
| Step Two: determining the individual's annual allowance | 7-022 |
| High-income individuals | 7-023 |
| "Adjusted" and "threshold" income | 7-024 |
| Anti-avoidance | 7-027 |
| The tapered annual allowance | 7-028 |
| Carry forward of unused annual allowance | 7-029 |
| Step Three: default chargeable amount | 7-031 |
| Step Four: member has flexibly accessed pension rights | 7-032 |
| Flexibly accessing pension rights | 7-033 |
| Application to non-UK schemes | 7-034 |
| The calculation | 7-035 |
| The money-purchase input sub-total | 7-037 |
| Relevant hybrid arrangements | 7-038 |
| Illustration | 7-041 |
| Pension rights are first flexibly accessed | 7-042 |
| The defined-benefit input sub-total | 7-048 |
| The annual allowance charge | 7-050 |
| The scheme pays option | 7-051 |
| Exceptions to liability of scheme administrator | 7-055 |
| Discharge of scheme administrator's liability | 7-056 |
| Reporting obligations | 7-057 |
| The money purchase annual allowance | 7-058 |

## OVERVIEW

In broad terms, the purpose of the annual allowance provisions is to restrict the cost to the Exchequer of tax relief provided in respect of contributions to registered

**7-001**

pension schemes.[1] The provisions achieve this, not by restricting tax relief, but by imposing a charge to income tax (called the annual allowance charge), at the member's marginal rate, to the extent that the member's rights under one or more registered pension schemes increase in excess of the member's annual allowance in a tax year. The charge arises whether or not any tax relief is actually obtained.

The provisions are in FA 2004 ss.227–238A.

### Development

**7-002**    In the 2006/07 tax year, each individual had an annual allowance of £215,000. This increased each tax year, peaking at £255,000 in the 2010/11 tax year.[2] Following the 2008 financial crisis, a much lower "special annual allowance" was introduced on a temporary basis for high earners in the 2009/10 and 2010/11 tax years.[3] The annual allowance was reduced to £50,000 for the 2011/12 tax year. To make the reduction more palatable, measures were introduced at the same time to allow individuals to carry forward unused annual allowance from the previous three tax years, and to permit the scheme to discharge the annual allowance charge in certain circumstances (referred to as the "scheme pays" option). The annual allowance was further reduced to £40,000 from 6 April 2014, and remained at £40,000 until the 2023/24 tax year. Since 6 April 2023, the annual allowance has been £60,000.

In the 2015/16 tax year, the pension input period of every arrangement was aligned with the tax year, and a new "money purchase annual allowance" of £10,000 (reduced to £4,000 from 6 April 2017, and then increased back to £10,000 from 6 April 2023) was introduced for individuals who have "flexibly accessed" money purchase benefits.

In the 2016/17 tax year a "tapered" annual allowance was introduced for high-income individuals, the effect of which is to reduce their annual allowance by £1 for each £2 of annual income over £150,000 (increased to £240,000 from 6 April 2020, and to £260,000 from 6 April 2023), subject to a minimum tapered allowance of £10,000 (reduced to £4,000 from 6 April 2020, and then increased back to £10,000 from 6 April 2023).

### Steps involved

**7-003**    The annual allowance charge is a charge on "chargeable amounts". The following steps are required to determine whether a chargeable amount arises in respect of an individual:

| | |
|---|---|
| *Step One:* | Calculate the "pension input amount" for each arrangement of which the individual is a member. Aggregate them to arrive at the member's total pension input amount for the tax year. |
| *Step Two:* | Determine the individual's annual allowance for the tax year. This is the standard annual allowance (£60,000) unless the individual is a high income individual or if he has unused an- |

---

[1] A modified version of the annual allowance provisions applies to "currently-relieved non-UK pension schemes". See Ch.30.
[2] For a table showing the annual allowance for each tax year since 2006, see Ch.1.
[3] FA 2009 Sch.35. See *Restricting pensions tax relief through existing allowances: a discussion document*, HM Treasury and HMRC (27 July 2010), and the summary of responses (October 2010). Also see *Catherine Vine Lott v HMRC* [2014] UKFTT 947.

|  | nual allowance which he can carry forwards from the previous three tax years. |
|---|---|
| *Step Three:* | Determine whether the total pension input amount exceeds the individual's annual allowance. Any excess is a chargeable amount, and is referred to as the "default chargeable amount". |
| *Step Four:* | If the member has "flexibly accessed" his pension rights, perform an additional calculation to determine if it produces a chargeable amount higher than the default chargeable amount. This is referred to as the "alternative chargeable amount". If the alternative chargeable amount is higher than the default chargeable amount then the alternative chargeable amount (and not the default chargeable amount) is subject to the annual allowance charge. |

**Pension input periods**

The provisions refer to "pension input periods" rather than tax years. The pension input period is the period of time over which the pension input amount is measured. Since 9 July 2015, the pension input period of every arrangement under a registered pension scheme is aligned with the tax year (i.e. 6 April to 5 April).[4] Prior to that date, a different pension input period could be nominated, and changed, during the period. Prior to the 2019/20 tax year, it was necessary to understand the pre-9 July 2015 position where a member wished to carry forward unused annual allowance from the 2015/16 tax year (or earlier).

7-004

## STEP ONE: PENSION INPUT AMOUNTS

The first step is to calculate the "pension input amount" in respect of each arrangement relating to the individual under all registered pension schemes (and certain non-UK schemes[5]) during the pension input period.[6] The total pension input amount is essentially the increase in the value of the member's rights under the arrangement during the pension input period. Death benefits are taken into account if payable in respect of a money purchase arrangement, but not if payable in respect of a defined benefits arrangement. The method for calculating the pension input amount depends on the category of arrangement. The pension input amounts in respect of each arrangement relating to the individual.

7-005

---

[4] FA 2004 s.238ZB.
[5] Pension input amounts in respect of arrangement under RNUKS are included if the RNUKS is a "currently-relieved non-UK pension scheme" and the individual is a "currently-relieved member". See Ch.30.
[6] FA 2004 s.229(1). For the meaning of "arrangement", see Ch.2.

### Exception: year of death or severe ill health

**7-006** An individual expressly has no pension input amount in the tax year in which he dies, or in which he satisfies the severe ill health condition.[7] An individual satisfies the severe ill health condition if:[8]

(a) he becomes entitled to all the benefits to which he is entitled under the arrangement as a result of the scheme administrator having received evidence from a registered medical practitioner that the individual is suffering from ill health which makes him unlikely to be able (otherwise than to an insignificant extent) to undertake gainful work (in any capacity) before reaching state pension age;[9]

(b) he becomes entitled to a serious ill-health lump sum under the arrangement; or

(c) he is a member of the armed forces of the Crown who becomes entitled under the arrangement to a benefit on which no liability to income tax arises by virtue of ITEPA 2003 s.641(1).[10]

**7-007** The rationale for this exception is presumably that it is reasonable for a pension scheme to provide exceptional benefits on death or severe ill health and in such circumstances, the annual allowance charge should not act as a deterrent. The exemption is most likely to be relevant for occupational schemes providing death in service and/or critical illness benefits. For example, if the pension scheme insures the member's life then the value of the right to those death benefits will usually increase significantly in the year of death and that increase could give rise to an annual allowance charge were it not for this exception. Similarly, on death or severe ill health, sums/assets may be reallocated to the member's arrangement from a general fund within the pension scheme.

---

[7] FA 2004 s.229(3).

[8] FA 2004 s.229(3) and (4).

[9] At PTM051200, HMRC acknowledge that gainful work will not include voluntary/unpaid work where out of pocket expenses are reimbursed or small amounts of travelling or subsistence payments are made. HMRC suggest that paid work is "insignificant" where it is infrequent or only for a few days during the year and the payment is small in amount, not just as a proportion of previous pay or salary.

[10] Pursuant to s.641(1), no liability to income tax arises on: (a) a wounds pension granted to a member of the armed forces of the Crown; (b) retired pay of a disabled officer granted on account of medical unfitness attributable to or aggravated by service in the armed forces of the Crown; (c) a disablement or disability pension granted to a member of the armed forces of the Crown, other than a commissioned officer, on account of medical unfitness attributable to or aggravated by service in the armed forces of the Crown; (d) a disablement pension granted to a person who has been employed in the nursing services of any of the armed forces of the Crown on account of medical unfitness attributable to or aggravated by service in the armed forces of the Crown; (e) […]; (f) an injury or disablement pension payable under any War Risks Compensation Scheme for the Mercantile marine; (g) a pension: (i) granted to a person on account of disablement; and (ii) payable under any scheme made under ss.3, 4 or 5 of the Pensions (Navy, Army, Air Force and Mercantile Marine) Act 1939; (h) a benefit under a scheme established by an order under s.1(2) of the Armed Forces (Pensions and Compensation) Act 2004 payable to a person by reason of his illness or injury: (i) by way of a lump sum; or (ii) following the termination of the person's service in the armed forces or reserve forces.

## STEP ONE: PENSION INPUT AMOUNTS 163

### Calculating the pension input amount

*Cash balance arrangements*

The pension input amount in respect of a cash balance arrangement is the amount by which the closing value of the individual's rights under the arrangement exceeds the opening value.[11]

**7-008**

The opening value of the individual's rights under an arrangement is the amount which would be available for the provision of benefits under the arrangement if the individual became entitled to the benefits at the end of the immediately preceding pension input period. The rights must be valued on the assumption that the individual has reached the age at which no reduction would apply to the payment of an immediate benefit (as a result of early retirement), and he is in good physical and mental health (and so the benefits are not calculated on the basis that they are paid on grounds of ill-health).[12] If the calculation relates to the first pension input period of an arrangement established on or after 6 April 2006, the opening value is nil. The opening value is then increased by the percentage by which the CPI for the September before the start of the pension input period is higher than it was for the previous September.[13]

**7-009**

The closing value of the individual's rights under the arrangement is the amount which would be available for the provision of benefits under the arrangement if the individual became entitled to the benefits at the end of the pension input period. The valuation assumptions referred to above must be applied. The closing value is then adjusted as follows, to take account of events that have occurred during the pension input period:[14]

**7-010**

(a) *Pension debits/credits:* if the rights of the individual under the arrangement are reduced by a pension debit, the amount of that reduction is added to the closing value. If his rights are increased by a pension credit, the amount of the increase is subtracted from the closing value.

(b) *Recognised transfers in/out:* if the rights of the individual under the arrangement are reduced by a recognised transfer from the scheme, the amount of that reduction is added to the closing value. If his rights are increased by a recognised transfer to the scheme, the amount of that increase is subtracted from the closing value. Where a transfer is made as part of a block transfer (i.e. a single transaction of all the sums or assets relating to more than one individual), and consequently the rights of the individual under the transferring/receiving arrangements are reduced/increased by an equal (or virtually equal[15]) amount, the amount of the reduction/increase is added/subtracted to/from the closing value.

(c) *Surrenders:* if the rights of the individual under the arrangement are reduced by any surrender made, or similar action taken, pursuant to an option available to the individual under the arrangement, the amount of the reduction is added to the closing value.[16]

---

[11] FA 2004 s.230.
[12] FA 2004 s.277.
[13] FA 2004 s.231.
[14] FA 2004 s.232.
[15] For HMRC guidance on the meaning of "virtually equal", see PTM053720.
[16] The terminology used here suggests that this is intended to reflect PA 1995 s.91. Any such surrender will of course reduce the closing value, and this adjustment adds it back on so that the surrender is neutral from an annual allowance perspective. If that were not the case, a surrender could

(d) *Benefit commencement:* if any of BCE 1, 2, 3 or 4[17] occurs in relation to the individual and the arrangement, the amount of the reduction in the amount of the rights available for the provision of benefits to or in respect of the individual occurring by reason of the BCE is added to the closing value. If BCE 6 occurs, in relation to the individual and the arrangement by virtue of the individual becoming entitled to a PCLS or a PCELS, the amount of the lump sum is added to the closing value.[18]

(e) *Allocations:* if there is an allocation of the individual's rights under the arrangement (other than on the occurrence of BCE 1, 2 or 4), the amount of any reduction in the amount of the rights available for the provision of benefits to or in respect of the individual occurring by reason of the allocation is added to the closing value.[19]

(f) *Payments under scheme pays option:* if an adjustment to the individual's rights under the arrangement is made in consequence of the scheme administrator satisfying a liability to the annual allowance charge under the scheme pays option (see below), and the adjustment is reflected in the closing amount, the amount of the adjustment is added to the closing amount. This is however disapplied where: (i) the individual becomes actually entitled to all of his benefits under the pension scheme; and (ii) the adjustment takes place after the individual becomes so entitled.

**7-011** Any guaranteed minimum pension[20] paid during the pension input period is subtracted from what would otherwise be the individual's pension input amount.

**7-012** The pension input amount is expressly nil where the member is a deferred member and the value of his rights under the arrangement does not increase by more than the CPI (or any RPI-related index specified in the scheme rules on 6 April 2012, or any other annual rate specified in the scheme rules on 14 October 2010).[21]

*Other money purchase arrangements*

**7-013** The pension input amount in respect of another money purchase arrangement is the total of:[22]

(a) Any "relievable pension contributions" paid by or on behalf of the individual under the arrangement.[23] It is important to appreciate that relievable pension contributions are taken into account whether or not the

---

potentially allow a member to benefit from tax relief in respect of contributions or accruals significantly in excess of his annual allowance.

[17] These BCEs are in FA 2004 Sch.32 para.A2, and they are the same as the pre-6 April 2024 BCEs applicable for lifetime allowance purposes (see Ch.10). They occur when: (a) sums/assets are designated as available for drawdown; (b) the individual becomes entitled to a scheme pension; (c) a scheme pension is increased in excess of a permitted amount; or (d) the individual becomes entitled to a lifetime annuity. Each of these events will reduce the value of the member's arrangement, so they are added back.

[18] BCE 6 occurs if the member becomes "entitled" to a PCLS, a serious ill-health lump sum, an UFPLS, or a PCELS (FA 2004 Sch.32 para.A2 and para.15). An individual becomes entitled to a PCLS or a PCELS immediately before he becomes entitled to the connected pension (FA 2004 s.166(2)(a)).

[19] FA 2004 s.232(8A)(d). It is not at all clear what sort of allocation the draftsman had in mind here. However, to be clear, the occurrence of such an allocation cannot cause an annual allowance charge to arise: the effect of this provision is to neutralise any annual allowance advantages created by such an allocation.

[20] As defined in PSA 1993 s.8.

[21] FA 2004 s.230(5B). HMRC refer to this as the "deferred member carve out" at PTM053910.

[22] FA 2004 s.233(1).

[23] For the meaning of "relievable pension contribution", see Ch.6.

individual obtained tax relief or the employer obtained a tax deduction.[24] In relation to contributions made by or on behalf of the individual, any relievable pension contributions that are subsequently refunded as a refund of excess contributions lump sum are disregarded for annual allowance purposes.[25]

(b) Contributions paid in respect of the individual under the arrangement by an employer of the individual, during the pension input period of the arrangement that ends in the tax year.

**7-014** Any employer contributions that are not made "in respect of any individual", but subsequently become held for the purposes of the provision of benefits under an arrangement, are deemed to be contributions paid at that time in respect of the individual under the arrangement.[26] This applies where a contribution is not immediately allocated to any particular member's arrangement under the scheme (e.g. a contribution that is unallocated, or allocated to a general fund), and is then subsequently so allocated.[27] The sums contributed do not count towards any member's pension input amount until the sums are allocated for a particular member. Section 233(3) applies only where *contributions* are so allocated; it has no application where sums within a general fund are invested and the investment growth is subsequently allocated to a member's arrangement.

*Defined benefits arrangements*

**7-015** The pension input amount in respect of a defined benefits arrangement is the amount by which the closing value of the individual's rights under the arrangement exceeds the opening value of the individual's rights.[28]

**7-016** To find the opening value of the individual's rights under the arrangement, one must ascertain the annual rate of the pension which would be payable to the individual if he became entitled to the pension at the end of the immediately preceding pension input period. That annual rate is then multiplied by 16 and added to the amount of any lump sum to which the individual would be entitled under the arrangement (otherwise than by commutation of pension) if he became entitled to it at the end of the immediately preceding pension input period.[29] In each case one must value the individual's rights on the assumption that he is at an age at which no reduction would apply to the payment of an immediate benefit (as a result of early retirement), and he is in good physical and mental health (and so the benefits are not increased as a result of being paid on grounds of ill-health).[30] If the calcula-

---

[24] In relation to contributions by or on behalf of the individual, tax relief is available under FA 2004 s.188(1) in respect of relievable pension contributions: (a) provided that the individual is a relevant UK individual; and (b) subject to an annual limit equal to the individual's chargeable relevant UK earnings (or £3,600 if greater). It follows that tax relief is not always available in respect of relievable pension contributions.

[25] FA 2004 s.233(4). The amount of any such lump sum is limited to that amount of contributions which exceed the individual relevant UK earnings for a tax year (of £3,600 if greater).

[26] FA 2004 s.233(3). It is likely that the deeming of the contribution to take place at the time of the allocation under s.233(3) is only relevant for the purposes of s.233(1). Otherwise there could be scope for double tax deductions: first, when the contribution is paid and secondly, on an allocation of the contribution in a subsequent year.

[27] The deemed unauthorised payment in s.172C applies in similar circumstances if the member is connected with the employer.

[28] FA 2004 s.234(1).

[29] These provisions are not concerned with any death benefits which may be paid in respect of the member (cf. the cash balance provisions).

[30] FA 2004 s.277.

tion relates to the first pension input period of an arrangement established on or after 6 April 2006, the opening value is nil. The opening value is then increased by the percentage by which the CPI for the September before the start of the tax year is higher than it was for the previous September.[31]

**7-017** To find the closing value of the individual's rights under the arrangement, one values his rights to a pension and lump sum in the same way as above at the end of the pension input period.[32] That annual rate of the pension is referred to as "PE" and the amount of the lump sum is referred to as "LSE". The closing value is then adjusted as follows, to take account of events that have occurred during the pension input period:[33]

(a) *Pension debits/credits:* if the annual rate of the pension, or the amount of the lump sum, to which the individual would be entitled under the arrangement is reduced by having become subject to a pension debit, the amount of the reduction is added to PE or LSE. If the annual rate or lump sum is increased by the individual having become entitled to a pension credit, the amount of the increase is subtracted from PE or LSE.

(b) *Recognised transfers in/out:* if the annual rate of the pension, or the amount of the lump sum, to which the individual would be entitled under the arrangement is reduced by reason of a recognised transfer[34] from the scheme, the amount of that reduction is added to PE or LSE. If the annual rate or lump sum is increased by reason of a recognised transfer to the scheme, the amount of that increase is subtracted from PE or LSE. Where a transfer is made as part of block transfer (i.e. a single transaction of all the sums or assets relating to more than one individual), and consequently the rights of the individual under the transferring/receiving scheme are decreased/increased by an equal (or virtually equal[35]) amount, then the amount of the reduction/increase is added/deducted to/from PE or LSE. For this treatment to apply, the transfer must not form part of an arrangement the main purpose (or one of the main purposes) of which is the avoidance of tax.

(c) *Surrenders:* if the annual rate of the pension, or the amount of the lump sum, to which the individual would be entitled under the arrangement is reduced by any surrender made in return for any other entitlement/allocation (or similar), pursuant to an option available to the individual under the arrangement, the amount of the reduction is added to PE or LSE.

(d) *Benefit commencement:* if BCE 2 occurs in relation to the individual and the arrangement, the annual rate of the pension to which the individual became entitled is added to PE or LSE.[36] If BCE 3 occurs in relation to the individual and the arrangement, the increase in the annual rate of the pension is added to PE or LSE.[37] If BCE 6 occurs in relation to the individual and the arrangement by virtue of the individual becoming entitled to a PCLS or a PCELS,

---

[31] FA 2004 s.235.
[32] As noted above, these provisions do not take into account any increase in the value of death benefits which may be paid in respect of the member (cf. the cash balance provisions, which relate to the increase in any benefits which may be paid to or in respect of the member).
[33] FA 2004 s.236.
[34] See FA 2004 s.169(1) and Ch.12.
[35] For HMRC guidance on the meaning of "virtually equal", see PTM053720.
[36] BCE 2 occurs when the individual becomes entitled to a scheme pension (FA 2004 Sch.32 para.A2(5)). This will reduce the value of the member's arrangement, so it is added back.
[37] BCE 3 occurs when the rate of a scheme pension, to which the individual is entitled, is increased in excess of a permitted amount (FA 2004 Sch.32 para.A2(3)). This is the same as BCE 3 for lifetime allowance purposes: see Ch.10.

the amount of the lump sum is added to PE or LSE.[38]

(g) *Payments under scheme pays option:* if an adjustment to the annual rate of the pension, or to the amount of the lump sum, to which the individual would be entitled to under the arrangement is made in consequence of the scheme administrator satisfying a liability to the annual allowance charge under the scheme pays option (see below), and the adjustment is reflected in PE or LSE, the amount of the adjustment is added to PE or LSE. This is however disapplied where: (i) the individual becomes actually entitled to all of his benefits under the pension scheme; and (ii) the adjustment takes place after the individual becomes so entitled.

7-018 Any guaranteed minimum pension[39] paid during the pension input period is subtracted from what would otherwise be the individual's pension input amount.

7-019 The method for calculating the pension input amount in respect of a defined benefits arrangement is modified if during the pension input period the individual enters into a "scheme" (which includes any arrangements, agreement, understanding, transaction or series of transactions, whether or not legally enforceable) for the making of an "avoidance-inspired post-entitlement enhancement". A "post-entitlement enhancement" is an increase in the annual rate of a scheme pension under the arrangement at any time after the member has become entitled to the scheme pension.[40] Such an enhancement is "avoidance-inspired" if the main purpose, or one of the main purposes, of the individual in entering into the scheme was to avoid or reduce a liability to the annual allowance charge. In these circumstances, the provisions described above relating to the adjustments of opening and closing values are disregarded, and one finds the opening and closing values by finding the expected cost (applying normal actuarial practice) of giving effect to the individual's rights under the arrangement at the applicable time.[41] The "expected cost" is likely to be similar to the cash equivalent transfer value (for the purposes of PSA 1993 s.93A).[42]

7-020 The pension input amount is expressly nil where the member is a deferred member and the value of his rights under the arrangement does not increase by more than the CPI (or any RPI-related index specified in the scheme rules on 6 April 2012, or any other annual rate specified in the scheme rules on 14 October 2010).[43]

*Hybrid arrangements*

7-021 To find the pension input amount in respect of a hybrid arrangement, one must calculate the pension input amount for each category of benefit which may be provided under the arrangement as per the provisions described above. The pension input amount for the arrangement is the greater or greatest of such pension input amounts.[44]

---

[38] BCE 6 occurs if the member becomes "entitled" to a PCLS, a serious ill-health lump sum, an UFPLS, or a PCELS (FA 2004 Sch.32 para.A2 and para.15). An individual becomes entitled to a PCLS or a PCELS immediately before he becomes entitled to the connected pension (FA 2004 s.166(2)(a)).
[39] As defined in PSA 1993 s.8.
[40] A person becomes *entitled* to a scheme pension when he acquires an *actual* rather than a *prospective* entitlement to the pension (FA 2004 s.165(3)(b)).
[41] FA 2004 s.236A.
[42] The Explanatory Notes to the Finance Bill 2011 refer to this being the valuation "based on the cash equivalent value". A CETV is calculated by the trustee after obtaining actuarial advice.
[43] FA 2004 s.234(5B). HMRC refer to this as the "deferred member carve out" at PTM053910.
[44] FA 2004 s.237(1).

## STEP TWO: DETERMINING THE INDIVIDUAL'S ANNUAL ALLOWANCE

**7-022** The second step is to determine the individual's annual allowance for the relevant pension input period. The standard annual allowance is £60,000 in the 2024/25 tax year.[45] An individual's annual allowance for a pension input period may be:

(a) reduced (although not below £10,000) if he is a "high-income individual" during the tax year;[46] and
(b) increased if he has unused annual allowance which may be carried forward from any of the previous three tax years.[47]

**High-income individuals**

**7-023** An individual is a high-income individual for a tax year if his "adjusted income" for the tax year exceeds £260,000 and his "threshold income" for the tax year exceeds £180,000.[48]

*"Adjusted" and "threshold" income*

**7-024** An individual's "adjusted income" for a tax year is:[49]

(a) the individual's net income for the year. This is the individual's total income (not merely his employment income) less any relief under ITA 2007 s.24 (which includes relief under FA 2004 ss.193(4) (excess relief under net pay arrangements) and 194(1) (relief on making a claim);[50]
(b) plus the amount of any relief obtained under FA 2004 ss.193(4) or 194(1) in the year;
(c) plus the amount of any deductions made from employment income of the individual for the year under net pay arrangements or under the transitional corresponding relief provisions;[51]
(d) plus an amount equal to: (i) the total pension input amount (see Step One); less (ii) the amount of any contributions paid by or on behalf of the individual during the year under registered pension schemes of which the individual is a member;
(e) less the amount of any LSDB which is subject to the charge to tax on pension income under ITEPA 2003 Pt 9 in the tax year.[52]

---

[45] FA 2004 s.228(1).
[46] Also see Step Four below, the effect of which may be to impose a lower "money purchase annual allowance".
[47] Or four tax years, if one of those years is the 2015/16 tax year, which is split into two tax years for annual allowance purposes. See earlier editions of this book.
[48] These amounts were respectively £150,000 and £110,000 prior to the 2020/21 tax year; £240,000 and £200,000 in 2020/2021 and 2021/22.
[49] FA 2004 s.228ZA(4).
[50] See steps 1 and 2 in ITA 2007 s.23. For FA 2004 ss.193(4) and 194(1) see Ch.6.
[51] i.e. relief under ITEPA 2003 Pt 5 Ch.2 in accordance with para.51(2) of Sch.36. See Ch.24.
[52] This applies to any authorised LSDB paid to an individual other than a charity LSDB or a trivial commutation LSDB in respect of a member who died on or after his 75th birthday. It also applies to the payment of the following LSBDs to an individual in respect of a member who died before his 75th birthday of not paid within the relevant two-year period: (a) drawdown pension fund LSDB; (b) flexi-access drawdown fund LSBD; (c) defined benefits LSBD; and (d) uncrystallised funds LSBD.

## STEP TWO: THE INDIVIDUAL'S ANNUAL ALLOWANCE

An individual's "threshold income" for a tax year is:[53] 

**7-025**

(a) the individual's net income for the year (see (a) above);
(b) plus any amount by which what would otherwise be general earnings or specific employment income of the individual for the year has been reduced by relevant salary sacrifice arrangements or relevant flexible remuneration arrangements made on or after 9 July 2015.[54] *Relevant salary sacrifice arrangements* are arrangements under which the individual gives up the right to receive general earnings or specific employment income in return for the making of relevant pension provision. *Relevant flexible remuneration arrangements* are arrangements under which the individual and an employer of the individual agree that relevant pension provision is to be made rather than the individual receive some description of employment income. *Relevant pension provision* is the payment of contributions (or additional contributions) to a pension scheme in respect of the individual or otherwise (by an employer of the individual or any other person) to secure an increase in the amount of the benefits to which the individual or any person who is a dependant of, or is connected with, the individual is actually or prospectively entitled under a pension scheme;
(c) less the gross amount of any contribution paid in the year in respect of which the individual is entitled to be given relief under FA 2004 s.192 (relief at source);[55]
(d) less the amount of any LSDB which is subject to the charge to tax on pension income under ITEPA 2003 Pt 9 in the tax year.[56]

The key distinction is therefore that adjusted income includes pension contributions whereas threshold income does not.

**7-026**

*Anti-avoidance*

Anti-avoidance provisions seek to prevent individuals from avoiding the tapered annual allowance by reducing their adjusted or threshold income for a tax year, and redressing that reduction by an increase in their adjusted or threshold income for a different tax year.[57] The provisions apply only if it is reasonable to assume that the main purpose or one of the main purposes of the arrangements[58] is to increase the tapered annual allowance.

**7-027**

---

[53] FA 2004 s.228ZA(5).
[54] Correspondence with HMRC regarding the date that an arrangement is "made" for these purposes is available on the Association of Consulting Actuaries website. Where an arrangement made before 9 July 2015 provides that it will automatically terminate unless the employee directs that it should continue, it is likely that any such direction will create a new arrangement.
[55] See Ch.6. If a member wants to make a total contribution of £100, he pays £80 to the scheme and the scheme administrator claims £20 from HMRC and adds it to the member's fund. The gross amount of the contribution is £100.
[56] As above, this applies to any authorised LSDB paid to an individual other than a charity LSDB or a trivial commutation LSDB in respect of a member who died on or after his 75th birthday. It also applies to the payment of the following LSDBs to an individual in respect of a member who died before his 75th birthday of not paid within the relevant two-year period: (a) drawdown pension fund LSDB; (b) flexi-access drawdown fund LSDB; (c) defined benefits LSDB; and (d) uncrystallised funds LSDB.
[57] FA 2004 s.228ZB.
[58] "Arrangement" includes any agreement, understanding, scheme, transaction or series of transactions (whether or not legally enforceable). This is of course different to the usual meaning of *arrangement* in FA 2004 Pt 4 when it is used in relation to a member of the pension scheme (see FA 2004 s.152(1)).

*The tapered annual allowance*

**7-028** The annual allowance for a high-income individual is reduced (but not below £10,000[59]) by deducting £260,000 from the individual's adjusted income for the tax year and dividing the result by two.[60] For example, if a high-income individual's adjusted income is £285,000 for the 2023/24 tax year, his annual allowance is reduced by £12,500 (i.e. £25,000/2). If his annual allowance would otherwise be £60,000, it is reduced to £47,500 for the 2023/24 tax year. Any unused tapered annual allowance may be carried forwards as usual.

**Carry forward of unused annual allowance**

**7-029** To the extent that an individual has not fully utilised his annual allowance in the previous three tax years, the unused annual allowance can be carried forwards to the current year.[61] The only requirement is that the individual was a member of a registered pension scheme (any registered pension scheme will suffice) during that previous period. If the individual is a member of a registered pension scheme, and he was a currently-relieved member of a currently-relieved non-UK pension scheme in any of the three immediately preceding tax years, the non-UK pension scheme is treated as a registered pension scheme for the purposes of the carry forward provisions.[62]

**7-030** The current year's annual allowance is utilised first. Once that is used up, the unused annual allowance from the earliest carry forwards year is utilised, then the subsequent carry forwards year, and then finally the most recent carry forwards year.

## STEP THREE: DEFAULT CHARGEABLE AMOUNT

**7-031** If the total pension input amount exceeds the individual's annual allowance for the year, the excess is a chargeable amount. This is referred to as the "default chargeable amount". Provided that the member has not (either in the current or a previous tax year) flexibly accessed his pension rights, it is not necessary to consider Step Four: the default chargeable amount will be subject to the annual allowance charge.

## STEP FOUR: MEMBER HAS FLEXIBLY ACCESSED PENSION RIGHTS

**7-032** If the individual has, either in the current or a previous tax year, "flexibly accessed his pension rights" then it is necessary to perform an additional calculation (using a £10,000 "money purchase annual allowance"[63]) to determine if it produces a higher chargeable amount than the default chargeable amount calculated at Step Three. This is referred to as the "alternative chargeable amount". If the alternative

---

[59] The minimum was £10,000 prior to the 2020/21 tax year, and £4,000 in 2020/21 and 2021/22.
[60] This is expressed by the formula "(AI - £260,000) × ½" where "AI" is the individual's adjusted income for the tax year.
[61] FA 2004 s.228A.
[62] FA 2004 Sch.34 para.9B. See Ch.30.
[63] "Money purchase annual allowance" is not a term used in FA 2004, but is frequently used by HMRC and others.

## STEP FOUR: FLEXIBLY ACCESSED PENSION RIGHTS

chargeable amount is higher than the default chargeable amount then the alternative chargeable amount is the individual's chargeable amount for the tax year (and so is subject to the annual allowance charge).

**Flexibly accessing pension rights**

An individual flexibly accesses his pension rights on the occurrence of the following events.[64] If he was in flexible drawdown prior to 6 April 2015 (so his drawdown pension fund automatically converted to a flexi-access drawdown fund on 6 April 2015), he flexibly accessed his pension rights on 6 April 2015. He otherwise flexibly accesses his pension rights immediately before payment of any of the following under a registered pension scheme:

(a) Income withdrawal under a member's flexi-access drawdown fund, or a payment of a short-term annuity purchased using sums or assets out of a member's flexi-access drawdown fund.[65]
(b) An UFPLS.
(c) A lifetime annuity under a "flexible annuity contract", which is a contract for a lifetime annuity that the member became entitled to on or after 6 April 2015 the terms of which are such that there will or could be decreases in the amount of the annuity (other than the usual permitted decreases which apply to pre-6 April 2015 lifetime annuities).
(d) A scheme pension in respect of a money purchase arrangement on or after 6 April 2015, at a time when fewer than 11 other individuals are entitled to the present payment of a scheme pension (including dependants' scheme pension), and the scheme pension is not payable under an annuity contract which is deemed to be a registered pension scheme.
(e) A stand-alone lump sum from a money purchase arrangement (when entitled to primary protection with a right to take a lump sum greater than £375,000).

7-033

*Application to non-UK schemes*

An individual also flexibly accesses his pension rights for the purposes of the money purchase annual allowance if any of the above events occur in relation to: (a) a currently-relieved non-UK pension scheme of which the individual is a currently-relieved member; or (b) a QROPS or former QROPS of which the individual is a transfer member, but only insofar as the event relates to the individual's relevant transfer fund or ring-fenced transfer funds under the scheme.[66]

7-034

**The calculation**

There are two parts to the calculation:

7-035

(a) First, determine whether the individual's "money-purchase input subtotal" exceeds £10,000.[67] If it does not, the chargeable amount (if any) is the default chargeable amount (per Step Three).

---

[64] FA 2004 s.227G. HMRC guidance is at PTM056520.
[65] This does not include payment at a time when the whole of the fund represents rights attributable to a disqualifying pension credit.
[66] FA 2004 Sch.34 para.9ZA(1) and para.9ZB(1). See Ch.30.
[67] This was £10,000 prior to 2017/18; £4,000 from 2017/18 to 2022/23. The £10,000 is a fixed amount; it cannot be increased by the carry forward provisions.

(b) If the individual's money-purchase input sub-total does exceed £10,000, one is required to:
  (i) identify the excess; and
  (ii) determine if the individual's "defined-benefit input sub-total" exceeds his "alternative annual allowance" for the year. The individual's alternative annual allowance is his annual allowance for the year (i.e. the result of the calculation at Step Two above) less £10,000. If his defined-benefit input sub-total exceeds his alternative annual allowance for the year then one is required to determine the excess.

**7-036** If the excess in (b)(i) and (b)(ii) above (if any) exceeds the default chargeable amount (at Step Three) then the individual's chargeable amount is determined by this Step Four and not by Step Three. This is referred to as the alternative chargeable amount.

For example, if an individual's annual allowance is £60,000 and his total pension input amount is £55,000 then his default chargeable amount is nil (because his default chargeable amount is less than £60,000). If he has flexibly accessed his pension rights and his money-purchase input sub-total is say £15,000 then the excess for the purposes of (b)(i) is £5,000. His alternative annual allowance is £50,000 (being his £60,000 annual allowance less £10,000). His defined-benefit input sub-total (explained below) must be £40,000, so the excess for the purposes of (b)(ii) is nil. Here the total excess under (b)(i) and (b)(ii) is £5,000, which is greater than his default chargeable amount and so the £5,000 alternative chargeable amount applies and is subject to the annual allowance charge.

**The money-purchase input sub-total**

**7-037** The money-purchase input sub-total is the total of the pension input amounts in respect of: (a) each money purchase arrangement relating to the individual; and (b) each hybrid arrangement that may provide money purchase benefits in respect of the individual.[68] Special rules apply:

(a) to relevant hybrid arrangements; and
(b) in the year in which the individual first flexibly accesses his pension rights.

*Relevant hybrid arrangements*

**7-038** This special rule applies to "prevent avoidance of the annual allowance charge through manipulation of the pension input amount in a hybrid arrangement".[69] Relevant hybrid arrangements are hybrid arrangements: (a) made on or after 14 October 2014 or having become a hybrid arrangement (whether or not for the first time) on or after that day; and (b) in respect of which the applicable pension input amount is the input amount relating to the possible defined benefits (see Step Two above).[70] In relation to each relevant hybrid arrangement in the "maximising set of relevant hybrid arrangements", one disregards the pension input amount relating to the possible defined benefits under the hybrid arrangement and instead takes into account the pension input amount relating to the possible money purchase benefits. The effect of this is to include the input amount relating to the hybrid arrangement in the money-purchase input sub-total rather than the defined-benefit input sub-total.

---

[68] FA 2004 s.227C.
[69] PTM056550.
[70] FA 2004 s.227D. See PTM056550 for HMRC guidance. For hybrid arrangements generally, see Ch.2.

# STEP FOUR: FLEXIBLY ACCESSED PENSION RIGHTS

For these purposes: (a) the maximising set contains no relevant hybrid arrangements; (b) a particular relevant hybrid arrangement makes up that set; or (c) two or more particular relevant hybrid arrangements make up that set, if the alternative chargeable amount with the maximising set so made up is not less than it would be with the maximising set made up in any other way.

**7-039**

The maximising set is identified by taking the following six steps:[71]

**7-040**

(a) Identify all of the relevant hybrid arrangements.
(b) Identify all of the different combinations of relevant hybrid arrangements (including the combination consisting of all of those arrangements, and the combination consisting of none of them, as well as every possible combination of each possible size in between).
(c) For each combination identified at (b) above, calculate what the money-purchase input sub-total would be if, in respect of each relevant hybrid arrangement in the combination, one disregarded the pension input amount relating to the possible defined benefits under the relevant hybrid arrangement and instead used the pension input amount relating to any possible cash balance benefits or (if greater) the input amount relating to any possible other money purchase benefits.
(d) If the result of each calculation at (c) above is less than or equal to £10,000 the chargeable amount is the default chargeable amount.
(e) If the amount calculated at (c) above for a combination is greater than £10,000 then calculate what the alternative chargeable amount would be if: (i) in relation to each relevant hybrid arrangement in the combination one disregarded the pension input amount relating to the possible defined benefits under the relevant hybrid arrangement and instead used the pension input amount relating to any possible cash balance benefits or (if greater) the input amount relating to any possible other money purchase benefits; and (ii) for each relevant hybrid arrangement not in the combination, the pension input amount relating to the possible defined benefits were included in the total.
(f) Identify the highest (or higher) of the amounts calculated at (e) above. The maximising set is made up of each relevant hybrid arrangement in the combination concerned.

*Illustration*

Suppose that A has four arrangements under registered pension schemes: two hybrid arrangements (both made after 14 October 2014, which may provide either defined benefits or money purchase benefits when A retires), a defined benefits arrangement, and a money purchase arrangement.[72] He flexibly accessed his pension rights in the previous pension input period. He is not a high-income individual and has no unused annual allowance to carry forward from previous years, so his annual allowance for the year is £60,000. The pension input amounts for each arrangement are:

**7-041**

---

[71] FA 2004 s.227D(4).
[72] This illustration is based on HMRC's example at PTM056590.

|  | Arrangement 1 (hybrid) | Arrangement 2 (hybrid) | Arrangement 3 (defined benefits) | Arrangement 4 (money purchase) |
|---|---|---|---|---|
| Defined benefits pension input amount | £20,000 | £25,000 | £29,000 | N/A |
| Money purchase pension input amount | £8,000 | £4,000 | N/A | £3,000 |

His total pension input amount is £77,000 (£20,000 plus £25,000 plus £29,000 plus £3,000). His default chargeable amount is therefore £17,000 (£77,000 less £60,000).

Both of the hybrid arrangements are relevant hybrid arrangement because the possible defined benefits are greater than the possible money purchase benefits. There are four possible combinations of relevant hybrid arrangements:

| Combination | Money purchase input sub-total |
|---|---|
| *One*: arrangement 1 (hybrid) only | £11,000 (£8,000 plus £3,000: arrangements 1 and 4) |
| *Two*: arrangement 2 (hybrid) only | £7,000 (£4,000 plus £3,000: arrangements 2 and 4) |
| *Three*: arrangements 1 (hybrid) and 2 (hybrid) | £12,000 (£8,000 plus £4,000 plus £3,000: arrangements 1, 2 and 4) |
| *Four*: disregard arrangements 1 (hybrid) and 2 (hybrid) | £3,000 (arrangement 4) |

Combinations One and Three result in a money purchase input in excess of the £10,000 money purchase annual allowance for the year.

Combination One exceeds the £10,000 "money-purchase input" by £1,000. The "other inputs" do not exceed the £50,000 alternative annual allowance. £54,000 (arrangement 2 using defined benefits pension input amount plus arrangement 3) exceeds the £50,000 alternative annual allowance by £4,000. The alternative chargeable amount for Combination One is therefore £4,000.

Combination Three exceeds the £10,000 "money-purchase input" by £2,000. The other inputs (£29,000 for arrangement 3) do not exceed the £50,000 alternative annual allowance. The alternative chargeable amount for Combination Three is therefore £2,000.

Combination One gives the greatest alternative chargeable amount (£4,000) for the current tax year. A's alternative chargeable amount found from Combination Three (£2,000) is less than his default chargeable amount (£17,000), so A is liable for the annual allowance charge on basis of his default chargeable amount for the tax year of £17,000.

*Pension rights are first flexibly accessed*

**7-042** The second special rule referred to above relates to the pension input period in which pension rights are first flexibly accessed. In that period, the money purchase

## STEP FOUR: FLEXIBLY ACCESSED PENSION RIGHTS

input sub-total ought to relate only to part of the pension input period (unless the individual first flexibly accesses his pension rights on 6 April[73]).

If the arrangement is a cash balance arrangement, the pension input amount in respect of that arrangement is (for the purposes of determining the money-purchase input sub-total) determined as follows. First, ascertain how much of the pension input period (as a fraction) occurred after the individual first flexibly accessed his pension rights. Secondly, multiply that fraction by the actual pension input amount in respect of that arrangement.[74]

**7-043**

If the arrangement is another money purchase arrangement, the pension input amount in respect of that arrangement (for the purposes of determining the money-purchase input sub-total) is treated as being the amount in respect of the arrangement that would be arrived at for a pension input period beginning with the day after that on which the individual first flexibly accesses pension rights, and ending at the end of the pension input period.[75]

**7-044**

In relation to any money purchase arrangement, the amount by which the (actual) pension input amount in respect of the arrangement exceeds the amount treated by the two paragraphs above (relating to cash balance and other money purchase arrangements) as being the pension input amount in respect of the arrangement, is required to be included in the defined-benefit input sub-total referred to below.

**7-045**

If the arrangement is a hybrid arrangement:

**7-046**

(a) input amount A is (for the purposes of determining the money-purchase input sub-total) treated as being equal to "F/(PIP x AAIAA)", where *AAIAA* is the (actual) amount of input amount A for the arrangement, *F* is the number of days in the period beginning with the day after that on which the individual first flexibly accesses pension rights, and ending at the end of the pension input period, and *PIP* is the number of days in that pension input period; and

(b) input amount B is (for the purposes of determining the money-purchase input sub-total) treated as being the amount for the arrangement that would be arrived at under s.233 for a pension input period beginning on the day after that on which the individual first flexibly accesses pension rights, and ending at the end of the pension input period.

In relation to hybrid arrangements, the amount (if any) by which the (actual) pension input amount in respect of the arrangement, exceeds the amount which, in accordance with the paragraph above, is (for the purposes of determining the money-purchase input sub-total) the pension input amount in respect of the arrangement, is required to be included in the defined-benefit input sub-total calculated referred to below.

**7-047**

### The defined-benefit input sub-total

The defined-benefit input sub-total is the total of:[76]

**7-048**

(a) the pension input amounts in respect of each defined benefits arrangement relating to the individual (per Step One);

---

[73] The provisions do not therefore have any application to a member who was in flexible drawdown (in respect of any arrangement) at any time before 6 April 2015 (FA 2004 s.227F).

[74] This is expressed as "(F/PIP) x APIA" where "APIA" is the (actual) pension input amount in respect of the arrangement, "F" is the number of days in the period beginning with the day after that on which the individual first flexibly accesses pension rights, and ending at the end of the pension input period, and "PIP" is the number of days in that pension input period.

[75] i.e. one applies the usual provisions relating to other money purchase arrangements.

[76] FA 2004 s.227B(3).

(b) the pension input amounts in respect of each hybrid arrangement which is capable of providing defined benefits relating to the individual (per Step Two). These are calculated as if the benefits provided to or in respect of the individual under the arrangement were defined benefits;[77] and

(c) any amounts required to be included by the provisions described above relating to pension input periods that end in the year and contain the day on which rights are first flexibly accessed.

**7-049**   If, in the case of a hybrid arrangement, the input amount relating to the possible defined benefits is a relevant input amount and is equal to the greater of the input amounts relating to the cash balance or other money purchase benefits, the pension input amount in respect of the arrangement is, for these purposes, treated as being the input amount relating to the cash balance or other money purchase benefits or, as the case may be, the greater of such input amounts (and, in either case, not the input amount relating to the possible defined benefits).

## THE ANNUAL ALLOWANCE CHARGE

**7-050**   The annual allowance charge arises to the extent that the individual has a "chargeable amount" for a tax year.[78] The chargeable amount is taxable as if it were taxable income of the member (i.e. the rate of tax is his marginal rate of income tax).[79]

The individual is liable for the charge.[80] He must pay it under self-assessment, subject to the application of the "scheme pays" option.

### The scheme pays option

**7-051**   If an individual becomes liable to an annual allowance charge in excess of £2,000 he may notify the scheme administrator that he and the scheme administrator are jointly and severally liable for some or all of the charge.[81]

The notice must usually be given by 31 July in the year following that in which the tax year ends, however an earlier or later deadline may apply in the following circumstances. Firstly, a notice may not be given after the individual becomes actually entitled to all of his benefits under the pension scheme. The intention is to avoid a situation whereby the scheme administrator becomes liable in circumstances that he is not holding sufficient scheme funds. Secondly, with effect from 6 April 2022, the deadline is extended where: (a) the member is given a pension savings statement for a tax year: (i) on or after 2 May in the year following that in which the tax year in question ends; and (ii) before the end of the period of six years beginning with the end of the tax year in question; (b) the scheme administrator is required to give the member that pension savings statement because of a change to the member's pension input amount for the tax year due to either the scheme administrator receiving additional information from a third party, or a change to the

---

[77] This is expressly subject to FA 2004 s.227D (pension input amounts for certain hybrid arrangements).
[78] FA 2004 s.227(1).
[79] FA 2004 s.227(4) and (4A). The chargeable amount is not however treated as income for tax purposes (s.227(5)).
[80] FA 2004 s.237A. It does not matter whether or not he or the scheme administrator are resident, ordinarily resident or domiciled in the UK.
[81] FA 2004 s.237B. The notice must contain the information and declarations prescribed in The Registered Pension Schemes (Notice of Joint Liability for the Annual Allowance Charge) Regulations 2011 (SI 2011/1793).

scheme rules; and (c) as a result of that change to the pension input amount, the member is able to use the scheme pays option for the tax year in question.[82] In these circumstances, the member must notify the scheme administrator: (a) within three months of the day on which the scheme administrator gives the member the pension savings statement due to the change to the member's pension input amount, or, if earlier; (b) within six years of the end of the tax year in question.

The individual can give such notice only to the scheme administrator of a scheme under which his pension input amount is more than the standard annual allowance (i.e. £60,000). The notice must specify the amount of the charge for which the scheme administrator is jointly and severally liable. Where the individual's annual allowance is lower than the standard annual allowance (because he is a high income individual and/or because the money purchase annual allowance applies), the amount specified in the notice cannot exceed the amount of the charge which would have arisen if the standard annual allowance applied to the individual.[83]

On receipt of the notice the scheme administrator and the individual become jointly and severally liable to pay the amount specified in the notice, subject to the exceptions below and subject to a discharge of the scheme administrator's liability under s.237D. Payment of the annual allowance charge in these circumstances is a payment *in respect of* the member, but it should be an authorised payment on the basis that it is a scheme administration member payment.[84] The member should report that he has incurred an annual allowance charge in his self-assessment return, indicating that he is making use of the scheme pays option.[85] The scheme administrator must account for the charge in its accounting for tax return.[86]

7-052

Where the scheme administrator satisfies such a liability in respect of the individual, consequential adjustment must be made to the individual's entitlement to benefits under the pension scheme on a basis that is just and reasonable having regard to normal actuarial practice.[87] In relation to a money purchase arrangement, one would expect this to involve a straightforward debit from the value of the member's arrangement. The position is less straightforward in relation to a cash balance or defined benefits arrangement. Where an adjustment is made to the entitlement of the member and his death beneficiaries, PTM056460 suggests that HMRC would expect it to be proportionate (i.e. the death beneficiaries should not suffer a disproportionate burden). There appears to be no time restrictions regarding the adjustment, so if HMRC challenge an adjustment then it may be possible to make a further adjustment at that time.

7-053

Where the scheme pays option is not available, the charge is a liability of the member only. HMRC consider that any voluntary discharge of this liability by the scheme administrator is an authorised payment provided that the member's rights under the scheme are reduced to take account of the tax paid.[88] This is presumably on the basis that the payment by the scheme is a scheme administration member

7-054

---

[82] FA 2004 s.237BA.
[83] FA 2004 s.237B(3)(a).
[84] For scheme administration member payments, see Ch.11.
[85] HMRC's pension schemes newsletter 86 (21 April 2017).
[86] For the accounting for tax return, see Ch.19.
[87] FA 2004 s.237E.
[88] PTM056410 says: "Where a member does not meet the conditions for 'Scheme Pays' to apply or they do not make their nomination in time then a scheme may decide to pay the member's annual allowance charge on a voluntary basis. Unlike with 'Scheme Pays' the scheme would not then have joint and several liability for the tax charge so the liability would remain with the member. The payment made by the scheme on a voluntary basis should therefore be paid to the member's normal Self Assessment deadline. Where the scheme does not reduce the member's benefits in the scheme to take

payment.[89] To be a scheme administration member payment, a payment: (a) must be on arm's length terms; and (b) must be made for the purpose of the administration or management of the scheme. It is not at all clear that either of these requirements is satisfied where the scheme administrator discharges a member's tax liability.

**Exceptions to liability of scheme administrator**

**7-055** The scheme administrator cannot become liable for the annual allowance charge during an assessment period in relation to the scheme, and if an assessment period begins when the scheme administrator is already so liable (but has not satisfied the liability), the liability ceases when the assessment period begins.[90] In addition, the scheme administrator cannot become liable if there is no power to make a consequential adjustment to the entitlement of the individual concerned as a result of PSA 1993 s.159.[91]

**Discharge of scheme administrator's liability**

**7-056** A scheme administrator who becomes liable for an annual allowance charge may apply to HMRC for the discharge of his liability on either of the following grounds: (a) that paying the amount to which the scheme administrator is liable would be to the substantial detriment of the interests of the members of the pension scheme; or (b) that in all the circumstances of the case it would not be just and reasonable for the scheme administrator to be liable to that amount.[92] If HMRC refuse, the scheme administrator can appeal to the FTT.[93]

# REPORTING OBLIGATIONS

**7-057** The following reporting obligations apply generally in connection with the annual allowance:

(a) The scheme administrator is required to provide a member with a "pension savings statement" if either: (i) the total pension input amounts for the relevant pension input period in respect of each arrangement under the pension scheme relating to the individual exceeds the annual allowance for that tax year; or (ii) the scheme administrator has reason to believe that the member has first flexibly accessed pension rights, and the pension input amount in respect of all money purchase arrangements (or hybrid arrange-

---

account of the tax the scheme has paid, then the member may also become liable to an unauthorised payments charge on the amount of their liability that the scheme has paid on their behalf".

[89] For scheme administration member payments, see Ch.11 and following.
[90] FA 2004 s.237C. These provisions are applicable where the Board of the Pension Protection Fund assumes responsibility for a scheme following insolvency of the scheme employer (see PA 2004 ss.132 and 159).
[91] Which prohibits the alienation of guaranteed minimum pension.
[92] FA 2004 s.237D.
[93] FA 2004 s.269(1)(a).

# REPORTING OBLIGATIONS

ment capable of proving money purchase benefits) exceeds £4,000[94] (or, presumably, £10,000 from 6 April 2023[95]).

(b) Any scheme administrator required to provide a member with a pension savings statement (as per the paragraph above) must file an event report to HMRC.[96]

(c) Following a written request by a member or former member, the scheme administrator must provide the member or former member with the information that must be contained in a pension savings statement.[97]

(d) A sponsoring employer must provide the scheme administrator such information as will enable the scheme administrator to calculate the pension input amount.[98]

**The money purchase annual allowance**

The following reporting obligations apply specifically in connection with the money purchase annual allowance:

7-058

(a) The scheme administrator must provide a member with a statement within 31 days of the member first flexibly accessing his pension rights.[99]

(b) Any member who receives such a statement from a scheme administrator must within 91 days pass it on to the scheme administrator of any other registered pension scheme of which he is an accruing member.[100]

(c) If there is a recognised transfer from one registered pension scheme to another or to a QROPS and the scheme administrator of the transferring scheme has reason to believes that the member first flexibly accessed his pension rights before the transfer, the scheme administrator of the transferring scheme must notify the scheme administrator of the receiving scheme of the date that it believes he first flexibly accessed his pension rights.[101]

(d) If the member was in flexible drawdown prior to 6 April 2015 and on or after that date is an accruing member of any registered pension scheme, the member must provide certain information to the scheme administrator of each registered pension that he is an accruing member of.[102]

(e) Where a member in capped drawdown prior to 6 April 2015 converts to flexi-access drawdown and accesses that flexi-access drawdown fund, and on the date that he first flexible access his pension rights he is an accruing member of any registered pension scheme, the member must provide certain information to the scheme administrator of each registered pension that he is an accruing member of.[103]

---

[94] The Registered Pension Schemes (Provision of Information) Regulations 2006 (SI 2006/567) reg.14A(1). The statement must contain the information specified in reg.14A(2) or (10).
[95] The Finance (No.2) Bill 2023 does not amend SI 2006/567. Presumably, amending regulations will be introduced in due course.
[96] SI 2006/567 reg.3 (reportable events 22 and 23).
[97] SI 2006/567 reg.14B(1).
[98] SI 2006/567 reg.15A(1).
[99] SI 2006/567 reg.14ZA(1).
[100] SI 2006/567 reg.14ZB(1).
[101] SI 2006/567 reg.14ZC(1).
[102] SI 2006/567 reg.14ZD(1).
[103] SI 2006/567 reg.14ZE(1).

# CHAPTER 8

# Scheme Investments (and Scheme Borrowing)

## TABLE OF CONTENTS

| | |
|---|---|
| Introduction and Overview | 8-001 |
|   Non-tax law | 8-002 |
|     Trusts law | 8-002 |
|     Pensions law | 8-003 |
|       Transactions involving scheme employers | 8-005 |
|     Financial Services and Markets Act 2000 | 8-006 |
|   Finance Act 2004 | 8-007 |
|     Transactions involving a member or sponsoring employer | 8-008 |
|     SDLT on the purchase of land from a connected partnership | 8-012 |
|     Unauthorised borrowing | 8-013 |
| Income of the Scheme | 8-014 |
|   Exemption for investment income | 8-014 |
|     Stock lending | 8-015 |
|     Futures contracts and options contracts | 8-016 |
|     Repos and manufactured payments | 8-017 |
|     "Investments" | 8-018 |
|     Trading income | 8-019 |
|     Stocks and shares | 8-023 |
|     Land | 8-025 |
|     FA 2016 transactions in land rules | 8-028 |
|     Circumstances other than the acquisition and disposal of assets | 8-030 |
|     Trading vehicles | 8-031 |
|     Income "derived from" investments | 8-033 |
|     Investments "held for the purposes of" a pension scheme | 8-035 |
|     Investment vehicles | 8-036 |
|     Underwriting commissions | 8-039 |
|     Property investment LLPs | 8-042 |
|     Taxable property | 8-045 |
|     Repayment of tax | 8-046 |
|   Other sources of income | 8-047 |
| Capital Gains | 8-048 |
| Unauthorised Borrowing | 8-051 |
|   "Borrowing" | 8-054 |
|     "By a registered pension scheme" | 8-056 |

| | |
|---|---|
| "In respect of an arrangement" | 8-058 |
| Application to general funds | 8-059 |
| Money purchase arrangements (other than collective money purchase arrangements) | 8-061 |
| Uncrystallised rights | 8-062 |
| The amount of the scheme chargeable payment | 8-063 |
| Other arrangements | 8-066 |
| The amount of the scheme chargeable payment | 8-068 |
| Valuation points | 8-071 |

## INTRODUCTION AND OVERVIEW

**8-001** The taxation of registered pension scheme investments is generally straightforward. Income received in respect of scheme investments is exempt from income tax, and any gain accruing on a disposal of such investments is exempt from CGT.[1] The distinction between investment income and trading income (the latter of which is not exempt from tax when carried on by a registered pension scheme) may in certain circumstances require consideration, but in most cases steps can be taken to make the position clear. Care is required regarding transactions between the pension scheme and any member or sponsoring employer (or any transactions with a third party which may indirectly provide a benefit to any member or sponsoring employer). In addition, if any members are able to influence scheme investments then the scheme will be an "investment-regulated pension scheme" and the taxable property provisions will apply.[2] These provisions can complicate matters considerably.

There are no tax reliefs or exemptions specifically for registered pension schemes in relation to SDLT, stamp duty, VAT or insurance premium tax.

**Non-tax law**

*Trusts law*

**8-002** The trusts of pension funds are in general governed by the ordinary law of trusts, and so the trustees are obliged to exercise their powers in the interests of the whole class of beneficiaries.[3] Trustees have a duty to invest the trust fund to produce a financial return, and a failure to do so may expose the trustee to a claim for breach of trust.[4] Trustees have a duty to take reasonable care and skill in discharging their powers and duties, and to act prudently and diligently like an ordinary man of business, using any special skill they possess.[5] The Trustee Act 2000 does not generally apply to occupational pension schemes that are established under trusts and subject to the law of England and Wales,[6] but a significant body of pension legislation does apply to such schemes.

---

[1] For issues relating to overseas investments, see Ch.20.
[2] For the taxable property provisions, see Ch.9.
[3] *Cowan v Scargill* [1985] Ch. 270 at 286–287.
[4] *Robinson v Robinson* (1851) 42 E.R. 547; (1851) 1 De G.M. & G. 247; *Stafford v Fiddon* (1857) 53 E.R. 151; (1857) 23 Beav. 386.
[5] See *Re Whitely* (1886) 33 Ch. D. 347; *Learoyd v Whiteley* (1887) 12 A.C. 727.
[6] Trustee Act 2000 s.36.

# INTRODUCTION AND OVERVIEW

*Pensions law*

Investment duties form a major part of the duties of a pension scheme trustee, and this is reflected in pension legislation restricting the class of investments that occupational pension schemes may acquire, the amount that such schemes may borrow, and regulating the decision-making process. In particular, PA 1995 ss.33–36 and the Occupational Pension Schemes (Investment) Regulations 2005 (SI 2005/3378) require consideration.

8-003

PA 1995 s.34 confers on the trustees the same power to make an investment of any kind as if they were absolutely entitled to the assets of the scheme, but SI 2005/3378 reg.4 imposes a number of requirements relating to the trustee's exercise of their investment powers. In particular, the assets of the scheme must consist predominantly of investments admitted to trading on regulated markets, and investment in assets which are not admitted to trading on such markets must in any event be kept to a prudent level.[7] In addition, the assets of the scheme must be properly diversified in such a way to avoid excessive reliance on any particular asset or issuer.[8] Regulation 4 does not apply to pension schemes with fewer than 100 members,[9] however where that is the case, the trustees (or fund manager) must have regard to the need for diversification of investments, in so far as appropriate to the circumstances of the scheme.[10]

8-004

**Transactions involving scheme employers** Certain pension provisions restrict transactions between the scheme and scheme employers.[11] In particular, PA 1995 s.40 and SI 2005/3378 reg.12 restricts employer-related investments. These provisions do not, however, apply to "small schemes".[12] A trustee who fails to take all reasonable steps to secure compliance with PA 1995 s.40 may be the subject of sanctions under PA 1995 s.3 (prohibition order) or PA 1995 s.10 (civil penalty). If the resources of a pension scheme are invested in contravention of PA 1995 s.40, a pension trustee who agreed in the determination to make the investment is guilty of an offence and is liable to a fine or imprisonment.[13]

8-005

*Financial Services and Markets Act 2000*

If the investment of the scheme assets involves a regulated activity under FSMA 2000 s.22, the trustee is required to appoint a fund manager in accordance with PA 1995 s.47. The fund manager must be authorised under FSMA 2000, or exempt. Again, there is an exception for certain small occupational schemes.[14]

8-006

---

[7] SI 2005/3378 reg.4(5) and (6).

[8] SI 2005/3378 reg.4(7).

[9] SI 2005/3378 reg.7(1). PA 1995 s.35 and regs 2 and 3 (which relate to statements of investment principles), and reg.5 (which restricts borrowing) are also disapplied for such schemes.

[10] SI 2005/3378 reg.7(2).

[11] And persons "connected" or "associated" with the employer as those terms are defined in Insolvency Act 1986 ss.249 and 435 (Pensions Act 1995 s.123). Those definitions are complex and sometimes difficult to apply in practice (see e.g. D. Pollard, "Who is 'connected' or 'associated' within the meaning of the Insolvency Act 1986?" (2009) 22(3) *Insolvency Intelligence* 33, 33-44).

[12] i.e. a scheme with fewer than 12 members, where all the members are trustees of the scheme (or directors of a corporate trustee) and all decisions of the trustees must be made by the unanimous agreement of the trustees (or directors) who are members of the scheme. Alternatively, the scheme may have an independent trustee (SI 2005/3378 reg.1(2)).

[13] PA 1995 s.40(5).

[14] The Occupational Pension Schemes (Scheme Administration) Regulations 1996 (SI 1996/1715) reg.3(3) and The Financial Services and Markets Act 2000 (Carrying on Regulated Activities by Way

184   SCHEME INVESTMENTS (AND SCHEME BORROWING)

**Finance Act 2004**

8-007   The purchase of an asset by a pension scheme from a person that is not a member or a sponsoring employer (or connected with a member or sponsoring employer) is neither an authorised nor an unauthorised payment.[15] The same analysis applies to a sale to such a person. FA 2004 Pt 4 is entirely silent regarding such transactions.

*Transactions involving a member or sponsoring employer*

8-008   In relation to transactions involving a member or sponsoring employer, the following provisions may require consideration:

(a) scheme administration employer payments;[16]
(b) scheme administration member payments;[17] and
(c) authorised employer loans.[18]

8-009   A scheme administration member/employer payment must be on arm's length terms and cannot be a loan. There are also restrictions on payments to the sponsoring employer to acquire shares in the sponsoring employer. Strictly speaking, it seems that an authorised employer loan need not be on arm's length terms (as far as FA 2004 is concerned), although there are a number of conditions which must be carefully followed.

8-010   As is explained in Ch.9, if the pension scheme is an investment-regulated pension scheme then the taxable property provisions will usually give rise to tax charges if the scheme invests in non-investment companies connected with scheme members. There is an exception where the investment is an authorised employer loan.

8-011   In addition, any transactions with third parties which have the effect of providing a benefit to a member or shifting value out of the scheme may constitute an unauthorised payment.[19]

*SDLT on the purchase of land from a connected partnership*

8-012   Where land in England or Northern Ireland is purchased by a pension scheme from a partnership comprising solely of persons connected with the trustee, the transaction will not be subject to any SDLT.[20] The connected persons test in CTA 2010 s.1122 is applied, with the omission of s.1122(7) (partners connected with

---

of Business) Order 2001 (SI 2001/1177) reg.4(4), which applies to an occupational scheme (a) constituted under an irrevocable trust, (b) with no more than 12 relevant members, (c) where all "relevant members", other than any relevant member who is unfit to act, or is incapable of acting, as trustee of the scheme, are trustees of it, and (d) all day to day decisions relating to the management of the assets of the scheme which are securities or contractually based investments are required to be taken by all, or a majority of, relevant members who are trustees of the scheme or by an authorised/exempt person acting alone or jointly with all, or a majority of, such relevant members. A person is a "relevant member" of a scheme if he is an employee or former employee by or in respect of whom contributions to the scheme are being or have been made and to or in respect of whom benefits are or may become payable under the scheme.

[15] Assuming that the payment to purchase the asset does not deplete the fund and is not otherwise on clearly uncommercial terms (see Ch.18).
[16] For scheme administration employer payments, see Ch.17.
[17] For scheme administration employer payments, see Ch.11.
[18] For authorised employer loans, see Ch.17.
[19] See FA 2004 ss.173 and 174, explained in Ch.18.
[20] See FA 2003 Sch.15 paras 18 and 20. Provided that all of the partners are connected with the trustees, the "sum of the lower proportions (SLP)" will be 100 per cent and no SDLT will be payable accord-

each other) and s.1122(6)(c)–(e) (trustee connected with settlement).[21] Although it is most unlikely that a pension scheme will be a "settlement" for the purposes of s.1122(6),[22] in many cases the members of a small occupational scheme will be connected with the persons who are the trustees.

The same analysis applies in principle where such land is purchased by two or more pension schemes carrying on business together in partnership, if the seller is connected with the trustees of each scheme.[23]

*Unauthorised borrowing*

Where a pension scheme borrows money, it will often be in connection with an investment. The FA 2004 provisions relating to unauthorised borrowing are explained below.

8-013

# INCOME OF THE SCHEME

## Exemption for investment income

FA 2004 s.186(1)(a) provides:

8-014

"No liability to income tax arises in respect of—

(a) income derived from investments or deposits held for the purposes of a registered pension scheme, or
(b) underwriting commissions applied for the purposes of a registered pension scheme which are not relevant foreign income and which would otherwise be chargeable to income tax under Chapter 8 of Part 5 of ITTOIA 2005 (income not otherwise charged)."

*Stock lending*

Stock lending often forms an integral part of the investment operations of a pension scheme.[24] The fees received from such operations are not received from investment or deposits "held for the purposes of the scheme", and so to address this the exemption in s.186(1)(a) is *deemed* to apply to relevant stock lending fees.[25] A relevant stock lending fee, in relation to any investments, means any amount, in the nature of a fee, which is payable in connection with any stock lending arrangement relating to investments. A stock lending arrangement means so much of any

8-015

---

ing to the formula "market value × (100–SLP)". Any actual chargeable consideration given by the trustees is disregarded".

[21] FA 2003 Sch.15 para.39.
[22] For "connected persons", see Ch.2.
[23] See FA 2003 Sch.15 paras 10 and 12. It is sometimes suggested that two or more members' funds under a single small occupational scheme may acquire property as a partnership, but that seems misconceived: unless each separate fund has its own trustees (which would be highly unusual), they are not different "persons" so they cannot form a partnership (see Partnership Act 1890 s.1(1)). Although the trustees of different sub-fund settlements (as defined in TCGA 1992 Sch.4ZA para.1) can be different persons (see CTA 2010 s.1122(6)(f) and (g)), as noted above a pension scheme will not usually be a "settlement".
[24] For further background, see *HMRC v Coal Staff Superannuation Scheme Trustees Ltd* [2022] UKSC 10, in which the Supreme Court held that the pre-2014 regime applicable to manufactured overseas dividends was not contrary to art.56 of the Treaty Establishing the European Community (now art.63 of the TFEU).
[25] ICTA 1988 s.129B.

arrangements between two persons (the "borrower" and the "lender") as are arrangements under which:[26]

(a) the lender transfers securities to the borrower otherwise than by way of sale; and
(b) a requirement is imposed on the borrower to transfer those securities back to the lender otherwise than by way of sale.

*Futures contracts and options contracts*

**8-016** FA 2004 s.186(3) and (4) extend the meaning of the term "investments" in limited circumstances. They provide that:

> "(3) In this Part "investments", in relation to a registered pension scheme, includes futures contracts and options contracts; and income derived from transactions relating to futures contracts or options contracts is to be treated as derived from the contracts.
> (4) For that purpose a contract is not prevented from being a futures contract or an options contract by the fact that a party is or may be entitled to receive or liable to make, or entitled to receive and liable to make, only a payment of a sum (as opposed to a transfer of assets) in full settlement of all obligations."

*Repos and manufactured payments*

**8-017** Any manufactured payment or deemed payment of interest on a sale and repurchase of securities made to a person for the benefit of a registered pension scheme is deemed to be comprised in income derived from investments for the purposes of FA 2004 s.186(1).[27]

*"Investments"*

**8-018** Section 186(1)(a) applies to income from "investments". The term *investments* does not have a precise legal meaning; it should be construed in a non-technical sense.[28] Its natural meaning in a financial context is an asset acquired to be used as a source of income[29] or with the intention of realising a capital profit.[30] This plainly includes a scheme pension purchased from an insurance company and payable to the scheme, notwithstanding that the receipts will usually be matched with payments of scheme pension to the member. It may be that unsecured personal loans are incapable of constituting *investments* as a matter of trusts law,[31] but such loans are clearly capable of constituting investments as a matter of tax law.[32]

---

[26] TCGA 1992 s.263B.
[27] SI 1995/3036 regs 3(1) and 4(1).
[28] *IRC v Desoutter Bros Ltd* [1946] 1 All E.R. 58; (1945) 29 T.C. 155 (Lord Greene MR); *McCall v HMRC* [2009] NICA 12; [2009] S.T.C. 990 per Girvan LJ at [11].
[29] Per Lord Walker in *Dominica Social Security Board v Nature Island Investment Co* [2008] UKPC 19. Also see *Re Wragg* [1919] 2 Ch. 58.
[30] *Marson v Morton* [1986] 1 W.L.R. 1343; [1986] S.T.C. 463.
[31] *Khoo Tek Keong v Ch'ng Joo Tuan Neoh* [1934] A.C. 529; *Re Peczenick's Settlement* [1964] 1 W.L.R. 720; [1964] 2 All E.R. 339.
[32] Assuming that the purpose of the loans is to obtain a return for the scheme. In *Dalriada v Faulds* [2011] EWHC 3391 (Ch); [2012] 2 All E.R. 734 it was argued by HMRC and accepted by the Court that certain loans "were not made for the purpose of obtaining a return for the lender ... whether by way of income or capital gain. Rather they were made to a member of another scheme for the purpose of procuring a reciprocal long-term loan from that scheme to A". The judge said that "I

## Trading income

The profits of a trade do not constitute income derived from investments. For income tax purposes, the term trade includes any venture in the nature of *trade*,[33] so an isolated transaction can give rise to a trading profit. The word *trade* should be given its ordinary dictionary sense, namely "a pecuniary risk, a venture, a speculation, a commercial enterprise".[34]

**8-019**

There is no single fixed rule to determine what is a trade; each case must be decided according to its own circumstances. The general approach of the courts has been to see whether a transaction that gives rise to a taxable profit bears any of the so-called "badges" of trade. In *Marson v Morton*,[35] Browne-Wilkinson VC identified nine badges of trade:[36]

**8-020**

"(i)     That the transaction in question was a one-off transaction. Although a one-off transaction is in law capable of being an adventure in the nature of trade, obviously the lack of repetition is a pointer which indicates there might not here be trade but something else.

(ii)    Is the transaction in question in some way related to the trade which the taxpayer otherwise carries on? For example, a one-off purchase of silver cutlery by a general dealer is much more likely to be a trade transaction than such a purchase by a retired colonel.

(iii)   The nature of the subject matter may be a valuable pointer. Was the transaction in a commodity of a kind which is normally the subject matter of trade and which can only be turned to advantage by realisation, such as referred to in the passage that the chairman of the commissioners quoted from *Inland Revenue Commissioners v Reinhold* 1953 S.C. 49. For example, a large bulk of whisky or toilet paper is essentially a subject matter of trade, not of enjoyment.

(iv)   In some cases attention has been paid to the way in which the transaction was carried through: was it carried through in a way typical of the trade in a commodity of that nature?

(v)    What was the source of finance of the transaction? If the money was borrowed that is some pointer towards an intention to buy the item with a view to its resale in the short term; a fair pointer towards trade.

(vi)   Was the item which was purchased resold as it stood or was work done on it or relating to it for the purposes of resale? For example, the purchase of second-hand machinery which was repaired or improved before resale. If there was such work done, that is again a pointer towards the transaction being in the nature of trade.

(vii)  Was the item purchased resold in one lot as it was bought, or was it broken down into saleable lots? If it was broken down it is again some indication that it was a trading transaction, the purchase being with a view to resale at profit by doing something in relation to the object bought.

(viii) What were the purchasers' intentions as to resale at the time of purchase? If there was an intention to hold the object indefinitely, albeit with an intention to make a capital profit at the end of the day, that is a pointer towards a pure investment as opposed to a trading deal. On the other hand, if before the contract of purchase is made a contract for resale is already in place, that is a very strong pointer towards a trading deal rather than an investment. Similarly, an intention to resell in the short term rather than the long term is some indica-

---

would characterise the purpose of the PRP as being not investment but disinvestment. The MPVA loans were accordingly outside the scope of the power of investment in the Schemes".

[33] ITA 2007 s.989.
[34] Per Scott LJ in *Smith Barry v Cordy* [1946] 2 All E.R. 396; (1946) 28 T.C. 250 at 258.
[35] *Marson v Morton* [1986] 1 W.L.R. 1343; [1986] S.T.C. 463.
[36] In 1955, the Royal Commission listed 6 badges of trade: Cmd.9474 (1955) para.116. Also see HMRC's commentary at BIM20200.

(ix) Did the item purchased either provide enjoyment for the purchaser, for example a picture, or pride of possession or produce income pending resale? If it did, then that may indicate an intention to buy either for personal satisfaction or to invest for income yield, rather than do a deal purely for the purpose of making a profit on the turn. I will consider in a moment the question whether, if there is no income produced or pride of purchase pending resale, that is a strong pointer in favour of it being a trade rather than an investment."

**8-021** These are objective tests of what is a trading adventure; the taxpayer's motive is not determinative. The badges are intended to provide a framework in which the existence of a trade can be determined. There is a substantial body of case law, but the courts have repeatedly stated that there are no absolute principles and each case must be decided on its own facts. The existence of a trade is a question of fact, so a finding of the First-tier Tax Tribunal can only be disturbed on *Edwards v Bairstow*[37] grounds (i.e. if the Tribunal can be shown to have committed an error of law which vitiates its decision or if its decision is one which no reasonable decision-maker on the finding of facts which the Tribunal made could have reached).

**8-022** If property that does not produce any income is acquired and disposed of, that may point towards a trade. However, it was stressed in *Marson v Morton* that this is just one factor. Some investments are specifically designed to produce capital growth rather than income. When considering the distinction between investment and trading stock, the nature of the asset is often a very important factor. If the property produces income then that is a strong indication of investment. Certain types of property commonly held by pension schemes, such as shares and land, can be held as investments or trading stock, and so the nature of the asset does not provide much assistance.

*Stocks and shares*

**8-023** In the case of stocks and shares, the number and frequency of transactions, and the organisation involved have been considered significant factors.[38] In relation to marketable securities, it is common practice for changes to be made to portfolios and the frequency of changes will not usually create an inference that trading has occurred. In *Cooper v C&J Clark Ltd*, Nourse J said:[39]

"First, marketable securities, being income-yielding assets usually capable of appreciating in value, are prima facie purchased and sold by way of investment and not by way of trade. Secondly, a series of purchases and sales may sometimes, if carried out pursuant to a deliberate and organised scheme of profit-making, amount to a trade. Thirdly, it is easier to characterise a series of purchases and sales as a trade in a case where they are made by a trading entity as opposed to an individual. Fourthly, in the case of a trading entity, that characterisation is more easily made where the purchases and sales are substantial in relation to its other activities, all the more so where they are of frequent occurrence and extend over a long period of time. Fifthly, it is sometimes helpful, although not decisive, to ask whether a series of sales and purchases is speculative or not. The

---

[37] *Edwards v Bairstow* [1956] A.C. 14; [1955] 3 W.L.R. 410. As it happens, *Edwards v Bairstow* was concerned with whether a purchase and sale of certain plant was an adventure in the nature of a trade.
[38] *Lewis Emanuel v White* (1965) 42 T.C. 369; *Cooper v C&J Clark Ltd* [1982] S.T.C. 335; 54 T.C. 670; *Salt v Chamberlain* [1979] S.T.C. 750; 53 T.C. 143.
[39] *Cooper v C&J Clark Ltd* [1982] S.T.C. 335; 54 T.C. 670 at 676.

reason why the question is sometimes helpful is that the answer may throw light in one direction or the other, but it is not decisive because according to the circumstances either a trade or a course of investment may be speculative."

In the context of financial instrument and shares, HMRC's position is that:[40]

**8-024**

"There is a strong presumption that a pension fund is an investment, not a trading vehicle. This is not to say that pension funds cannot undertake activities which amount to a trade. If such an activity is clearly trading, the status of the pension fund cannot change that. But if the position is unclear, it will be necessary to investigate the purpose of the transaction to see if it was a trading one or part of the investment activities."

*Land*

Many of the cases on the distinction between investment and trade relate to transactions in land. Particular problems arise where the property is developed or improved in some way and also let out for a time.[41] The acquisition of an asset in the expectation of making a profit on its sale does not necessarily signify a trade because a good investment should generate capital appreciation.[42] If a pension scheme lets land to a developer (including a company owned by the scheme) this should not involve any trading by the scheme.[43]

**8-025**

In *Simmons v IRC*, Lord Wilberforce provided the following helpful guidance:[44]

**8-026**

"One must ask, first, what the commissioners were required or entitled to find. Trading requires an intention to trade: normally the question to be asked is whether this intention existed at the time of the acquisition of the asset. Was it acquired with the intention of disposing of it at a profit, or was it acquired as a permanent investment? Often it is necessary to ask further questions: a permanent investment may be sold in order to acquire another investment thought to be more satisfactory; that does not involve an operation of trade, whether the first investment is sold at a profit or at a loss. Intentions may be changed. What was first an investment may be put into the trading stock—and, I suppose, vice versa. If findings of this kind are to be made precision is required, since a shift of an asset from one category to another will involve changes in the company's accounts, and, possibly, a liability to tax: see *Sharkey v Wernher* [1956] A.C. 58. What I think is not possible is for an asset to be both trading stock and permanent investment at the same time, nor to possess an indeterminate status—neither trading stock nor permanent asset. It must be one or other, even though, and this seems to me legitimate and intelligible, the company, in whatever character it acquires the asset, may reserve an intention to change its character. To do so would, in fact, amount to little more than making explicit what is necessarily implicit in all commercial operations, namely that situations are open to review."

Once it has been established that an asset is acquired as an investment, there must be a clear appropriation of that asset to trading stock before a tribunal can find that a subsequent sale was in the course of a trade.[45] In *Taylor v Good*, Russell LJ stated:[46]

**8-027**

"If of course you find a trade in the purchase and sale of land, it may not be difficult to

---

[40] BIM56930.
[41] See e.g. *Orchard Parks v Pogson* (1965) 42 T.C. 442; *Shadford v H Fairweather Ltd* (1966) 43 T.C. 291.
[42] *IRC v Reinhold* (1953) 34 T.C. 389; *Jenkinson v Freedland* (1961) 39 T.C. at 647.
[43] *IRC v Dean Property Co* (1939) 22 T.C. 706.
[44] *Simmons v IRC* [1980] 1 W.L.R. 1196 at 1199.
[45] *Dunn Trust Ltd v Williams* (1950) 31 T.C. 477.
[46] *Taylor v Good* [1974] 1 W.L.R. 556 at 560.

find that properties originally owned (for example) by inheritance, or bought for investment only, have been brought into the stock-in-trade of that trade. To such circumstances I would relate the dicta relied upon in the other three cases referred to by Megarry J. But where, as here, there is no question at all of absorption into a trade of dealing in land of lands previously acquired with no thought of dealing, in my judgment there is no ground at all for holding that activities such as those in the present case, designed only to enhance the value of the land in the market, are to be taken as pointing to, still less as establishing, an adventure in the nature of trade."

*FA 2016 transactions in land rules*

**8-028** FA 2016 replaced the transactions in land provisions with a new code, which applies, inter alia, where *one of the main purposes* of acquiring land is to realise a profit or gain from disposing it.[47] If these provisions apply, "the profit or gain is to be treated for income tax purposes as profits of a trade carried on by the chargeable person".[48] The previous provisions only applied where the *sole or main object* of acquiring the land was to realise a gain on its disposal and it was clear that land acquired as an investment (i.e. to produce rental income) was not caught by these provisions apply even if an expected gain on a future sale was a reason for buying the land. It is clear from case law that a taxpayer may have more than one *main purpose* and so there is a concern that if a registered pension scheme acquired land with a view to letting it out but where part of the motivation was an expected gain these provisions will apply.

**8-029** However, it is strongly arguable that these provisions do not affect the application of FA 2004 s.186(1). This is because s.86(1) refers to "income derived from investments", and it is likely that the term *investments* is not intended to have a technical tax meaning. Indeed, the new provisions do not have the effect of changing an investment transaction into a trading transaction; they have the effect of deeming the profits of certain investment transactions to be profits of a trade. This does not necessarily involve deeming the underlying transaction to be anything other than an investment, and hence s.186(1) should continue to apply.

*Circumstances other than the acquisition and disposal of assets*

**8-030** The badges of trade, and many of the leading cases on what constitutes a trade, are concerned with the acquisition and disposal of assets rather than with the provision of services or the acceptance or incurring of contingent liabilities. In *Ransom v Higgs*,[49] the House of Lords considered a situation where the taxpayer had neither bought nor sold anything. Lord Reid said this:

"As an ordinary word in the English language 'trade' has or has had a variety of meanings or shades of meaning. Leaving aside obsolete or rare usage, it is sometimes used to denote any mercantile operation, but it is commonly used to denote operations of a commercial character by which the trader provides to customers for reward some kind of goods or services."

*Trading vehicles*

**8-031** Where the trustees of a registered pension scheme are concerned that an activity may constitute a trade, they may wish to invest in an exempt unauthorised unit

---

[47] ITA 2007 s.517B(4).
[48] ITA 2007 s.517C(1).
[49] *Ransom v Higgs* 50 T.C. 1 at 7.8.

# INCOME OF THE SCHEME

trust, which can carry on the trading activity.[50] The profits of the unit trust are subject to income tax at the basic rate,[51] but tax relief is provided in respect of the amount distributed to unit holders.[52] The distributions paid to the pension scheme will be investment income rather than trading income.[53] This was highlighted as one of the key uses of such unit trusts in a 2012 consultation, and the decision to preserve the tax efficiency of trading income arising to such unit trusts for the benefit of exempt investors was quite deliberate.[54]

Investing in a trading partnership (including an LLP) will not assist because the share of profits arising to each partner does not lose its characterisation as trading income.[55]

**8-032**

*Income "derived from" investments*

In *Davenport v Chilver*,[56] Nourse J said that "I do not think that one thing can be said to derive from another unless it is in some sense the fruit of the tree". Income derives from the holding of an investment notwithstanding that the person holding the investment has to take active steps. For example, rental income derives from the holding of land as an investment notwithstanding that in order to obtain the income the holder carries out incidental maintenance and management work, finds tenants and grants leases etc.[57] The meaning of the word *derived* has been considered on a number of occasions in the context of TCGA 1992 s.22, which creates a deemed disposal where any capital sum is derived from assets. These cases suggest that *derived* means *immediately derived*.[58]

**8-033**

Where some form of statutory compensation is provided to trustees in their capacity as holder of an investment, it seems unlikely that the payment could be said to derive from the investments.[59] If trustees receive a compromise payment in negligence litigation arising in connection with an investment, it is likely that the sum received derives from the right to sue and not the investment.[60]

**8-034**

*Investments "held for the purposes of" a pension scheme*

Per FA 2004 s.150(1), the *pension scheme* is the arrangement(s) comprised in the instrument(s) which are capable of providing benefits in the specified circumstances, and so investments *held for the purposes of the scheme* must mean investments that may be used to provide the benefits. It follows that investments held by

**8-035**

---

[50] An "unauthorised unit trust" is a collective investment scheme under which property is held on trust for the participants, which is not an authorised unit trust (ITA 2007 ss.989 and 1007, applying FSMA 2000 s.237). "Collective investment scheme" is defined in FSMA 2000 s.235. An unauthorised unit trust is "exempt" if it satisfies the requirements in SI 2013/2819 reg.3. This includes a requirement that all of the unit holders are "eligible investors", which is the case where any gain accruing in the event of a disposal of its units would be wholly exempt from CGT (otherwise than by reason of residence).
[51] SI 2013/2819 reg.12(3)(d) disapplies ITA 2007 s.479, so only basic rate tax can apply.
[52] SI 2013/2819 reg.18(2).
[53] SI 2013/2819 reg.12(1).
[54] HMRC's Consultation on high-risk areas: Taxation of unauthorised unit trusts—proposals for change Annexe B, responses to Question 1 and Question 9.
[55] ITTOIA 2005 s.848.
[56] *Davenport v Chilver* [1983] Ch. 293 at 300.
[57] *McCall v HMRC* [2009] NICA 12; [2009] S.T.C. 990 per Girvan LJ at [14].
[58] *IRC v Montgomery* (1975) 49 T.C. 679.
[59] *Davis v Powell* (1977) 51 T.C. 492; *Davenport v Chilver* (1983) 57 T.C. 661; *Drummond v Brown* (1984) 58 T.C. 67.
[60] *Zim Properties v Procter* (1984) 58 T.C. 371.

persons other than the trustee or manager of the pension scheme may constitute investments held for the purposes of the scheme. This would clearly be the case where investments are held by a nominee for the trustees. The position is less clear where investments are held by an investment manager (for example) pursuant to the terms of a contract which does not place the beneficial ownership with the trustees. If the investment manager is in some sense holding specific investments for the trustees then s.186 should apply to exempt any income derived from those investments received by the investment manager. However, if the trustees provide funds to an investment manager and merely have a contractual right to receive funds calculated by reference to the value of underlying investments then it is difficult to see how those underlying investments could be described as being held for the purposes of the pension scheme.

*Investment vehicles*

8-036    The exemption in FA 2004 s.186 will not generally extend to investments held by investment vehicles owned by the scheme,[61] unless the *vehicle* is a mechanism through which the benefits are to be provided to members (so that the vehicle forms part of the *pension scheme*). This will not usually be the case, but conceivably an investment vehicle could be a mechanism for providing benefits. This would be the case where the contractual or other arrangements between the pension scheme and the vehicle are such that the provision of benefits to or in respect of a member is expressly anticipated. In such circumstances, investments held by the vehicle would be held for the purposes of the pension scheme.

8-037    If a pension scheme invests in shares issued by a company, an investment held by the company would not, without more, constitute an investment held for the purposes of the pension scheme.[62] The fact that the funds invested by the company may be derived from funds held for the purposes of a registered pension scheme is not sufficient to engage FA 2004 s.186. In any event, if the company was beneficially entitled to the income then it would be subject to corporation tax, and s.186(1) exempts income tax only.

8-038    Where trustees lend money to a person and that person invests it, any income received by that person is not derived from investments held for the purposes of a registered pension scheme even though that income must be used to repay the lender (i.e. the registered pension scheme). Similarly, where a registered pension scheme borrows money, HMRC cannot reasonably argue that the funds borrowed are not held for the purposes of the registered pension scheme, even though at least some of the income deriving from those funds must be used to repay the lender.

*Underwriting commissions*

8-039    FA 2004 s.186(1)(b) provides that no liability to income tax arises in respect of underwriting commissions applied for the purposes of a registered pension scheme

---

[61] FA 2004 s.161(3) and (4) have particular application to investment vehicles, but these provisions perform a limited function and they do not mean that investment held by the vehicle are deemed to be held by the scheme. They provide that payments or benefits provided under on in connection with investments acquired using scheme funds are deemed to be made or provided from sums or assets held for the purposes of the scheme.

[62] The property held for the purposes of the scheme cannot be both the shares *and* the property owned by the company.

# INCOME OF THE SCHEME

which are not relevant foreign income[63] and which would otherwise be chargeable to income tax under ITTOIA 2005 Pt 5 Ch.8 (income not otherwise charged).

Underwriting commissions are commissions received from undertaking to purchase any unsold shares, typically on a rights issue or initial public offering or takeover. If the rights issue or IPO is fully subscribed (as is usually the case) then the underwriters receive their commission without any further obligation. If the issue is not fully subscribed the issuer will require the underwriter to purchase the unsubscribed shares at the issue price.[64]

8-040

In *Clarke v British Telecom Pension Scheme Trustees*,[65] the trustees of exempt approved pension schemes received sub-underwriting commissions. The trustees claimed exemption under what is now FA 2004 s.186(1)(b) on the basis that the commissions would otherwise be chargeable under what is now ITTOIA 2005 Pt 5 Ch.8. The Revenue disallowed the claims on the grounds that the commissions were receipts of a trade and so the exemption did not apply. The Revenue argued that the sub-underwriting activities amounted to a trade because they were habitual, organised, for reward, extensive and business-like. This appears to have been largely accepted by the Special Commissioners, who found that the activity of underwriting issues of shares in return for a commission has features indicative of a trade. Its essence is the acceptance of a risk for reward. However, the Special Commissioners found that the trustees' sub-underwriting activities formed an integral part of their overall investment activities, and so took its colour from them. The trustees only entered into sub-underwriting contracts in respect of shares in companies in which they wished to invest, and their policy was to support the management of companies in which they held investments unless there was a contrary reason. In addition, sub-underwriting was viewed by the trustees as an integral part of their investment strategy and not as a means of making money, but as reducing the cost of shares which the schemes would acquire in any event. Accordingly, the Special Commissioners found that the trustees' activities did not amount to a trade.[66] The Court of Appeal, although critical of some aspects of the decision, found that the Special Commissioners were entitled to reach that decision.

8-041

*Property investment LLPs*

FA 2004 s.186(2) provides that:

8-042

"The exemption provided by subsection (1) does not apply to income derived from investments or deposits held as a member of a property investment LLP; and for this purpose 'income' includes relevant stock lending fees, in relation to any investments, to which subsection (1) would apply by virtue of section 129B of ICTA (inclusion of relevant stock lending fees in income)."

A *property investment LLP* is an LLP whose business consists wholly or mainly

8-043

---

[63] Relevant foreign income is income which arises from a source outside the UK and is chargeable under any of the provisions specified in ITTOIA 2005 s.830(2) (ITTOIA 2005 s.830(1)).
[64] For greater detail on how underwriting works see *BT Pension Scheme Trustees v Clarke* [1997] O.P.L.R. 279; [1998] Pens. L.R. 85 at 30–34.
[65] *Clarke v British Telecom Pension Scheme Trustees* [2000] S.T.C. 222. Also see Kerridge [2000] B.T.R. 397.
[66] It was accepted by counsel for the trustees that trading could occur in different factual circumstances, e.g. where: (a) the underwriter wanted the commission and not the shares; (b) there was an intention to sell the underwritten shares and not to hold them as a long-term investment; (c) there was an intention to generate income from the commissions; (d) there was a considerable degree of selectivity as to which shares to underwrite; and/or (e) the commissions were brought into a profit and loss account.

in the making of investments in land, and the principal part of whose income is derived from investments in land.[67] Whether an LLP is a property investment LLP is determined for each period of account of the partnership. HMRC take that view that, except in exceptional circumstances, letting a single commercial property to a single tenant will amount to a *business* for these purposes. Land includes "buildings and structures, land covered with water, and any estate interest, easement, servitude or right in or over land".[68] The *principal part* presumably means more than 50%, and *investments in land* are presumably to be distinguished from trading in land.

8-044　　The policy of this provision is to avoid having a UK tax transparent corporate property investment vehicle with tradable interests, because this could result in tax loss and distort the investment market. In particular, the concern appears to have been that LLPs would allow exempt bodies to invest more tax-efficiently than via a property investment company. Given that pension schemes may invest in property via limited partnerships and unit trusts, the restriction relating to LLPs is slightly puzzling.

*Taxable property*

8-045　　The exemption provided by s.186(1) does not prevent income from being charged to tax by virtue of FA 2004 s.185A,[69] which provides that an investment-regulated pension scheme is deemed to make a scheme chargeable payment if it holds an interest in taxable property. The taxable property provisions are considered in detail in Ch.9.

*Repayment of tax*

8-046　　If a registered pension scheme has had income tax deducted from its investment income, that tax can be reclaimed from HMRC.[70] This does not apply in relation to trading income, dividends from shares owned by the pension scheme or property investment limited liability partnerships.

**Other sources of income**

8-047　　In the context of a trust scheme, the normal trust rules apply to any income not exempted by s.186 (for example, trading income). Income arising to a UK resident pension scheme where no person has an immediate right to income will be taxed at the rate applicable to trusts (currently 45%).[71] Accordingly, it would usually be more tax-efficient for the trustees to incorporate an underlying company to carry on any trade. If the trustees were non-UK resident then non-UK income should not be subject to UK tax provided that the trustees are trading with the UK rather than in the UK and not through a permanent establishment.

---

[67] ITA 2007 s.1004.
[68] Interpretation Act 1978.
[69] FA 2004 s.186(2A).
[70] See PTM024400; form R63N; HMRC Guidance: *Reclaim tax deducted from pension scheme investments* (published 16 September 2014).
[71] ITA 2007 s.9(1).

## CAPITAL GAINS

TCGA 1992 s.271(1A) provides: 8-048

"A gain accruing to a person on a disposal of investments held for the purposes of a registered pension scheme or an overseas pension scheme is not a chargeable gain."

This language reflects that in FA 2004 s.186, and so the comments above regarding the meaning of *investments* and *held for the purposes of* are equally relevant for the purpose of TCGA 1992 s.271. Section 271 also contains provisions materially identical to those considered above relating to futures contracts and options contracts, and there is also an exception for gains accruing to a person from the acquisition and disposal by him of assets held as a member of a property investment LLP. 8-049

The exemption provided by TCGA 1992 s.271 does not prevent a gain from being treated as a chargeable gain for the purposes of FA 2004 ss.185F–185I. These provisions (explained in Ch.9) broadly provide that an investment-regulated pension scheme is deemed to make a scheme chargeable payment if it holds an interest in taxable property and a deemed gain accrues to the pension scheme. 8-050

## UNAUTHORISED BORROWING

FA 2004 ss.182–185 contain provisions relating to unauthorised borrowing. In broad terms, borrowing is unauthorised if the total amount borrowed is equal to or greater than half of the value of: (a) any money purchase arrangement(s) that the borrowing is in respect of; or (b) if the borrowing is in respect of an arrangement which is not a money purchase arrangement, all of the arrangements under the scheme which are not money purchase arrangements.[72] One is required to value the arrangement(s) immediately before the borrowing occurs. This has two consequences. First, the value does not include the money which will be received from the lender. Secondly, it does not matter if there is a subsequent reduction in the value of the scheme property (e.g. as a result of the provision of benefits under the scheme). 8-051

The rationale for penalising excessive borrowing in FA 2004 Pt 4 is slightly obscure. Certain pension legislation restricts pension scheme borrowing because it is associated with inappropriate speculation.[73] The purpose of the unauthorised borrowing provisions in FA 2004 Pt 4 may be to limit the extent to which a registered pension scheme can take advantage of the exemption in FA 2004 s.186(1) (relat- 8-052

---

[72] FA 2004 ss.183(2) and 185(2). PTM124000 states that a registered pension scheme is authorised to borrow an aggregate amount up to and including 50% of the net value of the fund. This is not strictly correct. To be authorised it must be less than 50%, so borrowing equal to 50% is not authorised (although the amount of the scheme chargeable payment in these circumstances is nil).

[73] PA 1995 s.36A (introduced by PA 2004 s.246) and SI 2005/3378 reg.5 prohibit an occupational pension scheme from borrowing any money except to the extent required to provide temporary liquidity (although reg.7 disapplies reg.5 in relation to any scheme with less than 100 members). These provisions were introduced as a result of European Pensions Directive art.18(2) (Directive 2003/41/EC), which was concerned with prudent investment (see EU Briefing 17 March 2006). Prior to the introduction of those provisions, it seems there were no specific restrictions: borrowing considered as part of investment strategy (see "Implementing the European Directive on the Activities and Supervision of Institutions for Occupational Retirement Provision: Government Response to Consultation" para.6.7, DWP).

ing to investment income).[74] If there were no limit, a scheme member could lend a significant sum to the scheme at little or no interest, which the scheme could invest and thereby cause the value of the member's arrangement under the scheme to grow exponentially.[75] Be that as it may, the provisions apply regardless of the identity of the lender or the terms on which the borrowing is made.[76]

8-053 Where scheme borrowing is contemplated, the trustees should check carefully that they have the power to do so.[77] Even an apparently unrestricted power to borrow may be exercised only for the purposes for which it is conferred and not for any extraneous or ulterior purpose.[78]

**"Borrowing"**

8-054 Despite the heading to FA 2004 s.163 (which is "meaning of 'borrowing' etc"), it does not seek to define "borrowing" for these purposes, so the term should be given its usual meaning. The general law meaning of "loan" is explained in Ch.2, and one would expect a "borrower" to be a person who has received a loan. Accordingly, transactions that have the same economic effect as borrowing, such as the purchase of an asset by a pension scheme for deferred consideration, should not involve any borrowing.[79] "Loan" is deemed under FA 2004 s.162(4) to include certain debts, but that extended meaning (of *loan*) is not expressly applied for the purposes of s.163, which is concerned only with the general law meaning of "borrowing". Notwithstanding this, HMRC assert that "a registered pension scheme is treated as borrowing or having a liability of an amount, if that amount is to be repaid or met from cash or assets held for the purpose of the pension scheme".[80] This is plainly not what the legislation says, and more importantly it seems quite clear that this is not what Parliament intended it to mean. The obligation to provide

---

[74] This would explain why the unauthorised borrowing provisions are not applied to RNUKS: s.186(1) does not apply to such schemes.

[75] This would be attractive where the annual allowance charge would apply to any contribution. A loan on commercial terms clearly cannot constitute a contribution, and it is strongly arguable that a beneficial loan (e.g. interest-free) does not constitute a contribution provided that the loan is repayable on demand. The key characteristic of a contribution is that it transfers value to the scheme. For inheritance tax purposes, HMRC accept (at IHTM14317) that "The grant of an interest free loan repayable on demand ... is not a transfer of value (because the value of the right to repayment of the loan is equal to the amount of it)". Similarly, although a beneficial loan to an employee may constitute earnings, if it is repayable on demand then it has no value (per Vinelott J in *O'Learly v Macinlay* [1991] S.T.C. 42; 63 T.C. 729). The analysis would be different if the loan were allowed to become statute-barred. The income tax settlement provisions (see Ch.25) should not have any application to such a loan.

[76] At PTM120000, HMRC state that a loan from a member or sponsoring employer (or connected person), must be at a commercial rate otherwise it will be subject to a tax charge. However the payment of interest at an uncommercially low rate would not itself give rise to a tax charge. The payment of interest by the scheme at an uncommercially high level would however constitute an unauthorised payment because the payment of interest will not be a scheme administration member/employer payment if it is not on arm's length terms.

[77] Trustees do not have an unrestricted power to borrow under general law (*Walker v Southall* (1887) 56 LT 882; *Re Suenson-Taylor's Settlement Trusts* [1974] 1 W.L.R. 1280; [1974] 3 All E.R. 397) and so they are usually given an express power to do so in the trust instrument.

[78] See e.g. *Re Courage Pension Schemes* [1987] 1 All E.R. 528 at 536 (Millett J).

[79] Section 163(3) provides that "a liability is a liability of a registered pension scheme if the liability is to be met from sums or assets held for the purposes of the pension scheme"; however s.161(3) has no application to the unauthorised borrowing provisions (it is relevant only for the purposes of the value shifting provisions in FA 2004 ss.174 and 181). The unauthorised borrowing provisions are concerned with borrowing rather than liabilities.

[80] PTM124000. Also see the Explanatory Notes to cl.153 of the Finance Bill 2004 (which became FA 2004 s.163): "a registered pension scheme is to be treated as having borrowed an amount if it is to be repaid from assets held for the purpose of the scheme".

pension benefits to and in respect of scheme members is, on any reasonable analysis, a liability of the pension scheme, so if Parliament had intended that liabilities (as distinct from borrowings) are to be taken into account for the purposes of the unauthorised borrowing provisions, there would be an express exception for a liability to pay benefits under the scheme.[81] There is no such exception.

8-055 Where borrowing is replaced or restructured, HMRC's view appears to be that it is not necessary to consider these provisions unless the amount of the borrowing increases.[82]

## "By a registered pension scheme"

8-056 Borrowing is "by a registered pension scheme" if the amount borrowed is to be repaid from sums or assets held for the purposes of the pension scheme.[83] It is thus irrelevant who receives the amount borrowed; one must determine who is responsible for repaying the lender. It is unclear if this condition is met where the trustees or managers of a pension scheme act as guarantor for a borrower (such as may be required where money is lent to a company owned by the scheme). The requirement is that the amount borrowed *is to be* repaid from scheme funds, which indicates a primary liability rather than a secondary liability. A guarantor is usually liable only if the person with the primary liability fails to discharge the debt, so the most that can be said where the trustees or manager act as guarantor is that the amount borrowed may be repaid from scheme funds.

8-057 Where a registered pension scheme holds shares in a company or units in a unit trust, any borrowing by the company or trust will plainly not involve any borrowing *by the scheme* provided that the scheme is not required to repay the lender. Sums or assets held by the company or trust are not "held for the purposes of the pension scheme".[84] There seems to be no reason in principle (at least from a tax perspective) that a sponsoring employer or scheme member could not act as guarantor for any borrowing by an underlying company or unit trust, if a guarantor is required by the lender.

## "In respect of an arrangement"

8-058 One is required to determine whether the proposed borrowing is *in respect* of: (a) a money purchase arrangement which is not a collective money purchase arrangement; or (b) an arrangement which is not such an arrangement. Borrowing is in respect of an arrangement if it is properly attributable to the arrangement in accordance with the provisions of the scheme and any just and reasonable apportionment.[85] It seems that all borrowing by a scheme will either be in respect of a money purchase arrangement or in respect of an arrangement that is not a money purchase arrangement: it is not possible for borrowing by a registered pension scheme to be otherwise. If borrowing relates specifically to a member's money

---

[81] Prior to 6 April 2006, liabilities were taken into account for the purposes of determining the amount which a SSAS was authorised to borrow, but there was an express exception for "liabilities to pay benefits under the scheme" (see The Retirement Benefits Schemes (Restriction on Discretion to Approve) (Small Self-administered Schemes) Regulations 1991 (SI 1991/1614) reg.4(1)(c)). The equivalent provisions for SIPPs focused instead on the value of the asset to be purchased with the borrowing, so this issue did not arise (see The Personal Pension Schemes (Restriction on Discretion to Approve) (Permitted Investments) Regulations 2001 (SI 2001/117) reg.6(4)).
[82] PTM124000.
[83] FA 2004 s.163(2).
[84] For the meaning of "held for the purposes of the pension scheme", see Ch.18.
[85] FA 2004 s.163(4).

purchase arrangement, in the sense that all loan repayments will reduce the value of his arrangement, the borrowing is clearly in respect of that member's arrangement. If borrowing is in respect of more than one such arrangement then the borrowing is apportioned on a just and reasonable basis. If, for example, £100,000 is borrowed to purchase an asset and the costs of repaying the loan are attributed 75% to one money purchase arrangement and 25% to another (e.g. for a husband and a wife) then one would expect this to be a just and reasonable method of apportioning the borrowing.[86] As is explained below, each arrangement must satisfy the 50% restriction: the value of the two arrangements are not aggregated for these purposes. The relevant time at which to determine which arrangement(s) any borrowing is in respect of is the time at which the borrowing occurs. Subsequent events (for example, loan repayments in different proportions) should not be relevant if the decisions are taken later on.[87]

*Application to general funds*

8-059　　Section 163(4) refers to "an arrangement". Normally, when the term "arrangement" is used in FA 2004 Pt 4, it is a reference to a member's arrangement under the scheme,[88] which may be distinguished from a general fund under the scheme (which does not relate to any particular member). Is borrowing within the scope of these provisions where it is properly attributable to a general fund (i.e. borrowing that cannot be apportioned to one or more members' arrangements under the scheme on any just and reasonable basis)? Sections 182 and 183 apply only to borrowing "in respect of a money purchase arrangement", and it is quite clear that a general fund is not a money purchase arrangement. Sections 184 and 185 apply to borrowing "in respect of any arrangement which is not a money purchase arrangement". It follows that if a general fund is an "arrangement", ss.184 and 185 can apply to it. For the purposes of FA 2004 Pt 4, the term "arrangement" is generally understood to mean an agreement under the scheme regarding the calculation of the benefits to be paid to or in respect of a particular member.[89] If that is correct then a general fund is not an arrangement, and the unauthorised borrowing provisions cannot apply to borrowing attributable to a general fund. However, the better view is likely to be that s.152 is relevant only where an arrangement *relates to a member*, and ss.184 and 185 do not refer to an arrangement *relating to a member*. Sections 184 and 185 therefore appear to be using the term *arrangement* in a different context, and so ss.184 and 185 can apply to borrowing in respect of general funds.

8-060　　It follows that any borrowing which is to be repaid with sums or assets held generally for the purposes of the pension scheme (and so cannot be apportioned to any money purchase arrangement) is *in respect of* an arrangement which is not a money purchase arrangement.

---

[86] In principle, the profits or losses relating to the asset may be apportioned differently between the two arrangements. The unauthorised borrowing provisions focus only on how the borrowing will be repaid.
[87] There may be a surrender for the purposes of FA 2004 s.172A if borrowing attributed to one arrangement is discharged from a different member's arrangement.
[88] See FA 2004 s.152(1).
[89] For the meaning of "arrangement", see FA 2004 s.152 and Ch.2.

## Money purchase arrangements (other than collective money purchase arrangements)

**8-061** A registered pension scheme is not authorised to borrow an amount in respect of a money purchase arrangement that is not a collective money purchase arrangement unless the arrangement borrowing condition is met.[90] The arrangement borrowing condition is met if the amount proposed to be borrowed in respect of the arrangement, plus any amounts previously borrowed in respect of the arrangement and not yet repaid,[91] is less than half of the value of the arrangement. The value of the arrangement is the total of:

(a) the amount of such of the sums and the market value of such of the assets as represent drawdown pension funds or flexi-access drawdown funds in respect of the arrangement;
(b) the total value of each scheme pension payable in respect of the arrangement;[92] and
(c) the value of any uncrystallised rights under the arrangement.

## Uncrystallised rights

**8-062** Rights are *uncrystallised* if no one has become entitled to the present payment of benefits in respect of the rights. For these purposes, a person is deemed to be entitled to the present payment of benefits in respect of any sums and assets representing the person's drawdown pension fund or the person's flexi-access drawdown fund. The value of any uncrystallised rights is equal to:

(a) if the arrangement is a cash balance arrangement, the amount which would on the valuation assumptions[93] be available for the provision of benefits in respect of those rights if a person became entitled to benefits in respect of those rights;
(b) for other money purchase arrangements, the total value of the sums and assets held for the purposes of the arrangement as represent those rights; or
(c) for hybrid arrangements under which either cash balance benefits or other money purchase benefits (but not defined benefits or collective money purchase benefits) may be provided, the greater of the above two calculations.

## The amount of the scheme chargeable payment

**8-063** If a scheme borrows in respect of a money purchase arrangement an amount that it is not authorised to borrow, the amount of the scheme chargeable payment is determined as follows. If immediately before the amount is borrowed, the total

---

[90] FA 2004 s.182.
[91] This includes amounts borrowed prior to 6 April 2006. The reference is to amounts previously borrowed; not the amount currently owed. Thus, if £10,000 was borrowed and the amount currently owed is £11,000 (including accrued but unpaid interest), only the £10,000 is taken into account.
[92] The value of a scheme pension payable in respect of the arrangement is the relevant valuation factor (see FA 2004 s.276) multiplied by the annual rate at which the pension is payable. Once it commences, a scheme pension is by its nature a defined benefit, but for the purpose of FA 2004 Pt 4, it is payable in respect of a money purchase arrangement if the member's arrangement under the scheme is a money purchase arrangement.
[93] The valuation assumptions require one to value the individual's rights on the assumption that the individual is at the age at which no reduction would apply to the payment of an immediate benefit, and the individual is in good physical and mental health at the time so the benefits would not be discounted under the scheme rules as a result of being paid as a result of ill-health (FA 2004 s.277).

amount previously borrowed in respect of the arrangement (excluding any amounts which have been repaid) is less than half of the value of the arrangement, the amount of the scheme chargeable payment is equal to: "APB + AB − VA/2" where:

- *APB* is the total amounts (if any) previously borrowed in respect of the arrangement, excluding any amounts which have been repaid;
- *AB* is the new amount borrowed; and
- *VA* is the value of the arrangement immediately before the new amount is borrowed.

8-064　For example, if an arrangement currently valued at £100,000 has previously borrowed £25,000 (and not repaid any of it), and then borrows a further £26,000, the amount of the scheme chargeable payment is: £25,000 + £26,000 − £100,000/2 = £1,000.

8-065　If the amount previously borrowed is equal to or greater than half of the value of the arrangement, the amount of the scheme chargeable payment is limited to the amount of the new borrowing. The reason for this favourable treatment is presumably because the excess may have been subject to tax as unauthorised borrowing when the previous borrowing occurred. Of course, the previous borrowing may not have been unauthorised, for example the value of the arrangement may have decreased since the previous borrowing. Where the value of the arrangement has decreased since the previous borrowing one might expect that the amount of new borrowing ought to be reduced accordingly, but that is not the case.

*Other arrangements*

8-066　A registered pension scheme is not authorised to borrow an amount in respect of any arrangement which is not a money purchase arrangement or a collective money purchase arrangement unless the scheme borrowing condition is met. The scheme borrowing condition is met if the total amounts previously borrowed by the pension scheme in respect of such arrangements (excluding any amounts which have been repaid) plus the amount proposed to be borrowed by the pension scheme, is less than half of the total amount of the *relevant sums and assets*.[94] The value of the relevant sums and assets is the total amount of the sums and the market value of the assets held for the purposes of such of the arrangements under the pension scheme as are not money purchase arrangements or collective money purchase arrangements.

8-067　As noted above, if any of the borrowing is attributable to any such arrangement then the amount of that borrowing must be less than half of the value of *all* arrangements under the scheme that are not money purchase arrangements or collective money purchase arrangements.

*The amount of the scheme chargeable payment*

8-068　The amount of the scheme chargeable payment is calculated in essentially the same way as for money purchase arrangements. If, immediately before the amount is borrowed, the total amount previously borrowed in respect of any non-money purchase arrangement(s) is less than half of the value of all such arrangements under the scheme, the amount of the scheme chargeable payment is equal to "APB + AB − AARAS/2" where:

- *APB* is the total amounts (if any) previously borrowed in respect of arrange-

---

[94] FA 2004 s.184.

ments which are not money purchase arrangements, excluding any amounts which have been repaid;
- *AB* is the new amount borrowed; and
- *AARA* is the total value of sums/assets held for the purposes of such of the arrangements under the pension scheme as are not money purchase arrangements.

For example, if the value of funds held for the purposes of arrangements that are not money purchase arrangements is £100,000 and the scheme has previously borrowed £25,000 in respect of such arrangements, and then borrows a further £26,000, the amount of the scheme chargeable payment is £25,000 + £26,000 − £100,000/2 = £1,000.

**8-069**

As above, if the amount previously borrowed (if any) in respect of such arrangement(s) is equal to or greater than half of the value of such arrangements, the amount of the scheme chargeable payment is limited to the amount of the new borrowing.

**8-070**

*Valuation points*

One determines the value of the arrangement(s) immediately before the amount is borrowed. Any subsequent reduction in value (e.g. because of the payment of benefits in respect of the arrangement, or because scheme assets subsequently decrease in value) cannot cause any previous borrowing to become unauthorised, unless further borrowing occurs. Valuing scheme assets almost certainly requires one to disregard any unsecured debt.[95] This means that borrowing on an unsecured basis has the effect of increasing the value of the arrangement, which in turn allows the scheme to borrow an additional amount without breaching the 50% limit (which in turn allows the scheme to borrow an additional amount, and so on). For example, if a money purchase arrangement has a value of £100,000 then up to £50,000 can be borrowed in respect of that arrangement.[96] If £50,000 is borrowed without giving security over the scheme assets, the arrangement will then have a value of £150,000, and so a further £25,000 can be borrowed without making a scheme chargeable payment. If £25,000 is then borrowed (and is unsecured), the arrangement will have a value of £175,000, and so a further £12,500 can be borrowed (etc.). This allows the scheme to borrow a total of £100,000, but only if it is done incrementally. If the scheme did borrow £100,000 on an unsecured basis, the value of the arrangement would be £200,000, so the amount of the debt would not exceed 50% of the value of the arrangement.

**8-071**

---

[95] The value of an asset is its market value, and market value is to be determined in accordance with TCGA 1992 s.272 (see FA 2004 s.278(1)). See the discussion in Ch.2.
[96] For borrowing to be authorised it must be less than 50%, so borrowing £50,000 will not be authorised, however the amount of the scheme chargeable payment will be £50,000 − £100,000/2 = £nil.

# CHAPTER 9

# Taxable Property

## TABLE OF CONTENTS

| | |
|---|---|
| Introduction | 9-001 |
| The provisions | 9-003 |
| "Investment-regulated pension scheme" (IRPS) | 9-005 |
| Occupational pension schemes | 9-008 |
| Non-occupational schemes | 9-009 |
| Sums/assets treated as held for the purposes of an arrangement | 9-010 |
| "Taxable property" | 9-011 |
| Residential property | 9-012 |
| Exceptions to "residential property" | 9-013 |
| Tangible moveable property | 9-016 |
| Exceptions to "tangible moveable property" | 9-020 |
| "Holding" taxable property | 9-026 |
| Direct holding | 9-027 |
| Paragraph 14(1) | 9-028 |
| Paragraph 14(3) | 9-032 |
| Exception for hotel accommodation | 9-037 |
| Exception to para.14(3) | 9-039 |
| Indirect holdings | 9-041 |
| "An interest in another person" | 9-044 |
| Exception for authorised employer loans | 9-054 |
| Interests in companies | 9-057 |
| Interests in collective investment schemes | 9-060 |
| Interests in trusts | 9-061 |
| "Relevant interest in a trust" | 9-063 |
| Para.19(7): "arm's length transaction" | 9-065 |
| Conclusions on "holding an interest in another person" (in para.16(2)) | 9-066 |
| Exceptions: indirect holding | 9-068 |
| "Vehicle" | 9-069 |
| Trading vehicles | 9-070 |
| Real Estate Investment Trusts | 9-072 |
| Diverse investment vehicles | 9-073 |
| Paragraph 24 | 9-074 |
| Life policies etc | 9-079 |
| "Associated persons" | 9-082 |
| Deemed unauthorised payment (s.174A) | 9-085 |
| Acquiring | 9-087 |
| Amount and timing of the unauthorised payment | 9-091 |
| The total taxable amount | 9-093 |

Direct acquisitions of taxable property .......... 9-097
Certain acquisitions for less than market value
   consideration ............................. 9-100
Paragraph 33 ............................... 9-102
Security interests .......................... 9-107
Paragraph 34 ............................... 9-109
Variations of leases ........................ 9-113
Indirect acquisitions of taxable property ......... 9-114
Deemed acquisitions of taxable property ......... 9-116
Improvements ................................. 9-118
Conversion or adaption as residential property ...... 9-119
   Timing ...................................... 9-124
Apportionment to the pension scheme ............. 9-125
   "Extent" of an interest ...................... 9-129
   Apportionment to member ..................... 9-133
Scheme chargeable payment under s.185A ............ 9-134
   Amount of the scheme chargeable payment ........ 9-135
   The annual profits .............................. 9-136
   The amount of the deemed profits ................ 9-138
   Leases of residential property .................. 9-141
   Apportionment to pension scheme ................. 9-144
   Credit for tax paid ............................. 9-146
Scheme chargeable payment under s.185F .............. 9-148
   The amount of the scheme chargeable payment ..... 9-150
      Disposal by person holding directly ............ 9-151
      Whether the transferor disposes of the taxable
         asset ...................................... 9-152
      When such a disposal occurs ................. 9-154
      Whether a chargeable gain or allowable loss ac-
        crues and, if so, the amount of the chargeable
        gain or allowable loss ..................... 9-155
   Disposal of interest in vehicle ................. 9-168
   Credit for tax paid ............................. 9-171

## INTRODUCTION

**9-001** The taxable property provisions, introduced by FA 2006, impose penal tax charges where certain types of registered pension scheme directly or indirectly hold taxable property (i.e. residential property or tangible moveable property, subject to certain exceptions).[1] In a Technical Note accompanying the 2005 Pre-Budget Report, the rationale for the taxable property provisions was explained thus:

> "… to prevent people benefiting from tax relief in relation to contributions made into self-directed pension schemes for the purpose of funding purchases of holiday or second homes and other prohibited assets for their or their family's personal use."

**9-002** It is suggested that the policy of the taxable property provisions is to prevent pen-

---

[1] For the transitional provisions applicable to pre-A Day holdings of taxable property, see Ch.3. In short, taxable property is not subject to the taxable property provisions if it was: (a) acquired before 6 April 2006 and not improved since that date; and (b) permitted under the rules in force at that time.

sion schemes from holding property which members or their families *might* be able to personally use or enjoy. The provisions are not concerned with benefit as such: that is the purpose of FA 2004 s.173, which imposes a charge where an asset is used to provide a benefit to a member.[2] Note also that, in contrast to the charge under s.173,[3] the charges imposed under the taxable property provisions are penal.

# THE PROVISIONS

Where an "investment-regulated pension scheme" holds an interest in "taxable property", the scheme may be deemed to make: (a) an unauthorised payment (FA 2004 s.174A); and (b) an annual scheme chargeable payment (FA 2004 s.185A). In addition, a scheme chargeable payment may arise under FA 2004 s.185F when such property is disposed of. Before considering in detail the requirements of these provisions, it is necessary to consider the meaning of:

(a) investment-regulated pension scheme;
(b) taxable property; and
(c) what it means for a pension scheme to "hold" an interest in taxable property.

The relevant provisions are in FA 2004 Sch.29A.

9-003

9-004

### "Investment-regulated pension scheme" (IRPS)

To determine whether or not a pension scheme is an IRPS, one must ascertain whether any member, or any person related to a member, can direct, influence, or advise on the manner of investment of any of the sums or assets held for the purposes of an arrangement under the pension scheme.[4] A person is "related" to a member if the person and the member are connected persons[5] or the person acts on behalf of the member or a person connected with the member.[6] The words "on behalf of" ordinarily suggest a relationship of agency[7] but where the context requires they have been read more widely as meaning "in the place of", or "for the benefit of" or "in the interests of".[8] In the present context, it is likely to be read more widely. The idea is that if a member can influence the manner of investment then he may be able to procure that the scheme property is invested in such a way that he can use or enjoy it. Even an entirely independent fund manager may be said to act in the interests of the scheme members but that cannot itself be objectionable: for the purpose of Sch.29A he acts "on behalf of" a member only where the member

9-005

---

[2] See Ch.18. Section 173 is disapplied where the asset is taxable property: s.173(7A).
[3] A deemed unauthorised payment under s.173 is subject to an unauthorised payments charge, and may also be subject to an unauthorised payments surcharge, by reference to the value of the benefit provided. It is not subject to a scheme sanction charge unless the asset is a wasting asset, so s.173 is not penal.
[4] FA 2004 Sch.29A Pt 1. The scheme administrator must notify HMRC if a registered pension scheme becomes or ceases to be an IRPS: The Registered Pension Schemes (Provision of Information) Regulations 2006 (SI 2006/567) reg.3, reportable event 10.
[5] Whether a person is "connected" with another person is determined in accordance with ITA 2007 s.993: see Ch.2.
[6] FA 2004 Sch.29A para.4.
[7] See *Gaspet Ltd v Elliss (Inspector of Taxes)* [1985] 1 W.L.R. 1214 at 1220 (Peter Gibson J); *Clixby v Pountney (Inspector of Taxes)* [1968] Ch. 719 at 728–729 (Cross J).
[8] See *R. (Cherwell DC) v First Secretary of State* [2004] EWCA Civ 1420; [2005] 1 W.L.R. 1128 at [56] (Chadwick LJ); *R. (S) v Social Security Commissioner* [2009] EWHC 2221 (Admin); [2010] P.T.S.R. 1785 at [27]–[28]; *Rochdale MBC v Dixon* [2011] EWCA Civ 1173; [2012] P.T.S.R. 1336 at [49]–[50] (Rix J).

can influence the manner of investment. The requirement is probably satisfied if the person can be relied upon to choose investments that the member would choose if he had the power and he wanted to personally use or enjoy them. In practice, the relationship may be inferred from the actual choice of investments: if the person chooses investments that a scheme member can personally use or enjoy, this may itself indicate that the member can influence the investments such that the scheme is an IRPS.

**9-006** The provisions are widely drawn. They apply if a member or related person:[9]

> "is or has been able (directly or indirectly) to direct, influence or advise on the manner of investment of any of the sums and assets held for the purposes of an arrangement under the pension scheme relating to the member."

**9-007** The reference to "has been able" is likely to be a reference to an ability *at the time at which the relevant decision to invest is made*. It will usually be clear if a person has the ability to "direct" (meaning a legal right to select the investment) or "advise" on the manner of investment. However, "influence" is a vague concept, especially as the requirement is merely that the person has the *ability* to influence (so actual influence is unnecessary). In a sense, anyone can be said to be *able* to influence other people, if only by voicing their opinions. It is suggested that "influence" for these purposes, must mean actual influence, in the sense that it must make a material difference to the trustees' decision. This is a question of fact; the drafting of the scheme documentation cannot determine the issue.

*Occupational pension schemes*

**9-008** In the case of an occupational pension scheme with 50 or fewer members, if any member or related person is able to direct, influence, or advise on the investment of *any* property held for the purposes of the pension scheme (even if the property does not relate to the member with that ability), the entire pension scheme is an IRPS.

In the case of an occupational pension scheme with more than 50 members, a member's arrangement under the pension scheme is itself deemed to be an IRPS if the member or any related person can direct, influence, or advise on the investment of any sums or assets "linked" to the member's arrangement. Sums or assets are "linked" to a member's arrangement if they are: (a) held for the purposes of the member's arrangement, but (b) not held for the purposes of the arrangement merely by virtue of a just and reasonable apportionment of the sums and assets held for the purposes of the pension scheme. In other words, sums or assets are "linked" with a member's arrangement where actual sums/assets are allocated for that member, and not where investments are held on a pooled basis and notionally allocated between several members' arrangements.

*Non-occupational schemes*

**9-009** A non-occupational scheme is an IRPS if any member or related person can direct, influence, or advise on the manner of investment of property held for the purposes of an arrangement relating to the member. Note that in these circumstances the entire pension scheme is an IRPS.

---

[9] FA 2004 Sch.29A paras 1(2) and 2(2).

# THE PROVISIONS

*Sums/assets treated as held for the purposes of an arrangement*

Sums or assets held for the purposes of an IRPS which are not in fact held for the purposes of any arrangement relating to a member (and not otherwise treated as so held) are treated as if they were held for the purposes of the arrangements under the pension scheme, by reference to the respective rights under the scheme of the members to which the arrangements relate. **9-010**

However, this deeming provision applies only if the sums or assets are held "otherwise than for the purposes of the administration[10] or management[11] of the pension scheme". A *payment* to buy or sell an investment asset is a payment made for the purposes of the administration or management of the pension scheme,[12] but it seems clear that investment assets are not *held* for the purposes of the administration or management of the scheme. It seems likely that this is a reference to, for example, money which is allocated within the pension scheme to pay trustee fees and assets such as an office used by the trustees for the purpose of administering the scheme.

**"Taxable property"**

Subject to the exceptions described below, property is "taxable property" if it is:[13] **9-011**

(a) "residential property"; or
(b) "tangible moveable property".

*Residential property*

"Residential property" is defined exhaustively as any of the following (whether in the UK or elsewhere):[14] **9-012**

(a) A building[15] used or suitable for use as a dwelling. "Dwelling" is not defined. Its usual meaning is a home. The term suggests a greater degree of settled occupation than the place in which one merely habitually sleeps and

---

[10] In *R. (Britannic Asset Management Ltd) v Pensions Ombudsman* [2002] EWHC 441 (Admin); [2002] O.P.L.R. 175, Lightman J said this, in the context of PSA 1993 s.146(4), "... 'administering the Scheme' means (in whole or in part) running the Scheme, e.g. inviting employees to join, keeping records of members, communicating with members, calculating benefits, providing benefit statements, paying benefits when due, keeping documentation up to date, dealing with governmental or regulatory agencies (Inland Revenue, DWP, OPRA) etc. In the case of a funded scheme, it will also no doubt involve running the fund and investing in managing the Scheme's assets".

[11] In *Century Life Plc v Pensions Ombudsman* [1995] C.L.C. 1276; [1995] Pens. L.R. 135 at 44 and 52, which concerned (amongst other things) the meaning of "manager" in PSA 1993 s.146, Dyson J accepted that "'Manager' is an ordinary English word. It means the person who is in fact running the scheme. This means, for example, calculating benefits, arranging for actuarial reviews, providing documentation and keeping it up to date, corresponding with the Inland Revenue and Department of Social Security, paying transfer values for early leavers, general administration and giving advice to the trustees in a funded scheme. It was accepted that under the trust deeds of funded schemes the ultimate responsibility lies with the trustees, and that it is against the trustees that members have enforceable rights. It does not, however, follow from this that the trustees will be running the scheme. In small insurance schemes, the insurance company almost invariably runs the scheme, and the role of the trustees in practice is likely to be little more than collecting and paying contributions, and taking whatever other steps the insurance company advises should be taken."

[12] See Ch.11.

[13] FA 2004 Sch.29A para.6.

[14] FA 2004 Sch.29A para.7.

[15] For these purposes a "building" includes: (a) a structure; and (b) part of a building or structure.

usually eats.[16] An overnight stay in a hotel or hostel does not amount to dwelling in that accommodation (hotel and similar accommodation is dealt with separately in (c) below).[17] An IRPS may buy land, obtain planning permission, and start to build a dwelling, provided that the land is disposed of prior to it being used, or becoming suitable for use, as a dwelling.[18]

(b) Any land consisting of, or forming part of, the garden or grounds of such a building (including a building on any such land) which is used or intended for use for a purpose connected with the enjoyment of the building.

(c) Hotel or similar accommodation.

(d) A beach hut.

**9-013** **Exceptions to "residential property"** A building used for any of the following purposes is expressly *not* residential property:[19]

(a) a home or other institution providing residential accommodation for children;

(b) a hall of residence for students;[20]

(c) a home or other institution[21] providing residential accommodation with personal care for persons in need of personal care by reason of old age, disability, past or present dependence on alcohol or drugs or past or present mental disorder;

(d) a hospital or hospice; and

(e) a prison or similar establishment.

**9-014** A building that is used, or was last used, for one of the above purposes and which is also suitable for use as a dwelling, will not constitute residential property by virtue of that suitability. Furthermore, any building which has not been used for any purpose, and is suitable for use as a dwelling, will not constitute residential property if it is *more* suitable for one of the above purposes than for any other purpose.

In addition, residential property is expressly not taxable property if the property is (or, if currently unoccupied, is to be) occupied by:[22]

(a) an employee who is not a member of the scheme nor connected with either any member or the employer, and is required as a condition of employment[23] to occupy the property; or

(b) a person who is not a member of the scheme nor connected with such a

---

[16] *Uratemp Ventures Ltd v Collins* [2001] UKHL 43; [2002] 1 A.C. 301 at [30] (Lord Millet).

[17] A useful review of a number of cases can be found in *R. (on the application of ZH and CN) v Newham LBC* [2014] UKSC 62; [2015] A.C. 1259.

[18] Although this may well constitute a trade, in which case the profits will not be exempt under FA 2004 s.186.

[19] FA 2004 Sch.29A para.8.

[20] cf. the SDLT provisions in FA 2003 s.116(3)(b) which are restricted to students "in further or higher education". PTM125200 sets out HMRC's view of the meaning of "hall of residence". It is unclear at precisely what point a dwelling becomes a hall of residence (see Taxation, 12 October 2006, 38, and Standing Committee A, 20 June 2006, cols 721–726).

[21] Here the word "home" must be interpreted with "or other institution" and so it is a reference to an institution such as a care home or nursing home rather than simply a place where one lives (*Pensioneer Trustees (London) Ltd v HMRC* [2016] UKFTT 0346).

[22] FA 2004 Sch.29A para.10.

[23] *J&A Young (Leicester) Ltd v HMRC* [2015] UKFTT 638. "Condition" in this context means a fundamental term of the employment contract i.e. a term so important that it usually gives one party the right to repudiate a contract if the obligation is breached (at [63]).

member, and used in connection with business premises held as an investment of the pension scheme.

9-015 The exception in (a) above will apply where there is a requirement to occupy the property in the employment contract.[24] There is no need to show that occupying the property is necessary to the employment or that occupying the property allows the employee to better perform his duties. In respect of the exception in (b) above, the breadth of the phrase "in connection with" means that there will be sufficient *connection* between the residential property and the business premises if residential property is acquired to provide accommodation to employees working in the business premises (and it is in fact so used and used for no other purpose).[25]

*Tangible moveable property*

9-016 "Tangible moveable property" is not defined. Property is "tangible" if it is a physical object. Determining whether or not property is "moveable" can be problematic. HMRC suggest that the distinction between moveable and immoveable is the same as the distinction, in property law, between chattels and fixtures.[26] As a matter of property law, a fixture is an object which, when attached physically to land, is regarded as forming part of the land. By contrast, chattels are physical objects which do not form part of the land. The distinction turns on the *degree* of annexation and the *purpose* of annexation, and the latter is more important than the former. In relation to the former (the degree of annexation), anything attached to land by bolts, screws or nails is prima facie a fixture, even if it is attached only slightly and can be easily removed. Objects which rest by their own weight are chattels.[27] In relation to the latter (the purpose of annexation), objects which are intended to form part of the land (even if not attached to the land) will be fixtures, and objects attached to land merely to facilitate enjoyment will be chattels.

9-017 As a matter of property law a number of important consequences flow from an object being found to constitute a "fixture" (and therefore "land"), and these consequences have naturally influenced the case law. It is not easy to see why they should be relevant to the taxable property provisions. Nonetheless, in *Morgan Lloyd Trustees Ltd and Ray Hallam v HMRC*[28] both sides agreed that the "general law" of fixtures applied, so the FTT was not required to consider whether or not this is the appropriate test. In that case, an IRPS acquired some printing presses and other machinery. Each of the presses weighed at least three tonnes, and one weighed over seven tonnes. The machinery was affixed to the floor, but, importantly, this was done in order to "facilitate their more effective operation as printing presses, and not in order to make a permanent improvement to the property where they were housed". The nature of the fixing was such that it would only have taken a matter of minutes to undo without any significant damage to the machines or the premises, and they could then be moved with a forklift truck. The FTT found that the presses were not fixtures and therefore concluded that they were tangible moveable property.

9-018 The real issue with tangible property is that a member may obtain some sort of use, or benefit, or enjoyment from the property. That being the case, one would

---

[24] *J&A Young (Leicester) Ltd v HMRC* [2015] UKFTT 638 at [68].
[25] *J&A Young (Leicester) Ltd v HMRC* [2015] UKFTT 638 at [102]. The legislation (in contrast to ITEPA 2003 s.99, for example) does not explicitly impose any requirements as to the necessity of any particular type or location of employee accommodation.
[26] PTM125100.
[27] *Holland v Hodgson* (1872) L.R. 7 C.P. 328 at 335 (Blackburn J).
[28] *Morgan Lloyd Trustees Ltd and Ray Hallam v HMRC* [2017] UKFTT 131.

expect the test to focus on whether it is possible for a member to obtain some use, benefit or enjoyment. Whether an object is moveable or not seems to focus on an arbitrary feature of the property.[29] Of course, personal use is perhaps more likely with moveable property because you can *do* things with it. In the *Morgan Lloyd Trustees* case, the taxpayers argued that, bearing in mind the penal tax charges that apply to an acquisition of taxable property, it could not have been intended by Parliament that machinery would constitute taxable property because it was not possible for the members to derive any benefit from it for as long as it belonged to the pension scheme. This was in contrast to "personal chattels" and residential property, which small schemes were not permitted to invest in under the pre-A Day regime: such property could be enjoyed by members even when owned by the scheme. However, the FTT found that it was not possible to interpret the legislation this way:

> "Parliament could very easily have retained the previous wording if it had wished to limit the new provisions to the same articles as before. Instead, it chose to adopt new wording which has a wider scope."

9-019 Of course, the test of being moveable will, in most cases, be clearer than a test based on ability to enjoy, so perhaps it can be justified on that basis.

9-020 **Exceptions to "tangible moveable property"** Each of the following is excepted from the definition of taxable property:[30]

(a) gold bullion; or
(b) any item of tangible moveable property with a market value[31] of less than £6,000 if:
  (i) it is held by a "vehicle" (see below) solely for the purposes of the administration or management of the vehicle;
  (ii) the IRPS does not hold an interest in the property directly; and
  (iii) no member of the IRPS or any person connected with such a member occupies or uses, or has any right to occupy or use, the property.

9-021 HMRC suggest that these items are removed from the definition of taxable property because they are of a type that are normally held as investments and do not provide any possibility of personal use or enjoyment.[32] This reflects the policy of the taxable property provisions, which is to prevent the scheme owning property from which a member *might* use or enjoy.

9-022 The exception in (b) above is necessary because the taxable property provisions apply where an IRPS holds taxable property indirectly, such as where the IRPS owns shares in a company (or other *vehicle*) and the company owns taxable property. It is common for companies to own small items of property such as furniture, computers etc which would be taxable property were it not for this exception.

9-023 On the face of it, the reference to "administration or management" in (b)(i) above imposes a significant restriction. The exception applies only where the property is held by a vehicle solely for the purposes of the administration or management of the vehicle. The exception will therefore apply to most tangible moveable property owned by an investment vehicle, and it will apply to property used to carry on a

---

[29] e.g. trees, whilst they are growing in the ground, are not moveable property, however, the act of felling the trees will convert them into movable property, and therefore taxable property. It is difficult to discern any rational reason for the difference in treatment.
[30] SI 2006/1959 art.2.
[31] "Market value" is determined in accordance with TCGA 1992 s.272 (FA 2004 s.278(3A)). See Ch.2.
[32] PTM125100.

management or administrative function within a trading vehicle, but it would appear to apply to little else. If this is correct, it creates a serious obstacle to investing in trading businesses. There is a separate exception for tangible moveable property held by trading vehicles (explained below), but that exception does not apply where a member is a controlling director of the vehicle.

What is meant in (b)(iii) above by "occupies or uses"?[33] The position is unclear but it is suggested that it does not include the use by a member of property (such as a computer) for the purposes of the member's occupation. If this were otherwise then (except where one of the exceptions for indirect holdings applies: see below) it would effectively mean that a pension scheme could never own shares in a company which employed a member of the IRPS, because almost all companies will own taxable property. That does not appear to be the policy of the taxable property provisions and so the better view is that "use" means personal use (i.e. using the property outside of work).[34]

**9-024**

Any company cars with a market value of £6,000 or more will be taxable property. Many companies own plant and machinery with a value far in excess of £6,000 and so investment in such companies by an IRPS will usually involve an indirect holding of taxable property (subject to the exceptions below).

**9-025**

**"Holding" taxable property**

The provisions apply where an IRPS holds an interest in taxable property "directly" or "indirectly". Where an IRPS holds an interest in taxable property indirectly, some other person holds the interest in taxable property directly, and the IRPS directly or indirectly holds an interest in that other person. For this reason, the provisions refer to a *person* (rather than the IRPS) holding an interest in property directly.

**9-026**

*Direct holding*

Paragraph 14 of Sch.29A explains what is meant by a direct holding. Broadly, it means actual ownership (para.14(1)) and in some cases contractual relationships which closely mirror the usual rights of an owner (para.14(3)).

**9-027**

**Paragraph 14(1)**  Paragraph 14(1) provides:

**9-028**

"For the purposes of the taxable property provisions a person holds an interest in property directly if (under the law of any country or territory) the person (whether jointly, in common or alone):
(a) holds the property or any estate, interest, right or power in or over the property,
(b) has the right to use, or participate in arrangements relating to the use of, that property or a description of property to which that property belongs, or
(c) has the benefit of any obligation, restriction or condition affecting the value of any estate, interest, right or power in or over the property, under the law of any country or territory."

---

[33] The word "occupies" is not a term of art; it takes its colour from the context of the statute in which it is found: *Lee-Verhulst (Investments) Ltd v Harwood Trust* [1973] Q.B. 204 at 217 (Stamp LJ).

[34] This analysis is reinforced by Sch.29A para.16(3), which provides an exception to the indirect holding provisions as a result of an authorised employer loan. In almost all cases of authorised employer loans, a member of the scheme will be employed by the sponsoring employer, but this provision expressly does not apply if the taxable property is occupied or used by a member of the pension scheme or a person connected with such a member, and so if the exception is to have any application at all the expression *occupy or use* in para.16(3) is very likely to relate to personal use only.

**9-029**  Paragraph 14(1)(a) and (c) are similar to FA 2003 s.48, which defines "chargeable interest" for SDLT purposes, but note that, in contrast to the SDLT provisions, there is no exception for security interests or licences.

**9-030**  Does "value" in para.14(1)(c) mean market value? Section 278(3B) provides that in the taxable property provisions, the market value of taxable property or an interest in taxable property is to be determined in accordance with FA 2004 s.272, but para.14(1) refers to *value* and not *market value*. The difference may be material: for example, a call option clearly affects the market value of an estate/interest, whereas an overage agreement which is personal to the grantor does not (it affects the value of the interest *to the grantor* of the overage, but it does not affect the market value). It seems likely that it is intended to be a reference to market value: the words focus on the property rather than the owner and so if something affects the value to the owner but not to anyone else then it should not be relevant for the purposes of para.14(1)(c).

**9-031**  If an IRPS enters into a partnership which invests in residential property (and title to the property is held by a partner other than the IRPS) the IRPS has a direct interest in the property because, as a matter of partnership law, the other partner holds the property as agent for the IRPS (thereby giving the IRPS an interest in the land).

**9-032**  **Paragraph 14(3)**  Paragraph 14(3) significantly extends para.14(1). It provides that:

> "A person holds an interest in property directly if the person is entitled (whether jointly, in common or alone) to receive payments determined by reference to the value of or the income from the property."

**9-033**  It is unclear if para.14(3) applies only where the payments are determined *solely* by reference to the value of or the income from the property, or if it also applies where the payments are also determined by other factors. "Income" is unlikely to mean "profit", because FA 2004 s.185A (which also relates to taxable property) draws a clear distinction between income and profit and was introduced at the same time as para.14(3).

**9-034**  There must be an entitlement to receive "payments",[35] so a call option to purchase taxable property would not normally bring one within the scope of para.14(3)[36] even though its value may well be determined by reference to the value of the property. Rent received by an IRPS as a partner in a general partnership or member of an LLP may be caught, depending on the circumstances. However, a joint venture to develop residential property may well not within para.14(3). The property will not normally receive any income, and the right to receive sale proceeds is different to the right to receive payments by reference to the value of the property, even though one would expect the sale proceeds to be similar to the value.

**9-035**  It is apparent from para.15 (see below) that insurance policies, annuities and capital redemption polices are intended to be caught by para.14(3). Clearly, para.14(3) will apply where the policyholder has a right to receive income from the policy or contract. But what of investment bonds, where the only payment that the holder (i.e. the IRPS) is entitled to receive is a payment on surrender, or part surrender, of the bond? The IRPS is clearly entitled to receive a payment by refer-

---

[35] The plural generally includes the singular (Interpretation Act 1978) so a right to receive even a single payment would be caught.

[36] Although if the property is land then the option would create an equitable interest in land, and so would be caught by para.14(1).

THE PROVISIONS 213

ence to the value of the underlying property and so para.14(3) seems to apply. The difficulty with this analysis is that, if it is correct, it suggests that owning 100% of the shares in a company will also be within para.14(3), on the basis that on a liquidation the shareholder would be entitled to a payment. This is plainly not intended. For example, if an IRPS owns 100% of a company which owns taxable property, the fact that the scheme can receive dividends, or liquidate the company and receive the profits does not make this a direct holding. It is intended to constitute an indirect holding.[37]

It may be that the key to understanding this aspect of para.14(3) is the words "entitled ... to receive payments". Under an annuity contract there is an entitlement, without having to *do* anything, to receive payments (e.g. periodic payments, and/or a lump sum on death). There may also be an option to surrender, however it seems arguable that the right to receive a payment on surrender is not within the scope of para.14(3) because there is no entitlement unless and until the option to surrender is exercised. For this same reason, the right of a 100% shareholder to liquidate or receive dividends from a company does not mean that the shareholder is not within para.14(3); there is no entitlement until some step is taken. The same may apply to an investment bond. If correct, this analysis significantly limits the ambit of para.14(3).

9-036

**Exception for hotel accommodation** As noted above, the definition of residential property includes hotel accommodation. However, a person does not hold an interest in residential property consisting of hotel accommodation directly unless:[38]

9-037

(a) the person holds part only of the hotel accommodation or any estate, interest, right or power in or over such a part and, as a result, any person has a right to use or occupy that or any other part of the hotel accommodation; or

(b) the person has a right to use, or participate in arrangements relating to the use of, part only of the hotel accommodation or a description of property to which that part belongs.

It follows that holding an entire hotel (including a joint holding with other persons) is not a direct holding of an interest in residential property. If no person holds such property directly then it will not be possible for an IRPS to hold an interest in that property indirectly.

9-038

**Exception to para.14(3)** A person does not hold an interest in taxable property directly by virtue of para.14(3) where three conditions are met:[39]

9-039

(a) the person is entitled to receive the payments by virtue of a policy of life insurance, a contract for a life annuity or a capital redemption policy, and the policy/contract is issued by an insurance company;

(b) the property does not constitute a linked asset, or has been appropriated by the insurance company to an internal linked fund; and

(c) one of the following applies:
    (i) where the person is an occupational pension scheme, the policy/

---

[37] HMRC agree that this is an indirect holding: PTM125400 states, "A pension scheme holds 100% of the shares in company A and the company owns a residential property. This demonstrates an indirect holding by the pension scheme, of 100%. The pension scheme indirectly holds an interest in the residential property owned by company A."

[38] FA 2004 Sch.29A para.14(2).

[39] FA 2004 Sch.29A para.15.

214    TAXABLE PROPERTY

        contract, either by itself or taken together with one or more associated policies, does not entitle the pension scheme, either alone or together with one or more associated persons, to receive payments representing 10% or more of the market value of or the income from the property,

(ii) where the person is a pension scheme other than an occupational pension scheme, the policy or contract, either by itself or taken together with one or more associated policies, does not entitle an arrangement under the pension scheme, either alone or together with one or more associated persons, to receive such payments, or

(iii) otherwise, the policy or contract does not entitle the person to receive such payments.

**9-040** This exception does not apply if the purpose or one of the purposes for which the person holds rights under the policy or contract is to enable a member of the pension scheme or a person connected with such a member to occupy or use the property.[40]

*Indirect holdings*

**9-041** Schedule 29A para.16(1) provides that:

"For the purposes of the taxable property provisions a person holds an interest in property indirectly if the person does not hold the interest directly but (whether jointly, in common or alone):
(a) holds an interest in a person who holds the interest in the property directly, or
(b) holds an interest in a person who holds the interest in the property indirectly by virtue of paragraph (a) or this paragraph."

**9-042** It does not matter how long the chain of ownership is. For example:
IRPS – Co1 – Co2 – Co3 – Co4 – Co5 – taxable property

**9-043** If Co1 holds an interest in Co2 and Co2 holds an interest in Co3, and so on, the IRPS will indirectly hold an interest in taxable property, because:
(a) Co5 directly holds an interest in taxable property;
(b) Co4 indirectly holds an interest in taxable property by virtue of para.16(1)(a);
(c) Co3 indirectly holds an interest in taxable property because it holds an interest in a person (i.e. Co4) who indirectly holds the interest in the property by virtue of para.16(1)(a). Therefore Co3 indirectly holds an interest in taxable property by virtue of para.16(1)(b);
(d) Co2 indirectly holds an interest in a person (i.e. Co3) who holds the interest in the property by virtue of para.16(1)(b); and
(e) Co1 indirectly holds an interest in a person (i.e. Co2) who holds the interest in the property by virtue of para.16(1)(b).

**9-044** **"An interest in another person"** Paragraph 16(2) provides:

"For the purposes of the taxable property provisions a person holds an interest in another person if:

---

[40] FA 2004 Sch.29A para.15(5), which commences with the words, "But for the purposes of applying paragraph 14(3) for determining whether a pension scheme holds an interest in taxable property directly or indirectly...". It is not at all clear what, if anything, these opening words are intended to add to the exception.

## THE PROVISIONS

(a) the person holds an interest, right or power in or over that other person, or
(b) the person lends money to that other person to fund the acquisition by that other person of an interest in taxable property."

Paragraphs 17–19 exhaustively explain what it means for a person to hold an interest in a company, a collective investment scheme, and a trust by virtue of para.16(2)(a) (see below). In other cases, it is less clear precisely how wide para.16(2)(a) is. Some conclusions on the scope of para.16(1) are suggested below, after first considering paras 17–19.

**9-045**

The word "interest" in para.16(2)(a) suggests a proprietary interest, but "right" and "power" on their own suggest mere contractual interests. However, the draftsman evidently considered that para.16(2)(a) was not wide enough to encompass a contractual right to repayment (as must always exist where there is a loan), otherwise para.16(2)(b) would be otiose. For this reason, it seems likely that para.16(2)(a) is referring to some proprietary interest in the person rather than a merely contractual right against that person. One difficulty with this analysis however is that, if it is correct, an investment bond that does not come with para.14(3) (see above) would also not be caught by para.16(1), which would be surprising to say the least.

**9-046**

Bearing in mind that the overriding purpose of the taxable property provisions is to prevent situations where members *might* be able to use or enjoy taxable property, the purpose of para.16 is to identify situations where an IRPS may be able to influence persons who directly hold taxable property. One would expect it to be interpreted broadly. There are other provisions (considered below) that reduce the charge where the level of influence is small.

**9-047**

Paragraph 16(2)(b) plainly does not apply where a loan is made to a person in order to refinance taxable property that the person already holds, because such a loan is not for the purpose of acquiring taxable property by the borrower. The rationale for such a limitation may be that if the loan is to be used to *purchase* taxable property, the IRPS (as the lender) may have some influence over the choice of property by the borrower, and may prefer a property which a member can use or enjoy. As this is not the case in a refinancing situation, it is logical that that is treated differently.

**9-048**

Similarly, if an IRPS makes a loan to person A and person A makes a loan to person B who uses it to acquire an interest in taxable property, that is not within para.16(2)(b).

**9-049**

It seems likely that in order for para.16(2)(b) to apply, the lender must be aware that the purpose of the loan is to acquire an interest in taxable property. If that is correct then a loan for general business purposes may not be caught even if it is in fact used to acquire an interest in taxable property. So if an IRPS wishes to invest in a fund that provides loans to borrowers for general purposes (or if the IRPS wishes to provide such loans directly), it need not be concerned with how the loans are in fact used.

**9-050**

Finally it should be noted that para.16(2)(b) uses the term "lend" and so this brings in FA 2004 s.162,[41] but only to the extent that the loan is by the IRPS.[42] Where a loan is made by a vehicle in which the IRPS holds an interest and the loan is not under or in connection with the investment then the term "lend" has its normal meaning (which is generally narrower than under s.162).

**9-051**

---

[41] Considered in Ch.2.
[42] Or "under or in connection with" an investment of the scheme: see FA 2004 s.161(3), explained in Ch.17.

**9-052**  If the above analysis is correct then para.16 is more limited than it may initially appear. Further support for this can be found in para.19(7): a person does not have an interest in a trust merely because of an arm's length transaction (which could include a loan to refinance), so it does not matter if the trust holds taxable property in these circumstances (see below).

**9-053**  Paragraph 16(4) specifies (non-exhaustively) what it means to "hold" an interest in another person in certain contexts.[43] It provides that:

(a) an IRPS holds an interest in another person if an interest in that person is held for the purposes of the scheme;

(b) an arrangement under a pension scheme holds an interest in another person if an interest in that person is held for the purposes of the arrangement; and

(c) a trust which is not a pension scheme holds an interest in another person if an interest in that person is held for the purposes of the trust.

**9-054**  **Exception for authorised employer loans**  Paragraph 16(3) provides that para.16(2)(b) does not apply to an authorised employer loan within FA 2004 s.179, provided that:

(a) the interest in the property is acquired so that the property may be used for the purposes of a trade, profession or vocation carried on by the sponsoring employer or for the purposes of the sponsoring employer's administration or management; and

(b) after the acquisition, the property is not occupied or used by a member of the pension scheme or a person connected with such a member.

**9-055**  The reference to "administration or management" might suggest that the focus is on the administrative elements of a business rather than its core business. However, that seems unlikely because SI 2006/1959 generally exempts such property. The term "administration or management" also appears in FA 2004 ss.171 and 180 in the context of arm's length payments from a pension scheme to a member or sponsoring employer. Both s.171 and s.181 explain, by way of example, that it includes purchasing assets to be held for the purposes of the pension scheme. Assuming that the same applies to para.16(3), this should mean that if the sponsoring employer buys residential property as an investment, para.16(2)(b) will apply provided that it is not occupied by a member or connected person.

**9-056**  The exclusion in para.16(3) relates only to para.16(2)(b), which strongly suggests that para.16(2)(a) is not capable of applying to an authorised employer loan. As the employer will usually be a company, this further suggests that a secured loan to a company is not within the scope of para.16(2)(a). This does not mean that secured loans are not caught (para.17 may well apply to secured loans: see below), but it does suggest a limit to the scope of para.16(2)(a), and this point is considered below.

**9-057**  **Interests in companies**

"A person holds an interest in a company if:[44]

(a) the person has, or is entitled to acquire, share capital or voting rights in the company;

(b) the person has, or is entitled to acquire, a right to receive or participate in distributions of the company;

---

[43] FA 2004 Sch.29A para.16(4) is the same as para.13(1) except that para.13(1) relates to interests in *property* rather than *persons*. It is curious that the draftsman did not put these two provisions together.

[44] FA 2004 Sch.29A para.17.

# THE PROVISIONS

(c) the person is entitled to secure that income or assets (whether present or future) of the company will be applied directly or indirectly for the person's benefit; or

(d) the person, either alone or together with other persons, has control[45] of the company."

For these purposes, a person is "entitled" to do something if he is currently entitled to do it at a future date, or will at a future date be entitled to do it.

**9-058**

The scope of (c) above is uncertain in the context of transactions that are not loans of money to fund the acquisition of taxable property (so para.16(2)(b) will not apply) but that have a similar economic effect to loans and so the IRPS has purely contractual rights against the company. The wording in (c) above suggests that some security is required, but if the company is contractually obliged to make payments to the IRPS (or other investor), can it be said that the investor is entitled to secure that income or assets (whether present or future) of the company will be applied directly or indirectly for the investor's benefit? The better view is that security is required and mere contractual rights are not enough to cause a person to have an interest in a company. If (c) above applied in the absence of any security, it would potentially create issues for all occupational IRPS where the employer is contractually obliged to pay contributions to the IRPS. Similarly, as noted above, if (c) above applied in the absence of any security, most authorised employer loans which are not within para.16(2)(b) would give rise to unauthorised payments unless one of the exceptions to indirect holding apply (see below) (e.g. because the sponsoring employer is a trading vehicle), which seems unlikely.

**9-059**

**Interests in collective investment schemes** A person holds an interest in a collective investment scheme if the person is a participant in the scheme.[46]

**9-060**

**Interests in trusts** A pension scheme[47] holds an interest in a trust (other than a unit trust scheme[48]) if Condition A or B is met:[49]

**9-061**

(a) *Condition A* is that: (i) the pension scheme has a "relevant interest" in the trust; (ii) the pension scheme, a member of the pension scheme or a person connected with such a member has made a payment to the trust on or after the acquisition of the interest; and (iii) the payment is not an arm's length transaction to which para.19(7) applies (see below).

---

[45] "Control" has the meaning given by CTA 2010 ss.450 and 451.
[46] FA 2004 Sch.29A para.18. See FSMA 2000 s.235 for the meanings of "collective investment scheme" and "participant".
[47] Paragraph 19 is concerned solely with whether a *pension scheme* has an interest in a trust (in contrast to paras 17 and 18, which are concerned with whether a *person* holds an interest in a company or collective investment scheme). At first glance, it may be assumed that the reason for this was because the definition of "relevant interest" essentially traced through everyone between the trust and the scheme, but that is not the case. A scheme has a *relevant interest* if it may receive property from the trust (e.g. it is a beneficiary or potential beneficiary, or it has for example made a loan to the trust (subject to para.19(7))) or the scheme receives a benefit deriving directly or indirectly from the settled property. If the IRPS owns a company which is a beneficiary or has made a loan that is not caught, but if a payment is made from the trust to the company it could be said that this indirectly benefited the IRPS. This suggests that para.19 does not apply where the IRPS has an interest in a person which has an interest in a trust. Although, it is possible that this is a typographical error, as para.16(5) lumps paras 17–19 together as explaining what it means for a *person* to hold an interest in a trust.
[48] Paragraph 19 does not apply to a unit trust scheme (within the meaning of FSMA 2000 s.237(1)), which will be a collective investment scheme and so within the ambit of para.18.
[49] FA 2004 Sch.29A para.19.

(b) *Condition B* is that: (i) a member of the pension scheme or a person connected with such a member has a relevant interest in the trust; (ii) the pension scheme has made a payment to the trust on or after the acquisition of the interest; and (iii) the payment is not an arm's length transaction to which para.19(7) applies.

9-062　For the purposes of these conditions, a person other than the pension scheme holds an interest in a trust if: (a) the person has a relevant interest in the trust; (b) the person has made a payment to the trust on or after the acquisition of the interest; and (c) the payment is not an arm's length transaction to which para.19(7) applies. So, if the IRPS owns shares in a company, and that company is a beneficiary of a trust that holds taxable property, the IRPS will indirectly hold taxable property.

9-063　**"Relevant interest in a trust"**　A person has a relevant interest in a trust if either: (a) any property which may at any time be comprised in the trust or any *derived property* is, or will or may become, payable to or applicable for the benefit of the person in any circumstances; or (b) the person enjoys a benefit deriving directly or indirectly from any property which is comprised in the trust or any derived property. "Derived property" means, in relation to any property, income from that property or any other property directly or indirectly representing proceeds of, or income from, that property.

9-064　The test for whether a person has a relevant interest in a trust is therefore extremely broad. For example, if a lender makes a loan to trustees, the lender has a relevant interest in the trust because trust property would become payable to the lender. However, that may not matter because a pension scheme will not have an interest in a trust for the purposes of para.19(1) as a result of an arm's length transaction.

9-065　**Para.19(7): "arm's length transaction"**　Neither of Conditions A or B will be satisfied where a person has an interest in a trust only as a result of an arm's length transaction to which para.19(7) applies. Paragraph 19(7) applies to a payment if: (a) it is made as part of an arm's length transaction by which property or a benefit is to be provided in return for the payment, and (b) it is made otherwise than for the purposes of enabling a member of the pension scheme or a person connected with such a member to occupy or use any property. The words "property" and "benefit" suggests para.19(7) is aimed at purchases of goods or services, but it may be broad enough to cover a loan: the promise to repay being property provided in return for the payment. It should be noted that it does not provide that the property/benefit needs to be provided to the person making the payment.

9-066　**Conclusions on "holding an interest in another person" (in para.16(2))**　One would expect para.16 to be fairly wide reaching. However, a careful reading of para.16, especially in the light of paras 17–19, suggests that it may in fact be quite narrow. Paragraph 16(2)(b) applies only to loans to acquire taxable property, and there is an *arm's length* exemption in para.19(7). The overall impression is that para.16 will apply only where the scheme has a direct *ownership* interest in a vehicle which holds taxable property.[50] Contractual rights do not appear to be caught

---

[50] Or that vehicle holds a direct "ownership" interest in some sort of vehicle which holds taxable property (or another vehicle, and so on).

THE PROVISIONS                                                219

except where there is a loan to acquire an interest in taxable property.[51] Paragraph 17 (which appears to be exhaustive) generally supports this: share capital, voting rights, participation in distributions, rights over property of the company, and control of the company are all ownership-type interests (i.e. rights of ordinary shareholders) or rights that an owner has over the property of the company. The precise ambit of para.17(1)(c) is a little unclear, but it is arguable that it relates only to *security* type interests that are proprietary.

One concern with contractual rights is para.14(3): it is not at all clear how wide this is intended to be. Indeed, if para.16 is narrow then that may support a broad interpretation of para.14(3). However, it does seem clear that para.14(3) does not apply to the holding of shares in a company (unless there is also, for example a loan to the company). If that is correct then if a company owned by an IRPS lends money to a person (who must not be connected with the member or sponsoring employer) for any reason other than to acquire an interest in taxable property, that should not result in the provisions applying.

**9-067**

**Exceptions: indirect holding**  In contrast to direct holdings (where there is just one, fairly limited, exception), there are four relatively helpful exceptions to indirect holdings.

**9-068**

An IRPS does not hold an interest in property indirectly through a "vehicle" through which the IRPS would otherwise hold the interest in the property indirectly where one of the following applies:

(a) paragraph 21 (trading vehicles);
(b) paragraph 22 (Real Estate Investment Trusts);
(c) paragraph 23 (diverse investment vehicles); and
(d) paragraph 26 (life policies etc).

**"Vehicle"**  A "vehicle" means a person through whom the IRPS holds the interest in the property. A person holds an interest in a vehicle directly if the person holds an interest of the kind mentioned in para.16(2) in the vehicle (see above). A person holds an interest in a vehicle indirectly if the person does not hold the interest directly but:

**9-069**

"(a) holds an interest in a person who holds an interest in the vehicle directly, or
(b) holds an interest in a person who holds the interest in the vehicle indirectly by virtue of paragraph (a) or this paragraph."

**Trading vehicles**  The exception in Sch.29A para.21 applies to a vehicle in which an IRPS directly or indirectly holds an interest where:

**9-070**

(a) the vehicle's main activity is the carrying on of a trade, profession or vocation;
(b) the IRPS does not, whether alone or together with one or more associated persons (see below), have control[52] of the vehicle; and
(c) neither a member of the IRPS nor a person connected with such a member is a controlling director[53] of the vehicle or any other vehicle which holds an interest in the vehicle directly or indirectly.

---

[51] For reasons that are not entirely clear, loans are often given special treatment in pension investment provisions. See PA 1995 s.40 and The Occupational Pension Schemes (Investment) Regulations 2005 (SI 2005/3378).
[52] "Control" has the same meaning as in CTA 2010 ss.450 and 451 (i.e. broadly, shareholder control). These provisions only appear to apply in the context of control over companies.
[53] A "controlling director", in relation to a vehicle, means a director to whom CTA 2010 s.452(2)(b)

**9-071**  The exception expressly does not apply if one of the purposes for which the pension scheme holds the interest in the vehicle is to enable a member, or a person connected with a member, to occupy or use the property. An IRPS or an arrangement under an IRPS has "control" of a vehicle if the IRPS or the arrangement holds such interest as would, if the IRPS or the arrangement were a person, mean that the person had control of the vehicle. As a result of (b) and (c) above, para.21 is unlikely to have much application to schemes investing in companies connected with a member.

**9-072**  **Real Estate Investment Trusts**  The exception in Sch.29A para.22 applies to a vehicle in which an IRPS directly or indirectly holds an interest where the vehicle is a company/group which is a Real Estate Investment Trust and para.24 applies to the scheme's interest in the vehicle (see below).

**9-073**  **Diverse investment vehicles**  The exception in Sch.29A para.23 applies to a vehicle in which a pension scheme directly or indirectly holds an interest where Conditions A to C are met in relation to the vehicle, and para.24 applies to the pension scheme's interest in the vehicle (see below):

(a) *Condition A* is that: (i) the total value of the assets held directly by the vehicle is at least £1 million; or (ii) the vehicle holds directly at least three assets which consist of an interest in residential property, and no asset held directly by the vehicle which consists of an interest in taxable property has a value which exceeds 40% of the total value of the assets held directly by the vehicle. For these purposes, assets must be valued in accordance with generally accepted accounting practice, and where generally accepted accounting practice offers a choice of valuation between cost basis and fair value, fair value must be used. Importantly, no account is to be taken of liabilities secured against or otherwise relating to assets (whether generally or specifically).

(b) *Condition B* is that, if the vehicle is a company: (i) it is resident in the UK and is not a close company; or (ii) it is not resident in the UK and would not be a close company if it were resident in the UK.

(c) *Condition C* is that the vehicle does not have as its main purpose, or one of its main purposes, the direct or indirect holding of an animal or animals used for sporting purposes.

**9-074**  **Paragraph 24**  In order for the exception in Sch.29A para.22 (REITs) or para.23 (diverse investment vehicles) to apply, para.24 must also apply to the pension scheme's interest in the vehicle. Paragraph 24 applies if Condition A is met, and either Condition B or C is met:

(a) *Condition A* is that the IRPS does not hold the interest in the vehicle for the purpose of enabling a member of the IRPS or a person connected with such a member to occupy or use the property.

(b) *Condition B* is that the IRPS is an occupational pension scheme, and the IRPS does not, either alone or together with one or more associated persons, directly or indirectly hold an interest in the vehicle to which the following applies, that is to say: (i) 10% or more of the share capital or issued share capital of the vehicle; (ii) 10% or more of the voting rights in the vehicle;

---

applies (i.e. he is the beneficial owner of, or directly or indirectly able to control, at least 20% of the ordinary share capital of the company).

# THE PROVISIONS

(iii) a right to receive 10% or more of the income of the vehicle; (iv) such interest in the vehicle as gives an entitlement to 10% or more of the amounts distributed on a distribution in relation to the vehicle; (v) such interest in the vehicle as gives an entitlement to 10% or more of the assets of the vehicle on a winding-up or in any other circumstances; (vi) such interest in the vehicle as gives rise to income or gains from a specific property.

(c) *Condition C* is that the IRPS is not an occupational pension scheme, and no arrangement under the IRPS, either alone or together with one or more associated persons, directly or indirectly holds an interest in the vehicle to which (i)–(vi) in Condition B apply.

**9-075** Paragraph 25 supplements para.24. It provides that where Condition C is not met by an IRPS that is not an occupational pension scheme:

"the interest in the property is to be treated as held through the vehicle for the purposes of another arrangement under the pension scheme only if that arrangement, either alone or together with one or more associated persons, directly or indirectly holds an interest in the vehicle to which [(a) to (f) in Condition B apply]."

**9-076** It is not at all clear what this is intended to mean. For example, is it saying that, where more than one arrangement holds an interest in the vehicle, the only arrangement that is relevant is the one to which (a)–(f) in Condition B apply? And if there is more than one arrangement to which (a)–(f) apply, how does one determine which one is relevant?

**9-077** Where it is necessary to determine the percentage of an interest held by a person in a vehicle at a time when the person holds that interest indirectly: that percentage is equal to the percentage of the total taxable amount that would be apportioned to the person under paras 41–43: (a) where the person is not the IRPS, if the person were the IRPS; and (b) in any case, if the person were treated as making an unauthorised payment by virtue of the vehicle coming to hold the interest in the property directly at that time.

**9-078** For the purposes of paras 24 and 25, any increase in the extent of the interest held directly in the vehicle without the acquisition of a further interest in the vehicle is ignored unless the event by which the extent of the interest held directly in the vehicle increases forms part of a scheme or arrangement the main purpose or one of the main purposes of which is: (a) to enable the amount of the unauthorised payment treated as arising on the original acquisition of the interest in the property by the pension scheme to be lower than it otherwise would have been; or (b) to prevent an unauthorised payment from being treated as made on that original acquisition.[54] HMRC provide the following example:[55]

"A person has an interest in an open ended investment company of 8% and, because other investors reduce their holdings in the company the interest rises to 40%. Unless this is part of a scheme to avoid an unauthorised payments charge this increase will not create an unauthorised payment."

**9-079 Life policies etc** The exception in Sch.29A para.26 applies to a vehicle in which a pension scheme directly or indirectly holds an interest where:

(a) the vehicle holds the interest in the property directly by virtue of para.14(3) merely because it does not meet Condition C in para.15(4), and (b) the following applies in relation to the pension scheme;

---

[54] FA 2004 Sch.29A para.29.
[55] See PTM125400.

(b) where the pension scheme is an occupational pension scheme, the pension scheme is not, either alone or together with one or more associated persons, deemed to be entitled to 10% or more of the market value of or the income from the property; or

(c) where the pension scheme is not an occupational pension scheme, no arrangement under the pension scheme, either alone or together with one or more associated persons, is deemed to be so entitled.

**9-080** The percentage of the market value of or the income from the property to which a person is deemed to be entitled at any time is equal to "IG x ITA", where:

- *IG* is the percentage of the market value of or the income from the property to which the vehicle that holds the interest in the property directly is entitled at that time; and
- *ITA* is the percentage of the total taxable amount that would be apportioned to the person at that time on the following assumptions:
  (a) if the person is not the pension scheme, that the person is the pension scheme; and
  (b) in any case, that the person is treated as making an unauthorised payment by virtue of the vehicle coming to hold the interest in the property directly at that time.

**9-081** For the purposes of para.26, any increase in the extent of the interest held directly in the vehicle without the acquisition of a further interest in the vehicle is ignored unless the event by which the extent of the interest held directly in the vehicle increases forms part of a scheme or arrangement the main purpose or one of the main purposes of which is: (a) to enable the amount of the unauthorised payment treated as arising on the original acquisition of the interest in the property by the pension scheme to be lower than it otherwise would have been; or (b) to prevent an unauthorised payment from being treated as made on that original acquisition.[56] HMRC provide the following example:[57]

> "A person has an interest in an open ended investment company of 8% and, because other investors reduce their holdings in the company the interest rises to 40%. Unless this is part of a scheme to avoid an unauthorised payments charge this increase will not create an unauthorised payment."

**9-082** **"Associated persons"** The following are "associated persons", in relation to a pension scheme:[58] (a) any member of the pension scheme; (b) any person connected with such a member; (c) any arrangement (under that or another pension scheme) relating to a member of the pension scheme; (d) any arrangement (under that or another pension scheme) relating to a person connected with such a member; and (e) any associated pension scheme.

**9-083** A pension scheme is associated with another pension scheme if members representing at least 10% by value of one pension scheme are members of the other pension scheme or connected with such members. The percentage by value represented by a member of a pension scheme is: "(AM/AA) x 100 where *AM* is an amount equal to the aggregate of the amount of the sums and the market value of the assets held for the purposes of an arrangement under the pension scheme relating to the member, and *AA* is an amount equal to the aggregate of the amount

---

[56] FA 2004 Sch.29A para.29.
[57] See PTM125400.
[58] FA 2004 Sch.29A para.30.

of the sums and the market value of the assets held for the purposes of the pension scheme".

An associated person, in relation to an arrangement under a pension scheme, means: (a) the member of the pension scheme to which that arrangement relates; (b) any person connected with such a member; (c) any arrangement (under that or another pension scheme) relating to a member of the pension scheme to which that arrangement relates; and (d) any arrangement (under that or another pension scheme) relating to a person connected with such a member.

9-084

## DEEMED UNAUTHORISED PAYMENT (S.174A)

By FA 2004 s.174A, an IRPS is deemed to make an unauthorised payment to a member of the scheme in the following three circumstances:

9-085

(a) the IRPS "acquires" an interest in taxable property, and the interest is held by the IRPS for the purposes of an arrangement under the IRPS relating to the member;
(b) an interest in taxable property is held by the IRPS for the purposes of an arrangement under the IRPS relating to the member, and the property is "improved"; or
(c) an interest in property which is not residential property is held by the IRPS for the purposes of an arrangement under the IRPS relating to the member, and the property is "converted or adapted" to become residential property.

Section 174A does not apply to taxable property held within a general fund under an IRPS, because such an interest is not "held for the purposes of an arrangement under the IRPS relating to a member".[59] However, in these circumstances a deeming provision applies unless the interest in taxable property is held "for the purposes of the administration or management of the pension scheme".[60]

9-086

### Acquiring

For the purposes of s.174A(1)(a), an IRPS "acquires" an interest in property if it comes to hold the interest, no matter how that happens.[61] An acquisition by a person in which the IRPS holds an interest (such as a company in which the IRPS owns shares), is an indirect acquisition by the IRPS. In addition, there are two circumstances in which an IRPS is *deemed* to acquire an interest in taxable property.

9-087

First, where an IRPS holds an interest in property which is not taxable property, and that property becomes taxable property otherwise than by reason of its conversion or adaptation as residential property,[62] the IRPS is deemed to acquire an interest in the property at that time.[63] This would happen, for example, where an IRPS holds an interest in residential property that is let to an employee of the sponsoring employer who is required to occupy it as a condition of his employment (so the exemption in Sch.29A para.10(2) applies) and the property is subsequently let to

9-088

---

[59] The meaning of "arrangement", see Ch.2.
[60] FA 2004 Sch.29A para.5. See above.
[61] FA 2004 Sch.29A para.12.
[62] Converting or adapting property so that it becomes residential property is dealt with separately in s.174A(3), so it is excluded from s.174A(1).
[63] FA 2004 Sch.29A para.27.

someone else so that the exemption ceases to apply.[64] It would also happen where tangible property is modified to become moveable property.

**9-089**  Secondly, an IRPS is deemed to acquire an interest in the taxable property if the IRPS holds an interest in taxable property indirectly, and there is:[65]

(a) an increase in the extent of the interest held directly by the IRPS; or
(b) an increase in the extent of the interest held directly by another vehicle in which the IRPS holds an interest.

**9-090**  This could happen, for example, where the IRPS owns some of the shares issued by a company that holds taxable property, and the IRPS acquires more shares in that company (or where the IRPS owns shares in a company and that company owns shares in a second company that holds taxable property, and the first company acquires more shares in the second company). However, if there is such an increase without the acquisition of a further interest in the vehicle, there is no deemed acquisition unless the event giving rise to the increase forms part of a scheme or arrangement the main purpose or one of the main purposes of which is to enable the amount of the unauthorised payment treated as arising on the original acquisition of the interest in the property by the pension scheme to be lower than it otherwise would have been (or to prevent an unauthorised payment on that original acquisition). HMRC suggest that an example of this would be where a pension scheme (or vehicle in which the pension scheme holds an interest) has an interest in an open-ended investment company of 8% and, because other investors reduce their holdings in the company the interest rises to 40%.[66] This increase will not constitute the acquisition of an interest in taxable property (and therefore, a deemed unauthorised payment) unless it is part of a scheme to avoid an unauthorised payments charge.

*Amount and timing of the unauthorised payment*

**9-091**  Once it is established that an IRPS holds taxable property for the purposes of a member's arrangement, s.174A applies to create a deemed unauthorised member payment. In order to calculate the unauthorised payments charge it is necessary to determine the *amount* of the unauthorised payment which is deemed to have been made to the member. Part 4 of Sch.29A, as modified by the Pension Schemes (Taxable Property Provisions) Regulations 2006 (SI 2006/1958), specify how to determine the amount of the unauthorised payment, and the time at which the payment is deemed to have been made.

**9-092**  In order to determine the amount of the unauthorised payment, the following four steps are involved:[67]

(a) find the total taxable amount in relation to the unauthorised payment;
(b) apportion the total taxable amount to the pension scheme;
(c) in a case where there is a deemed acquisition under para.28 (see above), adjust the amount in (b) above; and

---

[64] See PTM125300.
[65] FA 2004 Sch.29A para.28.
[66] PTM125400.
[67] FA 2004 Sch.29A para.31(2).

# DEEMED UNAUTHORISED PAYMENT (S.174A)

(d) apportion the amount to the relevant member(s).

*The total taxable amount*

It will be recalled that s.174A is concerned with: (a) the *acquisition* of taxable property; (b) the *improvement* of taxable property; and (c) the *conversion* of property into residential property. The method for determining the total taxable amount depends on which activity gives rise to the deemed unauthorised payment.

9-093

In the context of an acquisition, the method for determining the total taxable amount depends on how the interest in the property is acquired. In particular, it depends on whether the IRPS:

9-094

(a) directly acquires an interest in taxable property;
(b) indirectly acquires an interest in taxable property; or
(c) is deemed to acquire an interest in taxable property.

The relevant provisions are set out at Sch.29A paras 32–35 and SI 2006/1958 regs 3–9. In each case, the deemed unauthorised payment is made at the time that the interest in the property is acquired (or deemed to be acquired) by the IRPS.[68]

9-095

Where a part interest in taxable property is acquired, the total taxable amount only relates to "the interest" acquired. So, for example, if taxable property is held by the IRPS and another person as tenant in common in equal shares, the total taxable amount only relates to the part interest which is acquired by the IRPS. If property is held as joint tenants (which would be extremely unusual in this context) rather than tenants in common, it seems that the *interest* will be entire interest in the taxable property because, as a matter of general law, each joint tenant holds the entirety of the property. The provisions do not expressly make this point, but when read as a whole it becomes reasonably clear that this must be correct.

9-096

*Direct acquisitions of taxable property*

Where an interest in the property is acquired because the IRPS or another person comes to hold the interest *directly* the total taxable amount is the amount of consideration, in money or money's worth, given directly or indirectly for the interest, plus the amount of any fees and other costs incurred in connection with the acquisition.[69] So, in the context of a straightforward acquisition of taxable property (either by the IRPS or by a person in which the IRPS holds an interest), the total taxable amount is simply what is paid for the taxable property. However, special rules apply to determine the amount of the consideration given:

9-097

(a) in certain limited circumstances where the interest is acquired for less than its market value (in which case para.35 applies);
(b) if a chargeable interest is acquired and some or all of the consideration is not rent (in which case para.33 applies); or
(c) if a chargeable interest is acquired and some or all of the consideration is rent (in which case para.34 applies).

Although para.32(4) provides that the *money or money's worth* rule is "subject to" these special rules applying, it is reasonably clear that the draftsman intended this to mean, "subject to any increase" under those special rules. For example, in the context of a straightforward purchase of residential property for monetary consideration, para.33 would clearly apply, but the consideration as determined in

9-098

---

[68] FA 2004 Sch.29A para.32(2).
[69] FA 2004 Sch.29A para.32(3).

accordance with para.33 would be nil (because, as is explained below, para.33 only deals with non-standard consideration). In these circumstances, the *money or money's worth* rule must apply. This issue does not affect para.34 (where it applies), because the provisions in para.34 allow one to determine the consideration in all situations.

9-099 Where more than one of the special rules applies, it is not clear how the provisions are intended to interact. It seems likely that one determines the consideration in accordance with the *money or money's worth* rule and any applicable special rules to determine which produces the greatest amount of consideration, and that is the total taxable amount.

*Certain acquisitions for less than market value consideration*

9-100 If the interest is acquired for less than its market value,[70] and either: (a) immediately before the acquisition the interest was held by a registered pension scheme which was not an IRPS; or (b) tax relief is available under s.188 or s.196 in respect of the transfer of the interest,[71] the amount of the consideration for the interest is deemed to be the market value, at the date the interest is acquired, of the interest in the property held by the person who holds it directly.

9-101 However, if the interest in the property is a lease at a rent (i.e. the IRPS or other person acquires the lease directly and is required to pay rent to the lessee), the amount of the consideration for the interest is the amount of consideration that would be treated as given by the person for the lease by virtue of para.34 if it were assigned to the IRPS (or other person) at that time. This involves applying the provisions in para.34 (see below) to determine the rent payable under the lease and then using the formula in FA 2003 Sch.5 para.3 to calculate the relevant rental value.

*Paragraph 33*

9-102 Paragraph 33 of Sch.29A (and also para.34, considered below) incorporate a number of SDLT provisions. SDLT is chargeable by reference to the "chargeable consideration" given, or deemed to have been given, for the acquisition of a "chargeable interest". A *chargeable interest* means: (a) an estate, interest, right or power in or over land; or (b) the benefit of an obligation, restriction or condition affecting the value of any such estate, interest, right or power, other than an "exempt interest".[72] The following are exempt interests: any "security interest", a tenancy at will, an advowson, franchise or manor. A *security interest* means an interest or right (other than a rent charge) held for the purpose of securing the payment of money or the performance of any other obligation. As is explained below, the definition of chargeable interest is extended considerably for the purposes of the taxable property provisions.

9-103 Paragraph 33 of Sch.29A applies if the IRPS acquires an interest in taxable property because it acquires a *chargeable interest* in the property and some or all of the consideration for the interest is consideration other than rent. If it applies the

---

[70] The market value of taxable property is determined in accordance with TCGA 1992 s.272 (FA 2004 s.278(3A)). See Ch.2.
[71] This is a curious provision, because: (a) it is not possible to obtain tax relief under s.188 in respect of *in specie* contributions (except for eligible shares); and (b) s.196 does not have the effect of providing tax relief: it merely modifies some of the rules that apply to determine whether a tax deduction is available in respect of employer contributions to registered pension schemes. In order for this provision to make sense, (b) must be read as referring to a tax deduction under any relevant provision (rather than s.196).
[72] FA 2003 s.48.

amount of the consideration (or the part of the consideration that is not rent) is determined in accordance with the following provisions in FA 2003 as they apply for determining the amount of chargeable consideration for SDLT purposes: FA 2003 ss.51 and 52 and Sch.4 paras 2–8 and 9–19. In outline, these provisions contain special rules about how to determine the chargeable consideration where the consideration given: (a) includes VAT; (b) is postponed; (c) relates to more than one transaction; (d) comprises an exchange of property; (e) comprises a partition; (f) is non-monetary; (g) comprises of the satisfaction, release or assumption of debt; (h) comprises foreign currency; (i) consists of the provision of works or services; (j) relates to transactions entered into by reason of employment; and (k) consists of an indemnity. Section 51 applies where there is contingent, uncertain or unascertained consideration, and FA 2003 s.52 applies where the consideration consists of an annuity. So para.33 is only concerned with non-standard circumstances, where the usual *money or money's worth* rule is considered to be inappropriate and so is modified.

SI 2006/1958 reg.5 provides that para.33 applies to the following as it applies to a chargeable interest in property: (a) tangible moveable property; (b) a licence to use or occupy residential property if the consideration is wholly or partly other than rent; and (c) the right to use, or participate in arrangements relating to the use of, taxable property or a description of taxable property to which the property in question belongs, for a consideration which is wholly or partly rent. This regulation therefore dramatically extends the meaning of *chargeable interest*.   9-104

In order for para.33 to apply, the IRPS must acquire a chargeable interest in taxable property (para.33(1)(a)), and the interest must be acquired because the IRPS *or another person* comes to hold the interest directly (para.33(1)(b)). It is difficult to envisage a situation in which the IRPS acquires a chargeable interest (as defined above) without *directly* acquiring the taxable property. Accordingly, para.33 will have little application where the IRPS indirectly acquires the taxable property.   9-105

One point should be noted regarding the territorial application of these provisions. FA 2003 s.48 applies only to land in England and Northern Ireland, and for the purposes of the taxable property provisions, this is extended by SI 2006/1958 reg.3 to land "outside of the United Kingdom". Accordingly, para.33 (and also para.34, considered below) applies to an acquisition of land everywhere in the world except Scotland or Wales.[73]   9-106

*Security interests*

If an IRPS takes security over taxable property it will usually acquire an interest in that property[74] without giving any consideration for the acquisition. In such circumstances the total taxable amount is nil unless the IRPS incurs any fees or costs associated with putting the security in place.[75] A security interest is not a *chargeable interest* and so para.33 will not apply. If the IRPS enforces the security and thereby acquires a chargeable interest in the taxable property then para.33 will   9-107

---

[73] This is clearly an error. Prior to 1 April 2015, FA 2003 s.48 applied to land in Scotland in the same way as the rest of the UK. On that date, the Scotland Act 2012 introduced the Scottish land and buildings transaction tax, and removed land in Scotland from the scope of SDLT. FA 2003 s.48 ceased to apply to land in Wales from 1 April 2018 (Wales Act 2014 s.16(2)), whereupon the Welsh land transaction tax commenced). The Treasury has the power to introduce regulations remedying this under FA 2004 Sch.29A para.33(4). Until they do so, paras 33 and 34 do not apply to acquisitions of land in Scotland or Wales.

[74] Taking security over taxable property will involve a direct holding pursuant to FA 2004 Sch.29A para.14(1)(a) or (b).

[75] Pursuant to the basic position, set out in para.32(3) of Sch.29A.

apply at that time and the total taxable amount is the amount of the debt that is satisfied by the acquisition of the taxable property.[76] If enforcing the security does not discharge the debt (i.e. the debt continues to exist but the lender may use the sale proceeds to discharge the debt) para.33 would not appear to apply, and so the total taxable amount will be limited to the costs and expenses of enforcing security.[77]

**9-108** However, where security is taken over taxable property, there appears to be no reason that ss.185A and 185F FA 2004 would not apply (see below).

*Paragraph 34*

**9-109** Paragraph 34 of Sch.29A provides that if the IRPS acquires an interest in taxable property because it acquires a chargeable interest in the property and the whole or part of the consideration for the acquisition is rent, the amount of the consideration (or the part of the consideration that is rent) is the *relevant rental value* of the property. As with para.33, a number of SDLT provisions are incorporated. The relevant rental value is the net present value of the rent payable over the term of the lease[78] and the formula for calculating net present value is set out in FA 2003 Sch.5 para.3. This includes a *temporal discount rate* of 3.5%.[79] The way this formula works is complex, but HMRC have an online calculator that may be used to determine the net present value of rent for SDLT purposes.[80]

**9-110** "Chargeable interest" has the same meaning as in para.33, except that it does not include a licence to use or occupy residential property or the right to use, or participate in arrangements relating to the use of, taxable property.[81]

**9-111** The following provisions in FA 2003 apply for the purposes of determining the amount of rent payable as they apply for determining the amount of rent payable under a lease to which FA 2003 applies: paras 2, 5–7A, 9 and 16 of Sch.17A, and (subject to those provisions) paras 2–8 and 9–16 of Sch.4, s.51, and s.52 (all referred to in para.33 and outlined above). These provisions contain special rules about how to determine the amount of rent payable where: (a) a fixed-term lease contains a contingency; (b) there are successive linked leases; (c) the lease continues after a fixed term; (d) the rent is payable for other matters; (e) the rent is variable or uncertain; (f) there is a first rent review in final quarter of fifth year; (g) there is an overlap period in case of grant of further lease; or (h) there is a surrender of an existing lease in return for a new lease. Paragraphs 3(1), 3(2), 4(1), 4(2), 8(1) and 8(2) of Sch.17A, which contain provisions relating to leases that continue after a fixed period, and leases for an indefinite term, and an adjustment when rent ceases to be uncertain, also apply as modified by SI 2006/1958 regs 7 and 8. Where on an assignment of a lease the assignee assumes the obligation to pay rent, the assumption counts as consideration for the assignment.

**9-112** As with para.33, para.34 is only concerned with non-standard circumstances, where the usual "money or money's worth" rule is considered to be inappropriate and so is modified. If leasehold property is acquired for money consideration at a peppercorn rent, para.34 will have no application.

---

[76] FA 2003 Sch.4 para.8(1), as applied by FA 2004 Sch.29A para.33(3)(a).
[77] HMRC agree at PTM125300 (relating to charging orders).
[78] FA 2003 Sch.5 para.2(4)(a).
[79] FA 2003 Sch.5 para.8(1).
[80] See *https://www.tax.service.gov.uk/calculate-stamp-duty-land-tax/#/intro*.
[81] FA 2003 s.48(1), as extended by SI 2006/1958 reg.6.

# DEEMED UNAUTHORISED PAYMENT (S.174A)

*Variations of leases*

SI 2006/1958 reg.9 provides that an IRPS is deemed to make an unauthorised payment within s.174A(1) to a member of the IRPS if a lease of taxable property is varied so as to increase the amount of the rent and the increase is *abnormal*.[82] Such a variation is deemed to be a grant of a lease in consideration of the additional rent made payable by the variation. Regulation 9 does not say so expressly, but presumably it is only intended to apply where: (a) the interest in the lease is held by the IRPS; and (b) the interest is held by the IRPS for the purposes of an arrangement relating to a member.

**9-113**

*Indirect acquisitions of taxable property*

If the interest in the property is acquired because the IRPS or another person acquires an interest in a person that already holds an interest in the taxable property (directly or indirectly), the total taxable amount is the market value, at the date the interest in the person is acquired, of the interest in the property held by the person who holds it directly. So, for example, if two companies each own 50% of a residential property and an IRPS acquires all of the shares in one of those companies, the total taxable amount is the market value of the 50% of the taxable property held by that company at the time that the shares are acquired by the IRPS.

**9-114**

However, if the interest in the property is a lease at a rent, the total taxable amount is the amount of consideration that is deemed to be given by the person for the lease by virtue of para.34 if it were assigned to the person at that time. This involves applying the provisions in para.34 (see above) to determine the rent payable under the lease and then using the formula in FA 2003 Sch.5 para.3 to calculate the relevant rental value.

**9-115**

*Deemed acquisitions of taxable property*

If there is a deemed acquisition under para.27 (because property becomes taxable property otherwise than by reason of its conversion or adaption as residential property) or under para.28 (because the IRPS holds the interest indirectly and there is an increase in the extent of the interest), the total taxable amount is the market value, at the date the interest is deemed to be acquired, of the interest in the property held by the person who holds it directly.

**9-116**

However, as above, if the interest in the property is a lease at a rent, the total taxable amount in relation is the amount of consideration that would be treated as given by the person for the lease by virtue of para.34 if it were assigned to the person at that time. This involves applying the provisions in para.34 (see above) to determine the rent payable under the lease and then using the formula in FA 2003 Sch.5 para.3 to calculate the relevant rental value.

**9-117**

**Improvements**

Where s.174A applies because taxable property is *improved*, the total taxable amount is the amount of any payment made in connection with the improvement works.[83] The unauthorised payment is deemed to be made when a payment is made

**9-118**

---

[82] Within the meaning of FA 2003 Sch.17A para.15.
[83] FA 2004 Sch.29A para.38(3).

in connection with the improvement works.[84] There is no express requirement that the payment is made by the IRPS, although as a matter of principle there is no reason that a payment by anyone else should be relevant. No guidance is provided regarding the concept *of improvement*, and it is not difficult to envisage circumstances in which expenditure is incurred for works that do not involve any objective *improvement* of the property.

**Conversion or adaption as residential property**

9-119   Where s.174A applies because property is *converted* or *adapted* so as to become residential property, the method for determining the total taxable amount depends on *when* the work commenced. If the work commenced within 12 months of the acquisition of the interest in the property by the IRPS then the total taxable amount is the amount of consideration for the interest, determined in accordance with paras 32–36 (all considered above in the context of acquisitions), plus the development costs. If the work did not commence within 12 months, the total taxable amount is the relevant market value plus the development costs.

9-120   The *relevant market value* is the market value,[85] at the date the works began, of the interest in the property held by the person who holds it directly. However, if the interest in the property is a lease at a rent, it is the amount of consideration that would be treated as given by the person for the lease by virtue of para.34 if it were assigned to the person at that time. This involves applying the provisions in para.34 (see above) to determine the rent payable under the lease and then using the formula in FA 2003 Sch.5 para.3 to calculate the relevant rental value.

9-121   The *development costs* are the total cost of the works to convert or adapt the property at the time when the unauthorised payment is deemed to have been made. If any of the development costs are only payable if some uncertain future event occurs, or will cease to be payable if some uncertain future event occurs, the development costs are determined on the assumption that the amount will be payable or, as the case may be, will not cease to be payable. Where an amount payable depends on uncertain future events, or cannot otherwise be ascertained, that amount is determined on the basis of a reasonable estimate.

9-122   Where an amount estimated later becomes ascertained, and the ascertained amount is more than the estimated amount, an unauthorised payment is deemed to be made when the amount becomes ascertained. The total taxable amount is the difference between the ascertained amount and the estimated amount.[86] References in the taxable property provisions to unauthorised payments treated as made under s.174A include references to such unauthorised payments.

9-123   As with acquisitions within s.174A(1), it is important to appreciate that the total taxable amount relates to the *interest* converted or adapted, and this means the interest in taxable property held directly or indirectly by the IRPS. So, for example, if an IRPS and an unconnected person hold property as tenants in common with the IRPS owning 5% and it is converted into residential property, the total taxable amount only relates to the 5% interest. However, as with improvements within s.174A(2) there is no express requirement that the development costs must be paid by the IRPS, although as a matter of principle there is no reason that a payment by anyone else should be taxable.

---

[84] FA 2004 Sch.29A para.38(2).
[85] The market value of taxable property is determined in accordance with TCGA 1992 s.272 (FA 2004 s.278(3A)). See Ch.2.
[86] FA 2004 Sch.29A para.40.

## DEEMED UNAUTHORISED PAYMENT (S.174A)

*Timing*

For a conversion or adaptation as residential property within s.174A(3), the unauthorised payment is deemed to be made on the occurrence of whichever of the following first occurs after the property has become residential property: (a) the substantial completion of the works to convert or adapt the property; and (b) the interest in the property ceasing to be held by the pension scheme.[87] However, if the property becomes residential property after the end of the period of three years beginning with the date on which the first payment was made in connection with the works to convert or adapt the property, the unauthorised payment is treated as made when the property becomes residential property.[88]

**9-124**

**Apportionment to the pension scheme**

Paragraph 41 of Sch.29A prescribes how one is to apportion the total taxable amount to the IRPS. As one would expect, the whole of the total taxable amount is apportioned to the IRPS if the IRPS directly holds the interest in the taxable property, or if the IRPS holds the interest in the property indirectly through: (a) one vehicle and the vehicle is wholly owned by the IRPS; or (b) more than one vehicle and each vehicle in the *chain* is wholly owned by another vehicle in the chain or by the IRPS. For these purposes, a vehicle is *wholly owned* by a person if no other person directly holds an interest in that vehicle.

**9-125**

Where the IRPS holds the interest in the property indirectly through one vehicle, and the vehicle is not wholly owned by the IRPS, the amount apportioned to the IRPS is a proportion of the total taxable amount determined by reference to the extent of the pension scheme's interest in the vehicle. So, for example, where an IRPS is a beneficiary under a discretionary trust and the trustees purchase an interest in taxable property the total taxable amount relates to the entire interest acquired by the trust, but the amount apportioned to the IRPS under para.41 will be negligible.

**9-126**

Where the IRPS holds the interest in the property indirectly through one or more chains of vehicles, and one or more vehicles in such a chain is not wholly owned by another vehicle in the chain or by the IRPS, the amount of the unauthorised payment is the following amount or the total of all the following amounts for each chain through which the IRPS owns the interest in the property. The amount is a proportion of the total taxable amount determined by reference to the extent of the interest held directly by the IRPS or another vehicle in the chain in each vehicle in the chain: (a) starting with the vehicle which holds the interest in the property directly; and (b) ending with the vehicle in which the IRPS directly holds an interest.

**9-127**

However, where an IRPS is deemed to have acquired an interest in taxable property by virtue of para.28 (because the IRPS holds the interest indirectly and there is an increase in the extent of the interest: see above), the amount of the deemed unauthorised payment is equal to "UP - UPB", where:

**9-128**

- *UP* is the amount that would otherwise have been the amount of the unauthorised payment; and
- *UPB* is the amount that would have been the amount of any unauthorised payment treated as made by the IRPS if it had acquired the interest in the property immediately before the increase in the extent of the interest in the

---

[87] FA 2004 Sch.29A para.39(2).
[88] FA 2004 Sch.29A para.39(3).

vehicle (assuming the total taxable amount in relation to the unauthorised payment to be that given under para.32(5)).

*"Extent" of an interest*

**9-129** The extent of an interest held directly by a person in a vehicle *other than a company* is the proportion of the interests of everyone who directly holds an interest in the vehicle which on a just and reasonable apportionment is represented by that interest.[89]

**9-130** The extent of a person's interest *in a company* is determined by reference to whichever of the following gives the person the greatest interest in the company:[90]

(a) the percentage of the share capital or issued share capital of the company owned by the person;
(b) the percentage of the voting rights in the company owned by the person;
(c) the percentage of all the income of the company to which the person has a right;
(d) the percentage of the amounts distributed on a distribution in relation to the company to which the person has a right;
(e) the percentage of the assets of the company to which the person has a right on a winding-up or in any other circumstances; or
(f) where the person has a right to a percentage of a particular asset or description of assets of the company, or of the income or gains from such an asset or description (either generally or in particular circumstances), that percentage or the highest of all the percentages found under this paragraph.

**9-131** A person is treated as owning or having a right to anything which the person will only acquire at some future date, or if the person exercises a right to acquire it, or if some other uncertain future event occurs or does not occur.

**9-132** However, where a person has an interest in a company as a result of lending the company money to fund the acquisition of an interest in taxable property,[91] the extent of the person's interest in the company is determined by the proportion that the value of the loan bears to the total value of the assets held directly by the company, if that gives the person a greater interest in the company than any interest given above. For these purposes, assets must be valued in accordance with generally accepted accounting practice, no account is to be taken of liabilities secured against or otherwise relating to assets (whether generally or specifically), and where generally accepted accounting practice offers a choice of valuation between cost basis and fair value, fair value must be used.

*Apportionment to member*

**9-133** The whole of the unauthorised payment is deemed to have been made to the member if it is held by the IRPS for the purpose of an arrangement relating to the member.[92] If the interest is held by the IRPS for the purposes of more than one arrangement, the unauthorised payment is apportioned on a just and reasonable basis between those arrangements.

---

[89] FA 2004 Sch.29A para.42.
[90] FA 2004 Sch.29A para.43.
[91] See FA 2004 Sch.29A para.16(2)(b).
[92] FA 2004 Sch.29A para.45.

# SCHEME CHARGEABLE PAYMENT UNDER S.185A

If an IRPS directly or indirectly holds an interest in taxable property in a tax year it is deemed to make a scheme chargeable payment under FA 2004 s.185A.[93] These provisions apply irrespective of whether any actual income or profits relating to the taxable property are received by anyone. The term "scheme-held taxable property" is used frequently in these provisions. It means taxable property in which the IRPS directly or indirectly holds an interest. If the IRPS holds the interest in the property indirectly for the whole of the period in the tax year for which the property is scheme-held taxable property, then there is an apportionment to the IRPS.

9-134

### Amount of the scheme chargeable payment

If any person who holds an interest in the property directly receives profits arising from the interest in the tax year, the amount of the scheme chargeable payment is the greater of:

9-135

(a) the annual profits from the interest; and
(b) the amount of the deemed profits from the interest.

If no such person receives any profits arising from the interest in the tax year, the amount of the scheme chargeable payment is the amount of the deemed profits from the interest in the property for the year. So, in all cases one is simply concerned with the actual or deemed profits received by any person who holds a direct interest in the taxable property. Any profits received by any person who holds an indirect interest are not taken into account.

### The annual profits

The *annual profits* from the interest are the total profits received from the interest in the tax year by each person who holds the interest directly at a time when the property is scheme-held taxable property. The reference to *profits* rather than *income* indicates that any expenses associated with the income (for example, finance costs associated with rental income) will reduce the annual profits, but it is unfortunate that the legislation does not specify how one is to calculate the profits for these purposes.

9-136

If the taxable property forms part of the stock in trade of the person who directly holds the taxable property then it seems that the profits of the trader on a sale of the taxable property will be *annual profits*. However, profits are only annual profits if they are *from the interest* in taxable property. It seems clear that any profits received by a person in his capacity as owner of the interest in taxable property will be caught, but it may be possible in certain circumstances to separate the profits into *ownership* profits and *development* profits (for example) and argue that only the former profits are annual profits.

9-137

### The amount of the deemed profits

The amount of the deemed profits from the interest in the property for the tax year is 10% of the *deemed market value* of the taxable property. If the taxable property is not scheme-held taxable property for the entire year then it is apportioned on a

9-138

---

[93] The scheme administrator must notify HMRC of any scheme chargeable payments under SI 2006/567 reg.3.

time basis. There are special rules that apply where the person who holds the interest in the property directly does so by virtue of a lease of residential property, and these are considered below.

**9-139** In circumstances other than where the direct holder has a lease of the residential property, the deemed market value of the interest for the year is "(MV + UP) x (1 + RPI)", where:

- *MV* is the "opening market value", which means the deemed market value of the interest for the previous tax year. If the property was not scheme-held taxable property immediately before the beginning of the tax year, it means the market value of the interest in the property when the property first became scheme-held taxable property.
- *UP* is the total of any unauthorised payments treated as made by the pension scheme under s.174A in relation to the property in the tax year, other than any such payment treated as made by virtue of the property becoming scheme-held taxable property in the year. This will therefore be zero unless there has been any improvement to or further acquisition of an interest in the taxable property in the tax year. In which case it is the total of any unauthorised payments treated as made by the pension scheme in respect of the improvements or further interests acquired.
- *RPI* is the percentage increase in the retail prices index (expressed as a decimal) from the first day in the tax year that the scheme held the taxable property interest and the last day of that tax year. If there is no such increase, this is nil.

**9-140** For example,[94] suppose an IRPS acquires some plant and machinery on 1 September 2015 with a market value of £100,000. It is leased to a business at an initial rent net of expenses of £7,000 per annum. The net rent increases in 2016/17 to £10,500. The RPI increase from acquisition to 5 April 2016 is 5.3%. The RPI increase for 2016/17 is 6.2%.[95]

"The deemed value is (£100,000 + 0) x (1 + 0.053) = £105,300
Deemed income is £105,300 x 10% x 217/365 = £6,260
(The scheme only holds the taxable property for 217 days so the deemed income is apportioned)
Actual net income is £7,000 x 7/12 = £4,083
The scheme chargeable payment is the deemed net income received of £6,260 (the deemed income amount is greater than the actual net income received).
The deemed value is (£105,300 + 0) x (1 + 0.062) = £111,828
Deemed income is £111,828 x 10% = £11,182
Actual net income is £10,500
The scheme chargeable payment is the deemed net income received of £11,182 (the deemed income amount is greater than the actual net income received)."

### Leases of residential property

**9-141** Where a person who holds the interest in the property directly does so by virtue of a lease of residential property, the deemed market value of the interest for the year is the *relevant rental value* of the property. This is calculated in accordance with FA 2004 Sch.29A para.34 on the assumption that: (a) the lease was granted

---

[94] This example is based on an example provided by HMRC at PTM125300, however HMRC's example is liable to confuse as it appears to relate to a lease of residential property, where the calculation is different.

[95] Both RPI figures are used for illustrative purposes only.

when the property first became scheme-held taxable property; (b) the term of the lease is 50 years; (c) a fully commercial rent is payable for the first five years of that term; and (d) afterwards the rent is reviewed on an upwards-only basis.

As is explained above, Sch.29A para.34 incorporates a number of SDLT provisions from FA 2003. It provides that the *relevant rental value* of property is the net present value of the rent payable over the term of the lease[96] and the formula for calculating net present value is set out in FA 2003 Sch.5 para.3. This includes a *temporal discount rate* of 3.5%.[97] The way this formula works is complex, but HMRC have an online calculator that may be used to determine net present value of rent for SDLT purposes.[98]

9-142

By way of example, if the IRPS owns a lease of residential property, and the full commercial rent is £10,000 p/a for the first five years, the net present value (and therefore the deemed market value) is £234,560.

9-143

### Apportionment to pension scheme

If the IRPS holds the interest in the property indirectly for the whole of the period in the tax year for which the property is scheme-held taxable property, the amount that would otherwise be the amount of the scheme chargeable payment must be apportioned to the IRPS. This is achieved by applying paras 41–43 of Sch.29A to it as if it were the total taxable amount in relation to an unauthorised payment treated as made: (a) by the IRPS; (b) in connection with the acquisition of the interest in the property; and (c) at the end of the last day in the tax year on which the property is scheme-held taxable property. Paragraphs 41–43 of Sch.29A are explained above.

9-144

But where the amount found in relation to the IRPS on the last day in the tax year on which the property is scheme-held taxable property, differs from the amount that would be found in relation to the IRPS under the above paragraph on another day in the tax year on which the property is scheme-held taxable property, the amount to be apportioned to the IRPS is the average of the amounts produced by applying the above paragraph in relation to the IRPS on each day in the tax year on which the property is scheme-held taxable property.

9-145

### Credit for tax paid

If the IRPS holds the interest in the property indirectly in the tax year and a person who holds the interest directly pays tax on the profits arising from the interest at a time in the tax year when the property is scheme-held taxable property, the scheme is entitled to a credit against the scheme chargeable payment. The amount of the credit is a proportion of the tax paid determined by reference to the proportion of the amount that would otherwise be the amount of the scheme chargeable payment that is apportioned to the IRPS above.[99]

9-146

For example, an IRPS owns 50% of the shares in a company which owns taxable property worth £120,000 and the company receives rental profits of £5,000 and pays 20% corporation tax on this (i.e. £1,000). The amount of the scheme chargeable payment is the greater of the annual profits (£5,000) or the deemed profits

9-147

---

[96] FA 2003 Sch.5 para.2(4)(a).
[97] FA 2003 Sch.5 para.8(1).
[98] See *https://www.tax.service.gov.uk/calculate-stamp-duty-land-tax/#/intro*.
[99] Where an amount is allowed as a credit against the scheme sanction charge and the amount of tax paid by reference to which the amount of the credit was calculated is subsequently varied, the amount of the credit is to be varied accordingly, and any necessary adjustments are to be made to give effect to the variation (whether by making assessments or otherwise).

(£12,000, being 10% of the value of the property). This £12,000 must then be apportioned to the IRPS. As the IRPS owns 50% of the company, the amount of the scheme chargeable payment apportioned to the IRPS is £6,000, which gives rise to a scheme sanction charge of £2,400. However, the IRPS is then entitled to a credit against the scheme chargeable payment of 50% of £1,000 (i.e. £500).

## SCHEME CHARGEABLE PAYMENT UNDER S.185F

**9-148** Pursuant to FA 2004 s.185F, an IRPS makes a scheme chargeable payment[100] if it holds an interest in property which is or has been taxable property at any time whilst the interest has been held by the IRPS (this is referred to as a *taxable interest*) and: (a) a deemed gain accrues to the IRPS in respect of the taxable interest in the tax year; and (b) the total amount of such deemed gains exceeds the total amount of deemed losses accruing to the IRPS in respect of taxable interests in the tax year.

**9-149** These provisions apply only to capital gains. If the taxable property forms part of the stock in trade of the person who directly holds the taxable property, FA 2004 s.185A (see above) will apply rather than these provisions.[101] The provisions incorporate a number of provisions from TCGA 1992. The most relevant are referred to below but only by way of very brief outline; this is not intended to be a comprehensive explanation of the TCGA provisions.

### The amount of the scheme chargeable payment

**9-150** The amount of the scheme chargeable payment is the amount by which the deemed gains exceed the deemed losses. For these purposes, a deemed gain or loss accrues to an IRPS if:

(a) the person that directly holds the taxable interest disposes of it and a deemed chargeable gain or allowable loss accrues to that person; or

(b) a person (which may be the IRPS or another vehicle) ceases to hold some or all of an interest in a vehicle through which the IRPS indirectly holds the taxable interest.

*Disposal by person holding directly*

**9-151** The person (referred to as "the transferor") who holds the taxable interest directly is treated as holding an asset (referred to as a "taxable asset") consisting of the interest. Subject to a number of modifications mentioned below, TCGA 1992 is deemed to apply to the transferor and the taxable asset for the purpose of determining:

(a) whether the transferor disposes of the taxable asset;
(b) when such a disposal occurs; and
(c) whether a chargeable gain or allowable loss is treated for the purposes of s.185F as accruing to the transferor on a disposal of the taxable asset in a tax year and, if so, the amount of the chargeable gain or allowable loss.

**9-152** **Whether the transferor disposes of the taxable asset** The term *disposal* is not

---

[100] The scheme administrator must notify HMRC of any scheme chargeable payments under SI 2006/567 reg.3.
[101] This is because these provisions apply most of TCGA 1992, including TCGA 1992 ss.37 and 39 which generally exclude income transactions.

# SCHEME CHARGEABLE PAYMENT UNDER S.185F

defined in TCGA 1992. It will usually correspond to a change in beneficial ownership. In addition, it is extended as follows:

(a) The term *disposal* expressly includes a part disposal. A part disposal occurs where an interest or right in or over the asset is created by the disposal, as well as where it subsists before the disposal, and generally, there is a part disposal of an asset where, on a person making a disposal, any description of property derived from the asset remains undisposed of.[102]

(b) There is a disposal of assets where any capital sum is derived from assets notwithstanding that no asset is acquired by the person paying the capital sum.[103] This may be the case, for example, where a capital sum is received in return for a forfeiture or surrender of rights, or for refraining from exercising rights. It would also apply where a capital sum is received as consideration for use or exploitation of assets.

(c) The occasion of the entire loss, destruction, dissipation or extinction of an asset constitutes a disposal of the asset.[104]

(d) An appropriation to and from trading stock is deemed to constitute a disposal.[105]

(e) A lessor under a long funding lease is deemed to dispose of the plant and machinery on the commencement and the termination of the lease.[106]

(f) The grant of an option is the disposal of an asset (namely of the option).[107]

(g) There is a deemed disposal where value is passed out of the holder's shares or securities and into another person's shares or securities in the company.[108]

(h) A trustee is deemed to dispose of trust assets where a beneficiary becomes absolutely entitled to the settled property as against the trustee.[109]

**9-153** Conversely, certain transactions expressly do not involve a disposal. In particular, the reorganisation of a company's share capital is deemed not to involve a disposal of the original shares.[110]

**9-154** **When such a disposal occurs** In general the disposal takes place when the beneficial ownership changes. However, where an asset is disposed of under a contract, the disposal takes place at the time that the contract is made (and not, if different, the time at which the asset is conveyed or transferred). If the contract is conditional then the disposal takes place at the time that the condition is satisfied.[111]

**9-155** **Whether a chargeable gain or allowable loss accrues and, if so, the amount of the chargeable gain or allowable loss** The starting point is to ascertain the consideration given for the disposal. If the disposal is a bargain at arm's length then this is the actual consideration, and if it is not such a bargain then it is market value. Transactions between connected persons are assumed to be on non-arm's length

---

[102] TCGA 1992 s.21(2).
[103] TCGA 1992 s.22(1).
[104] TCGA 1992 s.24(1).
[105] TCGA 1992 s.161.
[106] TCGA 1992 s.25A.
[107] TCGA 1992 s.144(1).
[108] TCGA 1992 ss.29–34.
[109] TCGA 1992 s.71(1).
[110] TCGA 1992 s.127.
[111] TCGA 1992 s.28.

terms.[112] One then ascertains the allowable expenditure, which falls into the following five categories:[113]

(a) acquisition expenditure;
(b) the incidental costs of making the acquisition;
(c) expenditure incurred to enhance the value of the asset;
(d) expenditure incurred to establish or preserve title to the asset; and
(e) the incidental costs of making the disposal.

**9-156** If the taxable asset became taxable property whilst held directly by the IRPS, it is deemed to have been acquired by the transferor at the time it became taxable property, and the amount of allowable expenditure is the amount of the unauthorised payment treated as made by the IRPS at that time.

**9-157** Where the IRPS holds the taxable asset indirectly, the amount of allowable expenditure in respect of the disposal is: (a) the total amount of unauthorised payments treated as made by the IRPS in respect of the taxable asset up to the time of the disposal; less (b) the amount found under para.(a) to the extent that it has already been taken into account in calculating the gains or losses accruing to the IRPS in respect of the taxable asset by virtue of this section or s 185H. In the context of a part disposal, one applies TCGA 1992 s.42, but in doing so in relation to the taxable asset, the amount of the consideration for the disposal is taken to be that amount apart from the below paragraph relating to scaling down.

**9-158** TCGA 1992 s.42 contains provisions about part disposals. Where a person disposes of an interest or right in or over an asset, and generally wherever on the disposal of an asset any description of property derived from that asset remains undisposed of, the sums which under paras (a) and (b) of s.38(1) are attributable to the asset shall, both for the purposes of the computation of the gain accruing on the disposal and for the purpose of applying this part in relation to the property which remains undisposed of, be apportioned. The fraction of the said sums allowable as a deduction in the computation of the gain accruing on the disposal shall be determined by reference to the following formula (and the remainder is attributed to the property which remains undisposed of): "A/A+B", where:

- *A* is the amount or value of the consideration for the disposal on the one hand.
- *B* is the market value of the property which remains undisposed of on the other hand.

**9-159** Where the IRPS holds the taxable asset indirectly, the amount that would otherwise be the amount of the consideration for which the disposal is made (or treated as made) is to be scaled down by applying paras 41–43 of Sch.29A to it as if it were the total taxable amount in relation to an unauthorised payment treated as made: (a) by the pension scheme; (b) in connection with the acquisition of the interest in the property which constitutes the taxable asset; and (c) at the time of the disposal. Paragraphs 41–43 of Sch.29A are explained above.

**9-160** The difference between the disposal consideration and the allowable expenditure will usually represent the chargeable gain or allowable loss. However, this is subject to various provisions in TCGA which adjust either the disposal consideration or the allowable expenditure before arriving at the final result. For example, transfers of assets within a group of companies are deemed to take place on a *no gain no loss*

---

[112] TCGA 1992 s.18(1).
[113] TCGA 1992 s.38(1). In the case of a disposal by a company, the expenditure within (a)–(d) is normally indexed, but not for the purposes of the taxable property provisions.

## SCHEME CHARGEABLE PAYMENT UNDER S.185F

basis[114] however this is disapplied for the purposes of the taxable property provisions.

**9-161** Where the taxable asset was not taxable property for the whole period beginning with: (a) the time when the IRPS acquired the asset; or (b) if later, the time when the asset first became taxable property, and ending with the disposal, the amount that would otherwise be the amount of any chargeable gain or allowable loss treated as accruing on a disposal of the asset is to be reduced by reference to the proportion of the period for which the asset was not taxable property.

**9-162** The general position is that no chargeable gains accrue on the disposal of an asset which is tangible movable property and which is a wasting asset,[115] but this is disapplied for the purpose of the taxable property provisions. Instead, where: (a) the taxable asset is a wasting asset consisting of tangible moveable property; and (b) by virtue of s.185F, a loss is treated as accruing to the IRPS from a disposal of the asset in a tax year, the loss is only to be allowed as a deduction from any gains treated as accruing to the IRPS by virtue of that section from other disposals in the year of taxable assets which are wasting assets consisting of tangible moveable property.

**9-163** The general position is that if a beneficiary of a settlement occupies residential property such that primary residence relief applies, any gains on a disposal are not chargeable gains,[116] however this is disapplied for the purpose of the taxable property provisions.

**9-164** The chargeable gains accruing on all disposals taking place in a tax year (or accounting period for a company) are aggregated and allowable losses for that year or period are then deducted. One can usually also deduct unallowed losses from previous year, but this is disapplied for the purpose of the taxable property provisions.

**9-165** For the purposes of these provisions, the transferor is deemed to be resident and domiciled in the UK throughout the tax year.

**9-166** A gain accruing on a disposal of tangible movable property is not a chargeable gain if the amount of the consideration for the disposal does not exceed £6,000. Where the consideration exceeds £6,000, there is excluded from any chargeable gain accruing on the disposal so much of it as exceeds five-thirds of the difference between: (a) the amount of the consideration; and (b) £6,000.[117]

**9-167** A mechanically propelled road vehicle constructed or adapted for the carriage of passengers, except for a vehicle of a type not commonly used as a private vehicle and unsuitable to be so used, is not a chargeable asset; and accordingly, no chargeable gain or allowable loss accrues on its disposal.[118]

*Disposal of interest in vehicle*

**9-168** Where the IRPS or another vehicle ceases to hold all or part of an interest in a vehicle through which the IRPS holds the taxable interest indirectly, the IRPS is treated as disposing of the interest in the vehicle through which the IRPS holds the taxable interest indirectly. The amount of the gain or loss treated as accruing to the IRPS on the disposal of the interest in the vehicle is the difference between: (a) the

---

[114] TCGA 1992 s.171.
[115] TCGA 1992 s.45(1). A wasting asset is an asset with a predictable life not exceeding 50 years (TCGA 1992 s.44). Instead, the acquisition and enhancement expenditure on wasting assets is written down over its life.
[116] TCGA 1992 s.225.
[117] TCGA 1992 s.262.
[118] TCGA 1992 s.263.

deemed consideration received for the disposal of the interest; and (b) the deemed consideration given for the interest.

**9-169** The deemed consideration received for the disposal of the interest in the vehicle is the difference between: (a) the market value of the taxable interest at the time of the disposal, apportioned to the IRPS immediately before that time; and (b) the market value of the taxable interest at the time of the disposal, apportioned to the IRPS immediately after that time. Apportioning to the IRPS is achieved by applying paras 41–43 of Sch.29A to it as if it were the total taxable amount in relation to an unauthorised payment treated as made: (a) by the IRPS; (b) in connection with the acquisition of the taxable interest; and (c) at the time at which the amount is to be apportioned to the IRPS in accordance with that subsection.

**9-170** The deemed consideration given for the interest in the vehicle is: (a) the total amount of unauthorised payments treated as made by the IRPS in respect of the taxable interest up to the time of the disposal; less (b) the amount found under para.(a) to the extent that it has already been taken into account in calculating the gains or losses accruing to the pension scheme in respect of the taxable interest by virtue of s.185G or this section.

*Credit for tax paid*

**9-171** Where tax is payable (and is paid) in respect of the disposal by the person who makes the disposal, the following amount (as appropriate) is to be allowed as a credit against any income tax charged under s.239 in respect of the scheme chargeable payment:

(a) Where a chargeable gain is treated by virtue of s.185G as accruing to another person on a disposal of a taxable asset, that amount is a proportion of the amount of tax paid and payable determined by reference to the proportion of the amount of consideration for the disposal that is apportioned under s.185G(7).

(b) Where a gain is treated by virtue of s.185H as accruing to the IRPS as a result of another person disposing of an interest in a vehicle through which the pension scheme holds a taxable interest indirectly, that amount is the amount of tax paid and payable apportioned to the pension scheme by applying paras 41–43 of Sch.29A to it as if it were the total taxable amount in relation to an unauthorised payment treated as made: (i) by the IRPS; (ii) in connection with an acquisition of the taxable interest by the person disposing of the interest in the vehicle; and (iii) at the time of the disposal.

**9-172** Where an amount is allowed as a credit and the amount of tax payable and paid is subsequently varied, the amount of the credit will also be varied accordingly.

# CHAPTER 10

# The Lifetime Allowance (pre-6 April 2024)

## TABLE OF CONTENTS

| | |
|---|---|
| Introduction | 10-001 |
| BCES and amounts crystallised | 10-005 |
|     The "relevant pension schemes" | 10-007 |
|     The "relevant two-year period" | 10-008 |
|     "RVF": the relevant valuation factor | 10-009 |
|     Unauthorised payments | 10-013 |
|     Age 75 | 10-014 |
|     Credit for previous BCE | 10-015 |
|     "Relevant unused uncrystallised funds" | 10-016 |
|     "Remaining unused funds" | 10-017 |
|     "Threshold annual rate" and "permitted margin" | 10-018 |
|     BCE 9 | 10-019 |
| Amount of available lifetime allowance | 10-020 |
|     Fixed protection | 10-021 |
|         Benefit accrual | 10-023 |
|             The relevant percentage | 10-024 |
|             Comment | 10-028 |
|         Impermissible transfers | 10-029 |
|         Permitted transfers | 10-030 |
|         Arrangements made otherwise than in permitted circumstances | 10-031 |
|         Rescinding a protection-cessation event on the ground of mistake | 10-032 |
|     Individual protection | 10-040 |
|         Individual protection 2014 ("IP 2014") | 10-041 |
|             Effect of IP 2014 | 10-042 |
|             Pension debits | 10-043 |
|         Individual protection 2016 ("IP 2016") | 10-044 |
|     Lifetime allowance enhancement factors | 10-046 |
| Availability of lifetime allowance on a BCE | 10-049 |
| The lifetime allowance charge | 10-053 |
|     Scheme-funded tax payments | 10-056 |
|     The purpose of the charge | 10-057 |
|     Liability | 10-058 |
|         Relevant post-death crystallisation events | 10-059 |
|         Discharge of tax liability: good faith | 10-061 |
| Reporting obligations | 10-065 |

## INTRODUCTION

**10-001** The lifetime allowance charge was removed with effect from 6 April 2023, and the lifetime allowance was abolished altogether from 6 April 2024. But it remains relevant for any member in respect of whom a Benefit Crystallisation Event (BCE) occurred before 6 April 2024, because such BCEs may be taken into account for the purposes of determining the member's available LS allowance and LS&DB allowance.

**10-002** Prior to its removal, the lifetime allowance was an important concept for two main reasons:

(a) A lifetime allowance charge arose to the extent that the value of the member's benefits "crystallised" by a BCE exceed the member's available lifetime allowance.

(b) Certain categories of authorised lump sum could be paid only if the member had some lifetime allowance available at that time. A lump sum could be a PCLS or UFPLS only to the extent that the member had available lifetime allowance. A serious ill-health lump sum paid before the member's 75th birthday, was tax-free except to the extent that it exceeded the member's available lifetime allowance. A trivial commutation lump sum and winding-up lump sum (both tax-advantaged) could be paid only if the member had some available lifetime allowance at that time.

**10-003** A scheme administrator could not properly discharge its functions under FA 2004[1] without understanding:

(a) The events that were BCEs, and the amount crystallised by a BCE.
(b) The amount of a member's available lifetime allowance.
(c) The implications of an amount being crystallised by one or more BCEs.

**10-004** This chapter explains each of the above. The main provisions were in FA 2004 ss.214–226 and Sch.32.

## BCES AND AMOUNTS CRYSTALLISED

**10-005** Prior to 6 April 2024, there were 13 BCEs specified in FA 2004 s.216:

| BCE | Description | Amount crystallised |
|---|---|---|
| 1 | The designation of sums or assets held for the purposes of a money purchase arrangement under any of the relevant pension schemes as available for the payment of drawdown pension to the individual. | The amount of the sums and the market value of the assets designated. |

---

[1] On the occurrence of each BCE, the scheme administrator was required to provide information to the member and to HMRC. The scheme administrator was usually jointly and severally liable for the lifetime allowance charge.

| BCE | Description | Amount crystallised |
|---|---|---|
| 2 | The individual becoming entitled[2] to a scheme pension under any of the relevant pension schemes.<br><br>BCE 2 also occurs where the individual attains normal minimum pension age, if he became entitled to a lifetime annuity before normal minimum pension age.[3] | "RVF x P" where "P" is the total amount of the pension which will be payable to the individual in the first 12 months.[4] "RFF" is usually 20 (see below). "RVF v P", or, if greater, the amount that would have been crystallised by BCE 4.[5] |
| 3 | The individual, having become so entitled, becoming entitled[6] to payment of the scheme pension, otherwise than in excepted circumstances, at an increased annual rate which: (a) exceeds the "threshold annual rate"; and (b) exceeds by more than the "permitted margin" the rate at which it was payable on the day on which the individual became entitled to it. | "RVF x XP"[7] where "XP" is the amount by which the increased annual rate of the pension exceeds the rate at which it was payable when the individual first became entitled to it, increased by a "permitted margin". "RFF" is usually 20 (see below). |
| 4 | The individual becoming entitled[8] to a lifetime annuity purchased under a money purchase arrangement under any of the relevant pension schemes. | The amount of the sums and market value of the assets value of the assets, representing the individual's rights under the arrangement as are applied to purchase the lifetime annuity and any "related" dependants' or nominees' annuity. |

---

[2] A person becomes "entitled" to a scheme pension when he acquires an actual (rather than a merely prospective) right (FA 2004 s.165(3)(b)). If the individual becomes entitled to the scheme pension before reaching normal minimum pension age (including any protected pension age: see Ch.3) and he does not satisfy the ill-health condition, the individual is deemed to become entitled to it on reaching normal minimum pension age or satisfying the ill-health condition (FA 2004 Sch.32 para.8). Prior to that, each payment of pension will usually be an unauthorised payment.

[3] FA 2004 Sch.32 para.7. "Normal minimum pension age" includes any protected pension age (see Ch.3). Any payments of annuity before that age will be unauthorised payments.

[4] Sch.32 para.9. It is assumed that the pension will be payable throughout the 12-month period at the rate at which it is payable on the day that the member becomes entitled to it. If, prior to becoming entitled to a scheme pension, a member commutes part of it in order to pay a PCLS, only the reduced level of scheme pension is included (the PCLS is BCE 6).

[5] FA 2004 Sch.32 para.7(5).

[6] A person becomes "entitled" to an increased scheme pension when he acquires an actual (rather than a merely prospective) right to the increased pension (FA 2004 s.165(3)(b)).

[7] FA 2004 Sch.32 para.13.

[8] A person becomes "entitled" to an annuity when he acquires an actual (rather than prospective) right to the annuity (FA 2004 s.165(3)(b)).

| BCE | Description | Amount crystallised |
|---|---|---|
| 5 | The individual reaching the age of 75 when prospectively entitled[9] to a scheme pension or a lump sum (or both) under a defined benefits arrangement under any of the relevant pension schemes. If he is a member of a hybrid arrangement that may provide either money purchase benefits or defined benefits, assume the benefits will be defined benefits.[10] | "(RVF x DP) + DSLS" where "DP" is the annual rate of scheme pension to which the individual would be entitled if, on his 75th birthday, he acquired an actual right to receive it; "DSLS" is the amount of the lump sum that he would be entitled to in those circumstances.[11] "RVF" is usually 20 (see below). |
| 5A | The individual reaching the age of 75 having designated sums or assets held for the purposes of a money purchase arrangement under any of the relevant pension schemes as available for the payment of drawdown pension to the individual. | The amounts of the sums and market value of the assets representing the individual's drawdown pension fund, and/or the individual's flexi-access drawdown fund under the arrangement, less the amount previously crystallised by BCE 1. |
| 5B | The individual reaching the age of 75 when there is a money purchase arrangement relating to the individual under any of the relevant pension schemes. | The amount of any remaining unused funds. |
| 5C | The designation, on or after 6 April 2015 but before the end of the "relevant two-year period", of "relevant unused uncrystallised funds" as available for the payment, to a dependant or nominee of the individual, of (as the case may be) dependants' flexi-access drawdown pension or nominees' flexi-access drawdown pension. | The amount of the sums and the market value of the assets designated. |

---

[9] i.e. the pension has not yet commenced. "Prospective" entitlement is contrasted with "actual" entitlement in FA 2004 s.165(3).
[10] FA 2004 Sch.32 para.5.
[11] FA 2004 Sch.32 para.14(1) and (2).

| BCE | Description | Amount crystallised |
|---|---|---|
| 5D | A person becoming entitled, on or after 6 April 2015 but before the end of the "relevant two-year period", to a dependants' annuity or nominees' annuity in respect of the individual if: (a) the annuity is purchased using (whether or not exclusively) "relevant unused uncrystallised funds"; and (b) the individual died on or after 3 December 2014.[12] | The value of the "relevant uncrystallised funds" applied to purchase the annuity. |
| 6 | The individual becoming entitled[13] under any of the relevant pension schemes to: (a) a PCLS; (b) a serious ill-health lump sum; (c) an UFPLS; or (d) a lifetime allowance excess lump sum.[14]<br><br>But this BCE does not apply where the individual becomes entitled to a PCLS under a money purchase arrangement before his 75th birthday but it is not paid to him until after that day.[15] | The amount of the lump sum paid to the individual. |
| 7 | A person being paid: (a) a defined benefits lump sum death benefit; or (b) an uncrystallised funds lump sum death benefit, within the "relevant two-year period" in respect of the individual under any of the relevant pension schemes.[16] | The amount of the lump sum. |

---

[12] FA 2004 Sch.32 para.14C.
[13] A person becomes "entitled" to a serious ill-health lump sum and a lifetime allowance excess lump sum when he acquires an actual (rather than a merely prospective) right to receive the lump sum (FA 2004 s.166(2)(b)). A person becomes entitled to a PCLS immediately before he becomes entitled to the connected pension (FA 2004 s.166(2)(a)). A person becomes entitled to an UFPLS immediately before it is paid (FA 2004 s.166(2)(aa)).
[14] FA 2004 Sch.32 para.15.
[15] FA 2004 Sch.32 para.15A. Instead, one of BCE 5A or BCE 5B will apply, by virtue of the member reaching age 75.
[16] FA 2004 Sch.32 para.16.

| BCE | Description | Amount crystallised |
|---|---|---|
| 8 | The transfer[17] of sums or assets held for the purposes of, or representing accrued rights under, any of the relevant pension schemes so as to become held for the purposes of or to represent rights under a QROPS in connection with the individual's membership of that pension scheme. | The amount of the sums and market value of the assets transferred. |
| 9 | If regulations under s.164(1)(f) so provide, the happening of an event prescribed in the regulations in relation to a payment prescribed in the regulations. These payments are described below. | An amount determined in accordance with the regulations. |

10-006  It will be apparent that there were two main categories of BCE: (a) those that occurred when uncrystallised funds were applied to provide benefits to the member (or *in respect of* the member, following his death); and (b) those that occurred on the member's 75th birthday. The anomalous BCE 8 occurred where sums and assets are transferred to a QROPS, and thus, outside of the registered pension scheme regime.

### The "relevant pension schemes"

10-007  Each BCE referred to the "relevant pension schemes".[18] A relevant pension scheme was a registered pension scheme of which the individual is a member (or, in the case of BCE 5C, BCE 5D and BCE 7, *was* a member immediately before death).[19] The provisions described in this chapter could occur only in relation to a registered pension scheme.[20] A BCE could not occur in relation to sums or assets which had been transferred to a QROPS (which is why the transfer itself was a BCE).

### The "relevant two-year period"

10-008  For the purposes of the death benefit BCEs (BCE 5C, BCE 5D and BCE 7), the "relevant two-year period" was the period of two years beginning with the earlier of the day on which the scheme administrator first knew of the individual's death and the day on which the scheme administrator could first reasonably have been expected to have known of it. In most cases, the two-year period will commence on the day the administrator receives a copy of the death certificate.[21] The more objective part of this test ("or could first reasonably have been expected to have known of it") is likely to apply where the administrator has reason to suspect death but unreasonably fails to obtain knowledge of it.

---

[17] The date of the "transfer" must mean the date that the beneficial or equitable interest in the sums or assets passes to the receiving scheme (HMRC agree at PTM088690).

[18] In relation to BCE 5C and BCE 5D, the reference is incorporated in the definition of "relevant unused uncrystallised funds" in FA 2004 Sch.32 para.14C.

[19] FA 2004 Sch.32 para.1.

[20] A modified version of these provisions was applied to "relieved members" of "relieved non-UK pension schemes" as if the scheme were a registered pension scheme (see Ch.30).

[21] Plainly, there is a material distinction between "knowing" of someone's death (which suggests a high degree of certainty, e.g. because the administrator has received a copy of the death certificate), and

The relevant two-year period corresponded with the taxation of these death benefits: (a) if provided within the relevant two-year period, they were tax-free but subject to the lifetime allowance; (b) if provided after the expiration of the two-year period, they were taxable[22] but not subject to the lifetime allowance.

### "RVF": the relevant valuation factor

10-009 For the purposes of BCE 2, 3, and 5, "RVF" was 20 unless HMRC and the scheme administrator agreed that the "relevant valuation factor" in relation to the pension scheme, or any arrangement under the pension scheme, was a number greater than 20.[23]

10-010 The relevant valuation factor was applied to provide a capital value of a scheme pension. A pension of £10,000 p/a had a capital value of £200,000 unless HMRC agreed to a higher valuation factor. A PCLS is calculated by reference to the capital value of the scheme pension, so increasing the relevant valuation factor had the effect of increasing the amount of the available (tax-free) PCLS. If a higher valuation factor was agreed with HMRC then this will of course increase the capital value of all scheme pensions payable under the scheme. The reason a scheme administrator may be permitted to use a higher relevant valuation factor relates to BCE 3. If the scheme rules allow a scheme pension to increase annually by more than 5% or the increase in the RPI, and a relevant valuation factor of 20 is used, such increases are likely to constitute BCE 3 once the pension has commenced.[24]

10-011 HMRC's position[25] was that, except in exceptional circumstances, they will agree to the adoption of a higher relevant valuation factor only if all of the following conditions are satisfied:

(a) the scheme has at least 20 members;
(b) the proposed rate of increase of pensions will apply to all members of the scheme who start to receive a pension on or after the date of the agreement;
(c) HMRC are satisfied that the proposed non-standard valuation factor accurately reflects the value of pension to be paid, and the proposed rate of increase; and
(d) the proposal is not part of avoidance arrangements to increase the member's entitlement to a lump sum on which there is no liability to tax.

10-012 A higher relevant valuation factor meant that a greater amount was crystallised by BCE 2 when the entitlement to the scheme pension arose, but it could prevent a subsequent BCE 3 from occurring as and when increases were applied to that pension. If HMRC agreed a higher relevant valuation factor, then they would at the same time agree the "relevant percentage rate" that should be applied for the purpose of BCE 3.[26] The standard relevant percentage rate was 5%, but where a higher relevant valuation factor was agreed then a higher relevant percentage rate would also be agreed.

---

having reason to suspect someone's death (e.g. where the administrator has been notified of the death but received no evidence). On the face of it, knowledge requires proof.

[22] At the recipient's marginal rate (if the recipient is an individual) or subject to the 45% special lump sum death benefits charge (if the recipient is not an individual).
[23] FA 2004 Sch.32 para.6, applying FA 2004 s.276. For HMRC guidance, see PTM088620.
[24] See FA Sch.32 para.11(4).
[25] PTM088620. The application process is also set out on that page.
[26] PTM088630.

### Unauthorised payments

**10-013** Any BCE which involved a *payment* was a BCE only to the extent that it was an authorised payment. A payment was not a BCE if it is an unauthorised payment.

### Age 75

**10-014** Only BCE 3 could occur after the member's 75th birthday.[27] Once he had attained age 75, a lifetime allowance charge could not otherwise arise. However, certain categories of authorised lump sum could be paid only if the member had some lifetime allowance available at that time, and for the purpose of determining whether he had any available lifetime allowance, the amount that crystallised on his 75th birthday under BCE 5 or BCE 5B[28] was disregarded, and any events which would be BCEs if the member were under age 75 were treated as being BCEs.

### Credit for previous BCE

**10-015** Where a BCE occurred in relation to rights that had already crystallised, credit was provided for the previous BCE:

(a) In relation to BCE 1, where the designation was in connection with the winding-up of the scheme, and the sums or assets designated were sums or assets out of which benefits were provided under a collective money purchase arrangement, the amount crystallised under BCE 1 is reduced by the amount (or an appropriate proportion of the amount) previously crystallised on the individual becoming entitled to a scheme pension under the collective money purchase arrangement.

(b) In relation to BCE 2, where the scheme pension is funded by the application of sums or assets representing the individual's drawdown pension fund, the amount crystallised under BCE 2 is reduced by the amount (or an appropriate proportion of the amount) previously crystallised on the designation of the sums or assets as available for the payment of drawdown pension.[29] For example, if £500,000 is designated as available for the payment of drawdown pension and then sometime later, when the value of the fund is £650,000, the member decides to apply £325,000 to take a scheme pension of £17,500 p/a. The amount crystallised though BCE 2 is £17,500 x 20 = £350,000, but he gets credit for the previous BCE 1. As half of the drawdown fund is being applied, half of the BCE 1 can be credited (i.e. £250,000). This means that the amount crystallised under BCE 2 is £150,000 (£350,000 less £200,000). There does not appear to be any equivalent provision applicable where a scheme pension is paid from a flexi-access drawdown fund.

(c) Also in relation to BCE 2, a scheme pension may be paid before the member's normal minimum pension age[30] on grounds of ill-health. If the member's health subsequently recovers, and so the pension ceases, and then later re-commences when he reaches normal minimum pension age (for

---

[27] FA 2004 Sch.32 para.2.
[28] BCE 5 occurs if a member reaches age 75 when prospectively entitled to a scheme pension or a lump sum (or both) under a defined benefits arrangement, and BCE 5B occurs if a member reaches age 75 when there is a money purchase arrangement relating to him.
[29] FA 2004 Sch.32 para.3.
[30] This concept includes any protected pension age: see Ch.3.

# BCES AND AMOUNTS CRYSTALLISED 249

example), HMRC consider[31] that the re-commenced pension "represents" the original scheme pension and so is not BCE 2 (although, if the annual rate of the re-commenced pension is higher than the original pension, that may be BCE 3). Given that becoming "entitled" is BCE 2, and credit is not expressly given for any previous BCE 2, it is not at all clear that the provisions can withstand this interpretation. HMRC's position is therefore best treated as a concession. HMRC go on to add that if the member returns to work and becomes entitled to a further pension benefit in respect of his subsequent service, that entitlement is a new entitlement in its own right under the scheme and would therefore be BCE 2.

(d) In relation to BCE 3, where one or more BCE 3s have previously occurred in relation to the same scheme pension, XP does not include the amount of XP on those previous events.[32] For these purposes the amount of XP on a previous BCE 3 is increased by the greater of: (a) 5% per annum[33] for the period beginning with the month in which the previous BCE 3 occurred and ending with the month in which current BCE 3 occurs. Where the intervening period is not measured in whole years this is applied on a pro rata basis; (b) the increase in the RPI.[34]

(e) In relation to BCE 4, if the cash or assets used to purchase the lifetime annuity (and/or any related annuity) have previously been designated as available for the payment of drawdown pension, the amount crystallised by BCE 4 is reduced by the amount (or an appropriate proportion of the amount) previously crystallised by BCE 1.[35]

(f) In relation to BCE 8, where any of the sums or assets transferred represent the whole or part of the individual's drawdown pension fund or flexi-access drawdown fund, the amount that crystallises by BCE 8 is reduced by the amount (or the appropriate proportion of the amount) previously crystallised by BCE 1.[36] Where, after the transfer to a QROPS, a scheme pension to which the individual became entitled before the transfer is to be payable out of the sums or assets transferred, the amount crystallised by the transfer is reduced by the amount (or the appropriate proportion of the amount) previously crystallised under BCE 2 (and BCE 3 if applicable) in relation to the scheme pension.

---

[31] PTM088620.
[32] FA 2004 Sch.32 para.13(2).
[33] Unless the relevant valuation factor of the pension scheme, or the arrangement under the pension scheme, was more than 20. If it is more than 20 the relevant annual percentage rate was the annual rate agreed between HMRC and the scheme administrator.
[34] The relevant indexation percentage is: (a) if the RPI for the reference month is higher than the RPI for the base month, the percentage increase in the RPI; and (b) if it is not, 0%. The scheme administrator may select as the reference month any month in the period of 12 months ending with the month in which the individual becomes entitled to payment of the pension at the increased rate. The base month is the month which is the same number of months before the month in which the previous event occurred, as the reference month is before the month in which the individual becomes entitled to payment of the pension at the increased rate. The percentage is rounded up to one decimal place. Where the intervening period is not measured in whole years, this must be applied on a pro rata basis.
[35] FA 2004 Sch.32 para.4.
[36] FA 2004 Sch.32 para.17.

### "Relevant unused uncrystallised funds"

**10-016** For the purposes of BCE 5C and BCE 5D, funds were "relevant unused uncrystallised funds" if they were "unused uncrystallised funds" and the individual died before reaching age 75:

(a) In the case of a cash balance arrangement, funds held for the purposes of the arrangement after the individual's death were unused uncrystallised funds if:[37] (i) they represented the whole or any part of the sum that would have been available immediately before the individual's death for the provision of benefits to or in respect of the individual if entitlement had arisen at that time to all benefits under the arrangement to which entitlement had not previously arisen; and (ii) since the individual's death they have not been designated as available for the payment of dependants' drawdown pension or nominees' drawdown pension, and have not been applied towards the provision of a dependants' annuity or a nominees' annuity and have not been applied towards the provision of a dependants' scheme pension.

(b) In the case of another money purchase arrangement, funds held for the purposes of the arrangement after the individual's death are unused uncrystallised funds if:[38] (i) immediately before the individual's death they were held for the purposes of the arrangement and at that time had not been designated as available for the payment of drawdown pension, and had not been applied towards the provision of a scheme pension or dependants' scheme pension (or they arise or derive from such unused uncrystallised funds or from sums or assets which so arise or derive); and (ii) since the individual's death they have not been designated as available for the payment of dependants' drawdown pension or nominees' drawdown pension, and have not been applied toward the provision of a dependants' annuity or a nominees' annuity and have not been applied towards the provision of a dependants' scheme pension.

### "Remaining unused funds"

**10-017** For the purposes of BCE 5B, "remaining unused funds" means:[39] (a) in relation to a cash balance arrangement, a sum equal to what would, on the valuation assumptions in s.277(a),[40] be available for the provision of benefits to or in respect of the member if the member became entitled to them on his 75th birthday; and (b) in relation to another money purchase arrangement, such of the sums and assets held for the purposes of the arrangement as are not member-designated funds (i.e. held for the purposes of a drawdown pension fund)[41] and have not been applied towards the provision of a scheme pension or a dependants' scheme pension.

---

[37] FA 2004 Sch.32 para.14C, applying and modifying Sch.28 para.27E(4).
[38] FA 2004 Sch.32 para.14C, applying and modifying Sch.28 para.27E(5).
[39] FA 2004 Sch.32 para.14A.
[40] The valuation assumption in FA 2004 s.277(a) requires one to value the individual's rights on the assumption that the individual is at the age at which no reduction would apply to the payment of an immediate benefit. The other valuation assumption (not required here) is that the individual is in good physical and mental health at the time.
[41] There appears to be no reason that BCE 5B would not apply to newly designated funds (i.e. funds held for the purposes of a flexi-access drawdown fund).

## "Threshold annual rate" and "permitted margin"

In relation to BCE 3:

**10-018**

(a) Each time the annual rate of a scheme pension is increased, one must compare the new annual rate to the rate one year earlier.[42] The threshold annual rate is exceeded if the new rate exceeds the rate a year earlier by more than the greatest of: (a) 5%,[43] (b) the increase in the RPI; and (c) £250.[44] When determining the increase in the RPI, one may select any month in the 12-month period prior to the increase in pension as the reference month and then measure the increase in the index from the same month in the previous year. For example, if the increase occurred in December 2016 the scheme administrator may select any month as far back as January 2015 as the reference month. The percentage should be rounded up to one decimal place. If the individual became entitled to the increased pension less than 12 months after first becoming entitled to the pension, the threshold annual rate is the annual rate of the pension on the date on which the person became entitled to it, increased and rounded up as specified above. In other words, the 5% per annum is not applied on a pro rata basis where the increase takes place within the first year.

(b) In contrast to the threshold rate (which is concerned with the increase from one year to the next), the permitted margin is concerned with the total increase since the BCE 2 occurred. The method for calculating the permitted margin is different depending on whether the pension commenced before 6 April 2006 or on or after that date.[45] If the individual became entitled to the pension on or after 6 April 2006, the permitted margin is the amount by which the annual rate of the pension on the day on which the individual became entitled to it would be greater if it had been increased by whichever of calculation A and calculation B gives the greater amount.[46] Calculation A involves increasing that annual amount at the rate of 5% per annum[47] for the whole of the period beginning with the month in which the individual became entitled to the pension (i.e. when BCE 2 occurred), and ending with the month in which the individual becomes entitled to payment of the pension at the increased rate. Where the intervening period is not measured in whole years, this is applied on a pro-rata basis by measure of months (counting the months in which the two points occur in as completed months). Calculation B involves increasing that annual amount by the RPI. The scheme administrator may select as the reference month any

---

[42] Any abatement of the scheme pension is disregarded when determining the increased annual rate of the pension, and the rate at which it was payable on the day on which the individual became entitled to it (FA 2004 Sch.32 para.9A). Abatement is defined in s.279(1) but only in relation to public service pension schemes. It means a reduction of pension (under a public service pension scheme) in accordance with the rules of the pension scheme by reason of the person's employment in public service. Paragraph 9A is not, on the face of it, limited to public service pensions, and the meaning of abatement is presumably the same for private pension schemes.

[43] Unless a different rate is agreed by HMRC and the scheme administrator. This is referred to as the relevant percentage rate. If HMRC agree to a higher RVF than 20 for the purposes of BCE 2 then they will also agree to a relevant percentage rate in excess of 5%: see PTM088630.

[44] FA 2004 Sch.32 para.10A.

[45] For pre-6 April 2006, see Ch.3.

[46] FA 2004 Sch.32 para.11(2).

[47] Unless the relevant valuation factor of the pension scheme, or the arrangement under the pension scheme, is more than 20. If it is more than 20 then the relevant annual percentage rate is the annual rate agreed between HMRC and the scheme administrator.

month in the period of 12 months ending with the month in which the individual becomes entitled to payment of the pension at the increased rate. The base month is the month which is the same number of months before the month in which the individual became entitled to the pension, as the reference month is before the month in which the individual becomes entitled to payment of the pension at the increased rate. The percentage is rounded up to at least one decimal place. The reference month for the permitted margin need not be the same as the reference month for the threshold annual rate.

(c) The annual rate of a scheme pension may be increased above the threshold annual rate and the permitted margin without BCE 3 occurring where conditions A and B are met[48] Condition A is that (a) the entitlement to payment of a scheme pension at an increased annual rate is under an arrangement that is not a collective money purchase arrangement; (b) at the time of the increase there are at least 50 pensioner members[49] of the pension scheme; and (c) the individual is one of a class of at least 20 pensioner members of the pension scheme, and all the scheme pensions being paid to pensioner members of that class are at that time increased at the same rate. A class may consist of all the pensioner members of the pension scheme. If there is more than one such increase in any 12-month period either: (a) the class of 20 or more pensioner members referred to above must be the same class for each increase; or (b) it must not have been one of the main purposes of the individual's being included in the new class to increase the annual rate of the individual's pension without BCE 3 occurring. If the requirements in the paragraph above are satisfied in respect of the further increase, it is an increase in excepted circumstances. Condition B is that (a) the entitlement to payment of a scheme pension at an increased annual rate is under an arrangement that is a collective money purchase arrangement; and (b) at the time when the annual rate of the individual's pension is increased, all the scheme pensions being paid under collective money purchase arrangements are increased at the same rate.

**BCE 9**

10-019 The Registered Pension Schemes (Authorised Payments) Regulations 2009 (SI 2009/1171) provide that certain payments to or in respect of a member are payments of a prescribed description for the purposes of s.164(1)(f) (and are therefore authorised payments).[50] The regulations provide that the following are BCE 9:

(a) Payment of accrued arrears of scheme pension in respect of a defined benefits arrangement after the member's death.[51] If the member died after 5 April 2006 it is necessary that: (i) the member's entitlement to the pension was not established until after his death; (ii) the payment would not have been an unauthorised payment if it had been made immediately before his death and he had been entitled to it; and (iii) the scheme administrator could not reasonably have been expected to make the payment before the member's death. The amount crystallised is the amount of the payment.

---

[48] FA 2004 Sch.32 para.10.
[49] For the meaning of "pensioner member", see Ch.2.
[50] SI 2009/1171 regs 3–5B.
[51] SI 2009/1171 reg.16.

# AMOUNT OF AVAILABLE LIFETIME ALLOWANCE

(b) Payment of a commencement lump sum based on pension errors.[52] The crystallisation event occurs on the same date as the BCE 6 to which it is related. The amount crystallised is the amount by which the payment exceeds the permitted maximum.
(c) Payment of a commencement lump sum paid in error under a money purchase arrangement.[53] The BCE occurs on the same date as the BCE 6 to which it is related (i.e. immediately before the connected pension). The amount crystallised is the amount by which the payment exceeds the permitted maximum.[54]
(d) Payment of a commencement lump sum after death.[55] The amount crystallised is the amount of the payment.

## AMOUNT OF AVAILABLE LIFETIME ALLOWANCE

Each individual had one lifetime allowance. The standard lifetime allowance was £1,073,100 for the 2023/24 tax year.[56] An individual's lifetime allowance was less than the standard lifetime allowance if he was in receipt of a pension which commenced before 6 April 2006 or if he has a protected pension age of less than 50 and a BCE occurred before he reached normal minimum pension age.[57] An individual's lifetime allowance was greater than the standard lifetime allowance if the individual is entitled to:

(a) Enhanced protection.[58]
(b) Fixed protection (there are three versions: FP 2012, FP 2014 and FP 2016).
(c) Individual protection (there are two versions: IP 2014 and IP 2016).
(d) One or more lifetime allowance enhancement factors.

**Fixed protection**

There are three versions of fixed protection:

(a) FP 2012: an individual has FP 2012 if: (i) he had one or more arrangements under a registered pension scheme on 6 April 2012; (ii) he did not have primary protection or enhanced protection on that date; and (iii) he gave notice to HMRC by 5 April 2012.[59] In relation to an individual with FP 2012, ITEPA 2003 Ch.15A applies as if the individual's LS allowance were £450,000 and his LS&DB allowance were £1.8 million.
(b) FP 2014: an individual has FP 2014 if: (i) he had one or more arrangements under a registered pension scheme on 6 April 2014; (ii) he does not, on that date, have primary protection, enhanced protection or FP 2012; and (iii) he gave notice to HMRC by 5 April 2014.[60] In relation to an individual with FP 2014, ITEPA 2003 Ch.15A applies as if the individual's LS allowance were £375,000 and his LS&DB allowance were £1.5 million.

10-020

10-021

---

[52] SI 2009/1171 reg.17.
[53] SI 2009/1171 reg.18.
[54] See Ch.14.
[55] SI 2009/1171 reg.19.
[56] The Finance Act 2004 (Standard Lifetime Allowance) Regulations 2020 (SI 2020/342) reg.2 and FA 2021 s.28. For a table showing the standard lifetime allowance for each tax year since 2006, see Ch.1.
[57] See Ch.3.
[58] For enhanced protection, see Ch.3.
[59] FA 2011 Sch.18 para.14.
[60] FA 2013 Sch.22.

(c) FP 2016: an individual has FP 2016 if: (i) he had one or more arrangements under a registered pension scheme on 6 April 2016; (ii) he does not, on that date, have primary protection, enhanced protection or FP 2012, FP 2014 or IP 2014; and (iii) he gives notice to HMRC. There is no deadline for giving such notification to HMRC.[61] In relation to an individual with FP 2016, ITEPA 2003 Ch.15A applies as if the individual's LS allowance were £312,500 and his LS&DB allowance were £1.25 million.

**10-022** In each case, fixed protection ceases to apply if: (a) the relevant notice to HMRC is given on or after 15 March 2023;[62] and (b) any of the following events on or after the relevant date:[63]

(i) there is benefit accrual in relation to the individual under an arrangement under a registered pension scheme;

(ii) there is an impermissible transfer into any arrangement under a registered pension scheme relating to the individual;

(iii) a transfer of sums or assets held for the purposes of, or representing accrued rights under, any such arrangement is made that is not a permitted transfer; or

(iv) an arrangement relating to the individual is made under a registered pension scheme otherwise than in permitted circumstances.

*Benefit accrual*

**10-023** The meaning of "benefit accrual" depends on the category of arrangement:

(a) Benefit accrual occurs under another money purchase arrangement if a "relevant contribution" is paid under the arrangement. "Relevant contribution" has the same meaning as for enhanced protection (see Ch.3).[64]

(b) Benefit accrual occurs under a cash balance arrangement if there is an increase in the amount that would, on the valuation assumptions,[65] be available for the provision of benefits to or in respect of the member, and the increase in any tax year exceeds the "relevant percentage".

(c) Benefit accrual occurs under a defined benefits arrangement if there is an increase in the "benefits amount", and the increase in any tax year exceeds

---

[61] FA 2016 Sch.4 Pts 1 and 3. If an individual dies without making an application for FP 2016, and he satisfied the requirements, his personal representatives can apply (FA 2016 Sch.4 para.19). If HMRC refuse to issue a reference number, or withdraw a reference number which has been issued, the taxpayer may appeal to the FTT (FA 2016 Pt 4 para.16).

[62] The 15 March 2023 restriction is in Finance (No.2) Bill 2023 draft cl.23. As a result of this restriction, the protection-cessation event will rarely have any application to fixed protection. HMRC's pensions schemes newsletter 148 (March 2023) confirms that "Members who hold a valid enhanced protection or any valid fixed protections, where this protection was applied for before 15 March 2023, and a certificate or reference number subsequently issued, from 6 April 2023 will be able to accrue new pension benefits, join new arrangements or transfer without losing this protection. They will also keep their entitlement to a higher PCLS."

[63] Being 6 April 2012 for FP 2012, 6 April 2014 for FP 2014, and 6 April 2016 for FP 2016.

[64] HMRC accept that if the member has told their bank or building society in good time that they want to stop the payment but the bank or building society have failed to act on this then the member will not lose fixed protection. The member did not intend the payment to be made so HMRC will not consider such payments as contributions. The payments should be returned to the member although they will have to repay any tax relief they obtained in relation to them: PTM093800.

[65] The valuation assumptions require one to value the individual's rights on the assumption that the individual is at the age at which no reduction would apply to the payment of an immediate benefit (e.g. as a result of early retirement) and the individual is in good physical and mental health and so the benefits are not increased as a result of being paid on grounds of ill-health (FA 2004 s.277).

# AMOUNT OF AVAILABLE LIFETIME ALLOWANCE

the "relevant percentage". To find the "benefits amount", one multiplies the annual rate of the pension which would, on the valuation assumptions, be payable to the individual under the arrangement by 20,[66] and adds the amount of the lump sum to which the individual would, on the valuation assumptions, be entitled under the arrangement (otherwise than by commutation of pension).

(d) In relation to a hybrid arrangement, one must perform the above calculations in relation to each category of benefits which may be provided to determine whether benefit accrual has occurred.

**The relevant percentage** The "relevant percentage", in relation to a tax year, means: (a) where the arrangement (or a predecessor arrangement[67]) includes provision for the value of the rights of the individual to increase during the tax year at an annual rate specified in the rules of the pension scheme (or a predecessor registered pension scheme) on the relevant date:[68] (i) that percentage (or, where more than one arrangement includes such provision, the higher or highest of the percentages specified); plus (ii) the relevant statutory increase percentage; or (b) if no annual rate is specified in the rules: (i) the percentage by which the CPI for the month of September in the previous tax year is higher than it was for the September before that (or 0% if CPI has not increased);[69] or (ii) if higher, the relevant statutory increase percentage. **10-024**

For FP 2012 only, there is a further alternative, which is an annual rate specified by reference to the RPI which is used to increase the member's rights and was specified in the rules of the scheme (or a predecessor registered pension scheme) on 6 April 2012 and which does not exceed the RPI increase (or the highest percentage so specified for an arrangement where there is more than one arrangement and they have different annual rates) plus the "relevant statutory increase percentage". If this produces a higher percentage than (a) above, this may be used as the relevant percentage. The "relevant statutory increase percentage", in relation to a tax year, means the percentage increase in the value of the individual's rights under the arrangement during the tax year so far as it is attributable solely to one or more of the following: (a) an increase in accordance with PSA 1993 s.15;[70] (b) a revaluation in accordance with PSA 1993 s.16;[71] (c) a revaluation in accordance with the PSA 1993 Pt 4 Ch.2;[72] (d) a revaluation in accordance with the PSA 1993 Pt 4 Ch.3;[73] (e) the application of the Equality Act 2010 s.67.[74] **10-025**

Where the scheme's rules provide for the rights to increase each year by one of **10-026**

---

[66] Unless a higher relevant valuation factor has been agreed with HMRC.
[67] i.e. another arrangement (under the same or another registered pension scheme) from which some or all of the sums or assets held for the purposes of the arrangement directly or indirectly derive. A predecessor registered pension scheme means another registered pension scheme from which some or all of the sums or assets held for the purposes of the arrangement under the pension scheme directly or indirectly derive.
[68] Being 9 December 2010 for FP 2012, 11 December 2012 for FP 2014 and 9 December 2015 for FP 2016.
[69] Where the arrangement is under a deferred annuity contract treated as a registered pension scheme under FA 2004 s.153(8), if applicable, the relevant percentage will instead be an annual rate of increase provided for in the contract so long as this annual rate is limited to the percentage increase in the RPI over a 12-month period specified in the contract and ending in the 12-month period preceding the month in which the increase occurs.
[70] Increase of guaranteed minimum where commencement of guaranteed minimum pension postponed.
[71] Early leavers: revaluation of earnings factors.
[72] Early leavers: revaluation of accrued benefits.
[73] Early leavers: protection of increases in guaranteed minimum pensions.
[74] Sex equality rule for occupational pension schemes.

**10-027** a number of specified rates (for example, by a rate that is the greater/lesser of 5% and the increase in the RPI during a 12-month period defined in the rules), this amounts to a specified annual rate and the relevant percentage is the rate by which the rights are actually increased in any particular tax year. Accordingly, this will not involve benefit accrual.

**10-027** Where an active member becomes a deferred member during a tax year the relevant percentage will, until the time of the change in status, be the relevant percentage applying to an active member.[75] From the date that he becomes a deferred member the relevant rate will be that applicable to a deferred member. It is not permissible to anticipate a more advantageous rate before the change in status occurs. And as the test is by reference to the value of the individual's rights at the beginning of the tax year, any increase in those rights during the period of active membership will be taken into account when testing for benefit accrual during the period of deferred membership.

**10-028** **Comment** In the context of cash balance and defined benefits arrangements, benefit accrual occurs if the value of rights increases in excess of the relevant percentage. Where benefits under a cash balance arrangement crystallise (i.e. funds are designated as available for drawdown pension or they are applied to purchase an annuity or scheme pension) the value of the cash balance arrangement will reduce. HMRC accept that a subsequent increase in the value of rights to their pre-crystallisation value does not involve benefit accrual.[76] Similarly, if rights under a defined benefits arrangement increase above the relevant percentage but are shortly afterwards reduced (because the member takes an early pension, for example), that will involve benefit accrual even though the value of the benefits taken may at that stage be less than the value of those benefits when they were calculated under the benefit accrual test. Death benefits which are defined benefits (e.g. a fraction of salary on death in service) do not form part of a member's defined benefit pension rights and so increases in the value of such rights cannot cause fixed protection to cease.[77]

*Impermissible transfers*

**10-029** There is an impermissible transfer for the purposes of fixed protection in the same circumstances in which there is an impermissible transfer for the purposes of enhanced protection (see Ch.3).[78]

*Permitted transfers*

**10-030** A transfer of sum or assets held for the purposes of, or representing accrued rights under, an arrangement is a permitted transfer if the sums or assets are transferred so that one of the following provisions applies in relation to them, and the total value of the sums or assets is equivalent before and after the transfer.[79] The provisions apply in relation to sums or assets held for the purposes of, or representing accrued rights under, the arrangement if:

---

[75] i.e. the rate stated in the scheme rules as at 9 December 2010 for FP 2012, 11 December 2012 for FP 2014 or 9 December 2015 for FP 2016 or CPI for September prior to the tax year in question.
[76] PTM093700.
[77] HMRC accept this at PTM093520.
[78] The references in the enhanced protection provisions to the existing relevant arrangement should be read as referring to the arrangement and the references to 5 April 2006 should be read as the relevant date Being 6 April 2012 for FP 2012, 6 April 2014 for FP 2014 and 6 April 2016 for FP 2016.
[79] FA 2004 Sch.36 para.12(7), as applied by FA 2011 Sch.18 para.14(9).

# AMOUNT OF AVAILABLE LIFETIME ALLOWANCE

(a) They are transferred so as to become held for the purposes of another money purchase arrangement under a registered pension scheme or ROPS. Where such a permitted transfer occurs, fixed protection applies in relation to the transferee arrangement.
(b) Where the transfer occurs in connection with the winding up of the pension scheme and the arrangement is a cash balance or defined benefits arrangement, the sums or assets are transferred so as to become held for the purposes of, or to represent rights under, a cash balance or defined benefits arrangement relating to the same employment as the transferor arrangement made under a registered pension scheme or ROPS. Where there is such a permitted transfer, fixed protection applies in relation to the transferee arrangement as if it were the same as that from which it is made.
(c) Where the arrangement is a cash balance or defined benefits arrangement relating to a present or former employment, the sum or assets are transferred in connection with a "relevant business transfer" so as to become held for the purposes of, or to represent rights under, a cash balance or defined benefits arrangement made under a registered pension scheme or ROPS.[80] Where there is a such a permitted transfer, fixed protection applies in relation to the transferee arrangement as if it were the transferor arrangement and (if the employment is transferred) as if the employment with the transferee were the employment with the transferor.
(d) Where the arrangement is a cash balance or defined benefits arrangement, the sums or assets are transferred as part of a "retirement-benefit activities compliance exercise" so as to become held for the purposes of, or to represent rights under, a cash balance or defined benefits arrangement relating to the same employment as the transferor arrangement and made under a registered pension scheme or ROPS.[81]

*Arrangements made otherwise than in permitted circumstances*

Whether or not an arrangement is made in permitted circumstances is determined in accordance with the enhanced protection provisions (see Ch.3). **10-031**

### Rescinding a protection-cessation event on the ground of mistake

Where a contribution to a pension scheme is a protection-cessation event, it may be desirable to apply to the High Court to have the contribution (and any subsequent contributions) rescinded. Applying the principles established in *Pitt v Holt*,[82] a contribution may be set aside by a court where: **10-032**

(a) the contribution was a mistake; and
(b) an examination of the nature and seriousness of that mistake establishes that

---

[80] A "relevant business transfer" is a transfer of an undertaking or a business (or part of an undertaking or a business) from one person to another which involves the transfer of at least 20 employees, and in the case of which, if the transferor and the transferee are bodies corporate, they would not be treated as members of the same group for the purposes of CTA 2010 Pt 5.
[81] Sums or assets held for the purposes of, or representing accrued rights under, the old arrangement are transferred as part of a "retirement-benefit activities compliance exercise" if there is a prospective entitlement to authorised death benefits under both the old arrangement and the new arrangement, and the transfer constitutes or forms part of a transaction the purpose of which is to secure that the activities of the pension scheme under which the old arrangement was made are limited to retirement-benefit activities within the meaning of PA 2004 s.255.
[82] *Pitt v Holt* [2013] UKSC 26.

**10-033** it is appropriate to set aside the contribution. The gravity of the mistake must be assessed by a close examination of the facts.

**10-033** These requirements were considered in *Hymanson v HMRC*.[83] In that case, Mr Hymanson obtained FP 2012 and was advised that any further contributions would cause protection to cease, but he misunderstood that advice and concluded that he could continue to make the same contributions he had made before he obtained protection. The first monthly contribution after April 2012 (of £62.50) was a protection-cessation event, as a result of which he was around £50,000 worse off.

**10-034** A mistake as to the tax consequences of a transaction is sufficient, provided that the taxpayer actively believes that the contribution would not cause protection to cease. Mere ignorance, even if causative, is insufficient, but "the court, in carrying out its task of finding the facts, should not shrink from drawing the inference of conscious belief or tacit assumption when there is evidence to support such an inference".[84] In *Lobler v HMRC*[85] (a case concerning the chargeable event regime applicable to insurance policies), the taxpayer did not take any advice but the Upper Tribunal held that that did not mean he should be deprived of the remedy of rectification (the requirements for which are not, at least in this respect, materially different to those for the remedy of rescission). The Upper Tribunal said at [73]: "One does not seek advice on everything, the legislation is not at all intuitive and no reasonable man would have expected the outcome." The same may be said of the lifetime allowance provisions.

**10-035** In relation to the "sufficiently serious" aspect of the test, the FTT in *Hymanson* formulated the question thus: if the member had understood the tax consequences of making the contribution, would he have done so?[86] It was clear to the FTT that he would not.

**10-036** The FTT does not itself have jurisdiction to rescind a transaction, so historically it was thought to be necessary to apply to the High Court. However, the decision in *Hymanson* shows that it may be possible to sidestep that requirement on the basis that HMRC's decision to revoke the member's enhanced or fixed protection does not take into account relevant factors, and/or does take into account factors which are not relevant. Where a contribution to a pension scheme is a protection-cessation event, one of the factors HMRC should take into account is the possibility that the contribution may be void as a result of mistake.

**10-037** In *Hymanson* the FTT concluded that if an application were made to the High Court, the remedy of rescission would be granted in respect of the taxpayer's mistake and, applying the equitable maxim, "that which should be done should be treated as having been done" (or, in that case, "that which should not have been done should be treated as not having been done"), the FTT concluded that Mr Hymanson's tax position should be determined as if that remedy had been granted. The FTT found that HMRC should have, but did not, take into account any possibility that the contributions to the pension schemes might be void as a result of mistake, even though the relevant arguments had been put to them at that stage. The FTT therefore concluded that HMRC's decision was unreasonable and directed HMRC to issue a new certificate to Mr Hymanson.

**10-038** HMRC gave notice of its intention to appeal the decision, but decided not to

---

[83] *Hymanson v HMRC* [2018] UKFTT 667 (TC).
[84] *Pitt v Holt* [2013] UKSC 26 at [108].
[85] *Lobler v HMRC* [2015] UKUT 152.
[86] *Hymanson v HMRC* [2018] UKFTT 667 (TC) at [74].

AMOUNT OF AVAILABLE LIFETIME ALLOWANCE

proceed with the appeal. It is understood that this was because Mr Hymanson did in fact obtain an order from the High Court for rescission.[87]

**10-039** Note that, in practice, HMRC may invite the taxpayer to accept that protection has ceased. This should be resisted, as the decision in *Gough v HMRC* shows.[88] If HMRC can avoid making a decision, the taxpayer will have nothing he can appeal to the FTT.

### Individual protection

**10-040** There are two types of individual protection:

(a) *IP 2014:* when the lifetime allowance was reduced from £1.5 million to £1.25 million on 6 April 2014, IP 2014 was introduced in order to provide protection for members who had already accrued benefits of more than £1.25 million.

(b) *IP 2016:* when the lifetime allowance was reduced from £1.25 million to £1 million on 6 April 2016, IP 2016 was introduced in order to provide protection for members who had already accrued benefits of more than £1 million.

*Individual protection 2014 ("IP 2014")*

**10-041** IP 2014 applies to an individual if:[89]

(a) On 5 April 2014 he was a member of a registered pension scheme, or a relieved member of a relieved non-UK pension scheme.[90]
(b) He does not have primary protection.
(c) He gave notice to HMRC before 6 April 2017.
(d) The total of Amounts A, B, C and D (his "relevant amount") is greater than £1.25 million:
  (i) Amount A relates to the value of any pension under a tax-approved pension schemes, or any other "relevant existing pension",[91] to which the individual had an actual (rather than a merely prospective) right on 5 April 2006.[92] The method for determining Amount A depends on whether a BCE has occurred in relation to the individual between 6 April 2006 and 5 April 2014. If no such BCE has occurred, Amount A is equal to "25 x ARP", where ARP is an amount equal to the total annual rate at which all relevant existing pensions were payable to the individual on 5 April 2014. If on 5 April 2014, the member was in capped drawdown, ARP is the maximum amount of drawdown pension a member is able to take for his drawdown year which includes

---

[87] See *Gough v HMRC* [2021] UKFTT 273 at [50].
[88] *Gough v HMRC* [2021] UKFTT 273.
[89] FA 2014 Sch.6 para.1. Also see The Registered Pension Schemes and Relieved Non-UK Pension Schemes (Lifetime Allowance Transitional Protection) (Individual Protection 2014 Notification) Regulations 2014 (SI 2014/1842) and The Registered Pension Schemes (Provision of Information) (Amendment) Regulations 2014 (SI 2014/1843).
[90] For relieved non-UK pension schemes, see Ch.30.
[91] "Relevant existing pension" in defined in Sch.36 para.10(2). If before 6 April 2014, there was a recognised transfer of sums or assets representing a relevant existing pension, and those sums or assets were, after the transfer, applied towards the provision of a scheme pension, the new scheme pension is also a relevant existing pension. However a pension, annuity or right is not a relevant existing pension if entitlement to it was attributable to the death of any person.
[92] FA 2014 Sch.6 para.2.

5 April 2014. If the member was in flexible drawdown on that date, ARP is the maximum annual amount of capped drawdown pension that would have been payable in the drawdown pension year in which the flexible drawdown declaration was accepted by the scheme administrator, had that declaration not been made. If such a BCE has occurred, Amount A is equal to "25 x ARP x (1,500,000/SLT)" where SLT is an amount equal to what the standard lifetime allowance was at the time the BCE occurred, and ARP is an amount equal to the total annual rate at which all relevant existing pensions were payable to the individual at the time immediately before the BCE occurred. Where a relevant existing pension was drawdown pension: (a) if the BCE occurred before 6 April 2011, ARP is the maximum annual amount that could have been paid as either unsecured pension or alternatively secured pension in the pension year in which the first BCE occurred; (b) for capped drawdown between 6 April 2011 and 5 April 2014, ARP is the maximum amount that could have been paid in the pension year that contains the date of the first BCE; (c) for flexible drawdown between 6 April 2011 and 5 April 2014, ARP is the maximum annual amount that could have been paid as capped drawdown immediately before the BCE had a flexible drawdown declaration not been made. If the member has had more than one BCE before 6 April 2014, one uses the date of the first BCE for the purposes of the revaluation.

(ii) Amount B is the amount crystallised by each BCE that has occurred in relation to the individual between 6 April 2006 and 5 April 2014, multiplied by "1,500,000/SLT" where SLT is an amount equal to the standard lifetime allowance at the time that the BCE occurred.[93]

(iii) Amount C is the total value of the individual's uncrystallised rights on 5 April 2014 under registered pension schemes determined as follows.[94] The value of the member's uncrystallised rights under a cash balance arrangement is the amount which would, on the valuation assumptions,[95] be available for the provision of benefits in respect of those rights if the member became entitled to benefits in respect of those rights on 5 April 2014. The value of the member's uncrystallised rights under another money purchase arrangement on 5 April 2014 is the total value of the cash and assets held for the purposes of the arrangement on that date as represent those rights. The value of the member's uncrystallised rights under a defined benefits arrangement on 5 April 2014 is equal to "(20[96] x ARP) + LS" where: ARP is the annual rate of pension to which the member would, on the valuation assumptions, be entitled under the arrangement on 5 April 2014 if, on that date, the member acquired an actual (rather than a prospective) right to receive a pension in respect of the rights;

---

[93] FA 2014 Sch.6 para.3.
[94] FA 2014 Sch.6 para.4, applying FA 2004 s.212.
[95] The valuation assumptions require one to value the individual's rights on the assumption that the individual is at the age at which no reduction would apply to the payment of an immediate benefit (e.g. as a result of early retirement) and the individual is in good physical and mental health and so the benefits are not increased as a result of being paid on grounds of ill-health (FA 2004 s.277).
[96] Or such higher valuation factor agreed between HMRC and the scheme administrator under FA 2004 s.276.

# AMOUNT OF AVAILABLE LIFETIME ALLOWANCE

and LS is the amount of any lump sum to which the member would, on the valuation assumptions, be entitled under the arrangement on 5 April 2014 (otherwise than by way of commutation of pension) if, on that date, the member acquired an actual (rather than a prospective) right to payment of a lump sum in respect of the rights. The value of the member's uncrystallised rights under a hybrid arrangement on 5 April 2014 is the greater of whichever of the above may be applicable.

(iv) Amount D is applicable if the individual is, at the end of 5 April 2014, a relieved member of a relieved non-UK pension scheme.[97] In relation to each such scheme: (a) assume that a BCE occurs in relation to the individual at the end of 5 April 2014; and (b) determine what the "untested portion" of the "relevant relieved amount" would be immediately before the assumed BCE.[98] Amount D is the sum of those untested portions.[99]

**Effect of IP 2014** In relation to an individual with IP 2014, FA 2004 Pt 4 applies as if the standard lifetime allowance were: (a) if the individual's relevant amount is greater than £1.5 million, the greater of the standard lifetime allowance and £1.5 million; or (b) otherwise, the greater of the standard lifetime allowance and the individual's relevant amount. An individual with enhanced protection, FP 2012, or FP 2014 can also have IP 2014, but those provisions provide greater protection, and so take priority. **10-042**

**Pension debits** If the member's pension rights are subject to a pension debit then his protected lifetime allowance may be reduced or cease to apply altogether. If rights of an individual under a relevant arrangement become subject to a pension debit where the transfer day[100] is after 5 April 2014, the individual's relevant amount on and after the transfer day is reduced by an amount equal to "X − (Y x Z)", where: X is the appropriate amount;[101] Y is 5% of X; and Z is the number of tax years beginning after 5 April 2014 but ending on or before the transfer day. If the effect of this is that individual's relevant amount would be reduced to £1.25 million or less, IP 2014 ceases to apply on and after the transfer day. **10-043**

*Individual protection 2016 ("IP 2016")*

IP 2016 applies to an individual at any particular time on or after 6 April 2016 if:[102] **10-044**

(a) On 5 April 2016 he was a member of a registered pension scheme, or a relieved member of a relieved non-UK pension scheme.[103]
(b) He does not have primary protection.
(c) He does not have enhanced protection, FP 2012, FP 2014, IP 2014 or FP 2016 at the particular time.
(d) At the particular time or any later time he has a reference number.

---

[97] For relieved non-UK pension schemes, see Ch.30.
[98] For the meaning of "untested portion" of the "relevant relieved amount", see Ch.30.
[99] FA 2014 Sch.6 para.5.
[100] "Transfer day", in relation to a pension debit, has the same meaning as in WRPA 1999 s.29.
[101] "Appropriate amount", in relation to a pension debit, has the same meaning as in WRPA 1999 s.29.
[102] FA 2016 Sch.4 para.9.
[103] For relieved non-UK pension schemes, see Ch.30.

(e) The total of Amounts A, B, C and D (his "relevant amount") is greater than £1 million:
    (i) Subject to the following two points, amount A is determined in the same way as for IP 2014 (except that the relevant date is 5 April 2016 rather than 5 April 2014). Firstly, if a BCE occurred between 6 April 2006 and 5 April 2016, Amount A is equal to "25 x ARP x (1,250,000/SLT)". Secondly, in the case of drawdown pension, ARP is 80% of the maximum that could be paid.[104] Also, in the case of flexi-access drawdown (which did not exist when IP 2014 was introduced), ARP is determined as follows: (a) for flexi-access drawdown that was previously flexible drawdown, if on 5 April 2016 the drawdown pension was in flexi-access drawdown but the pension had previously been in flexible drawdown ARP is the maximum amount of capped drawdown pension that would have been payable in the drawdown pension year in which the flexible drawdown declaration was accepted by the scheme administrator, had that declaration not been made; (b) for flexi-access drawdown that was previously capped drawdown, where the member converted his capped drawdown fund to flexi-access drawdown after 5 April 2015 but before 6 April 2016 ARP is maximum annual capped drawdown pension that could have been paid in the drawdown pension year in which the conversion to flexi-access drawdown occurred, had that conversion not occurred.
    (ii) Amount B is the amount crystallised by each BCE that has occurred in relation to the individual between 6 April 2006 and 5 April 2016, multiplied by "1,250,000/SLT" where SLT is an amount equal to the standard lifetime allowance at the time that the BCE occurred.[105]
    (iii) Amount C is determined in the same way as for IP 2014, except that the relevant date is 5 April 2016 rather than 5 April 2014.
    (iv) Amount D is determined in the same way as for IP 2014, except that the relevant date is 5 April 2016 rather than 5 April 2014.

**10-045** In relation to an individual with IP 2016, FA 2004 Pt 4 applies as if the standard lifetime allowance were: (a) if the individual's relevant amount is greater than £1.25 million, the greater of the standard lifetime allowance and £1.25 million; or (b) otherwise, the greater of the standard lifetime allowance and the individual's relevant amount. An individual with enhanced protection, FP 2012, FP 2014, IP 2014, or FP 2016 can also have IP 2016 on a "dormant" basis for so long as the other protection remains valid.[106] This is because these other protections all protect a higher amount of lifetime allowance, so IP 2016 is not required while the other protection remains valid. The commentary above in relation to pension debits and IP 2014 is the same as for IP 2016 (except that the relevant date is 5 April 2016 rather than 5 April 2014).

**Lifetime allowance enhancement factors**

**10-046** A lifetime allowance enhancement factor applied where:

---

[104] FA 2016 Sch.4 para.10(3) and (4), applying FA 2004 Sch.36 para.20(4).
[105] FA 2016 Sch.4 para.11.
[106] FA 2016 Sch.4 para.14(7)–(9).

# AVAILABILITY OF LIFETIME ALLOWANCE ON A BCE

(a) The member is entitled to primary protection. This is referred to as the "primary protection factor" (see Ch.3).
(b) The member acquires a pension credit on or after 6 April 2006 in relation to rights under another registered pension scheme which consisted of or included rights to a pension already in payment and which came into payment on or after 6 April 2006 (the "pension credit factor") (see Ch.16).
(c) A pension credit was acquired before 6 April 2006 (the "pre-commencement pension credit factor") (see Ch.16).
(d) Certain benefits accrue under a registered pension scheme during a period in which the member is a relevant overseas individual (the "non-residence factor") (see Ch.20).
(e) Benefits accrue in a ROPS and are subsequently transferred to a registered pension scheme (the "recognised overseas scheme transfer factor") (see Ch.20).

In each case, the member must claim the lifetime allowance enhancement factor by notifying HMRC, and HMRC will provide the individual with a certificate confirming his entitlement.

**10-047**

If a lifetime allowance enhancement factor operates in relation to a BCE the individual's lifetime allowance at the time of the BCE is equal to "SLA + (SLA x LAEF)" where:

**10-048**

- *SLA* is the standard lifetime allowance at the time of the BCE, except in the case of the primary protection lifetime allowance enhancement factor, where SLA is £1.8 million if that is greater than the standard lifetime allowance at the time of the BCE. Other than in relation to primary protection, if the BCE occurred before 6 April 2012, SLA is £1.8 million if that is greater than the standard lifetime allowance at the time. If the event occurred between 6 April 2012 and 5 April 2014, SLA is £1.5 million if that is greater than the standard lifetime allowance at the time. If the event occurred between 5 April 2014 and 6 April 2016, SLA is £1.25 million if that is greater than the standard lifetime allowance at the time; and
- *LAEF* is the lifetime allowance enhancement factor which operates with respect to the BCE and the individual or (where more than one so operates) the aggregate of them.

# AVAILABILITY OF LIFETIME ALLOWANCE ON A BCE

On the occurrence of each BCE, it was necessary to calculate the individual's available lifetime allowance.[107] Prior to 6 April 2023, it was advisable for the scheme administrator to perform this calculation prior to making any payment so that a sum equal to any lifetime allowance charge arising as a result of the event could be retained and paid to HMRC.[108] The scheme administrator was not expressly required to do this, but as the scheme administrator was jointly liable for any lifetime allowance charge (except in relation to BCE 5C, BCE 5D and BCE 7), the administrator would usually wish to ensure that it was paid from scheme funds.

**10-049**

On the occurrence of the first BCE relating to the individual, the whole of his

**10-050**

---

[107] FA 2004 s.219.
[108] The scheme administrator is not obliged under FA 2004 to consider whether a charge arises but as the scheme administrator is jointly liable for any lifetime allowance charge (except in relation to BCE 7) he will usually be anxious to ensure that it is paid from scheme funds.

lifetime allowance is available. On the occurrence of a subsequent BCE, one reduces his available lifetime allowance by the amount(s) crystallised by the previous BCE(s). The amount available is then adjusted as follows. The amount crystallised on a previous BCE is that amount multiplied by "CSLA/PSLA", where CSLA is the individual's lifetime allowance at the time of the current BCE; and PSLA is the individual's lifetime allowance at the time of the previous BCE. The effect of this is that the amount crystallised as a result of a BCE is always shown as a percentage of the individual's lifetime allowance at the time of that BCE. The amount crystallised by subsequent BCEs is also shown as a percentage of the individual's lifetime allowance at the time of that subsequent BCE. The percentage remains constant even though the individual's lifetime allowance may change from one year to the next (e.g. because the standard lifetime allowance changes). This means that the member's available lifetime allowance is also shown as a percentage and so the actual amount available will increase or decrease with his lifetime allowance.

10-051 Where more than one BCE occurs in relation to an individual on the same day, he must decide the order in which they are to be treated as occurring for these purposes. This is subject to s.166(2), which provides that the entitlement to a PCLS always arises immediately before the entitlement to the connected pension.

10-052 Where more than one BCE occurs by reason of the payment of lump sum death benefits in respect of an individual, the BCEs are deemed to occur simultaneously immediately before the individual's death.

## THE LIFETIME ALLOWANCE CHARGE

10-053 As noted above, the lifetime allowance charge was removed with effect from 6 April 2023. The following commentary will therefore has no effect from that date.

10-054 Prior to 6 April 2023, the lifetime allowance charge arose where the amount crystallised by a BCE exceeded the amount of the individual's available lifetime allowance.[109] It was chargeable by reference to the "chargeable amount", meaning the "basic amount" plus any "scheme-funded tax payment" in respect of any "lump-sum amount" or any "retained amount".[110] The basic amount is the amount by which the amount crystallised by the BCE exceeds the amount of the individual's available lifetime allowance. The lump-sum amount means so much of the basic amount as is paid as a lump sum to the individual or a lump sum death benefit in respect of the individual. The retained amount means so much of the basic amount as is not paid as a lump sum.

10-055 The rate of the charge is 55% in respect of so much of the chargeable amount as is a lump-sum amount and 25% in respect of so much of the chargeable amount as is a retained amount. Only BCE 6 and BCE 7 (or some of the equivalent payments under BCE 9) can give rise to the 55% charge.[111] All other BCEs give rise to the 25% charge. A recognised transfer to a QROPS (which is BCE 8) does *not* involve a lump sum amount because it is not paid *to the individual* (such a payment in in

---

[109] FA 2004 s.214.
[110] FA 2004 s.215.
[111] Only the following can give rise to the 55% charge: a serious ill-health lump sum, a stand-alone lump sum, a lifetime allowance excess lump sum, a defined benefits LSDB, or uncrystallised funds LSDB. Neither a PCLS (except where protected lump sum of more than £375,000, or scheme specific protection lump sum of over 25%) nor an uncrystallised funds pension lump sum can give rise to a chargeable amount.

# THE LIFETIME ALLOWANCE CHARGE

respect of the member but not to him). It is therefore a retained amount and so is taxed at 25%.[112]

**Scheme-funded tax payments**

The scheme administrator may pay any lifetime allowance charge which arises, and where he does so this is referred to as a "scheme-funded tax payment".[113] In all cases other than BCE 2, BCE 3, and BCE 5 (which all involve scheme pension) where there is a scheme-funded tax payment, the amount that crystallises for lifetime allowance purposes is the net amount (i.e. the amount that is actually available to pay benefits) whereas the lifetime allowance charge is calculated by reference to the gross amount (i.e. the amount available to pay benefits plus the tax payable). HMRC accept that the lifetime allowance charge may be paid from the scheme's own resources[114] (i.e. without reducing the member's benefits under the scheme).[115] In relation to BCE 2, BCE 3, and BCE 5, if a scheme pension is reduced to fund the lifetime allowance charge, the amount that crystallises for lifetime allowance purposes is determined by reference to the original (unreduced) scheme pension.[116]

10-056

**The purpose of the charge**

The purpose of the lifetime allowance charge was to limit the total value of pension rights that a person can accrue tax-efficiently. HMRC assert that its purpose is to "broadly recover the tax reliefs those funds have benefited from over the years, both on the initial payments and the build-up of those funds or underlying investments over the years".[117] There is however no requirement that the funds actually benefitted from any tax relief.[118] The accrual of benefits may well have given rise to an annual allowance charge but there is nothing in the lifetime allowance provisions to make allowance for this. Accordingly it is quite possible for an individual's pension benefits to have been subject to the annual allowance charge as they accrued, and subject to the lifetime allowance charge on a subsequent BCE.[119]

10-057

**Liability**

The member[120] and the scheme administrator are both liable for the lifetime allowance charge on a joint and several basis,[121] except where the chargeable amount

10-058

---

[112] HMRC agree at PTM085000.
[113] FA 2004 s.215(9).
[114] PTM085000.
[115] This is because the scheme administrator is jointly and severally liable for the lifetime allowance charge. It should constitute a scheme administration member payment (and is therefore an authorised payment).
[116] For the purposes of BCE 2, BCE 3, and BCE 5, respectively, any such reduction is left out of account in determining the amount of "P" (FA 2004 Sch.32 para.9(2)), "XP" (Sch.32 para.13(4) and "DP" (Sch.32 para.14(2)).
[117] PTM083000.
[118] Although there is partial recognition of this for transfers from ROPS (see Ch.20).
[119] In 2006 the lifetime allowance was approximately seven times the annual allowance. Now the lifetime allowance is almost 26 times the annual allowance, making it much more difficult to reach the lifetime allowance without suffering an annual allowance charge.
[120] Where a BCE 9 occurs after the member's death, the scheme administrator has joint and several liability with the deceased member (through his personal representatives).
[121] Payment of the charge by the scheme administrator should always be a scheme administration member payment, and therefore an authorised payment (see Ch.11).

arises in respect of a "relevant post-death crystallisation event". As with the other tax charges imposed under FA 2004 Pt 4, liability is not affected by the residence or domicile status of the taxpayer. The scheme administrator accounts to HMRC for the lifetime allowance charge in the Accounting for Tax Return, which is due on a quarterly basis. The member is required to include his own liability to the charge on his personal self-assessment tax return and can claim a credit for the tax paid by the scheme administrator. The scheme administrator will provide a notice confirming the rate of charge due and the amount paid by the scheme to help the individual do this.

*Relevant post-death crystallisation events*

**10-059** BCE 5C, BCE 5D and BCE 7 relate to death benefits and are referred to as relevant post-death crystallisation events. The liability for any charge arising in respect of such events is solely a liability of the dependant/nominee (BCE 5C and BCE 5D) or recipient (BCE 7).[122] As the scheme administrator is not liable for any charge arising in these circumstances, any payment of the tax will effectively be a payment to the beneficiary (even if paid directly to HMRC). The member's personal representatives are responsible for determining whether a chargeable amount arises following a relevant post-death crystallisation event, and for informing HMRC. They only need to do this after the event occurs and HMRC will then assess the beneficiary.

**10-060** If the individual has some lifetime allowance available at death, but a chargeable amount arises as a result of more than one relevant post-death crystallisation events, the events are deemed to have occurred simultaneously immediately before death and each recipient is liable to such portion of the total amount of the tax payable by reason of their having been paid as appears to HMRC to be just and reasonable.[123]

*Discharge of tax liability: good faith*

**10-061** Where a scheme administrator becomes liable to pay a lifetime allowance charge he may apply to HMRC for the discharge of this liability if: (a) he reasonably believed that there was no such liability; and (b) in all the circumstances of the case, it would not be just and reasonable for the scheme administrator to be liable.[124] A scheme administrator may apply to HMRC for the discharge of *part* of his liability to the lifetime allowance charge in respect of the BCE if: (a) the scheme administrator reasonably believed that the amount of the lifetime allowance charge in respect of the BCE was less than the actual amount; and (b) in all the circumstances of the case, it would not be just and reasonable for the scheme administrator to be liable to an amount equal to the difference between the amount which the scheme administrator believed to be the amount of the charge and the actual amount.[125]

**10-062** Such an application must be made within six years of the end of the accounting period to which the application relates (for a corporate scheme administrator), or five years after 31 January next following the year of assessment to which the application relates (for a scheme administrator that is not a company). However, if

---

[122] FA 2004 s.217.
[123] At PTM087000.
[124] See FA 2004 s.267 and The Registered Pension Schemes (Discharge of Liabilities under ss.267 and 268 of the Finance Act 2004) Regulations 2005 (SI 2005/3452).
[125] FA 2004 s.267.

REPORTING OBLIGATIONS 267

there has been a discovery assessment[126] then the deadline is two years after the date on which the assessment was made. If HMRC refuse to discharge the scheme administrator from liability for the lifetime allowance charge, he can appeal to the FTT under FA 2004 s.269(2). The burden of proof is on the scheme administrator to satisfy the tribunal that it would be not be just and reasonable in all the circumstances for the scheme administrator to be liable to the charge (or part thereof).[127] The discharge of the scheme administrator's liability to the lifetime allowance charge (or part thereof) does not of course affect the liability of any other person to the lifetime allowance charge.

The only way that the scheme administrator can know how much of a member's lifetime allowance has been used up by previous BCE s occurring in relation to other pension schemes, is if the member informs him. If a BCE occurs and the scheme administrator does not withhold sufficient tax, he is jointly and severally liable for the outstanding amount, and there may not be any funds remaining in the scheme to pay the tax. If the scheme administrator has relied on a statement by the member then one would expect that it would be just and reasonable for him to be discharged, provided that it was reasonable for him to rely on the statement. If there is any reason to suspect that the member may be carelessly providing the information then the scheme administrator should look further.[128]

**10-063**

HMRC suggest that where a member fails to declare to the scheme administrator what his available lifetime allowance is, the scheme administrator should postpone the event triggering the BCE.[129] Where the event cannot be postponed (e.g. where the member is approaching his 75th birthday) HMRC suggest that the scheme administrator may assume the member has no available lifetime allowance, pay 25% tax to HMRC and retain the balance in the scheme.[130] They recommend that a lifetime allowance excess lump sum is not paid in these circumstances because it can only be paid if the member has no available lifetime allowance and if this is not the case then it may be an unauthorised member payment, and if so HMRC would not discharge the scheme administrator's liability to the scheme sanction charge because the scheme administrator acted on insufficient information and so there would not be reasonable belief.

**10-064**

## REPORTING OBLIGATIONS

The scheme administrator had the following reporting obligations in connection with the lifetime allowance:

**10-065**

(a) It must, within three months of each BCE occurring, notify the member (or his personal representatives) of the percentage of his lifetime allowance that has been used up.[131] If the member is receiving a pension from the scheme (including having designated sums or assets as available for the payment

---

[126] i.e. an assessment made under TMA 1970 s.36.
[127] FA 2004 s.269.
[128] The ground for relief is similar to the grounds applicable in respect of the unauthorised payments surcharge and the scheme sanction charge.
[129] At PTM086000.
[130] HMRC will repay any overpayment (with interest) to the scheme administrator (SI 2005/3454 regs 6 and 7). It is possible to pay any such repayment to the member as a PCLS notwithstanding that it is not paid within the usual 18-month window (see Ch.14).
[131] The Registered Pension Schemes (Provision of Information) Regulations 2006 (SI 2006/567) regs 8 and 14.

drawdown pension) the scheme administrator must notify him of his available lifetime allowance at least once each tax year.[132]

(b) If it has paid, or intends to pay, any lifetime allowance charge it must within three months of the BCE occurring notify the member of the chargeable amount.[133]

(c) It must, within three months of a recognised transfer, notify the administrator of the receiving scheme of the member's available lifetime allowance.[134]

(d) It must notify HMRC (in the annual event report) if a BCE occurs that exceeds the lifetime allowance and the member claims one or more of the available forms of protection.[135]

(e) It must notify HMRC of any payment of lump-sum death benefits exceeding 50% of the standard lifetime allowance.[136]

**10-066** The personal representatives of the member must notify HMRC where a relevant lump sum death benefit is paid in respect of a deceased member and the payment result in a lifetime allowance charge.[137]

---

[132] SI 2006/567 regs 8 and 14.
[133] SI 2006/567 reg.12.
[134] SI 2006/567 reg.15.
[135] SI 2006/567 reg.3 (reportable event 6).
[136] SI 2006/567 reg.3 (reportable event 2).
[137] SI 2006/567 reg.10.

# CHAPTER 11

# Authorised Member Payments

## TABLE OF CONTENTS

| | |
|---|---|
| Introduction | 11-001 |
| Scheme administration member payments | 11-002 |
|     "For the purposes of administration or management" | 11-004 |
|     "The amount which might be expected to be paid to a person ... at arm's length" | 11-010 |
|     Loans | 11-012 |

## INTRODUCTION

**11-001** A payment made to or in respect of a member or former member of a registered pension scheme is an authorised member payment if it is one of the following:[1]

(a) pensions permitted by the pension rules or pension death benefits rules to be paid to or in respect of a member (see Chs 13 and 15);
(b) lump sums permitted by the lump sum rule or lump sum death benefits rules to be paid to or in respect of a member (see Chs 14 and 15);
(c) recognised transfers (see Ch.12);
(d) scheme administration member payments (see below);
(e) payments pursuant to a pension sharing order or provision (see Ch.16); and
(f) certain other payments prescribed by regulations (see Chs 13 to 15).

This is an exhaustive list; any other payment to or in respect of a member is an unauthorised member payment.

## SCHEME ADMINISTRATION MEMBER PAYMENTS

**11-002** The purchase by a pension scheme of an asset from a scheme member, or the sale of an asset to a member (or, in either case, a person connected with a member), necessarily involves a payment by the scheme to or in respect of the member.[2] If the payment is on arm's length terms, and is made for the purposes of the administration or management of the scheme, it will usually be a scheme administration member payment, which is a type of authorised member payment. Section 171(1)–(4) provides that:

"(1) A "scheme administration member payment" is a payment by a registered pen-

---

[1] FA 2004 ss.160(1) and 164(1).
[2] "Payment" expressly includes the transfer of an asset (FA 2004 s.161(2)). A payment to a person connected with a member is deemed to be "in respect of" the member (FA 2004 s.161(5)).

sion scheme to or in respect of a person who is or has been a member of the pension scheme which is made for the purposes of the administration or management of the pension scheme.

(2) But if a payment falling within subsection (1) exceeds the amount which might be expected to be paid to a person who was at arm's length, the excess is not a scheme administration member payment.

(3) Scheme administration member payments include in particular—
  (a) the payment of wages, salaries or fees to persons engaged in administering the pension scheme, and
  (b) payments made for the purchase of assets to be held for the purposes of the pension scheme.

(4) A loan to or in respect of a person who is or has been a member of the pension scheme is not a scheme administration member payment."

**11-003** If the payment exceeds the amount which might be expected to be paid to a person who is at arm's length then only the excess is an unauthorised member payment. Thus, for example, if the trustees of a registered pension scheme purchase an asset with a value of £100 from a member, and they pay £110 to him, this is a scheme administration member payment to the extent of £100 but the additional £10 is an unauthorised member payment.

### "For the purposes of administration or management"

**11-004** It is unlikely that "administration"[3] and "management"[4] are intended to be construed separately: it is a single composite phrase with considerable overlap between the two words.[5] Any payment made for the purpose of running the scheme is within the scope of this provision. The payment must be either "to" or "in respect of" a member.[6] In addition to the purchase of investments from, or the sale of investments to, a scheme member (or connected persons), the payment of fees to administrators, trustees, investment managers, auditors, actuaries, advisers, and other persons involved in the administration or management of the scheme, are plainly within the scope of this provision.

---

[3] In *R. (Britannic Asset Management Ltd) v Pensions Ombudsman* [2002] EWHC 441 (Admin); [2002] O.P.L.R. 175, Lightman J said this, in the context of PSA 1993 s.146(4), "... "administering the Scheme" means (in whole or in part) running the Scheme, e.g. inviting employees to join, keeping records of members, communicating with members, calculating benefits, providing benefit statements, paying benefits when due, keeping documentation up to date, dealing with governmental or regulatory agencies (Inland Revenue, DWP, OPRA) etc. In the case of a funded scheme, it will also no doubt involve running the fund and investing in managing the Scheme's assets."

[4] In *Century Life Plc v Pensions Ombudsman* [1995] C.L.C. 1276; [1995] Pens. L.R. 135 at 44 and 52, which concerned (amongst other things) the meaning of "manager" in PSA 1993 s.146, Dyson J accepted that "'Manager' is an ordinary English word. It means the person who is in fact running the scheme. This means, for example, calculating benefits, arranging for actuarial reviews, providing documentation and keeping it up to date, corresponding with the Inland Revenue and Department of Social Security, paying transfer values for early leavers, general administration and giving advice to the trustees in a funded scheme. It was accepted that under the trust deeds of funded schemes the ultimate responsibility lies with the trustees, and that it is against the trustees that members have enforceable rights. It does not, however, follow from this that the trustees will be running the scheme. In small insurance schemes, the insurance company almost invariably runs the scheme, and the role of the trustees in practice is likely to be little more than collecting and paying contributions, and taking whatever other steps the insurance company advises should be taken".

[5] As Lord Roskill said of the composite phrase "repair or maintenance" in *ACT Constructions Ltd v Customs and Excise Comrs* [1981] 1 W.L.R. 1542.

[6] A payment to a person connected with a member is deemed to be "in respect of" the member (FA 2004 s.161(5)). Payments which deplete the value of a member's arrangement under the scheme are also made in respect of the member (see Ch.18).

11-005 The payment by a scheme administrator of a tax charge for which the member and scheme administrator are jointly and severally liable is a payment in respect of the member.[7] If the charge arises by virtue of an authorised payment, it seems that payment of the charge is regarded as forming part of the authorised payment, so it is not necessary to consider whether it is a scheme administration member payment.[8] In other circumstances, such as where a lifetime allowance charge arose before 6 April 2023 by virtue of the member reaching age 75 (i.e. BCE 5, 5A or 5B occurred), or where an annual allowance charge arises and the member exercises the scheme pays option, a payment of the charge should constitute a scheme administration member payment.[9] Such a payment is made for the purposes of the administration of the scheme, because the scheme administrator is jointly liable for the charge. The payment of a lifetime allowance charge or annual allowance charge by the scheme administrator does not give rise to a taxable benefit for the member (notwithstanding the member's joint liability) because, despite being charges to income tax, the events giving rise to these charges are expressly not treated as income for tax purposes.[10]

11-006 A payment by a scheme for the cost of pension advice provided to a member is a payment in respect of the member. Where such a payment is not within the pension advice allowance (which will be an authorised payment by virtue of SI 2009/1171), HMRC suggest that such a payment is a scheme administration member payment to the extent that the advice relates to the pension scheme and the cost of the advice is genuinely commercial.[11] HMRC must therefore consider that paying for the member to receive such advice properly forms part of the administration or management of the scheme. This indicates that HMRC interpret the phrase "administration" or "management" fairly broadly.[12]

11-007 If a scheme borrows money from a member, the payment of interest on arm's length terms is a scheme administration member payment. This may include payments in connection with a short service refund lump sum or a refund of excess

---

[7] The scheme administrator is exclusively liable for the scheme sanction charge and de-registration charge. If the payment of the charge depletes a member's scheme fund it will be a payment in respect of that member and will be a scheme administration member payment. If the payment does not deplete a member's scheme fund (e.g. it is paid from a general fund), it is not a payment "in respect of" a member so it is neither authorised nor unauthorised.

[8] The same analysis applies where the trustees pay income tax in respect of pension income to HMRC under the PAYE provisions. The payment of tax to HMRC is not materially different to the payment of benefits to the member, and so is an authorised payment for the same reason.

[9] As no payment is made to the member, the payment of tax cannot be said to form part of such a payment. Indeed, in the context of BCE 5 or 5B, the trustees could not make a payment to the member as the funds are currently uncrystallised; some additional step (such as a designating the funds as being available for the payment of drawdown) would need to be taken first.

[10] See e.g. FA 2004 s.227(5) in relation to the annual allowance charge.

[11] PTM143200.

[12] Also see PTM056410, which suggests HMRC think a voluntary payment of the annual allowance charge is a scheme administration member payment: "Unlike with 'Scheme Pays' the scheme would not then have joint and several liability for the tax charge so the liability would remain with the member. [...] Where the scheme does not reduce the member's benefits in the scheme to take account of the tax the scheme has paid, then the member may also become liable to an unauthorised payments charge on the amount of their liability that the scheme has paid on their behalf." HMRC do not expressly say that the payment of tax will be a scheme administration payment where the scheme reduces the member's benefits, but it is difficult to see how it could possibly be any other type of authorised payment. This suggests that the discharge of any tax liability which arises in connection with the scheme may be a payment for the purpose of the administration or management of the scheme.

contributions lump sum to reflect interest or investment growth.[13] Such payments will of course be taxable income of the recipient (as interest, for example). Compensation payments for distress, inconvenience or other non-financial loss may also be scheme administration member payments.[14]

**11-008** A payment to a member by a third party in connection with a scheme investment, such as a rebate of commission, may be deemed to be a payment by the pension scheme pursuant to FA 2004 s.161(3).[15] If the payment is at a commercial rate HMRC apparently accept that it is a scheme administration member payment.[16] It is unclear on what basis the payment of commission to a member could be described as being for the purposes of the administration or management of the scheme.

**11-009** The test is a subjective purpose test: was a particular payment made for the purposes of the administration or management of the pension scheme, or was it made for some other purpose? If, for example, the trustees agree to purchase an asset from a member for its market value but the trustees are motivated solely by a desire to provide money to the member rather than to purchase an appropriate investment for the scheme, the payment to the member would not satisfy the purpose test and so could not be a scheme administration member payment even though it is on arm's length terms.

### "The amount which might be expected to be paid to a person ... at arm's length"

**11-010** A payment will exceed the amount which might be expected to be paid to a person who was at arm's length if the amount exceeds the comparable market level as a result of the parties' relationship. In the VAT case, *Temple Finance Ltd v HMRC*,[17] Richards J said about the meaning of "arm's length":

> "As a matter of ordinary usage, a party will be transacting at "arm's length" with a counterparty if it is seeking to obtain the best deal for itself and without any intention to confer a gratuitous benefit on the counterparty. Where services or goods are supplied on "arm's length" terms, it would be normal for them to be charged for at [open market value or "OMV"] since, if less than OMV were charged, the counterparty would be receiving a gratuitous benefit. There may be exceptions to this rule. For example, a person urgently in need of money may decide, in an arm's length transaction, to sell property for less than OMV if he or she is more interested in getting money quickly than in getting the highest possible price for the property. However, I consider that such a situation is exceptional and that, in most cases, if goods or services are supplied on "arm's length" terms, they will be charged for at OMV."

**11-011** In *Boardman v HMRC*,[18] HMRC successfully argued that £288,750 paid to Mr Boardman from his SIPP to purchase 288,750 shares in a company called Omega

---

[13] HMRC accept this at PTM045000.
[14] HMRC accept this at PTM143300.
[15] See Ch.18.
[16] PTM143200.
[17] *Temple Finance Limited, Temple Retail Ltd v HMRC* [2016] UKFTT 41 (TC) at [51]. The decision was concerned with the meaning of "open market value" in VATA 1994 s.19(5), which provides, "... the open market value of a supply of goods or services shall be taken to be the amount that would fall to be taken as its value under subsection (2) above if the supply were for such consideration in money as would be payable by a person standing in no such relationship with any person as would affect that consideration."
[18] *Guy Boardman v HMRC* [2022] UKFTT 238.

4 Ltd, was not a scheme administration member payment because it was not on arm's length terms. Mr Boardman had purchased the shares for £1 each less than two months earlier, but with the benefit of a £255,000 limited recourse loan from a company (FCPF) controlled by the promoter of the Omega 4 investment (which was described as an investment opportunity connected with a hotel development project in Montenegro). When Mr Boardman asked the scheme administrator to buy the shares from him, the administrator obtained confirmation from FCP that the shares were still being sold in the market for £1 each, but they did not undertake any additional due diligence to determine their value.

The FTT noted that the legislation does not define what is an "amount which might be expected to be paid by the SIPP to a person who was at arm's length" and there is no useful case law on the point. However, it found some of the CGT case law on "market value" to be helpful, and in particular the summary in *Green v HMRC*:[19] "(1) the hypothetical vendor and purchaser should be assumed to do whatever reasonable people buying and selling the property in question would be likely to have done in real life;[20] (2) the purchaser is a willing purchaser who behaves reasonably and makes proper enquiries about the property and is cautiously optimistic about the company's future prospects;[21] (3) the only information available to the hypothetical purchaser is what is available to the open market;[22] (4) the vendor is a reasonable vendor, who goes about the sale as a prudent man of business, negotiating seriously without giving the impression of being overanxious or unduly reluctant;[23] ... (7) while a sale between parties acting at arm's length may provide evidence of the market value, it is a logical fallacy to assume that an arm's length price must equal the market value." The FTT held that the information available to a hypothetical purchaser would include all of the documents available to Mr Boardman. From these documents a hypothetical purchaser of the shares at arm's length would have been aware that the shares were acquired by Mr Boardman as part of a package which included a limited recourse loan and the acquisition of an LLP interest, and the overall effect of the arrangements was that the effective cost of the shares for Mr Boardman was apparently intended to be nil overall. Even a cautiously optimistic hypothetical purchaser would have considered that the prospect of any return on the shares was very remote and highly speculative. The FTT concluded that such a hypothetical purchaser would not have purchased the shares in circumstances where that purchase would not also include the acquisition of the vendor's related LLP interest, and so the price paid by the SIPP to Mr Boardman for his shares was in excess of the price which might have been expected to be paid for those shares to a person who was at arm's length. It was therefore an unauthorised payment.

**Loans**

Section 171(4) provides that a loan to or in respect of a member cannot be a scheme administration member payment. The meaning of "loan" is considered in Ch.2. As a loan to a member cannot constitute any other type of authorised payment, all loans to or in respect of scheme members are unauthorised payments.

Pursuant to s.162(4), a loan includes a debt which is not required to be discharged

**11-012**

**11-013**

---

[19] *Nicholas Green v HMRC* [2014] UKFTT 396 at [90].
[20] *IRC v Gray* [1994] S.T.C. 360 per Hoffmann LJ at 372.
[21] *Marks v Sherred* [2004] S.T.C. (S.C.D.) 362 at [26].
[22] *Lynall v IRC* [1972] A.C. 680; 47 T.C. 375.
[23] *IRC v Gray* [1994] S.T.C. 360 per Hoffmann LJ at 372.

by the relevant date (being the date on which a person at arm's length might be expected to require the debt to be discharged). Thus, for example, if the scheme sells an asset to the member on terms that he must pay for it at some specified date in the future, but the member fails to do so and the scheme does not enforce those terms, the debt is treated as a loan at that time. However, at the time that the actual payment was made to the member (i.e. when the asset was transferred to him), it was not a payment which was treated as a loan so it will have been a scheme administration member payment if it was on arm's length terms and made for the purposes of the administration or management of the scheme. Section 162(4) deems the debt to be a loan made by the scheme to the member on the relevant date, but if the intention is that such a deemed loan creates an unauthorised payment then it is not clear that it achieves this. Section 162(4) deems there to be a loan but it does not expressly deem there to have been a *payment*, nor does it have the effect of treating the actual payment (the transfer of the asset from the scheme to the member) as if it were a loan at that time. If s.162(4) does not create a deemed payment, and does not have the effect of converting a previous payment into a loan, it is difficult to see how the application of s.162(4) can give rise to an unauthorised payment.

**11-014** There may also be situations where the pension scheme does not make a payment to the member at all. For example, where an unconnected person makes a loan to the member and then sells the debt to the scheme. In these circumstances there is a debt, which is deemed to be a loan under s.162(4) if it is not enforced, but again it is difficult to see how that could involve an unauthorised payment unless the deemed loan to the member is interpreted as involving a deemed *payment* to the member. Section 160(2)(b) provides that an unauthorised member payment includes "anything which is to be treated as an unauthorised member payment to or in respect of a person who is or has been a member of the pension scheme under FA 2004". Could this be interpreted as meaning that a deemed loan is also a deemed payment? HMRC would no doubt contend that a deemed loan involves, by necessary implication, a deemed payment. Such an argument may well find favour with a tribunal, but it is not at all clear that it is correct. Such an argument would have more force if any other interpretation rendered s.162(4) otiose, but that is not the case because the existence of a loan (including a deemed loan) is material to the application of other provisions.[24]

---

[24] e.g. if a payment is not a loan then it cannot be an authorised employer loan; special rules apply to the valuation of any right or interest in respect of money lent to any relevant associated person (see FA 2004 s.278(2)); and certain parts of the taxable property provisions apply where lending is involved (FA 2004 Sch.29A paras 16 and 43).

# CHAPTER 12

# Pension Transfers

## TABLE OF CONTENTS

| | |
|---|---|
| Introduction | 12-001 |
| In specie transfers | 12-003 |
| Recognised transfers | 12-004 |
| Post-crystallisation transfers | 12-007 |
| Scheme pension | 12-007 |
| Lifetime annuity | 12-009 |
| Drawdown pension | 12-011 |
| Compliance | 12-013 |
| Transfers that are not recognised transfers | 12-014 |
| Discharge from scheme sanction charge | 12-015 |
| The overseas transfer charge | 12-018 |
| The main provisions: s.244AC | 12-022 |
| Exclusions | 12-023 |
| Member and receiving scheme in same country | 12-026 |
| Receiving scheme in EEA state or Gibraltar and member resident in UK or EEA state | 12-029 |
| Receiving scheme is an occupational pension scheme | 12-030 |
| Receiving scheme set up by international organisation | 12-031 |
| Receiving scheme is an overseas public service scheme | 12-032 |
| Transfers exceeding available overseas transfer allowance: s.244IA | 12-033 |
| Availability of member's overseas transfer allowance | 12-036 |
| The "transferred value" | 12-037 |
| Amount of the charge | 12-039 |
| Liability | 12-040 |
| Repayment of charge under s.244AC on subsequent excluding events | 12-043 |
| Discharge of liability | 12-048 |

## INTRODUCTION

**12-001** It is generally desirable for pension rights to be portable.[1] To that end, a member of a registered pension scheme will usually have a statutory right to direct the trustee or manager to transfer the cash equivalent of his accrued pension rights to a different pension scheme which is willing and able to accept the transfer.[2] Scheme rules also typically confer on each member a contractual right to a pension transfer.[3] The tax rules should not unduly impede portability.[4] In relation to FA 2004 Pt 4[5]:

(a) The payment by the transferring scheme will be an unauthorised payment unless it is a "recognised transfer".[6] If benefits have crystallised under the transferring scheme, the payment will be an unauthorised payment (even if it is a recognised transfer) unless additional requirements are satisfied.

(b) Prior to 6 April 2023, a recognised transfer was not a BCE for lifetime allowance purposes, unless it was a transfer to a QROPS (in which case it was BCE 8, assuming the member was under the age of 75). Therefore, a transfer to a QROPS could be subject to a lifetime allowance charge.[7]

(c) A transfer to a QROPS may be subject to the overseas transfer charge (see below).[8]

(d) Prior to 6 April 2023, if the member had a protected lifetime allowance, a transfer from one scheme to another could prejudice his protection.[9]

(e) If the member has a protected pension age, it will cease to apply unless the transfer is a block transfer.[10]

(f) If a registered pension scheme receives a transfer from a ROPS, a lifetime allowance enhancement factor could apply before 6 April 2024.[11]

(g) A transfer from a "pension scheme"[12] is expressly not a "contribution" for

---

[1] See e.g. D. Blake and J.M. Orzag, *Portability and Preservation of Pension Rights in the United Kingdom* (the Pensions Institute, 1998).

[2] See PSA 1993 Pt 4ZA Ch.1. The statutory right applies only to transfers to registered pension schemes; there is no statutory right to a transfer to a QROPS. In relation to defined benefits arrangements, cash equivalent transfer values must be calculated on a scheme specific basis on terms no less favourable than those specified in the Occupational Pensions (Transfer Values) Regulations 1996 (SI 1996/1847).

[3] The contractual right is often broader than the statutory right. Where no contractual right is conferred, the trustee will have discretion to permit such transfers, which one would expect to be exercised in the absence of any particular reason not to permit a transfer.

[4] This is recognised, e.g., in the OECD Commentary on the Model Treaty at paras 66–68.

[5] When referring to pension transfers, the FA 2004 Pt 4 refers to sums or assets "held for the purposes of" the pension scheme or "representing accrued rights under" the pension scheme. The former is presumably intended to relate to any funds held for the purposes of a money purchase arrangement, and the latter relates to the cash equivalent transfer value of any rights under a cash balance or defined benefits arrangement.

[6] As is suggested in Ch.17, such a transfer involves a payment "in respect of" the member, not merely because it is a payment relating to his fund, but because it has the effect of depleting the value of his fund. A transfer of funds from a general fund in which no member has any specific interest, to a person who is not a member or sponsoring employer or connected with a member or sponsoring employer does not appear to involve an unauthorised payment.

[7] See Ch.10.

[8] All overseas transfers must be reported to HMRC (see The Registered Pension Schemes (Provision of Information) Regulations 2006 (SI 2006/567) regs 3, 11BA, 11BB, 12A, 14ZC and 14ZCA).

[9] See e.g. Ch.3 (enhanced protection).

[10] See FA 2004 Sch.36 para.22.

[11] FA 2004 ss.224–226. See Ch.20.

[12] "Pension scheme" is defined in FA 2004 s.150(1). It includes unregistered pension schemes.

the purposes of FA 2004 s.188(1), so tax relief is not available.[13] It is likely that a transfer from an arrangement which is not a pension scheme (such as an employee benefits trusts, or a family trust, for example), *would* be a contribution for the purposes of s.188(1).

Pension transfers can also have inheritance tax implications, if the effect is to reduce the value of the member's estate (see Ch.21).

**In specie transfers**

The transfer of assets from one pension scheme to another *in specie* involves a disposal for CGT purposes, but the exemption in TCGA 1992 s.271(1A) will apply. The transfer of shares does not give rise to a charge to stamp duty.[14] The transfer of land does not give rise to a charge to SDLT,[15] unless there is an assumption of debt by the receiving scheme.[16] The transfer of commercial property will usually be a transfer of a going concern for VAT purposes.

# RECOGNISED TRANSFERS

A payment by a registered pension scheme to or in respect of a person who is or has been a member of the pension scheme is an unauthorised payment unless it is one of the six types of authorised payment. A pension transfer will generally involve a payment "in respect of" the scheme member, so express provisions are required to permit such transfers.[17] A recognised transfer is an authorised payment.[18]

A "recognised transfer" is a transfer of sums or assets held for the purposes of, or representing accrued rights under, a registered pension scheme so as to become held for the purposes of, or to represent rights under: (a) another registered pension scheme; or (b) a QROPS, in connection with a member of that pension scheme.[19] Two questions arise:

(a) Is the reference to "that" pension scheme (at the end of the definition) a reference to the transferring scheme or the receiving scheme? It is very likely that it is a reference to the receiving scheme, and so it necessary for the individual to join the receiving scheme *before* the transfer is made.[20]

(b) How broadly should the prepositional phrase "in connection with" be interpreted for the purposes of s.169(1)?[21] The phrase seems to be significantly broader than is required for the typical situation where the cash

---

[13] FA 2004 s.188(5).
[14] See Ch.6 (in relation to contributions rather than transfers but the position is not materially different).
[15] This is because the assumption of the obligation to provide retirement benefits (by the receiving scheme) is not chargeable consideration (HMRC agree at SDLTM31800). See Ch.6 (in relation to contributions rather than transfers but the position is not materially different).
[16] FA 2003 Sch.4 para.8.
[17] See Ch.17—a payment which deliberately depletes a scheme member's fund is a payment in respect of that member.
[18] FA 2004 s.164(1)(c).
[19] FA 2004 s.169(1).
[20] It is possible to make a recognised transfer of death benefits (this is expressly acknowledged in s.169(1C) and (1D)). Although it may be the case that a death beneficiary becomes a member (see Ch.2), it is quite likely that he does not (FA 2004 refers to death benefits being paid in respect of the member rather than to the member) and therefore s.169(1) only requires the death beneficiary to be a member of the receiving scheme.
[21] The phrase is considered in Ch.17 in the context of FA 2004 s.161(3). It does not pose a causal test but merely asks whether there is a link (per David Richards J, whose decision in the High Court was

equivalent of a member's accrued pension rights is transferred from one pension scheme to another pension scheme of which he is a member. Section 169(1) does not for example expressly require that the sums or assets transferred were, prior to the transfer, held for the purposes of an arrangement relating to the member under the transferring scheme.[22] Such sums or assets could therefore have been allocated to a general fund under the transferring scheme.[23]

**12-006** The following points may be observed:

(a) FA 2004 Pt 4 does not prescribe the amount which may be transferred as a recognised transfer. In relation to a money purchase arrangement, the amount transferred will be equal to the accrued fund. In relation to a defined benefits arrangements, there is more flexibility, however, the amount transferred must genuinely represent the member's accrued rights. HMRC are understood to accept that enhanced transfer values may be scheme administration member payments[24], which suggests that FA 2004 Pt 4 is relaxed regarding transfer values.

(b) A recognised transfer can occur at any time. There are no restrictions relating to the age of the member, and a transfer can occur after benefits have crystallised.[25]

(c) Partial transfers are permitted, except where a scheme pension has commenced.

(d) A recognised transfer can relate to death benefits.

(e) There is no requirement under FA 2004 Pt 4 that the member requests or consents to a recognised transfer.[26]

(f) A deferred annuity contract issued by an insurance company securing benefits under a registered pension scheme is deemed to be a registered pension scheme.[27] Section 169(1) will therefore apply on the purchase of a deferred annuity.

(g) Subject to any restrictions in the scheme rules, a registered pension scheme

---

affirmed by the Court of Appeal in *Barclays Bank Plc v HMRC* [2006] EWHC 2118 (Ch); [2007] S.T.C. 747). The phrase may describe a wide range of links and so one must look closely at the surrounding words and the context of the legislative scheme (per Arden J in *Barclays Bank Plc v HMRC* [2007] EWCA Civ 442; [2008] S.T.C. 476). It seems likely that it should be construed more narrowly than in s.161(3) (which is essentially an anti-avoidance provision).

[22] Suppose that A's funds were transferred to a registered pension scheme to be credited to B's account. Section 169(1) would on the face of it apply. It may be suggested that such a transfer would involve a surrender by A, and therefore a deemed unauthorised payment under FA 2004 s.172A, however the same could be said of any transfer between schemes, and it is implicit that an authorised member payment cannot also be a deemed unauthorised member payment (see Ch.17).

[23] Indeed, there is also no express requirement that the member referred to in s.169(1) is or was a member of the transferring scheme. If he was not a member of the transferring scheme (or connected with a member) then the payment would not be "to or in respect of" a member of the transferring scheme and so it could not be an unauthorised payment and so there is no reason that s.169 should apply to such a payment.

[24] See Ch.11.

[25] However, in order to avoid an unauthorised payment, additional requirements must be satisfied if the transfer relates to a scheme pension in payment or funds which have been designated as available for the payment of drawdown pension. For the reporting obligations relating to such transfers, see PTM109000.

[26] The preservation requirements in PSA 1993 Pt IV Ch.1 may however prevent a transfer from an occupational scheme without the member's consent.

[27] FA 2004 s.153(8).

# RECOGNISED TRANSFERS

can receive funds from an arrangement that is not a registered pension scheme.
(h) A registered pension scheme is not obliged to accept a transfer in (unless the scheme rules provide that it must).
(i) HMRC consider that a payment to induce a member to move from a defined benefits arrangement to a money purchase arrangement is made in connection with past service if the member is, at the time of the payment, a retired former employee.[28]

## Post-crystallisation transfers

### Scheme pension

A transfer of sums or assets held for the purposes of, or representing accrued rights under, a registered pension scheme to an insurance company is deemed to be a recognised transfer if the sums or assets had been applied by the pension scheme towards the provision of a scheme pension or a dependants' scheme pension.[29] A transfer of sums or assets which represent rights in respect of a scheme pension to which a member or dependant has become entitled[30] is not a recognised transfer unless those sums or assets are, after the transfer, applied towards the provision of a new scheme pension.[31] If the sums or assets are so applied, the new scheme pension is treated as if it were the original scheme pension for most purposes.[32] A deemed unauthorised payment will usually arise if the annual rate of the new scheme pension is less than the annual rate of the old scheme pension.[33] Following such a transfer, the original scheme pension will cease to be payable. This will necessarily involve a reduction in scheme pension and so it must come within one of the exceptions in para.2(4) (see Ch.13).

12-007

Where a scheme pension payable to a member or death beneficiary by an insurance company ceases to be payable and the insurance company consequently transfers sums or assets to a different insurance company or back to the registered pension scheme that purchased the scheme pension, the transfer is an unauthorised member payment unless a new scheme pension becomes payable.

12-008

### Lifetime annuity

If a lifetime annuity ceases to be payable and the insurance company consequently transfers funds to another insurance company and a new lifetime annuity becomes payable, the new lifetime annuity is deemed to be the original lifetime annuity for most purposes, to the extent that the amount of the sums or assets ap-

12-009

---

[28] EIM15155.
[29] FA 2004 s.169(1A).
[30] A person becomes entitled to a scheme pension when he first acquires an actual (rather than a merely prospective) right to receive the pension (FA 2004 s.165(3)).
[31] FA 2004 s.169(1B) and (1C) and The Registered Pension Schemes (Transfer of Sums and Assets) Regulations 2006 (SI 2006/499) regs 3 and 8.
[32] SI 2006/499 regs 3(2) and 4. The purposes are specified in table 1 of SI 2006/499. e.g. when the member becomes entitled to the scheme pension under the receiving scheme, it is not possible for him to receive another PCLS from the receiving scheme.
[33] See Ch.13. This would appear to be the case even where the old scheme pension is reduced (but continues) and a new scheme pension matches the reduction (notwithstanding that the member or dependant receives the same rate of scheme pension overall). In addition, when determining whether there has been a substantial reduction for the purposes of the anti-avoidance provisions described above, one is concerned with the rate of the original scheme pension and not the new scheme pension.

plied to purchase the new lifetime annuity are equal to the funds transferred.[34] If a member becomes entitled to an annuity which satisfies the post-6 April 2015 requirements (see Ch.13) and the annuity replaced a lifetime annuity which commenced before 6 April 2015, the new annuity is expressly not a lifetime annuity if the terms of the contract are such that there will or could be decreases in its amount, other than decreases that were permitted for pre-6 April 2015 lifetime annuities.[35] This is to prevent members within the old regime cancelling a lifetime annuity and having the insurance company apply the funds in respect of a new lifetime annuity after 6 April 2015 in order to come within the new (more flexible) regime.

**12-010** Where an annuity payable to a member or death beneficiary by an insurance company ceases to be payable and the insurance company consequently transfers sums or assets to a different insurance company or back to the registered pension scheme that purchased the annuity, the transfer is an unauthorised member payment unless a new annuity becomes payable.[36]

*Drawdown pension*

**12-011** Where any of the sums or assets transferred represent a drawdown pension fund or flexi-access drawdown fund (whether relating to a member, dependant, nominee or successor) the transfer will be a recognised transfer only if all of the sums and assets transferred become held under an arrangement under which no other sums or assets are held.[37] If the transferred sums and assets are so held under the transferee arrangement, they are treated as if they were held for the purposes of the transferor arrangement.[38]

**12-012** Where a short-term annuity ceases to be payable and sums or assets are consequently transferred to another insurance company, or sums or assets are transferred to the pension scheme that purchased the original annuity, the scheme is treated as making an unauthorised payment to the member of an amount equal to the value of the sums or assets transferred unless a new short-term annuity becomes payable. Where the member became entitled to the original short-term annuity before 6 April 2015, if the terms of the new short-term annuity are such that there will or could be decreases in its amount other than allowed decreases then the new annuity is not a short-term annuity.[39] This is to prevent members within the old (pre-6 April 2015) regime from cancelling an annuity and having the insurance company apply the funds in respect of a new annuity after 6 April 2015 in order to come within the new (more flexible) regime.

**Compliance**

**12-013** A scheme administrator making a recognised transfer to a fully insured pension scheme is liable to a penalty of up to £3,000 if the transfer is not made to either the

---

[34] SI 2006/499 reg.6.
[35] SI 2006/499 reg.13.
[36] See Ch.13.
[37] FA 2004 s.169(1D) and SI 2006/499 reg.12(1).
[38] SI 2006/499 reg.12(2). HMRC considers that a transfer of only part of a drawdown fund cannot be a recognised transfer (PTM104000). This is presumably because SI 2006/499 reg.12 refers to "all of those sums or assets", however this appears to be a reference to all of the sums or assets *transferred* rather than all of the sums or assets representing the drawdown fund.
[39] Decreases are *allowed decreases* if they are permitted by The Registered Pension Schemes (Prescribed Manner of Determining Amount of Annuities) Regulations 2006 (SI 2006/568) (FA 2004 Sch.28 para.6(1E)).

receiving scheme administrator or an insurance company that has issued any of the insurance policies that the scheme has invested in.[40]

**Transfers that are not recognised transfers**

A pension transfer is an unauthorised payment if it is not a recognised transfer. The member will be subject to an unauthorised payments charge and surcharge, and the scheme administrator will be liable for the scheme sanction charge.

12-014

*Discharge from scheme sanction charge*

Where a scheme administrator makes a pension transfer that is not a recognised transfer (and so is an unauthorised payment), he will be able to obtain a discharge from liability for the scheme sanction charge only if he reasonably believed that the transfer was a recognised transfer. His belief will be reasonable only if he carries out reasonable checks to determine whether the requirements are satisfied.[41] HMRC consider that there is no checklist of the acceptable due diligence requirements because each case will depend on the circumstances.[42] In practice, on receipt of a transfer request from a member, the trustees or managers of many registered pension schemes ask HMRC to confirm that the receiving scheme is a registered pension scheme. HMRC's current practice is to confirm the registration status of a receiving scheme only where: (a) the scheme is registered and is not subject to a de-registration notice; and (b) the information held by HMRC does not indicate a significant risk of the scheme being set up or being used to allow pension liberation. In any other case HMRC will state that they cannot confirm the status of the receiving scheme.

12-015

If the information held by HMRC indicates a significant risk of the scheme being set up or used to allow pension liberation, they will contact the receiving scheme to try to resolve any issues before responding to the transferring scheme's request. Examples which HMRC say cause concern are:

12-016

- the tax affairs of the scheme, its administrator or members are currently under consideration by HMRC for matters relating to pension liberation;
- HMRC has reason to suspect the scheme has made or proposed investments that have previously been used to release assets from a pension scheme;
- the scheme demonstrates one or more of the warning signs set out in the Pension Regulator's pension liberation fraud awareness leaflet;
- one or more of the names of the scheme or administrator or establisher or practitioner cause concern;
- the scheme or administrator or establisher is linked to a website that could be viewed as offering tax free cash;
- HMRC has received numerous requests to confirm the status of this scheme; and
- the promoter or practitioner is currently under enquiry with HMRC for reasons other than:
  — repayment claims;
  — relief at source claims;

---

[40] FA 2004 s.266.
[41] See Ch.5.
[42] PTM101000. As is explained at below, the scheme administrator may write to HMRC where he has any concerns about a proposed transfer.

- annual allowance;
- lifetime allowance;
- accounting for tax;
- property (commercial and residential);
- rent arrears; and
- scheme borrowing.

**12-017** If the issues cannot be resolved within three months HMRC will inform the transferring scheme that they cannot confirm the registration status of the receiving scheme. HMRC's views do not of course affect a member's statutory right to a transfer.

## THE OVERSEAS TRANSFER CHARGE

**12-018** FA 2017 created a new income tax charge under FA 2004 Pt 4 called the overseas transfer charge. The then Treasury Minister Jane Ellison referred to this new charge as "a significant anti-avoidance measure" designed to "deter those who seek to gain an unfair tax advantage by transferring their pensions abroad".[43] She did not however indicate what these unfair tax advantages may be.

**12-019** The effect (and presumably the purpose) of the charge is to restrict the circumstances in which it may be attractive to transfer a fund from a registered pension scheme to a QROPS, or to transfer a fund from one QROPS to another. The exclusions described below are instructive when considering the rationale for the overseas transfer charge. It is clear from the *same country* and *EEA states* exclusions that the intention is to discourage the use of third country non-EEA QROPS. The charge is effectively voluntary for anyone currently resident in the UK/EEA and not intending to leave the UK/EEA for five years: such an individual can transfer his accrued benefits under a registered pension scheme to a QROPS established in the EEA or Gibraltar now and retire outside of the EEA after five complete tax years. The member's fund can then be transferred to a QROPS established outside of the EEA after that period if the member so wishes. In these circumstances, the provisions encourage transfers to QROPS earlier than might otherwise be desirable. There is also an important compliance aspect to the overseas transfer charge: the exclusions are generally available only if the reporting obligations are satisfied.

**12-020** The charge will be a significant deterrent in most cases, but there are circumstances in which suffering the charge may be considered worthwhile.[44]

**12-021** With effect from 6 April 2024, the overseas transfer charge also arises where the amount transferred by a recognised transfer to a QROPS, or an onwards transfer, exceeds the member's available "overseas transfer allowance". These provisions are described below, after the main provisions, and the exclusions to the main provisions, have been described.

---

[43] *Hansard*, HC Vol.624, cols 1013–14 (25 April 2017).
[44] e.g. most benefits paid from a registered pension scheme with UK resident trustees or managers to a member resident in a jurisdiction with no tax treaty with the UK will be subject to UK income tax at up to 45%. If the member is resident in a very low or no tax jurisdiction, the overseas transfer charge will usually be lower than the UK income tax.

## The main provisions: s.244AC

Subject to the exclusions described below the overseas transfer charge arises where a recognised transfer is made to a QROPS.[45] These provisions also apply where an onward transfer is made from a QROPS during the relevant period for the original transfer (see Ch.33). The overseas transfer charge does not apply to any transfer which gives rise to the unauthorised payments charge.

12-022

## Exclusions

There are five exclusions to the overseas transfer charge:

12-023

(a) the member and receiving scheme are both in the same country;
(b) the receiving scheme is in the EEA or Gibraltar and the member is resident in the UK or EEA;
(c) the receiving scheme is an occupational pension scheme;
(d) the receiving scheme is set up by an international organisation; and
(e) the receiving scheme is an overseas public service scheme.

The requirements in (a) and (b) must continue to be met for the duration of the "relevant period" (i.e. five full tax years after the date of the original transfer) in order for the exclusion to apply. If the requirements cease to be satisfied at any time during the relevant period then the charge will arise at that time.

12-024

The above exclusions are available only if the member has, in connection with the transfer, complied with either of the following (to the extent that they are applicable)[46]:

12-025

(a) SI 2006/567 reg.11BA, which requires a member of a registered pension scheme to provide specified information to the scheme administrator in connection with a transfer request to a QROPS (including information relating to any applicable exclusion from the overseas transfer charge); and
(b) The Pension Schemes (Information Requirements—Qualifying Overseas Pension Schemes, Qualifying Recognised Overseas Pensions Schemes and Corresponding Relief) Regulations 2006 (SI 2006/208) reg.3AE, which requires a member of a QROPS or former QROPS to provide specified information to the scheme manager in connection with an onward transfer to a QROPS, except where it is excluded under the grandfathering or avoidance of double charge provisions, or where it takes place outside of the relevant period. Again, this includes information relating to any applicable exclusion from the overseas transfer charge.

*Member and receiving scheme in same country*

A recognised transfer to a QROPS is excluded from the overseas transfer charge if during the relevant period the member is resident in the country or territory in which the QROPS is established, and there is no onward transfer: (a) for which the

12-026

---

[45] FA 2004 s.244AA. A recognised transfer to a QROPS is excluded from the overseas transfer charge if it is made in execution of a request made before 9 March 2017 (s.244G(1)). HMRC's position is that "A transfer request is made when a member has made a substantive request to the scheme administrator of their pension scheme on which the scheme administrator is required to take action in relation to the transfer. This means an instruction from the member to transfer £X or X% of their pension funds to a named overseas pension scheme. A casual enquiry is not a transfer request". (PTM102300).
[46] FA 2004 s.244I.

recognised transfer is the original transfer; and (b) which is not excluded from the charge.[47]

**12-027** A scheme is established where its main administration is carried out.[48] "Residence", in relation to the member, is likely to mean residence for tax purposes.[49] HMRC consider that residence should be determined in accordance with the laws of the relevant country (which will vary from country to country), and where an individual is resident in more than one country in a tax year, the country of residence should be determined in accordance with article 4 of the OECD model tax convention.[50] The better view is that residence should be established by applying the UK common law test.[51]

**12-028** In order to satisfy the above test, it is not necessary to wait until the end of the relevant period: if the member is resident in that country or territory at the time of the recognised transfer or onward transfer then it is expressly assumed that the member will continue to be so resident during the relevant period. If during the relevant period the member ceases to be resident in the country or territory in which the QROPS is established (other than as a result of his death) the charge will apply at that time.

*Receiving scheme in EEA state or Gibraltar and member resident in UK or EEA state*

**12-029** A recognised transfer to a QROPS established[52] in an EEA state[53] or Gibraltar is excluded from the charge if during the relevant period the member is resident[54] in the UK or an EEA state, and there is no onward transfer: (a) for which the recognised transfer is the original transfer; and (b) which is not excluded from the charge.[55] If the member is resident in an EEA state at the time of the recognised transfer or onward transfer, it is expressly assumed that he will continue to be so

---

[47] FA 2004 s.244B.
[48] See PTM112200. In *Macklin v HMRC* [2015] UKUT 0039 at [28] and [46] the UT concluded that a pension scheme is established in the geographic location where it is set up, funded, managed and administered on a continuous and stable fashion through human and material resources. See *R. (Britannic Asset Management Ltd) v Pensions Ombudsman* [2002] EWHC 441 (Admin) at [20] for what it means to *administer* a scheme.
[49] This is also HMRC's view (see PTM102300). Curiously, HMRC's position regarding the requirement in FA 2004 Sch.33 para.4(1)(a) (that a relevant migrant member is *resident in the UK*) is that it is *not* a test for formal tax residence status for a tax year but is instead a test of whether the individual, as a question of fact, was actually UK resident at the particular date. There is no obvious reason why the tests should be different.
[50] PTM102300.
[51] The statutory residence test will not assist as it can only establish whether an individual is resident in the UK or not.
[52] A scheme is established where its main administration is carried out. See PTM112200. In *Macklin v HMRC* [2015] UKUT 0039 at [28] and [46] the UT concluded that a pension scheme is established in the geographic location where it is set up, funded, managed and administered on a continuous and stable fashion through human and material resources. See *R. (Britannic Asset Management Ltd) v Pensions Ombudsman* [2002] EWHC 441 (Admin) at [20] for what it means to *administer* a scheme.
[53] "EEA state" means: (a) a state which is a member of the EU; or (b) any other state which is a party to the agreement on the European Economic Area signed at Oporto on 2 May 1992, together with the Protocol adjusting that Agreement signed at Brussels on 17 March 1993, as modified or supplemented from time to time (see Interpretation Act 1978 Sch.1 and European Communities Act 1972 s.1 and Sch.1).
[54] As with the previous exclusion (see above), it is likely that "residence" should be established in accordance with the common law rules.
[55] FA 2004 s.244C. Prior to 11pm on 31 December 2020, this exclusion applied only where both the scheme and the member were in EEA states. Gibraltar has never been an EEA state but prior to 11pm on 31 December 2020 was treated as one by virtue of the Treaty on the Functioning of the EU.

resident. If at any time before the end of the relevant period he ceases to be so resident (otherwise than by reason of his death) the charge applies at that time. There is no express requirement that the QROPS continues to be established in an EEA state or Gibraltar for the duration of the relevant period. The member may move between the UK and EEA states throughout the relevant period.

*Receiving scheme is an occupational pension scheme*

**12-030** A transfer to a QROPS is excluded from the overseas transfer charge if the QROPS is an occupational pension scheme, and when the transfer is made the member is an employee of a sponsoring employer of the QROPS.[56] On the face of it, this exclusion appears to be generous, especially when one considers the very broad definition of occupational pension scheme.[57] There is no express requirement that the employer is carrying on business in the jurisdiction in which the QROPS is established (although many jurisdictions only permit an employer carrying on business in that jurisdiction to establish a tax-approved occupational scheme in that jurisdiction) or even that the employer is carrying on business on an international basis.[58]

*Receiving scheme set up by international organisation*

**12-031** A transfer to a QROPS is excluded from the overseas transfer charge if: (a) the QROPS is established by an international organisation and has effect so as to provide benefits for or in respect of past service as an employee of the organisation; and (b) when the transfer is made the member is an employee of the organisation.[59]

*Receiving scheme is an overseas public service scheme*

**12-032** A transfer to a QROPS is excluded from the overseas transfer charge if the QROPS is an overseas public service pension scheme, and when the transfer is made the member is an employee of an employer that participates in the scheme.[60] A QROPS is an "overseas public service pension scheme" if[61]: (a) either it is established by or under the law of the country or territory in which it is established, or it is approved by the government of that country or territory; and (b) it is

---

Gibraltar was added by regulations made on 18 February 2021 but with retrospective effect to 31 December 2020. Where a transfer was made between 11pm on 31 December 2020 and 18 February 2021, the scheme should have withheld an amount equal to the overseas transfer charge and then paid that amount as an additional transfer on or after 18 February 2021 (the charge need not be paid or reported to HMRC until April 2021, but if it was reported and paid prior to the due date, the scheme can apply for a repayment of the charge on or after 18 February 2021).

[56] FA 2004 s.244D.
[57] For the meaning of "occupational pension scheme", see Ch.2.
[58] Note HMRC's commentary at PTM102300: "This exclusion [...] is aimed at pension schemes set up by multi-national employers for their employees working in a branch, or for a subsidiary or other group company in another country. HMRC will be keeping the use of the term occupational pension scheme in this context, and the scope of this exemption from the tax charge, under review". Also note that PSA 1993 and PA 1995 apply (or purport to apply) to an occupational scheme with its main administration outside of the EEA (PSA 1993 s.1(1)).
[59] FA 2004 s.244E. An *international organisation* is an organisation to which the International Organisations Act 1968 s.1(1) applies by virtue of an Order in Council.
[60] An employer participates in a QROPS that is an overseas public service pension scheme if the scheme has effect so as to provide benefits to or in respect of any or all of the employees of the employer in respect of their employment by the employer.
[61] FA 2004 s.244F.

established solely for the purpose of providing benefits to individuals for or in respect of services rendered to that country or territory, or any political subdivision or local authority of that country or territory.

**Transfers exceeding available overseas transfer allowance: s.244IA**

**12-033** From 6 April 2024, the overseas transfer charge also arises in two circumstances where the transfer exceeds the member's available overseas transfer allowance.[62] A member's "overseas transfer allowance" is an amount equal to the member's LS&DB allowance.[63] This replaces the lifetime allowance charge which formerly arose where a transfer to a QROPS exceeded the member's available lifetime allowance.

**12-034** Firstly, the overseas transfer charge arises where: (a) a recognised transfer is made to a QROPS; (b) the transfer is excluded from the charge under s.244AC; and (c) the transferred value (see below) exceeds the member's available overseas transfer allowance.

**12-035** Secondly, the overseas transfer charge arises where: (a) a recognised transfer is made to a QROPS; (b) that transfer was subject to the overseas transfer charge under s.244AC ("the original charge"); (c) a person liable to the original charge becomes entitled under s.244M to a repayment in respect of the original charge; and (d) the transferred value exceeds the member's available overseas transfer allowance.

*Availability of member's overseas transfer allowance*

**12-036** On the making of a recognised transfer to a QROPS ("the current overseas transfer"), if no such transfer has been made in relation to the member before the current overseas transfer, the whole of the member's overseas transfer allowance is available.[64] Otherwise, the amount of the member's available overseas transfer allowance is: (a) so much of that allowance as is left after deducting the previously-used amount; or (b) if none is left after deducting that amount, nil. The "previously-used amount" is the aggregate of the transferred value (see below) of each such transfer (if any) that has been made in relation to the member before the current overseas transfer. However, only transfers made on or after 6 April 2024 are taken into account.

**The "transferred value"**

**12-037** If the transfer is from a registered pension scheme established in the UK, the "transferred value" is the value of the sums/assets transferred, subject to the provisos described below. If the transfer is from a registered pension scheme established outside the UK, the transferred value is the value of the cash and assets that are attributable to UK-relieved funds of the scheme, again subject to the provisos below.[65]

---

[62] FA 2004 s.244IA. This charge also applies to "relieved relevant non-UK scheme transfers" (i.e. transfers from RNUKS which have benefitted from UK tax relief): see Ch.30.
[63] FA 2004 s.244IB.
[64] FA 2004 s.244IC. "Relieved relevant non-UK scheme transfers" (i.e. transfers from RNUKS which have benefitted from UK tax relief) must also be included: see Ch.30.
[65] For the meaning of "UK-relieved funds", see Ch.20.

# THE OVERSEAS TRANSFER CHARGE

The provisos referred to above are:[66]

**12-038**

(a) If a transfer is one that is initially assumed to be excluded[67] but an event occurring before the end of the relevant period means that the transfer is not so excluded, the transferred value is the value of the cash or assets transferred which, at the time of the event, are represented in any of the member's ring-fenced transfer funds under any QROPS or former QROPS. If benefits have been provided since the transfer, this will reduce the amount of the charge.
(b) If the scheme administrator of the transferring scheme pays the charge on the transfer and does so: (i) otherwise than by deduction from the transfer; and (ii) out of sums and assets held for the purposes of the scheme from which the transfer is made,[68] the transferred value is the amount given by the above provisions grossed up by 25%.
(c) If the scheme administrator of the transferring scheme pays the overseas transfer charge on the transfer and deducts the amount of the charge from the transfer, the transferred value is the value of the cash and assets transferred before the deduction.
(d) If the member pays the charge on the transfer, the transferred value is the value of the cash and assets transferred without any deduction for the charge.

## Amount of the charge

Where the charge arises under s.244AC, the charge is equal to 25% of the "transferred value" (see above).[69]

**12-039**

Where the charge arises under s.244IA, the charge is 25% of so much of the transferred value as exceeds the amount of the member's available overseas transfer allowance.

### Liability

In the case of a recognised transfer to a QROPS, the scheme administrator of the registered pension scheme and the member are jointly and severally liable to the overseas transfer charge.[70] If a transfer is one that is initially assumed to be excluded[71] but an event occurring before the end of the relevant period means that the transfer is not so excluded, the member is jointly and severally liable with the scheme manager of any QROPS or former QROPS which is at that time holding the ring-fenced transfer funds[72] which have become subject to the charge.

**12-040**

---

[66] FA 2004 s.244K(6)–(9).
[67] i.e. the member and receiving scheme were both (at the time of the transfer) resident in the same country, or the scheme was in the EEA or Gibraltar and the member was in the UK or an EEA state.
[68] e.g. from the member's retained rights under the transferring scheme, or from a general fund under the transferring scheme.
[69] FA 2004 s.244JA.
[70] FA 2004 s.244J(1). The scheme administrator should report and pay the tax using the Accounting for Tax return. The member should report the tax charge, and pay any remaining tax, via his self-assessment tax return.
[71] i.e. the member and receiving scheme were both (at the time of the transfer) in the same country, or they were both in EEA states.
[72] A *ring-fenced transfer fund* in relation to a QROPS or former QROPS has the meaning in FA 2004 Sch.34 para.1.

**12-041**  As with the other charges under FA 2004 Pt 4, a person is liable to the overseas transfer charge whether or not that person, and any other person who is liable to the charge, are resident or domiciled in the UK.

**12-042**  The scheme manager must notify HMRC of the event causing the charge to apply, and HMRC will provide the scheme manager with an accounting reference for paying the charge. Payment is due within 91 days of the date of issue of the accounting reference.[73] If the charge is not paid within this period then it carries interest at the prescribed rate until payment.[74]

*Repayment of charge under s.244AC on subsequent excluding events*

**12-043**  Section 244M applies if: (a) the overseas transfer charge under s.244AC arose on a transfer at the time the transfer was made; and (b) at any time during the relevant period for the transfer, circumstances arise such that, had those circumstances existed at the time the transfer was made, the transfer would at the time it was made have been excluded from the charge by any of the five exclusions described above.[75] In these circumstances, HMRC will repay any amount paid in respect of charge on the transfer. This does not give rise to entitlement to repayment of, or cancellation of liabilities to, interest or penalties in respect of late payment of charge on the transfer. Any repayment is conditional on making a claim, which must be made within one year of the end of the relevant period for the transfer concerned.[76]

**12-044**  Section 244M applies, for example, where a transfer was subject to the charge only because the member failed to provide the scheme administrator or scheme manager with the required information before the transfer and the member has now provided that information, or where the QROPS is an occupational pension scheme and when the transfer was made the member was not employed by a scheme employer, and he is now so employed. It should be noted however that s.244M only applies if the charge arose on a transfer *at the time the transfer was made*. It follows that it does not apply if an exclusion applied at the time of the transfer and the exclusion ceases to apply during the five-year period. For example, if a transfer was made to a QROPS established in an EEA state at a time when the member was resident in an EEA state, and during the relevant period the member becomes resident outside of the EEA (thereby causing the charge to apply at that time), there could be no repayment if he subsequently became resident in an EEA state again during the five-year period.

**12-045**  Repayment to the scheme administrator is conditional on prior compliance with any requirements to give information to HMRC about the circumstances in which the right to repayment arises.[77] Repayment is not conditional on compliance with any time limits so imposed for compliance with any such requirements.

**12-046**  Any such repayments to the scheme are expressly not relievable pension contributions.

---

[73] SI 2006/208 reg.3AH.

[74] SI 2006/208 reg.3AJ. The *prescribed rate* means the rate applicable under FA 1989 s.178 for the purposes of TMA 1970 s.86, which is Bank of England base rate plus 2.5% (The Taxes (Interest Rate) Regulations 1989 (SI 1989/1297) reg.3(2)).

[75] Or as a result of the exercise by HMRC of the power in s.224H to make regulations providing for a recognised transfer to a QROPS, or an onward transfer, to be excluded from the overseas transfer charge.

[76] SI 2006/208 reg.3AL. Regulation 3AL specifies the information to be provided.

[77] Although only if the requirement is imposed under FA 2004 s.169 (which contains HMRC's powers to require person to provide information relating to QROPS and former QROPS) or FA 2004 s.251 (which contains HMRC's general powers to require a person to provide information).

Where an amount is repaid to the scheme administrator of a registered pension scheme, and there is a recognised transfer from that scheme to a QROPS of some or all of that amount, that transfer did not cause BCE 8 to occur before 6 April 2023 (but that did not affect the amount crystallised by the BCE consisting of the making of the transfer that originally gave rise to the charge). **12-047**

*Discharge of liability*

If a scheme administrator is liable for the charge, he may apply to HMRC for the discharge of his liability on the ground that: (a) he reasonably believed that there was no liability to the overseas transfer charge on the transfer concerned; and (b) in all the circumstances of the case, it would not be just and reasonable for him to be liable to the charge on the transfer.[78] If HMRC refuse, he can appeal to the tribunal.[79] **12-048**

---

[78] FA 2004 s.244N.
[79] FA 2004 s.269. The burden of proof is on the scheme manager or scheme administrator to satisfy the tribunal that it is not just and reasonable in all the circumstances for him to be liable to the charge. These provisions are materially identical to the circumstances in which a scheme administrator may be discharged from liability to the scheme sanction charge (see Ch.5).

# CHAPTER 13

# Authorised Pensions

## TABLE OF CONTENTS

| | |
|---|---|
| Authorised pensions | 13-001 |
|     The pension rules | 13-002 |
|         "Entitlement" and "payment" | 13-003 |
|         Normal minimum pension age | 13-004 |
|         The ill-health condition | 13-005 |
|         Post-death payments | 13-006 |
|         "In respect of" an arrangement | 13-007 |
|     Taxation of authorised pensions | 13-008 |
|         ITEPA 2003 Pt 9 | 13-009 |
|         National insurance contributions | 13-012 |
|         Interaction with lifetime allowance (pre-6 April 2024) | 13-013 |
| Scheme pension | 13-014 |
|     The meaning of "scheme pension" | 13-015 |
|         "Pension" | 13-017 |
|         Anti-avoidance | 13-018 |
|         Money purchase arrangements | 13-020 |
|         Associated death benefits | 13-022 |
| Lifetime annuity | 13-023 |
|     "Annuity" | 13-024 |
|         Post-6 April 2015 annuities | 13-025 |
|         Pre-6 April 2015 annuities | 13-027 |
|         Cessation | 13-028 |
|         Associated death benefits | 13-029 |
|     Comparing scheme pensions and lifetime annuities | 13-030 |
| Drawdown pension | 13-031 |
|     Short-term annuity | 13-032 |
|         Cessation | 13-034 |
|     Income withdrawal | 13-035 |
|     Flexi-access drawdown funds | 13-036 |
|         "Designate" | 13-038 |
|     Drawdown pension funds | 13-039 |
|         Pension rule 5 | 13-041 |
| Pensions paid in error | 13-042 |
|     Payments representing accrued arrears of pension | 13-043 |
|     Pensions paid in error (recipient is alive) | 13-044 |
|     Pensions paid after discovery of error | 13-045 |
|     Pensions continuing to be paid after death | 13-046 |
|     Payments of arrears of pension after death | 13-047 |
| Reporting obligations | 13-049 |

# AUTHORISED PENSIONS

**13-001** There are just three categories of authorised pension:[1]
(a) scheme pension;
(b) lifetime annuity; and
(c) drawdown pension, of which there are two sub-categories:
  (i) short-term annuity; and
  (ii) income withdrawal.

The terms of a scheme pension or annuity may also include the provision of certain death benefits.

This chapter is concerned with the meaning and taxation of each category of authorised pension, including the associated death benefits.

## The pension rules

**13-002** The list of authorised member payments in FA 2004 s.164(1) includes "pensions permitted by the pension rules ... to be paid to ... a member".[2] There are five pension rules:[3]

| Pension rule 1 | No payment of pension may be made before the day on which the member reaches normal minimum pension age, unless the ill-health condition was met immediately before the member became entitled to a pension under the pension scheme. |
|---|---|
| Pension rule 2 | If the member dies before the end of the period of ten years beginning with the day on which the member became entitled to a scheme pension or an annuity, and if in the case of an annuity that day was before 6 April 2015, payment of the scheme pension or annuity may continue to be made (to any person) until the end of that period.
If the member becomes entitled to an annuity on or after 6 April 2015 and the annuity is payable until the later of the member's death and the end of a term certain, payment of the annuity may continue to be made (to any person) until the end of that term.
Except as provided by the preceding provisions of this rule, no payment of the member's pension may be made after the member's death. |
| Pension rule 3 | No payment of pension other than a scheme pension may be made in respect of a defined benefits arrangement or a collective money purchase arrangement. |
| Pension rule 4 | No payment of pension other than: (a) a scheme pension; (b) a lifetime annuity; or (c) drawdown pension, may be made in respect of a money purchase arrangement that is not a collective money purchase arrangement; but a scheme pension may only be paid if the member had an opportunity to select a lifetime annuity instead. |

---

[1] In addition, certain pensions paid in error are treated as if they were authorised payments: see below.
[2] FA 2004 s.164(1)(a). "Pension" expressly includes an annuity and income withdrawal (FA 2004 s.165(2)).
[3] FA 2004 s.165(1).

| Pension rule 5 | The total amount of drawdown pension paid in each drawdown pension year from, or under a short-term annuity purchased using sums or assets out of, the member's drawdown pension fund in respect of a money purchase arrangement must not exceed 150% of the basis amount for the drawdown pension year.[4] |

*"Entitlement" and "payment"*

**13-003** There is an important distinction in the pension rules between: (a) entitlement to pension; and (b) payment of pension. The meaning of "payment" is considered in Ch.2. A person becomes *entitled* to a scheme pension or annuity when he first acquires an actual (rather than a prospective) right to receive the pension or annuity.[5] A person becomes *entitled* to income withdrawal when sums or assets are designated as available for the payment of drawdown pension. Entitlement that is conditional (for example, on reaching a specified age, retiring, or obtaining consent) is *prospective* until the condition is satisfied. Entitlement is *actual* if the member has the immediate right to benefit without having to satisfy any further conditions or take any further actions.[6] Thus, if a member becomes entitled under the rules of a scheme to a scheme pension on his or her 65th birthday, and the administrator has all of the information needed to make the payment, the member becomes actually entitled to the pension on his or her 65th birthday, even if administrative delays mean that he or she does not actually receive the first payment until a later time. A person cannot become actually entitled to an annuity until the premium is paid to the insurance company.[7]

*Normal minimum pension age*

**13-004** A pension paid to a member before he reaches "normal minimum pension age" will not comply with pension rule 1 unless the ill-health condition is met immediately before the member becomes entitled to the pension.[8] Normal minimum pension age is currently age 55,[9] unless the member has a "protected pension age".[10]

---

[4] Since April 2015, pension rule 5 applies only in very limited circumstances. It is addressed below when considering drawdown pension.

[5] FA 2004 s.165(3).

[6] *Devon and Somerset Fire and Rescue Authority v Howell* [2023] EWHC 257 (Ch) at [115], which goes on to explain that "a condition that requires consent or permission of a third party before there is any right to a pension will be a contingency that will result in there not being a 'prospective right to a benefit' within the meaning of [the provisions relating to protected pension ages]".

[7] Suppose that a person becomes entitled to a scheme pension on his 55th birthday but the first payment is not due until six months after his birthday and annually thereafter. When does he become entitled to the pension? If he has absolute entitlement to the payment (albeit in six months' time) then he becomes actually entitled on his 55th birthday. This can be tested by asking whether his estate would be able to sue for the payment (once the six months has elapsed) if the member died in the six-month period. If the first payment is conditional on the member being alive at the time of payment, he would not become actually entitled until that time.

[8] Four authorised *lump sums* may however be paid before normal minimum pension age: (a) serious ill health lump sums; (b) winding-up lump sums; (c) short service refund lump sums (and certain payments deemed to be short service refund lump sums); and (d) refund of excess contributions lump sums.

[9] FA 2004 s.279. Normal minimum pension age was age 50 before 6 April 2010. For everyone except members of "uniformed services pension schemes", it will increase to age 57 on 6 April 2028. In contrast to the pre-6 April 2006 position, it is not necessary for a member to retire before commencing benefits; hence the reference is to "pension age" rather than "retirement date".

*The ill-health condition*

**13-005** The ill-health condition is met if:

(a) the scheme administrator has received evidence from a registered medical practitioner that the member is (and will continue to be) incapable of carrying on the member's occupation because of physical or mental impairment; and

(b) the member has in fact ceased to carry on the member's occupation.[11]

The "evidence" need not be categorical: a statement from a medical practitioner that the member's incapacity is expected to continue ought to suffice. It is suggested that the words "and will continue to be" do not mean that the incapacity must be expected to continue for the rest of the member's life. Satisfying the ill-health condition permits pension benefits to commence prior to normal minimum pension age, so it is implicit that the incapacity need continue only until the member reaches normal minimum pension age.[12] If the member does in fact recover then he or she will at that time cease to satisfy the ill-health condition and so entitlement will cease. The fact that the member may be capable of carrying on a different occupation (following retraining, for example) is not material.[13] As a result, retired professional athletes, for example, will often be able to satisfy the ill-health condition long before they reach age 55.[14]

*Post-death payments*

**13-006** The final sentence of pension rule 2 ("no payment of the member's pension may be made after the member's death", other than the specified term guarantee) refers only to payments of pension which accrue after death.[15] This rule does not prevent payments of pension which accrued during the member's life but for some reason were not paid prior to death.[16]

*"In respect of" an arrangement*

**13-007** Pension rules 3 and 4 refer to pensions paid "in respect of" an arrangement.[17] This imposes a requirement that there is a material connection between the member's arrangement and the pension.

A pension is paid *in respect of* a defined benefits arrangement only if the annual rate of the pension is calculated in accordance with the terms of his arrangement. The money applied to provide or purchase the pension "represents" his accrued rights under the arrangement.[18]

A pension is paid "in respect of" a money purchase arrangement if the money ap-

---

[10] For protected pension ages, see Ch.3.
[11] FA 2004 Sch.28 para.1.
[12] See *Harris v Shuttleworth* [1994] I.C.R. 991; [1994] Pens. L.R. 47; *R. v Secretary of State for the Environment Ex p. McClorry* unreported 3 September 1998.
[13] See *Fernance v Wreckair* [1993] Pens. L.R. 191.
[14] Such individuals may also have a pre-2006 protected pension age: see Ch.3.
[15] PTM062800.
[16] This is supported by the fact that an income tax assessment may relate to the tax year in which the pension accrued rather than the date it was paid (ITEPA 2003 s.579B). Such payments will also usually be authorised payments under The Registered Pension Schemes (Authorised Payments) Regulations 2009 (SI 2009/1171) reg.15.
[17] For the meaning of "arrangement", see Ch.2.
[18] Thus, for example, a "recognised transfer" is defined as "a transfer of sums or assets held for the purposes of, *or representing accrued rights under*, a registered pension scheme so as to become held

plied to provide or purchase the pension accumulated in accordance with the terms of a money purchase arrangement. Once a member becomes entitled to a scheme pension or annuity, his entitlement is by its nature a defined benefit, but that does not prevent it from being paid in respect of a money purchase arrangement.

Ex-gratia benefits (i.e. benefits to which the member is not entitled) are not provided "in respect of" an arrangement. A payment to a member can be in respect of his arrangement only if he first becomes entitled to the payment.

### Taxation of authorised pensions

FA 2004 Pt 4 does not impose any tax charges in respect of authorised pensions. Such pensions are taxable only under ITEPA 2003 Pt 9. Where the scheme or member is resident outside of the UK, see Ch.20.

**13-008**

*ITEPA 2003 Pt 9*

ITEPA 2003 Pt 9 Ch.2 imposes the charge to tax on "pension income", excluding any "exempt income".[19] "Pension income" means any pension under a registered pension scheme, to the extent that it is not an unauthorised payment.[20] "Pension" expressly includes income withdrawal and an annuity under, or purchased with sums or assets held for the purposes of, or representing accrued rights under, a registered pension scheme.[21] "Exempt income" means pension income on which no liability to income tax arises as a result of any provision of ITEPA 2003 Pt 9 Ch.15A (lump sums under registered pension schemes), or Ch.17[22] or Ch.18,[23] which do not have much application to authorised pensions (although Ch.17 does contain an exemption for payments of lifetime annuity for the duration of a term certain (in accordance with pension rule 2) following the death of the member before his 75th birthday).[24]

**13-009**

---

for the purposes of, *or to represent rights under* another registered pension scheme ..." (s.169(1) FA 2004).

[19] ITEPA 2003 s.566(1).
[20] ITEPA 2003 s.579A.
[21] ITEPA 2003 s.579D. It may be possible in principle for an authorised lump sum to constitute pension for these purposes (e.g. this could conceivably be the case where say five annual payments of UFPLS are paid), however Pt 9 Ch.15A provides exhaustively for the chargeability of authorised lump sums, leaving no scope for such lump sums to be taxed under Ch.5A (except where Ch.5A is expressly applied by Ch.15A).
[22] ITEPA 2003 Pt 9 Ch.17 contains exemptions relating to awards for bravery, pensions in respect of death due to military or war service, lump sums provided under armed forces early departure scheme, wounds and disability pensions, compensation for National-Socialist persecution, Netherlands Benefit Act for Victims of Persecution 1940–1945, Malawi, Trinidad and Tobago and Zambia government pensions, pensions payable where employment ceased due to disablement, health and employment insurance payments, social security pensions: increases in respect of children, former miners etc.: coal and allowances in lieu, foreign pensions of consular employees, registered schemes: beneficiaries' annuities from unused funds, registered schemes: beneficiaries' annuities from drawdown funds, non-registered schemes: beneficiaries' annuities from unused funds, and non-registered schemes: beneficiaries' annuities from drawdown funds.
[23] ITEPA 2003 Pt 9 Ch.18 contains exemptions relating to pensions paid to non-UK residents under The Central African Pension Fund, Commonwealth government pension funds, the Oversea Superannuation Scheme, the Overseas Pensions Act 1973, the Overseas Service Act 1958, the Overseas Service Pensions Fund, and The Pensions (India, Pakistan and Burma) Act 1955.
[24] ITEPA 2003 s.646B(4) (applicable to deaths on or after 3 December 2014). There is no equivalent exception for scheme pension.

**13-010** The amount charged to tax is the "net taxable pension income" for the tax year, which means the "taxable pension income" less any allowable deductions.[25] "Taxable pension income" means the full amount of the pension that accrues in the year, irrespective of when it is actually paid.[26] Thus, liability arises even where pension is not paid (for example, because the trustees cannot trace the member). It is implicit that income withdrawal "accrues" when the trustees agree to pay it; no liability can arise before that time. "Allowable deductions" are those under ITEPA 2003 s.567A, and ITEPA 2003 Pt 12. The former applies a deduction to avoid double taxation where ITEPA 2003 Pt 7A has applied to the source of the pension income, and the latter applies to charitable gifts via payroll.

**13-011** The person liable for the tax is "the person receiving or entitled to the pension".[27] ITEPA 2003 Pt 9 does not impose any tax charges on the scheme administrator. If the member entitled to a pension directs the trustees or managers to pay it to another person, the member and recipient are both liable, but the member has credit for the tax paid by the recipient.[28]

*National insurance contributions*

**13-012** Authorised pensions under registered pension schemes are disregarded for NIC purposes.[29]

*Interaction with lifetime allowance (pre-6 April 2024)*

**13-013** Prior to 6 April 2024, for lifetime allowance purposes, becoming entitled to a scheme pension was BCE 2, becoming entitled to a lifetime annuity was BCE 4, and the designation of sums or assets as available for the payment of drawdown pension was BCE 1.[30] The only BCE that could occur after the member had reached age 75 was an "excessive" increase in the rate of a scheme pension (BCE 3). Prior

---

[25] ITEPA 2003 s.567(2).
[26] ITEPA 2003 s.579B.
[27] ITEPA 2003 s.579C. Liability for income tax is almost always imposed on the person "receiving or entitled" to the income: see e.g. ITTOIA 2005 s.8 (trading income), s.271 (property income), s.371 (interest), s.385 (dividends), s.685 (annual payments).
[28] TSEM9310 states: "The 'receiving' basis enables you to tax the person in receipt of the income, even if you cannot trace the person entitled to it. But ultimately you want to tax the person who is entitled. For example, in an interest in possession trust (TSEM1105), the trustees are initially taxable on the trust income because they receive it. But the IIP beneficiary is ultimately taxable on the trust income because he or she is entitled to it. So you tax the beneficiary on the income on the 'entitled' basis, and give credit for any tax paid by the trustees who received it. In sum, for the purpose of taxation of income, you want to establish who is 'entitled to' the income". Indeed, if the person so entitled directs the trustees to pay the pension to a third party then the person has exercised dominion over it and is thus taxable in any event: see e.g. *Meredith-Hardy v McLellan* [1995] S.T.C. (SC D) 270.
[29] Social Security (Contributions) Regulations 2001 (SI 2001/1004) Sch.3 Pt VI para.2. The provisions are poorly drafted. They provide that a payment is disregarded for NIC purposes if it is a payment by way of any benefit pursuant to a registered pension scheme to which: (a) FA 2004 s.204(1) and Sch.31 applies; or (b) FA 2004 s.208 or s.209 applies. Section 204(1) provides that "Schedule 31 contains provision about the taxation of pensions and lump sums which are authorised to be paid by this Part" so it is not at all clear how s.204(1) could be said to "apply" to a payment. Schedule 31 contains the provisions that amended ITEPA 2003 Pt 9 from 6 April 2006 to include the taxation of benefits from registered pension schemes. It does this primarily by inserting a new Ch.5A and a new Ch.15A into ITEPA Pt 9, and so it seems to be intended that any payments within Ch.5A or Ch.15A are disregarded for NIC purposes. Section 208 imposes the unauthorised payments charge and s.209 imposes the unauthorised payments surcharge. It is not possible for s.209 to apply without s.208 applying, so (b) above will apply to all unauthorised payments.
[30] With effect from 6 April 2024, BCE 1, BCE 2, BCE 3, BCE 4 (and also BCE 6) are applied only for annual allowance purposes: see Ch.7.

to 6 April 2023, a 25% lifetime allowance charge arose to the extent that the amount crystallised by such BCEs exceeded the member's available lifetime allowance.

## SCHEME PENSION

A "scheme pension" is a traditional pension paid directly from the pension scheme or from an insurance company until the member's death. It is the only type of authorised pension that may be provided in respect of a defined benefits arrangement.[31] A scheme pension may be paid in respect of a money purchase arrangement, provided that the member had an opportunity to select a lifetime annuity instead.[32] References to a scheme pension paid "in respect of" a money purchase arrangement or a defined benefits arrangement (e.g. in pension rules 2 and 3), are references to the category of arrangement under which the sums and assets accumulated prior to the application of the sums or assets to purchase or pay the scheme pension.

13-014

**The meaning of "scheme pension"**

A pension payable to the member is a "scheme pension" if:

13-015

(a) It is payable by the scheme administrator or by an insurance company[33] selected by the scheme administrator.
(b) It is payable at least annually.
(c) It is payable until the member's death, or until the later of the member's death and the end of a term certain not exceeding ten years.[34]

It is permissible however for such a scheme pension to terminate before the end of the term certain where it terminates after the death of the member on the recipient: (i) marrying; (ii) entering into a civil partnership; (iii) reaching the age of 18; or (iv) ceasing to be in full-time education.[35]

(d) The rate of pension payable at any time during any "relevant 12-month period" must not be less than the rate payable immediately before the beginning of that period (or, in the case of the first relevant 12-month period, the day on which the member became entitled to the pension).[36] A "relevant 12-month period" means any 12-month period which begins on or after the first anniversary of the day on which the member becomes entitled to the pension, and ends before the day on which the pension ceases to be payable.

The following are excepted:[37] (i) a reduction of the pension if the member

---

[31] Pension rule 3.
[32] Pension rule 4.
[33] "Insurance company" is defined in FA 2004 s.275(1). The policy may be in the name of the scheme trustees (in which case the insurance company will usually pay the pension to the trustees, although the insurance company may act as the trustees' paying agent and pay the member direct) or in the name of the member (in which case the insurance company will usually pay the pension directly to the member) (see PTM062310).
[34] A ten-year term certain mirrors pension rule 2. The term certain will usually be specified when the pension commences, but this is not an express requirement. If a member who is entitled to a scheme pension in respect of a defined benefits arrangement dies before receiving a specified minimum amount of pension, a pension protection LSDB (a type of authorised payment) may be paid (see Ch.15).
[35] FA 2004 Sch.28 para.2(6).
[36] See FA 2004 Sch.28 paras 2 and 2A.
[37] FA 2004 Sch.28 para.2(4).

became entitled to it by reason of the ill-health condition being met;[38] (ii) a reduction in the rate of the pension which applies to all the scheme pensions being paid to or in respect of members of the pension scheme; (iii) a reduction of the pension in consequence of a pension sharing order or provision;[39] (iv) forfeiture of entitlement to the pension in circumstances prescribed by regulations made by HMRC;[40] (v) a reduction of the pension in consequence of a court order; (vi) if the pension is under a public service pension scheme, its reduction by abatement; or (vii) a reduction of the pension in any other circumstances prescribed by regulations made by HMRC.[41]

**13-016** If any of the above requirements cease to be met after a scheme pension has commenced (because, for example, the annual rate of the pension is reduced), each payment after that time will not be scheme pension.

*"Pension"*

**13-017** A payment can be "scheme pension" only if it is "pension". The term "pension" is not defined for the purposes of FA 2004 Pt 4,[42] and has no clear meaning as a matter of general law. Certain case law suggests that for a payment to be "pension": (a) it must be income in the hands of the pensioner; and (b) it must be made in respect of an employment which has ceased (although the employment need not have ceased because of retirement).[43] But there is nothing in FA 2004 Pt 4 to suggest that there must be any employment nexus (and, where there happens to be an employment nexus, it is quite clear that the employment need not have ceased).[44] In *Westminster v Haywood*,[45] Millet LJ said that it is a perfectly accurate use of the word "pension" to mean periodic payments as distinguished from lump sum payments. It is suggested that any payment which satisfies the requirements in (a)–(d) above will be a pension.

---

[38] The ill-health condition is explained above. It is not uncommon for the rules of a scheme to provide that an enhanced scheme pension is payable to a member who is in ill-health. If he recovers from ill-health he will cease to be entitled to the enhanced scheme pension, and so this exception applies to the reduction in these circumstances.
[39] For pension sharing orders, see Ch.16.
[40] See The Pension Schemes (Reduction in Pension Rates) Regulations 2006 (SI 2006/138) reg.2 (forfeiture permitted under PA 1995 ss.92(2) or 93 (provided that the member is not connected with the sponsoring employer), or PA 1995 ss.92(4) or (5), or in any circumstances prescribed by The Occupational Pension Schemes (Assignment, Forfeiture, Bankruptcy etc.) Regulations 1997 (SI 1997/785).
[41] See SI 2006/138 reg.3 (reductions under PA 2004 s.138(2); Gender Recognition Act 2004 Sch.5 paras 14(3) or 15(3); FA 2004 s.237E(1); FA 2004 s.227(1) (annual allowance charge); reductions of pension during winding up); The Registered Pension Schemes (Authorised Reductions) Regulations 2006 (SI 2006/1465) reg.2 (reduction of scheme pension in connection with admission to Chelsea Hospital); The Registered Pension Schemes (Bridging Pensions) and Appointed Day Regulations 2016 (SI 2016/1005) regs 3 and 4; The Registered Pension Schemes (Transfer of Sums and Assets) Regulations 2006 (SI 2006/499) reg.5 (reduction relating to administration costs).
[42] Section 165(2) provides that "pension" includes an annuity and income withdrawal, but that is not a definition.
[43] *Johnson v Holleran* [1989] S.T.C. 1; 62 T.C. 428; *Mcmann v Shaw* [1972] 1 W.L.R. 1578; [1972] 3 All E.R. 732. The dictionary definition is "periodic payment made especially by a government or an employer, in consideration of past services or of relinquishment of rights etc.
[44] See e.g. *Simplifying the taxation of pensions: increasing choice and flexibility for all* 17 December 2002, para.1.10.
[45] *Westminster v Haywood* [1998] Ch. 377 at 409.

## SCHEME PENSION

*Anti-avoidance*

When a member becomes entitled to a scheme pension, the terms of the pension scheme will also usually confer a right to a PCLS. The maximum PCLS is determined by reference to the annual rate of the scheme pension. Because a PCLS is tax-free, anti-avoidance provisions prevent members taking a scheme pension which is initially high (when the amount of the PCLS is calculated) and is subsequently reduced. These provisions apply in any of the following circumstances:[46] **13-018**

(a) The pension is not payable (at least annually) until the member's death or until the later of the member's death and the end of a term certain not exceeding ten years.[47]
(b) The rate of pension payable at any time during any relevant 12-month period is less than the rate payable at the relevant time because a "substantial reduction" occurs in the rate of the pension. A substantial reduction occurs in the rate of a pension if the rate at which the pension is payable at any time during any "relevant 12-month period" is less than 80% of the rate payable when the member became entitled to the pension. A relevant 12-month period is any 12-month period which begins on or after the first anniversary of the day on which the member becomes entitled to the pension, and ends before the day on which the pension ceases to be payable.
(c) The pension is reduced by reason of the ill-health condition being met, and the reduction is part of "avoidance arrangements". Avoidance arrangements are defined (non-exhaustively) to include schemes, arrangements and understandings of any kind (whether or not legally enforceable) the main purpose, or one of the main purposes, of which is to increase the member's entitlement to a lump sum on which there is no liability to income tax.
(d) There is a reduction in the rate of the pension which applies to all the scheme pensions being paid to or in respect of members of the pension scheme and the reduction is part of "avoidance arrangements".

In the above circumstances, the pension scheme is deemed to make an unauthorised payment to the member of an amount equal to the amount of any lump sum on which there was no liability to tax to which the member became entitled in connection with the commencement of the scheme pension. Thus, in the context of a PCLS, the amount of the unauthorised payment is equal to the whole of the lump sum, not merely the amount of the lump sum corresponding to the subsequent reduction in scheme pension. These are therefore punitive provisions; alleviated only very slightly by para.2A(6), which provides that once these anti-avoidance provisions have applied in relation to a pension they cannot apply in relation to it again. This means that the scheme pension can be further reduced without giving rise to another unauthorised payment under para.2A. However, the further reduction must be in accordance with the exceptions above, otherwise each payment may constitute an unauthorised payment on the basis that it is not scheme pension (or any other category of authorised pension). **13-019**

---

[46] FA 2004 Sch.28 para.2A.
[47] This is necessary because a cessation is not itself deemed to be an unauthorised payment. A cessation will breach the "payable until the member's death" requirement, and so any future payments would not be scheme pension, but there will not be any future payments if it has ceased.

*Money purchase arrangements*

**13-020** Where a scheme pension is paid in respect of a defined benefits arrangement, the annual rate of scheme pension is determined in accordance with the terms of the arrangement. The commencement of the pension is the fruition of the arrangement. Where a scheme pension is paid in respect of a money purchase arrangement, the annual rate of the pension can be determined only at the time that the sums or assets held for the purposes of the money purchase arrangement are applied to pay or purchase the scheme pension. The annual rate will be determined by the amount of the sums and assets which are available to be so applied. Given that a scheme pension must be payable for the duration of the member's life, and cannot decrease except in limited circumstances, many money purchase schemes either purchase a scheme pension from an insurance company for the member, or purchase a scheme pension or annuity for the scheme (essentially as an investment, to fund the trustees' obligations to the member), but there is no requirement to do so.

**13-021** The legislation does not prescribe the process by which a scheme pension is provided in respect of a money purchase arrangement. The process is best characterised as a surrender of rights under the arrangement in return for an entitlement to the scheme pension.[48] The surrender may relate to the sums and assets of an uncrystallised fund, or to sums and assets which have been designated as available for drawdown pension.[49] Procedurally, where the pension is paid directly from the pension scheme, the sums and assets held for the purposes of the member's arrangement can be reallocated to a separate fund under the scheme (and can continue to be invested). Subject to the scheme rules, any surplus of that fund can be applied: (a) for the general purposes of the scheme (including the augmentation of any member's benefits under the scheme[50]); and/or (b) on the member's death to provide dependants' scheme pension.

*Associated death benefits*

**13-022** The terms of a scheme pension may include the payment of (a) a term certain guarantee; (b) a dependants' scheme pension; and/or (c) a pension protection LSDB (if the scheme pension is payable in respect of a defined benefits arrangement) or annuity protection LSDB (if the scheme pension is payable in respect of a money purchase arrangement). The undertaking by the trustees/managers or insurance company to provide such death benefits will usually arise when the scheme pension is purchased or otherwise comes into payment (or possibly later, but in any event before the member's death because otherwise the death benefits would not be paid "in respect of" the member's arrangement).

---

[48] Such a surrender will not be a deemed unauthorised payment under FA 2004 s.172A as a result of the exception in s.172A(5)(c), and it should not be made void by PA 1995 s.91(1) as a result of the exception in s.91(5)(b)(ii).

[49] HMRC agree at PTM062330. Also see e.g. The Taxation of Pension Schemes (Transitional Provisions) Order 2006 (SI 2006/572) reg.29(5), which expressly refers to a scheme pension and a lifetime annuity being funded by the "surrender" of funds in a drawdown fund. Prior to 6 April 2024, this would cause BCE 2 to occur, with credit given for the amount crystallised under BCE 1 when the funds were designated as available for the payment of drawdown pension (see Ch.10). Since 6 April 2024, these BCEs are relevant only for annual allowance purposes: see Ch.7.

[50] Such a surplus may arise during the life of the member (if the investment returns exceeds the pension paid) or on the member's death. In the latter case, if the deceased member and recipient member were connected persons immediately before death, note the possible application of FA 2004 s.172B. As is explained in Ch.17, s.172B should not usually apply where the augmentation occurs at the trustees' discretion.

# LIFETIME ANNUITY

The requirements an annuity must satisfy to be a "lifetime annuity" are different depending on whether the member becomes entitled[51] to the annuity: (a) before 6 April 2015; or (b) on or after that date.[52] A lifetime annuity can be purchased only in respect of a money purchase arrangement. The annuity may be purchased by the application of sums or assets: (a) which are uncrystallised; or (b) which have been designated as available for drawdown pension.

A lifetime annuity cannot be paid directly from the pension scheme: it must be purchased by the trustees or managers from an insurance company. It will therefore be paid by the insurance company to the member. However, each annuity payment by the insurance company to the member is deemed by FA 2004 s.161(4) to be paid by the pension scheme, even if the scheme has been wound up since it purchased the annuity.[53] For this reason, any payments or benefits other than authorised payments (such as the annuity payments) by the insurance company to or in respect of the member will be unauthorised payments by the pension scheme.[54]

**"Annuity"**

Payments can be a lifetime annuity only if they are properly characterised as an "annuity". The mere fact that an arrangement is described as an annuity does not necessarily make it so.[55] "Annuity" is not defined for the purposes of FA 2004 Pt 4. The case law on the meaning of "annuity" for income tax purposes[56] establish that:[57] (a) the payments must be income of the recipient and not a payment of capital by instalments;[58] (b) it must be pure income profit;[59] (c) there must be a legal obligation to pay the sum;[60] and (d) if not recurring, it is at least capable of recurrence.[61] The fact that such payments may be contingent and variable in character does not prevent them from being an annuity.[62]

13-023

13-024

---

[51] A person becomes "entitled" to a lifetime annuity when he first acquires an actual (rather than a prospective) right to receive the annuity (FA 2004 s.165(3)). In most cases, this will be when the annuity is purchased.
[52] For lifetime annuities which commenced prior to 6 April 2006, see Ch.3.
[53] FA 2004 s.161(3) and (4) (for which, see Ch.18).
[54] This explains why the payment of a lifetime annuity is itself shown as an authorised payment (even though it cannot in fact be paid by a registered pension scheme), and why the purchase of the lifetime annuity by the pension scheme is not itself shown as an authorised payment: it is treated as not being a payment at all.
[55] Secretary of State in *Council of India v Scobie* [1903] A.C. 299; *Perrin v Dickson* [1929] 2 K.B. 85; *Sothern-Smith v Clancy* [1941] 1 K.B. 276; [1941] 1 All E.R. 111.
[56] See *Foley v Fletcher and Rose* 157 E.R. 678; (1858) 3 H. & N. 768 (Watson J); *Perrin v Dickson* [1929] 2 K.B. 85 (Rowlatt J); *Sothern-Smith v Clancy* 24 T.C. 1 (Sir Wilfred Greene MR).
[57] "Annuity" is construed ejusdem generis with "annual payments".
[58] *Brodie's Will Trustees v IRC* (1933) 17 T.C. 432.
[59] *Hanbury, Re* (1939) 38 T.C. 588. So, e.g. agreeing to pay a garage £500 p/a for five years for the hire and upkeep of a car does not constitute an annuity: *Howe v IRC* [1919] 2 K.B. 336; 7 T.C. 289.
[60] See *Ridge Securities Ltd v IRC* (1964) 44 T.C. 373.
[61] See *IRC v Whitworth Park Coal Ltd* 38 T.C. 531.
[62] *Moss Empires Ltd v IRC* 21 T.C. 264.

## Post-6 April 2015 annuities

**13-025** An annuity to which the member becomes entitled on or after 6 April 2015 is a lifetime annuity if:[63]

(a) it is payable by an insurance company;[64] and
(b) it is payable until the member's death, or until the later of the member's death and the end of a term certain. A fixed term annuity is payable "until the end of a term certain" even if it may, after the death of the member during the term, end on the annuitant: (i) marrying; (ii) entering into a civil partnership; (iii) reaching the age of 18; or (iv) ceasing to be in full-time education.[65] In contrast to a scheme pension (and a pre-6 April 2015 lifetime annuity), the term certain may exceed ten years.

**13-026** The terms of a lifetime annuity may also (but need not) provide that:[66]

(a) following the member's death, a dependants' or nominees' annuity commences (this is called a "joint-life" annuity); or
(b) if the member dies before receiving a specified minimum amount of annuity, an annuity protection LSDB may be paid.

## Pre-6 April 2015 annuities

**13-027** If the member became entitled to the annuity before 6 April 2015, a lifetime annuity must satisfy the two requirements above (i.e. it must be payable by an insurance company until the member's death) and three further requirements:[67]

(a) the member must have had an opportunity to select the insurance company;[68]
(b) any term certain must not exceed ten years; and
(c) its amount either; (i) cannot decrease, except by reason of a pension sharing order or provision; or (ii) is determined in any manner prescribed by regulations made by HMRC. The applicable regulations are The Registered Pension Schemes (Prescribed Manner of Determining Amount of Annuities) Regulations 2006 (SI 2006/568), reg.2 of which prescribes that variable annuities are permissible in certain circumstances where the annuity payments fluctuate in accordance with changes to; (i) the RPI; (ii) the market value of any freely marketable assets; or (iii) an index reflecting the value of any freely marketable assets.

## Cessation

**13-028** The cessation of an annuity does not itself appear to have any tax consequences (cf. the position regarding scheme pensions) unless sums or assets are consequently transferred back to the pension scheme that purchased the original lifetime annuity. Where such a transfer occurs, the pension scheme is treated as making an

---

[63] FA 2004 Sch.28 para.3(1A). A term certain simply means a fixed period of time. The term certain will usually be specified when the annuity commences, but this is not an express requirement.
[64] "Insurance company" is defined in FA 2004 s.275(1).
[65] FA 2004 Sch.28 para.3(2).
[66] See Ch.15.
[67] FA 2004 Sch.28 para.3(1).
[68] Many providers of personal pensions are insurance companies, which also offer annuities, so this safeguard was to ensure that the pension providers did not force the member to buy one of their own annuities.

unauthorised payment to the member of an amount equal to the value of the sums and assets transferred.[69]

*Associated death benefits*

The terms of a lifetime annuity may include the payment of: 

13-029

(a) a term certain guarantee;
(b) a dependants' or nominees' annuity (where the lifetime annuity is a joint-life annuity); and/or
(c) the payment of an annuity protection LSDB.[70]

**Comparing scheme pensions and lifetime annuities**

There are four key differences between a lifetime annuity and a scheme pension:

13-030

(a) A lifetime annuity must be purchased from an insurance company whereas a scheme pension may be paid directly from the pension scheme.
(b) Since 6 April 2015 there are no restrictions on the maximum guaranteed term of a lifetime annuity, whereas any guaranteed term of a scheme pension cannot exceed ten years from commencement.
(c) Since 6 April 2015 the annual rate of a scheme pension can decrease only in very limited circumstances, whereas the annual rate of a lifetime annuity may be decreased without restriction.
(d) Before 6 April 2024, the amount which crystallised for lifetime allowance purposes on the purchase of a lifetime annuity was equal to the purchase price of the annuity (BCE 4), whereas the amount which crystallised on the member becoming entitled to a scheme pension was equal to the annual rate of the initial pension multiplied by 20 (BCE 2). This could be a significant difference in practice, because a scheme pension purchased from an insurance company may cost much more than the amount which crystallises under BCE 2, especially where the rate of the scheme pension increases by 5% p/a, and it includes a dependants' scheme pension for the life of the dependant. This therefore usually favoured scheme pension.

# DRAWDOWN PENSION

"Drawdown pension" means either:[71]

13-031

(a) a short-term annuity; or
(b) income withdrawal.

As will be seen below, drawdown pension may be paid in respect of a drawdown pension fund or a flexi-access drawdown fund. Pension rule 5 applies to the former but not the latter.

---

[69] FA 2004 Sch.28 para.3(2B) and SI 2006/499 reg.6. Where a lifetime annuity ceases and a new lifetime annuity becomes payable, see Ch.12.
[70] For annuity protection LSDBs, see Ch.15.
[71] FA 2004 Sch.28 para.4. The payment of drawdown pension (but not merely the creation of a flexi-access drawdown fund) causes the money purchase annual allowance provisions to apply (see Ch.7).

**Short-term annuity**

**13-032**  An annuity[72] to which the member becomes entitled[73] on or after 6 April 2015 is a short-term annuity if:[74]

(a) it is purchased using some or all of the sums or assets in the member's drawdown pension fund or flexi-access drawdown fund;
(b) it is payable by an insurance company;[75] and
(c) it is payable for a term which does not exceed five years. If the member dies during the term certain, the annuity may continue until the end of the term.

**13-033**  An annuity to which the member became entitled before 6 April 2015 is a short-term annuity if it satisfies the above three requirements and two further requirements:[76]

(a) the member must have had an opportunity to select the insurance company; and
(b) its amount either: (i) cannot decrease, except by reason of a pension sharing order or provision; or (ii) is determined in any manner prescribed by regulations made by HMRC.[77]

*Cessation*

**13-034**  Where a short-term annuity ceases to be payable and sums or assets are consequently transferred to another insurance company, or sums or assets are transferred to the pension scheme that purchased the original annuity, the scheme is treated as making an unauthorised payment to the member of an amount equal to the value of the sums or assets transferred unless a new short-term annuity becomes payable.[78]

**Income withdrawal**

**13-035**  Income withdrawal means an amount (other than an annuity) which the member is entitled to be paid from either his drawdown pension fund or his flexi-access drawdown fund.[79] There are no restrictions regarding the amount of income withdrawal which may be paid from a flexi-access drawdown fund: payments may

---

[72] The meaning of "annuity" is considered above. Typically an annuity will consist of at least three payments, but a single payment calculated by reference to the net profits for each of the three years following that date has been found to be an annuity (*IRC v Hogarth* 1940 23 T.C. 491).
[73] A member becomes "entitled" to a short-term annuity when he first acquires an actual right to receive the annuity (FA 2004 s.165(3)(b)). In most cases, this will be when the annuity is purchased.
[74] FA 2004 Sch.28 para.6(1ZA).
[75] "Insurance company" is defined in FA 2004 s.275(1).
[76] FA 2004 Sch.28 para.6(1).
[77] See The Registered Pension Schemes (Prescribed Manner of Determining Amount of Annuities) Regulations 2006 (SI 2006/568) reg.4. As with lifetime annuities, the regulations provide that variable annuities are permissible in certain circumstances where the annuity payments fluctuate in accordance with changes to (i) the RPI, (ii) the market value of any freely marketable assets or (iii) an index reflecting the value of any freely marketable assets.
[78] FA 2004 Sch.28 para.6(1B) and SI 2006/499 reg.7(1). Where a new short-term annuity becomes payable, see Ch.12.
[79] FA 2004 Sch.28 paras 7 and 8. The words "(other than an annuity)" may seem odd, given that an annuity cannot be paid from a pension scheme, but they are perhaps explicable on the basis that annuity payments by an insurance company to the member are deemed by FA 2004 s.161(4) to be paid by the pension scheme. Each payment under a lifetime annuity or short-term annuity purchased with sums or assets in a drawdown pension fund or flexi-access drawdown fund is therefore deemed to be a payment from the member's drawdown pension fund or flexi-access drawdown fund.

DRAWDOWN PENSION

be made as and when requested by the member (including a single payment of an amount equal to the entire flexi-access drawdown fund).

**Flexi-access drawdown funds**

A member's flexi-access drawdown fund consists of such sums and assets as are "newly designated funds".[80] Sums and assets are newly designated funds in any of five circumstances:   13-036

(a) The sums or assets are designated as available for the payment of drawdown pension on or after 6 April 2015 and they are not "member-designated funds" (i.e. they were not designated as available for the payment of drawdown pension before 6 April 2015: see below).

(b) The sums or assets were member-designated funds immediately before 6 April 2015 and the conditions for "flexible" drawdown (in FA 2004 s.165(3A): see below) applied to the arrangement at that time. Any such sums or assets automatically ceased to be member-designated funds on 6 April 2015.

(c) The sums or assets formed part of the member's "capped" drawdown fund prior to 6 April 2015 (see below) and on or after 6 April 2015 a payment of drawdown pension is made that would (were it not for the automatic conversion to flexi-access drawdown) breach the cap in pension rule 5.[81] In these circumstances, the sums and assets that make up the fund immediately before the payment is made become newly designated funds immediately before the payment is made.[82]

(d) The sums or assets formed part of the member's capped drawdown fund prior to 6 April 2015 and the member notifies the scheme administrator that he wishes the fund to become the member's flexi-access drawdown fund.[83] In these circumstances, the sums or assets become newly designated funds on the date that the scheme administrator accepts the notification (or 6 April 2015, if later).

(e) There is a recognised transfer of member-designated funds from one scheme to another and: (i) the sums or assets transferred are designated as available for the payment of drawdown pension under the receiving scheme; and (ii) the member notifies the scheme administrator of the receiving scheme that he wishes the sums or assets to be newly designated funds.[84] The sums or assets become newly designated funds so on the later of the date that the designation is made, or immediately after the transfer. If the member does not make such a notification then the sums or assets will become member-designated funds, and will do so on the later of the date that the designation is made or immediately after the transfer.

In addition, any sums or assets which arise or derive from newly designated funds (or from sums or assets which so arise or derive) are also newly designated funds. It follows that if any money which has been so designated is used to purchase assets, those assets are newly designated funds (they do not need to be separately designated). Similarly, if designated assets produce income, the income comprises   13-037

---

[80] FA 2004 Sch.28 para.8A.
[81] Schedule 28 para.8B. For pension rule 5, see below.
[82] It follows that the payment is made out of the member's flexi-access drawdown fund in respect of the arrangement and so is not part of the total capped by pension rule 5.
[83] FA 2004 Sch.28 para.8C.
[84] FA 2004 Sch.28 para.8D.

newly designated funds. If any designated assets are sold, the sale proceeds are newly designated funds.

*"Designate"*

**13-038** "Designate" is not defined. It is suggested that it requires nothing more than a written record that certain sums or assets will only be used for that purpose.[85] Prior to such designation, the sums or assets will have been uncrystallised.[86] It is unclear whether *specific* scheme sums or assets (i.e. the underlying investments) must be designated for this purpose.[87] If so, this may well be problematic where each member's fund or account is notional (as is often the case with larger occupational schemes where the members do not have any influence over the choice of investments).[88] In such schemes, the investments are held on a pooled basis and each member's fund under the scheme is notionally allocated for him. In such circumstances, the better view seems to be that the designation of some or all of a member's fund under the scheme (whether as a percentage of the member's total fund, or possibly by reference to a specified value on that date) as available for the payment of drawdown pension should be effective.[89]

It is implicit that once funds have been designated for a particular purpose they cannot be undesignated or redesignated for a different purpose during the life of the member. Designating funds as available for the payment of drawdown pension is therefore irrevocable. The legislation does not specify *who* must designate the sums and assets as available for drawdown pension. HMRC appear to assume that it will be the member rather than the trustees or managers.[90]

---

[85] HMRC's position (at PTM062510) is that "The member starts a drawdown pension by 'designating' part or all of their pension funds to provide them with a drawdown pension. This means that the member tells their scheme administrator that they want to use £y to provide them with a drawdown pension. The funds that have been put aside (designated) to provide a drawdown pension form the member's 'drawdown pension fund'. The member's drawdown pension will be paid from that drawdown pension fund".

[86] It is not possible to designate sums or assets that have been applied to pay a scheme pension as being available for the payment of drawdown pension (FA 2004 Sch.28 para.8(1A)(b)).

[87] FA 2004 Sch.28 para.8A refers to "such of the sums or assets held for the purposes of the arrangement", which suggests that the designation must apply to specific assets.

[88] This is an important point because if a member purports to create a drawdown fund but fails to do so, it will not be possible to pay income withdrawal or purchase a short-term annuity. Any such payments will need to be characterised as UFPLS in order to avoid an unauthorised payment. A failed designation would not be a BCE (although since 6 April 2024 this is relevant only for annual allowance purposes), and any investment growth will increase the value of uncrystallised funds rather than a drawdown fund.

[89] Indeed, given the fungible nature of money, a specific "sum" can be designated for any particular purpose only where the money is held physically in notes or coins, or possibly where it is held in a separate bank account (and thereby ring-fenced). Again, this strongly suggests that "designation" is not a reference to specific sums/assets. This is further supported by the terminology used in, e.g., FA 2004 s.169(1D), which refers to a transfer of sums/assets which "represent" a member's drawdown fund rather than "comprise" the drawdown fund.

[90] See PTM062730. This is perhaps influenced by the terminology: a member's drawdown pension fund consists of sums/assets that are "member-designated funds", which indicates that they are designated by the member. The terminology for flexi-access drawdown funds is "newly designated funds".

## Drawdown pension funds

Prior to 6 April 2015, there was only one type of drawdown pension fund. If the member met the conditions in FA 2004 s.165(3A),[91] he could be paid any amount under a short-term annuity or income withdrawal from the fund (usually referred to as "flexible" drawdown pension). If the member did not meet those conditions, limits were imposed on the annual amount that he could be paid under a short-term annuity or income withdrawal from the fund (usually referred to as "capped" drawdown pension). On 6 April 2015, drawdown pension funds paying flexible drawdown pension automatically became flexi-access drawdown funds. Since 6 April 2015 a member's drawdown pension fund can only pay capped drawdown pension, and it is only available to members who were in capped drawdown prior to 6 April 2015. No new drawdown pension funds can be created since 6 April 2015. As noted above, a drawdown pension fund will automatically become a flexi-access drawdown fund in a number of circumstances. The only attraction of retaining a drawdown pension fund rather than converting it into a flexi-access drawdown fund is that the payment of drawdown pension under a drawdown pension fund does not trigger the money purchase annual allowance.[92]

13-039

The member's drawdown pension fund consists of any sums or assets which were designated as available for the payment of capped drawdown pension prior to 6 April 2015 (and all sums or assets that arise or derive from such sums or assets, such as investment return). These are referred to as "member-designated funds".[93] If such sums or assets are transferred to a different pension scheme, they can be designated as available for the payment of drawdown pension under the transferee scheme (even on or after 6 April 2015), provided that such sums or assets had not previously been applied towards the provision of a scheme pension.

13-040

### *Pension rule 5*

Pension rule 5 provides that the total amount of drawdown pension paid in each "drawdown pension year" from, or under a short-term annuity purchased using sums or assets out of, the member's drawdown pension fund must not exceed 150% of the "basis amount" for the drawdown pension year. A "drawdown pension year" is the period of 12 months from the day on which the member first becomes entitled to drawdown pension in respect of the arrangement, and each succeeding period of 12 months[94] until the member's death. The "basis amount" is, broadly speaking, the annual amount of an annuity which could have been purchased by the application of the sums and assets representing the member's drawdown pension fund.[95]

13-041

---

[91] An individual met the conditions in s.165(3A) if he met the "flexible drawdown conditions", and he made a valid declaration to the scheme administrator to that effect which was accepted by the scheme administrator. An individual met the flexible drawdown conditions if: (a) he satisfied the minimum income requirement on the relevant day; (b) no relevant contributions were paid under another money purchase arrangement relating to the member under a registered pension scheme in the tax year in which the declaration was made; and (c) at the time of the declaration the member was not an active member of any registered pension scheme under which there was a defined benefits or cash balance arrangement relating to the member. These provisions were repealed by TPA 2014 Sch.1 para.32(1)(b) with effect from 6 April 2015.

[92] For the money purchase annual allowance, see Ch.7.

[93] FA 2004 Sch.28 para.8.

[94] FA 2004 Sch.28 para.9. This is subject to para.10B.

[95] The details are in FA 2004 Sch.28 paras 9-10B and 14 and The Registered Pension Schemes (Relevant Annuities) Regulations 2006 (SI 2006/129).

## PENSIONS PAID IN ERROR

**13-042**  The following payments, which as a result of some error do not satisfy the above requirements of a scheme pension, lifetime annuity or drawdown pension, are nevertheless treated as if they were authorised payments. Typically these will be inadvertent overpayments but the provisions apply equally to other errors. For the more general treatment of payments made in error, see Ch.18.

### Payments representing accrued arrears of pension

**13-043**  The payment by a pension scheme of an amount representing accrued arrears of pension to a member is an authorised payment to the extent that it does not exceed the amount that the member is entitled to under the rules of the scheme, and it constitutes taxable pension income within ITEPA 2003 s.579B.[96] Section 597B applies to all pension income paid under a registered pension scheme, so one would expect all payments of accrued arrears of pension to constitute taxable pension income within s.579B.

### Pensions paid in error (recipient is alive)

**13-044**  A payment is an authorised payment if it was intended to represent a payment permitted by the pension rules or the pension death benefit rules, and the scheme administrator or insurance company making the payment believed that the recipient was entitled to the payment.[97]

### Pensions paid after discovery of error

**13-045**  The above paragraph applies to payments made *before* the discovery of the error. Payments made *after* the discovery of an error can still be authorised member payments in two circumstances. The first is where the payment is made following a payment to which the above paragraph applies, to the same person and (apart from the discovery of the error) is of a similar nature to that payment. The second is where the above paragraph did not apply (because the error was discovered before the first payment was made) but that paragraph would have applied if the error had not been discovered until after the first payment. In each case, one of the following must also apply to the payment:[98] (a) it is made even though the payer took reasonable steps to prevent its being made or its being made in that amount; (b) it is made while the scheme administrator is considering whether the rules of the scheme should be amended so that such payments will be permitted by the pension rules or the pension death benefit rules (as the case may be), provided the scheme administrator has not taken an unreasonable amount of time to decide; or (c) it is made while the scheme administrator is in the process of amending the rules of the scheme so that such payments will be permitted by the pension rules or the pension death benefit rules (as the case may be), provided the scheme administrator has not taken an unreasonable amount of time to amend the rules.

---

[96] The Registered Pension Schemes (Authorised Payments—Arrears of Pension) Regulations 2006 (SI 2006/614) reg.2. Although this is not expressly limited to scheme pensions it is unlikely to have any application to other categories of authorised pension.
[97] SI 2009/1171 reg.13.
[98] SI 2009/1171 reg.14.

## Pensions continuing to be paid after death

Except in the case of pensions continuing under a term certain guarantee, scheme pension must cease on the death of the pensioner.[99] However a payment is an authorised member payment if it was intended to represent the payment of a pension permitted by the pension rules or the pension death benefit rules and:[100] (a) the member or dependant concerned has died; (b) the payment is made no later than six months after the date of the person's death; (c) the payment would not have been an unauthorised payment if it had been made on the day before the person died; and (d) either: (i) the scheme administrator or insurance company making the payment did not know, and could not reasonably have been expected to have known, that the person had died before the payment was made; or (ii) where the payer knew of the person's death before the payment was made, the payer took reasonable steps to prevent the payment's being made or its being made in that amount.

**13-046**

## Payments of arrears of pension after death

A payment of pension to or in respect of a member who has died is an authorised payment if:[101] (a) the payment is in respect of a defined benefits arrangement; (b) the member was not a controlling director of a sponsoring employer of this or any related scheme (or connected to such a person); and (c) either: (i) the member died before 6 April 2006, the payment represents accrued arrears of pension, the payment was allowed or required by the rules of this scheme as they stood immediately before the member died, and the existence of the rule or rules concerned would not have prejudiced approval of the scheme by HMRC;[102] or (ii) the member died on or after 6 April 2006, the payment represents accrued arrears of scheme pension the member's entitlement to which the scheme administrator had not established until after the member's death, the payment would not have been an unauthorised payment if the payment had been made immediately before the member's death and the member had been entitled to it, and the scheme administrator could not reasonably have been expected to make the payment before the member's death.

**13-047**

The payment is an authorised payment to the extent that it does not exceed the amount accrued during the period beginning with the earliest date on which the member could have required the scheme administrator to make the payment if the member had been entitled to it, and ending with the member's death.

**13-048**

---

[99] This is the effect of pension rule 2 in FA 2004 s.165. HMRC interprets this as referring only to payments of pension which accrue after death (PTM062800). Pension rule 2 does not prevent payment of pension that accrued during the member's life but was not paid prior to death (for whatever reason).
[100] SI 2009/1171 reg.15.
[101] SI 2009/1171 reg.16.
[102] Whether something would have prejudiced the approval of a scheme by HMRC is determined in accordance with IR 12 (2001) (see Ch.3) as it stood on the date of the members death (or 23 March 2001, if later).

## REPORTING OBLIGATIONS

**13-049** The scheme administrator will usually be required to report the provision of authorised pensions to HMRC in the pension scheme return.[103] In addition, it may be necessary to make an event report in connection with the provision of authorised pensions in certain circumstances.[104]

---

[103] For the pension scheme return, see Ch.19.
[104] For event reports, see Ch.19.

# CHAPTER 14

# Authorised Lump Sums

## TABLE OF CONTENTS

| | |
|---|---|
| Authorised lump sums | 14-001 |
|     The lump sum rule | 14-002 |
|     Taxation | 14-003 |
|         National insurance contributions | 14-004 |
|     The lump sum allowance | 14-005 |
|         The individual's "available" LS allowance | 14-007 |
|         Pre-6 April 2024 BCEs | 14-008 |
|         Pre-6 April 2006 pensions in payment | 14-010 |
|     The LS&DB allowance | 14-011 |
|         The individual's "available" LS&DB allowance | 14-013 |
|         Pre-6 April 2024 BCEs | 14-014 |
|         Pre-6 April 2006 pensions in payment | 14-016 |
|     Transitional tax-free amount certificates | 14-017 |
| Pension commencement lump sum | 14-018 |
|     The permitted maximum | 14-020 |
|         The applicable amount | 14-021 |
|         Anti-avoidance | 14-022 |
| Pension commencement excess lump sum | 14-023 |
| Uncrystallised funds pension lump sum | 14-025 |
| Serious ill-health lump sum | 14-027 |
| Short service refund lump sum | 14-030 |
| Refund of excess contributions lump sum | 14-032 |
| Trivial commutation lump sum | 14-034 |
|     Valuing the member's pension rights | 14-036 |
| Winding-up lump sum | 14-037 |
| Lifetime allowance excess lump sum (pre-6 April 2024) | 14-039 |
| Other authorised lump sums | 14-041 |
|     Small payments | 14-042 |
|         Relevant accretion following transfer | 14-042 |
|         Certain payments under the FSCS | 14-045 |
|         Occupational pension schemes | 14-046 |
|         Non-occupational schemes | 14-048 |
|     Lump sums paid in error | 14-051 |
|         Other lump sum errors | 14-053 |
|         Commencement lump sums paid after death | 14-055 |
| Enhanced Allowances | 14-056 |
|     Primary protection | 14-059 |
|     Enhanced protection | 14-062 |
|     Fixed protection | 14-064 |
|     Individual protection | 14-068 |

Other enhancement factors ..................... 14-070
Reporting obligations ............................. 14-072
    Provision of information by scheme administrators to members ................................. 14-073
    Statements for certain members who would not otherwise receive one in 2024/25 ............. 14-074

# AUTHORISED LUMP SUMS

**14-001** The list of authorised member payments in FA 2004 s.164(1) includes "lump sums permitted by the lump sum rule ... paid to ... a member".[1] Such lump sums are referred to as "authorised lump sums".[2] A payment of income withdrawal (even a single payment of the member's entire flexi-access drawdown fund) is a payment of pension and not a lump sum for the purposes of FA 2004 Pt 4 and ITEPA 2003 Pt 9.[3]

**The lump sum rule**

**14-002** The "lump sum rule" is that no lump sum may be paid to a member of a registered pension scheme other than one of the following:[4]

(a) Pension commencement lump sum (PCLS).
(b) Pension commencement excess lump sum (PCELS) (on or after 6 April 2024).
(c) Uncrystallised funds pension lump sum (UFPLS).
(d) Serious ill-health lump sum.
(e) Short service refund lump sum.
(f) Refund of excess contributions lump sum.
(g) Trivial commutation lump sum.
(h) Winding-up lump sum.
(i) Lifetime allowance excess lump sum (prior to 6 April 2024).

**Taxation**

**14-003**

| Lump sum | Taxation |
|---|---|
| PCLS | Tax-free.[5] |
| PCELS | Treated as pension income taxable under ITEPA 2003 s.579A.[6] |

---

[1] FA 2004 s.164(1)(b).
[2] FA 2004 Sch.29 para.12(6).
[3] FA 2004 s.165(2); ITEPA 2003 s.579D.
[4] FA 2004 s.166(1). Certain small lump sums and lumps sums paid in error are also authorised payments. Prior to 6 April 2015 the lump sum rule included a reference to a transitional 2013/14 lump sum (see FA 2004 Sch.29 para.11A, repealed by FA 2024). This was payable where a scheme paid a PCLS before 27 March 2014, but because of the increased trivial commutation lump sum limit with effect from that date, the scheme was subsequently able to commute the entirety of the member's pension.
[5] ITEPA 2003 s.637A.
[6] ITEPA 2003 s.637B.

# AUTHORISED LUMP SUMS

| Lump sum | Taxation |
|---|---|
| UFPLS | 25% is tax-free except to the extent that it exceeds the "permitted maximum"; remaining 75% is taxable as pension income under ITEPA 2003 s.579A.[7] The permitted maximum means the lower of: (a) so much of the member's LS allowance as is available immediately before he becomes entitled to the lump sum; and (b) so much of the member's LS&DB allowance as is available immediately before he becomes entitled to the lump sum. |
| Serious ill-health lump sum | Tax-free provided that: (a) the member is under the age of 75 at the time of the payment; and (b) the lump sum does not exceed the member's available LS&DB allowance.[8] Otherwise, taxable as pension income under ITEPA 2003 s.579A.[9] |
| Short service refund lump sum | Subject to a short service refund lump sum charge, but not otherwise taxable.[10] The scheme administrator is liable to the charge, the rate of which is 20% in respect of the first £20,000 and 50% thereafter. The charge is calculated by reference to the amount of the lump sum paid or, if the scheme administrator deducts the tax before payment, the amount of the lump sum before any such deduction. |
| Refund of excess contributions lump sum | Not subject to income tax[11] (to reflect the fact that no tax relief was available in respect of the contributions which are refunded). |
| Trivial commutation lump sum | Taxable as pension income under ITEPA 2003 s.579A, although if the member has any uncrystallised rights under one or more arrangements under the pension scheme, the taxable amount is reduced by 25% of the value of the uncrystallised rights extinguished by the lump sum.[12] |

---

[7] ITEPA 2003 s.637D(1).
[8] ITEPA 2003 s.637C(1).
[9] ITEPA 2003 s.637C(2).
[10] FA 2004 s.205 and ITEPA 2003 s.637E. It is not treated as income for any purpose of the Tax Acts.
[11] ITEPA 2003 s.637F.
[12] ITEPA 2003 s.637G. Rights are "uncrystallised" if the member is not entitled to the present payment of benefits in respect of the rights (FA 2004 s.212). He is treated as entitled to the present payment of benefits in respect of any sums or assets representing his drawdown pension fund or flexi-access drawdown fund.

| Lump sum | Taxation |
|---|---|
| Winding-up lump sum | Same as trivial commutation lump sum.[13] As there is no lower age limit, anti-avoidance provisions are required to prevent abuse. If the winding-up of a registered pension scheme has begun and HMRC consider that it is being wound up wholly or mainly to facilitate the payment of a winding-up lump sum, the scheme administrator is liable to a penalty of up to £3,000 in respect of each member to whom a winding-up lump sum is paid under the pension scheme.[14] |
| Certain small payments | Same as trivial commutation lump sum. |

*National insurance contributions*

**14-004**  All authorised lump sums are disregarded for NIC purposes.[15]

**The lump sum allowance**

**14-005**  A PCLS, and the tax-free part of an UFPLS, are limited by reference to the individual's LS allowance. The LS allowance is £268,275,[16] but this is reduced where any lifetime allowance BCEs occurred in relation to the individual, and is increased where the individual has an enhanced LS allowance.[17]

**14-006**  For the purposes of the LS allowance, a PCLS and an UFPLS are "relevant lump sums", and becoming entitled to a relevant lump sum on or after 6 April 2024 is a "relevant BCE".

*The individual's "available" LS allowance*

**14-007**  If no relevant BCE has already occurred in relation to the individual, on the occurrence of a relevant BCE, the whole of his LS allowance is available.[18]

If a relevant BCE *has* already occurred, his available LS allowance is so much

---

[13] ITEPA 2003 s.637G.
[14] FA 2004 s.265.
[15] Social Security (Contributions) Regulations 2001 (SI 2001/1004) Sch.3 Pt VI para.2(b). The provisions are poorly drafted. They provide that a payment is disregarded for class 1 NICs purposes if it is a payment "by way of any benefit pursuant to a registered pension scheme to which: (i) FA 2004 s.204(1) and Sch.31 applies; or (ii) FA 2004 s.208 or s.209 applies". FA 2004 s.204(1) provides that "Sch.31 contains provision about the taxation of pensions and lump sums which are authorised to be paid by this Part" so it is unclear how s.204(1) could be said to "apply" to a payment. FA 2004 Sch.31 amended ITEPA 2003 Pt 9 from 6 April 2006 to include the taxation of benefits from registered pension schemes, primarily by inserting a new Ch.5A and a new Ch.15A into ITEPA Pt 9. FA 2004 s.208 imposes the unauthorised payments charge and s.209 imposes the unauthorised payments surcharge. It is not possible for s.209 to apply without s.208 applying, so it is unclear why this is expressed as an alternative. It seems to be intended that any payments within Ch.5A or Ch.15A are disregarded for NIC purposes, as are all unauthorised payments. HMRC accept this at NIM02717: "In simple terms, this means that any payment out of a RPS is not liable for Class 1 NICs". This is extended to class 1A NICs by SI 2001/1004 reg.40(2)(a), which provides that "Class 1A contributions shall not be payable in respect of the [...] the general earnings [...] which are excluded from the calculation of a person's earnings in respect of any employed earner's employment by virtue of [...] Sch.3 Part VI para.2(b)...".
[16] ITEPA 2003 s.637P.
[17] For the circumstances in which an individual has an enhanced LS allowance, see "enhanced allowances" below.
[18] ITEPA 2003 s.637Q.

# AUTHORISED LUMP SUMS

of his LS allowance (if any) as is left after deducting the "non-taxable amount(s)" of each previous PCLS or UFPLS, meaning so much of each PCLS or UFPLS as was exempt from income tax under ITEPA 2003 Pt 9 Ch.15A (or the aggregate of such amounts, where more than one relevant BCE has already occurred).[19] This is referred to as the "previously-used amount".

*Pre-6 April 2024 BCEs*

**14-008** Where one or more BCEs occurred in relation to the individual before 6 April 2024, and no transitional tax-free amount certificate (see below) is in force in relation to the individual, on the occurrence of a relevant BCE it is necessary to calculate the member's "lifetime allowance previously-used amount".[20] This is the total amount(s) crystallised by BCEs prior to 6 April 2024. If his lifetime allowance previously-used amount is equal to or greater than his lifetime allowance, none of his LS allowance is available. Otherwise, his available LS allowance is reduced by 25% of his lifetime allowance previously-used amount (or, if that produces a negative result, nil). This is the default method of calculating an individual's lifetime allowance previously-used amount. An alternative method is used where a transitional tax-free amount certificate is in force in relation to the individual. As is explained below, before the occurrence of the first relevant BCE, the individual should consider whether the alternative method will produce a better result. The default method will be appropriate where: (a) the individual received 25% of the amounts crystallised by BCEs as a tax-free amount, and (b) the lifetime allowance at the time of the BCE was at least £1,073,100.

**14-009** Where a transitional tax-free amount certificate is in force in relation to the individual, on the occurrence of a relevant BCE the amount of his available LS allowance is reduced by his "lump sum transitional tax-free amount" (or, if that produces a negative result, nil). A lump sum transitional tax-free amount, in relation to an individual, means the total of any PCLS and any tax-free UFPLS to which the individual, before 6 April 2024, became entitled under a registered pension scheme.

*Pre-6 April 2006 pensions in payment*

**14-010** A transitional provision applies where: (a) on 5 April 2006, an individual had an actual (rather than a merely prospective) right to the payment of one or more relevant existing pensions, (b) no BCE occurred in relation to that individual between 6 April 2006 and 5 April 2024, and (c) a relevant BCE occurs on or after 6 April 2024.[21] For the purpose of determining his available LS allowance, immediately before the first relevant BCE occurs: (a) a relevant BCE is treated as having occurred in relation to the individual, and (b) the amount of the lump sum to which the relevant BCE relates was an amount equal to 25% of the value of the individual's pre-commencement pension rights immediately before the relevant BCE.

---

[19] ITEPA 2003 Pt 9 Ch.15A applies only to lump sums under registered pension schemes. A lump sum paid under an unregistered pension scheme (including a QROPS or other RNUKS, for example) is not a non-taxable amount, so such a lump sum does not impact the amount of the individual's available LS allowance.
[20] FA 2024 Sch.9 para.125.
[21] FA 2004 Sch.36 para.20.

**The LS&DB allowance**

**14-011** All tax-free lump sums (i.e. a PCLS, the tax-free part of an UFPLS, a serious ill health lump sum before the member's 75th birthday, and all LSDBs if the member dies before his 75th birthday) are limited by reference to the individual's LS&DB allowance. The LS&DB allowance is £1,073,100,[22] but this is reduced where any lifetime allowance BCEs occurred in relation to the individual before 6 April 2024, and is increased where the individual he has an enhanced LS&DB allowance.[23]

**14-012** For the purposes of the LS&DB allowance, a "relevant BCE" occurs on or after 6 April 2024, where:

(a) an individual becomes entitled to a PCLS, a serious ill-health lump sum, or an UFPLS (a "relevant lump sum"); or

(b) a person is paid a relevant LSDB in respect of the individual. "Relevant LSDB" means any authorised LSDB other than a charity LSDB or a trivial commutation LSDB.[24]

*The individual's "available" LS&DB allowance*

**14-013** On the occurrence of a relevant BCE, if no relevant BCE has already occurred in relation to the individual, the whole of his LS&DB allowance is available.[25] If a relevant BCE *has* already occurred, the amount of his available LS&DB allowance is so much of that allowance (if any) as is left after deducting the aggregate of the non-taxable amounts in relation to each relevant BCE that has previously occurred in relation to the individual. This is referred to as the "previously-used amount". The "non-taxable amount" means so much (if any) of the relevant lump sum, or relevant LSDB, as is exempt from income tax under ITEPA 2003 Pt 9 Ch.15A.[26]

Where the individual becomes entitled to more than one relevant lump sum on the same day, he can decide the order in which they are treated as occurring. Where more than one relevant LSDB is paid in relation to an individual, they are treated as occurring (a) immediately before the individual's death, (b) immediately after any PCLS to which the individual becomes entitled immediately before death, and (c) in such order as may be decided by the individual's personal representatives.

*Pre-6 April 2024 BCEs*

**14-014** Where one or more BCEs occurred in relation to an individual before 6 April 2024,[27] and a relevant BCE occurs in relation to the individual on or after that date:[28]

(a) If the individual's "lifetime allowance previously-used amount" is equal to or greater than his lifetime allowance, none of his LS&DB allowance is

---

[22] ITEPA 2003 s.637R.
[23] For the circumstances in which an individual has an enhanced LS&DB allowance, see "enhanced allowances" below.
[24] However, this does not include a lump sum death benefit if and to the extent that it is paid in respect of rights that were crystallised by a BCE before 6 April 2024 (FA 2024 Sch.9 para.131).
[25] ITEPA 2003 s.637S.
[26] Again, ITEPA 2003 Pt 9 Ch.15A applies only to lump sums under registered pension schemes, so a lump sum paid under an unregistered pension scheme (including an RNUKS, for example) is not a non-taxable amount, so such a lump sum does not impact the amount of the individual available LS&DB allowance.
[27] For pre-6 April 2024 BCEs, see Ch.10.
[28] FA 2024 Sch.9 para.126.

available on the occurrence of the relevant BCE. The lifetime allowance previously-used amount means the amount that would have been the previously-used amount for the purposes of FA 2004 s.219 (availability of individual's lifetime allowance) if a BCE had occurred immediately before 6 April 2024.

(b) Otherwise, the amount of the individual's LS&DB allowance that is available on the occurrence of the relevant BCE is (i) the amount of that allowance that is available in accordance with ITEPA 2003 s.637Q on the occurrence of that event; less (ii) an amount equal to the "appropriate percentage" of the individual's lifetime allowance previously-used amount; or, if that produces a negative result, nil. The appropriate percentage" means: (i) 100% in a case in which (a) the individual becomes entitled to a serious ill-health lump sum before 6 April 2024 and is under the age of 75 at the time of the payment; or (b) the individual dies before 6 April 2024 under the age of 75 and before that date a person is paid a LSDB in respect of the individual;[29] (ii) 25% in any other case.

**14-015** Where a transitional tax-free amount certificate (see below) is in force in relation to the individual, on the occurrence of the relevant BCE the amount of his available LS&DB allowance is (a) the amount of that allowance that is available in accordance with ITEPA 2003 s.637S on the occurrence of that event; less (b) the individual's "LS&DB transitional tax-free amount"; or, if that produces a negative result, nil. An "LS&DB transitional tax-free amount", in relation to an individual, means the total of (a) any relevant lump sum to which the individual, before 6 April 2024, became entitled under a registered pension scheme, so far as no charge to income tax under ITEPA 2003 Pt 9 or FA 2004 Pt 4 arose in respect of it; and (b) any relevant lump sum death benefit paid before 6 April 2024 by a registered pension scheme in respect of the individual so far as no charge to income tax under ITEPA 2003 Pt 9 or FA 2004 Pt 4 arose in respect of it. A lump sum is "relevant" if the individual becoming entitled to it constituted a BCE within the meaning of FA 2004 Pt 4. A lump sum death benefit is "relevant" if its payment constituted a BCE within the meaning of FA 2004 Pt 4.

*Pre-6 April 2006 pensions in payment*

**14-016** As with the LS allowance, a transitional provision applies where: (a) on 5 April 2006, an individual had an actual (rather than a prospective) right to the payment of one or more relevant existing pensions, (b) no BCE occurred in relation to the individual between 5 April 2006 and 5 April 2024, and (c) a relevant BCE occurs in relation to the individual on or after 6 April 2024.[30] For the purpose of determining the individual's LS&DB allowance, immediately before the first relevant BCE that occurs, a relevant BCE is treated as having occurred in relation to the individual. The amount of the lump sum or LSDB to which that deemed relevant

---

[29] In Pension Schemes Newsletter 159 (25 April 2024), HMRC acknowledge that FA 2024 Sch.9 para.126(4)(a)(ii) (relating to LSDBs paid before 6 April 2024 in respect of a member who died before his 75th birthday) contains an error. The appropriate percentage should be 100% only where the LSDB was an uncrystallised funds pension LSDB or a defined benefit LSDB. Those were the only LSDBs which were BCEs. The other four LSDBs which are relevant BCEs from 6 April 2024 were never BCEs and so would not have been paid tax-free up to the lifetime allowance. The government will amend Sch.9 para.126(4)(a)(ii) so that the 100% appropriate percentage is limited to uncrystallised funds pension LSDB or a defined benefit LSDBs.

[30] FA 2004 Sch.36 para.20

BCE relates is an amount equal to 25% of the value of the individual's pre-commencement pension rights immediately before the relevant BCE.

**Transitional tax-free amount certificates**

14-017   A "transitional tax-free amount certificate" is a certificate relating to an individual which certifies that the scheme administrator of the scheme is satisfied as to (a) the amount of the individual's LS transitional tax-free amount, and (b) the amount of the individual's LS&DB transitional tax-free amount. It can be issued by a registered pension scheme only following an application made in accordance with FA 2024 Sch.9 para.127.

An application for a certificate may be made by the individual (or his personal representatives, if he is deceased) to any registered pension scheme of which the individual is a member (or of which the individual was a member immediately before death). The application must be accompanied by complete evidence[31] as to the amount of the individual's LS&DB transitional tax-free amount. The application may not be made after the first LS&DB relevant BCE. The "LS&DB transitional tax-free amount" means the total of (a) each relevant lump sum (if any) to which the individual, before 6 April 2024, became entitled under a registered pension scheme, so far as no charge to income tax under ITEPA 2003 Pt 9 or FA 2004 Pt 4 arose, and (b) each relevant LSDB (if any) paid before 6 April 2024 by a registered pension scheme so far as no charge to income tax under ITEPA 2003 Pt 9 or FA 2004 Pt 4 arose in respect of it.

The scheme administrator of a registered pension scheme to which an application is made must, within three months of the date on which the scheme receives the application, determine the application by either issuing a certificate or notifying the applicant that the application is refused. A certificate must also contain: (a) the individual's name, address and national insurance number; (b) the individual's lifetime allowance previously-used amount expressed as a percentage of the standard lifetime allowance; (c) the amount that the scheme administrator is satisfied is the individual's LS transitional tax-free amount; and (d) the amount that the scheme administrator is satisfied is the individual's LS&DB transitional tax-free amount.

A certificate may be in such form as the scheme administrator may determine. If at any time it appears to the scheme administrator that the amount specified on a certificate does not accurately reflect the individual's LS transitional tax-free amount or LS&DB transitional tax-free amount, they must cancel the certificate by giving notice of the cancellation to the applicant (or to his personal representatives, if he is deceased). A certificate comes into force when it is issued, and ceases to be in force on the giving of a cancellation notice.

# PENSION COMMENCEMENT LUMP SUM

14-018   A lump sum is a PCLS if it satisfies five requirements:[32]

---

[31] "Complete evidence", in relation to an individual's LS&DB transitional tax-free amount, means evidence of (a) each lump sum (if any) to which the individual has become entitled; and (b) each lump sum death benefit (if any) that has been paid in respect of the individual, that is comprised, or any part of which is comprised, in the individual's lump sum and death benefit transitional tax-free amount.

[32] FA 2004 Sch.29 para.1(1) and (2). If one or more of these requirements is not satisfied, the pay-

# PENSION COMMENCEMENT LUMP SUM

(a) The member becomes entitled to it in connection with becoming entitled to income withdrawal, a lifetime annuity or a scheme pension,[33] under the same scheme (a "relevant pension"), or dies after becoming entitled to the lump sum but before becoming entitled to the intended relevant pension.[34]

A person becomes "entitled" to a PCLS immediately before he becomes entitled to the relevant pension.[35] A person becomes "entitled" to income withdrawal when sums or assets are designated as available for the payment of drawdown pension, and, in all other cases, a person becomes entitled to the pension when he acquires an actual rather than a prospective entitlement to the pension.[36] The maximum amount which may be paid as a PCLS is determined in part by reference to the commencement of a particular pension: the requisite "connection" is that the former is calculated by reference to the latter.

(b) The member has some LS allowance and some LSDB allowance immediately before the lump sum is paid.[37]

(c) It is paid within the period beginning six months before, and ending one year after, the day on which the member becomes entitled to it.[38]

(d) It is paid when the member has reached normal minimum pension age, unless the ill-health condition[39] is satisfied.

Normal minimum pension age is currently age 55, unless the member has a "protected pension age".[40]

(e) It is not an "excluded lump sum".[41]

A lump sum is an excluded lump sum if it is a CMP-derived drawdown pension.[42]

However, a lump sum that meets the above requirements will not be a PCLS to the extent that it exceeds the "permitted maximum", unless the individual has "protected lump sum right".[43] Where a payment in excess of the permitted maximum is made as a result of a genuine mistake, it is deemed to be a PCLS.[44]

**14-019**

---

ment will be an unauthorised payment, unless it satisfies the requirements of a different authorised lump sum (such as an UFPLS). For the provisions relating to the "recycling" of PCLS, see Ch.6.

[33] FA 2004 Sch.29 para.1(3). A person becomes entitled to income withdrawal when sums or assets are designated as available for drawdown pension so designating sums or assets as available for the payment of a short-term annuity is a relevant pension for these purposes, notwithstanding the reference to income withdrawal only.

[34] In these circumstances the member becomes entitled to the PCLS immediately before death (FA 2004 s.166(2)(a)).

[35] FA 2004 s.166(2)(a).

[36] FA 2004 s.165(3)(a) and (b).

[37] FA 2004 Sch.29 para.12(2)–(4). Note the reference to "payment" rather than "entitlement".

[38] This requirement was temporarily relaxed in certain circumstances to allow members to take advantage of the new flexibilities available from 6 April 2015 (see FA 2004 s.185J and FA 2004 Sch.29 paras 1A and 1B, the latter of which were removed by FA 2024).

[39] For the ill-health condition, see Ch.13.

[40] FA 2004 s.279. For protected pension ages, see Ch.3.

[41] FA 2004 Sch.29 para.1(4).

[42] A "CMP-derived drawdown pension" means a drawdown pension where (a) the sums or assets constituting the fund from which the pension is payable were transferred from another pension scheme; and (b) before the transfer, those sums or assets were held for the purposes of paying CMP periodic income. "CMP periodic income" means income payable by virtue of PSA s.36(7)(b) or s.87(7)(b) (FA 2004 s.279(1F) and (1G).

[43] For protected lump sum rights, see Ch.3.

[44] The Registered Pension Schemes (Authorised Payments) Regulations 2009 (SI 2009/1171) regs 17 and 18.

## The permitted maximum

**14-020** The permitted maximum means the lowest of:[45]

(a) the "applicable amount" in relation to the relevant pension;
(b) so much of the member's LS allowance as is available on the individual becoming entitled to the lump sum (see above); and
(c) so much of the member's LS&DB allowance (see above) as is available on the individual becoming entitled to the lump sum.

*The applicable amount*

**14-021** The method for calculating the applicable amount depends on the categorisation of the relevant pension:[46]

(a) If the member becomes entitled to income withdrawal, the applicable amount is one third of the value of the money and/or assets[47] designated as available for the payment of drawdown pension on that occasion.[48] The value of any such money/assets which represent rights attributable to a disqualifying pension credit are disregarded.
(b) If the member becomes entitled to a lifetime annuity, the applicable amount is one third of the annuity purchase price. This means the value of the money and/or assets that are applied in (or in connection with) the purchase of the lifetime annuity and any "related" dependants' or nominees' annuity.[49]

However, if any of the sums or assets applied to purchase the annuity represented some or all of the member's drawdown pension fund or flexi-access drawdown fund, such sums or assets are disregarded. In these circumstances, the member will have had the opportunity to take a PCLS by reference to the sums/assets designated as available for drawdown pension, so this reduction prevents the payment of another PCLS to the member when the annuity is purchased.[50] If any of the money/assets used to purchase the annuity represented rights which were attributable to a disqualifying pension credit, these are also disregarded.
(c) Where the member becomes entitled to a scheme pension under a defined benefits arrangement or a collective money purchase arrangement, the applicable amount is 25% of: (i) the amount of the lump sum; plus (ii) the aggregate of the relevant revaluation factor multiplied by the amount of the pension which will be payable to the member in the period of 12 months beginning with the day on which the member becomes entitled to the pension (assuming that it remains payable throughout that period at the rate at

---

[45] FA 2004 Sch.29 para.2.
[46] The provisions are set out in FA 2004 Sch.29 paras 2A–2D.
[47] This is referred to as the "scheme pension capital value". In relation to an asset, "value" means market value, and the market value of an asset held for the purposes of a pension scheme is determined in accordance with TCGA 1992 s.272 (FA 2004 s.278). See Ch.2.
[48] A member becomes entitled to income withdrawal when sums or assets are designated to provide a drawdown pension (FA 2004 s.165(3)(a)), even though the fund may be used to purchase a short-term annuity rather than pay income withdrawal.
[49] An annuity payable to a dependant or nominee of the member is *related* to a lifetime annuity payable to the member if they are purchased either in the form of a joint life annuity or separately in circumstances in which the day on which the one is purchased is no earlier than seven days before, and no later than seven days after, the day on which the other is purchased (FA 2004 s.278B).
[50] Such funds are disregarded even if the member did not receive a PCLS in connection with the designation.

which it is payable on that day); less (iii) so much (if any) of such amounts as represents rights which are attributable to a disqualifying pension credit.[51]

(d) Where the member becomes entitled to a scheme pension under a money purchase arrangement that is not a collective money purchase arrangement, the applicable amount is one third of the value of the money and/or assets as are applied in (or in connection with) the purchase or provision of the scheme pension and any related dependants' scheme pension.[52]

A scheme pension payable to a dependant of the member is "related" to a scheme pension payable to the member if the day on which one is purchased (or funds are applied for its provision) is no earlier than seven days before, and no later than seven days after, the day on which the other is purchased (or funds are applied for its provision).[53] If the scheme pension is funded (in whole or in part) by the application of sums or assets representing some or all of the member's drawdown pension fund or flexi-access drawdown fund, such sums or assets are disregarded. In addition, any of the scheme pension purchase price representing rights which were attributable to a disqualifying pension credit is also disregarded.

*Anti-avoidance*

An anti-avoidance provision applies where:[54]

**14-022**

(a) sums or assets held for the purposes of a money purchase arrangement are either: (i) surrendered in exchange for a corresponding increase in funds held for the purposes of, or representing rights under, a defined benefits arrangement relating to the member under the pension scheme; or (ii) transferred to a defined benefits arrangement relating to the member under a different registered pension scheme;
(b) the sole or main purpose of the surrender or transfer is to increase the applicable amount on the member becoming entitled to a scheme pension; and
(c) the member becomes entitled to a scheme pension under: (i) the defined benefits arrangement mentioned in (a) above; or (ii) any other defined benefits arrangement relating to the member if any of the sums or assets held for the purposes of the arrangement directly or indirectly represent sums or assets previously held for the purposes of the defined benefits arrangement so mentioned.

It seems likely that these anti-avoidance provisions will apply even if there are other schemes or arrangements interposed between the original money purchase arrangement and the final defined benefits arrangement.[55]

Where the provision applies the pension scheme to which the defined benefits arrangement relates is treated as making an unauthorised payment to the member. The

---

[51] FA 2004 Sch.29 para.2C. The formula is "(A + (B x C) - D)/4", where "A" is the amount of the lump sum; "B" is the relevant revaluation factor (see s.276); "C" is the amount of the pension which will be payable to the member in the period of 12 months beginning with the day on which the member becomes entitled to the pension (assuming that it remains payable throughout that period at the rate at which it is payable on that day); and "D" is so much (if any) of A or C as represents rights which are attributable to a disqualifying pension credit.
[52] FA 2004 Sch.29 para.2D.
[53] FA 2004 s.278B.
[54] FA 2004 Sch.29 para.3B. For the provisions relating to the "recycling" of PCLS in FA 2004 Sch.29 para.3A, see Ch.6.
[55] See the explanatory notes to the Finance (No.2) Bill 2006.

amount of the unauthorised payment is the amount by which the applicable amount in relation to the scheme pension calculated as per the defined benefits rules exceeds the applicable amount calculated as per the money purchase rules.

## PENSION COMMENCEMENT EXCESS LUMP SUM

**14-023** With effect from 6 April 2024, a lump sum is a PCELS if it satisfies five requirements:[56]

(a) The member becomes entitled to it in connection with becoming entitled to a relevant pension (or dies after becoming entitled to it but before becoming entitled to the relevant pension in connection with which it was anticipated that the member would become entitled to it).

(b) It is paid when none of the member's LS allowance is available (see above).
For the purpose of determining the member's available LS allowance, he is treated as having already become entitled to any PCLS that is paid in connection with the relevant pension.

(c) It is paid within the period beginning six months before, and ending one year after, the day on which the member becomes entitled to it.

(d) It does not reduce the rate of payment of any pension to which the member has become (actually) entitled, or extinguish the member's entitlement to payment of any such pension.

(e) It is paid when the member has reached normal minimum pension age (or the ill-health condition is met).

(f) It is not an excluded lump sum.

A lump sum is an excluded lump sum if (i) it could be paid as any other type of authorised lump sum;[57] or (ii) the pension in connection with which the member becomes entitled to it is a CMP-derived drawdown pension.

**14-024** But if such a lump sum exceeds the permitted maximum, the excess is not a PCELS. The "permitted maximum" means "$(A \times 4) - B$", where "A" is the "applicable amount" in relation to the relevant pension (see the PCLS provisions above); and "B" is the amount of the member's available LS&DB allowance. For the purpose of determining the member's available LS&DB allowance, he is treated as having already become entitled to any PCLS that is paid in connection with the relevant pension.

Prior to 6 April 2024, many pension schemes entitled members to a lump sum in excess of 25% where the member had no available lifetime allowance. This could be paid as a lifetime allowance excess lump sum lump sum. Such a lump sum can now be paid as a PCELS.[58]

---

[56] FA 2004 Sch.29 para.1(1) and (2). If one or more of these requirements is not satisfied, the payment will be an unauthorised payment, unless it satisfies the requirements of a different authorised lump sum (such as an UFPLS).

[57] It follows that a PCELS can be paid only from a crystallised fund (otherwise it would be an UFPLS).

[58] HMRC's Pension Schemes Newsletter 155 (7 February 2024).

## UNCRYSTALLISED FUNDS PENSION LUMP SUM

A lump sum is an UFPLS if:[59]  **14-025**

(a) It is paid on or after 6 April 2015 in respect of a money purchase arrangement that is not a collective money purchase arrangement.
(b) It is paid when the member has reached normal minimum pension age, or the ill-health condition is met.
(c) It is not a PCLS.[60]
(d) It is not a lump sum which is treated an authorised lump sum pursuant to regulations under ITEPA 2003 s.164(1)(f) and (2) (see 'other authorised lump sums' below).
(e) Immediately before the lump sum is paid,[61] the sums or assets that are to be used to provide it: (i) have not been designated as available for the payment of drawdown pension or applied to pay or purchase a scheme pension or lifetime annuity;[62] and (ii) do not to any extent represent rights attributable to a "disqualifying pension credit".[63]

There is no restriction on the amount which may be paid as an UFPLS, but the beneficial tax treatment will not apply to the extent that it exceeds the "permitted maximum" (being the lower of the member's available LS allowance or LS&DB allowance).[64]  **14-026**

## SERIOUS ILL-HEALTH LUMP SUM

A lump sum is a serious ill-health lump sum if:[65]  **14-027**

(a) Before it is paid the scheme administrator receives evidence from a registered medical practitioner that the member is expected to live for less than one year.[66]

---

[59] FA 2004 Sch.29 para.4A.
[60] In general, a lump sum that satisfies the other requirements of an UFPLS will be a PCLS if it is paid in connection with a relevant pension (see above).
[61] The legislation refers to "entitlement" rather than payment, but a person becomes entitled to an UFPLS immediately before it is paid (FA 2004 s.166(2)).
[62] Rights are *uncrystallised* if the member is not entitled to the present payment of benefits in respect of the rights. He is treated as entitled to the present payment of benefits in respect of any sums or assets representing his drawdown pension fund or flexi-access drawdown fund (FA 2004 s.212(1) and (2), applied by Sch.29 para.4A(1)(f)(i)).
[63] A pension credit (see Ch.16) is "disqualifying" if, when the member became entitled to it, the person subject to the corresponding pension debit had an actual (rather than a merely prospective) right to payment of a pension under that other arrangement (FA 2004 s.278A). Such pension credits are excluded because beneficial tax treatment is afforded to UFPLS, and if the credits came from a fund that has already crystallised then that other person would have become entitled to a PCLS. The restriction applies whether or not the other person actually received a PCLS.
[64] Prior to 6 April 2024, a lump sum could not be an UFPLS to the extent that it exceeded the member's available lifetime allowance.
[65] FA 2004 Sch.29 para.4.
[66] "Registered medical practitioner" is not defined. HMRC suggest (at PTM063400) that it means a fully registered person within the meaning of the Medical Act 1983. Where the member is in serious ill-heath overseas, HMRC will accept a certificate from someone with equivalent overseas qualifications.

(b) It is either:[67] (i) paid in respect of an uncrystallised arrangement (i.e. an arrangement under which the member has not previously become entitled to any pension or lump sum), and it extinguishes the member's entitlement to benefits under the arrangement; or (ii) paid in respect of uncrystallised rights of the member under an arrangement other than an uncrystallised arrangement, and it extinguishes the member's uncrystallised rights under the arrangement.[68] HMRC accept that a lump sum does not cease to be a serious ill-health lump sum solely because further entitlement is later created (e.g. through a pay revision) that could not have been known about at the time of the initial payment.[69] The member's arrangement includes any contingent dependant's benefits, so if any provisions prevent dependants' benefits from being commuted such benefits must be reallocated to a separate arrangement under the scheme so that the member's rights or entitlement can be extinguished.[70]

**14-028** In relation to a defined benefits arrangement, HMRC accept that it is for the scheme to attribute a capital value to the pension benefit entitlement being commuted.[71]

**14-029** The focus on rights being uncrystallised suggests that the intention is to make funds available which would not otherwise be available to the member (e.g. because he has not reached normal minimum pension age). It is therefore rational that sums or assets representing a flexi-access drawdown fund cannot be paid as a serious ill-health lump sum: the member can already access them. However, given that a serious ill-health lump sum is tax-free if paid to a member under age 75 (whereas drawdown pension is taxable at his marginal rate, even if he is in serious ill-health), this distinction does seem slightly arbitrary.[72]

## SHORT SERVICE REFUND LUMP SUM

**14-030** A lump sum is a short service refund lump sum if all of the following apply:[73]

(a) The pension scheme is an occupational pension scheme.
(b) The member's pensionable service was terminated before normal pension age in circumstances in which he is not entitled to short service benefit under PSA 1993 s.71.[74] PSA 1993 Pt IV and the Occupational Pension Schemes (Preservation of Benefit) Regulations 1991 (SI 1991/167) preserve

---

[67] Payments made before 16 September 2016 must satisfy (c)(i). Satisfying (c)(ii) was not an option at that time.
[68] Rights are uncrystallised if the member is not entitled to the present payment of benefits in respect of the rights. For this purpose he is treated as entitled to the present payment of benefits in respect of any sums or assets representing his drawdown pension fund or flexi-access drawdown fund (FA 2004 s.212(1) and (2), applied by Sch.29 para.4(2A)).
[69] PTM063400.
[70] HMRC confirm that "this requires no more than documenting the creation of a new arrangement in a manner which is considered acceptable under the scheme" (PTM063400).
[71] PTM063400.
[72] It might be possible for an individual to surrender his rights respect of sums or assets held for the purposes of a flexi-access drawdown fund in respect of an arrangement in circumstances that the rights are transferred so as to become rights under a different (uncrystallised) arrangement relating to the member (see FA 2004 s.172A(5)(c)).
[73] FA 2004 Sch.29 para.5.
[74] For the meaning of "pensionable service", "normal pension age" and "short service benefit" see PSA 1993 s.181(1).

minimum benefits for members of occupational schemes who leave pensionable service before reaching normal minimum pension age. A member is entitled to a short service benefit under PSA 1993 s.71 if he has at least two years' pensionable service. This two-year period is reduced to 30 days' pensionable service in relation to money purchase benefits for members who joined the scheme after 1 October 2015. If a member leaves pensionable service before acquiring rights to short service benefits, the scheme must provide him with the following options, provided that he has completed at least three months' pensionable service:[75] (a) a refund of contributions to the scheme made by or on behalf of the member; or (b) a transfer of the member's accrued rights (which is not expressly limited to contributions by or on behalf of the member, so may include employer contributions).

(c) The member has not previously become entitled to any pension or lump sum under the pension scheme (but such benefits may have been provided in relation to the member under a different scheme).

(d) The lump sum extinguishes the member's entitlement to benefits under the pension scheme. This includes any specifically identifiable contingent dependant benefits/rights. HMRC accept that a lump sum will not cease to be a short service refund lump sum solely because further entitlement is later created that could not have been known about at the time of the initial payment, for example through a pay revision.[76] Where the member's entitlement is not extinguished because the rules of the pension scheme prohibit it from being extinguished, this requirement is satisfied if:[77] (i) it does not exceed an amount equal to the aggregate of the member's contributions under the pension scheme;[78] (ii) the payment extinguishes the member's entitlement to benefits under the scheme to the extent that the entitlement is not prohibited from being extinguished by the rules of the pension scheme; and (iii) at the time that the lump sum is paid the rules of the pension scheme prohibit a member's entitlement to benefits from being extinguished by the payment of a lump sum, and at the time those rules took effect there was a legislative requirement prohibiting such lump sums,[79] and the legislative requirement has since been repealed or revoked or has otherwise ceased to apply.

(e) It is paid before the member reaches age 75.

But if such a lump sum is greater than the member's contributions under the pension scheme, the excess is not a short service refund lump sum. The following are included within the member's contributions: (a) any amount paid under the Social Security Act 1986 s.7;[80] (b) any rebate paid by HMRC under PSA 1993 s.42A(3); and (c) any amount recovered by the member's employer under regulations made under PSA 1993 s.8(3) in respect of minimum payments made to the scheme in rela-

**14-031**

---

[75] PSA 1993 ss.101AA(1) and 101AB(1).
[76] PTM045000.
[77] SI 2009/1171 reg.20.
[78] This is different to FA 2004 Sch.29 para.5(2), which provides that if a lump sum exceeds the member's contributions then the excess is not a short service refund lump sum. Here if the lump sum exceeds the member's contributions then no part of it is treated as a short service refund lump sum.
[79] e.g. prior to 6 April 2012, a contracted out money purchase scheme would be prevented from refunding protected rights as a short service refund lump sum. Many scheme rules do still prohibit such refunds, even though the legislation is no longer in force.
[80] These are incentive payments to schemes becoming contracted-out between 1986 and 1993 (claims for which were permitted until 5 April 2001).

## REFUND OF EXCESS CONTRIBUTIONS LUMP SUM

**14-032**  A lump sum is a refund of excess contributions lump sum if: (a) it is paid in respect of a tax year in which the amount of relievable pension contributions paid by or on behalf of the member in the tax year exceeded the maximum amount of relief to which the member was entitled for the tax year under FA 2004 s.190;[82] and (b) it is paid within six years of the last day of that tax year.[83] In other words, contributions were made for which tax relief would have been available had they not exceeded the individual's relevant UK earnings (or the basic amount, if greater). To the extent that such a lump sum exceeds the member's excess contributions for the tax year in respect of which it is paid, the excess is not a refund of excess contributions lump sum. It is not necessary for a refund of excess contributions lump sum to be paid from the pension scheme to which the contributions were made. If any refund of excess contributions lump sums have already been paid to the member (by any registered pension scheme) then the amount of such payments will reduce the member's available excess contributions. If any relief given under relief at source is in excess of the maximum amount of relief to which the member is entitled under s.190, the relievable pension contributions must also be reduced by the amount of that excess.

**14-033**  If the rules of a pension scheme prescribe that the trustees must refund excess contributions plus interest (to reflect the fact that the scheme has had the use of the money for a time), the interest, if paid on arm's length terms, will usually constitute a scheme administration member payment.[84]

## TRIVIAL COMMUTATION LUMP SUM

**14-034**  A lump sum is a trivial commutation lump sum if:[85]

(a) It is paid when no trivial commutation lump sum has previously been paid to the member (by any registered pension scheme) disregarding previous payments within the period of 12 months following the day on which a trivial commutation lump sum is first paid to the member (the "commutation period").

(b) It is paid in respect of (i) a defined benefits arrangement; (ii) a collective money purchase arrangement; (iii) a scheme pension payable by the scheme administrator to which the member has become entitled under a money

---

[81] See Ch.11. This is accepted by HMRC at PTM045000.
[82] See Ch.6.
[83] FA 2004 Sch.29 para.6.
[84] See Ch.11. HMRC accept this at PTM045000. Any such payment is taxable as interest under ITTOIA 2005 s.369 (and not as pension income under ITEPA 2003 Pt 9). Provided that the total payments (including any interest) do not exceed the excess contributions in respect of a tax year, and the interest is paid as part of the lump sum (rather than separately to it), HMRC accept that the interest element forms part of the (tax-free) refund of excess contributions lump sum and is not taxable as interest.
[85] FA 2004 Sch.29 para.7.

# TRIVIAL COMMUTATION LUMP SUM

purchase arrangement that is not a collective money purchase arrangement (referred to as an "in-payment money-purchase in-house scheme pension"); or (iv) any combination of such arrangement and scheme pensions.[86]

(c) On the nominated date, the value of the member's pension rights (see below) under all registered pension schemes does not exceed £30,000.[87] The nominated date is any day nominated by the member in the three months preceding the commencement of the commutation period (or, if no date is nominated, it is the first day of the commutation period).

(d) The member has some LS allowance available immediately before the lump sum is paid.[88] It extinguishes any entitlement that the member has under the pension scheme to: (i) defined benefits; (ii) collective money purchase benefits; and (iii) payments of in-payment money-purchase in-house scheme pensions. HMRC accept that a lump sum will not fail to be a trivial commutation lump sum solely because further entitlement is later created that could not have been known about at the time of the initial payment, for example, through a pay revision.[89] As noted above, if HMRC are correct that only those rights in existence on the nominated date can be commuted then it seems to follow that the lump sum only needs to extinguish those rights in existence on the nominated date, so it makes no difference whether the further entitlement was known about at that time of the payment. Where specifically identifiable contingent beneficiary's benefits or rights exist under the scheme in relation to the member's rights that are commutable, these must be extinguished along with the member's own entitlement to such benefits. If the contracting out requirements prevent dependants' benefits from being commuted, such benefits must be reallocated to a separate arrangement under the scheme so that the member's arrangement (which includes any contingent dependant's benefits) can be extinguished. HMRC accept that "this requires no more than documenting the creation of a new arrangement in a manner which is considered acceptable under the scheme".[90]

(e) It is paid when the member has reached normal minimum pension age or the ill-health condition is met.[91]

HMRC accept that it is for the scheme to attribute a capital value to the pension benefit being commuted.[92] One would expect the amount of the lump sum to be determined shortly before it is paid, and that could be up to 15 months after the nominated date. HMRC accept that any increase in the value of the commutable rights during this period may be included in the payment of the trivial commuta-

**14-035**

---

[86] Prior to 6 April 2015, these provisions were not restricted to defined benefits arrangements and in-payment money-purchase in-house scheme pensions. Since that date, money purchase arrangements not paying a scheme pension can provide the funds to the member as an UFPLS or flexi-access drawdown pension. However, in-payment money-purchase in-house scheme pensions were only added with effect from 16 September 2016.

[87] The scheme administrator will therefore need to rely on information provided by the member regarding the existence and value of rights under other registered pension schemes. The scheme administrator may be discharged from liability to the scheme sanction charge if he makes an unauthorised payment as a result of reasonably relying on incorrect information provided by the member: see Ch.5 and PTM063500. The limit was £18,000 prior to 28 March 2014.

[88] FA 2004 Sch.29 para.12(2)–(4).

[89] PTM063500.

[90] PTM063400.

[91] See above for an explanation of normal minimum pension age and the ill-health condition. Prior to 6 April 2015 a trivial commutation lump sum could not be paid to a member under the age of 60.

[92] PTM063500.

tion lump sum.[93] However HMRC's position is that only those rights in existence on the nominated date can be commuted, so any new rights that accrue after that date cannot be paid out in this way. This may not be correct but it is certainly arguable. If it is correct then it seems to follow that the requirement that the lump sum extinguishes the member's entitlement to relevant benefits under the pension scheme must also be limited to such rights in existence on the nominated date.

**Valuing the member's pension rights**

**14-036** For the purposes of the £30,000 limit, the value of the member's pension rights on the nominated date is the total value of his "relevant crystallised pension rights" and his "uncrystallised rights" on that date:

(a) The value of the member's "relevant crystallised pension rights" on the nominated date is the aggregate of the following:[94]
   (i) The value of his "crystallised pension rights" on 5 April 2006. This is the total annual rate at which all "relevant existing pensions" were payable to the member on 5 April 2006 multiplied by 25.[95] Relevant existing pensions means any pension or annuity under a pre-6 April 2006 tax-approved pension scheme (including a right to make income withdrawals under such a scheme) or an annuity under an approved retirement annuity contract or trust scheme. A pension, annuity or right is not a relevant existing pension if entitlement to it was attributable to the death of any person. In the case of income drawdown the annual rate at which the pension was payable on 5 April 2006 is the amount which, on that date, is the maximum annual amount that could have been drawn down by the individual as income in accordance with the pension scheme or contract concerned. In the case of a right to make income withdrawals, the annual rate at which the pension was payable on 5 April 2006 is the maximum amount of income withdrawals that could have been made by the individual in the 12 months referred to in ICTA 1988 s.634A(4) during which 5 April 2006 falls.
   (ii) An amount equal to "$((A - B) \times 4) + C$", where "A" is the member's LS allowance, "B" is the amount of the member's LS allowance that is available on the payment of the lump sum in question, and "C" is the amount of any serious ill health lump sum already paid to the member so far as it was not chargeable to income tax.
(b) The value of the member's "uncrystallised rights" on the nominated date is the total value of the member's uncrystallised rights on that date under each arrangement relating to the member under a registered pension scheme:[96]
   (i) The value of the member's uncrystallised rights under a cash balance arrangement on the nominated date is the amount which would, on the valuation assumptions,[97] be available for the provision of

---

[93] PTM063500.
[94] FA 2004 Sch.29 para.8. For commutation periods beginning before 27 March 2014, an adjustment factor applied to these valuations to take any changes to the standard lifetime allowance into account. This was repealed by FA 2014 s.42(2).
[95] FA 2004 Sch.36 para.10. Crystallised rights are valued at 25 x ARP (instead of 20 x ARP for uncrystallised rights) to take account of the fact that when the rights crystallised it is likely that a lump sum will have been paid.
[96] FA 2004 Sch.29 para.9, applying FA 2004 s.212.
[97] The valuation assumptions require one to value the individual's rights on the assumption that the

benefits in respect of those rights if the member became entitled to benefits in respect of those rights on the date.
(ii) The value of the member's uncrystallised rights under another money purchase arrangement on the nominated date is the total value of the sums or assets held for the purposes of the arrangement on the date as represent those rights.
(iii) The value of the member's uncrystallised rights under a defined benefits arrangement on the nominated date is: "(RVF x ARP) + LS" Where *RVF* is 20;[98] *ARP* is the annual rate of pension to which the member would, on the valuation assumptions, be entitled under the arrangement on the date if, on the date, the member acquired an actual (rather than merely a prospective) right to receive a pension in respect of the rights; and *LS* is the amount of any lump sum to which the member would, on the valuation assumptions, be entitled under the arrangement on the date (otherwise than by way of commutation of pension) if, on the date, the member acquired an actual (rather than a prospective) right to payment of a lump sum in respect of the rights.
(iv) If the arrangement is a hybrid arrangement (i.e. it can provide more than one category of benefit, for example cash balance and defined benefits), one must calculate the value of each possible benefit and use the value of whichever is the greatest.

## WINDING-UP LUMP SUM

The rules of a pension scheme will typically provide that the scheme will, or may, be wound up in specified circumstances, such as (a) the dissolution of the employer; (b) where notice is given to the trustees by the scheme's principal employer; (c) the termination of contributions by a participating employer; or (d) the failure by a participating employer to comply with its duties under the trust deed and rules.

**14-037**

Once the decision has been made to wind up the scheme, the trustees must secure the members' benefits, by (a) buying annuities for the members from an insurance company; (b) arranging for recognised transfers to other pension schemes; or (c) by commuting members' pension entitlements for: (i) a trivial commutation lump sum; (ii) a small lump sum; (iii) an UFPLS (with the member's consent); or (iv) a winding-up lump sum.

A lump sum is a winding-up lump sum if all of the following requirements are satisfied:[99]

(a) The pension scheme is an occupational pension scheme.
(b) The pension scheme is being wound up.[100] The term "wound up" is not

---

individual is at the age at which no reduction would apply to the payment of an immediate benefit (e.g. as a result of early retirement), and the individual is in good physical and mental health and so the benefits are not increased as a result of being paid on grounds of ill-health: FA 2004 s.277.

[98] Or such greater number as is agreed between the scheme administrator and HMRC: see FA 2004 s.276.
[99] FA 2004 Sch.29 para.10.
[100] Once a winding-up trigger event has occurred, the trustees may defer winding up the scheme, and instead run it as a "closed scheme" (PA 1995 s.38).

defined. HMRC accept that, in the context of a sectionalised master scheme, winding up a section of the scheme may meet these requirements.[101]

(c) Any employer of the member at the time when the lump sum is paid who has made contributions under the pension scheme in respect of the member within the five years before the lump sum is paid: (i) is not making contributions under any other registered pension scheme in respect of the member; and (ii) undertakes to HMRC not to make such contributions within one year of the day on which the lump sum is paid.[102]

(d) The member has some LS allowance available immediately before the lump sum is paid.

(e) It extinguishes the member's entitlement to benefits under the pension scheme.

However, such a lump sum is not a winding up lump sum to the extent that it exceeds £18,000.[103]

**14-038** HMRC accept that under a defined benefits arrangement it is for the scheme to attribute a capital value to the pension benefit entitlement being commuted for the purposes of deciding the size of the lump sum payment to be made.

## LIFETIME ALLOWANCE EXCESS LUMP SUM (PRE-6 APRIL 2024)

**14-039** Prior to 6 April 2024, a lump sum was a lifetime allowance excess lump sum if:[104]

(a) It was paid when none of the member's lifetime allowance was available.

(b) It was not a short service refund lump sum or a refund of excess contributions lump sum (these are the only other authorised lump sums that can be paid when the member has no available lifetime allowance).

(c) It did not reduce the rate of payment of any pension to which the member has become (actually) entitled, or extinguish the member's entitlement to payment of any such pension.

(d) It was paid when the member has reached normal minimum pension age (or the ill-health condition is met).

(e) It was paid before the member reaches age 75.

**14-040** HMRC accepted that under a defined benefits arrangement it was for the scheme to attribute a capital value to the pension benefit entitlement being commuted for the purposes of deciding the amount of the lump sum payment to be made.[105]

---

[101] See PTM063600.

[102] HMRC request (at PTM063600) that the undertaking is in writing and confirms that the employer will meet the condition in FA 2004 Sch.29 para.10(3)(c). It should be sent to Pension Scheme Services in Nottingham before the winding-up lump sum is paid. One declaration per employer listing all the members in respect of whom they give the undertaking at that time is sufficient.

[103] This limit applies to each member, rather than to the scheme. Prior to 6 April 2012 the limit was 1% of the standard lifetime allowance.

[104] FA 2004 Sch.29 para.11.

[105] PTM084000.

## OTHER AUTHORISED LUMP SUMS

Regulations made under FA 2004 s.164(1)(f) provide that certain lump sum payments are authorised member payments.[106] These may be split into two categories: **14-041**

(a) Small payments.
(b) Lump sums paid in error.

**Small payments**

*Relevant accretion following transfer*

Where *relevant accretion* occurs in respect of a member following a recognised transfer of that member's funds to another scheme or the purchase of a scheme pension or annuity for the member, an amount not exceeding the accretion may be paid to or in respect of the member as an authorised payment, provided that: (a) the payment extinguishes the member's entitlement to benefits under the pension scheme;[107] (b) it does not exceed £10,000;[108] and (c) it is made no later than six months after the date the accretion occurred (or 1 June 2010 if the accretion occurred at any time before 1 December 2009).[109] Such a payment is taxed as if it were a trivial commutation lump sum.[110] **14-042**

The following are relevant accretions:[111] **14-043**

(a) a payment is received by the scheme in respect of the member, other than a contribution or a recognised transfer, or any other transfer of funds held for the purposes of another pension scheme (including an unregistered scheme). The value of such a relevant accretion is the amount of the payment;
(b) there is an allocation to the arrangement in the amount by which the value of the sums and assets held for the purposes of the arrangement exceeds the value the scheme administrator had believed they had. The value of such a relevant accretion is the amount by which the value of the sums and assets exceeds the value they had been believed to have; and
(c) the scheme administrator becomes aware that the member is entitled to a benefit under the pension scheme, provided that the scheme administrator had not been aware of the entitlement before the recognised transfer or pension or annuity purchase, and the scheme administrator could not reasonably have been expected to be aware of it before that event. The value of

---

[106] See SI 2009/1171.
[107] Where the accretion occurs after the purchase of a scheme pension or annuity, the scheme pension or annuity is disregarded in determining whether the member's entitlement to benefits under the scheme are extinguished. Any specifically identifiable contingent beneficiary's benefits/rights must be extinguished along with the member's own entitlement to benefits. It is implicit from the definition of relevant accretion that the reference to extinguishing the member's entitlement to benefits is to all the rights that could reasonably have been known about at the time of the payment. This is accepted by HMRC (see PTM063700). The lump sum will not cease to be an authorised payment purely because further entitlement is later created that could not have been known about at the time of the initial payment, for example through a pay revision.
[108] The maximum was £2,000 for payments made before 27 March 2014.
[109] FA 2004 s.164(1)(f) and SI 2009/1171 reg.6.
[110] SI 2009/1171 reg.3.
[111] SI 2009/1171 reg.7.

such a relevant accretion is the value of the benefit to which the member is entitled.

**14-044** Typically, this may apply where contingent investment returns are received after the transfer out or purchase of the pension or annuity, or where the right to receive a future payment has been overlooked. Or where, for example, a valuation error caused an investment that provided part of the transfer value to be undervalued. A later correction in the valuation could result in there being further rights in the scheme relating to the member who had transferred out.

*Certain payments under the FSCS*

**14-045** Where a small lump sum is paid by a registered pension scheme by way of compensation under the Financial Services Compensation Scheme, to or in respect of a member, it will be an authorised member payment providing that certain conditions are met.[112] Such a payment is taxed as if it were a trivial commutation lump sum.[113]

*Occupational pension schemes*

**14-046** A payment by an occupational pension scheme to or in respect of a member is an authorised payment, provided that:[114] (a) the member has reached normal minimum pension age or the ill-health condition is met;[115] (b) the member is not a controlling director of a sponsoring employer of this or of any related scheme, and is not a person connected to such a person; (c) the payment does not exceed £10,000;[116] (d) the commutation value[117] of the benefits to which the member is entitled under this and any related scheme does not exceed £10,000 in total; (e) the payment extinguishes the member's entitlement to benefits under this scheme; and (f) no recognised transfer was made out of this or any related scheme in respect of the member during the three years preceding the date of the payment. Such a payment is taxable as if it were a trivial commutation lump sum.[118] These provisions permit a payment to the member without the need for that lump sum to satisfy the more onerous test for a trivial commutation lump sum. The rights commuted may be crystallised or uncrystallised.

**14-047** Where specifically identifiable contingent beneficiary's benefits/rights exist, these must be extinguished along with the member's own entitlement to benefits. HMRC accept[119] that the reference to extinguishing the member's entitlement to benefits is to all the rights that could reasonably have been known about at the time of the payment. The lump sum will not cease to be an authorised payment purely because further entitlement is later created that could not have been known about at the time of the initial payment, for example, through a pay revision.

---

[112] SI 2009/1171 reg.8. See PTM063700.
[113] SI 2009/1171 reg.3.
[114] SI 2009/1171 regs 10 and 11. Regulation 12 contains very similar provisions, restricted to payments from occupational schemes with 50 or more members.
[115] See FA 2004 Sch.28 para.1.
[116] The maximum was £2,000 for payments made before 27 March 2014.
[117] The commutation value is equal to the amount of the lump sum that, if paid, would extinguish the member's entitlement to benefits under the scheme concerned.
[118] SI 2009/1171 reg.3.
[119] PTM063700. This is also implicit from the definition of relevant accretion.

*Non-occupational schemes*

A payment by a non-occupational pension scheme to or in respect of a member is an authorised payment, provided that:[120] (a) the member has reached normal minimum pension age or the ill-health condition is met;[121] (b) the payment does not exceed £10,000; (c) the payment extinguishes the member's entitlement to benefits under the arrangement; and (d) the member has not previously received more than two payments under this provision. Such a payment is taxable as if it were a trivial commutation lump sum.[122] These provisions permit a payment to the member without the need for that lump sum to satisfy the more onerous test for a trivial commutation lump sum. The rights commuted may be crystallised or uncrystallised. **14-048**

The payment must extinguish the member's entitlement to benefits under the arrangement (per (c) above), but not necessarily the scheme. This appears to allow a reallocation to a new arrangement (or a consolidation of multiple arrangements) for the purposes of this provision. Up to three payments could be made from the same scheme to the member. Lump sum payments can be made (under SI 2009/1171 reg.11A) regardless of the individual's total pension savings in registered pension schemes and can be made in addition to any trivial commutation lump sum payment the individual may receive. **14-049**

Where specifically identifiable contingent beneficiary's benefits/rights exist, these must be extinguished along with the member's own entitlement to benefits. HMRC accept[123] that the reference to extinguishing the member's entitlement to benefits is to all the rights that could reasonably have been known about at the time of the payment. The lump sum will not cease to be an authorised payment purely because further entitlement is later created that could not have been known about at the time of the initial payment, for example, through a pay revision. **14-050**

**Lump sums paid in error**

A payment of a lump sum the whole of which is intended to represent a PCLS, but which exceeds the permitted maximum, is an authorised payment provided that:[124] **14-051**

(a) the lump sum exceeds the permitted maximum only because it has been calculated by reference to the amount of a connected pension; and
(b) either: (i) the payment of the connected pension is a pension paid in error within SI 2009/1171 reg.13 (or would be such a pension if the error had not been discovered until after the payment); or (ii) the following conditions apply: (a) the lump sum is paid before the pension by reference to which its amount was calculated; (b) the pension is not in the event paid, or paid in the amount originally intended, because an error is discovered; and (c) if the error had not been discovered and the pension had been paid as intended, its payment would have been a payment within SI 2009/1171 reg.13.

If it is discovered that the lump sum exceeds the permitted maximum before the payment, it will only be an authorised payment if the payer took reasonable steps **14-052**

---

[120] SI 2009/1171 regs 10 and 11A.
[121] See FA 2004 Sch.28 para.1.
[122] SI 2009/1171 reg.3.
[123] PTM063700. This is also implicit from the definition of relevant accretion.
[124] SI 2009/1171 reg.17.

to prevent its being made or its being made in that amount.[125]

*Other lump sum errors*

**14-053** A payment of a lump sum the whole of which is intended to represent a PCLS, but which exceeds the permitted maximum, is an authorised payment if:[126] (a) the lump sum exceeds the permitted maximum only because it has been calculated by reference to the annuity purchase price or the scheme pension purchase price; (b) an error in that calculation means that the amount concerned is greater than it would have been; and (c) the lump sum is paid before the lifetime annuity or scheme pension is purchased; and the lifetime annuity or scheme pension is not in the event purchased, or purchased for the amount originally intended, because the error is discovered.

**14-054** The discovery that the lump sum exceeds the permitted maximum before the payment is made does not prevent the payment from meeting the above requirements if the payer took reasonable steps to prevent its being made or its being made in that amount.[127]

*Commencement lump sums paid after death*

**14-055** A payment of a lump sum under the pension scheme to or in respect of a member who has died is an authorised payment if:[128] (a) the payment is in respect of a defined benefits arrangement; (b) the scheme administrator had not established the member's entitlement to the payment until after the member's death; (c) the scheme administrator could not reasonably have been expected to make the payment before the member died; (d) the payment would have been a PCLS if it had been made immediately before the member's death and the member had been entitled to it; (e) it is made within one year of the day on which the scheme administrator first knew of the member's death or (if earlier) the day on which the scheme administrator could first reasonably be expected to have known of it; and (f) the member was neither a controlling director of a sponsoring employer of this or any related scheme, nor connected to such a person.[129]

# ENHANCED ALLOWANCES

**14-056** Special provisions apply in relation to a relevant BCE occurring in relation to an individual, other than the individual becoming entitled to a PCLS or an UFPLS, where one or more LS&DB allowance "enhancement factors" operate in relation

---

[125] For lifetime allowance purposes (before 6 April 2024), BCE 9 occurred when the member became entitled to the PCLS that formed part of such a payment, and this did not prevent BCE 6 from occurring when the member became entitled to the PCLS. The amount crystallised was the amount by which the lump sum exceeds the permitted maximum.
[126] SI 2009/1171 reg.18.
[127] For lifetime allowance purposes (before 6 April 2024), BCE 9 occurred when the member became entitled to the PCLS that formed part of the payment meeting these requirements and the amount crystallised was the amount by which the lump sum exceeded the permitted maximum. That did not prevent BCE 6 occurring in relation to the PCLS.
[128] SI 2009/1171 reg.19.
[129] For lifetime allowance purposes (before 6 April 2024), the making of the payment was treated as BCE 9 and the amount crystallised was the amount of the payment.

ENHANCED ALLOWANCES

to the relevant BCE.[130] In those circumstances, ITEPA 2003 Pt 9 Ch.15A has effect in relation to the individual as if the individual's LS&DB allowance were an amount equal to "A + (A × B)" where "A" is (a) in the case of an individual in relation to whom a "relevant protection provision" applies, the individual's "protected LS&DB allowance"; (b) in any other case, £1,073,100; "B" is the aggregate of the LS&DB allowance enhancement factors that operate in relation to the relevant BCE.

The "relevant protection provisions" means primary protection, fixed protection 2011, fixed protection 2014, individual protection 2014, fixed protection 2016, and individual protection 2016. **14-057**

The individual's "protected LS&DB allowance" depends on the which protection provisions apply: see below. **14-058**

**Primary protection**

For an individual with primary protection, ITEPA 2003 Pt 9 Ch.15A has effect as if his LS allowance were £375,000 and his LS&DB allowance were £1.8m.[131] **14-059**

However, an LS&DB allowance enhancement factor (called the primary protection factor) operates in relation to any relevant BCE other than the payment of a PCLS or UFPLS.[132] The primary protection factor is "(RR − £1,500,000) / £1,500,000" where "RR" is the amount of the relevant pre-commencement pension rights of the individual. The amount of the relevant pre-commencement rights of the individual is the aggregate of (a) the value of the individual's relevant uncrystallised pension rights on 5 April 2006; and (b) the value of the individual's relevant crystallised pension rights on that date. This is subject to para.11 (pension debit on or after 6 April 2006) and para.11A (pension debit on or after 6 April 2006: lump sum death benefits). **14-060**

In relation to an individual with primary protection, a lump sum is not an UFPLS if (a) he has registered tax-free cash rights,[133] or (b) his available tax-free cash is less than 25% (e.g. because he has received a disqualifying pension credit). **14-061**

**Enhanced protection**

Enhanced protection is explained in Ch.3 **14-062**
For a member with enhanced protection: **14-063**

(a) The LS allowance is £375,000.[134]
(b) *PCLS*: the "permitted maximum" is not limited by reference to the member's available LS allowance or LS&DB allowance. It is limited to an amount equal to: (i) the maximum amount of a PCLS that could have been paid to the individual on 5 April 2023 under the arrangement pursuant to which the individual becomes entitled to the relevant pension, less, and (ii) the aggregate of the amounts of any PCLS to which the member has previously become entitled under that arrangement after that date.[135]
(c) *UFPLS*: in the definition of "permitted maximum", the reference to the member's available LS&DB allowance is replaced with a reference to the

---

[130] FA 2004 Sch.36 para.6A.
[131] FA 2004 Sch.36 para.7(2).
[132] FA 2004 Sch.36 para.7(3).
[133] i.e. the lump sum condition (see Sch.36 paras 24(2) and (3), 25 and 26) is met in relation to the individual.
[134] FA 2004 Sch.36 para.12(3E).
[135] FA 2004 Sch.36 para.27.

maximum amount of an UFPLS that could have been paid to the individual with no liability to income tax on 5 April 2024 under the arrangement pursuant to which the entitlement to the UFPLS arises. As noted above, the member's LS allowance is £375,000. However, where the individual has previously become entitled to a serious ill-health lump sum, the permitted maximum is nil.[136]

(d) *Serious ill-health lump sum*: the "permitted maximum" is not limited by reference to the member's available LS&DB allowance. It is limited to the maximum amount of a serious ill-health lump sum that could have been paid to the individual on 5 April 2024 under the arrangement.[137]

(e) *LSDBs*: in relation to the following LSDBs, the "permitted maximum" is not limited by reference to the member's available LS&DB allowance. It is limited to (i) the maximum amount of the relevant LSDB that could have been paid in respect of the individual on 5 April 2024 under the arrangement, less (ii) the aggregate of the non-taxable amounts[138] of each authorised LSDB (if any) previously paid in respect of the individual under that arrangement after that date:[139]

(i) Defined benefits LSDB.
(ii) Pension protection LSDB.
(iii) Uncrystallised funds LSDB.
(iv) Annuity protection LSDB.
(v) Drawdown pension fund LSDB.
(vi) Flexi-access drawdown LSDB.

**Fixed protection**

14-064 Fixed protection is explained in Ch.10.

14-065 In relation to an individual with FP 2012, ITEPA 2003 Pt 9 Ch.15A applies as if the individual's LS allowance were £450,000 and his LS&DB allowance were £1.8 million.[140]

14-066 In relation to an individual with FP 2014, ITEPA 2003 Pt 9 Ch.15A applies as if the individual's LS allowance were £375,000 and his LS&DB allowance were £1.5 million.[141]

14-067 In relation to an individual with FP 2016, ITEPA 2003 Pt 9 Ch.15A applies as if the individual's LS allowance were £312,500 and his LS&DB allowance were £1.25 million.[142]

**Individual protection**

14-068 In relation to an individual with IP 2014, ITEPA 2003 Pt 9 Ch.15A applies as if: (a) the individual's LS allowance were the lower of (i) 25% of the individual relevant amount (i.e. the value of his pension rights on 5 April 2014); and (ii)

---

[136] FA 2004 Sch.36 para.12(3B) amending ITEPA 2003 s.637D.
[137] FA 2004 Sch.36 para.12(3B) amending ITEPA 2003 s.637C.
[138] i.e. so much of the lump sum as is exempt from income tax under ITEPA 2003 Ch.15A Pt 9 (ITEPA 2003 s.637S(6)).
[139] FA 2004 Sch.36 para.12(3B) amending ITEPA 2003 ss.637H, 637I, 637J, 637K, 637L, and 637M. If this produces a negative result, the permitted maximum is nil.
[140] FA 2011 Sch.18 para.14, as amended by FA 2024 Sch.9 para.90(4).
[141] FA 2013 Sch.22 para.1, as amended by FA 2024 Sch.9 para.91(3).
[142] FA 2016 Sch.4 para.1, as amended by FA 2024 Sch.9 para.93(3).

£375,000; and (b) his LS&DB allowance were the lower of: (i) the individual's relevant amount; and (ii) £1.5 million.[143]

In relation to an individual with IP 2016, ITEPA 2003 Pt 9 Ch.15A applies as if: (a) the individual's LS allowance were the lower of (i) 25% of the individual relevant amount (i.e. the value of his pension rights on 5 April 2016); and (ii) £375,000; and (b) his LS&DB allowance were the lower of: (i) the individual's relevant amount; and (ii) £1.5 million.[144]

**Other enhancement factors**

An LS&DB enhancement factor also applies where:

14-069

14-070

(a) The member acquires a pension credit on or after 6 April 2006 in relation to rights under another registered pension scheme which consisted of or included rights to a pension already in payment and which came into payment on or after 6 April 2006 (the "pension credit factor") (see Ch.16).
(b) A pension credit was acquired before 6 April 2006 (the "pre-commencement pension credit factor") (see Ch.16).
(c) Certain benefits accrue under a registered pension scheme during a period in which the member is a relevant overseas individual (the "non-residence factor") (see Ch.20).
(d) Benefits accrue in a ROPS and are subsequently transferred to a registered pension scheme (the "recognised overseas scheme transfer factor") (see Ch.20).

In each case, the member must claim the enhancement factor by notifying HMRC, and HMRC will provide the individual with a certificate confirming his entitlement.

14-071

# REPORTING OBLIGATIONS

The scheme administrator will usually be required to report the provision of authorised lump sums to HMRC in the pension scheme return.[145] In addition, it may be necessary to make an event report in connection with the provision of authorised lump sums in certain circumstances.[146]

14-072

**Provision of information by scheme administrators to members**

A reference in the Registered Pension Schemes (Provision of Information) Regulations (SI 2006/567) to a relevant BCE is, in relation to times before 6 April 2024, a reference to a BCE.[147]

14-073

Sub-paragraph (3) applies where (a) one or more BCEs occurred in relation to a member of a registered pension scheme before 6 April 2024, and (b) it is necessary to determine, for the purposes of any provision of SI 2006/567 as that provision has effect for the 2024/25 tax year or a subsequent tax year, the amount of the member's LS allowance that has been expended by the events mentioned in paragraph (a). For those purposes, the amount of the member's LS allowance that

---

[143] FA 2014 Sch.6 para.1, as amended by FA 2024 Sch.9 para.92(3).
[144] FA 2016 Sch.4 para.9, as amended by FA 2024 Sch.9 para.93(4).
[145] For the pension scheme return, see Ch.19.
[146] For event reports, see Ch.19.
[147] FA 2024 Sch.9 para.128.

has been expended is: (a) if a transitional tax-free amount certificate is in force in relation to the member, so much of the member's LS transitional tax-free amount as is referable to those events; (b) otherwise, an amount equal to 25% of so much of the member's lifetime allowance previously-used amount as is referable to those events.

Sub-paragraph (5) applies where (a) one or more BCEs occurred in relation to a member of a registered pension scheme before 6 April 2024, and (b) it is necessary to determine, for the purposes of any provision of SI 2006/567 as it has effect for the 2024/25 tax year or a later tax year, the amount of the member's LS&DB allowance that has been expended by the events mentioned in paragraph (a). For those purposes, the amount of the member's LS&DB allowance that has been expended is (a) if a transitional tax-free amount certificate is in force in relation to the member, so much of the member's LS&DB transitional tax-free amount as is referable to those events; (b) otherwise, an amount equal to the appropriate percentage of so much of the member's lifetime allowance previously-used amount as is referable to those events. The "appropriate percentage" means (a) 100% in a case in which (i) the member becomes entitled to a serious ill-health lump sum under the scheme before 6 April 2024 and is under the age of 75 at the time of the payment, or (ii) the member dies before 6 April 2024 under the age of 75 and before that date a person is paid a lump sum death benefit under the scheme in respect of the individual; (b) 25% in any other case.

*Statements for certain members who would not otherwise receive one in 2024/25*

**14-074** The scheme administrator of a registered pension scheme must provide a statement to each relevant person before the end of the 2024/25 tax year.[148] "Relevant person" means: (a) any member of the scheme (i) in relation to whom one or more BCEs occurred before 6 April 2024; and (ii) who on that date does not have an actual (as opposed to prospective) entitlement to be paid a pension; or (b) the personal representatives of such a member who has died.

The statement must contain the information that would have been required to be provided under reg.14(1) of SI 2006/567 if such a requirement had arisen in relation to a BCE occurring immediately before 6 April 2024.

---

[148] FA 2024 Sch.9 para.130.

# CHAPTER 15

# Authorised Death Benefits

## TABLE OF CONTENTS

| | |
|---|---|
| Introduction and overview | 15-001 |
|     Money purchase arrangements | 15-003 |
|         The effect of death | 15-008 |
|         Nominations and expressions of wishes | 15-009 |
|     Defined benefits arrangements | 15-010 |
|     The relevant two-year period | 15-012 |
|     Interaction with the LS&DB allowance | 15-014 |
| Authorised pension death benefits | 15-015 |
|     Options available | 15-017 |
|     "Dependant" | 15-018 |
|     "Nominee" | 15-020 |
|     "Successor" | 15-021 |
|     Taxation of pension death benefits | 15-022 |
|         National insurance contributions | 15-023 |
|         Term certain payments | 15-024 |
|     Scheme pension | 15-025 |
|         The dependants' scheme pension limit | 15-026 |
|             Exception | 15-028 |
|     Annuities | 15-029 |
|         Related annuities | 15-030 |
|         Annuities acquired after death | 15-031 |
|     Drawdown pension | 15-032 |
|         Beneficiaries' short-term annuity | 15-033 |
|         Beneficiaries' income withdrawal | 15-034 |
|         Beneficiaries' flexi-access drawdown funds | 15-035 |
|         Dependants' drawdown pension funds | 15-039 |
|         Pension death benefit rule 4 | 15-043 |
| Authorised lump sum death benefits | 15-044 |
|     Taxation of authorised LSDBs | 15-046 |
|         The special LSDB charge | 15-047 |
|         "Non-qualifying person" | 15-049 |
|     Defined benefits LSDB | 15-052 |
|     Uncrystallised funds LSDB | 15-053 |
|         Permitted maximum | 15-055 |
|     Pension protection LSDB | 15-056 |
|     Annuity protection LSDB | 15-058 |
|     Drawdown pension fund LSDB | 15-060 |
|         Permitted maximum | 15-061 |
|     Flexi-access drawdown fund LSDB | 15-064 |
|         Permitted maximum | 15-065 |

| | |
|---|---|
| Charity LSDB | 15-066 |
| Uncrystallised funds | 15-068 |
| Drawdown funds | 15-069 |
| Trivial commutation LSDB | 15-072 |
| Paid to dependant | 15-073 |
| Paid to any individual | 15-074 |
| Life cover lump sum | 15-075 |
| Trusts of death benefits | 15-077 |
| Payments not subject to the special LSDB charge | 15-078 |
| Payments subject to the special LSDB charge | 15-079 |
| Disguised remuneration | 15-081 |

## INTRODUCTION AND OVERVIEW

**15-001** Most registered pension schemes provide for the payment of death benefits.[1] This chapter is concerned with authorised pension and lump sum death benefits.

**15-002** Authorised death benefits are generally tax-free if the member (or prior death beneficiary[2]) dies before his 75th birthday, and are otherwise:

(a) taxable at the recipient's marginal rate of income tax if paid to an individual; or

(b) subject to a 45% special LSDB charge if paid to a non-individual (including a trustee). Authorised *pension* death benefits may not be paid to a non-individual, but authorised *lump sum* death benefits may.

**Money purchase arrangements**

**15-003** The authorised death benefits payable on the death of a member of a money purchase arrangement depend to a large extent on whether the member's benefits crystallised before death, and if so which type of pension he was receiving, as the following table outlines:

| Circumstances immediately before death | Possible authorised death benefit |
|---|---|
| Uncrystallised sums or assets are held for the purposes of the member's arrangement | Such sums or assets may be:<br>(a) applied to pay or purchase a dependants' scheme pension;<br>(b) applied to purchase a dependants' or nominees' annuity;<br>(c) designated as available for dependants' or nominees' drawdown pension; |

---

[1] The trustee or manager of an occupational scheme that has its main administration in the UK must secure that the activities of the scheme are limited to "retirement benefit activities" (PA 2004 s.255). Death benefits are acceptable but only if they are ancillary to retirement benefits (see TPR Guidance on "lump sum death benefits" (June 2006)).

[2] In relation to money purchase arrangements, on the death of a dependant or nominee of the member, authorised death benefits may be paid to a successor of the member, and on the death of that successor death benefits may be paid to another successor of the member. In this chapter, the "prior death beneficiary" means the dependant, nominee, or immediately preceding the current successor.

# INTRODUCTION AND OVERVIEW

| Circumstances immediately before death | Possible authorised death benefit |
|---|---|
| | (d) paid as an uncrystallised funds LSDB; or<br>(e) paid as a charity LSDB (if no dependants). |
| Member is receiving a scheme pension | The terms of the scheme pension may specify:<br>(a) the continuation of the member's scheme pension for the duration of any remaining term certain (this is not a death benefit);<br>(b) the payment of a dependants' scheme pension; or<br>(c) the payment an annuity protection LSDB. |
| Member is receiving a lifetime annuity | The terms of the annuity may specify:<br>(a) the continuation of the member's annuity for the duration of any remaining term certain (this is not a death benefit);<br>(b) the payment of a dependants' or nominees' annuity (a "joint life" annuity);<br>(c) an annuity protection LSDB. |
| Member designated sums or assets as available for drawdown pension and there are sums or assets representing the member's drawdown pension fund or flexi-access drawdown fund | Such sums or assets may be:<br>(a) designated as available for dependants' or nominees' drawdown pension;<br>(b) applied to purchase an annuity for a dependant or nominee;<br>(c) applied to pay or purchase a dependants' scheme pension;<br>(d) paid as a drawdown pension fund LSDB or flexi-access drawdown fund LSDB; or<br>(e) paid as a charity LSDB (if no dependants). |

In each case, where a death beneficiary becomes entitled to a pension death benefit, he may be able to commute it for a trivial commutation LSDB.  **15-004**

Where the member is survived by one or more dependants, it will always be possible to pay a dependants' scheme pension, including on an ex gratia basis.[3]  **15-005**

A dependants' or nominees' flexi-access drawdown fund operates in the same way as a members' flexi-access drawdown fund. The dependant or nominee may also nominate a successor who can, following the death of the dependant or nominee, designate any undrawn sums or assets as available for the payment of successors' drawdown pension. And that successor can nominate a further successor, and so on. Thus FA 2004 Pt 4 expressly provides for the transfer of pension rights  **15-006**

---

[3] The definition of dependants' scheme pension does not impose a requirement that it is paid "in respect of" the member's arrangement, so it may be paid on an ex gratia basis (e.g. by the application of sums or asset held for the purposes of a general fund under the scheme).

from one generation to the next. There is no requirement to draw death benefits if the beneficiary does not wish to do so, and until such time as the fund is exhausted it will continue to benefit from tax-free investment return and the generous inheritance tax treatment afforded to registered pension schemes.

**15-007** For the purposes of FA 2004 Pt 4, all death benefits are paid "in respect of" the deceased member (including where they are paid following the death of a dependant, nominee or successor of the deceased member).

*The effect of death*

**15-008** The death of the member does not cause his arrangement under the scheme to cease to be an arrangement under a registered pension scheme for the purposes of FA 2004 Pt 4. In relation to uncrystallised sums and assets, the death of the member merely changes to whom the trustees can pay an authorised payment and in some cases *when* they can pay it (i.e. they do not need to wait until the death beneficiary attains any particular age). Similarly, a member's drawdown pension fund or flexi-access drawdown fund does not cease to exist on death; it can, in principle, continue indefinitely.[4]

*Nominations and expressions of wishes*

**15-009** Where a money purchase arrangement offers all of the death benefits permitted under FA 2004, the best course of action will usually be to give the trustees maximum flexibility, so death beneficiaries can keep the fund invested within the pension scheme (and outside of their estates) until such time as money is required. This can be achieved in a nomination and expression of wishes which identifies the desired death beneficiaries (and specifies the desired proportion of the fund for each beneficiary), and expressly nominates each of the identified beneficiaries "for the purposes of paragraph 27A of Schedule 28 to the Finance Act 2004 (and for the purposes of nominees' drawdown pension in particular)." It is also generally helpful to request that the trustees, before exercising their discretion, consult with each of the identified beneficiaries as to the form of benefit they would each wish to receive (i.e. lump sum, annuity, and/or drawdown pension). It may also be desirable to request that if any of the identified beneficiaries predecease the member leaving issue, such issue is provided with the death benefits which such beneficiary would have received had that beneficiary survived the member, and if there shall be more than one of such issue, they take such benefits in equal shares per stirpes.

**Defined benefits arrangements**

**15-010** Defined benefits arrangements typically provide for lump sum death in service benefits (often four times annual salary[5]). Once the member retires and starts to draw a scheme pension, the available death benefits usually reduce significantly (frequently limited to a pension for a surviving spouse). There is only one authorised pension death benefit that may be paid in respect of a defined benefits arrangement: dependants' scheme pension. Four types of authorised lump sum death benefit may be paid in respect of a defined benefits arrangement:

---

[4] Where the member dies before age 75, death benefits usually need to be provided within the relevant two-year period in order to be free of income tax. But where the member dies on or after age 75, there is no tax reason to provide death benefits within any particular period of time.

[5] Before 6 April 2006, this was the maximum death in service payment permitted under an approved scheme (IR12 para 11.2).

# INTRODUCTION AND OVERVIEW

(a) a defined benefits LSDB;
(b) a pension protection LSDB;
(c) a trivial commutation LSDB; or
(d) a life cover lump sum.

Authorised lump sum death benefits must be paid "in respect of" the member's defined benefits arrangement. This imposes a requirement that the death benefits form part of the member's arrangement under the pension scheme. The trustees may have discretion regarding the identity of the recipient, but they must be required (under the terms of the member's arrangement) to pay the death benefits to someone. Ex gratia death benefits are not provided "in respect of" a defined benefits arrangement.[6] **15-011**

## The relevant two-year period

The relevant two-year period is the period of two years beginning with the earlier of the day on which the scheme administrator first knew of the individual's death and the day on which the scheme administrator could first reasonably have been expected to have known of it. In most cases, the two-year period will commence on the day the administrator receives a copy of the death certificate.[7] The more objective part of this test ("or could first reasonably have been expected to have known of it") is likely to apply where the administrator has reason to suspect death but unreasonably fails to obtain knowledge of it. **15-012**

If the member dies before his 75th birthday, the application of uncrystallised sums or assets to provide authorised LSDBs is usually a relevant BCE (and so tested against the member's available LS&DB allowance) if the application occurs within the relevant two-year period (but not otherwise). Following such application within the relevant two-year period, authorised death benefits are usually free of income tax.[8] **15-013**

## Interaction with the LS&DB allowance

If the member dies prior to age 75 the following are tax-free if they occur within the relevant two-year period: **15-014**

(a) the designation of uncrystallised sums or assets as available for dependants' or nominees' drawdown pension;
(b) the purchase of a dependants' or nominees' annuity with uncrystallised sums or assets;
(c) the payment of a defined benefits LSDB; and
(d) the payment of an uncrystallised funds LSDB.

---

[6] That is not to say that ex gratia death benefits cannot be provided following the death of the member of a defined benefits arrangement. Although pension death benefit rule 2 provides that no payment of pension death benefit other than a dependants' scheme pension may be paid in respect of a defined benefits arrangement, a dependants' scheme pension need not be paid in respect of the member's arrangement. So a dependants' scheme pension may be provided on an ex gratia basis. By definition, ex gratia benefits are not provided "in respect of" the member's arrangement under the scheme. For the meaning of "arrangement", see Ch.2.

[7] Plainly, there is a material distinction between "knowing" of someone's death (which suggests a high degree of certainty, e.g. because the administrator has received a copy of the death certificate), and having reason to suspect someone's death (e.g. where the administrator has been notified of the death but received no evidence). On the face of it, knowledge requires proof.

[8] Exceptions apply to dependants' scheme pension (which is always taxable), pension protection LSDB and annuity protection LSDB (which are both tax-free even if they are not provided within the relevant two-year period), and charity LSDB (which is always free of tax).

To the extent that any of the above lump sums exceed the member's available LS&DB allowance, the lump sum is taxable as pension income of the recipient.[9] For the member's available LS&DB allowance, see Ch.14.

## AUTHORISED PENSION DEATH BENEFITS

**15-015** The list of authorised member payments in FA 2004 s.164(1) includes "pensions permitted by the pensions death benefit rules … to be paid … in respect of a member". There are six pension death benefit rules:[10]

| | |
|---|---|
| Pension death benefit rule 1 | No payment of pension death benefit may be made otherwise than to a dependant, or nominee or successor, of the member. |
| Pension death benefit rule 2 | No payment of pension death benefit other than a dependants' scheme pension may be made in respect of a defined benefits arrangement or a collective money purchase arrangement. |
| Pension death benefit rule 3 | No payment of pension death benefit other than (a) a dependants' scheme pension, (b) a dependants' annuity, or (c) dependants' drawdown pension, may be made to a dependant in respect of a money purchase arrangement that is not a collective money purchase arrangement; but a dependants' scheme pension may only be paid if the member or dependant had an opportunity to select a dependants' annuity instead. |
| Pension death benefit rule 3A | No payment of pension death benefit, other than a nominees' annuity in respect of a money purchase arrangement or nominees' drawdown pension in respect of a money purchase arrangement, may be made to a nominee of the member. |
| Pension death benefit rule 3B | No payment of pension death benefit, other than a successors' annuity in respect of a money purchase arrangement or successors' drawdown pension in respect of a money purchase arrangement, may be made to a successor of the member. |
| Pension death benefit rule 4 | The total amount of dependants' drawdown pension paid to a dependant in each drawdown pension year from, or under a dependants' short-term annuity purchased using sums or assets out of, the dependants' drawdown pension fund in respect of a money purchase arrangement must not exceed 150% of the basis amount for the drawdown pension year. |

---

[9] Prior to 6 April 2023, the recipient would have been subject to the lifetime allowance charge.
[10] FA 2004 s.167.

A "pension death benefit" means: (a) a pension payable on the death of the member; or (b) a pension payable in respect of the member on the death of a dependant, nominee or successor of the member.[11] The words "on the death" mean "as a result of the death".[12] One has regard to the reason that the benefits are provided, however death need not be the *sole* reason. Death benefits that can be paid only if, or to the extent that, the trustees exercise a discretion are still death benefits. The words "on the death" impose no temporal requirement (other than that such benefits cannot be provided before death). Such benefits need not commence on the day of death: there could conceivably be a considerable delay before death benefits are provided.

**15-016**

### Options available

The pension death benefit rules therefore permit the payment of:

**15-017**

(a) Dependants' scheme pension.
(b) Dependants' annuity, nominees' annuity, and successors' annuity.
(c) Dependants' drawdown pension, nominees' drawdown pension, and successors' drawdown pension.

### "Dependant"

The following individuals are dependants of a member:[13]

**15-018**

(a) A person who was married to, or a civil partner of the member at the date of the member's death.
(b) If the rules of the pension scheme so provide, a person who was married to, or a civil partner of, the member when the member first became entitled to a pension under the pension scheme.
(c) A child of the member, if the child is: (i) under the age of 23; or (ii) age 23 or over and, in the opinion of the scheme administrator, was at the date of the member's death dependent on the member as a result of physical or mental impairment.
(d) A child of the member, if the child is age 23 or over and was not, in the opinion of the scheme administrator, at the date of the member's death dependent on the member because of physical or mental impairment. However, this does not apply for the purposes of dependants' scheme pension, or charity LSDB, or for the definition of nominee.
(e) Any person who was not married to, or a civil partner of, the member at the date of the member's death and is not a child of the member if, in the opinion of the scheme administrator, at the date of the member's death: (i) the person was financially dependent on the member; (ii) the person's financial relationship with the member was one of mutual dependence; or (iii) the person was dependent on the member because of physical or mental impairment.

---

[11] FA 2004 s.167(2).
[12] A pension or annuity with a fixed minimum term which continues to be payable after the member's death (which is authorised under pension rule 2) is not paid "on" the death of the member, as it is a continuation of the member's pension/annuity. The fact that it is paid to a nominated beneficiary may create some uncertainty, so s.167(2) expressly provides that it is not a death benefit.
[13] FA 2004 Sch.28 para.15. There are also transitional provisions in The Taxation of Pension Schemes (Transitional Provisions) Order 2006 (SI 2006/572) art.34 (relating to benefits commencing prior to 6 April 2006) and 34A (relating to benefits commencing on or before 1 July 2008), inserting FA 2004 Sch.28 paras 15(2)(c) and (d) regarding child dependants aged 23 or over.

**15-019**   The references in (c), (d) and (e) to the "opinion of the scheme administrator" do not permit an entirely subjective approach, or suggest that the scheme administrator does not require evidence.[14]

**"Nominee"**

**15-020**   A "nominee" of the member means an individual who is nominated by the member or the scheme administrator, but is not a dependant of the member.[15] It is unclear whether a class of individuals (such as "my children") can be nominees, and HMRC's views on this point are unknown. It is therefore preferable to identify each individual by name. In relation to any particular benefits under an arrangement, no individual nominated by the scheme administrator can be a nominee of the member at any time when there is a dependant of the member, or an individual, or charity, nominated by the member in relation to the benefits. Thus the scheme administrator can nominate an individual only where the member: (a) has not nominated anyone; and (b) has no dependants. The power of the member to nominate an individual for this purpose need not of course confer on the member a general power of appointment for inheritance tax purposes.[16] The member will usually nominate individuals in a written statement of his wishes, on terms that do not fetter the trustees' discretion.

**"Successor"**

**15-021**   A successor of the member is an individual who is nominated by a beneficiary (i.e. a dependant, or nominee, or successor of the member), or is nominated by the scheme administrator.[17] However in relation to any particular benefits under an arrangement relating to a beneficiary in that capacity, no individual nominated by the scheme administrator counts as a successor of the member at any time after the beneficiary's death when there is an individual, or charity, nominated by the beneficiary in relation to the benefits. Where a successor of the member is also a dependant of the member, he is treated as not being a dependant.

**Taxation of pension death benefits**

**15-022**   As with authorised pensions, authorised pension death benefits are taxable in accordance with ITEPA 2003 Pt 9 Ch.2 unless exempt under ITEPA 2003 Pt 9 Ch.17[18]

---

[14] *Wild v Smith* [1996] 2 F.L.R. 680; [1996] Pens. L.R. 275 concerned a trustee decision to provide death benefits to a "common law spouse". The scheme rules defined *dependant* as "any person whom the trustees may consider to have been at the time of the member's death ... dependent on the member ... for all or any of the ordinary necessaries of life ...". Carnwath J observed that the primary decision is thus that of the trustees, but that decision may be reviewed by the court not as a court of appeal but with a limited role. The principles were summarised by Glidewell LJ in *Harris v Lord Shuttleworth* [1994] I.C.R. 991; [1995] OPLR 79 at p.86H: "(a) The trustees must ask themselves the correct questions. (b) They must direct themselves correctly in law; in particular, they must adopt a correct construction of the pension fund rules. (c) They must not arrive at a perverse decision, i.e. a decision at which no reasonable body of trustees could arrive, and they must take into account all relevant but no irrelevant factors".

[15] FA 2004 Sch.28 para.27A.

[16] For general powers of appointment, see Ch.21.

[17] FA 2004 Sch.28 para.27F.

[18] ITEPA 2003 Pt 9 Ch.17 contains exemptions relating to awards for bravery, pensions in respect of death due to military or war service, lump sums provided under armed forces early departure scheme, wounds and disability pensions, compensation for National-Socialist persecution, Netherlands Benefit Act for Victims of Persecution 1940–1945, Malawi, Trinidad and Tobago and Zambia

or Ch.18.[19] The amount charged to tax is the full amount of pension income for the tax year, less any deductions allowable under ITEPA 2003 s.567A (deduction to avoid double taxation where ITEPA 2003 Pt 7A has applied to the source of the pension income), or ITEPA 2003 Pt 12 (charitable gifts via payroll).[20] Authorised pension death benefits are subject to tax as follows:

| Pension death benefit | Member (or other prior beneficiary) dies before age 75 | Member (or other prior beneficiary) dies age 75 or over |
|---|---|---|
| Dependants' scheme pension | •Recipient's marginal rate.[21] | •Recipient's marginal rate.[22] |
| Dependants' annuity | •Exempt unless (a) any payments made before 6 April 2015, or (b) it is purchased with uncrystallised funds after the relevant two-year period. Otherwise taxable at recipient's marginal rate.[23] | •Recipient's marginal rate.[24] |
| Dependants' drawdown pension | •Exempt unless (a) any drawdown pension paid before 6 April 2015, or (b) it consists of previously uncrystallised funds not designated within relevant two-year period. Otherwise taxable at recipient's marginal rate.[25] | •Recipient's marginal rate.[26] |
| Nominees' annuity | •Exempt unless (a) any payments made before 6 April 2015, or (b) it is purchased with uncrystallised funds after the relevant two-year period. Otherwise taxable at recipient's marginal rate.[27] | •Recipient's marginal rate.[28] |

---

government pensions, pensions payable where employment ceased due to disablement, health and employment insurance payments, social security pensions: increases in respect of children, former miners etc: coal and allowances in lieu, foreign pensions of consular employees, registered schemes: beneficiaries' annuities from unused funds, registered schemes: beneficiaries' annuities from drawdown funds, non-registered schemes: beneficiaries' annuities from unused funds, and non-registered schemes: beneficiaries' annuities from drawdown funds.

[19] ITEPA 2003 Pt 9 Ch.18 contains exemptions relating to pensions paid to non-UK residents under the Central African Pension Fund, Commonwealth government pension funds, the Oversea Superannuation Scheme, the Overseas Pensions Act 1973, the Overseas Service Act 1958, the Overseas Service Pensions Fund, and the Pensions (India, Pakistan and Burma) Act 1955.
[20] ITEPA 2003 s.567(2).
[21] ITEPA 2003 s.579A.
[22] ITEPA 2003 s.579A.
[23] ITEPA 2003 s.646B.
[24] ITEPA 2003 s.579A.
[25] ITEPA 2003 s.579CZA(1), (3)–(6) and s.646C(1).
[26] ITEPA 2003 s.579A.
[27] ITEPA 2003 s.646B.
[28] ITEPA 2003 s.579A.

| Nominees' drawdown pension | •Exempt unless consists of previously uncrystallised funds and is not designated within relevant two-year period. Otherwise taxable at recipient's marginal rate.[29] | •Recipient's marginal rate.[30] |
|---|---|---|
| Successors' annuity | •Exempt.[31] | •Recipient's marginal rate.[32] |
| Successors' drawdown pension | •Exempt.[33] | •Recipient's marginal rate.[34] |

*National insurance contributions*

**15-023**   Authorised death benefits are disregarded for NIC purposes.[35]

*Term certain payments*

**15-024**   Where a scheme pension or annuity payable to the member before his death continues to be paid for the duration of a guaranteed term certain, such payments are authorised member payments (as a result of pension rule 2); they are not death benefits. Such payments are however taxable in the same way as most death benefits: if the member dies before his 75th birthday they are not taxable under ITEPA 2003 Pt 9.[36]

**Scheme pension**

**15-025**   A scheme pension may be paid only to a dependant of the member. It is the only authorised pension death benefit that may be paid in respect of a defined benefits arrangement.[37] A pension payable to a dependant is a dependants' scheme pension if it is payable by the scheme administrator or by an insurance company selected by the scheme administrator.[38] If it is payable in respect of a money purchase arrangement, the member or dependant must have had the opportunity to select a dependants' annuity instead.[39] There are no further requirements. In contrast to a members' scheme pension, there is no requirement that a dependants' scheme pension must continue for the duration of the dependant's life, or that it must be paid at least annually, or that its annual rate may not decrease. There is no requirement that it commences within a certain period of time following the member's death. It is unnecessary for the member to have been entitled to a scheme pension before death, but if the member was so entitled (whether actually or prospectively), and

---

[29]   ITEPA 2003 s.579CZA(1) and (6) and s.646C.
[30]   ITEPA 2003 s.579A.
[31]   ITEPA 2003 s.646B.
[32]   ITEPA 2003 s.579A.
[33]   ITEPA 2003 ss.579CZA(2) and 646C.
[34]   ITEPA 2003 s.579A.
[35]   Social Security (Contributions) Regulations 2001 (SI 2001/1004) Sch.3 Pt VI para.2.
[36]   ITEPA 2003 s.646B(4).
[37]   FA 2004 s.167(1) (pension death benefit rule 2).
[38]   FA 2004 Sch.28 para.16.
[39]   FA 2004 s.167(1) (pension death benefit rule 3).

he died on or after his 75th birthday, the maximum rate of dependants' scheme pension may be restricted by the "dependants' scheme pension limit".

*The dependants' scheme pension limit*

**15-026** Payments in excess of the dependants' scheme pension limit are unauthorised payments.[40] The limit applies if: (a) the member dies on or after 6 April 2006 and after attaining age 75; (b) at the time of the member's death he was actually or prospectively entitled to a scheme pension under the pension scheme;[41] (c) the member was not entitled to enhanced protection immediately before his death;[42] and (d) the total annual rate of all dependants' scheme pensions paid in respect of the deceased member during any 12-month period (commencing with the date of death) exceeds both the "general limit" and the "personal limit". The "general limit" was £25,000 for the 2016/17 tax year, and for each subsequent tax year it is equal to the previous tax year's general limit increased by the highest of 5% or the percentage increase in either the CPI or the RPI between the September in the previous tax year and the September prior to that, rounded up to the nearest £100. The general limit is therefore £30,500 for the 2020/21 tax year. The "personal limit" for the tax year in which death occurs is the annual rate of all scheme pensions to which the member was actually or prospectively entitled immediately before death. For each subsequent tax year, the personal limit is equal to the personal limit applicable for the previous tax year increased by the greater of: (i) 5%; or (ii) the percentage increase in either the CPI or the RPI between the September in the previous tax year and the September prior to that, rounded up to the nearest £100.

**15-027** If the dependants' scheme pension limit applies, each payment of pension is an unauthorised payment to the extent that it exceeds either the "initial member pension limit" in the 12 months following the member's death, or the "current member pension limit" in any 12-month period following the first 12 months after the member's death:

(a) The "initial member pension limit" is: (i) the amount of scheme pension that the member was actually or prospectively entitled in the 12 months before death, plus (ii) 5% of any tax-free lump sum paid in connection with the member's scheme pension.[43] For 12-month periods ending on or after 6 April 2016, this amount is increased by the greater of the percentage increase in the CPI or the RPI from the month that entitlement to the lump sum arose to the month in which the member died.

(b) The "current member pension limit" is the "initial member pension limit" increased by 5% p/a (or, if higher, the annual rate agreed by HMRC for the purposes of the relevant valuation factor) or the percentage increase in the RPI from the month in which the member died to the first month of the 12-month period in question.

**15-028** **Exception** However in the following circumstances the payment of a dependants' scheme pension in excess of the current member pension limit is not an unauthorised payment where, for any 12-month period ending on or after 6 April 2016 (except the post-death year) in which the dependants' scheme pension is

---

[40] FA 2004 Sch.28 paras 16A–16C.
[41] References to a scheme pension include a pension payable before 6 April 2006 which would be a scheme pension if payable after that date.
[42] FA 2004 Sch.28 para.16AA.
[43] FA 2004 Sch.28 para.16B.

increased: (i) there are at least 50 pensioner members of the pension scheme at the start of the 12-month period, (ii) the dependant is one of a group of at least 20 pensioner members of the scheme, and (iii) any increases to the dependants' scheme pensions in that period are at the same rate for all the pensioner members of that group.

**Annuities**

15-029   The trustees or managers of a money purchase arrangement may purchase an annuity from an insurance company for a beneficiary. Dependants' annuities, nominees' annuities, and successors' annuities are all authorised pension death benefits. Such annuities are referred to in this chapter collectively as "beneficiaries' annuities". Such annuities can be purchased in the following circumstances:

(a) A dependants' annuity or nominees' annuity may be purchased at the same time that a lifetime annuity is purchased for the member (see Ch.13), albeit that the beneficiaries' annuity will not commence until the member dies. Such annuities are referred to as "related" annuities.

(b) A dependants' annuity or nominees' annuity may be purchased following the member's death using the member's uncrystallised funds.

(c) A beneficiaries' annuity may be purchased following the death of the member, dependant, nominee, or successor using the deceased's unused drawdown funds.

(d) A beneficiaries' annuity may be purchased from a dependant's drawdown pension fund or a beneficiary's flexi-access drawdown fund.

*Related annuities*

15-030   A beneficiaries' annuity is "related" to a lifetime annuity if they are both purchased from an insurance company either: (a) in the form of a joint life annuity; or (b) separately, if that they are both purchased within a seven-day period.[44] An annuity is a beneficiaries' annuity if one of the following applies:

(a) It is payable to a dependant, and either: (i) the member became entitled to the related lifetime annuity on or after 6 April 2015;[45] or (ii) the member became entitled to the related annuity before 6 April 2015,[46] the member or dependant had an opportunity to select the insurance company,[47] and the amount of the annuity either cannot decrease, or is determined in any manner prescribed by regulations made by HMRC.[48]

(b) It is payable to a nominee, the member became entitled to the related

---

[44] FA 2004 s.278B.
[45] FA 2004 Sch.28 para.17(1ZA). A person becomes *entitled* to an annuity when he first acquires an actual (rather than a prospective) right to receive the annuity (FA 2004 s.165(3)).
[46] FA 2004 Sch.28 para.17.
[47] This was called the *open market option*. It was designed to prevent pension providers from purchasing annuities from connected insurance companies as a matter of course. If the member/dependant had the opportunity to select an insurance company but failed to do so, the scheme administrator or trustees could select the insurance company.
[48] An annuity does not fail to satisfy this condition by reason of the operation of a pension sharing order or provision. The regulations referred to are The Registered Pension Schemes (Prescribed Manner of Determining Amount of Annuities) Regulations 2006 (SI 2006/568) reg.3. The circumstances in which the annual rate of income provided under a dependants' annuity may be varied are essentially the same as the circumstances in which the income provided by a member's lifetime annuity may be varied: see Ch.13.

lifetime annuity on or after 6 April 2015,[49] and it is payable until the nominee's death or until the earliest of the nominee getting married, entering into a civil partnership or dying.[50]

*Annuities acquired after death*

An annuity is a beneficiaries' annuity if it is purchased from an insurance company after the death of the member or previous beneficiary and one of the following applies: **15-031**

(a) It is payable to a dependant, and the dependant becomes entitled to it on or after 6 April 2015. Alternatively, it is payable to a dependant and: (i) the dependant became entitled to it before 6 April 2015;[51] (ii) the member or dependant had an opportunity to select the insurance company;[52] and (iii) the amount of the annuity either cannot decrease, or is determined in any manner prescribed by regulations made by HMRC.[53] If the dependant is not the member's child, the annuity must be payable until the dependant's death or until the earliest of the dependant getting married, entering into a civil partnership or dying. Where the dependant is the member's child, the annuity must be payable until the earlier of the dependant ceasing to be a dependant or dying, or until the earliest of the dependant getting married, entering into a civil partnership, ceasing to be a dependant or dying.[54]

(b) It is payable to a nominee and: (i) is payable until the nominee's death or until the earliest of the nominee getting married, entering into a civil partnership or dying;[55] (ii) the member dies on or after 3 December 2014; and (iii) the nominee became entitled to the annuity on or after 6 April 2015.

(c) It is payable to a successor,[56] and: (i) the successor becomes entitled to it on or after 6 April 2015; (ii) it is payable until the successor's death or until the earliest of the successor's marrying, entering into a civil partnership or dying; (iii) the previous beneficiary dies on or after 3 December 2014; and (iv) it is purchased using "undrawn funds". Undrawn funds means sums or assets held for the purposes of an arrangement after the beneficiary's death if, immediately before the beneficiary's death, they represented some or all of the beneficiary's drawdown pension fund or flexi-access drawdown fund.

---

[49] A nominees' annuity is purchased *together with* a lifetime annuity if they are either: (a) purchased in the form of a joint life annuity; or (b) purchased separately within a seven-day period.

[50] FA 2004 Sch.28 para.27AA. If a lifetime annuity payable to the member before his death continues to be paid for the duration of the fixed term, such annuity payments are not taxable under ITEPA 2003 Pt 9 if the member died before reaching age 75: ITEPA 2003 s.646B(4). This is not a nominees' annuity and is referenced here for completeness.

[51] FA 2004 Sch.28 para.17.

[52] This was called the *open market option*. It was designed to prevent pension providers from purchasing annuities from connected insurance companies as a matter of course. If the member/dependant had the opportunity to select an insurance company but failed to do so, the scheme administrator or trustees could select the insurance company.

[53] An annuity does not fail to satisfy this condition by reason of the operation of a pension sharing order or provision. The regulations referred to are SI 2006/568 reg.3. The circumstances in which the annual rate of income provided under a dependants' annuity may be varied are essentially the same as the circumstances in which the income provided by a member's lifetime annuity may be varied.

[54] FA 2004 Sch.28 para.17(1ZA).

[55] FA 2004 Sch.28 para.27AA. If a lifetime annuity payable to the member before his death continues to be paid for the duration of the fixed term, such annuity payments are not taxable under ITEPA 2003 Pt 9 if the member died before reaching age 75: ITEPA 2003 s.646B(4). This is not a nominees' annuity and is referenced here for completeness.

[56] FA 2004 Sch.28 para.27FA.

Funds that arise or derive from such undrawn funds (such as investment returns) are also undrawn funds.

**Drawdown pension**

15-032  Dependants' drawdown pension, nominees' drawdown pension and successors' drawdown pension are all authorised pension death benefits. They are referred to collectively in this chapter as beneficiaries' drawdown pension. Beneficiaries' drawdown pension means either: (a) a beneficiaries' short-term annuity; or (b) beneficiaries' income withdrawal.[57]

*Beneficiaries' short-term annuity*

15-033  An annuity payable by an insurance company to a beneficiary is a beneficiaries' short-term annuity if:[58] (a) it is purchased by the application of sums or assets representing the whole or any part of the beneficiary's flexi-access drawdown fund (or, the case of a dependant, the dependant's drawdown fund); (b) the beneficiary becomes entitled to it on or after 6 April 2015; and (c) it is payable for a term which does not exceed five years and ends before the beneficiary dies. If a dependant became entitled to the annuity before 6 April 2015 it must satisfy the above requirements and, in addition, the dependant must have been given an opportunity to select the insurance company, and the amount of the annuity either: (a) cannot decrease; or (b) is determined in any manner prescribed by regulations made by HMRC.[59]

*Beneficiaries' income withdrawal*

15-034  Beneficiaries' income withdrawal means an amount, other than an annuity, which the beneficiary is entitled to be paid from the beneficiary's flexi-access drawdown fund (or, in the case of a dependant, his dependants' drawdown pension fund).[60]

*Beneficiaries' flexi-access drawdown funds*

15-035  A dependant's flexi-access drawdown fund consists of such of the sums or assets held for the purposes of the arrangement as are "newly designated dependant funds".[61] Sums or assets are newly designated dependant funds if: (a) they are designated as available for the payment of dependants' drawdown pension after 5 April 2015; or (b) they were designated before that time and the conditions for flexible drawdown applied; or (c) they formed part of the dependant's capped drawdown fund before that date and they have since been converted to newly designated dependant funds (either automatically or by notice). In addition, any funds which arise or derive from newly designated dependant funds (or from funds which so arise or derive), are also newly designated dependant funds.

15-036  A nominee's flexi-access drawdown fund in respect of an arrangement consists

---

[57] FA 2004 Sch.28 para.18 (dependants); para.27B (nominees); para.27G (successors).
[58] FA 2004 Sch.28 para.20(1ZA) (dependants); FA 2004 Sch.28 para.27C (nominees); FA 2004 Sch.28 para.27H (successors).
[59] An annuity does not fail to satisfy this condition by reason of the operation of a pension sharing order or provision. The regulations referred to are SI 2006/568 reg.4. The circumstances in which the annual rate of income provided under a short-term annuity may be varied are essentially the same as the circumstances where the income provided by a member's lifetime annuity may be varied.
[60] FA 2004 Sch.28 paras 21 and 22 (dependants); para.27D (nominees); para.27J (successors).
[61] FA 2004 Sch.28 paras 22A–22D. These provisions mirror the provisions applicable to members' flexi-access drawdown funds (see Ch.13 for more detail).

of such of the sums or assets held for the purposes of the arrangement as are "newly designated nominee funds".[62] Sums or assets held for the purposes of an arrangement are newly designated nominee funds if they are designated as available for the payment of nominees' drawdown pension on or after 6 April 2015. Immediately before being so designated, such sums or assets must have been either:

(a) unused drawdown funds. Sums or assets held for the purposes of an arrangement after the member's death are unused drawdown funds if:[63] (i) immediately before the member's death, they were held for the purposes of the arrangement and represented (whether alone or with other sums or assets) the member's flexi-access drawdown fund or drawdown pension fund, or they arise or derive from such unused drawdown funds or from sums or assets which so arise or derive;[64] and (ii) since the member's death they have not been crystallised (i.e. designated as available for the payment of dependants' drawdown pension or nominees' drawdown pension, or applied towards the provision of a dependants' annuity, a nominees' annuity, or a dependants' scheme pension).

(b) unused uncrystallised funds. In the case of a cash balance arrangement, sums or assets held for the purposes of the arrangement after the member's death are unused uncrystallised funds if:[65] (i) they represent the whole or any part of the sum that would have been available immediately before the member's death for the provision of benefits to or in respect of the member if entitlement had arisen immediately before the member's death to all benefits under the arrangement to which entitlement had not previously arisen; and (ii) since the member's death they have not been crystallised.[66] In the case of an other money purchase arrangement, sums or assets held for the purposes of the arrangement after the member's death are unused uncrystallised funds if:[67] (i) immediately before the member's death they were held for the purposes of the arrangement and at that time were uncrystallised;[68] or they arise or derive from such sums or assets or from sums or assets which so arise or derive; and (ii) since the member's death they have not been crystallised.

Any sums or assets which arise or derive from newly designated nominee funds (such as investment returns) are also newly designated nominee funds. Such sums or assets do not need to be separately designated. So, post-death investment growth is included within unused uncrystallised funds in the case of an other money purchase arrangement (provided that they derive from unused uncrystallised funds), but not in the case of a cash balance arrangement. **15-037**

A successor's flexi-access drawdown fund in respect of an arrangement consists of such of the sums or assets held for the purposes of the arrangement as are newly **15-038**

---

[62] FA 2004 Sch.28 para.27E(1).
[63] FA 2004 Sch.28 para.27E(3).
[64] Unused drawdown funds therefore include investment returns, provided that they derive from designated sums or assets. This includes returns relating to investment made after the death of the member.
[65] FA 2004 Sch.28 para.27E(4).
[66] i.e. designated as available for the payment of dependants' drawdown pension or nominees' drawdown pension, or applied towards the provision of a dependants' annuity, a nominees' annuity, or a dependants' scheme pension.
[67] FA 2004 Sch.28 para.27E(5).
[68] i.e. the sums or assets were not member-designated funds or newly designated funds, and had not been applied towards the provision of a scheme pension or a dependants' scheme pension.

designated successor funds.[69] Sums or assets held for the purposes of an arrangement are newly designated successor funds if: (a) they are designated as available for the payment of successors' drawdown pension at any time on or after 6 April 2015; and (b) they were, immediately before being so designated, *unused drawdown funds* of the same deceased dependant, nominee or successor of the member. Any sums or assets which arise or derive from newly designated successor funds (such as investment returns) are also newly designated successor funds. Sums or assets held for the purposes of an arrangement after the death of a beneficiary (i.e. a dependant, nominee or successor) are unused drawdown funds of the beneficiary's if: (a) immediately before the beneficiary's death, they were held for the purposes of the arrangement and represented (whether alone or with other sums or assets) the beneficiary's drawdown pension fund or flexi-access drawdown fund, or they arise or derive from such funds or from sums or assets which so arise or derive;[70] and (b) since the beneficiary's death they have not been designated as available for the payment of successors' drawdown pension or applied towards the provision of a successors' annuity.

*Dependants' drawdown pension funds*

**15-039** Prior to 6 April 2015 there was only one type of drawdown pension fund. If a dependant met the "flexible drawdown" conditions in FA 2004 s.167(2A), he could be paid any amount under a short-term annuity or income withdrawal from the fund, and if he did not meet those conditions then the "capped drawdown" limits were imposed on the annual amount that could be paid under a short-term annuity or as income withdrawal from the fund.[71]

**15-040** On 6 April 2015, dependants' drawdown pension funds paying flexible drawdown automatically converted to dependants' flexi-access drawdown funds. Since 6 April 2015, a dependants' drawdown pension fund can only pay capped drawdown and it is only available to dependants who were in capped drawdown prior to 6 April 2015. No new dependants' drawdown pension funds can be created since 6 April 2015. It is a much more restricted option than flexi-access drawdown. A dependants' drawdown pension fund will automatically convert into a dependants' flexi-access drawdown fund if the conditions for capped drawdown are breached. Breaching the cap has no other implications.

**15-041** So, the dependant's drawdown pension fund consists of any sums or assets which were designated as available for capped drawdown prior to 6 April 2015 (and all sums or assets that arise or derive from such funds, such as investment returns). If such sums or assets are transferred to a new scheme then the sums or assets can be designated as available for the payment of dependant's drawdown pension under the new scheme (even on or after 6 April 2015). The sums or assets must not have been applied towards the provision of a scheme pension.

**15-042** If any sums or assets representing a dependant's drawdown pension fund would otherwise come to represent another dependant's drawdown pension fund of his under the pension scheme, or a drawdown pension fund of his under the pension

---

[69] FA 2004 Sch.28 para.27K.
[70] Unused drawdown funds therefore include investment returns, provided that they derive from designated sums or assets. This includes returns relating to investment made after the death of the member.
[71] These provisions mirror those for member's capped and flexible drawdown: see Ch.13. The provisions were repealed by TPA 2014 Sch.1 para.32(1)(d) with effect from 6 April 2015.

scheme, they are treated as not doing so.[72] The same applies where such sums or assets are applied towards the provision of a scheme pension or a lifetime annuity.

**Pension death benefit rule 4**   The amount that the dependant is entitled to be paid under a dependants' short-term annuity purchased using sums or assets from the dependant's drawdown pension fund is restricted by pension death benefit rule 4. The annuity must not exceed 150% of the basis amount for the drawdown pension year. A drawdown pension year is the period of 12 months from the day on which the member first becomes entitled to drawdown pension in respect of the arrangement, and each succeeding period of 12 months[73] until the member's death. The basis amount is, broadly speaking, the annual amount of an annuity which could have been purchased by the application of the sums and assets representing the member's drawdown pension fund.[74] There is no upper limit on the amount that can be paid under a dependants' short-term annuity purchased by the application of funds representing the dependants' flexi-access drawdown pension fund.

15-043

## AUTHORISED LUMP SUM DEATH BENEFITS

The list of authorised member payments in FA 2004 s.164(1) includes "lump sums permitted by... the 'lump sum death benefit rule' to be paid... in respect of a member".[75] The "lump sum death benefit rule" is that no lump sum death benefit may be paid in respect of a member of a registered pension scheme other than:[76]

15-044

(a) a defined benefits LSDB;
(b) a pension protection LSDB;
(c) an uncrystallised funds LSDB;
(d) an annuity protection LSDB;
(e) a drawdown pension fund LSDB;
(f) a flexi-access drawdown fund LSDB;
(g) a charity LSDB; or
(h) a trivial commutation LSDB (before 6 April 2024).

A "lump sum death benefit" means a lump sum payable on the death of the member, or a lump sum payable in respect of the member on the subsequent death of a dependant, nominee or successor of the member.[77] An "authorised lump sum death benefit" means a lump sum death benefit authorised to be paid by the lump sum death benefit rule.[78] A lump sum is payable "on" the death of the member or other beneficiary if it is payable as a result of the death. The requirement for death benefits to be paid "on" death does not impose a requirement that they are paid, or are capable of being paid (e.g. where assets must first be liquidated), on the date of death or immediately afterwards.

15-045

---

[72] FA 2004 Sch.28 para.22(3).
[73] FA 2004 Sch.28 para.23. This is subject to para.24B.
[74] The details are in FA 2004 Sch.28 paras 23–24B and 14 and The Registered Pension Schemes (Relevant Annuities) Regulations 2006 (SI 2006/129).
[75] FA 2004 s.164(1)(b).
[76] FA 2004 s.168. It was also possible to pay a winding-up LSDB prior to 6 April 2015 (see PTM073800).
[77] FA 2004 s.168(2).
[78] FA 2004 Sch.29 para.22(3).

## Taxation of authorised LSDBs

**15-046** Authorised LSDBs are taxed as follows:

| Lump sum death benefit | Member (or other prior beneficiary) dies before age 75 | Member (or other prior beneficiary) dies age 75 or over: Individual recipient | Member (or other prior beneficiary) dies age 75 or over: Non-individual recipient |
|---|---|---|---|
| Defined benefits LSDB | Tax-free if the lump sum is: (a) paid within relevant two-year period; and (b) does not exceed so much of the member's LS&DB allowance as is available immediately before it is paid.[79] If it exceeds the member's available LS&DB allowance, the excess is taxed under s.579A. If not paid within relevant two-year period, it is taxed as if the member had died aged 75 or over. | Recipient's marginal rate.[80] | 45% special LSDB charge.[81] |
| Pension protection LSDB | Tax-free, except to the extent that it exceeds the member's available LS&DB allowance.[82] Any excess is taxed as pension income under s.579A. | Recipient's marginal rate.[83] | 45% special LSDB charge.[84] |

---

[79] ITEPA 2003 s.637H.
[80] ITEPA 2003 s.637H(5), applying s.579A.
[81] ITEPA 2003 s.637H(6), applying FA 2004 s.206.
[82] ITEPA 2003 s.637. It need not be paid within the relevant two-year period.
[83] ITEPA 2003 s.637I(3), applying s.579A.
[84] ITEPA 2003 s.637I(4), applying FA 2004 s.206.

| Uncrystallised funds LSDB | Tax-free if paid within relevant two-year period.[85] Any amount paid in excess of the member's available LS&DB allowance is taxable as pension income under ITEPA 2003 s.579A. If not paid within relevant two-year period, it is taxed as if the member had died aged 75 or over. | Recipient's marginal rate.[86] | 45% special LSDB charge.[87] |
|---|---|---|---|
| Annuity protection LSDB | Tax-free, except to the extent that it exceeds the member's available LS&DB allowance.[88] Any excess is taxed as pension income under s.579A. | Recipient's marginal rate.[89] | 45% special LSDB charge.[90] |
| Drawdown pension fund LSDB | Tax-free if paid within relevant two-year period.[91] Any amount paid in excess of the member's available LS&DB allowance is taxable as pension income under ITEPA 2003 s.579A. If not paid within relevant two-year period, it is taxed as if the member had died aged 75 or over. | Recipient's marginal rate.[92] | 45% special LSDB charge.[93] |

---

[85] ITEPA 2003 s.637J.
[86] ITEPA 2003 s.637J(5), applying s.579A.
[87] ITEPA 2003 s.637J(6), applying FA 2004 s.206.
[88] ITEPA 2003 s.637K. It need not be paid within the relevant two-year period.
[89] ITEPA 2003 s.637K(3), applying s.579A.
[90] ITEPA 2003 s.637K(4), applying FA 2004 s.206.
[91] ITEPA 2003 s.637L.
[92] ITEPA 2003 s.637L(5), applying s.579A.
[93] ITEPA 2003 s.637L(6), applying FA 2004 s.206.

| Flexi-access drawdown fund LSDB | Tax-free if paid within relevant two-year period.[94] Any amount paid in excess of the member's available LS&DB allowance is taxable as pension income under ITEPA 2003 s.579A. If not paid within relevant two-year period, it is taxed as if the member had died aged 75 or over. | Recipient's marginal rate.[95] | 45% special LSDB charge.[96] |
|---|---|---|---|
| Charity LSDB | Not subject to tax.[97] | Not subject to tax. | Not subject to tax. |
| Trivial commutation LSDB | Deemed to be pension income, so exempt (except possibly on commutation of dependants' scheme pension).[98] | Deemed to be pension income, so taxable at recipient's marginal rate.[99] | N/A: must be paid to individual.[100] |

*The special LSDB charge*

**15-047** FA 2004 s.206 contains provisions relating to the special LSDB (other than a charity LSDB) charge. The scheme administrator is liable for the charge,[101] and will typically deduct it from the payment of the lump sum death benefit and pay it to HMRC under the accounting for tax return procedure.[102] The rate of the charge is 45% of the amount of the lump sum paid.[103] If the rules of the pension scheme permit the scheme administrator to deduct the tax before payment, the charge applies to the amount of the lump sum before deduction of the tax.

**15-048** The charge arises where an authorised LSDB (other than a charity LSDB) is paid

---

[94] ITEPA 2003 s.637M.
[95] ITEPA 2003 s.637M(5), applying s.579A.
[96] ITEPA 2003 s.637M(6), applying FA 2004 s.206.
[97] This is not because any exemption applies, but because no provision subjects it to tax.
[98] ITEPA 2003 s.637N and the relevant provision for the pension that is commuted.
[99] ITEPA 2003 s.637N.
[100] FA 2004 Sch.29 para.20(1).
[101] In the case of a scheme which is a "split scheme" for the purposes of The Registered Pension Schemes (Splitting of Schemes) Regulations 2006 (SI 2006/569), references to the scheme administrator are read as references to the sub-scheme administrator (within the meaning of those regulations). An insurance company is treated as the scheme administrator for the purposes of FA 2004 s.206 (and so is responsible for paying the special LSDB charge) if it pays any of the following under an insurance contract or annuity purchased using funds held for the purpose of a registered pension scheme: (a) a pension protection LSDB; (b) an annuity protection LSDB; (c) a drawdown pension fund LSDB; or (d) a flexi-access drawdown fund LSDB (FA 2004 s.273A and The Pension Benefits (Insurance Company Liable as Scheme Administrator) Regulations 2006 (SI 2006/136).
[102] For the accounting for tax return, see Ch.19.
[103] The rate was 55% for lump sums paid before 6 April 2015. The provisions do not prescribe how to value benefits which are paid *in specie*.

to a "non-qualifying person":

(a) in respect of a member who had reached the age of 75 at the date of the member's death, or
(b) in respect of a member who had *not* reached the age of 75 at the date of the member's death, if the payment is not made with the relevant two-year period.[104]

**"Non-qualifying person"** A person is a non-qualifying person in relation to the payment of a lump sum if:[105]   **15-049**

(a) the person is not an individual; or
(b) the person is an individual and the payment is made to the person in the person's capacity as:
  (i) a trustee or personal representative;
  (ii) a director of a company;[106]
  (iii) a partner in a firm;[107] or
  (iv) a member of a LLP,
except that a person is not a non-qualifying person in relation to payment of a lump sum if the payment is made to the person in the person's capacity as a bare trustee.

A "bare trustee" means a person acting as trustee for: (a) an individual absolutely entitled as against the trustee; (b) two or more individuals who are so entitled; (c) an individual who would be so entitled but for being a minor or otherwise lacking legal capacity; or (d) two or more individuals who would be so entitled but for all or any of them being a minor or otherwise lacking legal capacity.   **15-050**

On its face, the exception for bare trustees applies to a payment to an individual as bare trustee for an individual within one of (i) to (iv), or as bare trustee for a company, but that is plainly not intended. The intention is that a payment is excepted if it is to a non-individual as bare trustee for an individual.   **15-051**

**Defined benefits LSDB**

A defined benefits LSDB means a lump sum death benefit:[108]   **15-052**

(a) paid in respect of a defined benefits arrangement; and
(b) not a pension protection LSDB, or a trivial commutation LSDB.

There are no restrictions relating to the amount of the lump sum, or the timing of the payment, or the identity of the recipient. In order for a lump sum to be paid "in respect of" a defined benefits arrangement, the lump sum must form part of the member's arrangement. In other words, the trustees must be legally obliged to make such a payment, although they may have some discretion regarding when and to whom it is paid.

---

[104] For the relevant two-year period, see para.15-012.
[105] FA 2004 s.206(9).
[106] "Director" is read in accordance with CTA 2010 s.452.
[107] References to a firm are read in the same way as references to a firm in ITTOIA 2005 Pt 9 (which contains special provision about partnerships).
[108] FA 2004 Sch.29 para.13.

### Uncrystallised funds LSDB

**15-053** A lump sum death benefit is an uncrystallised funds LSDB if it is paid in respect of "relevant uncrystallised funds" under a money purchase arrangement and it is not a charity LSDB.[109] "Relevant uncrystallised funds" means such of the sums and assets held for the purposes of the arrangement at the member's death as: (a) had not been applied for purchasing a scheme pension, a lifetime annuity, a nominees' annuity, a dependants' scheme pension or a dependants' annuity; and (b) had not been designated under the arrangement as available for the payment of drawdown pension.[110] It seems that any investment income received after the member's death relating to assets which are the relevant uncrystallised funds cannot be relevant uncrystallised funds. The definition does not include sums or assets which arise or derive from relevant uncrystallised funds. On the face of it, if an asset forming part of the relevant uncrystallised funds is sold after the member's death, the sale proceeds cannot be paid as an uncrystallised funds LSDB. Similarly, where the scheme holds a life policy insured on the member's life, the proceeds of that policy cannot be paid as an uncrystallised funds LSDB.

**15-054** In the following circumstances sums or assets contributed to a cash balance arrangement after the death of the member are expressly treated as relevant uncrystallised funds:[111] (a) under the arrangement, a dependant of the member is entitled to be paid after the member's death an amount by way of a lump sum; (b) the dependant's entitlement to a lump sum of that amount under the arrangement comes into being at a time no later than the member's death; (c) such of the sums and assets held for the purposes of the arrangement immediately after the member's death as are held for the purpose of meeting the liability to pay the lump sum are insufficient for that purpose (including where that is because none are held for that purpose); and (d) a person who was an employer in relation to the member pays a contribution to the scheme for or towards making good that insufficiency, and of no more than is needed for making good the insufficiency.

*Permitted maximum*

**15-055** A lump sum is not an uncrystallised funds LSDB to the extent that it exceeds the amount of the sums, and the market value of the assets, which constitute the relevant uncrystallised funds immediately before the payment is made. As noted above, sums and assets are relevant uncrystallised funds only if they are held for the purposes of the arrangement at the member's death. The value of those assets may increase after the member's death (as a result of investment return, for example), and where that is the case the full amount can be paid as an uncrystallised funds LSDB.

### Pension protection LSDB

**15-056** A lump sum death benefit is a pension protection LSDB if:[112] (a) it is paid in respect of a defined benefits arrangement; (b) it is paid in respect of a scheme pension to which the member was entitled at the date of his death; and (c) the member specified that it is to be treated as a pension protection LSDB (rather than a defined

---

[109] FA 2004 Sch.29 para.15.
[110] FA 2004 Sch.29 para.15(2).
[111] FA 2004 Sch.29 para.15(2A).
[112] FA 2004 Sch.29 para.14.

benefits LSDB).[113] But such a lump sum is a pension protection LSDB only to the extent that it does not exceed the "pension protection limit". The pension protection limit is equal to:[114]

(a) the amount crystallised when the member became entitled to the pension (or, where the member became so entitled after attaining age 75, the amount that would have crystallised if BCE 2 were capable of occurring after the member's 75th birthday); less
(b) the amount of the pension paid in respect of the period between the member becoming entitled to the pension and the member's death; less
(c) the amount of any pension protection LSDB previously paid in respect of the pension.

This authorised death benefit allows a pension scheme or insurance company to guarantee that if the member receives less scheme pension during his life than the amount which crystallised, the balance will be paid as a lump sum death benefit. HMRC suggest[115] that the promise must be put in place when the pension commences, and that will no doubt usually be the case, but it is not an express requirement. Therefore the lump sum must be paid "in respect of" a defined benefits arrangement, so the promise must be given to the member during his life. To the extent that the payment exceeds the pension protection limit, it will not be a pension protection LSDB but it may be a defined benefits LSDB.[116] If it does not satisfy the requirements of another authorised payment, it will be an unauthorised payment.

15-057

**Annuity protection LSDB**

A lump sum death benefit is an annuity protection LSDB if: (a) it is paid in respect of a money purchase arrangement; and (b) it is paid in respect of a scheme pension or lifetime annuity to which the member was entitled at the date of the member's death.[117] But such a lump sum is an annuity protection LSDB only to the extent that it does not exceed the "annuity protection limit", which is equal to:[118]

(a) the amount crystallised under BCE 2 or BCE 4 when the member became entitled to the pension or annuity[119] (or, where the member became so entitled after attaining age 75, the amount that would have crystallised if BCE 2 or BCE 4 could occur after the member's 75th birthday);[120] less

15-058

---

[113] To the extent that the payment exceeds the pension protection limit, it will be an unauthorised payment unless it satisfies the requirements of another type of authorised payment. There seems to be no reason that the excess could not be a defined benefits LSDB.
[114] FA 2004 Sch.29 para.14(3). These provisions are modified in relation to pensions that commenced before 6 April 2006 (see SI 2006/572 art.33).
[115] PTM073300.
[116] The fact that the member will have specified that it is to be treated as a pension protection LSDB rather than a defined benefits LSDB does not appear to preclude the excess from being a defined benefits LSDB.
[117] FA 2004 Sch.29 para.16.
[118] These provisions are modified by SI 2006/572 art.33 in relation to pensions and annuities that commenced before 6 April 2006.
[119] If the scheme pension or lifetime annuity is purchased from funds which were previously designated as available for the payment of drawdown, the amount that crystallises under BCE 2 or BCE 4 is reduced by the amount so designated (which is BCE 1). One disregards this reduction for the purposes of the annuity protection limit.
[120] BCE 2 or 4 cannot occur after the member's 75th birthday as a result of FA 2004 Sch.32 para.2. This is disregarded so that BCE 2 or 4 can apply for these purposes. Again, if the scheme pension or lifetime annuity is purchased from funds which were previously designated as available for the pay-

(b) the amount of the pension paid in respect of the period between the member becoming entitled to the pension or annuity and the member's death; less

(c) the amount of any annuity protection LSDB previously paid in respect of the pension or annuity.

**15-059** The purpose of this authorised payment is to permit a pension scheme or insurance company to provide the member with a promise that if he receives less than a minimum total amount of scheme pension or lifetime annuity during his life, the balance will be paid as a lump sum death benefit. HMRC suggest[121] that the promise must be put in place when the pension commences, and that will no doubt usually be the case, but that is not an express requirement. However, the requirement that it must be paid in respect of a scheme pension or lifetime annuity to which the member was entitled at death means that the promise must be given prior to the member's death.[122] To the extent that the payment exceeds the annuity protection limit, it will be an unauthorised payment unless it satisfies the requirements of another type of authorised payment.

**Drawdown pension fund LSDB**

**15-060** A lump sum death benefit is a drawdown pension fund LSDB if:[123] (a) it is not a charity LSDB; (b) it does not exceed the permitted maximum; and (c) it is paid either: (i) in respect of income withdrawal to which the member was entitled to be paid from the member's drawdown pension fund[124] at the date of the member's death; or (ii) on the death of a dependant of the member, and it is paid in respect of dependants' income withdrawal to which the dependant was entitled at the date of the dependant's death to be paid from his drawdown pension fund in respect of an arrangement relating to the member.

*Permitted maximum*

**15-061** A lump sum is not a drawdown pension fund LSDB to the extent that it exceeds the amounts of the sums and the market value of the assets representing the member's or dependant's drawdown pension fund in respect of the arrangement immediately before the payment is made. This is a reference to sums or assets: (a) which are held for the purposes of an arrangement immediately before the payment is made; and (b) were designated as available for the payment of capped drawdown pension, or arise or derive from such designated sums or assets.[125] Any such sums or assets which have been applied towards the provision of a scheme pension are expressly disregarded.

**15-062** Post-death investment return can be included within such a lump sum.[126] The permitted maximum is concerned with the value of the sums or assets im-

---

ment of drawdown, one disregards the reduction that would otherwise be made to reflect the previous BCE 1.

[121] PTM073400.

[122] The payment of a pension protection LSDB is tax-free even if not paid with the relevant two-year period (assuming the member died under the age of 75). This treatment makes sense only for sums and assets which crystallised prior to the member's death.

[123] FA 2004 Sch.29 para.17.

[124] A drawdown fund is a capped drawdown fund created before 6 April 2015 which has not been converted into a flexi-access drawdown fund. See Ch.13.

[125] FA 2004 Sch.28 paras 8 and 22.

[126] This is also HMRC's position. PTM073500: "... any growth in the value of the capped drawdown pension fund between the date of the member's or dependant's death and the date the lump sum is paid is part of the drawdown pension fund lump sum death benefit".

mediately before the payment is made (rather than immediately before death). The lump sum must be paid "in respect of" income withdrawal to which the member or dependant was entitled to be paid from the drawdown pension fund at the date of death, but this does not mean that income received post-death is not included. A lump sum is paid "in respect of" income withdrawal if the member or dependant was entitled to income withdrawal before death, and the lump sum comprises the sums and assets held for the purposes of the fund to which the entitlement related. If the assets include a life policy, the proceeds of such a policy could be paid as a drawdown pension fund LSDB.

The value of a lifetime annuity or short-term annuity purchased with sums or assets from the drawdown pension fund (which may form an asset of the drawdown pension fund) is not disregarded for the purposes of the permitted maximum. However, to the extent that a lump sum relates to the value of any such annuity, it would not be paid "in respect of" income withdrawal. This is because income withdrawal means an amount, *other than an annuity*, which the member or dependant is entitled to be paid from his drawdown pension fund.[127]

**Flexi-access drawdown fund LSDB**

A lump sum death benefit is a flexi-access drawdown fund LSDB if it is not a charity LSDB and one of the following applies:[128]

(a) it is paid in respect of income withdrawal to which the member was entitled to be paid from the member's flexi-access drawdown fund in respect of an arrangement at the date of the member's death; or

(b) it is paid on the death of a dependant of the member, and it is paid in respect of dependants' income withdrawal to which the dependant was at the date of the dependant's death entitled to be paid from the dependant's flexi-access drawdown fund in respect of an arrangement relating to the member; or

(c) it is paid on the death of a nominee of the member, and it is paid in respect of nominees' income withdrawal to which the nominee was at the date of the nominee's death entitled to be paid from the nominee's flexi-access drawdown fund in respect of an arrangement relating to the member; or

(d) it is paid on the death of a successor of the member, and it is paid in respect of successors' income withdrawal to which the successor was at the date of the successor's death entitled to be paid from the successor's flexi-access drawdown fund in respect of an arrangement relating to the member.

*Permitted maximum*

A lump sum is not a flexi-access drawdown fund LSDB to the extent that it exceeds the amounts of the sums and the market value of any assets representing the member's, dependant's, nominee's or successor's flexi-access drawdown fund in respect of the arrangement immediately before the payment is made. The analysis above relating to the permitted maximum in respect of drawdown pension fund

15-063

15-064

15-065

---

[127] FA 2004 Sch.28 paras 7 and 21. Any lifetime annuities could pay death benefits in the form of annuity protection LSDB. Short-term annuities cannot pay death benefits as such, but they can be guaranteed to continue making payments for a fixed period not exceeding five years (notwithstanding the death of the member).

[128] FA 2004 Sch.29 para.17A.

LSDB applies equally to flexi-access drawdown fund LSDB.[129] However, in contrast to the position regarding drawdown pension, there is nothing in the relevant provisions[130] which expressly excludes the value of sums and assets which have been applied towards the provision of a scheme pension. On the face of it, therefore, where sums or assets representing the member's flexi-access drawdown fund have been applied towards the provision of a scheme pension, it appears that the value of the pension is taken into account when calculating the permitted maximum.

**Charity LSDB**

15-066   On the death of a member a charity LSDB may be paid in respect of: (a) uncrystallised funds; or (b) drawdown funds. Such a lump sum may also be paid on the death of a dependant, nominee, or successor, from drawdown funds.

15-067   As will be seen below, the requirements of a charity LSDB are more restrictive than one would perhaps expect given that charitable giving is generally encouraged. Where the deceased has a dependant, the intention is perhaps that death benefits will be paid to the dependant who can then pay them to the charity (and would typically obtain tax relief).

*Uncrystallised funds*

15-068   A lump sum death benefit is a charity LSDB if:[131]

(a)   there are no dependants of the member;
(b)   it is paid in respect of "relevant uncrystallised funds" in respect of a money purchase arrangement at the date of the member's death; and
(c)   it is paid to a charity nominated by the member.

Sums or assets are "relevant uncrystallised funds" if they are held for the purposes of the arrangement at the member's death and have not been designated as available for the payment of drawdown pension, or applied to purchase a scheme pension, lifetime annuity, nominees' annuity, dependants' scheme pension or dependants' annuity.[132] This is the same definition as applies for the purposes of uncrystallised funds LSDB. As with uncrystallised funds LSDB, it seems that any investment income received after the member's death relating to assets which are the relevant uncrystallised funds cannot be relevant uncrystallised funds. There is however no permitted maximum for relevant uncrystallised funds paid as a charity LSDB.

*Drawdown funds*

15-069   A lump sum death benefit is a charity LSDB if:[133]

(a)   there are no dependants of the member;

---

[129] HMRC's position is set out at PTM073600 provides that "The maximum amount of lump sum payable is an amount equal to the combined total of all the sums and the market value of the assets representing the member's or appropriate beneficiary's flexi-access drawdown fund in respect of the arrangement immediately before the payment is made. So the maximum is effectively whatever was held in the fund at the date of payment".
[130] FA 2004 Sch.28 paras 8A, 22A, 27E and 27K.
[131] FA 2004 Sch.29 para.18(1). For payments before 16 September 2016 it was also a requirement that the member had reached the age of 75 at the date of his death.
[132] FA 2004 Sch.29 para.15(2).
[133] FA 2004 Sch.29 para.18(1A).

# AUTHORISED LUMP SUM DEATH BENEFITS

(b) it is paid in respect of "relevant uncrystallised funds" in respect of a money purchase arrangement at the date of the member's death; and

(c) it is paid to a charity nominated by the member.

**15-070** A lump sum death benefit is also a charity LSDB if: (a) it is paid on the death of a beneficiary (i.e. a dependant, nominee or successor) of the member; (b) there are no dependants of the member (or, where the beneficiary is a dependant, there are no *other* dependants of the member); (c) it is paid in respect of the beneficiary's flexi-access drawdown fund (or, in the case of a dependant, the dependant's drawdown pension fund), at the date of the beneficiary's death in respect of an arrangement relating to the member; and (d) it is paid to a charity nominated by the member or, if the member made no nomination, by the beneficiary.

**15-071** Where the lump sum is paid in respect of a drawdown fund or flexi-access drawdown fund, it is not a charity LSDB to the extent that it exceeds the amount of the sums and the market value of the assets representing the member's or other beneficiary's drawdown pension fund or flexi-access drawdown fund immediately before the payment is made. The analysis above relating to the permitted maximum in respect of drawdown pension fund LSDB and flexi-access drawdown fund LSDB applies equally here.

## Trivial commutation LSDB

**15-072** A lump sum is a trivial commutation LSDB if the amount of the lump sum is £30,000 or less and the requirements below are satisfied.[134] The £30,000 limit is per scheme. The requirements are different depending on whether the lump sum is paid to a dependant or another individual (it is not possible to pay such a lump sum to a non-individual). To the extent that such a lump sum exceeds £30,000, it is not a trivial commutation LSDB and so will be an unauthorised payment unless it can be paid as some other authorised payment.

### Paid to dependant

**15-073** A lump sum death benefit is a trivial commutation LSDB if it is paid to a dependant entitled under the scheme to pension death benefit in respect of the member, provided that the payment extinguishes the dependant's entitlement under the pension scheme to pension death benefit and lump sum death benefit in respect of the member.

### Paid to any individual

**15-074** A lump sum death benefit is a trivial commutation LSDB if it is paid to any individual provided that: (a) the individual is entitled to be paid a pension under the scheme which the member was entitled to be paid immediately before the member's death, and it is payable to the individual under pension rule 2;[135] (b) if the pension is an annuity or scheme pension payable by an insurance company, the lump sum extinguishes all entitlements in respect of the member under the contract concerned; and (c) if the pension is a scheme pension payable by the scheme administrator, the lump sum extinguishes all entitlements to receive a scheme pension in respect of the member from the scheme administrator under pension rule 2.

---

[134] FA 2004 Sch.29 para.20.
[135] For pension rule 2, see Ch.13.

**Life cover lump sum**

**15-075** Prior to 6 April 2006, it was permitted for a tax-approved retirement benefit scheme to pay a small lump sum death benefit to meet the cost of his funeral expenses. A lump sum death benefit is a life cover lump sum (and therefore an authorised payment) if all of the following requirements are satisfied:[136]

(a) the member died after attaining the age of 75;
(b) payment of the sum would not have prejudiced the tax-approval of the scheme if it had been made on 5 April 2006.
(c) the registered pension scheme was, immediately before 6 April 2006, a tax-approved retirement benefits scheme;
(d) the member had a right under the pension scheme to a life cover lump sum on 5 April 2006;
(e) the rules of the pension scheme on 10 December 2003 included provision conferring such a right on some or all of the persons who were then members of the pension scheme, and such a right was either then conferred on the member or would have been had the member been a member of the scheme on that date;
(f) the rules of the scheme in relation to life cover lump sums have not been changed since 10 December 2003; and
(g) the member was in receipt of benefits from the scheme on or before 5 April 2006, or entitled to one or more life cover lump sums amounting in total to £2,500 or less.

**15-076** A life cover lump sum is not subject to income tax.[137]

# TRUSTS OF DEATH BENEFITS

**15-077** In contrast to authorised *pension* death benefits, *lump sum* death benefits can be paid to a non-individual. A payment to trustees (even where the trustees are all individuals) is deemed to be a payment to a non-individual.[138] It is not uncommon for lump sum death benefits to be paid to a discretionary settlement established for the benefit of the member's family.[139] If the member dies before his 75th birthday then the payment is tax-free, and is otherwise subject to the 45% special LSDB charge.

**Payments not subject to the special LSDB charge**

**15-078** The source of the sums and assets in the settlement may be the pension scheme, but any distributions from such a settlement are not pension income for the purposes of ITEPA 2003 Pt 9 (unless exceptionally, the settlement is itself a pension scheme). The usual rules that apply to distributions from family discretionary settlements apply. Thus, if the payments are annual payments then they will be taxable under ITTOIA 2005 s.683. Any payment by trustees in exercise of a power over trust income will always be income in the hands of the recipient and taxed as an annual payment. Payments which are not annual payments and are paid in exercise of a

---

[136] FA 2004 Sch.29 para.21A, inserted by SI 2006/572 arts 6 and 8.
[137] ITEPA 2003 s.636(1)(g), inserted by SI 2006/572 art.7.
[138] FA 2004 s.206(9)(b).
[139] The inheritance tax implications of such settlements are considered in Ch.20.

power over trust capital (including accumulated income),[140] are capital and not income in the hands of the beneficiary[141] unless the purpose of the power/trust is to augment an income interest held by the beneficiary.[142] This is the case even if the payment is to satisfy an "income purpose" (e.g. the maintenance of a beneficiary), unless the terms of the trust require payments to be made expressly to supplement income.

**Payments subject to the special LSDB charge**

Special provisions apply where: (a) a lump sum death benefit that is subject to the special LSDB charge is paid to a trustee[143] (in his capacity as trustee); and (b) a payment of any part of the lump sum is made out of a settlement to a beneficiary who is an individual.[144] In these circumstances, the amount received by the beneficiary, together with the amount of the special LSDB charge that is attributable to the amount received by the beneficiary, is expressly income of the beneficiary for income tax purposes. This therefore effectively creates a double charge. However, the beneficiary may set off the amount of the special LSDB charge paid by the scheme administrator against his own tax due on the payment from the settlement.[145] 15-079

For example, if a registered pension scheme intends to pay £100 to a settlement, the scheme administrator will pay £45 to HMRC and £55 to the settlement. If the settlement subsequently pays the £55 to a beneficiary, the beneficiary is deemed to receive income of £100 but he may deduct £45 from his income tax liability for the year in which the payment is made. If the beneficiary is a basic rate taxpayer, and has no other tax liability for the year, his liability for £20 is reduced by the £45 paid by the scheme administrator of the registered pension scheme. Can the beneficiary claim the additional £25 from HMRC? FA 2004 s.206(8) refers to a "deduction" but not a "repayment". However, PTM073010 explains that HMRC will repay the £25. The overall tax liability is therefore equal to the beneficiary's marginal rate of income tax, as it would have been if he had received the payment directly from the registered pension scheme. 15-080

**Disguised remuneration**

In certain circumstances the disguised remuneration provisions in ITEPA 2003 Pt 7A could conceivably apply to trusts of death benefits. The exemptions applicable to registered pension schemes do not appear to apply to a discretionary settlement that has received death benefits from a registered pension scheme. That settlement will not itself be a "relevant arrangement" because it will not usually have any employment nexus, however if the registered pension scheme is an occupational scheme (and therefore a relevant arrangement) the effect of s.554A(11) 15-081

---

[140] *Stanley v IRC* [1944] K.B. 255; [1944] 1 All E.R. 230.
[141] *Stevenson v Wishart* 59 T.C. 740.
[142] *Cunard's Trustees v IRC* (1945) 27 T.C. 122.
[143] Other than a bare trustee (being a person acting as trustee for an individual absolutely entitled as against the trustee, or who would be so entitled but for being a minor or otherwise lacking legal capacity).
[144] FA 2004 s.206(8). This is only applicable to lump sums paid after 5 April 2016. The scheme administrator must provide prescribed information to the trustees of the settlement and the trustees must provide prescribed information to the beneficiary (SI 2006/567 reg.10A and 10B).
[145] The claim is made in the beneficiary's self-assessment tax return or using form R40.

appears to be that a step taken by the death benefits settlement may be a relevant step (see Ch.22). If correct, this is a very surprising and presumably unintended consequence. The disguised remuneration provisions are considered in detail in Ch.27.

# CHAPTER 16

# Pensions on Divorce

## TABLE OF CONTENTS

| | |
|---|---|
| Introduction | 16-001 |
| FA 2004 and pension sharing orders | 16-003 |
| The LS&DB allowance | 16-005 |
|     LS allowance and LS&DB allowance enhancement factors | 16-008 |
|     The pension credit factor | 16-009 |
|     The pre-commencement pension credit factor | 16-010 |
|     Debited member with primary protection | 16-012 |

## INTRODUCTION

There are three main methods by which a court may deal with pensions in divorce proceedings[1]: **16-001**

(a) By offsetting the member's pension rights against other assets (such as property or cash) of commensurate value. The scheme member retains his pension rights and the spouse is awarded other assets. This is the most straightforward and common method of dealing with pension rights, but it is not always satisfactory.

(b) By making a pension attachment order[2] (sometimes referred to as "earmarking"), directing the trustees to pay a percentage of the member's pension benefits (pension, and/or lump sum, and/or death benefits) to the former spouse at the time those benefits become payable. Attachment orders were introduced in July 1996 to address some of the perceived deficiencies of offsetting. Attachment orders are themselves frequently unsatisfactory in a number of respects, including that the recipient cannot compel the paying party to continue in pensionable service (or make further contributions), and cannot control when that person retires, any right to periodical payments will usually cease on the death or remarriage of the recipient,[3] and they inhibit a clean break between the parties. Although paid to the former spouse, the entire benefits are taxable on the member, which is usually tax-inefficient.

---

[1] For the purposes of this chapter, "spouse" and "divorce" include, respectively, civil partner and dissolution of a civil partnership. For more information on the treatment of pensions on divorce, see *A Guide to the Treatment of Pensions on Divorce*, Pension Advisory Group (July 2019).

[2] Under the Matrimonial Causes Act 1973 ss.25B–25D, or the Civil Partnership Act 2004 Sch.5 Pt 6 para.24.

[3] See Matrimonial Causes Act 1973 s.28.

(c) By making a pension sharing order, directing the trustees to reallocate a percentage of the member's rights for his spouse. The rights obtained by the former spouse are those of a scheme member, separate and distinct from those of the member. The spouse receiving the pension rights may either retain them in the same pension scheme as the former spouse, or direct the trustees to transfer them to another registered pension scheme. Pension sharing orders were introduced in December 2000, to address the deficiencies of attachment orders.

**16-002** In each case, the standard "cash equivalent transfer value" is usually used for valuation purposes.[4] There are no special provisions in FA 2004 Pt 4 relating to offsetting or earmarking, but there are various provisions relating to pension sharing.

## FA 2004 AND PENSION SHARING ORDERS

**16-003** Any order or provision mentioned in the Welfare Reform and Pensions Act ("WRPA") 1999 s.28(1)[5] is referred to in FA 2004 Pt 4 as a "pension sharing order or provision". A number of orders and provisions are mentioned in s.28(1); the most important for present purposes are pension sharing orders under: (a) the Matrimonial Causes Act 1973; and (b) the Civil Partnership Act 2004 Sch.5.[6] Each involves a court directing the trustees to reduce the rights of the member, and to allocate such rights to his former spouse. Such reallocation involves a "pension debit" and a "pension credit" for the purposes of WRPA 1999,[7] and these terms are incorporated directly into FA 2004 Pt 4.[8] The receiving spouse may (subject to the scheme rules and, where required, the agreement of the trustees) retain the pension credits in the same scheme, or may require the pension credits to be transferred to a different registered pension scheme. In this chapter, a "debited member" means the member whose rights have been reduced by a pension debit, and "credited ember" means the member whose rights have been increased by a pension credit.

---

[4] See the Pension Sharing (Valuation) Regulations 2000 (SI 2000/1052).
[5] FA 2004 s.279(1).
[6] The others are: (a) an order under Part III of the Matrimonial and Family Proceedings Act 1984 (financial relief in England and Wales in relation to overseas divorce etc) corresponding to an order made under the Matrimonial Causes Act 1973; (b) an order under the Civil Partnership Act (("CPA") 2004 Sch.7 (financial relief in England and Wales after overseas dissolution etc of a civil partnership) corresponding to an order made under CPA 2004 Sch.5; (c) a pension sharing order under the Family Law (Scotland) Act 1985; (d) provision which corresponds to the provision which may be made by such an order and which: (i) is contained in a qualifying agreement between the parties to a marriage or between persons who are civil partners of each other; (ii) is in such form as the Secretary of State may prescribe by regulations; and (iii) takes effect on the grant, in relation to the marriage, of decree of divorce under the Divorce (Scotland) Act 1976 or of declarator of nullity or (as the case may be) on the grant, in relation to the civil partnership, of decree of dissolution or of declarator of nullity; (e) an order under Pt IV of the Matrimonial and Family Proceedings Act 1984 (financial relief in Scotland in relation to overseas divorce etc.) or under CPA 2004 Sch.11 (financial provision in Scotland after overseas proceedings) corresponding to an order made under the Family Law (Scotland) Act 1985; (f) a pension sharing order under the Matrimonial Causes (Northern Ireland) Order 1978 (SI 1978/1045); (g) an order under Pt IV of the Matrimonial and Family Proceedings (Northern Ireland) Order 1989 (financial relief in Northern Ireland in relation to overseas divorce etc) corresponding to an order under the Matrimonial Causes (Northern Ireland) Order 1978; (h) a pension sharing order under CPA 2004 Sch.15; and (i) an order under CPA 2004 Sch.17 (financial relief in Northern Ireland after overseas dissolution etc of a civil partnership) corresponding to an order under CPA 2004 Sch.15.
[7] See WRPA 1999 s.46(1) and s.29(1).
[8] FA 2004 s.279(1). The recipient of pension credits is a "pension credit member" (FA 2004 s.151(5)).

# FA 2004 AND PENSION SHARING ORDERS

In outline, the implications under FA 2004 Pt 4 are as follows: **16-004**

(a) A payment to or in respect of a member pursuant to a pension sharing order is an authorised payment.[9]

(b) A pension credit is not a "contribution" for the purposes of s.188(1), so tax relief is not available.[10]

(c) Pension credits and debits are disregarded for annual allowance purposes. A debit does not reduce the closing value and a credit does not increase the closing value of cash balance or defined benefits arrangements.[11] It may be difficult to rebuild pension fund where the MPAA applies prior to a pension credit.

(d) Where the debited member's pension has commenced prior to the pension sharing order, the rate of a scheme pension, lifetime annuity, short-term annuity, capped drawdown, dependants' annuity, dependants' short-term annuity, and dependants capped drawdown may be reduced in consequence of a pension sharing order.[12] In relation to the credited member: (i) any sums or assets attributable to a "disqualifying" pension credit are disregarded when determining the value of the relevant pension for the purposes of the PCLS, and (ii) sums or assets cannot be paid as an UFPLS if they are attributable to a disqualifying pension credit. A pension credit is "disqualifying" if, when the member becomes entitled to it, the person subject to the corresponding pension debit has an actual (rather than a merely prospective) right to payment of a pension under the relevant arrangement.[13] The relevant arrangement is the arrangement to which the pension sharing order or provision, by virtue of which the member becomes entitled to the pension credit, relates.

(e) In relation to the LS&DB allowance: (i) an LS&DB allowance enhancement factor may apply where pension credits are received from rights which have already been crystallised;[14] (ii) the rights of members with primary protection are reduced by a pension debit, and one is required to recalculate the primary protection factor[15]; (iii) a transfer pursuant to a pension sharing order is not an impermissible transfer for the purposes of enhanced protection.[16]

## The LS&DB allowance

The payment of a pension credit is not a relevant BCE, so, where rights have not crystallised, there may be an opportunity to take advantage of two LS&DB allowances rather than one. The debited member can make further contributions (assuming no protection) to rebuild his fund. The credited member does not benefit from any protection that the debited member had. **16-005**

In relation to crystallised rights, the debited member's ability to rebuild his fund will be much restricted if the money purchase annual allowance applies. The **16-006**

---

[9] FA 2004 s.164(1)(e). It expressly does not involve an assignment within s.172 or a surrender within s.172A (see FA 2004 ss.172(2) and 172A(5)(a) respectively).
[10] FA 2004 s.188(4).
[11] FA 2004 s.232(2) and (3) (cash balance); s.236(2) and (3) (defined benefits).
[12] FA 2004 Sch.28 paras 2(4)(d), 3(2A), 6(1A), 10(4), 17(2), 20(1A), and 24(4) respectively.
[13] FA 2004 s.278A.
[14] FA 2004 Sch.36 para.18.
[15] FA 2004 Sch.36 para.11.
[16] FA 2004 Sch.36 para.17A(1).

credited member may be able to benefit from an LS&DB allowance enhancement factor.

**16-007** Where a pension sharing order is made following one or more relevant BCEs, the debited member does not benefit from an enhancement factor to reflect his loss of benefits.

*LS allowance and LS&DB allowance enhancement factors*

**16-008** An LS&DB allowance enhancement factor applies where: (a) a pension credit was acquired before 6 April 2006; or (b) the member acquires a pension credit on or after 6 April 2006 in relation to rights under another registered pension scheme which consisted of or included rights to a pension already in payment and which came into payment on or after 6 April 2006.[17]

**16-009 The pension credit factor** When calculating the amount crystallised by a relevant BCE, pension credits are treated no differently to any other funds. However if an ex-spouse or former civil partner has, at any time after 5 April 2006 but before 6 April 2024, acquired rights under a registered pension scheme by reason of having become entitled to a pension credit (whether deriving from the same or another registered pension scheme), and the rights under the scheme which became subject to the corresponding pension debit consisted of or included rights to a pension to which a person became (actually) entitled on or after 6 April 2006, the ex-spouse's or civil partner's LS&DB allowance factor is "A/£1m" where[18] $A$ is the amount of the pension credit awarded for the purposes of WRPA 1999 s.29(1).[19] This is referred to as the "pension credit factor". The rationale for this enhancement factor is that the pension rights/benefits will already have been tested against the ex-spouse's or former civil partner's LS&DB allowance when the pension began.

**16-010 The pre-commencement pension credit factor** An LS allowance enhancement factor (called the "pre-commencement pension credit factor") applies where the ex-spouse or former civil partner acquired a pension credit before 6 April 2006 under a pension scheme which automatically became a registered pension scheme on 6 April 2006.[20] The LS allowance of such an individual is the lower of: (a) £268,275 increased by the pre-commencement pension credit factor, and (b) £375,000. The pre-commencement pension credit factor is "A/£1.5 million" where $A$ is the amount of the pension credit awarded for the purposes of s.29(1) WRPA 1999, as increased by the percentage by which the RPI for April 2006 is greater than that for the month in which the rights were acquired. For example, if an individual was awarded a pension credit of £250,000 in June 2001, by applying the increase in the RPI from June 2000 to April 2006, the pension credit on that date was worth (say) £300,000. By applying the above formula to the standard lifetime allowance on 5 April 2006, it will be enhanced by a factor of 0.2 (£300,000/£1.5 million).

The pre-commencement pension credit factor is also an LS&DB allowance enhancement factor.

---

[17] FA 2004 s.220 and Sch.36 para.18.
[18] FA 2004 s.220.
[19] FA 2004 Sch.36 para.20A.
[20] See FA 2004 Sch.36 para.18.

# FA 2004 AND PENSION SHARING ORDERS

The individual must have given notice to HMRC prior to 5 April 2009 and HMRC will have issued a certificate showing the enhancement factor.[21]  **16-011**

*Debited member with primary protection*

A debited member with primary protection must notify HMRC, as his primary protection factor will be reduced. If the pension debit reduces the value of his fund below £1.5 million, his primary protection will cease. Individual protection works in a similar way, albeit the pension debit is reduced by 5% for each complete tax year after the date the protection was introduced.  **16-012**

---

[21] The Registered Pension Schemes (Enhanced Allowances) Regulations 2006 (SI 2006/131) reg.5.

# CHAPTER 17

# Authorised Employer Payments

## TABLE OF CONTENTS

| | |
|---|---|
| Introduction | 17-001 |
| Authorised Surplus Payments | 17-002 |
|     PA 1995 s.37 | 17-003 |
|     PA 1995 s.76 | 17-004 |
|     The authorised surplus payments charge | 17-005 |
| Compensation Payments | 17-007 |
| Authorised Employer Loans | 17-008 |
|     Loans which are not authorised: amount of unauthorised payment | 17-010 |
|     Amount 1 | 17-012 |
|     Amount 2 | 17-014 |
|     Amount A | 17-016 |
|     Amount B | 17-018 |
|     Amount C | 17-022 |
|     Loan ceasing to be secured by charge of adequate value | 17-025 |
|     Further reduction in value of charge which is not of adequate value | 17-026 |
|     Loans ceasing to comply with repayment terms | 17-028 |
|     Increase in extent to which loan does not comply with repayment terms | 17-029 |
|     Prevention of double charging | 17-032 |
| Scheme Administration Employer Payments | 17-033 |

## INTRODUCTION

A payment to or in respect of a sponsoring employer, or former sponsoring employer, of a registered pension scheme is an authorised employer payment if it is one of the following:[1]   **17-001**

(a) A public service scheme payment (not considered in this book).
(b) An authorised surplus payment.
(c) A compensation payment.
(d) An authorised employer loan.
(e) A scheme administration employer payment.

This is an exhaustive list. Any other payment to or in respect of a sponsoring

---

[1] FA 2004 s.175(1).

employer, or former sponsoring employer, is an unauthorised employer payment.

## AUTHORISED SURPLUS PAYMENTS

**17-002**   A payment is an authorised surplus payment if one of the following applies:[2]

(a) The payment is made in compliance with PA 1995 s.37 (which can only apply where the scheme is not being wound up).
(b) The payment is made in connection with the winding-up of a scheme which satisfies the requirements in PA 1995 s.76.
(c) The payment does not satisfy either (a) or (b) above, but it does satisfy all of the following conditions:[3]
  (i) the rules of the scheme permit such a payment to be made;
  (ii) the rules of the scheme contain a limit, calculated other than by reference to the size of the member's fund, on the maximum amount of benefits that may be paid to, or in respect of, members of the scheme;
  (iii) if the scheme is being wound up, the liabilities of the scheme have been fully discharged including any tax that may be due and there is a surplus of assets over liabilities; and
  (iv) if the scheme is not being wound up, the requirements in PA 1995 s.37 would have been met if the scheme had been one to which s.37 applied.

**PA 1995 s.37**

**17-003**   PA 1995 s.37 applies to a trust scheme if:

(a) under the scheme, power is conferred on the employer or any other person to make payments to the employer out of funds held for the purposes of the scheme;[4] and
(b) the scheme is not being wound up; and
(c) the payment is not a compensation payment or authorised employer loan.[5]

**PA 1995 s.76**

**17-004**   The requirements of PA 1995 s.76 are that: (a) the scheme is a trust scheme and is a registered pension scheme; (b) the scheme is being wound up; and (c) power is conferred on the employer or the trustees to distribute assets to the employer on

---

[2] FA 2004 s.177 and SI 2006/574 reg.2. A payment to a sponsoring employer solely in respect of the death of a member can only be an authorised surplus payment if, in addition to satisfying the conditions in (a) or (b), the member was not connected to the sponsoring employer at the date of the member's death.
[3] SI 2006/574 reg.3. A payment made to a sponsoring employer solely in respect of the death of a member can only be an authorised surplus payment if, in addition to satisfying the conditions in (a)–(d), the member was not connected to the sponsoring employer at the date of the member's death.
[4] This power must be exercised by the trustees, even if it is conferred by the scheme on a person other than the trustees. In addition, the power can only be exercised if the requirements in s.37(3) are satisfied. These relate to the need to obtain a written valuation and for there to be a certificate in force specifying the maximum amount of payment that may be made to the employer, and the trustees must be satisfied that it is in the interests of the members that the power is exercised in the manner proposed, and notice is given to the members etc.
[5] "Compensation payment" and "authorised employer loan" have the same meanings as in FA 2004 ss.178 and 179.

a winding-up. This power cannot be exercised unless: (i) the liabilities of the scheme have been fully discharged; (ii) where there is any power under the scheme, after the discharge of those liabilities, to distribute assets to any person other than the employer, the power has been exercised or a decision has been made not to exercise it; and (iii) notice has been given in accordance with prescribed requirements[6] to the members of the scheme of the proposal to exercise the power; and (iv) the Pensions Regulator is of the opinion that the above requirements are satisfied and any prescribed requirements are satisfied.[7]

### The authorised surplus payments charge

FA 2004 s.207 imposes an authorised surplus payments charge where an authorised surplus payment is made to a sponsoring employer by an occupational pension scheme that is a registered pension scheme. The scheme administrator is liable to the charge.[8] The rate of the charge is 25%[9] *in respect of* the authorised surplus payment.[10] The charge does not apply to any authorised surplus payment: **17-005**

(a) to the extent that (if FA 2004 s.207 had not been enacted) the sponsoring employer would have been exempt, or entitled to claim exemption, from income tax or corporation tax in respect of it; or
(b) if the sponsoring employer is a charity; or
(c) to the extent that the payment is funded (directly or indirectly) by a surrender of (or an agreement to surrender) benefits or rights which results in the registered pension scheme being treated as making an unauthorised payment under FA 2004 s.172A; or
(d) if the payment is made in pursuance of the winding-up of a pension scheme if the winding-up commenced before 19 March 1986.[11]

In relation to (a), it is possible that, if s.207 had not been enacted, a payment of surplus would not be an unauthorised payment because it would not be a payment "by" a registered pension scheme.[12] Prior to the introduction of a charge on payments to employers out of surplus (by FA 1986), such payments were simply taken into account when computing the employer's profits for tax purposes. If it is correct that such a payment would not otherwise be subject to tax then the reference to the sponsoring employer being exempt, or entitled to claim exemption, from income tax or corporation tax in respect of the payment, appears to be a reference to exemption from UK tax generally in respect of the payment. **17-006**

---

[6] These requirements are prescribed in The Occupational Pension Schemes (Payments to Employer) Regulations 2006 (SI 2006//802) regs 15 and 17.
[7] These requirements are prescribed in SI 2006//802 regs 16 and 17.
[8] Liability is not affected by the residence or domicile status of the scheme administrator or the sponsoring employer.
[9] The rate was 35% prior to 6 April 2024. The rate was amended by The Authorised Surplus Payments Charge (Variation of Rate) Order 2024 (SI 2024/335).
[10] It is not entirely clear what "in respect of" is intended to mean where the surplus payment comprises assets. It may relate to the market value of the assets, or it may relate to some other method of valuation.
[11] FA 2004 Sch.36 para.47.
[12] FA 2004 s.279(2) provides that a payment is by a registered pension scheme if the payment is made from sums held for the purposes of the pension scheme. A surplus is (by definition) money in excess of what is required for the purposes of the scheme (per Lord Hoffmann in *International Power v Healey* [2001] P.L.R. 121).

## COMPENSATION PAYMENTS

**17-007** Pursuant to FA 2004 s.178, a "compensation payment" means a payment from a pension scheme to a sponsoring employer in respect of a member's liability to that employer in respect of a criminal, fraudulent or negligent act or omission by the member.[13]

## AUTHORISED EMPLOYER LOANS

**17-008** A loan[14] made to or in respect of person who is or has been a sponsoring employer[15] is an authorised employer loan if:[16]

(a) The amount loaned does not exceed 50% of the amount of the sums and market value of the assets held for the purposes of the pension scheme immediately before the loan is made.[17]

(b) The loan is secured[18] by a "charge"[19] which is of "adequate value", meaning:[20]

(i) In the case of the first charge to secure the loan, at the time the charge is given, the market value of the assets subject to the charge is at least equal to the amount owing (including interest). In any other case, the market value of the assets must be at least equal to the lower of that amount and the market value of the assets subject to the previous charge.

(ii) If, at any time after the charge is given, the market value of the assets charged is less than would be required under (i) above if the charge were given at that time, the reduction in value is not attributable to any step taken by the pension scheme, the sponsoring employer or a person connected with the sponsoring employer.

---

[13] Although a compensation payment within s.178 is an authorised *employer* payment, such a payment would be in respect of a member and therefore it will usually be an unauthorised *member* payment.

[14] See above for the meaning of "loan" for the purposes of FA 2004 Pt 4. It seems clear that there must be an enforceable debt or a contractual obligation to repay debt. If the amount of a loan to or in respect of a sponsoring employer is increased, the amount of the increase is deemed to be a loan made on the date of the increase.

[15] It is clear that the loan need not be made to the sponsoring employer (or former sponsoring employer). A payment is made "in respect of" a sponsoring employer if it is made to any person connected with the sponsor employer, provided that the connected person is not a member (see FA 2004 s.161(5)).

[16] FA 2004 s.179. In addition to the FA 2004 requirements, any loans to a sponsoring employer must comply with PA 1995 s.40 and SI 2005/3378. This will only be possible if the scheme is a small scheme (i.e. a scheme with 12 members or less, where each member is a trustee): see reg.12.

[17] In the context of a sectionalised multi-employer scheme, the pension scheme is the entire scheme (not just the section relating to any given employer) so this 50% restriction can have arbitrary results. One determines the market value of assets in accordance with TCGA 1992 s.272 (FA 2004 s.278. See Ch.2).

[18] A loan made to a UK corporate employer is not "secured" unless it is registered at Companies House in accordance with s.859A CA 2006 (see *Nilebond Ltd v HMRC* [2023] UKFTT 14 (TC), in which the FTT also held that late registration is not sufficient if there is a period of time in which the loan is not secured).

[19] "Charge" includes a right in security or an agreement to create a right in security (s.179(7)). It does not appear to be necessary for the employer to own the charged property, so it seems that the security may by provided by a third party (such as a shareholder of the employer, for example).

[20] FA 2004 Sch.30 para.1.

(iii) The charge takes priority over any other charge over the assets. In *Eden Consulting Services (Richmond) Ltd v HMRC*,[21] the FTT found that an unregistered charge cannot satisfy this requirement, but this was criticised in *Bayonet Ventures LLP v HMRC*.[22]

(c) The rate of interest payable on the loan is not less than the "relevant interest rate" (currently 5.25% p/a[23]). A fixed rate of interest will satisfy this requirement provided that it is not less than the relevant rate at the time of the loan.

(d) The repayment date is less than five years from the date on which the loan is made. The repayment date may be postponed (once only) to a date not exceeding five years from the initial repayment date.

(e) The amount payable in each year is not less than the "required amount", which in relation to a period beginning with the date on which the loan is made and ending with the last day of a loan year, is[24] "[(L+TIP) / TLY] x NLY" where L is the amount of the loan; *TIP* is the total interest payable; *TLY* is the total number of loan years; and *NLY* is the number of loan years in the period. This generally requires the payments to be spread evenly.

It is very likely that the existence of a charge will reduce the market value of the asset charged,[25] so the above references to market value must mean market value disregarding any charges.[26]

**17-009**

### Loans which are not authorised: amount of unauthorised payment

If a loan is not an authorised employer loan at the time it is paid, it is an unauthorised payment, and the amount of the unauthorised payment is equal to the largest of such of Amount 1, Amount 2, Amount A, Amount B, or Amount C, as arise in relation to the loan.[27] However the total amount of the unauthorised payment in relation to a loan is expressly limited to the amount of the loan when it was made.[28]

**17-010**

If an authorised employer loan is made, but the employer fails to pay the "required amount" each year, the debt is itself treated (under FA 2004 s.162(4)) as a loan from the scheme to the employer, and that deemed loan cannot itself be an authorised employer loan, or a scheme administration employer payment, or any other type of authorised payment.[29]

**17-011**

*Amount 1*

Amount 1 arises if the amount of the loan exceeds 50% of the value of the sums and assets held for the purposes of the pension scheme immediately before the loan

**17-012**

---

[21] *Eden Consulting Services (Richmond) Ltd v HMRC* [2017] UKFTT 596 at [42].
[22] [2018] UKFTT 262 at para.28.
[23] The Registered Pension Schemes (Prescribed Interest Rates for Authorised Employer Loans) Regulations 2005 (SI 2005/3449), which prescribes that the relevant interest rate is 1% above the average clearing bank base rate for six nominated High Street Banks rounded up to the nearest 0.25%. The rate is the same as the interest charged by HMRC on underpaid corporation tax quarterly instalment payments, as set out here: *http://www.gov.uk/government/publications/rates-and-allowances-hmrc-interest-rates-for-late-and-early-payments/rates-and-allowances-hmrc-interest-rates*.
[24] FA 2004 Sch.30 para.4.
[25] See Ch.2.
[26] This is HMRC's position: PTM123200.
[27] FA 2004 Sch.30 para.5.
[28] FA 2004 Sch.30 para.11.
[29] For the meaning of "loan" in FA 2004, see Ch.2.

was made. Amount 1 is calculated as follows:[30]

$$\frac{(AL/VA \times 100) - 100}{100} \times VA$$

Where:
- AL is the amount of the loan; and
- VA is an amount equal to 50% of the total value of sums/assets held for the purposes of the pension scheme before the loan is made.

**17-013** This is the difference between the amount of the loan and 50% of the value of the sums and assets held for the purposes of the pension scheme before the loan was made. For example, if a scheme with assets valued at £360,000 makes a loan of £200,000 to the employer, the amount of the unauthorised payment is £200,000 – £180,000 (being 50% of £360,000) = £20,000.

*Amount 2*

**17-014** Amount 2 arises if the loan is not secured by charge of adequate value. To calculate Amount 2, one determines the amount owing (including interest) at the relevant time, and subtracts from that the market value at that time of the assets charged.[31] If the loan is not secured by a charge, or is secured by a charge which does not take priority over any other charge over the assets, the amount to subtract is nil.

**17-015** For example, a scheme makes a loan to a sponsoring employer of £500,000, and the employer provides a property as security that has a value of £600,000. The charge is of adequate value. However, the property is sold and security is provided over a property valued at £450,000 at a time when the amount outstanding on the loan is £460,000. This charge is not of adequate value and so an unauthorised payment occurs. The amount of the unauthorised payment is £10,000 (being the difference between the value of the security and the amount of the loan outstanding).

*Amount A*

**17-016** Amount A arises if the interest rate is less than the rate prescribed by SI 2005/3449. Amount A is:[32]

$$\frac{100 - [(IR/PIR) \times 100]}{100} \times AO$$

Where:
- IR is the rate of interest payable at the relevant time;
- PIR is the rate of interest prescribed by regulations; and
- AO is the amount owing (not including interest) at the relevant time.

**17-017** For example if a scheme borrows £100,000 at an interest rate of 1% p/a when

---

[30] FA 2004 Sch.30 para.12.
[31] FA 2004 Sch.30 para.13.
[32] FA 2004 Sch.30 para.4.

the prescribed rate is 1.25% this will give rise to an unauthorised payment of £20,000:

$$\frac{100 - [(1/1.25) \times 100]}{100} \times £100,000 = £20,000$$

*Amount B*

Amount B arises if the loan repayment date is not within five years of the date on which the loan is made. Amount B is:[33]  **17-018**

$$\frac{[(DLRP/DFY) \times 100] - 100}{100} \times AO$$

Where:

- *DLRP* is the number of days in the period which begins with the date on which the loan is made and ends with the loan repayment date;
- *DFY* is the number of days in the period which begins with the date on which the loan is made and ends five years after that date; and
- *AO* is the amount owing (including interest) at the relevant time.

But if the amount produced by the above fraction is greater than 1, Amount B is the amount owing (including interest) at the relevant time.  **17-019**

If the loan repayment date has been postponed under FA 2004 s.179(3), the above applies as if references to the date on which the loan is made were to the standard loan repayment date on which the loan repayment date was postponed.  **17-020**

For example, if a loan of £10,000 is made on 6 April 2017 with a repayment date of 5 October 2023 gives rise to an unauthorised payment of £823.67:  **17-021**

$$\frac{[(2373 \text{ days}/2191 \text{ days}) \times 100] - 100}{100} \times £10,000 = £830.67$$

*Amount C*

Amount C arises if the amount payable in each year is less than the required amount, and is calculated as follows. In relation to each period beginning with the date on which the loan is made and ending with the last day of a loan year, one calculates the required amount in relation to that period, and subtracts the amount payable during that period.[34] Amount C is the largest of the amounts calculated.  **17-022**

For example, if the required amount in each year is £28,000 and the loan agreement provides for the following payments to be made:  **17-023**

(a) Year 1: £20,000 (difference: £8,000).
(b) Year 2: total £56,000 (difference: nil).
(c) Year 3: total £80,000 (difference: £4,000).

---

[33] FA 2004 Sch.30 para.15.
[34] FA 2004 Sch.30 para.16.

(d) Year 4: total £108,000 (difference: £4,000).
(e) Year 5: total £140,000 (difference: nil).

**17-024** The amount of the unauthorised payment is the highest amount calculated of the five years, i.e. £8,000.

*Loan ceasing to be secured by charge of adequate value*

**17-025** If at any time after a loan is made it ceases to be secured by a charge of adequate value, there is an unauthorised payment equal to Amount 2 above.[35]

*Further reduction in value of charge which is not of adequate value*

**17-026** An unauthorised payment is made if at any time after a loan is made the loan is secured by a charge which is not of adequate value, and one of the following events occurs:[36]

(a) the loan ceases to be secured by a charge;
(b) a charge is given which does not comply with conditions A or C;
(c) there a reduction in the value of the assets charged which does not comply with condition B; and
(d) the charge ceases to comply with condition C.

**17-027** To determine the amount of the unauthorised payment, one calculates Amount 2 after the event and Amount 2 before the event and subtracts the latter from the former.

*Loans ceasing to comply with repayment terms*

**17-028** If at any time after a loan is made there is an alteration in the repayment terms, and as a result the repayment terms cease to comply with one or more paragraphs of s.179(2) (authorised repayment terms), there is an unauthorised payment of an amount equal to the larger of such of Amounts A, B, and C as arise when that paragraph or those paragraphs are not complied with.[37]

*Increase in extent to which loan does not comply with repayment terms*

**17-029** If at any time after a loan is made there is an alteration in the repayment terms, and as a result the "deterioration condition" is met in relation to one or more paragraphs of s.179(2) (authorised repayment terms) which were not complied with before the alteration, there is an unauthorised payment of an amount calculated in accordance with the provisions below.[38] The deterioration condition is met in relation to a paragraph if AAA > ABA, where:

- *AAA*, in relation to a paragraph of s.179(2) (authorised repayment terms) which was not complied with before the alteration in the repayment terms, is the amount arising when that paragraph is not complied with, calculated after the alteration in the repayment terms; and
- *ABA*, in relation to such a paragraph, is the amount arising when that paragraph is not complied with, calculated before the alteration in the repayment terms.

---

[35] FA 2004 Sch.30 para.6.
[36] FA 2004 Sch.30 para.7.
[37] FA 2004 Sch.30 para.8.
[38] FA 2004 Sch.30 para.9.

If the deterioration condition is met, for each paragraph in relation to which the deterioration condition is met, one calculates AAA – ABA. **17-030**

There is an unauthorised payment of an amount equal to the largest of the amounts calculated under the paragraph above. **17-031**

*Prevention of double charging*

If on any date there is an unauthorised payment under more the following provisions then there is a single unauthorised payment and the amount of the unauthorised payment is an amount equal to the amount of the greater or greatest of the unauthorised payments under those paragraphs:[39] **17-032**

(a) loans ceasing to be secured by charge of adequate value;
(b) further reductions in value of charge which is not of adequate value;
(c) loans ceasing to comply with repayment terms; or
(d) increases in extent to which loan does not comply with repayment terms.

## SCHEME ADMINISTRATION EMPLOYER PAYMENTS

FA 2004 s.180(1)–(5) provides as follows: **17-033**

"(1) A "scheme administration employer payment" is a payment made—
    (a) by a registered pension scheme that is an occupational pension scheme, and
    (b) to or in respect of a person who is or has been a sponsoring employer,
for the purposes of the administration or management of the pension scheme.

(2) But if a payment falling within subsection (1) exceeds the amount which might be expected to be paid to a person who was at arm's length, the excess is not a scheme administration employer payment.

(3) Scheme administration employer payments include in particular—
    (a) the payment of wages, salaries or fees to persons engaged in administering the pension scheme, and
    (b) payments made for the purchase of assets to be held for the purposes of the pension scheme.

(4) A loan to or in respect of a person who is or has been a sponsoring employer is not a scheme administration employer payment.

(5) Payments made to acquire shares in a sponsoring employer are not scheme administration employer payments if, when the payment is made—
    (a) the market value of shares in the sponsoring employer held for the purposes of the pension scheme is equal to or greater than 5% of the aggregate of the amount of the sums, and the market value of the assets, held for the purposes of the pension scheme, or
    (b) the total market value of shares in sponsoring employers held for the purposes of the pension scheme is equal to or greater than 20% of the aggregate of the amount of the sums, and the market value of the assets, held for the purposes of the pension scheme."

Section 180(1)–(4) are materially identical to the scheme administration member payment provisions considered in Ch.11, and the meaning of "administration or management" and "loan" will be the same. **17-034**

Note that s.180(5) does *not* mean that a pension scheme cannot hold more than 5% shares in a sponsoring employer. Section 180(5) is not engaged unless there is **17-035**

---

[39] FA 2004 Sch.30 para.10.

a payment by the scheme to or in respect of a sponsoring employer to purchase shares in the sponsoring employer. The mere fact that the value of such shares is equal to or exceeds 5% of the scheme assets (e.g. because the shares have increased in value, or because the other scheme assets have fallen in value) is not itself deemed to be an unauthorised payment. And where shares were acquired before A-Day, the payment to purchase the shares cannot have been an unauthorised payment. If, for example, the sponsoring employer issued the shares to the scheme for nil consideration then there would not be a payment by the scheme to or in respect of the sponsoring employer. If the scheme purchased shares issued to the scheme by a company connected with a sponsoring employer, that would involve a payment in respect of a sponsoring employer (so that s.180 is engaged) but the payment is not to acquire shares in a sponsoring employer. If the scheme bought shares in a sponsoring employer from a person who is unconnected with the sponsoring employer (which could include a member) the payment to purchase the shares is not a payment to or in respect of a sponsoring employer and so it does not engage s.180 (it cannot be an unauthorised employer payment).[40]

---

[40] One must also have regard to PA 1995 s.40 and reg.12 of the Occupational Pension Schemes (Investment) Regulations 2005 (SI 2005/3378), which restrict employer-related investments. Note there is an exception for "small schemes" i.e. schemes with fewer than 12 members where all the members are trustees of the scheme (or directors of a corporate trustee) and all decisions of the trustees must be made by the unanimous agreement of the trustees (or directors) who are members of the scheme (SI 2005/3378 reg.1(2)).

# CHAPTER 18

# Unauthorised Payments

## TABLE OF CONTENTS

| | |
|---|---|
| Overview | 18-001 |
|     Why penalise unauthorised payments? | 18-003 |
| Unauthorised payments | 18-009 |
|     Unauthorised member payments | 18-010 |
|     Unauthorised employer payments | 18-012 |
| Actual unauthorised payments | 18-014 |
|     "Payment" | 18-016 |
|     "By" a registered pension scheme | 18-017 |
|         Payments under or in connection with investments | 18-024 |
|         "Under" or "in connection with" | 18-030 |
|     Payments "to" or "in respect of" a member or employer | 18-042 |
|         Payments to connected persons | 18-049 |
|         Payments that deplete the fund | 18-050 |
|         Payments on uncommercial terms | 18-051 |
|         Requirement to have an identifiable member | 18-052 |
|         Summary | 18-058 |
| Deemed unauthorised member payments | 18-059 |
|     Can an authorised payment also be a deemed unauthorised payment? | 18-062 |
|     Can an actual unauthorised payment also be a deemed unauthorised payment? | 18-063 |
|     Implications of connected persons | 18-064 |
|     Assignment (FA 2004 s.172) | 18-065 |
|         The law of assignment | 18-066 |
|         FA 2004 treatment of assignments | 18-070 |
|         Exceptions | 18-074 |
|         The amount of the unauthorised payment | 18-075 |
|         PA 1995 s.91 | 18-077 |
|     Surrenders (FA 2004 s.172A) | 18-078 |
|         Surrenders by members | 18-083 |
|         Surrenders by non-members | 18-084 |
|         Exceptions | 18-088 |
|         Meaning of retirement-benefit activities compliance exercise | 18-091 |
|         Defined benefits and cash balance arrangements | 18-092 |
|         Amount of the unauthorised payment | 18-093 |
|         Pensions Act 1995 s.91 | 18-094 |
|     Increase in rights of connected person on death (FA 2004 s.172B) | 18-095 |

"Relevant member" .......................... 18-097
"Increased pension rights" ................... 18-099
The amount of the unauthorised payment ........ 18-101
Exceptions ................................. 18-102
Allocation of unallocated employer contributions (FA 2004 s.172C) ................................. 18-105
The deemed unauthorised payment ............ 18-109
The "permitted maximum" ................... 18-111
The amount of the unauthorised payment ........ 18-113
Limit on increase in benefits (FA 2004 s.172D) ...... 18-114
The deemed unauthorised payment ............ 18-115
The pension input amount ................... 18-116
The notional unconnected person input amount ... 18-117
The amount of the unauthorised payment ........ 18-118
Benefits (FA 2004 s.173) ....................... 18-119
The deemed unauthorised payment ............ 18-120
Meaning of "benefit" ........................ 18-121
Exceptions and limitations .................... 18-127
The amount of the unauthorised payment ........ 18-132
Dalriada v Faulds ........................... 18-137
Dalriada v HMRC ........................... 18-141
Value shifting (FA 2004 s.174) ................... 18-142
The deemed unauthorised payment ............ 18-144
The events ................................. 18-147
The amount of the unauthorised payment ........ 18-149
Holding taxable property (FA 2004 s.174A) ........ 18-150
The deemed unauthorised payment ............ 18-151
Deemed unauthorised employer payments ............ 18-153
Value shifting ................................. 18-153
The events ................................. 18-156
The amount of the unauthorised payment ........ 18-157
Transactions benefitting a sponsoring employer ..... 18-158
Taxation of unauthorised payments .................. 18-159
The unauthorised payments charge ............... 18-161
Reduction anticipating scheme sanction charge .... 18-165
Liability .................................. 18-166
Relief from the unauthorised payments charge .... 18-168
The unauthorised payments surcharge ............. 18-169
Surchargeable unauthorised member payments .... 18-170
Valuation of crystallised rights ............... 18-173
Valuation of uncrystallised rights ............. 18-174
Surchargeable unauthorised employer payments . 18-176
The rate of the charge ..................... 18-178
Liability .................................. 18-179
Discharge from liability for the surcharge ...... 18-180
Relief from the surcharge ................... 18-188
The scheme sanction charge ..................... 18-189
Genuine errors ................................. 18-192
Treatment by HMRC ........................... 18-192
The Roxburghe principle ...................... 18-194
Reporting obligations ............................... 18-195

# OVERVIEW

One of the chief concerns of FA 2004 Pt 4 is to prescribe whether a "payment" by a registered pension scheme is "authorised" or "unauthorised". This classification is of importance primarily in determining the tax consequences of the payment. All unauthorised payments are charged to tax under FA 2004 Pt 4, but are not otherwise chargeable.[1] All authorised pensions and lump sums are chargeable under ITEPA 2003 Pt 9, but not usually under FA 2004[2] or elsewhere. Most authorised payments other than pensions and lump sums are not subject to tax under ITEPA 2003 Pt 9 or FA 2004 Pt 4.[3] In addition to the tax consequences, making an unauthorised payment could, in extreme circumstances, result in de-registration (which would in turn give rise to further tax charges: see Ch.4). **18-001**

This chapter explains what an unauthorised payment is, and the tax consequences of making an unauthorised payment. As will be seen, the consequences are essentially penal; the provisions do not seek to simply reverse the benefit of any previously obtained tax relief.[4] **18-002**

### Why penalise unauthorised payments?

The rationale for penalising unauthorised payments was explained thus by Jonathan Cannan J:[5] **18-003**

> "to ensure that the tax reliefs and exemptions in respect of contributions to registered pension schemes are available only to the extent that the pension schemes genuinely make provision for the benefit of members on retirement, subject to various statutory limits."

It may be helpful to expand on this rationale slightly. The purpose of a pension scheme, generally speaking, is to provide benefits at a time when the member is less able to provide for himself. This may be as a result of advanced age or serious illness. Thus the pension fund is typically used to replace or augment employment or trading income. For various reasons the Government wishes to encourage pension saving, and it does this by providing certain tax reliefs and exemptions. Except in cases of serious ill-health, payments or benefits provided before normal pension age (currently age 55) are penalised because they have, or may have, the effect of depleting the fund available when it is required (i.e. on retirement). This is the main policy of the unauthorised payments regime. **18-004**

However, unauthorised payments are penalised even if they do not have the effect of depleting the scheme funds. In particular, investments by the pension scheme **18-005**

---

[1] FA 2004 s.208(8) provides that an unauthorised payment does not constitute income for tax purposes.

[2] There are two types of authorised lump sums that are subject to tax under FA 2004: short service refund lump sums (s.205) and special lump sum death benefits (s.206).

[3] Only two types of authorised payments other than pensions and lump sums are subject to tax under FA 2004: authorised surplus payments (s.207) and transfers to QROPS in certain circumstances (s.244A). Other authorised payments, such as scheme administration member payments see Ch.11), may give rise to other tax charges under general principles.

[4] In *Morgan Lloyd Trustees Ltd v HMRC* [2017] UKFTT 131 at [108] and [109], the FTT considered that the purpose of the unauthorised payments charge is to neutralise the tax relief that might have been given on the original contributions to the scheme, but the purpose of the unauthorised payments surcharge and the scheme sanction charge is to deter and punish. The latter charges should therefore be categorised as penalties.

[5] *Willey v HMRC* [2013] UKFTT 328 at [6]; approved by Poole J in *Danvers v HMRC* [2016] UKFTT 3 at [60].

on entirely arm's length terms may involve an unauthorised payment in the following four circumstances:

(a) the investment is a loan made to or in respect of a member;
(b) a payment or benefit is provided to a member under or in connection with the investment made by the scheme;
(c) the investment is used in some way to provide a benefit to a member; or
(d) the scheme is an investment-regulated pension scheme and it holds taxable property.

**18-006** The policy for this appears to be an extension of the aforementioned policy: the trustees' investment decisions should not be influenced by a desire to provide pre-retirement benefits, because there is an increased risk that such investments will not be appropriate and may have the effect of either depleting the scheme funds or causing the fund to grow more slowly than would otherwise be the case.

**18-007** In addition, it will be seen that the unauthorised payments regime penalises non-standard benefits taken even after the member has reached normal minimum pension age. The original policy for this may have been to ensure that a member's benefits continue until death. However, more recent developments in the context of money purchase schemes[6] make it clear that this is no longer a general policy: once a member has attained normal minimum pension age the member is free to take as much or as little of his fund as and when he wishes. In the light of these developments, what is the policy of penalising non-standard benefits once the member has reached normal minimum pension age? One might tentatively suggest that the policy for requiring benefits to be in a prescribed form is to ensure that they are appropriately taxed. This is not, of course, a policy, because it does not explain *why* they are penalised. Why not tax such benefits at the recipient's marginal rate, instead of imposing the unauthorised payments charge, surcharge, and scheme sanction charge? It is difficult to find any consistent policy currently reflected in FA 2004 Pt 4 insofar as it applies to the penalisation of non-standard benefits after normal minimum pension age.

**18-008** The position is ameliorated to some extent by the inclusion of a process whereby HMRC (and, on appeal, the FTT) can discharge a taxpayer from liability for the unauthorised payments surcharge and scheme sanction charge. In the context of an application to be discharged from the scheme sanction charge, Nugee J explained:[7]

> "The tax charged at stage (iv) [on pension benefits] will tend to be lower than the tax relief given at stage (i) [on pension contributions]. Parliament is content for the Exchequer to suffer these costs given the social utility of individuals saving for their retirement, but only where the entire bargain set out at [72] is respected. It is for this reason that different aspects of the unauthorised payments regime apply to different potential breaches of the bargain. For example, if a registered scheme impermissibly pays benefits to a member before he or she reaches 55, there is an unauthorised payment because the Exchequer has suffered the costs we have outlined, but since the funds have been drawn before retirement age, the social utility of funding retirement is not present. In a similar vein, if pension funds are lent by way of risky loans to an employer, the Exchequer is exposed to the risk that, even though it has given tax relief, and exempted income and gains of the scheme from tax, the funds are not ultimately available to pay pension benefits."

These observations also explain how the making of unauthorised payments can be more, or less, serious. For example, an extreme form of "pensions liberation"

---

[6] Notably the introduction of flexi-access drawdown funds, and the disapplication of IHTA 1984 s.3(3) in the context of omissions to exercise pension rights.
[7] *HMRC v Bella Figura Ltd* [2020] UKUT 120 (TCC) at [74] and [75].

might involve a co-ordinated attempt by an individual to access a pension fund held in a registered scheme before he or she reaches the age of 55 in a manner that escapes tax altogether. Such a scheme seeks to impose on the Exchequer the cost of deductions at stage (i) and exemptions at stage (iii) even though no retirement benefits are ultimately provided. In addition, were such a scheme successful the Exchequer would not even obtain tax at stage (iv) when the funds leave the scheme. Considerably less serious would be the making of a loan to an employer which, while it fails the requirements necessary to be an "authorised employer loan" (so exposing the Exchequer to a risk of loss) is ultimately repaid in full with a market rate of interest so that the Exchequer suffers no actual cost and the social utility of the provision of retirement benefits is preserved.

## UNAUTHORISED PAYMENTS

An "unauthorised payment" means either an unauthorised *member* payment or an unauthorised *employer* payment.[8] As will be seen below, each type of unauthorised payment may be further divided into *actual* and *deemed* unauthorised payments. Deemed unauthorised payments involve transactions that would not ordinarily constitute "payments" (or, if they do, they are not payments *by the pension scheme*).

**18-009**

### Unauthorised member payments

Section 160(2) provides that "unauthorised member payment" means:

**18-010**

"(a) a payment by a registered pension scheme to or in respect of a person who is or has been a member of the pension scheme which is not authorised by section 164, and
(b) anything which is to be treated as an unauthorised payment to or in respect of a person who is or has been a member of the pension scheme under this Part."

Payments within s.160(2)(a) are referred to in this chapter as "actual" unauthorised member payments, and payments within s.160(2)(b) are referred to as "deemed" unauthorised member payments.

**18-011**

### Unauthorised employer payments

Section 160(4) provides that "unauthorised employer payment" means:

**18-012**

"(a) a payment by a registered pension scheme that is an occupational pension scheme, to or in respect of a person who is or has been a sponsoring employer, which is not authorised by section 175, and
(b) anything which is to be treated as an unauthorised payment to a person who is or has been a sponsoring employer under section 181."

Payments within s.160(4)(a) are referred to in this chapter as "actual" unauthorised employer payments, and payments within s.160(4)(b) are referred to as "deemed" unauthorised employer payments.

**18-013**

---

[8] FA 2004 s.160(5).

## ACTUAL UNAUTHORISED PAYMENTS

**18-014** It is convenient to deal with actual unauthorised member payments and actual unauthorised employer payments together, as the provisions are very similar. The constituent parts of an actual unauthorised member/employer payment are:

(a) a payment;
(b) by a registered pension scheme;
(c) to or in respect of a member/employer;
(d) which is not one of the six types of authorised member payment listed in s.164(1) or one of the six types of authorised employer payment in s.175 (as the case may be).

**18-015** In most cases it will be clear whether these constituent parts are present. Where difficulties are encountered in practice, they usually relate to (c). Once it is established that a payment is *to or in respect of* a member/employer then it will always be an unauthorised payment unless it is one of the authorised payments listed in s.164(1) or s.175. Each constituent part is now considered.

### "Payment"

**18-016** The meaning of "payment" is considered in Ch.2.

### "By" a registered pension scheme

**18-017** A payment can be an actual unauthorised payment only if it is made "by" a registered pension scheme.[9] A payment is "by" a registered pension scheme if the payment is made from sums or assets held for the purposes of the pension scheme.[10] Per FA 2004 s.150(1), the "pension scheme" consists of all the arrangement(s) which are capable of having effect so as to provide benefits in the specified circumstances, and so "sums or assets held for the purposes of the scheme" must mean property that may be used to provide the benefits.

**18-018** It follows that payments by persons other than the trustee or manager of the pension scheme may be payments "by" the pension scheme. For example, it is quite common for the administrators of a pension scheme to have the ability to control payments of scheme property, and if they were to make a payment of scheme property that would clearly involve a payment by the pension scheme. The same would apply to payments of scheme property held by a nominee for the trustee or manager, such as an investment manager.

**18-019** In this respect, HMRC's position regarding investment vehicles appears to be misconceived. At PTM026000, HMRC state that if a pension scheme purchases an annuity, insurance contract or other "investment vehicle" and the vehicle remains in the ownership of the scheme (i.e. the vehicle is not bought in the name of the member) then a payment by the vehicle is a payment by the scheme even without the application of s.161(3) (see below). This seems wrong unless the vehicle is a mechanism through which pension benefits are to be provided to the member, because only in those circumstances will the vehicle form part of the "pension scheme". A vehicle may be a mechanism for providing pension benefits where the arrangements between the pension scheme and the vehicle are such that the provision of benefits to or in respect of a member is expressly anticipated. In such

---

[9] See FA 2004 s.160(2)(a) and s.161(4)(a).
[10] FA 2004 s.279(2).

## ACTUAL UNAUTHORISED PAYMENTS

circumstances a payment by the vehicle would amount to a payment "by" the pension scheme, because the property held by the vehicle would be held for the purposes of the pension scheme.

It should be stressed, however, that this will rarely be the case where a pension scheme invests in an "investment vehicle". For example, if a pension scheme invests in shares issued by a company, a payment by the company would not, without more, be a payment of property held for the purposes of the pension scheme. The property held for the purposes of the pension scheme cannot be both the shares *and* the property owned by the company.[11]

18-020

This analysis is further supported by FA 2004 s.186(1)(a), which uses the same terminology as s.279(2).[12] No one (least of all HMRC) would suggest that where a company owned by a registered pension scheme receives investment income it is exempt from tax under s.186(1)(a) on the basis that the company's property is held for the purposes of a registered pension scheme. There is no reason that the same phrase used in s.279(2) and s.186(1)(a) should have different meanings.

18-021

It follows that if a pension scheme buys shares in a sponsoring employer and the employer makes payments such as loans or distributions to its employees or shareholders who also happen to be members of the pension scheme, those loans or distributions should not be payments "by" the pension scheme.

18-022

Of course, if the pension scheme is entitled to payment from an investment vehicle and directs the vehicle to make a payment to a third party (including a member/sponsoring employer), that will be a payment "by" the pension scheme. In these circumstances, the property may be said to form part of the pension scheme when the pension scheme became entitled to direct the payment, because the property then became "held for the purposes of the pension scheme".

18-023

*Payments under or in connection with investments*

FA 2004 s.161(3) and (4) extend the circumstances in which a payment will be made "by" the pension scheme. They provide as follows:

18-024

"(3) Subsection (4) applies to a payment made or benefit provided under or in connection with an investment (including an insurance contract or annuity) acquired using sums or assets held for the purposes of a registered pension scheme.
(4) The payment or benefit is to be treated as made or provided from sums or assets held for the purposes of the pension scheme, even if the pension scheme has been wound up since the investment was acquired."

FA 2004 s.161(7) further extends the application of s.161(3) by providing that any increase in the value of an asset held by, or reduction in the liability of, a person connected with a current or former member is *treated* as an increase or reduction for the benefit of the member.

18-025

FA 2004 s.161(3) and (4) do not generally apply to annuities purchased before 6 April 2006 with property held for the purposes of a tax-approved scheme, unless the terms of the annuity contract are amended after 5 April 2006 to allow a payment that would be an unauthorised payment if it had been made by a registered pension scheme.[13]

18-026

The provisions appear to be aimed primarily at situations where a pension

18-027

---

[11] Payments by the company would usually be brought within FA 2004 Pt 4 by ss.161(3) and (4) (considered below).
[12] Section 186(1)(a) provides "No liability to income tax arises in respect of income derived from investments *held for the purposes of a registered pension scheme* ...".
[13] See The Taxation of Pension Schemes (Transitional Provisions) Order 2006 (SI 2006/572) art.2.

scheme has bought an annuity or scheme pension for a member (i.e. in the member's name) from an insurance company. The intention is to ensure that any payments or benefits from the insurance company to the member or a sponsoring employer are within the scope of the unauthorised payments regime.[14] As noted above, HMRC's statement at PTM026000 that payments from investment vehicles belonging to a pension scheme are usually "by" the scheme even without the application of s.161(3) is doubtful, and so s.161(3) plays a more significant role than HMRC acknowledge.

**18-028** As noted above, a payment cannot be an unauthorised payment unless it is made "by" a registered pension scheme, and FA 2004 s.279(2) provides that references to payments by a registered pension scheme mean payments made from property held for the purposes of the pension scheme. Curiously, s.161(4) deems the s.161(3) payment to be made "from sums or assets held for the purposes of the registered pension scheme", but there is nothing in FA 2004 Pt 4 which provides that a payment made from sums or assets held for the purposes of a registered pension scheme is the same as a payment "by" a registered pension scheme. The draftsman of s.161(4) may have assumed that the effect of s.279(2) is to make these two phrases interchangeable, but that is not what s.279(2) actually says. This is a drafting error, but the meaning is clear: a payment or benefit from a third party is deemed to be a payment "by" the pension scheme if the payment or benefit is connected with a scheme investment.

**18-029** FA 2004 s.161(3) applies only to "a payment made or benefit provided". This appears to be narrower than every unauthorised payment that may be made by a pension scheme.[15] In particular, a *deemed* payment within FA 2004 ss.172–174A and s.181 will not involve a payment and may or may not provide a benefit[16] depending on the circumstances.

*"Under" or "in connection with"*

**18-030** Section 161(3) applies only to a payment or benefit provided "under" or "in connection with" an investment. One would expect a payment or benefit to be provided *under* an investment if the payment or benefit is made pursuant to the terms of the investment.[17] If, for example, a pension scheme purchases an annuity in the name of the member then the payment of the annuity to the member is a payment *under* the annuity contract.

**18-031** The prepositional phrase "in connection with" is commonly used in anti-avoidance provisions and its meaning has been considered in a number of cases. In *Re Nanaimo Community Hotel Ltd*,[18] McFarlane J said, "one of the very generally accepted meanings of 'connexion' is 'relation between things one of which is

---

[14] Pursuant to FA 2004 s.153(8), a deferred annuity is deemed to be a registered pension scheme and so the unauthorised payment regime would apply to it for that reason. However, an immediate annuity is not deemed to be a registered pension scheme and so s.161(3) is intended to fill the gap.

[15] If all unauthorised payments had been the intention, s.161(3) could easily have been drafted along the lines of FA 2004 Sch.34 para.1, which applies the "member payment provisions" to payments from RNUKS.

[16] "Benefit" is not defined in FA 2004, but some guidance may be obtained from FA 2004 s.173 (see below).

[17] In *Danvers v HMRC* [2016] UKUT 569 at [52], the UT suggest that a payment is *under* an investment if it is paid *from* the investment vehicle. Also see *Trustees of Barclays Bank Pension Fund v HMRC* [2005] UKSPC SPC00520 at [72] to [79]: in order for a payment or benefit to be provided *under* an investment, the investment must have a commercial life separate from the mechanics of conferring the payment or benefit.

[18] *Re Nanaimo Community Hotel Ltd* [1944] 4 D.L.R. 638 at 639.

bound up with or involved in another'; or 'having to do with'. The words include matters occurring prior to as well as subsequent to or consequent upon so long as they are related to the principal thing. The phrase "having to do with" perhaps gives as good a suggestion of the meaning as could be had".[19] In *Emery v IRC*,[20] Nourse LJ said that it meant "a less definite causal link" (when contrasted with the causal link required by "whereby"). The phrase does not pose a causal test but simply asks whether there is a link.[21] It may describe a wide range of links and the court must look closely at the surrounding words and the context of the legislative scheme.[22]

In *J&A Young (Leicester) Ltd v HMRC*,[23] the FTT found that two propositions can be derived from the dozens of authorities which have considered those words in different contexts: 18-032

> "First, the words 'in connection with' generally have a very broad meaning. Secondly, the degree of connection—the remoteness, proximity and type of connection—required by the use of that phrase in a particular statute must be identified from the particular statutory context in which it is used."

In the context of s.161(3) the *link* must be between the payment or benefit and the investment. The noun "investment" has no precise legal meaning but usually means property acquired as a source of income[24] or to make a capital profit.[25] There is some authority that an unsecured loan, even at interest, does not constitute an investment (at least in a non-statutory context)[26] but it is extremely unlikely that an unsecured loan at interest would not be an investment for the purposes of s.161(3). However, an interest-free loan cannot be an investment because it is not a source of income. Similarly, property that is acquired by trustees for the use and enjoyment of a beneficiary could not normally be described as an investment.[27] On that basis, the purchase of an annuity for the member (i.e. in the member's name) would not be an "investment", because it will not produce any return for the pension scheme. Yet this seems to be precisely the sort of arrangement that s.161(3) is aimed at.[28] Perhaps anticipating this, s.161(3) expressly provides that "investment" includes an insurance contract or annuity. But that does not help us to understand what "investment" is intended to mean in cases other than insurance contracts and annuities.[29] To reconcile this difficulty it is necessary to interpret "investment" as meaning an application of property to produce a return for the pension scheme *or to produce an income for the member*. Whilst the application of property to produce an income for the member is clearly *not* an investment from the perspective of the pension scheme, it can be regarded as an investment from the member's perspective, and it is noteworthy that s.161(3) does not specify that the *investment* must be 18-033

---

[19] Cited with approval by Sommerville LJ in *Johnson v Johnson* [1952] 1 All E.R. 250.
[20] *Emery v IRC* [1981] S.T.C. 150 at 171.
[21] David Richards J, whose decision in the High Court was affirmed by the Court of Appeal in *Barclays Bank Plc v HMRC* [2007] S.T.C. 747.
[22] Per Arden J in *Barclays Bank Plc v HMRC* [2007] EWCA Civ 442.
[23] *J&A Young (Leicester) Ltd v HMRC* [2015] UKFTT 638 at [73].
[24] Per Lord Walker in *Dominica Social Security Board v Nature Island Investment Co* [2008] UKPC 19.
[25] See *Marson v Morton* (1986) 1 W.L.R. 1343.
[26] See e.g. *Khoo Tek Keong v Ch'ng Joo Tuan Neoh* [1934] A.C. 529 (Privy Council); and *re Peczenick's Settlement* [1964] 1 W.L.R. 720.
[27] *Re Power* [1947] 2 All E.R. 282; [1947] 2 All E.R. 282.
[28] If the pension scheme no longer exists, as is expressly anticipated by s.161(4), that will usually be because the scheme funds have been used to buy an annuity for the member. Also see the extract from PTM026000 cited in para.18-026.
[29] Section 186(3) and (4) provide that, for the purposes of FA 2004 Pt 4, *investments* includes futures contracts and options contracts, but that provides little assistance in interpreting s.161(3).

an investment from the perspective of the pension scheme. Although this interpretation involves a conflation of the pension scheme and the member, it seems to be the only way to reconcile this difficulty.

**18-034** When construing s.161(3), it should also be noted that it does not provide that a payment *by* an investment vehicle is deemed to be a payment *by* the pension scheme. There must be a "connection" between the investment and the payment or benefit, and the extent of the connection must be determined from the provisions. For example, if a pension scheme buys shares in a bank and the bank subsequently lends money to a member, there will be some sort of connection between the shares and the loan (because the shares were issued by the lender) but it is clearly not intended that the loan would be a payment by the pension scheme under s.161(4). In these circumstances s.161(3) does not apply because that connection is not the sort of connection that s.161(3) is concerned with. It is not a *relevant* connection.

**18-035** How does one determine what is a relevant connection? These are anti-avoidance provisions: the purpose of s.161(3) is to prevent taxpayers from circumventing the unauthorised payments regime in FA 2004 Pt 4. It achieves this by deeming certain payments made by third parties as having been made "by" the pension scheme. If a payment to the member is conditional on the pension scheme acquiring the investment, that is clearly a relevant connection. In the context of a series of steps with one overall purpose, one would expect the individual steps to be connected with each other. The purpose or motivation of the trustee or manager in acquiring the investment does not appear to be material, especially where other persons (such as the member) have significant influence over the choice of investment and are aware of the possibility of a connected payment to the member. Similarly, it is not necessary for the person making the payment to the member to have knowledge of the investment by the pension scheme (especially where there is more than one investment vehicle between the pension scheme and the person making the payment to the member).

**18-036** A straightforward example of the type of transaction to which s.161(3) commonly applies is where the trustees or managers acquire a particular investment and as a result the member receives some commission from a third party. The trustee or manager may not know about the commission, but there is clearly a connection because the member would not have received the commission but for the investment. If the trustee or manager is not aware of the payment of commission to the member then it may be assumed that the investment is on arm's length terms[30] and so, by definition, the commission or other payment to the member does not in any way detract from the investment.[31] The policy of s.161(3) is therefore not to prevent depletion of the scheme assets but to discourage the provision of non-standard benefits to members.

**18-037** In *Danvers v HMRC*[32] a pension scheme purchased preference shares in a company and that company lent money to another company and that second company made a loan to a member of the pension scheme. HMRC argued that the loan to the member was *in connection with* the investment by the pension scheme. In that case, the loan to the member was expressly conditional on the purchase of the preference shares, so it was not difficult to find a relevant connection between the payment and the investment. Indeed, the FTT found that the investment and the

---

[30] If that were not the case then it is likely that the purchase of the investment would be an unauthorised payment because it was a payment "in respect of" the member and it would not be a scheme administration member payment.

[31] HMRC do however accept that a payment of such commission may, in certain circumstances, be a scheme administration member payment (and therefore an authorised payment): PTM143200.

[32] *Danvers v HMRC* [2016] UKUT 569.

loan were "inextricably linked". The UT considered this to be another way of saying that Mr Danvers would not have received the loan if he had not promised that the pension scheme would purchase the preference shares and it was never going to be the case that having received the loan he did not ensure that the investment was made. The FTT also found that the entire arrangement was orchestrated from beginning to end to ensure that Mr Danvers received the loan. In that case there was a close association between the two companies, and the first company provided the second company with funds, and so this was a fairly clear example of the sort of mischief that s.161(3) is aimed at. But it is equally clear from the decision that there need not be any such association or flow of funds between the investment vehicle and the person making the payment to the member. It follows that if a person agrees to make a loan to a member of a pension scheme on condition that for the duration of the loan his pension fund invests in the shares of a particular FTSE 100 company then there will be the necessary connection between the investment and the payment and so s.161(3) will apply. At first glance, it is perhaps surprising that such an arrangement should be considered objectionable, however it is (just about) consistent with the policy of inappropriately influencing scheme investments.

*White v HMRC*[33] concerned essentially the same arrangement as in *Danvers*, except that the loan was not expressly conditional on the investment. The loan was, however, expressly connected with the pension scheme as it was intended that the loan would be repaid from funds paid from the scheme to Mr White on retirement. The FTT considered that the nature of the connection or link required by s.161(3) is primarily causal and found that the relevant question to be answered was: *would one have been made without the other*? In the absence of any evidence in the loan agreement itself, the FTT had to determine whether there was a relevant connection from the surrounding evidence. The intentions, expectations and understanding of Mr White were relevant, and presumably so too were the intentions and expectations of the lender (see [115] and [123]). The FTT found from the surrounding evidence that the investment and the loan were more likely than not to have been connected. The FTT inferred from the evidence (or lack thereof) that the arrangement had been suggested to Mr White by the lender and he took the necessary steps to transfer his pension funds to a pension scheme that would permit the proposed investment, and he regarded it as important and possibly essential that the pension scheme did acquire that investment in order for him to receive the loan.[34]

18-038

So the FTT in *White* interpreted the *in connection with* test as being primarily causal. Not, it should be noted, *exclusively* causal. It is clear from the other authorities cited above that the phrase is broader than a merely causal test.

18-039

A potential difficulty with s.161(3) arises where an authorised employer loan is made by a small occupational scheme where the same individuals are members, trustees and also control the sponsoring employer. Such a loan is clearly an investment, and the fact that it involves an authorised payment does not prevent s.161(3) from applying to any payments from the employer. Many payments by the sponsoring employer to a member, such as a payment by way of dividend (received in his capacity as shareholder) will not be within s.161(3) because there is no relevant connection between the loan to the employer and the payment of dividends (for example). But if the member would not have received the dividend (or other payment) were it not for the loan to the employer (because the employer did not have

18-040

---

[33] *White v HMRC* [2016] UKFTT 802.
[34] A number of other factors, including the following, were also found to suggest a relevant connection: (a) the loan and the investment were made on the same day; (b) the lender's recourse was limited to the funds in the pension scheme; and (c) the investment by the pension scheme did not seem like a compelling investment (and this suggested that the real reason was to procure the loan).

any money available to pay a dividend, for example) then it seems likely that s.161(3) would apply in principle. Similarly, if a member-trustee becomes aware of a potentially very profitable investment opportunity, he may arrange for the pension scheme to make an authorised employer loan and for the employer to use the borrowed money to acquire the investment. The pension scheme will receive some interest, but if the investment is successful the employer will make much more profit, and if this profit is subsequently paid to the member by way of dividend (for example) it seems arguable that s.161(3) would apply. There is a causal connection if the employer would otherwise have been unable to acquire the investment. There is no easy answer to this, but the better view is probably that there is no relevant connection between the loan to the employer and the payment to the member where the payment to the member is entirely dependent on external factors (such as the success of the investment). Penalising such payments is not consistent with any principles or policies on which the unauthorised payments regime is based. Also, it should be noted that in almost all cases one would expect an authorised employer loan to increase the profitability of the employer to some extent (otherwise why would the employer want the loan?) and so it is implicit that *some* benefit to the owners of the employer must be acceptable.

**18-041** As noted above, HMRC consider that s.161(3) and (4) are relevant only where the investment is not held by the scheme (e.g. an annuity bought by the scheme in the member's name), because payments by an investment vehicle held by the pension scheme are payments "by" the pension scheme.[35] It is doubtful that this is correct and it is noteworthy that HMRC argued that the opposite is correct in *Danvers*.

### Payments "to" or "in respect of" a member or employer

**18-042** A payment cannot be an actual unauthorised payment unless it is "to" or "in respect of" a member or sponsoring employer. As will be seen below, the (no doubt deliberate) ambiguity regarding the meaning of the term *in respect of* makes it difficult to delineate the scope of the unauthorised payments regime with any precision.

**18-043** HMRC do not appear to accept that the requirement that a payment must be "to" or "in respect of" a member or employer is a separate requirement within the concept of an unauthorised payment. It seems to be HMRC's view that the authorised and unauthorised payment dichotomy is exhaustive: all payments by a scheme must be one or the other (and this includes, presumably, payments to third parties to invest scheme property).[36] If that were correct then all payments by a pension scheme would be "to" or "in respect of" a member or sponsoring employer. This is very doubtful. If it were correct, all payments by the pension scheme by way of investment would need to come within ss.171 or 180[37] or else they would be unauthorised payments, and this would mean that a pension scheme could never make a loan except an authorised employer loan. This cannot be right and is contrary to HMRC's stated position on third party loans.[38] Indeed, when one considers that a deposit with a bank probably amounts to a *loan* for the purposes of FA

---

[35] PTM026000.
[36] PTM026000: "Any payment (or deemed payment) a scheme makes that doesn't fall within the defined list [of authorised payments] will be classed as an unauthorised payment and taxed accordingly".
[37] These are, respectively, scheme administration member payments and scheme administration employer payments. These are two categories of authorised payment, but neither can apply to a loan.
[38] PTM123100 provides that "There is no objection to a registered pension scheme making loans to

2004,[39] it is even clearer that HMRC's position cannot be correct. The better view is that a payment to an unconnected third party to acquire an investment (with no intention to benefit a member or sponsoring employer) is not paid "in respect of" a member or employer and accordingly it is neither authorised nor unauthorised: it is a "*nothing*".

**18-044** When is a payment "to" a member or employer? Plainly if it is paid to the member's or employer's bank account[40] or (in the context of a transfer of an asset) it is transferred into his name or he takes possession of it, such that he becomes the absolute owner of the property paid or transferred. This includes joint bank accounts and jointly owned assets, since joint tenants own the entirety of the property.

**18-045** When is a payment "in respect of" a member or employer? The legislation itself provides little guidance, although two points are clear. First, it is implicit from FA 2004 ss.167(1) and 168(1) that all authorised death benefits are payments made "in respect of" the (deceased) member. Second, s.161(5) provides that a payment to or in respect of a person who is not a member or sponsoring employer, but who is connected with a sponsoring employer or member (or was connected at the date of the member's death) is expressly *deemed* to be a payment made "in respect" of the connected member or sponsoring employer. "Connected" for these purposes is determined in accordance with the test in ITA 2007 s.993.

**18-046** In *Albon v Naza Motor Trading Sdn Bhd*,[41] Lightman J approved the following formulation of Mann CJ in the Supreme Court of Victoria case of *Trustees Executors & Agency Co Ltd v Reilly*:[42]

> "The words 'in respect of' are difficult of definition, but they have the widest possible meaning of any expression intended to convey some connection or relation between the two subject-matters to which the words refer."

**18-047** So plainly there must be some connection or relation between the payment and the member or employer. But what is the extent of the required relationship or connection for the purposes of FA 2004? For the reasons given above in relation to third party loans, it cannot simply be that the payment *relates to* the member in the sense that he has requested or directed it, or that it is his fund under the pension scheme that is being invested.

**18-048** The Explanatory Notes to the Finance Bill 2004 generally refer to payments to or *for the benefit of* a member or employer, and the relevant legislation prior to FA 2004 also generally used this terminology: unauthorised payments were either to or *for the benefit of* a member.[43] Although the phrase *in respect of* is clearly not limited to payments from which the member or employer derives some sort of benefit (otherwise ss.171 and 180 would be otiose) the overarching policy of the unauthorised payments regime is to prevent pre-retirement benefits and so it is a reasonably useful guide to the meaning of the term *in respect of*.

---

third parties i.e. persons not connected to members or sponsoring employers. Such loans are normally on an arm's length basis at a market rate".

[39] As Lord Millett explained in *Foskett v McKeown* [2001] 1 A.C. 102: "Money paid into a bank account belongs legally and beneficially to the bank and not to the account holder. [...]. There is merely a single debt of an amount equal to the final balance standing to the credit of the account holder".

[40] See *Simpson v Executors of Bonner Maurice as Executor of Edward Kay* (1929) 14 T.C. 580.

[41] *Albon v Naza Motor Trading Sdn Bhd* [2007] EWHC 9 (Ch) at [27].

[42] *Trustees Executors & Agency Co Ltd v Reilly* [1941] V.L.R. 110.

[43] See ICTA 1988 s.600.

*Payments to connected persons*

**18-049** Section 161(5) (see above) both enlarges and restricts the payment provisions: a payment *to* a member's spouse is deemed to be a payment *in respect of* the member (assuming that the spouse is not also a member of the pension scheme), but a payment *to* a sponsoring employer can never be deemed to be a payment *in respect of* a member who is connected with the sponsoring employer.[44] If a payment is made to a person who is not a member or a sponsoring employer, but he is connected with *both* a sponsoring employer and a member, it seems that this will be a payment in respect of both the member and the employer. There is no reason that the same payment cannot be both an unauthorised member payment and an unauthorised employer payment.[45]

*Payments that deplete the fund*

**18-050** Given the overarching policy of restricting pre-retirement benefits, it seems very likely that any payment that knowingly depletes the value of a pension scheme will be *in respect of* a member or sponsoring employer (assuming that there is an identifiable member: see below). It is difficult to think of any legitimate reason that the trustees or managers of a pension scheme could deliberately make such a payment unless it was for the benefit of a member or (possibly) a sponsoring employer. Thus a payment of authorised death benefits is *in respect of* the deceased member, even if the recipient was not connected with the member prior to the member's death. The application of scheme property to purchase benefits for a member (i.e. in the member's name) is a payment *in respect of* the member. A payment from a pension scheme to the administrators in order to pay their fees is a payment *in respect of* a member or employer.[46] A transfer of scheme property from one pension scheme to another is a payment *in respect of* the member.[47] Such payments are "in respect of" the member because they have the effect of depleting the member's fund. To reiterate the point made above, it makes no difference whether the member requested the payment (or even whether he has consented to it): it is a payment *in respect of* him. Nowhere in FA 2004 Pt 4 is this principle set out expressly. It applies by necessary implication.

*Payments on uncommercial terms*

**18-051** As with payments that knowingly deplete the scheme fund, it is difficult to think of any legitimate reason that a pension scheme could make a payment that is otherwise clearly on uncommercial terms, even if the payment doesn't strictly deplete the value of the scheme fund (such as where an interest-free loan is made to a third party) unless it is to provide some sort of benefit to a member or sponsor-

---

[44] It is for this reason that an authorised employer loan is not deemed to be an unauthorised payment to any member(s) connected with the employer.

[45] This will not however give rise to double taxation as there is clearly only one unauthorised payment. Pursuant to s.208(2) and (3), the member and employer will be jointly and severally liable for the charge in these circumstances.

[46] See FA 2004 s.171(3)(a) and s.180(3)(a).

[47] If such a transfer did not involve a payment to or in respect of a member then s.164(1)(c), which provides that a recognised transfer is an authorised member payment, would be otiose.

ing employer. It is therefore likely that any such payment will be found to be *in respect of* a member or sponsoring employer.[48]

*Requirement to have an identifiable member*

In the context of an unauthorised member payment, the member is liable for the unauthorised payments charge and surcharge,[49] and it follows that it must be possible to identify which member a given payment is *in respect of* at the time of the payment. That appears to have been one of the conclusions that Bean J reached in *Dalriada Trustees Ltd v Faulds*.[50] That case involved a so-called "pension reciprocation plan" under which a pension scheme made a loan to a member of a different pension scheme in the "hope and expectation" that the other scheme would make a loan to a member of the scheme making the loan. Counsel for the defendants argued that a loan to a member of a different scheme is not *in respect of* a member of the paying scheme because: (a) the loans were not paid from a member's account, they were paid from the fund of a scheme; and (b) they were not used to "buy" a reciprocal loan for a particular member because when a loan was made it was not possible to identify a member who would receive a loan back—there was no twinning of members. There is no record of the claimants arguing to the contrary, and the judge does not analyse the defendant's arguments, he simply finds that they are right to say that the loans were not "to" or "in respect of" a member of the paying scheme. But it is not clear if he is agreeing only with their conclusion or also their reasons. As noted above, a payment cannot be *in respect of* the member simply because it is from the member's account (i.e. his arrangement under the pension scheme) because otherwise a loan to an unconnected third party could never be made from a member's account (because a loan can never be an authorised member payment) and that plainly cannot be correct.

18-052

If a payment is made but the value of the pension scheme is not depleted as a result (because property of equal value is acquired by the pension scheme in exchange for the payment) it should not be *to or in respect of* a member/employer unless the payment is to the member/employer or a person connected with the member/employer. Thus payments to unconnected third parties to acquire investments are *"nothings"*. The fact that the member may have requested (or even directed) the payment cannot itself make the payment *in respect of* the member. Does it make any difference if it is intended (by the person controlling the payments, which may or may not be the trustees or manager) that the investment will ultimately benefit the member in some way outside of the scheme? If the payment does not have the effect of depleting the value of the pension scheme, and is not otherwise on clearly uncommercial terms, it is strongly arguable that an intention that the member may receive some sort of incidental benefit will not cause the payment to be *in respect of* the member.[51] The position is even stronger where the payment by the pension scheme is to acquire an investment on arm's length terms, because in those circumstances even if the payment is found to be in respect of the member, it will be a scheme administration member payment (unless it is a loan) and therefore an authorised payment pursuant to FA 2004 s.171.

18-053

---

[48] A payment on clearly uncommercial terms would not be an "investment" and so s.161(3) could not apply.
[49] See ss.208(2) and 209(3).
[50] *Dalriada Trustees Ltd v Faulds* [2011] EWHC 3391 (Ch); [2012] 2 All E.R. 734. Also see the Pension Regulator's Compulsory Review (case ref: C4177180).
[51] Of course, any payment or benefit provided under or in connection with the investment may be within the ambit of s.161(3). An intention to benefit a member may well provide the necessary connection.

**18-054**  It seems likely that a payment to a third party to enable, but not to bind, that third party to make a payment to a member or employer is not a payment in respect of the member or employer (assuming that the payment does not deplete the value of the pension scheme, and is not otherwise on clearly uncommercial terms).[52] The existence of FA 2004 s.161(3), which would normally apply in these circumstances, supports this analysis. However, in *Dalriada Trustees Ltd v HMRC*,[53] it was common ground that a payment to a member of a different pension scheme was "in respect of" an identifiable member of the paying scheme if the administrators *intended* the payment to be matched with a payment back to the member of the paying scheme.[54] In that case, the loans were not "investments" so s.161(3) could not apply.

**18-055**  In *Clark v HMRC*,[55] surplus funds were paid from a pension scheme to a sponsoring employer[56] in circumstances where the overall intention (by the member and the sponsoring employer, who together controlled the relevant payments) was for the funds to be passed from the employer to a trust arrangement that would in turn make loans to Mr Clark (a member of the pension scheme). As a result of this intention, the FTT found that the payment to the sponsoring employer was a payment "in respect of" the member: "the common thread running through all these arrangements, both as they were conceived and more particularly in the way they operated in practice, was Mr Clark".[57] There are a number of difficulties with this decision. In particular, if the payment to the employer was an authorised surplus payment then it would seem to be contrary to the overall policy of the legislation if the payment could also be *in respect of* the member merely because the sponsoring employer intended to use the funds to benefit the member: there is no reason that this should be relevant. An authorised member/employer payment cannot also be an unauthorised member/employer payment.[58] Once the property has ceased to be held for the purposes of the pension scheme the only way it can be brought within the unauthorised payments regime is via s.161(3). It must therefore be questionable whether this part of the decision is correct. Indeed, in the context of payment to invest the scheme property it seems clear that this part of the decision in *Clark* is unlikely to be sound: if scheme money is lent on arm's length terms to an unconnected third party and there is an intention that a member will ultimately receive a benefit, the decision in *Clark* suggests the payment to the third party will be a payment *in respect of* the member and it will therefore be an unauthorised payment (as a loan cannot be an authorised payment). But the subsequent benefit to the member will also be taxable by virtue of s.161(3) because it is provided in connection with an investment (i.e. the loan). This would therefore give rise to double taxation and that cannot have been Parliament's intention. The much better view is that an investment made on arm's length terms (and so does not knowingly deplete the

---

[52] See *In re O'Shea* [1911] 2 K.B. 981.
[53] *Dalriada Trustees Ltd v HMRC* [2023] UKFTT 314 (TC).
[54] See [201]. Given the focus on intention, the loan will be an unauthorised payment even if no loan back was in fact made.
[55] *Clark v HMRC* [2016] UKFTT 630 (TC). These points are unaffected by the subsequent decisions of the UT and Court of Appeal.
[56] So this did involve value leaving the pension scheme, but this does not appear to have been material to the decision.
[57] *Clark v HMRC* [2016] UKFTT 630 (TC) at [105].
[58] e.g. where authorised death benefits are paid to a beneficiary connected with a sponsoring employer (which is very common in the context of small occupational schemes), if the reasoning in *Clark v HMRC* [2016] UKFTT 630 (TC) were correct then the payment would constitute an unauthorised employer payment. This would be an absurd result, and is clearly wrong. It is wrong because if it is an authorised payment it cannot also be an unauthorised payment.

scheme funds) is "to" or "in respect of" a member only if it is paid to the member or a person connected with the member.

In certain contexts, a payment from A to B at the direction or request of C has been found to involve a payment *to* C.[59] In the context of FA 2004 Pt 4, it is arguable that such a payment would be neither "to" nor "in respect of" a member of a pension scheme (i.e. person C) because it is common for a member to request or direct that payment is made to a particular counterparty to acquire an investment. For the reasons given above, it is very likely that FA 2004 treats investments with unconnected third parties as "*nothings*".

18-056

One might expect that a payment from a pension scheme to a member as bare trustee for an unconnected person would be characterised as a payment to the unconnected person (rather than *to* or *in respect of* the member), and the same analysis to apply to a payment to a member or employer as trustee of a trust that is not a bare trust. This is because the member does not in reality receive anything of any value. However, for the reasons given in Ch.2, FA 2004 is generally concerned with "payments" rather than benefits. Such a payment will therefore be a payment to a member and will be an unauthorised payment unless FA 2004 ss.171 or 180 applies.

18-057

*Summary*

In summary:

18-058

(a) the fact that a payment is made from an identifiable member's arrangement under the pension scheme should not in itself cause the payment to be *in respect of* that member;

(b) if a payment has the effect of depleting the value of the pension scheme (i.e. the scheme does not acquire an asset of equal value in exchange for the payment) or is otherwise clearly uncommercial then the payment will be *in respect of* a member or employer, provided that there is an identifiable member or employer;

(c) if a payment to an unconnected third party is made on arm's length terms then the fact that a member or employer is intended to benefit should not in itself make the payment *in respect of* him (although FA 2004 s.161(3) is likely to apply in these circumstances);

(d) the fact that a member has requested or directed a payment should not in itself cause the payment to be *in respect of* that member;

(e) if a payment is an authorised payment (and therefore, by definition, *to or in respect of* a member/employer) then FA 2004 s.161(3) should have no application even if the payment is intended to, or indeed does, indirectly provide a benefit to the member/employer.

## DEEMED UNAUTHORISED MEMBER PAYMENTS

The following are the main deemed unauthorised member payments, each of which is considered in detail below:

18-059

(a) assignments within s.172;
(b) surrenders within s.172A;

---

[59] *Parsons v Equitable Investment Co Ltd* [1916] 2 Ch. 527 (Lord Cozens-Hardy MR); *Law v Coburn* [1972] 1 W.L.R. 1238.

(c) increases in rights of connected person on death within s.172B;
(d) allocation of unallocated employer contributions within s.172C;
(e) limit on increase in benefits within s.172D;
(f) benefits within s.173;
(g) value shifting within s.174; and
(h) holding taxable property within s.174A.

**18-060** In addition, an unauthorised payment is deemed to be made in the following circumstances:

(a) The annual rate of a scheme pension in payment is reduced.[60]
(b) Sums or assets held for the purposes of a money purchase arrangement are transferred to a defined benefits arrangement and the main purpose of the transfer is to increase the "applicable amount" on the member becoming entitled to a scheme pension, and the member becomes entitled to a scheme pension under the relevant defined benefits arrangement.[61] The transferee pension scheme is deemed to make the unauthorised payment to the member. These provisions also apply where there is a surrender (instead of a transfer) and, in consequence of the surrender, there is a corresponding increase in the sums or assets held for the purposes of, or representing rights under, a defined benefits arrangement relating to the member under the pension scheme.
(c) One of the following types of benefit ceases and is not replaced by the same type of benefit (see Ch.12):
  (i) lifetime annuity;[62]
  (ii) short-term annuity,[63] dependant's short-term annuity,[64] nominees' short-term annuity[65] or successors' short-term annuity;[66]
  (iii) dependants' annuity,[67] nominees' annuity[68] or successors' annuity;[69] or
  (iv) dependants' scheme pension.[70]
(d) A PCLS is "recycled" (i.e. contributed to a registered pension scheme).[71]

**18-061** The above transactions either do not involve a "payment" by the pension scheme, or they do involve a payment but it is not to or in respect of a member. If any of the above involved a payment by the pension scheme to or in respect of a member, it would be an actual unauthorised member payment because it is not in the list of authorised member payments in s.164(1).[72]

---

[60] FA 2004 Sch.28 para.2A. See Ch.13.
[61] FA 2004 Sch.29 para.3(10). See Ch.14.
[62] The Registered Pension Schemes (Transfer of Sums and Assets) Regulations 2006 (SI 2006/499) reg.6(2).
[63] FA 2004 Sch.28 para.6 and SI 2006/499 reg.7(1).
[64] FA 2004 Sch.28 para.20 and SI 2006/499 reg.11.
[65] FA 2004 Sch.28 para.27C and SI 2006/499 reg.17.
[66] FA 2004 Sch.28 para.27H and SI 2006/499 reg.18.
[67] SI 2006/499 reg.10.
[68] FA 2004 Sch.28 para.27AA and SI 2006/499 reg.19(2).
[69] FA 2004 Sch.28 para.27FA and SI 2006/499 reg.20(2).
[70] FA 2004 Sch.28 para.16 and SI 2006/499 reg.9.
[71] FA 2004 Sch.29 para.3A.
[72] Confirmed at para.192 of the explanatory notes to Finance (No.2) Bill 2005.

## Can an authorised payment also be a deemed unauthorised payment?

An authorised member/employer payment cannot be an actual unauthorised member/employer payment, because ss.160(2)(a) and 160(4)(a) preclude this. It is very likely that an authorised member/employer payment cannot also be a deemed unauthorised member/employer payment. If that were not correct, a recognised transfer (which is an authorised payment) would be a deemed unauthorised payment under s.172A (surrenders)[73] or possibly s.174 (value shifting), which is plainly not intended. The analysis of the FTT in *Clark v HMRC*[74] (that an authorised surplus payment to the employer was also an unauthorised payment *in respect of* the member, because the sponsoring employer intended to use the funds to benefit the member) seems wrong for the reasons given above.

**18-062**

## Can an actual unauthorised payment also be a deemed unauthorised payment?

As mentioned above, an unauthorised member payment may also be an unauthorised employer payment (but this will not give rise to double taxation as there is clearly only one unauthorised payment). However, an actual unauthorised member payment cannot also be a deemed unauthorised member payment. Of course, where there are two transactions (even if closely connected), it is possible for both transactions to be unauthorised payments. For example, in *Dalriada Trustees Ltd v HMRC*,[75] a pension scheme made a loan to a member of a different scheme and that second scheme made a loan to a member of the first scheme. The FTT held that: (a) each loan was an actual unauthorised payment because it was intended to be matched with a loan back to a member of the paying scheme (so it was *in respect of* that member); and (b) the loan back conferred a benefit on the same member, so it was a deemed unauthorised payment under s.173. It should be noted that the circumstances of that case were highly unusual.[76]

**18-063**

## Implications of connected persons

As is explained below, a number of provisions in FA 2004 Pt 4 apply where payments or benefits are provided to persons connected with members and/or sponsoring employers.[77] It is quite possible, especially in the context of small occupational schemes, for all of a pension scheme's members to be connected with each other and also connected with the sponsoring employer. A deemed unauthorised payment to one of the members will be also be a deemed unauthorised payment to all the other connected members and the sponsoring employer. This may appear to create multiple unauthorised payments, potentially giving rise to multiple tax charges, however the better view is that there is just one unauthorised payment

**18-064**

---

[73] HMRC agree (at IHTM17072) that a recognised transfer involves a surrender of rights under the transferring scheme.
[74] *Clark v HMRC* [2016] UKFTT 630 (TC). The point was not argued on appeal.
[75] *Dalriada Trustees Ltd v HMRC* [2023] UKFTT 314 (TC).
[76] In particular, in earlier proceedings the High Court applied a somewhat strained interpretation of s.173 to avoid the conclusion that the arrangement did not involve an unauthorised payment. It was an important part of the claimant's case that the loans were not "investments", thereby precluding any argument that s.161(3) applied. Before the FTT (12 years later) there was evidence that in fact the loans were intended to be paired, so the loans were "in respect of" the members of the lending scheme (and therefore actual unauthorised payments), but that did not affect the analysis of the High Court in relation to s.173.
[77] See s.161(5)–(7) in particular.

and all of the relevant persons are jointly and severally liable for the unauthorised payments charge.[78]

**Assignment (FA 2004 s.172)**

**18-065** Section 172 provides that an assignment by a beneficiary of a registered pension scheme of his entitlement to any benefits under the scheme is a deemed unauthorised payment by the scheme. Such a transaction involves a payment, but not by the pension scheme, so it cannot be an actual unauthorised payment. Section 172 therefore operates to create a deemed unauthorised payment. Before looking at s.172 in detail it is worth considering the general law of assignment. Section 172 does not appear to use the term *assignment* in any special way, so it may be assumed that it is using the term consistently with the general law.

*The law of assignment*

**18-066** An entitlement to receive money or assets under a pension scheme which is constituted as a contract, insurance policy or trust is a *chose in action*, meaning that it is recognised as a form of *property*. As such, such entitlement is, in principle, capable of assignment (i.e. transfer to another person), although the ability to assign may be restricted or prohibited by the terms of the pension scheme. Such entitlement is a current *chose in action* notwithstanding that the right may only be enforceable in the future (because it is not yet payable), and may be contingent (because entitlement may cease in certain circumstances, such as death).[79] This is in contrast to a *future chose* (also called a *mere expectancy*), which is not regarded as a form of property and is therefore in capable of assignment.[80] If the trustees or managers have discretion to benefit one or more persons from a class of beneficiaries then no one in that class has any entitlement until such time as the trustees exercise their discretion in his or her favour. Similarly, if the member retains the power to revocably nominate death beneficiaries, any person nominated will not have a chose in action during the life of the member because the member may subsequently nominate someone else. The nomination therefore has no effect until the death of the member[81] and so the death beneficiary has nothing which may be assigned until that time. By definition, a member can never be entitled to his own death benefits and so nominating a death beneficiary (even irrevocably) cannot involve an assignment by the member.

**18-067** That is the position where the nomination is revocable. If a death beneficiary obtains an irrevocable entitlement the rights of the death beneficiary should be a current *chose in action*, and are therefore capable of assignment, even though the entitlement may be conditional on the beneficiary surviving the member (i.e. if the death beneficiary dies before the member then the right to receive the death benefits will not pass under the beneficiary's will).

**18-068** It follows from the above analysis that the rights of a member to receive retirement benefits are almost always a current chose in action and the rights of death

---

[78] See s.208(2) and (3).
[79] See e.g. *Re Landau* [1998] Ch. 223 (Ch.D) at 232, confirming that a retirement annuity policy maturing in the future in a present chose in action.
[80] However, an agreement to assign or settle property will be enforceable if it is supported by consideration (under the doctrine in *Walsh v Lonsdale* (1882) 21 Ch. D. 9). In such a case, there will be an assignment of the right to receive the money the moment that the mere expectancy becomes a current chose in action.
[81] The position is similar to that of a beneficiary under a will. Such a beneficiary does not have a chose in action because a will is ambulatory until the testator's death.

beneficiaries are usually mere expectancies. Only the former are capable of assignment. Dealings in the latter (even if labelled as an assignment) do not involve an assignment.

However, it is not uncommon for the terms of certain pre-2006 schemes (especially schemes established as a contract or insurance policy) to provide that lump sum death benefits will be paid to the member's estate. In these circumstances the death benefits will be subject to inheritance tax on the member's death (subject to spouse relief etc), so it is common for the member to assign the contract/policy to trustees on terms that they will hold the right to receive the retirement benefits as bare trustee for the member, and the right to receive the death benefits on discretionary trusts. The pension provider should be notified of the assignment and the parties should confirm that the retirement benefits will be paid by the provider directly to the member. The whole contract/policy is assigned to trustees because the contract/policy is likely to be a single chose in action,[82] and one cannot at law assign part of a chose in action.[83] An assignment of only the death benefits may therefore be invalid at law, although such an assignment should be valid in equity and an equitable assignment should achieve the same outcome: the right to receive the death benefits should not form part of the member's estate for inheritance tax purposes.[84]

18-069

*FA 2004 treatment of assignments*

Pursuant to s.172(1) and (2), a pension scheme is deemed to make an unauthorised payment to a member if the member (or his personal representatives) assigns or agrees to assign:

18-070

(a) any benefit, other than an *excluded pension*,[85] to which the member (or any dependant, nominee or successor of the member) has an actual or prospective entitlement[86] under the scheme; or

(b) any right in respect of any sums or assets held for the purposes of any arrangement under the scheme.

It seems that all rights to receive normal pension benefits (whether pension, annuity or lump sum) will be within (a) above, as will any rights to receive non-standard benefits.[87] Any rights of a member under transactions with the pension scheme on arm's length terms should not be within (a) as they could not be described as a *benefit*. The reference in (b) to "sums or assets held for the purposes

18-071

---

[82] See e.g. *Foskett v McKeown* [2001] A.C. 102. If under the terms of the contract/policy the right to receive retirement benefits and the right to receive death benefits can be enforced by separate actions, they may be separate choses in action and therefore capable of separate assignment. But that is not usually the case.

[83] Because Law of Property Act 1925 s.136 does not apply to an assignment of part of a chose in action: *Williams v Atlantic Assurance Co Ltd* [1933] 1 K.B. 81.

[84] If it becomes necessary to sue the pension provider to enforce the right to receive the death benefits, the assignee of an equitable assignment must be joined by the assignor (in this case the member's personal representatives), whereas the assignee of a legal assignment can sue in his own name.

[85] An *excluded pension* is so much of any pension which under pension rule 2 may continue to be paid after the member's death as may be so paid. Such pensions are presumably excluded because otherwise the transition from paying them to the member to paying them to the dependant could be regarded as an assignment.

[86] The provisions do not explain the distinction between "prospective" and "actual" entitlement, but it seems clear that the former is conditional whereas the latter is unconditional. Both require current entitlement, so a mere expectancy (e.g. a right to receive benefits only if the trustees exercise a discretion) is neither an actual nor a prospective entitlement.

[87] The provision of which may be a deemed unauthorised payment under ss.173 or 174 (see below).

of an arrangement" suggests that it is concerned with money purchase arrangements. Perhaps therefore (b) simply relates to any right relating to funds within a money purchase arrangement that is not within (a). If that is the case then (b) could include rights of a member under transactions with the pension scheme on arm's length terms. For example, if a member lent money to the scheme on the basis that the funds are to be held for the purposes of his arrangement under the scheme, it is possible that an assignment by the member of the debt could be within (b).

**18-072** Pursuant to s.172(3) and (4), a pension scheme is deemed to make an unauthorised payment in respect of a member if a person (or the person's personal representatives) assigns or agrees to assign any benefit to which he had a prospective (but, note, not an *actual*) entitlement in respect of a member. The fact that these provisions only relate to the assignment of prospective entitlement suggests that it is focusing on the rights of death beneficiaries while the member is still alive. On the death of the member one would expect the entitlement of a death beneficiary to become actual rather than prospective.

**18-073** References to a benefit to which the member or other person has an entitlement *under the pension* scheme is expressly extended to include rights to payments under a scheme pension or a lifetime annuity purchased from an insurance company by the application of sums or assets held for the purposes of the pension scheme. This extension is necessary because such rights would not otherwise be *under the pension scheme*.

*Exceptions*

**18-074** There is only one exception to the deemed unauthorised payment under s.172. It applies when there is an assignment or agreement pursuant to a pension sharing order or provision.

*The amount of the unauthorised payment*

**18-075** The amount of the unauthorised payment is the consideration received in respect of the assignment or agreement, or if greater, the consideration which might be expected to be received in respect of the assignment or agreement if the parties to the transaction were at arm's length and any power to reduce the entitlement to the benefit or right did not exist. The reason that any power to reduce the rights or benefits is disregarded is to prevent the amount charged being reduced by the use of a discretionary power that is unlikely in practice to be used.[88]

**18-076** In order to avoid double taxation, if there is a deemed unauthorised payment under s.172 then payments by the pension scheme of the benefit or right assigned (or agreed to be assigned) are not themselves unauthorised payments.

*PA 1995 s.91*

**18-077** PA 1995 s.91 provides that (subject to certain exceptions) a member of an occupational pension scheme cannot assign, commute or surrender any benefits and any agreement to do so is void. There is an exception to this in s.91(5) for assignments in favour of the person's widow, widower, surviving civil partner or dependant (although not in respect of guaranteed minimum pension).[89] If s.91 applies to a

---

[88] See para.194 of the Explanatory Notes to the Finance (No.2) Bill 2005.
[89] See PSA 1993 s.159.

## Surrenders (FA 2004 s.172A)

**18-078** Section 172A provides that the surrender by a beneficiary of a registered pension scheme of his entitlement to any benefits under the scheme is a deemed unauthorised payment by the scheme. The deeming is necessary because a surrender would not usually involve a *payment*. The usual meaning of "surrender" is to *relinquish* or *give up* some entitlement. Section 172A(9) provides that, for the purposes of s.172A, the term *surrender*:

> "includes any schemes, arrangements or understandings of any kind (whether or not legally enforceable) the main purpose, or one of the main purposes, of which is to reduce the person's entitlement to the benefit or right."

**18-079** The Explanatory Notes to Finance (No.2) Bill 2005 provide that "the definition of 'surrender' is widely drawn, to ensure that all such avoidance transactions are caught whether or not undertaken at the explicit direction of the individual". However, if it was the intention that a surrender by someone other than the member (such as the trustees or managers) is caught then that is not very clearly reflected in the provisions. Section 172A(2) only imposes a deemed unauthorised payment "if a member of a registered pension scheme surrenders or agrees to surrender ...". It therefore seems that the person taking the action must be the member. This is supported by the choice of terminology: only a person that is entitled to a benefit can *surrender* it. If a person has the power to reduce another person's entitlement then it would not be appropriate to refer to the exercise of that power as a "surrender": the term *revoke* would perhaps be more appropriate. The better view is therefore that s.172A is limited to steps taken by the person entitled to the benefit and not by any other person.

**18-080** If a money purchase scheme is drafted so that the expenses of the scheme (such as trustee and administrator fees) are borne by the scheme (thereby reducing the benefits payable to a member under the scheme) unless paid by the employer or member, and they are in fact paid from the scheme, could this amount to a surrender? If the payment is a scheme administration member payment (which is an authorised payment under s.171) then it cannot be an unauthorised payment. However, even where it is not a scheme administration member payment, it should not be within s.172A because the purpose is not to reduce the member's benefits; it is to pay the fees. Similarly, if a member becomes liable to the annual allowance charge and exercises the *scheme pays* option, that will have the effect of reducing the member's benefits, but its purpose is to pay the tax and so this is not a surrender within s.172A.[90]

**18-081** Section 172A is aimed at members with accrued benefits in excess of the lifetime allowance surrendering accrued rights to someone else in order to avoid the lifetime allowance charge, or to create a larger PCLS than would otherwise be the case.[91]

**18-082** It is relatively clear that the provisions apply in relation to specific benefits or rights under the scheme. It follows that if rights under an arrangement are sur-

---

[90] Similarly, if a member has control over the timing of the provision of benefits from the scheme, it would be absurd if requiring the trustees to provide him with benefits constituted a surrender within s.172A. It would reduce the value of his rights under the scheme, but that cannot be determinative in these circumstances. In any event, if it is an authorised payment then it is likely that it cannot also constitute an unauthorised payment.

[91] Explanatory Notes to Finance (No.2) Bill 2005 para.197

rendered in exchange for rights under a different arrangement (e.g. part of a scheme pension is commuted for a lump sum), that involves a surrender of the rights to a pension, and the fact that the overall rights of the member may be of equal value before and after the surrender does not in itself prevent these provisions from applying.[92]

*Surrenders by members*

**18-083** A pension scheme is deemed to make an unauthorised payment to a member of the scheme if the member surrenders or agrees to surrender:

(a) any benefit, other than an *excluded pension*,[93] to which the member (or any dependant, nominee or successor of the member) has a prospective entitlement under an arrangement under the pension scheme;

(b) any rights to payments under a lifetime annuity or dependants' annuity[94] purchased by the application of sums or assets held for the purposes of the pension scheme; or

(c) any right in respect of any sums or assets held for the purposes of any arrangement under the pension scheme.

*Surrenders by non-members*

**18-084** A pension scheme is deemed to make an unauthorised payment to a person in respect of the member if the person surrenders or agrees to surrender:

(a) any benefit, other than an excluded pension, to which the person has a prospective entitlement under an arrangement under the pension scheme in respect of a member of a pension scheme; or

(b) any right in respect of any sums or assets held for the purposes of any arrangement relating to a member under the pension scheme.

**18-085** The language here is almost identical to that used in s.172 (assignments), and so there is the same difficulty with the precise ambit of (c) and (b) respectively. If the member is entitled to receive funds from the pension scheme and he then waives his rights, that waiver may well come within (c) or (b). For example, if a member lent money to the scheme on the basis that the funds are to be held for the purposes of his arrangement under the scheme, and he then releases the debt, that release would appear to involve a surrender of a right in respect of any sums or assets held for the purposes of his arrangement under the pension scheme. This is of course totally illogical—in this example, the surrender would have the effect of *increasing* the value of his pension rights under the scheme, whereas s.172A is clearly aimed at transactions with the opposite effect.

**18-086** One point to note is that, in contrast to s.172, (a) above (in respect of surrenders by both members and non-members) is only concerned with the surrender of *prospective* entitlement, and not *actual* entitlement. It is likely that in this context

---

[92] There is an exception in s.172A(5)(c) which appears to apply to such commutations, but the point being emphasised here is that s.172A applies even where the value of the member's overall rights under the scheme are not reduced.

[93] An *excluded pension* is so much of any pension which under pension rule 2 may continue to be paid after the member's death as may be so paid. Such pensions are presumably excluded because otherwise the transition from paying them to the member to paying them to the dependant could be regarded as a surrender.

[94] Or a replacement lifetime annuity, replacement dependants' annuity, replacement nominees' annuity, or successors' annuities (see, respectively, FA 2004 Sch.28 paras 3, 17, 27AA and 27FA and SI 2006/499 regs 6, 10, 19(1) and 20(1)).

## DEEMED UNAUTHORISED MEMBER PAYMENTS

*prospective* means conditional whereas *actual* means unconditional. This is particularly relevant in the context of scheme pensions: once a member becomes entitled to a scheme pension, s.172A can have no application.[95]

As with s.172, references to a benefit to which the person has an entitlement under the pension scheme is expressly extended to include rights to payments under a scheme pension or a lifetime annuity purchased from an insurance company by the application of sums or assets held for the purposes of the pension scheme. This extension is necessary because such rights would not otherwise be *under the pension scheme*.

**18-087**

*Exceptions*

The following are excepted from the above provisions:

**18-088**

(a) a surrender pursuant to a pension sharing order or provision;
(b) a surrender by the member in return for the conferring on a dependant or nominee of an entitlement to benefits after the member's death. For this exception to apply it is required that the entitlement is held by the dependant, or nominee, under an arrangement under the pension scheme relating to the member or dependant or nominee;
(c) a surrender by a dependant, nominee or successor of the member in return for the conferring, on a successor of the member, of an entitlement to benefits after the beneficiary's death. For this exception to apply it is required that the entitlement is held (or is to be held) by the successor under an arrangement under the pension scheme relating to the beneficiary or successor;
(d) a transfer of benefits or rights so as to become benefits or rights under another arrangement under the pension scheme relating to the member or dependant, nominee or successor;[96]
(e) a surrender of rights to payments under an annuity in any case covered by regulations under Sch.28 para.3(2B) or 17(3);[97]
(f) a surrender made as part of a retirement-benefit activities compliance exercise;
(g) a surrender of a prospective entitlement to pension death benefits within s.167(1) or lump sum death benefits within s.168(1) made in order to comply with the Employment Equality (Age) Regulations 2006;
(h) a surrender which constitutes an assignment within FA 2004 s.172; or
(i) any surrender prescribed by The Registered Pension Schemes (Surrender of Relevant Excess) Regulations 2006 (SI 2006/211). These regulations permit a surrender of rights under a scheme that existed prior to 6 April 2006 in order to qualify for enhanced protection under the lifetime allowance provisions.

---

[95] A reduction in scheme pension is dealt with in FA 2004 Sch.28 para.2B.

[96] Presumably this exception would apply where part of a scheme pension is commuted for a lump sum. One would not ordinarily regard a commutation as involving a *transfer* of benefits or rights, because the right to a lump sum is different to the right to a pension, but HMRC accept that such commutations do not give to an unauthorised payment and it is difficult to see how any of the other exceptions could apply to a commutation.

[97] These regulations apply where a lifetime annuity or a dependants' or nominees' annuity ceases to be payable by an insurance company and as a result the insurance company transfers sums and assets to another insurance company, which applies those sums or assets to provide a new lifetime or dependants' or nominees' annuity. In these circumstances the regulations treat the new annuity as if it were the original annuity.

**18-089** Prior to 21 March 2014, there was also an exception where entitlement was surrendered in favour of an employer to fund an authorised surplus payment.[98]

**18-090** As noted above, the Explanatory Notes to Finance (No.2) Bill 2005 explain that one of the purposes of s.172A is to discourage members surrendering accrued rights to someone else in order to avoid the lifetime allowance charge, but it is apparent from the exceptions in (b), (c) and (d) above that this is unobjectionable provided that the surrender is in return for the conferring on a dependant or nominee of an entitlement to benefits after the member's death under the same pension scheme.

*Meaning of retirement-benefit activities compliance exercise*

**18-091** In order for a surrender to be made as part of a retirement-benefit activities compliance exercise, the various conditions in s.172A(10A) must be met. The reason for this exception is to allow compliance with PA 2004 s.255, which provides that an occupational pension scheme must limit its activities to "retirement benefits activities". Schemes providing only non-retirement benefits (such as death benefits) may therefore need to be terminated and replaced with a scheme providing only retirement benefits.[99]

*Defined benefits and cash balance arrangements*

**18-092** In the context of defined benefits arrangements and cash balance arrangements, the charging provisions in s.172A do not apply to the surrender of a benefit unless:

(a) in consequence of the surrender, the actual or prospective entitlement of another member (or dependant of another member) of the pension scheme, or of another person in respect of another member, to benefits under the scheme is increased; and

(b) the two members are or have been connected persons.

*Amount of the unauthorised payment*

**18-093** The amount of the unauthorised payment is the consideration that might be expected to be received if the surrendered entitlement were assigned by a transaction between parties at arm's length and any power to reduce the entitlement did not exist. As with s.172, the reason that any power to reduce the rights or benefits is disregarded is to prevent the amount charged being reduced by the use of a discretionary power that is unlikely in practice to be used.

*Pensions Act 1995 s.91*

**18-094** PA 1995 s.91(1) provides that (subject to certain exceptions) a member of an occupational pension scheme cannot assign, commute or surrender any benefits and any agreement to do so is void. There are a number of exceptions to this in s.91(5), including a surrender for the purpose of providing benefits for the person's widow or dependant, or acquiring entitlement to further benefits under the scheme, and a commutation of benefits on or after retirement or in exceptional circumstances of serious ill health. If s.91 applies to a purported surrender then it seems unlikely that the arrangement would be caught by s.172A as that surrender would be void.

---

[98] This was removed following *Pensions Regulator v A Admin Ltd* [2014] EWHC 1378 (Ch).
[99] See the example at PTM133300.

## Increase in rights of connected person on death (FA 2004 s.172B)

**18-095** Section 172B applies if at any time after the death of a *relevant member* of a registered pension scheme, there is an increase in the pension rights of another member of the same scheme which is attributable to the death, and the deceased member and the other member were connected persons immediately before the death.

**18-096** These provisions are aimed at post-death reallocations between members of a pension scheme instead of paying death benefits. There are various circumstances in which this could be attractive, were it not for these provisions. For example, avoiding the payment of death benefits could avoid a lifetime allowance charge,[100] or allowing the recipient member to receive a larger (tax-free) PCLS than would otherwise be the case. The deeming is necessary because such an increase in rights will not be a *payment* and therefore could not be an actual unauthorised payment.

*"Relevant member"*

**18-097** Pursuant to s.172B(2), a member of a registered pension scheme is a *relevant member* if, immediately before his death, any of his rights under the pension scheme were:

(a) rights to benefit to which the member (or any dependant or nominee or successor of the member) has a prospective entitlement under an arrangement under the pension scheme;

(b) rights to payments under a scheme pension provided by the scheme administrator or as a result of the application of sums or assets held for the purposes of the pension scheme or under a lifetime annuity purchased by the application of sums or assets held for the purposes of the pension scheme;[101]

(c) rights representing the nominee's flexi-access drawdown fund or successor's flexi-access drawdown fund in respect of an arrangement under the pension scheme;

(d) rights representing the member's drawdown pension fund or dependant's drawdown pension fund in respect of an arrangement under the pension scheme; or

(e) rights representing the member's flexi-access drawdown fund or dependant's flexi-access drawdown fund in respect of an arrangement under the pension scheme.

**18-098** As with ss.172 and 172A, references to a benefit to which the member or a person has an entitlement *under the* pension scheme includes rights to payments under a scheme pension or a lifetime annuity purchased by the application of sums or assets held for the purposes of the pension scheme. The extension is necessary because such rights would not otherwise be *under the pension scheme*.

---

[100] Death itself is not a benefit crystallisation event, but the payment of certain death benefits may be if the member died before reaching age 75.

[101] As currently drafted, these provisions do not work properly for purchased scheme pensions or lifetime annuities that are not deemed to be registered pension schemes by FA 2004 s.150(8). A person can only be a "relevant member" if he is a member of a registered pension scheme. Section 172B does not deem such a person to be a member of a registered pension scheme if he is not otherwise such a member.

*"Increased pension rights"*

**18-099** There is an increase in the pension rights of the other member which is attributable to the death if, in consequence of the death:

(a) the consideration which might be expected to be received in respect of an assignment of the benefits to which he has an actual or prospective entitlement under the pension scheme at that time, exceeds;

(b) the consideration which might be expected to be received in respect of such an assignment immediately before that time.

**18-100** In both cases, any power to reduce the entitlement to the benefits is ignored. The requirement that the increase must be *in consequence of* the death suggests that the death must be the cause of the increase: the fact that the increase would not have occurred but for the death is unlikely to be sufficient.[102]

*The amount of the unauthorised payment*

**18-101** If s.172B(1) applies, the pension scheme is deemed to make an unauthorised payment to the other member (or to the other member's personal representatives) of an amount equal to the excess. However, this is reduced by so much of the excess as arises from the other member becoming entitled to pension death benefits or lump sum death benefits in respect of the deceased member.

*Exceptions*

**18-102** Section 172B does not apply if the benefits to which at least 20 members of the pension scheme have an actual or prospective entitlement under the pension scheme are increased at the same rate in consequence of the death.

**18-103** In addition, s.172B does do not apply if:

(a) the increase in pension rights is an increase in the rate of a dependants' annuity or dependants' scheme pension or in rights representing a dependant's drawdown pension fund or dependant's flexi-access drawdown fund; and

(b) the increase is attributable to rights of the dead member to payments under a dependants' annuity or dependants' scheme pension or rights representing a dependant's drawdown pension fund or dependant's flexi-access drawdown fund.

**18-104** In order to prevent double taxation, s.172B does not apply if the increase in the pension rights of the other member is brought about by an assignment within s.172.

## Allocation of unallocated employer contributions (FA 2004 s.172C)

**18-105** Section 172C applies where contributions are made by an employer which are initially unallocated (or allocated to a general fund) and are subsequently allocated to a particular member's arrangement. Such an allocation does not involve a *payment* and so it could not involve an actual unauthorised payment. Paragraph 197 of the Explanatory Notes to the Finance (No.2) Bill 2005 explains that s.172C addresses a potential avoidance opportunity whereby:

"employer's contributions intended for one individual are not allocated to a particular member as they are made. Then, before benefits are crystallised, these contributions are

---

[102] See *Harris (as trustee of the Harris Family Charitable Trust) v HMRC* [2010] UKFTT 385 at [58].

# DEEMED UNAUTHORISED MEMBER PAYMENTS

allocated between two or more individuals in a way that reduces exposure to the lifetime allowance charge and maximises the total pension commencement lump sums payable."

**18-106** It is not at all clear why this should be considered to be objectionable. In any event, as will be seen below, s.172C is not restricted to circumstances where the allocation is to two or more members, and it can apply where there is no reduced exposure to the lifetime allowance charge. The provisions can apply where funds are allocated to the same member in subsequent tax years.

**18-107** There is significant overlap between FA 2004 ss.172C and 233(3).[103] Section 233(3) provides that, for the purposes of the annual allowance provisions, there is deemed to be a *contribution* when unallocated employer contributions are subsequently allocated for a member. This overlap creates the potential for double tax charges: if the amount allocated exceeds both the member's annual allowance and the "permitted maximum" (see below), the same allocation will give rise to both an annual allowance charge and an unauthorised payments charge.

**18-108** Section 172C only applies to other money purchase arrangements, or hybrid arrangements capable of providing such benefits. Defined benefits arrangements and cash balance arrangements are dealt with separately in s.172D (whereas there is no equivalent provision for collective money purchase arrangements).

*The deemed unauthorised payment*

**18-109** Pursuant to s.172C(5), a pension scheme is deemed to make an unauthorised payment to the member (or to the member's personal representatives) if:

(a) contributions are paid under a scheme by an employer otherwise then in respect of any individual;
(b) the contribution becomes held for the purposes of the provision of benefits to or in respect of a member of the pension scheme under any relevant arrangement or arrangements[104] (the "allocated contributions");
(c) the amount of the allocated contributions exceeds the *permitted maximum*; and
(d) the member and the employer, or the member and any person connected with the employer at any time during the tax year, are connected persons at any time during the tax year.

**18-110** A contribution is paid "otherwise than in respect of any individual" if it is not allocated within the scheme for a particular member.[105] Such contributions may be allocated to a general fund under the pension scheme, until such time as they are allocated to a particular member's arrangement.

*The "permitted maximum"*

**18-111** The *permitted maximum* is the maximum amount of relief to which the member would be entitled under FA 2004 s.188 in respect of relievable pension contributions paid during the tax year, less the amount of any contributions paid by employers under any registered pension scheme in respect of the member in the tax year. So, if the member would have been entitled to tax relief in respect of the allocated amounts if they had been contributions by or on behalf of the member, there is no unauthorised payment under s.172C.

---

[103] See Ch.7.
[104] *Relevant arrangements* are other money purchase arrangements or hybrid arrangements capable of providing other money purchase benefits.
[105] See para.219 of the Explanatory Notes to the Finance (No.2) Bill 2005.

**18-112**  If the member is also a member of one or more other registered pension schemes, the permitted maximum in relation to each of the registered pension schemes of which he is a member is the amount arrived at above divided by the number of registered pension schemes of which he is a member.

*The amount of the unauthorised payment*

**18-113**  The amount of the unauthorised payment is the amount by which the allocated contributions exceeds the permitted maximum.

**Limit on increase in benefits (FA 2004 s.172D)**

**18-114**  If a member's rights under a defined benefits or cash balance arrangement are increased in excess of a specified limit and the member is connected with a sponsoring employer then s.172D will apply. As with s.172C, there is considerable overlap between s.172D and the annual allowance provisions, and this creates the potential for double tax charges: if the increase exceeds both the member's annual allowance and the "notional unconnected person input amount" (see below), the same increase will give rise to both an annual allowance charge and an unauthorised payments charge on the unauthorised payment under s.172D.

*The deemed unauthorised payment*

**18-115**  Pursuant to s.172D(2), a pension scheme is deemed to make an unauthorised payment to a member if, at any time during any pension input period in respect of a relevant arrangement[106] under an occupational pension scheme:

(a) the member and a sponsoring employer (or a person connected with a sponsoring employer), are connected persons; and
(b) the pension input amount for the pension input period in respect of the relevant arrangement, exceeds the notional unconnected person input amount for the pension input period in respect of the relevant arrangement.

*The pension input amount*

**18-116**  The pension input amount for a pension input period in respect of the relevant arrangement is determined in accordance with the *relevant annual allowance provisions*, which are ss.230–232 if the arrangement is a cash balance arrangement, ss.234–236A if it is a defined benefits arrangement, and s.237 if it is a hybrid arrangement (disregarding the references in s.237 to *input amount B*).[107]

*The notional unconnected person input amount*

**18-117**  The *notional unconnected person input amount* for the pension input period in respect of the relevant arrangement is what the pension input amount (determined as per the above paragraph), would have been had the member *not* been connected with a sponsoring employer (or a person connected with a sponsoring employer) at any time during the pension input period.

---

[106] A "relevant arrangement" means a defined benefits arrangement, a cash balance arrangement, or a hybrid arrangement capable of providing defined benefits or cash balance benefits.
[107] These provisions are explained in Ch.7.

# DEEMED UNAUTHORISED MEMBER PAYMENTS

*The amount of the unauthorised payment*

If s.172D applies, the pension scheme is deemed to make an unauthorised payment to the member (or to the member's personal representatives) of an amount equal to the excess. **18-118**

## Benefits (FA 2004 s.173)

Section 173 applies if an asset held for the purposes of the pension scheme is used to provide a benefit to or in respect of a member without making a payment to him. Section 173 is the only unauthorised payment (whether actual or deemed) that focuses on what is *received*, as opposed to what is *paid*.[108] **18-119**

*The deemed unauthorised payment*

Pursuant to s.173(1) a pension scheme is deemed to make an unauthorised payment to a person who is or has been a member if an asset held for the purposes of the pension scheme is used to provide a benefit (other than a payment) to the person, or a member of the person's family or household. Pursuant to s.173(4) a pension scheme is deemed to make an unauthorised payment to a person who is or has been a member if after the person's death an asset held for the purposes of the pension scheme is used to provide a benefit (other than a payment) to a person who, at the date of the person's death, was a member of the person's family or household. **18-120**

*Meaning of "benefit"*

"Benefit" is not defined in FA 2004. Although some sort of benefit may be said to arise in most commercial transactions,[109] in a tax context the term "benefit" usually connotes the provision of bounty,[110] and that is very likely to be required here. Once a benefit is identified, the amount of the deemed unauthorised payment is calculated by reference to the benefits code in ITEPA 2003.[111] Strictly speaking, the benefits code is not applied to determine whether a benefit has been provided in the first place, however, if the benefit is such that it would not produce a charge under the benefits code (for whatever reason), then the amount of the unauthorised payment is nil. It is meaningless to refer to an unauthorised payment of nil, and so the better view is that there is no unauthorised payment at all in such circumstances. **18-121**

Under the benefits code, a promise to provide a benefit is not itself a benefit. No **18-122**

---

[108] See the above discussion regarding the meaning of "payment". It is likely that there is no deemed unauthorised payment under s.173 if the member does not *receive* anything of any value, for example.

[109] In *IRC v Levy* [1982] S.T.C. 442, Nourse J said, "If a person buys a pair of socks from Marks & Spencer for a fair price, that is a benefit to him and to Marks & Spencer". In *Vestey v IRC* [1949] 1 All E.R. 1108; 31 T.C. 1, Lord Morton of Henryton said, "a loan may well benefit a person even if it is made at a commercial rate of interest, as it may tide him over a difficult period". In *IRC v Chappie* 46 R. & I.T. 418; 34 T.C. 509, Sir Raymond Evershed MR said, "it is I think, a truism that a person receiving a loan, albeit of a commercial character, can be said to receive a benefit". In *Medical Defence Union v Department of Trade* [1980] Ch. 82; [1979] 2 W.L.R. 686 at [95] Megarry VC commented that "Obviously much is a 'benefit' which is not money or money's worth, ranging from matters such as peace and quiet to the pleasure of listening to the argument of counsel in this case, and much besides".

[110] In other words, the member must receive something that the pension scheme would not be prepared to give as a fair bargain to an unconnected third party dealing on arm's length terms with the scheme. See e.g. *Mairs v Haughey* [1994] 1 A.C. 303; [1993] 3 W.L.R. 393.

[111] The benefits code comprises ITEPA 2003 Pt 3 Chs 2–7 and 10 and 11.

benefit is provided until the asset becomes available to be enjoyed by the taxpayer.[112] This is also likely to be the case under FA 2004 s.173.

18-123   A typical example of a benefit to which s.173 applies is where a pension scheme owns commercial real estate and the trustees allow a member to use the property on subsidised terms.[113] The property is the *asset* and the *benefit* is the ability to live in the property without paying a market rent. The asset is *used to provide* the benefit by making it available to the member. This does not involve a transaction that could be described as a *payment* by the pension scheme, and so the provision of such benefits cannot be an actual unauthorised payment. By contrast, the payment by a pension scheme of a member's rent directly to his landlord is not within s.173 because the benefit is a *payment*. The payment to the landlord is an actual unauthorised payment, because it is a payment *in respect of* the member.

18-124   Any asset held by a person connected with a member is treated as being held for the benefit of the member[114] and any increase in the value of an asset held by, or reduction in the liability of, a person connected with a member is treated as an increase or reduction for the benefit of the member.[115] It follows that the use of scheme property to increase the value of an asset held by, or reduce the liability of, a person connected with a member is deemed to provide a benefit to the member.

18-125   One point to note regarding s.173 is that, in contrast to most other unauthorised payments, it is not a scheme chargeable payment (and so does not give rise to a scheme sanction charge) unless the asset is a wasting asset.[116] A wasting asset is an asset with a predictable life span not exceeding 50 years.[117] All plant and machinery are deemed to have a life of less than 50 years. Wasting assets are treated more severely because owning them will usually have the effect of depleting the value of the pension scheme. Presumably the reason that s.173 is taxed more favourably than most other unauthorised payments is because (except in the case of wasting assets) it does not involve a depletion of the member's fund and it does not allow the member to pass his fund to other persons.[118]

18-126   Where s.173 applies, the benefit must be reported on the annual event report and the scheme administrator must provide certain information to the member to enable him to complete his self-assessment tax return.[119]

*Exceptions and limitations*

18-127   In order to avoid double taxation, s.173 does not apply if the pension scheme is an investment-regulated pension scheme and the asset consists of taxable property.

18-128   Section 173 does not apply to a benefit which is received by reason of an employment, unless the employment is an *excluded employment*. This exception is intended to avoid double charges, because if a benefit were received *by reason of an employment* then it would be taxable under the benefits code. This could arise, for example,

---

[112] *Templeton v Jacobs* [1996] 1 W.L.R. 1433; [1996] S.T.C. 991.
[113] The same issue could also arise with residential property, assuming that the taxable property provisions do not apply (e.g. because the pension scheme is not an investment-regulated pension scheme, or because an exemption applies).
[114] FA 2004 s.161(6).
[115] FA 2004 s.161(7).
[116] The full list of unauthorised payments that do not give rise to a scheme sanction charge is set out at FA 2004 s.241(2).
[117] TCGA 1992 s.44, as applied by FA 2004 s.241(3).
[118] The same could of course be said of the taxable property provisions, however they are best considered as standalone provisions.
[119] See The Registered Pension Schemes (Provision of Information) Regulations 2006 (SI 2006/567) reg.13.

# DEEMED UNAUTHORISED MEMBER PAYMENTS

where scheme property is leased to a sponsoring employer and the employer then allows an employee member to enjoy it.

**18-129** An employment is an *excluded employment* if it is undertaken by a lower paid employee (i.e. one whose earnings are less than £8,500 p/a) who is either not a director, or a full-time director with no material interest in the company.[120] Such employees are not generally taxable under the benefits code. If the benefit is received by reason of an excluded employment (and therefore not taxable under the benefits code), s.173(1) only applies if:

(a) it is a benefit to which Ch.6 (cars and vans) or Ch.10 (benefits not dealt with elsewhere in benefits code) of the benefits code would apply if the employment were not an excluded employment;
(b) the pension scheme is an occupational pension scheme; and
(c) the person, or a member of the person's family or household, is a director of, and has a material interest in, a sponsoring employer.

**18-130** If a benefit after the death of the member is received by reason of an excluded employment, s.173(1) only applies if:

(a) it is a benefit to which Ch.6 (cars and vans) or Ch.10 (benefits not dealt with elsewhere in benefits code) of the benefits code would apply if the employment was not an excluded employment;
(b) the pension scheme is an occupational pension scheme; and
(c) at the date of the person's death the person, or a member of the person's family or household,[121] was a director[122] of, and had a material interest in, a sponsoring employer.

**18-131** Section 173(5) provides that "the person who receives the benefit is to be treated as having received the unauthorised payment". This is clearly only intended to apply in the case of benefits provided after the death of the member. The deemed unauthorised payment is treated as being made to the member during his life, even if the benefit is provided to a member of his family or household.[123]

*The amount of the unauthorised payment*

**18-132** Section 173(8)(b) provides that the amount of the unauthorised payment deemed to be made under s.173 is:

"... the amount which would be the cash equivalent of the benefit under the benefits code if the benefit were received by reason of an employment and the benefits code applied to it."

**18-133** For these purposes, references in the benefits code to the *employee* are treated as references to the person who is or has been a member, and references in the benefits code to the *employer* are treated as references to the pension scheme.

**18-134** The final words of s.173(8)(b) cited above are that "the benefits code applied to it". Does this mean that any exemptions from the benefits code should be disregarded for the purposes of s.173? Where the exemption is itself within the benefits code then it should also apply for the purposes of s.173. HMRC seem to take the view that even exemptions outside of the benefits code apply for the purposes of s.173: PTM133940 states that the exemption in ITEPA 2003 s.316

---

[120] See ITEPA 2003 ss.63(4) and 216. "Material interest" is defined in ITEPA 2003 s.68.
[121] As defined in ITEPA 2003 s.721.
[122] As defined in ITEPA 2003 s.67.
[123] This is apparent from FA 2004 s.173(1).

(relating to accommodation, supplies and services used in employment duties) can apply where a scheme administrator uses an asset as a necessary part of his duties as a scheme administrator or trustee, but as ITEPA 2003 s.316 does not form part of the benefits code (as defined in FA 2004 s.173(10)) it is questionable whether such an exemption is applicable.

18-135 Each chapter of the benefits code prescribes how the *cash equivalent* for that category of benefit is to be calculated. For example, under ITEPA 2003 Pt 3 Ch.10 (which contains the residual provisions), the cash equivalent of the benefit is the cost incurred by the pension scheme less any part of that cost made good by the member.[124] *Making good* essentially involves paying for the benefit in some way. Where the asset (other than a car or living accommodation, which are dealt with separately) is placed at the disposal of a member or a member of his household, the cost of the benefit will usually be the *annual value* of the asset, plus any *additional expenses* incurred in connection with the provision of the benefit other than the cost of acquisition and any rent or hire charge.[125] The annual value is 20% of the market value of the asset at the first time that it is provided (except for land which has a separate annual value specified in ITEPA 2003 s.207).

18-136 Special rules apply to determine the amount of the unauthorised payment where living accommodation is held partly for the purposes of a pension scheme and partly for other purposes.[126] This will typically involve co-ownership.

*Dalriada v Faulds*

18-137 *Dalriada Trustees Ltd v Faulds*[127] involved a so-called "pension reciprocation plan" under which a pension scheme made a loan to a member of a different scheme and that second scheme made a loan to a member of the first scheme. Members of different schemes were apparently not paired in any way, and each scheme's assets (i.e. the right to repayment) were pooled amongst all of the members' funds so the risk of default by any particular borrower was shared. Importantly, the defendants asserted (and there is no record of the claimant disputing this) that a loan back was not guaranteed: there was a "hope" that a loan back would be made, but no legal entitlement.

18-138 It seems reasonably clear that s.161(3) would usually apply in these circumstances (see above), but it was an important part of the claimant's case that the loans were not *investments* (and were therefore made in breach of trust and so were void in equity), so instead of arguing that s.161(3) applied, the claimants argued that s.173 applied.

18-139 The judge agreed with the claimants. He found that the loan back was a "benefit" to the member who received it, and the assets of the member's scheme were used to provide that benefit. Presumably the *assets* here were the money in the pension scheme (or perhaps the debt), although this does not appear to have been considered in any detail. The judge notes that the wording is "used to provide" rather than simply "provides", and, in his view, it is clear from this choice of language that "indirect" benefits are also caught. The judge does not appear to have considered whether the words "used to provide" were chosen for the simple reason that the

---

[124] ITEPA 2003 s.203(2).
[125] The *annual value* is determined in accordance with ITEPA 2003 s.205(3). *Additional expenses* is defined in s.205(4).
[126] In these circumstances, the amount of the unauthorised payment is determined under The Registered Pension Schemes (Co-ownership of Living Accommodation) Regulations 2006 (SI 2006/133).
[127] *Dalriada Trustees Ltd v Faulds* [2011] EWHC 3391 (Ch). Also see the Pension Regulator's Compulsory Review (case ref: C4177180).

trustee must *do* something with the assets in order to provide the benefit. Returning to the example of residential property, it is not the owning of the property that provides the benefit; it is the making it available to the member. Hence the property must be *used* in such a way as to provide the benefit to the member.

**18-140** Because the judge did not consider s.161(3), to him there appeared to be a rather obvious gap in the legislation as it applied to indirect benefits. In finding a solution, he seems to have glossed over a number of difficulties. In particular, the judge's interpretation involves difficult issues of causation which are not addressed.[128] Where benefits are provided indirectly there must presumably be a causal connection between the action of the trustee or manager (the only person who can "use" the asset in order to provide the benefit, is the trustee or manager—and "use" indicates some action) and the receipt of the benefit.[129] Surprisingly, the decision suggests that the *connection* between the action taken by the trustees or managers and the benefit received by the member need not be very strong. It applies where the trustees or managers make a payment to a third party in the "hope" (see [47]) that the third party will provide a benefit to a member of the scheme.

## *Dalriada v HMRC*

**18-141** The *Faulds* litigation did not involve HMRC, and HMRC did not agree to be bound by the decision. It was concerned with s.173 only because that provision was material to the question of whether the trustees had power to make the loans. The tax case came 12 years later in *Dalriada Trustees Ltd v HMRC*.[130] By the time of this litigation, it had become apparent that in fact the matching of loans between members of different scheme *had* been intended (despite the fact that it appeared to be unnecessary), and the FTT therefore held that each loan was an actual unauthorised payment. But the FTT held that each loan back was *also* a deemed unauthorised payment under s.173, for the same reasons as the judge in *Faulds*. As no interest was paid on the loans, the amount of the deemed unauthorised payment was determined by reference to the official rate of interest.

The FTT also considered the effect of: (a) the repayment of a loan; and (b) the release or writing off of a loan. The FTT held that where a loan is repaid in an amount which exceeds the amount of the principal, s.191 ITEPA 2003[131] (incorporated by ss.173(8)(b) and 173(9) FA 2004), would not provide any relief because the excess (even if properly characterised as interest) did not accrue daily. Where a loan is released or written off, the FTT had no doubt that *should* be taxable in full, but it held that s.188 ITEPA 2003[132] did not apply, because the charge in s.188 is not imposed by reference to the "cash equivalent" of the benefit, and so it was not incorporated by s.173(8)(b).

---

[128] Counsel for the claimants suggested hypothetically that if the trustees of a pension scheme lent money to a complete stranger on beneficial terms and the stranger then lends that money to a member of the scheme on the same terms, or otherwise uses the money to confer some benefit on a member, that would be caught by s.173. The judge does not expressly confirm whether he agrees with this or not.

[129] *Dalriada Trustees Ltd v Faulds* [2011] EWHC 3391 (Ch) at [47] the judge uses the term "indirect causation".

[130] *Dalriada Trustees Ltd v HMRC* [2023] UKFTT 314 (TC).

[131] By ITEPA 2003 s.191(1) and (2), a claim for relief may be made where: (a) an employment-related loan has been taxed on an employee under s.175 because interest was not paid; and (b) the interest is subsequently paid.

[132] Which provides that where an employment-related loan is released or written off, the amount released or written off is treated as earnings from the employment.

**Value shifting (FA 2004 s.174)**

**18-142** If there were no value shifting provisions in FA 2004 Pt 4 then it would be easy to extract value from a registered pension scheme in a non-taxable form. HMRC give the following examples of value shifts:[133]

(a) Altering rights attached to shares: a pension scheme owns all the A shares in a company and a member owns all the B shares. The rights attached to the A shares are changed so that they no longer have right to dividends.

(b) Altering rights in a lease: a pension scheme sells the freehold of a property to a sponsoring employer for a nominal amount subject to a leaseback for 100 years at a peppercorn. The sponsoring employer subsequently increases the rent to £10,000 p/a.

(c) Removal of rights or restrictions: a pension scheme leases a property to a member subject to a restrictive covenant, and the scheme subsequently removes the restrictive covenant. This has the effect of reducing the value of the asset owned by the pension scheme and it can therefore reduce the rent.

**18-143** In each case, altering the rights does not involve a *payment* and so it cannot involve an actual unauthorised payment.

*The deemed unauthorised payment*

**18-144** A pension scheme is deemed to make an unauthorised payment to a person who is or has been a member of the scheme if, in connection with any of the events described below or a change in the value of any currency:[134]

(a) the value of an asset held for the purposes of the pension scheme is reduced or a liability of the pension scheme is increased; and

(b) the value of an asset held by or for the benefit of the person is increased, a liability of the person is reduced, or a liability of another person is reduced for the benefit of the person.

**18-145** If the event or the change in the value of the currency occurs after the person's death, the pension scheme is treated as having made an unauthorised payment *in respect of* the person (rather than *to* the person), and the person who holds the asset or is subject to the liability in relation to which (b) is satisfied is treated as having received the unauthorised payment.

**18-146** Any asset held by a person connected with a member is treated as being held for the benefit of the member[135] and any increase in the value of an asset held by, or reduction in the liability of, a person connected with a member is treated as an increase or reduction for the benefit of the member.[136]

*The events*

**18-147** Section 174(3) specifies the events, as follows:

"(a) the creation, alteration, release or extinction of any power, right, option or liability relating to assets held for the purposes of the pension scheme (whether or not provided for in the terms on which the asset is acquired or held),

---

[133] PTM133700.
[134] FA 2004 s.174(1).
[135] FA 2004 s.161(6).
[136] FA 2004 s.161(7).

(b) the creation, alteration, release or extinction of any power, right or option relating to a liability of the pension scheme (whether or not provided for in the terms on which the liability is incurred),
(c) the exercise of, or failure to exercise, any power, right or option in relation to assets held for the purposes of the pension scheme or a liability of the pension scheme, or
(d) the exercise of, or failure to exercise, any power, right or option which constitutes an asset held for the purposes of the pension scheme,

in a way which differs from that which might be expected if the parties to the transaction were at arm's length."

**18-148** The final words are important: it is only if the value shift is not on arm's length terms that the deemed unauthorised payment arises.

*The amount of the unauthorised payment*

**18-149** The amount of the unauthorised payment is the amount by which the reduction in value of the asset held for the purposes of the pension scheme, or the increase in the liability of the pension scheme, exceeds that which might be expected if the parties to the transaction were at arm's length. A liability is a liability of a registered pension scheme if the liability is to be met from sums or assets held for the purposes of the pension scheme.[137]

## Holding taxable property (FA 2004 s.174A)

**18-150** If an investment-regulated pension scheme holds an interest in taxable property for the purposes of a member's arrangement then the scheme is deemed to make an unauthorised payment to the member under FA 2004 s.174A. The meaning of "investment-regulated pension scheme", "taxable property", what it means for a pension scheme to "hold" an interest in taxable property, and the taxation consequences of it doing so, are all explained in Ch.9. In addition to the deemed unauthorised payment, a scheme sanction charge arises under FA 2004 ss.185A–185I in relation to actual or deemed income and gains relating to taxable property.

*The deemed unauthorised payment*

**18-151** Pursuant to s.174A, an investment-regulated pension scheme is deemed to make an unauthorised payment to a member of the scheme in the following three circumstances:

(a) the pension scheme acquires an interest in taxable property, and the interest is held by the pension scheme for the purposes of an arrangement under the pension scheme relating to the member;
(b) an interest in taxable property is held by the pension scheme for the purposes of an arrangement under the pension scheme relating to the member, and the property is improved; or
(c) an interest in property which is not residential property is held by the pension scheme for the purposes of an arrangement under the pension scheme

---

[137] FA 2004 s.163(3).

relating to the member, and the property is converted or adapted to become residential property.[138]

**18-152** In each case, the interest must be held for the purposes of an arrangement under the pension scheme relating to the member. It follows that s.174A does not apply to taxable property held within a general fund under a pension scheme.[139] However, if an interest in taxable property is held by the pension scheme "otherwise than for the purposes of the administration or management of the pension scheme" then it is deemed to be held for the purposes of the arrangements under the pension scheme by reference to the respective rights under the scheme of the members to which the arrangements relate.[140] As is explained in Ch.11 (in the context of scheme administration member payments), the activities of "administering" and "managing" a pension scheme include all the usual activities of a pension scheme, and so it is not at all clear when property will be held otherwise than for the purposes of the administration or management of the pension scheme.

## DEEMED UNAUTHORISED EMPLOYER PAYMENTS

### Value shifting

**18-153** There is only one type of deemed unauthorised employer payment: value shifting. The provisions (in FA 2004 s.181) are broadly equivalent to the deemed unauthorised member payment in s.174, and much of the above commentary relating to s.174 applies equally to s.181. The main difference is that s.181 applies to transactions by the scheme as a whole rather than transactions relating to a particular member's arrangement. This is to be expected, given that s.181 relates to the employer.

**18-154** A registered pension scheme is deemed to make an unauthorised payment to a sponsoring employer if, in connection with any of the events mentioned below or a change in the value of a currency:

(a) the value of an asset held for the purposes of the pension scheme is reduced or a liability of the pension scheme is increased; and
(b) the value of an asset held by or for the benefit of the sponsoring employer is increased, a liability of the sponsoring employer is reduced, or a liability of another person is reduced for the benefit of the sponsoring employer.

**18-155** Any asset held by a person connected with a current or former sponsoring employer is treated as being held for the benefit of the sponsoring employer.[141] Any increase in the value of an asset held by, or reduction in the liability of, a person connected with a current or former sponsoring employer is treated as an increase or reduction for the benefit of the sponsoring employer.[142]

---

[138] Residential property is a category of taxable property. Residential property is defined in FA 2004 Sch.29A Pt 2: see Ch.9.
[139] The meaning of a member's "arrangement" is explained in Ch.2.
[140] FA 2004 Sch.29A para.5.
[141] FA 2004 s.161(6).
[142] FA 2004 s.161(7).

## DEEMED UNAUTHORISED EMPLOYER PAYMENTS

*The events*

The events referred to above are the following, but only if the event occurs in a way which differs from that which might be expected if the parties to the transaction were at arm's length:

18-156

(a) the creation, alteration, release or extinction of any power, right, option or liability relating to assets held for the purposes of the pension scheme (whether or not provided for in the terms on which the asset is acquired or held);
(b) the creation, alteration, release or extinction of any power, right or option relating to a liability of the pension scheme (whether or not provided for in the terms on which the liability is incurred);
(c) the exercise of, or failure to exercise, any power, right or option in relation to assets held for the purposes of the pension scheme or a liability of the pension scheme; or
(d) the exercise of, or failure to exercise, any power, right or option which constitutes an asset held for the purposes of the pension scheme.

*The amount of the unauthorised payment*

The amount of the unauthorised payment is the amount by which the reduction in value of the asset held for the purposes of the pension scheme, or the increase in the liability of the pension scheme, exceeds that which might be expected if the parties to the transaction were at arm's length. A liability is a liability of a registered pension scheme if the liability is to be met from sums or assets held for the purposes of the pension scheme.[143]

18-157

### Transactions benefitting a sponsoring employer

It is perhaps surprising that there is no equivalent to s.173, creating a deemed unauthorised employer payment where scheme property is used to provide a benefit to a sponsoring employer. If, for example, the pension scheme owns offices and makes them available to a sponsoring employer rent-free, would that involve an unauthorised payment? It would not involve an actual payment, so it could only do so if it was one of the deemed unauthorised payments. It would not be a deemed unauthorised employer payment, because it does not involve a value shift: making the property available does not reduce its value. If the member is a shareholder in the employer, is it arguable that making the scheme property available to the employer provides a *benefit* to the member because it increases the value of his shares and therefore s.173 applies? Possibly, but any benefit *to the member* does not involve making an asset available or the transfer of a used or depreciated asset, and so the cost of the benefit is the expense incurred in connection with the provision of the benefit,[144] and in these circumstances the scheme will not incur any expense if it owns the property and it simply makes it available. In any event, the increase in the value of the shares owned by the member is deemed by s.161(7) to be an increase for the benefit of the sponsoring employer, because it is connected with the member, and so this would appear to dispose of any possible s.173 argument. It fol-

18-158

---

[143] FA 2004 s.163(3).
[144] ITEPA 2003 s.204.

lows that making property available to a sponsoring employer at less than market rent does not appear to involve an unauthorised payment.[145]

## TAXATION OF UNAUTHORISED PAYMENTS

**18-159** Unauthorised payments are subject to a 40% unauthorised payments charge (FA 2004 s.208). If the payment exceeds a certain threshold then it is also subject to a 15% unauthorised payments surcharge (FA 2004 s.209). Subject to a small number of limited exceptions, all unauthorised payments also give rise to a scheme sanction charge (in FA 2004 s.239) of 40%, which is reduced to 15% if the unauthorised payments charge is paid in full.

**18-160** An unauthorised payment is deemed not to be income for the purposes of the Tax Acts.[146] Several consequences follow from this. First, the payment will not otherwise be subject to income tax (for example under ITEPA 2003 Pt 9, which taxes pension income), so there will not be double taxation. Secondly, it will not be possible to offset the tax charges against personal allowances, losses, or tax relief (for example, in respect of pension contributions or EIS investments). Thirdly, no tax treaties will affect the taxation of unauthorised payments.

### The unauthorised payments charge

**18-161** The unauthorised payments charge arises whenever a registered pension scheme makes an unauthorised payment.[147] The rate of tax is 40% "in respect of" the unauthorised payment. It is not clear precisely what the words "in respect of" mean in this context. Presumably it means 40% of the *amount* of the unauthorised payment.[148] This is straightforward in the case of deemed unauthorised payments, because the provisions relating to each type of deemed unauthorised payment prescribe what is the *amount* of each deemed unauthorised payment. However, other than in relation to employer loans,[149] the provisions relating to actual unauthorised payments do not prescribe what is the amount of the unauthorised payment.[150] If an asset is transferred to a member, what is the amount of the unauthorised payment? One might naturally expect it to be the market value of the asset, but s.208 does not prescribe any method of valuation. If an asset is leased to a member on below market value terms, is the amount of the unauthorised payment equal to the value of the asset, or the value of the lease? Is the position any different for money? For example, if £1,000 is lent to a member on terms that it must be repaid within 24 hours, is the amount of the unauthorised payment £1,000, or is it the (much lower) value of the loan?

---

[145] Whether the trustees have the power to provide such a benefit under the scheme rules is another matter.
[146] FA 2004 s.208(8).
[147] FA 2004 s.208. It is sometimes suggested that the charge does not apply to member who has never been UK resident and has never received UK tax relief, but there does not appear to be any authority for this.
[148] The explanatory notes to the Finance Bill 2004 cl.197 explains that the unauthorised payments charge is "a charge, based on the amount of the payment received by [a member or a sponsoring employer], or paid to another person for that member or employer's benefit".
[149] For authorised employer loans, see Ch.17. If a loan meets some but not all of the requirements to constitute an authorised employer loan, the *amount* of the unauthorised payment is prescribed.
[150] The provisions relating to scheme administration member/employer payments provide only very limited assistance. They tell us that where a payment is made from a scheme to or in respect of a member/employer which exceeds the amount which might be expected to be paid to a person at arm's length, the excess is an unauthorised payment, but they do not tell us how to value the excess.

## TAXATION OF UNAUTHORISED PAYMENTS

In relation to loans, one might expect that very clear statutory language would be required in order to impose a charge on the full amount of the loan.[151] There is no such language in FA 2004 Pt 4, at least in relation to member loans. In the context of employer loans, the provisions in FA 2004 Sch.30 prescribe the amount of any unauthorised payment arising, which can in certain circumstances be equal to the amount of the loan.[152] These provisions therefore show that taxing loans in the same way as outright payments is something that Parliament does consider to be appropriate, at least in certain circumstances. Indeed, it does seem clear from the decisions relating to payments made in breach of trust[153] that once it has been established that a payment has occurred, the unauthorised payments charge is applied to the amount of the payment rather than the value conferred on the recipient.

**18-162**

In the context of assets, it does seem likely (given the clear intention of s.173) that if an asset is leased to a member on below market value terms,[154] the amount of the unauthorised payment is equal to the value of the lease, not the value of the asset. If that were not the case then transactions which are very similar in substance would be taxed in completely different ways, depending on whether or not s.173 applied.

**18-163**

These difficulties are exacerbated by the fact that the same phrase "in respect of" is also used to determine the amount of the unauthorised payments surcharge and the scheme sanction charge.[155] It is presumably intended to mean the same thing in each case, but as the purpose of the surcharge and scheme sanction charge is quite different to the purpose of the unauthorised payments charge, it is very difficult to approach this purposively.

**18-164**

*Reduction anticipating scheme sanction charge*

If the scheme administrator, anticipating a liability to the scheme sanction charge, reduces the amount of an unauthorised payment, the *amount* of the unauthorised payment is expressly increased by the amount of the reduction.[156] Were it not for this provision, payment of the scheme sanction charge would not itself be an unauthorised payment because the scheme administrator is solely liable for the charge and so paying it does not involve a payment "in respect of" the relevant member or employer. If the liability is subsequently found to be less than the amount of the reduction, and the scheme administrator pays the difference to or in respect of the same person within two years of the unauthorised payment, that payment will not itself be an unauthorised payment.[157]

**18-165**

*Liability*

If the payment is an unauthorised *member* payment made to or in respect of a member or former member during his life, the tax liability falls on that member or

**18-166**

---

[151] e.g. in the disguised remuneration provisions, the charge under ITEPA 2003 s.554Z2 is on the value of the relevant step and s.554Z3 provides that if the relevant step involves a sum of money, its value is the amount of the money. Section 554Z(7) provides that references to a payment of a sum of money include payments by way of loan. Thus there can be no doubt that loans are fully taxable under the disguised remuneration provisions.

[152] See Ch.17. This would be the case, e.g. where a loan was made to the employer without the provision of any security.

[153] Such as *Clark v HMRC* [2020] EWCA Civ 204, considered above.

[154] The assignment of a lease would involve a *payment* and so s.173 should not apply.

[155] Indeed, it is used for all of the tax charges imposed under FA 2004 Pt 4.

[156] FA 2004 s.160(4A).

[157] FA 2004 s.160(4B).

former member. If the payment is an unauthorised member payment made in respect of a member or former member after his death, the tax liability falls on the recipient. If the payment is an unauthorised *employer* payment, the sponsoring employer or former sponsoring employer to or in respect of whom the payment is made is liable for the tax charge. Where more than one person is liable, those persons are jointly and severally liable to the charge. Liability is not affected by the residence or domicile status of the taxpayer or the scheme administrator.

18-167    Given that the scheme administrator is not liable for the charge, it seems clear that any payment of the charge by the pension scheme (thereby discharging the member's liability) will be a payment "to" the member and so may itself be an unauthorised payment. However, if it is correct that a voluntary payment by the scheme of the annual allowance charge is an authorised payment provided that the member's rights under the scheme are reduced to take account of the tax paid (as HMRC suggest[158]), it is difficult to see why a voluntary payment of the unauthorised payments charge should be an unauthorised payment.

*Relief from the unauthorised payments charge*

18-168    Certain provisions in PA 2004 permit a court to make an order for funds to be restored to a pension scheme.[159] If such an order is made following an unauthorised member payment, and as a result of the order funds are transferred to a registered pension scheme, the taxpayer liable for the unauthorised payment charge[160] may claim relief from a proportion of the unauthorised payments charge, provided that no part of the unauthorised payment (or any sum or asset representing it):[161] (a) was received by or on behalf of the member (or any person connected with the member); and (b) has been held for more than 180 days by a person or succession of persons, other than the member or a person connected with the member, involved in any transaction by which the unauthorised member payment was made. The relevant proportion of the unauthorised payments charge is expressed by the formula "ASO/UMP" where *ASO* is the amount subject to the relevant order, that is the aggregate of the market value of any property and the amount of any money transferred, or the amount of the sum paid, towards a registered pension scheme pursuant to the relevant order in respect of the unauthorised member payment, and *UMP* is the amount of the unauthorised member payment. However, if ASO is greater than UMP then the relevant proportion of the unauthorised payments charge or the unauthorised payments surcharge is the whole of it. There is no requirement that the unauthorised payment was inadvertent.

**The unauthorised payments surcharge**

18-169    The unauthorised payments surcharge arises where a surchargeable unauthorised payment is made by a registered pension scheme.[162] A surchargeable unauthorised payment means either a surchargeable unauthorised *member* payment or a surchargeable unauthorised *employer* payment. In each case the surcharge applies if the amount of unauthorised payments exceeds 25% of the member's rights under the scheme, or 25% of the entire scheme in the case of an employer payment, are made within a 12-month period. Once this threshold is reached, all of the pay-

---

[158] See PTM056410 and Ch.7.
[159] See PA 2004 ss.16(1), 19(4) or 21(2)(a).
[160] i.e. the member or former member, or (after his death) the recipient.
[161] FA 2004 s.266A.
[162] FA 2004 s.209.

ments in the reference period are surchargeable (even those made before the threshold was reached).

*Surchargeable unauthorised member payments*

**18-170** Every unauthorised member payment (whether actual or deemed) made in a *surcharge period* is surchargeable if the *surcharge threshold* is reached within a period of 12 months beginning with a reference date.[163] The surcharge period is the period beginning with the reference date, and ending with the day on which the surcharge threshold is reached. The first reference date is the date on which the pension scheme first makes an unauthorised member payment in respect of the arrangement. Each subsequent reference date is the date, after the end of the previous reference period, on which the pension scheme next makes an unauthorised member payment in respect of the arrangement. The previous reference period is the period of 12 months beginning with the previous reference date or, if the surcharge threshold is reached in that period, is the surcharge period ending with the date on which it was reached.

**18-171** The surcharge threshold is reached if the unauthorised payments percentage reaches 25%. The percentage of the pension fund used up on the occasion of an unauthorised member payment is expressed by the formula "(UMP/VR) x 100", where *UMP* is the amount of the unauthorised member payment and *VR* is an amount equal to the total value of the member's rights under the arrangement when the unauthorised payment is made. If the unauthorised payment is made after the member's death, *VR* is the value of the member's rights at the date of the member's death.

**18-172** The method for valuing the member's rights under the arrangement depends on whether his rights are crystallised or uncrystallised. Rights are *crystallised* if the member is entitled to the present payment of benefits in respect of the rights. In other words, the member has an actual entitlement to a scheme pension or lifetime annuity or funds have been designated as available for drawdown pension.

**18-173** **Valuation of crystallised rights** The value of the member's crystallised rights under an arrangement is the total value of any scheme pension or lifetime annuity to which the member has an actual (rather than a merely prospective) entitlement under the arrangement, and the value of any sums and assets representing the member's drawdown pension fund or flexi-access drawdown fund in respect of the arrangement.[164] The value of a scheme pension or lifetime annuity is the annual rate of the pension or annuity multiplied by 20.[165]

**18-174** **Valuation of uncrystallised rights** The value of the member's uncrystallised rights under a cash balance arrangement on any date is the amount which would, on the valuation assumptions,[166] be available for the provision of benefits in respect of those rights if the member became entitled to benefits in respect of those rights

---

[163] FA 2004 s.210.
[164] FA 2004 s.211.
[165] Or such greater *relevant valuation factor* as is agreed between the scheme administrator and HMRC (see FA 2004 s.276 and PTM088620).
[166] The valuation assumptions require one to value the individual's rights on the assumption that the individual is at the age at which no reduction would apply to the payment of an immediate benefit (e.g. as a result of early retirement), and the individual is in good physical and mental health and so the benefits are not increased as a result of being paid as a result of ill-health (FA 2004 s.277).

on the date.[167] The value of the member's uncrystallised rights under an other money purchase arrangement on any date is the total value of the sums and assets held for the purposes of the arrangement on the date as represent those rights. The value of the member's uncrystallised rights under a defined benefits arrangement on any date is expressed by the formula "($20^{168}$ x ARP) + LS". *ARP* is the annual rate of pension to which the member would, on the valuation assumptions, be entitled under the arrangement on the date if, on the date, the member acquired an actual (rather than a prospective) right to receive a pension in respect of the rights. *LS* is the amount of any lump sum to which the member would, on the valuation assumptions, be entitled under the arrangement on the date (otherwise than by way of commutation of pension) if, on the date, the member acquired an actual (rather than a prospective) right to payment of a lump sum in respect of the rights.

**18-175** If the arrangement is a hybrid arrangement (i.e. it can, in any circumstances, provide more than one type of benefit, for example cash balance and defined benefits), one must calculate the value of each and apply the value which is the greatest.

**18-176 Surchargeable unauthorised employer payments** Every unauthorised employer payment (actual or deemed) made in a surcharge period is surchargeable if the surcharge threshold is reached within a period of 12 months beginning with a reference date.[169] The surcharge period is the period beginning with the reference date, and ending with the day on which the surcharge threshold is reached. The first reference date is the date on which the pension scheme first makes an unauthorised employer payment to or in respect of the employer. Each subsequent reference date is the date, after the end of the previous reference period, on which the pension scheme next makes an unauthorised employer payment to or in respect of the employer. The previous reference period is the period of 12 months beginning with the previous reference date or, if the surcharge threshold is reached in that period, is the surcharge period ending with the date on which it was reached.

**18-177** The surcharge threshold is reached if the unauthorised payments percentage reaches 25%. The percentage of the pension fund used up on the occasion of an unauthorised employer payment is expressed by the formula "(UEP/AA) x 100" where *UEP* is the amount of the unauthorised employer payment and *AA* is an amount equal to the total value of the sums and assets held for the purposes of the pension scheme at the time when the unauthorised employer payment is made.

**18-178 The rate of the charge** The rate of the charge is 15% "in respect of" the surchargeable unauthorised payment. As with the unauthorised payments charge, it is not clear precisely what the words *in respect of* mean in this context, although it presumably has the same meaning as for the unauthorised payments charge. As with the unauthorised payments charge, if the scheme administrator has reduced an unauthorised payment in order to pay the scheme sanction charge, the amount of the surchargeable unauthorised payment is deemed to be increased by the amount of the reduction.[170]

**18-179 Liability** The person liable for the unauthorised payments charge is also liable for the surcharge (including where liability is joint and several). As with the

---

[167] FA 2004 s.212.
[168] Or such greater number as is agreed between the scheme administrator and HMRC: see s.276.
[169] FA 2004 s.213.
[170] FA 2004 s.160(4A).

unauthorised payments charge, liability is not affected by the residence or domicile status of any person.[171]

**Discharge from liability for the surcharge**  Any person liable to pay the surcharge can apply to HMRC to be discharged on the grounds that, in all the circumstances, it would not be just and reasonable for him to be so liable.[172] If HMRC refuse, the taxpayer can appeal to the FTT. The burden of proof is on the taxpayer to satisfy the tribunal that the *just and reasonable* requirements are satisfied.[173]  **18-180**

In *Peter Browne v HMRC*,[174] a member of two registered pension schemes intended for his pension funds to be transferred to another pension scheme, but they were in fact transferred to him personally for a period of three years before being transferred to another registered pension scheme. The payment to the member gave rise to an unauthorised payments charge but the judge held that the intention to transfer the funds to another pension scheme (which did subsequently happen) justified discharging the member from liability to the surcharge. A consideration of what is just and reasonable in the circumstances involves having regard to the discernible purpose of the surcharge. The judge said (at [71]):  **18-181**

> "We consider that the purpose of the surcharge is to penalise unauthorised payments where they are made in order to frustrate the purposes of the pension scheme tax regime and abuse its tax reliefs and exemptions. Where, as we consider is the case with these appeals, the unauthorised payments were not made for that reason, and the funds concerned remain vested in a registered pension scheme (albeit with a three year interlude under the personal control of Mr Browne), we find, having considered all the circumstances, that it would not be just and reasonable for Mr Browne to be liable to the unauthorised payment surcharge in respect of the payments by the Pearl and Scottish Life, and we so decide. Among the circumstances relevant to our decision is the fact that at least some of the three year delay was caused by Mr Browne's anxiety and HMRC's criminal investigation into the matter."

In *O'Mara v HMRC*,[175] two members of a registered pension scheme honestly, but mistakenly, believed that loans to a company connected with them were not unauthorised payments. The FTT found that the circumstances were not such that it was just and reasonable to discharge them from liability to the surcharge. This was because their belief was not based upon reasonable grounds. They did not take independent advice or even make themselves familiar with the details notwithstanding that they were aware of certain "warning bells" from the outset and parts of the arrangement did not make commercial sense.[176] They relied on the salesman (who received sizable fees for their participation in the arrangement) who deceived them. It is not clear that it was appropriate for the FTT to incorporate a *reasonable belief* test into the *just and reasonable* requirement in s.268(3). It is quite clear from  **18-182**

---

[171] FA 2004 s.209(5). This also expressly refers to the residence of domicile of any "sub-scheme administrator", which is a reference to The Registered Pension Schemes (Splitting of Schemes) Regulations 2006 (SI 2006/569).
[172] FA 2004 s.268 and The Registered Pension Schemes (Discharge of Liabilities under ss.267 and 268 of the Finance Act 2004) Regulations 2005 (SI 2005/3452).
[173] FA 2004 s.269.
[174] *Peter Browne v HMRC* [2016] UKFTT 595.
[175] *O'Mara v HMRC* [2017] UKFTT 91.
[176] The arrangement involved, or purported to involve, a small investment in FX trading which would generate enough income to pay for the 5% p/a interest on the loans. The loans were therefore effectively interest-free from the perspective of the borrower. In addition, the lender did not prepare any loan documentation, meaning that there were no express repayment terms. Realising the inappropriateness of this, the members prepared their own loan documents.

s.268(7) (which relates to discharge from the scheme sanction charge) that a *reasonable belief* requirement is not intended to form part of the *just and reasonable* requirement. If it did then s.268(7)(a) would be otiose.

**18-183** In *Morgan Lloyd Trustees Ltd v HMRC*,[177] an investment-regulated pension scheme acquired taxable property shortly after 6 April 2006 that would have been permissible prior to that date. In relation to the taxpayers' application for discharge from the surcharge, the FTT said:

> "148. It is self-evident that the scheme of legislation for pensions remains immensely complicated, in spite of the Government's stated aim of simplifying it. Under the regime in force up to April 2006, the transactions the subject of this appeal would have been entirely uncontroversial, and (as we have found above) the way in which the rules were changed was unclear even to professionals operating in the field. The second appellant relied on advice from an apparently competent professional adviser in what he did. He was in our view entitled to do so in the circumstances of the case. We would observe that HMRC themselves only published any indication that such transactions might (contrary to previous indications) give rise to a problem in late July 2006, when the provisions themselves were expressed to come into force on 6 April 2006; and even then, their published commentary blew 'hot and cold' (see [46] above). We have no hesitation in finding that it would not be just and reasonable for him to be subject to the unauthorised payments surcharge."

**18-184** In *AIM (Perth) Ltd v HMRC*,[178] a registered pension scheme made two informal loans to a sponsoring employer as a temporary measure to keep the company out of financial difficulty. The loans were not authorised employer loans as they did not satisfy the requirements in FA 2004 s.179. The loans were apparently made with no real consideration of whether they were authorised or whether there were any formalities that should be adhered to. When the employer's auditors identified the problem, steps were taken to rectify it. In relation to the application for discharge of liability for the surcharge, the FTT found that it was just and reasonable for the taxpayer to be liable. In doing so, the FTT rejected the argument that liability to pay the surcharge ought to be discharged on the basis that there was ultimately no loss to the pension fund, because that is not the point of the legislation. The deterrent in the legislation is to ensure that there is minimal risk to any pension fund.

**18-185** In *HMRC v Bella Figura Ltd*,[179] the UT said:

> "[70] As to the considerations that should be taken into account in evaluating the question whether it is just and reasonable to set aside a scheme sanction charge or unauthorised payments surcharge, we would respectfully endorse what the First-tier Tribunal (Judge Rupert Jones and Mohammed Farooq) said in *O'Mara v HMRC* [2017] UKFTT 91 (TC):
> 152. The statutory test will not benefit from unnecessary gloss. It requires the Tribunal to examine all the circumstances and decide whether it would be just and reasonable for the appellants to be liable to surcharges.
> 153. It does not require any finding of dishonesty or negligence on part of the appellants. It allows the Tribunal to examine all the circumstances surrounding the making and receipt of the unauthorised payments in each appellant's case. This in turn allows the Tribunal to examine an appellant's conduct or any other relevant mitigating circumstances pertaining to the payments or the appellant's circumstances. It also allows the Tribunal to take account of the statutory scheme and mischief the surcharge is designed to prevent.

---

[177] *Morgan Lloyd Trustees Ltd v HMRC* [2017] UKFTT 131.
[178] *AIM (Perth) Ltd v HMRC* [2017] UKFTT 533.
[179] *HMRC v Bella Figura Ltd* [2020] UKUT 120 (TCC); [2020] S.T.C. 922 at [70]–[75]. Also see the following paragraphs of that decision.

# TAXATION OF UNAUTHORISED PAYMENTS 431

[71] Having been shown a number of FTT decisions in this area, we detect that there has been some difficulty in formulating precisely the 'nature of the statutory scheme and the mischief that the surcharge is designed to prevent'. Having rightly acknowledged an important point, namely that the aggregate of the three charges that HMRC can impose in connection with a scheme chargeable payment is either 70% or 95% of that payment and in either case more than the aggregate tax relief that an individual might be expected to obtain on a contribution to a registered pension scheme, tribunals have gone on to consider why that is the case. In some cases, they have posed the question whether the charges are 'penal' or intended simply to recover tax reliefs and exemptions previously given.

[72] We do not ourselves consider that whether the charges are described as 'penal' or not will serve as much of a guide to how to decide, in a particular case, whether it is 'just and reasonable' for a charge to be imposed. More important, in our view, is to consider the entire statutory scheme of which these charges form part. In essence, that scheme provides: (i) for contributions made by employers and employees to benefit from tax relief at the point of payment; (ii) for the funds contributed to be held securely to provide pension benefits that can, at least in usual cases, only be taken once an individual reaches the age of 55; (iii) for most income and gains received by the registered pension scheme in connection with the investments of contributions not to be subject to tax; but (iv) for amounts payable to an individual taking benefits to be subject, in most cases, to income tax (with the most important exception of the ability to take a tax-free lump sum equal to 25% of the accumulated fund).

[73] While conceptually it might be said that tax relief granted to individuals and employers at stage (i) is counteracted by the taxability of pension benefits at stage (iv), the overall scheme clearly involves a material cost to the Exchequer. First, the Exchequer suffers an obvious timing disbenefit as it gives relief at stage (i) a long time before it obtains tax at stage (iv). That timing benefit is not counteracted by a charge on income and gains of the pension scheme– see stage (iii). Second, a person's income in retirement will tend to be lower than income when working, so even in absolute terms the tax charged at stage (iv) will tend to be lower than the tax relief given at stage (i).

[74] Parliament is content for the Exchequer to suffer these costs given the social utility of individuals saving for their retirement, but only where the entire bargain set out at [72] is respected. It is for this reason that different aspects of the unauthorised payments regime apply to different potential breaches of the bargain. For example, if a registered scheme impermissibly pays benefits to a member before he or she reaches 55, there is an unauthorised payment because the Exchequer has suffered the costs we have outlined, but since the funds have been drawn before retirement age, the social utility of funding retirement is not present. In a similar vein, if pension funds are lent by way of risky loans to an employer, the Exchequer is exposed to the risk that, even though it has given tax relief, and exempted income and gains of the scheme from tax, the funds are not ultimately available to pay pension benefits.

[75] These observations also explain how the making of unauthorised payments can be more, or less, serious. For example, an extreme form of 'pensions liberation' might involve a co-ordinated attempt by an individual to access a pension fund held in a registered scheme before he or she reaches the age of 55 in a manner that escapes tax altogether. Such a scheme seeks to impose on the Exchequer the cost of deductions at stage (i) and exemptions at stage (iii) even though no retirement benefits are ultimately provided. In addition, were such a scheme successful the Exchequer would not even obtain tax at stage (iv) when the funds leave the scheme. Considerably less serious would be the making of a loan to an employer which, while it fails the requirements necessary to be an 'authorised employer loan' (so exposing the Exchequer to a risk of loss) is ultimately repaid in full with a market rate of interest so that the

Exchequer suffers no actual cost and the social utility of the provision of retirement benefits is preserved."

**18-186** Also see *Dalriada Trustees Ltd v HMRC*:[180] Ms Oades would've been discharged if she had applied.

**18-187** In *Curtis v HMRC*,[181] the FTT said:

> "[95] The burden is on Mrs Curtis to establish that it would not be just and reasonable for her to be liable to the surcharge. We have taken into account the statutory regime for pension tax relief and the various charges and surcharges that may be imposed as described at [71] - [75] of Bella Figura. We have also taken into account all our findings of fact as to the circumstances in which the unauthorised member payment came to be made. In our view there was nothing more that Mrs Curtis might reasonably be expected to do that would have avoided the unauthorised member payment. She obtained what she believed to be independent advice from an independent financial adviser who had been recommended to her by a colleague. It appears that she was the unfortunate victim of a scam.
>
> [96] HMRC say that Mrs Curtis did not obtain independent advice, because Mr Peacock was clearly obtaining some form of commission from the transactions he advised Mrs Curtis to enter into. That may be true, but it was not uncommon for financial advisers to be remunerated by way of commission.
>
> [97] HMRC say that Mrs Curtis did not take any steps to mitigate the risk of entering into the unauthorised member payment. In our view, that criticism is made with the benefit of hindsight. On the face of it, Mrs Curtis took advice from an independent financial adviser and was entitled to rely on that advice. We have found that there was no reason for Mrs Curtis to consider that the loan from Blu Funding was in any way connected with the transfer of her pension to Fast Pensions. HMRC say that Mrs Curtis should have been suspicious that Mr Peacock was able to secure a loan for her when she had a bad credit rating and had been unable to secure a loan from high street lenders. Again, we consider that criticism is made with the benefit of hindsight.
>
> [98] Overall, we are satisfied that it would be not be just and reasonable for Mrs Curtis to be liable to the unauthorised payments surcharge."

**18-188 Relief from the surcharge** Relief is available under FA 2004 s.266A in the same (very limited) circumstances as for the unauthorised payment charge. No other relief is available.

### The scheme sanction charge

**18-189** The scheme sanction charge arises where a scheme chargeable payment is made by a registered pension scheme.[182] All unauthorised payments other than the following "exempt" unauthorised payments are scheme chargeable payments:[183]

(a) a deemed unauthorised payment under FA 2004 s.173, provided that the asset used to provide the benefit is not a wasting asset.[184] Section 173 applies

---

[180] *Dalriada Trustees Ltd v HMRC* [2023] UKFTT 314 (TC) at [245].
[181] *Curtis v HMRC* [2022] UKFTT 172 (TC); [2022] Pens. L.R. 10 at [95]–[98].
[182] FA 2004 s.239.
[183] FA 2004 s.241(2). As scheme chargeable payments in excess of the de-registration threshold will allow HMRC to de-register the scheme, it is also important to consider the possible application of the provisions discussed in Ch.4.
[184] *Wasting asset* has the same meaning as in TCGA 1992 s.44, namely an asset with a predictable life of 50 years or less.

where scheme assets are used to provide benefits to a member. In contrast to the other unauthorised payments, the provision of such benefits will not usually have the effect of reducing the value of scheme property (unless the asset is a wasting asset) and so for this reason a deemed unauthorised payments within s.173 is not subject to a scheme sanction charge;[185]
(b) compensation payments within FA 2004 s.178. These are payments from a pension scheme to a sponsoring employer in respect of a member's liability to that employer in respect of a criminal, fraudulent or negligent act or omission by the member;[186]
(c) payments made to comply with an order of a court or of a person or body with power to order the making of the payment, or made on the ground that a court or any such person or body is likely to order the making of the payment (or would be likely to do so were it asked to do so);
(d) any part of an unauthorised payment that would be a PCLS if it did not exceed the *permitted maximum* in certain circumstances where the individual's lump sum rights exceeded £375,000 on 5 April 2006;[187] or
(e) an unauthorised payment made before 6 April 2011 which the rules of the scheme as they stood immediately before 6 April 2006 required the trustees or managers to make, to the extent that it is referable to subsisting rights which accrued under a defined benefits arrangement before 6 April 2006 or to contributions made to a money purchase arrangement before that date.[188]

Parliament evidently considers the above unauthorised payments to be less objectionable than the other unauthorised payments, presumably on the basis that they do not involve any failing by the scheme administrator. **18-190**

The rate of the scheme sanction charge is 40% "in respect of" the scheme chargeable payment.[189] This presumably means 40% of the *amount* of the scheme chargeable payment. Where some or all of the unauthorised payments charge has been paid, the scheme sanction charge is reduced by the lesser of: (a) 25% of the amount of the scheme chargeable payment(s) if the whole or any part of the unauthorised payments charge in relation to it has been paid; and (b) the amount of the unauthorised payments charge which has been paid in relation to the scheme chargeable payment. **18-191**

---

[185] The same could of course be said of loans to members, which are evidently considered to be highly objectionable under FA 2004, but loans are perhaps best thought of as sui generis as they could easily become of negligible value.
[186] Although a compensation payment within s.178 is an authorised *employer* payment, such a payment would be in respect of a member and therefore it will usually be an unauthorised *member* payment.
[187] See FA 2004 Sch.36 para.30. For the meaning of "permitted maximum" in this context, see Ch.14.
[188] The Registered Pension Schemes (Unauthorised Payments by Existing Schemes) Regulations 2006 (SI 2006/365) reg.2(1) applying The Registered Pension Schemes (Modification of the Rules of Existing Schemes) Regulations 2006 (SI 2006/364) reg.3(1) (made under FA 2004 Sch.36 para.3). "Subsisting rights" is construed in accordance with PA 1995 s.67A(6). A payment is not exempt to the extent that it includes a refund of additional voluntary contributions that could have been used to provide pension benefits for the member and his dependants without prejudicing approval of the scheme.
[189] FA 2004 s.240(1).

# GENUINE ERRORS

### Treatment by HMRC

**18-192** HMRC assert:[190]

> "An inadvertent payment made in the following circumstances will not be an unauthorised payment:
> - the payment is made in genuine error, such that there was no intention to make a payment to that extent or at all, and
> - the erroneous payment is spotted by someone involved with the management of the scheme (or the recipient of the payment or the recipient's adviser might have brought the matter to the attention of the scheme managers), and
> - the error is rectified as soon as reasonably possible.
>
> There is no requirement for the scheme administrator to report a payment made in these circumstances as an unauthorised payment, as the payment is not an unauthorised payment for the purpose of the tax rules relating to registered pension schemes."

**18-193** This has no statutory basis, but support for the general principle may be found in *Duke of Roxburghe's Executors v IRC*[191] (see below). The examples at PTM146200 relate to transposition errors resulting in overpayments (e.g. transferring £52,000 instead of £25,000), errors by third party valuers resulting in overpayments, and errors by the scheme bank resulting in early payments. The HMRC guidance (which to some extent may be concessionary) is aimed at payments made as a result of an inadvertent administrative failure or because of circumstances that were beyond the control of the trustees or managers making the payment. A payment which is made deliberately but on the basis of an incorrect understanding of the law (or where the payer is ignorant of the law) is not the sort of payment to which one would expect concessionary treatment to apply.[192] To the extent that this treatment is concessionary, a refusal by HMRC to exercise their discretion will not usually be capable of appeal to the FTT.[193]

### The *Roxburghe* principle

**18-194** In *Duke of Roxburghe's Executors v IRC*[194] a remittance basis taxpayer received (a) income which was subject to UK tax on the arising basis; and (b) income which was subject to UK tax only if remitted to the UK. The two categories of income were segregated in different accounts with the same non-UK bank. A remittance to the UK from the former account would not be taxable (because it had already been taxed as it arose), but a remittance from the latter account would be taxable. The taxpayer directed the bank to make a remittance to the UK out of her former account, but the bank mistakenly debited the latter account. The Court of Session held

---

[190] PTM146100.
[191] *Duke of Roxburghe's Executors v IRC* 20 TC 711.
[192] See Ch.13 for the statutory treatment of certain pensions paid in error, including payments made on the basis of an incorrect understanding of the law.
[193] The FTT's jurisdiction is limited to the terms of TMA 1970 s.50(6), which is to decide whether an appellant has been overcharged by an assessment (see *AIM (Perth) Ltd v HMRC* [2017] UKFTT 533 at [71] and [72]). Questions relating to fairness or HMRC's use of discretion are not within the jurisdiction of the FTT (*Eden Consulting Services (Richmond) Ltd v HMRC* [2016] UKFTT 656 at [23]). It may be possible in certain circumstances to argue that a legitimate expectation has arisen.
[194] *Duke of Roxburghe's Executors v IRC* 20 TC 711.

that this was in fact (contrary to the bank's records) a remittance from the former account because the *taxpayer* had *intended* the remittance to come from that account. The taxpayer was legally entitled to have the remittance debited against any account belonging to her and under her control, and she did so effectually by the instructions to debit it against the former account. The bank's records were therefore wrong and did not reflect the legal position. They could therefore be rectified by way of a simple amendment to book entries.[195]

For the principle to apply, the instructions to the bank or other agent (without which the bank or other agent would have no authority to make any payments) must make the taxpayer's intentions clear. The fact that the instructions may have been misunderstood by the bank or other agent does not necessarily preclude the application of the principle. In the *Roxburghe* case, it appears there was some confusion regarding the names of her accounts, and the bank's mistake was caused by a misunderstanding of the taxpayer's intentions.

In *Hymanson v HMRC*,[196] the FTT records HMRC's acceptance that if the taxpayer could prove that his bank had made the contributions to his pension scheme contrary to his instructions, they would be prepared to "reverse" the contributions (i.e. to treat the contributions as though they had not been made).

## REPORTING OBLIGATIONS

**18-195** The following reporting obligations arise in connection with unauthorised payments:

(a) The scheme administrator must notify HMRC of any unauthorised payment.[197]
(b) If an unauthorised employer payment is made to or in respect of a company, the company must provide specified information to HMRC no later than 31 January following the tax year in which the payment is made.[198]
(c) If a deemed unauthorised payment within FA 2004 s.173 (benefits) is made, the scheme administrator must provide specified information to the member before 7 July following the tax year in which the payment is made.[199]

---

[195] See RDRM33560: "Where a bank acts contrary to express instructions by an account holder, and that mistake inadvertently results in a taxable remittance to the UK by the account holder, the account holder and the bank may alter the transaction in line with the original instructions given. If the bank does this, HMRC will treat the earlier [mistaken] transaction as not having taken place, and the new transaction as being the original transaction in looking at whether there has been a taxable remittance from that account."
[196] *Hymanson v HMRC* [2018] UKFTT 667 (TC) at [86].
[197] SI 2006/567 reg.3 (reportable event no.1). See Ch.19.
[198] SI 2006/567 reg.5. The required information is: (a) the details of the scheme that made the payment; (b) the nature of the payment; (c) the amount of the payment; and (d) the date of the payment.
[199] SI 2006/567 reg.13. The required information is: (a) the nature of the benefit; (b) the amount of the unauthorised payment; and (c) the date of the benefit. The member will require this information to complete his tax return.

# CHAPTER 19

# Compliance

## TABLE OF CONTENTS

| | |
|---|---|
| Introduction and overview | 19-001 |
| Requirement to preserve documentation | 19-003 |
| Requirement to provide information and documentation | 19-008 |
| FA 2008 Sch.36 | 19-009 |
| The pension scheme return | 19-011 |
| Penalties | 19-012 |
| Event reports | 19-013 |
| Penalties | 19-015 |
| The accounting for tax return | 19-016 |
| Penalties | 19-020 |
| The Information Regulations (SI 2006/567) | 19-021 |
| Penalties | 19-022 |
| Breach of obligation to provide information or documentation | 19-023 |
| Making false statements etc. | 19-024 |
| Preparation of inaccurate documents | 19-025 |
| Assessments | 19-026 |
| Assessments under FA 2004 Pt 4 | 19-027 |
| Self-assessment | 19-032 |
| Enquiries | 19-034 |
| Discovery assessments | 19-039 |
| Appeals | 19-043 |

## INTRODUCTION AND OVERVIEW

Persons involved in the administration of registered pension schemes are required to provide information to HMRC on the occurrence of certain events. In addition, HMRC have extensive powers to require that information and documentation is provided to them. Penalties may be imposed for non-compliance. The primary purpose of these provisions is to make HMRC aware that a charge to tax has (or may have) arisen, so that HMRC can assess the taxpayer, or require the taxpayer to self-assess. HMRC are required to do so strictly in accordance with the relevant provisions, and HMRC's failure to do so may result in a purported assessment being found to be invalid. **19-001**

This chapter considers the requirements to preserve documentation, the requirement to provide information and documentation to HMRC, the penalties for failing to do so, and the provisions applicable to assessment and appeals. **19-002**

## REQUIREMENT TO PRESERVE DOCUMENTATION

**19-003** Scheme members and trustees have a general requirement under TMA 1970 s.2B to keep records relating to their own tax position. This requirement applies whether or not such persons normally file a tax return as any member or trustee may be sent a notice to file a tax return.[1]

**19-004** The following persons are required to preserve documentation relating to a registered pension scheme[2]:

(a) any person who is or has been a scheme administrator;
(b) any person who is or has been a trustee of the scheme;
(c) any person who provides or has provided administrative services to the scheme; and
(d) if the scheme is an occupational pension scheme, any person who is or has been a sponsoring employer or a director of an employer company.

**19-005** Such persons are obliged to preserve any documents in their possession or under their control relating to: (a) any monies received by or owing to the scheme; (b) any investments or assets held by the scheme; (c) any payments made by the scheme; (d) any contracts to purchase a lifetime annuity in respect of a member of the scheme; and (e) the administration of the scheme.

**19-006** Documents must be preserved for the tax year to which they relate and for a period of six years following that year. However, where a person ceases to act in relation to a scheme or ceases to provide administrative services to a scheme, he is not required to preserve documents where he has transferred all the documents to another person who has succeeded him in acting or providing services to the scheme.

**19-007** A penalty of up to £3,000 may be imposed for failure to comply with these requirements.[3]

## REQUIREMENT TO PROVIDE INFORMATION AND DOCUMENTATION

**19-008** The following are considered here:

(a) HMRC's general information and inspection powers under FA 2008 Sch.36;
(b) Pension scheme returns (FA 2004 s.250);
(c) Accounting for tax returns (FA 2004 s.254 and SI 2005/3454);
(d) Event reports (SI 2006/567 reg.3); and
(e) The Registered Pension Scheme (Provision of Information) Regulations 2006 (SI 2006/567) (made under FA 2004 s.251).

### FA 2008 Sch.36

**19-009** HMRC may by notice in writing require a person to provide information or to produce documentation if it is reasonably required by HMRC for the purpose of

---

[1] For more information on the general requirements, see CH11200 (what records should be kept) and CH14500 (how long records should be kept for).
[2] FA 2004 s.251(1)(b) and The Registered Pension Schemes (Provision of Information) Regulations 2006 (SI 2006/567) reg.18.
[3] FA 2004 s.258(2).

# REQUIREMENT TO PROVIDE INFORMATION

checking the taxpayer's tax position, or the tax position of another person whose identity is known to HMRC (a third party notice) or whose identity is not known to HMRC (including a class of persons whose individual identities are not known to HMRC).[4] Penalties may be imposed for failing to comply with an information notice or deliberately obstructing HMRC in the course of an inspection, or for providing inaccurate information or producing a document that contains an inaccuracy.[5]

The usual provisions in Sch.36 relating to third party notices and notices about persons whose identity is not known are modified as follows where such a notice refers only to information or documents that relate to a matter relating to a registered pension scheme, or an annuity purchased with sums or assets held for the purposes of a registered pension scheme or a pre-6 April 2006 pension scheme.[6] In relation to third party notices, Sch.36 para.3(1) (approval etc. of third party notices) and 4(1) (copying third party notices to taxpayer) do not apply, and para.30(1) (appeal) has effect as if it permitted an appeal on any grounds. In relation to notices about persons whose identity is not known, para.5(3) and (4) (approval of the FTT) have effect as if they permitted, but did not require, HMRC to obtain the approval of the FTT, and para.31 (appeal) has effect as if it permitted an appeal on any grounds. In relation to both types of notice, a person may not appeal against a requirement in the notice to provide any information, or produce any document, that forms part of any person's statutory records.

19-010

## The pension scheme return

Pursuant to FA 2004 s.250, HMRC may, in relation to any tax year, by notice require the scheme administrator: (a) to make and deliver to HMRC a return containing any information reasonably required by the notice; and (b) to deliver with the return any accounts, statements or other documents relating to information contained in the return which may reasonably be required by the notice. This return is generally referred to by HMRC as the "pension scheme return" (because the title to s.250 is "registered pension scheme return") but it is referred to as an "information return" in the legislation. HMRC may require the return to include any information relating to:

19-011

(a) contributions made under the pension scheme;
(b) transfers of sums or assets held for the purposes of, or representing accrued rights under, another pension scheme so as to become held for the purposes of, or to represent rights under, the pension scheme;
(c) income and gains derived from investments or deposits held for the purposes of the pension scheme;
(d) other receipts of the pension scheme;
(e) the sums and other assets held for the purposes of the pension scheme;
(f) the liabilities of the pension scheme;
(g) the provision of benefits by the pension scheme;
(h) transfers of sums or assets held for the purposes of, or representing accrued rights under, the pension scheme so as to become held for the purposes of, or to represent rights under, another pension scheme;
(i) other expenditure of the pension scheme;

---

[4] FA 2008 Sch.36 paras 1, 2 and 5.
[5] FA 2008 Sch.36 paras 39, 40 and 40A.
[6] FA 2008 Sch.36 para.34B.

(j) the membership of the pension scheme; or
(k) any other matter relating to the administration of the pension scheme.

*Penalties*

**19-012** If the scheme administrator fails to comply with a notice under s.250, the scheme administrator is liable to a penalty of £100, and then a further penalty of up to £60 for each day on which the failure continues after the day on which the £100 penalty was imposed.[7] If the scheme administrator fraudulently or negligently makes an inaccurate return, or delivers any inaccurate accounts, statements or other documents with the return, the scheme administrator is liable to a penalty of up to £3,000.[8]

**Event reports**

**19-013** The scheme administrator must provide event reports to HMRC in respect of the following reportable events listed in SI 2006/567 reg.3[9]:

(a) *Unauthorised payments:* the scheme makes an unauthorised payment.
(b) *Payments exceeding 50% of standard lifetime allowance:* the scheme pays a lump sum death benefit to a person in respect of the death of a member, and that payment, either alone or when aggregated with other such payments from that scheme, amounts to more than 50% of the standard lifetime allowance applicable at the time of the member's death.
(c) *Early provision of benefits:* the scheme provides benefits to a member who is under the normal minimum pension age and before the benefits were provided the member was, either in the year in which they were provided or any of the preceding six years: (i) in relation to the sponsoring employer, or an associated company of that employer, a director or a person connected with a director; (ii) whether alone or with others, the sponsoring employer; or (iii) a person connected with the sponsoring employer.
(d) *Serious ill-health lump sums:* a scheme pays a serious ill-health lump sum and before the payment was made the member was, either in the year in which it was provided or any of the preceding six years: (i) in relation to the sponsoring employer, or an associated company of that employer, a director or a person connected with a director; (ii) whether alone or with others, the sponsoring employer; or (iii) a person connected with the sponsoring employer.
(e) *Suspension of ill-health pension:* an ill-health pension which has been paid, pursuant to pension rule 1 in FA 2004 s.165(1), is not paid.
(f) *BCE where non-standard lifetime allowance:* a BCE occurs in relation to a member and in order to reduce or eliminate liability to the lifetime allowance charge the member relies on entitlement to an enhanced lifetime allowance, enhanced protection, FP 2012, FP 2014, IP 2014, FP 2016 or IP 2016.
(g) *PCLS:* the scheme pays a PCLS to a member which: (i) exceeds 25% of the amount found by adding the amount of the payment to the entitlement amount; and (ii) is more than 7.5%, but less than 25%, of the standard

---

[7] FA 2004 s.257(1) and (2).
[8] FA 2004 s.257(4).
[9] The information to be provided to HMRC in relation to each reportable event is specified in the second column of the table at SI 2006/567 reg.3. See PTM161000.

lifetime allowance for the tax year in which the sum is paid.[10]
- (h) *PCLS (primary and enhanced protection):* the scheme pays a PCLS which is an authorised payment by reason only of the application of FA 2004 Sch.36 paras 24-30 (i.e. the member has primary or enhanced protection).
- (i) *Stand-alone lump sum:* the scheme pays a stand-alone lump sum where: (i) circumstance A in SI 2006/572 art.25B(2) is met; (ii) circumstance B in SI 2006/572 art.25B(3) is met; or (iii) circumstance C in SI 2006/572 art.25B(4) is met and the payment is more than 7.5% of the standard lifetime allowance for the tax year in which the sum is paid.
- (j) *Transfers to QROPS:* the scheme makes a recognised transfer to a QROPS.
- (k) *Investment-regulated pension schemes:* the scheme becomes, or ceases to be, an investment-regulated pension scheme.
- (l) *Changes in scheme rules:* the scheme changes its rules to: (i) entitle any person to require the making of unauthorised payments; or (ii) permit investment other than in contracts or policies of insurance.
- (m) *Changes to rules of pre-commencement scheme treated as more than one scheme:* the scheme, being one which immediately before 6 April 2006 was treated in accordance with ICTA 1988 s.611 as two or more separate schemes, changes its rules in any way.
- (n) *Change in legal structure of scheme:* the legal structure of the scheme changes from one of the following categories to another: (i) a single trust under which all of the assets are held for the benefit of all members of the scheme (and which does not fall within the next category); (ii) a single trust under which all of the assets are held for the benefit of all members of the scheme and which provides benefits only in the event of the death of a member, and in respect of a sum assured under a policy of insurance which becomes payable on the death of that member; (iii) a body corporate; and (iv) other.
- (o) *Change in number of members:* the number of scheme members falls in a different band at the end of a tax year from that in which it fell at the end of the previous tax year. The bands are: (i) 0 members; (ii) 1 member; (iii) 2 to 11 members; (iv) 12 to 50 members; (v) 51 to 10,000 members; and (vi) more than 10,000 members.
- (p) *Scheme chargeable payments:* the scheme is treated as having made a scheme chargeable payment under s.185A (income from taxable property) or s.185F (gains from taxable property).
- (q) *Country or territory of establishment:* the scheme changes the country or territory in which it is established.
- (r) *Occupational pension scheme:* the scheme becomes, or ceases to be, an occupational pension scheme.
- (s) *Master trust scheme:* the scheme becomes, or ceases to be, a Master Trust scheme within the meaning of PSA 2017 s.1.
- (t) *Annual allowance:* the scheme administrator is required to provide a member with a pension savings statement under SI 2006/567 reg.14A(1) containing the information specified in reg.14A(2).[11]

---

[10] The entitlement amount is: (a) the amount crystallised by reason of the member becoming entitled to the pension with which the lump sum payment is associated; or (b) where a BCE did not occur by reason of the member becoming entitled to the pension with which the lump sum payment is associated, the amount that would have been so crystallised if the member had been under the age of 75 at the date the entitlement arose.

[11] This requirement arises where the aggregate pension input amounts for the pension input period in

(u) *Dual annual allowances:* the scheme administrator is required to provide a member with a pension savings statement under SI 2006/567 reg.14A(1) containing the information specified in reg.14A(10).[12]

**19-014** An event report in respect of (j) (transfer to QROPS) must be delivered within 60 days of the transfer, and an event report in respect of (s) (master trust schemes) must be delivered within 30 days of the event.[13] Event reports in respect of all other reportable events must be delivered prior to 31 January in the tax year following the tax year in which the reportable event occurs.[14]

*Penalties*

**19-015** The penalties which may be imposed in connection with event reports are[15]:

(a) a penalty of up to £300 for failure to provide the required information on time;

(b) where the initial failure to provide penalty has been levied and the information still has not been provided further penalties may be due. These penalties can include daily penalties of up to £60 for every day that the failure to provide the required information continues; and

(c) a penalty of up to £3,000 where incorrect information has been provided and the inaccuracy is due to either negligence or fraud.

## The accounting for tax return

**19-016** A scheme administrator must make returns to HMRC of the income tax to which he is liable under FA 2004 Pt 4, except for the scheme sanction charge.[16] This return is referred to by HMRC as the accounting for tax return.

**19-017** A return must be made within 45 days of the end of each quarter[17] if tax has been charged on the scheme administrator in that quarter (nil returns are not required). Where the scheme administrator is liable for the annual allowance charge under the *scheme pays* option in s.237B, the tax is charged on the scheme administrator in the period ending with 31 December in the year following that in which that tax year ended (or such earlier period as the scheme administrator may elect).[18]

**19-018** The return must show any income tax to which the scheme administrator is liable in respect of: (a) the authorised surplus charge; (b) the lifetime allowance

---

respect of each arrangement under the scheme relating to the member exceeds the annual allowance for that tax year.

[12] This requirement arises where the scheme administrator has reason to believe that the member has first flexibly accessed his pension rights and the total money purchase pension input amounts exceed £4,000.

[13] SI 2006/567 reg.3(7) and (8).

[14] SI 2006/567 reg.3(6). Where a scheme has been wound up, the event report must be delivered within three months of completion of the winding-up (if that is earlier than would otherwise be required) (reg.4(3)).

[15] FA 2004 s.258 and TMA 1970 s.98(1)(b) and (2).

[16] FA 2004 s.254(1), (8). Where a scheme has been de-registered, the person responsible for making returns is the person who was, or each of the persons who were, the scheme administrator immediately before the registration was withdrawn.

[17] i.e. for each period of three months ending with 31 March, 30 June, 30 September or 31 December.

[18] However if the notice which gave rise to the liability is amended in accordance with regulations under s.237B(5)(c), any additional tax to which the scheme administrator becomes liable is charged in the period in which the scheme administrator receives notice of the amendment (if later).

# REQUIREMENT TO PROVIDE INFORMATION 443

charge; (c) the annual allowance charge; (d) the de-registration charge; and (e) the overseas transfer charge.[19]

Any income tax payable is due at the time that the return is to be made. HMRC are not required to make an assessment. Tax paid late is subject to interest at the prescribed rate.[20] The scheme administrator must immediately make an amended return if he becomes aware of any omissions or errors in the return.[21]

**19-019**

*Penalties*

The penalties which may be imposed in connection with the accounting for tax returns are:

**19-020**

(a) a penalty of £100 for failure to deliver a return on or before the filing date.[22] Daily penalties may be imposed if the return is not delivered within three months of the penalty date (i.e. the day after the filing date), with further penalties if the return is not delivered within six months of the penalty date, and further penalties if the return is not delivered within 12 months of the penalty date.[23]
(b) A penalty of 5% of the unpaid tax 30 days after the filing date, with a further 5% penalty six months after that and a further 5% penalty 12 months after that.[24]
(c) A penalty of between 30% and 200% of the potential lost revenue if the return contains a careless or deliberate inaccuracy which amounts to, or leads to: (i) an understatement of a liability to tax; (ii) a false or inflated statement of a loss; or (iii) a false or inflated claim to repayment of tax.[25]

## The Information Regulations (SI 2006/567)

The following table summarises the obligations under SI 2006/567[26]:

**19-021**

| Event | Obligation |
| --- | --- |
| Scheme is wound up | Person who was scheme administrator immediately prior to the wind up must notify HMRC. |
| Scheme makes unauthorised employer payment to a company | Employer company must provide specified information to HMRC. |
| Unauthorised borrowing | Scheme administrator must provide specified information to HMRC. |

---

[19] The Registered Pension Schemes (Accounting and Assessment) Regulations 2005 (SI 2005/3454) reg.3. The return must include the particulars specified in column 2 of the table in SI 2005/3454 reg.3. See PTM162000.
[20] SI 2005/3454 regs 5 and 7(2). The "prescribed rate" means the rate applicable under FA 1989 s.178 for the purposes of TMA 1970 s.86.
[21] SI 2005/3454 reg.6.
[22] FA 2009 Sch.55 paras 1 and 3.
[23] FA 2009 Sch.55 paras 1, 4, 5 and 6.
[24] FA 2009 Sch.56 paras 1 and 3.
[25] FA 2007 Sch.24 paras 1 and 4.
[26] Event reports (which are in reg.3 of SI 2006/567) are detailed above. The obligations imposed on insurance companies have been omitted from this table (see regs 16–17C).

| Event | Obligation |
|---|---|
| Ceasing to be scheme administrator | Scheme administrator must notify HMRC when ceases to be scheme administrator. |
| Death of member | Scheme administrator must provide specified information to personal representatives. |
| Death of recipient of lifetime annuity or scheme pension from insurance company | Insurance company must provide specified information to personal representatives. |
| Death of member | Personal representatives must provide specified information to HMRC. |
| Payment of LSDB to trustees | Scheme administrator must provide specified information to trustee. |
| Provision of benefits by trustee of death benefits trust | Trustee must provide specified information to beneficiary. |
| Claiming entitlement to enhanced lifetime allowance, enhanced protection, fixed protection and individual protection | The member must give to the scheme administrator the reference number issued by HMRC. |
| Recycling of lump sums | Member must provide specified information to scheme administrator. |
| Intention to pay PCLS | Member must provide such information as will enable the scheme administrator to calculate the available portion of the member's lump sum allowance. |
| Member requests transfer to QROPS | Scheme administrator must notify member of requirement to provide specified information to scheme administrator. Member must provide the information to the scheme administrator. |
| Transfer to QROPS gives rise to overseas transfer charge or is initially assumed to be excluded | Member must provide specified information to scheme administrator. |
| Scheme administrator requires NI number | Individual must provide NI number to scheme administrator. |
| Scheme administrator intends to pay lifetime allowance charge except that a person is not a non-qualifying person in relation to payment of a lump sum if the payment is made to the person in the person's capacity as a bare trustee | Scheme administrator must provide specified information to member. |
| Transfer to QROPS is subject to overseas transfer charge | Scheme administrator must provide specified information to member. |
| Scheme makes unauthorised payment under FA 2004 s.173 (provision of benefits) | Scheme administrator must provide specified information to member. |
| Must be provided annually | Scheme administrator must provide specified information to member. |

# REQUIREMENT TO PROVIDE INFORMATION

| Event | Obligation |
|---|---|
| A BCE occurs | Scheme administrator must provide specified information to member. |
| It appears that member may be first flexibly accessing pension rights | Scheme administrator must provide notice containing specified information to member. |
| Member receives notice under reg.14ZA | Member must pass on information to scheme administrator of every other registered pension scheme that he is a member of. |
| Recognised transfer where it appears that member has first flexibly accessed pension rights | Scheme administrator of transferring scheme must provide specified information to scheme administrator of receiving scheme. |
| Transfer to QROPS | Scheme administrator of transferring scheme must provide specified information to scheme administrator of receiving scheme. |
| Flexible drawdown arrangements applied to individual before 6 April 2015 | Member must provide specified information to scheme administrator of every registered pension scheme that he is a member of. |
| Individual accesses flexi-access drawdown fund | Individual must provide specified information to scheme administrator of every registered pension scheme that he is active member of. |
| Annual allowance charge arises | Scheme administrator must provide pension saving statement to member. |
| Member requests information re pension input amount | Scheme administrator must provide specified information to member. |
| Member requests information re IP 2016 | Scheme administrator must provide specified information to member. |
| Transfer of crystallised rights between schemes | Scheme administrator of transferring scheme must provide specified information to scheme administrator of receiving scheme. |
| Recognised transfer of drawdown or flexi-access | Scheme administrator of transferring scheme must provide specified information to scheme administrator of receiving scheme. |
| Member is director of employer | Employer must provide specified information to scheme administrator. |
| Scheme purchases scheme annuity or lifetime annuity (other than from drawdown fund) from insurance company | Scheme administrator must provide specified information to insurance company. |
| Scheme purchases scheme annuity or lifetime annuity from drawdown fund from insurance company | Scheme administrator must provide specified information to insurance company. |

## PENALTIES

**19-022** Penalties relating to the pension scheme return, event report and accounting for tax return are set out above.

### Breach of obligation to provide information or documentation

**19-023** Failing to comply with SI 2006/567 could result in the following penalties[27]:
(a) a penalty of up to £300 for failure to provide the required information on time (this covers both non provision and late provision);
(b) where the initial failure to provide penalty has been levied and the information still has not been provided further penalties may be due. These penalties can be daily penalties of up to £60 for every day that the failure to provide the required information continues; and
(c) a penalty of up to £3,000 where incorrect information has been provided and the inaccuracy is due to either negligence or fraud.

### Making false statements etc.

**19-024** A person who fraudulently or negligently makes a false statement or representation is liable to a penalty of up to £3,000 if, in consequence of the statement or representation: (a) that person or any other person obtains relief from, or repayment of, tax chargeable under FA 2004 Pt 4 or ITEPA 2003 Pt 9 on pension income to which: (i) any provision of ITEPA 2003 Pt 9 Ch.15A applies; or (ii) s.579A applies by virtue of any provision of ITEPA 2003 Ch.5A; (b) or a registered pension scheme makes an unauthorised payment.[28]

### Preparation of inaccurate documents

**19-025** A person who assists in or induces the preparation of any document which the person knows is inaccurate, and will, or is likely to, cause a registered pension scheme to make an unauthorised payment, is liable to a penalty of up to £3,000.[29]

## ASSESSMENTS

**19-026** There are three stages in the imposition of a charge to tax: (a) establish liability; (b) assessment; and (c) collection/enforcement by HMRC if the taxpayer fails to pay.[30] HMRC are unable to enforce payment if they have not assessed the taxpayer in accordance with the relevant legislation.[31]

---

[27] TMA 1970 s.98.
[28] FA 2004 s.264(1).
[29] FA 2004 s.264(2).
[30] *Whitney v IRC* [1926] A.C. 37 at 52 (Lord Dunedin); *Hoey v HMRC* [2022] EWCA Civ 656 at [31].
[31] See, e.g. *John Mander Pension Scheme Trustees v HMRC* [2015] UKSC 56; [2015] 1 W.L.R. 3857 (assessment relating to wrong year); *Bayonet Ventures LLP v HMRC* [2018] UKFTT 262 (assessment issued to wrong taxpayer).

## Assessments under FA 2004 Pt 4

In the following circumstances, HMRC must issue an assessment to tax to the assessable person[32]:  **19-027**

| Case | Event |
|---|---|
| Case 1 | An unauthorised payments charge arises and the person liable to the charge is a company. The assessable person is the person liable to the charge under FA 2004 s.208(2). |
| Case 2 | An unauthorised payments surcharge arises and the person liable to the charge is a company. The assessable person is the person liable to the charge under FA 2004 s.209(3). |
| Case 3 | A charge to tax arises under FA 2004 s.217(2) (lifetime allowance charge on receipt of a lump sum death benefit). The assessable person is the person liable under FA 2004 s.217(2). |
| Case 4 | A scheme sanction charge arises. The assessable person is the scheme administrator, or the person or persons liable to the scheme sanction charge under s.239(3). |
| Case 5 | The correct tax due under FA 2004 s.254 (accounting for tax return) has not been paid on or before the due date. The assessable person is the scheme administrator. |
| Case 6 | FA 2004 s.272 (trustees etc liable as scheme administrator) applies. The assessable person is the person specified as assuming liability under s.272(4). |
| Case 6A | FA 2004 s.272C (former scheme administrator etc to retain liability) applies. The assessable person is the person or persons specified as assuming liability under s.272C(3), (4) or (7). |
| Case 7 | FA 2004 s.273 (members liable as scheme administrator) applies. The assessable person is the person liable under s.273(2). |
| Case 7A | A charge to tax arises under SI 2006/1958 reg.10 (income and gains from taxable property where scheme and property are outside the UK). The assessable person is the person liable to the charge. |

Tax assessed under cases 1 and 2 is payable on the day following the expiry of nine months from the end of the accounting period in which the unauthorised payment was made or, if later, within 30 days of the issue of the notice of assessment. Tax assessed under the other cases is payable within 30 days of the issue of the notice of assessment.  **19-028**

An assessment under case 3 may be made at any time not later than six years after HMRC are notified of the relevant lump sum death benefit, but cannot be made later than 20 years after 31 January following the end of the tax year in which the relevant lump sum death benefit was paid.  **19-029**

Any tax assessable under one or more of the above cases may be included in one assessment if the tax so included is all due on the same date.  **19-030**

Tax assessed under the above provisions carries interest at the prescribed rate until paid.[33]  **19-031**

---

[32] SI 2005/3454 reg.4, made under FA 2004 s.255.
[33] SI 2005/3454 regs 5 and 7(2). The "prescribed rate" means the rate applicable under FA 1989 s.178 for the purposes of TMA 1970 s.86.

**Self-assessment**

**19-032** Individuals liable for one of the tax charges in FA 2004 Pt 4 must, if they have not received a notification to file (or it has been withdrawn), notify HMRC of their chargeability to income tax within six months from the end of the tax year in which the tax liability arises.[34] HMRC will then issue a notice requiring the taxpayer to make and deliver to HMRC a return containing such information as may reasonably be required in pursuance of the notice, and to deliver with the return such accounts, statements and documents, relating to information contained in the return, as may reasonably be so required.[35] Every such return must include a self-assessment of the tax liability,[36] however the tax to be assessed on a person by a self-assessment does not include any tax which[37]:

(a) is chargeable on the scheme administrator of a registered pension scheme under FA 2004 Pt 4;
(b) is chargeable, on the scheme manager of a QROPS or a former QROPS, under FA 2004 Pt 4;
(c) is chargeable on the sub-scheme administrator of a sub-scheme under FA 2004 Pt 4 as modified by SI 2006/569;
(d) is chargeable on a person under FA 2004 s.217(2) (liability to lifetime allowance charge by reason of the payment of a relevant lump sum death benefit);
(e) is chargeable on a person or persons under FA 2004 s.272 (trustees etc. liable as scheme administrator); or
(f) is chargeable on a person or persons under FA 2004 s.273 (members liable as scheme administrator).

**19-033** If a taxpayer fails to file a self-assessment return by the due date, HMRC may within three years of the filing date make a determination (in estimated amounts) of the liability and notify the taxpayer.[38] A determination is not an assessment and may not be appealed, but it may be displaced by the delivery of a self-assessment (which must occur within 12 months of the issue of the determination).

*Enquiries*

**19-034** HMRC may check the completeness and accuracy of any return. If they think fit, they can serve formal notice on the taxpayer that they intend to make an enquiry into that return.[39] HMRC are likely to do so only where there are grounds for believing that there is a risk of tax loss. Notice must be served within 12 months of submission of the tax return (usually referred to as the *enquiry window*).[40]

**19-035** Where HMRC have given formal notice of their intention to make enquiries into a taxpayer's return, they may also require the taxpayer to produce such documents and information as they consider necessary to determine the accuracy of the return.[41] Such requirement can extend only to such documents as are in the taxpayer's pos-

---

[34] TMA 1970 s.7. Failure to do so may result in the imposition of penalties under FA 2008 Sch.41. The maximum penalty is the net amount of tax due, but unpaid, at 31 January following the tax year in which the liability arises (so if the tax is paid by 31 January the penalty is nil).
[35] TMA 1970 s.8. Failure to do so may result in the imposition of penalties under FA 2009 Sch.55.
[36] TMA 1970 s.9(1).
[37] TMA 1970 s.9(1A)
[38] TMA 1970 s.28C; FA 1998 Sch.18 para.36.
[39] TMA 1970 s.9A; TMA 1970 Sch.1A para.5; FA 1998 Sch.18 para.24.
[40] TMA 1970 s.9A(2)(a).
[41] FA 2008 Sch.36.

session or power.[42] A notice to produce material may be appealed (to the FTT) on the basis that it is not reasonably required.

The taxpayer may amend his self-assessment during the enquiry period.[43] HMRC may also do so by giving notice to the taxpayer within nine months of the day on which the return was delivered (or any subsequent amendment by the taxpayer), but this is of no effect if rejected by the taxpayer.[44]

19-036

An enquiry into a return is completed when HMRC notify the taxpayer that they have completed their enquiries and stated their conclusions.[45] Once issued, a closure notice prevents HMRC from making any further enquiries into that year except on the grounds of discovery.

19-037

Interest is charged automatically at the prescribed rate on all tax paid late, regardless of the reason for that late payment. Penalties may also be applied for incorrect returns.

19-038

*Discovery assessments*

Under self-assessment, once the enquiry window has closed or an enquiry has been finalised by means of a closure notice, the only way that HMRC can bring further items into charge is by the use of the discovery provisions.[46] HMRC may issue an assessment if they discover that an amount has not been self-assessed which should have been. HMRC may make an assessment if they discover, as regards any person (the taxpayer) and a year of assessment[47]:

19-039

(a) that any income which ought to have been assessed to income tax, or chargeable gains which ought to have been assessed to CGT have not been assessed; or
(b) that an assessment to tax is or has become insufficient; or
(c) that any relief which has been given is or has become excessive.

The amount of the assessment is the amount, or the further amount, which ought in HMRC's opinion to be charged in order to make good the loss of tax.

19-040

Paragraph (a) is modified by SI 2005/3454 reg.9 in relation to an assessment to tax under case 1, 2 or 3, to include unauthorised payments under FA 2004 s.208, surchargeable unauthorised payments under FA 2004 s.209 or relevant lump sum death benefit under FA 2004 s.217(2) which ought to have been assessed to income tax. Assessments to tax under cases 1, 2 or 3 can only apply to the unauthorised payments charge, the unauthorised payments surcharge, and the lifetime allowance charge. It follows that HMRC cannot raise a discovery assessment in respect of any of the other charges under FA 2004 Pt 4 where there has been a failure to assess. Thus in *Bella Figura Ltd v HMRC*,[48] the FTT held that HMRC was not competent to raise a discovery assessment in relation to a scheme sanction charge. However, on appeal,[49] the UT held that SI 2005/3454 reg.4 confers on HMRC "a freestanding power to assess the scheme sanction charge arising in these proceedings".[50] Observing that this conclusion gives rise to some related difficulties of interpretation, the UT expressly restricted it to the case in hand.

19-041

---

[42] FA 2008 Sch.36 para.1.
[43] TMA 1970 s.9B.
[44] TMA 1970 s.9C.
[45] TMA 1970 s.28A.
[46] TMA 1979 s.29.
[47] TMA 1970 s.29(1).
[48] *Bella Figura Ltd v HMRC* [2018] UKFTT 412.
[49] *HMRC v Bella Figura Ltd* [2020] UKUT 120.
[50] *HMRC v Bella Figura Ltd* [2020] UKUT 120 at [39] (emphasis in original).

# COMPLIANCE

**19-042**  In general, a discovery assessment must be made within four years of the end of the year of assessment to which it relates.[51] This is extended to six years where the loss of tax is brought about carelessly, and is extended to 20 years where the loss of tax is brought about deliberately.[52]

## APPEALS

**19-043**  Any appeal against a decision made by HMRC under FA 2004 Pt 4 must be made to "the tribunal".[53] This is a reference to the FTT or, where determined by or under the Tribunal Procedure Rules, the UT.[54] The Tribunal Procedure Rules are rules made by the Tribunal Procedure Committee governing the practice and procedure to be followed in the FTT and in the UT.[55] These are currently found in The Tribunal Procedure (First-tier Tribunal) (Tax Chamber) Rules 2009 (SI 2009/273) and The Tribunal Procedure (Upper Tribunal) Rules 2008 (SI 2008/2698).

**19-044**  In practice, all appeals are made to the FTT. A person making or notifying an appeal to the FTT starts proceedings by delivering a notice of appeal to the FTT.[56] The notice of appeal must include the information specified in SI 2009/273 rule 20(2). The FTT will then give notice of the proceedings to the respondent (i.e. HMRC).

**19-045**  When the FTT receives a notice of appeal, it will allocate the case to one of the following four categories[57]:

(a) default paper cases, which will usually be disposed of without a hearing;
(b) basic cases, which will usually be disposed of after a hearing, with minimal exchange of documents before the hearing;
(c) standard cases, which will usually be subject to more detailed case management and be disposed of after a hearing; and
(d) complex cases. This is only if the FTT considers that the case: (i) will require lengthy or complex evidence or a lengthy hearing; (ii) involves a complex or important principle or issue; or (iii) involves a large financial sum. If a case is allocated as a complex case, there are certain costs implications.[58] Rule 28 also applies, meaning that the FTT may, with the consent of the parties, refer a case or a preliminary issue to the President of the Tax Chamber of the FTT with a request that the case or issue be

---

[51] TMA 1970 s.34(1). An objection to the making of any assessment on the ground that the time limit for making it has expired can be made only on an appeal against the assessment.

[52] TMA 1970 s.36(1) and (1A).

[53] See FA 2004 ss.156 and 156A (registration), s.159 (de-registration), s.271 (liability of former scheme administrator) and Sch.33 para.6 (qualifying overseas pension schemes). In addition, s.269(1)(a) provides that an appeal may be made to the tribunal where HMRC decide to refuse an application under s.237D (discharge of scheme administrator's liability to annual allowance charge), s.244N (discharge of liability to overseas transfer charge), s.267(2) (discharge of liability to lifetime allowance charge) or s.268 (discharge of liability to unauthorised payments surcharge or scheme sanction charge). An appeal may also be made to the tribunal where HMRC on an application under s.267(5), decides to refuse the application or to discharge the applicant's liability to the lifetime allowance charge in respect of part of the excess amount (s.269(1)(b)).

[54] ITA 2007 s.989, which applies for the purposes of the "Income Tax Acts". FA 2004 Pt 4 is an Income Tax Act (see ITA 2007 s.1(2)(c); Interpretation Act 1978 Sch.1).

[55] Tribunals, Courts and Enforcement Act 2007 s.22.

[56] SI 2009/273 r.20.

[57] SI 2009/273 r.23.

[58] See SI 2009/273 r.10(1)(c).

considered for transfer to the UT. In such cases the President of the Tax Chamber may, with the concurrence of the President of the Tax and Chancery Chamber of the UT, direct that the case or issue be transferred to and determined by the UT.

# CHAPTER 20

# International Aspects

## TABLE OF CONTENTS

| | |
|---|---|
| Introduction | 20-001 |
|     A presumption of territoriality? | 20-002 |
| Non-UK registered schemes | 20-003 |
|     The annual allowance charge | 20-007 |
|     The taxable property provisions | 20-008 |
|     The overseas transfer charge | 20-009 |
| Contributions | 20-010 |
|     Non-UK members | 20-010 |
|     Non-UK schemes | 20-012 |
| The annual allowance | 20-013 |
| Scheme investments | 20-015 |
|     Tax treaties | 20-015 |
| The LS&DB allowance | 20-016 |
|     Relevant overseas individuals | 20-016 |
|         Cash balance arrangements | 20-019 |
|             Opening value | 20-020 |
|             Closing value | 20-021 |
|             Interaction with primary protection: modification of opening value | 20-022 |
|         Other money purchase arrangements | 20-024 |
|         Defined benefits arrangements | 20-026 |
|         Hybrid arrangements | 20-027 |
|     Transfers from ROPS | 20-029 |
|         Cash balance arrangements | 20-034 |
|         Other money purchase arrangements | 20-035 |
|         Defined benefits arrangements | 20-036 |
|         Hybrid arrangements | 20-037 |
| Benefits | 20-039 |
|     Scheme is established in the UK | 20-040 |
|     Scheme is established outside the UK | 20-041 |
|     PAYE provisions | 20-044 |
|         Non-UK members | 20-045 |
|         Non-UK trustees | 20-046 |

## INTRODUCTION

There are no restrictions in FA 2004 Pt 4 relating to the country or territory in which a registered pension scheme may be established, or in which any member

**20-001**

or sponsoring employer is resident.[1] This chapter considers a number of aspects of the registered pension scheme regime in an international context: (a) non-UK registered schemes; (b) contributions; (c) the annual allowance; (d) scheme investments; (e) the LS and LS&DB allowances; and (f) benefits.

**A presumption of territoriality?**

20-002    HMRC apparently accept that the tax charges under FA 2004 Pt 4 have never applied to non-UK resident members unless they received UK tax relief on contributions, and the reporting obligations under FA 2004 Pt 4 have never applied to non-UK resident schemes except in relation to members who received UK tax relief on contributions.[2] That is not as a result of any provision in FA 2004, but HMRC's practice of applying the presumption that UK legislation does not apply outside the UK. On that basis, Ch.5A (considered immediately below) merely clarified the law rather than introducing a new territorial restriction. However, that view has been rejected (or at least doubted) by the FTT.[3]

# NON-UK REGISTERED SCHEMES

20-003    FA 2017 introduced a new Ch.5A into FA 2004 Pt 4 containing provisions relating to registered pension schemes established in a country or territory outside the UK (referred to as "non-UK registered schemes").[4] New s.242C(1) provides that FA 2004 Pt 4 (so far as would not otherwise be the case) is to be read:

(a) as applying in relation to UK-relieved funds of a non-UK registered scheme as it applies in relation to sums or assets held for the purposes of, or representing accrued rights under, a registered pension scheme established in the UK;

(b) as applying in relation to a non-UK registered scheme, so far as the scheme

---

[1] cf. the position prior to 6 April 2006: see IR12 (2001) Pt 15. It is however necessary for the scheme administrator to be resident in the UK, an EU member state, or a non-member EEA state (FA 2004 s.270(2)(a)). Prior to 6 April 2006 it was necessary for the administrator to be resident in the UK (see IR12 (2001) para.2.7).

[2] See *BAV-TMW-Globaler-Immobilien Spezialfonds v HMRC* [2019] UKFTT 129 (TC); [2019] S.F.T.D. 631 at [86] and [87] and the HMRC guidance cited at [90].

[3] *BAV-TMW-Globaler-Immobilien Spezialfonds v HMRC* [2019] UKFTT 129 (TC): "[88] It is clear that, on its plain words, the provisions of the FA 2004 apply to registered pensions schemes whether or not they have members who are relevant UK individuals or any UK-situated assets. HMRC did not suggest otherwise. I was not shown any authority that established that the tax charges and reporting obligations imposed by the FA 2004 were subject to any territorial restriction nor do I consider that one can be implied. I was referred to passages in *Clark v Oceanic Contractors Inc* [1983] STC 35 and *Agassi v Robinson* [2006] STC 1056 which only serve to underline the difficulty of determining when the principle of territoriality is applicable in the context of tax as well as the relatively limited scope of the principle. I can see no reason why the provisions in the FA 2004 should be taken to be limited in their application so as to exclude non-UK pension schemes that had registered from liability to the tax charges and having to comply with the reporting obligations. [89] At the very least, I consider that there is a high degree of uncertainty about the applicability and scope of the principle of territoriality in relation to non-resident pension schemes registered under section 153 FA 2004. As [counsel for the taxpayer] submitted, I think that it is reasonably arguable that any non-resident pension scheme that chose to register would, by the fact of its registration, have established the necessary nexus to the UK and be subject to the consequences that flowed from registration under UK law."

[4] FA 2004 s.242A.

relates to the scheme's UK-relieved funds, as it applies in relation to a registered pension scheme established in the UK;
(c) as applying in relation to members of a non-UK registered scheme, so far as their rights under the scheme are represented by UK-relieved funds of the scheme, as it applies in relation to members of a registered pension scheme established in the UK; and
(d) as applying to relevant contributions to a non-UK registered scheme as it applies in relation to contributions to a registered pension scheme established in the UK.

Read literally, it seems that Ch.5A is intended to extend the reach of the tax charges in FA 2004 Pt 4. The words "This Part (so far as would not otherwise be the case) is to be read as applying …" can only mean that s.242C takes as its starting point that there is, or may be, some circumstances in which Pt 4 does not apply to UK relieved-funds, and where that is the case the purpose of Ch.5A is to make sure those charges apply. But there are no such circumstances, so s.242C is otiose if read literally. HMRC consider that s.242C should be read as restricting the tax charges in FA 2004 Pt 4,[5] apparently by reading in the word "only" (i.e., HMRC read s.242C(1)(a) as if it said, "This Part (so far as would not otherwise be the case) is to be read as applying only in relation to UK-relieved funds of a non-UK registered scheme…"). That interpretation seems to have been common ground in a case before the FTT.[6] But that is not what s.242C says, so the drafting of Ch.5A appears to be defective. The risk of HMRC taking a different view should be low.[7]

**20-004** The "UK-relieved funds" of a non-UK registered scheme are sums or assets held for the purposes of, or representing accrued rights under, the scheme[8]:

(a) that (directly or indirectly) represent sums or assets that at any time were held for the purposes of, or represented accrued rights under, a registered pension scheme established in the UK;
(b) that (directly or indirectly) represent sums or assets that at any time formed the UK tax-relieved fund under an RNUKS of a relieved member of that scheme; or
(c) that: (i) are held for the purposes of, or represent accrued rights under, an arrangement under the scheme relating to a member of the scheme who on any day has been an accruing member of the scheme; and (ii) in accordance with regulations made by HMRC,[9] are to be taken to have benefited from relief from tax.

**20-005** A relevant contribution means: (a) a relievable pension contribution by or on behalf of the individual under an other money purchase arrangement; (b) a contribution in respect of the individual by his employer under an other money purchase arrangement; or (c) a contribution which is: (i) paid under the scheme by an employer

---

[5] HMRC Guidance, *Pension Tax for overseas pensions* (3 January 2017) says "With the exceptions of the annual allowance and taxable property provisions, the general rule is that Part 4 Finance Act 2004 and supporting regulations will [after the introduction of Ch.5A] apply to non-UK registered schemes only to the extent of the UK-relieved funds."
[6] *BAV-TMW-Globaler-Immobilien Spezialfonds v HMRC* [2019] UKFTT 129 (TC) at [85]: "[Counsel for the taxpayer] said that […] Chapter 5A of Part 4 of FA 2004 […] introduced a territorial limitation on charges by providing that they only applied to UK relieved funds, ie funds which derived from assets that have benefited from relief from UK tax."
[7] Although, as the decision in *HMRC v Sippchoice Ltd* [2020] UKUT 149 shows, HMRC are quite prepared to argue that their guidance is wrong where it is in their interests to do so.
[8] FA 2004 s.242B.
[9] HMRC have not yet made any such regulations.

of the individual otherwise than in respect of any individual; and (ii) subsequently becomes held for the purposes of an other money purchase arrangement relating to the individual.[10]

**20-006** An individual is an "accruing member" of a registered pension scheme on any particular day if the individual is an active member under a cash balance arrangement or hybrid arrangement, or a relevant contribution is made under the scheme on that day.[11]

### The annual allowance charge

**20-007** Pension input amounts in respect of arrangements relating to an individual under a non-UK registered scheme are taken into account in applying the provisions for a tax year in relation to the individual only if, in accordance with regulations made by HMRC,[12] relieved inputs are to be taken to have been made in respect of the individual under the scheme in the year.[13]

### The taxable property provisions

**20-008** For the purposes of the application of the taxable property provisions in relation to a non-UK registered scheme, property is taxable property in relation to the scheme if it would be taxable property in relation to the scheme were the scheme a registered pension scheme established in the UK.[14]

### The overseas transfer charge

**20-009** The overseas transfer charge (see Ch.12) is equal to 25% of the "transferred value". Where an overseas transfer charge arises on a transfer from a registered pension scheme established outside the UK, the "transferred value" is limited to the value of the cash and assets that are attributable to UK-relieved funds of the scheme.[15] The UK-relieved funds of such a registered pension scheme are the sums or assets held for the purposes of the scheme:[16]

  (a) that (directly or indirectly) represent sums or assets that at any time were held for the purposes of a registered pension scheme established in the UK;
  (b) that (directly or indirectly) represent sums or assets that at any time formed the UK tax-relieved fund under an RNUKS of a relieved member of that scheme; or
  (c) that are held for the purposes of an arrangement under the scheme relating to a member of the scheme who on any day has been an accruing member of the scheme, and in accordance with regulations made by HMRC, is to be taken to have benefited from relief from tax.

---

[10] The Registered Pension Schemes (Provision of Information) Regulations 2006 (SI 2006/567) reg.14ZB(8).
[11] SI 2006/567 reg.14ZB(7).
[12] HMRC have not yet made any such regulations.
[13] FA 2004 s.242D.
[14] FA 2004 s.242E.
[15] See Ch.12.
[16] FA 2004 s.242B.

## CONTRIBUTIONS

### Non-UK members

Where an employee is non-UK resident but performs some of his duties in the UK, his earnings relating to those UK duties will usually be subject to UK tax (subject to the application of a double tax treaty providing otherwise). If a contribution were made to a registered pension scheme by or on behalf of such an individual, would he obtain UK tax relief that can be used to reduce his UK tax liability? The requirements that must be satisfied are discussed in Ch.6. These include a requirement that the member is a "relevant UK individual" for that year. If the individual has not been resident in the UK at some point during the tax year or the previous five tax years and at the time he became a member of the scheme, he will be a relevant UK individual only if he has relevant UK earnings chargeable to income tax for that year. Relevant UK earnings are: (a) employment income; (b) trading income; (c) property income in respect of a UK or EEA furnished holiday lettings business; and (d) patent income. In the circumstances envisaged here, the individual will have employment income chargeable to income tax and so he may be able to obtain UK tax relief in respect of contributions. 

20-010

The maximum amount of UK tax relief available is limited to the amount of the individual's relevant UK earnings which are chargeable to income tax for the tax year or the basic amount (currently £3,600). Relevant UK earnings are "chargeable to income tax" even if there is no charge to UK tax as a result of personal allowances (for example).[17]

20-011

### Non-UK schemes

It should be noted that PA 2004 s.253 applies to an occupational pension scheme that has its main administration outside the EEA states. An employer based in the UK[18] may cause a contribution to be paid to the scheme in respect of an employee (whether or not employed in the UK) only if, at the time of payment: (a) the scheme is established under irrevocable trusts; and (b) a trustee of the scheme is resident in the UK. The same conditions apply where an employer based outside the UK may cause a contribution to be paid to the scheme in respect of an employee employed in the UK. An exemption applies for split approved schemes and to unregistered occupational pension schemes (i.e. EFRBS) which have their main administration outside of the EEA.[19]

20-012

## THE ANNUAL ALLOWANCE

The method for determining the individual's pension input amount is the same irrespective of whether he is resident in the UK or not. In the context of other money

20-013

---

[17] A non-UK resident individual will have a UK personal allowance in a number of circumstances, including where he is a national of an EEA state, or he is resident in the Isle of Man or Channel Islands, or if he was previously UK resident and is now resident abroad for the sake of his health (ITA 2007 s.56). Alternatively, a tax treaty may provide that he is to have the benefit of the UK personal allowance.

[18] In relation to a corporate employer, based in the UK means incorporated in the UK, and in relation to any other employer means resident in the UK.

[19] The Occupational Pension Schemes (Non-European Schemes Exemption) Regulations 2008 (SI 2008/624) reg.2.

purchase arrangements, contributions by a non-UK resident member will not usually be *relievable pension contributions* and where that is the case they will not be taken into account for annual allowance purposes.[20] However, any contributions by his employer (no matter where the employer is resident) will be taken into account.

20-014 If an annual allowance charge arises, it is treated as being the top slice of the member's income. But, as the charge does not constitute income (it is merely calculated as if it were income), the member will not usually be able to take advantage of his personal allowance etc.[21]

## SCHEME INVESTMENTS

### Tax treaties

20-015 If an approved pension scheme located in one territory invests in property in a different territory, some tax treaties operate to exempt the investment from any tax in the second territory.[22] This is considered in Ch.29.

## THE LS&DB ALLOWANCE

### Relevant overseas individuals

20-016 A LS&DB allowance enhancement factor applies to a relevant BCE occurring in relation to an individual who: (a) is or has been a relevant overseas individual during any part of the active membership period; and (b) gives notice to HMRC.[23] A "relevant overseas individual" means an individual who is, at any time, either:

(a) not a relevant UK individual[24]; or
(b) a relevant UK individual only by virtue of FA 2004 s.189(1)(c)[25] and is not employed by a person resident in the UK.

20-017 The "active membership period" is the period beginning with the date on which the benefits first began to accrue to or in respect of the individual under the arrangement (or, if later, 6 April 2006) and ending on 5 April 2024. But if benefits ceased to accrue to or in respect of the individual under the arrangement at a time before 5 April 2024, the active membership period ended at that time. The rationale for this enhancement factor is that a relevant overseas individual will not have benefitted from UK tax relief during his period of non-residence and so his LS&DB allowance should be increased to this extent. The factor depends on the type of arrangement.

20-018 Where para.20B applies, a lump sum is not an UFPLS if, immediately before the

---

[20] If they are relievable then they will be taken into account, even if tax relief is not claimed.
[21] In these circumstances, it may be preferable for contributions to be made to an unregistered pension scheme (which may need to be approved in the jurisdiction in which the member is resident in order to obtain tax relief) and for such contributions to be transferred to the registered pension scheme, because such a transfer will not constitute a contribution (FA 2004 s.188(5)) or otherwise be taken into account for annual allowance purposes.
[22] See e.g. the UK/Ireland Tax Treaty art.14A.
[23] FA 2004 Sch.36 para.20B.
[24] For the meaning of "relevant UK individual", see Ch.6.
[25] i.e. the individual was resident in the UK both at some time during the five tax years immediately before that year and when the individual became a member of the pension scheme.

lump sum is paid, the amount given by the following formula is less than 25% of the lump sum. The formula is "(A − B) / 4" where "A" is: (a) in the case of an individual in relation to whom a relevant protection provision applies, the individual's protected LS&DB allowance;[26] (b) in any other case, £1,073,100; "B" is the amount that would be the previously-used amount within the meaning of ITEPA 2003 s.637S (availability of individual's LS&DB allowance) if a relevant BCE had occurred immediately before the lump sum is paid.

*Cash balance arrangements*

The "cash balance arrangement non-residence factor" is the factor arrived at by the application of the following formula in relation to the part of the active membership period during which the individual was a relevant overseas individual.[27] The formula is "A-B/£1m" where: "A" is the closing value of the individual's rights under the arrangement; and "B" is the opening value of the individual's rights under the arrangement.[28] **20-019**

**Opening value** The "opening value" of the individual's rights under the arrangement is the amount which would, on the valuation assumptions,[29] be available for the provision of benefits to or in respect of the individual under the arrangement if the individual became entitled to the benefits at the beginning of that part of that period. So, one obtains a valuation of the individual's rights under the cash balance arrangement at the latest of the following to occur: (a) the date when the individual became a relevant overseas individual; (b) the date when benefits first began to accrue to or in respect of the individual under the cash balance arrangement; and (c) 6 April 2006. **20-020**

**Closing value** The "closing value" of the individual's rights under the arrangement is the amount which would, on the valuation assumptions, be available for the provision of benefits to or in respect of the individual under the arrangement if the individual became entitled to the benefits at the end of that part of that period. Here one obtains a valuation of the individual's rights under the cash balance arrangement as at the earliest of the following dates: (a) immediately before the relevant BCE; (b) the date when the individual ceased to be a relevant overseas individual; and (c) the date when benefits ceased to accrue to or in respect of the individual under the cash balance arrangement. **20-021**

**Interaction with primary protection: modification of opening value** Where the individual is also claiming primary protection, the calculation of the opening value is modified if the individual would have been a relevant overseas individual in the 2005/06 tax year and either[30]: (a) the individual has notified HMRC of his entitlement to a non-residence factor where the active membership period in relation to **20-022**

---

[26] For relevant protection provisions, and enhanced LS&DB allowances, see Ch.14.
[27] If there have been two or more parts of that period during which the individual was a relevant overseas individual, the factor is the aggregate of the factors arrived at by the application of the formula in relation to each of those parts of that period.
[28] FA 2004 Sch.36 para.20C(3).
[29] The valuation assumptions require one to value the individual's rights on the assumption that the individual is at the age at which no reduction would apply to the payment of an immediate benefit (e.g. as a result of early retirement), and the individual is in good physical and mental health and so the benefits are not increased as a result of being paid on grounds of ill-health (FA 2004 s.277).
[30] The Registered Pension Schemes (Enhanced Allowances) Regulations 2006 (SI 2006/131) arts 12 and 13.

the cash balance arrangement began on 6 April 2006, and notifies, or has notified, HMRC of his intention to rely on primary protection; or (b) the individual has notified HMRC of his intention to rely on primary protection, and notifies, or has notified, HMRC of his entitlement to a non-residence factor where the active membership period in relation to the cash balance arrangement began on 6 April 2006.

20-023　In these circumstances the opening value is equal to "OVA x (SLA/£1.5 million)" where OVA is the value of the individual's rights under the arrangement on 5 April 2006 calculated as above; and SLA is the standard lifetime allowance at the time when the part of the active membership period referred to above ended.

*Other money purchase arrangements*

20-024　The "other money purchase arrangement non-residence factor" is the factor arrived at by the application of the following formula in relation to the part(s) of the active membership period during which the individual was a relevant overseas individual. The formula is "C/£1m" where "C" is the amount of the contributions made under the arrangement by or in respect of the individual in any part of the active membership period during which the individual was a relevant overseas individual.[31]

20-025　In other words, "C" is the total amount of contributions made by or in respect of the individual to the other money purchase arrangement between the following dates:

(a) the latest of: (i) the date when the individual became a relevant overseas individual; (ii) the date when benefits first began to accrue to or in respect of the individual under the other money purchase arrangement; and (iii) 6 April 2006.

(b) the earliest of: (i) the date immediately before the relevant BCE; (ii) the date when the individual ceased to be a relevant overseas individual; and (iii) the date when benefits ceased to accrue to or in respect of the individual under the other money purchase arrangement.

*Defined benefits arrangements*

20-026　The "defined benefits arrangement non-residence factor" is the factor arrived at by the application of the formula below in relation to the part(s) of the active membership period during which the individual was a relevant overseas individual.[32] The formula is "[(A x B + C) – (A x D + E)]/£1m" where:

- "A" is the relevant valuation factor, i.e. 20;[33]
- "B" is the amount of the annual rate of the pension which would, on the valuation assumptions,[34] be payable to the individual under the arrangement if the individual became entitled to payment of it at the end of that part of that period;
- "C" is the amount of the lump sum to which the individual would, on the valuation assumptions, be entitled under the arrangement (otherwise than

---

[31] FA 2004 Sch.36 para.20C(6).
[32] FA 2004 Sch.36 para.20D(2).
[33] Or such greater number as is agreed between the scheme administrator and HMRC (see PTM88620).
[34] The valuation assumptions require one to value the individual's rights on the assumption that the individual is at the age at which no reduction would apply to the payment of an immediate benefit (e.g. as a result of early retirement), and the individual is in good physical and mental health and so the benefits are not increased as a result of being paid on grounds of ill-health (FA 2004 s.277).

by commutation of pension) if the individual became entitled to payment of it at the end of that part of that period;
- "D" is the amount of the annual rate of the pension which would, on the valuation assumptions, be payable to the individual under the arrangement if the individual became entitled to payment of it at the beginning of that part of that period;
- "E" is the amount of the lump sum to which the individual would, on the valuation assumptions, be entitled under the arrangement (otherwise than by commutation of pension) if the individual became entitled to payment of it at the beginning of that part of that period.

*Hybrid arrangements*

The "hybrid arrangement non-residence factor" is the greatest of such of the following as are "relevant factors" in relation to the arrangement:[35]

(a) what would be the cash balance arrangement non-residence factor if the arrangement were a cash balance arrangement;
(b) what would be the other money purchase arrangement non-residence factor if the arrangement were a collective money purchase arrangement;
(c) what would be the other money purchase arrangement non-residence factor if the arrangement were a money purchase arrangement other than a collective money purchase arrangement; and
(d) what would be the defined benefits arrangement non-residence factor if the arrangement were a defined benefits arrangement.

A factor is a "relevant factor" in relation to a hybrid arrangement if, in any circumstances, the benefits that may be provided to or in respect of the individual under the arrangement may be benefits linked to that factor. For that purpose, cash balance benefits are linked to the cash balance arrangement non-residence factor, other money purchase benefits are linked to the other money purchase arrangement non-residence factor, and defined benefits are linked to the defined benefits arrangement non-residence factor.

**Transfers from ROPS**

A LS&DB allowance enhancement factor applies to a relevant BCE occurring in relation to an individual where: (a) at any time after 5 April 2006 but before 6 April 2024, there has been a recognised overseas scheme transfer; and (b) notice has been given to HMRC.[36]

There is a recognised overseas scheme transfer if any sums or assets held for the purposes of an arrangement under a ROPS (or representing accrued rights under such an arrangement) are transferred so as to become held for the purposes of an arrangement under a registered pension scheme relating to the individual.

Sums or assets which are transferred from a ROPS[37] to a registered pension scheme will not usually have benefitted from UK tax relief, and this enhancement factor is designed to reflect that.

The LS&DB allowance enhancement factor is the "recognised overseas scheme transfer factor", which is "$(A - B)/£1m$" where: "A" is the total amount of any

---

[35] FA 2004 Sch.36 para.20D(5).
[36] FA 2004 Sch.36 para.20E.
[37] For ROPS, see Ch.32.

**20-032** money and the market value of any assets transferred on the recognised overseas scheme transfer and "B" is the relevant relievable amount.

The way in which the relevant relievable amount is determined depends on the type of arrangement under the recognised overseas scheme arrangement. In each case, it is necessary to determine the "overseas arrangement active membership period", which is the period beginning with the date on which the benefits first began to accrue to or in respect of the individual under the recognised overseas scheme arrangement (or, if later, 6 April 2006), and ending on 5 April 2024. But if benefits ceased to accrue to or in respect of the individual under the recognised overseas scheme arrangement before 6 April 2024, the overseas arrangement active membership period is treated as having ended at that time.

**20-033** Where para.20E applies, a lump sum is not an UFPLS if, immediately before the lump sum is paid, the amount given by the following formula is less than 25% of the lump sum. The formula is "(A − B) / 4" where "A" is: (a) in the case of an individual in relation to whom a relevant protection provision applies, the individual's protected LS&DB allowance;[38] (b) in any other case, £1,073,100; "B" is the amount that would be the previously-used amount within the meaning of ITEPA 2003 s.637S (availability of individual's LS&DB allowance) if a relevant BCE had occurred immediately before the lump sum is paid.

*Cash balance arrangements*

**20-034** If the arrangement under the recognised overseas scheme is a cash balance arrangement, the relevant relievable amount is the cash balance relevant relievable amount.[39] This is the amount arrived at by the application of the following formula in relation to the part of the overseas arrangement active membership period during which the individual was not a relevant overseas individual. The formula is "A − B" where:

- "A" is the closing value of the individual's rights under the recognised overseas scheme arrangement. This is the amount which would, on the valuation assumptions,[40] be available for the provision of benefits to or in respect of the individual under the arrangement if the individual became entitled to the benefits at the end of that part of that period; and
- "B" is the opening value of the individual's rights under the arrangement. This is the amount which would, on the valuation assumptions, be available for the provision of benefits to or in respect of the individual under the arrangement if the individual became entitled to the benefits at the beginning of that part of that period.

*Other money purchase arrangements*

**20-035** If the arrangement under the recognised overseas scheme is an other money purchase arrangement, the relevant relievable amount is the other money purchase relevant relievable amount.[41] This is the amount of the contributions made under the arrangement by or in respect of the individual in any part of the overseas ar-

---

[38] For relevant protection provisions, and enhanced LS&DB allowances, see Ch.14.
[39] FA 2004 Sch.36 para.20F(3).
[40] The valuation assumptions require one to value the individual's rights on the assumption that the individual is at the age at which no reduction would apply to the payment of an immediate benefit (e.g. as a result of early retirement), and the individual is in good physical and mental health and so the benefits are not increased as a result of being paid on grounds of ill-health (FA 2004 s.277).
[41] FA 2004 Sch.36 para.20F(6).

rangement active membership period during which the individual was not a relevant overseas individual.

*Defined benefits arrangements*

In the case of a recognised overseas scheme arrangement that is a defined benefits arrangement, the relevant relievable amount is the defined benefits relevant relievable amount.[42] This is the amount arrived at by the application of the following formula in relation to the part of the overseas arrangement active membership period during which the individual was not a relevant overseas individual. If there have been two or more parts of that period during which the individual was not a relevant overseas individual, the amount is the aggregate of the amounts arrived at by the application of the formula in relation to each of those parts of that period. The formula is "$(A \times B + C) - (A \times D + E)$" where: 

**20-036**

- "A" is the relevant valuation factor, i.e. 20;[43]
- "B" is the annual rate of the pension which would, on the valuation assumptions, be payable to the individual under the recognised overseas scheme arrangement if the individual became entitled to payment of it at the end of that part of that period;
- "C" is the amount of the lump sum to which the individual would, on the valuation assumptions, be entitled under the arrangement (otherwise than by commutation of pension) if the individual became entitled to payment of it at the end of that part of that period;
- "D" is the annual rate of the pension which would, on the valuation assumptions, be payable to the individual under the arrangement if the individual became entitled to payment of it at the beginning of that part of that period; and
- "E" is the amount of the lump sum to which the individual would, on the valuation assumptions, be entitled under the arrangement (otherwise than by commutation of pension) if the individual became entitled to payment of it at the beginning of that part of that period.

*Hybrid arrangements*

In the case of a recognised overseas scheme arrangement that was a hybrid arrangement, the relevant relievable amount is the hybrid relevant relievable amount.[44] This is the greater or greatest of such of the following as are relevant to that arrangement:

**20-037**

(a) what would be the cash balance relevant relievable amount if the recognised overseas scheme arrangement had been a cash balance arrangement;
(b) what would be the other money purchase relevant relievable amount if that arrangement had been a collective money purchase arrangement;
(c) what would be the other money purchase relevant relievable amount if that arrangement had been a money purchase arrangement other than a collective money purchase arrangement; and
(d) what would be the defined benefits relevant relievable amount if that arrangement had been a defined benefits arrangement.

---

[42] FA 2004 Sch.36 para.20G(3).
[43] Or such greater number as is agreed between the scheme administrator and HMRC (see FA 2004 s.276).
[44] FA 2004 Sch.36 para.20G(5).

**20-038** An amount is "relevant" to a hybrid arrangement if, in any circumstances, the benefits that may be provided to or in respect of the individual under the arrangement may be benefits linked to that amount. For that purpose, cash balance benefits are linked to the cash balance relevant relievable amount, other money purchase benefits are linked to the other money purchase relevant relievable amount, and defined benefits are linked to the defined benefits relevant relievable amount.

## BENEFITS

**20-039** ITEPA 2003 Pt 9 Ch.5A applies to "any pension under a registered pension scheme". Thus, on the face of it, it applies to UK resident and non-UK resident members, and to UK resident and non-UK resident schemes.

### Scheme is established in the UK

**20-040** Subject to the application of a double tax treaty, pension income paid from a registered pension scheme that is established in the UK to a member who is non-UK resident is taxable under Ch.5A of Pt 9.[45] Most double tax treaties provide that pension income is taxable only in the jurisdiction in which the member is resident.

### Scheme is established outside the UK

**20-041** Pension income paid from a non-UK registered pension scheme to a UK resident beneficiary is taxable under Ch.5A of Pt 9 on an arising basis. "Foreign pension" (taxable under Pt 9 Ch.4) is taxable on the remittance basis, but pension under a registered pension scheme can never be foreign pension because Ch.5A takes priority to Ch.4.[46] The jurisdiction in which the scheme is resident may also impose a tax charge (usually be collected via deduction at source), subject to any applicable double tax treaty between the UK and that jurisdiction.

**20-042** Is a pension paid from a non-UK registered pension scheme to a non-UK resident member subject to UK tax? Clearly it would not be taxable if a tax treaty between the UK and the jurisdiction in which the member is resident confers exclusive taxing rights on the latter jurisdiction in respect of pensions and other similar remuneration.[47] In other circumstances the position is less clear, because Ch.5A is not subject to any express territorial limitations. There is a presumption that all UK legislation is subject to territorial limits[48] and there appears to be nothing in ITEPA

---

[45] A non-UK resident individual will have a UK personal allowance in a number of circumstances, including where he is a national of an EEA state, or he is resident in the Isle of Man or Channel Islands, or if he was previously UK resident and is now resident abroad for the sake of his health (ITA 2007 s.56). Alternatively, a tax treaty may provide that he is to have the benefit of the UK personal allowance.

[46] ITEPA 2003 s.573(2).

[47] In this context "other similar remuneration" will cover non-periodic payments, including income withdrawal and lump sum payments (including death benefit lump sums) (see Ch.29).

[48] In *Colquhoun v Brooks* (1889) 14 App. Cas. 493; 2 T.C. 490 (at 503) Lord Herschell said that the Income Tax Acts "impose a territorial limit; either that from which the taxable income is derived must be situate in the United Kingdom or the person whose income is to be taxed must be resident there". Also see *Whitney v CIR* 10 T.C. 88 at 113; *Clark v Oceanic Contractors Inc* [1983] 2 A.C. 130; [1983] S.T.C. 35; *Re Sawers Ex p. Blain* (1879) 12 Ch. D. 522; *Agassi v Robinson* [2006] UKHL 23; [2006] 1 W.L.R. 1380.

2003 Pt 9 Ch.5A to rebut that presumption.[49] The source of pension scheme benefits is likely to be the pension scheme itself,[50] and if that is the case then pension income from a non-UK scheme should have a non-UK source. It should make no difference that the funds in the scheme may have been contributed to the scheme when the member and his employer were resident in the UK.

However, it may be argued that the fact that the scheme is registered with HMRC causes the pension income to have a UK source, or otherwise rebuts the presumption of territoriality. It is possible that a court would accept such an argument. Given the ease with which a non-UK resident member may require his registered pension scheme funds to be transferred to a QROPS (so that Pt 9 Ch.4 applies instead of Ch.5A, and Ch.4 is expressly limited to pensions paid to UK resident individuals), this may not be an important point in practice.

20-043

**PAYE provisions**

ITEPA 2003 Pt 11 creates the mechanism for taxing "PAYE income" at source, and this includes "PAYE pension income".[51] All pension under a registered pension scheme is PAYE pension income,[52] as is pension treated as arising from the payment of a trivial commutation lump sum, trivial commutation lump sum death benefit, winding-up lump sum or winding-up lump sum death benefit.[53] Any person making such payments is required, under the PAYE provisions, to withhold tax from each payment and pay it to HMRC. If the amount withheld does not discharge the recipient's liability in full then he is required to pay the balance under self-assessment.

20-044

*Non-UK members*

UK resident trustees are required to operate PAYE notwithstanding that the member is non-UK resident, unless there is a tax treaty between the UK and the jurisdiction in which the member is resident, which confers exclusive taxing rights on the jurisdiction of the member's residence, or the pension arises wholly from an employment carried out abroad.[54] PAYE pension income for a tax year does not include any taxable pension income that is treated as accruing in that tax year under s.579CA.[55] Section 579CA provides that any pension income in excess of £100,000 paid to a taxpayer in a period of non-residence is treated as accruing (and therefore taxable) in the year that they return to the UK, if it was not subject to tax under ITEPA Pt 9 when it was paid.

20-045

---

[49] Part 9 Ch.5A is different, e.g. to the legislation considered in *Agassi v Robinson* [2006] UKHL 23; [2006] 1 W.L.R. 1380, because that legislation was expressly aimed at payments to foreign taxpayers, and if the presumption of territoriality applied in such cases then that would render the charge to all intents voluntary.
[50] *Wales v Tilley* [1943] A.C. 386.
[51] ITEPA 2003 s.683(1)(b).
[52] ITEPA 2003 s.683(3), referring to s.579B.
[53] Under ITEPA 2003 ss.636B and 636C.
[54] The Income Tax (Pay As You Earn) Regulations 2003 (SI 2003/2682) reg.57. HMRC accept this at PAYE81750. The pension will remain taxable under the self-assessment unless it is exempted by a tax treaty.
[55] ITEPA 2003 s.683(3B).

*Non-UK trustees*

**20-046** The House of Lords in *Clark v Oceanic Contractors*[56] considered the territorial limitations of the PAYE system. In that case their Lordships held by a 3:2 majority that a non-UK resident company had brought itself within the scope of PAYE, but the precise reasons given differed. All of their Lordships agreed that the PAYE provisions can only apply to a person with a "tax presence" in the UK. It follows that a payment by a person (whether he is the trustee or the scheme administrator) who is not resident in the UK and has no permanent establishment in the UK should not be subject to PAYE.

---

[56] *Clark v Oceanic Contractors* [1983] 2 A.C. 130; (1982) 56 T.C. 1873.

# CHAPTER 21

# Inheritance Tax

## TABLE OF CONTENTS

| | |
|---|---|
| Introduction | 21-001 |
|     Overview of inheritance tax | 21-002 |
|         Interests in possession | 21-008 |
|     Typical application to pension schemes | 21-009 |
| Contributions | 21-014 |
|     Contributions by a business | 21-015 |
|         IHTA 1984 s.12 | 21-016 |
|         Contributions in respect of partners | 21-018 |
|     Contributions by scheme members | 21-019 |
|         HMRC practice: the two-year rule | 21-022 |
|         IHTA 1984 s.12 | 21-025 |
|         IHTA 1984 s.10 | 21-029 |
|             Intended to confer any gratuitous benefit on any person | 21-032 |
|             Made in a transaction intended to confer any gratuitous benefit on any person | 21-036 |
|             A transaction at arm's length between unconnected persons | 21-037 |
|         IHTA 1984 s.11 | 21-040 |
|         IHTA 1984 s.18 | 21-044 |
|         IHTA 1984 s.21 | 21-045 |
|         IHTA 1984 s.28 | 21-047 |
|         Settlement powers | 21-048 |
|         Reservation of benefit provisions | 21-051 |
|     Contributions by other persons | 21-056 |
| Disposals of scheme interests | 21-059 |
| Devaluing interests | 21-061 |
|     Interests in possession | 21-069 |
| Relevant property | 21-070 |
|     Nature of scheme | 21-071 |
|         Scheme funds on death of member | 21-073 |
|         Trusts of lump sum death benefits | 21-075 |
|         Who is the settlor? | 21-078 |
|         Calculating periodic and exit charges | 21-080 |
|         Distributions from the settlement | 21-082 |
|     Retaining death benefits within the pension scheme | 21-083 |
| Omitting to exercise rights | 21-084 |
| Death of a beneficiary | 21-086 |
|     Entitlement immediately before death | 21-089 |
|         The general position | 21-089 |

> Pensions and annuities ceasing on death ......... 21-091
> Interests in possession ...................... 21-097
> Benefits continuing after death ................... 21-099
> Changes occurring by reason of the death .......... 21-101
> Protected rights ............................... 21-104
> Powers of nomination ........................ 21-105
> General powers of appointment ............... 21-105
> The meaning of "general power" .............. 21-107
> Contributions, transfers, disposals etc. before death .. 21-110
> Form IHT409 .................................... 21-112

# INTRODUCTION

**21-001** This chapter explains how the relevant inheritance tax provisions apply to registered pension schemes.

### Overview of inheritance tax

**21-002** Where a person makes a "disposition", and as a result of that disposition the market value of his estate is reduced, the disposition will (subject to certain exceptions) be a "transfer of value".[1] Any transfer of value by an individual is a "chargeable transfer", unless it is an exempt transfer.[2] Inheritance tax is payable in respect of chargeable transfers at the rate of 20% (for lifetime transfers) or 40% (for transfers that are deemed to take place on death) to the extent that the disposition and any other transfers of value in the previous seven years exceed the individual's nil rate band and any available annual exemptions.[3]

**21-003** "Disposition" is not defined, and its precise meaning is unclear. In practice, virtually any act by which a person intentionally divests himself of his beneficial ownership of property is likely to involve a disposition.[4] The term expressly includes a disposition effected by associated operations[5] and certain deemed dispositions.[6]

**21-004** A person's "estate" consists of all the property to which he is beneficially entitled, except for an interest in possession in settled property in certain circumstances.[7] "Property" includes rights and interests of every kind but expressly does not include a "settlement power".[8] It follows that a right to receive property is itself property, but a right to receive property only if a third party exercises his discretion is not

---

[1] IHTA 1984 s.3(1).
[2] IHTA 1984 s.2(1).
[3] IHTA 1984 s.7(2).
[4] *McCutcheon on Inheritance Tax*, 7th edn (London: Sweet & Maxwell, 2016), para.2–06.
[5] IHTA 1984 s.272.
[6] e.g. in certain circumstances a person is deemed to make a disposition if he deliberately omits to exercise a right (IHTA 1984 s.3(3)).
[7] IHTA 1984 s.5(1).
[8] IHTA 1984 s.272. A "settlement power" is any power over, or exercisable (directly or indirectly) in relation to settled property (IHTA 1984 s.47A). Settled property includes any property held in trust for persons in succession (IHTA 1984 s.43(1) and (2)).

property.[9] A person's estate is deemed to include any property over which he has a general power of appointment.[10]

The value of property for inheritance tax purposes is the price which the property might reasonably be expected to fetch if sold in the open market at that time.[11] This predicates a hypothetical sale.[12] One is required to establish what someone would pay to step into the shoes of the deceased.[13] The fact that the sale is hypothetical has certain consequences. In particular, the property is assumed to be capable of sale in the open market, even if (as is the case with most interests under retirement benefits schemes[14]) the property is inherently unassignable.[15]

21-005

"Exempt transfers" include transfers between spouses, transfers that do not exceed the annual exemption (currently £3,000), and transfers of surplus income. A gift to another individual is a potentially exempt transfer, which becomes an exempt transfer if the transferor survives for seven years after the transfer.

21-006

Where there is a transfer of value, one must determine the value transferred by the transfer. The value transferred is not the value of the property disposed of; it is the loss in value to the disponer's estate.[16] Thus, if a contribution to a pension scheme is a chargeable transfer, the value transferred must take into account the value of the right to receive benefits "received" by the disponer under the pension scheme.[17]

21-007

*Interests in possession*

Special rules apply to interests in possession in settled property. An "interest in possession" is a present right to present enjoyment of the settled property,[18] so a pension or annuity in payment gives the member an interest in possession. Since 22 March 2006, most interests in possession are treated in the same way as any other form of property: one owns a right to receive an income stream, the value of which is the net present value of that income stream. However, pre-22 March 2006 interests in possession (referred to as "qualifying" interests in possession) are treated quite differently. A beneficiary with a qualifying interest in possession is deemed to own the settled property in which the interest in possession subsists. It follows that a disposal or termination of the interest is deemed to be a disposition of the underlying settled property (and not simply a disposition of the right to receive the income). The loss to the disponer's estate will therefore usually be much higher than if one merely took the right to receive the income produced by that property into account. Similarly, on the death of a member with a qualifying interest in possession, the settled property (and not simply the right to receive the income) is deemed to form part of his estate. These provisions are considered in more detail in Ch.28. They are not considered in greater detail here because the rules that apply to

21-008

---

[9] Per Lord Walker in *Schmidt v Rosewood Trust Ltd* [2003] UKPC 26 at [40]: "the object of a discretionary trust has no more of an assignable or transmissible interest than the object of a mere power".
[10] IHTA 1984 s.5(2).
[11] IHTA 1984 s.160.
[12] See e.g. *Duke of Buccleuch v IRC* [1967] 1 A.C. 506.
[13] *Att-Gen (I) v Jameson* [1905] 2 Ir. R. 201 at [230].
[14] The provisions of most pension schemes expressly prohibit the assignment by a beneficiary of his interests under the scheme, and there are restrictions in PA 1995 s.91 relating to the assignment of interests under occupational pension schemes.
[15] See *IRC v Crossman* [1937] A.C. 26 and *Lynall v IRC* [1972] A.C. 680.
[16] IHTA 1984 s.3(1).
[17] See e.g. *Postlethwaite v HMRC* [2006] UKSPC SPC00571 at [9] and [10].
[18] *Pearson v IRC* [1981] A.C. 753.

interests in possession are disapplied in relation to registered pension schemes, so qualifying interests in possession are treated in the same way as any other item of property.

**Typical application to pension schemes**

**21-009** In a pensions context, the following may give rise to a chargeable transfer by a person (X):

(a) X makes a contribution to a pension scheme;
(b) X disposes of his interest under a pension scheme;
(c) There is a reduction in the value of X's interest under a pension scheme (e.g. changes are made to the benefit structure of the scheme, or funds are transferred to a second scheme with a different benefit structure);
(d) X is a beneficiary and he deliberately omits to exercise a right under a pension scheme. Such an omission may be deemed to constitute a disposition; and
(e) X is a beneficiary of a pension scheme and he dies. A beneficiary could include the member or anyone else with rights under the pension scheme (such as a person entitled to death benefits).

**21-010** In addition, if the scheme property is held on trust, it may constitute "relevant property", and so may be subject to periodic (ten yearly) and exit charges.

**21-011** As a result of the following provisions, inheritance tax rarely affects registered pension schemes:[19]

(a) IHTA 1984 s.12(1): a disposition is not a transfer of value if it is allowable in computing the disponer's profits or gains for tax purposes.
(b) IHTA 1984 s.12(2): a contribution for the benefit of the employees of the disponer is not a transfer of value.
(c) IHTA 1984 ss.12(2ZA) and 12A(1): an omission to exercise a right under the scheme is not deemed to be a disposition by virtue of s.3(3). In relation to a drawdown pension fund or flexi-access drawdown fund, this expressly applies to an omission that results in the fund not being used up in the person's lifetime.
(d) IHTA 1984 s.58(1)(d): scheme property held on trust is not relevant property.
(e) IHTA 1984 s.151(3): Qualifying interests in possession are treated as if they were non-qualifying (during the life and on the death of a beneficiary).
(f) IHTA 1984 s.151(2) and (3): on the death of a beneficiary, any rights to pension or annuity which cease on death are disregarded.

**21-012** In addition, there is an important general exception in IHTA 1984 s.10 which applies where a disponer does not intend the disposition to confer gratuitous benefit on any person. This general exception is particularly important in the context of contributions to pension schemes.[20] In practice, HMRC appear to assume (unless there is clear evidence to the contrary) that s.10 will apply to a disposition, such as a contribution, by the member if he was in good health at the time of the disposi-

---

[19] The same exceptions apply to QNUPS and s.615 funds so this chapter applies equally to such schemes. For inheritance tax purposes, "registered pension scheme" has the same meaning as in FA 2004 Pt 4 (IHTA 1984 s.272),

[20] Where there is any intention to confer gratuitous benefit, one must also have regard to the income tax settlements provisions in ITTOIA 2005 Pt 5 Ch.5 (see Ch.22), which can apply to registered and unregistered schemes.

tion, and HMRC will also apparently assume that he was in good health if he lives for at least two years after the disposition.

These exceptions are clearly intended to ensure that registered pension schemes and their beneficiaries are not, in the normal course, subject to inheritance tax. This is consistent with the income tax and CGT exemptions that apply to such schemes. Indeed, given that most death benefits will be subject to income tax when paid,[21] it would be most unfair if they were also subject to inheritance tax. As a result of the above exceptions, it is only the following circumstances that tend to cause inheritance tax issues in practice:

(a) a contribution is made in circumstances that the member's estate is reduced;
(b) the value of the member's interest under the scheme is devalued in some way;
(c) a beneficiary of a pension scheme dies and:
   (i) his personal representatives are entitled to the death benefits arising as a result of his death;
   (ii) immediately before he died he had a general power over the death benefits; or
   (iii) immediately before he died he was entitled to a pension or annuity that is guaranteed for a minimum term.

21-013

# CONTRIBUTIONS

It is convenient to consider contributions by a business (usually—but by no means exclusively—for one or more of its employees) and contributions by a scheme member separately, before considering contributions by other individuals such as family members.

21-014

### Contributions by a business

A disposition by a sole trader, as with any other disposition by an individual, may give rise to a chargeable transfer if the estate of the sole trader (i.e. all of the property to which the sole trader is entitled—whether the property is connected with the business or not) is consequently devalued. Partnerships are transparent for inheritance tax purposes and LLPs are deemed to be transparent[22] so a disposition by a partnership or LLP is a disposition by its partners/members and one must consider the effect of the disposition on the value of their estates.[23] A company cannot make a chargeable transfer,[24] but if a close company makes a transfer of value then some or all of that transfer of value may be apportioned to its participators under IHTA 1984 s.94.[25] A company makes a transfer of value if the estate of the company (i.e. all of the property to which the company is beneficially entitled) is

21-015

---

[21] On the death of a member on or after his 75th birthday, death benefits paid to an individual are taxable at the recipient's marginal rate of tax and death benefit paid to a non-individual are subject to the special lump sum death benefits charge (see Ch.15).
[22] IHTA 1984 s.267A(d).
[23] The transparency of partnerships follows from the fact that a partnership is not a legal entity distinct from its partners (see Partnership Act 1890 s.1(1)). For LLPs see IHTA 1984 s.267A.
[24] Pursuant to IHTA 1984 s.2(1), "a chargeable transfer is a transfer of value which is *made by an individual* …".
[25] Close company has the same definition as in CTA 2010 s.439 (see IHTA 1984 s.102(1)). If the company is not a close company there is no mechanism to tax a transfer of value.

reduced as a result of the contribution.[26] As a result of the exemptions in IHTA 1984 s.12(1) and (2) it is not usually necessary to consider this point in any detail.[27]

*IHTA 1984 s.12*

**21-016** IHTA 1984 s.12(1) provides that a disposition is not a transfer of value if it is allowable in computing the disponer's profits or gains for tax purposes. The circumstances in which a business will obtain a tax deduction in respect of a contribution to a registered pension scheme are considered in Ch.6. In practice, given the very clear exemption in s.12(2) for contributions in respect of employees, s.12(1) is important only for contributions in respect of non-employees such as self-employed consultants. IHTA 1984 s.12(2) provides that a disposition made by any person is not a transfer of value if it is a contribution under a registered pension scheme in respect of an employee of the disponer. It follows that any contribution by an employer in respect of an employee (even one that is wholly uncommercial) is not a transfer of value. Section 12(2) does not apply to a contribution relating solely to the provision of death benefits to a non-employee dependant of an employee, but one would expect s.12(1) to apply.

**21-017** Sections 12(1) and (2) apply to dispositions made by "any person". There should be no scope for HMRC to argue that even if s.12(1) or (2) prevents a contribution from being a transfer of value by the *employer*, it may still be a disposition by the *member* by associated operations (where the member is the beneficial owner of the employer, for example).

*Contributions in respect of partners*

**21-018** Section 12 cannot apply to contributions by a partnership or LLP in respect of a partner.[28] Such contributions will not usually involve a transfer of value, since the value of each partner's estate will be increased by his pension rights. Where there is a reduction in the value of a partner's estate, s.10 may assist. To the extent that a scheme provides death in service benefits in respect of the partners, contributions are likely to involve a transfer of value unless s.21 (normal expenditure out of surplus income) applies (see below).

**Contributions by scheme members**

**21-019** A pension scheme generally consists of two distinct interests: retirement benefits and death benefits.[29] In relation to a contribution to a typical money purchase arrangement, the member is entitled to the retirement benefits, so if there is a reduc-

---

[26] See IHTA 1984 s.3(1), which applies to *persons* and therefore includes companies. The value transferred by a participator is a proportionate amount of the value transferred by the company, less the amount (if any) by which the value of his estate is more than it would have been but for the company's transfer (s.94(1)).

[27] If neither ss.12(1) nor (2) apply, consideration may be given to ss.10 and 13. Section 10 is considered in more detail below in the context of member contributions. If the pension scheme is a trust for the benefit of employees within IHTA 1984 s.86 then a contribution by a close company is not a transfer of value if the restrictions in IHTA 1984 s.13 apply. Given the broad exemptions in s.12 it is unlikely that one would ever need to rely on s.13 in the context of registered pension schemes. IHTA 1984 ss.13 and 86 are considered in detail in Ch.27.

[28] No tax deduction is available for such a contribution, for the same reason that no deduction is available for salaries paid to equity partners (in their capacity as such): such payments are an allocation of the firm's profits, rather than an expense of the business. Section 12(1) will not therefore apply.

[29] This is also the way that HMRC has traditionally approached pension schemes (see *IR Tax Bulletin* 2 (February 1992)).

A contribution by a member to a pension scheme does not reduce the value of **21-020** his estate if he is entitled to the retirement benefits and his personal representatives are entitled to the death benefits.[30] This is a straightforward valuation point. Although certain pension rights may be excluded from the value of an individual's estate immediately before death, they are not excluded at other times. The fact that the individual may not be *immediately* entitled to the benefits does not reduce the value of those benefits for inheritance tax purposes, provided that the future benefits include investment return.

Suppose a member makes a contribution to a registered pension scheme under **21-021** which he is presently entitled to direct the trustees to pay his entire fund to him as an uncrystallised funds pension lump sum. The member has the option to receive all of the funds back immediately, and so the contribution itself does not reduce the value of his estate (even if his personal representatives are not entitled to the death benefits).

*HMRC practice: the two-year rule*

HMRC appear to accept that contributions made by the member when he is in **21-022** good health do not give rise to a transfer of value. This seems to be on the basis that any dispositions before that time are likely to have been of nominal value (or, possibly, because IHTA 1984 s.10 will apply). Furthermore, HMRC will assume (unless there is evidence to the contrary) that a member was in good health at the time of a contribution provided that he lives for at least two years afterwards.[31] IHTM17042 provides that:

"There are two situations where contributions may result in a lifetime transfer;
- the transferor contributes to their own pension scheme whilst in ill-health and the death benefits are payable outside the estate, or
- the transferor contributes to a pension scheme for someone else."

HMRC's reference to "ill-health" means terminally ill or such poor health that **21-023** the member's life is uninsurable.[32] If a member makes a contribution at a time when he is in ill-health, but he is at that time entitled to direct the trustees to pay his entire fund to him as an uncrystallised funds pension lump sum, the contribution itself does not reduce the value of his estate.[33]

This *two-year rule* has no basis in law. It is merely HMRC's current practice **21-024** regarding the circumstances in which they are likely to want to investigate a disposition. Details of all contributions in the two years before death must be disclosed on the form IHT409. HMRC suggest that they will only take an interest if the contributions are substantial and unusual (by which they mean that the contributions are not made under regular arrangements that have been in exist-

---

[30] HMRC appear to agree at IHTM17042.
[31] See IHTM17043: "Any transfer of value depends on the health of the scheme member at the time the contributions were made. In general, where contributions are made more than 2 years before a death you can assume that the member was in normal health, unless there is evidence that suggests they were not. If the member is in normal health there is no transfer of value".
[32] IHTM17104.
[33] Assuming that the tax payable in respect of the lump sum is less than the tax relief obtained in respect of the contribution.

ence for more than two years).[34] If there is evidence that the member was in good health at the time of the contribution and his death was unexpected, HMRC accept that any transfers of value are likely to have been of nominal value (or IHTA 1984 s.10 will have applied). Any contributions involving a transfer of value more than two years before death (but less than seven years before death) must be disclosed in the IHT403.

*IHTA 1984 s.12*

**21-025** IHTA 1984 s.12(1) and (2) are considered in para.21-016 in the context of employer contributions. They are set out in full here because their application to member contributions (if any) is less clear:

> "(1) A disposition made by any person is not a transfer of value if it is allowable in computing that person's profits or gains for the purposes of income tax or corporation tax or would be so allowable if those profits or gains were sufficient and fell to be so computed.
> (2) Without prejudice to subsection (1) above, a disposition made by any person is not a transfer of value if it is a contribution under a registered pension scheme, a qualifying non-UK pension scheme, or section 615(3) scheme in respect of an employee of the person making the disposition."

**21-026** Section 12(1) does not apply to contributions by a member; it can only apply to contributions by a business. This is because s.12(1) relates to dispositions that are allowable in computing the disponer's "profits or gains" for the purposes of income tax. Any tax relief given to the member under FA 2004 s.188 is in the form of a deduction or set off against the relevant earnings of the member[35] and these are calculated after computing the person's profits for income tax purposes.[36] A contribution by a member is therefore *not* allowable in computing his profits for income tax purposes.

**21-027** In relation to s.12(2), it is unclear if the words "in respect of an employee of the person making the disposition" relates to s.615 funds only, or also to registered pension schemes and QNUPS. The omission of a comma between "section 615(3) scheme" and "in respect of an employee of the person making the disposition" suggests that the latter words only relate to contributions to s.615 funds. HMRC consider that s.12(2) relates only to employer contributions.[37] It is difficult to think of any cogent reason why such an exemption *should* apply only to employers, especially as that means that there is no express exemption for member contributions to registered pension schemes, which seems surprising given the other exceptions. However, on balance, the better view is that s.12(2) does apply only to employer contributions.[38]

---

[34] IHTM17015. HMRC's *two-year rule* is presumably predicated on the terms of the pension scheme being typical. If, for example, the scheme rules provide that the member cannot take benefits until he reaches age 100 then one would expect HMRC to adopt a different position, as it is fairly unlikely that the member will live long enough to take retirement benefits.
[35] See Ch.6.
[36] This is also HMRC's position: see IHTM17043.
[37] See IHTM17035.
[38] Prior to 6 April 2006 (when the current wording of s.12(2) was introduced), there was no doubt that s.12(2) only applied to contributions by employers, and there was no express intention to change that.

CONTRIBUTIONS 475

In the context of a salary sacrifice arrangement,[39] the employer is the disponer.[40] **21-028**
The member gives up any future rights to the earnings in exchange for pension contributions. At the time of the sacrifice, the employee is not entitled to the earnings sacrificed (no one is entitled to future earnings: they are always contingent upon continuing to work for the employer). There will therefore usually be no scope for HMRC to argue that the employee is the disponer and so s.12(2) does not apply.

*IHTA 1984 s.10*

If a contribution does reduce the value of the member's estate, IHTA 1984 s.10 **21-029**
will apply provided that his motivation was to provide pension benefits for himself (rather than to pass on death benefits to his family, for example). IHTA 1984 s.10(1) provides that:

> "(1) A disposition is not a transfer of value if it is shown that it was not indented, and was not made in a transaction intended, to confer any gratuitous benefit on any person and either—
> 
> (a) that it was made in a transaction at arm's length between persons not connected with each other, or
> 
> (b) that it was such as might be expected to be made in a transaction at arm's length between persons not connected with each other."

There are three parts to s.10. In order for it to apply, the taxpayer must show that, **21-030**
on a balance of probabilities, the contribution was:

(a) not intended to confer any gratuitous benefit on any person;
(b) not made in a transaction (including either a series of transactions or any associated operations) intended to confer any gratuitous benefit on any person; and
(c) either made in a transaction at arm's length between persons not connected with each other, or was on such terms as might be expected in such a transaction.

Both (a) and (b) refer to the taxpayer's intention at the time the contribution is **21-031**
made. These provisions therefore pose a subjective test. It will frequently be the case that the taxpayer has died by the time of any challenge by HMRC, so contemporaneous evidence (such as correspondence between the member and his advisers) demonstrating the member's motivation for making a contribution to the pension scheme should be retained.[41]

**Intended to confer any gratuitous benefit on any person** Section 10 is likely **21-032**
to apply to a contribution if the member is in good health and expects to take retirement benefits. If contributions are proportionate to the member's net income, lifestyle and general wealth, evidence of this will support the taxpayer's position. If the reason the member made the contribution was to benefit other persons (other than his spouse: see IHTA 1984 s.18, discussed in para.21-044) by passing on the death benefits to such persons, this may prevent s.10 from applying.

In the context of a typical money purchase arrangement, any sums or assets not **21-033**
provided as retirement benefits will be available to be paid as death benefits. One would expect the existence of such death benefits to be a relevant factor when a

---

[39] For salary sacrifice arrangements, see Ch.6.
[40] It may well be the case that the employee is the settlor of any contributions which become settled property, but that not relevant for the purposes of s.12(2).
[41] See *Postlethwaite's Executors v RCC* [2007] S.T.C. (S.C.D.) 38 at [80].

member is considering whether to contribute to a pension scheme. It is unrealistic to expect a member to be entirely disinterested in the existence of death benefits, even when he is in good health and fully intends to take all of his retirement benefits. Unless there is some evidence that the member does not intend to take the retirement benefits, the fact that the existence of death benefits is an important factor to him should not be relevant when considering whether s.10 applies.

**21-034** If the same individuals are beneficiaries under the taxpayer's will and also death beneficiaries under the pension scheme, it may be argued that a contribution to the scheme, even in ill-health, does not involve an intention to confer any benefit on those individuals, as the death beneficiaries would have otherwise received the funds under the taxpayer's will. This was accepted by the Supreme Court in *HMRC v Parry*[42] (in the context of a transfer rather than a contribution), but only because the deceased was unaware of the inheritance tax benefits. The Court held that one must ask whether the overall effect of the contribution was intended to be favourable to, or advantageous to, the individuals. Section 10 could be applicable unless the taxpayer intended to put the individuals in a better position than they would otherwise have been in (i.e. under the taxpayer's will).

**21-035** In *Postlethwaite's Executors v RCC*,[43] HMRC argued that IHTA 1984 s.10 did not apply to a contribution by an employer to a FURBS because the member's family could benefit from the death benefits and therefore there was intention to confer gratuitous benefit on the taxpayer's family. HMRC were unsuccessful as the member was only aged 49 and in good health at the time of the contribution, so he was not expected to die before taking significant benefits. The same reasoning would apply to member contributions.

**21-036 Made in a transaction intended to confer any gratuitous benefit on any person** If the disposition is not itself intended to confer gratuitous benefit, but it is made as part of a transaction or series of transactions which is intended to confer gratuitous benefit, s.10 does not apply to the disposition. For example, suppose that a member made a contribution with no intention to confer gratuitous benefit, but then subsequently omits to take benefits in order to confer gratuitous benefit (e.g. in order to prevent his taxable estate from increasing in value). This was essentially the situation in *Parry*, and HMRC argued that the transfer and the omission should be regarded as a single transaction, and the taxpayer's intention to provide gratuitous benefit by the omission "tainted" the previous contribution. "Transaction" includes a series of transactions and any associated operations. Operations are "associated" if they affect the same property, and "operation" includes an omission.[44] Mrs Staveley's decision to omit was intended to benefit her sons, so if it was an operation associated with the pension transfer, the executors would fail the second part of the test in s.10. For the purposes of s.10 operations are associated only if they "form a part of and contribute to a scheme which [is intended to confer gratuitous benefit]".[45] The Supreme Court considered that Mrs Staveley's "essential scheme" was her decision to omit in June 2006, which continued until her death. The transfer did not contribute to that scheme because the decision was made prior to the transfer, and the sons would have benefitted from the decision to omit without the transfer.

**21-037 A transaction at arm's length between unconnected persons** In *Parry*, the UT

---

[42] *HMRC v Parry* [2020] UKSC 35 at [61].
[43] *Postlethwaite's Executors v RCC* [2007] S.T.C. (S.C.D.) 38.
[44] IHTA 1984 s.268.
[45] *IRC v Macpherson* [1989] A.C. 159, per Lord Jauncey

found that the only parties to the transfer were the pension provider and the taxpayer. Although the taxpayer's sons were named in the statement of wishes, it could not be said that any part of the relevant transaction was *between* the taxpayer and her sons.[46]

**21-038** IHTA 1984 s.10(1)(a) cannot apply to a member contribution to a pension scheme established under trusts because the scheme is a settlement for inheritance tax purposes and the member is a settlor, and so he is connected with the trustees.[47] If the scheme is not a settlement for inheritance tax purposes one would expect s.10(1)(a) to apply to all member contributions provided that the main requirement in s.10(1) is met.

**21-039** Section 10(1)(b) requires one to consider what benefits the member can expect to receive under the terms of the pension scheme. By definition, a member cannot receive his own death benefits, and if his estate cannot benefit from the death benefits then only the retirement benefits can be taken into account for the purpose of s.10. If the member is in good health at the time of the contribution and can be expected to live long enough to take significant benefits from the pension scheme then one would expect s.10(1)(b) to apply.

*IHTA 1984 s.11*

**21-040** In certain circumstances it may be arguable that, to the extent that s.10 does not apply (e.g. because a contribution is made when in ill health or the benefit structure of the pension scheme is unusually restrictive etc.), then s.11 may apply. Section 11(1) provides that:[48]

> "A disposition is not a transfer of value if it is made by one party to a marriage or civil partnership in favour of the other party or of a child of either party and is—
> (a) for the maintenance of the other party, or
> (b) for the maintenance, education or training of the child for a period ending not later than the year in which he attains the age of eighteen or, after attaining that age, ceases to undergo full-time education or training."

**21-041** Although it is not entirely clear what *in favour* of means for the purposes of s.11(1), it is plainly intended to be broader than *to*, and it seems arguable that it could include a contribution by a member to a pension scheme if the death benefits are held on trusts exclusively for the member's spouse, children and dependent relatives (if any) and must be used for their maintenance, care, education etc.

**21-042** A terminally ill individual may be able to dispose of a substantial amount of property if he has young children or elderly parents and it is reasonable to assume that such relatives will need paid care in the near future. Section 11 does not pose an all or nothing test, so where an excessive (i.e. unreasonable) gift is made, only the excessive part of the gift is chargeable. In *McKelvey v RCC*[49] the taxpayer (who was expected to live for only a few months) gifted two properties to her elderly and dependant mother with the intention that they should be sold when necessary and

---

[46] *HMRC v Representatives of Staveley (deceased)* [2017] UKUT 4 at [59]. Neither the Court of Appeal (*HMRC v Parry* [2018] EWCA Civ 2266) nor the Supreme Court (*HMRC v Parry* [2020] UKSC 35) commented on this analysis (presumably because HMRC accepted that if the second part of the test in s.10 was satisfied, this third part of the test was also satisfied).

[47] See IHTA 1984 s.270, applying a modified version of TCGA 1992 s.286.

[48] Subsections (2)–(4) contain similar provisions relating to dispositions in favour of: (a) children not in the care of the parent for their maintenance, education or training; (b) dependent relatives for the reasonable provision for their care and maintenance; and (c) illegitimate children for their maintenance, education or training.

[49] *McKelvey v RCC* [2008] S.T.C. (S.C.D.) 944.

the proceeds used to meet the cost of her mother's paid care. In the event, the properties were not required because the mother refused to accept paid care and the taxpayer's siblings took care of her instead. Nevertheless, at the time of the gift it was reasonable for the taxpayer to conclude that her mother would require paid care in the near future, and so s.11 applied to the extent that the value of the properties was not excessive.

**21-043** HMRC consider that *maintenance* means "the supply of necessaries, such as food or clothing, so as to maintain a qualifying beneficiary in the condition of life which is appropriate to a dependant of the transferor", and *education and training* means "dispositions for a child's education or training whilst the child is under the age of 18. After the age of 18, the requirement is that the education or training shall be full-time".[50]

*IHTA 1984 s.18*

**21-044** Pursuant to IHTA 1984 s.18, a transfer of value is an exempt transfer to the extent that the value transferred is attributable to property which becomes comprised in the estate of the transferor's spouse or civil partner. If a member's spouse is entitled to the death benefits, s.18 will apply to any transfer of value on a contribution by the member (e.g. where the member is in poor health). The exemption is limited to the nil rate band at the time of the transfer if, immediately before the transfer, the transferor but not the transferor's spouse or civil partner is domiciled in the UK.

*IHTA 1984 s.21*

**21-045** Pursuant to IHTA 1984 s.21, a transfer of value is an exempt transfer to the extent that: (a) it was made as part of the normal expenditure of the transferor; (b) (taking one year with another) it was made out of his income; and (c) after allowing for all transfers of value forming part of his normal expenditure, the transferor was left with sufficient income to maintain his usual standard of living. It is generally helpful, if one wishes to place reliance on s.21, for the member to write to the trustees or managers of the pension scheme expressing an intention to make regular contributions out of surplus income, and to then pay regular contributions from surplus income.

**21-046** Suppose that in some (but not all) of the seven years prior to death there is insufficient surplus. Does that mean that all payments fail, on the basis that s.21(1) seems to be looking at all of the payments over the seven-year period? The better view is that the relief should apply whenever there is a surplus. It may also be the case that surplus income in one year can be accumulated and used in a subsequent year.

*IHTA 1984 s.28*

**21-047** If the pension scheme is a trust for the benefit of employees within IHTA 1984 s.86, then an *in specie* contribution of shares by any individual is an exempt transfer if the restrictions in IHTA 1984 s.28 apply.[51]

---

[50] IHTM04172.
[51] IHTA 1984 s.86 is considered in Ch.27. It may also be possible for the individual to obtain roll over relief for CGT purposes under TCGA 1992 s.239.

*Settlement powers*

As noted above, a person's *estate* consists of all the property to which he is beneficially entitled (except for an interest in possession in settled property in certain circumstances)[52] and *property* includes rights and interests of every kind but does not include a settlement power.[53] It follows that when considering to what extent the value of a person's estate is reduced by a disposition such as a contribution, one does not take into account the value of any settlement power held or acquired by the member. A settlement power is defined (exhaustively) as:[54]

21-048

> "any power over, or exercisable (whether directly or indirectly) in relation to, settled property or a settlement."

The precise scope of the term is uncertain. On the face of it, it applies to *any* power granted to the member under the scheme (including, for example, a power to designate funds as available for drawdown pension). If that is correct then it may well be the case that a member's most valuable rights under a registered pension scheme established under trusts are settlement powers. Where that is the case, it seems that a contribution by the member will *always* involve a diminution in the value of his estate for inheritance tax purposes, because he is contributing money (which is property within his estate) and increasing the value of his rights under the pension scheme (which, to the extent that they are settlement powers, are not property and so do not form part of his estate). A diminution in the value of his estate will not be a transfer of value if s.10 applies to the contribution, but where there is a concern that s.10 may not apply, it may be prudent to ensure, insofar as is possible, that the member's rights under the scheme are not settlement powers.

21-049

Separately to the above, IHTA 1984 s.55A provides that if a person makes a disposition by which he acquires a settlement power for consideration in money's worth then IHTA 1984 s.10(1) is expressly disapplied, so the disposition is a transfer of value and the value transferred is determined without bringing into account the value of any property acquired by the disposition.[55] Although it seems likely that some of the member's rights under a pension scheme may be settlement powers, they will be granted to the member under the terms of the scheme. Provided that he does not acquire a settlement power by reason of a contribution, s.55A should have no application.

21-050

*Reservation of benefit provisions*

The gift with reservation of benefit provisions in FA 1986 s.102 can in principle apply in respect of a contribution by a member to a pension scheme, if the death benefits may be paid otherwise than to his personal representatives. Such a contribution conceivably involves a gift of the death benefits and a reservation of benefit in the retirement benefits. If these provisions apply at the time of the member's death (or at any time in the seven years preceding death) then, on his death, the property is deemed to be within his estate for inheritance tax purposes.[56] The property deemed to be within the member's estate should be only the gifted ele-

21-051

---

[52] IHTA 1984 s.5(1).
[53] IHTA 1984 s.272.
[54] IHTA 1984 s.47A.
[55] IHTA 1984 s.55A.
[56] FA 1986 s.102(3).

**21-052** ment (rather than the entire fund), but the position is unclear and may depend on the circumstances.[57]

**21-052** The reservation of benefit provisions apply only to gifts by individuals, so they ought to have no application to contributions by a company. HMRC consider that the member is the "settlor" of all contributions relating to him (even if wholly funded by his employer),[58] and they presumably consider that this analysis extends to the reservation of benefit rules.

**21-053** In most cases, the reservation of benefit provisions will not apply to a contribution to a pension scheme, either because the contribution is not a "gift", or (to the extent that it is a gift) the *carve out principle* applies. In order for a contribution to be a *gift* for these purposes, it is likely that there must be an intention to confer gratuitous benefit (so it cannot apply where IHTA 1984 s.10 applies). In relation to the carve-out principle, Lord Hoffmann in *Ingram v IRC*[59] explained that the reservation of benefit provisions:

> "laid down a rule that if the donor continued to derive any benefit from the property in which an interest had been given, it would be treated as a pretended gift unless the benefit could be shown to be referable to a specific proprietary interest which he had retained."

**21-054** One must therefore draw a distinction between a benefit "retained" and a benefit "reserved". A benefit is *retained* if it is an interest which is intended to have a separate existence to the interest gifted (and it is capable of independent existence) and is not gifted to anyone. *Ingram* further made clear that the carve-out principle does not require a prior independent transaction creating the two interests and then a distinct gift of one of them.[60] The interest of a member under a pension scheme will usually be a specific proprietary interest.[61] There are generally two separate interests under the scheme: retirement benefits and death benefits. The interest of a member in the retirement benefits is an interest retained, and not an interest reserved. There may be a gift of the death benefits, but the provisions will not apply because there is no reservation of benefit in the property gifted.[62]

**21-055** In any event, HMRC's longstanding practice is to treat the gift with reservation of benefit provisions as not applying to registered pension schemes, even where the death benefits are held on discretionary trusts under the scheme rules and the member (or his personal representatives) are potential beneficiaries.[63]

**Contributions by other persons**

**21-056** A contribution by an individual other than the member, such as a spouse, parent or grandparent, is a transfer of value unless an exception applies. Section 10 cannot apply because the disponer intends to gratuitously benefit the member, but s.18 (spouse exemption), s.21 (surplus income), and/or s.19 (annual exemption) will usually apply. In certain circumstances, s.11 may be found to apply. IHTA 1984 s.18 will typically apply to contributions by an individual in respect of his or her spouse,

---

[57] See *Dymond's Capital Taxes* (London: Sweet & Maxwell), para.5A.294.
[58] See IHTM17085. This is discussed below.
[59] *Ingram v IRC* [1999] S.T.C. 1234.
[60] Contrary to the dicta of Goff J in *Nichols v IRC* [1975] W.L.R. 534.
[61] It is a current chose in action (see e.g. *Re Landau (a bankrupt)* [1998] Ch. 223).
[62] This appears to be HMRC's position (see IHTM14392). If the member made an *in specie* contribution of an interest in land to the scheme, this may however complicate matters (see FA 1986 ss.102A–102C).
[63] See Statement of Practice 10/86 and IHTM17073.

because the loss to the estate of the disponer is the same as the increase in the value of the estate of the spouse.[64] The comments above regarding settlement powers should however be borne in mind: to the extent that the value of a settlement power is increased by a contribution, s.18 will not apply.

If such a contribution does involve a transfer of value, it will be a potentially exempt transfer rather than a chargeable transfer if it is a "gift to another individual" for the purposes of IHTA 1984 s.3A(1A)(c)(i). Section 3A(2) provides that a transfer of value is a gift to another individual:  **21-057**

"(a) to the extent that the value transferred is attributable to property which, by virtue of the transfer, becomes comprised in the estate of that other individual, or

(b) so far as that value is not attributable to property which becomes comprised in the estate of another person, to the extent that, by virtue of the transfer, the estate of that other individual is increased."

If £100 is contributed to a pension scheme by a person other than the member one would expect the value of the member's estate to increase by at least £100.[65] The contribution is therefore a potentially exempt transfer by virtue of s.3A(2)(b), provided that the £100 does not become comprised in the estate of any other person. One would expect this proviso to be satisfied where the contribution is made to a scheme established under trusts, but not where it is contract-based (because the £100 will become comprised in the estate of the pension provider).  **21-058**

## DISPOSALS OF SCHEME INTERESTS

It will not usually be possible to assign an interest under a registered pension scheme to another person.[66] Where it is possible, an assignment to an individual is a potentially exempt transfer.  **21-059**

The value transferred by the disposal (or termination) by a member of a qualifying interest in possession is equal to the actual loss to his estate (not the value of the settled property in which the interest in possession subsisted, as would otherwise by the case where a qualifying interest in possession is disposed of). This is because s.151(3) disapplies IHTA 1984 ss.49–53 in relation to registered pension schemes. Section 151(3) has no application to non-qualifying interests in possession, which continue to be disregarded as a result of IHTA 1984 s.5(1).[67]  **21-060**

---

[64] If H contributes £100 for the benefit of his wife, clearly the loss to his estate is £100. It is equally clear that the value of her estate increases by £100 if she is in good health and can be expected to take full retirement benefits: that fact that interests under pension schemes are generally disregarded on death does not mean that they are disregarded at other times. The value of her chose in action increases by £100.

[65] Under the relief at source method, where a contribution of £100 is made, HMRC will usually add £25, so the value of the member's estate may be increased by up to £125. The member may also obtain an additional 20% tax relief in his self-assessment tax return, but that would not appear to increase the value of his estate.

[66] The provisions of most pension schemes expressly prohibit the assignment by a beneficiary of his interests under the scheme, and there are restrictions in PA 1995 s.91 relating to the assignment of interests under occupational pension schemes. Such an assignment may be deemed to be an unauthorised payment under FA 2004 s.172.

[67] To be clear, this does not treat a qualifying interest in possession in the same way as a non-qualifying interest in possession. If it did, there would be no transfer of value at all as a result of IHTA 1984 s.5(1).

## DEVALUING INTERESTS

**21-061** The following dispositions may result in a diminution in the value of the estate of a beneficiary of a pension scheme:[68]

(a) transfers between pension schemes;
(b) amendments to the terms of a pension scheme; or
(c) a surrender of rights or a value shift.

**21-062** Subject to the application of IHTA 1984 ss.10–17 (dispositions that are not transfers of value) and IHTA 1984 Pt II Ch.1 (exempt transfers), such dispositions are potentially exempt transfers if they constitute a gift to an individual (see Ch.21), and are otherwise chargeable transfers. The analysis above relating to member contributions (see Ch.21) also applies to such dispositions. If the value of a member's estate is reduced then one must consider if the disposition involves a transfer of value and if so whether it is exempt.

**21-063** The exercise by a member of a right to transfer scheme funds involves a surrender of rights under the first scheme in return for rights under the second scheme.[69] If under the terms of the first scheme the death benefits have been irrevocably assigned to a separate discretionary settlement (for example), but there has been no such assignment in relation to the second scheme, any subsequent nomination by the member could involve a transfer of value at that time.[70]

**21-064** Pursuant to FA 2004 s.172A(5), a member may surrender his interests under a registered pension scheme in various circumstances which will not constitute an unauthorised payment.[71] It will frequently be the case that, to the extent that a member's estate is reduced in consequence of a surrender, his spouse's estate will be increased, and in these circumstances the spouse exemption in IHTA 1984 s.18 should apply.

**21-065** Any transfers, amendments or disposals must be disclosed on form IHT409 if they occur in the two years before death.

**21-066** In *HMRC v Parry*,[72] the taxpayer's pension funds were transferred from a deferred annuity to a personal pension scheme less than two months before her death, at a time when she understood that she had terminal cancer. The Supreme Court held that the transfer was a disposition, and that the disposition gave rise to a diminution in the value of her estate. This was because the deferred annuity granted the taxpayer a general power of appointment over the death benefits (and so, pursuant to IHTA 1984 s.5(2), the value of the death benefits under the deferred annuity were included within her estate), whereas under the personal pension scheme the scheme administrator had discretion to pay death benefits to any of a class of beneficiaries. The taxpayer's personal representatives argued that this disposition was not a transfer of value because IHTA 1984 s.10 applied (for the reasons explained below). In addition to procuring the transfer, the taxpayer also omitted to access the pension despite being entitled to do so, and so HMRC argued that s.3(3) applied. It was common ground that the reason that the taxpayer omitted to access her pension rights was because accessing the benefits would cause a significant reduction in death benefits.

---

[68] Of course, the payment of benefits to the member will devalue his interest under the scheme (assuming it is a money purchase arrangement) but there is no loss to his estate because the benefits paid to him are of equal value.
[69] HMRC agree with this analysis (IHTM17072). In *HMRC v Parry* [2018] EWCA Civ 2266 at [43], Arden LJ referred to a transfer as *extinguishing* rights under the transferor scheme.
[70] See IHTM17072. It may depend on the terms of the scheme/policy.
[71] In the context of scheme pensions in payments, see FA 2004 Sch.28 paras 2 and 2A.
[72] *HMRC v Parry* [2020] UKSC 35.

In relation to the transfer, the Supreme Court considered the three parts to IHTA 1984 s.10 (set out above) and found that: **21-067**

(a) The transfer was not intended to confer any gratuitous benefit on any person. There was contemporaneous written advice to the taxpayer from just before the time of the transfer making it clear that her sole motive in making the transfer was to ensure that the company run by her former husband did not benefit from any surplus on her death (as she believed might have been the case under the deferred annuity). The Court of Appeal and Supreme Court agreed with this analysis.

(b) The transfer was not made in a transaction (including either a series of transactions or any associated operations) intended to confer any gratuitous benefit on any person. The Supreme Court considered that Mrs Staveley's "essential scheme" was her decision to omit in June 2006, which continued until her death. The pension transfer did not contribute to that scheme because the decision was made prior to the transfer, and the sons would have benefitted from her decision to omit without the transfer.

Suppose that a member makes a contribution to a registered pension scheme, and that contribution is a transfer of value to which s.10 applies, and then sometime later the member realises that his circumstances have changed such that he no longer requires the pension benefits and so he decides that he will omit to take benefits in order to confer a benefit on his death beneficiaries. Any such omission should not have any inheritance tax consequences.[73] However, as the decision in *Parry* demonstrates, if the member transfers his funds to a new scheme (in order to obtain a better return, for example) after having made the decision to omit, and that transfer involves a transfer of value to which s.10 applies, the transfer and the omission may well be associated operations such that s.10 does not apply to the overall transaction. **21-068**

**Interests in possession**

As with disposals of scheme interests, the devaluation (or termination) of a qualifying interest in possession may give rise to a transfer of value if it reduces the value of a person's estate, but this is based on the actual loss to his estate (not the value of the settled property, as would otherwise by the case where a qualifying interest in possession is disposed of). This is because s.151(3) disapplies IHTA 1984 ss.49–53. **21-069**

# RELEVANT PROPERTY

Settled property that is relevant property for inheritance tax purposes is subject to a periodic charge every ten years, and may also be subject to an exit charge when the settled property ceases to be relevant property. **21-070**

**Nature of scheme**

If the pension fund is held in trust for persons in succession, or for any person subject to a contingency, it is *settled property* and the pension scheme is a *settle-* **21-071**

---

[73] If this were not correct then the disapplication of s.3(3) by s.12(2ZA) would not serve much purpose.

ment for inheritance tax purposes.[74] All funded occupational pension schemes that have their main administration in the UK must be established under trusts.[75] Property is also settled property if it is charged or burdened (otherwise than for full consideration in money or money's worth paid for his own use or benefit to the person making the disposition) with the payment of any annuity or other periodical payment (including, for example, a pension) payable for a life or any other limited or terminable period.[76] Subject to certain exceptions, all settled property is relevant property unless a qualifying interest in possession subsists in it.

**21-072** Property held for the purposes of a registered pension scheme is expressly not relevant property.[77] A right to receive benefits from a registered pension scheme (such as the right to receive death benefits) is a chose in action which will itself be relevant property if held by a separate discretionary settlement. In such circumstances the value of the settled property (i.e. the chose in action) in the discretionary settlement will depend on how likely the member is to die at any given time.

*Scheme funds on death of member*

**21-073** IHTA 1984 s.58(2A)(a) provides that, for the purposes of IHTA 1984 s.58(1)(d):

"... property applied to pay lump sum death benefits within section 168(1) of the FA 2004 in respect of a member of a registered pension scheme is to be taken to be held for the purposes of the scheme from the time of the member's death until the payment is made ..."

**21-074** Scheme property does not normally automatically cease to be held for the purposes of a registered pension scheme on the death of the member. This is clearly the case as far as *pension* death benefits are concerned, as such benefits may continue to be provided for many years after the death of the member. To the extent that a scheme can only provide *lump sum* death benefits it may be suggested that on the death of the member the death benefits are no longer held for the purposes of the scheme. If the trustees have any discretion regarding the identity of the death beneficiaries, the property will continue to be held for the purposes of the registered pension scheme until such time as the discretion is exercised. It was previously necessary to exercise such discretion and pay authorised lump sum death benefits within a two-year period. There is currently no such requirement, although it may be more tax-efficient to pay death benefits within the relevant two-year period.[78] If the trustees do not have any discretion, or they have discretion but have exercised it, it is possible that the property to be provided as lump sum death benefits may cease to be held for the purposes of the registered pension scheme at that time. Where that is the case, s.58(2A)(a) will assist.[79]

---

[74] IHTA 1984 s.43(2)(a).
[75] PA 2004 s.252.
[76] IHTA 1984 s.43(2)(c). Property is also settled property if it would be so held or charged or burdened if the disposition creating the settlement was regulated by the law of any part of the UK, or whereby, under the law of any other country, the administration of the property is for the time being governed by provisions equivalent in effect to those which would apply if the property were so held, charged or burdened.
[77] IHTA 1984 s.58(1)(d). '
[78] Lump sum death benefits paid on the death of a member who died before his 75th birthday are tax-free only if paid within the relevant two-year period.
[79] One difficulty with s.58(2A)(a) is that it refers to lump sum death benefits within FA 2004 s.168(1) rather than s.168(2). For a lump sum death benefit to be within s.168(1) it must be paid by a registered pension scheme, whereas IHTA 1984 s.58(2A) can only have any application to property

## Trusts of lump sum death benefits

**21-075** Section 58(2) provides that:

"The reference in subsection (1)(d) above to property which is held for the purposes of a scheme does not include a reference to a benefit which, having become payable under the scheme, becomes comprised in a settlement."

**21-076** The precise scope of s.58(2) is uncertain. If the pension scheme trustees exercise a discretion to pay lump sum death benefits to a separate settlement (which does not form part of the registered pension scheme and is not itself a registered pension scheme), the exemption in s.58(1)(d) will clearly not apply to the separate settlement and so the property held for the purposes of that separate settlement will be relevant property.[80] This is not as a result of the application of s.58(2); it is simply because the property subject to the trusts of the separate settlement is not held for the purposes of a registered pension scheme. Section 58(2) refers to a benefit which "has become payable" rather than "is paid", so it may be intended to apply where a death benefit becomes payable but the trustees of the scheme declare that they are holding it on discretionary trusts. In any event, s.58(2) seems unnecessary.

**21-077** If the pension scheme trustees *must* pay the death benefits to a specific settlement, or must hold the death benefits on the terms of a separate settlement, it may be the case that the settlement is properly viewed as forming part of the registered pension scheme, on the basis that the definition of *pension scheme* in FA 2004 s.150(1) includes the entire arrangement for the provision of benefits (including death benefits). Where that is the case, the property comprised in the settlement is still held for the purposes of the registered pension scheme, and so the exemption in s.58(1)(d) would ordinarily continue to apply to it. Section 58(2) disapplies s.58(1)(d) in these circumstances. If this analysis is correct then it presents a trap for the unwary. The settlement containing the death benefits forms part of a registered pension scheme for the purposes of FA 2004 Pt 4, so the unauthorised payments regime will apply to it (so, for example, a loan to any person connected with a member would be an unauthorised payment and be taxable as such). However, as a result of s.58(2), the settled property constitutes relevant property rather than the usual beneficial treatment afforded to property held for the purposes of a registered pension scheme.

## Who is the settlor?

**21-078** The settlor of the settled property held for the purposes of the registered pension scheme will usually be the scheme member, on the basis that he has directly or indirectly provided the property.[81] HMRC appear to take a fairly extreme position, but they do accept that the employer can be the settlor in some circumstances (such as in relation to insured death benefits[82]). The settlor of the contributions to

---

which is *not* held for the purposes of a registered pension scheme. By contrast, FA 2004 s.168(2), which actually defines "lump sum death benefit" is not limited to benefits paid by a registered pension scheme.

[80] Unless some other exemption applies, e.g. it may be excluded property. Such a payment will give rise to a 45% special lump sum death benefits charge (which is an income tax charge) if the member died after reaching age 75 (see Ch.15).

[81] IHTA 1984 s.44(1).

[82] IHTM17091.

the pension will usually also be the settlor of the lump sum death benefits which become comprised in a separate settlement.[83]

**21-079** Where a benefit has become payable under a registered pension scheme and the benefit becomes comprised in a settlement made by a person other than the person entitled to the benefit (such as the trustees of the scheme), the settlement is treated as being made by the person so entitled.[84]

*Calculating periodic and exit charges*

**21-080** If the registered pension scheme is not established under trusts, the ten-year anniversary of the separate settlement is determined by reference to the date that the settlement was established by the member (either during his life or under his will).[85] If the pension scheme is established under trusts, the property will have moved from one settlement to another and so the date of the ten-year anniversary is determined by reference to the date the member first joined the pension scheme.[86]

**21-081** HMRC give the following example at IHTM17084:

- "Hilary became a member of a trust based pension scheme on 15 May 1974
- She set up a new discretionary trust on 2 September 2007 with £100 and completed a letter of wishes nominating the trust to receive any death benefits from the pension scheme
- Hilary died on 3 January 2012
- The death benefit is paid at the discretion of the pension scheme trustees to the new trust on 4 August 2012."

"The lump sum death benefit is relevant property from the date of payment on 4 August 2012. However, the ten-year anniversary is based on the date Hilary joined the pension scheme on 15 May 1974, so will first apply to these funds on 15 May 2014. The ten-year anniversary charge relating to the initial £100 used to set up the trust is based on the date the trust was set up, so it will first apply on 2 September 2017."

*Distributions from the settlement*

**21-082** Distributions from the separate settlement may be subject to exit charges under IHTA 1984 s.65.[87]

### Retaining death benefits within the pension scheme

**21-083** If a member of a money purchase arrangement dies with uncrystallised funds or unused drawdown funds, the trustees may create a dependant's or nominee's flexi-access drawdown fund. If the member dies after reaching age 75, there is no reason

---

[83] The definition of *settlor* in s.44(1) may well be broad enough to include the deceased pension scheme member in these circumstances. In any event, for the purposes of calculating the periodic and exit charges applicable to the separate settlement, the property is deemed by IHTA 1984 s.81(1) to remain in the transferor settlement (i.e. the pension scheme), and so the settlor of the transferor settlement is deemed to be the settlor of the transferee settlement. Section 81 does not of course deem the property to continue to be held for the purposes of a registered pension scheme (such that s.58(1)(d) would continue to apply to it).

[84] IHTA 1984 s.151(5). The word "made" is linked with s.44. The registered pension scheme is made by its settlor and any transferee settlement will have the same settlor. The purpose of s.151(5) seems to be to ensure that, where the employer is the settlor of the registered pension scheme, it is not also the settlor of the transferee settlement.

[85] For the periodic charge, see Ch.27.

[86] IHTA 1984 s.81.

[87] For the exit charge, see Ch.27.

to create such drawdown funds within any particular timeframe.[88] The funds can continue to be invested within the registered pension scheme until such time as death benefits are required, at which point they can be designated as available for drawdown pension.

## OMITTING TO EXERCISE RIGHTS

**21-084** Where a person omits to exercise a right and, as a result of that omission, the value of his estate is diminished and the value of any other person's estate or any settled property is increased, the omission is treated as if it were a disposition by IHTA 1984 s.3(3). This could be the case, for example, where a pension scheme member omits to exercise a right to elect to receive pension benefits. Subject to the application of IHTA 1984 ss.10–17 (dispositions that are not transfers of value) and IHTA 1984 Pt II Ch.1 (exempt transfers), such deemed dispositions are potentially exempt transfers if they constitute a gift to an individual (see above), and are otherwise chargeable transfers. The analysis relating to member contributions (see above) also applies to such deemed dispositions. However, Since 6 April 2011, s.3(3) does not apply in relation to any pension or lump sum under a registered pension scheme.[89] Nor does s.3(3) apply in relation to any omission that results in a drawdown pension fund or flexi-access drawdown fund under a registered pension scheme not being used up in the person's lifetime.[90] It follows that a deliberate omission to exercise a right to pension benefits is not a disposition, even where the member is in ill health and does so solely in order to increase the amount of death benefits payable after his death.

**21-085** However, if the omission forms part of a scheme which includes a disposition which is a transfer of value to which IHTA 1984 s.10 applies,[91] the disposition and omission may be associated operations such that s.10 does not apply to the overall transaction.

## DEATH OF A BENEFICIARY

**21-086** On the death of a pension scheme beneficiary (i.e. the member or a death beneficiary), it is necessary to consider the following:

(a) Was the beneficiary entitled to receive any benefits from the scheme immediately before his death? If so, what was the value of those benefits at that time?

(b) Did any changes to the value of the beneficiary's estate occur by reason of his death? If so, are such changes deemed by IHTA 1984 s.171 to have occurred before his death?

(c) Did the beneficiary hold a general power of appointment immediately before death, or did he exercise such a power in the seven years before his death?

---

[88] If the member dies before reaching age 75 with unused uncrystallised funds, income withdrawal is tax-free only if the flexi-access drawdown fund is created within the relevant two-year period.

[89] IHTA 1984 s.12(2ZA). *Pension* has the same meaning as in FA 2004, and so includes an annuity and income withdrawal.

[90] IHTA 1984 s.12A(1).

[91] As was the case in *HMRC v Parry* [2018] EWCA Civ 2266 (see para.21-066), where the omission was found to form part of the same scheme as the previous transfer to the pension scheme.

(d) Were any contributions, transfers, disposals or changes to the benefits structure made in the two years before death? If so, they must be reported on form IHT409. Any such transactions involving a transfer of value more than two years before death (but less than seven years before death) must be disclosed in the IHT403.

**21-087** On the death of a member of a money purchase arrangement, the rules of the scheme typically provide that the trustees may provide death benefits to one or more of a wide class of beneficiaries (including the member's personal representatives), and the member will usually provide the trustees with a written statement or memorandum providing non-binding guidance explaining how the member wishes the trustees to exercise their discretion following his death.[92] Provided that the statement is not binding on the trustees it will not prejudice the discretionary nature of the trusts.[93] If the intention is for the trustees to decide merely who should receive lump sum death benefits then the statement will typically say who the member wishes to benefit and what, as a percentage or fraction of his fund, the member wishes them to receive.[94] Where the trustees have genuine discretion, there should be no question of (b) or (c) above applying. However, in extreme cases, such as where the member only had one possible living beneficiary who is nominated in a statement of wishes (other than a charity, perhaps), HMRC could convincingly argue that the trustees did not in reality have any discretion.

**21-088** Where the trustees have discretion about whether or not to pay death benefits (to the member's widow, for example), the position is less clear.[95] Although in some older cases the purported discretion was accepted,[96] in more recent cases the courts have made it clear that members of occupational pension schemes are not volunteers and that has influenced the court's attitude to the obligations of trustees.[97]

---

[92] For an explanation of the proper decision-making process trustees should follow, see *Punter Southall Governance Services Ltd v Benge* [2022] EWHC 193 (Ch). A statement of wishes does not involve a disposal of an equitable interest and so it need not be in writing (see LPA 1925 s.53(1)(c)). It will not normally constitute a testamentary disposition, and so does not require attestation in accordance with the statutory requirement for execution of a will, provided that the member's interest under the scheme is non-assignable (see *Baird v Baird* [1990] 2 A.C. 548; *Re Danish Bacon Company Ltd v Staff Pension Fund Trusts* [1971] 1 W.L.R. 248).

[93] For an example of a statement of wishes that the court found to be binding, see *Chen v Wong* [2006] T.L.I. 262.

[94] See J. Kessler, *Drafting Trusts and Will Trusts*, 9th edn (London: Sweet & Maxwell, 2008), para.7.16. The author also provides examples of strongly worded statements of wishes, which may be used where appropriate. There is no reason in principle that a registered pension scheme could not be designed to provide benefits in the same way as a discretionary settlement of the death benefits. In such cases the statement of wishes may be more general, and may, for example, request that the member's spouse is reasonably provided for during his or her life and subject to that the member's children should be regarded as the principal beneficiaries.

[95] See Hayton, [2005] Conv. PL Lawyer; Moffatt [1993] 56 M.L.R. 471, 488.

[96] e.g. in *Re J Bibby & Sons Ltd (Pension Trust Deed)*, also known as *Davies v IRC* [1952] 2 All E.R. 483 at 486, Harman J observed that although "everybody knows that a good employer will not see the widow of his faithful employee left in the street with nothing", having regard to the deed "... I can only come to the conclusion that this is a purely discretionary trust deed. It is true it is a trust, but it is a trust under which, so far as any employee is concerned, it seems to me the trustees have an absolute discretion either to give or to withhold a pension according to their views of the desirability of paying it ...". The decision that the widow had no beneficial interest in the scheme "sounds incredible to pensions practitioners bought up on the modern concept of pensions as deferred pay" and is "not a line of reasoning one would expect to be adopted today, even if the pension scheme were identically worded". Tennet, [2007] *Trust Law International*.

[97] *Kerr v British Leyland (Staff) Trustees* 26 March 1986; *Milhenstedt v Barclays Bank International* [1989] I.R.L.R. 522; *Stannard v Fisons Pensions Trust* [1992] I.R.L.R. 27.

## DEATH OF A BENEFICIARY

### Entitlement immediately before death

*The general position*

A right to receive a benefit from a pension scheme is potentially very valuable. However, if the interest terminates on death (i.e. the beneficiary's personal representatives are not entitled to the benefit), HMRC consider that it has no value.[98] The requirement in IHTA 1984 s.4(1) is to value the person's estate *immediately* before death. In almost all circumstances, it will be apparent immediately before death (i.e. the very moment before death occurs) that the person is about to die. This is not a case of valuing the rights with the benefit of hindsight: even sudden deaths are clearly foreseeable in the moment before death legally occurs.[99] The value of his right to receive the benefit is the price which that right might reasonably be expected to fetch if sold in the open market at that time.[100] No reasonable purchaser would buy the property without some indication of that person's state of health, which indicates that the value for the purposes of s.160 would be very low. This analysis is supported by the approach of the Court of Appeal in *Powell v Osbourne*.[101] In that case, the Court considered the requirement, in the Inheritance (Provision for Family and Dependants) Act 1975 s.9(1), to value certain property "immediately before [the deceased's] death". Simon Brown LJ observed that "immediately before death the fact of imminent death is by definition inevitable ..." and there was no reason that the Court should ignore the imminence of death.

21-089

There are however some difficulties with HMRC's position.[102] First, the sale referred to in s.160 is an entirely hypothetical sale. The parties to the sale are hypothetical, and, in particular, the characteristics and circumstances of the person who actually owns or owned the property in question are ignored.[103] That indicates that the deceased's state of health should also be ignored for the purposes of s.160 (although it might also be suggested that their age should be ignored). Second, if HMRC's position were correct, there is no obvious reason why a joint tenancy of land would not also have a nil value immediately before death. Third, the closing words to s.171(2) ("but the termination on the death of any interest [...] does not fall within this subsection") would be otiose. Fourth, HMRC's interpretation seems to render s.151(2) (see below) otiose.

21-090

*Pensions and annuities ceasing on death*

IHTA 1984 s.151(2) provides that:

21-091

"(2) An interest in or under a registered pension scheme, a qualifying non-UK pen-

---

[98] See *McCutcheon on Inheritance Tax*, 7th edn (London: Sweet & Maxwell, 2016) para.25–56, and *Dymond's Capital Taxes* (London: Sweet & Maxwell), para.23.153–159, although neither provides any authority for this statement. None of the IHT400, IHT409 or IHT410 request information relating to pensions or annuities which cease on death.

[99] Which may well be some moments *after* the heart ceases to beat. As Lord Goff observed in *Airedale NHS Trust v Bland* [1993] A.C. 789 at 863, "... doctors no longer associate death exclusively with breathing and heart beat, and it has come to be accepted [by the medical profession] that death occurs when the brain, and in particular the brain stem, has been destroyed".

[100] IHTA 1984 s.160.

[101] *Powell v Osbourne* [1993] 1 F.L.R. 1001.

[102] See E. Chamberlain and C. Whitehouse, *Trust Taxation and Estate Planning* 4th edn (London: Sweet & Maxwell, 2014), para.61–40; *McCutcheon on Inheritance Tax*, 7th edn (London: Sweet & Maxwell, 2016), paras 25–50 to 25–57.

[103] Plowman J in *Lynall v IRC* [1969] 1 Ch. 421 (affirmed by the House of Lords in *Lynall v IRC* [1972] A.C. 680).

sion scheme or section 615(3) scheme which comes to an end on the death of the person entitled to it shall be left out of account in determining for the purposes of this Act the value of his estate immediately before his death, if the interest—
  (a) is, or is a right to, a pension or annuity, and
  (b) is not an interest resulting (whether by virtue of the instrument establishing the scheme or otherwise) from the application of any benefit provided under the scheme otherwise than by way of a pension or annuity."

**21-092** Section 151(3) (considered below) is concerned with interests within s.151(2)(a) or (b) which are qualifying interests in possession in settled property (which will usually mean pre-22 March 2006 interests in possession). It is therefore implicit that s.151(2) is aimed at interests which are not qualifying interests in possession (including, for example, annuity contracts where there is no settled property).

**21-093** In contrast to other provisions within IHTA 1984 (such as s.12, for example), neither "pension" nor "annuity" is defined for the purposes of s.151. These terms are considered in Ch.13 Clearly a scheme pension, lifetime annuity and short-term annuity are covered, but income withdrawal under a flexi-access drawdown fund could not normally be described as a *pension* unless there is some promise to make regular payments from the fund. However, one would expect a tribunal to find that, for the purposes of s.151(2)(a), "pension" does include income withdrawal.

**21-094** Section 151(2)(b) could conceivably apply where a person surrenders a lump sum in exchange for an annuity. Such an annuity is an interest arising from the application of a lump sum (i.e. not a pension or annuity) and so the annuity is not protected by s.151(2). It could also apply where a lump sum death benefit is settled on trusts (which form part of the registered pension scheme) to pay a pension or create an annuity. In these circumstances the pension or annuity will be taxable in the usual way. Given the general position regarding the value of interests that terminate on death, it seems unlikely that s.151(2) will, in the normal course, have much application.

**21-095** HMRC note that lump sum death benefits do not fall within the exclusion in s.151(2),[104] and the same must apply to a lump sums such as a PCLS or an UFPLS to which the member was entitled immediately before death. A *right* to a lump sum (including a right to commute part of a pension) is therefore not excluded by s.151(2). It is likely that a lump sum can form part of a person's estate if he was absolutely entitled to the lump sum, such that it must be paid to his estate if he dies before receiving it. The fact that the member may have the power to elect to receive a lump sum at any time should not itself be problematic if the power ceases on death. It is therefore generally unnecessary for s.151(2) to apply to lump sums. Pensions and annuities require special treatment because it is possible to become absolutely entitled to a stream of payments prior to death.

**21-096** Similarly, the right to receive a pension or annuity purchased with a lump sum from the scheme (or payable from a trust of which the lump sum is the settled property) is not excluded by s.151(2). This would include a situation where the post-death payments are made, not to the deceased, but at the direction of the deceased.

*Interests in possession*

**21-097** IHTA 1984 s.151(3) disapplies ss.49–53 in relation to any qualifying interest in possession satisfying the conditions of s.151(2)(a) and (b). The disapplication of s.49 means that in the event of a chargeable transfer on the death of the person

---

[104] IHTM17036.

entitled to the interest, inheritance tax is charged on the value of the interest, not the value of the settled property (which is usually much greater). As noted above, the value of an interest which ends on death is nil.

Section 151(3) has no application to non-qualifying interests in possession, which continue to be disregarded under s.5(1). To be clear, the effect of s.151(3) is not to treat a qualifying interest in possession in the same way as a non-qualifying interest in possession; if it did, there would be no transfer of value at all as a result of s.5(1).

21-098

**Benefits continuing after death**

If a beneficiary dies when entitled to a fixed-term pension or annuity (i.e. it will continue to be paid to his personal representatives after his death for the duration of the term), or when he has a general power over such payments, the value of the rights relating to the unexpired term on death is included within his estate. The same analysis applies to any arrears of pension or short service refund lump sum or refund of excess contributions lump sum that the member was entitled to immediately before his death.[105]

21-099

Any retirement benefits mistakenly provided after death as a result of the trustee or manager being unaware of the death are not taken into account for inheritance tax purposes. Such benefits are repayable to the trustee or manager, although HMRC accept that small overpayments may occasionally be written off.[106]

21-100

**Changes occurring by reason of the death**

IHTA 1984 s.171 provides that:

21-101

"(1) In determining the value of a person's estate immediately before his death changes in the value of his estate which have occurred by reason of the death and fall within subsection (2) below shall be taken into account as if they had occurred before the death.

(2) A change falls within this subsection if it is an addition to the property comprised in the estate or an increase or decrease of the value of any property so comprised, other than a decrease resulting from such an alteration as is mentioned in section 98(1) above;[107] but the termination on the death of any interest or the passing of any interest by survivorship does not fall within this subsection."

As a result of IHTA 1984 s.171, in determining the value of the member's estate immediately before his death any changes in the value of his estate which occur by reason of his death are taken into account as if they occurred before his death. It follows that any death benefits which *must* be paid to the member's personal representatives on his death are deemed to form part of his estate immediately before death.[108] HMRC have confirmed that death benefits payable to the member's personal representatives as of right are not regarded as property comprised in a

21-102

---

[105] See Ch.14.
[106] IHTM17055.
[107] IHTA 1984 s.98 relates to alterations in so much of a close company's share or loan capital as does not consist of quoted shares or quoted securities, and alternations in any rights attaching to unquoted shares in or unquoted debentures of a close company.
[108] The same analysis applies to any short service refund lump sum that the member's personal representatives become entitled to as a result of the member's death (see Ch.14).

settlement.[109] Section 171 does not apply to death benefits paid to the member's personal representatives following the exercise of a discretion by the pension scheme trustees, because such death benefits are not paid to his personal representatives "by reason of his death", but by reason of the trustees exercising their discretion.

**21-103** If an individual dies when entitled to receive death benefits (either in respect of someone else, or where his personal representatives are entitled to the death benefits) it is necessary to consider if that right had any value immediately before death. Again, if the trustees have discretion there is nothing that can be included within anyone's estate.

### Protected rights

**21-104** Prior to 6 April 2012, if a member died before taking retirement benefits or with unsecured pension rights, any death benefits which were protected rights (i.e. rights derived from a contracted-out scheme) needed to be used to provide benefits for certain family members only. If there were no such family members then the cash value of the protected rights may have been payable to nominated beneficiaries or the member's estate, and so it may have been liable to inheritance tax. The position depends on the precise terms of the scheme rules. The taxpayer or agent should give details on the form IHT409.[110]

### Powers of nomination

*General powers of appointment*

**21-105** Pursuant to IHTA 1984 s.5(2), a "general power" is "a power or authority enabling the person by whom it is exercisable to appoint or dispose of property as he thinks fit". A power to specify the recipient of death benefits may be a general power. A person who has a general power which enables him, or would if he were sui juris enable him, to dispose of any property in or under a registered pension scheme is treated as beneficially entitled to the property.[111] The consequences of this are:

(a) If a person irrevocably exercises a general power during his life he will make an actual transfer of value if it diminishes the value of his estate (which it would do if omitting to exercise it means that it is paid to his personal representatives).[112]

(b) If a person dies without having irrevocably exercising the power (i.e. he still holds the general power) he will be chargeable under s.4(1) on the value of the property.

---

[109] See the guidance notes reproduced in *McCutcheon on Inheritance Tax*, 7th edn (London: Sweet & Maxwell, 2016), para.23–15.

[110] See IHTM17056.

[111] IHTA 1984 s.5(2) (modified in relation to settled property by s.151(4)). Where on a person's death an annuity becomes payable under a registered pension scheme to a death beneficiary and under the terms of the scheme a sum of money might at his option have become payable instead to his personal representatives, he is not, by virtue of s.5(2), treated as having been beneficially entitled to that sum (IHTA 1984 s.210).

[112] However, IHTA 1984 s.10 may apply to the exercise of such a power by a scheme member in favour of persons who would otherwise benefit under the member's will, if the member was unaware of the inheritance tax advantages of exercising the power (*HMRC v Parry* [2018] EWCA Civ 2266 (Newey LJ and Birss J; Arden LJ dissenting) at [89]).

# DEATH OF A BENEFICIARY

This presents a trap for the unwary. It is the one instance in which IHTA 1984 creates the possibility of an inheritance tax charge in respect of registered pension schemes which would not otherwise exist. As is explained below, it is straightforward to avoid the conferral of a general power, and so it is important that a member of a registered pension scheme is not given a general power at any time when the death benefits have any value (such as when the member is in ill-health).[113]

**21-106**

*The meaning of "general power"*

The definition of "general power" in s.5(2) suggests that if the power is limited in any way then it will not be a general power. HMRC accept that if the power does not allow a member to nominate himself then if he dies while owning it that will not form part of his estate unless as a result of the failure to exercise it, it forms part of his estate. Typically, a general power will be an express power to nominate, but the definition will plainly include a situation where the trustee or manager has no choice and effectively must pay the benefits in accordance with the member's directions.

**21-107**

On the death of a member of a registered pension scheme, authorised pension death benefits can be paid only to a nominee or a dependant of the member.[114] A "nominee" is an individual nominated by the member or the scheme administrator, who is not a dependant of the member.[115] A *nomination* for these purposes does not require a binding nomination. Typically, the scheme provisions will permit the trustees to pay death benefits to one or more of a broad class of beneficiaries and the member will nominate one or more individuals, but without imposing any obligation on the trustees to pay the death benefits to those individuals. Those individuals are *nominees* for the purposes of FA 2004 Sch.28 para.27A(1).

**21-108**

A general power is an actual power, not merely a non-binding nomination such as an expression of wishes. If the trustee or manager has discretion regarding to whom the death benefits are to be paid then no one has a general power and so there is nothing which may form part of any individual's estate. It is irrelevant that the trustees may in fact decide to pay the death benefits to the deceased member's personal representatives. The person with the power could conceivably be a death beneficiary (such as the member's spouse).

**21-109**

## Contributions, transfers, disposals etc. before death

If any contributions, transfers, disposals or changes to the benefits structure are made in the two years before death, they must be reported on form IHT409. Any such transactions involving a transfer of value more than two years before death (but less than seven years before death) must be disclosed in the IHT403. HMRC will want to know about the deceased's state of health at the time of any dispositions and will apparently assume that the value transferred was nominal (or, possibly, that s.10 applied) provided that the deceased survived for at least two years afterwards.[116]

**21-110**

Where, under the terms of a pension scheme, the death benefits are to be paid to the member or his spouse, it may be desirable to assign the death benefits to a

**21-111**

---

[113] It is of course possible that someone other than the member has a general power, and in these circumstances it is not clear how one would value the death benefits assuming that on the death of that person the member was still alive.
[114] See Ch.15.
[115] FA 2004 Sch.28 para.27A(1).
[116] See IHTM17015.

discretionary settlement. It is not possible under English law to assign only part of a chose in action, so this is usually achieved by transferring the entire contract/policy to trustees to hold the retirement benefits on bare trust for the member and the death benefits on discretionary trusts for the member's estate and his family. The assignment will be a transfer of value but HMRC accept that it will of nominal value if the member is in good health. The property held on discretionary trusts is relevant property, but has only a nominal value until death.

## FORM IHT409

**21-112** An IHT409 must be completed on the death of any person who has made private pension provision. The form requests information on four areas:

(a) Payments made under a pension arrangement that continue after a death;
(b) Payments of lump sum death benefits;
(c) Changes, transfers, disposals and contributions made within two years of death; and
(d) Alternatively secured pensions and corresponding dependants' pensions (for deaths between 6 April 2006 and 5 April 2011).

**21-113** In relation to (c) above, suppose that the deceased made a contribution at a time when he understood that he was terminally ill, but did not die within the two-year period. The contribution should clearly not be disclosed in the IHT409, but if it involved a transfer of value then it should be disclosed in the IHT403. If the position is unclear, or if there is reason to think that HMRC may disagree, it may be appropriate to draw that to HMRC's attention in a covering letter.

# CHAPTER 22

# Miscellaneous Topics

## TABLE OF CONTENTS

| | |
|---|---|
| Introduction | 22-001 |
| VAT and pension schemes | 22-002 |
| Overview of VAT | 22-003 |
| Input tax | 22-005 |
| Person to whom supply is made | 22-006 |
| Business purpose | 22-008 |
| HMRC practice | 22-009 |
| Management/administration costs | 22-009 |
| Investment costs | 22-010 |
| Services attributable to both administration and investment | 22-011 |
| Services supplied to the employer: tripartite contracts | 22-013 |
| Anti-avoidance provisions | 22-017 |
| The income tax settlement provisions | 22-018 |
| Disguised remuneration | 22-020 |
| Section 554E(1)(g) | 22-021 |
| Section 554E(1)(h) | 22-023 |
| Relevant steps following unauthorised payment | 22-026 |
| Trusts of death benefits | 22-027 |
| The chargeable event regime | 22-028 |
| Compensation payments for loss of pension rights | 22-029 |

## INTRODUCTION

This chapter considers a number of unrelated aspects of the taxation of registered pension schemes and their beneficiaries. **22-001**

## VAT AND PENSION SCHEMES

There are no VAT reliefs or exemptions that apply specifically to registered pension schemes. The trustee or manager of a pension scheme may register for VAT purposes if they make taxable supplies. This will not usually be the case except where they hold UK commercial real estate. If the trustees are VAT registered they can reclaim VAT to the extent that it relates to that business (e.g. on conveyancing costs). The trustees will not be able to recover VAT paid on supplies relating to the scheme generally (e.g. in respect of legal, actuarial/consulting, administration and **22-002** investment management services), because such supplies do not relate to that business. In the context of an occupational pension scheme, it may however be possible for a sponsoring employer to recover such VAT.

## Overview of VAT

**22-003** UK VAT is charged on any supply of goods or services made in the UK, if it is a taxable supply made by a taxable person in the course or furtherance of any business carried on by him.[1] A "taxable person" means a person who is VAT registered, or is required to be VAT registered (e.g. because the value of his annual taxable supplies exceed £85,000).[2] A "taxable supply" means a supply of goods or services in the UK other than an exempt supply.[3] A supply is "exempt" if it is of a description specified in Sch.9.[4]

**22-004** VAT is a liability of the supplier, who usually adds it to the consideration to be paid by the recipient. VAT on supplies made by a taxable person is referred to as "output tax".[5] Where a taxable person pays VAT on goods or services supplied to it ("input tax"), only the net amount of VAT (i.e. output tax less input tax) must be paid to HMRC. If input tax exceeds output tax, HMRC will repay the difference.

### Input tax

**22-005** Tax is input tax if: (a) it is VAT on the supply to a taxable person of any goods or services, (b) the goods or services are used or to be used for the purpose of any business carried on or to be carried on by that person, and (c) the tax is chargeable, paid or payable under the UK VAT legislation.[6] So, in order for an employer to reclaim input tax, it must be the case that the goods or services are:

(a) supplied "to" the employer; and
(b) used for the purposes of the employer's business.

*Person to whom supply is made*

**22-006** When determining to whom a supply is made for VAT purposes, one must consider the economic and commercial realities.[7] The contractual position between the parties normally reflects the economic and commercial reality of the transactions,[8] so that is the most useful starting point.[9] The aim of that enquiry is to determine whether there is a supply of services affected for a consideration. This will be the case only if there is a legal relationship between the provider of the service and the recipient pursuant to which there is reciprocal performance, the remuneration received by the provider of the service constituting the value actually given in return for the service supplied to the recipient.[10] It is only if the contractual position does not reflect the economic reality that it is appropriate to

---

[1] VATA 1994 s.4(1).
[2] VATA 1994 s.3(1) and Sch.3 para.1
[3] VATA 1994 s.4(2).
[4] VATA 1994 s.31(1).
[5] VATA 1994 s.24(2).
[6] VATA 1994 s.24(1).
[7] *Airtours Holidays Transport Ltd v HMRC* [2016] UKSC 21 at [42]–[51].
[8] *HMRC v Newey* (C-653/11) [2013] S.T.C. 2432 at [42]–[43].
[9] *WHA Ltd v HMRC* [2013] UKSC 24 at [27] (Lord Reed).
[10] *Tolsma v Inspecteur der Omzetbelasting Leeuwarden* (C-16/93) [1994] S.T.C. 509 at [14]; *HMRC v Newey* (C-653/11) [2013] S.T.C. 2432 at [40].

## VAT AND PENSION SCHEMES

depart from that approach. That may occur where the contractual terms constitute a "purely artificial arrangement" which does not correspond with the economic and commercial reality of the transactions.[11]

If the employer contracts directly with the supplier (such that the employer has the right to require the supplier to supply the services to the trustees and the supplier has a corresponding obligation to the employer to do so), the employer will usually be regarded as a recipient of the supply.[12] The trustee will also be a recipient of a supply, but there is no reason that a single supply cannot be made to more than one person.[13] Where the employer does not contract directly with the supplier, the position is less clear. Simply paying the supplier's fees will not on its own cause the employer to be the recipient of the supply.[14] Regard must be had to the economic and commercial realities of the arrangements under consideration.

22-007

*Business purpose*

A supply is treated as being used for the purpose of the employer's business if there is a "direct and immediate link" between the supply and one or more output transactions or between the supply and the employer's economic activity as a whole.[15] The activity of providing and setting up an occupational pension fund is a function of the employer's business.[16] Once the scheme has been established, it may be the case that services relating to the management of the scheme and supplied to the trustees are found to be used by the employer for the purposes of its business.[17] Where the employer is also the trustee, or associated with the trustee, it may be clearer that supplies are made to the employer.[18]

22-008

*HMRC practice*[19]

**Management/administration costs** HMRC accept that the management/administration of an occupational pension scheme is part of the employer's normal business activities, so the VAT incurred on administrative services is the employer's input tax, even where the responsibility for the general management of the scheme rests with the trustee, or the trustees pay for the services supplied. HMRC consider that the following are administrative services:

22-009

(a) making arrangements for setting up a pension fund;
(b) management of the scheme, that is the collection of contributions and payment of pensions;
(c) advice on reviewing the scheme and implementing changes to it;

---

[11] *HMRC v Newey* (C-653/11) [2013] S.T.C. 2432 at [45].
[12] *Airtours Holidays Transport Ltd v HMRC* [2016] UKSC 21.
[13] *CCE v Redrow Group Plc* [1999] UKHL 4.
[14] *HMRC v Aimia Coalition Loyalty UK Ltd* [2013] UKSC 42.
[15] *Finanzamt Koln-Nord v Becker* (C-104/12) [2013] B.V.C. 565 at [19] and [20].
[16] *Linotype and Machinery Ltd v C&E Comrs* (1978) V.A.T.T.R. 123. In that case the Tribunal found that the supplies (paid for by the employer) relating to the management and administration of the scheme were not made to the employer.
[17] *Manchester Ship Canal Co v C&E Comrs* [1982] S.T.C. 351. In that case, the employer had an interest in the scheme actuary's report because the employer was required to make good any deficiency.
[18] See *C&E Comrs v British Railways Board* [1976] 1 W.L.R. 1036; [1976] S.T.C. 359, CA; *BOC International Ltd v C&E Comrs* (1982) V.A.T.T.R. 84. Also see VIT44800.
[19] For HMRC practice in relation to defined benefits schemes, see VIT44600 to VIT45510. For recent developments see VAT Notice 700/17, Brief 6 (2014), Brief 43 (2014), Brief 8 (2015), Brief 17 (2015) and Brief 14 (2016). In relation to money purchase schemes see VATFIN5120 and Brief 44 (2014).

(d) accountancy and auditing relating to management of the scheme, such as preparation of the annual accounts;
(e) actuarial valuation of the assets of a fund;
(f) general actuarial advice connected with administration of the fund;
(g) providing general statistics in connection with the performance of a fund's investments or properties; and
(h) legal instructions and general legal advice, including drafting trust deeds, insofar as it relates to the management of the scheme.[20]

HMRC accept that the following services are attributed only to administration activity: (a) regular meetings with consulting actuaries; (b) submission of data to independent performance monitoring service; and (c) programming and provision of relevant computer support for valuations and performance statistics.[21]

**22-010** **Investment costs** However, HMRC consider that input tax relating to investment costs cannot be reclaimed by the employer, on the basis that such costs are separate from the employer's business.[22] HMRC consider that investment services include:

(a) advice connected with making investments;
(b) brokerage charges;
(c) rent and service charge collection for property holdings;
(d) producing records and accounts in connection with property purchases, lettings and disposals or investments;
(e) trustee services, that is services of a professional trustee in managing the assets of the fund;
(f) legal services paid on behalf of representative beneficiaries in connection with changes in pension fund arrangements; and
(g) custodian charges.[23]

HMRC consider that the following services are attributed only to investment activity: investment management—asset allocation and stock selection; investment research, including relevant travel—(UK and overseas); economic research, including relevant travel—(UK and overseas); dealing in securities in UK and overseas markets on behalf of clients; keeping detailed accounts of all investments, receipts, disbursements other transactions; review and control of investment portfolios; preparation of contract notes; preparation of schedules of transactions; preparation of specialist market commentaries; safekeeping of property and securities in own name or name of nominee or in bearer form; appointment of and responsibility for sub-custodians domestic or foreign; provision of nominee service; maintenance of securities accounts, stock registration and transfer; collection of dividends and interest and obtaining new coupon sheets; recovery of tax; and administration in respect of: (i) capital repayments; and (ii) capitalisation issues; administration in respect of company meetings and, in particular, execution of forms of proxy as appropriate; conversions; exchanges; liquidation; distributions; redemptions; right issues; and payment of calls; programming and provision of relevant computer support for: (i) investment management; and (ii) investment administration and control.

---

[20] VIT44700.
[21] VIT44750.
[22] For a list of services that HMRC consider to be administrative services, and those that HMRC consider to be investment services, see VIT44700 and VIT44750.
[23] For a list of services that HMRC consider to be administrative services, and those that HMRC consider to be investment services, see VIT44700 and VIT44750.

**Services attributable to both administration and investment** HMRC consider that the following services are to be attributed to both administration and investment: regular meetings with clients; cash management; preparation of performance statistics; and preparation of valuations.

**22-011**

Where a supplier issues a single tax inclusive invoice for both kinds of services, allowing no means of separately identifying the management services, HMRC are prepared to accept that 30% of the invoice relates to administration and is therefore recoverable by the employer.[24]

**22-012**

**Services supplied to the employer: tripartite contracts** In relation to defined benefits schemes, HMRC consider that VAT will be deductible by the employer only if the employer is a party to the contract for the supply of those services and has paid for them.[25] Where the trustees are required to be a party,[26] HMRC suggest the use of a tripartite contract between the service provider, the trustee and the employer which evidences, as a minimum, that[27]:

**22-013**

(a) the service provider makes supplies to the employer (albeit that the contract may recognise that the service provider may be appointed by, or on behalf of, the pension scheme trustees);

(b) the employer directly pays for the services that are supplied under the contract;

(c) the service provider will pursue the employer for payment and only in circumstances where the employer is unlikely to pay (for example, because it has gone into administration) will it recover its fees from the scheme's funds or the pension scheme trustees;

(d) both the employer and the pension scheme trustees are entitled to seek legal redress in the event of breach of contract, albeit that the liability of the service provider need not be any greater than if the contract were with the pension scheme trustees alone and any restitution, indemnity or settlement payments for which the service provider becomes liable may be payable in whole to the pension scheme trustees for the benefit of the pension scheme (for example in circumstances where the scheme is not fully funded);

(e) the service provider will provide any service-related reports, such as fund performance reports, to the employer on request (subject to the pension scheme trustees being able to stipulate that reports are withheld, for example where there could be a conflict of interest);

(f) the employer is entitled to terminate the contract, although that may be subject to a condition that it should not do so without the pension scheme trustees prior written consent (this can be in addition to any right that the pension scheme trustees may have to terminate the contract unilaterally).

In addition to the above, HMRC suggest that evidence that the pension scheme trustees agree that it is the employer who is entitled to deduct any VAT incurred on the services will reduce the potential for disputes.

**22-014**

HMRC consider that the above analysis does not apply to money purchase schemes, because the employer does not bear the same level of risks and benefits

**22-015**

---

[24] VIT45000.
[25] VIT44650.
[26] e.g. to comply with PA 1995 s.47.
[27] VIT45400. HMRC acknowledge that such contracts may give rise to a conflict of interests in some circumstances. Other possible solutions include: (a) the supply of scheme administration services from the trustees to the employer; and (b) VAT grouping (see Brief 17 (2015)).

associated with the performance of the fund.[28] However, supplies are exempt if they are made to a "qualifying pension fund", which means a pension fund established in the UK which satisfies the following conditions: (a) it is solely funded, whether directly or indirectly (e.g. by an employer) by pension members; (b) the pension members bear the investment risk; (c) the fund contains the pooled contributions of more than one pension member; and (d) the risk borne by the pension members is spread over a range of investments.[29] Where individual investors exercise an option to give directions as to how their contributions are invested (e.g. in specific assets and/or funds external to the pension fund) that overrides the investment powers of the trustee or manager, the exemption may still apply provided that the management costs relating to such investors can be identified and excluded from the exemption.

**22-016** HMRC guidance at VATFIN5350 says:

> "The CJEU judgment in *ATP Pension Services* found that management and administration services that are integral (i.e. specific and essential) to the operation of a qualifying pension fund will fall within the exemption.
>
> Exemption will only apply to charges made by third parties for services provided in connection with the management or administration of the contributions held in the pension fund itself. It will not apply to services provided in connection with any other funds in which the contributions paid into the pension funds may have been invested; although the management of such funds may qualify for exemption on the basis that the fund is a special investment fund in its own right (e.g. an Authorised Unit Trust). The fact that some or all of the costs of managing a fund in which a qualifying pension fund has invested is being charged onto a pension scheme, and therefore borne ultimately by the pension customers, will not bring services supplied in connection with non-qualifying investment funds within the fund management exemption."

## ANTI-AVOIDANCE PROVISIONS

**22-017** In general, one would not expect anti-avoidance provisions to have much application to registered pension schemes. However this should not be taken for granted, especially where any non-standard transactions are contemplated. The income tax settlements provisions and the disguised remuneration provisions are considered here. Both contain exceptions applicable to registered pension schemes.

### The income tax settlement provisions

**22-018** The income tax settlements provisions in ITTOIA 2005 Pt 5 Ch.5 are considered in detail in Ch.25.[30] Subject to the relatively minor exception explained below, these provisions apply equally to registered schemes. ITTOIA 2005 s.627(2)(c) provides that the rule in s.624(1) (i.e. that income which arises under a settlement is treated for income tax purposes as the income of the settlor and of the settlor alone) does not apply to income which consists of a benefit under one of the following pension schemes:

---

[28] VIT45400.
[29] VATA 1994 Sch.9 Group 5 item 9(k), which essentially reflected HMRC's previous practice relating to "special investment funds" as set out in VATFIN5120 and Brief 44 (2014), following the decision of the CJEU in *ATP PensionService A/S v Skatteministeriet* (C-464/12) [2014] S.T.C. 2145. The argument that a defined benefits scheme may be a special investment fund was rejected in *Wheels Common Investment Fund Trustees Ltd v HMRC (C-424/11)*.
[30] Per Lord Hoffmann in *Jones v Garnett* [2007] UKHL 35; [2007] 1 W.L.R. 2030, these are anti-avoidance provisions.

# ANTI-AVOIDANCE PROVISIONS

(a) a registered pension scheme;
(b) a pension scheme established by a government outside the UK for the benefit, or primarily for the benefit, of its employees (or an annuity acquired using funds held for the purposes of such a pension scheme); or
(c) any pension arrangements of any description prescribed by regulations made under the WRPA 1999.

This exception does *not* provide that if a registered pension scheme is a settlement then any investment income arising to the scheme cannot be attributed to the settlor under s.624(1). It provides that the rule in s. 624(1) does not apply to income *which consists of a benefit under* a registered pension scheme. Its meaning becomes clearer when one looks at the predecessor legislation,[31] which provided that "The reference in [what is now s. 624(1)] to a settlement does not include an irrevocable allocation of pension rights by one spouse to the other in accordance with the terms of a relevant statutory scheme (within the meaning of Chapter I of Part XIV)". This was replaced by FA 2000 with provisions substantially the same as they are now. Therefore the circumstances envisaged are that a member of the pension scheme arranges for his pension rights to be transferred or allocated under the registered pension scheme for the benefit of another person. It would also appear to apply to an irrevocable nomination relating to death benefits. The transfer or allocation is the *settlement* and the income arising under *that* settlement is not the income of the registered pension scheme, it is the benefits paid to the other person. This exception is therefore of fairly limited application.

22-019

## Disguised remuneration

The disguised remuneration provisions in ITEPA 2003 Pt 7A are considered in detail in Ch.27. Although they were originally conceived of as anti-avoidance provisions, they apply in principle to any arrangement that is designed to provide rewards to employees. Were it not for the exceptions described below these provisions would apply to all occupational pension schemes.

22-020

### *Section 554E(1)(g)*

Pursuant to s.554E(1)(g), the charging provision in Pt 7A Ch.2 does not apply by reason of a relevant step if the step is taken "under" a registered pension scheme. What does *under* mean in this context? In particular, is it a reference merely to the provision of benefits, or does it also include relevant steps made in exercise of administrative powers, such as to invest scheme funds? It is very likely that this exception must apply to an investment. If this were not the case then Pt 7A would create a tax charge whenever there is an authorised employer loan and the employer is linked with a member (which will usually be the case in the context of small occupational schemes).

22-021

Section 554E(1)(g) clearly applies where the step is taken *by* a registered pension scheme, and it may also apply where a payment is made *to* a registered pension scheme, provided that the step is in some sense *pursuant to* the registered pension scheme. In a pensions context, there are a number of statutory provisions in which a reference to a payment *under* a pension scheme means a payment *pursuant to and in consequence of* the scheme.[32] It would be unusual for Pt 7A to be engaged in respect of a contribution to a registered pension scheme (because steps

22-022

---

[31] In ICTA 1988 s.660A(7).
[32] e.g. IHTA 1984 s.12 provides that "a disposition made by any person is not a transfer of value if it

taken by the employer are generally disregarded for the purposes of Pt 7A), however it may be arguable that the exemption in s.554E(1)(g) applies where an employee requests that a contribution is made to a registered pension scheme and the person making the contribution is someone other than the employer (such as the trustees of an EFRBS, for example).

*Section 554E(1)(h)*

**22-023** Pursuant to s.554E(1)(h), the charging provision in Pt 7A Ch.2 does not apply by reason of a relevant step if the step is taken under an arrangement the sole purpose of which is the making of *payments*[33]:

(a) to which FA 2004 s.161(4) applies in relation to a registered pension scheme (or a registered pension scheme which has been wound up); and
(b) which are authorised in relation to that scheme by FA 2004 s.160(1).

**22-024** The effect of s.554E(1)(h) is not to exempt relevant steps taken by a pension scheme the sole purpose of which is to make payments which would be authorised payments if the scheme were a registered pension scheme. Section 554E(1)(h) can apply only where FA 2004 s.161(4) applies. Section 161(4) applies to any payment or benefit provided under or in connection with an investment acquired using sums or assets held for the purposes of a registered pension scheme.[34] It is aimed primarily at situations where the registered pension scheme has purchased an annuity or scheme pension for a member (i.e. in the member's name) from an insurance company. Its purpose is to ensure that any payments or benefits by the insurance company are within the scope of the unauthorised payments regime. It achieves this by deeming such payments or benefits to have been made by the registered pension scheme. The disguised remuneration provisions do not apply to relevant steps taken by the insurance company as a result of s.554E(1)(h).

**22-025** However, the inclusion of a "sole purpose" test in s.554E(1)(h) may be problematic, because there is no such test in FA 2004 Pt 4. Suppose that an occupational registered pension scheme acquires an interest in an investment vehicle such as a unit trust. Can it be said that the sole purpose of that "arrangement" is the making of payments which are: (a) connected with the investment in the unit trust by the scheme; and (b) authorised by FA 2004 s.160(1)? The main purpose of the unit trust is likely to be to make and manage investments. The payment of money to acquire an investment will not usually be authorised by s.160(1).[35] On its face, the test in s.554E(1)(h) cannot be satisfied even if "arrangement" is interpreted very narrowly, to include only the payments to the registered pension scheme from the unit trust, because a payment to a registered pension scheme can never be an authorised payment. The provisions relating to authorised payments are concerned only with payments *by* a registered pension scheme. If the exception in s.554E(1)(h) does not apply, any investment of the money by the unit trust in accordance with the member's request will be a taxable relevant step. It is most unlikely that this was intended by Parliament.

---

is a contribution *under* a registered pension scheme ...". Similarly, FA 2004 s.246 and Sch.36 para.56 both refer to contributions made "under" a scheme, and it is clear that this is a reference to contributions "pursuant to" the scheme.

[33] "Payment" has the same meaning as in FA 2004 s.161(2), so the analysis in Ch.2 applies here.
[34] See FA 2004 s.161(3). Section 161(3) and (4) are considered in Ch.18.
[35] See Ch.18. A payment to acquire an investment will usually be neither authorised nor unauthorised: it is a "nothing".

## COMPENSATION PAYMENTS FOR LOSS OF PENSION RIGHTS

*Relevant steps following unauthorised payment*

Part 7A Ch.2 does not apply by reason of a relevant step if the subject of the relevant step is a sum of money or asset which has (wholly or partly) arisen or derived (directly or indirectly) from a payment made by a registered pension scheme that was subject to the unauthorised payments charge.[36] If the subject of the relevant step only partly arises or derives from such a payment then the relevant step is treated as being two separate relevant steps (apportioned on a just and reasonable basis) and only the relevant step relating to the sum of money or asset so far as it arises or derives from such a payment.

22-026

*Trusts of death benefits*

Conceivably, the disguised remuneration provisions could apply to trusts of death benefits. Although that trust would not itself be a relevant arrangement (because it will not usually have any employment context), if the registered pension scheme is an occupational scheme then the scheme *will* be a relevant arrangement, and any relevant step taken by the trustees of the death benefit trust will be within the scope of Pt 7A if it is reasonable to suppose that, "in essence" there is some connection (direct or indirect) between the relevant step and the relevant arrangement.[37] ITEPA 2003 s.554A(11) provides that there is such a connection where the relevant step is taken (wholly or partly) in pursuance of an arrangement at one end of a series of arrangements with the relevant arrangement being at the other end. Does the exemption in s.554E(1)(g) apply to a step taken under a discretionary trust that has received death benefits from a registered pension scheme? In some cases the death benefits trust may be found, on a proper analysis, to form part of the registered pension scheme. In other cases, it may be necessary to argue that a step taken by the trust is a step "under" the registered pension scheme.

22-027

## THE CHARGEABLE EVENT REGIME

The chargeable event regime in ITTOIA 2005 Pt 4 Ch.9 (including the provision relating to personal portfolio bonds) does not apply to a policy of insurance which: (a) constitutes a registered pension scheme; or (b) is issued or held in connection with such a scheme.[38] The phrase *in connection with* is extremely broad.[39] It seems quite clear that the policy need not be held for the purposes of the scheme.

22-028

## COMPENSATION PAYMENTS FOR LOSS OF PENSION RIGHTS

Suppose that a UK trading company agrees to contribute £10,000 per annum to a registered pension scheme for the benefit of an employee. The company subsequently wishes to cease these contributions and offers to pay him £50,000 as

22-029

---

[36] The Employment Income Provided Through Third Parties (Excluded Relevant Steps) Regulations 2011 (SI 2011/2696) reg.4.
[37] See Ch.27.
[38] ITTOIA 2005 s.479.
[39] See Ch.17.

compensation.[40] The tax analysis may be summarised as follows:

(a) The company will be able to deduct the £50,000 compensation payment in the calculation of its profits for corporation tax purposes provided that the payment is: (a) a revenue and not a capital payment; and (b) made wholly and exclusively for the purposes of its trade.[41] Contributions to a pension scheme are of course revenue payments,[42] and so a lump sum paid to extinguish a contractual obligation to make contributions is prima facie a revenue payment.[43] If the compensation payment is made to rid the company of a drain on its resources, but in such a way that the employee remains content, and for no other purpose, then that is a trading purpose. In most cases the company can therefore expect to obtain a tax deduction for the compensation payment.

(b) On the basis of the decision of the UT in *E.ON UK Plc v HMRC*,[44] it appeared that payments made solely to compensate the employee for the loss of pension rights were not earnings from the employment, and were therefore not taxable as employment income.[45] However, that was subsequently rejected by the Court of Appeal.[46]

(c) A compensation payment itself is neither a pension nor a lump sum paid "under a registered pension scheme", so it cannot be taxed under ITEPA 2003 Pt 9 Ch.5A or Ch.15A have any application. ITEPA 2003 Pt 9 Ch.3 applies only to pension, which is not defined and so must be given its usual meaning (which plainly does not include a lump sum compensation payment). The fact that the compensation payment is made in substitution for pension benefits should not cause the payment to be characterised as pension income under ITEPA 2003 Pt 9.[47]

(d) The disguised remuneration provisions in ITEPA 2003 Pt 7A do not apply to the compensation payment.[48]

(e) As the employee is still employed at the time of the compensation payment, it will not constitute a "relevant benefit" under an EFRBS for the purposes of ITEPA 2003 s.393B unless it is made in anticipation of retirement or a change in the nature of service.

(f) The compensation payment should not be subject to NIC.[49]

---

[40] Issues relating to auto-enrolment are disregarded for the purposes of this supposition.
[41] See CTA 2009 ss.46(1), 53 and 54(1)(a).
[42] With the possible exception of the very first contribution (*British Insulated and Helsby Cables v Atherton* [1926] A.C. 205; 10 T.C. 155 (although see FA 2004 s.196(2)(a)).
[43] Per Millett J in *Vodafone Cellular Ltd v Shaw* [1997] S.T.C. 734; 69 T.C. 376. Also see *Hancock v General Reversionary and Investment Company Ltd* [1919] 1 K.B. 25.
[44] *E.ON UK Plc v HMRC* [2022] UKUT 196 (TCC).
[45] *Tilley v Wales* [1943] A.C. 386; [1943] 1 All E.R. 280; *Kuehne & Nagel Drinks Logistics Ltd v HMRC* [2012] EWCA Civ 34.
[46] *HMRC v E.ON UK Plc* [2023] EWCA Civ 1383. The Court held that the ratio in *Tilley v Wales* [1943] A.C. 386 was restricted to sums paid in commutation of *accrued* pension rights.
[47] In *Mairs v Haughey* [1994] 1 A.C. 303; [1993] 3 W.L.R. 393, Lord Woolf said "[a] payment made to satisfy a contingent right to a payment derives its character from the nature of the payment which it replaces". However, the House of Lords in *Tilley v Wales* rejected the argument that a commutation payment should be taxable under the same schedule as the pension commuted. In *Kuehne & Nagel*, HMRC did not even attempt to argue that the compensation payments were pension income for the purposes of ITEPA 2003 Pt 9.
[48] Because the payment is by the employer, and the employer is not a relevant third person (see s.554A(7)). Part 7A Ch.3 does not apply because there is no relevant undertaking (see s.554Z16).
[49] In *Kuehne + Nagel* it was common ground that the test to be applied for NIC is, in substance, the same as that under ITEPA 2003 Pt 2 (earnings). Before the FTT, HMRC had argued that the test in

(g) The compensation payment should not be subject to CGT[50] as a result of the exception in TCGA 1992 s.237(a), which applies on the disposal of a right to any allowance, annuity or capital sum payable out of any superannuation fund, or under any superannuation scheme, established solely or mainly for employees and their dependants.

PA 1995 s.91(1)(a) (which provides that where a person is entitled to any benefit under an occupational pension scheme or has a right to a future benefit under such a scheme, the entitlement or right cannot be assigned, commuted or surrendered, and any agreement to do so is unenforceable) should not have any application because the employee is not giving up anything that he already has. He has no more than a mere hope or expectation of continuing to be employed.

**22-030**

---

SSCBA 1992 s.6(1) is broader than that in ITEPA 2003 s.9 but that was rejected and there was no appeal on that point. It follows that payments made solely to compensate employees for the loss of pension rights are not "remuneration or profit derived from an employment" for NIC purposes. This reflects HMRC's position in the NIC manual that compensation payments are not generally subject to NIC (see NIM2010 and NIM02540, albeit in slightly different contexts).

[50] Contractual rights are "assets" for CGT purposes (*Underwood v HMRC* [2009] S.T.C. 239; *Lloyd-Webber v HMRC* [2019] UKFTT 717), including rights under an employment contract (*O'Brien v Benson's Hosiery (Holdings) Ltd* [1980] A.C. 562; [1979] 3 W.L.R. 572), and there is a disposal for CGT purposes where a capital sum is derived from an asset, notwithstanding that no asset is acquired by the person paying the capital sum (TCGA 1992 s.22). This applies in particular to capital sums received in return for forfeiture or surrender of rights, or for refraining from exercising rights (s.22(1)(c)). However, s.22 is expressly subject to any exception in TCGA 1992 (including the exception in s.237).

# PART TWO: UNREGISTERED PENSION SCHEMES

# CHAPTER 23

# Introduction and Overview

## TABLE OF CONTENTS

| | |
|---|---|
| Overview of part two | 23-001 |
| Recent developments | 23-002 |
| Provisions with general application | 23-003 |
| Contributions | 23-003 |
| Scheme investments | 23-004 |
| Benefits | 23-005 |
| Disguised remuneration | 23-006 |
| Inheritance tax | 23-007 |
| Categories of pension scheme | 23-008 |
| Relevant non-UK schemes (RNUKS) | 23-009 |
| Overseas pension schemes and ROPS | 23-010 |
| Qualifying recognised overseas pension schemes (QROPS) | 23-011 |
| Qualifying non-UK pension schemes (QNUPS) | 23-012 |
| Employer-financed retirement benefit schemes (EFRBS) | 23-013 |
| Excepted group life schemes | 23-014 |
| Section 615 funds | 23-015 |
| FURBS | 23-016 |
| Corresponding schemes | 23-017 |
| Overview of current issues | 23-018 |

## OVERVIEW OF PART TWO

Part Two of this book deals with the taxation of unregistered pension schemes and their beneficiaries. **23-001**

### Recent developments

FA 2017 made a number of important changes, primarily in relation to the taxation of non-UK pensions, with effect from 6 April 2017: **23-002**

(a) UK residents are taxed on 100% rather than 90% of any foreign pensions received;
(b) provisions relating to optional remuneration arrangements were inserted into the benefits code;[1]

---

[1] For optional remuneration arrangements, see Ch.24.

(c) a number of amendments were made to the disguised remuneration provisions;[2]
(d) certain lump sums are expressly now taxable under ITEPA 2003 Pt 9, in some cases even where they are paid to non-UK residents;
(e) it is not generally possible to accrue further benefits under s.615 funds;
(f) a new tax charge, called the overseas transfer charge, potentially applies to transfers to QROPS;
(g) the circumstances in which foreign service relief is available under EFRBS is restricted to payments to non-UK residents; and
(h) in relation to RNUKS, the residency condition has been extended from five to ten years for funds which have benefitted from tax relief or are transferred to a QROPS on or after 6 April 2017.

## PROVISIONS WITH GENERAL APPLICATION

### Contributions

**23-003**   Since 6 April 2006 UK income tax relief is available only in respect of contributions by an individual to: (a) a qualifying overseas pension scheme, in circumstances that migrant member relief is available; (b) a corresponding scheme, in circumstances that transitional corresponding relief is available; and (c) a non-UK scheme in circumstances in which relief under a double tax treaty is available. In each case, a UK employer will also usually obtain a tax deduction in respect of such contributions. If tax relief is obtained, the pension scheme will be an RNUKS and the regime in FA 2004 Sch.34 will apply. It is not possible for a member to obtain UK tax relief in respect of contributions to an unregistered pension scheme in any other circumstances. It may be possible for an employer to obtain a tax deduction in respect of contributions to other schemes, but CTA 2009 s.1290 will usually defer the tax deduction until such time as taxable benefits are provided under the scheme.

### Scheme investments

**23-004**   Other than in relation to s.615 funds,[3] there are no special provisions that apply to the income of unregistered pension schemes. Capital gains accruing on a disposal of investments held for the purposes of a s.615 scheme or an overseas pension scheme are exempt from CGT,[4] but there are no other special CGT provisions. If the scheme is established under trusts, the income and gains are taxed in accordance with the usual rules applicable to trusts (which are quite different for UK resident trusts than for non-UK resident trusts). Investment income and gains received by unregistered pension schemes established in the UK are taxed at comparatively high rates, and this is one reason that most unregistered pension schemes are established outside of the UK. The usual rules are considered in Ch.25, as are the following anti-avoidance provisions that frequently need to be considered in practice:

(a) the income tax settlements provisions;
(b) the transfer of assets abroad provisions; and

---

[2] For the disguised remuneration provisions, see Ch.27.
[3] For s.615 funds, see Ch.37.
[4] TCGA 1992 ss.271(1)(c)(ii) and 271(1A).

(c) the CGT settlements provisions (TCGA 1992 ss.86 and 87).

**Benefits**

Pension benefits are typically taxable under ITEPA 2003 Pt 9. Until 6 April 2017, lump sum benefits were frequently not subject to tax under Pt 9, but the position has now changed. If the scheme is an occupational scheme then the EFRBS provisions and the disguised remuneration provisions also require consideration. The taxation of benefits under unregistered pension schemes is explained in Ch.26. 23-005

**Disguised remuneration**

The disguised remuneration provisions in ITEPA 2003 Pt 7A were introduced on 9 December 2010. The original motivation for introducing this new regime was to counter the use of employee benefit trust arrangements (including EFRBS) to provide tax-efficient benefits to employees and former employees. The provisions will prima facie apply to any *relevant step* taken in connection with any sort of funded occupational pension scheme or retirement benefit scheme, however there are a number of exclusions applicable to pension schemes. 23-006

**Inheritance tax**

The inheritance tax provisions as they apply to registered pension schemes are considered in Ch.21, and the same provisions are also generally applicable to QNUPS and s.615 funds. The position in relation to all other unregistered pension schemes is discussed in Ch.28. Much of the background commentary in Ch.21 is also applicable to unregistered pension schemes, and so in order to avoid unnecessary repetition, Ch.28 focuses exclusively on those provisions which are different for unregistered schemes. 23-007

## CATEGORIES OF PENSION SCHEME

Part B of Part Two of this book deals with a number of statutory regimes. It should be emphasised that these regimes are not mutually exclusive (there is significant overlap). For example, a QROPS will be a ROPS, a QNUPS, an RNUKS, and could also be an EFRBS. Section 615 schemes, FURBS and corresponding schemes are now available only on a transitional basis. 23-008

**Relevant non-UK schemes (RNUKS)**

The most significant category of unregistered pension scheme is that of RNUKS. RNUKS are non-UK pension schemes holding funds that have benefitted from UK tax relief in specified circumstances. The UK tax relief may have been provided in respect of contributions to the scheme, or in respect of contributions to a different scheme which were subsequently transferred to the current scheme (or both). To the extent that such schemes hold UK tax-relieved funds, FA 2004 Sch.34 applies a modified version of the main tax charges applicable to registered pension schemes, some of which only apply if *UK residency condition* is satisfied. The provisions do not generally apply to the extent that the scheme holds funds which have not benefitted from UK tax relief (such as investment returns received by the RNUKS). It is not generally advantageous for a scheme to be an RNUKS: the provisions 23-009 potentially expose the scheme and its members to tax charges that would not otherwise apply.

**Overseas pension schemes and ROPS**

**23-010** The provisions relating to overseas pension schemes and ROPS are explained in Ch.31 and Ch.32 respectively.

**Qualifying recognised overseas pension schemes (QROPS)**

**23-011** A QROPS is a ROPS in respect of which the scheme manager has provided certain information and undertakings to HMRC. The principal significance of a scheme being a QROPS is that it can receive a recognised transfer from a registered pension scheme,[5] which is a type of authorised payment. That does not mean that such a transfer will not give rise to any tax charges: if the amount transferred before 6 April 2023 exceeded the member's available lifetime allowance then a 25% lifetime allowance charge applies to the excess, and since April 2017 a transfer to a QROPS may give rise to the overseas payments charge. With effect from 6 April 2024, the overseas transfer charge also arises where the amount transferred by a recognised transfer to a QROPS exceeds the member's available "overseas transfer allowance". If a QROPS receives a recognised transfer (either from a registered pension scheme or another QROPS), it will become an RNUKS and thus many of the registered pension scheme provisions in FA 2004 Pt 4 and ITEPA 2003 Pt 9 apply to it. As a result of the RNUKS provisions applying, the QROPS will only be able to make a recognised transfer to a registered pension scheme or to another QROPS.[6]

**Qualifying non-UK pension schemes (QNUPS)**

**23-012** Favourable inheritance tax treatment is afforded to pension schemes that are QNUPS. There is no wider significance of a pension scheme being a QNUPS; it is not a term used in any income tax or CGT provisions. Most of the requirements which must be satisfied in order for a scheme to be a QNUPS are identical to those relating to overseas pension schemes.

**Employer-financed retirement benefit schemes (EFRBS)**

**23-013** Almost all unregistered pension schemes with any connection to employment are EFRBS, meaning that the provisions in ITEPA 2003 Pt 6 Ch.2 apply to any relevant benefits provided under the scheme. The EFRBS provisions replaced the FURBS and UURBS provisions from 6 April 2006. Any charge under the disguised remuneration provisions has priority over any charge under the EFRBS provisions and so the disguised remuneration provisions have significantly affected the taxation of funded EFRBS and also some unfunded EFRBS.

**Excepted group life schemes**

**23-014** Many employers agree to provide lump sum death in service benefits in respect of their employees, and will typically secure their obligation by purchasing life assurance. If provided under a registered pension scheme, such death in service

---

[5] FA 2004 s.169(1).
[6] For recognised transfers, see Ch.12.

## Section 615 funds

23-015 A s.615 fund is a retirement benefit fund that is designed to provide benefits to former employees in respect of duties performed outside of the UK. The fund must be established in connection with some trade or undertaking carried on wholly or partly outside the UK. Typically, the employer and the trustees will be resident in the UK but this need not be the case. Until 6 April 2017, such funds were, in appropriate circumstances, remarkably tax-efficient. The employer would usually obtain a tax deduction in respect of contributions, but without causing any of the registered pension scheme provisions to apply (unlike RNUKS). Investment income and gains are generally free of tax even where the trustees are resident in the UK, and such funds enjoy the same favourable inheritance tax treatment as registered pension schemes and QNUPS. In addition, benefits may be taken on ceasing to work for the relevant employer at any age (it is not necessary to retire from work altogether), and lump sum benefits received by a UK resident member are not usually subject to tax. Any "benefit accrual" on or after 6 April 2017 is attributed to a different fund (referred to as the "shadow fund" for the actual fund), and the shadow fund is expressly not a s.615 fund. The shadow fund is therefore an EFRBS, and so the provisions described in Ch.35 will apply to it.

## FURBS

23-016 The EFRBS provisions described in Ch.35 have applied to retirement benefit schemes since 6 April 2006. Prior to that date, a quite different tax regime applied to schemes that were usually referred to as either funded unapproved retirement benefits schemes (FURBS) or unfunded unapproved retirement benefits schemes (UURBS). The commentary in Ch.38 is primarily concerned with the former. Since 6 April 2006, all such schemes are subject to the EFRBS provisions, with transitional provisions applying after that date to retain certain aspects of the previous regime. In order to distinguish pre-April 2006 EFRBS from post-April 2006 EFRBS, the former are generally referred to in this book as FURBS.

## Corresponding schemes

23-017 A corresponding scheme is a retirement benefit scheme established prior to 6 April 2006 by a non-UK employer for UK resident but non-UK domiciled employees. Such schemes are unapproved retirement benefit schemes (i.e. FURBS) but they are sufficiently similar to an approved scheme to be afforded special tax treatment. In particular, employer and member contributions could benefit from a tax deduction or tax relief. The regime described in Ch.39 existed until 6 April 2006, with transitional provisions permitting a tax deduction or tax relief in respect of contributions after that date. Any such contributions on or after 6 April 2006 will cause the scheme to become an RNUKS.[7] The regime applicable to corresponding schemes has been replaced by migrant member relief.[8]

---

[7] For RNUKS, see Ch.30.
[8] For migrant member relief, see Ch.24.

## OVERVIEW OF CURRENT ISSUES

**23-018** In February 2023, the CIOT made the following suggestions[9] to rectify certain issues relating to the "relevant lump sum" provision in ITEPA 2003 s.574A:

(a) Limitations to the scope of s.574A which cause the disguised remuneration provisions and the EFRBS provisions to apply instead, and the consequential detrimental impact on foreign service relief. The CIOT believes that the legislation on foreign service relief needs to be amended so that the individuals that would expect to have full grandfathered relief are able to claim the full relief to which the CIOT believes they should properly be entitled in their particular circumstances. The CIOT did not suggest how this may be achieved.

(b) Lack of offset for employee contributions paid out of UK taxed income where s.574A applies to tax the lump sum. This could be addressed by amending s.577A to allow an offset for employee contributions that have been made out of pay that has already been subject to UK tax, in the same way that the law in s.554Z5 and s.395 allows such an offset.

(c) Transitional provisions from Sch.36 FA 2004 not applying to lump sums taxed under ITEPA 2003 s.574A. This could be resolved by the offsets provided for in paras 53–55 Sch.36 FA 2004 being replicated in a new s.567B, which in turn could be included as a permitted deduction under s.567(5).

(d) The exclusion of UK excepted group life policies from relevant lump sum treatment, by adding a new s.574A(1)(a)(iv) ITEPA 2003 covering death in service benefits from UK excepted group life policies. Or, alternatively, to make clear in guidance that the reference to UK EFRBS is intended to include such arrangements.

---

[9] *Employment Taxes and Pensions Tax Regime: Spiring Budget 2023 representations by the Chartered Institute of Taxation* (1 February 2023).

# PART A: PROVISIONS WITH GENERAL APPLICATION

# CHAPTER 24

# Contributions

## TABLE OF CONTENTS

| | |
|---|---|
| Introduction | 24-001 |
| Tax-advantaged arrangements | 24-002 |
| EU law | 24-004 |
| Non-tax advantaged arrangements | 24-005 |
| Relief in respect of relevant migrant members | 24-006 |
| Qualifying overseas pension schemes | 24-007 |
| Relevant migrant members | 24-008 |
| "Resident" in the UK | 24-010 |
| Transferee schemes | 24-011 |
| Replacement schemes | 24-012 |
| Member contributions | 24-013 |
| Relievable pension contributions | 24-014 |
| Relevant UK earnings | 24-015 |
| Annual limit for relief | 24-019 |
| Claiming relief | 24-020 |
| Prohibition on deductions under ITEPA 2003 s.355 | 24-021 |
| Employer contributions | 24-022 |
| CTA 2009 s.1290 | 24-023 |
| Taxable benefits | 24-024 |
| National insurance contributions | 24-025 |
| Transitional corresponding relief | 24-026 |
| Member contributions | 24-027 |
| Transferee schemes | 24-029 |
| Claiming the relief | 24-030 |
| Employer contributions | 24-031 |
| ITEPA 2003 s.308A | 24-034 |
| CTA 2009 s.1290 | 24-035 |
| National insurance contributions | 24-036 |
| Relief under double tax treaties | 24-037 |
| Non-tax advantaged arrangements | 24-038 |
| Employer contributions | 24-038 |
| Rules relating to unpaid remuneration | 24-039 |
| Rules relating to employee benefit contributions | 24-043 |
| "Employee benefit contribution" | 24-044 |
| "Employee benefit scheme" | 24-045 |
| Effect of s.1290 applying | 24-046 |
| "Qualifying benefits" | 24-047 |
| Exceptions | 24-051 |
| Taxation of the employee | 24-053 |
| The earnings charge | 24-053 |

        The benefits code ........................... 24-057
    National insurance contributions ..................... 24-058
        Employer-financed pension only schemes .......... 24-060
    Salary sacrifice ................................. 24-061
        Optional remuneration arrangements .............. 24-063
            Exemptions ............................... 24-066
        Application of certain anti-avoidance provisions .... 24-068
        Inheritance tax ............................. 24-069
        Discretionary bonuses ....................... 24-070
    Annual payments ................................. 24-071
    In specie contributions ........................... 24-072
    Tax on pre-owned assets ......................... 24-073
        Land ..................................... 24-075
        Chattels .................................. 24-079
        Intangible property ......................... 24-082

# INTRODUCTION

**24-001** This chapter is concerned with the taxation of contributions to unregistered pension schemes, and focuses in particular on the circumstances in which tax relief or a tax deduction will be available for contributions by members and their employers. It also considers the circumstances in which contributions by an employer may give rise to a tax charge on the employee.

**Tax-advantaged arrangements**

**24-002** Income tax relief is available in respect of contributions by a scheme member to one of the following schemes. The relief is provided by applying certain provisions in FA 2004 Pt 4 as they apply to contributions to registered pension schemes. The schemes are:

(a) "Qualifying overseas pension schemes" if the member is a "relevant migrant member".
(b) "Corresponding schemes" in circumstances that "transitional corresponding relief" is available.
(c) Non-UK schemes in circumstances in which tax relief under a double tax treaty is available.

**24-003** An employer will also usually obtain an immediate UK tax deduction in respect of contributions to such schemes in the above circumstances. This is achieved primarily by disapplying CTA 2009 s.1290, which would otherwise defer a tax deduction until such time as qualifying benefits are provided under the scheme. As with contributions to registered pension schemes, a tax deduction is not automatic; it must be available on general principles.[1] One therefore starts by determining the

---

[1] The statutory provisions relating to the calculation of trading profits are contained in CTA 2009 Pt 3 (for companies) and ITTOIA 2005 Pt 2 (for unincorporated traders such as sole traders and partnerships). The statutory provisions relating to the calculation of profits are contained in CTA 2009 Pt 16 (for companies) and the relevant part of ITTOIA 2005 (e.g. Pt 3 relates to property income and Ch.2 of Pt 5 relates to intellectual property).

accounting treatment[2] and then considers if any adjustments are required or authorised by law.[3] The obtaining of tax relief causes the pension scheme to become an RNUKS and the provisions in FA 2004 Sch.34 therefore apply.[4]

*EU law*

The requirements which must be satisfied before tax relief or a tax deduction is available are explained below. It is likely that these requirements infringe EU law to the extent that they are more onerous than the requirements under the registered pension scheme regime.[5] Indeed, even where the requirements are not more onerous than the requirements under the registered pension scheme regime they may still infringe EU law. In November 2008, the European Commission formally requested[6] that the UK amend its legislation which denies deductibility of pension contributions paid to pension funds established outside the UK. The Commission objected in particular to the requirement for the overseas scheme to provide information to HMRC. In cases where the foreign pension provider is unwilling or unable to provide the required information, the non-availability of tax relief may in practice oblige the employee to replace his foreign pension scheme with one provided in the UK in order to be eligible for tax relief in the UK. A person resident in another Member State may thus be dissuaded from exercising his right of free movement by taking up employment in the UK. The Commission also considered that the information requirements constitute a costly formality, particularly for foreign pension providers that do not wish to enter the UK market but merely provide services to existing scheme members who have exercised their right of free movement. Consequently, the Commission considered that the legislation was not compatible with EU Treaty arts 39, 43 and 49 and the EEA Agreement arts 28, 31 and 36. However, following HMRC's response the matter was not referred to the ECJ and proceedings against the UK were closed in October 2009.

24-004

**Non-tax advantaged arrangements**

It is not possible for a member to obtain income tax relief in respect of contributions to an unregistered pension scheme other than in the circumstances listed above. It may be possible for an employer to obtain a tax deduction in respect of contributions to other schemes, but CTA 2009 s.1290 will usually defer the tax deduction until such time as taxable benefits are provided under the scheme.

24-005

---

[2] As with contributions to registered pension schemes, the starting point will usually be FRS 105 or FRS 102 (see Ch.6).

[3] CTA 2009 s.46(1).

[4] For RNUKS, see Ch.30.

[5] See *Wielockx v Inspecteur der Directe Belastingen* (C-80/94) [1996] 1 W.L.R. 84; [1995] S.T.C. 876 ECJ; *Rolf Dieter Danner* (C-136/00) [2002] 3 C.M.L.R. 29; *Safir v Skattemyndigheten I Dalarnas Lan* (C-118/96) [1999] Q.B. 451; [1998] P.L.R. 161 ECJ; *Skandia/Ramstedt* (C-422/01) [2003] S.T.C. 1361. Infringement proceedings were taken in February 2003 by the EU against a number of member states for failing to extend the tax advantages granted to pension schemes in their own countries to those established in others. Also see *Commission of the European Communities v Kingdom of Denmark (supported by Kingdom of Sweden)* (C-150/04) [2007] S.T.C. 1392 ECJ.

[6] The request took the form of a reasoned opinion (which is the second step of the infringement procedure of the EU Treaty art.226), meaning that if no satisfactory response was received within two months the Commission would consider referring the matter to the ECJ. EC Case No.2005/2320.

## RELIEF IN RESPECT OF RELEVANT MIGRANT MEMBERS

**24-006**  Tax relief (or a tax deduction) is available in respect of member contributions to "qualifying overseas pension schemes" in respect of "relevant migrant members".[7]

### Qualifying overseas pension schemes

**24-007**  An overseas pension scheme[8] is a "qualifying" overseas pension scheme if[9]:

(a) The scheme manager has notified HMRC that it is an overseas pension scheme and has provided such evidence as is required.

(b) The scheme manager has undertaken to inform HMRC if it ceases to be an overseas pension scheme.

(c) The scheme manager has undertaken to comply with the "benefit crystallisation information requirements", which are a requirement to provide specified information to HMRC on the occurrence of a relevant event.[10] An event is a relevant event if it is a relevant BCE or an occasion that is, or could (depending on its timing) be an occasion on which an individual first flexibly accesses pension rights for the purposes of ss.227B–227F. This information is necessary because the scheme will be an RNUKS and so a modified version of the LS&DB allowance applies to it.[11] The information to be provided is the name and address of the relevant migrant member in respect of whom there has been a relevant BCE in the tax year, and the date, amount and nature of the relevant BCE. The information must be provided by 31 January following the end of the tax year in which the relevant BCE occurs. HMRC can require the information to be provided within 30 days of the issue of the notice if they have reasonable grounds for believing that the scheme: (i) has failed, or may fail, to comply with the benefit crystallisation information requirements; and (ii) such failure is likely to have led, or to lead, to serious prejudice to the proper assessment or collection of tax.[12]

(d) The overseas pension scheme is not excluded from being a qualifying

---

[7] FA 2004 Sch.33. These terms are relevant only to the application of Sch.33; they have no wider significance. These provisions replaced corresponding relief from 6 April 2006, which continues on a transitional basis for members and employers that obtained such relief in the 2005/06 tax year. For corresponding schemes, see Ch.39. The provisions in Sch.33 are less restrictive than corresponding relief in three respects: (a) a relevant migrant member need not be non-UK domiciled; (b) the employer need not be a foreign employer; and (c) there are no restrictions regarding where the scheme is established. Under the corresponding relief provisions, except in "exceptional circumstances" (IR 12 para.15.17), the scheme must be established where the member worked or was resident immediately before moving to the UK or in a jurisdiction in which the employer had an operating presence. In practice, many corresponding schemes were established for career expatriates in jurisdictions in which they had no operating presence and in which no employees had worked or been resident. The provisions are more restrictive in one respect, namely that relief in respect of member contributions cannot be claimed where the employee is not resident in the UK. The draftsman of Sch.33 may have assumed that no UK income tax liability can arise (and thus no relief is possible) unless the employee is resident in the UK. This is not the case (see ITEPA 2003 s.27).

[8] For the meaning of "overseas pension scheme", see Ch.31.

[9] FA 2004 Sch.33 para.5. The scheme manager may give the required notification and the undertakings referred to in (b) and (c) above to HMRC on Form APSS 250. The notification and undertakings must be sent to Pension Schemes Services in Nottingham. See PTM111400.

[10] See The Pension Schemes (Information Requirements—Qualifying Overseas Pension Schemes, Qualifying Recognised Overseas Pensions Schemes and Corresponding Relief) Regulations 2006 (SI 2006/208) reg.2.

[11] See Ch.30.

[12] SI 2006/208 reg.4. The required information can be provided to HMRC on Form APSS 252.

overseas pensions scheme. An overseas pension scheme is so excluded if HMRC has decided, and notified the scheme manager, that: (i) there has been a failure to comply with the benefit crystallisation information requirements and the failure is "significant"; and (ii) by reason of the failure it is not appropriate that relief from tax should be given in respect of contributions under the pension scheme.[13] A failure to comply with the benefit crystallisation information requirements is significant if the amount of information which has not been provided is substantial, or the failure to provide the information is likely to result in serious prejudice to the assessment or collection of tax.[14] The scheme manager may appeal against any decision of HMRC to the FTT.[15]

## Relevant migrant members

A member of an overseas pension scheme is a "relevant migrant member", in relation to any contributions, if he[16]: **24-008**

(a) was not resident in the UK when he first became a member of the pension scheme;
(b) was a member of the pension scheme at the beginning of the period of residence in the UK which includes the time when the contributions are paid[17];
(c) was, immediately before the beginning of that period of residence, entitled to tax relief in respect of contributions paid under the pension scheme under the law of the jurisdiction in which the individual was then resident. Alternatively, he was at any time in the ten years before the beginning of that period of residence entitled to tax relief in respect of contributions paid under the pension scheme under the law of the country or territory in which the individual was then resident.[18] This is a reference to tax relief in respect of member contributions and contributions by the member's employer (i.e. employer contributions are not a taxable benefit of the employee).[19] It is not a reference to a tax deduction that the employer may be entitled to in respect of contributions. The requirement is that the member was "entitled" to such relief in that other jurisdiction; it is irrelevant whether any such tax relief was in fact obtained (because he didn't make any contributions, for example). It is not necessary for the scheme to be established in the overseas country in which the individual was resident and entitled to tax relief prior to becoming resident in the UK. If before coming to the UK he was working in a country which does not relieve pension contributions or does not have any system of personal taxation, he may still be able to satisfy this requirement if he was working in that country for less than ten years; and
(d) has been notified by the scheme manager that information concerning

---

[13] FA 2004 Sch.33 para.5(3).
[14] FA 2004 Sch.33 para.5(4).
[15] See FA 2004 Sch.33 para.6.
[16] FA 2004 Sch.33 para.4.
[17] If an individual first becomes a member of a scheme when non-UK resident (so (a) is satisfied) and then ceases to be a member, and then becomes a member again after arriving in the UK, (b) would not appear to be satisfied.
[18] This alternative is specified in The Pension Schemes (Relevant Migrant Members) Regulations 2006 (SI 2006/212) reg.2.
[19] HMRC have confirmed that (as far as they are aware) there is no country within the EEA which does not meet this requirement (PTM111300).

relevant BCEs[20] relating to the individual and the pension scheme will be given to HMRC.

**24-009**    Merely joining a pension scheme (in the sense of completing the necessary paperwork and being accepted by the trustees or managers) does not in itself make a person a *member* for these purposes. Benefits must have accrued in respect of the member under the scheme or there must be arrangements for the future accrual of benefits under the scheme.[21]

*"Resident" in the UK*

**24-010**    HMRC's position is that the above references to "resident in the UK" and "residence in the UK" are not to be determined in accordance with the statutory residence test, but instead impose a test of whether the individual, as a question of fact, was actually resident in the UK at the relevant time.[22] The better view seems to be that, in relation to 2013/14 and subsequent tax years, whether or not an individual is resident in the UK should be determined in accordance with the statutory residence test.[23] In relation to tax years prior to the 2013/14 tax year, it should be determined in accordance with the common law test of residence, which established the following. To *reside* means "to dwell permanently or for a considerable time, to have one's settled or usual abode, to live in or at a particular place".[24] Physical presence in a particular place does not necessarily amount to residence in that place where, for example, a person's physical presence there is no more than a stop gap measure.[25] In considering whether a person's presence in a particular place amounts to residence there one must consider the amount of time that he spends in that place, the nature of his presence there and his connection with that place.[26] Residence in a place connotes some degree of permanence, some degree of continuity or some expectation of continuity.[27] However, short but regular periods of physical presence may amount to residence, especially if they stem from performance of a continuous obligation (such as business obligations) and the sequence of visits excludes the elements of chance and of occasion.[28] A person may simultaneously reside in more than one place, or in more than one country.[29]

*Transferee schemes*

**24-011**    The requirements in (a), (b) and (c) para.24-008 are extended so that a person is a relevant migrant member in relation to any transferee pension scheme, provided

---

[20] "Relevant BCE" has the same meaning as in ITEPA 2003 s.637S (in relation to the LS&DB allowance), namely: (a) the member becoming entitled to a PCLS, UFPLS, or serious ill-health lump sum; or (b) a person being paid an authorised lump sum death benefit in respect of the member, other than a charity LSDB or a trivial commutation LSDB.
[21] "Member" is defined in FA 2004 s.151. See Ch.2.
[22] PTM111300.
[23] See FA 2013 Sch.45 paras 1(4), 2(1) and 2(5). Subject to any express provision to the contrary, in enactments relating to income tax, a reference to being resident in the UK is a reference to being resident in the UK in accordance with the statutory residence test.
[24] *Levene v IRC* (1928) 13 T.C. 486 at 505; [1928] A.C. 217 at 222.
[25] *Goodwin v Curtis (Inspector of Taxes)* [1998] S.T.C. 475 at 480; 70 T.C. 478 at 510.
[26] *IRC v Zorab* (1926) 11 T.C. 289 at 291.
[27] *Fox v Stirk; Ricketts v Registration Officer for the City of Cambridge* [1970] 3 All E.R. 7 at 13; [1970] 2 Q.B. 463 at 477; *Goodwin v Curtis (Inspector of Taxes)* [1998] S.T.C. 475 at 481; 70 T.C. 478 at 510.
[28] *Lysaght v IRC* (1928) 13 T.C. 511 at 529; [1928] A.C. 234 at 245.
[29] *Levene v IRC* (1928) 13 T.C. 486 at 505; [1928] A.C. 217 at 223.

that the funds are transferred as part of a block transfer on or after 6 April 2006.[30] There is no limit to the number of permitted transfers, provided that each one is a block transfer. A transfer is a block transfer if[31]: (a) it involves the transfer in a single transaction of all the sums and assets held for the purposes of, or representing accrued rights under, the arrangements under the pension scheme from which the transfer is made which relate to the individual and at least one other member of that pension scheme; and (b) either: (i) the individual was not a member of the transferee pension scheme before the transfer; or (ii) he has been a member of that pension scheme for no more than 12 months before the transfer.[32]

*Replacement schemes*

**24-012** Where the requirements in (a)–(d) para.24-008 are met and the pension scheme is closed to new accruals and a replacement scheme is established to provide future benefits to members of the original scheme, and more than one member becomes a member of the replacement scheme, the requirements are deemed to be satisfied by the replacement scheme.

## Member contributions

**24-013** A relevant migrant member of a qualifying overseas pension scheme is entitled to relief under FA 2004 s.188 in respect of "relievable pension contributions" paid during a tax year if the individual[33]:

(a) has relevant UK earnings chargeable to income tax for that year;
(b) is resident in the UK when the contributions are paid[34]; and
(c) has notified the scheme manager of his intention to claim relief under s.188.

*Relievable pension contributions*

**24-014** A "relievable pension contribution" means a contribution by or on behalf of an individual under the pension scheme other than:

(a) any contributions paid after the individual has reached the age of 75;
(b) any contributions which are life assurance premium contributions[35];
(c) any contributions paid by an employer of the individual; and
(d) any contributions made pursuant to an order under certain provisions in PA 2004.[36]

*Relevant UK earnings*

"Relevant UK earnings" means: **24-015**

(a) employment income;

---

[30] The Registered Pension Schemes (Extension of Migrant Member Relief) Regulations 2006 (SI 2006/1957) reg.2. Becoming a member of a transferee scheme when resident in the UK is therefore permitted.
[31] FA 2004 Sch.36 para.22(6).
[32] The Registered Pension Schemes (Block Transfers) (Permitted Membership Period) Regulations 2006 (SI 2006/498) reg.2.
[33] FA 2004 Sch.33 para.1(1).
[34] No such restriction applies in relation to contributions to registered pension schemes, so this may be contrary to EU law. It prejudices individuals who are not resident in the UK but are subject to UK tax on their earnings in respect of duties performed in the UK (see ITEPA 2003 s.27).
[35] See FA 2004 s.195A.
[36] FA 2004 s.188(2), (3) and (3A).

(b) trading income which is chargeable under ITTOIA 2005 Pt 2 and is immediately derived from the carrying on or exercise of a trade, profession or vocation (whether individually or as a partner acting personally in a partnership);
(c) property income which is chargeable under ITTOIA 2005 Pt 3 and is immediately derived from the carrying on of a UK furnished holiday lettings business or an EEA furnished holiday lettings business (whether individually or as a partner acting personally in a partnership); and
(d) patent income, but only if the individual, alone or jointly, devised the invention for which the patent in question was granted.[37]

**24-016** Relevant UK earnings are treated as not being chargeable to income tax if, in accordance with an applicable tax treaty, they are not taxable in the UK.[38]

**24-017** The meaning of "relievable pension contribution" and "relevant UK earnings" is explained in more detail in Ch.6 (as are other relevant concepts such as the meaning of "under the pension scheme" and "paid"). FA 2004 s.195 (which permits tax relief in respect of contributions of eligible shares) also applies for these purposes.[39]

**24-018** The scheme must be a qualifying overseas pension scheme before the individual claims relief on his contributions to it, but it need not be when the contributions are made, provided that it is at that time an overseas pension scheme.[40]

*Annual limit for relief*

**24-019** The maximum amount of relief to which an individual is entitled under FA 2004 s.188(1) for a tax year is the greater of: (a) the amount of the individual's relevant UK earnings which are chargeable to income tax for the tax year; or (b) £3,600.[41]

*Claiming relief*

**24-020** The member must complete a tax return and claim the relief in accordance with FA 2004 s.194 (even if he has already received tax relief under an in-year claim or under a modified PAYE arrangement).[42] Tax relief is not available under the relief at source or net pay arrangement methods.

*Prohibition on deductions under ITEPA 2003 s.355*

**24-021** If the qualifying overseas pension scheme is also a corresponding scheme (see below) then tax relief in respect of contributions may in principle be available under both FA 2004 s.188 and ITEPA 2003 s.355. Where that is the case, no relief is allowed under s.355.[43]

---

[37] FA 2004 s.189(2)–(7).
[38] Where a UK resident individual performs some or all of his duties outside of the UK, a tax treaty between the UK and that other country will frequently provide that earnings relating to those services are taxable in the country in which the services are performed, and not in the UK (where he is resident for tax purposes).
[39] FA 2004 Sch.33 para.1(4).
[40] HMRC agree (PTM111200).
[41] FA 2004 s.190(1) and (2), applied by FA 2004 Sch.33 para.1(2).
[42] FA 2004 Sch.33 para.1(3). See PTM111700 for guidance on completing the tax return, and on in-year claims and modified PAYE arrangements.
[43] FA 2004 Sch.33 para.1(5).

## Employer contributions

FA 2004 ss.196–202 contain provisions relating to the availability of a tax deduction in respect of contributions by employers to registered pension schemes.[44] Sections 196(2)–(5) and 200 are applied to contributions paid by an employer under a qualifying overseas pension scheme in respect of an individual who is a relevant migrant member of the pension scheme in relation to the contributions.[45] These provisions can apply only to an employer that is within the scope of UK income tax or corporation tax. The effect of FA 2004 s.196 is to modify the normal rules for tax deductions in two ways. First, pension contributions are not treated as payments of a capital nature if they otherwise would be. Secondly, if they are deductible, they can be deducted only for the period of account in which the contribution is paid. The primary effect of s.200 appears to be that no deduction is permitted until a contribution is paid.[46] Section 196 relates to contributions "in respect of any individual" and s.200 applies to unfunded and defined benefits arrangements, which do not involve contributions in respect of any particular individual. All of the other provisions in FA 2004 ss.196–202 are *not* applied to contributions to qualifying overseas pension schemes. This means that the following provisions, all of which have the effect of restricting tax deductions in respect of contributions to registered pension schemes, do not apply: (a) s.196A (contributions in connection with EFRBS); (b) ss.196B–196L (employer asset-backed contributions); (c) ss.197 and 198 (spreading of relief); (d) s.199 (deemed contributions); or (e) s.199A (indirect contributions).

24-022

### *CTA 2009 s.1290*

CTA 2009 s.1290 normally defers a tax deduction in respect of employer contributions to employee benefit schemes, but there is an exception in s.1290(4)(c) for contributions under a qualifying overseas pension scheme in respect of an individual who is a relevant migrant member.[47] Notwithstanding the reference to "an individual" it seems unlikely that this is intended to restrict the application of this exception to contributions that are made in respect of a particular individual (as opposed to contributions on a general basis, as is often the case under defined benefits schemes).[48]

24-023

### *Taxable benefits*

No liability to income tax arises in respect of earnings where an employer makes contributions under a qualifying overseas pension scheme in respect of an employee

24-024

---

[44] These provisions do not provide a tax deduction; they modify the usual rules that apply to tax deductions in certain circumstances. See Ch.6 for an explanation of these provisions as they apply to registered pension schemes.
[45] FA 2004 Sch.33 para.2(1).
[46] The precise scope of s.200 is uncertain. See Ch.6.
[47] Identical exceptions are found in ITTOIA 2005 s.866(5)(c) (for non-trades and non-property businesses) and ITTOIA 2005 s.38(4)(c) (trade profits). Section 1290 is explained in more detail below.
[48] cf. FA 2004 s.196(1) discussed in Ch.6. In the case of s.196(1), the words "in respect of any individual" would be otiose unless they were intended to restrict the scope of the previous words. By contrast, the words "in respect of an individual" in CTA 2009 s.1290(4)(c) are necessary in order to give the sentence a proper structure: if they were missed out the provision would still have broadly the same meaning but it would not be grammatically sound.

who is a relevant migrant member of the pension scheme.[49] The benefits code should also not apply to any such contributions.[50]

**National insurance contributions**

24-025   Any such employer contributions are disregarded for NIC purposes.[51]

# TRANSITIONAL CORRESPONDING RELIEF

24-026   Individuals who received corresponding relief in respect of contributions to a corresponding scheme in the 2005/2006 tax year, and employers that obtained a tax deduction in respect of such contributions made between 1 April 2005 and 5 April 2006, may be entitled to receive transitional corresponding relief in respect of contributions made in subsequent tax years. Any such contributions will cause FA 2004 Sch.34 to apply as if the contributions obtained relief as a result of the application of Sch.33 (relief in respect of relevant migrant members), meaning that the scheme will be an RNUKS[52] and so the member payment charges, annual allowance provisions and the LS and LS&DB allowances will apply to it.

**Member contributions**

24-027   If HMRC allowed tax relief for contributions in the 2005/06 tax year in accordance with ITEPA 2003 s.355, the relief will continue to be available for contributions in subsequent years provided that[53]:

(a)   the conditions in s.355 continue to be met[54]; and
(b)   the scheme manager provides prescribed information to HMRC on the individual becoming entitled to a benefit under a pension scheme.[55]

24-028   For tax years subsequent to 2005/06, if the remittance basis applies to the earnings concerned, the relief is limited to the amount of the relevant UK earnings which are chargeable to UK income tax for the tax year.

*Transferee schemes*

24-029   The relief applies, not only to contributions to the relevant scheme, but also to contributions to any transferee pension scheme to which funds are transferred as

---

[49]   ITEPA 2003 s.308A.
[50]   *Templeton v Jacobs* [1996] 1 W.L.R. 1433; *Dextra Accessories Ltd v MacDonald* [2003] EWHC 872 (Ch); [2003] S.T.C. 749; *OCO Ltd v HMRC* [2017] UKFTT 589 at [348]. There is also an express exemption in ITEPA 2003 s.307. See Ch.30 for more detail.
[51]   The Social Security (Contributions) Regulations 2001 (SI 2001/1004) Sch.3 Pt VI para.3(1)(a).
[52]   FA 2004 Sch.36 para.51(3).
[53]   FA 2004 Sch.36 para.51(1) and (2).
[54]   The conditions, as at 6 April 2006, are explained at paras 39-004 and following. The conditions have not changed since that date, except that the requirement that the employee is not domiciled in the UK now (since F(No.2)A 2017) includes a requirement that he is not deemed to be so domiciled for income tax purposes (pursuant to ITA 2007 s.835BA).
[55]   FA 2004 Sch.36 para.51(4). The information to be provided is the name and address of the individual in respect of whom there has been a relevant BCE in the tax year, and the date, amount and nature of the relevant BCE (SI 2006/208 reg.2). The information must be provided by 31 January following the end of the tax year in which the relevant BCE occurs.

part of a block transfer.[56] There is no limit on the number of such transfers provided that each one is a block transfer. A transfer is a block transfer if[57]:

(a) it involves the transfer in a single transaction of all the sums and assets held for the purposes of, or representing accrued rights under, the arrangements under the pension scheme from which the transfer is made which relate to the individual and at least one other member of that pension scheme; and

(b) either the individual was not a member of the pension scheme to which the transfer is made before the transfer or he has been a member of that pension scheme for no more than 12 months before the transfer.[58]

*Claiming the relief*

24-030  An individual can obtain tax relief only by making a claim to HMRC. Tax relief cannot be given under relief at source or net pay arrangements. The process is the same as for claiming relief as a result of the application of Sch.33 (relevant migrant members).[59]

**Employer contributions**

24-031  If HMRC allowed a tax deduction in respect of employer contributions between 1 April 2005 and 5 April 2006 for the benefit of an employee, HMRC may allow contributions in respect of such employees in subsequent years to be treated as if they were relevant migrant member contributions under Sch.33 para.2 if[60]:

(a) HMRC are satisfied that the contribution consists of the expenses of paying any sum or of providing benefits pursuant to a pension scheme which is established outside the UK;

(b) HMRC are satisfied that the scheme corresponds to a registered pension scheme; and

(c) the scheme manager complies with any prescribed benefit crystallisation information requirements imposed on the scheme manager.[61]

24-032  As above, these provisions apply to contributions to the relevant scheme and also to any transferee scheme that has received a block transfer.

24-033  The effect of treating such contributions as if they were relevant migrant member contributions under Sch.33 para.2 is that FA 2004 s.196(2)–(5) and s.200 are applied to the contributions (see above).

*ITEPA 2003 s.308A*

24-034  ITEPA 2003 s.308A (exemption of contributions to overseas pension schemes) also applies to such contributions provided that HMRC allowed the employee to be exempted from income tax under ITEPA 2003 s.390 in relation to contributions made between 6 April 2005 and 5 April 2006.[62]

---

[56] FA 2004 Sch.36 para.51(5).
[57] FA 2004 Sch.36 para.22(6).
[58] SI 2006/498 reg.2.
[59] Guidance is at PTM111700.
[60] The Taxation of Pension Schemes (Transitional Provisions) Order 2006 (SI 2006/572) art.15.
[61] The prescribed benefit crystallisation information requirements imposed on the scheme manager are the same as for qualifying overseas pension schemes: see above.
[62] SI 2006/572 art.17.

*CTA 2009 s.1290*

**24-035** CTA 2009 s.1290 (which defers a tax deduction until qualifying benefits are provided under the scheme) does not apply in respect of contributions which have been given relief under FA 2004 s.196 as applied by Sch.33 para.2 and modified by SI 2006/572 art.15.[63] It is unclear whether this requirement is satisfied by all contributions to corresponding schemes that are treated as if they were relevant migrant member contributions, or whether FA 2004 s.196 must also apply to the contributions. Section 196 only applies to contributions "in respect of any individual"[64] and so does not apply to contributions made on a general basis. The better view seems to be that CTA 2009 s.1290 is disapplied in relation to all contributions to corresponding schemes that are treated as if they were relevant migrant member contributions.

*National insurance contributions*

**24-036** Any such employer contributions are disregarded for NIC purposes.[65]

## RELIEF UNDER DOUBLE TAX TREATIES

**24-037** Contracting states may wish to accommodate individuals working abroad by allowing them and their employers to continue to contribute to a scheme in their home country rather than switching schemes (which can lead to a loss of rights and benefits) or having pension arrangements in a number of different countries (which can lead to practical difficulties).[66] See Ch.29.

## NON-TAX ADVANTAGED ARRANGEMENTS

**Employer contributions**

**24-038** As with contributions to tax-advantaged arrangements, one must start by determining the accounting treatment,[67] and then consider if any adjustments are required or authorised by law.[68] In relation to contributions to an unregistered pension scheme, the following may require or authorise adjustments: (a) the "wholly and exclusively" rule[69]; (b) the rules relating to capital expenditure[70]; (c) the rules relating to unpaid remuneration[71]; and (d) the rules relating to employee benefit contributions.[72] The "wholly and exclusively" rule and the rules relating to capital expenditure are the same as for registered pension schemes, for which see Ch.6.

---

[63] SI 2006/572 art.16.
[64] The reference to "in respect of any individual" is in FA 2004 s.196(1).
[65] 2001/1004 Sch.3 Pt VI para.3(1)(b).
[66] See para.32 of the OECD commentary on art.18 of the Model Treaty.
[67] As above, the starting point will usually be FRS 105 or FRS 102. See Ch.6.
[68] CTA 2009 s.46(1).
[69] CTA 2009 s.54. See Ch.6.
[70] CTA 2009 s.53. See Ch.6.
[71] CTA 2009 s.1288.
[72] CTA 2009 s.1290.

## Rules relating to unpaid remuneration

CTA 2009 s.1288 applies if: (a) an amount is charged in respect of employees' (including office-holders') remuneration in a company's accounts for a period; (b) the amount would, apart from this provision, be deductible in calculating income from any source for corporation tax purposes; and (c) the remuneration is not paid before the end of the period of nine months immediately following the end of the period of account.[73] Where it applies, no deduction is allowed in respect of the contribution except to the extent that such benefits are provided within nine months of the year-end. A deduction will be allowed for any such benefits provided after that time only in the year that it is paid. If the remuneration is never paid then the employer will never obtain a deduction. For these purposes remuneration is paid when it is treated as received by an employee for the purposes of ITEPA 2003 ss.18 or 19 (receipt of money and non-money earnings) or would be so treated if it were not exempt income.

24-039

"Remuneration" means an amount which is or is treated as earnings for the purposes of ITEPA 2003 Pts 2–7. In the present context, this is a reference to earnings under ITEPA 2003 s.62 or benefits which are deemed to be earnings under the benefits code.[74] Benefits from a retirement benefit scheme should not constitute earnings,[75] and the benefits code can only apply to benefits provided in a tax year in which the employee is employed by the relevant employer, so if the scheme is incapable of providing such benefits then these provisions should not have any application.

24-040

Even if a retirement benefits scheme is capable of providing remuneration, it does not necessarily follow that a contribution is charged in respect of employees' remuneration in the company's accounts. If it is unclear whether any remuneration will be provided, it is strongly arguable that the amounts charged in the accounts are not "in respect of" remuneration. In this context, it is notable that the previous version of these provisions[76] expressly included "potential emoluments" and that would not have been necessary if benefits which may or may not constitute remuneration were already caught. In general, it is most unlikely that these provisions could apply to a contribution to a retirement benefits scheme unless there was a clear intention to provide pre-retirement benefits (i.e. remuneration).

24-041

Indeed, given that there is no express exception for contributions under registered pension schemes or s.615 funds, it seems highly unlikely that these provisions were intended to have any application to pension schemes.

24-042

## Rules relating to employee benefit contributions

CTA 2009 s.1290 applies if, in calculating for corporation tax purposes the profits of a corporate employer, a deduction would otherwise be allowable in respect of

24-043

---

[73] For the equivalent provisions applicable in relation to expenses of management of a company's investment business, see CTA 2009 s.1249.
[74] In the context of EFRBS, although the charge under ITEPA 2003 s.394 "counts as employment income", it does not appear to be "treated as earnings" for these purposes.
[75] The distinction between a pension and emoluments (or earnings) was explained by Viscount Dunedin in *Stedeford v Beloe* [1932] A.C. 388; 16 T.C. 505 at 520 (a case concerning a pension payable to the former headmaster of a school) thus: "It [the pension] is not given to him in respect of his office of headmaster, because he no longer holds that office of headmaster. It [the pension] is only given to him because he no longer holds that office of headmaster".
[76] FA 1989 s.43.

employee benefit contributions.[77] The purpose of the provisions is to introduce tax symmetry to such arrangements: the employer should not get a tax deduction until taxable benefits are provided, but when they are provided a deduction should be available.[78] Various attempts have been made to sidestep these provisions[79] and they have accordingly been amended on several occasions.

24-044 **"Employee benefit contribution"** An "employee benefit contribution" is made if, as a result of any act or omission: (a) property is held, or may be used, under an employee benefit scheme; or (b) there is an increase in the total value of property that is so held or may be so used (or a reduction in any liabilities under an employee benefit scheme).[80] The employee benefit contribution is the "act or omission" which leads to the results in (a) or (b). In *NCL Investments Ltd v HMRC*[81] the FTT found that, although these provisions are drawn very widely, the grant of share options by trustees to employees did not constitute an employee benefit contribution because the result of the grant of the options was not that property was held, or may be used, *under* an employee benefit scheme. One would expect a similar analysis to apply in the context of an unfunded promise to provide retirement benefits.

24-045 **"Employee benefit scheme"** An "employee benefit scheme" is a trust, scheme or other arrangement for the benefit of persons who are, or include, present or former employees[82] of the employer, or persons linked[83] with present or former employees of the employer.[84] In addition the term expressly includes an arrangement: (a) concerned with the provision of rewards or recognition or loans in connection with an employee's employment, or former or prospective employment, with an employer; or (b) concerned with the provision of payments or benefits or loans to or in respect of an employee who has some influence over their close company employer,[85] or any other arrangement connected (directly or indirectly) with that arrangement.

24-046 **Effect of s.1290 applying** The effect of s.1290 applying to a contribution is that a tax deduction is not allowed in respect of the contribution except so far as: (a) "qualifying benefits" are provided or *qualifying expenses*[86] are paid, out of the contribution during the period or within nine months from the end of it; or (b) if the making of the contribution is itself the provision of qualifying benefits, the

---

[77] The equivalent income tax provisions are in ITTOIA 2005 s.38. These provisions were originally enacted in FA 2003 Sch.24.
[78] See *Dextra Accessories Ltd v MacDonald* [2002] S.T.C. (S.C.D.) 413; (2002) Sp. C. 331, which led to the introduction of the predecessor of s.1290.
[79] See *Sempra Metals Ltd v HMRC* [2008] S.T.C. (S.C.D.) 1062; *Alway Sheet Metal Ltd v HMRC* [2017] UKFTT 0198; *Scotts Atlantic v HMRC* [2015] UKUT 0066; *OCO Ltd v HMRC* [2017] UKFTT 589; *Landid Property Ltd v HMRC* [2017] UKFTT 0692.
[80] CTA 2009 s.1291(1).
[81] *NCL Investments Ltd v HMRC* [2017] UKFTT 495 at [92]–[100].
[82] "Employee" includes an office holder: s.1296(1).
[83] ITEPA 2003 s.554Z1 (see Ch.27) applies for the purposes of determining when two persons are linked (but as if references to A were to a present or former employee of the employer).
[84] CTA 2009 s.1291(2).
[85] In relation to the close company arrangements, s.1291(4)(a)(ii) refers to s.554AA(1)(b) and (c), but query whether this should read s.554AA(1)(a) and (b). For the disguised remuneration provisions, see Ch.27.
[86] "Qualifying expenses" include any expenses of a scheme manager (i.e. a person who administers an employee benefit scheme, and acting in that capacity) other than the provision of benefits to employees of the employer: (a) which are incurred in operating the employee benefit scheme; and (b) which, if incurred by the employer, would be deductible in calculating for corporation tax purposes the employer's profits of any period of account (CTA 2009 s.1296(1)).

# NON-TAX ADVANTAGED ARRANGEMENTS

contribution is made during the period or within nine months from the end of it. Any amount disallowed is allowed as a deduction for a subsequent period of account so far as: (a) qualifying benefits are provided out of the contributions before the end of the subsequent period; or (b) if the making of the contributions is itself the provision of qualifying benefits, the contributions are made before the end of the subsequent period.

**"Qualifying benefits"** Qualifying benefits are provided if there is a payment of money or a transfer of assets (otherwise than by way of loan) which meets any of the following conditions[87]: 24-047

(a) *Condition A:* the payment or transfer gives rise both to an employment income tax charge[88] and a NIC charge[89];
(b) *Condition B:* the payment or transfer would give rise to both charges if: (i) the duties of the employment in respect of which the payment or transfer was made were performed in the UK; and (ii) the person in respect of whose employment the payment or transfer was made met at all relevant times the conditions as to residence or presence in the UK[90];
(c) *Condition C:* the payment or transfer is made in connection with the termination of the recipient's employment with the employer[91]; or
(d) *Condition D:* the payment or transfer is made under an EFRBS and the payment or transfer: (i) gives rise to an employment income tax charge under ITEPA 2003 Pt 6 Ch.2 or a tax charge under ITEPA 2003 Pt 9[92]; or (ii) is an excluded benefit as defined in ITEPA 2003 s.393B(3).[93]

Qualifying benefits are also provided if a relevant step within the meaning of ITEPA 2003 Pt 7A is taken, and Ch.2 of Pt 7A applies by reason of the step.[94] 24-048

In relation to employee benefit contributions made on or after 1 April 2017, qualifying benefits must be provided within five years of the employee benefit contribution. Where qualifying benefits are provided on or after 1 April 2017, any tax and NIC charges must be paid within 12 months.[95] 24-049

Difficulties may be encountered in practice where employer contributions are paid to an employer-financed pension only scheme. Such a scheme may not be an EFRBS, and, where that is the case, the provision of benefits may well not satisfy any of conditions A to D.[96] 24-050

---

[87] CTA 2009 s.1291.
[88] An "employment income tax charge" is a charge to tax under ITEPA 2003 (whether on the recipient or on someone else).
[89] A "NIC charge" is a liability to pay NIC under SSCBA 1992 s.6 (Class 1 contributions), s.10 (Class 1A contributions) or s.10A (Class 1B contributions).
[90] Such conditions are prescribed under SSCBA 1992 s.1(6).
[91] The meaning of *termination* was considered in *HMRC v Colquhoun* [2010] UKUT 431. The Tribunal noted (at [13]) that in the context of ITEPA 2003 s.401 "an individual's employment will always terminate eventually either by dismissal, death or retirement (on account of age or some other reason)." It follows that "termination" does not simply mean early dismissal; it means ceasing to work for the employer for any reason.
[92] These provisions actually provide that "the payment or transfer gives rise to an employment income tax charge under Chapter 2 of Part 6 of ITEPA 2003 or Part 9 of that Act", but given that it is not possible for an employment income tax charge to arise under ITEPA 2003 Pt 9 this must be a reference to taxable pension income under Pt 9.
[93] For excluded benefits, see Ch.35.
[94] For the disguised remuneration provisions, see Ch.27.
[95] New s.1290(1A), (2A), (2B) and (3A)–(3H), inserted by F(No. 2)A 2017 s.37.
[96] The trustee could deliberately earmark the sum of money before paying it to member, which would

**24-051** **Exceptions** There are a number of important exceptions, including any deduction that is allowable[97]:

(a) for anything given as consideration for goods or services provided in the course of a trade or profession;
(b) for contributions under a registered pension scheme or under a s.615 scheme;
(c) for contributions under a qualifying overseas pension scheme in respect of an individual who is a relevant migrant member of the pension scheme in relation to the contributions; or
(d) for contributions under an accident benefit scheme.[98]

**24-052** The exception in (a) above is of uncertain scope. The rationale may be that consideration given for goods or services will usually be taxable in the hands of the recipient, and so the payee should not be prevented from obtaining an immediate tax deduction. There seems to be no reason that it should not apply to the payment by an employer of premium under a relevant life policy (for example), and so may well have some application to pension schemes.

### Taxation of the employee

*The earnings charge*

**24-053** ITEPA 2003 imposes a charge to income tax on *earnings* from an employment.[99] It is therefore necessary to consider in what circumstances a contribution by an employer to a pension scheme may constitute earnings from an employment.[100] Earnings, in relation to an employment, means[101]:

(a) any salary, wages or fee;
(b) any gratuity or other profit or incidental benefit of any kind obtained by the employee if it is money or money's worth. *Money's worth* means something that is of direct monetary value to the employee, or capable of being converted into money or something of direct monetary value to the employee[102]; or
(c) anything else that constitutes an emolument of the employment.

**24-054** It seems that (a) and (c) above are intended to encompass all contractual or non-contractual but regular employee rewards, whereas (b) includes casual or informal benefits. It is apparent from (b) that the benefit must be obtained *by the employee* and it must be capable of being converted into money.

**24-055** Whether a contribution to a pension scheme by an employer constitutes earn-

---

arguably create a charge under ITEPA 2003 s.554B and so would constitute a qualifying benefit under s.1292(6A). However, this would give rise to a charge to NIC, whereas a pension may not do.

[97] CTA 2009 s.1290(4).
[98] An accident benefit scheme is an employee benefit scheme under which benefits may be provided only by reason of a person's disablement, or death, caused by an accident occurring during the person's service as an employee of the employer (CTA 2009 s.1296(1)).
[99] ITEPA 2003 ss.1(1)(a), 6(1)(a), 7(3) and 9(2).
[100] ITEPA 2003 ss.308 and 308A respectively exempt from the earnings charge contributions to registered pension schemes and contributions in respect of relevant migrant members of qualifying overseas pension schemes.
[101] ITEPA 2003 s.62(2) and (3).
[102] This principle was originally established in *Tennant v Smith* [1892] A.C. 150. In *Abbott v Philbin* [1961] A.C. 352 (at 378) Lord Radcliffe explained the principle in *Tennant v Smith* thus: "if [the benefits] are by their nature incapable of being turned into money by the recipient they are not taxable, even though they are in any ordinary sense of the word valuable to him".

ings from an employment depends on the facts. Earnings are *from an employment* if they are paid in return for acting as or being an employee.[103] A contribution to a pension scheme will not constitute earnings from an employment provided that each of the following four conditions is satisfied:

(a) The contribution to the scheme must not, on a true construction of the facts, be a payment out of the employee's salary.[104] Salary to which an employee is entitled does not cease to be his taxable income merely because he has committed himself to applying it in a particular way such that he is prevented from its immediate, or indeed any, enjoyment.[105]

(b) At the time of the contribution, the employee does not have a vested interest in the assets of the scheme. This condition will be satisfied where the employee's interest is contingent upon the occurrence of some event, such as the attainment of a specified age.[106] A contingency is not strictly required if the contribution is casual/informal and the employee does not receive money's worth.[107]

(c) The contribution does not discharge a pecuniary liability of the employee.[108] This condition will not be satisfied, for example, where the employee commits personally to making the contributions which are in fact made by his employer.[109]

(d) The employee does not have the option to receive some other taxable benefit (such as money) instead of the employer making a contribution.[110] This is particularly relevant in a salary sacrifice context.

Employer contributions to pension schemes will frequently meet the above conditions, and where that is the case an earnings charge in respect of such contributions will not arise.[111] Indeed, given that an earnings charge in respect of a contribution to a pension scheme would give rise to double taxation (on the contribution and then again on the receipt of the pension income under ITEPA 2003 Pt 9), it is most unlikely that an earnings charge will be found to apply.[112] The possibility of double taxation was considered to be an important factor by the Supreme Court in *HMRC*

**24-056**

---

[103] Per Lord Radcliffe in *Hochstrasser v Mayes* [1960] A.C. 376 at pp.391–392. In other words, payments as a reward or remuneration for the exertions of the employee (per Lord Hodge in *RFC 2012 Plc v Advocate General for Scotland* [2017] UKSC 45 at [35] and [58]).

[104] As in *Smyth v Stretton* (1904) 5 T.C. 36. In that case the employee's salaries were increased by £35 and required to become members of a retirement scheme and the £35 would be paid to the trustees of the retirement fund.

[105] See *Hudson v Gribble* 4 T.C. 522.

[106] *Edwards v Roberts* (1935) 19 T.C. 618; *HMRC v Forde and McHugh* [2014] UKSC 14. In the latter case the contingency was relatively weak, because the member controlled the employer and so he had the power to change the retirement age.

[107] Rights under an occupational pension scheme that has its main administration in the UK or outside the EEA are not assignable (PA 1995 s.91), so they may not constitute money's worth. This will also usually be the case in other jurisdictions, including in relation to non-occupational schemes.

[108] Per Viscount Cave LC in *Hartland v Diggines* [1926] A.C. 289.

[109] Prior to being amended by FA 2004, ITEPA 2003 s.308 was limited to employer contributions "under approved personal pension arrangements made by the employee", where employer contributions would frequently discharge a pecuniary liability of the employee.

[110] Per Lord Reid in *Heaton v Bell* [1970] A.C. 728.

[111] Prior to 6 April 2006, ITEPA 2003 s.386 imposed an income tax charge on payments by employers to non-approved retirement benefit schemes, and the fact that such a provision was considered necessary strongly supports the view that such contributions are not generally taxable. HMRC accept this at TSEM5300: "From 6 April 2006 there is no [earnings] charge on contributions to an EFRBS made by an employer".

[112] This presumption against double taxation was emphasised in *HMRC v Forde and McHugh Ltd* [2014] UKSC 14.

*v Forde and McHugh*.[113] Although it is in some respects difficult to reconcile *Forde and McHugh* with the more recent decision of the Supreme Court in *RFC 2012 Plc v Advocate General for Scotland*,[114] it is clear that a payment which does not give the intended recipient an immediate vested beneficial interest but only a contingent interest is not within the charge to tax as earnings.[115] This of course will typically be the case where a contribution is made to a retirement benefits scheme.

*The benefits code*

**24-057** ITEPA 2003 Pt 3 Ch.10 (the residual head of the benefits code) applies to *employment-related benefits*. These are benefits (other than excluded benefits) which are provided in a tax year for an employee, or for a member of an employee's family or household, by reason of the employment.[116] A contribution to a retirement benefit scheme will not usually involve the provision of a benefit for the purposes of the benefits code.[117] Notwithstanding this, ITEPA 2003 s.307 provides that no liability to income tax arises under Ch.10 of Pt 3 in respect of provision made by an employee's employer under a registered pension scheme or otherwise for a retirement or death benefit. For these purposes, "retirement or death benefit" is defined as a pension, annuity, lump sum, gratuity or other similar benefit which will be paid or given to the employee or a member of the employee's family or household in the event of the employee's retirement or death. This exemption does not however apply to provision made for insuring against the risk that a retirement or death benefit under an EFRBS cannot be paid or given because of the employer's insolvency.[118]

# NATIONAL INSURANCE CONTRIBUTIONS

**24-058** In *HMRC v Forde and McHugh Ltd*[119] HMRC argued that a contribution to a FURBS by an employer in respect of its sole member amounted to "earnings paid" for the benefit of the employee and was therefore subject to Class 1 NIC. If HMRC were correct then "earnings" would be paid to an earner both when contributions are made to such a scheme and also when payments are made from the scheme. Lord Hodge considered this stance to be remarkable and the fact that double counting would be avoided in this case by an exception did not stop it from being so. The Supreme Court rejected HMRC's argument for three reasons:

(a) it is counter-intuitive that a person would earn remuneration both when his

---

[113] *HMRC v Forde and McHugh* [2014] UKSC 14. This was a decision concerning earnings for NIC purposes, which has a wider meaning than for income tax purposes.
[114] *RFC 2012 Plc v Advocate General for Scotland* [2017] UKSC 45. The judgment has been criticised (see e.g. Mulley [2017] C.L.J. 502; Goldberg and Doran [2017] *Tax Journal*, issue 1362, 8; Blackwell [2017] B.T.R. 4, 398), largely on the basis that it fails to address the relevant question. The Supreme Court held that remuneration paid to a third party is taxable as earnings, which is well established. The question that the court was required to answer was: did certain payments to an employee trust constitute earnings?
[115] See [41] and [47] in particular.
[116] ITEPA 2003 s.201.
[117] *Templeton v Jacobs* [1996] 1 W.L.R. 1433; *Dextra Accessories Ltd v MacDonald* [2003] EWHC 872 (Ch); [2003] S.T.C. 749; *OCO Ltd v HMRC* [2017] UKFTT 589 at [348]. See Ch.30 for more detail.
[118] The rationale for excluding the cost of insurance from the exemption appears to be that where an employer promises to provide a benefit and also insures against the risk of insolvency, the insurance is an additional and immediate benefit and so there is no double taxation when the retirement or death benefits are subsequently provided.
[119] *HMRC v Forde and McHugh Ltd* [2014] UKSC 14.

employer paid money into a trust to create a fund for his benefit and again when at a later date that trust fund was paid out to him. Giving the words their ordinary meaning, it is clear that a retired earner receives "earnings" in respect of his employment in the form of deferred remuneration when he receives his pension;

(b) SSCBA 1992 s.6(1) is looking at what the employee receives and HMRC's argument was sustainable if one looks only at what the employer paid; and

(c) the employee's interest under the fund was contingent on him attaining a specified age and if he had died before that time then the fund would be paid to someone else. So if the contribution is assessable the amount assessed must be the value of the employee's contingent rights under the trust fund at the time of the contribution. That calculation would not be a simple exercise, and HMRC's approach failed to address this.

In the course of making the first point above, Lord Hodge said that he would characterise the payment from a pension scheme as "deferred earnings". This is a reference to the NIC position only; it is well settled that a payment from a pension scheme will not normally constitute earnings for income tax purposes.[120] In the lower courts much of the argument had focussed on whether earnings for NIC purposes is different to emoluments (now *earnings*) for income tax purposes. That argument was not advanced in the Supreme Court, but Lord Hodge took the opportunity to confirm that they are different. It was accepted by the parties that earnings for NIC purposes is broader and the Supreme Court appears to have agreed with this. It therefore seems likely that where a contribution does give rise to an earnings charge (for the reasons set out above), it will also be subject to NIC.[121]

**Employer-financed pension only schemes**

The NIC provisions introduce the concept of an "employer-financed pension only scheme". This is a scheme: (a) financed by payments made by or on behalf of the employer; and (b) providing only a pension. The provisions expressly state that such a scheme is not an EFRBS on the basis that a pension is not a relevant benefit (as defined in ITEPA 2003 s.393B). That does not appear to be strictly correct: a pension *may* be a relevant benefit if it is not charged to tax under ITEPA 2003 Pt 9.[122] In any event, a payment by way of an employer's contribution to an employer-financed pension only scheme is expressly disregarded for NIC purposes.[123]

# SALARY SACRIFICE

A salary sacrifice arrangement is an arrangement under which the employee and employer agree that henceforth the employee will receive a reduced salary, but with some other additional benefit.[124] It is therefore more accurate to describe the arrangement as a *variation* of the rights of the employee. Such an arrangement can

24-059

24-060

24-061

---

[120] *Wales v Tilley* [1943] A.C. 386.
[121] e.g. it is clear from *R. v Department of Social Security Ex p. Overdrive Credit Card Ltd* [1991] 1 W.L.R. 635 that a contribution that discharges a pecuniary liability of the employee constitutes earnings for NIC purposes.
[122] See ITEPA 2003 s.393B(2)(a). Curiously, HMRC explain that "for NICs purposes only, the meaning of "EFRBS" does not include an employer-financed pension only scheme" (NIM02756).
[123] SI 2001/1004 Sch.3 Pt VI para.9.
[124] The reduction in salary and the value of the other benefit need not be equal, but some benefit must be received by the employee. In *Reed Employment Plc v HMRC* [2012] UKFTT 28 (TC) at [225]

only be effective for tax purposes in relation to salary which has not been earned at the time of the variation; otherwise the employee is simply directing the employer to pay his earnings to a third party.[125] In a pensions context, the additional benefit is usually a contribution by the employer to a pension scheme for the employee's benefit or an unfunded promise by the employer to provide pension benefits in the future. If the benefit does not give rise to an income tax charge (as earnings or a benefit in kind) and/or NIC then it will be more tax-efficient for the employee to do this when compared to receiving taxable earnings and then making a contribution to a pension scheme himself (especially if he will not obtain tax relief will be available in respect of such a contribution). The employer saves 13.8% employer's NIC but, unless the scheme is one of the tax-advantaged schemes mentioned above, a tax deduction will not usually be available until such time as taxable benefits are provided from the scheme.

**24-062** In order to achieve this saving, the contributions must not constitute earnings of the employee (see above). So, for example, if there is an arrangement under which the benefit can be unilaterally surrendered by the employee and the salary restored then he will be taxed on the salary foregone.[126] An understanding that the salary will be restored if the employer and the employee agree at some future date should not present any problems. If the employer's contribution discharges a contractual obligation of the employee, the contribution will constitute earnings of the employee for tax and NIC purposes.[127]

**Optional remuneration arrangements**

**24-063** FA 2017 inserted provisions relating to optional remuneration arrangements into the benefits code in ITEPA 2003. The provisions apply only where the benefit does not otherwise give rise to a charge to earnings under general principles. If the provisions apply, the employee is deemed to receive earnings equal to the "amount forgone", unless the cash equivalent of the benefit under the benefits code is greater, in which case the benefits code will continue to apply.[128] The provisions apply for both income tax and NIC purposes.

**24-064** A benefit provided for an employee is provided under optional remuneration arrangements insofar as it is provided under:

(a) arrangements under which, in return for the benefit, the employee gives up the right (or a future right) to receive an amount of taxable earnings ("type A arrangements"); or

(b) arrangements (other than type A arrangements) under which the employee agrees to be provided with the benefit rather than an amount of taxable earnings ("type B arrangements").[129]

So, type A arrangements are traditional salary sacrifice arrangements, and type B

---

the Tribunal stated that: "In our view a salary sacrifice implies reciprocity: the employee gives up a portion of his or her earnings, even if the portion is variable, in exchange for an identified benefit provided by the employer. Reed, however, did not provide any benefit at all ...". Normally this will not create any difficulties, but if the scheme is essentially discretionary it may be necessary for the member to receive some sort of consideration for the sacrifice.

[125] As in *Smyth v Stretton* (1904) 5 T.C. 36.
[126] See *Heaton v Bell* [1970] A.C. 728.
[127] *Nicoll v Austin* (1935) 19 T.C. 531; and see *ITC v Sutherland 1952*. It is understood that HMRC are prepared to confirm the position in writing where the sacrifice relates to a contribution to a bona fide pension scheme.
[128] See e.g. ITEPA 2003 s.203A(2).
[129] ITEPA 2003 s.69A.

arrangements are where the employee does not *sacrifice* a prior entitlement. As the name suggests, both types of arrangement require that the remuneration arrangement is "optional" in the sense that the employee is given some sort of choice.

The "amount foregone" means the amount of earnings given up (under type A arrangements) or the amount of earnings that the employee would have received if he had not agreed to receive the benefit (under type B arrangement). In relation to a benefit provided for an employee partly under type A arrangements and partly under type B arrangements, the amount foregone is the amounts foregone under the arrangements of each type.[130]

24-065

*Exemptions*

The only exemptions under the benefits code that apply to benefits provided under optional remuneration arrangements are those which are "special case" exemptions and "excluded" exemptions.[131] The only excluded exemptions that are relevant to unregistered pension schemes are: (a) ITEPA 2003 s.307, to the extent that it relates to provision made for retirement benefits (but *not* death benefits); and (b) ITEPA 2003 s.308A (exemption of contributions to qualifying overseas pension schemes).

24-066

In the context of a contribution to a pension scheme, the relevant part of the benefits code is ITEPA 2003 s.203(1). New s.203A provides that where an employment-related benefit is provided pursuant to optional remuneration arrangements: (a) the relevant amount is treated as earnings from the employment; and (b) s.203(1) does not apply. To find the relevant amount, one must determine which (if any) is the greater of the cost of the employment-related benefit, and the amount foregone with respect to the benefit (the amount foregone is explained above). If the cost of the employment-related benefit is greater than or equal to the amount foregone, the relevant amount is the cash equivalent. Otherwise, the relevant amount is the amount foregone with respect to the employment-related benefit, less any part of the cost of the benefit made good by the employee to the person providing the benefit on or before 6 July following the tax year in which it is provided.

24-067

**Application of certain anti-avoidance provisions**

The income tax settlement provisions will not usually apply to a contribution by an employer because a company cannot be a settlor.[132] However, in the context of a salary sacrifice arrangement, the contributions are provided indirectly by the employee. In addition, if the transfer of assets abroad provisions apply, the employee rather than the employer will be the transferor in a salary sacrifice context.[133]

24-068

**Inheritance tax**

In the context of unregistered pension schemes, it is not uncommon for a member to sacrifice his salary in return for a benefit of a lower market value (such as where the trustees have some discretion, for example). This should not involve a transfer of value by the employee for two reasons. First, the member's estate is not reduced

24-069

---

[130] ITEPA 2003 s.69B.
[131] ITEPA 2003 s.228A.
[132] ITTOIA 2005 s.627(4)(b). The income tax settlement provisions are explained in Ch.25.
[133] The transfer of assets abroad provisions are explained in Ch.25.

in value as a result of the decision to sacrifice his salary.[134] By definition, he has not earned that salary at the time he agrees to sacrifice it; there is simply an expectation that his estate will be worth less in the future as a result of the sacrifice, and that does not give rise to a transfer of value. Secondly, if the employee expects that he will receive benefits from the scheme then, even if there was a reduction in the value of his estate, it is not intended to be gratuitous.[135]

### Discretionary bonuses

**24-070** A contribution to a pension scheme at the discretion of the employer (such as a discretionary bonus payment) does not involve a salary sacrifice. It also does not involve an optional remuneration arrangement because the remuneration arrangement must be optional in the sense that there is some sort of choice. In most cases discretionary bonuses are less problematic than salary sacrifice arrangements from a tax perspective.

## ANNUAL PAYMENTS

**24-071** If the trustee is contractually entitled to receive contributions from a sponsoring employer or member, the contributions could conceivably be taxed as income of the trustees under ITTOIA 2005 Pt 5 Ch.7 or Ch.8.[136] This should not be the case where the trustees are not a party to any agreement to make contributions. In addition, a contribution will not usually constitute "pure income profit" because the trustee is obliged to use the contribution to provide benefits to the members, especially if the contribution can be viewed as the purchase of benefits. This depends to an extent on the drafting of the scheme, but it is less likely to be the case where benefits are discretionary, and discretionary benefits are more common under an unregistered pension scheme than under a registered pension scheme.

## IN SPECIE CONTRIBUTIONS

**24-072** In principle it should make no difference to the tax consequences whether cash or an asset is contributed. In relation to CGT or chargeable gains and SDLT, the analysis is the same as for registered pension schemes.[137]

## TAX ON PRE-OWNED ASSETS

**24-073** FA 2004 Sch.15 imposes an income tax charge where (broadly): (a) an individual occupies land and either the disposal condition or the contribution condition is met; (b) an individual is in possession of or has the use of a chattel and either the disposal condition or the contribution condition is met; or (c) an individual settles any property other than land or chattels (referred to as intangible property) and the set-

---

[134] See IHTA 1984 s.3(1).
[135] See IHTA 1984 s.10. IHTA 1984 s.21 may also be relevant in appropriate circumstances. Provided that the member does not have a right to revert to the pre-salary sacrifice situation, he cannot be said to have a right which he omits to exercise (see IHTA 1984 s.3(3)).
[136] These provisions are considered in more detail at Ch.6.
[137] See Ch.6.

tlement is such that any income arising from that intangible property would be treated as the income of the settlor by virtue of ITTOIA 2005 s.624.

There is an important exception in Sch.15 para.11(1), which provides that these provisions do not apply to a person at a time when his "estate" for the purposes of IHTA 1984 includes:

24-074

(a) the relevant property; or
(b) other property:
   (i) which derives its value from the relevant property; and
   (ii) whose value, so far as attributable to the relevant property, is not substantially less than the value of the relevant property.

In most cases, where these provisions would otherwise apply, one would expect the value of a member's rights under a pension scheme to derive their value from the relevant property and for the value of the rights to not be substantially less than the value of the relevant property. However, although this may well be the case where the member is in good health, it may be otherwise if at any time it appears that he will not be in a position to take the full retirement benefits.

**Land**

"Occupation" is not defined for these purposes. HMRC explain that[138]:

24-075

"The meaning of the word 'occupies' should be taken quite widely. It goes wider than the [individual] being physically present at the property concerned. Case law suggests that the word 'occupy' requires some element of control. So a visitor may not be in occupation (even someone who stays for an extended period of time due to illness) but someone who has a key and can freely enter and leave premises as they please is more likely to be in occupation; even if they are absent for significant periods. It does not necessarily mean the place you reside which implies a greater level of permanence so a lower threshold is required to satisfy the occupation condition.

A person may be in occupation if they are storing possessions in a property—but only if they also had the right of access to the property to use it as they wished—or if they were the only person with the means of access and used the property from time to time. Storing possessions on its own is not occupation, but may be evidence of occupation. The chargeable person would not be regarded as occupying a property from which they were receiving rental payments from the person(s) actually in occupation."

Does an individual occupy an office building or other commercial property leased to his employer? If so, these provisions could have extremely wide application (including to registered pension schemes). The better view seems to be that this will not constitute "occupation" for these purposes.

24-076

The disposal condition is that[139]:

24-077

(a) at any time after 17 March 1986 the individual owned an interest: (i) in the land; or (ii) in other property the proceeds of the disposal of which were (directly or indirectly) applied by another person towards the acquisition of an interest in the land; and
(b) the individual has disposed of all, or part of, his interest in the land or the other property, otherwise than by an excluded transaction.

A sale for market value from the member to the trustees will not meet the disposal condition: arm's length sales are excluded transactions. It follows that the disposal condition will usually only be satisfied if land is contributed by the member to the scheme *in specie* (including where there is a sale at an undervalue).

---

[138] IHTM44003.
[139] FA 2004 Sch.15 para.3(2)(a) and (b).

**24-078** The contribution condition is that at any time after 17 March 1986 the individual has directly or indirectly provided, otherwise than by an excluded transaction, any of the consideration given by another person for the acquisition of an interest in the land or an interest in any other property the proceeds of the disposal of which were (directly or indirectly) applied by another person towards the acquisition of an interest in the land.[140] So if the member contributes cash to the pension scheme and the scheme then buys land from him and he occupies it, the contribution condition may be satisfied. If there is a gap of at least seven years between the contribution and the occupation then it will be an excluded transaction provided that the contribution(s) constituted an "outright gift of money". One would not normally consider a contribution by the member to be a gift.

**Chattels**

**24-079** "Possession" and "has the use of" are not defined and so bear their normal meaning.

**24-080** The disposal condition is that[141]:

(a) at any time after 17 March 1986 the individual had (whether alone or jointly with others) owned the chattel or any other property the proceeds of the disposal of which were (directly or indirectly) applied by another person towards the acquisition of the chattel; and

(b) the individual disposed of all or part of his interest in the chattel or other property otherwise than by an excluded transaction. Arm's length sales are excluded transactions, so a sale for market value from the member to the trustees will not meet the disposal condition.

**24-081** The contribution condition is that at any time after 17 March 1986 the individual had directly or indirectly provided, otherwise than by an excluded transaction, any of the consideration given by another person for the acquisition of the chattel or any other property the proceeds of the disposal of which were (directly or indirectly) applied by another person towards the acquisition of the chattel.[142] This gives rise to similar issues as for land.

**Intangible property**

**24-082** Schedule 15 applies where an individual settles intangible property and the settlement is such that any income arising from that intangible property would be treated as the income of the settlor by virtue of ITTOIA 2005 s.624.[143] ITTOIA 2005 s.624 will not usually apply to a pension scheme.[144]

**24-083** In relation to insurance-based pension policies, HMRC consider that the pension and other lifetime benefits for the member are either unsettled property or held in a trust separate from that on which the death benefits are held.[145] They say that "both parts can be treated as mutually exclusive and therefore provided the scheme member could not benefit from the trusts governing the death benefits, a POA charge will not arise". In circumstances other than where a pension policy is settled, it will often not be the case that the lifetime benefits under the pension scheme

---

[140] FA 2004 Sch.15 para.3(3).
[141] FA 2004 Sch.15 para.6(2).
[142] FA 2004 Sch.15 para.6(3).
[143] FA 2004 Sch.15 para.8.
[144] These provisions are explained in Ch.25.
[145] IHTM44114.

could be described as being held on bare trust for the settlor (the intangible property is the scheme property, not a policy giving the member a right to receive a pension). It will also usually be difficult to see how analysing the member's fund as two separate trusts will assist, as it suggests that the charge would still apply to the valuable trust of lifetime benefits. What HMRC are presumably saying here is that they will treat such arrangements in the same way as carve-outs for reservation of benefit purposes[146] so that there is no charge under Sch.15 on the lifetime benefits retained and no charge in respect of the death benefits as the member cannot benefit from them.[147]

---

[146] For the reservation of benefit provisions, see Ch.21.
[147] In relation to registered pension schemes, HMRC consider that no charge will arise under these provisions (see IHTM44114). That does not appear to be a concession, so presumably the same analysis should apply to unregistered schemes.

# CHAPTER 25

# Scheme Investments

## TABLE OF CONTENTS

| | |
|---|---|
| Introduction | 25-001 |
| UK schemes | 25-002 |
|     Income tax | 25-003 |
|         The taxation of trusts | 25-003 |
|         Contract-based schemes | 25-006 |
|     Capital gains tax | 25-007 |
| Non-UK schemes | 25-009 |
|     Income tax | 25-010 |
|     Capital gains tax | 25-015 |
|         Overseas pension schemes | 25-016 |
| The income tax settlements provisions | 25-017 |
|     Background | 25-017 |
|         Non-domiciled settlors | 25-020 |
|     "Settlement" | 25-022 |
|         "Bounty" | 25-025 |
|     "Settlor" | 25-027 |
|     "Income arises under the settlement" | 25-029 |
|     The income arises from property in which the settlor has an interest | 25-032 |
|         "Property in which the settlor has an interest" | 25-034 |
|         Exception for outright gifts between spouses or civil partners | 25-036 |
|         Exception for benefits under certain pension schemes | 25-038 |
|         Exception where settlor is not an individual | 25-041 |
|     Trust income paid for the benefit of a minor child | 25-043 |
|     Capital sum is paid to the settlor or spouse | 25-045 |
|     The taxation of the settlor | 25-049 |
| The transfer of assets abroad provisions | 25-050 |
|     Relevant transfers | 25-052 |
|         Associated operations | 25-055 |
|     Transferors with power to enjoy | 25-058 |
|         Power to enjoy | 25-059 |
|         Transferors and quasi transferors | 25-061 |
|         Application to retirement benefit schemes | 25-062 |
|     Transferors in receipt of capital sums | 25-063 |
|     Persons who receive a benefit | 25-066 |
|     Non-domiciled transferors | 25-068 |
|     Exemptions | 25-071 |
|     The "no tax avoidance purpose" exemption | 25-072 |

|    |    |
|---|---|
| The "commercial transaction" exemption | 25-081 |
| The "genuine transaction" exemption | 25-084 |
| The CGT settlements provisions | 25-089 |
| TCGA 1992 s.86 | 25-092 |
| "Settlement" and "settlor" | 25-093 |
| Corporate settlors | 25-094 |
| The settlor has an interest in the settlement | 25-096 |
| The effect of s.86(1) applying | 25-100 |
| TCGA 1992 s.87 | 25-102 |
| Settlement | 25-104 |
| Capital payment | 25-105 |
| The s.1(3) amount | 25-106 |
| Matching | 25-107 |
| Non-UK beneficiaries | 25-108 |
| The supplementary charge | 25-111 |

# INTRODUCTION

**25-001** Other than in relation to s.615 funds,[1] there are no special provisions relating to the income of unregistered pension schemes. Capital gains accruing on a disposal of investments held for the purposes of a s.615 scheme or an overseas pension scheme are exempt from CGT,[2] but there are no other special CGT provisions applicable specifically to pension schemes. If the scheme is established under trusts, the income and gains are taxable in accordance with the usual provisions applicable to trusts. In this chapter the usual rules are outlined and then the following anti-avoidance provisions are considered in greater detail:

(a) the income tax settlements provisions;
(b) the transfer of assets abroad provisions; and
(c) the CGT settlements provisions (TCGA 1992 ss.86 and 87).

# UK SCHEMES

**25-002** In the context of a retirement benefit scheme, the trustee or manager of which is resident in the UK, the taxation aspects are quite different depending on the legal structure of the scheme, and in particular whether the scheme is established under trusts or not.

**Income tax**

*The taxation of trusts*

**25-003** ITA 2007 Pt 9 contains provisions relating to the taxation of settlements and trustees. The fund of a retirement benefits scheme established under trusts constitutes "settled property" for income tax purposes because it is property "held

---

[1] For s.615 funds, see Ch.37.
[2] TCGA 1992 ss.271(1)(c)(ii) and 271(1A). The exemptions do not apply to gains accruing on a disposal of assets held as a member of a property investment LLP.

in trust" and is not held as nominee or bare trustee.[3] The fund is therefore property comprised in a settlement. A person is a "settlor" in relation to a settlement if the settlement was "made", or is treated as having been made, by that person.[4] A person is treated as having made a settlement if he entered into it or if he provided property for the purposes of the settlement (directly or indirectly). Where property is transferred from one settlement to another for less than full consideration (e.g. where there is a transfer between pension schemes), a settlor of the property transferred by the transferring scheme is treated as a settlor of the receiving scheme.[5] For income tax purposes, the trustees of a settlement are together treated as if they were a single person (distinct from the persons who are the trustees of the settlement from time to time).[6] Trustees are thus a person for income tax purposes, and not individuals.[7] That single person is UK resident if: (a) all of the trustees are UK resident; or (b) at least one trustee is UK resident and a settlor in relation to the settlement was resident or domiciled in the UK (including deemed domiciled for income tax purposes) when he made the settlement.[8] Where there is a transfer of funds between pension schemes, the transferee settlement is resident in the UK if at least one trustee is UK resident and a settlor is resident or domiciled in the UK (including deemed domiciled) *at the time of the transfer*.

In the case of an English law settlement, if any beneficiary has an interest in possession in any income of the settlement (i.e. he is entitled to it as it arises) the beneficiary is treated as directly entitled to the underlying income.[9] It follows that the income is deemed to arise or accrue to that beneficiary rather than to the trustees.[10] If the income is interest or rent the beneficiary is deemed to receive interest or rent (and not, for example, pension income). If the trust investments are located in the UK the beneficiary has UK source income and if they are located out of the UK the beneficiary has non-UK source income. If that beneficiary is a non-UK resident then the income does not arise or accrue to a UK resident, and if he is a remittance basis taxpayer and the investments are not located in the UK the income will only be subject to UK tax to the extent that it is remitted to the UK. In these circumstances, the residence status of the body of trustees is irrelevant. However, although such income arises to the beneficiary, if it is received by the trustees they may be assessed to UK tax in a representative capacity,[11] at the basic rate[12] (currently 20%) or the dividend ordinary rate (7.5%).[13] Any tax paid by the trustees should be given as a credit to the member. An annuitant under a trust is not treated as being entitled to the income as it arises.

25-004

If accumulated or discretionary income (i.e. income to which no beneficiary is entitled[14]) arises to the trustees of a settlement, it is charged at the trust rate or the

25-005

---

[3] ITA 2007 s.466(2).
[4] ITA 2007 s.467.
[5] ITA 2007 s.471.
[6] ITA 2007 s.474(1).
[7] It follows that certain reliefs are not available to trustees (e.g. ITA 2007 s.24). Trustees are also not entitled to certain rates of tax, such as the starting rate for savings (ITA 2007 s.12).
[8] ITA 2007 ss.475 and 476.
[9] *Baker v Archer-Shee* [1927] A.C. 844. Certain other jurisdictions, including Jersey, Guernsey and the Isle of Man are the same.
[10] *Williams v Singer* [1921] 1 A.C. 65.
[11] See, e.g. ITTOIA 2005 s.371 (interest) and ITTOIA 2005 s.385 (dividends): liability attaches to the person(s) receiving or entitled to the income. Also see TMA 1970 s.71.
[12] ITA 2007 s.11(1).
[13] ITA 2007 s.14.
[14] ITA 2007 s.480.

dividend trust rate,[15] meaning that the first £1,000 is taxed at 20% (savings income) or 7.5% (dividends)[16] and then 45% thereafter (or 38.1% for dividends).[17]

*Contract-based schemes*

**25-006** It is not uncommon for retirement benefits scheme to be established under contract rather than under trusts. Income arising to the issuer of the contract is taxable in accordance with the usual rules relating to the taxation of income received by such a person (e.g. a company, often an insurance company).

**Capital gains tax**

**25-007** TCGA 1992 Pt III Ch.2 contains provisions relating to the taxation of settlements and trustees. The definition of "settled property", and "settlor" are the same as for income tax (see above).[18] As with the income tax provisions, the trustees of a settlement are together treated as if they were a single person, and that person is UK resident if: (a) all the trustees are UK resident; or (b) at least one trustee is UK resident and a settlor in relation to the settlement was resident or domiciled in the UK (including deemed domiciled for CGT purposes) when he made the settlement.[19]

**25-008** Chargeable gains accruing to a UK resident person on a disposal of an asset (no matter where the asset is located) are subject to CGT.[20] Trustees are entitled to an annual exemption equal to one half of the exempt amount for individuals[21] (i.e. £6,150 for the 2020/21 tax year). The rate of CGT paid by trustees is 20%, except for residential property gains which are subject to 28% CGT.[22]

# NON-UK SCHEMES

**25-009** In relation to the taxation of scheme investments, the distinction between trust schemes and non-trust schemes is less significant in the context of non-UK schemes (although the inheritance tax position may be quite different).

**Income tax**

**25-010** Non-UK source income received by a non-UK person is not subject to UK income tax under general principles.[23]

**25-011** UK source investment income received by non-UK resident trustees is in principle subject to UK income tax. If the trust has no UK resident beneficiaries the

---

[15] ITA 2007 s.479.
[16] ITA 2007 s.491.
[17] ITA 2007 s.9.
[18] TCGA 1992 ss.68, 68A and 68B.
[19] TCGA 1992 s.69. As with the income tax provisions, where there is a transfer of funds between pension schemes, the transferee settlement is resident in the UK if at least one trustee is UK resident and a settlor is resident or domiciled in the UK (including deemed domiciled) *at the time of the transfer.*
[20] TCGA 1992 s.1A.
[21] TCGA 1992 Sch.1C para.5(2).
[22] TCGA 1992 s.1H.
[23] *Colquhoun v Brooks* (1889) 14 App. Cas. 493; 2 T.C. 490. A person other than the recipient may however be subject to UK tax as a result of the application of the anti-avoidance provision considered below.

tax liability is generally limited to any amounts deducted at source insofar as it relates to *disregarded income*.[24] Any income which is not disregarded income is taxable in full. If the trust has one or more UK resident beneficiaries during a tax year, all UK source investment income is taxable in full for that tax year[25] (subject to the application of a double tax treaty providing otherwise). The rate of income tax is 45% (or 38.1% for dividends).[26]

For these purposes, a person is *beneficiary* if: (a) the person is an actual or potential beneficiary; and (b) either: (i) the person is, or will become, entitled under the trust to receive some or all of any income under the trust; or (ii) some or all of any income under the trust may be paid to or used for the benefit of the person in the exercise of a discretion conferred by the trust.[27] *Income* includes capital so far as it represents accumulated income. In the context of a typical discretionary settlement, it is likely that *actual beneficiary* is intended to mean a person who has received a benefit, and potential beneficiary is intended to mean a member of the class who can benefit under the terms of the settlement but has not yet received a benefit.[28] Whether or not a death beneficiary under a pension scheme is a beneficiary for these purposes is unclear. Pension scheme rules typically provide that death benefits must be paid to one or more of a fairly wide class of beneficiary, and the member provides guidance to the trustees in a statement of wishes. Such death beneficiaries are different to potential beneficiaries under a discretionary settlement because there is no power to benefit them immediately. They may perhaps be classified as *future* potential beneficiaries as opposed to current potential beneficiaries. In the context of a money purchase arrangement, they may never become current potential beneficiaries because the member may exhaust the funds during his life. Whether or not it is material to draw a distinction between future and current potential beneficiaries remains to be seen. 25-012

Each member's fund under a pension scheme is likely to be a separate settlement as a matter of general law,[29] and it ought to follow that it is a separate settlement for the purposes of ITA 2007 s.466.[30] ITA 2007 s.812 refers to *trust* rather than settlement, but given that the definition of settled property for these purposes is "any property held in trust", it would be odd if trust (in s.812) was found to be broader than settlement (in s.466).[31] Indeed, if settlement and trust are intended to mean dif- 25-013

---

[24] ITA 2007 s.811. Disregarded income is defined in ITA 2007 s.813. Most investment income is disregarded income, except for rental income.

[25] ITA 2007 s.812(1), disapplying s.811.

[26] ITA 2009 ss.9 and 479. Credit is given for any tax deducted at source. Any tax paid by the trustees may be given as a credit to the member under ESC B18.

[27] ITA 2007 s.812(2).

[28] It was in this sense that Lord Wilberforce used the terms actual and potential beneficiary in *Vestey v IRC* [1980] A.C. 1148; [1980] S.T.C. 10, 15.

[29] See *Air Jamaica Ltd v Charlton* [1999] 1 W.L.R. 1399 at 1409; Law Commission report "*The Rules against Perpetuities and Excessive Accumulations*" (1998) (Law Com No.251), p.38; Thomas "Trusts of Death Benefits under Occupational Pension Schemes—Deep Waters for Advisers: Part 1" [1995] P.C.B. 133, 144.

[30] There does not appear to be any direct authority in an income tax context, but it is clear that a settlement for CGT purposes follows the general law position (see *Trennery v West* [2005] UKHL 5 at [26] (Lord Walker)) and given that the definition of settlement for CGT purposes is materially identical to the definition for income tax purposes, one would expect the income tax position to be the same.

[31] This analysis is supported by other parts of the legislation. For example, it is clear from ITA 2007 s.478(b) that if it were possible for income to arise to a trust which is not a settlement, such income could not be taxable at the higher rates of income tax (ITA 2007 s.479 applies only to settlements). It is therefore most unlikely that trust is broader than settlement.

ferent things, one would expect trust to be a narrower concept than settlement.[32] If this analysis is correct, the higher rates of UK income tax will not apply to any UK source income relating to non-UK resident beneficiaries, even where the pension scheme has other beneficiaries who are resident in the UK. However, HMRC's position is understood to be that a pension scheme is one trust for the purposes of ITA 2007 s.812, meaning that one UK resident beneficiary causes the UK source income of the entire scheme to be taxable at the higher rates of income tax. Where a member and his death beneficiaries are not resident in the UK, the trustees may elect for that member's fund to be treated as a separate settlement for income tax purposes.[33]

25-014 The trustees may incorporate a non-UK company, and invest the scheme funds via the company. Provided that the company is not resident in the UK, and does not trade in the UK through a permanent establishment, it will be subject to income tax only in respect of its UK-source investment income. The rate of income tax is the basic rate or the dividend ordinary rate.[34] However, most forms of investment income (with the notable exception of rent) are *disregarded company income* meaning that UK tax is limited to the amount of any UK tax deducted at source or treated as deducted at source.[35] With effect from April 2020, non-UK companies carrying on a UK property business will be brought within the scope of UK corporation tax.

**Capital gains tax**

25-015 Unless carrying on a trade in the UK,[36] a non-UK resident is currently subject to CGT only on a disposal of UK real estate and substantial interests in UK property rich entities.[37]

*Overseas pension schemes*

25-016 A gain accruing to a person on a disposal of investments[38] held for the purposes of an overseas pension scheme[39] is not a chargeable gain.[40] For these purposes, investments include futures contracts and options contracts, and a contract is not prevented from being a futures contract or an options contract by the fact that any party is or may be entitled to receive or liable to make, or entitled to receive and liable to make, only a payment of a sum (as opposed to a transfer of assets other than money) in full settlement of all obligations. Therefore for CGT purposes an

---

[32] However, for a decision in which each member's fund under a pension scheme as found to not be a separate trust as a matter of general law, see *Dalriada Trustees Ltd v Woodward* [2012] EWHC 21626 (Ch) at [19], [29] and [33].
[33] See ITA 2007 s.477. The election is made under TCGA 1992 Sch.4ZA.
[34] ITA 2007 ss.11 and 14. The basic rate is currently 20% (FA 2020 s.3, once it receives royal assent). The dividend ordinary rate is currently 7.5% (ITA 2007 s.8(1)).
[35] ITA 2007 ss.815 and 816. UK source interest is disregarded income but the payer is required deduct basic rate tax at source if it is yearly interest (ITA 2007 s.874). Where a non-resident person receives UK dividends, is deemed do have paid tax at the dividend ordinary rate on the distribution (ITTOIA 2005 s.399(2)), so there is no tax due by the company. UK dividends are also disregarded income. Basic rate tax on UK rental income must be deducted at source unless the non-resident landlord scheme applies (ITA 2007 ss.971–972 and The Taxation of Income from Land (Non-residents) Regulations 1995 (SI 1995/2902)).
[36] See TCGA 1992 s.10.
[37] TCGA 1992 s.14B.
[38] For the meaning of "investments", see Ch.8.
[39] For the meaning of "overseas pension scheme", see Ch.31.
[40] TCGA 1992 s.271(1A). This does not apply to gains accruing to a person from the acquisition and disposal by him of assets held as a member of a property investment LLP: TCGA 1992 s.271(12).

overseas pension scheme is treated in the same way as a registered pension scheme.[41]

## THE INCOME TAX SETTLEMENTS PROVISIONS

### Background

ITTOIA 2005 Pt 5 Ch.5 applies where: 25-017

(a) there is a "settlement";
(b) income arises under the settlement; and
(c) one of the following applies:
  (i) the income arises from property in which the settlor has an interest;
  (ii) trust income is paid to or for the benefit of a minor child of the settlor; or
  (iii) a capital sum is paid to the settlor or his spouse.

If the above conditions are met any income arising under the settlement is deemed to have arisen to the settlor and is accordingly taxable on the settlor (and the settlor alone). In relation to (c) above, if (i) applies then the settlor is taxed as the income arises and it follows that (ii) and (iii) can only apply if the settlor has not retained an interest. 25-018

Subject to one relatively minor exception,[42] these provisions apply in relation to registered and unregistered schemes. Given that they are essentially anti-avoidance provisions,[43] one would not expect them to have much application to registered pension schemes, and it should follow that they ought not have much application to unregistered pension schemes which do not differ markedly from registered pension schemes. In a pensions context, it will usually be desirable to establish that either there is no settlement, or if there is a settlement then the member is not the settlor. 25-019

### Non-domiciled settlors

The above provisions do not apply to income which arises under a settlement if it is "protected foreign-source income" for a tax year.[44] Income arising under a settlement in a tax year is protected foreign-source income for the tax year if the following conditions are met[45]: 25-020

(a) the income would be relevant foreign income if it were income of a UK resident individual.
(b) the income is from property originating from the settlor.
(c) when the settlement is created the settlor (i) is not domiciled in the UK, and

---

[41] For which, see Ch.8.
[42] In ITTOIA 2005 s.627(2)(c), which applies where a member of the pension scheme arranges for his pension rights to be transferred or allocated under the registered pension scheme for the benefit of another person. The transfer/allocation is the settlement and the income arising under that settlement is the income paid to the other person. This exception does not provide that if a registered pension scheme is a settlement then any income arising under the scheme cannot be attributed to the settlor under s.624(1).
[43] Per Lord Hoffmann in *Jones v Garnett* [2007] UKHL 35.
[44] ITTOIA 2005 ss.628A, 630A, and 635.
[45] ITTOIA 2005 s.628A.

(ii) if the settlement is created on or after 6 April 2017, is not deemed to be so domiciled.
(d) there is no time in the tax year when the settlor is: (a) domiciled in the UK; or (b) deemed domiciled in the UK by virtue of Condition A in ITA 2007 s.835BA.[46]
(e) the trustees of the settlement are not UK resident for the tax year.
(f) the settlement has not been tainted on or after 6 April 2017[47];

**25-021** Instead, a charge arises where the settlor or a close family member receives a benefit provided out of protected foreign-source income, or where such a benefit is provided to someone else who then makes on onward gift to the settlor or a close family member.[48]

**"Settlement"**

**25-022** ITTOIA 2005 s.620(1) provides that:

"'settlement' includes any disposition, trust, covenant, agreement, arrangement or transfer of assets (except that it does not include a charitable loan arrangement)."

**25-023** This is a broad and non-exhaustive definition. Any disposal or transfer of property (including, for example, a contribution to a pension scheme) is, on the face of it, a settlement. If a number of transactions are envisaged and one or more of the transactions are settlements then all of the transactions may together form an *arrangement* and therefore one settlement.[49] One must take a broad and realistic view of the matter in order to determine what the arrangement is.[50] For example, if an individual subscribes for shares in a company that he wholly owns and controls, with the intention that the company will contribute that money to a pension scheme established for the employees of the company (including the individual) the arrangement would likely include both the initial subscription and the contribution, and the individual (rather than the company) is the settlor of that arrangement.

**25-024** It was accepted in *Copeman v Coleman*[51] that bona fide commercial transactions are not settlements for these purposes. In *CIR v Leiner*,[52] the bona fide commercial transaction test in *Copeman* was reformulated as a requirement that a settlement requires some element of *bounty* and Plowman J attributed this requirement to the word "provided" in the legislation.[53] This was approved by the House of

---

[46] i.e. he was born in the UK and has a UK domicile of origin.
[47] A settlement is tainted if property or income is provided (directly or indirectly) for the purposes of the settlement by the settlor (or another settlement of which he is the settlor or a beneficiary), and at the time of the provision the settlor is UK domiciled or deemed UK domiciled (s.628A(8)). For this purpose, the transactions listed in s.628B are disregarded (e.g. property or income provided under a transaction, other than a loan, where the transaction is entered into on arm's length terms).
[48] ITTOIA 2005 ss.643A–643N.
[49] In *Jones v Garnett* [2007] UKHL 35, a husband and wife incorporated a company (each owning 50% of the shares) and the husband generated income for the company and received a modest salary, and the company paid substantial dividends to the husband and wife in their capacity as shareholders. The House of Lords held that all of these transactions were an arrangement, because it was envisaged at the outset.
[50] *Crossland v Hawkins* [1961] Ch. 537; (1961) 39 T.C. 493, approved in *Jones v Garnett* [2007] UKHL 35.
[51] *Copeman v Coleman* [1939] 2 K.B. 484; (1935–1939) 22 T.C. 594.
[52] *CIR v Leiner* (1964) 41 T.C. 589.
[53] Now in ITTOIA 2005 s.620(3), which relates to the definition of settlor.

Lords in *IRC v Plummer*.[54] Accordingly a settlement for these purposes must include some element of bounty.

*"Bounty"*

The term "gratuitous intent" was preferred in *Jones v Garnett*. One test is whether the recipient obtains a benefit without the assumption of any correlative obligation.[55] In *Jones v Garnett*, Lord Hoffmann said that the general effect of the cases is that, under the arrangement, the settlor must provide a benefit which would not have been provided in a transaction at arm's length. One must take a broad and realistic view of the matter.[56] **25-025**

The bounty test is very similar (although not identical) to the test in IHTA 1984 s.10, which applies where there is no intention to confer gratuitous benefit on any person.[57] Provided that the intention is for the member to take retirement benefits then any contributions he makes to the scheme should not involve any gratuitous intent. An intention to take reduced retirement benefits in order to pass death benefits to family members is an intention to gratuitously benefit the family members. The relevant time at which to consider intention is the time at which the funds are provided (i.e. when they are contributed to the scheme). If the member has no gratuitous intent at that time but subsequently decides not to take benefits in order to benefit his death beneficiaries, the (bounteous) decision not to take the benefits cannot convert the previous contribution into a settlement unless the contributions and the later decision form part of the same arrangement. **25-026**

**"Settlor"**

The settlor, in relation to a settlement, is any person by whom the settlement is *made*.[58] A person is, in particular, deemed to have made a settlement if he[59]: **25-027**

(a) has made or entered into the settlement;
(b) has provided or undertaken to provide funds directly or indirectly for the purposes of the settlement. This requires that there is at least be a conscious association of the provider of the funds with the settlement in question. It is not sufficient that the settled funds should historically have been derived from the provider of them[60]; or
(c) has made with any other person a reciprocal arrangement for that other person to make or enter into the settlement. A salary sacrifice arrangement clearly involves a reciprocal arrangement, so (if the contribution is a settlement) the employee is the settlor.

In relation to any particular settlor the property and income comprised in the settlement are restricted to the property originating from him.[61] "Originating" means property which the settlor himself provided, directly or indirectly, together with property representing that property and income derived therefrom.[62] **25-028**

---

[54] *IRC v Plummer* [1980] A.C. 896; [1979] UKHL T.C. 54 1.
[55] *Chinn v Collins* [1981] A.C. 533; (1979–1983) 54 T.C. 311 and *IRC v Levy* [1982] S.T.C. 442.
[56] Lord Hoffmann in *Jones v Garnett* [2007] UKHL 35 at [11].
[57] For IHTA 1984 s.10, see Ch.21.
[58] ITTOIA 2005 s.620(1).
[59] ITTOIA 2005 s.620(2) and (3).
[60] Per Lord Keith in *Fitzwilliam v IRC* [1993] 1 W.L.R. 1189; [1993] S.T.C. 502.
[61] ITTOIA 2005 s.644(3).
[62] ITTOIA 2005 s.645.

### "Income arises under the settlement"

**25-029** References to income arising under a settlement include all income chargeable to income tax by deduction or otherwise other than income which satisfies the following conditions[63]:

(a) had the income in fact arisen to the settlor he would not have been chargeable to income tax by deduction or otherwise; and

(b) the reason why he would not have been so chargeable is that he is not UK resident or domiciled.

**25-030** It follows that if the settlor is not resident in the UK, non-UK source income is not treated as his but UK source income is. If the settlor is non-UK domiciled and a remittance basis taxpayer, foreign income is excluded unless remitted to the UK.[64]

**25-031** The income of a company owned by a settlement is not income of the settlement (assuming that the company does not itself form part of the arrangement).[65] This is on the basis that transferring the assets to the company is merely an investment and is not essential to the continuation of the settlement. As such, the assets in the settlement are the shares in and loans to the company, not the company's assets. Such a company could however form part of the settlement if it was envisaged by the settlor that the trustees would transfer trust assets to the company (usually in exchange for shares or loan stock) or if the settlor made a bounteous disposal directly to the company.

### The income arises from property in which the settlor has an interest

**25-032** Income which arises under a settlement is treated for income tax purposes as the income of the settlor and of the settlor alone if it arises: (a) during the life of the settlor; and (b) from property in which the settlor has an interest.[66]

**25-033** A bounteous assignment of the right to receive death benefits is a settlement, but the income arising under the settlement (i.e. the payment of pension death benefits) will not arise during the life of the settlor.

#### "Property in which the settlor has an interest"

**25-034** A settlor is treated as having an interest in property if there are any circumstances[67] in which the property or any related property will or may become payable to, or applicable for the benefit of, the settlor or the settlor's spouse or civil partner.[68] Related property, in relation to any property, means income from that property or any other property directly or indirectly representing proceeds of, or of income from, that property or income from it.[69] The fact that the settlor could benefit by the independent act of a third party does not mean that he has an interest in the

---

[63] ITTOIA 2005 s.648(1).
[64] ITTOIA 2005 s.648.
[65] *Chamberlain v IRC* (1943) 25 T.C. 317. This is also implicit from the decisions in *IRC v Levy* [1982] S.T.C. 442 and *Jones v Garnett* [2007] UKHL 35, neither of which applied to the income arising to the company.
[66] ITTOIA 2005 s.624(1).
[67] Other than the fairly remote circumstances specified in s.625(2) and (3), which rarely have any application in a pensions context.
[68] ITTOIA 2005 s.625(1). References to the settlor's spouse or civil partner do not include a spouse or civil partner from whom the settlor is separated or the widow or widower or surviving civil partner of the settlor.
[69] ITTOIA 2005 s.625(5).

THE INCOME TAX SETTLEMENTS PROVISIONS 553

settlement,[70] otherwise there would never be any property in which the settlor does not have an interest.

25-035 The provisions do not expressly require the payment to the settlor to be pursuant to the terms of the settlement, but it seems that they are limited to cases where the income or property may become payable under the terms of the settlement or under some collateral agreement having legal force.[71] It follows that if a beneficial loan (e.g. interest-free) is made to a pension scheme by someone other than the member (so the loan is bounteous in favour of the member, and is therefore a settlement), the rights of the lender to be repaid from the scheme means that the lender has an interest in the settlement.[72] But a payment to the settlor pursuant to a commercial transaction does not cause the settlor to have an interest in a settlement.[73]

*Exception for outright gifts between spouses or civil partners*

25-036 The rule in s.624(1) (i.e. that income which arises under a settlement is treated for income tax purposes as the income of the settlor and of the settlor alone) does not apply in respect of an outright gift[74]:

(a) of property from which income arises;
(b) made from one spouse to the other (or one civil partner to the other);
(c) where the gift carries a right to the whole of the income; and
(d) the property is not wholly or substantially a right to income.

25-037 A contribution to a pension scheme by an individual for the benefit of his spouse appears to satisfy all of the above requirements, with the possible exception of (d). The property gifted (which must be the rights acquired by the spouse under the scheme) does entitle the spouse to income (i.e. a pension), but is it substantially a right to income? In *Jones v Garnett*, the House of Lords held that an ordinary share is not substantially a right to income.[75] Such a share confers a right to vote, to participate in the distribution of assets on a winding up, to block a special resolution, to complain under CA 2006 s.994, and these are all rights over and above the right to income. Depending on the terms of the scheme, it may well be arguable that the rights of the member are such that (d) is satisfied.[76]

*Exception for benefits under certain pension schemes*

25-038 The rule in s.624(1) does not apply to income which consists of a benefit under one of the following pension schemes[77]:

(a) a registered pension scheme;
(b) a pension scheme established by a government outside the UK for the

---

[70] *West v Trennery* [2003] EWHC 676 (Ch); [2003] S.T.C. 580 at [601].
[71] *Muir v IRC* [1966] 1 W.L.R. 1269; (1966) 43 T.C. 367 per Pennycuick J.
[72] See *Jenkins v IRC* (1944) 26 T.C. 265; *IRC v Watchel* (1970) 46 T.C. 543.
[73] *Lord Vestey's Executors v IRC* [1949] 1 All E.R. 1108; (1949) 31 T.C. 1 at 83.
[74] ITTOIA 2005 s.626. A gift is not an outright gift if it is subject to conditions, or there are any circumstances in which the property, or any related property will or may become payable to the giver, or is applicable for the benefit of the giver.
[75] In contrast to a non-voting preference share, which is substantially a right to income (*Young v Pearce* [1996] S.T.C. 743; (1996) 70 T.C. 331 (Ch)).
[76] Rights entitling the member to receive benefits which are not income, and rights relating to death benefits, and to influence investments, should be taken into account. If the scheme is established in jurisdiction which provides rights to scheme members as a matter of trusts law or pensions law, those rights should also be taken into account.
[77] ITTOIA 2005 s.627(2)(c).

554    SCHEME INVESTMENTS

        benefit of its employees (or an annuity acquired using funds held for the purposes of such a pension scheme); or

(c) any pension arrangements of any description prescribed by regulations made under WRPA 1999 s.11(2)(h).

**25-039** The pension arrangements prescribed for the purposes of WRPA 1999 s.11(2)(h) are arrangements (including an annuity purchased for the purpose of giving effect to rights under any such arrangement)[78]:

(a) to which: (i) the holder of an office or employment has contributed by way of payments out of earnings which have been allowed as a deduction under FA 2004 Sch.36 para.51 (transitional corresponding relief); (ii) art.17A of the Convention set out in the Schedule to the Double Taxation Relief (Taxes on Income) (Republic of Ireland) Order 1976 (pension scheme contributions) applies[79];

(b) made with a scheme which is an occupational pension scheme which is registered under FA 2004 s.153 or automatically became a registered pension scheme on 6 April 2006[80];

(c) to which ITEPA 2003 s.308A applies. Section 308A applies to employer contributions under a qualifying overseas pension scheme in respect of an employee who is a relevant migrant member[81];

(d) which are exempt or qualify for relief from, or are not liable to charge to, income tax by virtue of ICTA 1988 ss.614 or 615,[82] or ITEPA 2003 ss.629, 630 or 643 (pre-1973 pensions paid under the Overseas Pensions Act 1973 and Malawi, Trinidad and Tobago and Zambia government pensions);

(e) made with: (i) a public service pension scheme; or (ii) an occupational pension scheme established under the auspices of a government department or by any person acting on behalf of the Crown. This does not apply to any EFRBS which has been provided to an employee as part of or in addition to any such pension arrangement.

**25-040** As is explained in Ch.22, this exception appears to be of fairly limited application. In particular, it does *not* provide that if one of the pension schemes referred to above is a settlement then any investment income arising to the scheme cannot be attributed to the settlor under s.624(1).

*Exception where settlor is not an individual*

**25-041** Any income which arises on or after 21 March 2012 under a settlement and originates from a settlor who is not an individual is not treated as arising to the settlor.[83] The reference to income originating from a settlor means income from property originating from the settlor and income provided directly or indirectly by

---

[78] The Occupational and Personal Pension Schemes (Bankruptcy) (No. 2) Regulations 2002 (SI 2002/836) reg.2.
[79] It is implicit that (i) and (ii) are alternatives.
[80] For the deemed registration of existing schemes on 6 April 2006, see Ch.3.
[81] These provisions are considered in Ch.24. Given that s.627(2)(c) refers to different categories of pension schemes, it is arguable that the inclusion of arrangements to which s.308A applies means that s.627(2)(c) applies to all qualifying overseas pension schemes whether or not s.308A actually applied to any contributions (which will only be the case where the employee was a relevant migrant member).
[82] For ICTA 1988 s.615, see Ch.37.
[83] ITTOIA 2005 s.627(4).

the settlor.[84] For these purposes, references to property or income which a settlor has provided directly or indirectly: (a) include property or income which has been provided directly or indirectly by another person under reciprocal arrangements with the settlor; but (b) do not include property or income which the settlor has provided directly or indirectly under reciprocal arrangements with another person.

It follows that s.624(1) should not apply to corporate contributions to retirement benefit schemes (even if they are bounteous) provided that the company is the settlor. This was probably also the case prior to 21 March 2012 as it is implicit from various parts of the settlement provisions that the settlor must be an individual.[85] If an individual provides funds to a company which he controls with the intention that the company will bounteously contribute those funds to a pension scheme under which the individual is a beneficiary, the arrangement (and therefore the settlement) is likely to include both the payment to the company and the contribution to the pension scheme. The individual, not that company, is the settlor of that arrangement.

25-042

### Trust income paid for the benefit of a minor child

Income which arises under a settlement is treated for income tax purposes as the income of the settlor and of the settlor alone for a tax year if, in that year and during the life of the settlor, it: (a) is paid to, or for the benefit of, a relevant child of the settlor; or (b) would otherwise be treated (apart from this provision) as income of a relevant child of the settlor.[86]

25-043

Income which is accumulated and distributed to the child as capital is within these provisions save to the extent that it exceeds retained income in the settlement which has not been applied towards income expenses or otherwise treated as the income of the settlor.[87] The only circumstances in which a payment could be made from a pension scheme to a minor child would be the provision of death benefits. Assuming that the deceased member was the settlor then this provision would not apply because it could not happen during the life of the settlor. If the deceased member was not the settlor (e.g. a gift was made to the pension scheme by the deceased member's spouse) then this provision could apply, but it is unlikely to have much application in practice.

25-044

### Capital sum is paid to the settlor or spouse

Any capital sum paid directly or indirectly in any tax year by the trustees of a settlement[88] to the settlor is treated as the income of the settlor, but only insofar as the amount of the sum falls within the amount of income available up to the end of the year.[89] This also applies where the capital sum is paid by a company connected with the settlement if an associated payment is made to the company by the trustees. A capital sum is carried forwards to the extent that it exceeds the amount of income available.

25-045

A capital sum means: (a) any sum paid by way of loan or repayment of a loan;

25-046

---

[84] ITTOIA 2005 s.645(2).
[85] HMRC accept this at TSEM4016.
[86] ITTOIA 2005 s.629(1). A relevant child means a child (including a stepchild) that is under the age of 18 and unmarried (and not in a civil partnership).
[87] ITTOIA 2005 s.631.
[88] ITTOIA 2005 s.641(1).
[89] ITTOIA 2005 s.633.

556   SCHEME INVESTMENTS

and (b) any other sum which is paid otherwise than as income and is not paid for full consideration in money or money's worth.[90]

**25-047** The "income available" is the income arising under the settlement in the current year and any previous year which has not been distributed, less the amount of income already taken into account under s.633 or treated as the settlors under ss.624 or 629, less an amount equal to tax at the trust rate on the income otherwise available.[91]

**25-048** If the settlor is able to benefit under the settlement then s.624 will apply rather than s.633, so s.633 can only be concerned with capital sums paid to the settlor pursuant to a commercial transaction, such as where the trustees of a settlement make a loan to the settlor or repay a loan made by the settlor to the settlement. Lump sum death benefits paid to the settlor's widow should not be within the scope of this provision.

**The taxation of the settlor**

**25-049** There is no mechanism under these provisions for taxing anyone other than the settlor. If the settlor pays the tax he may recover it from the trustees.[92] Any tax paid by the trustees is treated as paid by them in a representative capacity on behalf of the settlor. Any income treated as that of the settlor cannot also arise to a person abroad for the purposes of the transfer of assets abroad provisions.[93]

# THE TRANSFER OF ASSETS ABROAD PROVISIONS

**25-050** The transfer of assets abroad provisions in ITA 2007 Pt 13 Ch.2 are extremely important in the context of non-UK retirement benefit schemes. There are three separate charging heads:

(a) Sections 720–726 (transferors with power to enjoy).
(b) Sections 727–730 (transferors in receipt of capital sums).
(c) Sections 731–735 (persons who receive a benefit[94]).

**25-051** These provisions apply only if a "relevant transfer" occurs, and they operate by reference to the income of a person abroad that is connected with that relevant transfer or another relevant transaction.[95]

**Relevant transfers**

**25-052** A transfer is a relevant transfer if all of the following requirements are satisfied[96]:

(a) it is a transfer of assets;
(b) income becomes payable to a person abroad; and
(c) the income becomes so payable as a result of: (i) the transfer; (ii) one or

---

[90] ITTOIA 2005 s.634(1).
[91] ITTOIA 2005 s.635.
[92] ITTOIA 2005 s.646.
[93] Since 2013 this has been made express: ITA 2007 ss.721(3C) and 728(2A).
[94] Prior to 6 April 2017, this third head was limited to non-transferors. Since that date it is capable of applying to transferors who are neither domiciled in the UK nor deemed to be so domiciled as long-stayers.
[95] ITA 2007 s.714(2). The requisite connection is not specified.
[96] ITA 2007 s.716(1).

more associated operations; or (iii) the transfer and one or more associated operations.

**25-053** A "transfer" expressly includes the creation of rights[97] and "assets" includes property or rights of any kind.[98] This could include the situation where a UK employee enters into an employment contract with a non-UK employer.[99] A person abroad means a person who is resident outside the UK or an individual who is domiciled outside the UK.[100] The relevant transfer need not have the effect of transferring the assets abroad[101] so the relevant transfer could be a transfer between persons who are both abroad (for example, the transfer of assets from a non-UK pension scheme to an underlying non-UK company).

**25-054** The income must become payable to the person aboard as a result of the relevant transfer or associated operations (or both). Thus the transaction(s) must *cause* the income to become so payable. If the person abroad purchases shares in a company then any income that would have been received by the company irrespective of the share purchase has not become payable as a result of the transfer or associated operations.[102]

*Associated operations*

**25-055** An associated operation, in relation to a transfer of assets, means an operation of any kind effected by any person in relation to: (a) any of the assets transferred; (b) any assets directly or indirectly representing any of the assets transferred; (c) the income arising from any assets within (a) or (b); or (d) any assets directly or indirectly representing the accumulations of income arising from any assets within (a) or (b).[103] It does not matter whether the associated operation is effected before, after or at the same time as the transfer (provided that it *relates* to the assets transferred). References to assets representing any assets, income or accumulations of income include: (a) shares in or obligations of any company to which the assets, income or accumulations are or have been transferred; or (b) obligations of any other person to whom the assets, income or accumulations are or have been transferred.[104]

**25-056** Death is not an associated operation, but making a will is.[105] It therefore seems likely that the application of the death benefits provisions under a pension scheme will be an associated operation. An omission is not an operation for these purposes.

**25-057** A literal reading of the associated operation provisions suggests that entirely unconnected operations may be associated simply because they relate to the same assets.[106] However, there are indications that operations are taken into account only

---

[97] ITA 2007 s.716(2).
[98] ITA 2007 s.717.
[99] *IRC v Brackett* [1986] S.T.C. 521; *Boyle v HMRC* [2013] UKFTT 723.
[100] ITA 2007 s.718. This includes a person treated as non-UK resident under ITA 2007 s.475(3).
[101] *IRC v Willoughby* [1995] S.T.C. 143 at 161.
[102] See *Vestey v IRC* [1980] A.C. 1148.
[103] ITA 2007 s.719.
[104] ITA 2007 s.717.
[105] *Bambridge v IRC* [1955] 1 W.L.R. 1329; [1955] 3 All E.R. 812.
[106] In *Corbett's Executrices v IRC* [1943] 25 T.C. 305 the taxpayers transferred some investments to a UK company and, two years later, the UK company transferred some of the investments to a Canadian company. The Court of Appeal found that the latter transfer was an operation associated with the former.

558 SCHEME INVESTMENTS

if they, in conjunction with the transfer, give the taxpayer the power to enjoy the income of the person abroad.[107]

**Transferors with power to enjoy**

**25-058** A charge to UK income tax is imposed on a UK resident individual under ITA 2007 s.720 if:

(a) the individual (or his spouse or civil partner) has power in the tax year to enjoy income of a person abroad;

(b) the power to enjoy is as a result of: (i) a relevant transfer; (ii) one or more associated operations; or (iii) a relevant transfer and one or more associated operations; and

(c) the income would be chargeable to income tax if it were the individual's and received by the individual in the UK.

*Power to enjoy*

**25-059** An individual has power to enjoy the income of the person abroad if any of Conditions A to E are met[108]:

(a) *Condition A* is that the income is in fact so dealt with by any person as to be calculated at some time to ensure for the benefit of the individual, whether in the form of income or not.

(b) *Condition B* is that the receipt or accrual of the income operates to increase the value to the individual: (i) of any assets the individual holds; or (ii) of any assets held for the individual's benefit.

(c) *Condition C* is that the individual receives or is entitled to receive at any time any benefit provided or to be provided out of the income or related money. Money is related money if it is or will be available for the purpose of providing the benefit as a result of the effect or successive effects: (i) on the income; and (ii) on any assets which directly or indirectly represent the income, of the associated operations referred to in s.721(2).

(d) *Condition D* is that the individual may become entitled to the beneficial enjoyment of the income if one or more powers are exercised or successively exercised. It does not matter who may exercise the powers or whether they are exercisable with or without the consent of another person.

(e) *Condition E* is that the individual is able in any manner to control directly or indirectly the application of the income.

**25-060** In determining whether any of these conditions are met, regard must be had to the substantial result and effect of all the relevant transactions. All benefits which may at any time accrue to the individual as a result of the transfer and any associated operations must be taken into account, irrespective of the nature or form of the benefits, or whether the individual has legal or equitable rights in respect of the benefits.[109] If s.720 applies, the amount of income of the person abroad taken into account is the income which the transferor has power to enjoy.

---

[107] *Herdman v IRC* (1967) 45 T.C. 394 (especially as summarised in *Macpherson v IRC* [1989] A.C. 159; [1988] S.T.C. 362 at 398); *Carvill v IRC* [2000] S.T.C. 143 at 165.

[108] ITA 2007 ss.722 and 723.

[109] ITA 2007 s.722(3) and (4).

## THE TRANSFER OF ASSETS ABROAD PROVISIONS

*Transferors and quasi transferors*

The individual referred to in the legislation is the individual that effected the relevant transfer, and he is referred to in this chapter as the "transferor". A company cannot be a transferor but its individual shareholders can be.[110] In addition, a person who procures the transfer (sometimes referred to as a quasi-transferor) may himself constitute a transferor.[111] In relation to a transfer by a company, the individual is required to have control of the company.[112]

25-061

*Application to retirement benefit schemes*

Individuals with power to enjoy the income of the person abroad will typically include the member, the death beneficiaries and anyone else who may receive a benefit from the scheme. In the straightforward case of a contribution to non-UK resident trustees by a UK resident individual, all of the enjoyment conditions A to E will usually be met. In relation to contributions by a company, the provisions will not apply unless one or more individuals (such as the shareholders) are transferors on the basis that they have procured or been associated with the transfer. This is only likely to be the case where there is a controlling shareholder or a small group of controlling shareholders. If such persons are excluded from benefiting then there should be no power to enjoy. Otherwise it may be necessary to place reliance of one of the exemptions below.

25-062

### Transferors in receipt of capital sums

Any income that has not been taxed under s.720 may be taxed under ITA 2007 s.727, which provides that a charge to UK income tax is imposed on a UK resident individual if:

25-063

(a) income has become the income of a person abroad as a result of: (i) a relevant transfer; (ii) one or more associated operations; or (iii) a relevant transfer and one or more associated operations;
(b) the individual (or his spouse or civil partner) receives or is entitled to receive a capital sum in the current or a previous tax year; and
(c) the payment of that sum is (or, in the case of an entitlement, would be) in any way connected with any relevant transaction.

A sum is a capital sum if it is: (a) paid or payable by way of loan or repayment of a loan[113]; and (b) paid or payable otherwise than as income, and not for full consideration in money or money's worth.[114] A sum is treated as a capital sum which the individual receives or is entitled to receive if another person receives or is entitled to receive it at the individual's direction or as a result of the assignment by the individual of his right to receive it.[115] A capital distribution from a pension scheme could clearly constitute a capital sum.

25-064

If s.727 applies, the transferor is taxed on all of the income of the person abroad from the assets that he transferred. It is irrelevant that he may only have received a small capital sum. If s.727 applies at any time then it continues to apply to the

25-065

---

[110] As was the case in *IRC v Pratt* [1982] S.T.C. 756 and *Fisher v HMRC* [2014] UKFTT 804.
[111] *Vestey v IRC* [1980] A.C. 1148; *IRC v Pratt* [1982] S.T.C. 756.
[112] *IRC v Pratt* [1982] S.T.C. 756; *Carvill v IRC* [2000] S.T.C. (S.C.D.) 143. cf. *Fisher v HMRC* [2014] UKFTT 804.
[113] Loans must be distinguished from other economically similar transactions: see Ch.2.
[114] ITA 2007 s.729(3).
[115] ITA 2007 s.729(4).

income of the person abroad in the future even if he never receives another capital sum. However there is an exception where a loan is made to the transferor and it is repaid, in which case liability ceases in the following tax year.

**Persons who receive a benefit**

**25-066** Income arises under ITA 2007 s.732 if:

(a) a relevant transfer occurs;
(b) an individual receives a benefit in that tax year;
(c) the benefit is provided out of assets which are available for the purpose as a result of the transfer or one or more associated operations;
(d) where there is a time in the year when the individual is UK domiciled or deemed to be so domiciled under Condition A of ITA 2007 s.835BA,[116] the individual is not liable to income tax under s.720 or s.727 by reference to the transfer; and
(e) the individual is not liable to income tax on the amount or value of the benefit (apart from ITA 2007 s.731 or certain provision in the income tax settlements provisions).

**25-067** If the requirements are met, the individual is charged to tax under s.731. The identity of the transferor is irrelevant (and so the transferor need not have any connection with the UK). *Benefit* is not defined but it seems clear that transactions on arm's length terms do not confer a benefit. It may be said that some sort of benefit arises in most commercial transactions[117] but in a tax context the term benefit usually connotes the provision of bounty[118] and that is very likely to be necessary for the purposes of s.732. The benefit here could be a capital distribution, or the provision of property on beneficial terms (e.g. rent-free accommodation or an interest-free loan, where the value of the benefit is the market value of the benefit received).[119] Any income which is deemed to have arisen to the individual under s.732 is calculated pursuant to six steps set out in s.733(1).

**Non-domiciled transferors**

**25-068** Since 6 April 2017, the charges under ITA 2007 ss.720 and 727 do not apply where the income of the person abroad is protected foreign-source income. In both cases the exemption applies only where the person abroad is a settlement or a company in which the trustees of the settlement are participators (or the ultimate participators) and the trustees of the settlement are non-UK resident for the tax year. Where the transferor is non-UK domiciled, such income is protected foreign-source income if it would be relevant foreign income if it were the actual income

---

[116] i.e. the individual was born in the UK, has a domicile of origin in the UK, and is resident in the UK for the relevant tax year.

[117] In *IRC v Levy* [1982] S.T.C. 442, Nourse J said, "If a person buys a pair of socks from Marks & Spencer for a fair price, that is a benefit to him and to Marks & Spencer". In *Vestey v IRC* [1949] 1 All E.R. 1108; 31 T.C. 1, Lord Morton of Henryton said, "a loan may well benefit a person even if it is made at a commercial rate of interest, as it may tide him over a difficult period". In *IRC v Chappie* 34 T.C. 509 Sir Raymond Evershed MR said, "it is I think, a truism that a person receiving a loan, albeit of a commercial character, can be said to receive a benefit".

[118] In other words, the member must receive something that the pension scheme would not be prepared to give as a fair bargain to an unconnected third party dealing on arm's length terms with the scheme. See e.g. *Mairs v Haughey* [1994] 1 A.C. 303.

[119] See *IRC v Botnar* [1998] S.T.C. 38 and *Billingham v Cooper* [2001] EWCA Civ 1041; [2001] S.T.C. 1177, which both concern different, but comparable, provisions. Also see *Tax Bulletin 40* (April 1999) p.651.

# THE TRANSFER OF ASSETS ABROAD PROVISIONS

of the transferor. Where the transferor is deemed to be non-domiciled as a long stayer such income is protected foreign-source income only if: (a) when the settlement is created, the individual is: (i) not domiciled in the UK; and (ii) if the settlement is created on or after 6 April 2017, not deemed domiciled in the UK as a longstayer; and (b) the settlement is not tainted on or after 6 April 2017.[120]

Income which is not protected foreign-source income constitutes relevant foreign income (and so is charged under ITTOIA 2005 s.832 when remitted to the UK) if the transferor is a remittance basis taxpayer in the tax year in which the income arises, and the actual income of the person abroad would be relevant foreign income if it were in fact the transferor's.[121]

25-069

To the extent that the exemption for protected foreign-source income applies, the charge under s.731 arises where the transferor or a close family member receives a benefit provided out of protected foreign-source income, or where such a benefit is provided to someone else who then makes on onward gift to the transferor or a close family member.

25-070

## Exemptions

There are three exemptions to the heads of charge considered above:

25-071

(a) the "no tax avoidance purpose" exemption (s.737(3));
(b) the "commercial transaction" exemption (s.737(4)); and
(c) the "genuine transaction" exemption (s.742A).

## The "no tax avoidance purpose" exemption

This exemption, often referred to as the motive defence, is satisfied if it would not be reasonable to draw the conclusion, from all the circumstances of the case, that the purpose of avoiding liability to taxation was the purpose, or one of the purposes, for which the relevant transactions or any of them were effected.[122]

25-072

The intention and purpose of any person who designs or effects or provides advice in relation to any of the relevant transactions is taken into account for these purposes.[123] The reference to taxation means UK tax (including NIC), so if the sole purpose of the relevant transactions is to avoid foreign tax then this exemption will apply.[124] The "avoidance" of tax for these purposes means a course of action designed to conflict with or defeat the evident intention of Parliament.[125]

25-073

For this exemption to apply there must be no tax avoidance purpose whatever,

25-074

---

[120] A settlement is tainted if property or income is provided (directly or indirectly) for the purposes of the settlement by the settlor (or another settlement of which he is the settlor or a beneficiary), and at the time of the provision the settlor is UK domiciled or deemed UK domiciled (s.721A(3)(e)). For this purpose, the transactions listed in s.721B are disregarded (e.g. property or income provided under a transaction, other than a loan, where the transaction is entered into on arm's length terms).

[121] ITA 2007 ss.726, 730 and 735.

[122] ITA 2007 s.737(3). This relates to transactions after 4 December 2005. A similar exemption in s.739 applies to transactions before 5 December 2005.

[123] ITA 2007 s.737(6).

[124] ITA 2007 s.737(7); *IRC v Herdman* [1969] 1 W.L.R. 323; [1969] 1 All E.R. 495.

[125] *IRC v Willoughby* [1997] 1 W.L.R. 1071; [1997] S.T.C. 995 per Lord Nolan. In that case counsel for HMRC said (and Lord Nolan accepted) that "The hallmark of tax avoidance is that the taxpayer reduces his liability to tax without incurring the economic consequences that Parliament intended to be suffered by any taxpayer qualifying for such reduction in his tax liability. The hallmark of tax mitigation, on the other hand, is that the taxpayer takes advantage of a fiscally attractive option afforded to him by the tax legislation, and genuinely suffers the economic consequences that Parliament intended to be suffered by those taking advantage of the option. Where the taxpayer's chosen course is seen upon examination to involve tax avoidance (as opposed to tax mitigation), it follows

regarding the contributions or transfers to the pension scheme or the investments of the pension scheme. One must first consider what the purpose of the contribution or transfer is, and if UK tax considerations is among those purposes, one must consider if a purpose of the contribution or transfer was to avoid tax. There are a number of non-tax reasons for establishing and contributing to a pension scheme outside of the UK.[126] The decision in *Willoughby* indicates that there are two tests potentially applicable in distinguishing avoidance from mitigation:

(a) Has the taxpayer, in economic terms, genuinely incurred the consequences of what, in tax terms, he has done?
(b) Does what he has done conflict with or defeat the intention of Parliament?

**25-075** Using dual contracts in order to benefit from the remittance basis of taxation on foreign earnings has been found to be tax mitigation rather than tax avoidance.[127] The creation by a non-UK resident settlor of a non-UK discretionary settlement in favour of his UK resident granddaughter, following UK tax advice, has been found to not be tax avoidance[128], but the creation of a non-UK settlement by a UK resident remittance basis taxpayer in order to protect the fund from IHT has been found to be tax avoidance.[129]

**25-076** In *Fisher v HMRC*[130] the FTT, after reviewing the case law, summarised the position in relation to the motive defence as follows:

(a) the test is subjective[131];
(b) evidence of a person's reactions to what is said to them and circumstances as well what they say their purpose is may be relevant[132];
(c) it is not enough to show a tax avoidance effect;
(d) knowledge that less tax is paid does not equate to a tax avoidance purpose (but knowledge is a pre-requisite to having a purpose);
(e) awareness of tax aspects does not equate to having a tax avoidance motive[133];
(f) the mere fact of taking tax advice does not mean there is a tax avoidance motive[134]; and
(g) picking a lower tax route over a higher tax route does not equate to tax avoidance (but equally does not preclude tax avoidance).[135]

**25-077** Consider, for example, a contribution to a QNUPS by a UK resident and domiciled individual. It may be argued that IHTA 1984 ss.58(1)(d) and 151 offer a very clear exemption from inheritance tax for QNUPS, and simply taking advantage of these exemptions cannot be said to defeat Parliament's intention. A QNUPS can-

---

that tax avoidance must be at least one of the taxpayer's purposes in adopting that course, whether or not the taxpayer has formed the subjective motive of avoiding tax".

[126] e.g. it may be desirable to avoid the application of PA 1995 (see the definition of occupational pension scheme in PSA 1993 s.1(1), applied by PA 1995 s.176) or to avoid the application of the Matrimonial Causes Act 1973 (see *Goyal v Goyal* [2016] EWCA Civ 792).

[127] *Carvill v IRC* [2000] S.T.C. (S.C.D.) 143.

[128] *Beneficiary v IRC* [1999] S.T.C. (S.C.D.) 134. The settlor's purpose was to secure the financial independence of his granddaughter and ensure she did not have to rely on her mother.

[129] *Rialas v HMRC* [2020] S.F.T.D. 106. On appeal, the UT decided against HMRC on other points and so did not find it necessary to consider the motive defence (*Rialas v HMRC* [2020] UKUT 367).

[130] *Fisher v HMRC* [2014] UKFTT 804 at [287].

[131] *Carvill v IRC* [2000] S.T.C. (S.C.D.) 143.

[132] *Philippi v IRC* [1971] 1 W.L.R. 1272; 47 T.C. 75.

[133] *IRC v Willoughby* [1997] 1 W.L.R. 1071; [1997] S.T.C. 995.

[134] *Beneficiary v IRC* [1999] S.T.C. (S.C.D.) 134.

[135] *IRC v Brebner* [1966] S.L.T. 208; (1966) 43 T.C. 705; *IRC v Willoughby* [1997] 1 W.L.R. 1071; [1997] S.T.C. 995.

not be established in the UK so the only way to utilise a QNUPS is to make a transfer to a person abroad. Any income tax efficiencies arising in respect of scheme investments follow as a consequence of the scheme being non-UK resident and a bona fide pension scheme. The taxpayer has, in economic terms, genuinely incurred the consequences of what, in tax terms, he has done, and it does not conflict with or defeat the intention of Parliament. As was the case in *Willoughby* (in relation to life policies), the UK tax code contains provisions applicable to non-UK pension schemes (in ITEPA 2003 Pt 9 Ch.4, for example) and so these provisions should apply rather than the transfer of assets abroad provisions. In *IRC v Brebner*[136] (cited in *Willoughby* in the Court of Appeal), Lord Upjohn confirmed that in the context of commercial transactions and what is now ITA 2007 s.685 (the transactions in securities provisions), the fact that there may be more than one way of carrying out a transaction, one of which is more tax efficient than the others, does not necessarily mean that tax avoidance is one of the main objects. No reasonable person should choose any other cause of action. Therefore, the fact that the individual could have joined a UK resident unregistered pension scheme should not be a relevant consideration.

It is strongly arguable that making contributions to an offshore scheme with a benefit structure which would be permitted under a registered pension scheme does not constitute tax avoidance.[137] Provided that the member is entitled to receive benefits, any subsequent decision to defer drawing benefits would be entirely consistent with the registered pension scheme regime and so should not be objectionable. The registered pension scheme tax charges (for example, in relation to investment in taxable property) would not apply to such a scheme, but that is reasonable given that no tax relief would be available in respect of contributions to such a scheme.

**25-078**

If the exemption in s.737 applies in respect of a contribution or transfer, it may cease to apply if the trustees take steps to avoid UK tax on investment income. For example, if the trustees were to transfer UK land to an underlying company in order to reduce the higher rate of income tax on rental income, this, according to a Special Commissioner, may constitute tax avoidance.[138] It is also an associated operation for the purposes of the transfer of assets abroad provisions, and therefore, if it does constitute tax avoidance then it could result in the income of the member's fund under the scheme being taxed on the member under ITA 2007 s.720. The better view is likely to be that this does not constitute avoidance. UK source income is generally taxable at 45% if received by a trust and only 20% if received by a non-UK company, so investing via a company to take advantage of the lower rates is entirely consistent with Parliament's intention. The trustees may also of course have commercial reasons for purchasing land via a company, in which case the *commercial transaction* exemption may be relevant.

**25-079**

If the s.737 exemption is claimed it should be shown on the individual's tax return.

**25-080**

---

[136] *IRC v Brebner* [1967] 2 A.C. 18.
[137] In the past, this generally required one to ensure that benefits must commence no later than age 75 and approximately 70% must be applied to pay an income for life. Given the flexibility regarding benefits under registered pension scheme regime since April 2015, this should no longer be material.
[138] See *Burns v RCC* [2009] S.T.C. (S.C.D.) 165 at [58].

### The "commercial transaction" exemption

**25-081** This exemption is satisfied if the *no tax avoidance purpose* exemption does not apply (i.e. it starts from the premise that there is an intention to avoid UK tax) and[139]:

(a) all the relevant transactions are genuine commercial transactions; and
(b) it would not be reasonable to draw the conclusion, from all the circumstances of the case, that any one or more of those transactions was more than incidentally designed for the purpose of avoiding liability to taxation.

**25-082** A commercial transaction is a transaction on arm's length terms and effected: (a) in the course of a trade or business and for its purposes; or (b) with a view to setting up and commencing a trade or business and for its purposes.[140] In addition to being on arm's length terms, the transaction must not be a transaction that would not have been entered into between such persons so dealing.

**25-083** This exemption will usually be applicable only in the context of occupational pension schemes, although it could conceivably apply to a non-occupational scheme if the intention is for the trustees of the scheme to carry on a business, for example. A trade or business can include making and managing investments provided that the manager is not connected with the investor, and they are dealing at arm's length. If the purpose of the scheme is to provide funds for the purposes of retirement, and the benefit structure does not differ markedly from a registered pension scheme, one would expect this exemption to apply.

### The "genuine transaction" exemption

**25-084** If the relevant transaction takes place on or after 6 April 2012, and both of the conditions below are satisfied, the deemed income of the transferor is left out of account so far as it is attributable to the transaction. This exemption is sometimes referred to as the European defence, because its introduction was prompted by infraction proceedings initiated by the European Commission against the UK in connection with the transfer of assets abroad provisions breaching EU law. The conditions are that:

(a) viewed objectively, the transaction is considered to be a genuine transaction having regard to any arrangements under which it is effected and any other relevant circumstances; and
(b) on the assumption that (a) above is satisfied, the second condition is that if the individual were liable to tax under the transfer of assets abroad provisions by reference to the transaction, the individual's liability to tax would, in contravention of a relevant treaty provision, constitute an unjustified and disproportionate restriction on a freedom protected under that relevant treaty provision. A relevant treaty provision means Title II or IV of Part Three of the TFEU or Pt II or III of the EEA agreement.[141]

**25-085** In order for the transaction to be considered to be a genuine transaction, it must be on arm's length terms and must not be a transaction that would not have been entered into between such persons so dealing, having regard to any arrangements under which the transaction is effected and any other relevant circumstances. In the

---

[139] ITA 2007 s.737(4). This relates to transactions on or after 5 December 2005. A similar exemption in ITA 2007 s.739 applies to transactions before 5 December 2005.
[140] ITA 2007 s.738.
[141] Title IV includes the freedom of establishment and the freedom of movement of capital.

context of a retirement benefit scheme, provided that the member is entitled to retirement benefits, and expects to receive them, one would expect contributions to satisfy this requirement.

There is an additional requirement that must be satisfied in order for the transaction to be considered a genuine transaction where any assets or income derived from the relevant transfer are used for the purposes of, or received in the course of, a business establishment[142] in a territory outside the UK. The activities of such business must consist of the provision by the relevant person of goods or services to others on a commercial basis and involve: (a) the use of staff in numbers, and with competence and authority; (b) the use of premises and equipment; and (c) the addition of economic value, by the relevant person, to those to whom the goods or services are provided, commensurate with the size and nature of those activities. Staff means employees, agents or contractors of the relevant person. 25-086

This additional requirement does not apply if: 25-087

(a) the relevant transfer is made by an individual who makes it wholly for personal reasons (and not commercial reasons) and for the personal benefit (and not the commercial benefit) of other individuals; and
(b) no consideration is given (directly or indirectly) for the relevant transfer or otherwise for any benefit received by any of those other individuals and all of the following assets and income are dealt with accordingly: (i) any of the assets transferred by the relevant transfer; (ii) any assets directly or indirectly representing any of the assets transferred; (iii) any income arising from any assets within (i) or (ii); (iv) any assets directly or indirectly representing the accumulations of income arising from any assets within (i) or (ii).

It is very unlikely that the additional requirement above would have much application to retirement benefit schemes. 25-088

## THE CGT SETTLEMENTS PROVISIONS

The CGT settlements provisions are in: 25-089

(a) TCGA 1992 s.86 and Sch.5; and
(b) TCGA 1992 ss.87–97.

Section 86 taxes a UK resident settlor on an arising basis where non-UK resident trustees realise a gain, and s.87 taxes UK resident beneficiaries when, following a disposal of property at a gain, distributions are made to them. Section 87 can apply only to the extent that s.86 has not already applied to any gains. 25-090

If the non-UK scheme is an overseas pension scheme[143] any gains accruing on a disposal of scheme investments are not chargeable gains.[144] Therefore, for CGT purposes, an overseas pension scheme is treated in the same way as a registered pension scheme. Strictly speaking this may not in itself prevent ss.86 or 87 from 25-091

---

[142] To determine if a person has a business establishment in a territory outside the UK, one applies CTA 2010 ss.1141, 1142(1) and 1143 as if in those provisions references to a company were to a person, and references to a permanent establishment were to a business establishment.
[143] For the meaning of "overseas pension scheme", see Ch.31.
[144] TCGA 1992 s.271(1A). This does not apply to gains accruing to a person from the acquisition and disposal by him of assets held as a member of a property investment LLP: TCGA 1992 s.271(12).

applying[145] but it is strongly arguable that these provisions should not have any application to such a scheme.

**TCGA 1992 s.86**

**25-092**  If TCGA 1992 s.86 applies then any gains are taxed on the settlor on an arising basis, irrespective of whether he actually receives any sort of benefit from the scheme. In outline, s.86(1) applies where the following conditions are satisfied in relation to a *settlement* in a particular year of assessment:

(a) the trustees are not resident in the UK at any time in the year;
(b) a settlor in relation to the settlement is resident in the UK for the tax year and either: (i) domiciled in the UK at some time during the tax year or deemed to be so domiciled as a returner[146]; or (ii) the settlement has been tainted on or after 6 April 2017[147];
(c) at any time during the year the settlor has an interest in the settlement; and
(d) by virtue of disposals of any of the settled property originating from the settlor, there is an amount on which the trustees would be chargeable to CGT for the year under TCGA 1992 s.1(3) (i.e. the basic CGT charging provision) if they were resident in the UK (and any double taxation relief arrangements did not apply).

*"Settlement" and "settlor"*

**25-093**  For the purposes of TCGA 1992 s.86, settled property means any property held in trust (other than nominee and bare trust arrangements), and references to property comprised in a settlement are references to settled property.[148] A person is a settlor in relation to a settlement if the settled property consists of or includes property originating from him.[149] Property originates from a person if he *provided* the property (including any property representing the property provided, such as property representing accumulated income from that other property), and reciprocal arrangements are also included.[150] So, as with the income tax settlements provisions considered above, there is a requirement for property to have been provided. In *IRC v Leiner*,[151] Plowman J held that, for the purposes of the income tax settlement provisions, the term provided imports a requirement that the transfer of property must be bounteous. In practice, HMRC accept that s.86 requires bounty.[152] The Revenue have confirmed that s.86 does not normally apply to an overseas retirement benefit scheme if it is part of a normal arrangement for remunerating

---

[145] The position is not clear because each of ss.86 and 87 require one to determine the CGT that would be payable if the trustees were resident in the UK. Although it may be possible in principle for an overseas pension scheme to have UK resident trustees, it is arguable ss.86 and 87 require one to proceed on the basis that the scheme cannot satisfy the requirements in TCGA 1992 s.271(1A).

[146] i.e. he was born in the UK and has a UK domicile of origin.

[147] i.e. property or income is provided (directly or indirectly) for the purposes of the settlement by the settlor (or another settlement of which he is the settlor or a beneficiary), and at the time of the provision the settlor is UK domiciled or deemed UK domiciled (Sch.5 para.5A). For this purpose, the transactions listed in Sch.5 para.5B are disregarded (e.g. property or income provided under a transaction, other than a loan, where the transaction is entered into on arm's length terms).

[148] TCGA 1992 s.68.

[149] TCGA 1992 Sch.5 para.7.

[150] TCGA 1992 Sch.5 para.8(1), (3) and (6). Where there are reciprocal arrangements with another person, property or income provided by the other person are deemed to have been provided by the settlor.

[151] *IRC v Leiner* (1964) 41 T.C. 589.

[152] CG38445.

employees[153] or to a "genuine commercial arrangement to attract and motivate good quality staff".[154]

*Corporate settlors*

A company may be a settlor for the purposes of s.86. Provided that the company is excluded from benefitting then it will not have an interest in the settlement, however where the settlor is a close company or a company which would be a close company if it were resident in the UK (referred to as a *qualifying company*) the application of these provisions is greatly extended. Where property is provided by a qualifying company[155]:

25-094

(a) controlled by one person alone at the time it is provided, that person is taken to have provided that property;
(b) controlled by two or more persons (taking each one separately) at the time it is provided, those persons are taken to have provided the property and each one is taken to have provided an equal share of it; or
(c) controlled by two or more persons (taking them together) at the time it is provided, the persons who are participators in the company at the time it is provided are taken to have provided the property and each one is taken to have provided so much of it as is attributed to him on the basis of a just apportionment. However this does not apply to a person who would be taken to provide less than one-twentieth of such property.

Control of a company is construed in accordance with CTA 2010 ss.450 and 451[156] except that no rights or powers of (or attributed to) any associates of a person are attributed to him if he is not a participator in the company. Participator has the same meaning as in CTA 2010 s.454. A person is not regarded as a participator in a company controlled by the trustees of a settlement where the person has a share or interest in the capital or income of the company solely because of an interest which the person has under the settlement.

25-095

*The settlor has an interest in the settlement*

A settlor has an interest in a settlement if[157]:

25-096

(a) any property or income originating from the settlor is or will or may become applicable for the benefit of or payable to a defined person in any circumstances whatever; or
(b) any defined person enjoys a benefit directly or indirectly from any property or income originating from, or arising under, the settlement. It is implicit, given (a) above, that this relates primarily to benefits provided in breach of trust, and so simply excluding all defined persons would not in itself ensure that this cannot apply.

---

[153] *Law Society Gazette*, 29 January 1992.
[154] *Tax Bulletin 16*, April 1995, p.204.
[155] TCGA 1992 Sch.5 para.8(4).
[156] i.e. control at the level of general meetings (*Steele v EVC International NV* [1996] S.T.C. 785).
[157] TCGA 1992 Sch.5 para.2(1). As with the income tax settlement provisions, an exception applies where a defined person can benefit only in the event of: (i) the bankruptcy of a beneficiary; (ii) an assignment of, or a charge on, the property by a beneficiary; (iii) in the case of a marriage settlement the death of both parties to, and any children of, the marriage; or (iv) the death of a beneficiary under the age of 25 who would be beneficially entitled to the property on attaining that age (TCGA 1992 Sch.5 para.2(4)).

**25-097** Each of the following is a defined person[158]: (a) the settlor; (b) the settlor's spouse or civil partner; (c) any child of the settlor or of the settlor's spouse or civil partner; (d) the spouse or civil partner of any such child; (e) any grandchild of the settlor or of the settlor's spouse or civil partner; (f) the spouse or civil partner of any such grandchild; (g) a company controlled by person(s) within (a)–(f) above; and (h) a company associated with a company within (g) above.

**25-098** Where there is more than one settlor in respect of a settlement, each settlor is chargeable only in relation to gains accruing on disposals of property originating from him.[159] On the face of it (and in contrast to the income tax settlement provisions), if a defined person can benefit from derived property that should not cause the settlor to have an interest in the settlement. The fact that the settlor could benefit by the independent act of a third party does not mean that he has an interest in the settlement,[160] otherwise there would be no property in which the settlor does not have an interest.

**25-099** The provisions do not expressly require the payment to the settlor to be pursuant to the terms of the settlement but it seems that this is limited to cases where the income or property may become payable under the terms of the settlement or under some collateral agreement having legal force.[161]

*The effect of s.86(1) applying*

**25-100** Where s.86(1) applies, one is required to calculate the CGT that the trustees would have paid if they were UK resident.[162] Where trustees are participators in a non-UK resident close company, gains of the company may be treated as gains of the settlement if: (a) the gains would be attributed to the trust by virtue of TCGA 1992 s.13 if the trust were UK resident; and (b) the settlement's interest in the company originated from the settlor.[163]

**25-101** The gains are then attributed to the settlor under TCGA 1992 s.1(3). The settlor has a statutory right to recover from the trustees any tax he pays under s.86[164] and HMRC consider that any provision in the trust instrument to this effect does not constitute: (a) an interest in the settlement for the purposes of the income tax settlements provisions; (b) power to enjoy for the purposes of the transfer of assets abroad provisions; or (c) a reservation of benefit for inheritance tax purposes.[165] Nor does any reimbursement constitute a capital payment for the purposes of TCGA 1992 s.87.

**TCGA 1992 s.87**

**25-102** If s.86 does not apply to a non-UK resident settlement at the time that gains are realised by the trustees[166] then TCGA 1992 s.87 may have application. If it does, any gains realised by the settlement are subject to UK tax when capital payments are made to UK resident persons.

---

[158] TCGA 1992 Sch.5 para.2(3).
[159] TCGA 1992 s.86(1)(e).
[160] *West v Trennery* [2003] EWHC 676 (Ch); [2003] S.T.C. 580 at 601.
[161] *Muir v IRC* [1966] 1 W.L.R. 1269; (1966) 43 T.C. 367 per Pennycuick J.
[162] For this purpose, no annual exemption is available but current year losses are allowed (TCGA 1992 Sch.5 para.1).
[163] TCGA 1992 Sch.5 para.1(3).
[164] TCGA 1992 Sch.5 para.6.
[165] Statement of Practice 5/92 paras 8–10.
[166] e.g. because the settlor is dead, non-UK domiciled, or non-UK resident, or the settlement is not settlor-interested or it is not a trust.

## THE CGT SETTLEMENTS PROVISIONS

Section 87 applies to a settlement for a tax year if there is no time in that year when the trustees are resident in the UK. Where it applies, chargeable gains are treated as accruing in the relevant tax year to a beneficiary of the settlement who has received a capital payment from the trustees in the relevant tax year or any earlier tax year if all or part of the capital payment is matched with the s.1(3) amount for the relevant tax year or any earlier tax year.

25-103

### Settlement

For the purposes of s.87, *settlement* has the same meaning as in the income tax settlements provisions, and settled property and references to property comprised in a settlement are construed accordingly.[167] Therefore, unlike s.86, this is not restricted to trusts.[168] Incorporating the definition in the income tax settlements provisions puts it beyond doubt (again, in contrast to s.86) that bounty is required. In principle, the residence and domiciles status of the settlor is irrelevant, although in practice if he is both UK domiciled and resident then one would expect s.86 rather than s.87 to apply.

25-104

### Capital payment

A capital payment means any payment which is not chargeable to income tax on the recipient or, in the case of a recipient who is not resident in the UK, any payment received otherwise than as income. However this does not include a payment under a transaction entered into at arm's length.[169] Payment includes the transfer of an asset and the conferring of any other benefit (e.g. loans at less than the official rate of interest or occupation of trust property on non-arm's length terms). The amount of a capital payment made by way of loan, or of any other capital payment which is not an outright payment of money, is equal to the value of the benefit conferred by it.[170]

25-105

### The s.1(3) amount[171]

For each year that s.87 applies to a settlement, the trustees are required to determine the s.1(3) amount.[172] The s.1(3) amount is the amount upon which the trustees of the settlement would be chargeable to CGT under TCGA 1992 s.1(3) for that year if they were resident in the UK. If s.86 applies to the settlement for that year, the amount is reduced by the total amount of chargeable gains treated under s.86 as accruing in that year. If there is a transfer between settlements then some or all of the s.1(3) amount is carried across to the receiving settlement.

25-106

---

[167] TCGA 1992 s.97(7).
[168] Where there are no trustees the references to trustees are to any person in whom the property is vested or who has management of the property (TCGA 1992 s.97(7A)).
[169] TCGA 1992 s.97(1), applicable to payments received on or after 19 March 1991.
[170] TCGA 1992 s.97(4).
[171] Often referred to as trust gains or stockpiled gains.
[172] Although it is not necessary to do this on an annual basis (it frequently does not happen until a capital payment is made to a UK resident beneficiary), it is good practice to do so because it is otherwise easy to fail to obtain the necessary valuations etc. In addition, the s.1(3) amount must be computed according to the provisions applicable in that year, and so attempting to do so many years afterwards (when the tax provisions will no doubt be different) is much more difficult.

## Matching

**25-107** In order for s.87 to apply, the capital payment must be matched with a s.1(3) amount. If trust gains exceed capital payments, there are *unmatched* gains, and the trustees must keep a separate record of unmatched gains for each tax year (they are not pooled). Unmatched gains can be matched against capital payments in subsequent years (on a last in, first out basis). If capital payments exceed trust gains the unmatched payments can be used to attribute trust gains to beneficiaries in future years. Personal capital losses made by a beneficiary cannot be set against a beneficiary's trust gains arising under s.87 (in contrast to the position under s.86).

## Non-UK beneficiaries

**25-108** Prior to 6 April 2018, capital payments made to non-UK resident beneficiaries were matched with gains (and the payment thereby reduced trust gains), but the matched gains were not chargeable to CGT. For this reason, trustees often made capital payments to non-chargeable beneficiaries first, to reduce the *stockpile* of capital gains on which chargeable beneficiaries will pay tax in subsequent years. With effect from 6 April 2018, capital payments made to non-residents are disregarded.[173]

**25-109** In addition, with effect from 6 April 2018:

(a) A capital payment to a beneficiary who is a close family member of the settlor's family is deemed to be a capital payment to the settlor if the settlor is UK resident at any time in that tax year.[174]

(b) Where a capital payment is made to a non-UK person who then makes on onward gift to a UK person, the latter is deemed to have received the payment from the settlement.[175]

**25-110** Prior to 6 April 2018, if the beneficiary was a remittance basis taxpayer, s.87 applied only to the extent that the capital payment was remitted to the UK.[176]

## The supplementary charge

**25-111** Section 91 increases the tax due under s.87 where gains are not distributed in either the tax year in which they are realised or the following tax year. The supplementary charge is 10% of the CGT on a capital payment multiplied by the number of years in the chargeable period. The supplemental charge will therefore be 20%, 30%, 40%, 50% or 60%. The chargeable period cannot exceed six years (so the rate cannot exceed 60%). A chargeable period runs from 1 December following the tax year in which the gain arose to 30 November in the tax year after that in which the gain is distributed.

---

[173] New s.87D, inserted by FA 2018 Sch.10 Pt 1.
[174] TCGA 1992 s.87G.
[175] TCGA 1992 s.87I.
[176] TCGA 1992 ss.87B(2) and 12.

# CHAPTER 26

# Benefits

## TABLE OF CONTENTS

| | |
|---|---|
| Overview | 26-001 |
| Income tax | 26-003 |
|    ITEPA 2003 Pt 9 | 26-003 |
|    The amount charged to tax | 26-004 |
|       Exempt income | 26-006 |
| Foreign pensions | 26-007 |
|    Definition | 26-007 |
|    "Pension" | 26-008 |
|    Relevant lump sums | 26-010 |
|       Application of Pt 9 to relevant lump sums | 26-011 |
|       Amount of pension income | 26-014 |
|          Step 2: EFRBS foreign service relief | 26-015 |
|          Step 2: application to investment growth since 6 April 2017 | 26-018 |
|          Step 2: application to partial lump sums | 26-019 |
|          Step 3: is the deduction limited by reference to the LS allowance? | 26-020 |
|          Step 3: what lump sums would not be liable to income tax under ITEPA 2003 Pt 9 if the scheme were a registered pension scheme? | 26-021 |
|       Comment on the relevant lump sum provisions | 26-025 |
|    Exceptions | 26-026 |
|       RNUKS and overseas pension schemes | 26-027 |
|       Beneficiaries' income withdrawal | 26-029 |
|       Beneficiaries' annuities | 26-031 |
|    Taxable pension income | 26-032 |
|       Remittance basis taxpayers | 26-033 |
|    Liability | 26-034 |
|       Temporary non-residents | 26-035 |
| UK pensions | 26-039 |
|    Temporary non-residents | 26-040 |
| Employment-related annuities | 26-041 |
|    Annuities for the benefit of dependants | 26-043 |
|    Annuities under non-registered occupational pension schemes | 26-044 |
|    Annuities in recognition of another's services | 26-045 |
|       Exceptions | 26-046 |
|       Taxable pension income | 26-047 |
|       Liability | 26-050 |
| Voluntary annual payments | 26-051 |

572                                BENEFITS

        Taxable pension income ....................... 26-052
    Exempt pensions ................................ 26-053
        Disablement pensions ......................... 26-053
        Pensions paid under health and employment insurance
           policies ..................................... 26-055
           Genuine arm's length insurance ............... 26-058
    Other provisions which could apply to lump sums ....... 26-059
        Annual payments ............................ 26-060
        Transfer of assets abroad provisions ............. 26-064
        Capital gains tax ............................ 26-066
    Tax treaties .................................... 26-068
    Unilateral relief for foreign tax paid ................. 26-069
    National insurance contributions .................... 26-070
        Foreign service ............................. 26-072
        Qualifying overseas pension schemes ............. 26-073
        Employer-financed pension only schemes .......... 26-074
           The conditions ............................. 26-076
        Double taxation agreements .................... 26-077

## OVERVIEW

**26-001** This chapter considers the general taxation of benefits received under unregistered pension schemes. The chapter focuses in particular on UK resident beneficiaries, but comments where appropriate on non-UK resident beneficiaries. The NIC provisions are considered separately at the end of the chapter.

**26-002** In many cases, unregistered pension schemes can provide a much wider range of benefits than registered pension scheme, and such flexibility may complicate the tax analysis of such benefits.

## INCOME TAX

**ITEPA 2003 Pt 9**

**26-003** ITEPA 2003 Pt 9 contains provisions relating to the taxation of "pension income", which means the pensions, annuities and income of other types to which the provisions listed in s.566(4) apply (including pensions under registered pension schemes). In this chapter the following are considered:

(a) Foreign pensions (Pt 9 Ch.4);
(b) UK pensions (Pt 9 Ch.3);
(c) Certain employment-related annuities (Pt 9 Ch.10); and
(d) Voluntary annual payments (Pt 9 Ch.15).

Two exemptions in Pt 9 Ch.17 are also considered in this chapter: (a) disability pensions paid due to injury or illness at work; and (b) pensions paid under health and employment insurance policies.

# INCOME TAX

**The amount charged to tax**

In relation to each pension, annuity or other item of pension income, the amount charged to tax is the "net taxable pension income" for the tax year.[1] This is the amount of "taxable pension income" for that pension, annuity or item of pension income for that year, less any allowable deductions. "Allowable deductions" are those under ITEPA 2003 s.567A, and ITEPA 2003 Pt 12: the former applies a deduction to avoid double taxation where ITEPA 2003 Pt 7A has applied to the source of the pension income, and the latter applies to charitable gifts via payroll.

26-004

Under s.567A, if the taxable pension income includes an amount which accrues or arises out of rights (the "relevant rights") which represent or have arisen or derived from a sum of money or asset which was the subject of a relevant step to which Pt 7A Ch.2 applied, the taxable pension income is reduced by the amount which counted as employment income under Pt 7A Ch.2.[2] If such employment income exceeds the taxable pension income, the excess is carried forward to future tax years in order to reduce future taxable pension income until all such employment income has been offset. If it is determined on a just and reasonable basis that the relevant rights represent or have arisen or derived from only part of the sum of money or asset which was the subject of the relevant step, the amount of employment income that may be offset against taxable pension income is a corresponding proportion of the amount which counted as employment income.

26-005

*Exempt income*

The way that taxable pension income is determined depends on which of Chs 3–15A of Pt 9 is applicable, but in each case one disregards any "exempt income". "Exempt income" means pension income on which no liability to income tax arises as a result of any provision of ITEPA 2003 Pt 9 Ch.15A (lump sums under registered pension schemes) or Ch.17[3] or Ch.18.[4]

26-006

---

[1] ITEPA 2003 s.567.
[2] ITEPA 2003 s.567A.
[3] ITEPA 2003 Pt 9 Ch.17 contains exemptions relating to awards for bravery, pensions in respect of death due to military or war service, lump sums provided under armed forces early departure scheme, wounds and disability pensions, compensation for National-Socialist persecution, Netherlands Benefit Act for Victims of Persecution 1940–1945, Malawi, Trinidad and Tobago and Zambia government pensions, pensions payable where employment ceased due to disablement, health and employment insurance payments, social security pensions: increases in respect of children, former miners etc: coal and allowances in lieu, foreign pensions of consular employees, registered schemes: beneficiaries' annuities from unused funds, registered schemes: beneficiaries' annuities from drawdown funds, non-registered schemes: beneficiaries' annuities from unused funds, and non-registered schemes: beneficiaries' annuities from drawdown funds.
[4] ITEPA 2003 Pt 9 Ch.18 contains exemptions relating to pensions paid to non-UK residents under The Central African Pension Fund, Commonwealth government pension funds, the Oversea Superannuation Scheme, the Overseas Pensions Act 1973, the Overseas Service Act 1958, the Overseas Service Pensions Fund, and The Pensions (India, Pakistan and Burma) Act 1955.

# FOREIGN PENSIONS

### Definition

**26-007** ITEPA 2003 Pt 9 Ch.4 applies to "foreign pensions", meaning any "pension" paid by or on behalf of[5] a person who is outside the UK to a person who is resident in the UK, unless any of Chs 5–14 of Pt 9 apply.[6] It has an extended meaning in relation to "relevant lump sums", considered below. It usually applies to pensions under RNUKS (including QROPS) and QNUPS, so it is the most significant category of pension income after pensions under registered pension schemes.

### "Pension"

**26-008** For the purposes of Pt 9 Ch.4 "pension" expressly includes:[7]

(a) an annuity under, or purchased with sums or assets held for the purposes of an RNUKS or an overseas pension scheme;[8]
(b) a relevant lump sum (see below);
(c) an amount paid under an RNUKS or an overseas pension scheme which, if the scheme were a registered pension scheme, would be income withdrawal;[9] and
(d) if either of the following conditions are met, a pension which is paid voluntarily or is capable of being discontinued:[10]
  (i) the pension is paid to a former employee or office-holder,[11] or the widow or widower (or surviving civil partner) of such a person, or any child, relative or dependant of such a person; or
  (ii) the pension is paid by or on behalf of the former employer (or other person under whom the former office-holder held the office), or the successors of that employer (or other person).

**26-009** The list is not intended to be exhaustive; these are payments which may not otherwise be considered to be pension.[12]

---

[5] The person paying the pension may be within the UK if it is paid on behalf of a person outside of the UK. The words "on behalf of" ordinarily suggest a relationship of agency (*Gaspet Ltd v Elliss (Inspector of Taxes)* [1985] 1 W.L.R. 1214 at 1220 (Peter Gibson J); *Clixby v Pountney (Inspector of Taxes)* [1968] Ch. 719 at 728–729 (Cross J), but, where the context requires, they have been read more widely as meaning "in the place of" (*R. (S) v Social Security Commissioner* [2009] EWHC 2221 (Admin); [2010] P.T.S.R. 1785 at [27]–[28]). In most cases, where a UK administrator makes a payment of pension income relating to a scheme the trustees or managers of which are outside the UK, the payment will potentially be foreign pension.

[6] ITEPA 2003 s.573(1) and (2). In the context of private pension schemes, this means that Ch.4 will not apply to a foreign scheme which is a registered pension scheme (because Pt 9 Ch.5A will apply) or to the employment-related annuities described below (because Pt 9 Ch.10 will apply).

[7] ITEPA 2003 s.574(1).

[8] For "overseas pension schemes", see Ch.31.

[9] The reference to income withdrawal here includes dependants' income withdrawal, nominees' income withdrawal and successors' income withdrawal.

[10] Pensions which are paid voluntarily are referenced specifically because voluntary payments do not constitute income for tax purposes (*Stedeford v Beloe* [1932] A.C. 388).

[11] For these purposes, *office* includes in particular any position which has an existence independent of the person who holds it and may be filled by successive holders.

[12] In *Sinnamon v HMRC* [2016] UKFTT 168 at [78] the FTT appears to have concluded that, to be "foreign pension", it must be paid from an "overseas pension scheme": (as defined in FA 2004 s.150(7)). That is not a requirement.

## Relevant lump sums

A lump sum paid under a pension scheme[13] to a member of the scheme, or to a person in respect of a member, is a relevant lump sum if:[14]

26-010

(a) the scheme is not: (i) a registered pension scheme; (ii) an RNUKS; or (iii) an EFRBS established in the UK; and
(b) the payment of the lump sum is not a relevant step by reason of which Pt 7A Ch.2 applies.[15]

In relation to RNUKS, a lump sum paid to or in respect of a member[16] is a relevant lump sum if the member payment provisions do not apply in relation to the payment of the lump sum.[17] This will be the case where either the UK residency condition[18] does not apply or the payment is not referable to the member's tax-relieved fund or relevant transfer fund under the RNUKS. However, in relation to transfer members of an RNUKS, there is an exception for: (a) serious ill-health lump sums; and (b) authorised lump sum death benefits if the member died under the age of 75. Such lump sums are not relevant lump sums.

### *Application of Pt 9 to relevant lump sums*

ITEPA 2003 Pt 9 Ch.4 applies to a relevant lump sum paid by or on behalf of[19] a person who is outside the UK: (a) to a person who is resident in the UK;[20] or (b) to a person who is not resident in the UK if the lump sum is paid to that person in respect of a member of the scheme, and the member is, or immediately before the member's death was, resident in the UK. So, where a lump sum death benefit is a relevant lump sum, it will be taxable under Pt 9 Ch.4 if it is paid to: (a) a UK resident person; or (b) any person in respect of a UK resident member.

26-011

"Lump sum" is not defined. It is suggested that the payment of a lump sum involves the conferral of a benefit to or in respect of the member. Hence the purchase by the trustees or managers of an asset from the member on arm's length terms does not involve the payment of a lump sum. It seems reasonably clear that a transfer of the member's fund from one pension scheme to another does not involve the payment of a lump sum in respect of a member, especially where the rules of the transferor scheme do not refer to such a transfer as a benefit to the member. If a pension transfer is not the payment of a lump sum the relevant lump sum provisions can be sidestepped by transferring the member's fund to an unregistered pension scheme established in the UK, because a lump sum paid by a UK pension scheme cannot be a relevant lump sum. Alternatively, if it is possible to bring the non-UK pension scheme onshore by replacing the trustees with UK residents, the relevant lump sum provisions will not then apply.

26-012

---

[13] "Pension scheme" is defined in FA 2004 s.150(1). See Ch.2.
[14] ITEPA 2003 s.574A(1).
[15] See Ch.27.
[16] "Member", in relation to a pension scheme, is defined in FA 2004 s.151. See Ch.2.
[17] ITEPA 2003 s.574A(2).
[18] i.e. the member has not been resident in the UK at any time in the previous five full tax years (or ten full tax years for funds which have benefitted from tax relief or are transferred to a QROPS after 6 April 2017).
[19] As above, the words "on behalf of" ordinarily suggest a relationship of agency, but are likely to be interpreted more broadly here. In most cases, where a UK administrator makes a payment of pension income relating to a scheme the trustees or managers of which are outside the UK, the payment will potentially be foreign pension.
[20] ITEPA 2003 s.573.

**26-013** Where a non-UK resident member dies leaving UK resident beneficiaries, these provisions may be avoided if the relevant lump sum is paid to a non-UK resident settlement (e.g. a pilot trust established by the member). The relevant lump sum provision will not apply to a payment from the settlement provided that the settlement is not itself a pension scheme and cannot be said to form part of the non-UK pension scheme.

*Amount of pension income*

**26-014** If it is a foreign pension, the amount of the relevant lump sum which is taxable pension income is the amount of the lump sum, reduced in accordance with the following three steps.[21]

(a) *Step 1:* Deduct so much of the lump sum as is payable by reason of commutation of rights to receive pension income which would, if received as pension, constitute "exempt income" as a result of Pt 9 Ch.17.[22]

(b) *Step 2:* If the lump sum is paid under a pension scheme that was an EFRBS on 5 April 2017, deduct so much of the lump sum as qualifies for "foreign service relief" in accordance with the provisions described below.

If the lump sum is not paid under a pension scheme that was an EFRBS on 5 April 2017, deduct so much of the lump sum as is paid in respect of the value on 5 April 2017 of rights, accrued by then, specifically to receive benefits by way of lump sum payments.[23]

(c) *Step 3:* If the lump sum is paid under an overseas pension scheme,[24] deduct so much of the lump sum as would, if the scheme were a registered pension scheme, not be liable to income tax under ITEPA 2003 Pt 9. For this purpose, all amounts not included in taxable pension income as a result of s.637G(2)[25] are treated as being not liable to tax, and all of the member's LS allowance is deemed to be available. Two questions arise in relation to Step 3. First, when determining the amount which could be paid if the scheme were a registered pension scheme, is the deduction under Step 3 limited by reference to the LS allowance? Second, if the scheme were a registered pension scheme, what lump sums would not be liable to income tax under ITEPA 2003 Pt 9? These questions are considered below.

**26-015 Step 2: EFRBS foreign service relief** If at least 75% of pre-6 April 2017 reckonable service is made up of foreign service, the deductible amount is the value on 5 April 2017 of the rights then accrued to payment of so much of the "relevant amount" as is paid in respect of pre-6 April 2017 reckonable service. This also applies where: (a) the period of pre-6 April 2017 reckonable service exceeds 10 years and the whole of the last 10 years of that period is made up of foreign service; or

---

[21] ITEPA 2003 s.574A(3).
[22] For exempt income, see above.
[23] One might expect that this would not have much application to lump sum death benefits where the death occurs after 5 April 2017 because the death beneficiary will not usually have any right to death benefits before the member's death. However, the wording here is similar to that in ITEPA 2003 ss.554V and 554W, in relation to which HMRC take a generous view (see Ch.27).
[24] For "overseas pension schemes", see Ch.30.
[25] ITEPA 2003 s.636B applies if a trivial commutation lump sum or winding-up lump sum is paid to a member. Section 636B(3) provides that if, immediately before the lump sum is paid, the member has uncrystallised rights under any one or more arrangements under the pension scheme, the amount of the taxable pension income: (a) if all his rights under the pension scheme are uncrystallised rights, is 75% of the lump sum; and (b) otherwise, is reduced by 25% of the value of any uncrystallised rights extinguished by the lump sum.

(b) the period of pre-6 April 2017 reckonable service exceeds 20 years and at least 50% of that period, including any ten of the last 20 years, is made up of foreign service.

**26-016** The "relevant amount" means so much of the lump sum as is left after Step 1 as is paid in respect of rights specifically to receive benefits by way of lump sum payments. "Pre-6 April 2017 reckonable service" means reckonable service that is service before 6 April 2017, and "pre-6 April 2017 reckonable foreign service" means pre-6 April 2017 reckonable service that is foreign service. "Foreign service" means, broadly, service consisting of duties performed outside of the UK at a time when the individual was not resident in the UK.[26] "Reckonable service" means service in respect of which the rights to receive the relevant amount accrued (whether or not service in the same employment or with the same employer, and even if the rights originally accrued under a different EFRBS established in or outside the UK).

**26-017** If the pre-6 April 2017 reckonable service does not include sufficient foreign service for the above to apply, the deductible amount is the appropriate fraction of the value immediately before 6 April 2017 of the rights then accrued to payment of so much of the relevant amount as is paid in respect of pre-6 April 2017 reckonable service. The "appropriate fraction" is "F/R" where $F$ is the period of pre-6 April 2017 reckonable foreign service, and $R$ is the period of pre-6 April 2017 reckonable service.

**Step 2: application to investment growth since 6 April 2017** Under step 2, if **26-018** the pension scheme was an EFRBS on 5 April 2017, we are required deduct "the value immediately before 6 April 2017 of the rights then accrued to payment of so much of the relevant amount as is paid in respect of pre-6 April 2017 reckonable service". If the pension scheme was not an EFRBS on that date, we are required to deduct so much of the lump sum as is paid "in respect of the value on 5 April 2017 of rights, accrued by then, specifically to receive benefits by way of lump sum payments". Does this mean that we are required to determine the value on 6 April 2017, and the step 2 deduction does not apply to any growth since that date? That appears to be HMRC's position: "The deduction is limited to the value of the rights immediately before that date and does not include any investment growth thereafter".[27] The better view is that investment growth since 6 April 2017 is included in the step 2 deduction. Step 2 does not apply to post-6 April 2017 "accrual" and investment growth is not accrual. The drafting is very similar to ITEPA 2003 ss.554W, which provides an exception to the disguised remuneration provisions for a lump sum under an EFRBS paid out of "rights, which accrued before 6 April 2011, specifically to receive relevant benefits by way of lump sum payments". HMRC accept that "In general, investment returns from funds held on 5 April 2011 can be taken into account when valuing the relevant step treated as relating to the lump sum paid out of pre-6 April 2011 lump sum rights".[28] It is highly unlikely that these provisions are intended to mean different things.

**Step 2: application to partial lump sums** Where step 2 applies to some but not **26-019** all of a member's fund (i.e. it includes some post-6 April 2017 accrual), and he receives a lump sum of part of his fund, it is unclear how the provisions are intended to apply. Is the lump sum referrable to his pre-6 April 2017 accrual in priority to

---

[26] See ITEPA 2003 s.395C and Ch.35.
[27] EIM75550.
[28] EIM45635.

his post-6 April 2017 accrual (a "first in, first out" basis), or the other way round ("last in, last out"), or rateably from both (a pari passu basis)? If rateably, is this on the basis of the respective values, or on the basis of time? The legislation does not provide any indication,[29] and this point is not addressed in HMRC guidance. A similar issue arises in relation to post-6 April 2017 benefit accrual under s.615 funds and in that context HMRC are understood to consider that the rule in *Clayton's* case[30] dictates a first in, first out approach.[31] That will usually be the taxpayer's preferred answer, but it is suggested that a pari passu approach (by reference to the respective values of pre- and post-6 April 2017 accrual, or by reference to the amount of time that the taxpayer was a member pre- and post-6 April 2017) would not be unreasonable.

**26-020** **Step 3: is the deduction limited by reference to the LS allowance?** The assumption that we are required to make is not expressly limited to the time *before* the payment; it appears on its face to apply both before and after the payment. If that is correct, it seems that a payment cannot exhaust the member's LS allowance; it is effectively an instruction to disregard the application of the LS allowance for the purposes of the Step 3 deduction. It is arguable that that is the correct analysis. Suppose that a UK resident individual has 50% of the standard lifetime allowance (currently £1,073,100) available. The trustees of an overseas pension scheme wish to pay £1 million to him as a lump sum which would be an UFPLS if the scheme were a registered pension scheme. If such a lump sum were paid by a registered pension scheme, it would be limited to the amount of the member's available lifetime allowance (i.e. £536,550, in this example). If the trustees made two payments of UFPLS, each of £500,000, it is very clear that the limit does not apply, because the first payment (not being a payment under a registered pension scheme) will not use up any of the member's lifetime allowance. Prior to the second payment, the member still has 50% of the standard lifetime allowance (i.e. £536,550) available. It follows that 25% of each payment will be tax-free. It would be absurd if making two payments rather than one should make any difference to the tax analysis, which strongly suggests that the lifetime allowance is disregarded for the purposes of the deduction at Step 3. Now suppose that, instead of making two payments, the trustees made a single payment of £1 million. In these circumstances £463,450 could not (if the scheme were a registered pension scheme) be an UFPLS because it would exceed the amount of the member's lifetime allowance available at that time. If the scheme were a registered pension scheme, the £463,450 would normally be paid as a lifetime allowance excess lump sum. Such a lump sum is subject to tax under FA 2004 s.214, *not ITEPA 2003 Pt 9*.[32] The £463,450 therefore arguably benefits from a full Step 3 deduction. In this example, therefore, unless one disregards the lifetime allowance provisions when determining the amount of the Step 3 deduction, the £463,450 escapes UK tax altogether (as opposed to 25% being tax free). Again, this strongly suggests that the lifetime allowance is disregarded for these purposes (and HMRC would be unlikely to argue to the contrary).

**26-021** **Step 3: what lump sums would not be liable to income tax under ITEPA 2003**

---

[29] Cf. the RNUKS provisions in FA 2004 Sch.34, which prescribe that where a member's arrangement under an RNUKS comprises a UK tax-relieved fund and a non-relieved fund, benefits are first treated as made from the UK tax-relieved fund, and only once that fund is exhausted are benefits treated as made from the non-relieved fund.
[30] *Devaynes v Noble* 35 E.R. 767; (1816) 1 Mer. 529.
[31] See Ch.37 for more information on the application of *Clayton's* case.
[32] ITEPA 2003 s.636A(5).

## FOREIGN PENSIONS 579

**Pt 9 if the scheme were a registered pension scheme?** The following lump sums are expressly not liable to tax under ITEPA 2003 Pt 9 if paid by a registered pension scheme:

(a) a PCLS;[33]
(b) 25% of an UFPLS;[34]
(c) a serious ill-health lump sum paid to a member who has not reached age 75;[35]
(d) a refund of excess contributions lump sum;[36]
(e) a short service refund lump sum;[37] and
(f) all lump sum death benefits if the member (or other previous beneficiary) died before his 75th birthday and the lump sum is paid within the relevant two-year period.[38]

It follows that such a payment by an overseas pension scheme (even if it is an EFRBS), in relation to which an exemption from the disguised remuneration provisions applies, may be paid free of UK tax.

The deduction under Step 3 broadly aligns the tax treatment of lump sums received under overseas pension schemes with the tax treatment of lump sums received under registered pension schemes. However, the above payments are not the only lump sums which would not be liable to income tax under ITEPA 2003 Pt 9 if paid by a registered pension scheme. In particular, the following are not so liable:

26-022

(a) a lifetime allowance excess lump sum;[39]
(b) all authorised lump sum death benefits paid to a non-individual (including trustees), if the lump sum is not paid within the relevant two-year period, or the member dies on or after his 75th birthday;[40] and
(c) any lump sum that is an unauthorised payment.[41]

These payments *are* chargeable to income tax if they are paid by a registered pension scheme, but that liability arises under FA 2004 Pt 4 rather than under ITEPA 2003 Pt 9. The FA 2004 Pt 4 liability is referred to in ITEPA 2003 Pt 9,[42] but Pt 9 does not in any sense *cause* the FA 2004 Pt 4 charge to arise. The natural way to interpret the words "not be liable under Pt 9" (in Step 3) is that liability is not imposed by a provision in Pt 9. If that is correct, the fact that a charge to income tax is imposed under different legislation ought to be irrelevant. Perhaps HMRC

---

[33] ITEPA 2003 s.636A(1)(a).
[34] ITEPA 2003 s.636A(1A); ITEPA 2003 s.579A.
[35] ITEPA 2003 s.636A(1)(b).
[36] ITEPA 2003 s.636A(1).
[37] ITEPA 2003 s.636A(3)
[38] ITEPA 2003 s.636A(4). See Ch.15. The relevant two-year period is the period of two years beginning with the earlier of the day on which the scheme administrator first knew of the individual's death and the day on which the scheme administrator could first reasonably have been expected to have known of it.
[39] ITEPA 2003 s.636A(5). Such a lump sum cannot be paid from the relevant transfer fund of a QROPS or the UK tax-relieved fund of an RNUKS (The Pensions Schemes (Application of UK Provisions to Relevant Non-UK Schemes) Regulations 2006 (SI 2006/207) reg.15(8), modifying FA 2004 Sch.29 para.11), but there is no reason that such a lump sum could not otherwise be paid.
[40] Such lump sum death benefits are subject to tax under FA 2004 s.206 (not ITEPA 2003 Pt 9) (see ITEPA 2003 s.636A(4)).
[41] Such payments are not income for income tax purposes (FA 2004 s.208(8)). Section 579A(2) also supports this analysis.
[42] e.g. s.636A(5) provides that "a lifetime allowance excess lump sum is chargeable to income tax under sections 214 to 226 of FA 2004 (Lifetime allowance charge) but not otherwise".

would contend that the Step 3 deduction applies only to payments which are expressly referred to in Pt 9 as being not liable to income tax under any legislation (i.e. they are exempt from income tax). That might limit the Step 3 deduction to those payments referred to above. But as a matter of construction, that seems wrong. It also doesn't seem to fully address the position of unauthorised payments, because s.579A(2) does not expressly refer to such payments as not being liable under Pt 9.[43]

**26-023** In addition, where a lump sum death benefit is paid under a registered pension scheme established outside of the UK to a non-UK resident beneficiary (in respect of a beneficiary who was resident in the UK immediately before death), one would not expect any liability to arise *under ITEPA 2003 Pt 9*. This is not because of any express exemption in ITEPA 2003 Pt 9, but as a result of the territorial limitations of Pt 9 Ch.5A.[44] The position is even clearer where an applicable double tax treaty confers exclusive taxing rights on the country of residence.

**26-024** If a lump sum is not expressly taxable as a relevant lump sum (on the basis that it would not be taxable under ITEPA 2003 Pt 9 if received from a registered pension scheme), that does not mean that the lump sum is not otherwise subject to tax. The circumstances in which a lump sum may be subject to tax are considered below.

*Comment on the relevant lump sum provisions*

**26-025** The relevant lump sum provisions have extended the scope of ITEPA 2003 Pt 9 Ch.4 considerably. This is generally advantageous for non-UK EFRBS which are overseas pension schemes, because a lump sum paid to a UK resident is now chargeable under ITEPA 2003 Pt 9 rather than under ITEPA 2003 s.394[45] and the deduction permitted under Step 3 will usually result in a lower charge than would be the case under s.394. However in most other cases the provisions are likely to result in higher tax charges. Particular problems may arise where lump sums are paid to persons who are not resident in the UK in respect of a deceased beneficiary who was resident in the UK immediately before death. Such a lump sum may be taxable in the recipient's country of residence, and any double tax treaty between the UK and that country will assist only if the pension article is not restricted to income paid from a scheme in one jurisdiction to a beneficiary resident in the other (as that will clearly not be the case here: neither the scheme nor the beneficiary will be in the UK).

**Exceptions**

**26-026** There are no exceptions to the tax charge applicable to pension income paid to the member, but there are a number of exceptions relating to lump sums and death benefits.

*RNUKS and overseas pension schemes*

**26-027** In relation to RNUKS and overseas pension schemes, in most cases pension death benefits in the form of income withdrawal or an annuity will not be subject to tax under ITEPA 2003 Pt 9 provided that the member (or prior death beneficiary) dies

---

[43] If this analysis is correct, one would need to consider whether this is a 'shortcoming' in the legislation for the purposes of the general anti-abuse rule in FA 2013 Pt 5.
[44] For the implied territorial limits of Pt 9 Ch.5A, see Ch.20.
[45] See ITEPA 2003 s.393B(2)(a), which applies where benefits are charged to tax under ITEPA 2003 Pt 9 *or would be were it not for the three deductions under ITEPA 2003 s.574A(3)*.

before reaching age 75. These are exceptions rather than exemptions; the effect is that no charge under Pt 9 arises, but they do not expressly provide that such benefits are not otherwise taxable. In general, lump sum payments are unlikely to be subject to UK tax[46] but income payments could be.

These exceptions incorporate a number of concepts from FA 2004 Pt 4. References below to members, dependants, nominees and successors are to the persons that would be members, dependants, nominees or successors if the scheme was a registered pension scheme. Similarly, references to drawdown pension etc, are to what would be drawdown pension if the scheme was a registered pension scheme.

26-028

*Beneficiaries' income withdrawal*

Where the member (or dependant or nominee) of an RNUKS or overseas pension scheme dies before reaching age 75, there are two exceptions that apply to beneficiaries' income withdrawal. The first exception applies to dependants' and nominees' income withdrawal if:

26-029

(a) no pension payments were paid to the dependant or nominee before 6 April 2015 in respect of the deceased member out of the fund from which the pension is paid (or any fund represented to any extent by that fund);[47] and

(b) if the member died with uncrystallised funds which are designated on or after 6 April 2015 as available for the payment of dependants' or nominees' drawdown pension, the designation must occur within two years of earlier of the scheme manager becoming aware of the member's death or the date that the scheme manager could first reasonably have been expected to have become aware of it.[48]

The second exception applies to successors' income withdrawal. The only requirement is that the dependant or nominee died before reaching age 75.[49]

26-030

*Beneficiaries' annuities*

A number of exceptions apply to beneficiaries' annuities purchased[50] using sums or assets held for the purposes of an RNUKS or overseas pension scheme. The exceptions apply to beneficiaries' annuities purchased with unused drawdown funds, unused uncrystallised funds, or undrawn funds. In most cases, such annuities are not subject to tax under ITEPA 2003 Pt 9 provided that the member (or dependant or nominee) dies on or after 3 December 2014 before reaching age 75 and no payment of the annuity (or any prior annuity) was made before 6 April 2015.[51]

26-031

---

[46] Subject to the application of the transfer of assets abroad provisions, or TCGA 1992 s.87: seeCh.25.
[47] ITEPA 2003 s.573(2A).
[48] ITEPA 2003 s.573(2D). If the designation does not occur within the two-year period, the exception will not apply to any income withdrawal subsequently paid and so it will be taxable under s.575.
[49] ITEPA 2003 s.573(2B).
[50] Such annuities must be purchased from an insurance company, which has its usual FA 2004 s.275 meaning and also includes a person whose normal business includes the activity of providing annuities and who carries on that activity outside the UK, provided that it is regulated to do so in its home country, or is lawful under the law of that country because it is regulated in another country. An activity is regulated in a country if it is regulated by the government of that country or by a body established under the law of that country for the purpose of regulating the activity.
[51] The exceptions are in ITEPA 2003 ss.646D and 646E and are materially identical to the exceptions applicable to registered pension schemes in ss.646B and 646C (see Ch.15), except that they are less

### Taxable pension income

**26-032**   If Pt 9 Ch.4 applies the taxable pension income for the tax year is the full amount of the pension income "arising" in the tax year,[52] unless the taxpayer is a remittance basis taxpayer or temporarily non-resident.[53] The reference to pension "arising" in a tax year suggests (in contrast to the position regarding pensions under registered pension schemes)[54] that the pension must actually be paid to someone before any liability can arise.[55] If a person is entitled to a pension but it is not paid (for example, because the trustees cannot trace him) no liability should arise.[56]

*Remittance basis taxpayers*

**26-033**   The full amount of the pension income arising in the tax year, or (as the case may be) the UK part of the tax year, constitutes relevant foreign income for the purposes of ITTOIA 2005 Pt 8 Chs 2 and 3.[57] It follows that such income paid to a remittance basis taxpayer is chargeable only to the extent that it is remitted to the UK.

### Liability

**26-034**   The person liable for any tax charged under Pt 9 Ch.4 is the person receiving or entitled to the pension.[58] Typically, the person who receives the pension will also be the person that is entitled to it. The person entitled to the pension will either be the member or (after the member's death) a death beneficiary, but if he directs it to be paid to another person HMRC have a choice: they can tax the other person (who received the pension) or the member (or death beneficiary) who was entitled to the pension.[59] If one of those persons is outside the charge to UK income tax, or pays income tax at a lower marginal rate than the other, one would expect HMRC to pursue the greater liability. The meaning of *entitled* must be construed consistently with the fact that the taxable pension income for a tax year is the amount of the pension *arising* in that year. It follows that the pension must actually be paid to someone before any liability can arise.[60] For example, a member with a flexi-access drawdown fund could be said to be *entitled* to the sums and assets held for the purposes of that fund (in the sense that if he demanded them the trustees would be obliged to pay them to him) but no liability arises until such time as they are paid.

---

restrictive than for registered pension schemes, because such annuities may be purchased with unused uncrystallised funds outside of the relevant two-year period.

[52] ITEPA 2003 s.575(1). If the tax year is a split year as respects that individual, the taxable pension income for the tax year is the full amount of the pension income arising in the UK part of the year (subject to the temporary non-residence provisions: see below).

[53] Prior to 6 April 2017, this was calculated on the basis that the pension was 90% of its actual amount.

[54] Which applies to all such pension "that accrues in that year irrespective of when any amount is actually paid": ITEPA 2003 s.579B.

[55] *Dewar v IRC* [1935] 2 K.B. 351; (1935) 19 T.C. 561 CA.

[56] An amount deducted from a pension payment to reflect a debt owed to the scheme constitutes an application of the pension so the full amount is taxable (see e.g. *Magraw v Lewis* 18 T.C. 222).

[57] ITEPA 2003 s.575(3).

[58] ITEPA 2003 s.576.

[59] Indeed, if the member directs the trustees to pay the pension to a third party then he has exercised dominion over it and is thus taxable in any event: see e.g. *Meredith-Hardy v McLellan* [1995] S.T.C. (S.C.D.) 270.

[60] *Dewar v IRC* [1935] 2 K.B. 351; (1935) 19 T.C. 561 CA.

FOREIGN PENSIONS 583

If the member disclaims, surrenders or assigns his rights to a pension then he ceases to be entitled to it.[61]

*Temporary non-residents*

Section 576A applies to any "relevant withdrawals" paid to a person during a period of temporary non-residence,[62] which (were it not for these special provisions) would not be chargeable to tax under Pt 9 (including where it would not be if a claim under a double tax treaty were made in respect of it).[63] If s.576A applies, the relevant withdrawal(s) are treated for the purposes of s.575 as if they arose in the period of return. This expressly overrides any double taxation relief arrangements which would otherwise prevent the individual from being so chargeable. Since 6 April 2015, s.576A has been subject to a de minimis of £100,000, which includes relevant withdrawals from registered pension schemes during the temporary period of non-residence.[64] **26-035**

However, s.576A does not apply to a relevant withdrawal if: (a) it is paid to or in respect of a relieved member of the scheme and is not referable to the member's UK tax-relieved fund under the scheme;[65] or (b) it is paid to or in respect of a transfer member of the scheme and is referable neither to the member's relevant transfer fund, nor to the member's ringfenced transfer funds, under the scheme.[66] **26-036**

A "relevant withdrawal" is an amount paid under an RNUKS that would, if the RNUKS were a registered pension scheme, constitute:[67] (a) income withdrawal paid from a flexi-access drawdown fund; (b) short-term annuity purchased using sums or assets out of a flexi-access drawdown fund; (c) income withdrawal or dependants' income withdrawal paid before 6 April 2015 to the member or dependant in respect of an arrangement to which FA 2004 s.165(3A) or 167(2A) (flexible drawdown) applied; (d) lifetime annuity or dependants' annuity paid to the member or dependant, if the terms of the contract under which it is paid are such that there will or could be decreases in the amount of the annuity;[68] or (e) scheme pension paid to the member under a money purchase arrangement, to which the member became entitled to or after 6 April 2015 at a time when fewer than 11 other individuals were entitled to present payment of a scheme pension under the scheme. The payment of a relevant lump sum (see above) is also a relevant withdrawal. **26-037**

If the person is a remittance basis taxpayer for the year of return, any relevant withdrawal paid during the temporary period of non-residence that would not be chargeable under ITEPA 2003 Pt 9 (or would not be if a claim under a double tax treaty were made in respect of it) were it not for the temporary non-residence provi- **26-038**

---

[61] Note that once a pension commences, it may not be capable of assignment or being made subject to a trust: *Davis v Duke of Marlborough* (1818) 1 Swans. 74; *Cooper v Reilly* (1829) 2 Sim. 560; *Grenfell v Dean and Canons of Windsor* (1840) 2 Beav. 544.
[62] See FA 2013 Sch.45 Pt 4 (statutory residence test), which explains: (a) when a person is to be regarded as "temporarily non-resident"; and (b) what "the temporary period of non-residence" and "the period of return" mean.
[63] The provisions described here apply if the year of departure is the 2013/14 tax year or subsequent. For prior years, see the previous versions of s.576A.
[64] Any relevant withdrawal paid in a currency other than sterling is translated into sterling using the average exchange rate for the year ending with 31 March in the tax year in which the relevant withdrawal is paid.
[65] For "UK tax-relieved fund", see Ch.30.
[66] For "relevant transfer fund" and "ringfenced transfer funds", see Ch.30.
[67] ITEPA 2003 s.576A(4).
[68] Other than decreases which would be decreases from time to time allowed by regulations under FA 2004 Sch.28 para.3(1)(d) or 17(1)(c) (and any such regulations are to be treated as having effect for this purpose).

sions, and is remitted to the UK[69] in the temporary period of non-residence is treated as remitted to the UK in the period of return.[70]

## UK PENSIONS

**26-039** ITEPA 2003 Pt 3 Ch.3 applies to any pension paid by or on behalf of a person who is in the UK, unless any of Pt 9 Chs 5 to 14 apply to it.[71] For the purposes of Ch.3, *pension* expressly includes a pension which is paid voluntarily or is capable of being discontinued.[72] The taxable pension income for a tax year is the full amount of the pension accruing in that year irrespective of when any amount is actually paid, and the person liable for any tax is the person receiving or entitled to the pension. The remittance basis cannot apply to a UK pension, so it is taxable on an arising basis and the trustees will need to operate PAYE. As such a pension has a UK source (because it is paid by or on behalf of a person who is in the UK), this is so even if the pension income is paid to a non-UK resident (subject to any applicable tax treaty).

### Temporary non-residents

**26-040** If a UK pension is paid "in the form of a lump sum" which accrues in a temporary period of non-residence and would not otherwise be chargeable to tax under Ch.3 as a result of any double taxation relief arrangements,[73] the lump sum is treated for the purposes of Ch.3 as if it accrued in the period of return.[74] This expressly overrides any double taxation relief arrangements which would otherwise prevent the individual from being so chargeable.

## EMPLOYMENT-RELATED ANNUITIES

**26-041** ITEPA 2003 Pt 9 Ch.10 contains provisions relating to three types of employment-related annuity:

(a) annuities for the benefit of dependants (s.609);
(b) annuities under non-registered occupational pension schemes (s.610); and
(c) annuities in recognition of another's services (s.611).

**26-042** In each case, these provisions expressly do not apply to an annuity which arises from a source outside the UK unless it is paid to a person resident in the UK.

---

[69] See ITA 2007 Pt 14 Ch.A1 for the meaning of "remitted to the UK".
[70] ITEPA 2003 s.576A(5).
[71] ITEPA 2003 s.569. So, for example, if the scheme is a registered pension scheme Ch.5A will apply instead of Ch.3.
[72] Pensions which are paid voluntarily are referenced specifically because voluntary payments do not constitute income for tax purposes (*Stedeford v Beloe* [1932] A.C. 388).
[73] This includes a case where the charge could be prevented by making a claim for relief under TIOPA 2010 s.6, even if no claim is in fact made. *Double taxation relief arrangements* means arrangements that have effect under TIOPA 2010 s.2(1).
[74] ITEPA 2003 s.572A.

## Annuities for the benefit of dependants

Section 609 applies to any annuity granted for consideration consisting in whole or in part of sums which, in or after the 2013/14 tax year,[75] satisfied the following conditions:

26-043

(a) the consideration was paid by an individual, or was deducted from an individual's earnings, under an Act or the individual's terms and conditions of employment;[76]
(b) the consideration was for the purpose of securing a deferred annuity after the individual's death for the individual's surviving spouse or civil partner, or making provision after the individual's death for his children; and
(c) the individual was UK resident for the tax year in which the consideration was paid or deducted, or at any time in that tax year the individual:[77]
    (i) was resident in the Isle of Man or the Channel Islands;
    (ii) has previously resided in the UK and is resident abroad for the sake of the health of the individual or a member of the individual's family who is resident with the individual;
    (iii) is a person who is or has been employed in the service of the Crown;
    (iv) is employed in the service of any territory under Her Majesty's protection;
    (v) is employed in the service of a missionary society; or
    (vi) is a person whose late spouse or late civil partner was employed in the service of the Crown.

## Annuities under non-registered occupational pension schemes

Section 610 applies to: (a) any annuity paid under an occupational pension scheme[78] that is not a registered pension scheme; and (b) any annuity acquired using funds held for the purposes of such an occupational pension scheme.

26-044

## Annuities in recognition of another's services

Section 611 applies to any annuity purchased by any person in recognition of another person's services in any office or employment. Office includes in particular any position which has an existence independent of the person who holds it and may be filled by successive holders. Section 611 does not apply to any annuity provided under a registered pension scheme (because Pt 9 Ch.5A will apply).

26-045

*Exceptions*

The above exceptions applicable to death benefit annuities under RNUKS and overseas pensions schemes also apply to these employment-related annuities.[79] A similar exception applies where such annuities were purchased to secure or provide benefits under a tax-approved scheme prior to 6 April 2006.[80]

26-046

---

[75] Or, in or before the 2012/13 tax year, satisfied the conditions for relief under ICTA 1988 s.273 or ITA 2007 s.459 (obligatory contributions to secure an annuity for the benefit of dependants).
[76] This paragraph does not cover contributions paid by a person under SSCBA 1992 Pt 1.
[77] ITA 2007 s.460(3)(a)–(f).
[78] "Occupational pension scheme" is defined in FA 2004 s.150(5). See Ch.2.
[79] ITEPA 2003 s.611A(1).
[80] FA 2004 Sch.36 para.45A. It is a requirement that no payment of the annuity was made before 6 April

*Taxable pension income*

**26-047** The taxable pension income for a tax year in respect of an employment-related annuity arising from a source in the UK is the full amount of the annuity arising in that year.[81]

**26-048** Unless the taxpayer is a remittance basis taxpayer, the taxable pension income in respect of an employment-related annuity arising from a source outside the UK is the full amount of the annuity arising in the tax year.[82] The annuity is treated as relevant foreign income for the purposes of ITTOIA 2005 Pt 8 Ch.3 (relevant foreign income charged on arising basis: deductions and reliefs), but if the annuity arises in the Republic of Ireland, ITTOIA 2005 s.839 (which allows a deduction from relevant foreign income for annual payments other than interest under certain conditions) is modified.

**26-049** If the taxpayer is a remittance basis taxpayer, the full amount of the pension income arising in the tax year is treated as relevant foreign income for the purposes of ITTOIA 2005 Pt 8 Ch.2.

*Liability*

**26-050** The person liable for any tax charged under Pt 9 in respect of the above employment-related annuities is the person receiving or entitled to the annuity.[83]

# VOLUNTARY ANNUAL PAYMENTS

**26-051** Part 9 Ch.15 applies to an annual payment which: (a) is paid voluntarily; or (b) is capable of being discontinued, if Conditions A and B are satisfied:[84] *Condition A* is that the payment is paid to a former employee or a former office-holder[85] (or the widow, widower, surviving civil partner, child, relative or dependant of such a person); *Condition B* is that the payment is paid by or on behalf of the employer or other person under which the former office-holder held the office, or the successors of that employer or other person. If such a payment is made by or on behalf of a person who is outside the UK, Ch.15 applies only if it is paid to a person

---

2015, and the annuity must have satisfied the conditions specified in The Taxation of Pension Schemes (Transitional Provisions) Order 2006 (SI 2006/572) art.2(3) at all times since 6 April 2006. The conditions are that: (a) the annuity was purchased from an insurance company; (b) the annuity was purchased by a pension scheme which at the time of purchase fell within one of the categories set out in Sch.36 para.1(1)(a)–(g); (c) the annuity was purchased in order to secure or provide benefits under that scheme; (d) the terms of the annuity, or of any arrangement or agreement made in connection with that annuity do not permit a payment, the making of which would have given HMRC grounds for withdrawing approval of the pension scheme under ICTA 1988 s.591B if it had been made before 6 April 2006; (e) the terms of the annuity contract have not been altered on or after 6 April 2006 to allow a payment that would be an unauthorised payment if it had been made by a registered pension scheme.

[81] ITEPA 2003 s.612.
[82] ITEPA 2003 s.613. Prior to 6 April 2017 the pension income arising in the tax year was calculated on the basis that the pension was 90% of its actual amount.
[83] ITEPA 2003 s.614.
[84] ITEPA 2003 s.633. Pensions which are paid voluntarily are referenced specifically because voluntary payments do not constitute income for tax purposes (*Stedeford v Beloe* [1932] A.C. 388).
[85] For these purposes, the term office includes in particular any position which has an existence independent of the person who holds it and may be filled by successive holders.

resident in the UK. The person liable for any tax is the person receiving or entitled to the payment.

**Taxable pension income**

If Ch.15 applies to payments made by or on behalf of a person who is in the UK, the taxable pension income for a tax year is the full amount of the payments accruing in that year irrespective of when any amount is actually paid.[86] If Ch.15 applies to payments made by or on behalf of a person who is outside the UK, the taxable pension income for a tax year is the full amount of the pension income arising in the tax year[87] unless the taxpayer is a remittance basis taxpayer. The annuity is treated as relevant foreign income for the purposes of ITTOIA 2005 Pt 9 Ch.3 (relevant foreign income charged on arising basis: deductions and reliefs), but if the annuity arises in the Republic of Ireland, ITTOIA 2005 s.839 (which allows a deduction from relevant foreign income for annual payments other than interest under certain conditions) is modified. The full amount of the pension income arising in the tax year is treated as relevant foreign income for the purposes of ITTOIA 2005 Pt 8 Ch.2 (relevant foreign income charged on remittance basis).

26-052

# EXEMPT PENSIONS

**Disablement pensions**

By s.644 ITEPA 2003, the "exempt amount" of a "disablement pension" is tax-free. A pension is a "disablement pension" if:

26-053

(a) the pension is payable because a person has ceased to hold an employment or office because of disablement;
(b) that disablement is attributable to: (i) performance of the duties of the employment or office, or (ii) war injuries; and
(c) the pension is not paid under a registered pension scheme.

For these purposes, "office" includes, in particular, any position which has an existence independent of the person who holds it and may be filled by successive holders.

"Disablement" is not defined for these purposes. HMRC's guidance in the context of termination payments (which are tax-free if made on account of the disability of an employee) is likely to be relevant. In that guidance (Statement of Practice 10 (1981)) HMRC accept that "disability" covers not only a condition resulting from a sudden affliction, but also continuing incapacity to perform the duties of an employment arising out of the culmination of a process of deterioration of physical or mental health caused by chronic illness. It, therefore, seems clear that incapacity to perform the duties of an employment as a result of stress should constitute a "disablement".

"Disablement" does not of course include death. A pension payable to a

---

[86] ITEPA 2003 s.634.
[87] ITEPA 2003 s.635. Prior to 6 April 2017 this was calculated on the basis that the pension was 90% of its actual amount.

beneficiary following the death of the person who has suffered illness or injury is not a disablement pension.[88]

**26-054** To determine the "exempt amount" of a disablement pension, it is necessary to determine what pension would have been payable if: (a) the person had ceased to hold the employment because of the disablement, but (b) the disablement had not been attributable to performance of the duties of the employment or office. If no pension would have been payable, the exempt amount is the full amount of the disablement pension. If a pension of a smaller amount than the disablement pension would have been payable, the exempt amount is the amount by which the disablement pension exceeds the smaller amount. In any other case, the exempt amount is nil.

### Pensions paid under health and employment insurance policies

**26-055** Where the requirements in s.644A ITEPA 2003 are satisfied, a pension or annuity paid from an insurance policy taken out to protect a person from sickness, disability or unemployment, to which an employee has contributed, is exempt from tax (without limit). By s.644A ITEPA 2003, a pension or annuity payment is tax-free to the extent that it satisfies three requirements:

(a) Were the payment an annual payment falling within ITTOIA 2005 Pt 5 Ch.7, it would be exempt from income tax under s.735 ITTOIA 2005 (health and employment insurance payments).

(b) The payments are made to a person ("the pensioner") who made payments or contributions in respect of premiums under an insurance policy which another person took out wholly or partly for the pensioner's benefit, or to the pensioner's spouse or civil partner.

(c) The payments are attributable on a just and reasonable basis to the payments or contributions in respect of premiums.

**26-056** ITTOIA 2005 s.735 provides that no liability to income tax arises under this Act in respect of an annual payment under an insurance policy if: (a) the payment is a benefit provided under so much of the policy as insures against a health or employment risk (see s.736); (b) no part of any premiums under the policy has been deductible in calculating the income of the insured for income tax purposes; and (c) the conditions in ss.737 and 738 and, so far as applicable, those in ss.739 and 740 are met in relation to the policy.

For these purposes, a policy insures against a health risk if it insures against the insured becoming, or becoming in any specified way, subject to: (a) any physical or mental illness, disability, infirmity or defect; or (b) any deterioration in a condition resulting from any such illness, disability, infirmity or defect.

A policy insures against an employment risk if it insures against circumstances arising as a result of which the insured ceases to: (a) be employed or hold office; or (b) carry on any trade, profession or vocation.

References to insurance against a risk include insurance providing for benefits payable otherwise than by way of indemnity if the circumstances insured against occur.

The exemption in ITTOIA 2005 s.735 applies where payments received from an insurance policy are exempt from tax if:

(a) the insured person (see below) did not receive income tax relief for the premiums paid for the policy: this means UK income tax, so the exemp-

---

[88] EIM75080.

tion is still available if relief has been given outside the UK against foreign taxes;
(b) the policy insures against a qualifying health or employment risk;
(c) the payments are made during the qualifying period; and
(d) the policy is a genuine insurance policy issued on arm's length terms (see below).

There is no limit on the amount of payments that can be received free of tax.

By s.742 ITTOIA 2005, the "insured person" includes: spouse or civil partner child (under 21) spouse's child (under 21), and any person who is jointly liable for the expense that is insured, for example a joint borrower on a mortgage. Without these extensions to the definition of insured person a payment from a policy because of the sickness disability or unemployment of one person would be taxable on another person to the extent that they benefited from the payment. This extension allows such payments to come within the exemption.

*Genuine arm's length insurance*

There are rules aimed at preventing abuse of the exemption. For investments presented as insurance policies, see IPTM6130. For single policies providing different types of benefits or policies linked to other policies, see IPTM6135.

## OTHER PROVISIONS WHICH COULD APPLY TO LUMP SUMS

Where a lump sum paid under a pension scheme is not taxable as a relevant lump sum under ITEPA 2003 Pt 9 Ch.4, or under the disguised remuneration provisions or ITEPA 2003 s.394, it is necessary to consider if a lump sum paid to a UK resident individual may be taxable under any other provisions. In general, for the reasons given below, one would not expect such a lump sum to be taxable.

### Annual payments

ITTOIA 2005 s.683 provides that income tax is charged on *annual payments* that are not charged elsewhere. Case law has established that a payment is an annual payment[89] if: (a) the payments are income of the recipient, and not a payment of capital by instalments;[90] (b) it is "pure income profit";[91] (c) there is a legal obligation to pay the sum;[92] and (d) it recurs or is capable of recurrence.[93] The fact that

---

[89] *Annual payment* is construed *ejusdem generis* with *annuity*.
[90] *Brodie's Will Trustees v IRC* (1933) 17 T.C. 432.
[91] *Re Hanbury* (1939) 38 T.C. 588. Annual payments are inseparably associated with payments from which tax is deducted at source, and that mechanism can operate properly only if the payments are a taxable receipt in the hands of the payee without any deduction for expenses or the like (*IRC v Whitworth Park Coal Ltd* [1961] A.C. 31; 38 T.C. 531 at 575 (Lord Radcliffe); *Campbell v IRC* [1970] A.C. 77; 45 T.C. 427 at 475 (Lord Donovan)). Thus, agreeing to pay a garage £500 p/a for five years for the hire and upkeep of a car does not constitute an annuity: *Howe v IRC* [1919] 2 K.B 336. A payment subject to a condition or counter-stipulation that the payee provides good or services is not pure income profit. Typically, the payee satisfies his substantive obligations at the outset of the contract. The provision of any benefit under a pension scheme is likely to be pure income profit.
[92] See *Ridge Securities Ltd v IRC* [1964] 1 W.L.R. 479; 44 T.C. 373.
[93] See *IRC v Whitworth Park Coal Ltd* [1961] A.C. 31; 38 T.C. 531. The authorities identify the characteristic of recurrence in the context of establishing that a payment is not a one-off payment

such payments may be contingent and variable in character does not prevent them from being annual payments.[94]

**26-061** If a lump sum payment is entirely distinct from the member's right to receive a pension or annuity it will not be an annual payment because the above requirements will not be satisfied. However, a payment by trustees in exercise of a power over trust income will always be income in the hands of the recipient, and taxed as an annual payment even if the above tests are not met. A payment which does not satisfy all of the above four tests and is paid in exercise of a power over trust capital (including accumulated income), will be capital and not income in the hands of the member, unless the purpose of the power/trust is to augment an income interest held by the recipient. This remains the case even if the payment is to satisfy an income purpose (e.g. maintenance of a beneficiary), unless the terms of the trust require payments to be made expressly to supplement income.[95] It does not matter if the money paid can be traced to trust income; it is the purpose of the power/trust which is important,[96] not whether the money actually paid is the same money which was contributed or has been received as income, and not the reasons that the trustees exercised it.

**26-062** ITEPA 2003 s.636A lists a number of lump sum payments from registered pension schemes which are exempt from income tax, and it may be suggested that this creates an inference that lump sums not listed are subject to income tax. If s.636A referred to capital distributions rather than lump sums then this suggestion would perhaps have some force, because if the above analysis is correct then capital distributions should not be taxable. *Lump sum* is not a technical term. It is quite clear that a pension commencement *lump sum* could be paid in exercise of a power over trust income, and in such circumstances the exemption in s.636A is necessary to ensure that the lump sum is not taxable.

**26-063** Further support for the conclusion that lump sum payments are not generally taxable can be found in the FURBS provisions. Lumps sums from FURBS are generally taxable under ITEPA 2003 s.394 but there is an exception for lump sums paid in respect of certain pre-6 April 2006 contributions. The exception provides that s.394 does not apply, but it does not expressly say that such lump sums are tax-free. It is accepted by HMRC that lump sums from FURBS are tax-free if they are not taxed under s.394, and the reason they are tax-free is because there isn't any provision which taxes them (subject to the point above relating to distributions of trust income). In addition, if lump sums were generally taxable (whether or not capital distributions), the provisions relating to relevant lump sums would be otiose.

### Transfer of assets abroad provisions

**26-064** As is explained at in Ch.25 and following, ITA 2007 s.727 imposes a charge to tax on income treated as arising under s.728 (unless it has been taxed under s.720). Section 729 provides that the capital receipt conditions will be met in respect of the individual in the relevant year the individual receives or is entitled to receive any capital sum, whether before or after the relevant transfer, or the payment of that sum is (or, in the case of an entitlement, would be) in any way connected with any relevant transaction.

---

in the nature of capital, but has the quality of a payment which will or may recur (*Hargreaves Lansdown Asset Management Ltd v HMRC* [2018] UKFTT 127 at [73]). The fact that payments may be made weekly or monthly does not prevent them from being "annual" provided that the payments may continue beyond the year (*Smith v Smith* [1923] P. 191 (CA)).

[94] *Moss Empires Ltd v IRC* [1937] 21 T.C. 264.
[95] HMRC agree with this at TSEM3758.
[96] *Stevenson v Wishart* [1987] 1 W.L.R. 1204; 59 T.C. 740.

In addition, ITA 2007 s.732 imposes a charge to income tax on persons receiving a benefit as a result of relevant transactions (unless it has been taxed under s.720). This section applies if a relevant transfer occurs, and an individual who is ordinarily UK resident receives a benefit and the benefit is provided out of assets which are available for the purpose as a result of the transfer. If the member has not already been charged then a payment to a beneficiary on death could be charged to income tax as it could be matched with relevant income.

26-065

### Capital gains tax

If the pension scheme is a settlement to which TCGA 1992 s.87 applies then gains realised by the trustees will be apportioned to UK resident beneficiaries when a capital sum is subsequently paid to such a beneficiary.[97]

26-066

In relation to commutation payments, TCGA 1992 s.237 provides that no chargeable gain accrues to any person on the disposal of a right to, or any part of: (a) any allowance, annuity or capital sum payable out of any superannuation fund, or under any superannuation scheme, established solely or mainly for persons employed in a profession, trade, undertaking or employment, and their dependants;[98] or (b) annual payments which are due under a covenant made by any person and which are not secured on any property. The existence of a CGT exemption where a pension or annuity is disposed of suggests that a disposal (such as a commutation) is prima facie within the CGT regime, and this in turn further supports the analysis above that lump sum commutation payments are not generally subject to income tax.

26-067

## TAX TREATIES

Where pension benefits are paid by a scheme in one jurisdiction to a beneficiary resident in a different jurisdiction, it is not uncommon for the domestic legislation of both jurisdictions to claim taxing rights over the benefits. Treaty articles relating to the following items of income may be relevant in determining how such taxing rights should be allocated: (a) pensions and other similar remuneration; (b) pensions (without a reference to other similar remuneration); (c) exempt pensions; (d) other income; (e) annuities; and (f) double tax relief. This is considered in Ch.29.

26-068

## UNILATERAL RELIEF FOR FOREIGN TAX PAID

Where a tax treaty does not eliminate any double taxation (or there is no applicable treaty), credit for foreign tax paid may be available unilaterally under TIOPA 2010 s.9(1). This is similar to the double tax relief provision in many tax treaties but it is provided as a matter of domestic legislation and outside of any treaty.[99] Credit for tax paid under the law of the territory, which is calculated by reference to income arising in the territory, and corresponds to UK tax, is allowed

26-069

---

[97] These provisions are explained in Ch.25.
[98] "Superannuation" is not defined. It generally refers to the provision of benefits to a person upon retirement from employment (see, e.g., the definition of *sponsored superannuation scheme* in ICTA 1988 s.624(1) prior to 6 April 2006).
[99] TIOPA 2010 ss.112 and 113 offer an alternative to unilateral relief under s.9 but do not have much application to pension schemes.

against any income tax calculated by reference to that income or gain.[100] Such credit is not permitted if any credit for that tax is allowable in respect of that income under a tax treaty made in relation to the territory, or if a tax treaty contains an express prohibition on relief by way of credit.[101] The requirement that income must arise in the territory means that this is potentially applicable where benefits are taxed at source, but not where the liability in the other territory arises as a result of the individual being dual resident and the income arises in a third territory. HMRC accept[102] in the context of gains that it is not necessary for the tax liabilities to arise at the same time or for the same person to be liable, and one would expect the same analysis to apply to income.

# NATIONAL INSURANCE CONTRIBUTIONS

**26-070**  Payments from occupational pension schemes are "deferred earnings" for NIC purposes.[103] SI 2001/1004 Sch.3 Pt VI contains provisions relating to pensions and pension contributions. The provisions applicable to benefits from EFRBS, FURBS, corresponding schemes and s.615 funds are considered in the relevant chapter of this book dealing with those schemes.

**26-071**  If the member is resident in a jurisdiction with an international social security agreement with the UK, this would override the UK's ability to charge NIC on benefits.

### Foreign service

**26-072**  Where pension benefits are received by a UK resident individual but relate to former employment exercised outside of the UK when the individual was subject to foreign social security legislation, it is arguable that the payments are not subject to NICs on the basis that the earnings do not derive from "employed earner's employment" in Great Britain. "Employed earner's employment" means a person who is gainfully employed in Great Britain under a contract of service, or in an office with general earnings. This is arguably supported by an EU sourcing principle adopted following a meeting of the EC Administrative Commission in 1997 (known as 310/97). At this meeting, it was agreed in relation to a termination payment that the social security legislation of the country where the activity was exercised in respect of the employment to which the payment relates, rather than the social security legislation of the country where the person is insured at the time of payment, was applicable. HMRC follow this sourcing principle. It should, however, be noted that taking this position is not without risk of potential challenge from HMRC who may seek to argue that the sourcing principle does not apply to pension payments, and that such payments paid to an individual who is resident and present in Great Britain is earnings subject to NICs.

---

[100] TIOPA 2010 s.9(1).
[101] TIOPA 2010 s.11.
[102] INTM169040.
[103] Per Lord Hodge in *HMRC v Forde and McHugh Ltd* [2014] UKSC 14. This can only refer to the NIC position; it is well settled that a payment from a pension scheme is not earnings for income tax purposes.

## Qualifying overseas pension schemes

**26-073** Any benefit referable to an employer's contribution to which Sch.33 para.2 applies is disregarded for NIC purposes.[104]

## Employer-financed pension only schemes

**26-074** The NIC provisions introduce the concept of an *employer-financed pension only scheme*. This is a scheme: (a) financed by payments made by or on behalf of the employer; and (b) providing only a pension. The provisions expressly state that such a scheme is not an EFRBS on the basis that a pension is not a relevant benefit (as defined in ITEPA 2003 s.393B). That does not appear to be strictly correct: a pension may constitute a relevant benefit if it is not charged to tax under ITEPA 2003 Pt 9[105] (which would be the case, for example, where the scheme and the member are both resident outside of the UK).

**26-075** A payment of pension, pursuant to an employer-financed pension only scheme, which is income charged to tax pursuant to ITEPA 2003 Pt 9, is disregarded for NIC purposes provided that the pension:[106]

(a) would have been an authorised member payment (other than a recognised transfer or a scheme administration member payment) if the scheme had been a registered pension scheme;
(b) would satisfy any of the conditions below if the scheme had been a registered pension scheme;
(c) is made at a time when the individual is no longer employed by the employer, or a subsidiary of the employer, or a person connected with the employer or a subsidiary of the employer; and
(d) is not payable in respect of a period during which an earner is engaged as a self-employed earner under a contract for services with, or re-employed as an employed earner by, the employer from employment with whom the benefits were derived.

*The conditions*

**26-076** The conditions referred to in (b) above are that, if the scheme had been a registered pension scheme: (a) any pension payable under its rules would have satisfied pension rules 1, 3 and 4;[107] or (b) any pension is payable until the member's death in instalments at least annually.

---

[104] The Social Security (Contributions) Regulations 2001 (SI 2001/1004) Sch.3 Pt VI para.3(1)(a). See Ch.24 for an explanation of Sch.33.
[105] See ITEPA 2003 s.393B(2). Curiously, HMRC explain that "for NICs purposes only, the meaning of "EFRBS" does not include an employer-financed pension only scheme" (NIM02756).
[106] SI 2001/1004 Sch.3 Pt.VI paras 9 and 10.
[107] For the pension rules, see Ch.13. Pension rule 1 is that no payment of pension may be made before the member reaches normal minimum pension age (unless the ill-health condition is met). Pension rule 3 is that no payment of pension other than a scheme pension may be made in respect of a defined benefits arrangement. Pension rule 4 is that no payment of pension other than: (a) a scheme pension; (b) a lifetime annuity; or (c) drawdown pension, may be made in respect of a money purchase arrangement; but a scheme pension may only be paid if the member had an opportunity to select a lifetime annuity instead (FA 2004 s.165).

## Double taxation agreements

**26-077** Benefits referable to employer contributions to a pension scheme which was afforded relief under any of the following provisions are disregarded for NIC purposes:[108]

(a) Article 25(8) of the Convention set out in the Schedule to the Double Taxation Relief (Taxes on Income) (France) Order 1968;[109]

(b) Article 17A of the Convention set out in the SSchedule to the Double Taxation Relief (Taxes on Income) (Republic of Ireland) Order 1976.[110] Article 17A was added by art.1 of the Protocol set out in the Schedule to Double Taxation Relief (Taxes on Income) (Republic of Ireland) Order 1995;[111]

(c) Article 27(2) of the Convention set out in the Schedule to the Double Taxation Relief (Taxes on Income) (Canada) Order 1980;[112]

(d) Article 28(3) of the Convention set out in the Schedule to the Double Taxation Relief (Taxes on Income) (Denmark) Order 1980;[113]

(e) Article 18 of the Convention set out in the Schedule to the Double Taxation Relief (Taxes on Income) (The United States of America) Order 2002;[114]

(f) Article 17(3) of the Convention set out in the Schedule to the Double Taxation Relief (Taxes on Income) (South Africa) Order 2002;[115] and

(g) Article 17(3) of the Convention set out in the Schedule to the Double Taxation Relief (Taxes on Income) (Chile) Order 2003.[116]

---

[108] SI 2001/1004 Sch.3 Pt VI para.7.
[109] Double Taxation Relief (Taxes on Income) (France) Order 1968 (SI 1968/1869).
[110] Double Taxation Relief (Taxes on Income) (Republic of Ireland) Order 1976 (SI 1976/319).
[111] Double Taxation Relief (Taxes on Income) (Republic of Ireland) Order 1995 (SI 1995/764).
[112] Double Taxation Relief (Taxes on Income) (Canada) Order 1980 (SI 1980/709).
[113] Double Taxation Relief (Taxes on Income) (Denmark) Order 1980 (SI 1980/2877).
[114] Double Taxation Relief (Taxes on Income) (The United States of America) Order 2002 (SI 2002/2848).
[115] Double Taxation Relief (Taxes on Income) (South Africa) Order 2002 (draft).
[116] Double Taxation Relief (Taxes on Income) (Chile) Order 2003 (SI 2003/3200).

# CHAPTER 27

# Disguised Remuneration

## TABLE OF CONTENTS

| | |
|---|---|
| Overview | 27-001 |
| Recent developments | 27-005 |
| Pt 7A Ch.1: the general provisions | 27-008 |
| Relevant arrangements | 27-008 |
| Who is A? | 27-010 |
| Persons linked with A | 27-012 |
| Who is B? | 27-013 |
| "Concerned with ... rewards in connection with A's employment with B" | 27-014 |
| Relevant third person | 27-016 |
| When is a relevant step "connected with" the relevant arrangement? | 27-017 |
| Relevant steps | 27-019 |
| Exemption for certain relevant steps taken after A's death | 27-020 |
| Earmarking etc | 27-021 |
| "With a view to a later relevant step" | 27-024 |
| Payments and transfers | 27-029 |
| Relevant persons | 27-030 |
| Loans and debts | 27-032 |
| Changing trustees and transferring between trusts | 27-033 |
| Making assets available | 27-035 |
| Exceptions | 27-040 |
| General exclusions | 27-041 |
| Income arising from earmarked funds | 27-042 |
| Earmarking replacement funds | 27-043 |
| Loan repayments | 27-044 |
| Arrangements for the provision of excluded benefits | 27-045 |
| Sole purpose | 27-046 |
| Exclusions under ITEPA 2003 Pt 4 | 27-048 |
| Pensions chargeable under ITEPA 2003 Pt 9 | 27-051 |
| Employee pension contributions | 27-056 |
| FURBS | 27-059 |
| Purchased annuities | 27-063 |
| Pre-6 April 2011 annuity rights | 27-066 |
| Pre-6 April 2011 lump sums | 27-067 |
| "Pre-6 April 2011 lump sum rights" | 27-069 |
| Transfers relating to corresponding schemes | 27-072 |
| Transferred rights derive from contributions by B which are not tax-relieved | 27-074 |

Relevant non-UK schemes ........................ 27-076
Part 7A Ch.2: the charge to tax ...................... 27-079
   The value of the relevant step .................... 27-081
     Residence issues ........................... 27-083
     ITEPA 2003 s.16 ........................... 27-084
     ITEPA 2003 s.17 ........................... 27-087
     Rights to lump sum benefits accruing on or after 6
       April 2017 ............................. 27-089
     Overlap with money or asset subject to earlier tax
       liability .................................. 27-090
     Overlap with certain earnings ................. 27-092
     Consideration given for relevant step ........... 27-093
     A is selling an asset to P ..................... 27-094
     A is buying an asset from P ................... 27-096
     Tax avoidance arrangements ................... 27-098
   Remittance basis taxpayers ...................... 27-100
     A meets the s.26A requirement ................ 27-101
     A does not meet the s.26A requirement ......... 27-102
     Section 24: related employments ............... 27-103
     Associated employments ...................... 27-104
     Overlap provisions .......................... 27-105
     Temporary non-residents ..................... 27-106
   Liability ..................................... 27-107
     Liability after A has died ..................... 27-108
     The application of the PAYE system ............ 27-110
   Subsequent income tax liability ................... 27-116
   Relief where earmarking not followed by further
     relevant step ............................... 27-117
Part 7A Ch.3 ..................................... 27-118
   Effect of B making ss.554Z18 or 554Z19 relevant step . 27-120
   The basic requirements: relevant undertaking ....... 27-121
     "Undertaking" ............................. 27-123
     Relevant benefits ........................... 27-124
     Tax-relieved contributions and tax-exempt
       provisions .............................. 27-126
   Section 554Z18: earmarking etc .................. 27-127
   Section 554Z19: provision of security ............. 27-129
     Valuation of step within s.554Z19 .............. 27-130
     Anniversary steps ........................... 27-131
   Relief for earmarking or security not followed by
     contribution or relevant benefit ................ 27-132
Interaction with other legislation ..................... 27-133
   General earnings charge ........................ 27-133
   The benefits code ............................. 27-134
   ITEPA 2003 s.394 ............................. 27-136
   Pension income ............................... 27-137
National insurance contributions ..................... 27-139
   The Social Security (Contributions) Regulations 2001 . 27-140
   Differences between income tax and NIC .......... 27-142

# OVERVIEW

The disguised remuneration provisions in ITEPA 2003 Pt 7A were introduced on 9 December 2010.[1] The main rules apply to "relevant steps" taken on or after 6 April 2011, with anti-forestalling provisions applicable from 9 December 2010 to 5 April 2011.[2] The original motivation for the introduction of this regime was to counter the use of employee benefit trust arrangements (including EFRBS) provide tax-efficient benefits to employees and former employees. In the context of pension schemes, the policy objective, according to the HM Treasury commentary accompanying the 9 December 2010 draft legislation, is to support:

27-001

> "the Government's objective of a fairer tax system by ensuring that ... contributions to unregistered pension schemes do not benefit from tax advantages on pension savings beyond the annual and lifetime allowances available in registered pension schemes."

The provisions apply in principle to any relevant step taken in connection with any sort of funded occupational pension scheme or retirement benefit scheme, although there are a number of exclusions applicable to certain categories of pension schemes, including registered pension schemes. The provisions may also apply to any arrangement that holds funds received from such a scheme, such as a trust holding death benefits.[3] The provisions are particularly penal in relation to loans, which are taxable in the same way as outright payments with no relief given when the loan is repaid.

27-002

The provisions are organised as follows:

27-003

(a) Part 7A Ch.1 determines if Ch.2 applies to a step taken by a "relevant third person" (which is, broadly, any person other than the employer or the employee);
(b) Part 7A Ch.2 causes that tax charge to arise and prescribes how one is to determine the amount of the charge; and
(c) Part 7A Ch.3 contains special provisions relating to undertakings given by employers (and others) in relation to retirement benefits. If Ch.3 applies then Chs 1 and 2 are deemed to apply, in modified form, to the step taken by the employer as if the employer were a relevant third person.

The provisions are detailed and highly prescriptive. In this chapter the general provisions are outlined and then the provisions that are most relevant to retirement benefit schemes are described in more detail.

27-004

### Recent developments

FA 2017 introduced a number of new provisions, including those relating to transferring, releasing or writing off loans on or after 6 April 2017.[4] The overlap provisions in s.554Z5 were also replaced in their entirety, and are now limited to circumstances in which the tax charge associated with the previous relevant step has been paid in full (within similar provisions in new ss.554Z11B and 554Z11C). In addition, there are new exclusions relating to relevant steps involving the acquisition of debt in certain circumstances (new s.554OA), relevant steps involving the

27-005

---

[1] HMRC guidance is at EIM45000.
[2] See FA 2011 Sch.2 paras 52 to 59.
[3] See ITEPA 2003 s.554A(11), explained below.
[4] ITEPA 2003 s.554C(1)(aa) and (ab).

repayment of a loan where the sum repaid is earmarked (new s.554RA), and relevant steps involving the payment of a tax liability (new s.554XA).

**27-006** F(No.2)A 2017 Sch.11 contains provisions pursuant to which a creditor is deemed to take a relevant step on 5 April 2019 where any loan (including any form of credit and anything purporting to be a loan) or quasi-loan[5] made on or after 10 December 2010 was outstanding immediately before the end of 5 April 2019. If the other requirements in ITEPA 2003 s.554A were satisfied then Pt 7A Ch.2 will have applied by reason of that deemed relevant step on 5 April 2019. The amount of the relevant step is equal to the value of the outstanding debt. There are six exclusions set out in Sch.11 Pt 3, five of which are identical to exclusions which apply to the main provisions described below.[6] The additional exclusion relates to loans used solely to purchase employer shares.

**27-007** FA 2018 amended the disguised remuneration provisions by inserting:

(a) new s.554A(5A)–(5C), which provide that "redirected-earnings arrangements" remain within the scope of s.554A; and

(b) new ss.554AA–AF and s.554Z2A, which contain special provisions relating to employees with some influence over their close company employer (including non-UK resident close companies). New s.554AA applies, broadly, where there is an arrangement which has as one of its main purposes the avoidance of tax and which is intended to benefit such an employee, and the employer makes a payment under that arrangement to a third party and a third party takes a relevant step deriving from that payment.

## PT 7A CH.1: THE GENERAL PROVISIONS

**Relevant arrangements**

**27-008** ITEPA 2003 s.554A provides, insofar as is material, as follows:

"(1) Chapter 2 applies if—

(a) a person ('A') is an employee, or a former or prospective employee, of another person ('B'),

(b) there is an arrangement ('the relevant arrangement') to which A is a party or which otherwise (wholly or partly) covers or relates to A,

(c) it is reasonable to suppose that, in essence—

(i) the relevant arrangement, or

(ii) the relevant arrangement so far as it covers or relates to A, is (wholly or partly) a means of providing, or is otherwise concerned (wholly or partly) with the provision of, rewards or recognition or loans in connection with A's employment, or former or prospective employment, with B,

(d) a relevant step is taken by a relevant third person, and

(e) it is reasonable to suppose that, in essence—

(i) the relevant step is taken (wholly or partly) in pursuance of the relevant arrangement, or

---

[5] A quasi-loan is made where a right to a payment or a transfer of assets is acquired in connection with a loan to a relevant person or a transfer of assets to a relevant person.

[6] These exclusions relate to: (a) loans on ordinary commercial terms; (b) transfers of employment-related loans of no more than £10,000; (c) transactions under employee benefit packages; (d) cases involving employment-related securities; and (e) employee car ownership schemes.

## PT 7A CH.1: THE GENERAL PROVISIONS

    (ii)  there is some other connection (direct or indirect) between the relevant step and the relevant arrangement."

So, there must be an "arrangement"[7] which relates to "A" and is concerned with the provision of rewards or recognition or loans in connection with[8] A's employment, or former or prospective employment, with "B". A relevant step must be taken by a "relevant third person" and there must be some connection between the relevant step and the arrangement.

*Who is A?*

It will usually be relatively clear who A is. He must either be a party to the arrangements or the arrangements must otherwise relate to him, in the sense that the arrangement is concerned with the provision of rewards or recognition or loans in connection with his employment, or former or prospective employment, with B. Employment includes an office, so employee includes an office-holder (such as a director).[9]

The references to A in s.554A(1)(b) and (c)(ii) (but not s.554A(1)(a)) expressly include any person "linked" with A. So it must be possible to identify an actual employee, even if the relevant arrangement is a means of providing benefit to persons other than A (e.g. his family members).[10]

*Persons linked with A*

Section 554Z1 explains when a person is linked with A. It includes any person who is or has been "connected" with A for the purposes of ITA 2007 s.993, which is expanded to include a man and woman living together as if they were spouses or two people of the same sex living together as if they were civil partners.[11] It also includes a close company in which A or any person linked with A is or has been a participator (or would be if it were a UK resident company) and a company which is a 51% subsidiary of such a company.

*Who is B?*

It will also usually be relatively clear who B is. Where the same arrangement has been used to reward the employee of more than one employer, it seems that both employers are B in relation to that arrangement. There is no reason that there can only be one person who is B in respect of a relevant arrangement: s.554A(1)(c), which defines *B*, does not limit the definition to a single employer.

---

[7] "Arrangement" includes any agreement, scheme, settlement, transaction, trust or understanding (whether or not it is legally enforceable): s.554Z(3).

[8] For the meaning of "in connection with", see Chs 18 and 35.

[9] ITEPA 2003 ss.4 and 5. It seems reasonably clear that shadow directors are not office holders, and so are not within the scope of the main disguised remuneration provisions (although they are included for the purposes of the close company disguised remuneration provisions: see s.554AD, which defined director to include "any person in accordance with whose directions or instructions the directors of the company […] are accustomed to act."

[10] As was the case in *Sempra Metals Ltd v HMRC* [2008] S.T.C. (S.C.D.) 1062, for example.

[11] The precise scope of this is unclear. There are likely to be differences of opinion regarding the fundamental characteristics of persons living together "as if they were" spouses or civil partners, and this phrase is not found in any other tax legislation. It is however used in non-tax legislation (e.g. The National Health Service Pension Scheme Regulations 2015 (SI 2015/94); the Housing and Regeneration Act 2008; The Child Benefit (General) Regulations 2006 (SI 2006/223).

*"Concerned with ... rewards in connection with A's employment with B"*

**27-014** It must be reasonable to suppose that, in essence, the relevant arrangement (insofar as it relates to A) is concerned with the provision of rewards or recognition or loans *in connection with* A's employment, or former or prospective employment, with B. All relevant circumstances must be taken into account in order to get to the essence of the matter. It does not matter if the relevant arrangement does not include details of the steps which will or may be taken in connection with the provision of rewards etc. (for example, details of any sums of money or assets which will or may be involved or details of how or when or by whom or in whose favour any step will or may be taken).

**27-015** The prepositional phrase "in connection with" is commonly used in anti-avoidance provisions.[12] It does not pose a causal test but simply requires a link.[13] It may describe a wide range of links and so one must look closely at the surrounding words and the context of the legislative scheme.[14] In relation to s.554A(1), the *link* must be between the arrangement and the employment.

*Relevant third person*

**27-016** A relevant third person means: (a) A acting as a trustee; (b) B acting as a trustee; or (c) any person other than A and B.[15] It follows that the provisions will not generally apply to steps taken by the employer (although Pt 7A Ch.3 modifies this in certain circumstances: see below).

*When is a relevant step "connected with" the relevant arrangement?*

**27-017** Section 554A(11) provides that:

"For the purposes of subsection (1)(e)—
(a) the relevant step is connected with the relevant arrangement if (for example) the relevant step is taken (wholly or partly) in pursuance of an arrangement at one end of a series of arrangements with the relevant arrangement being at the other end, and
(b) it does not matter if the person taking the relevant step is unaware of the relevant arrangement."

**27-018** The precise scope of this provision is unclear. Consider, for example, a discretionary trust that holds death benefits received from a registered pension scheme. That trust will not itself be a relevant arrangement because it will not usually have any employment context, however if the registered pension scheme is an occupational scheme (and therefore a relevant arrangement) the effect of s.554A(11) appears to be that any relevant step taken by the trustees of the death benefits trust is *connected with* the relevant arrangement and therefore taxable under Pt 7A Ch.2. This would perhaps be a surprising result, but it does appear to be precisely the type of arrangement that s.554A(11) is aimed at, and none of the exemptions applicable to registered pension schemes appear to apply to relevant steps taken by

---

[12] See Ch.18.
[13] D. Richards J, whose decision in the High Court was affirmed by the Court of Appeal in *Barclays Bank Plc v HMRC* [2006] EWHC 2118 (Ch); [2007] S.T.C. 747.
[14] Per Arden J in *Barclays Bank Plc v HMCR* [2007] EWCA Civ 442.
[15] ITEPA 2003 s.554A(7).

such a trust,[16] and so on the face of it any relevant steps[17] taken by the trustees of the death benefits trust would be subject to tax and NIC under Part 7A Ch.2 and the associated NIC provisions.[18]

# RELEVANT STEPS

A "relevant step" means a step within s.554B, s.554C or s.554D. The fact that taking such a step, or some aspect of the step, may constitute a breach of trust or is a constituent part of a breach of trust, or is void as a result of breach of trust does not prevent it from being a relevant step.[19]

27-019

### Exemption for certain relevant steps taken after A's death

Part 7A Ch.2 does not apply by reason of a relevant step taken on or after A's death if the relevant step is within s.554B or s.554C(1)(ab) (which applies where a person writes off or releases a loan or other right to receive money or assets from a relevant person). All other relevant steps remain chargeable after A's death.

27-020

### Earmarking etc

Section 554B provides that:

27-021

"(1) A person ('P') takes a step within this section if—
(a) a sum of money or asset held by or on behalf of P is earmarked (however informally) by P with a view to a later relevant step being taken by P or any other person (on or following the meeting of any condition or otherwise) in relation to—
 (i) that sum of money or asset, or
 (ii) any sum of money or asset which may arise or derive (directly or indirectly) from it, or
(b) a sum of money or asset otherwise starts being held by or on behalf of P, specifically with a view, so far as P is concerned, to a later relevant step being taken by P or any other person (on or following the meeting of any condition or otherwise) in relation to—
 (i) that sum of money or asset, or
 (ii) any sum of money or asset which may arise or derive (directly or indirectly) from it."

Section 554B(1)(a) requires P to earmark funds with a view to a later relevant step (the later relevant step will usually be a s.554C or s.554D relevant step) and s.554B(1)(b) requires P to start to hold funds (without earmarking them) with a view to a later relevant step. It expressly does not matter whether or not the sum of money or asset in question has previously been held by or on behalf of P on a basis which is different to that mentioned in s.554B(1)(b). In the context of a money purchase

27-022

---

[16] See Ch.22.
[17] Other than the payment of taxable pension income: see ITEPA 2003 s.554S, considered below.
[18] In certain circumstances a payment from the death benefits trust to an individual may be deemed to be income of the individual under FA 2004 s.206(8) (see Ch.15), so the potential for double taxation may arise.
[19] These words were inserted into s.554A(2) by the FA 2017 Sch.6 para.2 and are expressed to have effect in relation to relevant steps taken on or after 6 April 2017. This suggests a tacit acceptance that such steps would not be relevant steps if taken prior to that date.

scheme where contributions are allocated for a particular member, the allocation will clearly involve a s.554B relevant step if the intention is to provide pension benefits from those funds in the future (the provision of benefits will usually constitute a s.554C relevant step[20]).

**27-023** "Earmarked" is not defined.[21] It is likely to mean *allocated* or *set aside* for a particular purpose. It probably requires a recorded decision of P (although the decision need not be irrevocable and need not be made in accordance with the scheme rules). Where there is more than one person comprising *P*, or P is a company with more than one director, it is very difficult to see how an informal decision of one of the persons comprising P (or one of the directors of P) could be within s.554B unless the decision is communicated to the other persons comprising P (or the directors of P).

*"With a view to a later relevant step"*

**27-024** It is likely that a step is taken "with a view to" a later relevant step if the later relevant step is a realistic possibility.[22] It expressly does not matter[23]:

(a) if details of the later relevant step have not been worked out (for example, details of the sum of money or asset which will or may be the subject of the step or details of how or when or by whom or in whose favour the step will or may be taken);

(b) if any condition which would have to be met before the later relevant step is taken might never be met; or

(c) if A, or any person linked with A, has no legal right to have a relevant step taken in relation to any sum of money or asset.

**27-025** It seems to follow that, focusing solely on s.554B, the question one needs to address is whether there is a realistic possibility that the trustee will use the funds to take a relevant step in the future. Even if the trustee has no power to take steps which are relevant steps, this will not prevent s.554B from applying if it is reasonably likely that the trustees will in fact take such steps. However, when one broadens one's focus to include the charging provisions in Pt 7A Ch.2, it becomes reasonably clear that one must be able to identify who A is. For example, if a contribution were made to a defined benefit scheme with numerous members, although the funds may be, in some sense, earmarked with a view to a later relevant step (such as the provision of benefits), if it is not possible to identify A or a group of persons that all could constitute A then it is difficult to see how Pt 7A Ch.2 can apply to such a step. The same analysis should apply where funds are contributed to a general fund under a money purchase scheme with numerous members.

**27-026** The reference to a "later" relevant step strongly suggests that there must be a material time delay between the earmarking and the relevant step. This is because, if s.554B were taken at face value, a s.554C or s.554D relevant step would *always* be preceded by a s.554B relevant step because immediately prior to taking the step

---

[20] The fact that s.554S (for example) may exempt the future benefits from tax under Part 7A Ch.2 does not prevent s.554B from applying, because the payments will still involve a relevant step.

[21] In a different context, there is some discussion of the term "earmark" in *Alan David Cameron v M & W Mack (ESOP) Trustee Ltd* [2002] W.T.L.R. 647, but there is otherwise little or no judicial guidance regarding the meaning of the term.

[22] In a similar context, the words *with a view to* were considered by the House of Lords in *MacDonald v Dextra Accessories Ltd* [2005] UKHL 47. Their Lordships agreed with the Court of Appeal that, in the context of the now repealed FA 1989 s.43, the expression "with a view to" was "... apt to embrace the whole ranges of realistic possibilities available to the trustee ...".

[23] ITEPA 2003 s.554B(2).

the trustee will start to hold the property which is the subject of the step with a view to the taking of the step. If a material time delay were not required then s.554C and s.554D would have almost no application because s.554B would always cause Pt 7A Ch.2 to apply (except where the s.554B relevant step occurred prior to 6 April 2011). This is clearly not intended and the much better view is that s.554B will only apply where it is not immediately followed by a s.554C or s.554D relevant step.

27-027

The only sums or assets that can be the subject of a s.554B relevant step are those held by or on behalf of the person taking the step. In the context of a trust, this will be the trustee and any person holding the funds on the trustee's behalf, such as an investment manager. If a different person records how the funds held by the trustee are to be allocated between the members then such recording should not amount to a s.554B relevant step.

27-028

It is implicit that once funds have been earmarked (including where funds were earmarked prior to 6 April 2011) then it should not be possible to earmark such funds again, unless they are "un-earmarked" in the meantime.

**Payments and transfers**

Section 554C provides that:

27-029

"(1) A person ('P') takes a step within this section if P—
(a) pays a sum of money to a relevant person,
(aa) acquires a right to a payment of a sum of money, or to a transfer of assets, where there is a connection (direct or indirect) between the acquisition of the right and—
  (i) a payment made, by way of a loan or otherwise, to a relevant person, or
  (ii) a transfer of assets to a relevant person,
(ab) releases or writes off the whole or a part of—
  (i) a loan made to a relevant person, or
  (ii) an acquired right of the kind mentioned in paragraph (aa)
(b) transfers an asset to a relevant person,
(c) takes a step by virtue of which a relevant person acquires an asset within subsection (4),[24]
(d) makes available a sum of money or asset for use,[25] or makes it available under an arrangement which permits its use—
  (i) as security for a loan made or to be made to a relevant person, or
  (ii) otherwise as security for the meeting of any liability, or the performance of any undertaking, which a relevant person has or will have, or
(f) grants to a relevant person a lease of any premises the effective duration of which is likely to exceed 21 years."

*Relevant persons*

A "relevant person" means A or any person chosen by A or within a class of person chosen by A. It also includes, if P is taking a step on A's behalf or otherwise at A's direction or request, any other person. References to A include any person

27-030

---

[24] This is a reference to "securities", "interests in securities", and "securities options", as defined in ITEPA 2003 s.420.
[25] Including making it available in an informal way. It does not matter if the relevant person has no legal right to have the sum of money or asset used as mentioned, and it does not matter if the sum of money or asset is not actually used as mentioned.

linked with A. So in order to avoid a payment or transfer being made to a relevant person, A must not choose the recipient, or direct or request that the payment/transfer is made to the recipient. In order to *choose* a recipient or class, A must be given a choice, and that would be unusual in practice. In order to *direct* a payment it seems likely that A would need to have a (legal) right to direct payment, which again would be unusual. If A has a power of veto which he decides not to exercise then that could not normally be described as a request.

**27-031** It is quite common for a member of a pension scheme to also be a trustee. For income tax purposes, trustees are treated as if they were a single person distinct from the persons who, from time to time, are trustees,[26] and it seems to follow that any decisions taken by the trustees as a body cannot be attributed to A in his individual capacity.[27]

*Loans and debts*

**27-032** For the purposes of the disguised remuneration provisions generally, references to the payment of a sum of money include (in particular) a payment by way of a loan.[28] For the purposes of s.554C(1) specifically, "loan" includes any form of credit, and a payment that is purported to be made by way of a loan.[29] Prior to 6 April 2017 the creation or assumption of debt by a relevant third person did not appear to involve a relevant step, but the introduction of s.554C(1)(aa) now expressly deals with this. New s.554C(1)(ab) also deals with the situation where loans are written off or released.[30] Such transactions would usually give rise to a charge under ITEPA 2003 s.188, but only during the life of the employee. Section 554C(1)(ab) also only applies during A's life.[31] The discharge of a debt for arm's length consideration should not amount to a release. However, where debt is transferred to the debtor (whether or not for consideration) that is deemed to constitute a release of the debt.[32]

*Changing trustees and transferring between trusts*

**27-033** HMRC accept that Pt 7A does not apply where there is a change of trustees.[33] They do not expressly comment on whether the transfer of trust property which will inevitably follow such a change of trustees (from the old trustee to the new trustee) is a relevant step, but given that for income tax purposes, the trustees of a settlement[34] are together treated as if they were a single person (distinct from the persons who are the trustees of the settlement from time to time),[35] it seems very likely that transactions between different trustees of a single settlement cannot constitute relevant steps. If that is correct then it does not matter if A requests the transfer, or if the recipient trustees are linked with A: there is no payment to a relevant person.

---

[26] ITA 2007 s.465(4).
[27] Notwithstanding that A, when acting as trustee, may constitute a relevant third person (s.554A(7)).
[28] ITEPA 2003 s.554Z(7).
[29] ITEPA 2003 s.554C(3A).
[30] For the meaning of "release" and "writing off", see *Collins v Addies* [1992] S.T.C. 746.
[31] See ITEPA 2003 s.554A(4).
[32] ITEPA 2003 s.554C(3B) and (3C).
[33] EIM45125.
[34] i.e. property held in trust (ITA 2007 s.466).
[35] ITA 2007 s.474.

RELEVANT STEPS 605

However, it seems clear that a transfer between separate trusts does involve a s.554C relevant step if A requests it.[36] The fact that A does not in any sense benefit from such a transfer is immaterial.[37]

**Making assets available**

Section 554D applies in two separate circumstances. The first involves a person making an asset available in a way which is substantially similar to ownership, and the second involves a person making assets available in any circumstances (i.e. circumstances which need not be substantially similar to ownership) but only once two years have elapsed from the end of the employment.

Section 554D(1) provides that:

"(1) A person ('P') takes a step within this section if, without transferring the asset to the relevant person, P—
   (a) at any time, makes an asset available for a relevant person to benefit from in a way which is substantially similar to the way in which the relevant person would have been able to benefit from the asset had the asset been transferred to the relevant person at that time, or
   (b) at or after the end of the relevant period, makes an asset available for a relevant person to benefit from."

This expressly includes making assets available in any way, however informal. It does not matter if the relevant person has no legal right to benefit from the asset, and it is irrelevant whether he does in fact benefit from the asset. The factors to take into account for the purposes of the *substantially similar* test include: (a) any limitations on the way in which the relevant person may benefit from the asset; (b) the period over which the asset is being made available and (if relevant) the extent to which that period covers the expected remaining useful life of the asset; (c) the extent to which the relevant person has, or is to have, a say over the disposal of the asset; and (d) the extent to which the relevant person may benefit from any proceeds arising.

Section 554D(2) provides that:

"(2) If—
   (a) before the end of the relevant period, P makes available an asset for a relevant person to benefit from, and
   (b) at the end of the relevant period, P continues to make the asset available for the relevant person to benefit from,
P is treated as taking a step within this section by virtue of subsection (1)(b) at the end of the relevant period."

The "relevant period" means the period of two years starting with the day on which A's employment with B ceases. The purpose of this appears to be to ensure that benefits in kind remain taxable after the employment has ended (which is not the case under the benefits code).

27-034

27-035

27-036

27-037

27-038

27-039

---

[36] If transfers between trusts were not chargeable then s.554X would be otiose (see below).
[37] cf. the EFRBS provisions, which focus on the provision of a benefit. For this reason, a transfer between trusts is not generally taxable under the EFRBS provisions.

# EXCEPTIONS

**27-040** There are a large number of exceptions, including the following which are particularly relevant to private retirement benefit schemes:

(a) arrangements the sole purpose of which is the provision of excluded benefits[38];
(b) registered pension schemes[39];
(c) arrangements the sole purpose of which is the making of payments within FA 2004 s.161(4)[40];
(d) exclusions applying to employment income exemptions under ITEPA 2003 Pt 4[41];
(e) pension taxable under ITEPA 2003 Pt 9[42];
(f) employee pension contributions[43];
(g) pre-6 April 2006 EFRBS (i.e. FURBS)[44];
(h) annuities purchased from pre-6 April 2011 rights[45];
(i) lump sums paid from pre-6 April 2011 rights (EFRBS and s.615 funds)[46];
(j) transfers between corresponding schemes[47]; and
(k) relevant non-UK schemes.[48]

### General exclusions

**27-041** In addition to the specific exceptions listed in para.27-040, there are some general exclusions which are outlined below.[49]

*Income arising from earmarked funds*

**27-042** Earmarking any income which arises from an earmarked sum or asset does not itself give rise to a s.554B relevant step provided that the income is not excessive and Pt 7A Ch.2 applied on the earmarking of the sum or asset,[50] and the sum or asset is still earmarked immediately before the income arises.[51]

---

[38] ITEPA 2003 s.554E(1)(d).
[39] ITEPA 2003 s.554E(1)(g). See Ch.22.
[40] ITEPA 2003 s.554E(1)(h). See Ch.22.
[41] ITEPA 2003 s.554P.
[42] ITEPA 2003 s.554S.
[43] ITEPA 2003 s.554T.
[44] ITEPA 2003 s.554U.
[45] ITEPA 2003 s.554V.
[46] ITEPA 2003 s.554W.
[47] ITEPA 2003 s.554X. See Ch.39.
[48] The Employment Income Provided Through Third Parties (Excluded Relevant Steps) Regulations 2011 (SI 2011/2696) reg.3.
[49] In addition to those referred to here, there are numerous other exclusions (relating, e.g. to commercial transactions (s.554F), transactions under employee benefit packages (s.554G), and earmarking of deferred remuneration (s.554H)) which are unlikely to be directly relevant to retirement benefit schemes.
[50] Or, where the earmarking took place before 6 April 2011 (and so Pt 7A Ch.2 did not apply), Pt 7A Ch.2 would have applied if Pt 7A did apply to relevant steps before 6 April 2011: FA 2011 Sch.2 para.56.
[51] ITEPA 2003 s.554Q.

## EXCEPTIONS

*Earmarking replacement funds*

If a sum or asset is earmarked and then a different sum or asset is acquired *wholly out of*[52] the earmarked sum or asset, and the new sum or asset is itself then earmarked, the latter earmarking will not give rise to a s.554B relevant step provided that[53]:

27-043

(a) the replacement sum or asset is not acquired from A or any person linked with A;
(b) it is reasonable to suppose that, in essence, the replacement assets are of equivalent value;
(c) Pt 7A Ch.2 applied on the earmarking of the former sum or asset; and
(d) the former sum or asset is still earmarked immediately before the acquisition.

*Loan repayments*

If a loan is repaid and the proceeds are the subject of a s.554B relevant step, Pt 7A Ch.2 does not apply to that relevant step provided that the proceeds are held on the same basis on which the right to repayment was held before the repayment.[54]

27-044

**Arrangements for the provision of excluded benefits**

Part 7A Ch.2 does not apply by reason of a relevant step if the step is taken under an arrangement the sole purpose of which is the provision of excluded benefits as defined in ITEPA 2003 s.393B(3).[55]

27-045

*Sole purpose*

The sole purpose test requires one to look at the purpose of the scheme: is it only to provide excluded benefits or does the scheme have some other purpose? Purpose tests such as this one are usually interpreted as posing a subjective rather than an objective test.[56] It is a continuing test, so one must inquire into the state of mind of the person establishing the scheme and also the person administering the scheme from time to time. The purpose cannot be determined by looking only at the scheme documentation.[57]

27-046

Prior to 6 April 2006, HMRC would not grant tax approval to an occupational pension scheme unless it was "bona fide established for the sole purpose of provid-

27-047

---

[52] By way of example, where the original sum or asset is sold, the sale proceeds are a sum or asset "wholly out of" the original sum or asset (s.554R(4)).
[53] ITEPA 2003 s.554R.
[54] ITEPA 2003 s.554RA.
[55] ITEPA 2003 s.554E(1)(d). For the meaning of "excluded benefits", see Ch.35.
[56] cf. *Pi Consulting (Trustee Services) Ltd v the Pensions Regulator* [2013] EWHC 3181 (Ch) at [39].
[57] PSI2.2.2 provided that "Section 590(2)(a) ICTA 88 requires that a retirement benefits scheme be 'bona fide established for the sole purpose of providing relevant benefits'. It has been argued that the purpose of a scheme is determined solely by reference to its documentation and that the Inland Revenue cannot question other aspects, such as the scheme's investments. The Board's Solicitor disagrees and has advised that where something is to be done 'bona fide', the requirement must be genuinely met and not just met on paper. It is up to the trustees of a scheme to prove, where necessary, that the scheme is genuine and has the provision of relevant benefits as its sole purpose". Section 554E(1)(d) does not expressly include a "bona fide" requirement, but will not make any difference: it is implicit that the requirements of any exemption must be genuinely satisfied, and not merely "on paper".

ing relevant benefits".[58] HMRC considered that the sole purpose test may be breached if the scheme invests in property from which a member was able to derive a benefit, because such a benefit would not be a relevant benefit.[59] But it is sometimes necessary to distinguish a person's purpose from the consequences of his actions. The fact that a member obtains a benefit which is not an excluded benefit does not, without more, show that the test is failed. But if the purpose of the investment (which may be inferred from the circumstances) is to provide such a benefit, it must follow that the *sole* purpose of the scheme is not the provision of excluded benefits.

### Exclusions under ITEPA 2003 Pt 4

**27-048** ITEPA 2003 Pt 4 contains a large number of exemptions from employment income, such as mileage allowance, travel and subsistence and work-related training etc. Some of these exceptions are "earnings-only exceptions" and some are "employment income exceptions". An employment income exemption means an exemption from income tax which prevents liability to tax arising in respect of employment income of any kind at all (and not merely earnings).[60]

**27-049** Section 554P provides that Pt 7A Ch.2 does not apply by reason of a relevant step if an employment income exemption under Pt 4 applies to the subject of the relevant step. ITEPA Pt 4 Ch.9 contains the following exemptions which are relevant in a pensions context:

(a) section 307, which provides that no liability to income arises under the residual head of the benefits code in respect of provision made for a retirement or death benefit (under a registered pension scheme or otherwise);

(b) section 308, which provides that no liability to income tax arises in respect of earnings where an employee's employer makes contributions under a registered pension scheme in respect of the employee;

(c) section 308A, which provides that no liability to income tax arises in respect of earnings where an employer makes contributions under a qualifying overseas pension scheme in respect of an employee who is a relevant migrant member of the pension scheme; and

(d) section 308B, which provides that no liability to income tax arises in respect of the provision to an employee of independent advice in respect of conversion and transfer of pension scheme benefits.

**27-050** Only s.308B is an employment income exception.

### Pensions chargeable under ITEPA 2003 Pt 9

**27-051** Section 554S provides that:

"(i) Chapter 2 does not apply by reason of a relevant step within section 554C or 554D if the step is the provision of pension income which is chargeable to income tax under Part 9 or is exempt income (within the meaning of that Part).

(ii) Sections 554T, 554U, 554V, 554W,[61] and 554X contain further provision relating to retirement benefits etc and are to be applied, so far as applicable, in that order."

---

[58] ICTA 1988 s.590 and IR12 (2001). Similar requirements were imposed in respect of personal pension schemes under ICTA 1988 s.630.

[59] IR76 (2000) paras 11.8 and 11.9.

[60] ITEPA 2003 s.227(3).

[61] For the purposes of applying the Employment Income Provided Through Third Parties (Excluded

ITEPA 2003 Pt 9 imposes the charge to tax on pension income.[62] Section 554S 27-052
applies if the pension income is "chargeable" under Pt 9; it need not be "charged"
under Pt 9.[63] A foreign pension paid to a UK resident remittance basis taxpayer is
chargeable under ITEPA 2003 Pt 9 notwithstanding that it will only be subject to
UK tax to the extent that it is remitted to the UK. It is also likely that pension
income paid from a UK scheme to a non-UK resident member which is not subject
to UK tax a result of a double tax treaty is "chargeable under Pt 9".[64] It seems
unlikely that pension income paid from a non-UK scheme to a non-UK resident
member could be described as being chargeable under Pt 9 (because Pt 9 Ch.4 applies to pension income only if the member is resident in the UK).[65]

Since 6 April 2017, for the purposes of ITEPA 2003 Pt 9 Ch.4 (foreign pension), pension income includes a "relevant lump sum". However, a lump sum can 27-053
only be a relevant lump sum if the payment of the lump sum is not a relevant step
by reason of which Pt 7A Ch.2 applies.[66] This requires one to determine whether
the payment of the lump sum is a relevant step to which Pt 7A Ch.2 applies,
disregarding the possible application of s.554S if it is found to be a relevant lump
sum. If Pt 7A Ch.2 does not apply then the lump sum may be a relevant lump sum
(and therefore taxable under Pt 9 Ch.4).

"Exempt income" means pension income on which no liability to income tax 27-054
arises as a result of any provision of ITEPA 2003 Pt 9 Chs 16 to 18.[67]

Section 554S only excludes a relevant step within s.554C or s.554D. One would 27-055
expect any provision of pension income to be preceded by a s.554B relevant step
(unless the funds have already been earmarked). The fact that s.554S does not
exclude a s.554B relevant step supports the proposition advanced above that there
is no s.554B relevant step unless there is a material time delay. If this were not correct then s.554S would only ever provide an exception to funds earmarked before
6 April 2011, as the earmarking immediately preceding the payment would still be
taxable under Pt 7A Ch.2. It is therefore arguable that the payment of pension
income does not involve a s.554B relevant step unless there is a material time delay
between the earmarking and the payment.

**Employee pension contributions**

Part 7A Ch.2 does not apply by reason of a s.554B relevant step if the sum of 27-056
money or asset which is the subject of the step arises or derives (whether wholly
or partly, directly or indirectly) from an excluded pension contribution paid by A
on or after 6 April 2011.[68] In addition, Part 7A Ch.2 does not apply by reason of a
s.554C or 554D relevant step if the sum of money or asset which is the subject of
the step represents relevant benefits[69] and arises or derives (whether wholly or partly
or directly or indirectly) from an excluded pension contribution paid by A.

---

Relevant Steps) Regulations 2011 (SI 2011/2696) (see below), s.554(2) is modified so that after the
reference to s.554W (and before the reference to s.554X), there was a reference to SI 2011/2696.
[62] For an analysis of ITEPA 2003 Pt 9, see Ch.26.
[63] cf. the exclusion to the EFRBS provisions in ITEPA 2003 s.393B(2)(a) which only applies if benefits
are "charged" (not merely "chargeable") to tax under ITEPA 2003 Pt 9: see Ch.35.
[64] See ITEPA 2003 ss.569(1) and 572A.
[65] See ITEPA 2003 s.573(1).
[66] ITEPA 2003 s.574A(1)(b).
[67] ITEPA 2003 s.566(3). See Ch.26.
[68] ITEPA 2003 s.554T(1).
[69] The term "relevant benefits" has the same meaning as in ITEPA 2003 s.393B, but ignoring
s.393B(2)(a). This means that the following benefits are relevant benefits for this purpose: benefits

**27-057** In each case, if the sum of money or asset only partly arises or derives from the excluded pension contribution, the relevant step is treated as being two separate relevant steps: one in relation to the sum of money or asset so far as it arises or derives from the excluded pension contribution, and one in relation to the sum of money or asset so far as it does not arise or derive from the excluded pension contribution, with s.554T(1) applying only in relation to the former. The sum of money or asset which is the subject of the relevant step is apportioned between the two separate relevant steps on a just and reasonable basis.

**27-058** An *excluded pension contribution* means a contribution:

(a) made to an arrangement by A by way of a payment of a sum of money;

(b) by virtue of which A acquires rights to receive relevant benefits under the arrangement, and nothing else;

(c) which is neither a *relievable pension contribution* nor a *tax-relieved contribution*[70]; and

(d) which is not a repayment of any loan and otherwise has nothing to do with any loan and has nothing to do with a sum of money or asset which has been the subject of a relevant step within s.554C(1)(d).

### FURBS

**27-059** Section 554U(1)–(3) provides that:

"(1) This section applies if the subject of a relevant step is a sum of money or asset which has (wholly or partly) arisen or derived (directly or indirectly) from a sum of money ('the taxed sum')—

(a) which was paid by B in accordance with an employer-financed retirement benefits scheme (within the meaning of Chapter 2 of Part 6) with a view to the provision of benefits under the scheme, and

(b) in respect of which A is taxed.

(2) For the purpose of determining whether A is taxed in respect of a sum of money, paragraph 53(3) of Schedule 36 to FA 2004 applies as it applies for the purpose of determining whether an employee is taxed for the purposes of paragraph 53(1)(b) of that Schedule.

(3) Chapter 2 does not apply by reason of the relevant step."

**27-060** FA 2004 Sch.36 para.53(3) provides that:

"(3) …an employee is taxed in respect of a sum or sums if—

(a) the employee is assessed to tax by virtue of section 595(1) of ICTA (charges on payments) in respect of the sum or sums, or

(b) the sum or sums counts or count as employment income of the employee under section 386(1) of ITEPA 2003 (charges on payments)."

**27-061** It follows from the above that if the money or asset which is the subject of a relevant step meets the following three conditions, Pt 7A Ch.2 will not apply to it:

(a) it has arisen or derived from a sum of money (the "taxed sum") paid in ac-

---

charged to tax under Pt 9, or that would be charged to tax under Pt 9 but for s.573(2A) or (2B), 646D or 646E or any deductions under s.574A(3). See Ch.35 and Ch.26.

[70] A relievable pension contribution is a contribution in respect of which an individual is entitled to relief under FA 2004 s.188. A tax-relieved contribution has the meaning given by FA 2004 Sch.34 para.3(3), which relates to contributions in respect of which relief from tax has been given by virtue of Sch.33 (migrant member relief), or has been given at any time after 5 April 2006 under double tax arrangements (see respectively Ch.24 and Ch.29). This includes transitional corresponding relief.

cordance with a FURBS with a view to the provision of benefits under the FURBS;
(b) the taxed sum was paid by B[71]; and
(c) A was taxed under ITEPA 2003 s.386(1)[72] in respect of the taxed sum. This can only be the case in relation to contributions made prior to 6 April 2006.[73]

If the sum of money or asset which is the subject of the relevant step only partly arises or derives from the taxed sum then the relevant step is treated as being two separate relevant steps: one in relation to the sum of money or asset so far as it arises or derives from the taxed sum, and one in relation to the sum of money or asset so far as it does not arise or derive from the taxed sum, with the exemption applying only in relation to the former. In order to give effect to this, the sum of money or asset which is the subject of the relevant step is apportioned between the two separate relevant steps on a just and reasonable basis.

27-062

## Purchased annuities

Section 554V applies if: (a) an annuity contract[74] is purchased from an insurance company[75] wholly out of rights which A has under a pension scheme[76]; and (b) A's rights out of which the annuity contract is purchased are, wholly or partly, pre-6 April 2011 annuity rights. Part 7A Ch.2 does not apply by reason of a relevant step taken by the purchaser for the sole purpose of purchasing the annuity contract or transferring the beneficiary's rights under the annuity contract to A or a person linked with A. Part 7A Ch.2 also does not apply if the purchaser, on the purchase of the annuity contract, otherwise takes a s.554B relevant step the subject of which is the beneficiary's rights under the annuity contract.

27-063

If the insurance company takes a relevant step for the sole purpose of selling the annuity contract, or on the sale of the annuity contract, otherwise takes a s.554B relevant step the subject of which is a sum of money or asset representing the purchase price received for the annuity contract Pt 7A Ch.2 does not apply by reason of the relevant step.

27-064

If A's rights out of which the annuity contract is purchased are only partly pre-6 April 2011 annuity rights then the relevant step is treated as being two separate relevant steps: one in relation to the annuity contract so far as it is purchased out of rights which are pre-6 April 2011 annuity rights, and one in relation to the annuity contract so far as it is purchased out of rights which are not pre-6 April 2011 annuity rights, with the exemption applying only in relation to the former. In order to give effect to this, the sum of money or asset which is the subject of the relevant step is apportioned between the two separate relevant steps on a just and reasonable basis. What is *just and reasonable* will depend on the facts, but one would

27-065

---

[71] Or a company which is a member of the same group as B at the relevant time.
[72] Or, prior to 2003, under ICTA 1988 s.595(1).
[73] For the circumstances in which the charge in s.386(1) arose, see Ch.38.
[74] An annuity contract is a contract for the provision of an annuity: (a) granted for consideration in money or money's worth in the ordinary course of a business of granting annuities on human life; and (b) payable for a term ending at a time ascertainable only by reference to the end of a human life (although it does not matter that the annuity may in some circumstances end before or after the life).
[75] An *insurance company* is: (a) a person or EEA firm within FA 2004 s.275(1)(a) or (b); or (b) a person resident in a territory outside the EEA: (i) whose normal business includes the provision of annuities; and (ii) who is regulated in the conduct of that business by the government of that territory or by a body established under the law of that territory for the purpose of regulating such business.
[76] Pension scheme has the same meaning as in FA 2004 s.150(1) (see s.554Z(8)).

expect[77] that the value of pre-6 April 2011 annuity rights would include investment growth after that date to the extent that the growth relates to funds held on 5 April 2011.

*Pre-6 April 2011 annuity rights*

**27-066**  Rights are *pre-6 April 2011 annuity rights* if they accrued before 6 April 2011 specifically to receive an annuity. Does the term *accrued* require the right to be absolute, or does it include a contingent right, or a right which is vested subject to be divested? HMRC take a relatively generous view[78]:

> "Section 554V uses the concept of 'pre-6 April 2011 annuity rights' to prevent people from obtaining an exclusion from Part 7A income by converting rights to other types of benefits held before 6 April 2011 into rights to receive an annuity on or after that date.
> The term "rights" includes both actual rights and prospective rights.
> The term "pre-6 April 2011 annuity rights" includes both actual rights and prospective rights accrued by that time. In this context, 'accrued by that time' refers to the fund value at that time plus later investment growth up to the time of the annuity purchase.
> Suppose that on 5 April 2011 a member had the actual or prospective right to receive an annuity:
> 
> - unconditionally,
> - under a member's election, or
> - at the option or discretion of the trustee.
> 
> Then the intention is that the value of relevant steps taken in the process of purchasing, transferring or paying the annuity will be excluded from Part 7A income but only to the extent that no other rights are involved (such as those arising from contributions paid after 5 April 2011).
> The detailed time-test for whether the member had such a right to receive an annuity (whether by explicit provision, by election, by trustee's option or by discretion) is that the right to receive an annuity:
> 
> - could have been exercised at 5 April 2011, or
> - could have been exercised at that date had the member met the sufficient conditions (for example, around age).
> 
> For the purposes of this test, it does not matter if:
> 
> - the right is exercised later, or
> - the purchase amount includes growth occurring after 5 April 2011."

**Pre-6 April 2011 lump sums**

**27-067**  Section 554W provides that Pt 7A Ch.2 does not apply by reason of a relevant step which is the provision of a relevant benefit under an EFRBS or a s.615 scheme[79] by way of a payment of a lump sum wholly out of rights which A has under the scheme if:

(a) A's rights out of which the lump sum is paid are, wholly or partly, pre-6 April 2011 lump sum rights; and
(b) the payment of the lump sum is a relevant step within s.554C.

---

[77] As HMRC note at EIM45625.
[78] EIM45625.
[79] For the meaning of "relevant benefits", see Ch.35.

# EXCEPTIONS

27-068 This exclusion will not of course prevent a relevant benefit under an EFRBS from being taxable in accordance with ITEPA 2003 s.394.[80]

*"Pre-6 April 2011 lump sum rights"*

27-069 Rights are "pre-6 April 2011 lump sum rights" if they accrued before 6 April 2011 specifically to receive relevant benefits by way of lump sum payments. As with pre-6 April 2011 annuity rights under s.554V (considered above), HMRC take a relatively generous view of this.[81] HMRC's position is that if the trustees had the power to provide lump sum relevant benefits to the member on 5 April 2011, or they would have had the power if the member had met any applicable conditions (e.g. relating to age), then that is a pre-6 April 2011 lump sum right.

27-070 What is a "lump sum" for these purposes? In particular, given the main focus of Pt 7A, does it include a payment by way of loan? A loan could be a relevant benefit, and it would clearly be a s.554C relevant step, so if it is a lump sum then s.554W could apply to it. In general, it is probably implicit that a lump sum involves an outright payment, but Pt 7A deliberately obscures the distinction between outright payments and loans and so it does appear to be arguable that, for the purposes of s.554W, a lump sum may include a payment by way of loan.

27-071 If A's rights out of which the lump sum is paid are only partly pre-6 April 2011 lump sum rights, the relevant step is treated as being two separate relevant steps: one in relation to the lump sum so far as it is paid out of rights which are pre-6 April 2011 lump sum rights, and one in relation to the lump sum so far as it is paid out of rights which are not pre-6 April 2011 lump sum rights, with the exemption only applying in relation to the former. The lump sum must be apportioned between the two separate relevant steps on a just and reasonable basis. What is *just and reasonable* will depend on the facts, but one would expect[82] that the value of pre-6 April 2011 lump sum rights would include investment growth after that date to the extent that it relates to funds held on 5 April 2011.

## Transfers relating to corresponding schemes

27-072 Section 554X applies in the following circumstances:

(a) Rights which A has under a "s.390 scheme" are transferred to: (i) another s.390 scheme; or (ii) an overseas pension scheme.[83] A "s.390 scheme" is a scheme in relation to which a claim was accepted under ITEPA 2003 s.390.[84]
(b) Rights which A has under an overseas pension scheme are transferred to another overseas pension scheme, and all of the rights transferred are "section 390 scheme rights". "Section 390 scheme rights" are rights which A has under an overseas pension scheme and which have been transferred to the scheme (directly or indirectly) from a s.390 scheme, or have arisen or derived (directly or indirectly) from rights that have been so transferred.
(c) Rights which A has under an overseas pension scheme are transferred to another overseas pension scheme, and some (but not all) of the rights transferred are s.390 scheme rights.

27-073 If s.554X applies, Pt 7A Ch.2 does not apply to a s.554C relevant step taken for

---

[80] For ITEPA 2003 s.394, see Ch.35.
[81] EIM45635.
[82] As HMRC note at EIM45635.
[83] "Overseas pension scheme" has the same meaning as in FA 2004 s.150(7). See Ch.31.
[84] For ITEPA 2003 s.390, see Ch.39.

the sole purpose of transferring the rights, or a s.554B relevant step taken by the transferee in relation to the transferred rights on their transfer. Where (c) above applies the s.554C or s.554B relevant step is treated as being two separate relevant steps: one in relation to the s.390 scheme rights, and one in relation to the rest of the transferred rights, with the exception applying only in relation to the former. For these purposes, the sum of money or asset which is the subject of the relevant step is apportioned between the two separate relevant steps on a just and reasonable basis.

*Transferred rights derive from contributions by B which are not tax-relieved*

**27-074** If any of the transferred rights arise or derive (directly or indirectly) from contributions to any scheme which are paid by B[85] on or after 6 April 2006, and are neither tax-relieved contributions nor tax-exempt provision,[86] any s.554C or s.554B relevant step is treated as being two separate relevant steps. One relevant step relates to the rights just mentioned, and the other relevant step relates to the rest of the transferred rights, with the exception for s.554C or 554B relevant steps applying only in relation to the latter relevant step. For these purposes, the sum of money or asset which is the subject of the relevant step is apportioned between the two separate relevant steps on a just and reasonable basis.

**27-075** Where both of the above apportionments apply, the second apportionment only applies to the s.390 scheme rights.

**Relevant non-UK schemes**

**27-076** SI 2011/2696 reg.3(1) relates to RNUKS. It provides that:

"Chapter 2 of Part 7A (treatment of relevant steps for income tax purposes) does not apply by reason of a relevant step if the subject of the relevant step is a sum of money or asset which represents or which has (wholly or partly) arisen or derived (directly or indirectly) from a sum of money or assets which represents or has represented—

(a) a UK tax-relieved fund under a relevant non-UK scheme, or
(b) a relevant transfer fund under a relevant non-UK scheme."

**27-077** "UK tax-relieved fund", "relevant non-UK scheme" and "relevant transfer fund" have the same meanings as in FA 2004 Sch.34.[87] Note that the exception does *not* expressly apply to a ring-fenced transfer fund, i.e., broadly, a fund comprising sums or assets transferred (a) from a registered pension scheme on or after 9 March 2017; or (b) from another RNUKS on or after 6 April 2017.[88] This omission is presumably unintended and hopefully will be corrected in due course.

If the sum of money or asset which is the subject of the relevant step only partly represents,[89] or arises/derives from a sum of money or assets which represents or has represented, a UK tax-relieved fund or a relevant transfer fund under an RNUKS then the relevant step is deemed to be two separate relevant steps. One

---

[85] If B is a member of a group of companies the reference to B includes a reference to any other company which is a member of that group.
[86] "Tax-exempt provision" and "tax-relieved contribution" have the meaning given by FA 2004 Sch.34 para.3(3) and (4) (see Ch.30).
[87] See FA 2004 Sch.34 paras 3(2) and 4(2), explained in Ch.30.
[88] SI 2006/207 reg.3B and FA 2004 Sch.34 para.1(6B), explained in Ch.30.
[89] HMRC consider that "Whether a sum or money or asset can be said to "represent" a particular fund or part of a particular fund, should be considered using the normal dictionary meaning of the word. It will typically apply where the sum or asset is actually held within such a fund for the purposes of

# PART 7A CH.2: THE CHARGE TO TAX

relevant step relates to the sum of money or asset so far as it represents or arises or derives from a sum of money or assets which represents or has represented the UK tax-relieved fund or relevant transfer fund, and one relates to the sum of money or asset so far as it does not represent or arise or derive from a sum of money or assets which represents or has represented such a fund, with the exemption applying only in relation to the former. In order to give effect to this, the sum of money or asset which is the subject of the relevant step is apportioned between the two separate relevant steps on a just and reasonable basis.[90]

Sums or assets "represent" one of the above funds if the sums or assets are held for the purposes of such a fund. The reference to sums or assets *arising* from such a fund appears to include investment growth relating to such funds. The reference to sums or assets *deriving* from such a fund will include sums or assets held by a third party such as an investment manager. If sums or assets representing such a fund are transferred to a scheme which is not an RNUKS (i.e. where the residency exemption is met at that time), does the exception apply to the transferred sums and assets (which will clearly not represent either of the above funds under the transferee scheme) on the basis that they *have represented* one of the above funds under an RNUKS, or they *derive* from one of the above funds? On the face of it, the exception will apply.

27-078

## PART 7A CH.2: THE CHARGE TO TAX

If Pt 7A Ch.2 applies, the *value* of the relevant step counts as employment income of A in respect of A's employment with B for the tax year in which the relevant step is taken.[91] If the relevant step is taken before A's employment with B starts, it counts as employment income for the tax year in which the employment starts. Where the value of a relevant step would otherwise count as employment income of more than one person, the value of the relevant step is apportioned between each of those persons on a just and reasonable basis.

27-079

Part 7A Ch.2 is not itself a charging provision: it causes a relevant step to be taxable by providing that it counts as employment income of A. Any amount which counts as employment income is *specific employment income* for the purposes of ITEPA 2003 s.7(4), and is therefore charged under ITEPA 2003 s.9(4), which provides that the amount charged is the "net taxable specific income" from the employment in the tax year. Section 12(1) provides that net taxable specific income is the amount of any taxable specific income from the employment for the tax year less any permitted deductions.

27-080

### The value of the relevant step

Section 554Z3 prescribes how one is to determine the value of the relevant step. If the relevant step involves a sum of money, its value is the amount of the sum. References to the payment of a sum of money expressly include a payment by way of a loan,[92] so a loan is taxed in the same way as an outright payment (with no relief

27-081

---

such a fund, or where the sum or asset has been produced to meet an unfunded benefit promise of such a "fund", for example on transfer." (EIM45655).
[90] SI 2011/2696 reg.3(3)–(4).
[91] ITEPA 2003 s.554Z2(1).
[92] ITEPA 2003 s.554Z(7).

given when the loan is repaid).[93] If the relevant step does not involve a sum of money, the value of the relevant step is the market value when the relevant step is taken of the asset which is the subject of the step. If the cost of the relevant step is higher than the market value of the asset, that is the value of the relevant step.[94] It makes no difference that sums or assets comprised in a relevant step relate partly (or even wholly) to investment returns rather than contributions.

**27-082** Section 554Z3 is subject to the following provisions, which, if applicable, are applied in the following order. Each may have the effect of reducing the value of the relevant step:

(a) If the value of the relevant step is "for" a tax year in which A was non-UK resident, and is not in respect of UK duties, it may be reduced under s.554Z4.
(b) If there is an overlap between the sums or assets forming the subject of the relevant step and an earlier relevant step, the value of the later relevant step may be reduced under s.554Z5.
(c) If the relevant step gives rise to taxable earnings then the value of the relevant step may be reduced under s.554Z6.
(d) If the relevant step involves an earmarking of share options then the value of the relevant step may be reduced under s.554Z7.
(e) If the relevant step is a payment to A on arm's length terms, the value of the relevant step may be reduced under s.554Z8.

*Residence issues*

**27-083** Once one has identified a relevant step and ascertained its value one must determine the particular tax year(s) which the value of the relevant step is "for".[95] This is achieved by applying ITEPA 2003 s.16(1)–(4). If the relevant step is for a year in which the employment is not held, one applies ITEPA 2003 s.17(1)–(3). If the value of the relevant step, or a part of it, is *for* a tax year for which A is non-UK resident, then the value, or the part of it, is reduced by so much of the value, or the part of it, as is not in respect of duties performed in the UK.[96] Section 554Z4 does not change the tax year for which the value of the relevant step counts as employment income under s.554Z2(1); it merely permits a reduction in the value of the relevant step to the extent that it relates to duties performed outside of the UK during periods of non-residence.

*ITEPA 2003 s.16*

**27-084** ITEPA 2003 s.16(1)–(4) provides that:

**"Meaning of earnings 'for' a tax year**

**16**(1) This section applies for determining whether general earnings are general earnings 'for' a particular tax year for the purposes of this Chapter.

---

[93] Although if the loan is subsequently released or written off then that relevant step is reduced by the amount of the loan under ITEPA 2003 s.554Z5.
[94] ITEPA 2003 s.554Z3.
[95] ITEPA 2003 s.554Z4.
[96] If the value of the relevant step, or a part of it, is *for* a tax year that is a split year as respects A then the value, or the part of it, is to be reduced by so much of the value, or the part of it, as is both attributable to the overseas part of the tax year, and not in respect of duties performed in the UK. This is determined on a just and reasonable basis.

"(2) General earnings that are earned in, or otherwise in respect of, a particular period are to be regarded as general earnings for that period.

(3) If that period consists of the whole or part of a single tax year, the earnings are to be regarded as general earnings 'for' that tax year.

(4) If that period consists of the whole or parts of two or more tax years, the part of the earnings that is to be regarded as general earnings 'for' each of those tax years is to be determined on a just and reasonable apportionment."

**27-085** Pursuant to s.16(2), the relevant step is *for* the period in which it is *earned in or otherwise in respect of*. If the contribution is made to reward the employee for his performance during a particular period, then one would expect that to be the period that the relevant step is *for*.[97] It follows that if a contribution is for a period in which the employee is non-UK resident, and the contribution is in respect of duties performed outside of the UK, the effect of s.554Z4(4)(a) is to reduce the value of any subsequent relevant step to nil. For example, if a contribution is made to a pension scheme and is earmarked for a member (a s.554B relevant step), and then sometime later is paid as a lump sum to the member (a s.554C relevant step), it makes no difference if the employee is resident in the UK when the relevant step is taken. The fact that the s.554C relevant step is *received* in a later year does not affect the year this it is *for*.[98]

**27-086** In *Mackay v HMRC*,[99] the taxpayer received £500,000 from his UK employer in the 2005/06 tax year as compensation for discontinuing his rights under an UURBS. His rights under the scheme had accrued over almost ten years, during which period he had spent 80% of his time working outside of the UK. It was accepted that the payment constituted earnings, but the FTT had to determine whether the payment was "for" the 2005/06 tax year (when it was received, as HMRC contended—because the taxpayer was resident in the UK during that tax year) or whether it was "for" the ten years in which the entitlement to the pension rights accrued, and therefore needed to be apportioned across those years (most of which were periods of non-residence). The FTT concluded that the £500,000 reflected both the value of the rights that had accrued over the ten years and also the future rights which were likely to accrue. It found that £400,000 related to the renunciation of the vested rights which had been earned in the years 1999 to 2005 (and so should be spread over those years). The other £100,000 was in respect of, and should be apportioned to, the renunciation of the earning of future enhanced pension entitlements, and this was earned in 2005/06, in respect of the renunciation of those rights in that year.

*ITEPA 2003 s.17*

**27-087** If a relevant step is *for* a tax year after the employment had ceased then ITEPA 2003 s.17 applies. This provides as follows:

"(1) This section applies for the purposes of this Chapter in a case where general earnings from an employment would otherwise fall to be regarded as general earnings for a tax year in which the employee does not hold the employment.

---

[97] In *Bray v Best* [1989] 1 W.L.R. 167 Lord Oliver said this: "In the Court of Appeal it was said that there is a prima facie presumption that an emolument is paid 'for' the year of assessment in which the payee becomes entitled to receive it. I would prefer, however, to say simply that the period to which any given payment is to be attributed is a question to be determined as one of fact in each case, depending upon all the circumstances, including its source and the intention of the payer so far as it can be gathered either from direct evidence or from the surrounding circumstances".

[98] Again, per Lord Oliver in *Bray v Best* [1989] 1 W.L.R. 167. HMRC agree with this analysis: see EIM40008.

[99] *Mackay v HMRC* [2017] UKFTT 441.

(2) If that year falls before the first tax year in which the employment is held, the earnings are to be treated as general earnings for that first tax year.

(3) If that year falls after the last tax year in which the employment was held, the earnings are to be treated as general earnings for that last tax year."

**27-088**   So, if s.17 applies the position is straightforward: the relevant step is deemed to be *for* the last year of his employment. If he was UK resident in the last year of his employment then s.554Z4 will not have any application. If he was non-UK resident at that time, and the step is in respect of duties performed outside of the UK, the effect of s.554Z4(4)(a) is to reduce the value of the relevant step to nil.

*Rights to lump sum benefits accruing on or after 6 April 2017*

**27-089**   The above reduction does not apply to the payment of a lump sum relevant benefit[100] under an EFRBS to a UK resident person if the lump sum is wholly in respect of rights which have accrued on or after 6 April 2017.[101] If the lump sum is wholly or partly in respect of rights which accrued before 6 April 2017, the amount of any reduction is given by the formula "R x (A/LS)", where:

- *A* is so much of the lump sum as is in respect of rights which accrued before 6 April 2017;
- *LS* is the amount of the lump sum; and
- *R* is the amount of the reduction above (i.e. disregarding the requirement to reduce the reduction in accordance with this formula).

*Overlap with money or asset subject to earlier tax liability*

**27-090**   Section 554Z5 (which was substituted in its entirely by FA 2017) is intended to prevent double taxation where it is just and reasonable to conclude that a relevant step is taken in relation to a sum or asset which has already been the subject of a previous relevant step (including sums or assets which directly or indirectly represent the sums or assets which were the subject of the previous relevant step). However, this is only applicable if the earlier relevant step created an income tax liability and that tax has either been paid or terms have been agreed with HMRC for the discharge of that liability.

**27-091**   This typically arises where a sum or asset is earmarked and then subsequently paid or transferred to A. If there is any investment growth between the two relevant steps, the amount of the investment growth will remain taxable on the second relevant step.

*Overlap with certain earnings*

**27-092**   If the relevant step gives rise to relevant earnings[102] of A from A's employment with B *for* a tax year in which A is: (a) UK resident[103]; or (b) non-UK resident but which are in respect of duties performed in the UK, then the value of the relevant

---

[100] For the meaning of "relevant benefit", see Ch.35.
[101] ITEPA 2003 s.554Z4(7).
[102] Including earnings within ITEPA 2003 s.62 and deemed employment payments under ITEPA s.50 (which relates to the intermediaries or "IR35" provisions). Anything which is exempt income is not "relevant".
[103] And, in the case of a tax year that is a split year as respects A, are not "excluded".

step (after any reductions under s.554Z4 or 554Z5) is reduced by the amount of the relevant earnings.[104] This is intended to avoid double taxation.

*Consideration given for relevant step*

If P were to buy an asset from a relevant person, or sell an asset to such a person, that would involve P making a s.554C relevant step. There is an important exception in s.554Z8 for arm's length transactions, which will apply if a number of conditions are satisfied. The conditions are slightly different depending on whether A is selling an asset to P or buying an asset from P. In these provisions, all references to A include any person linked with A.

27-093

*A is selling an asset to P*

Section 554Z8(2) applies if:

27-094

(a) the relevant step is a step within s.554C(1)(a)–(c);
(b) the relevant step is for consideration given by A in the form of the transfer of an asset to P from A;
(c) the transfer by A of the asset is made before, or at or about, the time the relevant step is taken and is not by way of a loan; and
(d) there is no connection (direct or indirect) between the transfer by A of the asset and a tax avoidance arrangement. It is expressly assumed that the transfer is connected with a tax avoidance arrangement if: (i) before the transfer, the asset was transferred to A by another person by way of a loan; or (ii) the asset is, or carries with it, any rights or interests under the relevant arrangement or any arrangement which is connected with the relevant arrangement.

If s.554Z8(2) applies then the value of the relevant step (after any reductions under ss.554Z4–554Z6) is reduced by the market value of the asset transferred by A at the time of its transfer. However if the value of the relevant step has been reduced under s.554Z4, then the value of the relevant step is reduced by X% of that market value, where "X%" means the proportion of the value of the relevant step (as determined under s.554Z3) left after the reduction under s.554Z4.

27-095

*A is buying an asset from P*

Section 554Z8(6) applies if:

27-096

(a) the relevant step is a step within s.554C(1)(b) or (c) or (e) or 554D and does not also involve a sum of money;
(b) the relevant step is for consideration given by A in the form of the payment of a sum of money to P by A;
(c) the payment is made before, or at or about, the time the relevant step is taken; and
(d) there is no connection (direct or indirect) between the payment and a tax avoidance arrangement.

If s.554Z8(6) applies then the value of the relevant step (after any reductions under ss.554Z4–554Z6) is reduced by the amount of the consideration given. However if the value of the relevant step was reduced under s.554Z4, then the value of the relevant step is reduced by X% of the amount of that consideration. "X%"

27-097

---

[104] ITEPA 2003 s.554Z6.

means the proportion of the value of the relevant step (as determined under s.554Z3) left after the reduction under s.554Z4.

*Tax avoidance arrangements*

**27-098** In each case there must be no connection between the relevant step and a tax avoidance arrangement. Simply bringing oneself within the terms of a relief could not normally be described as tax avoidance, provided that one genuinely suffers the economic consequences of doing so. Section 554Z(13)–(16) provide that an arrangement is a "tax avoidance arrangement" if it has a tax avoidance purpose, and an arrangement has a tax avoidance purpose if the main purpose, or one of the main purposes, of any party in entering into the arrangement is the avoidance of tax or NIC. A step is *connected* with a tax avoidance arrangement if (for example) the step is taken wholly or partly in pursuance of: (a) the tax avoidance arrangement; or (b) an arrangement at one end of a series of arrangements with the tax avoidance arrangement being at the other end. It does not matter if the person taking the step is unaware of the tax avoidance arrangement.

**27-099** Section 554Z8 does not appear to have any application where P transacts with a person who is not A and is not linked with A, but is a relevant person because the payment or transfer is made at A's request. In these circumstances, additional steps may be required in order to bring the transaction within the scope of s.554Z8.

**Remittance basis taxpayers**

**27-100** Sections 554Z9–Z11A contain provisions applicable to remittance basis taxpayers.[105] If A is a remittance basis taxpayer in the year in which the relevant step is "for" (referred to as the "relevant tax year") then these provisions may be applicable. As with the usual earnings provisions,[106] there are two slightly different regimes depending on whether ITEPA 2003 s.26A applies in the relevant tax year or not. Section 26A applies in the relevant tax year if, broadly, A has been UK resident for no more than three tax years (including the relevant tax year) and the tax year(s) of UK residence follow at least three tax year of non-UK residence.

*A meets the s.26A requirement*

**27-101** If s.26A applies in the relevant tax year then the charge under s.554Z2 only applies to the overseas portion of the amount of the relevant step to the extent that it is remitted to the UK in that year.[107] The *overseas portion* means so much of the amount of the relevant step as is not in respect of duties performed in the UK, determined on a just and reasonable basis.

*A does not meet the s.26A requirement*

**27-102** If s.26A does not apply in the relevant tax year then the remittance basis will apply if[108]: (a) A's employment with B in the relevant tax year is employment with a foreign employer[109]; (b) the duties of A's employment with B in the relevant tax year

---

[105] i.e. non-UK domiciliaries who have either made a claim under ITA 2007 s.809B for the remittance basis to apply, or who are not required to make a claim because either s.809D or 809E applies.
[106] In ITEPA 2003 ss.20–41ZA.
[107] ITEPA 2003 s.554Z10. See ITA 2007 Pt 14 Ch.A1 for the meaning of remitted to the UK.
[108] ITEPA 2003 s.554Z9.
[109] A foreign employer is one that is not resident in the UK (ITEPA 2003 s.721(1)).

## PART 7A CH.2: THE CHARGE TO TAX

are performed wholly outside the UK; and (c) ITEPA 2003 s.24A does not apply in relation to A's employment with B for the relevant tax year.

*Section 24: related employments*

If s.26A does not apply then all of A's duties must be performed wholly outside of the UK, and so it is common practice to enter into dual contracts. The purpose of s.24A is to restrict the amount of earnings that are chargeable overseas earnings (and therefore within the remittance regime) where the two associated employments are *related* to each other and the earnings are not subject to a prescribed amount of foreign tax.

27-103

*Associated employments*

Where A is employed by two (or more) *associated* employers, and his duties in respect of one of those employments are performed in the UK, the remittance basis will apply only to so much of the relevant step as is just and reasonable, having regard to all of the relevant circumstances. In particular, one has regard to A's total employment income for the relevant tax year from all associated employments, and the nature of and time devoted to the duties performed outside the UK, and those performed in the UK, in the relevant tax year.

27-104

*Overlap provisions*

Sections 554Z11B–554Z11G prevent double taxation where it is just and reasonable to conclude that a relevant step is taken in relation to a sum or asset which has already been the subject of a previous relevant step (including sums or assets which directly or indirectly represent the sums or assets which were the subject of the previous relevant step). However, this is only applicable if the earlier relevant step created an income tax liability, and that tax has either been paid or terms have been agreed with HMRC for the discharge of that liability.

27-105

*Temporary non-residents*

If A is temporarily non-resident[110] when the funds are remitted to the UK, they are deemed to be remitted in the period of return if[111]: (a) it is all or part of a lump sum relevant benefit[112] provided to a relevant person under an EFRBS or s.615 scheme[113]; (b) it is remitted to the UK in the temporary period of non-residence; and (c) disregarding this provision, no charge to tax would arise by virtue of s.554Z9 or 554Z10 in respect of it,[114] as a result of the application of a double tax treaty. If the effect of any applicable double tax treaty would prevent the above from applying in the period of return, the treaty is expressly overridden.

27-106

---

[110] See FA 2013 Sch.45 Pt 4.
[111] ITEPA 2003 s.554Z11A.
[112] "Relevant benefit" has the same meaning as in ITEPA 2003 Pt 6 Ch.2. See Ch.35.
[113] For s.615 funds, see Ch.37.
[114] Including a case where the charge could be prevented by making a claim for relief under TIOPA 2010 s.6, even if no claim is in fact made.

**Liability**

**27-107** If Pt 7A Ch.2 applies, the *value* of the relevant step counts as employment income of A.[115] Any amount which counts as employment income is "specific employment income".[116] The person liable for the tax on specific employment income is A, because he is the person in relation to whom the income, by virtue of Pt 7A, counts as employment income.[117]

*Liability after A has died*

**27-108** A s.554B relevant step cannot occur after A has died. If a s.554C or s.554D relevant step is taken after A has died, and the relevant person is A, then A's personal representatives are liable.[118] If the relevant person is an individual other than A then the relevant person is liable. If the relevant person is not an individual, then P is liable if he is resident in the UK. If P is not resident in the UK then B is liable. If B no longer exists then P (who must in these circumstances be non-UK resident) is liable. The rate of tax is 45%.[119]

**27-109** If there is more than one relevant person in relation to the relevant step, the taxable amount is apportioned between the relevant persons on a just and reasonable basis.[120]

*The application of the PAYE system*

**27-110** Although A is liable for the tax, B will usually be required to discharge that liability under the PAYE system (even where A is no longer employed by B).[121] The basic principle of PAYE is that where an employer makes a payment of taxable earnings to an employee, the employer deducts the tax and pays it to HMRC. The employee's self-assessment (if he is required to make one) should show his or her liability to income tax on the employment income but should then claim the PAYE amount deducted by the employer, as a credit for the PAYE that has been paid (referred to as the "PAYE credit").

In the context of the disguised remuneration provisions, B is treated as making the payment unless P accounts for the tax in accordance with the PAYE regulations.[122] PAYE employment income does not include any taxable specific income brought into charge by s.554ZA4 (temporary non-residents),[123] so A must self-assess where a charge arises in these circumstances.

**27-111** If B does not have a UK presence, but A worked for a person in the UK who does (referred to as the "relevant person"), the relevant person must pay the tax under the PAYE provisions.[124]

---

[115] ITEPA 2003 s.554Z2(1).
[116] ITEPA 2003 s.7(4).
[117] ITEPA 2003 s.13(3).
[118] ITEPA 2003 s.554Z12.
[119] ITEPA 2003 s.554Z12(7), applying ITEPA 2003 s.394(4).
[120] ITEPA 2003 s.554Z12(8).
[121] Any amount which counts as employment income under Pt 7A is *specific employment income* (per s.7(4)) and therefore *taxable specific income* (per s.10(3)) and therefore *PAYE employment income* (per s.683(2)(b)).
[122] ITEPA 2003 ss.687A and 695A.
[123] ITEPA 2003 s.683(3ZA).
[124] ITEPA 2003 s.689.

A may become directly liable for the tax in the following circumstances:[125]   **27-112**

(a) B is outside of the scope of PAYE because it has no UK tax presence. Where it is not possible to transfer liability to a relevant person under s.689, A must self-assess. No Class 1 NIC liability will arise for A. Where it is possible to transfer liability to a relevant person under s.689, HMRC must do so, unless they exercise the power under s.684(7A)(b) ITEPA 2003, which permits HMRC to not require a person to comply with the PAYE regulations where it would not be appropriate for that person to do so. If HMRC exercise that power, A must self-assess.[126]

(b) B is unable to pay. Liability will be transferred in accordance with The Income Tax (Pay As You Earn) Regulations 2003 (SI 2003/2682) reg.81. The process is for HMRC to issue reg.80 determination, and, if that remains unpaid, HMRC will issue a reg.81 direction to transfer liability to A.

(c) HMRC issue a direction transferring the liability to A under reg.72. HMRC may do so only if they are satisfied that either: (i) B took reasonable care and the failure to deduct was an error made in good faith; or (ii) A knew that B wilfully failed to deduct tax. If a trustee is required to pay the tax under the scheme documentation, or otherwise has the power and has agreed to do so, but fails to do so, it is unlikely that B will be found to have taken reasonable care.

(d) B no longer exists. In these circumstances the PAYE provisions cannot apply to a payment and so A is required to declare the taxable amount in his self-assessment tax return. No Class 1 NIC liability will arise for A.

In relation to (a) and (d) above, A's obligation to self-assess arises under TMA 1970 ss.7–9.   **27-113**

It is not uncommon for scheme documentation to require trustees to either account for PAYE or pay to the employer an amount equal to the tax. Where there is no such requirement in the scheme documentation, the trustees will usually be able to do so only at the request of the member.   **27-114**

If B (or the relevant person) does discharge A's liability: (a) the payment of the tax by B will itself constitute employment income of A, unless A "makes good" the tax paid by B within 90 days of the end of the tax year in which the charge arises[127]; and (b) B (or the relevant person) will usually have a common law restitutionary claim against A in respect of the tax paid by B.[128]   **27-115**

**Subsequent income tax liability**

Section 554Z13 applies to prevent double taxation where a relevant step is taken and then another event occurs which would (were it not for this provision) give rise to a liability for income tax of A or any other person and it is just and reasonable that the tax on the later event should be reduced in order to avoid a double charge to income tax. This does not however apply where the later event gives rise to a charge under ITEPA 2003 Pt 7A Ch.2 or Pt 9 (pension income).   **27-116**

---

[125] See e.g. HMRC's technical consultation document, *Tackling disguised remuneration* (10 August 2016).
[126] For an example, see *Hoey v HMRC* [2022] EWCA Civ 656.
[127] ITEPA 2003 s.222. This charge is not within the scope of the PAYE provisions so A must self-assess.
[128] Following *McCarthy v McCarthy & Stone Plc* [2007] EWCA Civ 664. The decision has been criticised (see, e.g. K. Gordon, "A McCarthy witchhunt—was the Court of Appeal correct in McCarthy v McCarthy & Stone Plc?" (2011) 14(1) P.T.P.R. 21–34).

### Relief where earmarking not followed by further relevant step

**27-117** A claim for relief may be made if[129]: (a) Pt 7A Ch.2 has applied by reason of a s.554B relevant step taken by a person ("P"); (b) there occurs an event which is not a relevant step in relation to a relevant sum or asset; (c) by reason of the event no further relevant step is or will be taken by P or any other person in relation to any relevant sum or asset; and (d) there is no connection between the event and a tax avoidance arrangement (which expressly includes the avoidance of tax by way of obtaining relief under this provision). One might expect there to be some relief where a s.554B relevant step occurs in relation to an asset, and the asset is subsequently distributed to a different beneficiary, however s.554Z14 has no application in such circumstances.

# PART 7A CH.3

**27-118** ITEPA 2003 Pt 7A Chs 1 and 2 do not apply to steps taken by the employer, because the employer is not a *relevant third person* unless acting as trustee.[130] However, Pt 7A Ch.3 creates two relevant steps that, if taken by the employer, are treated as being s.554B relevant steps and therefore cause most of Pt 7A Chs 1 and 2 to apply.

**27-119** Nothing in Part 7A Ch.3 applies to B acting as a trustee (because Pt 7A Ch.1 will apply). If B is a company and is a member of a group of companies, references to B include any other company which is a member of that group. If B is a LLP, references to B include any company which is a wholly-owned subsidiary[131] of B.

### Effect of B making ss.554Z18 or 554Z19 relevant step

**27-120** If the employer takes a step within ss.554Z18 or 554Z19, Pt 7A Chs 1 and 2 apply to the step as if the employer were a relevant third person and the step were a s.554B relevant step (if it would not otherwise be).[132] For the purpose of determining whether Ch.2 applies by reason of the step, most of the exclusions in Ch.1 are disregarded. If Ch.2 applies, a number of provisions that have the effect of reducing the value of the step (e.g. because the remittance basis applies) are also disregarded.

### The basic requirements: relevant undertaking

**27-121** Part 7A Ch.3 applies if there is an undertaking (referred to as the "relevant undertaking") that:

(a) a contribution will be paid to an arrangement which is not a registered pension scheme;

(b) in connection with that arrangement, relevant benefits are to be provided out of the contribution by a relevant third person[133];

(c) the provision of the relevant benefits would be a relevant step; and

---

[129] ITEPA 2003 s.554Z14. The application for relief must be made within four years of the relevant event.
[130] ITEPA 2003 s.554A(7)(b).
[131] As defined in CA 2006 s.1159(2).
[132] ITEPA 2003 s.554Z17.
[133] *Relevant third person* means a person within ITEPA 2003 s.554A(7)(a)–(c) (ignoring Pt 7A Ch.3).

## PART 7A CH.3

(d) the contribution would be neither a tax-relieved contribution nor a tax-exempt provision.

In a typical unfunded retirement benefit scheme, the employer will undertake to pay relevant benefits to the employee. Part 7A Ch.3 will not apply to such an undertaking because it is not an undertaking to make a contribution to an arrangement. **27-122**

*"Undertaking"*

The usual meaning of "undertaking" is a promise. One would typically expect to see an undertaking to make contributions in an employment contract. The term expressly includes undertakings which are not legally enforceable, and undertakings which are conditional.[134] One would typically expect the employer to be the person giving the undertaking, but that is not a requirement. If an employer unilaterally decides to make such a contribution then these provisions should not apply.[135] Given that such a contribution would generally give rise to a s.554B relevant step when received by the trustees, Ch.3 seems to be aimed at situations where there is a material delay between the promise and the contribution and the undertaking itself has some value to A. Indeed, it seems likely that the main purpose of Ch.3 is to counter attempts at avoiding Pt 7A by not contributing funds to a relevant arrangement until such time as benefits are to be provided. **27-123**

*Relevant benefits*

"Relevant benefits" has the same meaning as in ITEPA 2003 s.393B,[136] except that pension income charged to tax under Pt 9 is also included. The requirement above is that relevant benefits "are" to be provided, which suggests that there must be no power to provide benefits which are not relevant benefits. It is possible that in order for these provisions to apply there may need to be a contractual right to receive the relevant benefits. As noted above, the undertaking need not be legally enforceable and may be conditional, but the undertaking only relates to the contributions and not to the provision of benefits, and the wording in (b) above suggests that something close to contractual rights to receive the relevant benefits may be required. **27-124**

A promise by an employer to make a contribution to a scheme which can only pay pension income to which s.554S applies will still be caught if there is a s.554Z18 or 554Z19 step. This is because s.554S does not prevent the payment of a pension being a relevant step; it is simply that Pt 7A Ch.2 does not apply to such a relevant step. **27-125**

*Tax-relieved contributions and tax-exempt provisions*

A contribution is a tax-relieved contribution if tax relief is given for the contribution under: **27-126**

---

[134] This seems to expressly anticipate that in a normal employment or salary sacrifice context, contributions will be subject to the employee continuing to work for the employer.
[135] A resolution by an employer to make a discretionary contribution could not normally be described as an undertaking (although resolutions are sometimes drafted to create "constructive obligations" where the intention is to make a contribution after the year end, and this could amount to an undertaking).
[136] For "relevant benefits", see Ch.35.

(a) FA 2004 Sch.33 (migrant member relief)[137]
(b) FA 2004 Sch.36 para.51 or The Taxation of Pension Schemes (Transitional Provisions) Order 2006 (SI 2006/572) art.15 (transitional corresponding relief)[138]; or
(c) double tax arrangements (at any time after 5 April 2006).[139]

A contribution is a tax-exempt provision if the contribution was exempt from liability to tax by virtue of ITEPA 2003 s.307 in respect of provision made under the scheme at any time after 5 April 2006 when the scheme was an overseas pension scheme.[140]

### Section 554Z18: earmarking etc

**27-127**  The employer takes a step within s.554Z18 if sums or assets are earmarked, or otherwise start being held, with a view to the relevant undertaking being performed at a later time with those funds or funds representing those funds. The reference to "at a later time" strongly suggests that an undertaking which is performed immediately afterwards is not caught; there must be a material time delay (or at least the intention of a material time delay) between the undertaking and the payment. This is an important point because any payment or transfer to a retirement benefit scheme will always necessarily involve some sort of informal earmarking immediately before the payment or transfer. Given the draconian consequences of the earmarking provisions it seems quite likely that a tribunal or court will construe it strictly.

**27-128**  Sections 554Q and 554R (which apply, respectively, where income arises from earmarked funds and is itself earmarked, and where property is acquired "out of" earmarked funds) apply for these purposes.

### Section 554Z19: provision of security

**27-129**  The employer takes a step within s.554Z19 if it provides security in any way (however informal) for the performance of the relevant undertaking. In order for *security* to be provided, it seems likely that the employer must grant a present right to have a specified asset (or class of assets) appropriated in satisfaction of the relevant undertaking.[141] Typically one would expect the security to be provided to A but that is not expressly required.

*Valuation of step within s.554Z19*

**27-130**  The value of the relevant step is the lower of: (a) the amount to be paid as a contribution under the relevant undertaking determined on a just and reasonable basis assuming that any condition to be met before any payment is made will be met; or (b) the value of the security.[142] The value of the security consists of the sums and the market value of the assets which are the subject of the step, subject to a just and reasonable reduction to take account of any term of the security which limits the total amount which may be made available under the security.

---

[137] See Ch.24.
[138] See Ch.24.
[139] See Ch.29.
[140] See Ch.30.
[141] *National Provisional & Union Bank of England v Charnley* [1924] 1 K.B. 431.
[142] ITEPA 2003 s.554Z20(3).

*Anniversary steps*

**27-131** If the employer continues to provide the security for the performance of the relevant undertaking, there is a new s.554Z19 step (called an "anniversary step") on each anniversary provided that A has not died.[143]

**Relief for earmarking or security not followed by contribution or relevant benefit**

**27-132** A claim for relief may be made if[144]: (a) ss.554Z18 or 554Z19 have applied; (b) there occurs an event which is neither the payment of the relevant contribution (or any part of it) nor the provision of any relevant benefit; (c) by reason of the event the relevant contribution (or any part of it) will not be paid or a relevant benefit will not be provided; and (d) there is no connection between the event and a tax avoidance arrangement (which expressly includes the avoidance of tax by way of obtaining relief under this provision).

# INTERACTION WITH OTHER LEGISLATION

### General earnings charge

**27-133** The general earnings charge takes priority to any charge under Pt 7A Ch.2 and the value of the relevant step is reduced by the amount of the earnings.[145]

### The benefits code

**27-134** If a relevant step would otherwise be treated as earnings of A under the benefits code, Pt 7A Ch. applies instead of the benefits code.[146] It follows that in a case in which the relevant step is the making of an employment-related loan, the loan is not treated for any tax year as a taxable cheap loan for the purposes of the benefits code.

**27-135** The same applies to any income of A which would be dealt with under ITTOIA 2005 Pt 4 Ch.3.[147]

### ITEPA 2003 s.394

**27-136** The charge under Pt 7A Ch.2 takes priority to the charge under ITEPA 2003 s.394 (which applies where relevant benefits are provided under an EFRBS) and the charge under s.394 is reduced by any tax paid under Pt 7A.[148]

---

[143] ITEPA 2003 s.554Z20(6).
[144] ITEPA 2003 ss.554Z14 and 554Z21. The application for relief must be made within four years from the time when the relevant event occurs.
[145] ITEPA 2003 s.554Z6.
[146] ITEPA 2003 s.554Z2(2).
[147] Which applies to dividends etc from UK resident companies and tax treated as paid in respect of certain distributions.
[148] ITEPA 2003 s.394(4B).

### Pension income

**27-137** The provision of pension income which is chargeable to income tax under ITEPA 2003 Pt 9 is not chargeable under Pt 7A Ch.2.[149]

**27-138** If taxable pension income (under ITEPA 2003 Pt 9) accrues or arises out of rights which represent, or have arisen or derived (directly or indirectly) from, a sum of money or asset which was the subject of a relevant step to which Pt 7A Ch.2 applied, the taxable pension income is reduced by the amount which counted as employment income of A under Pt 7A.[150]

## NATIONAL INSURANCE CONTRIBUTIONS

**27-139** The provisions relating to the application of NIC to relevant steps came into force on 6 December 2011. They are not retrospective so if Pt 7A Ch.2 applied before that time the relevant step was not subject to NIC unless the usual NIC provisions applied to it.

### The Social Security (Contributions) Regulations 2001

**27-140** Any amount which counts as employment income of the employee by virtue of Pt 7A Ch.2 is treated as remuneration derived from an employment, provided that the relevant step would not otherwise give rise to earnings (i.e. there must be no double taxation).[151] Where an amount is treated as remuneration under reg.22B, and a payment is subsequently made, the subject of which represents or arises or derives (whether wholly or partly or directly or indirectly) from the amount already treated as remuneration, the latter payment is disregarded in the calculation of earnings.[152] However, this does not apply to the extent that the value of the latter payment exceeds the value of the prior payment.

**27-141** The intention appears to be that if an income tax charge arises under Pt 7A then it will also be subject to NIC unless it already constitutes earnings for NIC purposes. Contributions to retirement benefit schemes will not usually constitute earnings, but benefits may be deferred earnings for NIC purposes.[153] Many pension benefits are disregarded for NIC purposes,[154] in which case reg.22B does not apply.[155] It follows that many s.554C and s.554D relevant steps under retirement benefit schemes will not be subject to NIC. This is unlikely to assist a s.554B relevant step (earmarking etc), or a s.554Z18 or s.554Z19 relevant step as such steps would not normally constitute earnings for NIC purposes and so there are no disregards that apply. However, it should be noted that reg.22B is not a charging provision. It merely provides that the amount which counts as employment income of the employed earner by virtue of Pt 7A Ch.2 is treated as earnings for the purposes of Class 1 NIC.

---

[149] ITEPA 2003 s.554S. For ITEPA 2003 Pt 9, see Ch.26.
[150] ITEPA 2003 s.567A.
[151] Social Security (Contributions) Regulations 2001 (SI 2001/1004) reg.22B.
[152] Social Security (Contributions) Regulations 2001 Sch.3 Pt 10 paras 1 and 2A.
[153] *HMRC v Forde & McHugh Ltd* [2014] UKSC 14 at [16].
[154] See Ch.26.
[155] NIM52900 provides that "Although an amount may be disregarded from earnings when assessing Class 1 NIC the amount is earnings. Regulation 22B of the SS(C)R 2001 only applies where the amount is not already earnings. So, if an amount is earnings but it has been disregarded, regulation 22B does not apply".

A charge arises only if earnings are *paid* to or for the benefit of an earner.[156] As the regulations do not create a deemed payment, a charge to NIC will arise as a result of reg.22B only where the relevant step involves an actual payment.

**Differences between income tax and NIC**

The main differences between income tax and NIC are as follows: **27-142**

(a) There is no remittance basis in the NIC provisions, so the employer must apply NIC to the full amount counting as employment income without any reduction for the remittance basis.

(b) There is no equivalent to s.554Z12 (which applies to relevant steps taken after A's death) in the NIC provisions. However, if the relevant third person takes the relevant step after the employed earner's death, there is no Class 1 NIC liability in any event.[157]

(c) In relation to s.554Z13 (which prevents a further income tax charge arising after Pt 7A income has arisen, if certain conditions are met), although the Social Security (Contributions) Regulations 2001 Sch.3 Pt 10 para.2A performs a similar function it is not a direct equivalent.

(d) There is no equivalent to s.554Z14 (which permits an application for income tax relief to be made where earmarking is not followed by a further relevant step)[158] in the NIC provisions. The only circumstances in which Class 1 NIC are refundable is where the NIC have been paid in error.

One other difference relates to the territorial limitations of the NIC regime. For **27-143** NIC purposes the relevant step is not related back to the period that it is "for": one simply looks at the period in which the relevant step takes place. If the member is non-UK resident at that time, the relevant step should not be subject to NIC.

---

[156] SSCBA 1992 s.6.
[157] NIM52600.
[158] ITEPA 2003 s.554Z21 performs the same function where earmarking or provision of security is not followed by payment of a contribution or provision of a benefit.

# CHAPTER 28

# Inheritance Tax

## TABLE OF CONTENTS

| | |
|---|---|
| Overview | 28-001 |
| Interests in possession | 28-003 |
| Qualifying interests in possession | 28-005 |
| Non-qualifying interests in possession | 28-008 |
| The extent of the interest in possession | 28-009 |
| Excluded property | 28-010 |
| Sponsored superannuation schemes | 28-012 |
| Application of IHTA 1984 s.3(3) | 28-013 |
| Meaning of "sponsored superannuation scheme" | 28-014 |
| Effect of pension transfers | 28-018 |
| Transitional provisions | 28-019 |
| Contributions | 28-021 |
| Non-application of s.12(2) | 28-022 |
| IHTA 1984 s.12(1) | 28-023 |
| IHTA 1984 s.10 | 28-025 |
| IHTA 1984 s.13 | 28-029 |
| Business property relief | 28-033 |
| Disposals of scheme interests | 28-034 |
| Interests in possession | 28-034 |
| Relevant property | 28-035 |
| The relevant property regime | 28-036 |
| Who is the settlor? | 28-037 |
| Periodic charges | 28-039 |
| Exit charges | 28-045 |
| Exit event before first ten-year anniversary | 28-049 |
| Exit event after first ten-year anniversary | 28-053 |
| Sponsored superannuation schemes | 28-057 |
| IHTA 1984 s.86 | 28-061 |
| Omitting to exercise rights | 28-067 |
| Non-application of IHTA 1984 s.12(2ZA) | 28-067 |
| IHTA 1984 s.3(3) | 28-068 |
| Death of a beneficiary | 28-071 |
| Non-application of s.151(2) and (3) | 28-071 |
| Sponsored superannuation schemes | 28-073 |
| Powers of nomination (settlement powers/general powers) | 28-076 |

## OVERVIEW

**28-001** The application of the inheritance tax provisions to registered pension schemes is considered in Ch.21. Subject to one exception, those provisions apply equally to QNUPS and s.615 funds.[1] Much of the background commentary in Ch.21 is applicable to unregistered pension schemes and so to avoid unnecessary repetition this chapter focuses exclusively on those provisions which are different for unregistered schemes. The differences considered in this chapter are as follows:

(a) *Contributions:* IHTA 1984 s.12(2) (which provides that an employer contribution under a registered pension scheme is not a transfer of value) cannot apply, so it is necessary to consider the possible application of IHTA 1984 ss.12(1), 10 and 13 in greater detail;

(b) *Relevant property:* IHTA 1984 s.58(1)(d) (which provides that settled property held for the purposes of a registered pension scheme is not relevant property) cannot apply, so the provisions relating to excluded property, and also the possible application of IHTA 1984 s.86, are considered;

(c) *Omitting to exercise rights:* IHTA 1984 s.12(2ZA) (which provides that an omission to exercise a right under a registered pension scheme is not deemed to be a disposition under s.3(3)) cannot apply, so the circumstances in which IHTA 1984 s.3(3) applies are considered;

(d) *Death of a beneficiary:* IHTA 1984 s.151(2) (which provides that on the death of a beneficiary, any rights to pension or annuity under a registered pension scheme which cease on death are disregarded for inheritance tax purposes) cannot apply so it is necessary to consider what the value of such rights may be immediately before death; and

(e) *Interests in possession:* IHTA 1984 s.151(3) (which provides that qualifying interests in possession are disregarded for inheritance tax purposes) cannot apply, so the usual rules that apply to qualifying interests in possession (in IHTA 1984 ss.49 to 53) are considered in greater detail.

**28-002** In addition, the transitional provisions applicable to sponsored superannuation schemes are considered below. These provisions apply to certain occupational schemes established before 6 April 2006, and are relevant to (b), (d) and (e) above.

### Interests in possession

**28-003** IHTA 1984 s.151(3) does not apply to unregistered schemes (other than QNUPS and s.615 funds), so the existence (or otherwise) of interests in possession is more important than in the case of registered pension schemes.[2] For inheritance tax purposes, an interest in possession is a present right to the present enjoyment of property.[3] The enjoyment often relates to the income of a settlement, but a right to income is not essential. The words "in possession" mean that your interest enables you to claim now "whatever may be the subject of your interest".[4] So, for example, the right under a settlement to use and enjoy chattels or live rent-free in a house gives the beneficiary an interest in possession. If a beneficiary has a present right

---

[1] The exception is that IHTA 1984 s.58(2A)(a) applies only to registered pension schemes, and s.58(2A)(b) applies to QNUPS and s.615 funds (see Ch.34).
[2] Section 151(3) disapplies ss.49–53 in relation to qualifying interests in possession, so inheritance tax is charged on the value of the interest, not the value of the settled property (see Ch.21).
[3] *Pearson v IRC* [1981] A.C. 753.
[4] *Gartside v IRC* [1968] A.C. 553 at 607 (Lord Reid).

to receive a pension of £X per annum payable from settled property, he is beneficially entitled to an interest in possession which subsists in that settled property.

In the inheritance tax provisions described below, an interest in possession is material only if it is an interest in possession in "settled property". A purchased annuity (i.e. a contract) may create an interest in possession, but it will not usually be an interest in possession in settled property.[5] This should be the case even where settled property is applied to purchase the annuity.

*Qualifying interests in possession*

An interest in possession is a qualifying interest in possession if either: (a) the person became entitled to the interest in possession before 22 March 2006; or (b) the person became entitled to the interest in possession on or after 22 March 2006 and it is an immediate post-death interest, a disabled person's interest or a transitional serial interest.[6] It is unlikely that a beneficiary under a pension scheme will have an immediate post-death interest[7] or a disabled person's interest,[8] but a pension death benefit payable to the spouse or civil partner of a member may be a transitional serial interest where the member was entitled to a qualifying interest in possession.[9]

A person beneficially entitled to a qualifying interest in possession in settled property is deemed to be beneficially entitled to the property in which the interest subsists (and not merely to the interest in possession, i.e. the right to enjoy the property).[10] This has two important consequences:

(a) First, the creation of a qualifying interest in possession is a potentially exempt transfer rather than a chargeable transfer.

(b) Secondly, where a qualifying interest in possession terminates (for example on the death of the beneficiary), or where a person disposes of a qualifying interest in possession (which is deemed to be a termination under IHTA 1984 s.52),[11] that will usually give rise to a transfer of value (it could be a potentially exempt transfer or a chargeable transfer) and in valuing the transfer of value one looks at the value of the underlying property. So it is the notional transfer of the settled property, and not the actual transfer of the interest, which is relevant. In contrast, a non-qualifying interest in possession does not form part of a person's estate and so the termination or disposal of a non-qualifying interest in possession is disregarded.[12] Where the qualifying interest in possession is in part only of the income (if any) or where the entitlement is not to income but is to the use and enjoyment

---

[5] IHTA 1984 s.43(2)(c) provides that *settlement* includes any disposition of property, whereby the property is for the time being charged or burdened (otherwise than for full consideration in money or money's worth paid for his own use or benefit to the person making the disposition) with the payment of any annuity or other periodical payment payable for a life or any other limited or terminable period. This will usually have no application to annuities purchased from insurance companies.

[6] IHTA 1984 s.59(1).

[7] See IHTA 1984 s.49A. The settlement must be effected by will, meaning that new property would need to be contributed to the scheme under the will.

[8] See IHTA 1984 s.89B.

[9] See IHTA 1984 s.49D.

[10] IHTA 1984 s.49(1).

[11] IHTA 1984 s.51.

[12] IHTA 1984 s.5(1).

of property, the settled property *in which the interest subsists* forms part of the person's estate for the purposes of s.4(1).[13]

28-007    In addition, settled property in which a qualifying interest in possession subsists is not relevant property,[14] so the relevant property charges do not apply to the settled property.

*Non-qualifying interests in possession*

28-008    Interests in possession created since 22 March 2006 are non-qualifying interests in possession (assuming that they are not an immediate post-death interest, a disabled person's interest or a transitional serial interest). Section 49(1) does not apply to such interests[15] and so the beneficiary is *not* deemed to be beneficially entitled to the property in which the interest subsists. Indeed, a non-qualifying interest in possession (i.e. the right to enjoy the property) does not form part of the beneficiary's estate.[16] It follows that a disposal or termination of that interest does not cause the value of his estate to reduce. The settled property will however be relevant property.

*The extent of the interest in possession*

28-009    In the context of a pension scheme, the interest in possession (i.e. the present right to present enjoyment of settled property) will typically involve a present right to receive a pension. In relation to a pension scheme providing money purchase benefits, the amount of the pension will usually be calculated (at least in part) by reference to the amount of income that the fund is expected to produce. If the amount of the pension to which the beneficiary is entitled is equal to or exceeds the income of the settlement then the interest in possession subsists in all of the settled property. Where the income of the settlement exceeds the amount of the pension to which the beneficiary is entitled, his interest in possession subsists in so much of the settled property as is required to produce income equal to the pension.[17]

**Excluded property**

28-010    Property situated outside the UK is excluded property if the person beneficially entitled to it is an individual domiciled outside the UK.[18] Where property comprised in a settlement is situated outside the UK, the property (but not a reversionary interest in the property) is excluded property unless the settlor was domiciled in the UK at the time the settlement was made.[19]

28-011    The main consequences of property being excluded property are:

(a) No account is taken of the value of excluded property which ceases to form

---

[13] IHTA 1984 s.50.
[14] IHTA 1984 s.58(1): "relevant property means settled property in which no qualifying interest in possession subsists …".
[15] IHTA 1984 s.49(1A).
[16] IHTA 1984 s.5(1).
[17] IHTA 1984 s.50(2). If a pension is provided on terms that it is paid solely out of capital (so the member has no entitlement to income of the settled property), s.50(2) and (3) would appear to be inapplicable, as there would be no clear way of measuring "the property in which the interest subsists" (see C. Whitehouse, E. Chamberlain and R. Greenfield, *Dymond's Capital Taxes* (London: Sweet & Maxwell), para.16.514).
[18] IHTA 1984 s.6(1).
[19] IHTA 1984 s.48(3)(a). This is subject to the anti-avoidance provisions in s.48(3B) and (3E). It is also subject to Sch.A1, which provides that an interests in close companies and partnerships are not

part of a person's estate as a result of a lifetime disposition.[20] This would be the case for example, where a non-UK domiciled person contributes excluded property (e.g. money in a non-UK bank account) to a pension scheme.
(b) The estate of a person immediately before his death does not include excluded property,[21] so such property is disregarded in calculating the inheritance tax liability arising on death.[22]
(c) Excluded property comprised in a settlement is not relevant property.[23]
(d) There is no exit charge where relevant property becomes excluded property by reason only of it ceasing to be situated in the UK.[24]
(e) The termination or disposal of a qualifying interest in possession is not deemed to be a transfer of value by reference to the value of the property in which the interest subsisted (as would usually be the case under IHTA 1984 s.52(1) or (2A)), where the settled property is excluded property.[25]

**Sponsored superannuation schemes**

If, prior to 6 April 2006, a scheme was a "sponsored superannuation scheme":   28-012

(a) IHTA 1984 s.58(1)(d) applied, meaning that the settled property was not relevant property for inheritance tax purposes, and so it was not subject to periodic or exit charges; and
(b) IHTA 1984 s.151 applied, meaning that on the death of the member: (i) any right to a pension or annuity was disregarded for inheritance tax purposes; and (ii) qualifying interests in possession were not deemed not to be qualifying interests in possession.

*Application of IHTA 1984 s.3(3)*

Note that IHTA 1984 s.3(3) (see below) is not disapplied in relation to sponsored   28-013
superannuation schemes, which may be problematic where the member dies at a time when he is entitled to draw lump sum benefits. One way to address this may be for the member to transfer his fund to a QNUPS, because s.3(3) is disapplied in relation to QNUPS. However, if the sponsored superannuation scheme is a FURBS, and a lump sum would be tax-free if paid from that scheme, that will not be the case once the fund is transferred to the QNUPS.[26] One way to address the s.3(3) issue without prejudicing the preferential treatment of lump sums by amending the scheme so that the member is entitled to draw benefits only with the consent of the trustees, however in many cases the scheme rules and/or PA 1995 s.91 will prevent such an amendment. A better way to address those issue may be to transfer the member's fund to a new UK EFRBS under which the member is entitled to draw benefits only with the consent of the trustees. Such a transferee scheme should still be a sponsored superannuation scheme (as is explained below), and the income tax

---

excluded property to the extent that the value of the interest is attributable to UK residential property, and nor is certain property relating to loans used to finance the acquisition of UK residential property.
[20] IHTA 1984 s.3(1) and (2).
[21] IHTA 1984 s.5(1)(b).
[22] IHTA 1984 s.4(1).
[23] IHTA 1984 s.58(f).
[24] IHTA 1984 s.65(7).
[25] IHTA 1984 s.53(1).
[26] A lump sum paid from the QNUPS will be taxable as a relevant lump sum (see ITEPA 2003 Pt 9 Ch.4).

exceptions should apply.[27] Such a pension transfer may significantly reduce the value of the member's estate (since the value of his rights under the transferee scheme will be much reduced, as he has no absolute right to draw benefits), in which case it may be subject to 20% inheritance tax as a lifetime chargeable transfer. But in most cases the member's right to draw lump sum benefits will be a "settlement power" for inheritance tax purposes, meaning that it is ignored for inheritance tax purposes, so the transfer should not reduce the value of his estate for inheritance tax purposes.[28]

*Meaning of "sponsored superannuation scheme"*

**28-014** ICTA 1988 s.624(1) provided that:

"(1) … 'a sponsored superannuation scheme' means a scheme or arrangement—
  (a) relating to service in particular offices or employments, and
  (b) having for its object or one of its objects to make provision in respect of persons serving in those offices or employments against future retirement or partial retirement, against future termination of service through death or disability, or against similar matters,
being a scheme or arrangement under which any part of the cost of the provision so made is or has been borne otherwise than by those persons by reason of their service (whether it is the cost or part of the cost of the benefits provided, or of paying premiums or other sums in order to provide those benefits, or of administering or instituting the scheme or arrangement)."

**28-015** So, an occupational scheme will be a sponsored superannuation scheme if a person who is not a member (e.g. a sponsoring employer) pays any of the costs of establishing or administering the scheme. Is this requirement satisfied by reason of an employer contribution in respect of a member? ICTA 1988 s.624(2) provided:

"a person shall be treated as bearing by reason of his service the cost of any payment made or agreed to be made in respect of his service, if that payment or the agreement to make it is treated under the Income Tax Acts as increasing his income, or would be so treated if he were chargeable to tax under section 15 of ITEPA 2003 in respect of his general earnings from that service."

**28-016** Prior to 6 April 2006, employer contributions to a FURBS with a view to the provision of relevant benefits were deemed under ITEPA 2003 s.386(1) to increase the employee's income, so employer contributions would cause a FURBS to become a sponsored superannuation scheme only if part of the sums contributed did not relate to the provision of relevant benefits.[29] This would be the case, for example, where any contributions related to the costs of setting up or running the FURBS. It was not uncommon for the employer to make relatively modest contributions (so that the scheme became a sponsored superannuation scheme), followed by beneficial loans to the scheme for the trustees to invest.

---

[27] See ITEPA 2003 s.554U (exception to the disguised remuneration provisions) and FA 2004 Sch.36 para.53-58 (exception to the charge under the EFRBS provisions). The relevant lump sum provision will not apply if the transferee scheme is established in the UK.

[28] For settlement powers, see below. In most cases, the member's right to draw a lump sum will not be a "a general power" (because he cannot appoint or dispose of the property as he thinks fit: see IHTA 1984 s.5(2)), so the underlying property will not form part of his estate for that reason.

[29] See the Inland Revenue booklet, *The Tax Treatment of Top-Up Pension Schemes*, para.2.2.4.

## OVERVIEW

It was not uncommon for an employer to establish a separate sponsored superannuation scheme for each relevant employee.[30]

28-017

### *Effect of pension transfers*

Where the cash equivalent of a member's accrued rights has been transferred from a sponsored superannuation scheme to a scheme which does not satisfy the requirements in s.624(1), the transferee arrangement may be found, on a proper analysis, to form part of the sponsored superannuation scheme (the transferee arrangement being merely the mechanism by which the benefits are provided). In such cases, it should follow that the transferred property continues to be "held for the purposes of a sponsored superannuation scheme" for the purposes of ss.58(1)(d) and 151.

28-018

### *Transitional provisions*

If the scheme was a sponsored superannuation scheme prior to 6 April 2006 then, provided that no contributions are made under the scheme on or after that date, the above inheritance tax provisions continue to apply to the entire fund.[31] Where any contributions are made to the scheme on or after 6 April 2006, the above provisions will apply to part only of the fund (see below). It is suggested that the defining characteristic of a contribution is that there is a transfer of value to the scheme. One would therefore expect that a transfer from one pension scheme to another would involve a *contribution* to the transferee scheme.[32] However HMRC's position is that "a transfer from one pension scheme to another is not a new contribution, so the funds in one protected scheme may be transferred to another protected scheme without the exclusion being lost".[33] If a transfer from one pension scheme to another is not a contribution for these purposes then it seems to follow that property transferred to a sponsored superannuation scheme from an EFRBS (for example) would be similarly protected. Conversely, if HMRC's position is correct, transferred funds will not be protected if any contributions (no matter how small) are made to the transferee scheme,[34] which would be an arbitrary result. It is very unlikely that this was Parliament's intention.

28-019

Provided that the scheme satisfied the requirements in ICTA 1988 s.624(1) immediately before 6 April 2006, the transitional provisions apply on and after that date even if the scheme ceases to satisfy the requirements of s.624(1).

28-020

---

[30] cf. the requirements of IHTA 1984 s.86 (considered below).
[31] FA 2004 Sch.36 para.56.
[32] It is for this reason that FA 2004 s.188(5) provides that a transfer to a registered pension scheme from another pension scheme is expressly not a contribution, and ICTA 1988 s.615(13) provides that a transfer from one s.615 fund to another is expressly not a contribution. These provisions are necessary because such transfers would ordinarily constitute contributions.
[33] IHTM17039. The reference to a "protected scheme" is presumably a reference to the scheme being a sponsored superannuation scheme.
[34] As is explained below, where a contribution is made on or after 6 April 2006, the part of the fund that continues to be protected is determined by reference to the value of the scheme property held for the purposes of the scheme (i.e. the transferee scheme) on 5 April 2006.

## CONTRIBUTIONS

**28-021** There are no special rules that apply to member contributions to registered pension schemes, so the commentary in Ch.21 applies to unregistered schemes.

**Non-application of s.12(2)**

**28-022** IHTA 1984 s.12(2) provides that a disposition made by any person is not a transfer of value if it is a contribution under a registered pension scheme in respect of an employee of the person making the disposition. This does not apply to contributions to unregistered schemes (other than QNUPS and s.615 funds) so the possible application of IHTA 1984 ss.12(1), 10 and 13 is considered below.

*IHTA 1984 s.12(1)*

**28-023** Section 12(1) provides as follows:

"A disposition made by any person is not a transfer of value if it is allowable in computing that person's profits or gains for the purposes of income tax or corporation tax or would be so allowable if those profits or gains were sufficient and fell to be so computed."

**28-024** Section 12(1) cannot have any application to a contribution by a non-UK employer that is outside the scope of UK corporation tax or income tax.[35] But if an employer obtains a UK tax deduction in respect of a contribution then the contribution will not be a transfer of value. The circumstances in which a business will obtain a tax deduction in respect of a contribution to an unregistered pension scheme are explained in Ch.24. In particular, an employer will obtain a tax deduction in respect of contributions to: (a) qualifying overseas pension schemes if the member is a relevant migrant member; (b) corresponding schemes, in circumstances that transitional corresponding relief is available; and (c) non-UK schemes in circumstances in which relief under a double tax treaty is available. In most other cases, CTA 2009 s.1290 will defer the tax deduction until such time as qualifying benefits are paid from the scheme. IHTA 1984 s.12(1) only looks at the year of the contribution; if the employer does not obtain a deduction during that year then it seems unlikely that s.12(1) can apply.

*IHTA 1984 s.10*

**28-025** IHTA 1984 s.10 is extremely important in the context of contributions to unregistered pension schemes. This is examined in some detail in Ch.21 in relation to contributions by individuals to registered pension schemes, and the same principles apply to employer contributions.

**28-026** It is generally preferable for contributions to be made pursuant to a binding legal agreement in consideration for future service.[36]

---

[35] e.g. because it is non-UK resident and not trading in the UK, as was the case in *Postlethwaite's Executors v HMRC* [2007] S.T.C. (S.C.D.) 83.

[36] Per the Special Commissioners in *Postlethwaite v HMRC* [2006] UKSPC SPC00571 at [85]: "It is clear that if [the employer] had agreed at an early stage of Dr Postlethwaite's employment to pay £700,000 to a FURBS on 31 August 2003 provided he completed 20 months service that such payment would not have been intended to confer a gratuitous benefit. The fact is however that it did not so agree. The consequence is that when agreed and paid the payment was substantially if not entirely in consideration of past service. However, in our judgment the fact that on legal analysis the pay-

CONTRIBUTIONS 639

If the employer would have obtained a tax deduction for the contribution were it not for CTA 2009 s.1290, it is very likely that s.10 will apply.[37]  **28-027**

In *Postlethwaite's Executors v HMRC*,[38] HMRC argued that s.10 did not apply to an employer contribution to a FURBS because there was intention to confer gratuitous benefit on Dr Postlethwaite's family. This was rejected on the basis that Dr Postlethwaite was aged 49 and in good health at the time of the contribution and so he was not expected to die before taking benefits.  **28-028**

*IHTA 1984 s.13*

IHTA 1984 s.13 contains provisions relating to dispositions by close companies[39] to trusts for the benefit of employees. Insofar as is material, it provides as follows:  **28-029**

"(1) A disposition of property made to trustees by a close company whereby the property is to be held on trusts of the description specified in section 86(1) below is not a transfer of value if the persons for whose benefit the trusts permit the property to be applied include all or most of either—
  (a) the persons employed by or holding office with the company or
  (b) the persons employed by or holding office with the company or any one or more subsidiaries of the company.
(2) Subsection (1) above shall not apply if the trusts permit any of the property to be applied at any time (whether during any such period as is referred to in section 86(1) below or later) for the benefit of—
  (a) a person who is a participator in the company making the disposition, or
  (b) any other person who is a participator in any close company that has made a disposition whereby property became comprised in the same settlement, being a disposition which but for this section would have been a transfer of value, or
  (c) any other person who has been a participator in any such company as is mentioned in paragraph (a) or (b) above at any time after, or during the ten years before, the disposition made by that company, or
  (d) any person who is connected with any person within paragraph (a), (b) or (c) above.
(4) In determining whether the trusts permit property to be applied as mentioned in subsection (2) above, no account shall be taken—
  (a) of any power to make a payment which is the income of any person for any of the purposes of income tax, or would be the income for any of those purposes of a person not resident in the United Kingdom if he were so resident, ..."

A contribution by a close company to a trust satisfying the requirements of IHTA 1984 s.86(1) (see below) is not a transfer of value if the beneficiaries include all or most of the employees or office holders of the company (or the employees or office holders of any subsidiary of the company). Pursuant to s.13(2), the trust must not permit any of the settled property to be applied for the benefit of a participa-  **28-030**

---

ment was for past consideration does not mean that it was made with the intention of conferring a gratuitous benefit".

[37] That is to say, if a contribution is wholly and exclusively for the purposes of the employer's trade then it is difficult to see how there could be an intention to confer gratuitous benefit on anyone.

[38] *Postlethwaite's Executors v HMRC* [2007] S.T.C. (S.C.D.) 83.

[39] "Close company" means a company within the meaning of the Corporation Tax Acts which is (or would be if resident in the UK) a close company for the purposes of those Acts (see IHTA 1984 ss.13(5) and 102(1)).

tor,[40] however a participator is disregarded if: (a) he is not beneficially entitled to, or to rights entitling him to acquire, 5%, or more of, or of any class of the shares comprised in, its issued share capital; and (b) on a winding-up of the company would not be entitled to 5% or more of its assets.[41] As a result of s.13(4), any power of the trustees to apply property for the benefit of a participator is disregarded if the payment is the income of any person for tax purposes (or would be income of a non-UK resident person if he were UK resident).[42] The restrictions therefore apply only to capital benefits.

**28-031** Section 13(2)(d) extends the restrictions to persons connected[43] with a participator. One might expect that the relevant time at which to determine whether or not a person is connected with a participator is the time that the capital benefit is to be provided (with connection at any other time, such as of the time of the disposition, being irrelevant). Such analysis is supported by the judgment of Roth J in *Barker v Baxendale Walker Solicitors*[44] however the Court of Appeal disagreed.[45] On the interpretation favoured by the Court of Appeal, once a participator has died it is not possible to provide capital benefits to his family members even if they are not at that time participators or connected to a participator.

**28-032** *Benefit* is not defined for the purposes of s.13(2). It may be said that some sort of benefit arises in most commercial transactions,[46] but in a tax context the term usually connotes the provision of bounty,[47] and that is very likely to be necessary for the purposes of s.13(2).[48] Arm's length transactions between the trustees and a participator are not restricted under IHTA 1984 s.13.

---

[40] "Participator", in relation to any company, means any person who is (or would be if the company were resident in the UK) a participator in relation to that company within the meaning of CTA 2010 s.454, other than a person who would be such a participator by reason only of being a loan creditor (see IHTA 1984 ss.13(5) and 102(1)).

[41] IHTA 1984 s.13(3).

[42] It has been suggested that s.13(4) does not prevent an interest-free loan being made to a participator, on the basis that the benefit of the loan is taxed as income under the benefits code (see R. Mullan, *A series of unfortunate misconceptions, Taxation, 23 June 2010*). HMRC would no doubt argue that the payment of the capital sum is not itself taxed as income; it is the failure of the borrower to pay interest which is deemed to be income.

[43] The test of connection is the test in TCGA 1992 s.286, but as if relative included uncle, aunt, nephew and niece and "settlement", "settlor" and "trustee" had the same meanings as in IHTA 1984 (IHTA 1984 s.270).

[44] *Barker v Baxendale Walker Solicitors* [2016] EWHC 664 at [156]–[166] in relation to IHTA 1984 s.28(4), which is materially identical to s.13(2). Also see the GAAR Guidance para.D29.5.1, which is predicated on the basis that this analysis is correct.

[45] *Barker v Baxendale Walker Solicitors* [2017] EWCA Civ 2056 at [42]–[48]. This is a professional negligence case rather than a tax case (the taxpayer had already conceded that the gift to the trust was ineffective and paid the tax), and so is primarily concerned with whether the advice should have included a specific warning that there was a significant risk that the arrangement would fail to be tax effective on the basis that persons connected with a participator at the time of the disposition could receive benefits once they were no longer connected with any participator.

[46] In *IRC v Levy* [1982] S.T.C. 442, Nourse J said, "If a person buys a pair of socks from Marks & Spencer for a fair price, that is a benefit to him and to Marks & Spencer". In *Vestey v IRC* [1949] 1 All E.R. 1108; 31 T.C. 1, Lord Morton of Henryton said, "a loan may well benefit a person even if it is made at a commercial rate of interest, as it may tide him over a difficult period". In *IRC v Chappie* 34 T.C. 509, Sir Raymond Evershed MR said, "it is I think, a truism that a person receiving a loan, albeit of a commercial character, can be said to receive a benefit".

[47] In other words, the member must receive something that the pension scheme would not be prepared to give as a fair bargain to an unconnected third party dealing on arm's length terms with the scheme (see e.g. *Mairs v Haughey* [1994] 1 A.C. 303).

[48] The counterargument is that s.13 may be contrasted with IHTA 1984 s.10. The latter refers to "gratuitous" benefit, which very clearly suggests bounty (see *Jones v Garnett*), so the absence of the word "gratuitous" in s.13 may suggest that it is intended to include benefits which do not confer

*Business property relief*

If business property relief applies to the property contributed, it will not give rise to a chargeable transfer.[49] It is arguable that business property relief may apply to money which was used for business purposes.[50] In *Nelson Dance Family Settlement Trustees v HMRC*[51] Sales J held that business property relief can apply to property which is not a business or part of a business.

**28-033**

## DISPOSALS OF SCHEME INTERESTS

### Interests in possession

Because IHTA 1984 s.151(3) will not apply, if a member disposes of a qualifying interest in possession during his life then, in determining whether that disposition involves a transfer of value (and if so, determining the value transferred) one looks at the value of the settled property in which the interest subsists, and not the actual loss to his estate. The value of the settled property in which the interest in possession subsists will usually be greater than the value of the interest in possession.

**28-034**

## RELEVANT PROPERTY

Subject to the exceptions in IHTA 1984 s.58(1), all settled property is relevant property unless a qualifying interest in possession subsists in it. One exception applies to excluded property.[52] Another exception applies to registered pension schemes, QNUPS and s.615 funds.[53] In other circumstances it is necessary to consider the possible application of:

**28-035**

(a) the relevant property regime;
(b) the transitional provisions relating to sponsored superannuation schemes; and
(c) IHTA 1984 s.86.

### The relevant property regime

If the settled property is relevant property it will be necessary to consider whether an inheritance tax periodic or exit charge may arise. The provisions described below apply to taxable events (ten-year anniversary or exit event) occurring on or after 18 November 2015, in relation to settlements which commenced on or after 27 March 1974.

**28-036**

---

bounty. See Brief 49/2009 (12 August 2009) for HMRC's view that loans may be a benefit. This is unlikely to be the case if they are on arm's length terms (in relation to interest and security in particular).

[49] IHTM17082 provides that when property is contributed to an EFRBS "it is likely that business property relief will be available".
[50] See *Brown v IRC* [1996] S.T.C. (S.C.D.) 277.
[51] *Nelson Dance Family Settlement Trustees v HMRC* [2009] EWHC 71 (Ch).
[52] See IHTA 1984 ss.48(3) and 58(1)(f). See above.
[53] IHTA 1984 s.58(1)(d).

*Who is the settlor?*

**28-037** For the purposes of the provision described below, it is necessary to determine who is the settlor. The settlor of settled property includes any person who provided the property directly or indirectly.[54] In HMRC's view, the member of a retirement benefits scheme is a settlor of *all* contributions made for his benefit, including employer contributions.[55] However, it is very doubtful that the member will *always* be the settlor.[56] The better view is likely to be that the member will be a settlor only where: (a) the employer agrees to contribute property in consideration of the member's services; (b) the member is entitled to receive a sum as earnings and he requests the employer pays it to the scheme; or (c) the member is a majority shareholder of the employer and he exercises his power as shareholder to procure that the employer makes the contributions. Where an employer makes an entirely gratuitous contribution to a pension scheme for the benefit of an employee, one would expect the employer to be the settlor.

**28-038** Each member's fund under a pension scheme is likely to be a separate settlement as a matter of general law,[57] and therefore for inheritance tax purposes.[58] In any event, where there is more than one settlor in relation to a settlement, IHTA 1984 generally has effect in relation to it as if the settled property were comprised in separate settlements.[59]

*Periodic charges*

**28-039** Where immediately before a ten-year anniversary all or part of the property comprised in a settlement is relevant property, inheritance tax is charged on the value of the property at that time.[60] To calculate the amount of tax charged, one is required to find the value transferred by a hypothetical chargeable transfer made by a hypothetical transferor immediately before the ten-year anniversary.[61]

**28-040** The amount of the *hypothetical chargeable transfer* is equal to: (a) the value of the relevant property immediately before the ten-year anniversary; plus (b) the value, immediately after a related settlement commenced, of the relevant property then comprised in it; plus (c) the value of any same-day additions to another settle-

---

[54] IHTA 1984 s.44(1).
[55] IHTM17085, which states that the scheme member is a settlor of "contributions made by their employer (even where this is non-contributory for the employee (member) and is wholly financed by the employer). This is because pension rights and benefits are derived from payments by the employer as deferred or delayed remuneration for the employee's current work. This principle was established in *Parry v Cleaver* [169] 1AER 555 and *The Halcyon Skies* [1976] 1 AER 856. In this way, the scheme member has provided funds directly or indirectly and is the settlor for IHT purposes." These decisions established that employer contributions are "wages" for certain purposes. They are not tax cases.
[56] See C. Whitehouse, E. Chamberlain and R. Greenfield, *Dymond's Capital Taxes* (London: Sweet & Maxwell, 2019), para.11.509.
[57] See *Air Jamaica Ltd v Charlton* [1999] 1 W.L.R. 1399 at 1409; Law Commission report "*The Rules against Perpetuities and Excessive Accumulations*" (1998) (Law Com No.251), p.38; Thomas "Trusts of Death Benefits under Occupational Pension Schemes—Deep Waters for Advisers: Part 1" [1995] P.C.B. 133, 144.
[58] *Rysaffe Trustees Co (CI) Ltd v IRC* [2002] EWHC 1114 at [17] approved in [2003] EWCA Civ 356 at [25]; *Barclays Wealth Trustees (Jersey) Ltd v HMRC* [2017] EWCA Civ 1512 at [52]. HMRC's views are set out at IHTM42232.
[59] See IHTA 1984 ss.44(2) and 201(4).
[60] IHTA 1984 s.64(1).
[61] IHTA 1984 s.66(1) and (3).

ment[62] and the value, immediately after that other settlement commenced, of the relevant property then comprised in it.[63] Settlements are *related* if they have the same settlor and they commenced on the same day.[64]

**28-041** The *hypothetical transferor* is a person who has in the preceding seven years made chargeable transfers having a value equal to the aggregate of[65]:

(a) the values transferred by any (actual) transfers made by the settlor in the seven years prior to the day on which the settlement commenced, disregarding transfers made on that day.[66] However, if s.67(1) applies and the value specified in s.67(3)(b) is greater, one uses the value in s.67(3)(b) instead. Section 67(1) applies where, after the settlement commenced but before the anniversary, the settlor made a chargeable transfer as a result of which the value of the property (note that this is not limited to relevant property) comprised in the settlement was increased.[67] The value in s.67(3)(b) is the aggregate of the values transferred by any chargeable transfers made by the settlor in the seven years ending with the day on which the s.67(1) chargeable transfer was made: (i) disregarding transfers made on that day; and (ii) excluding any value attributable to property whose value has been taken into account in determining the amount of the hypothetical chargeable transfer; and (iii) excluding any value attributable to property in respect of which an exit charge was imposed in respect of the settlement in the ten years before the anniversary; and

(b) the amounts on which any exit charges were imposed in respect of the settlement in the ten years before the anniversary.

**28-042** One is then required to find the *effective rate* at which tax would be charged on the value transferred by the hypothetical chargeable transfer made by the hypothetical transferor immediately before the ten-year anniversary.[68] To find the effective rate it is necessary to calculate the amount of tax which would be charged (at the rate applicable to lifetime transfers, i.e. 20%)[69] on that hypothetical chargeable transfer, and then express that tax as a percentage of the amount of the hypothetical charge transfer.

**28-043** The rate of the charge is the effective rate multiplied by 3/10. To the extent that the relevant property was not relevant property comprised in the settlement throughout the ten-year period, the rate of the charge is reduced by 1/40 for each of the successive quarters in that period which expired before the property became, or last became, relevant property comprised in the settlement.[70]

**28-044** It follows from the above that the amount of the periodic charge cannot exceed 6% (being 3/10 of 20%) of the value of the relevant property immediately before the ten-year anniversary, and will be less than 6% if any of that property was not relevant property comprised in the settlement for the full ten years.

---

[62] For the meaning of *same-day additions*, and the value thereof, see IHTA 1984 s.62A.
[63] IHTA 1984 s.66(4).
[64] IHTA 1984 s.62(1).
[65] IHTA 1984 s.66(3)(b) and (5).
[66] A company is not able to make a chargeable transfer, so where the transferor is a company the hypothetical transferor must presumably have a full nil rate band available, irrespective of any previous transfers of value. It will also have two annual exemptions.
[67] If the settlor made more than one s.67(1) chargeable transfer, s.67(3)(b) relates to the transfer in relation to which the aggregate there mentioned is the greatest.
[68] IHTA 1984 s.66(1).
[69] IHTA 1984 s.66(3)(c), applying s.7(2).
[70] IHTA 1984 s.66(2).

## Exit charges

**28-045** IHTA 1984 s.65(1) imposes an inheritance tax charge where relevant property ceases to be relevant property, for example because it is paid to a beneficiary, or because an event causes the scheme to satisfy the requirements of a QNUPS.

**28-046** IHTA 1984 s.65(1) also imposes an inheritance tax charge where the trustees of the settlement make a disposition as a result of which the value of relevant property comprised in the settlement is less than it would be but for the disposition. For this purpose, trustees are treated as making a disposition if they deliberately omit to exercise a right.[71] However, no tax is charged if the disposition is such that, were the trustees beneficially entitled to the settled property, IHTA 1984 s.10 would prevent the disposition from being a transfer of value.[72]

**28-047** Tax is not charged under s.65(1) if the event occurs in a quarter[73] beginning with the day on which the settlement commenced or with a ten-year anniversary, or where relevant property becomes excluded property in specified circumstances.[74] Tax is also not charged under s.65(1) in respect of: (a) a payment of costs or expenses (so far as they are fairly attributable to relevant property); or (b) a payment which is (or will be) income of any person for any of the purposes of income tax or would for any of those purposes be income of a person not resident in the UK if he were so resident, or in respect of a liability to make such a payment. *Payment* includes a transfer of assets other than money.[75] It follows that any payment which is pension income for the purposes of ITEPA 2003 Pt 9 (or would be if the individual were resident in the UK), or which counts as employment income as a result of the application of the disguised remuneration or EFRBS provisions,[76] will not give rise to an exit charge. Since 6 April 2017, pension income paid by a non-UK scheme to a UK resident individual will in most cases include the payment of a lump sum, so an exit charge will rarely apply to a distribution from a retirement benefits scheme.

**28-048** Where the charge does apply (for example, because an event causes the scheme to satisfy the requirements of a QNUPS), the value on which tax is charged is the amount by which the value of relevant property comprised in the settlement is less immediately after the event. The amount on which tax is charged is reduced to the extent that it is attributable to relevant business property or agricultural property.[77]

### Exit event before first ten-year anniversary

**28-049** Where the event occurs before the first ten-year anniversary, the rate of tax is the appropriate fraction of the amount of tax which would be charged (at the rate applicable to lifetime transfers, i.e. 20%)[78] on the value transferred by a hypothetical chargeable transfer made by a hypothetical transferor.[79]

**28-050** The value transferred by the hypothetical chargeable transfer is equal to the aggregate of:

(a) the value of the property comprised in the settlement immediately after it commenced; plus

---

[71] IHTA 1984 s.65(9).
[72] IHTA 1984 s.65(6). For s.10, see Ch.21.
[73] A "quarter" is a period of three months (IHTA 1984 s.63).
[74] IHTA 1984 ss.65(4) and (6)–(8).
[75] IHTA 1984 s.63.
[76] See ITEPA 2003 s.7(2)(c) and (6).
[77] IHTA 1984 ss.103(1) and 115(1).
[78] IHTA 1984 s.68(4)(c), incorporating IHTA 1984 s.7(2).
[79] IHTA 1984 s.68(1).

# RELEVANT PROPERTY

(b) the value of any related settlements immediately after they commenced. Settlements are related if they have the same settlor and they commenced on the same day[80]; plus

(c) the value of any added property. Property is added property if the settlor made a chargeable transfer by which the value of the settled property was increased.[81]

The hypothetical transferor is a transferor who, in the seven years before the creation of the settlement, made chargeable transfers equal to the (actual) chargeable transfers made by the actual transferor in the seven years before the settlement commenced. **28-051**

The *appropriate fraction* is 3/10 multiplied by n/40 where "n" is: (a) the number of completed quarters in the period beginning with the day on which the settlement commenced[82] and ending the day before the exit event[83]; less (b) the complete quarters when the property was not relevant property comprised in the settlement.[84] **28-052**

## Exit event after first ten-year anniversary

Where the event occurs after the first ten-year anniversary, the rate of tax is the appropriate fraction of the rate at which it was charged on the most recent ten-year anniversary (or would have been charged had the relevant property been relevant property comprised in the settlement for the full ten years).[85] **28-053**

However, if any relevant property has become comprised in the settlement since the last ten-year anniversary, one is required to recalculate the effective rate for the last periodic charge as if that property had been relevant property comprised in the settlement immediately before the ten-year anniversary. For the purposes of that recalculation, one also includes any same-day additions.[86] **28-054**

The *appropriate fraction* is n/40 where "n" is: (a) the number of completed quarters in the period beginning with the most recent ten-year anniversary and ending the day before the exit event[87]; less (b) the complete quarters when the property was not relevant property comprised in the settlement.[88] **28-055**

The appropriate fraction is then multiplied by the rate for the most recent periodic charge (recalculated as above if any relevant property has become comprised in the settlement since the last ten-year anniversary), to give the percentage rate at which tax is charged. **28-056**

## Sponsored superannuation schemes

If the scheme was a sponsored superannuation scheme (see above) prior to 6 April 2006 then, provided that no contributions are made under the scheme on or after that date, the previous exclusion from the relevant property regime in s.58(1)(d) continues to apply to the entire fund.[89] If any contributions are made on or after 6 April 2006, only the *protected percentage* of the settled property is **28-057**

---

[80] IHTA 1984 s.62.
[81] IHTA 1984 s.67(1).
[82] A settlement commences when property first becomes comprised in it (IHTA 1984 s.60).
[83] IHTA 1984 s.68(2).
[84] IHTA 1984 s.68(3).
[85] IHTA 1984 s.69(1).
[86] For the meaning of "same-day additions", and the value thereof, see IHTA 1984 s.62A.
[87] IHTA 1984 s.69(4).
[88] IHTA 1984 s.68(3).
[89] FA 2004 Sch.36 para.56.

protected from the relevant property regime under these provisions.[90] One finds the protected percentage of the settled property as follows. Firstly, one must find the market value of the assets of the scheme on 5 April 2006 and:

(a) increase that value by the percentage by which the RPI for the month of September immediately preceding the time in question is greater than that for April 2006; and

(b) reduce that value by the amount of any previous payments made under the scheme on or after 6 April 2006, other than payments of costs or expenses, or payments which are (or will be) income of any person for any of the purposes of income tax.

**28-058** The aggregate value is referred to in Sch.36 para.57 as "ACV". Secondly, one must find the current market value of the assets of the scheme (referred to as "V"). To find the protected percentage one divides ACV by V and multiplies the result by 100.

**28-059** For example, suppose that the market value of scheme property was £1 million on 5 April 2006, and since that date contributions of £100,000 have been made to the scheme, and tax-free lump sum benefits of £500,000 have been paid under the scheme. The value of the settled property in February 2020 is £800,000 (meaning that there is £200,000 of investment growth). The protected percentage of the settled property is determined as follows:

- AVC is £1 million increased by 148.6% (RPI was 196.5 in April 2006 and 292 in February 2020) less £500,000 equals £986,000
- V is £800,000
- £986,000/£800,000 x 100 = 123.25% of the settled property is protected

**28-060** As will be apparent, to the extent that investment returns have fallen short of the increase in the RPI, contributions can be made on or after 6 April 2006 without causing any loss of protection.

### IHTA 1984 s.86

**28-061** Settled property is not relevant property if it is property to which IHTA 1984 s.86 applies.[91] Insofar as is material, s.86 provides as follows:

> "(1) Where settled property is held on trusts which, either indefinitely or until the end of a period (whether defined by a date or in some other way) do not permit any of the settled property to be applied otherwise than for the benefit of—
> 
> (a) persons of a class defined by reference to employment in a particular trade or profession, or employment by, or office with, a body carrying on a trade, profession or undertaking, or
> 
> (b) persons of a class defined by reference to marriage to or civil partnership with, or relationship to, or dependence on, persons of a class defined as mentioned in paragraph (a) above,
> 
> then, subject to subsection (3) below, this section applies to that settled property or, as the case may be, applies to it during that period.

---

[90] FA 2004 Sch.36 para.57. The settled property does not constitute relevant property irrespective of these provisions if the settlor was non-UK domiciled and the settled property is non-UK situs, or if IHTA 1984 s.86 applies to it (see below), or if the scheme is a QNUPS, for example.

[91] IHTA 1984 s.58(1)(b). This is subject to s.58(1A), which provides that such settled property is relevant property if an interest in possession subsists in the property in certain circumstances.

(3) Where any class mentioned in subsection (1) above is defined by reference to employment by or office with a particular body, this section applies to the settled property only if—
    (a) the class comprises all or most of the persons employed by or holding office with the body concerned ..."

The trusts may also permit the settled property to be applied for charitable purposes.[92]  **28-062**

Section 86(1)(a) applies to the employees of a particular employer carrying on a trade profession or undertaking[93] and also "persons of a class defined by reference to employment in a particular trade or profession" which is clearly not limited to employees as such. A sole trader or partner can be *employed* in a trade or profession. Given the separate reference to office holders, an executive pension plan for the provision of benefits to directors and other office holders should fall within s.86(1)(a). It is not necessary for the settlement to be established by the employer (or other body), and it is not unusual in practice for such settlements to be established by a shareholder or group company.  **28-063**

Where the beneficiaries are the employees of a particular employer (so IHTA 1984 s.86(3) is applicable), it is usually preferable to include all employees as beneficiaries rather than have a process whereby employees are invited to join the scheme.[94] If settled property is formally and irrevocably allocated within the scheme for individual members then s.86(3) may not be satisfied in relation to such property, and so informal earmarking may be preferable. It is however arguable that if there are circumstances in which any property formally allocated may in certain circumstances become available for the benefit of the class of employees generally then any such allocations should not prevent s.86 from applying. There would appear to be no difficulty with the creation of sub-funds with preferred beneficiaries (such as a specified member and his family) and other beneficiaries (e.g. all other employees). If there are restrictions, such that the other beneficiaries can only benefit in specified circumstances, s.86 may well not apply.  **28-064**

A separate single member scheme would be similarly problematic. This is in contrast to the position relating to sponsored superannuation schemes where it may be arguable that there is just one scheme. Section 86 looks at the trusts on which the settled property is held, leaving no scope for such arguments.  **28-065**

Where s.86 applies to settled property, the property is deemed to be comprised in one settlement, and an interest in possession in any part of the settled property is disregarded for the purposes of IHTA 1984 (except s.55) if that part is less than 5% of the whole.[95] The usual periodic and exit charges under IHTA 1984 ss.64 or 65 do not apply to any property to which s.86 applies (because it is not relevant property), but a special exit charge may arise under IHTA 1984 s.72(2). A charge arises under s.72 where there is a payment out of settled property, or property otherwise ceases to be settled property, or where the trustees otherwise make a disposition as a result of which the settled property the value of settled property is less than it would be but for the disposition. An omission to exercise a right is  **28-066**

---

[92] IHTA 1984 s.86(2).
[93] *Trade* has a fairly restricted meaning, (see *Ransom v Higgs* [1974] 1 W.L.R. 1594; (1974) 50 T.C. 1) but undertaking is much broader. Any commercial activity (including investment business) is likely to suffice (see *Baytrust Holdings Ltd v IRC* [1971] W.L.R. 1333).
[94] If this had been the case in *Postlethwaite v HMRC* [2006] UKSPC SPC00571 it seems that ss.13 and 86 may have been available: see [72].
[95] IHTA 1984 s.86(4).

deemed to be a disposition for these purposes.[96] The charitable trust provisions in s.70(3)–(10) are incorporated. The amount on which tax is charged is equal to the reduction in value of the settled property.[97] Any payments which are income of the recipient for tax purposes (or would be if he were resident in the UK) are exempted, as are any payments to a beneficiary who is not a settlor or a participator of a close company settlor (or connected with a participator).[98]

# OMITTING TO EXERCISE RIGHTS

### Non-application of IHTA 1984 s.12(2ZA)

**28-067** Since 6 April 2011, where a member of a registered pension scheme omits to exercise pension rights under the pension scheme, s.3(3) does not apply in relation to the omission.[99]

*IHTA 1984 s.3(3)*

**28-068** An omission to exercise a right is not generally a disposition, because no property is disposed of. However, pursuant to IHTA 1984 s.3(3), an omission is deemed to be a disposition if: (a) the omission is deliberate[100]; (b) the omission resulted in the value of the disponor's estate being diminished; and (c) the omission led to the value of another person's estate, or the value of settled property in which no interest in possession subsists, becoming increased. The disposition is deemed to occur at the latest time that the disponer could have exercised the right. As a result of s.3(3) it is usually desirable to ensure that the member does not have the right to select the retirement date.[101] Where there is a fixed retirement date then any deferral could be caught by s.3(3).

**28-069** In *HMRC v Parry*,[102] a member of a pension scheme with terminal cancer was entitled to benefits but omitted to access the pension. After her death, the scheme administrator (who had discretion to pay death benefits to one or more of a class of beneficiaries) paid the death benefits to her two sons. It was common ground that the omission was deliberate, and the value of her estate was diminished by that omission, but the executors argued that s.3(3) did not apply for two reasons:

(a) First, they said s.3(3) could apply only where the increase in the sons' estates occurs immediately after the diminution in Mrs Staveley's estate, and here the sons' estates were not increased until six months after her death. This was rejected: s.3(3) imposes no temporal requirement.

(b) Second, the value of the sons' estates was not increased "by" the omission;

---

[96] IHTA 1984 s.70(10), applied by s.72(5).
[97] IHTA 1984 s.70(5).
[98] IHTA 1984 s.72(2) and (3).
[99] IHTA 1984 s.12(2ZA).
[100] The words are "... unless it is shown that the omission was not deliberate", so an omission is to be treated as deliberate unless it can be shown not to have been deliberate. The burden of showing this (i.e. proving the negative) falls on the disponer or the disponer's personal representatives; it is not for HMRC to prove that the omission was deliberate.
[101] This can be achieved either by providing the trustees or managers of the scheme with the power to select the retirement date (within a prescribed range, typically age 50 to 75), or by providing that the member may select the retirement date only with the consent of the trustees.
[102] *HMRC v Parry* [2020] UKSC 35. The earlier decision in *Fryer v HMRC* [2010] UKFTT 87 involved similar issues.

the immediate and proximate cause of the increase was the exercise of the trustee's discretion. This was also rejected: the omission yielded the death benefits which increased the sons' estates, and the "limited discretion" of the scheme administrator (which it was obliged to exercise) did not interrupt the chain of causation, which began with the omission and ended with the receipt by the sons.

A deemed disposition under s.3(3) will not involve a transfer of value if IHTA 1984 s.10 applies.[103] This will usually be the case where the member intends to take the benefits, but does not currently require them and so elects to defer taking them until a later time (so that the fund can continue to be invested tax-efficiently, for example). Where such an election is exercised, it will usually be preferable for the commencement date to be deferred until age 75 (for example) or earlier with the agreement of the trustee. If a situation were to arise whereby the member can elect to receive the benefits whenever he wishes, but he fails to do so during his life, one would expect there to have been a time before he died where he was in ill-health and deliberately omitted to exercise his rights in order to benefit his death beneficiaries.

28-070

## DEATH OF A BENEFICIARY

### Non-application of s.151(2) and (3)[104]

As noted in Ch.21, HMRC consider that the value of an interest which terminates on death is nil, and so the non-application of s.151(2) is unlikely to have much significance. The non-application of s.151(3) means that on the death of a beneficiary with a qualifying interest in possession, the usual rules applicable to qualifying interests in possession apply. This means that the qualifying interest in possession beneficiary is deemed to own the underlying settled property[105] and so if it is terminated (on death) he is treated by ss.51 and 52 and making a transfer of value of the property in which the interest subsists (and not the value of the qualifying interest in possession, which will usually have a much lower value, and if it ends on death it will have no value). Non-qualifying interests in possession are disregarded as a result IHTA 1984 of s.5(1)(a)(ii).

28-071

A right to a pension or death benefits is a future interest and therefore a *reversionary interest* for the purposes of IHTA 1984 s.47. It follows that it is *excluded property* unless: (a) the interest has at any time been acquired (whether by the person entitled to it or by a person previously entitled to it) for a consideration in money or money's worth; or (b) it is one to which either the settlor or his spouse

28-072

---

[103] IHTA 1984 s.10(3) states expressly that s.10(1) can apply to a deemed disposition under s.3(3). See Ch.21 for an explanation of s.10 in the context of a contribution to a pension scheme. The same principles apply to a deemed disposition under s.3(3). At first sight, the references in s.10 to "a transaction" may appear to be problematic in the context of an omission. For the purposes of s.10, "transaction" includes a series of transactions and any associated operations (s.10(3)), and an "operation" includes an omission (s.268(1)). But what transaction is the omission associated with? In *Parry* the FTT considered that the transaction was the transfer between pension schemes.

[104] IHTA 1984 s.153 provides that, in determining the value of a person's estate immediately before his death there shall be left out of account any pension payable under various overseas public sector schemes.

[105] IHTA 1984 s.49(1).

or civil partner is or has been beneficially entitled.[106] If such an interest is excluded property then it is disregarded on death (but not at any other time).[107]

**Sponsored superannuation schemes**

**28-073** As noted above, if the scheme is a sponsored superannuation scheme and no contributions are made on or after 6 April 2006, IHTA 1984 s. 151 will continue to apply in full. Pursuant to FA 2004 Sch.36 para.58, if any contributions are made on or after 6 April 2006, IHTA 1984 s.151 will only continue to apply (by virtue of these provisions[108]) only to so much of the assets of the scheme as does not exceed the "protected amount".

**28-074** If para.58 has not previously applied to the scheme, and inheritance tax has not previously been chargeable by reference to the value of the assets of the scheme on or after 6 April 2006, the protected amount is equal to the market value of the assets of the scheme on 5 April 2006:

(a) increased by the percentage by which the retail prices index for the month of September immediately preceding the time in question is greater than that for April 2006; and

(b) reduced by the amount of any previous payments made under the scheme on or after 6 April 2006, other than payments of costs or expenses, or payments which are (or will be) income of any person for any of the purposes of income tax.

**28-075** If para.58 has previously applied to the scheme, and inheritance tax would otherwise (were it not for the application of para.58) have been chargeable by reference to the value of the assets of the scheme, the protected amount is what it was immediately before the occasion, or (where there has been more than one) the last occasion, on which inheritance tax would have been so chargeable (the "relevant tax occasion"):

(a) reduced by the value of the property on which inheritance tax would have been chargeable on the relevant tax occasion;

(b) increased by the percentage by which the retail prices index for the month of September immediately preceding the time in question is greater than that for the month in which the relevant tax occasion fell; and

(c) reduced by the amount of any previous payments, other than payments of costs or expenses, or payments which are (or will be) income of any person for any of the purposes of income tax, made under the scheme since the relevant tax occasion.

**Powers of nomination (settlement powers/general powers)**

**28-076** In relation to settled property, a power to specify who will receive death benefits is likely to be a settlement power[109] and so is not *property* for the purposes of IHTA 1984 s.5(1).[110] It follows that the value of the power is not included in the transfer of value that is deemed to occur immediately before death under s.4(1). However,

---

[106] IHTA 1984 s.48.
[107] IHTA 1984 s.5(1)(b).
[108] Section 151 would apply in any event if the scheme was a QNUPS, for example.
[109] A *settlement power* means any power over, or exercisable (whether directly or indirectly) in relation to, settled property or a settlement (IHTA 1984 s.47A).
[110] For inheritance tax purposes, *property* includes rights and interests of any description but expressly does not include a settlement power (s.272).

## DEATH OF A BENEFICIARY

if the power is a general power[111] which enables him, or would if he were sui juris enable him, to dispose of any property other than settled property, he is treated as beneficially entitled to the death benefits.[112] Thus, in *Kempe v IRC*,[113] the deceased had a general power under a life policy paid for by his former-employer. Although the deceased had exercised the power before his death, he could change his beneficiary designations at any time. The Special Commissioner found that the power was a general power and so the death benefits formed part of his estate.[114]

Section 151(4) modifies s.5(2) in relation to interests under registered pension schemes, such that s.5(2) also applies to a general power relating to settled property.[115] As s.151(4) does not apply to unregistered schemes (other than QNUPS and s.615 funds), s.5(2) does not cause any problems if a member of a scheme established under trusts has a general power.

**28-077**

---

[111] For these purposes, a *general power* means a power or authority enabling the person by whom it is exercisable to appoint or dispose of the property as he thinks fit (s.5(2)).
[112] IHTA 1984 s.5(2).
[113] *Kempe v IRC* [2004] S.T.C. (S.C.D.) 467. The employer was based in the US, and the policy was not taxable as a matter of US legislation. The decision demonstrates the importance of making sure that non-UK pension schemes are drafted to reflect UK law if any members are UK domiciled.
[114] The employer was based in the US, and the policy was not taxable under US legislation, but it was included within the employee's estate as a result of IHTA 1984 s.5(2). This case demonstrates the importance of making sure that non-UK pension schemes are drafted to reflect UK law if any members are UK domiciled.
[115] See Ch.21.

# CHAPTER 29

# Double Tax Treaties

## TABLE OF CONTENTS

| | |
|---|---|
| Introduction | 29-001 |
|     Tax treaties | 29-003 |
|     Interpreting tax treaties | 29-004 |
|         Article 3(2) | 29-006 |
|         Application to domestic deeming provisions | 29-008 |
|     Incorporation into UK law | 29-009 |
|     Requirement to make a claim | 29-011 |
|     Double tax relief | 29-013 |
| Application to Retirement Benefit Schemes | 29-014 |
|     Definitions of "pension scheme" | 29-015 |
| Cross Border Contributions | 29-017 |
|     Where is a pension scheme established? | 29-020 |
|     "Resident" | 29-023 |
|     "Recognised for tax purposes" | 29-024 |
|     "Generally corresponding to a pension scheme…" | 29-025 |
|     Articles which differ from the OECD Model | 29-027 |
|     Claiming relief | 29-029 |
|     National insurance contributions | 29-030 |
| Cross Border Investment Income/gains | 29-031 |
| Pension Transfers | 29-032 |
| Cross Border Pension Benefits | 29-034 |
|     The OECD Model | 29-035 |
|     Pension article, employment article, or other income article? | 29-037 |
|     "Pensions and other similar remuneration" | 29-041 |
|         Vested benefits vehicles | 29-042 |
|     "In consideration of past employment" | 29-044 |
|         Transferee pension schemes | 29-049 |
|     Provisions which differ from the OECD Model | 29-050 |
|     "In consideration of past service(s)" | 29-050 |
|     "Pensions" (without a reference to "other similar remuneration") | 29-051 |
|     Pensions "subject to tax" in the state of residence | 29-053 |
|         Are remittance basis taxpayers "subject to tax" in the UK? | 29-056 |
|     Annuities | 29-057 |
|     Payments which are "exempt" from tax in the source state | 29-063 |
|     Lump sums | 29-065 |
|     Saving clauses | 29-067 |

Articles conferring source taxation rights ........ 29-068
"Arising" .............................. 29-069
TIOPA 2010 s.130A ..................... 29-071
"Derived from" ......................... 29-072
The "other income" article ..................... 29-074

# INTRODUCTION

**29-001** All tax regimes contain implicit or explicit territorial limitations regarding their ability to tax persons and transactions. Tax is usually imposed by reference to the place in which a person is resident or the place in which a source of income exists.[1] In the context of cross-border transactions, this gives rise to the possibility of the same income being taxed twice. Double tax treaties address this issue.

**29-002** The UK has entered into more than 130 tax treaties, most of which broadly follow the OECD Model Treaty, but there are many differences.

### Tax treaties

**29-003** A treaty is "an international agreement concluded between states in written form and governed by international law, whether embodied in a single instrument, or in two or more related instruments and whatever its particular designation".[2]

Traditionally, the main objective of tax treaties was to prevent double taxation in circumstances where a particular source of income could give rise to liabilities in both states. A treaty may prevent double taxation by conferring exclusive taxing rights on State A, or by capping the amount of tax which may be imposed by State B ("distributive articles"), or by prescribing that State B must allow a credit for any tax suffered in State A ("credit articles").

### Interpreting tax treaties

**29-004** A frequently cited summary of the approach to be adopted by English courts when interpreting tax treaties is found in the judgment of Mummery J in *IRC v Commerzbank AG*.[3] Mummery J explained that, in the light of the decision of the House of Lords in *Fothergill v Monarch Airlines Ltd*,[4] the following principles apply:

---

[1] In *Colquhoun v Brooks* (1889) 2 T.C. 490, 499 Lord Herschell said "The Income Tax Acts [...] themselves impose a territorial limit; either that from which the taxable income is derived must be situate in the United Kingdom or the person whose income is to be taxed must be resident there". In *Whitney v CIR* 10 T.C. 88, 113 Lord Wrenbury said, "As regards the word 'income' [...] It means such income as is within the Act taxable under the Act. [...] The Act nowhere purports to tax income which is neither derived from property in the United Kingdom nor income received by a person resident in the United Kingdom. The word 'income' wherever found in the statute is to be understood as excluding income neither so derived nor so received". The references to being "situate" in the UK (Lord Herschell) and property "in" the UK (Lord Wrenbury) are reference to the source of the income.
[2] Article 2(1)(a) of the Vienna Convention on the Law of Treaties.
[3] *IRC v Commerzbank AG* [1990] S.T.C. 285, 297–298. This approach was endorsed by the Court of Appeal in *Smallwood v HMRC* [2010] EWCA Civ 778 at [26] and *Bayfine UK v HMRC* [2011] EWCA Civ 304.
[4] *Fothergill v Monarch Airlines Ltd* [1981] A.C. 251.

(a) One looks for the clear meaning of the words used in context, adopting a purposive approach.[5]
(b) The language of a treaty should be interpreted, not as an English statute, but "unconstrained by technical rules of English law, or by English legal precedent, [and] on broad principles of general acceptation."[6]
(c) A treaty should be interpreted "in good faith and in accordance with the ordinary meaning to be given to the terms of the treaty in their context and in the light of its object and purpose".[7] The "essential quest in the application of treaties" is to "search for the real intention of the contracting parties in using the language employed by them".[8]
(d) In cases of ambiguity or manifest absurdity, recourse may be had to supplementary means of interpretation including *travaux préparatoires*.[9]
(e) Subsequent commentaries on a convention or treaty have persuasive value only, depending on the cogency of their reasoning.
(f) Aids to the interpretation of a treaty such as *travaux préparatoires*, international case law and the writings of jurists are not a substitute for study of the terms of the treaty.

**29-005** HMRC approve the OECD Commentary on the Model Treaty as an aid to interpretation of tax treaties. Logically, the OECD Commentary can be relevant to the interpretation of a treaty only where it had been published at the time that the particular treaty was negotiated, but the Supreme Court recently accepted it may be appropriate to consider OECD Commentary which post-dates a treaty.[10]

*Article 3(2)*

**29-006** Many treaties contain a provision similar to art.3(2) of the OECD Model, which provides that any term not defined in the treaty shall, unless the context otherwise requires, have the meaning that it has for tax purposes in the state applying the treaty.[11]

**29-007** In what circumstances does "the context otherwise require"? In *Fowler*,[12] Marcus Smith J held that, although the term "requires" might be said to import a degree of necessity, he did not consider this to be consistent with his duty to construe the treaty as a whole. To his mind, when considering whether a definition ought to be supplied by art.3(2), it is necessary to have regard to the effect of that definition on the treaty as a whole. If the definition supplied by art.3(2) results in an unreasonable outcome it should be disapplied. Neither the Court of Appeal nor the Supreme Court expressly commented on this approach.

---

[5] *IRC v Commerzbank AG* [1990] S.T.C. 285, 297–298.
[6] Per Lord Wilberforce in *James Buchanan & Co Ltd v Babco Forwarding & Shipping (UK) Ltd* [1978] A.C. 141 at 152.
[7] Article 31(1) of the Vienna Convention on the Law of Treaties.
[8] Citing McNair's *The Law of Treaties* (1961) p.365.
[9] *Fothergill v Monarch Airlines Ltd* [1981] A.C. 251.
[10] *Fowler v HMRC* [2020] UKSC 22 at [18].
[11] See e.g. *Pirelli Cable Holding NV v HMRC* [2006] UKHL 4, where the "tax credit" was interpreted in accordance with UK legislation relating to advance corporation tax.
[12] *HMRC v Fowler* [2017] UKUT 219 (TCC) at [34].

*Application to domestic deeming provisions*

**29-008**  Treaties should be interpreted by giving the words their ordinary meaning. In *Fowler*,[13] the Supreme Court made clear that where UK income tax legislation contains a deeming provision, unless art.3(2) applies, the treaty applies to the real-world transaction and not the fictional, deemed world created by UK income tax legislation. The Court emphasised the importance of first identifying the purpose of a deeming provision (and for that reason reached a different conclusion to the Court of Appeal). However, the analysis of the court in *Fowler* may have been influenced to some extent by a desire to avoid a situation in which payments were not taxable in either state (in that case the UK and South Africa), and a court may see fit to depart from the reasoning where the real-world transactions results in no taxation in either state.

### Incorporation into UK law

**29-009**  Treaties are not self-executing as a matter of UK law.[14] They are incorporated into UK law by TIOPA 2010 ss.2(1)[15] and 6(1), which provides that "... double taxation arrangements have effect ... despite anything in any enactment". In relation to income tax and CGT, treaties have effect so far as they provide: (a) for relief from income tax or CGT; (b) for taxing income/gains of non-UK resident persons that arises from sources in the UK or accruing on the disposal of assets in the UK; (d) for determining the income or chargeable gains to be attributed to non-UK resident persons; (e) for determining the income or chargeable gains to be attributed to agencies, branches or establishments in the UK of non-UK resident persons; or (f) for determining the income or chargeable gains to be attributed to UK resident persons who have special relationships with non-UK resident persons.[16]

**29-010**  Treaties therefore override domestic legislation, subject to implicit[17] or explicit exceptions.[18] Overriding a treaty will of course breach the treaty.

### Requirement to make a claim

**29-011**  Pursuant to TIOPA 2010 s.6(6), relief under s.6(2)(a) (relief from income tax), and s.6(3)(a) (relief from CGT) requires a claim. Although this might suggest it is not otherwise necessary to make a claim in order to rely on a treaty,[19] the better view

---

[13] *Fowler v HMRC* [2020] UKSC 22 (at [30] in particular).
[14] See *Boake Allen Ltd v HMRC* [2006] EWCA Civ 25.
[15] Which provides that "If Her Majesty by Order in Council declares—(a) that arrangements specified in the Order have been made in relation to any territory outside the UK with a view to affording relief from double taxation in relation to [specified taxes, including income tax]; and (b) that it is expedient that those arrangements should have effect, those arrangements have effect". TIOPA 2010 s.2(1) has retrospective effect and applies whether or not the income/gains are subject to double taxation (s.3(1) and (2)).
[16] TIOPA 2010 s.6(2) and (3).
[17] This is especially the case where tax avoidance is involved, and the domestic provision postdates the treaty. See *Padmore v IRC* [2001] S.T.C. 280, where the court found that if the domestic provision did not override the treaty then the domestic provision would have no effect.
[18] See e.g. the temporary non-residence rules and also the general anti-abuse rule in FA 2013 s.212.
[19] This is supported by the content of Form DT-Individual, which suggests the Form is required only to claim relief where there would otherwise be an obligation to withhold UK tax at source (which will rarely apply to non-UK trustees), or where a taxpayer wishes to make a claim for repayment of UK tax.

seems to be that a claim is always required.[20] Claims are usually made in form DT-Individual or in the whitespace of a self-assessment tax return. It is not necessary to make the claim before the relevant transaction, but where there is an obligation to withhold tax, or where the trustee or administrator is required under the term of the scheme rules to discharge the PAYE liability of an employer under the disguised remuneration or EFRBS provisions, the claim usually will be made before the relevant transaction occurs. If the claim is denied, the member can reconsider his or her options. Alternatively, the member can make a claim for repayment of the tax after the relevant transaction has occurred.

Where a trustee or administrator intends to provide to a non-UK resident member benefits in circumstances that would require the withholding of tax were it not for a treaty, the trustee may request a written notice from HMRC directing it not to withhold.[21] In order to provide such a direction, HMRC require evidence, usually in the form of a certificate issued by the tax authority of the country of residence, that the member is resident in the relevant country. The certificate must cover the date on which the distribution is made, but that does not cause any difficulties where the certificate covers the entire tax year. Typically, the member requests a distribution and the trustee defers making any resolution to pay the distribution until the member has claimed relief and HMRC have issued the direction. This procedure will not work where a certificate of residence is issued only in arrears (for example, some tax authorities will issue a certificate for the 12-month period ending the day before the application is made). In these circumstances, the trustee should consider paying the distribution to an escrow account on terms that either (a) the full amount will be released to the member upon receipt by the trustee of a direction from HMRC, or (b) tax and NIC will deducted and paid to HMRC and the net amount released to the member if HMRC refuse to provide a direction.[22]

29-012

**Double tax relief**

Any double taxation remaining after the distributive articles of a treaty have been applied is usually addressed by a double tax relief article.[23] The UK treaty approach (which is wider than the OECD Model approach) provides relief, in principle, even where the liabilities arise at different times in each territory and different persons are taxed in respect of the income.[24] Matching the foreign income and tax with a UK liability is achieved in most UK treaties by providing the credit against UK tax computed by reference to "the same profits or income by reference to which the [foreign tax] is computed".

29-013

## APPLICATION TO RETIREMENT BENEFIT SCHEMES

In relation to retirement benefit schemes, tax treaties are particularly important in the following four circumstances:

29-014

(a) *Cross border contributions:* State A permits tax relief in respect of contributions to domestic pension schemes only. A tax treaty between State A and

---

[20] *Davies v HMRC* [2020] UKUT 67 (TCC) at [83]–[85].
[21] Such a direction is provided in accordance with the Double Taxation Relief (Taxes on Income) (General) Regulations 1970 (SI 1970/488).
[22] For a summary, see *JTC Employer Ser Trustees Ltd v Khadem* [2021] EWHC 2929 (Ch), which concerned a payment from an EFRBS to a member who was resident in the UAE.
[23] OECD Model art.23.
[24] See INTM169040.

State B may allow a member or employer in State A to obtain tax relief or a tax deduction in respect of contributions to pension schemes in State B.

(b) *Cross border investment income/gains:* State A imposes tax at source on investment income paid to non-residents. A tax treaty between State A and State B may allow pension schemes resident in State B to invest in property located in State A without the imposition of withholding tax.

(c) *Cross border pension transfers:* State A permits pension schemes which are tax-approved in State A to make pension transfers only to other pension schemes which are tax-approved in State A. A tax treaty between State A and State B may allow members resident in State B to procure pension transfers from tax-approved pension schemes in State A to pension schemes in State B.

(d) *Cross border pension benefits:* State A imposes a charge to tax on pension benefits paid from pension schemes established in State A, and/or pension benefits paid in respect of employments exercised in State A, and State B taxes pension benefits paid to residents of State B. A tax treaty between State A and State B may provide that pension benefits paid to a resident of State B are taxable only in State B.

**Definitions of "pension scheme"**

29-015   Some treaties contain a definition of "pension scheme". For example, art.3(1)(o) of the UK/US Treaty defines "pension scheme" as "any plan, scheme, fund, trust or other arrangement established in a Contracting State which is: (i) generally exempt from income taxation in that State; and (ii) operated principally to administer or provide pension or retirement benefits or to earn income for the benefit of one or more such arrangements."

29-016   One of the issues in *Macklin v HMRC*[25] (considered below) was whether the World Bank scheme satisfied this definition of "pension scheme". HMRC argued that, although the scheme was generally exempt from income tax, this was by virtue of immunities from tax contained in the treaty establishing the World Bank as an international organisation, and the treaty required that the exemption should be conferred under the US tax rules on pension plans. This was rejected by the UT. It found that "generally exempt" does not mean generally exempt "as a pension scheme". That is the ordinary meaning of the words used and HMRC's interpretation involved reading in a number of words that were not in the treaty and this was not justified.

# CROSS BORDER CONTRIBUTIONS

29-017   Contracting states may wish to accommodate individuals working abroad by allowing them and their employers to continue to contribute to a scheme in their home country rather than switching schemes (which can lead to a loss of rights and benefits) or having pension arrangements in a number of different countries (which can lead to practical difficulties).[26] To address this the following treaty provision is

---

[25] *Macklin v HMRC* [2015] UKUT 39 (TCC).
[26] See para.32 of the OECD commentary on art.18 of the Model Treaty.

suggested by the OECD Commentary:[27]

"(1) Contributions to a pension scheme established in and recognised for tax purposes in a Contracting State[28] that are made by or on behalf of an individual who renders services in the other Contracting State shall, for the purposes of determining the individual's tax payable and the profits of an enterprise which may be taxed in that State, be treated in that State in the same way and subject to the same conditions and limitations as contributions made to a pension scheme that is recognised for tax purposes in that State, provided that:
  (a) the individual was not a resident of that State, and was participating in the pension scheme, immediately before beginning to provide services in that State, and
  (b) the pension scheme is accepted by the competent authority of that State as generally corresponding to a pension scheme recognised as such for tax purposes by that State.
(2) For the purposes of paragraph 1:
  (a) the term "a pension scheme" means an arrangement in which the individual participates in order to secure retirement benefits payable in respect of the services referred to in paragraph 1, and
  (b) a pension scheme is recognised for tax purposes in a State if the contributions to the scheme would qualify for tax relief in that State."

**29-018** Where this provision applies, contributions will be treated in that state in the same way and subject to the same conditions and limitations as contributions made to a pension scheme that is recognised for tax purposes in that state. From a UK perspective this means:

(a) income tax relief is available where a UK resident member makes a contribution to a pension scheme in the other state (as per FA 2004 s.188(1)[29]);
(b) a UK resident employer will be able to obtain a corporation tax deduction in respect of a contribution to a pension scheme in the other state as if FA 2004 ss.196–200 and the exemption from CTA 2009 s.1290 applied;[30] and
(c) employer contributions to non-UK pension schemes in respect of UK resident employees are exempt from income tax.[31]

**29-019** More generally, it means that relief will be subject to the scheme manager undertaking to provide the same information to HMRC about the member's BCEs as would be required if the scheme were a qualifying overseas pension scheme.[32] So the scheme manager will need to provide the name and address of the member

---

[27] OECD (2017), *Model Tax Convention on Income and on Capital: Condensed Version 2017*, OECD Publishing, Paris, http://dx.doi.org/10.1787/mtc_cond-2017-en para.37 of the commentary on art.18.

[28] The OECD provides an alternative provision (at para.38) to permit schemes established in third States.

[29] It should be noted that relevant UK earnings are treated as not being chargeable to income tax if, in accordance with an applicable tax treaty, they are not taxable in the UK. Where a UK resident individual performs some or all of his duties outside of the UK, a tax treaty between the UK and that other country will frequently provide that earnings relating to those services are taxable in the country in which the services are performed, and not in the UK (where he is resident for tax purposes). This differs from the situation where the treaty provides for credit to be given for tax paid to the other country on earnings; in such circumstances the UK has subsidiary taxing rights (see PTM111600).

[30] PTM111600.

[31] This is the equivalent of ITEPA 2003 s.308. See the tax treaties with Canada (art.27(7)), Chile (art.17(3)), Denmark (art.28(3)), France (art.25(6)), Ireland (art.17A), Moldova (art.17(3)), Slovenia (art.26(6)), South Africa (art.17(3)) and the United States (art.18(2)).

[32] PTM111600 and PTM111800.

in respect of whom there has been a BCE in the tax year, and the date, amount and nature of the BCE.[33]

### Where is a pension scheme established?

**29-020** It is likely that a pension scheme is "established" in the country or territory in which its main administration is carried out.[34] This is the place in which any decisions relating to the administration of a scheme are made.[35] Activities which are purely incidental to the administration of the scheme or could reasonably be expected to be carried out by a third party should not be material.

**29-021** *Macklin v HMRC*[36] was concerned with whether the World Bank pension scheme was established in the US for the purposes of the UK/US Treaty art.17(1)(b).[37] The scheme was set up, managed and administered by the World Bank at its headquarters in Washington DC. However, HMRC argued that, for the purposes of the Treaty, "established in [the US]" means being established under and in conformity with the US tax legislation relating to pension schemes, which was not the case with the World Bank scheme. The UT, rejecting HMRC's arguments, held that a pension scheme is established in the geographic location where it is set up, funded, managed and administered on a continuous and stable fashion through human and material resources.

**29-022** It seems that the place in which a scheme is established is fluid; it can change over time and is not limited to the place where the scheme was originally administered.[38]

### "Resident"

**29-023** Most treaties provide that residence is essentially a domestic concept.[39] Article 4(1) of the OECD Model provides that "resident of a Contracting State" means any

---

[33] See SI 2006/208 reg.2. The information must be provided by 31 January following the end of the tax year in which the BCE occurs.

[34] HMRC's views, in relation to the place in which an "overseas pension scheme" is established, are set out at PTM112200: "Normally, a scheme will be treated as established in the country where its registered office is and main administration is carried out. If there is no registered office, then the location where its main administration is carried out will guide matters. The scheme's location of main administration is where the scheme's decisions are made. In the case of a trust-based scheme, that would normally be determined by reference to where the scheme trustees are resident as that is where the decision-making responsibilities in respect of the scheme will lie. It should be noted that the country in which a scheme is established may change if the location of the main administration and decision-making changes".

[35] Lightman J found (in the context of PSA 1993 s.146(4)) that "administering" a scheme means (in whole or in part) running the Scheme, e.g. inviting employees to join, keeping records of members, communicating with members, calculating benefits, providing benefit statements, paying benefits when due, keeping documentation up to date, dealing with governmental or regulatory agencies etc. In the case of a funded scheme, it will also involve running the fund and investing in managing the scheme's assets (*R. (Britannic Asset Management Ltd) v Pensions Ombudsman* [2002] EWHC 441 (Admin)).

[36] *Macklin v HMRC* [2015] UKUT 39 (TCC).

[37] Which requires that where a pension is paid from a pension scheme "established" in one state that would be exempt if the recipient were resident in that state, the pension shall also be exempt if it is paid to a resident of the other state. A pension from the World Bank scheme would have been exempt if received by a resident of the US, so the question was whether art.17(1)(b) applied to exempt the pension from UK tax.

[38] If this were not correct then SI 2006/567 reg.3 (number 19) would be otiose. Reg.3 imposes an obligation on the scheme administrator of a registered pension scheme to notify HMRC if the territory in which the scheme is established changes.

[39] e.g. UK/Israel Treaty art.II provides that "(h)(i) The terms 'resident of the UK' and 'resident of Israel'

person who, under the laws of that state, is liable to tax therein by reason of his domicile, residence, place of management or any other criterion of a similar nature, and also includes a recognised pension fund of that state. This term, however, does not include any person who is liable to tax in that state in respect only of income from sources in that state or capital situated therein.

### "Recognised for tax purposes"

A pension scheme is "recognised for tax purposes" if the contributions to the scheme would qualify for tax relief in that state. On its face, this suggests that one does not simply look at whether tax relief is available in respect of contributions to the scheme generally (as one might perhaps expect), instead one must consider whether tax relief would be available in respect of "the" contributions under consideration. This suggests that a scheme may be recognised for tax purposes in respect of some contributions but not others.

29-024

### "Generally corresponding to a pension scheme…"

The pension scheme must be accepted by the competent authority of that state as generally corresponding to a pension scheme recognised as such for tax purposes by that state.[40] When claiming tax relief, HMRC request that the individual confirms that the scheme has been accepted by Pension Schemes Services as corresponding to a registered pension scheme, or:

29-025

(a) in the case of a claim made under the UK/US Treaty, the US scheme is of a type specified in the Exchange of Notes of 24 July 2001 as being a pension scheme under the UK/US Treaty art.3.1(o); or
(b) in the case of a claim made under the UK/Ireland Treaty, the scheme is tax-approved, or registered for tax approval, in Ireland.[41]

Other than in relation to US or Irish pension schemes, relief is not available unless and until HMRC accept that the scheme corresponds to a registered pension scheme, as the decision in *Haseldine v HMRC*[42] makes clear.

29-026

### Articles which differ from the OECD Model

Some treaties also require that the member was participating in the scheme before beginning employment in the UK, or the member was not resident in the UK immediately before beginning employment in the UK, or the member is employed by the same person who was his employer immediately before beginning employment in the UK.

29-027

HMRC's guidance suggests that where a tax treaty provides relief in respect of contributions by UK employers to overseas pension schemes for the benefit of their employees, such contributions are relieved on the same basis as employer contributions to a registered pension scheme, meaning that the extent to which they are

29-028

---

mean respectively any person who is resident in the UK for the purposes of UK tax and any person who is resident in Israel for the purposes of Israel tax …".

[40] For a case in which this requirement (in the UK/Switzerland Treaty) was not satisfied, see *Haseldine v HMRC* [2012] UKFTT 480.
[41] PTM111700.
[42] *Haseldine v HMRC* [2012] UKFTT 480 (TC), which concerned contributions by a UK resident individual to a Swiss pension scheme.

deductible is determined as if FA 2004 ss.196–200 applied.[43] Whether or not that is correct depends on the terms of the applicable treaty. Some treaties provide that contributions to applicable schemes "shall be allowed as a deduction in computing the profits of the [employer]".[44] On its face, such contributions need not be wholly and exclusively for the purposes of the employer's trade,[45] and are not subject to any of the restrictions in FA 2004, such as the spreading rules.[46] Such treaties do not say *when* such contributions shall be allowed as a deduction, but it is implicit that the treaty provisions override CTA 2009 s.1290,[47] otherwise the treaty provisions would very rarely have any effect.

### Claiming relief

**29-029**  An individual[48] can obtain tax relief under a tax treaty only by making a claim to HMRC, specifying the relevant treaty and article in the "additional information" box of his tax return.[49] The process is the same as for claiming "migrant member" relief.[50] In the first year of making a treaty claim HMRC request that the individual also provides the name of the scheme, the amount of the contributions that he will make to the scheme in the tax year, and whether or not the claim is for one year only.[51] HMRC also request that the individual provides a copy of a letter from Pension Schemes Services stating that the scheme has been accepted as corresponding, or provides the SF74 reference number given to the scheme by Pension Schemes Services when accepting it as corresponding to a registered pension scheme.

### National insurance contributions

**29-030**  An employer contribution to a pension scheme which is afforded relief under any of the following provisions is disregarded for NIC purposes:[52]

(a) Convention set out in the Schedule to the Double Taxation Relief (Taxes on Income) (France) Order 1968 art.25(8);[53]

(b) Convention set out in the Schedule to the Double Taxation Relief (Taxes on Income) (Republic of Ireland) Order 1976 art.17A.[54] Article 17A was added

---

[43] PTM111600.
[44] e.g. art.25(7) of the UK/France Tax Treaty and art.17A of the UK/Ireland Tax Treaty.
[45] Although this may now seem surprising, this reflects the provisions applicable to contributions to tax-approved pension schemes prior to 6 April 2006.
[46] HMRC may disagree: PTM111600 says, "Some [treaties] provide for an employer's contribution to an overseas pension scheme for their employees' benefit to qualify for tax relief if certain conditions are met. Such contributions are relieved on the same basis as employer contributions to a registered pension scheme (see PTM043000) so the extent to which they are deductible is determined as if sections 196 to 200 Finance Act 2004 applied".
[47] Which defers a tax deduction until such time as qualifying benefits are provided from the scheme. See Ch.24.
[48] Presumably it is not necessary for an employee to claim relief regarding employer contributions (i.e. the equivalent to ITEPA 2003 s.308).
[49] PTM111700.
[50] For migrant member relief, see Ch.24.
[51] PTM111700.
[52] The Social Security (Contributions) Regulations 2001 (SI 2001/1004) Sch.3 Pt VI para.7.
[53] Double Taxation Relief (Taxes on Income) (France) Order 1968 (SI 1968/1869).
[54] Double Taxation Relief (Taxes on Income) (Republic of Ireland) Order 1976 (SI 1976/319).

by art.1 of the Protocol set out in the Schedule to the Double Taxation Relief (Taxes on Income) (Republic of Ireland) Order 1995;[55]
(c) Convention set out in the Schedule to the Double Taxation Relief (Taxes on Income) (Canada) Order 1980 art.27(2);[56]
(d) Convention set out in the Schedule to the Double Taxation Relief (Taxes on Income) (Denmark) Order 1980 art.28(3);
(e) Convention set out in the Schedule to the Double Taxation Relief (Taxes on Income) (The United States of America) Order 2002 art.18;[57]
(f) Convention set out in the Schedule to the Double Taxation Relief (Taxes on Income) (South Africa) Order 2002 art.17(3);[58] and
(g) Convention set out in the Schedule to the Double Taxation Relief (Taxes on Income) (Chile) Order 2003 art.17(3).[59]

## CROSS BORDER INVESTMENT INCOME/GAINS

**29-031** Where an approved pension scheme established in State A invests in property located in State B, some tax treaties operate to exempt the income from any withholding tax in the State B. In addition, some tax treaties exempt double tax on investments in one territory by a scheme in another.[60] The OECD Commentary suggests the following:

> "Notwithstanding any provision of this Convention, income arising in a Contracting State that is derived by a resident of the other Contracting State that was constituted and is operated exclusively to administer or provide pension benefits and has been accepted by the competent authority of the first-mentioned State as generally corresponding to a pension scheme recognised as such for tax purposes by that State, shall be exempt from tax in that State."

## PENSION TRANSFERS

**29-032** Some tax treaties contain provisions to allow funds held for the purposes of a pension scheme in State A to be transferred to a scheme in State B without any tax charges (such as where the individual moves from one employer to another in a different state).[61] Such provisions are not common in a UK context, so one must consider the usual QROPS regime. Where there are no domestic or treaty provisions permitting an overseas transfer, a member may be able to insist on a transfer to a scheme in anther EU state on the basis that any restrictions breach his right to free movement of capital under EU law.[62]

The Commentary suggests the following: **29-033**

---

[55] Double Taxation Relief (Taxes on Income) (Republic of Ireland) Order 1995 (SI 1995/764).
[56] Double Taxation Relief (Taxes on Income) (Canada) Order 1980 (SI 1980/709).
[57] Double Taxation Relief (Taxes on Income) (The United States of America) Order 2002 (SI 2002/2848).
[58] Double Taxation Relief (Taxes on Income) (South Africa) Order 2002 (draft).
[59] Double Taxation Relief (Taxes on Income) (Chile) Order 2003 (SI 2003/3200).
[60] e.g. art.14A of the UK/Ireland tax Treaty.
[61] See paras 66–68 of the commentary on art.18.
[62] See the Irish case of *Michael O'Sullivan v Canada Life Assurance (Ireland) Ltd* [2014] IEHC 217 in which the High Court found that an Irish resident member was entitled to have his fund transfer to a Maltese scheme notwithstanding that the member had no employment or residency connection with Malta.

"Where pension rights or amounts have accumulated in a pension scheme established in and recognised for tax purposes in one Contracting State for the benefit of an individual who is a resident of the other Contracting State, any transfer of these rights or amounts to a pension scheme established in and recognised for tax purposes in that other State shall, in each State, be treated for tax purposes in the same way and subject to the same conditions and limitations as if it had been made from one pension scheme established in and recognised for tax purposes in that State to another pension scheme established in and recognised for tax purposes in the same State."

# CROSS BORDER PENSION BENEFITS

29-034   State A imposes a charge to tax on pension benefits paid from pension schemes established in State A, and/or pension benefits paid in respect of employments exercised in State A, and State B taxes pension benefits received by residents of State B. A tax treaty between State A and State B may provide that pension benefits paid to residents of State B are taxable only in State B.

**The OECD Model**

29-035   Article 18 of the OECD Model provides:

"Subject to the provisions of paragraph 2 of Article 19,[63] pensions and other similar remuneration paid to a resident of a Contracting State in consideration of past employment shall be taxable only in that State."

29-036   Note:
(a) Exclusive taxing rights are conferred on the territory of residence.[64]
(b) The article is not limited to benefits paid to the member; it applies also to death benefits paid in respect of a member.
(c) The article does not have any application to non-occupational arrangements, which the OECD Commentary calls "individual retirement schemes".[65] In the absence of any express provision, benefits under individual retirement schemes will usually be dealt with in the "other income" article.
(d) The article is not restricted to benefits paid from a scheme established in, or otherwise connected with, either of the contracting states. The benefits must be paid in consideration of past employment, but it matters not where in the world the employment duties were performed.

**Pension article, employment article, or other income article?**

29-037   In the OECD Model, the pension article takes priority to the employment article,[66] so where the pension article applies it is unnecessary to consider the employment article.

---

[63] Paragraph 2 of art.19 relates to Government service, and so art.18 relates to private employment. Many treaties treat government pensions differently from other pensions.
[64] For the policy and administrative considerations which support giving exclusive taxing rights to the country of residence, see para.1 of the OECD Commentary to the Model.
[65] Paragraph 30 of the OECD Commentary suggests that individual retirement schemes should be provided for separately in a treaty, and suggests possible drafting.
[66] Article 15 (income from employment) commences, "Subject to the provisions of Articles 16, 18 [the pension article] and 19, salaries, wages and other similar remuneration...".

**29-038** The purpose of pension income is to provide income when the member's ability to earn income is reduced as a result of events which are inevitable, such as advanced age or death. Vogel suggests that the pension article can apply only to benefits which provide insurance against certain risks to the employee, such as longevity, premature death and disability.[67]

**29-039** The employment article of the OECD Model applies to "salaries, wages and other similar remuneration derived ... in respect of an employment". These terms are undefined and so art.3(2) prescribes that, where HMRC assert that a charge to UK tax arises, we apply the UK domestic meaning. Where a benefit is provided under a retirement benefits scheme and a charge arises in accordance with ITEPA 2003 s.394(1) (EFRBS) or Pt 7A (disguised remuneration), the income "counts as employment income" for UK tax purposes. Does that mean we ought to apply the employment article, or the pension article? The answer is almost certainly that the employment article does not apply. Where HMRC assert that a charge arises in accordance with the EFRBS or the disguised remuneration provisions, they are asserting that the income is not earnings (since a charge on general earnings would take priority to the EFRBS and disguised remuneration provisions). Thus, for example, an ex gratia termination payment for injury to feelings (which counts as employment income in accordance with ITEPA 2003 s.401) comes within the scope of the other income article rather than the employment article.[68] This analysis is generally supported by the approach in *Fowler*, in which the Supreme Court held that ITEPA 2003 s.15(2) (which provides that employed divers are deemed to be carrying on a trade for certain purposes) does not mean that qualifying divers are treated as carrying on a trade for treaty purposes such that income is within the scope of art.7 (business profits) rather than art.15 (income from employment). HMRC accept this in practice.[69]

**29-040** In some treaties, the pension article is restricted in some way, meaning that pension or similar remuneration paid in consideration of past employment falls outside the scope of the pension article because, for example, the pension scheme is not established in either of the two states.[70] Where the pension article for that reason does not apply, some commentators take the view that the employment article applies,[71] but the better view seems to be that the other income article applies.[72]

### "Pensions and other similar remuneration"

**29-041** "Pension" is not defined for treaty purposes and has no clear meaning as a matter of UK law. What little case law there is suggests that a payment is "pension" if: (a) it is income in the hands of the recipient; and (b) it is made in respect of an employment which has ceased (although the employment need not have ceased

---

[67] *Klaus Vogel on Double Tax Conventions*, 4th edn (Kluwer Law International), p.1440.
[68] *Resolute Management Services Ltd v HMRC* [2008] S.T.C. (S.C.D.) 1202 at [32]–[40].
[69] See Hennelly (deputy director, HMRC central policy), *Disguised Revealed*, Taxation, 20.09.11. Also see Q52 of HMRC's *FAQs on third party earnings: general*, 05.07.11: "To the extent that other payments under retirement benefit plans might come within the ambit of new Part 7A, would they also retain their character as pension/retirement income under the UK's double tax treaties? The legislation does not alter the character of pension/retirement income under double taxation treaties. It would not therefore change the way the UK's treaties allocate taxing rights".
[70] e.g. art.17(1)(b) of the UK/US Treaty, which applies only where the scheme is established in either the UK or the US.
[71] See e.g. *Klaus Vogel on Double Tax Conventions*, 4th edn (Kluwer Law International), p.1439, which suggests that employment-related pensions would fall within art.15 were it not for art.18.
[72] For the same reason that the other income article, and not the employment article, applied to a termination payment in *Resolute Management Services Ltd v HMRC* [2008] S.T.C. (S.C.D.) 1202 (see [35]–[40]).

because of retirement).[73] The words "other similar remuneration" are plainly broad enough to include benefits in kind, non-periodic (including income withdrawal and death benefit lump sums), or ex gratia payments.[74] A reimbursement of pension contributions (e.g. after a temporary employment) is not "other similar remuneration".[75] It is possible that a pension transfer may be "remuneration", but it is unlikely to be "similar".

*Vested benefits vehicles*

29-042   In some countries (Switzerland and Ireland, for example), it is not uncommon on retirement for a member's fund to be transferred from a pension scheme to a "vested benefits vehicle". It is important to understand how the tax authorities of such countries apply treaties to such vehicles. For example, in Ireland such vehicles ("approved retirement funds": ARFs) are essentially bare trust arrangements but taxed in the same way as pension funds (so a transfer to an ARF is not taxable, and nor is any investment income/gains accruing to the ARF, but distributions are taxable, with tax withheld at source). But the Irish Revenue consider that a distribution from an ARF is not within the scope of any treaty:

> "As the ARF owner is the beneficial owner of the ARF capital and any income and gains arising, he or she should be treated as such for the purposes of applying the various articles of the DTA [double tax agreement] between Ireland and the country of residence. Therefore, to determine where the taxing rights lie in relation to a distribution from an ARF, the distribution should be broken down between the underlying income, gains or capital which it represents. The appropriate articles in the DTA should then be applied accordingly as at the dates on which the income or gains arose to the ARF. If the individual was a resident of Ireland at those dates, the DTA does not apply. Where a distribution involves the return of all or part of the original capital invested in an ARF, then, unless there is a capital article in the DTA, any Irish tax charge under Part 30 TCA that relates to a capital disbursement is not limited by the DTA."[76]

29-043   Distributions to UK residents will therefore be subject to tax withheld at source in Ireland, notwithstanding the treaty. Distributions should also be subject to UK tax, with credit given for the Irish tax under art.21 (elimination of double taxation).

**"In consideration of past employment"**

29-044   "Consideration" is not here being used in a technical legal sense; the article imposes a requirement that there is a relevant causal connection with past employment.[77] The Commentary states[78] that a pension is paid in consideration of past employment if employment is a condition for that pension, such as where the amount of the pension is determined on the basis of: (a) either or both the period of employment and the employment income so that years when the individual was not employed do not give rise to pension benefits; (b) contributions to the scheme that are made under the condition of employment and in relation to the period of employment; or (c) the period of employment and either or both the contributions to the scheme and the investment income of the scheme.

---

[73] *Johnson v Holleran* [1989] S.T.C. 1; 62 T.C. 428; *Mcmann v Shaw* [1972] 1 W.L.R. 1578; [1972] 3 All E.R. 732. The dictionary definition is "periodic payment made especially by a government or an employer, in consideration of past services or of relinquishment of rights etc.
[74] Paragraph 5 of the OECD Commentary on art.18.
[75] Paragraph 6 of the OECD Commentary on art.18.
[76] Chapter 23 of the *Irish Revenue Pensions Manual*.
[77] *Klaus Vogel on Double Tax Conventions*, 4th edn (Kluwer Law International), p.1445.
[78] Paragraph 24 of the OECD Commentary on art.18 (in the context of social security pensions).

Benefits are paid in consideration of past employment if they have been earned and are in a sense a form of deferred remuneration. The requirement is most clearly satisfied where benefits are paid under a defined benefits scheme (whether it is contributory or not). Under a money purchase scheme, it would be more natural to say that employer contributions are made in consideration of employment and benefits are paid merely because the individual is entitled to them, but there can be no doubt that such benefits are within the scope of the article. **29-045**

Benefits which are compensatory in nature, such as benefits provided because of injury, or for death in service, may not be within the scope of the article. **29-046**

Benefits which derive from member contributions under a money purchase occupational scheme do not appear to be within the scope of this article. However, there is no requirement that the pension or other remuneration is paid "solely" in consideration of past employment, and the fact that the article does not expressly prescribe or permit any apportionment where only part of a benefit is paid in consideration of past employment perhaps indicates that benefits will qualify if they are in part paid in consideration of past employment. **29-047**

The meaning of "employment" in the article may conceivably be broader than its meaning for UK tax purposes,[79] but art.18 probably does not apply to benefits paid in respect of past self-employment. The employment must be "past" in the sense that it has terminated, so benefits provided under a pension scheme whilst the member is still employed do not appear to be within the scope of art.18. There is no suggestion that the recipient must have retired from employment generally. **29-048**

*Transferee pension schemes*

Benefits paid from individual retirement schemes, to the extent that they derive from employer contributions to that scheme or to a transferee occupational scheme, ought to be within the scope of the article. Similarly, benefits paid under an occupational scheme are not paid in consideration of past employment to the extent that they accrued under an individual retirement scheme before being transferred to the occupational scheme. **29-049**

## Provisions which differ from the OECD Model

*"In consideration of past service(s)"*

The pension article in some treaties applies to benefits paid in consideration of past "services" rather than past employment. As a matter of ordinary usage, "services" seems broad enough to include: (a) past self-employment; and (b) benefits paid in circumstances that the employment/self-employment has not terminated.[80] **29-050**

---

[79] It is perfectly proper, for example, to refer to a sole trader or partner as being "employed" in a trade or profession (see e.g. IHTA 1984 s.86(1), which refers to "persons of a class defined by reference to employment in a particular trade or profession", and is plainly not limited to individuals who are "employees" for UK tax purposes).

[80] Although a reference to past "service" (singular) rather than "services" seems more apt to describe a situation in which there has been a termination.

*"Pensions" (without a reference to "other similar remuneration")*

**29-051**  Some pension articles do not refer to past employment or services, and so are not limited to pensions from occupational schemes.[81] As noted above, a "pension" involves periodic payments. It is unclear if a reference in a treaty to a pension includes lump sum benefits (whether paid as a commutation of pension or as a stand-alone benefit). In *Westminster v Haywood*,[82] Millet LJ said that it is a perfectly accurate use of the word "pension" to mean periodic payments as distinguished from lump sum payments. In the Canadian case of *The Queen v John Cruikshank*,[83] a resident of France received a lump sum payment from a Canadian company to commute a pension. Gibson J held that, for the purposes of the treaty, "pension" should be given a wider meaning than its ordinary dictionary meaning, to include a lump sum payment. The Commentary suggests that pensions includes annuities.[84]

**29-052**  In practice, one would expect HMRC to accept that any benefits which can be provided under a registered pension scheme are within scope of pension article rather than employment article. Income withdrawal under a registered pension scheme should constitute a pension even if it is paid as a single payment.[85]

*Pensions "subject to tax" in the state of residence*

**29-053**  Some treaties include alternative provisions designed to secure either exclusive or limited source taxation rights (see below), but only where the state of residence does not tax these payments. The Commentary suggests the following wording to follow the standard article:

> "(2)   However such pensions and other similar remuneration may also be taxed in the Contracting State in which they arise if these payments are not subject to tax in the other Contracting State under the ordinary rules of its tax law."[86]

**29-054**  What is the meaning of "subject to tax"? HMRC guidance at INTM332210 suggests that the expression usually means that the person must actually pay tax on the income in their country of residence, but they accept that a person is still regarded as "subject to tax" even where he does not pay tax because, for example, his income is sufficiently small that it is covered by personal allowances that are available to set against liability to tax in the other country. HMRC consider that a person is not "subject to tax" if the income in question is exempted from tax because the law of the other country provides for statutory exemption from tax (e.g. the income is that of a charity or an exempt approved pension scheme (pension fund).

In *Paul Weiser v HMRC*,[87] a UK pension was paid to a resident of Israel which was exempt from tax in Israel on the basis that the recipient had been resident in Israel for less than ten years. The taxpayer argued that the pension was subject to tax in Israel on the basis that he was resident in Israel and therefore generally within the ambit of Israeli tax and the fact that Israel chose to provide an exemption did not detract from this. HMRC argued that there is an internationally recognised distinction between the expressions "subject to tax" and "liable to tax" as employed

---

[81] See e.g. UK/Isle of Man Treaty para.5A.
[82] *Westminster v Haywood* [1998] Ch. 377 at 409.
[83] *The Queen v John Cruikshank* (1977) 77 DTC 5226 at 5227.
[84] Paragraph 3 of the OECD commentary on art.18.
[85] The safer option may be to ensure that the payments are recurring, but that may be undesirable where lump sums are taxed more efficiently in the state of residence.
[86] See e.g. art.XI(2) of the UK/Israel Treaty before it was amended in 2019; art.19(1) of the UK/Cyprus Treaty, before it was amended by the 2019 Protocol.
[87] *Paul Weiser v HMRC* [2012] UKFTT 501 (TC).

in double tax treaties, and the taxpayer was confusing these two expressions. Being "liable to tax" requires only an abstract liability to taxation on income in the sense that a contracting state may exercise its right to tax the income in question (whether or not the exercise of that right actually results in an amount of tax becoming payable), and "subject to tax" requires income actually to be within the charge to tax in the sense that a contracting state must include the income in question in the computation of the individual's taxable income with the result that tax will ordinarily be payable subject to deductions for allowances or reliefs etc.

The FTT considered that the purpose of the treaty (as set out in its preamble) was the allocation of taxing rights as between the UK and Israel to avoid double taxation and prevent the "fiscal evasion" of tax. Its purpose is not to enable double non-taxation of the relevant income. The FTT then looked for a clear meaning of the words in the relevant article that is consistent with the purpose of the treaty and found that HMRC's interpretation (which was supported by certain non-UK decisions, academic writings, and the OECD commentary) was the correct one. In addition, the requirement that an individual must be subject to tax "in respect of" the relevant income must mean something more than simply being resident in that territory otherwise the words "and subject to Israel tax in respect thereof" would be otiose.

29-055

**Are remittance basis taxpayers "subject to tax" in the UK?** It is suggested that UK remittance basis taxpayers are "subject to tax" in the UK notwithstanding that the income will be taxed only if remitted.

29-056

*Annuities*

The Commentary suggests that "pensions" includes annuities,[88] but many treaties deal separately with annuities. For example art.18 of the UK/Italy Treaty provides:[89]

29-057

"(1) [...] pensions and other similar remuneration paid in consideration of past employment to a resident of a Contracting State and any annuity paid to such a resident shall be taxable only in that State.

(2) The term "annuity" means a stated sum payable periodically at stated times during life or during a specified or ascertainable period of time under an obligation to make the payments in return for adequate and full consideration in money or money's worth."

In the UK, historically, "pension" suggested an employment nexus and "annuity" suggested the equivalent for the self-employed and partners. In the UK, prior to the introduction of personal pension schemes in July 1988, the only tax-approved pension arrangements available to the self-employed were retirement annuity contracts. Under the above provision, an annuity need not be paid in consideration of past employment.

29-058

A pension paid by a UK personal pension scheme, for example, could be within the scope of this provision.

29-059

In the above provision, "annuity" is exhaustively defined. In principle, payments need not constitute an "annuity" as a matter of UK law (and/or the law of the other contracting state), however it will usually be desirable to ensure that it is. The mere fact that an arrangement is described as an annuity does not of course

29-060

---

[88] Paragraph 3 of the OECD commentary on art.18.
[89] Many other treaties are materially identical (e.g. art.18 of the UK/Malta Treaty; art.17 of the UK/Ireland Treaty).

make it so.[90] As a matter of UK law, payments are annuity payments provided that: (a) they are income of the recipient and not a payment of capital by instalments;[91] (b) they are "pure income profit";[92] (c) there is a legal obligation to pay the sum;[93] and (d) it recurs or is at least capable of recurrence.[94] To be an annuity, the capital must have "gone and [...] ceased to exist, the principal having been converted into an annuity".[95] It seems to follow that lump sum death benefits should not be payable under the terms of an annuity. The fact that such payments may be contingent and variable in character does not prevent them from being an annuity.[96]

**29-061** Such an annuity may be purchased by the pension scheme from an insurance company, but there seems to be no reason in principle that it cannot be paid directly from the pension scheme. The "specified or ascertainable period of time" should normally be at least three years, and five years is generally recommended.[97] Payments should be made at least annually. The payments need not be of an equal amount (they may, for example, reduce over time) provided that are not in fact a series of lump sums. A "stated sum" usually means an actual amount (rather than a fraction of the member's fund, for example).

**29-062** The obligation to make the payments must be "in return for adequate and full consideration in money or money's worth". Where the annuity is purchased, the premium will satisfy this requirement. Where the annuity is paid directly from the pension scheme, the contributions were the consideration (it should not be necessary for any new consideration when the annuity comes into payment).

*Payments which are "exempt" from tax in the source state*

**29-063** Certain schemes or categories of pension income are exempt from tax if received by a member who is resident in the state in which the scheme is established.[98] Some treaties preserve this exempt treatment of pensions when the recipient is resident in the other state. Paragraph 23 of the OECD commentary to art.18 suggests the following:

"Notwithstanding any provision of this Convention, any pension or other similar remuneration paid to a resident of a Contracting State in respect of past employment exercised in the other Contracting State shall be exempt from tax in the first-mentioned

---

[90] Secretary of State in *Council of India v Scobie* [1903] A.C. 299; *Perrin v Dickson* [1929] 2 K.B. 85; *Sothern-Smith v Clancy* [1941] 1 K.B. 276; [1941] 1 All E.R. 111.
[91] *Brodie's Will Trustees v IRC* (1933) 17 T.C. 432.
[92] *Hanbury, Re* (1939) 38 T.C. 588. Annuity payments are inseparably associated with payments from which tax is deducted at source, and that mechanism can operate properly only if the payments are a taxable receipt in the hands of the payee without any deduction for expenses and the like (*IRC v Whitworth Park Coal Ltd* (1961) 38 T.C. 531 at 575 (Lord Radcliffe); *Campbell v IRC* [1968] UKHL T.C. 427 at 475 (Lord Donovan). So e.g. agreeing to pay a garage £500 p/a for five years for the hire and upkeep of a car does not constitute an annuity (*Earl Howe v IRC* [1919] 2 K.B. 336; 7 T.C. 289). The provision of any benefit under a pension scheme is likely to be pure income profit.
[93] See *Ridge Securities Ltd v IRC* (1964) 44 T.C. 373.
[94] See *IRC v Whitworth Park Coal Ltd* (1961) T.C. 531. The authorities identify the characteristic of recurrence in the context of establishing that a payment is not a one-off payment in the nature of capital but has the quality of a payment which may recur (*Hargreaves Lansdown Asset Management Ltd v HMRC* [2018] UKFTT 127 (TC) at [73]). The fact that payments may be made weekly or monthly does not prevent them from being "annual" provided that the payments may continue beyond a year (*Smith v Smith* [1923] P.191 (CA)).
[95] *Foley v Fletcher and Rose* 157 E.R. 678; (1858) 3 Hurl. & N. 769 (Watson J).
[96] *Moss Empires Ltd v IRC* 21 T.C. 264.
[97] A five-year annuity is recognised as a short-term annuity for the purposes of FA 2004.
[98] e.g. a PCLS paid from a registered pension scheme to a UK resident member is not subject to tax in the UK.

State if that pension or other remuneration would be exempt from tax in the other State if the recipient were a resident of that other State."

To be "exempt", the income should be taxable in principle but expressly exempted (as opposed to income which is simply not subject to tax). **29-064**

*Lump sums*

Some pension articles treat lump sums differently to pensions and other similar remuneration. For example, art.17(2) of the UK/US Treaty provides: **29-065**

> "Notwithstanding the provisions of paragraph 1 of this Article, a lump-sum payment derived from a pension scheme established in a Contracting State and beneficially owned by a resident of the other Contracting State shall be taxable only in the first-mentioned State."

If the scheme is established in a state which taxes lump sums more favourably than pension income, this treatment usually works to the taxpayer's advantage. **29-066**

*Saving clauses*

Treaties sometimes include saving clauses, such as art.1(4) of the UK/US Treaty, under which each territory reserves the right to tax its own residents/citizens as if the treaty had not come into effect. **29-067**

*Articles conferring source taxation rights*

Some treaties confer exclusive or limited source taxation rights with respect to pensions paid in consideration of past employment. Conceptually, the state of source might be considered to be the state in which: **29-068**

(a) The fund is established.
(b) The relevant work has been performed.
(c) Tax deductions have been claimed.

**"Arising"** The pension article in some treaties applies only to payments which "arise" in one state and are paid to an individual resident in the other state. For example, art.17 of the UK/Hong Kong Treaty provides: **29-069**

> "Pensions and other similar remuneration (including a lump sum payment) arising in a Contracting Party and paid to a resident of the other Contracting Party in consideration of past employment or self-employment and social security pensions shall be taxable only in the first-mentioned Party."

The OECD commentary (at para.19) notes that "a mere reference to a pension 'arising in' a Contracting State could be construed as meaning either a pension paid by a fund established in that State or a pension derived from work performed in a State" and suggests that "States using such wording should clarify how it should be interpreted and applied". There is no such clarification in the UK/Hong Kong Treaty, so how should one interpret art.17? The Hong Kong Inland Revenue Department consider that a pension "arises" in Hong Kong if the fund from which it is paid is situated in Hong Kong.[99] HMRC's position is unknown. In UK tax legislation, the word "arising" usually signifies the time at which an item is recognised as **29-070**

---

[99] The Hong Kong Inland Revenue Department has stated in an annual general meeting of the HK

income,[100] but that tells us nothing about the state in which it arises. HMRC are likely to assert that pensions and other similar remuneration paid in consideration of past employment "arise" in the UK if either the scheme is established in the UK,[101] or the past employment was performed in the UK.

**29-071** **TIOPA 2010 s.130A** An anti-avoidance provision, TIOPA 2010 s.130A, applies where a UK resident member transfers his pension fund to a state (such as Hong Kong[102]) with a tax treaty with the UK which confers exclusive taxing rights on the source state. If s.130A applies, pension benefits are chargeable to UK income tax. It applies where both of the following conditions are met:

(a) Pension or other similar remuneration is paid out of sums or assets that were the subject of a relevant transfer or related sums or assets. A "relevant transfer" means a transaction or series of transactions as a result of which: (i) the sums or assets are transferred out of a pension scheme; and (ii) the sums or assets or related sums or assets (or both) are transferred into the pension scheme under which the pension or other similar remuneration is paid. "Related sums or assets", in relation to other sums or assets, means sums or assets which arise, or (directly or indirectly) derive, from those other sums or assets or from sums or assets which so arise or derive.

(b) The relevant transfer or any transaction forming part of that transfer was, or formed part of, a tax avoidance scheme. A scheme is a "tax-avoidance scheme" if the main purpose, or one of the main purposes, of any party to the scheme in entering into the scheme is to secure an income tax advantage for any person under TIOPA 2010 Pt 2 (which relates to double taxation relief) by virtue of the relevant provision made by double taxation arrangements.

**29-072** **"Derived from"** The pension article in some treaties applies only to payments which "derive from" a pension scheme established in one state. For example, art.18(2) of the UK/Switzerland Treaty provides:

"Notwithstanding the provisions of paragraph 1, a lump sum payment derived from a pension scheme established in a Contracting State and beneficially owned by a resident of the other Contracting State shall be taxable only in the first-mentioned State."

**29-073** Sometimes, the word "derived" in a treaty seems to mean the same as "arising",[103] but it is suggested that its use in the above provision is to emphasise that it includes indirect payments. In Switzerland, it is common for benefits which accrue under a pension scheme to be transferred to a "vested benefits vehicle" on

---

Institute Certified Public Accountants (HKICPA) that in determining the source of pensions for the purpose of art.17, the decisive factor is the place where the pension fund was managed and controlled (see HKICPA Tax Bulletin 2014; Annual Meeting 2014; pp.15–16). The IRD explains that this does not necessarily mean the place where the assets comprising the fund were physically situated.

[100] e.g. the DIMF rules apply where inter alia a management fee "arises" to the individual directly or indirectly from the scheme. HMRC guidance states that "43. Sums "arising" are not defined, so the word will take its usual meaning in legislation. Sums will arise when the individual actually has access to them. This will be when they are allocated to the individual, and the individual can access them. 44. If the sums are allocated, but not accessible to the individual, for example, they are deferred for a period of time, then they will not arise to the individual until he or she can actually access them." (HMRC, Investment Managers: Disguised Fee Income, Technical Note 29 March 2015).

[101] As TIOPA 2010 s.103A makes clear.

[102] The provision appears to have been aimed in particular at the UK/Hong Kong Treaty art.17 (the Treaty and s.130A both took effect on the same date: 6 April 2011).

[103] Kessler App. 5.8.1.

retirement. A vested benefits vehicle is not a "pension scheme" as defined in art.18 of the Treaty, but a vested benefits vehicle is little more than a conduit, and it is quite clear that benefits provided under a vested benefit vehicle "derive from" the pension scheme under which the benefits accrued.

### The "other income" article

Article 21 of the Model Treaty provides: 29-074

"(1) Items of income of a resident of a Contracting State, wherever arising, not dealt with in the foregoing Articles of this Convention shall be taxable only in that State.
(2) The provisions of paragraph 1 shall not apply to income, other than income from immovable property as defined in paragraph 2 of Article 6, if the recipient of such income, being a resident of a Contracting State, carries on business in the other Contracting State through a permanent establishment situated therein and the right or property in respect of which the income is paid is effectively connected with such permanent establishment. In such case the provisions of Article 7 shall apply."

As noted above, benefits provided under individual retirement schemes will usually fall within the scope of this article. In some treaties the other income article does not apply to income paid out of trusts,[104] in which case it may be desirable for the member to transfer his fund to a contract-based pension scheme. 29-075

---

[104] e.g. UK/France Tax Treaty art.23.1; UK/Switzerland Treaty art.21(1).

PART B: CATEGORIES OF PENSION SCHEME

# CHAPTER 30

# Relevant Non-UK Schemes

## TABLE OF CONTENTS

| | |
|---|---|
| Overview | 30-001 |
| What is a relevant non-UK scheme? | 30-004 |
|     Pre-A Day UK tax-relieved funds | 30-006 |
|         Migrant member relief, corresponding relief, relief under tax treaties | 30-007 |
|         ITEPA 2003 s.307 | 30-008 |
|         QROPS | 30-016 |
| Taxation of RNUKS | 30-017 |
|     Terminology | 30-022 |
|     Summary of the taxation of benefits | 30-023 |
|         National insurance contributions | 30-028 |
| The member payment charges | 30-029 |
|     The member payment provisions | 30-033 |
|     Relieved members | 30-036 |
|     Transfer members | 30-038 |
|         Relevant transfer funds | 30-039 |
|         Ring-fenced transfer funds | 30-043 |
|     Attributing payments to particular funds | 30-048 |
|         Payments prior to 6 April 2017 | 30-049 |
|         Payments and crystallisation events since 6 April 2017 | 30-050 |
|     The application of the member payment provisions | 30-058 |
|         Non-EEA annuity providers | 30-059 |
|         Recognised medical practitioners | 30-060 |
|         Determining a member's available LS allowance and LS&DB allowance | 30-061 |
|         Pension commencement excess lump sum | 30-062 |
|         Uncrystallised funds pension lump sum | 30-063 |
|         Serious ill-health lump sums | 30-064 |
|         Lifetime allowance excess lump sums (pre-6 April 2024) | 30-065 |
|     The UK residency condition | 30-066 |
|         Five-year rule funds | 30-067 |
|         Ten-year rule funds | 30-068 |
|         Ring-fenced funds with key date of 6 April 2017 or later | 30-069 |
|         Transfers to schemes that are not QROPS | 30-071 |
|     The UK residency condition and deceased members | 30-072 |
|     Liability | 30-073 |
|         Double tax treaties | 30-075 |

                Credit for overseas tax paid ................... 30-076
                Interaction with the EFRBS provisions ........... 30-077
                Interaction with disguised remuneration provisions .. 30-078
            The taxable property provisions ...................... 30-079
                TAFT and RFTATF ................................ 30-081
                The modifications ............................... 30-084
                    FA 2004 ss.185A–185I ........................ 30-085
                    The consideration is rent ................... 30-086
                    UK residency condition not relevant ......... 30-087
                Liability ....................................... 30-088
                Attributing payments to particular funds .......... 30-089
                    Payments made before 6 April 2017 ........... 30-089
                        Rule 1 .................................. 30-090
                        Rule 2 .................................. 30-093
                        Rule 3 .................................. 30-094
                        Rule 4 .................................. 30-095
                    Payments and crystallisation events since 6 April
                        2017 .................................... 30-097
            The annual allowance provisions ...................... 30-100
                The modifications ............................... 30-101
                    Cash balance and defined benefits arrangements ... 30-102
                    Other money purchase arrangements ............ 30-104
                    Member first flexibly accesses pension savings .... 30-106
                    Hybrid arrangements .......................... 30-107
                    Carry forwards of unused annual allowance ...... 30-108
                    Pension input amounts expressed in a foreign
                        currency ................................. 30-110
                    Enhancement of LS and LS&DB allowances ..... 30-112
                Liability ....................................... 30-113
            The overseas transfer charge ......................... 30-114
                "Relieved relevant non-UK scheme transfer" ....... 30-115
                The main provisions: s.244AC .................... 30-118
                Transfers exceeding available overseas transfer
                    allowance: s.244IA ........................... 30-119
            The lifetime allowance (pre-6 April 2024) ............ 30-120
                The modifications ............................... 30-121
                    The amount crystallising on a BCE ............ 30-121
                    Paragraph 15 BCEs ............................ 30-122
                    Block transfers .............................. 30-123
                    Modification of BCE 3 ........................ 30-125
                    Relevant valuation factor .................... 30-126
                UK residency exemption not relevant .............. 30-127
                Liability ....................................... 30-128

# OVERVIEW

**30-001**   Relevant non-UK schemes (RNUKS) are non-UK pension schemes holding funds that have benefitted from UK tax relief in specified circumstances. The UK tax relief may have been provided in respect of contributions to the scheme, or in respect of contributions to a different scheme which were subsequently transferred

## WHAT IS A RELEVANT NON-UK SCHEME?

to the current scheme (or both). To the extent that such schemes hold UK tax-relieved funds, FA 2004 Sch.34 applies a modified version of the main tax charges and protections that apply to registered pension schemes under FA 2004 Pt 4 and ITEPA 2003 Pt 9. Some of these tax charges do not apply if the member has not been resident in the UK for a specified period of time. Schedule 34 will not generally apply to the extent that the RNUKS holds funds which have not benefitted from UK tax relief, such as investment return received by the RNUKS.

It is not generally advantageous for a scheme to be an RNUKS: the provisions potentially expose the scheme and its members to tax charges which would not otherwise apply. However, in limited circumstances it can be desirable for an EFRBS to be an RNUKS, because there are exemptions that apply to the disguised remuneration regime and the charge under ITEPA 2003 s.394.

30-002

The relevant provisions are found primarily in FA 2004 Sch.34 and the Pensions Schemes (Application of UK Provisions to Relevant Non-UK Schemes) Regulations 2006 (SI 2006/207).

30-003

## WHAT IS A RELEVANT NON-UK SCHEME?

A "pension scheme"[1] is an RNUKS if one or more of the following applies:[2]

30-004

(a) The scheme is a qualifying overseas pension scheme and relief from tax has been given in respect of contributions paid under the scheme by virtue of FA 2004 Sch.33.[3] This is deemed to include contributions to a corresponding scheme on or after 6 April 2006 if HMRC have allowed tax relief in respect of the contribution.[4]

(b) Relief from tax has been given in respect of contributions paid under the scheme at any time on or after 6 April 2006 under double tax arrangements.[5]

(c) One or more members of the scheme have been exempt from liability to tax by virtue of ITEPA 2003 s.307 in respect of provision made under the scheme at any time on or after 6 April 2006 when the scheme was an overseas pension scheme.[6]

(d) The scheme has received a "relevant transfer" at any time on or after 6 April 2006 when the scheme was a QROPS.

In this chapter, the reliefs in (a) and (b) above and the exemption in (c) above are collectively referred to as RNUKS Tax Relief. The application of any of (a)–

30-005

---

[1] "Pension scheme" is defined in FA 2004 s.150(1) (see Ch.2).
[2] FA 2004 Sch.34 para.1(5).
[3] See Ch.24 for an explanation of these provisions. It is unlikely that this includes the 'relief' under ITEPA 2003 s.308A (available by virtue of Sch.33 para.3), for two reasons. First, s.308A is an exemption rather than relief, and Sch.34 generally maintains a distinction between exemptions and reliefs (see e.g. Sch.34 para.1(7)). Secondly, although Sch.33 inserts s.308A, it is still s.308A rather than Sch.33 that provides the exemption. This may be important where the member is resident in the UK but the employer is not (and so the employer does not obtain relief under Sch.33 para.2), although only if s.307 does not apply.
[4] See FA 2004 Sch.36 para.51(3) regarding employee contributions, and The Taxation of Pension Schemes (Transitional Provisions) Order 2006 (SI 2006/572) art.15(2) regarding employer contributions. These provisions are discussed in Ch.24.
[5] Paragraph 1(5)(b) does not expressly refer to tax relief in respect of contributions; instead it refers to tax relief "so given" and the natural meaning of this when read in conjunction with para.1(5)(a) is that it is a reference to contributions (and not for example, withholding tax on payments of benefits). The definition of "relieved member" (considered below) puts the matter beyond doubt.
[6] For the meaning of "overseas pension scheme", see Ch.31.

(d) above cause the entire scheme to become an RNUKS, however the RNUKS provisions apply only to those members and to the extent that RNUKS Tax Relief has been obtained.

**Pre-A Day UK tax-relieved funds**

30-006    Prior to the commencement of the QROPS regime on 6 April 2006, sums/assets could be transferred from UK tax-approved schemes to overseas unapproved schemes in very limited circumstances.[7] Such transferee schemes hold UK tax-relieved funds but they are not, by virtue of such transfers, RNUKS. Similarly, contributions to corresponding schemes prior to 6 April 2006 will have benefitted from UK tax relief, but such contributions do not cause the scheme (or any transferee scheme) to be an RNUKS.[8]

*Migrant member relief, corresponding relief, relief under tax treaties*

30-007    For the circumstances in which migrant member relief, transitional corresponding relief and relief under double tax treaties is available, see Ch.24.

*ITEPA 2003 s.307*

30-008    A usually benign provision, ITEPA 2003 s.307 takes on a special significance as a result of the RNUKS provisions. Insofar as is material, it provides that:

"(1) No liability to income tax arises by virtue of Chapter 10 of Part 3 (taxable benefits: residual liability to charge) in respect of provision made by an employee's employer under a registered pension scheme or otherwise for a retirement or death benefit.
(2) In this section "retirement or death benefit" means a pension, annuity, lump sum, gratuity or other similar benefit which will be paid or given to the employee or paid or given in respect of the employee to any other individual or to a charity in the event of the employee's retirement or death."

30-009    Given that such retirement or death benefits will normally be subject to tax when received, it is unsurprising that the benefit to the employee of his employer making provision for such benefits should not itself be a taxable benefit.

30-010    On the face of it, s.307 is aimed at the accrual of benefits under a retirement benefits scheme.[9] However, for the reasons that follow, the accrual of benefits under a retirement benefit scheme will not usually involve the provision of a "benefit" for the purposes of the benefits code. Ordinarily, a taxpayer may be content for s.307 to put the matter beyond doubt, but if the scheme is an overseas pension scheme it may be desirable to ensure that s.307 does *not* apply to any provision made by his employer so that the RNUKS provisions do not apply to the sums or assets representing such provision.

30-011    Given that s.307 can apply only if ITEPA 2003 Pt 3 Ch.10 would otherwise apply, it is necessary to consider in what circumstances Pt 3 Ch.10 could apply to provision made by an employer under a retirement benefits scheme. ITEPA 2003

---

[7] See IR12 (2001) Appendix VI and IR76 (2000) Appendix 22.
[8] For corresponding schemes, see Ch.39.
[9] In relation to another money purchase arrangement, benefit accrual involves the making of contributions to the scheme. In relation to cash balance and defined benefits arrangements, benefit accrual occurs when there is an increase in the value of the member's rights under the scheme.

## WHAT IS A RELEVANT NON-UK SCHEME? 681

Pt 3 Ch.10 applies to benefits (other than certain excluded benefits)[10] which are provided in a tax year for an employee, or for a member of an employee's family or household, by reason of the employment.[11]

In *Templeton v Jacobs*,[12] an employer paid for a loft conversion at the house of a prospective employee. The benefits code, as it stood at the time, could not apply to a benefit provided in a tax year before the employment was held, and so the Revenue argued that the benefit was not provided until the tax year in which the work was completed (by which time the employment had commenced). The taxpayer contended that the benefit was "provided" when the company paid for it, and this was not in any tax year in which the employment was held. Jonathan Parker J held that a benefit is not "provided" for the purposes of what is now ITEPA 2003 Pt 3 Ch.10 until it becomes available to be enjoyed by the taxpayer, and prior to that time there can be no benefit in respect of which a charge to tax can arise. The arrangements made between the employer and the builder for the carrying out of and payment for the conversion work were not relevant in determining whether a benefit had been provided. Accordingly, the benefit of the loft conversion was not provided until it was completed.

**30-012**

In *Dextra Accessories Ltd v MacDonald*,[13] HMRC argued that an allocation of funds under an employee benefits trust to a sub-fund involved the provision of a benefit for the purposes of what is now Pt 3 Ch.10. The taxpayer argued (following *Templeton v Jacobs*) that Pt 3 Ch.10 requires actual benefits rather than potential benefits and any other interpretation would result in double taxation since the benefit could be charged when the sub-fund was created, and again if subsequently distributed as an emolument. HMRC's arguments were rejected by the special commissioners and this aspect of the decision was not appealed by HMRC.[14]

**30-013**

It follows that the accrual of benefits under a pension scheme should not involve the provision of a benefit for the purposes of Pt 3 Ch.10, provided that the member's rights under the scheme are not available to be enjoyed by the member until benefits are provided under the scheme. The provision of additional benefits by the employer (such as insurance), which are not merely a right to receive future benefits, could perhaps fall within the scope of Pt 3 Ch.10, and it is noteworthy in this regard that the exemption in s.307 expressly does not apply to provision made for insuring against the risk that a retirement or death benefit under an EFRBS cannot be paid or given because of the employer's insolvency.[15]

**30-014**

Given that benefit accrual under a UK scheme does not cause the scheme (or any transferee scheme) to become an RNUKS, notwithstanding the application of s.307, Sch.34 para.1(5)(c) creates a disincentive to use non-UK schemes and so may well be vulnerable to challenge on EU law grounds (at least in relation to benefit accrual when the UK comprised part of the EU).[16]

**30-015**

---

[10] Excluded benefits primarily comprise benefits to which a different part of the benefits code applies, or would apply but for an exception (ITEPA 2003 s.202).
[11] ITEPA 2003 s.201. Such benefits are referred to as "employment-related benefits".
[12] *Templeton v Jacobs* [1996] 1 W.L.R. 1433.
[13] *Dextra Accessories Ltd v MacDonald* [2003] EWHC 872 (Ch); [2003] S.T.C. 749 at [9].
[14] Also see *OCO Ltd v HMRC* [2017] UKFTT 589 at [348].
[15] ITEPA 2003 s.307(1A). The rationale for excluding the cost of insurance from the exemption is presumably that where an employer promises to provide a benefit and also insures against the risk of insolvency, the insurance is an additional and immediate benefit and so there is no double taxation when the retirement or death benefits are subsequently provided.
[16] A contribution arguably involves a movement of capital and so engages TFEU art.63, which prohibits restrictions on movements of capital between member states and between member states and third countries.

*QROPS*

**30-016**   A QROPS is a ROPS in relation to which the scheme manager has provided certain undertakings to HMRC.[17] A QROPS is an RNUKS if it has received a "relevant transfer" (and there would be little point in a scheme becoming a QROPS if such a transfer were not anticipated). A relevant transfer means a direct or indirect[18] transfer of sums or assets held for the purposes of a registered pension scheme or another RNUKS.[19] Paragraph 1(5)(d) applies if the scheme was a QROPS at the time of the relevant transfer; if that scheme subsequently ceases to be a QROPS that will not affect its status as an RNUKS.

## TAXATION OF RNUKS

**30-017**   FA 2004 Sch.34 and SI 2006/207 contain provisions relating to the application of the following registered pension scheme provisions to RNUKS:

(a) The member payment provisions.[20]
(b) The taxable property provisions.[21]
(c) The annual allowance provisions.[22]
(d) The lifetime allowance provisions (pre-6 April 2024).[23]

**30-018**   These provisions apply to transfer members and relieved members of RNUKS.

**30-019**   The member payment provisions do not apply unless the UK residency condition is satisfied, but the other provisions below apply irrespective of the residency status of the member.[24]

**30-020**   Other than in relation to the taxable property provisions, HMRC have discretion following a request by the member to ignore any non-compliance which results in tax charges applying under the above provisions provided that the non-compliance does not materially affect the nature of a payment or the member in respect of whom it is payable.[25]

**30-021**   The following registered pension scheme provisions are not applied to RNUKS:

(a) The provisions relating to authorised and unauthorised *employer* payments[26] notwithstanding that many RNUKS are occupational pension schemes.

---

[17] See Ch.33.
[18] The inclusion of "indirect" transfers appears to be to accommodate jurisdictions (such as the US) which permit funds to be transferred, or rolled over, into a transferee pension scheme via the member whose rights are being transferred.
[19] FA 2004 Sch.34 para.1(6).
[20] FA 2004 Sch.34 paras 1–7, supplemented by SI 2006/207.
[21] FA 2004 Sch.34 para.7A, supplemented by SI 2006/207 (see regs 3A, 4A, 4B, 4C and 4D in particular).
[22] FA 2004 Sch.34 paras 8–12.
[23] FA 2004 Sch.34 paras 13–19.
[24] Where RNUKS Tax Relief was obtained before 6 April 2017, the UK residency condition is that the member is or has been UK resident in the current tax year or in any of the previous five tax years. It is otherwise satisfied if he is or has been UK resident in the current tax year or in any of the previous ten tax years.
[25] SI 2006/207 reg.17, inserting a new para.19A into Sch.34.
[26] Of course, if the employer is connected with a member then any payment to the employer is made *in respect of* the connected member, so the member payment provisions will apply.

# TAXATION OF RNUKS

(b) The scheme sanction charge.[27] This charge applies to most unauthorised payments made by a registered pension scheme and also unauthorised borrowing by the scheme, and so the fact that it does not apply to RNUKS means that: (i) unauthorised payments are not taxed to the same extent as they are under registered pensions schemes;[28] and (ii) there are no UK tax consequences of excessive borrowing by an RNUKS. The scheme sanction charge also applies to income (including deemed income) and gains received in respect of taxable property, and a modified version of these provisions *does* apply to RNUKS, except that they give rise to a deemed unauthorised payment rather than a scheme chargeable payment.

(c) The de-registration charge.[29] There is no equivalent to this charge in relation to RNUKS because it is not possible for an RNUKS to cease to be an RNUKS.

## Terminology

FA 2004 Sch.34 introduces a number of new terms, most of which have little or no application outside of the RNUKS provisions. The following table briefly summarises the meaning of the each of the main terms introduced:

**30-022**

| Term | Summary | Application |
|---|---|---|
| Relieved member | Member in respect of whom contributions benefitting from RNUKS Tax Relief have been made to the scheme. | Member payment charges |
| UK tax-relieved fund | Sums/assets representing contributions benefitting from RNUKS Tax Relief. | Member payment charges |
| Transfer member | Member in respect of whom sums/assets have been received from a registered pension scheme or an RNUKS. | Member payment charges |
| Relevant transfer fund | Sums/assets transferred from a registered pension scheme and any UK tax-relieved fund and/or relevant transfer fund transferred from another RNUKS before 6 April 2017. | Member payment charges |
| Ring-fenced transfer fund | Same as a relevant transfer fund, but transferred on or after 9 March 2017 (for QROPS) or 6 April 2017 (for other RNUKS). | Member payment charges |
| Taxable asset transfer fund | Sums/assets previously held for the purposes of a registered pension scheme, transferred to the RNUKS or to another RNUKS that are subsequently transferred to the current RNUKS. | Taxable property provisions |
| Ring-fenced taxable asset transfer fund | Same as a taxable asset transfer fund, but transferred on or after 9 March 2017 (for QROPS) or 6 April 2017 (for other RNUKS). | Taxable property provisions |

---

[27] In FA 2004 s.239. See Ch.5.

[28] An unauthorised payment made by a registered pension scheme gives rise to a 40% unauthorised payments charge, a 15% unauthorised payments surcharge (if the value of the unauthorised payment exceeds 25% of the members rights under the scheme) and a 40% scheme sanction charge (reduced to 15% if the unauthorised payments charge is paid in full). The amount of tax is therefore equal to 70% of the payment. The same payment made by an RNUKS would be subject to 55% tax.

[29] In FA 2004 s.242. See Ch.4.

| Term | Summary | Application |
|---|---|---|
| Currently relieved member | A member who has paid some of the tax-relieved contributions or who has been exempt under ITEPA 2003 s.307 in respect of his employer's provision. | Annual allowance provisions |
| Currently relieved non-UK pension scheme | A scheme where RNUKS Tax Relief is given in respect of member or employer contributions during the tax year. | Annual allowance provisions |
| Relieved member of a relieved non-UK pension scheme | Member in respect of whom contributions benefitting from RNUKS Tax Relief have been made. | Lifetime allowance provisions (pre-6 April 2024) |
| Relieved non-UK pension scheme | A scheme holding contributions benefitting from RNUKS Tax Relief. | Lifetime allowance provisions (pre-6 April 2024) |

**Summary of the taxation of benefits**

30-023   Pension income paid by an RNUKS to a person resident in the UK is chargeable under ITEPA 2003 Pt 9 Ch.4.[30] This includes "relevant lump sums" paid under RNUKS unless the member payment provisions apply to the payment.[31] To the extent that the member payment provisions apply, a number of registered pension scheme charges may be imposed.

30-024   Authorised pension death benefits paid in respect of a member who died before his 75th birthday are tax-free.[32] If the member died on or after his 75th birthday, such benefits paid to a UK resident individual are taxable at the recipient's marginal rate.[33] If the recipient is not resident in the UK such benefits should not be subject to UK tax.[34]

30-025   Authorised lump sum death benefits paid in respect of a member who dies before his 75th birthday are tax-free if paid within two years of death. If not paid within two years of death such lump sums are taxable as if the member had died after on or after his 75th birthday.

30-026   If the member dies on or after his 75th birthday, the member payment provisions are applicable (assuming that the deceased member satisfies the UK residency condition),[35] but only insofar as the lump sum is referable to the member's UK tax-relieved fund, transfer fund or ring-fenced transfer fund. The effect of the member payment provisions applying is that such benefits are taxable at the recipient's marginal rate in accordance with ITEPA 2003 Pt 9 Ch.15A, or are subject to the 45% special LSDB charge under FA 2004 s.206 if paid to a non-individual. To the

---

[30] For the taxation of such pension income, see Ch.26.
[31] See ITEPA 2003 s.574A(2).
[32] ITEPA 2003 s.573(2A)–(2D).
[33] ITEPA 2003 s.573.
[34] ITEPA 2003 Pt 9 Ch.4 applies only to foreign pension paid to UK residents (other than certain LSDBs). Temporary non-residents are taxable under ITEPA 2003 s.567A in the period of return.
[35] However, if the recipient is not resident in the UK the member payment charges under ITEPA 2003 Pt 9 arguably do not apply (even without a tax treaty).

extent that lump sum benefits are not referable to such a fund, they are taxable at the recipient's marginal rate under ITEPA 2003 Pt 9 Ch.4, but only if the member was resident in the UK immediately before his death.[36]

There are a number of exceptions for death benefits from RNUKS (and overseas pension schemes) which are explained in Ch.26 and following.

**30-027**

*National insurance contributions*

As is explained in Ch.26, benefits referable to contributions that have benefitted from migrant member relief, transitional corresponding relief or relief under double tax treaties will usually be disregarded for NIC purposes. Benefits subject to the unauthorised payment charge imposed by FA 2004 s.208 as applied to an RNUKS under FA 2004 Sch.34 are also disregarded for NIC purposes.[37]

**30-028**

# THE MEMBER PAYMENT CHARGES

The "member payment charges" apply to a payment by an RNUKS to or in respect of:

**30-029**

(a) a relieved member, to the extent that the payment is referable to the member's UK tax-relieved fund under the RNUKS; and
(b) a transfer member, to the extent that the payment is referable to the member's relevant transfer fund or ring-fenced transfer fund under the RNUKS.

The member payment charges are the following charges under FA 2004 Pt 4 and ITEPA 2003 Pt 9 that apply to registered pension schemes:[38]

**30-030**

(a) The unauthorised payments charge in FA 2004 s.208 (except the charge on taxable property: special provisions apply regarding taxable property).
(b) The unauthorised payments surcharge in FA 2004 s.209.
(c) The short service refund lump sum charge in FA 2004 s.205.
(d) The special LSDB charge in FA 2004 s.206.
(e) The charge to tax under ITEPA 2003 Pt 9 on pension income to which: (i) any provision of ITEPA 2003 Ch.15A (lump sums) applies; or (ii) ITEPA 2003 s.579A (pension income) applies by virtue of any provision of Ch.15A.

The charges referred to in (a)–(d) above are all of the tax charges that apply under FA 2004 Pt 4 when a payment is made to or in respect of a member (other than the scheme sanction charge, which is not applied to RNUKS). In relation to (e) above, Ch.15A applies to authorised lump sums and lump sum death benefits under

**30-031**

---

[36] This is taxable as a relevant lump sum (ITEPA 2003 s.573(4)). The amount chargeable is the amount of the lump sum less the value of any right to receive the lump sum that accrued before 6 April 2017 and so much of the lump sum as would not be taxable under ITEPA 2003 Pt 9 if the scheme were a registered pension scheme.

[37] The Social Security (Contributions) Regulations 2001 (SI 2001/1004) Sch.3 Pt VI para.3(1)(e).

[38] In addition, the serious ill-health lump sum charge is a member payment charge if the lump sum was paid before 15 September 2016 (see FA 2004 s.205A, repealed with effect from that date). Since that date, a serious ill-health lump sum paid under a registered pension scheme to a member on or after his 75th birthday is taxable as pension income under ITEPA 2003 s.579A (ITEPA 2003 s.637C). As ITEPA 2003 s.637C is not applied to RNUKS, a serious ill-health lump sum is not now taxable under the RNUKS regime. It may however be taxable under ITEPA Pt 9 Ch.4 as a relevant lump sum if paid after the member has attained age 75.

registered pension schemes (and would not otherwise apply to lump sums under RNUKS). If such charges apply, the payment is taxable under Pt 9 Ch.5A rather than Pt 9 Ch.4.[39]

**30-032** The member payment provisions apply only in relation to a payment if the "UK residency condition" is satisfied at that time (see below).

### The member payment provisions

**30-033** For the purposes of the member payment charges, the member payment provisions apply to payments made to or in respect of a relieved member or a transfer member of an RNUKS.[40] The member payment provisions are:

(a) the provisions of FA 2004 Pt 4 (other than the taxable property provisions) relating to actual or deemed payments made to or in respect of a member of a registered pension scheme; and

(b) ITEPA 2003 Pt 9 Ch.15A (lump sums under registered pension schemes).

**30-034** Therefore all of the provisions in FA 2004 Pt 4 "relating to" payments made by a registered pension scheme apply (although only for the purposes of the member payment charges)[41] to payments made to or in respect of a relieved member of an RNUKS or a transfer member of an RNUKS. Clearly, this includes the member payment charges themselves, and also all of the provisions relating to the circumstances in which they apply (and do not apply). This means that any payment (or deemed payment) by an RNUKS to or in respect of a member who satisfies the UK residency condition will be an unauthorised payment (and therefore give rise to the unauthorised payments charge and surcharge) unless it is one of the authorised payments listed in FA 2004 s.164.[42]

**30-035** Under ITEPA 2003 Pt 9 Ch.15A, most lump sum death benefits paid to an individual in respect of a member who died after reaching age 75 are taxable at the recipient's marginal rate of income tax. The relieving provisions in ITEPA 2003 s.637A–s.637N (as they apply to registered pension schemes) are not applied to RNUKS. These include provisions which provide that a lump sum is tax-free if it is: (a) a PCLS; (b) a serious ill-health lump sum paid to a member before his 75th birthday; or (c) a refund of excess contributions lump sum. If a payment made by an RNUKS is taxable under ITEPA 2003 s.579A, it cannot also be taxable under Pt 9 Ch.4.[43]

However, in relation to transfer members of an RNUKS, the provisions of Ch.15A are disapplied in the case of: (a) a serious ill-health lump sum; or (b) an authorised lump sum death benefit if the member died under the age of 75.[44]

### Relieved members

**30-036** A member of an RNUKS is a "relieved member" of the scheme if: (a) any contributions paid by or on behalf of, or in respect of, him benefitted from RNUKS

---

[39] ITEPA 2003 s.573(2).
[40] FA 2004 Sch.34 para.1(1).
[41] Certain provisions under FA 2004 Pt 4 relate to payments by a registered pension scheme but are not material to the member payment charges e.g. FA 2004 s.273B provides the trustees of a registered pension scheme with the power to make various payments (such as drawdown pension) notwithstanding any provision of the scheme documentation prohibiting such payments. Section 273B clearly forms part of the member payment provisions but it does not have any application to RNUKS because it is immaterial to the member payment charges.
[42] For such authorised payments, see Ch.11.
[43] ITEPA 2003 s.573(2).
[44] FA 2004 Sch.34 para.5ZA, added by FA 2024.

# THE MEMBER PAYMENT CHARGES

Tax Relief; or (b) he is the member who has been exempt from liability to tax under ITEPA 2003 s.307 in respect of provision made under the scheme.[45] In contrast to transfer members (considered below) the focus is entirely on contributions to (or other benefit accrual under) the scheme in question.

A member's "UK tax-relieved fund" under an RNUKS is so much of the sums or assets relating to the member that represent any of the contributions that benefitted from RNUKS Tax Relief.[46] In order to determine the amount of the sums or assets that "represent" such contributions, a modified version of the annual allowance provisions is utilised.[47] These provisions are explained in detail below. In outline, if the arrangement under the RNUKS relating to the member is another money purchase arrangement, the provisions are concerned solely with *contributions* under the RNUKS. So a member's UK tax-relieved fund under the RNUKS is equal in value to such contributions. Investment return does not form part of a member's UK tax-relieved fund in respect of another money purchase arrangement.[48] If the arrangement under the RNUKS relating to the member is a cash balance or defined benefits arrangement, the provisions are concerned with the greater of: (a) the increase in the value of the member's rights under the scheme during the year; and (b) contributions by the member during the year.

30-037

**Transfer members**

A member of an RNUKS is a "transfer member" of the scheme if a "relevant transfer" related to the member. A relevant transfer is a (direct or indirect) transfer of sums or assets held for the purposes of a registered pension scheme or another RNUKS so as to become held for the purposes of an arrangement under the RNUKS relating to the member. The sums or assets transferred by a relevant transfer create either:

30-038

(a) a "relevant transfer fund", if the relevant transfer took place before 6 April 2017; or
(b) a "ring-fenced transfer fund", if the relevant transfer took place on or after 6 April 2017.

*Relevant transfer funds*

A member's relevant transfer fund under an RNUKS is so much of the scheme funds as represents "relevant transferred sums or assets".[49] These are sums or assets transferred (directly or indirectly) to the RNUKS from a registered pension scheme or another RNUKS at any time on or after 6 April 2006 when the transferee RNUKS was an overseas pension scheme. Any funds in any of the member's ring-fenced transfer funds under the scheme are expressly not included in the member's relevant transfer fund.

30-039

The value taken into account when determining the amount of a member's relevant transfer fund is the total of:[50]

30-040

(a) the amount crystallised on any transfer from a registered pension scheme to the RNUKS, meaning the amounts of the sums and the market value of the assets so transferred; and

---

[45] FA 2004 Sch.34 para.1(7).
[46] FA 2004 Sch.34 para.3(2).
[47] SI 2006/207 reg.2.
[48] This is accepted by HMRC (PTM113230).
[49] FA 2004 Sch.34 para.4(2).
[50] SI 2006/207 reg.3.

(b) so much of the member's UK tax-relieved fund under any other RNUKS as has been transferred to the RNUKS without being subject to the unauthorised payments charge; and

(c) so much of the member's relevant transfer fund under any other RNUKS as has been transferred to the RNUKS without being subject to the unauthorised payments charge.

**30-041** HMRC provide the following example:[51]

"Gillian transferred £500,000 from a registered pension scheme (scheme A) to a QROPS (scheme B). This is the amount crystallised by virtue of BCE 8. Her relevant transfer fund in scheme B is therefore £500,000.

Gillian then transfers £150,000 from another RNUKS (scheme C) to scheme B. She has received migrant member relief on contributions of £50,000 to scheme C and £100,000 was contributed without UK tax relief whilst she was resident in Japan. So her UK tax-relieved fund under that scheme amounted to £50,000. The transfer was not subject to the unauthorised payments charge.

Her relevant transfer fund in scheme B is therefore increased to £550,000."

**30-042** The £100,000 is not included in Gillian's relevant transfer fund in scheme B because it was not transferred from: (a) a registered pension scheme; or (b) a UK tax-relieved fund under another RNUKS; or (c) a relevant transfer fund under another RNUKS. If several years later the value of the sums and assets in scheme B has increased to £700,000 as a result of investment growth, and Gillian then transfers the £700,000 in scheme B to another QROPS (scheme D), the value of the relevant transfer fund under scheme D is still £550,000.

*Ring-fenced transfer funds*

**30-043** A new concept of a "ring-fenced transfer fund" was introduced on 6 April 2017 to serve two primary purposes:

(a) in order to distinguish those funds in respect of which the overseas transfer charge may apply (ring-fenced transfer funds) from those in respect of which it cannot apply (relevant transfer funds); and

(b) in the context of the member payment provisions, in order to distinguish funds in respect of which the five-year residency rules apply (relevant transfer funds) from those in respect of which the ten-year residency rules apply (ring-fenced transfer funds) for the purposes of the UK residency condition described below.

**30-044** A ring-fenced transfer fund comprises the sums or assets transferred as a result of an "original relevant transfer" or a "subsequent relevant transfer" without being subject to the unauthorised payments charge.[52] An original relevant transfer is:[53]

(a) a relevant transfer of sums or assets held for the purposes of a registered pension scheme on or after 9 March 2017;

(b) a relevant transfer of sums or assets held for the purposes of another RNUKS on or after 9 March 2017, of the whole or part of the UK tax-relieved fund of a relieved member of a QROPS; or

(c) a relevant transfer of sums or assets held for the purposes of another

---

[51] At PTM113230.
[52] SI 2006/207 reg.3B.
[53] FA 2004 Sch.34 para.1(6B).

RNUKS on or after 6 April 2017, of the whole or part of the UK tax-relieved fund of a relieved member of an RNUKS that is not a QROPS.

**30-045** The "key date" for a ring-fenced transfer fund is the date of the transfer. This is relevant to the application of the UK residency condition described below, and also to the rules prescribing how a payment made by an RNUKS is attributed to a particular fund under the scheme.

**30-046** Where there is a relevant transfer of the whole or part of a ring-fenced transfer fund, the sums or assets transferred as a result of the transfer constitute a ring-fenced transfer fund under the transferee scheme and that fund has the same key date as under the transferor scheme. Such a transfer is a "subsequent relevant transfer" and is not an original relevant transfer.[54]

**30-047** Returning to the example above, in which Gillian has a total fund value of £700,000 in scheme D, but the amount of her relevant transfer fund is only £550,000. Now suppose that Gillian transfers £100,000 from a registered pension scheme to scheme D on 20 March 2017 and £200,000 from a registered pension scheme to scheme D on 1 June 2017. These transfers create two ring-fenced transfer funds and the key dates for those funds are 20 March 2017 and 1 June 2017 respectively. If Gillian were to then transfer the entire £1 million fund under scheme D to another QROPS (scheme E), the various funds under scheme E would be precisely the same as under scheme D. She would have a relevant transfer fund of £550,000, a ring-fenced transfer fund of £100,000 with a key date of 20 March 2017, and a ring-fenced transfer fund of £200,000 with a key date of 1 June 2017.

## Attributing payments to particular funds

**30-048** It may be the case that a member's arrangement(s) under an RNUKS comprise a UK tax-relieved fund and a relevant transfer fund and/or a ring-fenced transfer fund, and also sums or assets which are not comprised in any such funds (such as investment return received by the scheme, or contributions made when the member was not UK resident). It is necessary to determine to which fund each payment is referable.

### Payments prior to 6 April 2017

**30-049** Payments made prior to 6 April 2017 by an RNUKS to or in respect of a member are made out of the member's UK tax-relieved fund in priority to any other fund under that scheme, and the amount of the UK tax-relieved fund is reduced by the amount of that payment.[55] Once the member's UK tax-relieved fund is exhausted, payments are attributed to his relevant transfer fund until that is exhausted,[56] and then to his ring-fenced transfer fund. Once the member's ring-fenced transfer fund is exhausted, the member payment provisions cannot apply to any subsequent payments to or in respect of the member. If a member has more than one ring-fenced transfer fund under the RNUKS, these provisions apply in order of priority from the ring-fenced transfer fund with the earliest key date to the ring-fenced transfer fund with the latest key date.

---

[54] FA 2004 Sch.34 para.1(6D).
[55] SI 2006/207 reg.4(2). The amount of a member's UK tax-relieved fund expressly cannot be reduced below nil. This is presumably intended to ensure that subsequent contributions will be within the member's UK tax-relieved fund in all cases.
[56] Special rules apply where the RNUKS holds taxable property (see below).

*Payments and crystallisation events since 6 April 2017*

**30-050** In relation to payments made on or after 6 April 2017, only the following payments have the effect of reducing the member's UK funds (i.e. his UK tax-relieved fund, relevant transfer fund or ring-fenced transfer funds):[57]

(a) Unauthorised payments.
(b) Recognised transfers.
(c) The purchase of a lifetime annuity where the member has reached normal minimum pension age or meets the ill-health condition.
(d) The purchase of a lifetime annuity where the member has not reached normal minimum pension age and does not meet the ill-health condition and the contract does not provide for payment, and is not able to be amended to provide for payment before normal minimum pension age (unless the ill-health condition is met).
(e) The purchase of a dependants' or nominees' annuity, to the extent that the sums or assets applied to purchase the annuity are unused uncrystallised funds.[58]
(f) A payment pursuant to a pension sharing order or provision, to the extent that the pension debit derives from uncrystallised rights.[59]
(g) A defined benefits LSDB.
(h) An uncrystallised funds LSDB.
(i) So much of a charity LSDB paid in respect of relevant uncrystallised funds.[60]
(j) A payment that is an authorised lump sum payment. In the case of a trivial commutation lump sum and a winding up lump sum, the payment only reduces the member's UK funds to the extent that it is provided from uncrystallised rights under the scheme.
(k) An authorised lump sum under SI 2009/1171 regs 11, 11A or 12,[61] to the extent that the lump sum is provided from uncrystallised rights under the scheme.
(l) A tax liability of the scheme manager.

**30-051** In each case, the member's UK funds are reduced by the amount of the payment.

**30-052** The payment on or after 6 April 2017 of scheme pension is treated as being on the above list if the member became entitled to the scheme pension before 6 April 2017 and it is paid from sums and assets applied before 6 April 2017 towards the provision of the scheme pension.[62] The payment on or after 6 April 2017 of drawdown pension is also treated as being on the above list if it relates to a designation made before 6 April 2017. In each case, the member's UK funds are reduced by the amount the payment.

**30-053** In addition, the following crystallisation events on or after 6 April 2017 reduce

---

[57] SI 2006/207 reg.4ZA(3)(a) and reg.4ZB. For the purposes of determining if a payment is of a particular type, the RNUKS is treated as a registered pension scheme (reg.4ZA(2)).
[58] For the meaning of "unused uncrystallised funds", see Ch.15.
[59] For the meaning of "uncrystallised rights", see Ch.14.
[60] "Relevant uncrystallised funds" are such of the sums and assets held for the purposes of the arrangement at the member's death as: (a) had not been applied for purchasing a scheme pension, a lifetime annuity, a nominees' annuity, a dependants' scheme pension or a dependants' annuity; and (b) had not been designated under the arrangement as available for the payment of drawdown pension (FA 2004 Sch.29 para.15(2)).
[61] These are trivial commutation payments. See Ch.14.
[62] SI 2006/207 reg.4ZF.

the member's UK funds:[63]

(a) The designation of sums or assets as available for the payment of drawdown pension by an individual who has reached normal minimum pension age or meets the ill-health condition. The member's UK funds are reduced by the value of the sums and assets so designated.

(b) The designation of sums or assets as available for the payment of dependants' drawdown pension or nominees' drawdown pension. The member's UK funds are reduced by the amount of newly designated dependant funds or newly designated nominee funds that are unused uncrystallised funds.[64]

(c) A payment of scheme pension to an individual who has reached normal minimum pension age or meets the ill-health condition. The member's UK funds are reduced by an amount equal to "20 x P" where $P$ is the amount of the pension which will be payable to the individual in the 12 months following the day on which he becomes entitled to it (assuming it remains payable throughout that period at the rate at which it is payable on that day).

(d) An individual becoming entitled to a dependants' scheme pension. The amount of the reduction is equal to the value of the sums and assets as are applied in the purchase or provision of the dependants' scheme pension. The amount of the reduction is nil: (i) if the dependants' scheme pension is related to the member's scheme pension;[65] or (ii) to the extent that the dependants' scheme pension is funded by the application of sums or assets representing the whole or part of the member's or dependant's drawdown pension fund or flexi-access drawdown fund.

**30-054** All crystallisation events, and all payments (including deemed payments) except for transfers, are made out of the member's UK funds in the following order of priority:[66]

(a) so much of the member's UK tax-relieved funds made under the scheme before 6 April 2017;

(b) the member's relevant transfer fund;

(c) the member's ring-fenced transfer funds with a key date of 5 April 2017 or earlier, and where the member has more than one such fund the payment is referable in priority of the ring-fenced transfer fund with the earliest key date to the latest key date;

(d) so much of the member's UK tax-relieved funds made under the scheme on or after 6 April 2017;

(e) the member's ring-fenced transfer funds with a key of 6 April 2017 or later, in priority of the ring-fenced transfer fund with the earliest key date to the latest key date;

(f) any other funds under the scheme.

---

[63] SI 2006/207 reg.4ZA(3)(b) and reg.4ZB.

[64] For the meaning of "unused uncrystallised funds", see Ch.15.

[65] For these purposes a dependants' scheme pension is *related* to a member's scheme pension if: (a) the day on which one is purchased or sums or assets are applied for its provision is no earlier than seven days before, and no later than seven days after, the day on which the other is purchased or sums or assets are applied for its provision; and (b) the dependants' scheme pension will be payable to a dependant of the member (FA 2004 s.278B).

[66] SI 2006/207 reg.4ZC. Special rules apply where the RNUKS holds taxable property (see below).

**30-055** Payments which is are transfers are made out of the member's UK funds in the following order of priority:[67]

(a) the member's ring-fenced transfer funds made under the scheme (including such funds with a key date of before 6 April 2017) in priority of the latest key date to the earliest key date of the fund;
(b) so much of the member's UK tax-relieved funds made under the scheme before 6 April 2017;
(c) the member's relevant transfer fund;
(d) so much of the member's UK tax-relieved funds made under the scheme on or after 6 April 2017; and
(e) any other funds under the scheme.

**30-056** Any repayment of overseas transfer charge from HMRC to a scheme manager is attributed back to the particular fund or funds from which it was referable.[68]

**30-057** In the following circumstances an amount is attributed back to the member's UK funds:[69]

(a) The scheme makes a transfer and the member's UK funds have previously been reduced by a crystallisation even. The amount attributed back to the member's funds is equal to: (i) the value (if any) of the sums and asset designated as available for the payment of drawdown pension less the aggregate amount of drawdown pension paid from that flexi-access drawdown fund; plus (ii) the amount (if any) by which the fund was reduced if the individual became entitled to a scheme pension less the aggregate amount of the scheme pension payments made to the member; less (iii) the amount (if any) of any pension debit paid from that flexi-access drawdown fund, or sums and assets that have been applied towards the provision of scheme pension, on or after 6 April 2017. The amount is attributed back to the member's UK funds immediately before the transfer is made.
(b) The scheme receives a transfer and after receipt of that transfer the member's funds have been reduced by a crystallisation event, and the overseas transfer charge becomes due as a result of a change in circumstances after a transfer. The amount attributed back to the member's UK funds is determined in the same way as (a) above. The amount is attributed back immediately before the even causing the transfer to not be excluded from the charge.
(c) The scheme is treated as making an unauthorised payment in accordance with FA 2004 Sch.28 para.2A[70] and the member's funds have previously been reduced as a result of a crystallisation event occurring on the first payment of scheme pension. The amount attributed back to the member's UK funds is equal to the reduction when the individual became entitled to the scheme pension less the amount of scheme pension paid to the member. Any pension debit paid from the sums or assets applied on or after 6 April 2017 to provide the scheme pension is also attributed back. The amount is at-

---

[67] Special rules apply where the transfer is a payment treated as made by virtue of s.174A (see the taxable property provision below).
[68] SI 2006/207 reg.4ZE. For the circumstances in which the charge may be repaid, see Ch.12.
[69] SI 2006/207 reg.4ZD. These provisions do not apply in respect of any sums and assets: (a) designated before 6 April 2017 for the payment of drawdown pension; or (b) applied before 6 April 2017 towards the provision of a scheme pension (reg.4ZF(6)).
[70] i.e. where there is a significant reduction in the rate of payment of scheme pension.

THE MEMBER PAYMENT CHARGES 693

tributed back immediately before the deemed unauthorised payment is made, and is attributed back to the member's UK funds in the following order:
   (i) to the member's ring-fenced transfer funds, and where the member has more than one such fund the payment is referable in priority of the ring-fenced transfer fund with the latest key date to the earliest key date;
   (ii) to so much of the member's UK tax-relieved funds made under the scheme on or after 6 April 2017;
   (iii) to the member's relevant transfer fund; and
   (iv) to so much of the member's UK tax-relieved funds made under the scheme before 6 April 2017.
(d) The member's UK funds have been reduced as a result of a crystallisation event occurring on the first payment of scheme pension and no scheme pension has been paid in a period of 12 months for any reason, other than the death of the member or a recognised transfer. The amount attributed back, and the order of attribution, is the same as for (c) above.

## The application of the member payment provisions

**30-058** SI 2006/207 Pt 3 contains a number of modifications to the FA 2004 Pt 4 member payment provisions as they apply to RNUKS. Most are relatively minor[71] but the following are noteworthy.

### Non-EEA annuity providers

**30-059** In FA 2004 Pt 4, an annuity must be purchased from an "insurance company" (as defined in FA 2004 s.275). In relation to RNUKS established outside the EEA, any reference in FA 2004 Pt 4 to an insurance company includes a "non-EEA annuity provider".[72] A non-EEA annuity provider is a person resident in a country or territory outside the EEA whose normal business includes the provision of annuities and who is regulated in the conduct of that business: (a) by the government of that country or territory; or (b) a body established under the law of that country or territory for the purpose of regulating such business.[73]

### Recognised medical practitioners

**30-060** In relation to RNUKS, the ill-health condition may be satisfied by obtaining evidence from either a registered medical practitioner or a "recognised medical practitioner".[74] A recognised medical practitioner is a medical practitioner practising outside the UK who is authorised, licensed or registered to practise medicine in the country or territory outside the UK, in which either the scheme or the member is resident.

---

[71] e.g. a beneficiary need not be offered the opportunity of purchasing an annuity before a scheme pension can be paid (see pension rule 4 in FA 2004 s.165 and pension death benefit rule 3 in s.167) (SI 2006/207 regs 6 and 7).
[72] SI 2006/207 reg.14(6), inserting a new para.28 into FA 2004 Sch.28.
[73] SI 2006/207 reg.11.
[74] SI 2006/207 regs 14 and 15(4). The ill-health condition is explained in Ch.13.

*Determining a member's available LS allowance and LS&DB allowance*

**30-061** On the payment of a PCLS, trivial commutation lump sum, or winding-up lump sum, for the purposes of determining whether all or part of a transfer member's LS allowance or LS&DB allowance is available, ITEPA 2003 ss.637Q and 637S are applied as if references in those sections to relevant BCEs were only to relevant BCEs: (a) occurring in relation to the recognised overseas pension scheme; and (b) in respect of lump sums referable to the member's relevant transfer fund.[75]

*Pension commencement excess lump sum*

**30-062** To be a PCELS, a lump sum must satisfy two additional requirements:[76]

(a) it must not be paid from the relevant transfer fund of a QROPS; and
(b) it must not be paid from the UK tax-relieved fund of a relevant non-UK scheme.

*Uncrystallised funds pension lump sum*

**30-063** Where an UFPLS is paid to a transfer member of a ROPS, in determining the amount of the "permitted maximum", ITEPA 2003 ss.637Q and 637S are applied as if references to relevant BCEs were only to relevant BCEs: (a) occurring in relation to the ROPS; and (b) in respect of lump sums referable to the member's relevant transfer fund.[77]

*Serious ill-health lump sums*

**30-064** In the case of a serious ill-health lump sum from an RNUKS, the scheme manager may obtain the necessary evidence from either a registered medical practitioner or a "recognised medical practitioner".[78] A recognised medical practitioner is a medical practitioner practising outside the UK who is authorised, licensed or registered to practise medicine in the country or territory outside the UK, in which either the scheme or the member is resident.

*Lifetime allowance excess lump sums (pre-6 April 2024)*

**30-065** A lifetime allowance excess lump sum could not be paid from the relevant transfer fund of a QROPS or the UK tax-relieved fund of an RNUKS.[79]

**The UK residency condition**

**30-066** The member payment provisions (and therefore the member payment charges) apply to a payment to or in respect of a relieved member or transfer member only if the UK residency condition is satisfied.[80] There are separate rules for applying the residency condition in relation to:

(a) five-year funds, being funds which benefitted from RNUKS Tax Relief before 6 April 2017;

---

[75] SI 2006/207 reg.15(1C).
[76] SI 2006/207 reg.15(1A), modifying FA 2004 Sch.29 para.3C.
[77] SI 2006/207 reg.18.
[78] SI 2006/207 reg.15(1B).
[79] SI 2006/207 reg.15(8), modifying FA 2004 Sch.29 para.11.
[80] FA 2004 Sch.34 para.2.

# THE MEMBER PAYMENT CHARGES

(b) ten-year funds, being funds which benefitted from RNUKS Tax Relief on or after 6 April 2017; and
(c) ring-fenced transfer funds with a key date of 6 April 2017 or later.

*Five-year rule funds*

**30-067** The UK residency condition, in relation to a payment to or in respect of a relieved member or a transfer member, is satisfied in relation to five-year rule funds if the member is UK resident at the time the payment is made or was so resident earlier in the tax year or in any of the five tax years immediately preceding the tax year in which the payment is made. "Five-year rule funds" means:

(a) in relation to a payment to or in respect of a relieved member of an RNUKS, so much of the member's UK tax-relieved fund under the scheme as represents contributions benefitting from RNUKS Tax Relief made under the scheme before 6 April 2017; and
(b) in relation to a payment to or in respect of a transfer member of an RNUKS, the member's relevant transfer fund under the scheme and any of the member's ring-fenced transfer funds under the scheme that has a key date earlier than 6 April 2017.

*Ten-year rule funds*

**30-068** The UK residency condition, in relation to a payment to or in respect of a relieved member, is satisfied in relation to ten-year rule funds if he is UK resident at the time the payment is made, or was so resident earlier in the tax year or in any of the ten tax years immediately preceding the tax year in which the payment is made. "Ten-year rule funds" means so much of the member's UK tax-relieved fund under the scheme as represents contributions benefitting from RNUKS Tax Relief made under the scheme on or after 6 April 2017. The ten-year rule funds concept does not apply to transfer members (because the ring-fenced funds concept applies instead).

*Ring-fenced funds with key date of 6 April 2017 or later*

**30-069** The UK residency condition, in relation to a payment to or in respect of a transfer member, is satisfied in relation to any particular ring-fenced transfer fund of the member's under the scheme which has a key date of 6 April 2017 or later if the member is resident in the UK at the time of the payment. If the member is not resident in the UK at that time, the condition is satisfied if he was resident in the UK earlier in the tax year in which the payment is made, or he was so resident in any of the ten tax years immediately preceding that tax year, or the payment is no later than the end of five years beginning with the key date for the particular fund.

**30-070** The key date of a ring-fenced transfer fund is the date of the original transfer.[81] So the effect of having a ring-fenced fund with a key date of 6 April 2017 or later is that, in order to avoid the member payment charges, the member must be non-UK resident for ten complete tax years *and* the original transfer must have taken place at least five years previously (note: not *tax years*).

---

[81] FA 2004 Sch.34 para.1(6C).

*Transfers to schemes that are not QROPS*

**30-071**  A transfer of sums or assets held for the purposes of an RNUKS to a scheme which is not a QROPS or a registered pension scheme is an unauthorised payment.[82] If the UK residency condition is not satisfied at that time, the member payment provisions cannot apply and so the transfer will not cause any FA 2004 tax charges to arise. Given that such a transfer would not cause the transferee scheme to become an RNUKS,[83] this course of action may be attractive for two reasons. First, if the sums or assets were to remain in an RNUKS and the member subsequently becomes resident in the UK, the member payment charges will apply in full once again (but they cannot apply to any sums or assets which are not at that time held in an RNUKS). Secondly, the taxable property provisions always apply to an RNUKS (even if the UK residency condition is not satisfied), whereas they have no application to a scheme which is not an RNUKS.

**The UK residency condition and deceased members**

**30-072**  Where a payment of five-year rule funds is made six years after the death of a member who was resident in the UK immediately before death, it is difficult to see how, at the time of the payment, the member could be said to satisfy the UK residency condition. The deceased member has not been resident in the UK in the year of the payment or in any of the five tax years prior to the payment.[84] It follows that, in principle, the member payments provisions should not apply to the payment.

**Liability**

**30-073**  The member is liable for the unauthorised payments charge and surcharge if the payment is made during his life, and the recipient is liable if the payment is made after the member's death.[85] In relation to the short service lump sum charge and the special LSDB charge, the recipient is liable.[86] The person liable for the charge under ITEPA 2003 s.579A is the person receiving or entitled to the sum.[87]

**30-074**  Liability for the member payment charges that arise under FA 2004 Pt 4 is not affected by the residency status of any person (assuming that the UK residency condition is satisfied), however liability for the member payment charges that arise under ITEPA 2003 Pt 9 should not arise if the recipient is not resident in the UK.[88]

---

[82] See Ch.12.
[83] Sch.34 para.1(5)(d) provides that a scheme is an RNUKS if there has been a relevant transfer at any time on or after 6 April 2006 when the scheme was a QROPS. If the transferee scheme is not a QROPS it cannot be an RNUKS.
[84] This analysis is supported by FA 2004 ss.244B and 244C, which relate to certain exclusions from the overseas transfer charge. These both provide that the exclusions do not apply if the member ceases to be resident in a particular country of territory "otherwise than by reason of [his] death". These provisions therefore acknowledge that when an individual dies he ceases to be resident in the country or territory in which he was resident immediately before death.
[85] FA 2004 ss.208(2) and 209(3).
[86] FA 2004 Sch.34 para.5. In relation to registered pension schemes, the scheme administrator is liable for such charges.
[87] ITEPA 2003 s.579C.
[88] See Ch.20. The ITEPA 2003 member payment charges are chargeable under Pt 9 Ch.5A rather than Pt 9 Ch.4, so they are not taxable on the remittance basis.

*Double tax treaties*

If a payment (or part of a payment) to or in respect of a member of an RNUKS would give rise to a member payment charge were it not for the operation of double taxation arrangements, the payment: (a) is "pension" for the purposes of ITEPA 2003 Pt 9 Ch.4; and (b) is treated as included in the list in ITEPA 2003 s.576A of payments that are relevant withdrawals.[89] The effect of this is that the provisions relating to temporary non-residents apply to such a payment. This can only have any application to the ITEPA 2003 member payment charges, because the FA 2004 charges are not income for tax purposes and so are not within the scope of any double taxation arrangements.[90]

**30-075**

*Credit for overseas tax paid*

Where an individual is subject to a member payment charge in respect of a payment and the payment also gives rise to overseas tax (in the jurisdiction in which the individual is resident, for example), the member payment charge is reduced by the foreign tax paid. Where foreign tax is paid after the member payment charge has been paid an appropriate adjustment is made in the individual's liability to tax (by way of discharge or repayment of the UK tax).[91]

**30-076**

### Interaction with the EFRBS provisions

Many RNUKS are EFRBS.[92] Where that is the case, the provision of benefits may be chargeable in accordance with ITEPA 2003 s.394. However, benefits "chargeable to tax" under Sch.34 are expressly not "relevant benefits" and are therefore not within the scope of s.394.[93] For the reasons given in Ch.35, it is likely that this exclusion applies to any benefit to which the member payment charges can apply. Given that the member payment charges apply only to a payment to or in respect of a relieved member or transfer member of an RNUKS if the UK residency condition is satisfied, it seems unlikely that such a benefit could properly be described as being "chargeable to tax by virtue of Sch.34" unless the UK residency condition is satisfied. However the contrary is not unarguable.

**30-077**

### Interaction with disguised remuneration provisions

ITEPA 2003 Pt 7A Ch.2 does not apply to a relevant step if the subject of the relevant step is a sum of money or asset which represents or which has arisen or derived from a UK tax-relieved fund under an RNUKS or a relevant transfer fund under an RNUKS.[94]

**30-078**

# THE TAXABLE PROPERTY PROVISIONS

In relation to registered pension schemes that are investment-regulated pension schemes, a deemed unauthorised payment arises under FA 2004 s.174A where the

**30-079**

---

[89] FA 2004 Sch.34 para.5A.
[90] HMRC agree at PTM113210.
[91] FA 2004 Sch.34 para.6.
[92] Migrant member relief, corresponding relief and the exemption in ITEPA 2003 s.307 all have an employment context and so the schemes will usually constitute EFRBS.
[93] ITEPA 2003 s.393B(2)(b).
[94] The Employment Income Provided Through Third Parties (Excluded Relevant Steps) Regulations 2011 (SI 2011/2696) reg.3(1). See Ch.27.

scheme directly or indirectly holds an interest in taxable property for the purposes of an arrangement relating to a member under the scheme, and ss.185A–185I impose a scheme sanction charge where such a scheme receives any income (including deemed income) or gains relating to taxable property. Subject to the modifications described below, the taxable property provisions apply to a transfer member of an RNUKS in relation to deemed payments which are referable to the member's "taxable asset transfer fund" (TATF) or "ring-fenced taxable asset transfer fund" (RFTATF) under the RNUKS.[95]

**30-080** There is no express requirement for the RNUKS to be an investment-regulated pension scheme before the taxable property provisions can apply. HMRC take the view that an RNUKS must be "the equivalent of an investment-regulated pension scheme".[96] This is presumably on the basis that Sch.34 para.7A only authorises HMRC to make regulations that impose a liability "in the same or similar circumstances" to those in which a member would be liable under a registered pension scheme.

### TAFT and RFTATF

**30-081** A member's TATF is the total of: (a) the amount crystallised on the transfer from a registered pension scheme to the RNUKS;[97] and (b) so much of the member's TATF under any other RNUKS as has been transferred to the current RNUKS without being subject to an unauthorised payments charge.[98] A member's RFTATF under a ring-fenced transfer fund is the total of: (a) the value of the sums and assets transferred as a result of an original relevant transfer (see above) from a registered pension scheme to the RNUKS; and (b) so much of the member's RFTATF under any other RNUKS as has been transferred to the RNUKS without being subject to an unauthorised payments charge.[99]

**30-082** So the member's TATF or RFTATF is limited to so much of the fund as was formerly held for the purposes of a registered pension scheme before being transferred to an RNUKS. The taxable property provisions have no application to a member's UK tax-relieved fund. The amount of the member's relevant transfer fund or ring-fenced transfer fund may exceed the amount of his TATF or RFTATF, because the member's relevant transfer fund or ring-fenced transfer fund could also represent UK tax relieved funds contributed to an unregistered pension scheme (e.g. as a result of migrant member relief) before being transferred to the RNUKS.

**30-083** Given that a registered pension scheme can transfer sums or assets only to another registered pension scheme or a QROPS without being subject to an unauthorised payments charge, the taxable property provisions can apply only to RNUKS that are QROPS (or former QROPS).

### The modifications

**30-084** The two main modifications that are made to the taxable property provisions are: (a) the scheme chargeable payments that would ordinarily arise under FA 2004

---

[95] SI 2006/207 reg.4A (made pursuant to the power in FA 2004 Sch.34 para.7A). The "taxable property provisions" are: (a) FA 2004 s.173(7A) (exception from benefit charge where taxable property held by IRPS); (b) s.174A and Sch.29A; (c) ss.185A–185I (income and gains from taxable property); (d) s.273ZA (member liability for scheme sanction charge where pension scheme non-UK resident); (e) Sch.36 paras 37A–37I (transitional provisions); and (f) regulations made under Sch.29A para.37 or Sch.34 para.7A.
[96] See PTM113220.
[97] Meaning the amounts of the sums and the market value of the assets so transferred.
[98] SI 2006/207 reg.3A.
[99] SI 2006/207 reg.3C.

ss.185A–185I are deemed to be unauthorised payments; and (b) a different method is prescribed for calculating the amount of consideration given where some or all of the consideration is rent.[100]

*FA 2004 ss.185A–185I*

The scheme chargeable payment provisions in FA 2004 ss.185A–185I do not apply to RNUKS (because they are not member payment charges). However during such time as an "appropriated asset" forms the whole or part of a transfer member's TATF or RFTATF, the RNUKS is deemed to make unauthorised payments to that member equal in amount to the scheme chargeable payments which would have arisen under ss.185A–185I if the RNUKS were a registered pension scheme.[101] The transfer member is liable to pay the unauthorised payments charge in respect of such deemed payments.[102] Where the scheme's interest in taxable property is not wholly referable to the transfer member's TATF or RFTATF, the amount of the unauthorised payment is proportionately reduced.[103]

30-085

*The consideration is rent*

If an RNUKS acquires an interest in taxable property in certain circumstances[104] and some or all of the consideration given for the acquisition is rent, the amount of the consideration (or the part that is rent) is not the *relevant rental value* of the property (as it ordinarily would be under Sch.29A para.34(2)).[105] Instead, the total amount of rent paid during a year is deemed for the purposes of the taxable property provisions, as being consideration paid by the pension scheme or other person who acquired the interest, for the grant of a lease for the period for which the rent is paid.[106]

30-086

*UK residency condition not relevant*

It is irrelevant whether the member satisfies the residency condition in Sch.34 para.2, because the taxable property provisions are expressly not member pay-

30-087

---

[100] In addition, when applying Sch.29A para.15 to an RNUKS, the term *insurance company* is extended by SI 2006/207 reg.4C to include any person resident in a country or territory outside the EEA whose business consists of, or includes, the effecting or carrying out of contracts of long-term insurance (within the meaning in The Financial Services and Markets Act 2000 (Regulated Activities) Order 2001 (SI 2001/544) Sch.1 Pt 2) and who is regulated in the conduct of that business by the government of that country or territory or a body established under the law of that country or territory for the purpose of regulating such business. This is therefore more restrictive than the "Non-EEA annuity provider" concept considered above. Schedule 29A para.15 provides that a person does not hold an interest in taxable property directly where certain conditions are met, one of which is that the person is entitled to receive the payment by virtue of a policy or contract issued by an insurance company (see Ch.9).

[101] See Ch.9.

[102] SI 2006/207 reg.4B(2).

[103] SI 2006/207 reg.4B(3).

[104] The circumstances are the one of the following applies: (a) the interest in the property is acquired because the pension scheme or another person comes to hold the interest directly; (b) the interest in the property is acquired because the pension scheme or another person comes to hold an interest in a person who already holds the interest in the property directly or indirectly; or (c) the interest in the property is treated as acquired by the pension scheme by virtue of Sch.29A para.27 (which applies where property becomes taxable property otherwise than by reason of its conversion or adaption as residential property) or para.28 (which applies where the scheme holds the interest indirectly and there is an increase in the extent of the interest).

[105] See Ch.9.

[106] SI 2006/207 reg.4D.

ment provisions.[107] Accordingly, if an RNUKS directly or indirectly holds taxable property referable to a member's TATF or RFTATF it will always give rise to tax charges. It is therefore common, once the member ceases to satisfy the UK residency condition, to transfer his sums and assets from the RNUKS to a scheme that is not an RNUKS. The taxable property provisions will not apply to the transferee scheme even if the member subsequently satisfies the UK residency condition. The fact that the sums or assets comprising a member's UK tax-relieved fund or relevant transfer fund (or TATF or RFTATF) are transferred from the RNUKS to the transferee scheme does not cause the transferee scheme to become an RNUKS, provided that the transferee scheme is not a QROPS.

### Liability

**30-088** An unauthorised payment arising under the taxable property provisions is subject to the unauthorised payments charge and surcharge in the usual way (see above).

### Attributing payments to particular funds

*Payments made before 6 April 2017*

**30-089** The taxable property provisions can apply only in relation to deemed payments which are referable to the member's TATF or RFTATF. Once the member's UK tax-relieved fund (if any) is exhausted, special rules apply to attribute the deemed unauthorised payments to particular funds under the RNUKS. The following Rules apply (with an earlier Rule applying in preference to a later Rule).[108]

**30-090** **Rule 1** Where an RNUKS is deemed to make an unauthorised payment by virtue of FA 2004 s.174A,[109] the deemed payment is treated as being made out of the member's relevant transfer fund and TATF, but the interest in taxable property "represents" the deemed payment and forms part of the member's relevant transfer fund and TATF, up to an amount equal to the amount of that payment. The taxable property acquired, improved or converted in these circumstances is referred to an "appropriated asset". The effect of this is that the deemed unauthorised payment reduces the value of the relevant transfer fund or TATF, and the appropriated asset then forms part of the relevant transfer fund and TATF so there is no overall reduction in the value of the member's relevant transfer fund or TATF.

**30-091** For example, where an RNUKS has no UK tax-relieved fund, but has a relevant transfer fund and TATF of £250,000 and it then spends £500,000 converting scheme property to residential property, that will give rise to a deemed unauthorised payment of £500,000 but the deemed payment under s.174A cannot exceed the amount of the member's TATF (i.e. £250,000). Therefore this will give rise to a deemed unauthorised payment of £250,000. The taxable property is an appropriated asset, but only up to £250,000, which remains within the member's relevant transfer fund and TATF.

**30-092** If both the member's UK tax-relieved fund and relevant transfer fund are nil, the payment is treated as made out of the member's ring-fenced transfer fund and RFTATF, and the appropriated asset forms part of those funds.

---

[107] FA 2004 Sch.34 para.1(4)(a).
[108] SI 2006/207 reg.4(3). Also see the examples at the bottom of PTM113240.
[109] FA 2004 s.174A applies where an investment-regulated pension scheme acquires or improves taxable property, or where property held by an investment-regulated pension scheme is converted or adapted to become residential property. In each case, the provisions apply only if the property is held for the purposes of an arrangement relating to a member under the scheme.

# THE TAXABLE PROPERTY PROVISIONS

**Rule 2** If some or all of an appropriated asset (or an interest in a vehicle through which the scheme holds the interest in the taxable property indirectly) is transferred from the RNUKS to another pension scheme, the transfer is deemed to be a transfer of the whole or part of the member's relevant transfer fund and TATF, or ring-fenced transfer fund and RFTATF as the case may be, (limited to the amount of the unauthorised payment) to that other scheme. If the transferee scheme is an RNUKS and the transfer is not subject to an unauthorised payments charge then the appropriated asset form parts of the member's TATF or RFTATF under the transferee scheme.

**30-093**

**Rule 3** If an RNUKS disposes of all or part of an appropriated asset (or an interest in a vehicle through which the scheme holds the interest in the taxable property indirectly), then any other property which directly or indirectly represents proceeds of either of those interests (limited to the amount of the unauthorised payment) forms part of the member's relevant transfer fund and TATF (or ring-fenced transfer fund and RFTATF as the case may be). However, this does not apply if the disposal is to another pension scheme (because Rule 2 applies instead).

**30-094**

**Rule 4** Rule 4 applies to payments made by the RNUKS to or in respect of the member, other than a transfer of an interest in taxable property (or an interest in a vehicle through which the scheme holds the interest in the taxable property indirectly), and payments deemed to be made under FA 2004 s.174A. Rule 4 therefore relates to any payment (or deemed payment) to or in respect of a member that is not within Rules 1 to 3.

**30-095**

So far as the member's relevant transfer fund and TATF are not represented by appropriated assets, where the amount of a member's relevant transfer fund exceeds the amount of his TATF, a payment to which Rule 4 applies is, to the extent of that excess, treated as made out of his relevant transfer fund (but not his TATF) and as reducing his relevant transfer fund. After that, such payments are made out of the member's relevant transfer fund and TATF in priority to any other fund under that scheme, and reduce (but not below nil) the amount of the relevant transfer fund and TATF. The same applies where the amount of a member's ring-fenced transfer fund exceeds the amount of his RFTATF. Once the funds are of equal value, payments are made out of the member's ring-fenced transfer fund and RFTATF in priority to any other fund under that scheme, and reduce (but not below nil) the amount of the ring-fenced transfer fund and RFTATF.

**30-096**

*Payments and crystallisation events since 6 April 2017*

Since 6 April 2017 the payments and crystallisation events referred to above and following reduce a member's TATF and RFTATF. If the payment is a transfer, to the extent that the transfer is a payment treated as made by virtue of s.174A, it is attributed in the following order of priority: (a) the member's RFTATF and ring-fenced transfer fund in priority of the ring-fenced transfer fund with the latest key date to the earliest key date of the fund; (b) if the RFTATF is nil, the member's relevant transfer fund and TATF.

**30-097**

If the payment is an unauthorised payment by virtue of s.174A, or a payment other than a transfer, treated as made by virtue of s.174A, it is treated as referable to the member's UK funds in the following order of priority: (a) the payment is first treated as referable to the member's relevant transfer fund and TATF; (b) if the member's TATF is nil, or has been reduced to nil, the payment shall be treated as referable to the member's ring-fenced transfer fund, in priority of the ring-fenced transfer fund with the earliest key date to the latest key date, and the RFTATF.

**30-098**

702     RELEVANT NON-UK SCHEMES

30-099     Where a payment or crystallisation event is referable to the member's TATF or RFTATF, the funds are reduced in accordance with the four Rules referred to above.

## THE ANNUAL ALLOWANCE PROVISIONS

30-100     A modified version of the annual allowance provisions applies in relation to an individual who is a "currently relieved member" of a "currently relieved non-UK pension scheme" (and its scheme manager) as if the currently relieved pension scheme were a registered pension scheme.[110] An RNUKS is a currently relieved non-UK pension scheme if RNUKS Tax Relief is given in respect of member or employer contributions paid during the tax year.[111] A currently relieved member is a member who has paid some of the tax-relieved contributions or who has been exempt under ITEPA 2003 s.307 in respect of his employer's provision.[112]

**The modifications**

30-101     The modifications are set out at FA 2004 Sch.34 paras 9–12. They do not substantively change the annual allowance provisions as they apply to registered pension schemes;[113] they are generally required in order to make the usual annual allowance provisions make sense in the context of RNUKS.

*Cash balance and defined benefits arrangements*

30-102     When applying FA 2004 ss.230(1) and 234(1), the increase in the value of the individual's rights under a cash balance or defined benefits arrangement is the greater of: (a) the "appropriate fraction" of what it otherwise would be; and (b) the amount of any contributions paid under the arrangement during the tax year by or on behalf of the individual (otherwise than by an employer) in respect of which RNUKS Tax Relief other than under ITEPA 2003 s.307 is given.[114] The appropriate fraction is "(TE + TSI)/EI", where: *EI* is the total amount of employment income of the individual from any relevant employment[115] or employments for the tax year, excluding any such income which is exempt as a result of any exemption in ITEPA 2003 Pt 4 or elsewhere;[116] *TE* is so much of EI as constitutes taxable earnings[117] from any such employment; and *TSI* is so much of EI as constitutes taxable specific income[118] from any such employment.

30-103     When uprating the opening value under cash balance or defined benefits arrangements, instead of applying the CPI[119] one applies the "relevant index". If there is an index of the movement of consumer prices maintained or officially recognised by the government of the country or territory in which the recognised overseas

---

[110] FA 2004 Sch.34 para.8.
[111] FA 2004 Sch.34 para.8(3).
[112] FA 2004 Sch.34 para.8(4).
[113] The annual allowance provisions are explained in detail in Ch.7.
[114] FA 2004 Sch.34 para.10.
[115] An employment is a relevant employment if it is an employment with an employer who is a sponsoring employer in relation to the currently relieved non-UK pension scheme.
[116] See ITEPA 2003 s.8.
[117] Within the meaning of ITEPA 2003 s.10(2).
[118] Within the meaning of ITEPA 2003 s.10(3)–(5).
[119] See s.231(1) for cash balance and s.235 for defined benefits schemes.

scheme[120] is established, that index is the relevant index. If there is no such index, the CPI is the relevant index.[121]

*Other money purchase arrangements*

**30-104** When applying s.233(1)(a), "relievable pension contributions" means those contributions in respect of which RNUKS Tax Relief other than under ITEPA 2003 s.307 is given. When applying s.233(1)(b), the contributions paid in respect of the individual by his employer means the "appropriate fraction" of contributions so paid.[122] The purpose of the appropriate fraction concept is to exclude from the pension input amount those employer contributions that are deemed to relate to income which is not chargeable to UK tax. The appropriate fraction is "(TE + TSI)/EI", where: *EI* is the total amount of employment income of the individual from any employment or employments with the employer for the tax year, excluding any such income which is exempt income;[123] *TE* is so much of EI as constitutes taxable earnings[124] from any such employment; and *TSI* is so much of EI as constitutes taxable specific income[125] from any such employment.

**30-105** HMRC provide the following example:[126]

"Mark has received migrant member relief on his contributions of £15,000 to an overseas pension scheme. Mark's employer has contributed £25,000 to that scheme in respect of him, and Mark is exempted from liability to UK income tax on that contribution under section 307 Income Tax (Earnings and Pensions) Act 2003 (ITEPA 2003).

Mark has total income (EI) from his employment with the employer in that year of £125,000 (including non-remitted relevant foreign earnings not chargeable in that year but excluding the employer contribution). Only £95,000 of that income is UK taxable earnings (TE) under section 10(2) ITEPA 2003. Mark also has £5,000 taxable specific income which is UK taxable under Part 7 ITEPA in relation to an employment related share option scheme.

The appropriate fraction of the employer contribution is
(TE + TSI) / EI
(95,000 + £5,000) / 125,000 = 4/5 or 80 per cent
Mark's pension input amount in respect of the overseas pension scheme is Mark's individual contributions plus the appropriate fraction of the employer contribution.
£15,000 + £20,000 (25,000 x 4/5) = £35,000
Mark's pension input amount is £35,000."

*Member first flexibly accesses pension savings*

**30-106** For the purposes of determining whether a member has first flexibly accessed pension rights, one is required to take into account years prior to when the scheme was a currently relieved non-UK pension scheme.[127] In the following circumstances, FA 2004 s.227G (which sets out the five circumstances in which an individual flexibly accesses his pension rights) applies in the individual's case as if the scheme, so far as relating to the individual's relevant transfer fund or ring-fenced transfer

---

[120] "Recognised overseas scheme" is not a defined term. Presumably this should be a reference to the RNUKS.
[121] SI 2006/207 regs 9 and 10.
[122] FA 2004 Sch.34 para.11.
[123] See ITEPA 2003 s.8.
[124] Within the meaning of ITEPA 2003 s.10(2).
[125] Within the meaning of ITEPA 2003 s.10(3)–(5).
[126] At PTM113330.
[127] FA 2004 Sch.34 para.9ZA.

funds under the scheme, were a registered pension scheme at the particular time.[128] The circumstances are that, at any particular time: (a) the individual is a transfer member of the RNUKS; (b) the scheme is or has been a QROPS; and (c) the particular time is not in a tax year in relation to which the scheme is a currently relieved non-UK pension scheme of which the individual is a currently relieved member.

*Hybrid arrangements*

**30-107** FA 2004 s.237 applies to RNUKS in the same way as to registered pension schemes, except that one applies the modified version of the annual allowance provisions set out above in order to determine the greatest pension input amount.

*Carry forwards of unused annual allowance*

**30-108** FA 2004 s.228A allows a member of a registered pension scheme to carry forwards any unused annual allowance from the three immediately preceding tax years. Section 228A applies to a currently relieved member of a currently relieved non-UK pension scheme by virtue of Sch.34 paras 8–12. Where the individual is a currently relieved member of a currently relieved non-UK pension scheme, and was a member (but not a currently relieved member) of the scheme in relation to any one or more of the three immediately preceding tax years (referred to as a "relevant tax year"), s.228A has effect in relation to the individual for the tax year as it would if the individual had been a currently relieved member of the pension scheme for the relevant tax year (or each of the relevant tax years) and Sch.34 paras 10 and 11 were omitted.[129] The effect of omitting paras 10 and 11 is that the "appropriate fraction" does not apply, so employer contributions that might otherwise be disregarded are included (thereby reducing the amount which may be carried forwards).

**30-109** Where an individual is a member of a registered pension scheme in relation to a tax year, and was a currently relieved member of a currently relieved non-UK pension scheme in relation to any one or more of the three immediately preceding tax years (a "relevant tax year"), s.228A has effect in relation to the individual for the tax year as it would if the currently relieved non-UK pension scheme had been a registered pension scheme for the relevant tax year (or each of the relevant tax years).[130]

*Pension input amounts expressed in a foreign currency*

**30-110** PTM113330 provides that:

"If the date on which each contribution was made is known then the spot rate for that date of payment should be used, or each contribution should be added up and the total converted using the spot rate for either:

(a) 6 April (the spot rate at the start end of the pension input period), or
(b) 5 April (the spot rate at the end of the pension input period), or
(c) the average exchange rate over the entire pension input period.

However, the chosen method must be used on a consistent basis. If the exact date on which each contribution was paid is not known, the same spot rate that was used to convert

---

[128] FA 2004 Sch.34 para.9ZB.
[129] FA 2004 Sch.34 para.9A.
[130] FA 2004 Sch.34 para.9B.

the salary on which the contribution was based should be used. That salary may have been converted using the spot rate for the dates on which it was received or another method that HMRC has agreed in the particular case."

This does not appear to be based on any legislation so it is a statement of HMRC practice. **30-111**

*Enhancement of LS and LS&DB allowances*

The provisions of Sch.36 relating to the enhancement of an individual's LS allowance and LS&DB allowance ("the enhancement of allowances provisions") apply to an individual who is a relieved member of a relieved non-UK pension scheme as if the relieved non-UK pension scheme were a registered pension scheme.[131] **30-112**

A pension scheme is a relieved non-UK pension scheme if: (a) relief from tax has been given in respect of contributions paid under the pension scheme by virtue of Sch.33 (overseas pension schemes: migrant member relief); (b) relief from tax has been so given at any time after 5 April 2006 under double tax arrangements; or (c) a member of the pension scheme has been, or members of the pension scheme have been, exempt from liability to tax by virtue of ITEPA 2003 s.307 (exemption for provision made by employer for retirement or death benefit) in respect of provision made under the pension scheme at any time after 5 April 2006 when the pension scheme was an overseas pension scheme.

An individual is a relieved member of a relieved non-UK pension scheme if: (a) any of the contributions in respect of which relief has been given as mentioned in subpara.(2)(a) or (b) were contributions paid by or on behalf of, or in respect of, the individual; or (b) the individual is the member, or one of the members, who has been exempt from liability to tax as mentioned in subpara.(2)(c).

**Liability**

The individual is liable for the annual allowance charge, and his residency and domicile status are irrelevant.[132] As with the other charges under FA 2004 Pt 4 the chargeable amount does not constitute income for tax purposes[133] and so the annual allowance charge is not within the scope of any double tax treaties. Individuals who are liable to an annual allowance charge should declare it on their self-assessment tax return for the tax year in which the annual allowance charge arises. The "scheme pays" option applies in the same way as for registered pension schemes,[134] and the process under which the scheme manager of an RNUKS must notify HMRC is the same (using form APSS210). **30-113**

# THE OVERSEAS TRANSFER CHARGE

The overseas transfer charge is considered in more detail in Ch.12. The main provision (in s.244AC) imposes a charge where: (a) a relieved relevant non-UK **30-114**

---

[131] FA 2004 Sch.34 para.12A.
[132] FA 2004 s.237A.
[133] FA 2004 s.227(5).
[134] For the "scheme pays" option, see para.7-058.

scheme transfer is made from an RNUKS to a QROPS; or (b) an "onward transfer" is made during the "relevant period" for the "original transfer".[135]

With effect from 6 April 2024, the overseas transfer charge also arises where the amount transferred by a relieved relevant non-UK scheme transfer to a QROPS, or an onwards transfer, exceeds the member's available "overseas transfer allowance".

### "Relieved relevant non-UK scheme transfer"

**30-115** A "relieved relevant non-UK scheme transfer" means a transfer, other than a "block transfer", of sums or assets held for the purposes of, or representing accrued rights under, an arrangement under a relieved relevant non-UK scheme in relation to a relieved member of the scheme so as to become held for the purposes of, or to represent rights under, an arrangement under a QROPS in relation to that person as a member of that QROPS.[136]

A "relieved relevant non-UK scheme" means a pension scheme that is an RNUKS in respect of which at least one of paras (a)–(c) of Sch.34 para.1(5) applies.

**30-116** A transfer is "a block transfer" in relation to a member of a pension scheme if it involves the transfer, in a single transaction, of all the sums and assets held for the purposes of, or representing accrued rights under, the arrangements under the scheme which relate to the member and at least one other member of the scheme.

**30-117** An individual is "a relieved member" of a relieved relevant non-UK scheme if: (i) any of the contributions in respect of which relief has been given as mentioned in para.(a) or (b) of the definition of "relevant non-UK scheme" in para.1(5) of Sch.34 were contributions paid by or on behalf of, or in respect of, the individual; or (ii) the individual is the member, or one of the members, who has been exempt from liability to tax as mentioned in para.(c) of that definition.

### The main provisions: s.244AC

**30-118** Subject to the exclusions described in Ch.12, the overseas transfer charge arises where a relieved relevant non-UK scheme transfer is made from an RNUKS to a QROPS.[137] These provisions also apply where an onward transfer is made from a QROPS during the relevant period for the original transfer (see Ch.33). The overseas transfer charge does not apply to any transfer which gives rise to the unauthorised payments charge.

### Transfers exceeding available overseas transfer allowance: s.244IA

**30-119** From 6 April 2024, the overseas transfer charge also arises in two circumstances where the transfer exceeds the member's available overseas transfer allowance.[138] A member's "overseas transfer allowance" is an amount equal to the member's LS&DB allowance.[139]

---

[135] FA 2004 s.244A. For onwards transfers, see Ch.33.
[136] FA 2004 s.244AB(1).
[137] FA 2004 s.244AA.
[138] FA 2004 s.244IA. This charge also applies to "relieved relevant non-UK scheme transfers" (i.e. transfers from RNUKS which have benefitted from UK tax relief): see Ch.30.
[139] FA 2004 s.244IB.

# THE LIFETIME ALLOWANCE (PRE-6 APRIL 2024)

Prior to 6 April 2024, a modified version of the lifetime allowance provisions applied to a "relieved member" of a "relieved non-UK pension scheme" as if the scheme were a registered pension scheme.[140] A relieved non-UK pension scheme is a scheme in respect of which contributions have benefitted from RNUKS Tax Relief, and a relieved member is a member who has benefited from such relief or exemption. The lifetime allowance provisions therefore had no application to transfer members as such.

**30-120**

## The modifications

### The amount crystallising on a BCE

Where a BCE occurred under a relieved non-UK pension scheme, the amount which crystallised was not the full value; it was only the "untested portion" of the "relevant relieved amount" immediately before the BCE.[141] The relevant relieved amount was the total of all of the member's pension input amounts for the period from 6 April 2006 until the BCE occured, calculated using the modified annual allowance provisions set out above.[142] The intention was that the lifetime allowance provisions should apply only to UK tax-relieved funds. If the BCE occured part way through a tax year, the part of the year was treated as if it were a full tax year. The untested portion of the relevant relieved amount was so much of the relevant relieved amount as exceeded the total of the amounts crystallised as a result of previous BCEs in relation to the individual and the relieved non-UK pension scheme. If there had been no previous BCEs, the untested portion was the whole of the relevant relieved amount.

**30-121**

### Paragraph 15 BCEs

A relieved member of a relieved non-UK pension scheme could elect for a BCE to occur under Sch.34 para.15 (a "para.15 BCE"). The amount crystallised by a para.15 BCE was equal to the untested portion of the relevant relievable amount. The event was deemed to occur on a specified date by giving notice to HMRC. HMRC suggest that the purpose of the para.15 BCE was to encourage individuals who are leaving the UK to get their affairs in order (and pay any resulting tax charges) sooner rather than later.[143] The para.15 BCE election did not affect the application of the member payment provisions (or the annual allowance provisions).

**30-122**

### Block transfers

BCE 8 occurred when scheme funds were transferred from a registered pension scheme to a QROPS, and so (by virtue of Sch.34 para.13(1)) BCE 8 occurred when funds relating to a relieved member were transferred from a relieved non-UK pension scheme to a QROPS. However BCE 8 was expressly disapplied in respect of a member of a relieved non-UK pension scheme if the transfer was a block

**30-123**

---

[140] FA 2004 Sch.34 para.13(1). The modifications are in Sch.34 paras 14–19.
[141] FA 2004 Sch.34 para.14(2).
[142] FA 2004 Sch.34 para.14(3). This means that in relation to an other money purchase arrangement, only contributions are included (investment growth is disregarded).
[143] PTM113430.

transfer.[144] A block transfer is a single transfer (in one transaction), of all of the sums and assets in the relieved non-UK pension scheme relating to the member plus at least one other member of that scheme. The other member need not be a relieved member. The block transfer provisions were aimed at situations where a scheme was wound up or where members were obliged to transfer to a new scheme because of a company take-over or re-organisation, but this need not be the case.

30-124   Where a block transfer took place, the transferee scheme was deemed to be a relieved non-UK pension scheme, the member was deemed to be a relieved member of that scheme, and the amount transferred (which would otherwise have crystallised under BCE 8) was treated as part of his relevant relieved amount in the transferee scheme for the purposes of any subsequent BCEs under that scheme.[145]

*Modification of BCE 3*

30-125   BCE 3 applied where the annual rate of a scheme pension was increased above a permitted amount. The relevant provisions[146] referred to the RPI. SI 2006/207 reg.16 modified these provisions so that the references to the RPI were read as references to the *relevant index*. If there was an index of the movement of retail prices maintained or officially recognised by the government of the country or territory in which the recognised overseas scheme[147] was established, that is the relevant index. If there was no such index, the relevant index is the RPI.

*Relevant valuation factor*

30-126   FA 2004 s.276(2) provided that HMRC and the scheme administrator may agree to a relevant factor of greater than 20. This was modified to refer to the scheme manager instead of the scheme administrator.[148]

**UK residency exemption not relevant**

30-127   The lifetime allowance provisions applied to an RNUKS even after the member has ceased to satisfy the UK residency condition.

**Liability**

30-128   The relieved member of the relieved non-UK pension scheme was solely liable for any lifetime allowance charge arising.[149] His residency and domicile status were irrelevant. As with the other charges under FA 2004 Pt 4 the chargeable amount did not constitute income for tax purposes and so the lifetime allowance charge was not within the scope of any double tax treaties. Individuals who were liable to a lifetime allowance charge were required to declare it on their self-assessment tax return for the tax year in which the BCE occured.

---

[144] FA 2004 Sch.34 para.16.
[145] FA 2004 Sch.34 para.18.
[146] In FA 2004 Sch.32 paras 9A–13.
[147] "Recognised overseas scheme" is not a defined term. Presumably this should be a reference to the RNUKS.
[148] SI 2006/207 reg.12.
[149] FA 2004 s.217, as modified by Sch.34 para.17. The charge was removed with effect from 6 April 2023.

# CHAPTER 31

# Overseas Pension Schemes

## TABLE OF CONTENTS

| | |
|---|---|
| Introduction and overview | 31-001 |
|     Development | 31-005 |
|     Contrast with QNUPS | 31-006 |
| What is an overseas pension scheme? | 31-007 |
|     "Established" outside the UK | 31-008 |
|     The requirements prescribed by regulations | 31-009 |
|         International organisations | 31-010 |
|     Regulation 2(2) | 31-011 |
|         Regulatory bodies | 31-013 |
|     Regulation 2(3) | 31-014 |
|         Condition 1 | 31-015 |
|         Condition 2 | 31-021 |
|             "A system of taxation of personal income" | 31-023 |
|             "Tax relief is available in respect of pensions" | 31-024 |
|         Condition 2(a) and (b) | 31-025 |
|             Summary | 31-034 |
|             "Serious ill-health" | 31-035 |
|         Condition 3 | 31-036 |
| Taxation | 31-039 |
|     Capital gains tax | 31-039 |
|     Inheritance tax | 31-040 |
|     Income tax | 31-041 |
|     Interaction with RNUKS provisions | 31-042 |

## INTRODUCTION AND OVERVIEW

If a pension scheme satisfies the requirements of an "overseas pension scheme": **31-001**

(a) Gains accruing on the disposal of investments held for the purposes of the scheme are exempt from CGT.[1]

(b) A "relevant lump sum" paid under the scheme may be wholly or partly exempt from tax.[2] Up to 25% of a member's fund under an overseas pension scheme may be paid to a UK resident as a tax-free lump sum (even if the overseas pension scheme is an EFRBS), and death benefits paid under an overseas pension scheme in respect of a UK resident member who dies before reaching age 75 are expressly free of tax.

---

[1] TCGA 1992 s.271(1A).
[2] ITEPA 2003 s.574A(3) (step 3).

(c) The scheme may, if certain further steps are taken, qualify as a QROPS or a qualifying overseas pension scheme.[3]

**31-002** The relevant provisions are in FA 2004 s.150(7) and the Pension Schemes (Categories of Country and Requirements for Overseas Pension Schemes and Recognised Overseas Pension Schemes) Regulations 2006 (SI 2006/206).

**31-003** In outline, a pension scheme is an overseas pension scheme if it satisfies all of the following requirements:

(a) It is established outside the UK.
(b) It is either: (i) regulated by a local regulatory body; or (ii) there is no local body which regulates the type of scheme in question (i.e. either occupational or non-occupational). Unregulated non-occupational schemes must either be established in the EU/EEA, or the provider must be regulated for the purposes of establishing the scheme in question.
(c) Membership is genuinely open to local residents.
(d) The local jurisdiction provides tax relief in respect of pensions and either: (i) tax relief is not available to the member in respect of contributions; or (ii) most benefit are subject to tax.
(e) It is approved, recognised, or registered, with the local tax authorities as a pension scheme.

**31-004** Special rules apply to non-UK schemes established by international organisations and to certain Australian schemes. Each of the above requirements is considered in detail below.

**Development**

**31-005** The provisions were introduced with effect from 6 April 2006, and amended significantly in 2012 and 2017. Prior to 6 April 2012, it was unnecessary for an overseas pension scheme to be approved, recognised, or registered with the local tax authority as a pension scheme provided that: (a) no system existed for approval, recognition or registration;[4] (b) at least 70% of a member's UK tax-relieved scheme funds would be designated for the purpose of providing the member with an income for life; and (c) the benefits payable to the member under the scheme were payable no earlier than they would be if pension rule 1 in FA 2004 s.165 applied. Since 6 April 2012, an overseas pension scheme must be approved, recognised, or registered with the local tax authorities as a pension scheme. On 6 April 2017 the requirements relating to overseas pension schemes established by international organisations and overseas public service schemes were generally relaxed, and all requirements to use 70% of a member's fund to provide an income for life were removed.

**Contrast with QNUPS**

**31-006** All QNUPS are overseas pension schemes, but, since 6 April 2017, not all overseas pension schemes are QNUPS. Prior to that date, the requirements were identical. On that date, the regulations were amended to reflect the flexibilities avail-

---

[3] For QROPS see Ch.33; for qualifying overseas pension schemes see Ch.24.
[4] The meaning of this requirement, in the context of a jurisdiction which has a system of approval but not relating to the type of scheme in question, was considered in *TMF Trustees Singapore Ltd v HMRC* [2012] EWCA Civ 192 at [35]–[46].

able to money purchase registered pension schemes since April 2015[5] by removing all requirements to use 70% of a member's fund to provide him with an income for life. As the QNUPS regulations have not been amended, the following differences now exist:

(a) If there is no local regulator of occupational pension schemes, an occupational pension scheme may be an overseas pension scheme but it cannot be a QNUPS unless it is established in the EU/EEA or it satisfies the 70% income for life requirement.
(b) An unregulated scheme can be a QNUPS only if there is no regulator of occupational pension schemes or non-occupational pension schemes, whereas it may be an overseas pension scheme provided that there is no local regulator of the particular category of scheme in question.
(c) The provisions relating to schemes established by international organisations are different, and again include a 70% income for life requirement for QNUPS but not for overseas pension schemes.

## WHAT IS AN OVERSEAS PENSION SCHEME?

Pursuant to FA 2004 s.150(7) an overseas pension scheme is a pension scheme[6] (other than a registered pension scheme) which:  **31-007**

(a) is established in a country or territory outside the UK; and
(b) satisfies any requirements prescribed for the purposes of s.150(7) by regulations made by HMRC.

### "Established" outside the UK

It is likely that a pension scheme is "established" in the country or territory in which its main administration is carried out.[7] This is the place in which any decisions relating to the administration of a scheme are made.[8] Activities which are purely incidental to the administration of the scheme or could reasonably be expected to be carried out by a third party should not be material. In *Macklin v*  **31-008**

---

[5] Introduced primarily by TPA 2014.
[6] "Pension scheme" has the same meaning as in FA 2004 s.150(1). See Ch.2.
[7] HMRC's views are set out at PTM112200: "Normally, a scheme will be treated as established in the country where its registered office is and main administration is carried out. If there is no registered office, then the location where its main administration is carried out will guide matters. The scheme's location of main administration is where the scheme's decisions are made. In the case of a trust-based scheme, that would normally be determined by reference to where the scheme trustees are resident as that is where the decision-making responsibilities in respect of the scheme will lie. It should be noted that the country in which a scheme is established may change if the location of the main administration and decision-making changes. In such a case, the scheme manager would have to revisit whether the scheme still meets the requirements to be an overseas pension scheme. The scheme manager is the person or persons administering, or responsible for the management of the pension scheme."
[8] Lightman J found (in the context of PSA 1993 s.146(4)) that "administering" a scheme means (in whole or in part) running the Scheme e.g. inviting employees to join, keeping records of members, communicating with members, calculating benefits, providing benefit statements, paying benefits when due, keeping documentation up to date, dealing with governmental or regulatory agencies etc. In the case of a funded scheme, it will also involve running the fund and investing in managing the scheme's assets (*R. (Britannic Asset Management Ltd) v Pensions Ombudsman* [2002] EWHC 441 (Admin)).

*HMRC*[9] the UT found that, in the context of the UK-USA double tax treaty, a pension scheme is established in the geographic location where it is set up, funded, managed and administered on a continuous and stable fashion through human and material resources. It seems that the place in which a scheme is established is fluid; it can change over time and is not limited to the place where the scheme was originally administered.[10]

**The requirements prescribed by regulations**

**31-009**  The applicable regulations are in SI 2006/206. Regulation 2(1) prescribes that the pension scheme must either:

(a) be established (outside the UK) by an international organisation for the purpose of providing benefits for, or in respect of, past service as an employee of the organisation; or

(b) satisfy the requirements of regs 2(2) and 2(3).[11]

*International organisations*

**31-010**  An international organisation is any organisation to which the International Organisations Act 1968 s.1 applies by virtue of an Order in Council. This includes organisations such as the United Nations and the EU.

**Regulation 2(2)**

**31-011**  If the pension scheme is an occupational pension scheme,[12] reg.2(2) is satisfied if either:

(a) there is, in the country or territory in which the scheme is established, a body which regulates occupational pension schemes *and* which regulates the scheme in question; or

(b) no such regulatory body exists in the country or territory.

**31-012**  If the scheme is not an occupational pension scheme, reg.2(2) is satisfied if either:[13]

(a) there is in the country or territory in which it is established, a body which regulates pension schemes other than occupational pension schemes *and* which regulates the scheme in question; or

(b) no such regulatory body exists in the country or territory and: (i) the scheme is established in another member State,[14] Norway, Iceland or Liechtenstein; or (ii) there is in the country or territory in which the scheme is established

---

[9] *Macklin v HMRC* [2015] UKUT 39.
[10] If this were not correct then SI 2006/567 reg.3 (number 19) would be otiose. Reg.3 imposes an obligation on the scheme administrator of a registered pension scheme to notify HMRC if the territory in which the scheme is established changes.
[11] Unless the scheme is an overseas public service pension scheme within reg.3(1B) (see reg.2(2A)).
[12] "Occupational pension scheme" has the same meaning as in FA 2004 s.150(5), which is a very broad definition (see Ch.2). Members need not be employed by, or have any connection with, a sponsoring employer.
[13] Regulation 2(2)(b) and (d).
[14] i.e. a member of the EU (see European Communities Act 1972 s.1 and Sch.1, applied by Interpretation Act 1978 Sch.1). Gibraltar forms part of the same Member State as the UK and so cannot satisfy (i).

## WHAT IS AN OVERSEAS PENSION SCHEME?

a body which regulates providers of pension schemes and which regulates the provider for the purpose of establishing the scheme in question.

*Regulatory bodies*

31-013 HMRC suggest that this test looks not only at whether or not a pension scheme is regulated, but also *how* it is regulated.[15] That seems wrong—the test does not on its face impose any requirements regarding how a pension scheme is regulated. Provided that a pension scheme can be said to be "regulated", no minimum qualitative standard is imposed. The test refers to the regulation of pension schemes rather than the regulation of pension providers or pension trustees, but that can be a difficult distinction in practice: only the activities of persons can be regulated. The purpose of this requirement may be to ensure merely that the scheme is subject to the highest level of regulation available in the country in which it is established. If, for example, single-member occupational pension schemes are unregulated (as is the case in the UK), that would appear to be problematic for single-member schemes.

The minutes of a Joint Expatriate Forum Pensions Sub-group meeting held on 20 May 2016 record that it was put to HMRC that the uncertainty regarding the meaning of "regulated as a pension scheme" is particularly acute in federal systems. Sometimes different bodies undertake different aspects of regulation. For instance, regulatory duties might be split between prudential regulation, product and market conduct and administration/independence issues. HMRC explained that whether the pension regulation test is met will depend on the facts. Being regulated in some ways, but not as a pension scheme, is not enough. Some arrangements ultimately end up in companies, which means that they are regulated as a company rather than a pension scheme. HMRC were asked which were the more important factors. For instance, is protection of member interests counted as more significant than corporate governance or prudential regulation? HMRC responded that HMRC would consider the sort of regulation that they would normally expect a pension scheme to be subjected to, and then compare it to the regulation that is actually in place. The type of regulation that applies will be a matter of fact.

### Regulation 2(3)

31-014 Regulation 2(3) is satisfied if the scheme meets the following three conditions.

*Condition 1*

31-015 Condition 1 is that "the scheme is open to persons resident in the country or territory in which it is established".

31-016 In *Equity Trust (Singapore) Ltd v HMRC*,[16] Judge Hodge QC found (and the

---

[15] PTM112200: "This test looks at whether or not and how a pension scheme is regulated. The test is aimed at identifying a regulator in the other country that oversees legislation/guidelines that impacts directly on the operation of the pension scheme, to ensure that pension schemes are administered soundly in order to protect members' interests. Regulation tends to vary from country to country but such regulation might extend to submitting accounts, investment guidelines, rules on trustees, etc. In considering this test, HMRC would expect the scheme to be fully subject to the regulation in that country that covers these aspects. If a pension scheme is regulated but then opts out of the regulation so that it is exempt from providing some or all of the information that other regulated pension schemes are required to provide, it cannot meet this test".

[16] *Equity Trust (Singapore) Ltd v HMRC* [2011] EWHC 1463 at [59].

Court of Appeal subsequently accepted)[17] that although there was nothing in the scheme documentation preventing Singapore residents from becoming members (indeed the scheme documentation expressly provided that the scheme was open to Singapore residents), and notwithstanding that six members gave addresses in Singapore when applying to join the scheme, he was not satisfied on a balance of probabilities that the trustees would have knowingly accepted any Singapore resident members. This was because accepting Singapore residents would result in the scheme ceasing to be a "foreign trust", and that would cause investment income of the scheme to be taxable in Singapore. The scheme was marketed as a foreign trust and presented to the Singapore tax authorities as such.

**31-017** The test of whether a scheme is open to residents is therefore a broad practical one. In relation to jurisdictions in which schemes with resident members are treated in the same way as schemes without resident members, one would expect a court to be more willing to find that a scheme is open to local residents (subject to any evidence to the contrary).[18]

**31-018** It is most unlikely that the pension scheme must be "open" in the sense that new members must be able to join the scheme. A scheme which is closed to new members may satisfy Condition 1 if it was formerly open to residents. For example, HMRC consider that a scheme which is capable of having only one member can satisfy Condition 1, but only if the member is resident in the country in which the scheme is established.[19] If a pension scheme is established on terms that only one or more named individuals may join, that scheme will not satisfy Condition 1 unless at least one of those individuals is, or (arguably) intends to become, a local resident. Where the named individuals are non-resident, the fact that their membership of the scheme could continue if they decided (contrary to expectations) to become resident in the future does not appear to be material if there is no intention for that to happen. One is required to ask whether the particular pension scheme is open to residents, rather than the category of pension scheme.

**31-019** It is not uncommon for international pension plans (especially, but not limited to, those established by multinational employers) to be sectionalised, with a different section applicable to each different jurisdiction in which the scheme members are resident. It is quite possible that Condition 1 requires the *entire* scheme to be open to residents of the country in which the scheme is established, but each section may be found on a proper analysis to constitute a separate pension scheme.[20] Where that is the case, the sections relating to non-resident members may fail Condition 1.

**31-020** In most cases, a court will readily accept that a non-sectionalised pension scheme established under trusts is a single pension scheme. Difficulties may arise in relation to contract-based schemes, where the provider enters into a separate contract

---

[17] *TMF Trustees Singapore Ltd v HMRC* [2012] EWCA Civ 192 at [60].
[18] HMRC's views are set out at PTM112200: "... membership of the scheme should be genuinely available to residents of the country or territory in which it is established. If there are membership criteria, it would be of concern if these only applied to residents of the country of establishment".
[19] PTM112200: "If a scheme is designed to have only one member the 'open to residents' requirement means that only residents of the country or territory in which it is established can join single member schemes".
[20] See e.g. *PI Consulting (Trustee Services) Ltd v Pensions Regulator* [2013] EWHC 3181 at [46]; *Barclays Bank v Holmes* [2001] O.P.L.R. 37; [2000] Pens. L.R. 339; *Kemble v Hicks (No.2)* [1999] O.P.L.R. 1; *Reichhold v Wong* [2000] Pens. L.R. 277 Superior Court of Justice, Ontario. For a case in which separate arrangements were found to constitute a single pension scheme, see *Westminster City Council v Haywood* [1996] 3 W.L.R. 563; [1996] 2 All E.R. 467 at 477.

# WHAT IS AN OVERSEAS PENSION SCHEME?

with each member.[21] If each contract is, on a proper analysis, found to be a separate pension scheme, any contract issued to a non-resident member is unlikely to satisfy Condition 1.

*Condition 2*

Condition 2 is that:  31-021

"The scheme is established in a country or territory where there is a system of taxation of personal income under which tax relief is available in respect of pensions and—

(a) tax relief is not available to the member on contributions made to the scheme by the individual or, if the individual is an employee, by their employer, in respect of earnings to which benefits under the scheme relate;
(ab) the scheme is liable to taxation on its income and gains and is of a kind specified in Schedule 1 to these Regulations;[22] or
(b) all or most of the benefits paid by the scheme to members who are not in serious ill-health are subject to taxation.

For the purposes of this condition 'tax relief' includes the grant of an exemption from tax."

The purpose of Condition 2 is to ensure that the regime applicable to the pension scheme in question is broadly equivalent to the UK regime applicable to registered pension schemes.[23] As a matter of principle, one would expect that a regime offering no tax advantages not available under the registered pension scheme regime will not be objectionable.[24]  31-022

**"A system of taxation of personal income"** There must be, in the county or territory in which the scheme is established, a system under which individuals are taxable in respect of their income. The tax relief (or exemption) must relate to the taxation of individuals (as opposed to their corporate employers, for example).  31-023

**"Tax relief is available in respect of pensions"** Tax relief (which includes an exemption from tax) must be available in respect of "pensions". What is meant by *pensions* in this context? In general, one would expect this to be a reference to the income received under a pension scheme. However, the context suggests it is intended to have a broader meaning here. It seems likely that any tax incentive given in respect of pension *schemes* or pension *benefits* will suffice: the purpose of the condition is to demonstrate that the jurisdiction gives some special tax treatment to pension schemes and/or pension benefits.[25] The tax incentive could relate to local tax relief in respect of contributions to pension schemes, for example, or to investment income received by pension schemes, or to benefits (such as a tax-free lump sum) received from pension schemes in that jurisdiction.  31-024

---

[21] The fundamental differences between contract-based schemes and trust-based schemes are not always appreciated (see e.g. *RP Medplant Ltd v The Financial Conduct Authority* [2017] UKUT 385).
[22] Schedule 1 refers to a complying superannuation plan as defined in the Income Tax Assessment Act 1997 of Australia s.995–1.
[23] See *TMF Trustees Singapore Ltd v HMRC* [2012] EWCA Civ 192 at [21] (Lloyd LJ).
[24] Any restrictions not applicable to registered pension schemes may be vulnerable to challenge on EU law grounds (notwithstanding the UK's departure from the EU).
[25] HMRC also appear to take this view: see PTM112200.

*Condition 2(a) and (b)*

**31-025** Unless the scheme is a complying superannuation plan as defined in the Australian Income Tax Assessment Act 1997 s.995–1, the requirements in either of Condition 2(a) or (b) must be met in order for the scheme to be an overseas pension scheme.

**31-026** Condition 2(a) relates to tax relief available to the member, either in respect of contributions by the member, or in respect of contributions made by the member's employer.[26] It is irrelevant whether a tax deduction is available to the employer in respect of contributions. In many jurisdictions, employer contributions are not taxable as employment income on general principles (e.g. because the member has not received any employment income), rather than as a result of any express relief or exemption.

**31-027** At first glance, Conditions 2(a) and (b) appear to be relatively straightforward. As HMRC explain:[27]

> "So tax relief, or an exemption from tax, either applies at the point money goes into the scheme as a contribution, or the point it leaves as a benefit payment. It cannot be exempt at both of these points. Either the contribution into the scheme or most of the benefit payments out of it (excepting serious ill-health benefits) must be taxable."

**31-028** However, Condition 2(a) asks whether tax relief is available to "the member", and so it is necessary to determine who is "the member". Practitioners will rarely approach Condition 2 with any particular member in mind; they will usually need to determine whether or not the scheme as a whole is an overseas pension scheme.[28] Many jurisdictions (including the UK) provide tax relief for contributions to approved pension schemes, but this is usually subject to restrictions.[29] If the scheme has both resident and non-resident members then it will frequently be the case that some members will satisfy Condition 2(a) and some will not. Does that mean that Condition 2(a) is not satisfied at all, or is one required to split the scheme into one part comprising those members who satisfy Condition 2(a) and another part comprising those who do not, and only consider Condition 2(b) in the context of those members who do not satisfy Condition 2(a)?

**31-029** Condition 2(a) makes much more sense if the reference to "the member" is interpreted as meaning "any member". When one reads Condition 2 as a whole it is clear that it is not concerned with specific members. Given that Condition 2(a) is framed in the negative, by reading "the member" as "any member" it is apparent that Condition 2(a) is not satisfied if it is possible in principle for a hypothetical member (whether or not resident or in the local jurisdiction) to obtain tax relief. If it is not possible for any member to obtain tax relief in the local jurisdiction in respect of contributions to that scheme then Condition 2(a) is satisfied. This should be a straightforward question to answer: one simply needs to look at the local legislation. If Condition 2(a) is not satisfied (and most pension regimes are EET (exempt-exempt-taxed) systems, so Condition 2(a) will usually *not* be satisfied in practice) then one proceeds to Condition 2(b).

---

[26] The provision seems to have in mind something equivalent to ITEPA 2003 s.308.
[27] See PTM112200.
[28] It seems unlikely that a scheme can be an overseas pension scheme in relation to some members but not in relation to others.
[29] In particular, tax relief will never be available in practice to a person who doesn't have any local tax liability (there is no liability to relieve), and even if they do have local tax liability it will usually be subject to a number of requirements (e.g. being resident in that jurisdiction).

## WHAT IS AN OVERSEAS PENSION SCHEME?

**31-030** Condition 2(b) refers to "members" rather than "the member", however, this is not straightforward because in most jurisdictions (again, including the UK) the answer to this is likely to depend on the members' circumstances. For example, in the UK, benefits from registered pension schemes are generally subject to UK tax under the PAYE system, but not where they are paid to a non-resident member if a double tax treaty confers exclusive taxing rights on the country of residence.[30] So, as with Condition 2(a), the application of Condition 2(b) will frequently depend on the members' circumstances and so again one must determine what that means in the context of satisfying Condition 2(b).

**31-031** Some advisers appear to take the view that Condition 2 will be satisfied provided that no member can fail both Condition 2(a) and Condition 2(b). On that basis, it does not matter if some members fail Condition 2(b) provided that those same members do not also fail Condition 2(a). That approach requires one to read a number of additional words into Condition 2, and it also gives rise to practical problems. Firstly, it requires one to look at the circumstances of every single member (or perhaps, every class of member) including the effect of different double tax treaties. Secondly, if a member's circumstances change over time, that could affect whether Condition 2 is satisfied (and one will never know at the time of a contribution what the member's circumstances will be when he receives benefits). Thirdly, if a single member fails both (a) and (b), it appears that the entire scheme will fail to be an overseas pension scheme, which could be disastrous for a putative QROPS (because transfers to the scheme from registered pension schemes or RNUKS would involve an unauthorised payment) even for those members who do meet the requirements of Condition 2. Finally, if that were the correct way to interpret Condition 2, it would be more restrictive than the regime in the UK. For example, consider the position of a non-UK resident individual in receipt of profits of a furnished holiday lettings business in the UK. Such profits would be subject to UK tax[31] and if he were to make a contribution to a registered pension scheme he would obtain tax relief[32] notwithstanding his non-UK residence. However, benefits could be paid from the scheme without any UK tax provided that the jurisdiction in which he is resident has a suitable double tax treaty with the UK. If this approach were correct then such an individual would fail Condition 2(a) and (b), and so this very strongly suggests that it is not correct.

**31-032** Condition 2(b) makes much more sense if one reads the reference to "members" as a reference to "resident members".[33] This is the only way that the question can be answered with any degree of certainty (and, again, it should be noted that the same could be said of the registered pension scheme regime). Indeed, there are suggestions that when Condition 2 was drafted the draftsman assumed that a person would only join an overseas scheme if he was resident in the jurisdiction of the scheme.

---

[30] It is quite clear that Condition 2 is only concerned with tax in the jurisdiction of the scheme, so it is not necessary to consider whether the member actually pays tax in his country of residence.
[31] See ITTOIA 2005 Pt 3.
[32] See FA 2004 s.189(2)(ba).
[33] It is legitimate for a court to supply missing words in a statutory provision in plain cases of drafting mistakes, provided that the court is sure: (a) of the intended purpose of the statute or provision in question; (b) that by inadvertence the draftsman and Parliament failed to give effect to that purpose in the provision in question; and (c) that the substance of the provision Parliament would have made, although not necessarily the precise words Parliament would have used, had the error been noticed (*Inco Europe Ltd v First Choice Distribution* [2000] 1 W.L.R. 586 per Lord Nichols). It is therefore suggested that a court would be permitted to interpret the reference to "members" as "resident members".

31-033 This means disregarding the local tax position of non-residents. There is no reason to think that this approach could give rise to any difficulties. For example, if a jurisdiction taxed resident members but not non-resident members, Condition 2(b) would be satisfied even if most of the members were non-resident. There is no reason to think that HMRC would object to this. Indeed, reg.3(6)[34] (relating to ROPS) expressly envisages this sort of situation, so the draftsman evidently thought that it had not already been addressed. Furthermore, there are a number of jurisdictions with precisely this sort of system, and there has never been any suggestion that they are not compliant with Condition 2.[35]

31-034 **Summary** In summary, it is suggested that the reference to "the member" in Condition 2(a) should be interpreted as meaning "any member", and the reference to "members" in Condition 2(b) should be interpreted as meaning "resident members".

31-035 **"Serious ill-health"** "Serious ill-health" is not defined for the purposes of SI 2006/206. Nor is it defined in FA 2004 Pt 4, although that legislation does prescribe circumstances in which a serious ill-health lump sum (which is a type of authorised payment) may be paid. The main requirement in FA 2004 is that the scheme administrator has received evidence from a registered medical practitioner that the member is expected to live for less than one year.[36] Whilst it is clear that the term "serious ill-health" in SI 2006/206 must be interpreted from a UK perspective, there is no reason to expect the FA 2004 provisions to be used as an aid to construction. The term "serious ill-health" should therefore be given its natural meaning, which is likely to be broader than the circumstances in which a serious ill-health lump sum can be paid for the purposes of FA 2004.[37]

*Condition 3*

31-036 The pension scheme must be approved or recognised by, or registered with, the relevant tax authorities as a pension scheme in the country or territory in which it is established. It will usually be clear enough whether a scheme is approved by, or registered with, the local tax authorities, but it is less clear precisely what is required for a scheme to be "recognised" by a tax authority. If there are local tax incentives that apply to pension schemes (as is required by Condition 2) and those tax incentives are capable of applying to the scheme in question, it may be arguable that the scheme is recognised by the relevant tax authorities on the basis that it is recognised as a pension scheme by the local legislation. The better view is probably that the requirement is satisfied only if there is some mechanism by which the tax authori-

---

[34] Inserted by The Registered Pension Schemes and Overseas Pension Schemes (Miscellaneous Amendments) Regulations 2012 (SI 2012/884) reg.4(d), with effect from 6 April 2012.
[35] e.g. prior to 6 April 2012 (when SI 2006/206 reg.3(6) became effective) many Guernsey retirement annuity trust schemes (approved under the Income Tax (Guernsey) Law 1975 s.157A(4)) were accepted as being QROPS notwithstanding the existence of s.40(ee) of that Law (which provides, broadly, that tax is not chargeable in respect of an annuity or lump sum paid to an individual who is not resident in Guernsey).
[36] FA 2004 Sch.29 para.4.
[37] cf. HMRC's views: "Any serious ill-health provision ... under the pension tax regime of the country or territory in which the scheme is established must reflect the provision applying in respect of a member of a registered pension scheme. The provision does not have to apply the same conditions as are set out in PTM063400, but the approach must be fundamentally similar ..." (PTM112200).

TAXATION 719

ties expressly recognise (or accept) that the particular scheme qualifies for tax relief.[38]

PTM112200 suggests that if a jurisdiction has a system of approval or registration, and also some other form of recognition, Condition 3 is not satisfied if the scheme is recognised but not also approved or registered. The better view is probably that a scheme need not satisfy every available form of approval, registration or recognition in a jurisdiction; it merely needs to satisfy one such form. **31-037**

As with Condition 1 (see below), difficulties can arise in relation to international sectionalised schemes. In such cases typically only part of the scheme is approved in the jurisdiction in which the scheme is established. It is possible that Condition 3 may be breached on the basis that it requires the *entire* scheme to be approved, registered or recognised. **31-038**

## TAXATION

### Capital gains tax

A gain accruing to a person on a disposal of investments held for the purposes of an overseas pension scheme is not a chargeable gain.[39] Therefore, for CGT purposes, an overseas pension scheme is treated in the same way as a registered pension scheme. **31-039**

### Inheritance tax

An overseas pension scheme will usually be a QNUPS and so will benefit from the favourable inheritance tax treatment afforded to such schemes. **31-040**

### Income tax

Special provisions in ITEPA 2003 Pt 9 apply to overseas pension schemes. The effect of these provisions is that:[40] (a) it is possible for a UK resident individual to receive up to 25% of a member's fund as a tax-free lump sum, even if the scheme is an EFRBS or FURBS (and so may otherwise be taxable in full); and (b) death benefits received by UK residents in respect of a member (or other beneficiary) who dies before age 75 are expressly free of tax. **31-041**

### Interaction with RNUKS provisions

It will be apparent that it is generally desirable from a tax perspective for a scheme to be an overseas pension scheme. There is however one exception to this. **31-042**

---

[38] This is supported by the drafting of reg.2(3) prior to 6 April 2012. At that time, what is now Condition 3 was referred to as Condition A, and was followed by a Condition B (revoked from that date by SI 2012/884 reg.3(2)(d)), which referred to a "system" of approval, recognition or registration. The intention was that Condition A (now Condition 3) could only apply where there was such a system, and Condition B could only apply where there was no such system—there was no lacuna between the two conditions.

[39] TCGA 1992 s.271(1A). Gains accruing on the disposal of assets held as a member of a property investment LLP are excepted (TCGA 1992 s.271(12)).

[40] See Ch.26.

If ITEPA 2003 s.307 applies in respect of a contribution to an overseas pension scheme, such a contribution will cause the scheme to become an RNUKS and to that extent the (generally undesirable) regime described in Ch.30 will apply.

# CHAPTER 32

# Recognised Overseas Pension Schemes

## TABLE OF CONTENTS

| | |
|---|---|
| Introduction and overview | 32-001 |
| Development | 32-004 |
| What is a ROPS? | 32-005 |
| Regulation 3 | 32-006 |
| Schemes falling within reg.3(1A) | 32-007 |
| The requirements of reg.3(6) | 32-008 |
| The position in Guernsey | 32-011 |
| The requirements of reg.3(6A) | 32-012 |
| Relevant transfer fund or ring-fenced transfer funds | 32-014 |
| Pension rule 1 | 32-015 |
| Authorised member payments | 32-016 |
| The scheme must be established in a country or territory in reg.3(2) | 32-017 |
| Guernsey schemes | 32-018 |
| Taxation | 32-020 |

## INTRODUCTION AND OVERVIEW

The main significance of an overseas pension scheme satisfying the requirements of a "recognised overseas pension scheme" (ROPS) is that a QROPS is merely a ROPS in relation to which the scheme manager has given certain undertakings to HMRC.[1] The relevant provisions are in FA 2004 s.150(8) and the Pension Schemes (Categories of Country and Requirements for Overseas Pension Schemes and Recognised Overseas Pension Schemes) Regulations 2006 (SI 2006/206). **32-001**

In outline, an overseas pension scheme is a ROPS if: **32-002**

(a) any tax relief available to non-residents in respect of benefits paid from the scheme is also available to residents;
(b) benefits, to the extent that they consist of a member's relevant transfer fund or ring-fenced transfer funds, cannot commence earlier than age 55 (except in cases of ill-health), except where such benefits would be authorised payments if made by a registered pension scheme; and
(c) the scheme is established in the EU/EEA or in a jurisdiction with a tax information exchange agreement with the UK.

Special rules apply to certain schemes established in Guernsey, overseas public **32-003**

---

[1] See FA 2004 s.169 and Ch.33.

722    RECOGNISED OVERSEAS PENSION SCHEMES

service schemes, and schemes established by international organisations. Each of the above requirements is considered in detail below.

**Development**

32-004    The ROPS requirements did not change materially between 6 April 2006 and 5 April 2012. During that period the only requirements were that the overseas pension scheme: (a) was either established in the EU/EEA or any country with a UK tax treaty containing provisions about the exchange of information and non-discrimination; or (b) 70% of a member's fund must be used to provide the member with an income for life and benefits could not commence earlier than under a registered pension scheme. The following developments have since occurred:

(a) On 6 April 2012, the requirement that any tax relief available to non-residents in respect of benefits paid from the scheme is also available to non-residents was added.

(b) On 25 May 2012, the requirement that certain Guernsey schemes must not be open to non-residents of Guernsey was added.

(c) On 6 April 2015, the requirement that benefits, to the extent that they consist of the member's relevant transfer fund, are payable no earlier than they would be if pension rule 1 (in FA 2004 s.165) applied, except where such benefits would be authorised payments if they were made by a registered pension scheme was added.

(d) On 6 April 2017, the requirement that 70% of a member's fund must be used to provide an income for life was removed.

# WHAT IS A ROPS?

32-005    A ROPS is an "overseas pension scheme"[2] which satisfies the requirements of SI 2006/206 reg.3.[3]

**Regulation 3**

32-006    Pursuant to SI 2006/206 reg.3(1), a ROPS must:

(a) satisfy the requirements in reg.3(6) and (6A), *unless* it falls within reg.3(1A);
(b) be established in a country or territory mentioned in reg.3(2); and
(c) if it is established in Guernsey, satisfy the requirement in reg.3(4).

*Schemes falling within reg.3(1A)*

32-007    A pension scheme falls within reg.3(1A) if either:

(a) It is established (outside the UK) by an international organisation for the purpose of providing benefits for, or in respect of, past service as an employee of the organisation.

(b) It is an overseas public service pension scheme. A pension scheme is an overseas public service pension scheme if:

---

[2] For the meaning of "overseas pension scheme" see Ch.31.
[3] FA 2004 s.150(8).

(i) it is established in a country or territory outside the UK[4] and is either so established by or under the law of that country or territory, or approved by the government of that country or territory; and
(ii) it is established for the purpose of providing benefits to individuals for or in respect of services rendered to that country or territory or any political subdivision or local authority thereof.

*The requirements of reg.3(6)*

Regulation 3(6) provides that: 32-008

"Where tax relief in respect of benefits paid from the scheme is available to a member of the scheme who is not resident in the country or territory in which the scheme is established, the same or substantially the same tax relief must—
(a) also be available to members of the scheme who are resident in the country or territory; and
(b) apply regardless of whether the member was resident in the country or territory—
   (i) when the member joined the scheme; or
   (ii) for any period of time when they were a member of the scheme."

For these purposes "tax relief" means any tax relief that is available under the system of taxation of personal income in the country or territory in which the scheme is established, and includes the grant of an exemption from tax other than an exemption which applies by virtue of double taxation arrangements.[5] The disregard for double taxation arrangements is important because otherwise this would create a regime that was more restrictive than that applicable to registered pension schemes.[6] 32-009

The existence of any tax relief which breaches reg.3(6) is problematic only if that tax relief can apply to benefits paid under the scheme in question. Pension schemes that are incapable of providing such benefits to non-residents will always satisfy reg.3(6).[7] HMRC consider that there must be no qualification affecting whether residents actually or readily receive the tax relief as compared to non-residents, and provide the following example of an unacceptable qualification:[8] 32-010

"Country X does not tax benefits paid out of a scheme established in Country X if they are paid to a non-resident. It is also possible for residents of Country X to claim exemption from tax on such benefits, provided they did not contribute to the scheme in any period in which they were resident in Country X. As the exemption in relation to residents is qualified, the benefits tax relief test cannot be met."

---

[4] See Ch.31 for the meaning of the words "established in a country or territory outside the UK".
[5] Regulation 3(7). Double taxation arrangements are arrangements made between the country or territory in which the scheme is established and another country or territory with a view to affording relief from double taxation (reg.3(8)).
[6] See Ch.20 for the taxation of benefits paid from registered pension schemes to non-UK resident members.
[7] It is unclear if HMRC agree with this. PTM112300 provides that "Whilst the test is expressed in the context of the scheme and its members, it is always within the greater context of the country's tax rules. If the country's tax regime does not provide the conditions for the necessary availability of tax relief to both residents and non-residents, then schemes based in that country will not be able to meet this condition to be a [ROPS]".
[8] PTM112300.

### The position in Guernsey

**32-011** The historical position in Guernsey provides an illustration of the application of reg.3(6). Prior to the introduction of reg.3(6), most Guernsey ROPS were established under s.157A(4) of the Income Tax (Guernsey) Law 1975. This provides for a typical EET system, which includes an obligation to withhold 20% income tax on pensions paid to residents but not to non-residents (see s.40(ee) of the 1975 Law). Section 40(ee) breaches reg.3(6), and so Guernsey introduced a new regime (under s.157E of the 1975 Law) so that Guernsey schemes could continue to satisfy the ROPS requirements in relation to non-residents of Guernsey (primarily of course so that they could continue to constitute QROPS). Section 157E introduced a TEE system, under which no (Guernsey) tax relief was available in respect of contributions, but investment return and benefits were exempt from tax. Residents and non-residents were taxed in precisely the same way, so reg.3(6) was satisfied.

### The requirements of reg.3(6A)

**32-012** Regulation 3(6A) provides that:

"The benefits payable to the member under the scheme, to the extent that they consist of the member's relevant transfer fund or ring-fenced transfer funds—
(a) are payable no earlier than they would be if pension rule 1 in section 165 applied; or
(b) if payable earlier, are only payable in circumstances in which they would be authorised member payments if they were made by a registered pension scheme."

**32-013** This is an on-going test, so if the scheme satisfies the test when it receives a transfer (which is the main purpose of the QROPS regime: to receive a transfer from a registered pension scheme or RNUKS) but is then amended so that benefits can be paid at an earlier age it will cease to satisfy the test at that time.

### Relevant transfer fund or ring-fenced transfer funds

**32-014** The terms "relevant transfer fund" and "ring-fenced transfer funds" are not expressly defined in SI 2006/206. They are presumably intended to have the same meanings as in FA 2004 Sch.34 paras 1 and 4 (relating to RNUKS).[9] The scheme rules only need to restrict the minimum pension age as it applies to such funds; reg.3(6A) has no application to other funds under the scheme and it is not improper for a scheme to have different rules applicable to different categories of fund.

### Pension rule 1

**32-015** The reference is to benefits "payable" rather than "paid". If benefits are capable of being paid earlier than if pension rule 1 applied, it is irrelevant that no such benefits are in fact paid. Pension rule 1 in FA 2004 s.165 provides that no payment of pension may be made before the day on which the member reaches normal minimum pension age, unless the ill-health condition is met. Normal minimum pension age is currently age 55, unless the member has a protected pension age.[10] It is

---

[9] See Ch.30.
[10] FA 2004 s.279(1). For protected pension ages, see Ch.3. A member can have a protected pension age only if the funds in the ROPS derive from a pre-A Day tax-approved scheme where the member was

## WHAT IS A ROPS?

unnecessary for the scheme rules to expressly incorporate the provisions of pension rule 1 if the effect of local legislation restricts the payment of benefits from the scheme to circumstances which comply with pension rule 1.[11] It is quite clear that this requirement can be satisfied even where some members can receive benefits earlier than if pension rule 1 applied: the restriction applies only to the extent that the benefits consist of a member's relevant transfer fund or ring-fenced transfer funds.

*Authorised member payments*

The following authorised member payments can be paid from a registered pension scheme before the member reaches normal minimum pension age[12]: (a) a serious ill health lump sum; (b) a winding-up lump sum; (c) a short service refund lump sum (and certain payments that are deemed to be short service refund lump sums); and (d) a refund of excess contributions lump sum. **32-016**

*The scheme must be established in a country or territory in reg.3(2)*

The countries and territories mentioned in reg.3(2) are: **32-017**

(a) the Member States of the EU (other than the UK)[13];
(b) Iceland, Liechtenstein and Norway; and
(c) any country or territory in respect of which there is in force an Order in Council under FA 2006 s.173 (which relates to international tax enforcement arrangements, including tax information exchange agreements) or TIOPA 2010 s.2 (which relates to double taxation arrangements) giving effect in the UK to an agreement which contains provision about the exchange of information between the parties.

*Guernsey schemes*

Regulation 3(4) provides that: **32-018**

"At the time of the transfer of sums or assets which would, subject to these Regulations, constitute a recognised transfer, where the pension scheme is an exempt pension contract or an exempt pension trust within the meaning of section 157E of the Income Tax (Guernsey) Law, 1975, the scheme must not be open to non-residents of Guernsey."

The regulations do not define the term "recognised transfer". It is of course defined in FA 2004 s.169(1),[14] but that definition is not expressly incorporated into SI 2006/206. As noted above, Guernsey enacted the s.157E in response to the introduction of reg.3(6). Very shortly after it did so, HMRC (which has the power to amend SI 2006/206) introduced reg.3(4) aimed expressly at s.157E schemes. **32-019**

---

entitled to receive benefits before age 55 (see FA 2004 Sch.36 paras 21-23). Prior to 6 April 2015, protection did not apply to a transferee scheme unless the transfer formed part of a block transfer (FA 2004 Sch.36 paras 22(5) and 23(5)). Since 6 April 2015 the protected pension age will apply to a transferee scheme provided that the transfer was a recognised transfer (FA 2004 Sch.36 para.23ZA. See Ch.12 for recognised transfers). A ROPS must be a QROPS for a recognised transfer to be made to it.

[11] HMRC agree: see PTM112300.
[12] See Ch.13.
[13] Gibraltar forms part of the same Member State as the UK and so does not fall within (a) (but it is understood to fall within (c)).
[14] See Ch.12.

## TAXATION

**32-020**  All ROPS are overseas pension schemes and so benefit from the CGT and income tax treatment of such schemes.[15] Most ROPS are QNUPS and so benefit from the favourable inheritance tax treatment afforded to such schemes. In addition, the following tax points are specific to ROPS:

(a) Where funds are transferred from a ROPS to a registered pension scheme, an LS&DB allowance enhancement factor can be claimed in relation to any subsequent relevant BCE.[16]

(b) In the context of pension sharing orders, the concept of a "pension credit" is modified in certain circumstances so that it applies to an increase under a ROPS.[17]

(c) Any available tax deduction in respect of employer contributions to a registered pension scheme is restricted if benefits under the scheme are only paid if benefits under an EFRBS are not paid.[18] However, these provisions are disapplied if the EFRBS is a ROPS which meets certain requirements.[19]

**32-021**  Finally, and more generally, it is perhaps arguable that certain anti-avoidance provisions are less likely to apply to a ROPS on the basis that it is in some sense *recognised* for tax purposes.[20]

---

[15] See Ch.31.
[16] See Ch.20.
[17] The Pensions Schemes (Application of UK Provisions to Relevant Non-UK Schemes) Regulations 2006 (SI 2006/207) reg.13.
[18] FA 2004 s.196A and The Registered Pension Schemes (Restriction of Employers' Relief) Regulations 2005 (SI 2005/3458).
[19] See SI 2005/3458 reg.2.
[20] e.g. the transfer of assets abroad provisions, the income tax settlements provisions, and TCGA 1992 ss.86 and 87. These are all discussed in Ch.22.

# CHAPTER 33

# Qualifying Recognised Overseas Pension Schemes

## TABLE OF CONTENTS

| | |
|---|---|
| Introduction and overview | 33-001 |
|     The purpose of the QROPS regime | 33-004 |
|     HMRC's list of QROPS | 33-007 |
|         Transfers to schemes that are on the list but are not QROPS | 33-008 |
|         Designer legislation | 33-010 |
|         Former QROPS | 33-011 |
|         QROPS and EU law | 33-012 |
|     What is a QROPS? | 33-016 |
|     Exclusion under s.169(5) | 33-017 |
|     Residency of member | 33-021 |
| Taxation | 33-022 |
| The overseas transfer charge | 33-023 |
|     "Onward transfer", "relevant period", and "original transfer" | 33-024 |
|     The main provision: s.244AC | 33-028 |
|     Pre-9 March 2017 grandfathering | 33-029 |
|     Exclusions | 33-030 |
|         Member and receiving scheme is same country | 33-031 |
|         Member and receiving scheme in EEA States | 33-032 |
|         Transfers exceeding available overseas transfer allowance: s.244IA | 33-033 |
|         Availability of member's overseas transfer allowance | 33-036 |
|     The "transferred value" | 33-037 |
|     Amount of the charge | 33-038 |
|         Liability | 33-039 |
|         Avoidance of double charge | 33-042 |
| Information requirements | 33-043 |
|     Obligations of the scheme manager | 33-044 |
|         Subsequent changes or corrections | 33-045 |
|         Non-compliance | 33-046 |
|         Former QROPS | 33-047 |
|     Obligations of the member | 33-049 |

## INTRODUCTION AND OVERVIEW

**33-001** A qualifying recognised overseas pension schemes (QROPS) is a ROPS[1] in respect of which the scheme manager has provided specified information and undertakings to HMRC. The main provisions relating to QROPS are in FA 2004 s.169(2)–(8) and the Pension Schemes (Information Requirements for Qualifying Overseas Pension Schemes, Qualifying Recognised Overseas Pension Schemes and Corresponding Relief) Regulations 2006 (SI 2006/206).

**33-002** The principal significance of a ROPS being a QROPS is that it can receive a recognised transfer from a registered pension scheme or an RNUKS.[2] A recognised transfer is a type of authorised payment, but that does not mean that such a transfer cannot give rise to any tax charges: prior to 6 April 2023, the transfer was a BCE and so if the amount transferred exceeded the member's available lifetime allowance then a 25% lifetime allowance charge applied to the excess,[3] and a transfer to a QROPS may also give rise to the overseas transfer charge (see below). With effect from 6 April 2024, the overseas transfer charge also arises where the amount transferred by a recognised transfer to a QROPS exceeds the member's available "overseas transfer allowance".

**33-003** If a QROPS receives a recognised transfer (whether from a registered pension scheme or an RNUKS), it will become an RNUKS (in addition to being a QROPS) and accordingly many of the registered pension scheme provisions in FA 2004 Pt 4 and ITEPA 2003 Pt 9 will be applied to it.[4] As a result of the RNUKS provisions applying, the QROPS will be able to make a recognised transfer only to a registered pension scheme or another QROPS.

### The purpose of the QROPS regime

**33-004** The QROPS regime commenced on 6 April 2006.[5] Prior to that date, funds could be transferred from approved schemes to non-UK schemes only in very limited circumstances.[6] Apart from transfers to schemes established in one of the small number of jurisdictions with a reciprocal arrangement with the UK,[7] and transfers to certain schemes for staff of EU institutions, transfers often required specific HMRC consent and were subject to restrictions. It was usually necessary for the transferee scheme and the member to be resident in the same jurisdiction, which in some cases was inappropriate or impossible. By imposing restrictions that did not apply to transfers between UK tax-approved schemes, the previous regime was inconsistent with the free movement of capital that forms a central part of EU law.

**33-005** HMRC explain the purpose of the QROPS regime thus[8]:

---

[1] For ROPS, see Ch.32.
[2] FA 2004 s.169(1)(b). See Ch.12.
[3] See Ch.10.
[4] For RNUKS, see Ch.30.
[5] The number of transfers from registered pension schemes to QROPS in each tax year since 6 April 2006 are recorded in HMRC's publication *Transfers to Qualifying Recognised Overseas Pension Scheme: July 2018, Official Statistics.*
[6] See HMRC's *Occupational Pension Schemes Practice Notes IR12* (2001) Appendix VI; IR76 (2000) *Personal Pension Schemes Guidance Notes (Including Stakeholder Pension Schemes)* Appendix 22.
[7] Being Jersey, the Isle of Man, Guernsey and the Republic of Ireland. For a case in which the requirements of the reciprocal agreement between the UK and Guernsey were not satisfied, see *Gratton v HMRC* [2010] UKFTT 521.
[8] PTM112010.

# INTRODUCTION AND OVERVIEW

"The Government allows transfers to QROPS to be made free of UK tax because they enable people permanently leaving the UK to simplify their affairs by taking their pension savings with them to their new country of residence. This is intended to enable them to continue to save to provide an income when they retire.

An individual who leaves the UK and transfers their pension savings should be in broadly the same position as someone who remains in the UK with their pension savings."

In the past, HMRC have considered it to be an abuse of the QROPS regime if a transfer facilitates the subsequent withdrawal of funds as a 100% lump sum.[9] Since April 2015, all money purchase arrangements under registered pension schemes have been capable of providing a 100% lump sum at age 55, so presumably HMRC will not now consider it to be abusive for a QROPS to facilitate such a payment.

**33-006**

## HMRC's list of QROPS

HMRC maintains a list of schemes (available on its website), the managers of which have informed HMRC that they meet the conditions to be a ROPS and have asked to be included on the list. On 24 September 2008 HMRC prefaced the list with a caveat explaining that: (a) the list is based on information provided by scheme managers; (b) inclusion on the list does not mean that HMRC had verified all the information provided; and (c) a transfer could give rise to tax charges on the member. The caveat has remained in place since that date although the wording has changed slightly. It is therefore important to appreciate that the list serves a very limited function, and the fact that a scheme is on the list does not prove that it is a QROPS. From time to time, HMRC appear to audit certain jurisdictions, and if they take the view that certain regimes in those jurisdictions are not compatible with the ROPS regime then they will remove those schemes from the list. This suggests that, in relation to those jurisdictions (rather than the individual schemes) on the list, HMRC are not aware of any information to suggest that they are incompatible with the ROPS requirements.

**33-007**

*Transfers to schemes that are on the list but are not QROPS*

If property held for the purposes of a registered pension scheme is transferred to a scheme that is not another registered pension scheme or a QROPS, the transfer is an unauthorised payment and so gives rise to an unauthorised payments charge, an unauthorised payments surcharge (unless, exceptionally, less than 25% of a member's fund was transferred) and a scheme sanction charge.

**33-008**

HMRC accept that prior to 24 September 2008 (when the caveat was added) the list might "have given the impression that HMRC was satisfied that any scheme that had been included on the list was a QROPS so that there should not be any tax charges in respect of the transfer".[10] HMRC have accordingly agreed not to raise or pursue assessments where the transfer took place before 24 September 2008 to a pension scheme that was included on the QROPS list when the transfer took place but the scheme was not a QROPS and there is no evidence of dishonesty, abuse, artificiality or any similar circumstances relating to the transfer. Since 24 September 2008, HMRC will pursue any tax charges that arise from a transfer to a scheme that is not a QROPS. It is very unlikely that any relief from the unauthorised payments

**33-009**

---

[9] See e.g. HMRC's statement *Purpose of the QROPS regime* (6 December 2011).
[10] See HMRC's *Guidance for individuals, pension schemes and advisers on the taxation of unauthorised transfers to schemes included on the QROPS list* (published November 2013).

charge will be available,[11] however HMRC have the power to discharge any liability for the unauthorised payments surcharge[12] and the scheme sanction charge[13] on the grounds that it is not just and reasonable to be so liable. It is arguable that it is neither just nor reasonable to be liable for these charges where HMRC's list has been relied upon in good faith.

*Designer legislation*

**33-010** Where a country or territory makes legislation or otherwise creates or uses a pension scheme to provide tax advantages that are not intended to be available under the QROPS regime, the UK government has indicated that it will act so that the relevant types of pension scheme in those countries or territories will be excluded from being QROPS.[14]

*Former QROPS*

**33-011** The requirements which must be satisfied in order for a pension scheme to be a ROPS have changed over time, resulting in a number of QROPS becoming *former QROPS*[15] (sometimes referred to as *de-listed* QROPS). A former QROPS cannot of course receive a recognised transfer, but there are no penalties or other disadvantages associated with a scheme ceasing to be a QROPS.[16] Such schemes do not cease to be RNUKS,[17] so there are also no tax advantages of ceasing to be a QROPS. However, the information requirements described below apply only to former QROPS that ceased to be QROPS on or after 14 October 2013.

*QROPS and EU law*

**33-012** A transfer of pension funds involves a movement of capital and so engages TFEU art.63, which prohibits restrictions on movements of capital between Member States and between Member States and third countries. There are at least three aspects of the QROPS regime that may be vulnerable to challenge on EU law grounds. In relation to each aspect it may be objected (by HMRC) that it is possible to establish a registered pension scheme anywhere in the world, and so the QROPS regime is in a sense optional. However, it is a requirement that the scheme administrator of a registered pension scheme is resident within the EU or EEA,[18] and this is unlikely

---

[11] Relief from the unauthorised payment charge is available under FA 2004 s.266A but it seems unlikely that the relief could apply in these circumstances. See Ch.18.
[12] FA 2004 ss.267, 268 and 269 and SI 2005/3452. See Ch.18.
[13] See FA 2004 s.268. See Ch.5.
[14] See the Explanatory Memorandum to The Pension Schemes (Categories of Country and Requirements for Overseas Pension Schemes and Recognised Overseas Pension Schemes) (Amendment) Regulations 2012 (SI 2012/1221) para.7.8.
[15] Former QROPS are sometimes referred to as "de-listed", which is unhelpful because it suggests that HMRC's list determines whether or not a scheme is a QROPS.
[16] There would be tax implications of the scheme ceasing to be an overseas pension scheme. e.g. the CGT exemption (in TCGA 1992 s.271(1A)) would cease to apply to the scheme.
[17] FA 2004 Sch.34 para.1(5)(d) refers to a scheme which received a *relevant transfer* at any time after 5 April 2006 when the scheme was a QROPS. The fact that the scheme has subsequently ceased to be a QROPS is therefore irrelevant.
[18] FA 2004 s.270(2)(a).

## INTRODUCTION AND OVERVIEW

to be possible in practice where the scheme is established outside of the EU or EEA.[19]

The first, and perhaps the clearest, vulnerability relates to the overseas transfer charge. This is essentially an exit charge that has no application to transfers between registered pension schemes. Although there is an exclusion where the member is resident in an EEA state and the scheme is established in an EEA state, this is too restrictive. Article 63 prohibits restrictions on movements of capital between Member States *and between Member States and third countries*. It follows that if a UK resident individual wishes to transfer the funds in his registered pension scheme to a QROPS established in New Zealand (for example), the overseas transfer charge would apply in circumstances that would appear to breach art.63.

33-013

The second vulnerability relates to the fact that a transfer to a QROPS was a benefit crystallisation event (BCE 8) for lifetime allowance purposes, whereas a transfer between registered pension schemes was not. Prior to 6 April 2023, if the funds transferred exceeded the member's available lifetime allowance, the transfer gave rise to a 25% lifetime allowance charge at that time. Therefore, where it applied as a result of BCE 8, the lifetime allowance charge operated as an exit charge. The counter argument was that BCE 8 simply brought forward the time at which a BCE will occur in any event, but it remained arguable that this was discriminatory. It may have been otherwise if the charge was deferred until one of the other BCEs occurred.[20]

33-014

The final aspect that may be vulnerable to challenge relates to the administration of the QROPS regime generally. It is almost always certain whether a scheme is a registered pension scheme or not,[21] whereas it is frequently uncertain whether a scheme is a QROPS or not.[22] It is difficult to reconcile this with the principle of legal certainty, which is a general principle of EU law.[23]

33-015

### What is a QROPS?

A ROPS is a QROPS if[24]:

33-016

(a) the scheme manager has notified HMRC that it is a ROPS and has provided

---

[19] Many jurisdictions do not permit an approved local scheme to be administered in a different jurisdiction.

[20] See *X and Y, Riksskatteverket* (C-436/00) [2004] S.T.C. 1271; *N v Inspecteur van de Belastingdienst Oost/kantoor Almelo (C-470/04)*.

[21] If a pension scheme is registered with HMRC then it is a registered pension scheme (FA 2004 s.150(2)). The only prerequisites are that the scheme is a *pension scheme* (as defined in s.150(1)), and, unless it is a personal pension scheme it must be an occupational pension scheme (as defined in s.150(5)) if a valid application to register the scheme is to be made. If it subsequently became apparent that a scheme did not in fact meet these prerequisites then it seems that it could not have been a registered pension scheme, but the definition of pension scheme and occupational pension scheme are so broad that this is very unlikely to cause any difficulties in practice.

[22] *TMF Trustees Singapore Ltd v HMRC* [2012] EWCA Civ 192 serves as an illustration of this point. The court found (on a balance of probabilities), and following analysis of information that would not realistically have been available to any member, that the scheme was not open to residents of Singapore and so did not meet the requirements of an overseas pension scheme.

[23] *Commission v Spain (C-151/12)* 24 October 2013 ECJ at [28]; *Commission v Spain (C-71/92)* 17 November 1993 ECJ at 25; *Ålands Vindkraft, (C-573/12)* 1 July 2014 ECJ at [125]–[128]. The general principle requires "that rules of law be clear and precise and predictable in their effect, so that interested parties can ascertain their position in situations and legal relationships governed by EU law": *Parliament v Council (C-48/14)* 12 February 2015 ECJ at [45].

[24] FA 2004 s.169(2). The requirements in (a), (b) and (c) are usually satisfied in the original notification to HMRC by the scheme manager.

any such evidence that it is a ROPS as HMRC may require.[25] The "scheme manager" is the person(s) administering, or responsible for the management of, the pension scheme[26];

(b) the scheme manager has undertaken to inform HMRC if it ceases to be a ROPS.

(c) the scheme manager has confirmed to HMRC that the scheme manager understands the scheme manager's potential liability to overseas transfer charge and has undertaken to operate the charge including by meeting the scheme manager's liabilities to the charge;

(d) the scheme manager has undertaken to HMRC to comply with various information requirements imposed by regulations made under s.169(4), and to provide evidence of such compliance where required by HMRC. These information requirements are explained below; and

(e) the ROPS is not excluded from being a QROPS by s.169(5).

**Exclusion under s.169(5)**

33-017  Pursuant to s.169(5), a ROPS is excluded from being a QROPS if HMRC decide that:

(a) one or more of the following conditions is met in relation to the scheme:
  (i) there has been a failure to comply with a relevant requirement and the failure is significant. A failure is "significant" if there is a failure to give information or evidence that may be of significance, or there are reasonable grounds for believing that the failure might prejudice the assessment or collection of tax by HMRC;
  (ii) any information given pursuant to a relevant requirement is inaccurate in a material respect;
  (iii) any declaration given pursuant to a relevant requirement is false in a material respect;
  (iv) there is no scheme manager; and

(b) by reason of that condition being met it is not appropriate that transfers of sums or assets held for the purposes of, or representing accrued rights under, registered pension schemes so as to become held for the purposes of, or to represent rights under, the ROPS should be recognised transfers; and

(c) HMRC has notified the person(s) appearing to be the scheme manager of that decision.

33-018  HMRC may subsequently decide that the pension scheme is to cease to be so excluded.[27] They must notify the scheme manager of any such decision.

33-019  The scheme manager may appeal any decision made by HMRC within 30 days under FA 2004 s.170(2). On an appeal the tribunal will decide if the ROPS ought to have been excluded as a QROPS. If the tribunal concludes that the scheme ought not to have been excluded then the scheme is deemed to have never ceased to be a QROPS (subject to any appeal by HMRC).

---

[25] See Form APSS 251. It is necessary to specify which sections of the local tax legislation provide either for the tax relief on contributions or for the taxation of benefits paid (which must be the case in order for the scheme to be a ROPS).

[26] FA 2004 s.169(3). It is thus a broader concept than the scheme administrator as defined in FA 2004 s.270, which is the person(s) responsible for very specific functions.

[27] FA 2004 s.169(7).

# TAXATION

There is no suggestion in the legislation (or in HMRC guidance[28]) that a scheme can be excluded on a retrospective basis, so exclusion under s.169(5) should not cause any previous transfers to the scheme to cease to be recognised transfers.

**33-020**

### Residency of member

There is no express requirement that a member of a QROPS has ceased to be resident in the UK, or that he has any intention of leaving the UK in the future.

**33-021**

## TAXATION

The following points may be noted:

**33-022**

(a) A registered pension scheme can make a recognised transfer (which is an authorised payment) to a QROPS, and an RNUKS can transfer funds to a QROPS without an unauthorised payments charge applying.[29] This is the only reason for a ROPS to seek QROPS status.

(b) Making such a transfer will cause the QROPS to become an RNUKS (in addition to being a QROPS), and so a modified form of the main FA 2004 Pt 4 provisions will apply to such transferred funds.[30]

(c) Prior to 6 April 2024, for lifetime allowance purposes, a transfer from a registered pension scheme to a QROPS was a BCE (BCE 8),[31] but such transferred funds could not be subject to a further BCE, meaning that investment growth in the QROPS was not tested against the member's lifetime allowance.[32] The rationale for this was that any investment growth applicable to the funds transferred to the QROPS will not benefit from UK tax relief and so there should be no further testing against the lifetime allowance.

(d) Prior to 6 April 2017, all QROPS were QNUPS because the requirements to be a ROPS were identical to the QNUPS requirements.[33] Since that date, the QNUPS requirements are in certain respects more onerous than the ROPS requirements, so it is possible (although very uncommon[34]) for a scheme to be a QROPS but not a QNUPS.

(e) A QROPS will be an EFRBS if it is an occupational scheme.[35] A QROPS may also form part of an EFRBS where funds are transferred to the QROPS from an occupational scheme.

(f) Pension income received by a UK resident from a QROPS is taxable under

---

[28] See PTM112500.
[29] A transfer from an RNUKS to a QROPS is not a recognised transfer (see FA 2004 s.169(1)), but the application of the member payment provisions means that a transfer under an RNUKS which would be a recognised transfer if made by a registered pension scheme does not give rise to an unauthorised payments charge.
[30] For RNUKS, see Ch.30.
[31] For the lifetime allowance, see Ch.10.
[32] The various BCEs could occur only under a registered pension scheme (see Ch.10). The lifetime allowance provisions as they were applied to RNUKS only applied to a member's UK tax-relieved fund (and not a member's transfer fund or ring-fenced transfer funds).
[33] For QNUPS, see Ch.34.
[34] See Ch.31.
[35] For EFRBS, see Ch.35. The charge under ITEPA 2003 s.394 will not generally apply to the extent that the RNUKS tax charges apply. There is a wider exception from the disguised remuneration provisions.

ITEPA 2003 Pt 9 Ch.4 (foreign pensions). Remittance basis taxpayers are taxable only to the extent that the income is remitted to the UK.[36]

(g) If a member of a QROPS ceases to satisfy the UK residency condition, the member payment charges cease to apply.[37] This means that, inter alia, any funds in a QROPS may be transferred to a scheme which is neither a registered pension scheme nor a QROPS without giving rise to an unauthorised payments charge.

(h) Since 9 March 2017, a recognised transfer to a QROPS, or a transfer from one QROPS to another, may give rise to an overseas transfer charge.

## THE OVERSEAS TRANSFER CHARGE

**33-023** The overseas transfer charge is considered in more detail in Ch.12. The main provision (in s.244AC) imposes a charge where: (a) a recognised transfer is made from a registered pension scheme to a QROPS, or a relieved relevant non-UK scheme transfer is made from an RNUKS to a QROPS;[38] or (b) an "onward transfer" is made during the "relevant period" for the "original transfer".[39]

With effect from 6 April 2024, the overseas transfer charge also arises where the amount transferred by a recognised transfer to a QROPS, or a relieved relevant non-UK scheme transfer is made from an RNUKS to a QROPS; or an onwards transfer, exceeds the member's available "overseas transfer allowance".

This chapter is concerned only with onward transfers.

### "Onward transfer", "relevant period", and "original transfer"

**33-024** An "onward transfer" means a transfer of sums or assets held for the purposes of, or representing accrued rights under, an arrangement under a QROPS or a former QROPS in relation to a member so as to become held for the purposes of, or to represent rights under, an arrangement under another QROPS in relation to that person as a member of that other QROPS. Where there is an onward transfer, it is necessary to identify the "original transfer" in relation to that onward transfer, so that one can determine the "relevant period". This involves tracing the sums/assets transferred by the onward transfer back to a previous recognised transfer or relieved relevant non-UK scheme transfer from a registered pension scheme or RNUKS to a QROPS. If there has been more than one such transfer, the original transfer is the most recent transfer.[40] If there has not been any such recognised transfer or relieved relevant non-UK scheme transfer, the sums/assets must be traced back to a previous "relevant transfer", meaning a transfer of sums or assets from

---

[36] See Ch.26. In addition, prior to 6 April 2017 only 90% of a pension received by a UK resident from a non-UK scheme (such as a QROPS) was subject to UK tax. Such pension income is now fully taxable.

[37] See Ch.30. In relation to funds transferred to a QROPS before 6 April 2017, the residency condition is satisfied if the member has been non-UK resident for five complete tax years, and in relation to funds transferred on or after that date it is satisfied if he has been non-UK resident for ten complete tax years.

[38] For the application of the overseas transfer charge to relieved relevant non-UK scheme transfers from RNUKS, see Ch.30.

[39] FA 2004 s.244A.

[40] For example, where there is a recognised transfer to a QROPS and the sums/assets are subsequently transferred from the QROPS to a registered pension scheme, and then there is another recognised transfer from the registered pension scheme to a QROPS, the latter recognised transfer is the original transfer.

## THE OVERSEAS TRANSFER CHARGE

an RNUKS to a QROPS, which transferred some or all of the member's "UK tax-relieved fund".[41] A member's UK tax-relieved fund comprises the sums/assets representing contributions made to the transferring RNUKS which benefitted from any of the following on or after 6 April 2006[42]:

(a) tax relief by virtue of FA 2004 Sch.33 (migrant member relief), including transitional corresponding relief[43]; or
(b) tax relief under double tax arrangements; or
(c) exemption from tax by virtue of ITEPA 2003 s.307 (see Ch.30) when the RNUKS was an overseas pension scheme.

**33-025** If the sums/assets cannot be traced back to either a recognised transfer or a relevant transfer (for example, the sums/assets in the QROPS derive from an EFRBS that is not an RNUKS), the overseas transfer charge will not apply to those sums/assets. This is presumably because those sums/assets will not (usually)[44] have benefitted from any UK tax relief.

**33-026** The previous recognised transfer or relevant transfer (as the case may be) is the "original transfer". Where there are different original transfers for different parts of an onward transfer, each such part of the onward transfer is deemed to be a separate onward transfer.

**33-027** The relevant period begins with the date of the onward transfer and ends five complete tax years after the original transfer.[45] That is to say, the relevant period ends five years from the 6 April following the original transfer (or, where the original transfer is made on 6 April, five years from that date).

### The main provision: s.244AC

**33-028** As noted above, the main provision in s.244AC imposes a charge (subject to the exclusions described below) where either: (a) a recognised transfer is made from a registered pension scheme to a QROPS, or a relieved relevant non-UK scheme transfer is made from an RNUKS to a QROPS;[46] or (b) an "onward transfer" is made during the "relevant period" for the "original transfer".[47]

*Pre-9 March 2017 grandfathering*

**33-029** An onward transfer is excluded from the overseas transfer charge under s.244AC to the extent that the transfer is not made out of the member's *ring-fenced transfer funds* under the scheme.[48] The member's ring-fenced transfer fund means the sums or assets transferred as a result of an original relevant transfer or a subsequent

---

[41] FA 2004 Sch.34 para.1(6).
[42] See FA 2004 Sch.34 para.3.
[43] See FA 2004 Sch.36 para.51(3) regarding employee contributions and The Taxation of Pension Schemes (Transitional Provisions) Order 2006 (SI 2006/572) art.15(2) regarding employer contributions. These provisions are discussed in Ch.24.
[44] Undoubtedly, some employers will have obtained a tax deduction for contributions to unregistered pension schemes notwithstanding certain provisions designed to defer the deduction until such time as benefits are provided under the scheme (see Ch.24).
[45] FA 2004 s.244A(4). It seems inevitable that Parliament will increase the length of the relevant period in due course.
[46] For the application of the overseas transfer charge to relieved relevant non-UK scheme transfers from RNUKS, see Ch.30.
[47] FA 2004 s.244A.
[48] FA 2004 s.244G(3).

relevant transfer.[49] An original relevant transfer means[50]: (a) a (direct or indirect) transfer of sums or assets from a registered pension scheme to an RNUKS in relation to a member on or after 9 March 2017; (b) a (direct or indirect) transfer of sums or assets from one RNUKS to another in relation to a member on or after 9 March 2017, of the whole or part of the UK tax-relieved fund of a relieved member of a QROPS; or (c) a (direct or indirect) transfer of sums or assets from one RNUKS to another in relation to a member, on or after 6 April 2017, of the whole or part of the UK tax-relieved fund of a relieved member of an RNUKS that is not a QROPS. Where a ring-fenced transfer fund is subsequently transferred from one RNUKS to another in relation to a member, the sums and assets transferred as a result of the transfer also constitute a ring-fenced transfer fund. Such a transfer is a *subsequent relevant transfer*, and is not an original relevant transfer.[51]

**Exclusions**

33-030    There are five exclusions to the overseas transfer charge under s.244AC: (a) the member and receiving scheme are both in the same country; (b) the member and the receiving scheme are both in EEA states; (c) the receiving scheme is an occupational pension scheme; (d) The receiving scheme set up by international organisation; and (e) The receiving scheme is an overseas public service scheme. The requirements in (a) and (b) must continue to be met for the duration of the relevant period (i.e. five full tax years after the date of the original transfer) in order for the exclusion to apply. If the requirements cease to be satisfied at any time during the relevant period then the charge will arise at that time.

*Member and receiving scheme is same country*

33-031    An onward transfer to a QROPS is excluded from the charge if during so much of the relevant period as is after the time of the onward transfer: (a) the member is resident in the country or territory in which the QROPS is established; and (b) there is no subsequent onward transfer that: (i) is of sums and assets which derive from those transferred by the prior onward transfer; and (ii) is not excluded from the charge. If there is an onward transfer which is not excluded, the onward transfer will itself be subject to the charge. If an onward transfer causes an exclusion to cease to apply in respect of the original transfer, this creates two charges and relief is given provided that one of them is paid. However, the significance of this is that if the fund reduces in value after the recognised transfer (e.g. as a result of the provision of benefits) and there is a subsequent transfer to another QROPS that is not excluded then the charge will be on the higher of the two values transferred. If the member is resident in that country or territory at the time of the onward transfer then it is expressly assumed that the member will continue to be so resident during the relevant period. If during the relevant period the member ceases to be resident in the country or territory in which the QROPS is established (other than as a result of his death) the charge will apply at that time.

*Member and receiving scheme in EEA States*

33-032    An onward transfer is excluded from the charge if during the remaining relevant period the member is resident in an EEA state, and there is no subsequent onward

---

[49] FA 2004 Sch.34 para.1(6A).
[50] FA 2004 Sch.34 para.1(6B).
[51] FA 2004 Sch.34 para.1(6D).

transfer that: (a) is of sums or assets which, in whole or part, directly or indirectly derive from those transferred by the onward transfer; and (b) is not excluded from the charge. Provided that the member is resident in an EEA state at the time of the onward transfer, it is expressly assumed that he will continue to be so resident. If at any time before the end of the relevant period he ceases to be so resident (otherwise than by reason of his death) the charge applies at that time. There is no express requirement that the QROPS continues to be established in an EEA state for the duration of the relevant period. The member need not be resident in the same EEA state throughout the relevant period, and there is no requirement that the QROPS and the member are resident in the same EEA state. This exception will be modified with effect from 31 December 2020 to apply where the member is resident in the UK or an EEA State.[52]

**Transfers exceeding available overseas transfer allowance: s.244IA**

From 6 April 2024, the overseas transfer charge also arises in two circumstances where an onwards transfer made during the relevant period for the original transfer exceeds the member's available overseas transfer allowance.[53] A member's "overseas transfer allowance" is an amount equal to the member's LS&DB allowance.[54]  33-033

Firstly, the overseas transfer charge arises where: (a) an onwards transfer is made to a QROPS during the relevant period for the original transfer; (b) the transfer is excluded from the charge under s.244AC; and (c) the transferred value (see below) exceeds the member's available overseas transfer allowance.  33-034

Secondly, the overseas transfer charge arises where: (a) an onwards transfer is made to a QROPS during the relevant period for the original transfer; (b) that transfer was subject to the overseas transfer charge under s.244AC ("the original charge"); (c) a person liable to the original charge becomes entitled under s.244M to a repayment in respect of the original charge; and (d) the transferred value exceeds the member's available overseas transfer allowance  33-035

*Availability of member's overseas transfer allowance*

For the purposes of s.244IA, on the making of an onwards transfer made during the relevant period for the original transfer ("the current overseas transfer"), the amount of the member's available overseas transfer allowance is: (a) so much of that allowance as is left after deducting the previously-used amount; or (b) if none is left after deducting that amount, nil.[55] The "previously-used amount" is the aggregate of the transferred value (see below) of each such transfer (if any) that has been made in relation to the member before the current overseas transfer. However, only transfers made on or after 6 April 2024 are taken into account.  33-036

**The "transferred value"**

If the transfer is from a QROPS or former QROPS, the transferred value is the value of the cash and assets transferred that are attributable to the member's ring-fenced transfer funds under the scheme, subject to the following provisos:  33-037

---

[52] The Taxes (Amendments) (EU Exit) Regulations 2019 (SI 2019/689) reg.12(2).
[53] FA 2004 s.244IA. This charge also applies to "relieved relevant non-UK scheme transfers" (i.e. transfers from RNUKS which have benefitted from UK tax relief): see Ch.30.
[54] FA 2004 s.244IB.
[55] FA 2004 s.244IC. "Relieved relevant non-UK scheme transfers" (i.e. transfers from RNUKS which have benefitted from UK tax relief) must also be included: see Ch.30.

(a) If a transfer (before 6 April 2023) gave rise to a lifetime allowance charge which was deducted from the amount transferred, the transferred value is the value of the cash and assets transferred after deduction of the lifetime allowance charge.[56]
(b) If the scheme manager of the transferring scheme pays the overseas transfer charge on the transfer and deducts the amount of the charge from the transfer, the transferred value is the value of the cash and assets transferred before the deduction.
(c) If the member pays the charge on the transfer, the transferred value is the value of the cash and assets transferred without any deduction for the charge.
(d) If the scheme manager of the transferring scheme pays the charge on the transfer and does so: (a) otherwise than by deduction from the transfer; and (b) out of sums and assets held for the purposes of the scheme from which the transfer is made,[57] the transferred value is the amount given by the above provisions grossed up by 25%.
(e) If a transfer is one that is initially assumed to be excluded[58] but an event occurring before the end of the relevant period means that the transfer is not so excluded, the transferred value is the value of the cash or assets transferred which, at the time of the event, are represented in any of the member's ring-fenced transfer funds under any QROPS or former QROPS. If benefits have been provided since the transfer this will reduce the amount of the charge, as will a transfer to a registered pension scheme. So, where it becomes apparent that an exclusion is likely to cease within the five-year period, a charge can be avoided by distributing the fund to the member or transferring the fund to a registered pension scheme before the exclusion ceases.[59]

**Amount of the charge**

**33-038** Where the charge arises under s.244AC, the charge is equal to 25% of the "transferred value" (see above).[60] However, where the transfer is an onward transfer and the charge in s.244IA(1) arose in relation to the original transfer (i.e. the original exceeded the member's available overseas transfer allowance: see Ch.12), the charge is 25% of so much of the "transferred value" of the original transfer as did not exceed the amount of the member's available overseas transfer allowance.[61]

Where the charge arises under s.244IA, the charge is 25% of so much of the transferred value as exceeds the amount of the member's available overseas transfer allowance.

*Liability*

**33-039** In the case of an onward transfer, the scheme manager of the transferring QROPS or former QROPS and the member are jointly and severally liable. If a transfer is

---

[56] FA 2004 s.244K(5).
[57] e.g. from the member's retained rights under the transferring scheme, or from a general fund under the transferring scheme.
[58] i.e. the member and receiving scheme were both (at the time of the transfer) resident in the same country, or they were both in EEA states.
[59] FA 2004 s.244K(6).
[60] FA 2004 s.244JA.
[61] FA 2004 s.244JA(1).

one that is initially assumed to be excluded[62] but an event occurring before the end of the relevant period means that the transfer is not so excluded, the member is jointly and severally liable with the scheme manager of any QROPS or former QROPS which is at that time holding the ring-fenced transfer funds[63] which have become subject to the charge.

The scheme manager of a former QROPS is liable to the overseas transfer charge in the case of a transfer only if the former QROPS: (a) was a QROPS when a relevant inward transfer[64] was made; and (b) where a relevant inward transfer was made before 9 March 2017, was a QROPS on 9 March 2017. **33-040**

The scheme manager must notify HMRC of the event causing the charge to apply, and HMRC will provide the scheme manager with an accounting reference for paying the charge. Payment is due within 91 days of the date of issue of the accounting reference.[65] If the charge is not paid within this period then it carries interest at the prescribed rate until payment.[66] **33-041**

*Avoidance of double charge*

An onward transfer is excluded from the overseas transfer charge (under s.244AC and s.244IA) if: (a) the charge was paid on the original transfer and the amount paid is not repayable; or (b) the charge was paid on a previous onward transfer, the amount paid is not repayable, the previous onward transfer was made after the original transfer, and all the sums and assets transferred by the current onward transfer directly or indirectly derive from those transferred by the previous onward transfer.[67] **33-042**

# INFORMATION REQUIREMENTS

The information requirements for QROPS and former QROPS are found primarily in the Pension Schemes (Information Requirements for Qualifying Overseas Pension Schemes, Qualifying Recognised Overseas Pension Schemes and Corresponding Relief) Regulations 2006 (SI 2006/208). These provisions have only limited application to former QROPS which ceased to be QROPS prior to 14 October 2013. In addition, HMRC can issue an information notice at any time under FA 2008 Sch.36.[68] **33-043**

**Obligations of the scheme manager**

Information requirements apply to a scheme manager of a QROPS (and in most cases a former QROPS) in relation to the following: **33-044**

---

[62] i.e. the member and receiving scheme were both (at the time of the transfer) in the same country, or they were both in EEA states.
[63] A "ring-fenced transfer fund" in relation to a QROPS or former QROPS has the meaning in FA 2004 Sch.34 para.1.
[64] A "relevant inward transfer" means a recognised or onwards transfer to the former QROPS (at a time when it was a QROPS) of sums and assets which, to any extent, are represented by sums or assets transferred by the transfer concerned.
[65] SI 2006/208 reg.3AH.
[66] SI 2006/208 reg.3AJ. The "prescribed rate" means the rate applicable under FA 1989 s.178 for the purposes of TMA 1970 s.86, which is Bank of England base rate plus 2.5% (The Taxes (Interest Rate) Regulations 1989 (SI 1989/1297) reg.3(2)).
[67] FA 2004 s.244G(2).
[68] Penalties may be imposed for failing to comply with an information notice.

(a) *The scheme:* information relating to the scheme must be provided periodically (generally every five years) to HMRC.[69] HMRC may also require the information specified in reg.3(1) to be provided at any time.[70]

(b) *Payments:* information must be provided to HMRC when an actual or deemed payment[71] is made in respect of[72] a member in respect of whom there is any ring-fenced transfer funds[73] or a relevant transfer fund.[74] The information must be provided within 90 days of the payment, or by such other time as is agreed with HMRC. This requirement ceases once, in broad terms, more than ten years has elapsed since the transfer to the scheme provided that the member does not at that time satisfy the UK residency condition in Sch.34 para.2.[75]

(c) *Transfers:* information must be provided[76]:
   (i) to HMRC, where a recognised transfer is made to the scheme, or an onward transfer is made by the scheme, and an event occurring during the relevant period means that the transfer ceases to be excluded from the overseas transfer charge, or that entitlement to repayment under s.244M arises.[77] This requirement ceases once, in broad terms, more than ten years has elapsed since the transfer to the scheme provided that the member does not satisfy the UK residency condition in Sch.34 para.2 at that time[78];
   (ii) to HMRC, where a recognised transfer is made to the scheme, or an onward transfer is made by the scheme, and the scheme manager becomes aware that the member has during the relevant period acquired a new residential address that is neither in the country or territory in which the scheme is established, nor in an EEA state[79];
   (iii) to HMRC, where sums or assets are received by the scheme from: (a) a registered pension scheme; or (b) another QROPS if those sums or assets have at any time been held for the purposes of a registered pension scheme.[80] This obligation arises only if HMRC require the information to be provided;
   (iv) to the scheme manager of a transferee QROPS, where sums or as-

---

[69] SI 2006/208 reg.3(1A) to (1D) (with effect from 6 April 2016). The information is provided in form APSS 251. See PTM112600.
[70] See SI 2006/208 reg.3(1)(g) and PTM112720.
[71] Most, but not all, deemed unauthorised payments are reportable: only those within FA 2004 ss.172-174A (see Ch.18), Sch.28 para.2A (reduction in rate of scheme pension as part of avoidance arrangements: see Ch.13), or Sch.29 para.3A (PCLS is recycled: see Ch.6).
[72] Regulation 3(2) does not expressly apply where a payment is made "to" a member (only where it is "in respect of" a member: see Ch.18 for the distinction). This is a drafting error.
[73] The term "ring-fenced transfer fund" is not defined for these purposes. It is presumably intended to have the same meaning as in FA 2004 Sch.34 para.1(6C) (see Ch.30).
[74] SI 2006/208 reg.3(2). The information is provided in form APSS253. See PTM112700). In the case of a payment by way of a pension the obligation applies only to the first such payment. Given that each purchase or sale of an investment involves a *payment*, it seems that, strictly speaking, it should be reported to HMRC.
[75] SI 2006/208 reg.3(3).
[76] A transfer will involve a payment, so the requirements in (b) above may also apply.
[77] SI 2006/208 reg3(2B). See PTM112700.
[78] SI 2006/208 reg.3(3A).
[79] SI 2006/208 reg.3(2C). See PTM112700.
[80] SI 2006/208 reg.3A. See PTM112720. No obligation arises where the transferring scheme is a former QROPS.

# INFORMATION REQUIREMENTS 741

(v) sets comprised in a member's UK tax-relieved fund, relevant transfer fund or any ring-fenced transfer funds are transferred[81];

(v) to the member, where an onward transfer is made and either the overseas transfer charge arises on the transfer, or an exclusion to the charge applies[82];

(vi) to the member, where, following a recognised transfer or onward transfer to the QROPS, an event occurs during the relevant period which causes either an exclusion to the overseas transfer charge to cease to apply, or entitlement to repayment to arise[83]; and

(vii) to the scheme manager or scheme administrator of a transferee QROPS or registered pension scheme, where: (a) there is a transfer of the whole or part of a member's UK tax-relieved fund or relevant transfer fund; and (b) there is reason to believe that the member first flexibly accessed his pension rights before the transfer; and (c) at the time the member first flexibly accessed his pension rights he was UK resident or was so resident in any of the five tax years preceding that time.[84]

(d) *The money purchase annual allowance:* information must be provided to a member if he flexibly accesses his pension rights and either: (i) the scheme is a currently-relieved non-UK pension scheme and the individual is a currently-relieved member of the scheme; or (ii) the member has a relevant transfer fund or ring-fenced transfer funds under the scheme.[85]

(e) *Ceasing to be a QROPS:* information must be provided to HMRC if the scheme ceases to be a QROPS.[86]

## Subsequent changes or corrections

In relation to the obligations in (a), (b), (c)(i) and (e) above, HMRC must be notified if there is a material change affecting information previously provided, or if it becomes apparent that the information is incomplete or contains a material inaccuracy.[87] This obligation does not however arise if the scheme is a former QROPS and at least one of the following applies:

**33-045**

(a) the scheme ceased to be a QROPS prior to 14 October 2013[88];
(b) there is no relevant transfer fund or ring-fenced transfer funds under scheme; or
(c) the member payment provisions do not apply to the member[89] and more than ten years have elapsed since the member's relevant transfer fund came into existence or, where the information relates to a ring-fenced transfer fund in

---

[81] SI 2006/208 reg.3AD. See PTM112750.
[82] SI 2006/208 reg.3AG(1) and (2). See PTM112750.
[83] SI 2006/208 reg.3AG(4). See PTM112750.
[84] SI 2006/208 reg.3AC.
[85] SI 2006/208 reg.3AA, applying FA 2004 Sch.34 paras 9ZA and 9ZB. These terms are explained in Ch.30. This obligation does not arise if: (a) the scheme manager has already so notified the member, or is aware that the member flexibly accessed his pension rights on a previous occasion; or (b) the member is not UK resident when he flexibly accesses his pension rights, and has not been UK resident in any of the five previous tax years.
[86] SI 2006/208 reg.3B. See PTM112700.
[87] SI 2006/208 reg.3C. See PTM112700. The information must be provided in form APSS 251A.
[88] The Registered Pension Schemes and Overseas Pension Schemes (Miscellaneous Amendments) Regulations 2013 (SI 2013/2259) reg.5.
[89] This is a reference to the residency condition in FA 2004 Sch.34 para.2 (see Ch.30).

respect of the relevant member, more than ten years has elapsed beginning with the date on which that ring-fenced transfer fund came into existence.

*Non-compliance*

**33-046** In relation to the obligations in (a), (c)(iii) and (e) above, failing to provide the information within the prescribed time limits, or providing materially inaccurate information, may result in HMRC excluding the scheme from being a QROPS under FA 2004 s.169(5) (see above).

*Former QROPS*

**33-047** The above information requirements apply to QROPS and former QROPS. Most of the provisions in SI 2006/208 do not however apply where the scheme ceased to be a QROPS before 14 October 2013.[90] HMRC may however issue an information notice under FA 2008 Sch.36 to a QROPS or former QROPS no matter when it ceased to be a QROPS.[91]

**33-048** In relation to former QROPS only, penalties are imposed under FA 2008 Sch.36 Pt 7 where the scheme manager (but not a member) of a former QROPS fails to comply with the above obligations other than those in (a) above.[92] To achieve this the provisions in FA 2008 Sch.36 Pt 7 are applied in a slightly modified form as if the information had been required to be provided by an information notice given to the scheme manager and the information notice had specified that the information had to be provided by the time required under the relevant provision.

**Obligations of the member**

**33-049** In outline, information must be provided by a member of a QROPS or former QROPS:

(a) To the scheme manager or scheme administrator of each QROPS (or former QROPS) which is an RNUKS, or registered pension scheme, of which he is an accruing member, where he receives a statement under reg.3AA (see above).[93]

(b) To the scheme manager, where the member requests an onward transfer to a QROPS and the transfer will take place during the relevant period.[94]

---

[90] See SI 2013/2259 regs 4 and 5. The provisions relating to the overseas transfer charge are not excluded but they plainly cannot have any application to schemes which ceased to be QROPS prior to 9 March 2017. The obligations in (c)(iv) and (d) above appear to be the only provisions which apply to all former QROPS no matter when they ceased to be QROPS.
[91] Penalties may be imposed for failing to comply with an information notice.
[92] SI 2006/208 reg.5.
[93] SI 2006/208 reg.3AB.
[94] SI 2006/208 reg.3AE. No obligation arises if the transfer will be excluded from the overseas transfer charge by FA 2004 s.244G (i.e. the charge has already been paid and is not repayable, or the original transfer was made in execution of a request made before 9 March 2017, or the transfer is made otherwise than out of the member's ring-fenced transfer funds).

(c) To the scheme manager, where: (a) a recognised transfer or onward transfer is made to a QROPS; (b) either the overseas transfer charge arises on the transfer or ss.244B or 244C apply; and (c) the member becomes resident in a country or territory or ceases to be resident in a country or territory.[95]

---

[95] SI 2006/208 reg.3AF. Sections 244B and 244C apply where the member and receiving scheme are both in the same country, or the member and receiving scheme are both in EEA states (so the transfer is initially assumed to be excluded from the overseas transfer charge).

# CHAPTER 34

# Qualifying Non-UK Pension Schemes

## TABLE OF CONTENTS

| | |
|---|---|
| Introduction and overview | 34-001 |
|     Contrast with overseas pension schemes | 34-007 |
|     Reporting obligations | 34-008 |
| What is a QNUPS? | 34-009 |
|     "Established" outside the UK | 34-010 |
|     The regulations | 34-011 |
|         International organisations | 34-012 |
|     Recognised for tax purposes | 34-013 |
|         Primary Condition 1 | 34-014 |
|         Primary Condition 2 | 34-015 |
|         Primary Condition 2(a) and (c) | 34-018 |
|         Condition A | 34-019 |
|         Condition B | 34-020 |
|         "Relevant scheme funds" | 34-027 |
|         Pension rule 1 | 34-031 |
|     Regulation 6 | 34-035 |
| Taxation | 34-041 |
|     Inheritance tax | 34-041 |
|     CGT and income tax | 34-043 |
|         Anti-avoidance provisions | 34-044 |

## INTRODUCTION AND OVERVIEW

**34-001** Favourable inheritance tax treatment is afforded to qualifying non-UK pension schemes (QNUPS). There is no wider significance of a pension scheme being a QNUPS; it is not a term used in any income tax or CGT provisions. The primary purpose of the QNUPS provisions appears to be to provide the same inheritance tax treatment to QROPS (and, perhaps to a lesser extent, other types of RNUKS) as applies in relation to registered pension schemes.

**34-002** The relevant provisions are in IHTA 1984 s.271A and the Inheritance Tax (Qualifying Non-UK Pension Scheme) Regulations 2010 (SI 2010/51).[1]

**34-003** There is no mechanism by which QNUPS can be approved by HMRC. In outline, a pension scheme is a QNUPS if:

---

[1] Section 271A was inserted into IHTA 1984 by FA 2008 Sch.29 para.18(6) with effect from 6 April 2008, but is treated as having come into force on 6 April 2006. A draft version of the regulations, together with explanatory notes, were first issued in May 2008. SI 2010/51 came into force on 15 February 2010 but are expressed to have had effect from 6 April 2006. The provisions have not been amended since they were introduced.

(a) it is established outside of the UK;
(b) membership is genuinely open to persons resident in the jurisdiction in which it is established;
(c) the jurisdiction in which it is established provides tax relief in respect of pensions and: (i) tax relief is not available to the member in respect of contributions to the scheme; or (ii) most benefits paid by the scheme are subject to tax;
(d) it is either: (i) approved, recognised, or registered with the local tax authorities as a pension scheme; or (ii) no system for approval, recognition, or registration exists and 70% of each member's relevant scheme funds must be used to provide an income for life and pension benefits cannot commence earlier than age 55 (except in cases of ill-health); and
(e) the scheme is either: (i) regulated by a regulatory body; or (ii) no regulatory body exists and the scheme is either established in the EEA or 70% of each member's relevant scheme funds must be used to provide an income for life and pension benefits cannot commence earlier than age 55 (except in cases of ill-health).

**34-004** Special rules apply to schemes established by international organisations and to certain Australian plans. Each of the above requirements is considered in detail below.

**34-005** It is quite common for certain non-UK schemes to be marketed specifically as being QNUPS. What is usually meant is a non-occupational scheme which satisfies the QNUPS requirements and is not a QROPS or other RNUKS. Such schemes will inevitably be "overseas pension schemes", and thus certain CGT advantages apply.[2] Such schemes may be particularly attractive to UK domiciled individuals[3] who have already used up their annual allowance for a tax year or have reached their lifetime allowance under registered pension schemes or RNUKS, or who want the scheme to make investments that would not be tax-efficient if made by a registered pension scheme or QROPS (such as taxable property).

**34-006** Since April 2017, there has been increased interest in QNUPS holding residential property, even for non-UK domiciled individuals. Until April 2017, foreign domiciliaries were chargeable to inheritance tax only in respect of UK situs assets held directly or held by a trust set up by the foreign domiciled settlor. Such assets were therefore frequently held by a non-UK company. The foreign domiciled individual or trust would then hold non-UK situs assets (i.e. the shares in the non-UK company), which were therefore excluded property for inheritance tax purposes. The effect of IHTA 1984 Sch.A1 is that if a such an individual or trust owns any interests in non-UK assets which derive their value (directly or indirectly) from UK residential property then such property is not excluded property. It also applies where such an individual or trust holds any loans (whether held directly or through companies) to acquire, maintain or improve UK residential property. The favourable inheritance tax treatment afforded to QNUPS is unaffected by IHTA 1984 Sch.A1.

---

[2] See Ch.31.
[3] Settled property contributed by non-UK domiciled individuals will usually be excluded property for inheritance tax purposes (provided that it does not have a UK situs), and as such will benefit from favourable inheritance tax treatment.

## Contrast with overseas pension schemes

All QNUPS are overseas pension schemes, but since 6 April 2017 not all overseas pension schemes are QNUPS. Prior to that date, the requirements were identical.[4] On that date the provisions relating to overseas pension schemes were amended by removing any requirement to use 70% of a member's fund to provide the member with an income for life (to reflect the flexibilities available to money purchase registered pension schemes since April 2015). As the QNUPS regulations have not been amended, it is now possible that an overseas pension scheme may not be a QNUPS.

**34-007**

## Reporting obligations

There are no HMRC reporting requirements relating specifically to QNUPS.

**34-008**

# WHAT IS A QNUPS?

Pursuant to IHTA 1984 s.271A(1), a QNUPS is a pension scheme[5] (other than a registered pension scheme) which:

**34-009**

(a) is established in a country or territory outside the UK; and
(b) satisfies any requirements prescribed for the purposes of s.271A by regulations made by HMRC.[6]

## "Established" outside the UK

It is likely that a pension scheme is "established" in the country or territory in which its main administration is carried out.[7] This is the place in which any decisions relating to the administration of a scheme are made.[8] Activities which are purely incidental to the administration of the scheme or could reasonably be

**34-010**

---

[4] See Ch.31.
[5] "Pension scheme" has the same meaning as in FA 2004 s.150(1). See Ch.2.
[6] In the period between 6 April 2008 (when s.271A was introduced) and 15 February 2010 (when 2010/51 came into force), no requirements were "prescribed by HMRC", so it seems that any pension scheme established outside of the UK satisfied the requirements in s.271A and was a QNUPS. Where a non-UK pension scheme held relevant property prior to 6 April 2008, this may have caused an inheritance tax exit charge on that date. Any non-UK pension scheme which did not satisfy SI 2010/51 on 15 February 2010 would cease to be QNUPS on that date, thereby causing the settled property to become relevant property once again. Ceasing to be a QNUPS will not itself have caused any inheritance tax charges to arise, because it does not involve a disposition. HMRC are not known to have taken this point.
[7] HMRC's views are set out at PTM112200: "Normally, a scheme will be treated as established in the country where its registered office is and main administration is carried out. If there is no registered office, then the location where its main administration is carried out will guide matters. The scheme's location of main administration is where the scheme's decisions are made. In the case of a trust-based scheme, that would normally be determined by reference to where the scheme trustees are resident as that is where the decision-making responsibilities in respect of the scheme will lie. It should be noted that the country in which a scheme is established may change if the location of the main administration and decision-making changes. In such a case, the scheme manager would have to revisit whether the scheme still meets the requirements to be an overseas pension scheme. The scheme manager is the person or persons administering, or responsible for the management of the pension scheme".
[8] Lightman J found (in the context of PSA 1993 s.146(4)) that *administering* a scheme means (in whole or in part) running the Scheme, e.g. inviting employees to join, keeping records of members, communicating with members, calculating benefits, providing benefit statements, paying benefits when

expected to be carried out by a third party should not be material. In *Macklin v HMRC*[9] the UT found that, in the context of the UK-USA double tax treaty, a pension scheme is established in the geographic location where it is set up, funded, managed and administered on a continuous and stable fashion through human and material resources. It seems that the place in which a scheme is established is fluid; it can change over time and is not limited to the place where the scheme was originally administered.[10]

### The regulations

**34-011**    The applicable regulations are SI 2010/51. Regulation 4 prescribes that the pension scheme must either:

(a) be established by an international organisation for the purpose of providing benefits for, or in respect of, past service as an employee of the organisation and satisfy reg.7; or
(b) be recognised for tax purposes under the tax legislation of the country or territory in which it is established (per reg.5) and satisfy reg.6.

*International organisations*

**34-012**    An international organisation is an organisation to which the International Organisations Act 1968 s.1 applies by virtue of an Order in Council. This includes organisations such as the United Nations and the EU. Regulation 7 is satisfied if: (a) the scheme rules provide that at least 70% of a member's "relevant scheme funds" (see below) will be designated by the scheme manager for the purpose of providing the member with an income for life, or, in the case of a member who has died, so provided immediately before the member's death; and (b) the pension benefits payable to the member under the scheme (and any lump sum associated with those benefits) are payable no earlier than they would be if pension rule 1 applied (see below).

### Recognised for tax purposes

**34-013**    Regulation 5 provides that a pension scheme is recognised for tax purposes under the tax legislation of a country or territory in which it is established if:

(a) Primary Condition 1 *and* Primary Condition 2 are satisfied; and
(b) Condition A *or* Condition B is satisfied.

Primary Condition 1, Primary Condition 2 and Condition A are identical to Conditions 1 to 3 in The Pension Schemes (Categories of Country and Requirements for Overseas Pension Schemes and Recognised Overseas Pension Schemes) Regula-

---

due, keeping documentation up to date, dealing with governmental or regulatory agencies etc. In the case of a funded scheme, it will also involve running the fund and investing in managing the scheme's assets (*R. (Britannic Asset Management Ltd) v Pensions Ombudsman* [2002] EWHC 441 (Admin)).

[9] *Macklin v HMRC* [2015] UKUT 39.
[10] See PTM112200: "[...] the country in which a scheme is established may change if the location of the main administration and decision-making changes". For this reason, the information to be provided periodically to HMRC by the scheme manager of a QROPS includes the country or territory in which it is established (The Pension Schemes (Information Requirements—Qualifying Overseas Pension Schemes, Qualifying Recognised Overseas Pensions Schemes and Corresponding Relief) Regulations 2006 (SI 2006/208) reg.3(1A)). This would not be necessary if the place was static.

WHAT IS A QNUPS? 749

tions 2006 (SI 2006/206) reg.2(3), relating to overseas pension schemes.[11] There is no reason to interpret SI 2010/51 any differently.

*Primary Condition 1*

Primary Condition 1 is that the scheme is open to persons resident in the country or territory in which it is established. This is the same as Condition 1 in SI 2006/206 reg.2(3).[12] The test of whether a scheme is open to residents is a broad practical one: it must be the case that the scheme is genuinely available to local residents.[13]

34-014

*Primary Condition 2*

Primary Condition 2 is that:

34-015

"The scheme is established in a country or territory where there is a system of taxation of personal income under which tax relief is available in respect of pensions and—

(a) tax relief is not available to the member on contributions made to the scheme by the member or, if the member is an employee, by their employer, in respect of earnings to which benefits under the scheme relate;
(b) the scheme is liable to taxation on its income and gains and is of a kind specified in the Schedule to these Regulations[14]; or
(c) all or most of the benefits paid by the scheme to members who are not in serious ill-health are subject to taxation.

For the purposes of this condition 'tax relief' includes the grant of an exemption from tax."

This is the same as Condition 2 in SI 2006/206 reg.2(3).[15] The intention is to ensure that the tax regime applicable to the pension scheme in question is broadly equivalent to the UK regime applicable to registered pension schemes.[16]

34-016

Tax relief (which includes an exemption from tax) must be available in respect of "pensions". What is meant by "pensions" in this context? For the reasons given below it is suggested that the term is being used in a broad sense, such that any tax incentive given in respect of pension *schemes* or pension *benefits* will suffice: the purpose of the condition is to demonstrate that the country or territory is one in which some special tax treatment is given to pension schemes and/or pension benefits.[17] The tax incentive may, for example, relate to contributions to pension schemes, or to investment income received by pension schemes, or to benefits (such as a tax-free lump sum) received from pension schemes in that country or territory.

34-017

---

[11] See the commentary in Ch.31.
[12] For which, see Ch.31.
[13] *Equity Trust Singapore Ltd v HMRC* [2012] EWCA Civ 192; [2012] S.T.C. 998. HMRC's views are set out at PTM112200.
[14] Schedule 1 refers to a complying superannuation plan as defined in the Income Tax Assessment Act 1997 of Australia s.995–1.
[15] For which, see Ch.31.
[16] See *TMF Trustees Singapore Ltd v HMRC* [2012] EWCA Civ 192 at [21] (Lloyd LJ).
[17] HMRC also appear to take this view at PTM112200: "It is necessary for the country or territory (as part of its tax regime for taxing personal income) to give some tax relief incentive in respect of pensions".

*Primary Condition 2(a) and (c)*

**34-018** Unless the pension scheme in question is a complying superannuation plan as defined in the Australian Income Tax Assessment Act 1997 s.995–1, the requirements in either Primary Condition 2(a) or (c) must be met. The difficulties associated with interpreting the identical provisions in SI 2006/206 are discussed in detail below. For the reasons given there, it is suggested that the reference to "the member" in Primary Condition 2(a) should be interpreted as meaning "any member", and the reference to "members" in Primary Condition 2(c) should be interpreted as meaning "resident members".

*Condition A*

**34-019** Condition A is that the scheme is approved or recognised by, or registered with, the relevant tax authorities as a pension scheme in the country or territory in which it is established. This is the same as Condition 3 in SI 2006/206 reg.2(3).[18] It will usually be clear enough whether a scheme is approved by, or registered with, the local tax authorities, but it may be less clear whether a scheme is *recognised* by a tax authority. If there are local tax incentives that apply specifically to pension schemes (as is required in order to satisfy Primary Condition 2) and those tax incentives are capable of applying to the scheme in question, it may be arguable that Condition A is satisfied on the basis that the scheme is *recognised* by the local tax legislation as a pension scheme (and therefore would be recognised as such by the relevant tax authorities). However, the better view is probably that the requirement is satisfied only if there is some mechanism by which the tax authorities can expressly recognise, or acknowledge, that a scheme qualifies for the tax relief, and the scheme in question is so recognised. This is supported by the reference in Condition B to a *system* of recognition. The intention is that Condition A can apply only where there is a system of approval, recognition or registration, and Condition B can apply only where there is not such a system. There should be no gap between Conditions A and B.

*Condition B*

**34-020** Condition B is that:

"(3) If no system applies for the approval or recognition by, or registration with, relevant tax authorities of pension schemes in the country or territory in which it is established—
(a) the scheme must be resident there;
(b) the scheme rules must provide that at least 70% of a member's relevant scheme funds will be designated by the scheme manager for the purpose of providing the member with an income for life, or, in the case of a member who has died, so provided immediately before the member's death; and
(c) the pension benefits payable to the member under the scheme (and any lump sum associated with those benefits) must be payable no earlier than they would be if pension rule 1 applied."

**34-021** There is currently no equivalent of Condition B in SI 2006/206.[19]

**34-022** Notwithstanding the opening words of Condition B ("*If* no system applies…"),

---

[18] For which, see Ch.31.
[19] Whereas a QNUPS need not satisfy Condition A if it satisfies Condition B, an overseas pension scheme must satisfy the equivalent of Condition A (being SI 2006/206 reg.2(3)).

## WHAT IS A QNUPS?

it clearly requires that there is no such system in that county or territory. It uses the word *applies* rather *exists*. If such a system exists but does not apply to the scheme in question, can Condition B be satisfied? The subsequent reference to pension schemes, in the plural, makes it clear that "applies" means "exists".

The provisions do not specify how one is to determine where a scheme is resident. Primary Condition 1 (considered above) refers to the place that a scheme is *established* (and HMRC consider this to be the place that the scheme is administered) and the difference in terminology is presumably intended to have some significance. It may mean that the trustees of the scheme should be resident for tax purposes in that country or territory.

34-023

Paragraph (b) of Condition B specifies that the scheme rules must provide that at least 70% of a member's relevant scheme funds will be designated for the purpose of providing the member with an income for life. Where the scheme rules do not expressly contain such a restriction, one would expect this requirement to be satisfied if the scheme rules provide that benefits must be consistent with the applicable local approval regime, and that regime requires that at least 70% of a member's fund must be used to provide him with an income for life.

34-024

One might expect that the designation of 70% of a member's scheme funds should not occur before the time that benefits commence, but that is not an express requirement. It has been suggested that it may be permissible, for example, to designate 70% of the member's scheme funds for this purpose at the time of each contribution to the scheme, or at the time of a pension transfer to the scheme, such that subsequent investment growth does not have the effect of increasing that designated fund (thereby increasing the amount which may be provided as a lump sum). This is not obviously wrong. The test is plainly not an ongoing test, since the amount so designated will usually be closer to 100% once any lump sum has been paid.

34-025

"Income for life" is undefined. In the context of a pension or annuity payable on an annual basis it seems clear that, once it commences, it must continue until the death of the member. Provided that the payments constitute income of the recipient, there is no requirement in SI 2010/51[20] that such payments are made annually or that the payments are of equal amounts. The income for life requirement may therefore be more flexible than it perhaps appears at first sight. A form of income drawdown should be acceptable provided that it is capped so that the fund cannot be exhausted during the member's life.

34-026

*"Relevant scheme funds"*

Sums or assets are "relevant scheme funds" if they are held under the QNUPS and would be subject to inheritance tax if the scheme were not a QNUPS.[21] The statutory inheritance tax exceptions applicable to QNUPS are as follows:

34-027

(a) a contribution to a QNUPS in respect of an employee of the person making the contribution is expressly not a transfer of value[22];

(b) an omission to exercise pension rights under a QNUPS is not deemed to be a disposition under IHTA 1984 s.3(3)[23];

---

[20] There may well be requirements in the legislation of the jurisdiction in which the scheme is established.
[21] SI 2010/51 reg.2.
[22] IHTA 1984 s.12(2). See Ch.21.
[23] IHTA 1984 s.12(2ZA). See Ch.21.

(c) property held for the purposes of a QNUPS is not relevant property[24];
(d) the provisions which would ordinarily apply to qualifying interests in possession do not apply to interests under QNUPS (both during the life of the beneficiary and on his death)[25]; and
(e) on the death of a beneficiary of a QNUPS, any rights to pension or annuity ceasing on death are disregarded.[26]

**34-028** The exceptions in (a) and (b) above are clearly immaterial to the relevant scheme funds concept. Although (d) and (e) could conceivably be material, it would be more natural to describe those exceptions as applying to the member's rights under the scheme rather than the sums or assets held under the scheme. It therefore seems that the "relevant scheme funds" are those to which (c) applies. The provisions are here assuming that the scheme property is settled property for inheritance tax purposes,[27] and so "subject to inheritance tax" is a reference to the periodic (ten-yearly) charge under IHTA 1984 s.64. If the QNUPS is not established under trusts (e.g. it is a contract-based scheme) then the scheme property may not be settled property, meaning that there are no relevant scheme funds under the scheme.[28] Where the scheme property is settled property, the charge under s.64 applies only if the settled property is relevant property. In the following circumstances any settled property would not be relevant property (irrespective of the QNUPS provisions):

(a) If the settlor is non-UK domiciled, and not deemed to be UK domiciled for inheritance tax purposes, any non-UK situs property held for the purposes of a settlement will constitute excluded property,[29] which is not relevant property.[30]
(b) To the extent that IHTA 1984 s.86 applies the settled property will not be relevant property.[31] It is immaterial to the relevant scheme funds concept that there could be an inheritance tax exit charge (in this case, under IHTA 1984 s.72) because that is a charge on funds leaving the scheme, when they can no longer be described as being "held under a pension scheme".
(c) Any settled property in which a qualifying interest in possession subsists is not relevant property.[32]

**34-029** In the above circumstances, any scheme property that is settled property would not be relevant property, even if the scheme were not a QNUPS, and so the 70% income for life requirement need not apply to such property.

**34-030** There is no reason that a scheme should not have one set of rules applying to

---

[24] IHTA 1984 s.58(1)(d). See Ch.21 and following. This is relevant if only the scheme is established under trusts.
[25] IHTA 1984 s.151(3).
[26] IHTA 1984 s.151(2) and (3).
[27] i.e. the property is either: (a) held in trust for persons in succession or for any person subject to a contingency; or (b) charged or burdened (otherwise than for full consideration in money or money's worth paid for his own use or benefit to the person making the disposition) with the payment of any annuity or other periodical payment payable for a life or any other limited or terminable period. Property is also settled property if it would be so held or charged or burdened if the disposition creating the settlement was regulated by the law of any part of the UK, or whereby, under the law of any other country, the administration of the property is for the time being governed by provisions equivalent in effect to those which would apply if the property were so held, charged or burdened (IHTA 1984 s.43(2)(a) and (c)). See Ch.21.
[28] IHTA 1984 s.43(2)(c) should not apply to a pension or annuity contract because it will have been purchased for full consideration.
[29] IHTA 1984 s.48(3).
[30] IHTA 1984 s.58(1)(f).
[31] IHTA 1984 s.58(1)(d).
[32] IHTA 1984 s.58(1). See Ch.28.

relevant scheme funds and other rules applying only to sums and assets that are not relevant scheme funds. The 70% income for life requirement need apply only to the former.

*Pension rule 1*

Paragraph (c) of Condition B requires that the benefits payable to the member under the scheme are payable no earlier than they would be if pension rule 1 applied. The reference is to benefits *payable* rather than *paid*. If benefits are capable of being paid earlier than if pension rule 1 applied, it is irrelevant that no such benefits are in fact paid. It is unnecessary for the scheme rules to expressly incorporate the provisions of pension rule 1 if the effect of local legislation restricts the payment of benefits from the scheme to circumstances which comply with pension rule 1.[33] It seems reasonably clear that this requirement must be satisfied in respect of every member of the pension scheme (and not merely those members with relevant scheme funds). 34-031

Pension rule 1 (in FA 2004 s.165) provides that no payment of pension may be made before the day on which the member reaches normal minimum pension age unless the ill-health condition was met immediately before the member became entitled to a pension under the scheme. Normal minimum pension age is currently age 55, subject to the member having a protected pension age.[34] 34-032

The ill-health condition is met if the scheme administrator has received evidence from a registered medical practitioner[35] that the member is, and will continue to be, incapable of carrying on his occupation because of physical or mental impairment, and he has in fact ceased to carry on his occupation.[36] Many jurisdictions permit the early provision of benefits in circumstances similar, but not identical, to these. Condition B is not satisfied if benefits may be provided before normal minimum pension age where the ill-health condition is not met. 34-033

A short service refund lump sum, refund of excess contributions lump sum, and a winding-up lump sum may be paid as an authorised payment under a registered pension scheme prior to normal minimum pension age. It seems likely that the possibility of such benefits under a non-UK pension scheme would breach Condition B, especially when contrasted with the similar ROPS provisions in SI 2006/206 reg.3(6A).[37] 34-034

---

[33] HMRC agree at PTM112300.
[34] FA 2004 s.279. See Ch.3. A member of a QNUPS may have a protected pension age only if the funds in the QNUPS derive from a pre-A Day tax-approved scheme where the member was entitled to receive benefits before age 55 (see FA 2004 Sch.36 paras 21 to 23). Prior to 6 April 2015, protection did not apply to a transferee scheme unless the transfer formed part of a block transfer (FA 2004 Sch.36 paras 22(5) and 23(5)). Since 6 April 2015 the protected pension age will apply to a transferee scheme provided that the transfer was a recognised transfer (FA 2004 Sch.36 para.23ZA. For recognised transfers, see Ch.12). A QNUPS must be a QROPS for a recognised transfer to be made to it.
[35] This is not defined. HMRC suggest (at PTM063400) that it means a fully registered person within the meaning of the Medical Act 1983. Where the member is in serious ill-heath overseas, HMRC will accept a certificate from someone with equivalent overseas qualifications. In relation to RNUKS, the relevant provisions are expressly extended to include a medical practitioner practising outside the UK who is authorised, licensed or registered to practise medicine in the country or territory, outside the UK, in which either the scheme or the member is resident (SI 2006/207 regs 14 and 15(4)).
[36] FA 2004 Sch.28 para.1. These requirements are considered in more detail in Ch.13.
[37] SI 2006/206 reg.3(6A) requires that "The benefits payable to the member under the scheme […] (a) are payable no earlier than they would be if pension rule 1 in section 165 applied; or (b) if payable

## Regulation 6

**34-035** Regulation 6 is satisfied if one of reg.6(2), 6(3) or 6(4) applies. The application (or otherwise) of these regulations depends upon whether there is, in the country or territory in which the scheme is established, a body which regulates pension schemes. There is a distinction between the regulation of pension schemes and the regulation of pension providers or trustee companies.[38]

**34-036** Regulation 6(2) is satisfied if there is, in the country or territory in which the scheme is established, a body which regulates occupational pension schemes *and* which regulates the scheme in question.[39]

**34-037** Regulation 6(3) is satisfied if there is in the country or territory in which it is established a body which regulates pension schemes other than occupational pension schemes *and* which regulates the scheme in question.

**34-038** Regulation 6(4) applies if neither 6(2) nor 6(3) applies by reason only that no such regulatory body exists in the country or territory and:

"(a) the scheme is established in another member State, Norway, Iceland or Liechtenstein; or
(b) the scheme is one where—
　(i) the scheme rules provide that at least 70% of a member's relevant scheme funds will be designated by the scheme manager for the purpose of providing the member with an income for life, or, in the case of a member who has died, so provided immediately before the member's death, and
　(ii) the pension benefits payable to the member under the scheme (and any lump sum associated with those benefits) are payable no earlier than they would be if pension rule 1 applied."

**34-039** "Member State" means a member of the EU.[40] The requirements in (b) above are the same as in paragraphs (b) and (c) of Condition B, considered above.

**34-040** Regulation 6 is almost identical to SI 2006/206 reg.2(2).[41] There are two differences. First, in relation to occupational pension schemes, SI 2010/51 is currently more onerous than SI 2006/206 where there is no local regulator. In such circumstances an occupational pension scheme will always satisfy SI 2006/206 reg.2(2), but it will satisfy SI 2010/51 reg.6 only if it is established in the EU/EEA or it satisfies the 70% income for life requirement. Second, SI 2010/51 reg.6(4) applies only if there is no regulator of occupational pension scheme or non-occupational pension schemes,[42] whereas SI 2006/206 is satisfied if there is no local regulator of the particular category of scheme in question.

---

earlier, are only payable in circumstances in which they would be authorised member payments if they were made by a registered pension scheme."

[38] See PTM112200 and Ch.31.
[39] "Occupational pension scheme" has the same meaning as in FA 2004 s.150(5). See Ch.2. The definition in s.150(5) is extremely broad (members need not be employed by, or have any connection at all with, a sponsoring employer).
[40] See European Communities Act 1972 s.1 and Sch.1, applied by Interpretation Act 1978 Sch.1.
[41] See Ch.31.
[42] Paragraph 6(4) can apply only if *neither* 6(2) nor 6(3) applies, and so if there is a regulator of either occupational or non-occupational schemes then it seems that para.6(4) cannot apply.

# TAXATION

## Inheritance tax

**34-041** Subject to one relatively minor exception, IHTA 1984 applies to QNUPS in the same way it applies to registered pension schemes.[43] The minor exception is that IHTA 1984 s.58(2A)(a) applies only to registered pension schemes.[44] Instead, s.58(2A)(b) applies to QNUPS (and s.615 funds). It provides that, for the purposes of s.58(1)(d):

> "property applied to pay lump sum death benefits in respect of a member of a qualifying non-UK pension scheme or a section 615(3) scheme is to be taken to be so held if the benefits are paid within the period of two years beginning with the earlier of the day on which the member's death was first known to the trustees or other persons having the control of the fund and the day on which they could first reasonably be expected to have known of it."

**34-042** As is explained in Ch.21, s.58(2A)(a) appears to have practical application only where the trustees do not have any discretion regarding the identity of a death beneficiary (including where they had discretion but have exercised it). The effect of s.58(2A)(a) is that, until the death benefits are paid, the scheme property will continue to benefit from the exemption in s.58(1)(d). In relation to QNUPS, s.58(2A)(b) imposes a two-year restriction that s.58(2A)(a) does not.

## CGT and income tax

**34-043** There are no special income tax or CGT provisions that apply specifically to QNUPS. All QNUPS are "overseas pension schemes", and for that reason gains accruing on a disposal of investments held for the purposes of the scheme are exempt from CGT.[45] It is important to appreciate that any pension income (including "relevant lump sums") paid to a UK resident member is subject to UK tax,[46] notwithstanding that no UK tax relief may have been available in respect of contributions to the scheme.[47] Pension income paid from a QNUPS to a person resident in the UK is taxable under ITEPA 2003 Pt 9 Ch.4 (foreign pensions).[48] Prior to 6 April 2017, lumps sums paid from a QNUPS to a UK resident were not normally subject to UK tax unless the QNUPS held UK tax-relieved funds or was

---

[43] See Ch.21. The statutory inheritance tax exceptions for QNUPS are set out above.

[44] IHTA 1984 s.58(2A)(a) provides that, for the purposes of IHTA 1984 s.58(1)(d) (i.e. the exemption from the relevant property charges): "... property applied to pay lump sum death benefits within section 168(1) of the FA 2004 in respect of a member of a registered pension scheme is to be taken to be held for the purposes of the scheme from the time of the member's death until the payment is made ...".

[45] TCGA 1992 s.271(1A). This does not apply to gains accruing on the disposal of assets held as a member of a property investment LLP (TCGA 1992 s.271(12)).

[46] Under ITEPA 2003 Pt 9 Ch.4. As the FTT noted in *Haseldine v HMRC* [2012] UKFTT 480 at [37], "There is no applicable principle of symmetry in the construction of the legislation which allows us to disapply a charge on pension income on the basis that no relief is available for the relevant contributions". If the member is a remittance basis taxpayer pension income is taxable only to the extent that it is remitted to the UK.

[47] See Ch.24 for the circumstances in which tax relief is available for contributions to unregistered pension schemes. A QNUPS may also receive UK tax-relieved funds from a registered pension scheme if it is a QROPS. A QNUPS that is not a QROPS may receive UK tax-relieved funds from a QROPS if the residency exemption in FA 2004 Sch.34 para.2 is met (see Ch.30).

[48] See Ch.26.

an occupational scheme.[49] Since 6 April 2017, a lump sum paid from a QNUPS to a UK resident will usually be a "relevant lump sum" for the purposes of ITEPA 2003 Pt 9 Ch.4 and therefore taxable in the same way as pension income, subject to certain permitted deductions.[50]

*Anti-avoidance provisions*

**34-044** If the scheme is regulated in its local jurisdiction then (subject to any local restrictions, or any restrictions in the scheme rules) it is possible for a QNUPS to pay an amount equal to the entirety of a member's fund under the scheme once the member attains minimum pension age. Prior to April 2015, one would have been concerned, in such circumstances, about the application of certain anti-avoidance provisions.[51] Given that such payments are now capable of being authorised payments under a registered pension scheme, it is strongly arguable that these anti-avoidance provisions should not apply to an unregistered pension scheme simply because it is capable of making such payments. As a matter of principle, if the benefit structure of a QNUPS does not differ markedly from a registered pension scheme then it is difficult to see how such anti-avoidance provisions could have any application.

**34-045** Many jurisdictions permit loans to be made from a pension scheme to a scheme member. Does the availability of such loans cause these anti-avoidance provisions to apply? Whilst the position is clearer if loans are not available, it seems likely that the availability of loans on clearly commercial terms should be acceptable. This should be the case where, for example, loans are made on terms broadly similar to authorised employer loans under FA 2004 Pt 4.[52] It is implicit that authorised employer loans do not detract from the bona fides of a registered pension scheme, and so the same ought to apply to a loan to a member of a QNUPS.

---

[49] That is to say: (a) the QNUPS was an RNUKS and the payment was referable to the member's UK tax-relieved fund or relevant transfer fund (see Ch.30); (b) the QNUPS was an EFRBS and the lump sum was a relevant benefit (see Ch.35); or (c) the disguised remuneration provisions applied (see Ch.27).

[50] See Ch.26. The deductions include so much of the lump sum as is paid in respect of the value on 5 April 2017 of rights, accrued by then, specifically to receive benefits by way of lump sum payments. In addition, if the QNUPS is an overseas pension scheme (which most QNUPS will be), one deducts so much of the lump sum as would not be liable to tax under ITEPA 2003 Pt 9 if the scheme were a registered pension scheme. In most cases it should be relatively straightforward to pay lump sum death benefits (perhaps via a death benefits trust) in such a way that this latter deduction will reduce the taxable value to nil.

[51] Namely the income tax settlements provisions, the transfer of assets abroad provisions and the CGT settlements provisions (see Ch.25).

[52] See Ch.11.

# CHAPTER 35

# Employer-Financed Retirement Benefits Schemes

## TABLE OF CONTENTS

| | |
|---|---|
| Introduction | 35-001 |
|     Interaction with other Parts of ITEPA 2003 | 35-002 |
|     EFRBS in practice | 35-005 |
|     Pension transfers | 35-008 |
| What is an EFRBS? | 35-009 |
|     "For" the provision of benefits including relevant benefits | 35-011 |
|     "To or in respect of" | 35-012 |
|     "Scheme" | 35-014 |
| Relevant benefits | 35-019 |
|     Lump sum, gratuity or other benefit | 35-021 |
|     "On" | 35-022 |
|     "In anticipation of" | 35-023 |
|     "Retirement" | 35-024 |
|     "In connection with past service" | 35-031 |
|     "A change in the nature of service" | 35-041 |
|     Pension sharing orders | 35-043 |
|     Exclusions | 35-044 |
|         "Charged to tax" under Pt 9 | 35-046 |
|         "Chargeable" by virtue of FA 2004 Sch.34 | 35-051 |
|         Excluded benefits | 35-054 |
|             Ill-health, disablement and accidental death | 35-055 |
|             Regulations made by HMRC under s.393B(3) | 35-056 |
| Taxation | 35-058 |
|     Employer contributions | 35-059 |
|         CTA 2009 s.1290 | 35-059 |
|         FA 2004 s.246 | 35-060 |
|         CTA 2009 s.868 | 35-063 |
|         FA 2004 s.246A | 35-064 |
|         Employer contributions: taxation of the employee | 35-066 |
|     Taxation of relevant benefits | 35-068 |
|         Relevant benefit is provided to an individual | 35-069 |
|             Liability (and application of PAYE) | 35-070 |
|         Relevant benefit is provided to a non-individual | 35-071 |
|             The responsible person | 35-072 |
|         Territorial limitations | 35-074 |
|         Temporary non-residents | 35-078 |
|         Employee contributions | 35-080 |

758    EMPLOYER-FINANCED RETIREMENT BENEFITS SCHEMES

>                Grandfathering of old s.222 schemes ........... 35-081
>                Exemption or reduction for foreign service ....... 35-082
>                Valuing relevant benefits .................... 35-089
>                Employment-related loans .................... 35-090
>                Remittance basis taxpayers ................... 35-091
>         National insurance contributions ................ 35-092
>                Pension commencement lump sums ........... 35-096
>                Serious ill-health lump sum .................. 35-100
>         Inheritance tax ............................. 35-101
>     Reporting obligations ............................. 35-103
>         Special provisions in FA 2008 Sch.36 ............. 35-105

# INTRODUCTION

**35-001**   ITEPA 2003 Pt 6 Ch.2 imposes a charge to income tax where relevant benefits are provided under an employer-financed retirement benefits scheme (EFRBS).[1] Benefits are disregarded to the extent that they derive from employee contributions, and some measure of relief is provided for benefits relating to foreign service (much restricted since 6 April 2017). Where such benefits are provided to an individual, the recipient is liable for the charge. Otherwise, the "responsible person" (usually the trustee or manager of the EFRBS) is liable. In most cases, however, the member's employer will be liable under the PAYE provisions in the first instance.

### Interaction with other Parts of ITEPA 2003

**35-002**   The EFRBS provisions were originally introduced in order to bring within the scope of income tax certain benefits which would not otherwise be taxable. But there is considerable overlap, even with provisions which predate the EFRBS provisions. The order of priority is as follows:

(a)   ITEPA 2003 Pt 2 (earnings).
(b)   Benefits charged to tax under ITEPA 2003 Pt 9, disregarding the relevant lump sum provisions.
(c)   Benefits chargeable under FA 2004 Sch.34 (RNUKS).[2]
(d)   ITEPA 2003 Pt 7A.[3] Any charge in accordance with s.394 is reduced by any tax paid under Pt 7A.[4] Section 394 applies only to the extent that it is greater than a charge under Part 7A.[5]

---

[1]   Prior to 6 April 2006, ITEPA 2003 Pt 6 Ch.1 created an income tax charge on contributions to unapproved retirement benefit schemes, and Pt 6 Ch.2 imposed a tax charge on benefits received from such schemes (with an important exception for lump sums). Such schemes that were funded were commonly referred to as FURBS. Part 6 Chs 1 and 2 were repealed on 6 April 2006. Many FURBS still exist and the EFRBS provisions now apply to such schemes, subject to transitional provisions. For FURBS, see Ch.38.

[2]   Such benefits are expressly not relevant benefits for the purposes of the EFRBS provisions, nor are they taxable under the disguised remuneration provisions.

[3]   As is explained in Ch.27, certain provisions relate specifically to EFRBS: (a) s.554U (pre-6 April contributions to EFRBS (i.e. FURBS)); (b) s.554W (pre-6 April 2011 lump sums); (c) s.554Z4(7) (disapplication of s.554Z4(4) in relation to lump sums accruing on or after 6 April 2017); (d) s.554Z4A (temporary non-residents); and (e) s.554Z11A (temporary non-residents).

[4]   ITEPA 2003 s.554Z2 *overrides* any charge under the benefits code (i.e. the benefits code cannot apply to a relevant step) but not a charge arising in accordance with s.394.

[5]   ITEPA 2003 s.394(4C).

# INTRODUCTION

(e) The relevant lump sum provisions in ITEPA 2003 Pt 9.
(f) The EFRBS provisions.

No liability to income tax arises by virtue of any other provision of ITEPA 2003 in respect of a relevant benefit provided under an EFRBS.[6] **35-003**

If the receipt of a relevant benefit under an EFRBS gives rise to any of the following types of income of the employee or former employee, the charge in accordance with s.394 applies to the amount of the benefit only so far as that amount exceeds the other income:[7] **35-004**

(a) an amount which would count as employment income of the employee or former employee under Pt 7A Ch.2 but for the application of s.554Z5 (overlap with earlier relevant step); or
(b) an amount which would be within (a)–(c) above apart from the employee or former employee having been non-UK resident for any tax year, or any tax year having been a split year as respects the employee or former employee.

## EFRBS in practice

All occupational retirement benefit schemes are EFRBS unless they are either registered pension schemes or s.615 funds. Many foreign occupational pension schemes (quite unintentionally) are s.615 funds.[8] All other foreign occupational schemes are EFRBS; it is irrelevant that they may have no connection with the UK, or that they may be tax-approved in the jurisdiction in which they are established. **35-005**

In addition to foreign occupational schemes, many UK employers have established EFRBS as an alternative (or in addition) to a registered pension scheme.[9] As EFRBS are not subject to the unauthorised payments regime in FA 2004 Pt 4, they are frequently established on much more flexible terms than registered pension schemes. The ability to make loans to members (whether or not on beneficial terms) and to provide benefits in kind is not uncommon. **35-006**

It is also not uncommon for EFRBS, particularly where they are established for the owner managers of a smaller business, to have a more significant discretionary aspect than is found in most registered pension schemes. Instead of allocating scheme property for the benefit of any particular member, the property may simply remain unallocated,[10] or allocated to a general fund, or may be notionally allocated subject to being reallocated, or may be allocated for the benefit of an employee and his entire family (sometimes under a sub-fund or sub-trust). In such cases the benefit structure may resemble a family discretionary settlement. Such schemes may not have any formal process whereby individuals are granted membership; they are simply within the class of beneficiaries (often comprising all employees and former employees of the sponsoring employer). One reason for these unusual features is the tax treatment of EFRBS. In particular, in order to ensure that the scheme property is not relevant property for inheritance tax purposes, it is often necessary to rely on IHTA 1984 s.86, which generally requires the settled property **35-007**

---

[6] ITEPA 2003 s.394(5).
[7] ITEPA 2003 s.394(4A)–(4C).
[8] See Ch.37. It is not necessary for a s.615 fund to be approved or registered with HMRC. Any benefit accrual on or after 6 April 2017 expressly accrues to a separate fund which is not a s.615 fund.
[9] Some of which have been the focus of HMRC attention: see HMRC's Spotlights 5 and 6, and the 4th to the 9th GAAR Opinion Notices.
[10] For an example of this, see *Philpott v HMRC* [2014] UKFTT 853.

to be held for the benefit of all or most of the employees of an employer.[11] Also, concerns relating to the application of the benefits code have tended to discourage the structuring of EFRBS along the lines of traditional pension schemes. The disguised remuneration provisions also discourage the earmarking of sums or assets.

**Pension transfers**

**35-008** A pension transfer from an EFRBS to another EFRBS (or any similar arrangement), is not a relevant benefit.[12] Given the broad definition of "scheme" (see below), it seems quite clear that following a pension transfer from an EFRBS to a personal pension arrangement (including, for example, a QROPS), the transferee scheme will form part of the EFRBS.

# WHAT IS AN EFRBS?

**35-009** ITEPA 2003 s.393A(1) provides:

"In this Chapter 'employer-financed retirement benefits scheme' means a scheme for the provision of benefits consisting of or including relevant benefits to or in respect of employees or former employees of an employer."

**35-010** Registered pension schemes and s.615 funds are not EFRBS, but all other categories of pension scheme (including, for example, QROPS and other RNUKS) may be. The scheme need not be in any sense "employer-financed", and it need not provide benefits connected with "retirement". It does not matter by whom the scheme is established or funded, so schemes established or funded by third parties (such as group companies or shareholders of the employer company) may be EFRBS. There plainly must be *some* connection with employment,[13] but in practice the connection need be only very slight. A contribution by an employer to an employee's non-UK personal pension arrangement (assuming the scheme is not an RNUKS) would plainly provide the necessary connection. As is apparent from the reference to "*employees* or former employees", a scheme designed to provide pre-retirement benefits may be an EFRBS.

**"For" the provision of benefits including relevant benefits**

**35-011** A scheme will be an EFRBS only if it is "for" the provision of benefits consisting of or including relevant benefits.[14] This suggests it is necessary to determine what is the purpose of the scheme. Some commentators take the view that a scheme can be an EFRBS only if the provision of relevant benefits is the primary or substantial purpose of the scheme. The better view is likely to be that a scheme is

---

[11] See Ch.28.
[12] HMRC accept this in their Spotlight 6: "Neither an employer contribution to an EFRBS, nor a transfer between EFRBS gives rise to a possible employment Income Tax charge on the employee". It is for this reason that such a transfer is not, in HMRC's view, a "qualifying benefit" entitling the employer to a tax deduction. A pension transfer may well however be taxable in accordance with the disguised remuneration provisions.
[13] HMRC suggest at EIM15010 that all unregistered schemes are EFRBS, but that is plainly incorrect. If any authority for this statement is required, see step two of ITEPA 2003 s.574A(3), which applies differently depending upon whether or not the (unregistered) pension scheme is an EFRBS.
[14] cf. PSA 1993 s.1 and FA 2004 s.150(1), which refer to a scheme "having or capable of having effect" of providing benefits.

## WHAT IS AN EFRBS?

an EFRBS if it can, according to its terms, provide relevant benefits. On this basis, a scheme the primary purpose of which is to provide pre-retirement benefits is an EFRBS unless it is incapable of providing relevant benefits. Not every benefit provided under such a scheme will be a relevant benefit under an EFRBS; one must look closely at the circumstances in which the benefit is provided.

### "To or in respect of"

The precise scope of the phrase "to or in respect of" is unclear. The same phrase is used in FA 2004 Pt 4,[15] but its meaning is likely to be narrower in s.393A, because the latter is concerned only with benefits whereas the former is concerned with all payments whether or not they confer a benefit. The trustees or managers of an EFRBS will not be empowered to benefit any person other than a beneficiary or any persons materially connected with a beneficiary. Such benefits are plainly provided "in respect of" the beneficiary.   **35-012**

It is quite clear from s.393A(1) that an EFRBS may also be *for* the provision of benefits which are not to or in respect of employees or former employees. If the class of beneficiaries includes persons who are not employees or former employees but do have some connection with the employer (for example, shareholders who have never been employed by the employer) then benefits provided to such persons will be under an EFRBS, but such benefits are unlikely to constitute relevant benefits.   **35-013**

### "Scheme"

"Scheme" includes a deed, agreement, series of agreements, or other arrangements.[16] This is a non-exhaustive definition.[17] The "scheme" comprises all of the "arrangements" which are "for" the provision of benefits consisting of or including relevant benefits to or in respect of employees or former employees of an employer. It follows that the scheme may (and often will) include resolutions of the employer relating to the provision of benefits, and any undertakings given by the employer to make contributions to the scheme (often found in employment contracts or inside letters). This includes verbal promises to provide relevant benefits if the promise amounts to an "agreement". This is because there are no restrictions regarding the type of "agreements" which comprise the scheme.[18] The scheme could consist of a resolution by an employer to make a payment to a former employee.   **35-014**

In *Barclays Bank Pension Fund*,[19] the trustees contended that a one-off gratuitous payment did not constitute a "scheme" because there was no deed, and a unilateral act cannot be an agreement or series of agreements; a bi-lateral agreement is required. The Special Commissioner held that "arrangement" should be given its normal dictionary meaning as extended by the words which capture the sources of   **35-015**

---

[15] See FA 2004 s.161(3), which is considered in Ch.17. The meaning is not clear in that context either, but the provisions of FA 2004 Pt 4 do at least allow one to draw some tentative conclusions. Unfortunately, the EFRBS provisions, being much more concise than FA 2004 Pt 4, provide less material by which one may draw any conclusions. The meanings are unlikely to be coterminous.
[16] ITEPA 2003 s.393A(4).
[17] The suggestion that it is exhaustive was rejected in *Trustees of Barclays Bank Pension Fund v HMRC* [2005] UKSPC SPC00520.
[18] Although note that most—if not all—EFRBS will be *occupational pension schemes* for the purposes of PSA 1993 s.1(1), and such schemes (unless unfunded) must be established under irrevocable trusts if they have their main administration in the UK (PA 2004 s.252).
[19] *Trustees of Barclays Bank Pension Fund v HMRC* [2005] UKSPC SPC00520 at [39]–[44].

the relevant benefits (such as "deed"). He also held that for the purposes of ICTA 1988 s.611(2) (the predecessor to ITEPA 2003 s.393A(4)), an arrangement need not be bilateral, because a deed can be a unilateral instrument, and a deed is expressly an arrangement for the purposes of s.611(2). More helpfully, the Special Commissioner also held that the *arrangement* must be distinct from the *benefit*. The scheme must have a commercial life separate from the mechanics of conferring the benefit.[20] The payments implemented a *plan* or arrangement constituted for their payment. By way of contrast, in *Allum v Marsh* no prior expectation of payment had been raised; hence the payments were not received *under* a retirement benefits scheme.

**35-016** The Special Commissioner in *Barclays* [2005] UKSPC SPC00520 held that the only conceptual limitation of principle is that an "arrangement" must be capable of being put into effect.[21] Thus an *arrangement* must have terms. An *arrangement* must be an arrangement to achieve a particular objective. There can be no *arrangement* in the abstract, which cannot be fructified according to its terms. Equally, there can be no *arrangement* which cannot be implemented on its terms because, say there is a legal or factual impediment which prevents its implementation. He said (at [79]):

"In this case there was an 'arrangement' (and therefore a 'scheme'). The work done to calculate the quantum of the Payments does not of itself constitute a 'scheme' or 'arrangement'. However the letter by Sally Bott on 18 December 1997 informing the Pensioners that BPTS was to be sold, that the tax services would be withdrawn and that one off payments would be made by plc to the Pensioners constituted the framework, distinct from the mechanics of calculating and implementing the mechanics of the Payments, "under" which the Payments were made. This letter of 18 December 1997 raised an expectation of the Payments. It revealed a 'plan' (to enable the Payments to be made). That plan was distinct from the mere mechanics of making the Payments. So when the Payments arrived, the Payments fructified the 'plan' embodied in the letter of 18 December 1997. That letter articulated and constituted an 'arrangement' within Section 611(2). Contrast *Allum v Marsh* where a voluntary payment out of the blue did not fructify any prior expectation that had been raised (and so were not benefits received 'under' a 'retirement benefits scheme'). So the benefits in *Allum v Marsh* were not made under a 'scheme' within section 611(1). Here, in this case, however, the Payments were made under an 'arrangement' (and therefore under a 'scheme'). But since the Payments were not 'relevant benefits' the Payments were not made 'under' a 'retirement benefits scheme'. The letter of 18 December 1997 did not confer any 'relevant benefits' (within section 611(1)) at all and so the 'scheme' or 'arrangement' embodied in that letter could not amount to a 'retirement benefits scheme' within Section 611."

**35-017** Section 393(1) provides that the EFRBS provisions apply to relevant benefits provided "under" an EFRBS, and it is apparent from the extract above that whether or not a benefit is provided *under* a scheme is closely related to the question of whether there is a scheme.[22] In this context, one would expect "under" to mean "pursuant to the terms of".

**35-018** An ex gratia (i.e. voluntary) payment from an employer to a former employee is likely to constitute an "other arrangement", and therefore a scheme,[23] but such a payment may not be a benefit "under" the scheme (as was the case in *Allum v Marsh*).

---

[20] See *Allum v Marsh* [2005] S.T.C. (S.C.D.) 191 at [76].
[21] Citing *Scottish and Universal Newspapers Ltd v Fisher* [1996] S.T.C. (S.C.D.) 311 at [16].
[22] See *Barclays Bank Plc v RCC* [2006] S.T.C. (S.C.D.) 100 at [72]–[79].
[23] *Moffat v Revenue & Customs* [2006] S.T.C. (S.C.D.) 380; [2006] UKSPC SPC00538.

# RELEVANT BENEFITS

Given the broad definition of EFRBS, it is important to determine whether or not a particular benefit is a relevant benefit. ITEPA 2003 s.393B provides: **35-019**

"(1) In this Chapter "relevant benefits" means any lump sum, gratuity or other benefit (including a non-cash benefit) provided (or to be provided)—
  (a) on or in anticipation of the retirement of an employee or former employee,
  (b) on the death of an employee or former employee,
  (c) after the retirement or death of an employee or former employee in connection with past service,
  (d) on or in anticipation of, or in connection with, any change in the nature of service of an employee, or
  (e) to any person by virtue of a pension sharing order or provision relating to an employee or former employee."

The circumstances in (a)–(e) relate to the reason that the benefit is provided. The circumstances in (a), (b) and (d) are such that the employee's ability to earn income is significantly reduced or eradicated. It is implicit that (c) relates to benefits that are *not* provided in connection with retirement or death; they are provided after retirement or death for some other reason, and so the scope of (c) may be significantly broader. Benefits provided in the circumstances envisaged in (e) need not have any connection with retirement, death or past service: if they are provided under an EFRBS then they are relevant benefits. **35-020**

### Lump sum, gratuity or other benefit

A "lump sum" is likely to mean a standalone payment (i.e. not part of a series of payments). "Sum" suggests a payment of money but there can be little doubt that the transfer of an asset can constitute a lump sum.[24] "Gratuity" is likely to mean a payment to which the recipient does not have any entitlement.[25] In practice, the reference to *lump sum* and *gratuity* probably add very little to the word *benefit*. However, *lump sum* must be construed ejusdem generis with *other benefit*, so it must be beneficial; a payment on arm's length terms to a former employer (e.g. to purchase an asset from him) may be a lump sum but it is not a relevant benefit[26] even if it is paid by an EFRBS and it is made following retirement or death.[27] Although there are some indications that *pension* (i.e. income as opposed to a lump sum) may not be a relevant benefit,[28] the better view is that pension is a relevant benefit unless expressly excluded (otherwise the exclusion in s.393B(2)(a) would be otiose). **35-021**

---

[24] See *Irving v HMRC* [2008] EWCA Civ 6; [2008] B.T.C. 36.
[25] See, e.g. *Resolute Management Services Ltd v HMRC* [2008] S.T.C. (S.C.D.) 1202, which considered the meaning of *gratuity* in ITEPA 2003 s.62. The term was considered in a NIC context in *HMRC v Knowledgepoint 360 Group Ltd* [2013] UKUT 007.
[26] This is supported by the use of the word *provided* in s.393B, which suggests that an element of bounty is required (*CIR v Leiner* (1964) 41 T.C. 589; *IRC v Plummer* [1980] A.C. 896).
[27] e.g. the employer may be contractually obliged to buy certain assets used in its business and owned by the employee when he dies or retires.
[28] The Social Security (Contributions) Regulations 2001 (SI 2001/1004) Sch.3 Pt VI para.9(2) provides that a scheme providing only a pension is "not an [EFRBS] because it does not provide relevant benefits".

### "On"

**35-022** A benefit is provided "on" retirement or death if there is a material connection between the provision of the benefit and the retirement or death. The existence of a connection may be determined by examining the terms of the EFRBS. Where the trustees have discretion to provide a benefit, it is necessary to determine for what purpose the trustees exercised their discretion. If they would not have exercised their discretion but for the retirement then that is likely to suffice. The provision of benefits very soon after retirement may suggest, in the absence of any evidence to the contrary, that retirement was the reason that the benefits were provided. But a benefit is not provided *on* retirement simply because it is provided at or around the time of retirement, otherwise it would be very easy to avoid the provision of benefits on retirement (or death) simply by delaying payment, which cannot have been intended.

The fact that a benefit happens to be provided after retirement or death (such as the release or writing off of a loan made before retirement or death) does not necessarily mean it is a relevant benefit. If the loan would have been released irrespective of the retirement/death then such a benefit is not provided "on" retirement/death.

### "In anticipation of"

**35-023** It is less clear precisely how wide are the words "in anticipation of". Any payment to an employee by reason of that employee reaching an advanced age may be said to be in anticipation of retirement. HMRC consider that a payment to induce a member to move from a defined benefits arrangement to a money purchase arrangement is made in anticipation of retirement if it is paid to an existing employee or a former employee (who have left the employment other than by retirement).[29]

### "Retirement"

**35-024** Does "retirement" in s.393B mean: (a) ceasing to work for a particular employer; or (b) ceasing employment altogether? "Retirement" ordinarily describes the period of time after active employment has ceased at the end of a person's working life. Its meaning has been considered in a number of cases where it has been used in scheme documentation (usually in the context of early retirement)[30] rather than in a statute. This is a question of construction of the scheme documentation, but the courts have generally rejected the proposition that retirement means giving up all work on a permanent basis.[31] This is because the employer will not usually be concerned with whether the employee has given up work entirely or not, and on a practical level (especially in relation to early retirement) it may not be straightforward to determine if someone has ceased to work permanently. What is often much less clear, when construing scheme documentation, is whether *retirement* necessarily involves the employee giving up all work for the employer,[32] and whether the

---

[29] EIM15155.
[30] See Nugee and Asplin, *Retires, retiring, retired*, APL Seminar (21 April 2004).
[31] *Brooks v National Westminster Bank* unreported 8 November 1983 CA; *Hoover Ltd v Hetherington* [2002] EWHC 1052 (Ch).
[32] As was the case in *Venables v Hornby* [2001] S.T.C. 1221.

member must have left voluntarily (especially in the context of ill-health early retirement[33] or redundancy).[34]

**35-025** In a statutory context, the position was clearer prior to 6 April 2006, because ICTA 1988 s.612 (which contained the definition of relevant benefits) expressly provided that 'service' meant service as an employee of the employer in question and 'retirement' was to be construed accordingly".

**35-026** However, there are several strong indications in ITEPA 2003 s.393B(1) that *retirement* means retirement from employment generally. For example, consider s.393B(1)(b) (benefits provided on the death of an employee or former employee). Where this applies, the individual must have died, and so it is necessary to consider what the distinction between *employee* and *former employee* can mean in that context. If the member has died, the only way he could be described as an *employee*, is if *employee* means an employee at death. In which case *former employee* must mean a person who was not employed by the employer when he died. The term *former employee* is also used in s.393B(1)(a) and (c), and, as a matter of principle, it ought to mean the same thing in those provisions. If that is correct then, in the context of s.393B(1)(a) (benefits provided on or in anticipation of the retirement of an employee or former employee), an *employee* must mean a person who was an employee before the *retirement* referred to in s.393B(1)(a), and *former employee* must mean something else: it must mean a person who ceased to work for the employer in the past but did not cease work altogether. In such cases, s.393B(1)(a) applies where the person who ceased to work for the employer some time ago, retires from employment generally. HMRC seem to accept that retirement means retirement from employment generally.[35]

**35-027** In *Ballard*,[36] the taxpayer was made redundant at the age of 48 and a payment was made to him under a FURBS. The taxpayer argued that the payment was a relevant benefit within s.393B(1)(c),[37] and HMRC contended that the payment was a redundancy payment and so should be assessed under ITEPA 2003 s.401.[38] The taxpayer had decided not to seek further employment and the judge concluded that, for this reason, the taxpayer had retired for the purposes of s.393B. In that case, the taxpayer had still not sought further employment by the time of the hearing, but presumably if he had that could not retrospectively re-characterise his previous status of being retired (it is not an improper use of the term to describe a person returning to work as "coming out" of retirement). Whether a person has retired or not is a question of fact. The circumstances in which the employment terminated

---

[33] See *Brooks v National Westminster Bank* unreported 8 November 1983 CA; *Dorrell v May & Baker* [1991] Pens. L.R. 31; *Harris v Shuttleworth* [1993] EWCA Civ 29.

[34] See *Young v Associated Newspapers Ltd* [1971] 11 K.I.R. 413; *Spooner v British Telecommunications Plc* [2000] O.P.L.R. 189; [2000] Pens. L.R. 65; *AGCO Ltd v Massey Ferguson Pension Trustees* [2003] EWCA Civ 1044; [2003] Pens. L.R. 241.

[35] Thus, at EIM15155, HMRC explain that inducement payments are paid "in anticipation of retirement" if paid to a former employee who left the employment other than by retirement, and are "in connection with past service" if paid to a former employee who left the employment as a result of retirement.

[36] *Ballard v HMRC* [2013] UKFTT 087.

[37] i.e. a benefit provided after the retirement or death of an employee or former employee in connection with past service. Under the regime applicable before 6 April 2006, most contributions to FURBS were taxable on the employee under ITEPA 2003 s.386(1) but lump sum relevant benefits were tax free. See Ch.38.

[38] Which applies to payments and other benefits received in connection with: (a) the termination of a person's employment; (b) a change in the duties of a person's employment; or (c) a change in the earnings from a person's employment.

are not generally relevant.[39] In *Ballard*, the taxpayer had been forced to accept redundancy, but that did not mean that he was not entitled to retire from employment. In *Venables v Hornby*,[40] Laurence Collins J (with whom the higher Courts agreed) held that:

> "the word retire is not a term of art and ... It is to be given its ordinary and natural meaning. It is a matter of fact whether, in any particular circumstances, someone can be said to have 'retired', and the answer will depend upon the context ... every case has to be considered on its merits."

**35-028** In *Hoover v Hetherington*,[41] Pumfrey J said this, regarding the normal meaning of retirement:

> "I do not accept ... that the normal understanding of 'retirement' or 'retired' relates to a situation in which a person has ceased to be in employment, or at most has taken up part-time, and usually unpaid, employment as a 'retirement job', and does not relate to a situation in which a person has left the employment of one employer and taken up full-time employment with another employer. This is making the word do too much work. The word signifies final withdrawal from some office, or business, or employment, without necessarily saying anything about any other office, business, employment or occupation."

**35-029** In *Hoover*, the judge went on to conclude that "retire from service" in that particular scheme meant ceasing to work for that employer, because this was the only construction that was workable if it is otherwise necessary to determine the member's intention at a particular time.

**35-030** As is evident from the decision in *Ballard*, the interaction between ITEPA 2003 s.394 and s.401 does support the view that *retirement* for the purposes of s.393B does not simply mean ceasing to work for a particular employer. Section 401 applies to benefits received in connection with (inter alia) the termination of a person's employment.[42] That being the case, it seems that if *retirement* in s.393B included ceasing to work for a particular employer then s.401 would rarely apply in practice because s.394 would take priority. It is therefore arguable that s.393B is concerned with retirement from employment generally and s.401 is concerned with a specific employment. However, the position is not clear.

### "In connection with past service"

**35-031** As noted above, s.393B(1)(c) may be significantly broader than the rest of s.393B(1). The meaning of "in connection with past service" was considered in

---

[39] In *Harris v Shuttleworth* [1993] EWCA Civ 29, Gibson LJ considered whether someone suffering incapacity had retired. He said: "If an employee before reaching normal pension age is incapacitated from following her employment by a physical or mental disability or ill-health which renders it improbable that she will be able to follow her present or similar employment during any part of the period until she reaches normal pension age and if as a result her employment with the Society comes to an end it matters not how the employment is terminated. In my judgement whether she gives notice of her intention to leave or the Society gives notice dismissing her the termination can still properly be described as "retirement from the Service by reason of incapacity" ... if Mrs Harris was dismissed from the Society's service by reason of her incapacity this would constitute "retirement by reason of incapacity as I have defined the phrase".

[40] *Venables v Hornby* [2001] S.T.C. 1221 at 1230(a).

[41] *Hoover Ltd v Hetherington* [2002] EWHC 1052 (Ch) at [26].

[42] See *RCC v Colquhoun* [2010] UKUT 431 at [13]: in the context of ITEPA 2003 s.401 "an individual's employment will always terminate eventually either by dismissal, death or retirement (on account of age or some other reason)".

*Barclays Bank*.⁴³ In that case, in addition to providing its pensioners (former employees and their widows/widowers) with their contractual pension benefits, Barclays also provided pensioners with free tax-related services on a discretionary basis. Barclays decided to sell the business which provided those tax-related services, and therefore withdrew the provision of such services to those pensioners. In order to avoid hostile action by the pensioners and trade union and negative media coverage, the scheme made one-off ex gratia payments to compensate the pensioners. All eligible pensioners received a payment, but the amount paid to a particular pensioner depended upon whether he had used the service in the past and how complex his affairs were. The question for the court to determine was whether these payments were made in connection with past service, and so were relevant benefits.

In the Court of Appeal, Arden LJ observed that the expression "in connection with" could describe a range of links, and so one must look at the surrounding words and the context of the legislative scheme.⁴⁴ The purpose of the definition of relevant benefits is to identify the taxable payments under a retirement benefits scheme, and it may be assumed that Parliament would not have intended to limit connections to direct connections (because that would be easy to circumvent), and replacement benefits or compensation for ceasing other benefits would have been foreseen by Parliament. She also considered it significant that Parliament did not limit the provisions to payments in consideration for services. In that case, the class of recipients was limited to those who had been employees or who had connections through an employee by being the surviving spouse or personal representatives. No one else could come within the class of beneficiaries. The criterion for selection of the recipients is a strong factor to which substantial weight should be given. It is possible for a benefit to be in connection with more than one thing, and where that is the case the past service needs only to be one of those things. However, it is necessary to see whether the connections can co-exist, or whether one will exclude or displace the other.

35-032

The fact that the recipients were chosen because of their connection to the scheme was just one factor to take into account, but Arden LJ considered that it should be given significant weight. There were other relevant factors, such as the fact that the amount of each payment was calculated by reference to the age of the recipient and the complexity of his tax affairs, but these were subsidiary matters which are secondary to the selection of the class of recipients. Once it is shown that the recipients of the benefits were chosen because of their connection with the scheme, it will be very rare for the connection with past service to be displaced.⁴⁵

35-033

In addition, Arden LJ expressly rejected the suggestion by the Special Commissioner that there was a requirement that the benefit was a deferred reward. The expressions *pension* and *gratuity* do not entail any necessary element of reward and

35-034

---

⁴³ *Barclays Bank Plc v RCC* [2006] S.T.C. (S.C.D.) 100. The meaning of "in connection with" is considered in Ch.18 in the context of payments or benefits provided in connection with registered pension scheme investments.

⁴⁴ Per Lord Hope in *Coventry Waste Ltd v Russell* [1999] 1 W.L.R. 2093.

⁴⁵ However, Arden LJ does provide the following as a possible example: "the [employer] company, without any obligation to do so, decides one year as a one-off event to invite pensioners to an evening at a hotel at which it conducts a quiz. The winners of the quiz are given cash prizes. The pensioners are invited because of their link through past service with the company. However, when they win cash prizes, the prizes are given for their performance in the quiz. The winning of the prize is random so far as the company is concerned and prizes are given in the spirit of gamesmanship. The participation of the recipient is voluntary". One wonders if the designers of the tax scheme litigated in *Root 2 Tax Ltd v HMRC* [2019] UKFTT 744 had Arden LJ's example in mind.

so the expression *other like payment* cannot do so either. ICTA 1988 s.612(1) used the words "given ... in connection with past services" and Arden LJ thought that the word "given" creates a requirement for the maker of the payment to have known the facts constituting the link with past service. The current provisions (in ITEPA 2003 s.393B) do not use the word *given* (they use the word *provided*) but it would be very surprising if such knowledge by the maker of the payment is unnecessary.[46]

35-035　　According to Arden LJ's analysis, where you have a funded scheme established to provide benefits to former employees, the provision of any benefit after the death or retirement of the relevant employee to a person solely because he is a beneficiary will be in connection with past service.

35-036　　In *Forsyth*,[47] £29,700 was paid by an employer to a former employee in exchange for him surrendering his membership of the employer's healthcare scheme. The FTT found that the agreement between the employer and the retired employee was an EFRBS and the payment was in connection with past service because the payment would not have arisen but for his employment with the company. The judge therefore applied a "but for" test. If this is the correct test, it may have very important implications in relation to the taxation of termination payments under ITEPA 2003 s.403. Under that regime, the first £30,000 is not taxable, but those provisions will not apply if the benefit is taxable in accordance with s.394. It is therefore implicit that some payments from an employer to a former employee (which would not have arisen but for the employment) do not constitute relevant benefits. The decision in *Forsyth* can be criticised in a number of respects. First, given that there was no suggestion that the £29,700 was intended to benefit the taxpayer, it is not at all clear that the agreement was an EFRBS. Second, even if the payment was intended to benefit the taxpayer, the entire payment was clearly not a benefit since his rights to health care plainly had *some* value and therefore some attempt should have been made to find the amount of the benefit (only the "benefit" is taxable: s.394(1) and s.398(1)).[48] That is quite different to the position in *Barclays* where the benefits were provided on a discretionary basis and so could have been withdrawn at any time.

35-037　　In *Executors of Clark*,[49] an employee received £18 million under a settlement agreement on the termination of his employment, of which £15.7 million was to "buy out the rights of the Executive and the Executive's wife under Clauses 4.3 and 4.4 of the Service Agreement". Clauses 4.3 and 4.4 of the service agreement conferred on the employee a right to receive a pension until his death and on his wife the right to receive a pension until her death if she survived him. The employer's pension obligations were unfunded. Anne Scott J held that the settlement agreement was a "scheme", the £15.7 million was paid on or in anticipation of retirement (given that he was age 65 and did in fact retire), and it was paid in commutation of his pension rights and so was a benefit. The executors had argued that the £15.7 million was not a commutation: it was paid in exchange for the surrender of his pension rights, and it was not a benefit to the extent that it did not exceed the capitalised value of those rights.

35-038　　A payment under an EFRBS on arm's length terms (e.g. to buy an asset from a

---

[46] In a number of cases (in a different context) the word *provided* has been held to suggest that an element of bounty is required (*CIR v Leiner* (1964) 41 T.C. 589; *IRC v Plummer* [1980] A.C. 896).
[47] *Graeme Forsyth v HMRC* [2014] UKFTT 915 (T.C.).
[48] Given that the provision of the original benefit will generally be taxable, if a payment is made in consideration of the former employee surrendering that benefit it is illogical that the payment should also be taxable. That would represent double taxation.
[49] *The Executors of John Clark (deceased) v HMRC* [2019] UKFTT 473 (Anne Scott J).

beneficiary) is not a relevant benefit, but the same does not apply to a payment made in consideration of the beneficiary surrendering his rights under the EFRBS. For tax purposes, the "benefit" is the money or assets ultimately distributed under the EFRBS;[50] it is not the accrual of rights under the EFRBS (e.g. when contributions are made), so it is not appropriate to treat the accrual as the benefit and the payment as an arm's length transaction. Indeed, in the context of an unfunded arrangement, there may be no material difference between a payment for the surrender of rights and a payment in commutation of rights. Is the position any different where a beneficiary sells his rights under an EFRBS to a third party?[51] TCGA 1992 s.237(a)[52] indicates that such a transaction is at least capable of being subject to CGT rather than income tax. If the beneficiary's interest is expressly assignable under the terms of the EFRBS, one would expect a tribunal to hold that a payment received in consideration of an assignment is a benefit provided under the EFRBS. But the contrary is not unarguable, especially where there was never any intention for the beneficiary to benefit in this way.[53]

In *Moffat*,[54] a pension scheme was wound up following the privatisation of a Scottish bus company, and the surplus was passed to the UK Treasury. Ex gratia payments were subsequently made to former members of the pension scheme in order to bring about equal treatment of Scottish bus company employees and former employees with their equivalents in England and Wales. The taxpayer submitted that, in the case of the payment, the causal link between employer and employee was lacking, in that a third, disinterested party (the government) had been instrumental in making the payment. The special commissioner found that there was a scheme for the provision of benefits consisting of or including relevant benefits because there existed arrangements providing for relevant benefits. The payment to the taxpayer was in connection with his past service because that was how he qualified to receive the payment, and it was on the basis of his past service that the amount of the payment was arrived at. 35-039

HMRC consider that a payment to induce a member to move from a defined benefits arrangement to a money purchase arrangement is made in connection with past service if the member is, at the time of the payment, a retired former employee.[55] 35-040

### "A change in the nature of service"

What is the "nature" of an employee's service? Presumably a change from full time to part time would be a change in the nature of service of the employee. The 35-041

---

[50] As Lord Hodge suggested in *Forde & McHugh*.
[51] Assuming it is not made void by PA 1995 s.91.
[52] TCGA 1992 s.237(a) provides: "No chargeable gain shall accrue to any person on the disposal of a right to, or to any part of—(a) any allowance, annuity or capital sum payable out of any superannuation fund, or under any superannuation scheme, established solely or mainly for persons employed in a profession, trade, undertaking or employment, and their dependants...".
[53] The disguised remuneration provisions would require consideration. The payment to the beneficiary from the third party will be a s.554C relevant step, so the question is whether "it is reasonable to suppose that, in essence ... there is some ... connection (direct or indirect) between the relevant step and the [EFRBS]". One would expect there to be a relevant connection here, given that the payment is to acquire rights under the EFRBS. If they are relevantly connected, the payment would be within the scope of the disguised remuneration provisions, subject to any applicable exceptions (but note that the usual exception in s.554Z8 for arm's length transactions will not apply (see s.554Z8(3)(b)).
[54] *Moffat v HMRC* [2006] S.T.C. (S.C.D.) 380; [2006] UKSPC SPC00538.
[55] EIM15155.

770   EMPLOYER-FINANCED RETIREMENT BENEFITS SCHEMES

assumption seems to be that the change is detrimental to the earning ability of the employee (and hence the benefit is intended to redress that detriment), however taken literally it could include a benefit provided on the promotion of an employee, although it seems unlikely that this could have been intended. What does the prepositional phrase "in connection with" add here?[56] In the context of s.393B(1)(d), it must mean that the change in the nature of service has not itself triggered the benefit but the benefit is still somehow linked with the change.

35-042   Although a cessation of employment (for whatever reason) could be described as a change in the nature of service, it is more natural to read this head as applying only where the service continues but the nature is somehow different.[57] This could perhaps include where the employer is different (e.g. a group company).

### Pension sharing orders

35-043   A pension sharing order or provision means any such order or provision as is mentioned in WRPA 1999 s.28(1).[58]

### Exclusions

35-044   Pursuant to s.393B(2), the following are not relevant benefits:

(a) benefits charged to tax under Pt 9 (pension income), or that would be charged to tax under that Part but for ss.573(2A) or (2B), 646D or 646E or any deductions under s.574A(3);
(b) benefits chargeable to tax by virtue of FA 2004 Sch.34 (RNUKS); and
(c) excluded benefits.

35-045   It follows that a scheme cannot be an EFRBS if it can provide only one or more of the above benefits.[59]

*"Charged to tax" under Pt 9*

35-046   ITEPA 2003 Pt 9 imposes a charge to tax on "pension income".[60] Section 393B(2)(a) applies to benefits that are "charged to tax" under Pt 9. Pursuant to ITEPA 2003 s.567(2), the amount charged to tax under Pt 9 is the "net taxable pension income, which means the "taxable pension income" determined in accordance with the applicable chapter of Pt 9, less certain deductions.[61] For example, where pension is provided under a non-UK EFRBS to a person resident in the UK (so, Pt 9 Ch.4 (foreign pensions) applies), s.575(1) provides that the taxable pension income is the full amount of the pension income arising in the tax year (or, where split year treatment applies, the pension income arising in the UK part of the year, and in the case of temporary non-residence, the pension income arising in the year of return). In the case of a remittance basis taxpayer, the full amount of the pension income arising in the tax year is treated as relevant foreign income (and

---

[56] The phrase may describe a wide range of links and the court must look closely at the surrounding words and the context of the legislative scheme (per Arden LJ in *Barclays Bank Plc v CIR* [2007] EWCA Civ 442).
[57] See *Ballard v HMRC* [2013] UKFTT 87 at [26].
[58] ITEPA 2003 s.393B(5). See Ch.16.
[59] Such a scheme may also be beneficial under the disguised remuneration provisions: see s.554E(1)(d), discussed in Ch.27.
[60] ITEPA 2003 ss.565 and 566(1). See Ch.26 for the analysis of ITEPA 2003 Pt 9.
[61] ITEPA 2003 s.567(3) and (4). ITEPA 2003 s.393B(2)(a) therefore uses the expression "charged to tax" because that is the expression used in s.567(1).

therefore taxable only if remitted), which suggests that unremitted foreign pension is taxable pension income, and therefore "charged to tax" under Pt 9. It is therefore quite clear that benefits may be "charged to tax" under Pt 9 even where no charge actually arises.

Benefits paid from a non-UK EFRBS to a non-UK resident member are not taxable pension income (because none of the chapters in Pt 9 apply to such benefits) so the exclusion in s.393B(2)(a) cannot apply to such benefits.

An exclusion for pension income is consistent with the fact that a charge in accordance with s.394 is a charge on earnings,[62] whereas Pt 9 is concerned with pension income. A scheme which can pay only a pension is referred to as an "employer-financed pension only scheme" in the NIC provisions.[63] Although the NIC provisions expressly refer to such a scheme not being an EFRBS, on the basis that it can pay only a pension, it seems that such a scheme *would* be an EFRBS unless either: (a) the scheme is established in the UK; or (b) it was capable of providing pension income only to UK resident persons.[64] 35-047

Pursuant to s.573(2A) and (2B), the payment of death benefits in the form of income withdrawal under an RNUKS or an overseas pension scheme in respect of a member (or other beneficiary) who died before his 75th birthday is not subject to tax under ITEPA 2003 Pt 9 Ch.4.[65] The reference to these provisions in ITEPA 2003 s.393B(2) means that any such benefits will also not be taxable in accordance with s.394. 35-048

Pursuant to s.646D and 646E, the payment of death benefits in the form of an annuity purchased with unused funds or drawdown funds under an overseas pension schemes or RNUKS are exempt from tax under ITEPA 2003 Pt 9.[66] 35-049

ITEPA 2003 Pt 9 applies to lump sums paid under an EFRBS established outside of the UK, if the payment of the lump sum is not a relevant step by reason of which Pt 7A Ch.2 (disguised remuneration) applies. Section 574A(3) provides that the full amount of the lump sum is taxable, but this is reduced in certain circumstances.[67] This includes in particular, if the EFRBS is an overseas pension scheme, a reduction equal to so much of the lump sum as would, if the scheme were a registered pension scheme, not be liable to income tax under Pt 9. This will typically allow a deduction equal to 25% of a member's fund under the EFRBS. The reference to s.574A(3) in ITEPA 2003 s.393B(2) means that any such benefits will also not be taxable in accordance with s.394.[68] 35-050

---

[62] It "counts as employment income" where the recipient is an individual, and the title of Pt 6 (of which Ch.2 relates to EFRBS) is "employment income: income which is not earnings or share-related".

[63] An employer's payment into such a scheme is disregarded in the calculation of earnings for the purposes of Class 1 NIC (SI 2001/1004 Sch.3 Pt VI para.9(1)(a)). As such a contribution will not be a benefit in kind, it will also not attract Class 1A NIC (SSCBA 1992 s.10). A payment out of such a scheme will be disregarded provided that: (a) it is charged to tax under ITEPA 2003 Pt 9; (b) it would be an authorised member payment if received under a registered pension scheme; (c) it is made after the employment has ceased; (d) it would satisfy pension rules 1, 3 and 4 if received under a registered pension scheme; and (e) the pension is payable until the member's death in instalments at least annually (SI 2001/1004 Sch.3 Pt VI para.9(1)(b)).

[64] HMRC accept that "for NICs purposes only, the meaning of "EFRBS" does not include an employer-financed pension only scheme" (NIM02756).

[65] See Ch.26.

[66] See Ch.26.

[67] See Ch.26.

[68] However, such a lump sum will be taxable under the disguised remuneration provisions unless an exemption applies (e.g. under s.554U (for FURBS) or s.554W (for pre-6 April 2011 rights to the lump sum)).

*"Chargeable" by virtue of FA 2004 Sch.34*

**35-051** FA 2004 Sch.34 applies, in slightly modified form, the FA 2004 member payment provisions (including the member payment charges), the annual allowance, lifetime allowance (pre-6 April 2024) and taxable property provisions to RNUKS.[69] The exclusion in s.393B(2)(b) is important because many EFRBS are RNUKS, and a broad exclusion from the disguised remuneration provisions applies to RNUKS so in many cases, benefits will be taxed under s.394 unless an exclusion applies.

**35-052** In contrast to the immediately preceding provision in s.393B(2)(a) (relating to pension income), s.393B(2)(b) uses the term "chargeable" rather than "charged". This exclusion is plainly intended to apply to benefits which may not involve an actual charge to tax. Relevant benefits are chargeable to tax by virtue of Sch.34 only if they involve a payment from an RNUKS to or in respect of:

(a) a relieved member, to the extent that the payment is referable to the member's UK tax-relieved fund under the RNUKS; or
(b) a transfer member, to the extent that the payment is referable to the member's relevant transfer fund or ring-fenced transfer funds under the RNUKS.

**35-053** Does it make any difference whether the UK residency condition is satisfied at the time of the payment? The position is unclear, but it is at least arguable that a benefit is chargeable to tax by virtue of Sch.34 even if the UK residency condition is not satisfied. The expression "chargeable to tax" has no fixed meaning: its meaning in a particular provision must be determined from the context in which it is used.[70] The purpose of the exclusion in s.393B(2)(b) appears to be to recognise that a special tax regime applies to RNUKS, as a result of which members of RNUKS are subject to tax constraints which are similar those suffered by members of registered pension schemes.[71] To the extent that a benefit under an RNUKS is not referable to the member's UK tax-relieved fund or relevant transfer fund, it is outside that regime (so plainly not "chargeable" by virtue of that regime). By contrast, where a benefit is referable to the member's UK tax-relieved fund or relevant transfer fund, the regime itself provides an exception where the UK residency condition is not met. So, arguably, such benefits are chargeable by virtue of Sch.34 because they are within the scope of that regime.

*Excluded benefits*

**35-054** The following are excluded benefits:[72]

(a) Benefits in respect of ill-health or disablement of an employee during service.
(b) Benefits in respect of the death by accident of an employee during service.
(c) Benefits under a relevant life policy (see Ch.36).
(d) Benefits of any description prescribed by regulations made by HMRC.

**35-055** **Ill-health, disablement and accidental death** The exclusions in (a) and (b)

---

[69] See Ch.31.
[70] *Whitney v IRC* [1926] A.C. 37; 10 T.C. 88; *R. v Kensington Income Tax Commissioners Ex p. Aramayo* [1914] 3 K.B. 429; 6 T.C. 613; *Nicholas Barnes v HMRC* [2014] EWCA Civ 31 at [38]; *Prudential Assurance Co Ltd v Bibby* [1999] S.T.C. 153 at [34].
[71] For this reason, a charge under s.394 can never arise in respect of a registered pension scheme: s.393A(2)(a) provides that a registered pension scheme is not an EFRBS.
[72] ITEPA 2003 s.393B(3).

above apply to benefits provided in respect of ill-health and death. "Service" is not defined but it seems likely that it is simply a reference to employment.[73] To come within (b), death in service benefits must be restricted to death by accident, but one would expect most non-accidental deaths to be preceded by ill-health or disablement, so (a) and (b) together permit benefits in a reasonably broad range of circumstances.

Suppose that an individual (T) is a member of an EFRBS funded by his former employer, which expressly permits the provision of benefits at any age on the ground of ill health. Sometime later, when T is employed by an unconnected company, T ceases to work on the ground of ill health and a lump sum is provided to him under the EFRBS. Is that an excluded benefit by virtue of (a) above? More specifically, does the reference to "an employee" mean an employee of *any* employer, or only an employee of the employer which funded the EFRBS? The provision in (a) above (as with (b) above) does not expressly refer to a former employee. This may be contrasted with s.393B(1), for example, which defined "relevant benefits" and repeatedly refers to "an employee or former employee". As a matter of policy, there appears to be no reason that s.393B(3)(a) should be limited in that way. That is especially true if T is expected to live for less than one year, given that a distribution from a registered pension scheme in those circumstances would be a "serious ill-health lump sum" and therefore tax-free if T is under the age of 75. However, it is perhaps finely balanced. Note that any such payment may be taxable as a termination payment under s.401 ITEPA 2003 (if T's employment with his current employer does in fact cease), subject to the exception in s.406(1)(b) for benefits provided "on account of injury to, or disability of, an employee".[74]

**Regulations made by HMRC under s.393B(3)**  HMRC have made a number of regulations under s.393B(3). The most significant in the context of private pension schemes are in The Employer-Financed Retirement Benefits (Excluded Benefits for Tax Purposes) Regulations 2007 (SI 2007/3537).[75] Regulation 3 provides that any relevant benefit within s.393B(1)(a)–(c)[76] and described below is an excluded benefit if it is provided to a qualifying person: 35-056

| Benefit | Qualifying person |
| --- | --- |
| Accommodation provided for performance of duties—employees | The employee. |
| Accommodation provided for performance of duties—members of employees' families | A member of the employee's family. |

---

[73] Prior to 6 April 2006, "service" was expressly defined as "service as an employee of the employer in question" (ICTA 1988 s.612, which went on to say "and other expressions, including 'retirement', shall be construed accordingly").

[74] See EIM15044 and EIM13610.

[75] Also see The Armed Forces and Reserve Forces (Compensation Scheme) Order 2005 (Revoked 9.5.2011) (SI 2005/439) and The Armed Forces and Reserve Forces (Compensation Scheme) (Excluded Benefits for Tax Purposes) Regulations 2006 (SI 2006/132). SI 2007/3537 also contain provisions relating to: (a) accommodation provided by local authority; (b) accommodation provided for ministers of religion; (c) Tuition fees for armed forces personnel; (d) Armed Forces Resettlement Commutation and Resettlement Grants Schemes; (e) Armed Forces Gratuity Earnings Scheme; and (f) Independent Inquest Advice Service.

[76] These are benefits provided: (a) on or in anticipation of the retirement of an employee or former employee; (b) on the death of an employee or former employee; or (c) after the retirement or death of an employee or former employee in connection with past service. Benefits provided: (a) on or in anticipation of, or in connection with, any change in the nature of service of an employee; or (b) to any person by virtue of a pension sharing order or provision relating to an employee or former employee are not within the scope of the regulations.

| Benefit | Qualifying person |
| --- | --- |
| Accommodation provided as result of security threat | As above. |
| Removal expenses | As above. |
| Repairs and alterations to living accommodation | As above. |
| Council tax etc. paid for living accommodation | As above. |
| Non-cash benefits received before 6 April 1998 | The employee, and, if the employee has died, a member of the employee's family. |
| Welfare counselling | As above. |
| Recreational benefits | As above. |
| Annual parties and similar functions | As above. |
| Writing of wills etc | As above. |
| Equipment for disabled employees | The employee. |
| Health-screening and medical check-ups | The employee. |
| Trivial benefits | The employee and a member of the employee's family or household. |

**35-057** In addition, any lump sum benefit paid in respect of the non-accidental death of an employee during service and is already provided for under the rules of a scheme (as defined) on 6 April 2006 is an excluded benefit.[77]

# TAXATION

**35-058** Tax relief is not available in respect of member contributions to an EFRBS unless the EFRBS is one of the tax-advantaged arrangements described at Ch.24. There are no special rules that apply in relation to investment income or gains received by the EFRBS, so the provisions described in Ch.25 are generally applicable. The position in relation to employer contributions, and benefits provided under EFRBS, is considered immediately below.

### Employer contributions

*CTA 2009 s.1290*

**35-059** CTA 2009 s.1290 is considered in Ch.24. It operates to defer a tax deduction which would otherwise be available in respect of employer contributions to employee benefit schemes (including EFRBS), until such time as qualifying benefits are provided under the scheme. Qualifying benefits include a payment of money or a transfer of assets under an EFRBS if the payment or transfer gives rise to an employment income tax charge in accordance with ITEPA 2003 s.394 or is an

---

[77] The Employer-Financed Retirement Benefits (Excluded Benefits for Tax Purposes) Regulations 2006 (SI 2006/210) reg.2.

excluded benefit for the purpose of ITEPA 2003 s.393B(3), or gives rise to a tax charge under ITEPA 2003 Pt 9.[78]

*FA 2004 s.246*

CTA 2009 s.1290 only applies to defer a tax deduction in respect of a *contribution*. It is possible for an employer to obtain a tax deduction (in accordance with generally accepted accounting practice) in respect of the expenses of providing benefits under an EFRBS even where those expenses do not consist of making contributions under the EFRBS. This could be the case, for example, in the context of a defined benefits scheme or an unfunded scheme. FA 2004 s.246 applies in relation to an employer's expenses of providing benefits to or in respect of present or former employees under an EFRBS in a case where: (a) the expenses do not consist of the making of contributions under the scheme; but (b) in accordance with generally accepted accounting practice they are shown in the employer's accounts. If s.246 applies, it denies the tax deduction in respect of the expenses unless the benefits are ones in respect of which a person is, on receipt, chargeable to income tax. If the benefits are benefits in respect of which a person is, on receipt, chargeable to income tax then the employer's expenses are deductible (assuming that they are otherwise deductible)[79] but only for the period of account in which they are actually paid by the employer. It is generally unlikely that any person will be chargeable to income tax until benefits are actually provided under the EFRBS.[80]

**35-060**

A number of questions arise in relation to these provisions. Does FA 2004 s.246 apply to prevent a tax deduction where an employer pays the trustees' fees or other costs associated with administering the EFRBS? It may be argued that such costs relate to the EFRBS itself rather than the provision of benefits under the EFRBS, but the position is unclear. The interaction between CTA 2009 s.1290 and s.246 is also not entirely clear in one respect. Consider the following example. An employer agrees, unconditionally, to apply £50,000 to pay a pension to an employee once he reaches age 55 (in, say, ten years' time), and then three years later the employer pays £50,000 to an EFRBS in order to fund this obligation. When the employer makes the promise, no immediate deduction is available as a result of s.246, and when the employer makes the contribution no deduction is available as a result of s.1290. When the pension comes into payment a deduction will be allowed under both s.1290[81] and s.246. However, whereas s.1290 provides that the tax deduction is available in the year that the qualifying benefits are provided, s.246 provides that the deduction is available when the employer pays the expenses (i.e. in this example it is retrospectively applied to year three). Presumably they cannot both be correct, but it is unclear which is applicable.

**35-061**

In addition, s.246 does not (in contrast to CTA 2009 s.1290) expressly provide that the deduction is only available to the extent that benefits are subject to tax. Returning to the example in the previous paragraph, if say £4,000 of pension is paid

**35-062**

---

[78] CTA 2009 s.1292(1) and (5). These provisions actually provide that "the payment or transfer gives rise to an employment income tax charge under Chapter 2 of Part 6 of ITEPA 2003 or Part 9 of that Act", but given that it is not possible for an employment income tax charge to arise under ITEPA 2003 Pt 9 this must be a reference to taxable pension income under Pt 9. Until amended by FA 2011 (with effect from 6 April 2011), the requirement was simply that the payment or transfer is made under an EFRBS, which suggested that even a transfer payment from an EFRBS would be a qualifying benefit.

[79] See Ch.6.

[80] ITEPA 2003 s.307; *Templeton v Jacobs* [1996] 1 W.L.R. 1433; *RFC 2012 Plc (in liquidation) v Advocate General for Scotland* [2017] UKSC 45.

[81] See CTA 2009 s.1292(5)(a).

to the individual in the first year that it comes into payment, s.1290 allows a tax deduction in respect of £4,000. However, it is not clear from s.246 whether the entire £50,000 is allowed at that time or only £4,000. The *benefit* referred to is presumably the relevant benefit provided under the EFRBS. The expense itself need not be a benefit.

*CTA 2009 s.868*

**35-063**  If a debit in respect of expenses within FA 2004 s.246(3) is recognised by a company for accounting purposes, and the expenses are not paid until after the end of the period of account in which the debit is recognised, the expenses may be brought into account for the purposes of CTA 2009 Pt 8 (intangible fixed assets) only when they are paid. Any adjustment required by s.868 of an accounting debit that is partly referable to an amount to which s.868 applies and partly to other matters must be made on a just and reasonable basis.

*FA 2004 s.246A*

**35-064**  An employer's expenses of providing relevant benefits to or in respect of a present or former employee under an EFRBS (whether or not by the making of contributions under the scheme) are not subject to a tax deduction if:[82]

(a) the provision of the relevant benefits results in a reduction in the benefits payable to or in respect of the employee under a registered pension scheme; or

(b) a reduction in the benefits payable to or in respect of the employee under a registered pension scheme results in the provision of the relevant benefits.

**35-065**  But if the extent to which contributions paid by the employer under the registered pension scheme in respect of the employee are subject to relief has been restricted in accordance with regulations under s.196A, the employer's expenses of providing the relevant benefits are not prevented from being subject to relief to the extent that is just and reasonable.[83]

*Employer contributions: taxation of the employee*

**35-066**  ITEPA 2003 s.307(1) provides an exemption from the residual charge under the benefits code (i.e. ITEPA 2003 Pt 3 Ch.10) in respect of provision made by an employee's employer under a registered pension scheme or otherwise for a retirement or death benefit. *Retirement or death benefit* is expressly defined as a pension, annuity, lump sum, gratuity or other similar benefit which will be paid or given to the employee or a member of the employee's family or household in the event of the employee's retirement or death. However, there is an exception to this exemption where provision is made for insuring against the risk that a retirement or death benefit under an EFRBS cannot be paid or given because of the employer's insolvency.[84]

**35-067**  ITEPA 2003 s.401 only applies to a benefit that is not taxed elsewhere (e.g. in

---

[82] FA 2004 s.246A.
[83] See Ch.6.
[84] The rationale for excluding the cost of insurance from the exemption is presumably that where an employer promises to provide a benefit and also insures against the risk of insolvency, the insurance is an additional and immediate benefit and so there is no double taxation when the retirement or death benefits are subsequently provided.

accordance with Pt 7A Ch.2, or in accordance with s.394).[85] It expressly does not apply to a contribution to a registered pension scheme or an EFRBS if the contribution is made:[86]

(a) as part of an arrangement relating to the termination of a person's employment; and
(b) in order to provide benefits for the person in accordance with the terms of the scheme.

Given that the right to receive a benefit is not itself a benefit for the purposes of s.401,[87] it is unlikely that s.401 would apply to a contribution to a typical EFRBS in any event. However, there is no reason that s.401 could not apply to a benefit *from* an EFRBS. A payment in connection with the termination of a person's employment should not constitute a relevant benefit, but it will often be the case that an individual receives a termination payment at the same time as becoming entitled to benefits under an EFRBS, and this concurrence frequently complicates matters.

**Taxation of relevant benefits**

Relevant benefits provided under EFRBS are taxable in accordance with ITEPA 2003 s.394.[88] The charging mechanism operates differently depending on whether the recipient is an individual or a non-individual. 35-068

*Relevant benefit is provided to an individual*

Where a relevant benefit is provided under an EFRBS to an individual, the amount of the benefit "counts as employment income" of the individual for the year in which the benefit is received.[89] In contrast to s.394(2) (considered below), s.394(1) is not itself a charging provision; it merely provides that the amount of the relevant benefit *counts as employment income*. On receipt of an amount which counts as employment income, the amount charged to tax is the amount of the "taxable specific income" from the employment for the tax year less any permitted deductions.[90] 35-069

**Liability (and application of PAYE)** The recipient is liable for any charge arising in accordance with s.394(1),[91] but the employer (if it has a UK presence) or any entity for which the employee worked in the UK (the "relevant person") will be required to discharge the employee's liability for the charge under the PAYE 35-070

---

[85] ITEPA 2003 s.401(3).
[86] ITEPA 2003 s.408. The same exception applies to registered pension schemes.
[87] ITEPA 2003 s.402(4).
[88] ITEPA 2003 s.394 applies to "benefits to which this Chapter applies" and s.393(1) provides that "this Chapter applies to relevant benefits provided under an EFRBS". Therefore only relevant benefits are chargeable in accordance with s.394.
[89] ITEPA 2003 s.394(1). This is subject to a de minimis of £100 received in any given tax year. If more than £100 is paid the total (and not merely the excess) is subject to tax.
[90] ITEPA 2003 ss.7(4), 9(4) and 12(1). The deductions are those listed in s.327(3) and (4), namely those allowed under ITEPA 2003 Ch.2 (deductions for employee's expenses), Ch.3 (deductions from benefits code earnings), Ch.4 (fixed allowances for employee's expenses), Ch.5 (deductions for earnings representing benefits or reimbursed expenses), and s.232 (giving effect to mileage allowance relief), and s.262 CAA 2001 (capital allowances to be given effect by treating them as deductions from earnings).
[91] ITEPA 2003 s.13(3).

provisions.[92] Until recently, it was thought that HMRC are unable to transfer the liability under the PAYE provisions to the employee provided that the employer (if it has a UK presence) or the relevant person, exists and is able to pay the tax. But in *Hoey v HMRC*,[93] the Court of Appeal held that HMRC do in fact have power to transfer to an employee the obligation to meet a tax liability which falls to the employer under the PAYE Regulations.

The trustee will usually have no power under the instruments governing the scheme to discharge another person's tax liability. If either the employer or the relevant persons pays the tax, a further tax charge will arise under ITEPA 2003 s.222 unless the employee "makes good" the tax paid within 90 days of the end of the tax year in which the charge arises. A s.222 charge is not within the scope of the PAYE provisions so the employee is liable for it under self-assessment. If the employer or the relevant person does account for PAYE, it will have a common law restitutionary remedy against the employee.[94] The PAYE provisions do not apply where the charge arises in accordance with s.394A (temporary non-residents),[95] so the recipient must self-assess.

*Relevant benefit is provided to a non-individual*

35-071 Where a relevant benefit is provided under an EFRBS to a person who is not an individual, the "responsible person" in relation to the EFRBS is chargeable to income tax on the amount of the benefit for the year in which the benefit is received. The rate of tax is 45%.[96]

35-072 **The responsible person** There are five different categories of responsible persons (Heads One to Five) in relation to an EFRBS.[97] If a person is the responsible person by virtue of being specified under one head, no-one is the responsible person in relation to the scheme by virtue of being specified under a later head. The heads are:

| | |
|---|---|
| *Head one* | Each of the UK resident trustees of the scheme. |
| *Head two* | Each of the persons who control the management of the scheme. |
| *Head three* | If alive or still in existence, any of the employers who established the scheme and any person by whom that employer, or any of those employers, has been succeeded in relation to the provision of benefits under the scheme. |
| *Head four* | Any employer of employees to or in respect of whom benefits are, or are to be, provided under the scheme. |
| *Head five* | Each of the non-UK resident trustees of the scheme. |

35-073 If an EFRBS is established as a trust, and has non-UK resident trustees, can the trustees come within Head Two, or only Head Five? This is often important in practice, because if the trustees can come within Head Two then they will usually

---

[92] See ITEPA 2003 ss.10(3), 683(2)(b) and 687.
[93] *Hoey v HMRC* [2022] EWCA Civ 656.
[94] Following *McCarthy v McCarthy & Stone Plc* [2007] EWCA Civ 664. For criticism of the decision, see e.g. Gordon, "*A McCarthy witchhunt—was the Court of Appeal correct in McCarthy v McCarthy & Stone Plc?*" P.T.P.R. 2011, 14(1), 21–34.
[95] ITEPA 2003 s.683(3ZA).
[96] ITEPA 2003 s.394(4).
[97] ITEPA 2003 s.399A.

be liable, whereas if they can only come within Head Five then the employer will usually be liable (assuming the employer still exists). The trustees will control the management of the scheme and so they could in principle come within Head Two, however if they come within Head Two then Head Five would be otiose. For this reason, the better view is that Head Two applies only to non-trust schemes.

*Territorial limitations*

**35-074** Relevant benefits provided under an EFRBS are chargeable for the year in which the benefit is received. These provisions therefore appear to be concerned with the year in which the benefits are received rather than the year(s) in which the benefits accrued. Does the charge apply where the trustee/manager of the EFRBS and the beneficiary are both non-UK resident in that year, if the relevant employment duties were performed in the UK? Plainly, the charge will not apply if a tax treaty between the UK and the jurisdiction in which the beneficiary is resident confers exclusive taxing rights on the latter jurisdiction in respect of pensions and other similar remuneration.[98] In other circumstances the position is much less clear, because s.394 is not subject to any express territorial limitations.[99] If it had no such limitations then a relevant benefit provided under an EFRBS would be taxable in accordance with s.394 even if there were no connection whatsoever with the UK.[100] It is quite clear that there must be *some* territorial limit to the application of s.394.[101] HMRC rightly accept that a charge can arise only "where there is either a person or a source of income in the UK".[102]

**35-075** The source of earnings from employment is the employee's services, and so earnings have a source in the UK to the extent that the services are or were performed in the UK.[103] But the source of a pension paid after employment has ceased (and any lump sum paid in commutation of such a pension) is not the employee's services.[104] Such benefits are not provided in respect of employment; they are provided because the employment has ceased.[105] If the pension is payable under a pension scheme, the source must be the scheme.[106] The beneficiary's rights under the scheme are a chose in action and so situated in the country where the benefits

---

[98] In this context "other similar remuneration" will cover non-periodic payments, including income withdrawal and lump sum payments (including death benefit lump sums) (see Ch.29).
[99] Although the charge in s.394 does now have territorial limitations in the form of foreign service relief, the original provisions (in ICTA 1988 ss.596A and 596B, inserted by FA 1989 Sch.6 para.9) were silent on territoriality. The Inland Revenue subsequently amended ESC A10 to provide relief for foreign service, and this was codified in ITEPA 2003 s.395B with effect from 5 February 2014. The later addition of foreign service relief cannot of course be taken as any indication that those were the territorial limitations that Parliament intended when introducing the charge.
[100] e.g. a retirement benefit scheme with French trustees, established by a French employer in respect of French employees, none of which have ever worked in the UK.
[101] The Income Tax Acts "impose a territorial limit; either that from which the taxable income is derived must be situate in the United Kingdom or the person whose income is to be taxed must be resident there" (per Lord Herschell in *Colquhoun v Brooks* (1889) 14 App. Cas. 493; 2 T.C. 490 at 503). Also see *Whitney v CIR* (1924) 10 T.C. 88 at 113; *Agassi v Robinson* [2006] UKHL 23.
[102] EIM 15055. cf. *Nichols v Gibson* [1996] S.T.C. 1008, in which the Court of Appeal suggested that the provisions relating to termination payments (now in ITEPA 2003 s.401) may not be subject to any territorial limitations.
[103] *Hochstrasser v Mayes* [1960] A.C. 376; *Shilton v Wilmurst* [1991] 1 A.C. 684; ITEPA 2003 s.27.
[104] *Wales v Tilley* [1943] A.C. 386.
[105] *Stedeford v Beloe* [1932] A.C. 388 at 390 (Viscount Dunedin).
[106] This is largely reflected in ITEPA 2003 Pt 9. Each chapter of Pt 9 (apart from Ch.5A, relating to registered pension schemes) requires one to look at the location of the payer. There is no reference to any external relationship (such as employment) that would allow an argument that that relationship is the source.

are recoverable and the beneficiary's rights can be enforced.[107] Having regard to the scheme (as opposed to the services) is consistent with s.393(1): the EFRBS provisions apply only to a relevant benefit that is provided under a scheme which is an EFRBS. Thus, for example, a gratuitous payment by an employer to a former employee in respect of past employment is a relevant benefit, but is not subject to tax in accordance with s.394 because it is not provided under an EFRBS.[108] In this respect the charge in accordance with s.394(1) is fundamentally different to the general earnings charge and the charge on termination payments, which focus exclusively on the reason that the payment is made. For these reasons, it seems that the scheme is the source.

**35-076** Territorial limits may be implied only in the absence of any contrary intention. HMRC may assert that the existence of express territorial limitations (i.e. foreign service relief) leaves no scope for any to be implied. Such an argument was accepted by the Court of Appeal in relation to the provisions relating to termination payments,[109] however those provisions[110] have always included relief for foreign service, whereas the EFRBS provisions[111] were entirely silent on territoriality until February 2014. Prior to that date, implied territorial limitations would inevitably have applied, to avoid the absurd result that a charge may arise where there is no UK connection whatever. Following the introduction of the original EFRBS provisions, the Inland Revenue amended the terms of ESC A10 to provide relief for foreign service, and it is this concession that was ultimately codified in ITEPA 2003 s.395B with effect from 5 February 2014. The subsequent addition of express territorial limitations does not necessarily displace the limitations that Parliament may be presumed to have intended apply in relation to the original provisions. It therefore remains arguable, notwithstanding the existence of s.395B, that s.394 is subject to additional territorial limitations.

**35-077** If the above analysis is correct, then if the EFRBS and the beneficiary are both outside of the UK, and the scheme is not subject to English law or the UK courts, there should be neither a person nor a source in the UK (even if the funds held for the purposes of the ERFBS relate to employment in the UK and/or were contributed by a UK resident employer) and so s.394 should not apply. This is supported by the wording of s.394(1), which provides that the benefit counts as employment income "for" the tax year in which the benefit is received, suggesting that if both the member and the EFRBS are non-UK resident in *that* year and the employment has ceased, there is no charge in accordance with s.394(1) even if the benefit relates to duties that were performed in the UK. However, there is considerable uncertainty regarding the correct analysis, and HMRC's position is understood to be that such benefits are taxable in accordance with s.394. Importantly, as is explained below, the draftsman of the temporary non-residence provisions in s.394A (introduced by FA 2013) has assumed that relevant benefits referable to contributions made in respect of UK service do have a UK source,[112] and for that reason it would not be surprising for a tribunal or court to hold that, since 6 April 2013 at least, s.394 has no such territorial limitations.

---

[107] Dicey, Morris & Collins, *The Conflict of Laws*, 14th edn (London: Sweet & Maxwell, 2006), r.120. Also see *Alloway v Phillips* [1980] 1 W.L.R. 888; [1980] S.T.C. 490.
[108] See *Allum v Marsh* [2005] S.T.C. (S.C.D.) 191 at [76].
[109] In *Nichols v Gibson* [1996] S.T.C. 1008 at 1014.
[110] Originally in FA 1960 ss.37 and 38.
[111] Originally in ICTA 1988 ss.596A and 596B, inserted by FA 1989 Sch.6 para.9.
[112] See s.394A(3)(d) in particular.

## Temporary non-residents

**35-078** The receipt by an individual of a lump sum relevant benefit under an EFRBS when he is temporarily non-resident[113] is deemed to be received by the individual in the period of return if:[114] (a) no charge to tax would otherwise arise in accordance with s.394(1) (including where the charge could be prevented by making a claim for double taxation relief under TIOPA 2010 s.6, even if no claim is in fact made); but (b) such a charge would arise if the existence of any double taxation relief arrangements were disregarded. If the effect of any applicable double tax treaty would prevent the above from applying in the period of return, the treaty is expressly overridden.

**35-079** If the analysis above relating to the territorial limitations of the s.394 charge is correct, the temporary non-resident provisions will only have any application where benefits are provided from UK resident EFRBS. This would perhaps be surprising, and this suggests that the draftsman may have assumed that relevant benefits referable to contributions made in respect of UK service have a UK source. Later legislation cannot of course affect the interpretation of earlier legislation, but it seems likely that a tribunal would find this to be material when considering to what extent the charge in accordance with s.394 is subject to territorial limitations.

## Employee contributions

**35-080** If a lump sum relevant benefit is provided under an EFRBS, the amount chargeable in accordance with s.394 is reduced by any sum(s) contributed by the employee to the provision of the lump sum.[115] It is expressly assumed, unless the contrary is shown, that no such reduction is applicable. If the lump sum is provided wholly out of funds contributed by an employee then there will be 100% relief. It seems likely that this should be the case even if such funds are only segregated from employer contributions (even notionally) at a much later time, and in preparation for the payment of the lump sum.

## Grandfathering of old s.222 schemes

**35-081** Section 394 does not apply to a benefit provided under an EFRBS if:[116] (a) immediately before 6 April 1980, the scheme was approved under ICTA 1970 s.222; (b) the scheme was not approved under FA 1970 Pt 2 Ch.2; (c) no material changes have been made to the terms on which benefits are provided under the scheme after 5 April 1980; and (d) no contributions have been paid under the scheme after that date.

## Exemption or reduction for foreign service

**35-082** If relevant benefits accrue *entirely* in respect of foreign service and are provided under a non-UK EFRBS to a non-UK resident individual, no liability to UK tax can

---

[113] For the meaning of *temporarily non-resident and period of return* see FA 2013 Sch.45 Pt 4 (statutory residence test).
[114] ITEPA 2003 s.394A. This does not affect the *relevant tax year* for the purposes of the £100 de minimis in s.394(1A). It remains the tax year in which the benefit is actually received.
[115] ITEPA 2003 s.395. The legislation says "paid any sum or sums by way of contributions". The word "sum" suggests cash, but see *Irving v HMRC* [2008] EWCA Civ 6; [2008] B.T.C. 36. There is no reason in principle that an *in specie* contribution by an employee should not have the same effect as a cash contribution for the purpose of this relief.
[116] ITEPA 2003 s.395A.

782   EMPLOYER-FINANCED RETIREMENT BENEFITS SCHEMES

arise. This is not as a result of any express exemption; it is merely an application of the inherent territorial limitations of UK tax. There is an express exemption in ITEPA 2003 s.395B[117] which applies where a lump sum[118] is provided from a non-UK EFRBS to a non-UK resident individual if:

(a) three-quarters or more of the period of *reckonable service* (i.e. the service in respect of which rights to receive the lump sum accrued) is made up of foreign service;
(b) if the period of reckonable service exceeds ten years, the whole of the last ten years of that period is made up of foreign service; or
(c) if the period of reckonable service exceeds 20 years, one-half or more of that period, including any ten of the last 20 years, is made up of foreign service.

**35-083** Where more than one of (a)–(c) applies, they are alternatives (for example, if the period of service was 15 years then the condition is satisfied if the taxpayer meets either (a) or (b)). If none of the above apply, the amount chargeable in accordance with s.394 is reduced by the proportion of the relevant part of the lump sum equal to the proportion that the period of foreign service included in the reckonable service bears to the period of reckonable service. In determining the service in respect of which rights to receive the relevant part of the lump sum accrued, service in a previous employment or with a previous employer is taken into account if rights to receive the relevant part of the lump sum also accrued in respect of that service. It does not matter if the rights originally accrued under a different EFRBS (whether it was established in the UK or not).

**35-084** Service is "foreign service" to the extent that it consists of duties performed outside of the UK in respect of which earnings would not be relevant earnings, or if a deduction equal to the whole amount of the earnings from the employment was or would have been allowable under ITEPA 2003 Pt 5 Ch.6 (deductions from seafarers' earnings). Earnings are "relevant earnings" if they are earnings in relation to which ITEPA 2003 s.15 applies and to which s.15 would apply even if the employee made a claim for the remittance basis under ITA 2007 s.809B for that year.[119] Section 15 generally applies to earnings for a tax year in which the employee is UK resident.

**35-085** Section 395B applies only if the lump sum is received by the employee or former employee or a "related person". A related person, in relation to an employee or former employee means: (a) the employee's spouse, civil partner, widow, widower or surviving civil partner; (b) a person who is financially dependent on the employee, whose financial relationship with the employee is one of mutual dependence or who is dependent on the employee because of physical or mental impairment (or, if the lump sum is paid after the employee's death, anyone who was such a person at the time of the employee's death); or (c) the employee's personal representatives.

**35-086** Until 6 April 2017, there was no requirement for the beneficiary to be non-UK

---

[117] Section 393B was inserted in February 2014 pursuant to the Enactment of Extra-Statutory Concessions Order 2014 (SI 2014/211), as a codification of ESC A10. For rights to receive a lump sum that accrued before 6 April 2011, see ESC A10.
[118] *Lump sum* is not defined. In this context, it is likely to simply mean a standalone payment (i.e. not part of a series of payments). Given that a pension and annuity usually require annual payments, it is arguable that payments every other tax year will be lump sums, however that may not be the case if the payments were contractually due every other year. If each payment is a "one off" (i.e. ad hoc) then that would suggest it is not income, and the position is even clearer if such ad hoc payments are not made in successive tax years.
[119] ITEPA 2003 s.395C. This relates to service in or after the 2013/14 tax year; equivalent provisions relate to previous years.

# TAXATION

resident, and so prior to that date s.395B[120] appeared to be aimed primarily at payments to UK resident beneficiaries. If the analysis above relating to the territorial limitations of the s.394 charge is correct, then, since 6 April 2017, it is difficult to see how the relief in s.395B will ever have any application. Given that the title to the amending provisions in the FA 2017 Sch.3 para.5 is "ending of foreign-service relief", this is perhaps unsurprising. And given the uncertainty regarding the territorial limitations of s.394, it may also be suggested that it is unsurprising that s.395B was not simply repealed; the clarification is welcome.[121]

It should be noted that an individual becoming resident in the UK will usually benefit from split year treatment (i.e. he will be treated as non-UK resident for part of the tax year even if he would, on normal principles, be UK resident for the entire tax year). However, there are no split year rules under the EFRBS provisions, so benefits received when non-resident may become taxable as a result of a subsequent move to the UK.

35-087

Given that employer pension contributions are taxable as income of the employee in some jurisdictions, it is potentially extremely unfair that benefits relating to such contributions should also be subject to tax in the UK. A payment to a UK resident individual from an employee benefits trust in respect of foreign service would not be subject to UK tax (whether under the disguised remuneration provisions or the general earnings provisions), and so the April 2017 changes to the foreign service provisions applicable to EFRBS have the effect of penalising retirement benefits when compared to earnings.

35-088

## Valuing relevant benefits

In the case of a cash benefit, the amount of the benefit is the amount received.[122] In the case of a non-cash benefit, the amount of a benefit is the greater of:

35-089

(a) the amount of *earnings* that the benefit would give rise to if it were received for performance of the duties of an employment. *Earnings* is defined in ITEPA 2003 s.62, and in the context of non-cash benefits means any benefit obtained by the employee in money or money's worth. *Money's worth* is defined as anything of direct monetary value to the employee, or capable of being converted into money or something of direct monetary value to the employee. It is the value that the employee receives rather than the cost to the employer which is taxable,[123] except where the employer discharges a liability of the employee.[124] The measure of value received is the difference between the price the employee could get for the property and the price that he paid for it (if any).[125] That is to say, there is a hypothetical sale by that employee (so individual circumstances and market conditions are taken into account).[126] If the benefit is fettered in some way (e.g. it is forfeit if the

---

[120] ITEPA 2003 s.395B was originally added in February 2014 pursuant to the Enactment of Extra-Statutory Concessions Order 2014 (SI 2014/211). It was a codification of ESC A10.

[121] Indeed, it should be noted that s.395 does purport to provide relief for benefits which are clearly not taxable. This is the case where a benefit is provided under a non-UK EFRBS to a non-UK resident member and *all* of the reckonable service is foreign service. Section 395B(1)(e) expressly envisages these circumstances, and to the extent that s.395B purports to have any application in these circumstances its purpose can be nothing more than to put the position beyond doubt.

[122] ITEPA 2003 s.398.

[123] *Wilkins v Rogerson* [1961] Ch. 133; 39 T.C. 344.

[124] *Nicoll v Austin* (1933–1935) 19 T.C. 531.

[125] *Weight v Salmon* [1935] UKHL T.C. 19 174.

[126] Support for this can be found in *Wilkins v Rogerson* [1961] Ch. 133; 39 T.C. 344 (it was what he

employee ceases to be employed) then the fetter will reduce the taxable value; or

(b) the cash equivalent of the benefit under the benefits code if it were so received and the code applied to it.[127] The benefits code comprises a number of different chapters each dealing with a different category of benefit. In each case the code prescribes what the cash equivalent of the benefit is, and that cash equivalent is subject to tax. In contrast to the earnings provisions above, the benefits code is concerned with the cost (or deemed cost) to the employer of providing the benefit, and not the value that the employee receives.

*Employment-related loans*

**35-090** If s.394 applies to the benefit of a loan, the individual or the responsible person is treated for all purposes of the Tax Acts (other than the EFRBS provisions) as having paid interest on the loan in the tax year equal to the amount representing the cash equivalent of the loan.[128] The interest is treated as accruing during the period in the tax year during which the loan is outstanding, and as paid at the end of the period. The purpose of this is so that the taxpayer can claim tax relief on the deemed payment if actual interest would have qualified for relief.[129]

*Remittance basis taxpayers*

**35-091** The remittance basis applies to taxable pension income under ITEPA 2003 Pt 9 Ch.4.[130] Benefits chargeable under ITEPA 2003 s.394 are not pension income but rather "count as employment income", so they are specific employment income.[131] The remittance basis applies for the purposes of the charge to tax on general earnings but not specific employment income,[132] so the remittance basis does not apply to the charge in accordance with s.394.

**National insurance contributions**

**35-092** A payment by way of an employer's contribution towards an EFRBS is disregarded for NIC purposes.[133]

**35-093** A benefit paid under an EFRBS is disregarded for NIC purposes if the payment:[134]

---

could get for the suit as soon as he received it) and *Ede v Wilson* [1945] 1 All E.R. 367 (the taxable value may vary according to the employee's circumstances).

[127] For these purposes, the benefits code is modified so that references to the "employee" are read as references to the person by whom the benefit is received, and references to the employer are read as including references to the former employer. Where s.106 (cash equivalent: cost of accommodation over £75,000) applies, and the amount referred to in s.105(2)(b) (the sum made good) exceeds the amount referred to in s.105(2)(a) (the rental value), the amount subtracted under paragraph (b) of step 4 of the calculation in s.106(2) is that excess (and not only the excess rent referred to there).

[128] ITEPA 2003 s.399. The interest is not treated as income of the lender, or as relevant loan interest to which ICTA 1988 s.369 applies (mortgage interest payable under deduction of tax).

[129] See the Explanatory Notes to ITEPA 2003 s.399.

[130] ITEPA 2003 s.575(3). Also see ITA 2007 s.809F(3) and ITTOIA 2005 s.830(4)(c).

[131] ITEPA 2003 ss.7(4) and 6(c).

[132] ITEPA 2003 s.6(3).

[133] SI 2001/1004 Sch.3 Pt VI para.8(a). Such a contribution would not usually be subject to NIC in any event (*HMRC v Forde and McHugh* [2014] UKSC 14).

[134] SI 2001/1004 Sch.3 Pt VI paras 8(b) and 10.

TAXATION 785

(a) would have been an authorised pension or lump sum if the scheme had been a registered pension scheme;[135]
(b) would satisfy any of the conditions described below if the scheme had been a registered pension scheme;
(c) is made at a time when the individual is no longer employed by the employer, or a subsidiary of the employer, or a person connected with the employer or a subsidiary of the employer; and
(d) is not payable in respect of a period during which an earner is engaged as a self-employed earner under a contract for services with, or re-employed as an employed earner by, the employer from employment with whom the benefits were derived.

The conditions referred to in (b) above are that, if the scheme had been a registered pension scheme: 35-094

(a) any pension payable under its rules would have satisfied pension rules 1, 3 and 4;[136] or
(b) in relation to any lump sum payable under its rules, s.166(1)(a) (PCLS) and Sch.29 paras 1–3, as modified below, would have been satisfied; or
(c) in relation to any lump sum payable under its rules, s.166(1)(b) (serious ill-health lump sum) and Sch.29 para.4, as modified below, would have been satisfied; or
(d) any pension is payable until the member's death in instalments at least annually.

Although these conditions focus on the scheme rather than any particular payments, the main requirement (set out above) relates to each payment and so each payment must satisfy one of these conditions in order to be disregarded for NIC purposes. Provided that any pension payable under the rules of the EFRBS must satisfy pension rules 1, 3 and 4, there seems to be no reason that the EFRBS could not pay income withdrawal under a flexi-access drawdown fund (notwithstanding that such pension may not satisfy (d) above). An UFPLS paid under an EFRBS would not satisfy these requirements. 35-095

*Pension commencement lump sums*

A lump sum satisfies FA 2004 Sch.29 paras 1–3, as modified by SI 2001/1004 Sch.3 Pt VI para.10(6)(a)–(c), if it is a PCLS (as described below) that does not exceed the permitted lump sum. If a lump sum exceeds the permitted lump sum no part of it is disregarded.[137] 35-096

For these purposes a lump sum is a PCLS if: 35-097

(a) the member becomes entitled to it in connection with becoming entitled to

---

[135] There is no reference to death benefits, presumably because such benefits should not in any event be subject to NIC.
[136] For the pension rules, see Ch.13. Pension rule 1 is that no payment of pension may be made before the member reaches normal minimum pension age unless the ill-health condition is met. Pension rule 3 is that no payment of pension other than a scheme pension may be made in respect of a defined benefits arrangement. Pension rule 4 is that no payment of pension other than: (a) a scheme pension; (b) a lifetime annuity; (c) drawdown pension, may be made in respect of a money purchase arrangement; but a scheme pension may only be paid if the member had an opportunity to select a lifetime annuity instead (FA 2004 s.165).
[137] This is in contrast to the usual provisions relating to PCLS, which provide that a lump sum is not a PCLS *to the extent that* it exceeds the permitted maximum (FA 2004 Sch.29 para.1(2)).

a relevant pension[138] (or dies after becoming entitled to it but before becoming entitled to the relevant pension in connection with which it was anticipated that the member would become entitled to it);

(b) it is paid within the period beginning six months before and ending one year after the day on which the member becomes entitled to it; and

(c) it is paid when the member has reached normal minimum pension age or the ill-health condition is satisfied.

**35-098** The permitted lump sum is the higher of:

(a) 25% of the market value of the employee's fund under the EFRBS at the time the benefit is paid to the individual; and

(b) 5% of the value of the employee's rights under the EFRBS, multiplying the maximum annual pension which could be paid to the member under the arrangement by a factor of 20 and adding the amount of any lump sum entitlement.

**35-099** If, as is often the case, there is no mechanism in the rules of an EFRBS to determine the maximum annual pension which may be paid to the member then presumably one must calculate it (or simply follow (a) above). These provisions have not been updated to reflect the introduction of flexi-access drawdown funds, so if the EFRBS permits such funds then it seems that the maximum annual pension is the full amount of the member's fund, which would in turn result in a permitted lump sum far in excess of the member's fund.

*Serious ill-health lump sum*

**35-100** A lump sum satisfies FA 2004 Sch.29 para.4, as modified by SI 2001/1004 Sch.3 para.10(6)(d), if: (a) before it is paid the responsible person has received evidence from a registered medical practitioner that the member is expected to live for less than one year; and (b) either: (i) it is paid in respect of an uncrystallised arrangement and it extinguishes the member's entitlement to benefits under the arrangement; or (ii) it is paid in respect of uncrystallised rights of the member under an arrangement other than an uncrystallised arrangement, and it extinguishes the member's uncrystallised rights under the arrangement.[139]

**Inheritance tax**

**35-101** If the EFRBS is established under trusts, the scheme property will be relevant property unless:[140]

(a) the settlor is (at the time of making the settlement) non-UK domiciled,[141] and not deemed to be UK domiciled for inheritance tax purposes (in which case only UK situs property is relevant property);[142]

(b) IHTA 1984 s.86 applies to the EFRBS;[143]

---

[138] A pension is a relevant pension if it is income withdrawal, a lifetime annuity or a scheme pension, and the member becomes entitled to it under the pension scheme under which the member becomes entitled to the lump sum.
[139] See Ch.14.
[140] See Ch.28.
[141] A company is domiciled where it is registered: *Gasque v IRC* [1940] 2 K.B. 80.
[142] IHTA 1984 s.48(3) and s.58(1)(f).
[143] IHTA 1984 s.58(1)(d). See Ch.28.

(c) the EFRBS is a QNUPS;[144] or
(d) a qualifying interest in possession subsists in the settled property.[145]

HMRC's technical department are automatically notified where a person dies with an interest under an EFRBS.[146]

**35-102**

## REPORTING OBLIGATIONS

The responsible person[147] is required to provide the following information to HMRC:

**35-103**

(a) no later than 31 January following the end of the year of assessment during which the scheme first came into operation, the name of the scheme, the address of the responsible person, and the date the scheme came into operation;[148] and
(b) no later than 7 July following the end of the year of assessment in which a relevant benefit is provided, the identity of the recipient, and the nature and amount of the relevant benefit.[149] This information is expressly not required in respect of pensions which are chargeable to tax under ITEPA 2003 Pt 9.[150]

Where relevant benefits are paid to an individual (and are therefore taxable in accordance with s.394(1)), the trustee is usually required to operate PAYE. Where PAYE does not apply (e.g. because the benefits are not readily convertible assets, or because the trustee does not have a presence in the UK), the individual must self-assess. Where relevant benefits are provided to a non-individual (and therefore taxable under s.394(2)), HMRC are required to issue an assessment to the responsible person(s).[151]

**35-104**

### Special provisions in FA 2008 Sch.36

HMRC's general information and inspection powers are contained in FA 2008 Sch.36.[152] Schedule 36 applies to payments to and from EFRBS to the extent that such payments give rise to tax charges or reliefs. These powers permit HMRC to require a taxpayer or third party to provide information and/or documentation where it is reasonably required to check the taxpayer's position. Schedule 36 para.34B contains special provision relating to *pensions matters* which includes any matter relating to an EFRBS. HMRC may issue a third-party notice without the approval of the taxpayer or the tribunal. In addition, HMRC do not need to give a copy of

**35-105**

---

[144] See Ch.34.
[145] IHTA 1984 s.58(1). See Ch.28.
[146] IHTM17014.
[147] As defined in ITEPA 2003 s.399A (see above).
[148] The Employer-Financed Retirement Benefits Schemes (Provision of Information) Regulations 2005 (SI 2005/3453) reg.4, made under FA 2004 s.251. A scheme "comes into operation" at any time on or after 6 April 2006 on the day that an employer first makes a contribution to that scheme or (if earlier) the day that relevant benefits are provided.
[149] SI 2005/3453 reg.5.
[150] SI 2005/3453 reg.5(2). The reference is to pensions *chargeable* under Pt 9 notwithstanding that such pensions will usually be relevant benefits unless they are actually *charged* to tax under Pt 9.
[151] The Registered Pension Schemes (Accounting and Assessment) Regulations 2005 (SI 2005/3454) reg.4, made under FA 2004 s.255. Self-assessment is not required (TMA 1970 s.9(1A)).
[152] See Ch.19 for an overview of these powers.

the notice to the taxpayer whose tax position is being checked. The third party can appeal against the notice on any grounds, except the requirement to produce its statutory records. If the notice is issued to anyone other than the responsible person then a copy must be given to the responsible person.

# CHAPTER 36

# Excepted Group Life Schemes

## TABLE OF CONTENTS

| | |
|---|---|
| Introduction | 36-001 |
|     Excluded benefits | 36-004 |
|         Excepted group life schemes | 36-006 |
| Relevant life policies | 36-007 |
|     Excepted group life policies | 36-008 |
|         "Group life policies" | 36-008 |
|         "Excepted" group life policies | 36-009 |
|         A tax avoidance purpose | 36-010 |
|         Excepted group life schemes | 36-013 |
|         Drafting excepted group life schemes | 36-015 |
|     Excluded single life policies | 36-016 |
| Taxation | 36-017 |
|     The payment of premiums | 36-017 |
|     The provision of benefits | 36-019 |
|     Inheritance tax | 36-021 |

## INTRODUCTION

**36-001** Many employers agree to provide lump sum death in service benefits in respect of their employees.[1] Such employers typically secure their obligation by purchasing life assurance. Death in service benefits can be provided under a registered pension scheme, but this may be unattractive for two main reasons:

(a) The death benefits will be taken into account for the purposes of the employee's lifetime allowance (if he dies before age 75).

(b) The provision of such benefits in respect of an individual with enhanced or fixed protection may cause that protection to cease, for two reasons. Firstly, a *new* agreement to provide death benefits under a registered pension scheme will almost invariably involve the making of an arrangement "otherwise than in permitted circumstances". No difficulties arise where the agreement existed *prior* to the commencement of the protection. Secondly, depending on the type of arrangement under the registered pension scheme, an agreement to provide death benefits may also involve "benefit accrual". An unqualified agreement in the scheme rules to pay a lump sum death benefit of an amount calculated by reference to salary (or of a fixed amount),

---

[1] This chapter focuses on death in service benefits provided to employees, but a similar analysis applies where a partnership or LLP provides such benefits in respect of its partners.

is a defined benefits arrangement.[2] Death benefits do not form part of a member's defined benefit pension rights and so increases in the value of such rights cannot constitute benefit accrual (see PTM093520).[3] But if, as is often the case, the agreement to pay death benefits is qualified by reference to the amount (if any) made available to the trustees under an insurance policy, that is a hybrid arrangement, which will become either a defined benefits arrangement or an other money-purchase arrangement at the time that benefits are provided, depending on the circumstances. Thus, an agreement to pay death benefits equal to the lesser of 4x salary or the amount received by the trustees under the assurance policy relating to the life assured is a hybrid arrangement. In relation to fixed protection (but not enhanced protection), the payment of a premium in respect of a hybrid arrangement is likely to involve benefit accrual. (A contribution by an employer to an employee's money purchase arrangement so that the trustees can purchase life insurance would plainly involve benefit accrual, but death in service benefits are rarely provided in this way.)

**36-002** Two further complications may arise if the member's arrangement under the scheme is a hybrid arrangement. Firstly, employer contributions in respect of a hybrid arrangement are taken into account for annual allowance purposes. Secondly, if the hybrid arrangement becomes a money purchase arrangement,[4] it is not at all clear that the proceeds of an insurance policy can be paid as an authorised LSDB.[5] The proceeds of a policy could be paid as scheme pension or drawdown pension to a dependant of the member, but not to a nominee.

**36-003** This chapter is concerned with the taxation of death in service benefits provided outside of a registered pension scheme. Such benefits are generally within the scope of the disguised remuneration provisions and the EFRBS provisions unless they are "excluded benefits".[6]

## Excluded benefits

**36-004** "Excluded benefits" means: (a) benefits in respect of ill-health or disablement of an employee during service; (b) benefits in respect of the death by accident of an employee during service; (c) benefits under a "relevant life policy"; and (d) benefits of any description prescribed by regulations made by HMRC.[7] Most death in service benefits are provided under life policies. It is usually much more cost-effective to purchase group life insurance rather than single life insurance. To be a "relevant life policy" (and therefore an excluded benefit), a group life policy must be an "excepted group life policy".

---

[2] For the meaning of "defined benefits arrangement", see Ch.2.
[3] HMRC accept this at PTM093520.
[4] This will happen where e.g. there is an agreement to pay death benefits equal to the lesser of 4x salary or the amount received by the trustees under the assurance policy relating to the life assured, and the trustees receive (and therefore are required to pay) less than 4x the life assured's salary.
[5] e.g. an uncrystallised funds LSDB may consist only of "the sums and assets held for the purposes of the arrangement at the member's death". Although the *policy* will be held for the purposes of the arrangement at the member's death, it is difficult to see how the *proceeds* could be properly described as being so held. In contrast to other provisions in FA 2004, it does not expressly include "sums or assets deriving or arising from" the sums or assets held at death.
[6] Excluded benefits are not relevant benefits for the purposes of the EFRBS provisions (and so are not taxable in accordance with ITEPA 2003 s.394), and an arrangement the sole purpose of which is to provide excluded benefits is expressly excepted from the disguised remuneration provisions (ITEPA 2003 s.554E).
[7] ITEPA 2003 s.393B(3).

## INTRODUCTION

Life policies are within the scope of the chargeable event regime in ITTOIA 2005 Pt 4 Ch.9. A charge may arise under those provisions if one uses a group life policy other than an excepted group life policy.[8] Gains treated as arising on life insurance policies are subject to income tax under ITTOIA 2005 Pt 4 Ch.9.[9] Death giving rise to benefits under a life policy is a chargeable event.[10] Gains are calculated by reference to the surrender value of the policy immediately before the death,[11] plus any capital sum(s) paid under the policy before the death.[12] Life policies do not have a surrender value, so where there is a separate policy for each employee, death will not give rise to any gain. But where a group life policy (i.e. a single policy relating to more than one employee) is used, the death of every employee other than the first will give rise to a gain. However, an express exception under the chargeable event regime applies to excepted group life policies.[13]

36-005

### Excepted group life schemes

Although it is possible for the employer to hold an excepted group life policy directly, it is more common for the policy to be held on discretionary trusts for the benefit of the family and nominees of each life assured. In this chapter, such trusts are referred to as excepted group life schemes ("EGLS"). There are three main reasons to establish an EGLS rather than hold the policy directly:

36-006

(a) Some insurance companies refuse to provide benefits to the deceased individual's personal representatives, despite the fact that HMRC accept this is unobjectionable.[14]

(b) A policy needs to specify the death beneficiary: it is not possible (without creating a trust) for the insurance company to choose from amongst a class of beneficiaries. An EGLS therefore provides flexibility: the trustees can take into account all facts before deciding to whom to pay the benefits. This might be important, for example, if the death beneficiary were in very ill-health, or bankrupt.

(c) There are also inheritance advantages of using an EGLS. If the policy is held directly, the life assured may have a general power of appointment, and if so it will be desirable for that power to be exercised irrevocably (thereby reducing the flexibility even further). It is then necessary to consider if the right to receive the death benefits forms part of the death beneficiary's estate for inheritance tax purposes. If the death beneficiary were to die at a time when the death benefits are valuable (such as when the life assured is ill), his rights could be very valuable (although spouse exemption may be available). And if the beneficiary died shortly after the life assured, the benefits would form part of the beneficiary's estate.

---

[8] Indeed, the excepted group life policy concept was first introduced (by FA 2003, and now forming ITTOIA 2005 ss.480–482) specifically to address this issue.

[9] See ITTOIA 2005 ss.461(1) and 473(1)(a).

[10] ITTOIA 2005 s.484(1)(b).

[11] ITTOIA 2005 s.493(7).

[12] ITTOIA 2005 s.492(1)(b).

[13] ITTOIA 2005 ss.473(3) and 480. Alternatively, the disregard in s.485(2) could apply where the employer is not a company. There is a separate exception in s.479 for policies which are issued or held in connection with a registered pension scheme.

[14] HMRC accept this at IPTM7035.

# RELEVANT LIFE POLICIES

**36-007**  Pursuant to ITEPA 2003 s.393B(4), "relevant life policy" means:

(a) an excepted group life policy as defined in ITTOIA 2005 s.480;

(b) a policy of life insurance the terms of which provide for the payment of benefits on the death of a single individual and with respect to which the conditions described below are satisfied. Such policies are referred to in this chapter as "excluded single life policies"; or

(c) a policy of life insurance that would be within (a) or (b) but for the fact that it provides for a benefit which is an excluded benefit under or by virtue of ITEPA 2003 s.393B(3)(a), (b) or (d).[15]

## Excepted group life policies

*"Group life policies"*

**36-008**  A "group life policy" is a policy of life insurance[16] whose terms provide: (a) for the payment of benefits on the death of more than one individual; and (b) for those benefits to be paid on the death of each of those individuals.[17] A policy which insures the lives of two individuals (for example), but provides benefits only on the death of the last of those individuals to die, is not a group life policy. This requirement focuses on the *terms* of the policy, so a policy will not cease to be a group life policy merely because the number of individuals insured falls to one (e.g. because the other individuals previously insured have since died or otherwise ceased to be eligible for cover).[18] Whether a policy is a group policy or a series of individual policies is a matter of construction.[19]

---

[15] i.e. benefits in respect of ill-health or disablement of an employee during service, or benefits in respect of the death by accident of an employee during service, or benefits of any description prescribed by regulations made by HMRC. These are discussed in Ch.35.

[16] "Policy of life insurance" is not defined for these purposes. Any contract providing for the payment of a sum of money on the death of a person (as is anticipated here) is likely to be a policy of life insurance.

[17] ITTOIA 2005 s.480(2).

[18] HMRC agree at IPTM7020.

[19] Guidance issued by the Association of British Insurers in 1992 is reproduced at IPTM7015. It provides that any interconnection between insurances would indicate a single group policy contract rather than a series of individual contracts. Factors indicating that a policy is not a group policy are where: (a) there was individual rating of risk such that there was no cross-subsidy between scheme members. The application of free cover limits does not necessarily imply that rating is on anything other than an individual basis provided similar non-medical limits are applied generally. This would mean that individuals are able to secure insurances of the same type by reference to the same non-medical limits. By contrast, if a particular master/subordinate group policy is written by reference to non-medical limits which are generally not available, such as better non-medical limits, that is indicative of some interdependence between the policies and suggests a single contract; (b) the insurance is of a type which might be effected by an individual independently of any group arrangement; (c) membership of the scheme is not compulsory. Membership should also be open to all within the relevant class or category. In the case of schemes for employees, it is clearer if membership is open to all within the relevant class or category. In the case of schemes for employees, it is clearer if membership is open to all employees, although it is probably possible to make a case for membership being open to a particular class or category of employee; (d) the insured benefits are independent of benefits under any other contract; (e) the terms of the contract or options under the contract can be exercised independently of the terms of any other contract. It must be possible to terminate some contracts without having any effect or bearing on other contracts. In the extreme, termination of all but one contract should have no effect on the ability to continue the one remain-

## "Excepted" group life policies

An "excepted group life policy" is a group life policy which satisfies all of the following conditions[20]: **36-009**

(a) Under the terms of the policy a sum or other benefit of a capital nature must be payable or arise. A series of capital instalments is permissible but an income stream is not.[21] Benefits may take the form of money or a different benefit.
(b) That benefit must be provided on the death of each of the lives insured.
(c) The benefit must be provided on death in any circumstances. Alternatively, if benefits are not paid on death in certain circumstances (e.g. suicide), all of the lives insured must be subject to the same restriction(s).
(d) The terms of the policy must specify an age, which must not exceed 75 years,[22] after which no benefits will be paid on the death of an insured individual. An age lower than 75 years is frequently specified in practice. The specified age need not be the same for all lives assured. For example, the maximum age may be set by reference to retirement age, which may be different between the individuals insured.
(e) Under the terms of the policy, the same method must be used for calculating the benefits in respect of each life assured. Benefits may, for example, be calculated by reference to the age of the life assured at death, or the age of the beneficiary.[23] Benefits based on a specified multiple of salary are typical. It is not permissible for benefits to be a multiple of four times salary in respect of some lives assured, and a multiple of five times salary in respect of other lives assured under the same policy.
(f) Under the terms of the policy, any limitation on the benefits must be the same in the case of any death. It is thus permissible to limit the maximum payment that will be made in respect of any single death (e.g. to £1.5 million) even though this may only affect some of the lives insured (i.e. higher earners). Similarly, it is permissible to discriminate between employees, for example, additional benefits may be provided in respect of all employees who die leaving a spouse, or who die leaving dependants. It is also permissible for different benefits to be provided depending on the age of the employee at death, or of the beneficiary. Whatever the restrictions are, they must apply to all lives assured.
(g) The policy must not have, or be capable of having, on any day, a surrender value other than a refund of premiums for any unexpired period. Thus, for example, if a premium of £100 is required to be paid annually in advance, and the policy is cancelled after six months, a refund of no more than £50

---

ing insurance without any implications for premium rates, benefits, options and the like; (f) the member pays the premiums under the contract or is chargeable to tax on the premiums paid; and (g) dependants of the member and the like are entitled to receipt of the benefits for which insurance is provided for the member.

[20] ITTOIA 2005 s.480(3). The conditions are conditions A–D in s.481 and conditions A–C in s.482. These conditions apply continuously, not merely at the inception of the policy. HMRC guidance is at IPTM7025–IPTM7050.
[21] HMRC accept this at IPTM7030.
[22] Death in service benefits in respect of an individual on or over age 75 can be provided via a registered pension scheme. No lifetime allowance issues will arise.
[23] HMRC accept that "this condition may stretch quite widely so long as the method is predetermined and consistently applied" (IPTM7025).

is permissible. The purpose of this condition is to ensure that the policy has no investment element.

(h) No benefits may be provided under the policy other than those which satisfy the conditions above. The policy must not, for example, provide additional benefits on the redundancy or disability of an insured individual.

(i) Any benefits under the policy must be provided directly or indirectly to (or applied at the direction of) an individual or charity beneficially entitled to the benefits. Alternatively, benefits may be provided to a trustee or other person acting in a fiduciary capacity who will secure that the benefits are provided to (or applied in favour of) an individual or charity beneficially. A payment to the deceased individual's personal representatives will plainly satisfy this condition.[24] A company cannot be a beneficiary of the policy, so, if a corporate employer (for example) has agreed to pay death benefits, and it secures that obligation by purchasing a policy, it cannot receive the benefit (except as trustee) and then pay the benefits to the death beneficiary. HMRC consider that a "loan protection collective life policy", where the lending company has first call on the death benefit to pay off an outstanding loan, will not qualify.

(j) No person who is, or is connected with, an insured individual may, as a result of a group membership right relating to that individual, receive (directly or indirectly) any death benefit in respect of another individual whose life is so insured. A "death benefit in respect of an individual" means any sums or other benefits payable or arising under the policy on the individual's death or anything representing any such sums or benefits. A "group membership right", in relation to an individual insured by a group life policy, means any right (including the right of any person to be considered by trustees in their exercise of a discretion) that is referable to that individual being one of the individuals whose lives are insured by the policy. The provision of benefits to persons who also happen to be insured under the policy (e.g. where spouses are employed by the same employer) does not offend this condition because such benefits are received as a result of being nominated by the insured, and not as a result of a group membership right relating to that individual. This condition is intended to prevent business cover type policies which pay benefits on the death of a business owner (partner or shareholder) so that the other business owners can buy out the share of the deceased. There seems to be no reason that an insured individual could not nominate other business owners. HMRC appear to consider that benefits must be paid only to persons related to the insured individual, but that is not an express requirement.[25]

(k) A tax avoidance purpose must not be the main purpose, or one of the main purposes, for which a person is at any time: (i) the holder, or one of the holders, of the policy; or (ii) the person, or one of the persons, beneficially entitled under the policy. The meaning of this condition is considered immediately below.

---

[24] HMRC accept this at IPTM7035.
[25] IPTM7035 provides that "In general, the exception from the chargeable event rules only applies to policies where the beneficiaries on death are the families, dependants or nominated charities of the deceased".

## RELEVANT LIFE POLICIES

*A tax avoidance purpose*

A "tax avoidance purpose" means any purpose that consists in securing a "tax advantage" (whether for the holder of the policy or any other person). A "tax advantage" includes the avoidance or reduction of a charge to tax or an assessment to tax, and the avoidance of a possible assessment to tax.[26] For these purposes, "tax" means either income tax or corporation tax.[27] The existence of any advantage must be judged by reference to the transaction that the parties would have undertaken if they had no interest in tax.[28] A "main purpose" means an important purpose.[29] The test is subjective: what were the objectives of the actual parties involved?[30] Although the condition expressly refers to the holders and beneficiaries of the policy, one is required to find the subjective intentions of those in control.[31] This may include the subjective intentions of any advisers, to the extent that their advice affected the shape and structure of the arrangement.[32] In determining whether there is a tax avoidance purpose, one must consider the purpose of the entire arrangement; it is not appropriate to isolate individual transactions which were inserted to obtain the tax advantage.[33]

**36-010**

One of the main reasons for establishing an EGLS (as opposed to providing death in service benefits under a registered pension scheme) may be to avoid the possible application of the lifetime allowance provisions.[34] Where that is the case, it may be conceded that the appropriate comparator is the provision of benefits via a registered pension scheme. Is the obtaining of a tax advantage (for any person) one of the main purposes for which the trustee holds the policy? The test is subjective but the answer will usually be "no" for the following reasons:

**36-011**

(a) The scheme will be established by the employer. The employer's purpose will usually be to provide a satisfactory remuneration package for its employees (at least comparable with its competitors). That is a commercial purpose. Holding the policy is merely the method by which that commercial purpose is achieved. Choosing the most tax-efficient method of achieving a commercial purpose is not a tax avoidance purpose (provided

---

[26] CTA 2010 s.1139
[27] CTA 2010 s.1119. Any inheritance tax advantage (of holding the policy in a trust, for example) is therefore not a tax advantage for these purposes.
[28] See e.g. *IRC v Parker* [1966] A.C. 141 and *CIR v Tai Hing Cotton Mill* FACV No 2 of 2007. This is accepted by HMRC: "The concept of a 'tax advantage' is common in UK tax legislation. The language suggests that in deciding whether an advantage arises the actual tax position should be compared with another tax position. The appropriate comparison or alternative tax position will depend on the facts, but will usually derive from the arrangements that would have occurred without the abusive tax purpose (which may include no arrangement at all)". (GAAR Guidance para.C2.5).
[29] In *Travel Document Service & Ladbroke Group International v HMRC* [2018] EWCA Civ 549 at [48], Newey LJ rejected the submission by counsel for HMRC that "main", as used in FA 1996 Sch.9 para.13(4) means "more than trivial". He said, "A 'main' purpose will always be a 'more than trivial' one, but the converse is not the case. A purpose can be 'more than trivial' without being a 'main' purpose. 'Main' has a connotation of importance".
[30] *Travel Document Service & Ladbroke Group International v HMRC* [2018] EWCA Civ 549 at [41] (Newey LJ), following *IRC v Brebner* [1967] 2 A.C. 18. *Brebner* was concerned with whether transactions had as "their main object, or one of their main objects, to enable tax advantages to be obtained". Lord Pearce concluded (at 27) that "[t]he 'object' which has to be considered is a subjective matter of intention", and Lord Upjohn (with whom Lord Reid agreed) said (at 30) that "the question whether one of the main objects is to obtain a tax advantage is subjective, that is, a matter of the intention of the parties".
[31] *Addy v IRC* [1975] S.T.C. 601 at 610d.
[32] *Iliffe News and Media Ltd v HMRC* [2012] UKFTT 696 at [293].
[33] *IRC v Brebner* [1967] 2 A.C. 18.
[34] Which is a charge to income tax, and therefore within the scope of the *tax advantage* requirement.

that the obtaining of the tax advantage does not become the main purpose of the overall arrangement).[35]

(b) Given that the no tax avoidance purpose relates solely to the chargeable event gain regime, it seems likely that the test is primarily concerned with avoidance of the chargeable events regime. There was no equivalent of the exception to the EFRBS provisions when the EGLPs provisions were introduced, so Parliament cannot have had that in mind. Same with the LA. Both of those provisions were introduced in 2006. Indeed, given that Condition C forms part of s.482, which expressly relates to "conditions about persons intended to benefit" (the no tax avoidance requirement is not a standalone provision), which suggests that this is concerned with who benefits.

(c) No tax advantage is, or can be, obtained merely by holding the policy. Indeed, it is the benefits payable under the policy that create the possible tax disadvantage. If there is a tax advantage, it arises as a result of the trustee omitting to hold the policy under a registered pension scheme.

(d) If there is a tax avoidance purpose, it relates only to an individual transaction which is inserted to obtain the tax advantage, and that should not be objectionable.

(e) It cannot be relevant to ask why the trustees hold an excepted group life policy rather than a different type of policy. A group life policy which is not an excepted group life policy would give rise to chargeable event gains on the second and subsequent deaths. The exception from the chargeable event gain regime for excepted group life policies was introduced precisely to stop that, so it can hardly be objectionable to take advantage of it. If that amounted to a tax avoidance purpose then it seems unlikely that the exception for excepted group life policies would ever apply, which is plainly not intended.

**36-012** It may also be observed, more generally, that the conditions expressly acknowledge that an excepted group life policy may be held by trustees. This cannot be a reference to the trustees of a registered pension scheme, because there is a separate exception from the chargeable event gain regime where a policy is held in connection with a registered pension scheme,[36] so the exception for excepted group life policies is intended to be available only where a policy is *not* held in connection with a registered pension scheme. If it is not inherently objectionable for an excepted group life policy to be held by trustees outside of a registered pension scheme, there seems to be little reason that an EGLS should be considered objectionable.

HMRC are understood to accept the above analysis in practice, on the basis that the purpose of s.482(5) is to ensure that excepted group life policies cannot become, or have properties similar to, investment life insurance policies.

---

[35] *IRC v Brebner* [1967] 2 A.C. 18 (Lord Upjohn). The position is perhaps clearest where the employer agrees to provide the death benefits under the employment contract, and the EGLS is merely the mechanism by which the employer secures its obligation. In those circumstances it may be arguable that a registered pension scheme is not an appropriate comparator, because providing the benefits via a registered pension scheme would create a lifetime allowance issue.

[36] ITTOIA 2005 s.479.

## Excepted group life schemes

**36-013** It is permissible for a number of policies to be held by the same EGLS. This is common where the employer wishes to provide different amounts of cover for different employees (e.g. one policy may provide three times salary and another may provide four times salary). The only requirement is that each policy must cover at least two lives when the policy is set up.

**36-014** The requirements above generally relate to the policy rather than the terms of any EGLS, however HMRC consider that the policy and the scheme should be interdependent, so that the scheme reflects the above requirements. It is therefore generally helpful to draft an EGLS on this basis. But it should be noted that the above conditions are ongoing tests, and whether they are met are questions of fact. As HMRC note, "it is neither necessary nor sufficient that the trustees declare that they will only distribute death benefits to beneficiaries in accordance with the conditions".[37] If the trustees do in fact provide benefits to a person who was not an individual or a charity then the policy would cease to be an excepted group life policy at that time. However, HMRC suggest that such a declaration might be helpful: (a) in ensuring that the trustees are aware of the restrictions on the exercise of their powers needed if the policy is to remain excepted; and (b) for the insurer, who needs to know whether the policy is excepted for the purposes of determining whether they need to issue chargeable event certificates. HMRC accept that an insurer is entitled to assume that the trustees will comply with the conditions when distributing benefits paid under the policy unless it becomes aware of information to the contrary.

## Drafting excepted group life schemes

**36-015** An EGLS is typically governed by a trust deed and rules. It is generally helpful to include in the trust deed and rules:

(a) A declaration that the scheme is established for the sole purpose of providing benefits under one or more excepted group life policies.
(b) A statement that the employer is establishing the scheme for commercial reasons.
(c) A statement that the employer will pay the premiums to the insurance company—they will not form part of the trust fund. This is more important where the employer is the trustee.
(d) A declaration that the trustees will secure that the benefits are provided to (or applied in favour of) an individual or charity beneficially.
(e) A charity will usually be the default beneficiary of the trust to ensure that nothing can pass to the employer.
(f) No beneficiary who is, or is connected with, an insured individual may, as a result of a group membership right relating to that individual, receive (directly or indirectly) any death benefit in respect of another individual whose life is so insured. A *death benefit in respect of an individual* means any sums or other benefits payable or arising under the policy on the individual's death or anything representing any such sums or benefits. A *group membership right*, in relation to an individual insured by a group life policy, means any right (including the right of any person to be considered by trustees in their exercise of a discretion) that is referable to that individual being one of the individuals whose lives are insured by the policy.

---

[37] IPTM7040.

### Excluded single life policies

**36-016**  An excluded single life policy is a policy of life insurance the terms of which provide for the payment of benefits on the death of a single individual and which satisfies the following conditions:

- (a) Under the terms of the policy a benefit of a capital nature is provided on the death of an individual either: (i) in any circumstances; or (ii) except in specified circumstances.
- (b) The policy may not have, or be capable of having, on any day, a surrender value other than a refund of premiums for any unexpired period.
- (c) No benefits may be provided under the policy other than those which satisfy the conditions in (a) and (b) above.
- (d) Any benefits arising under the policy must (whether directly or indirectly) be paid to or for, or conferred on, or applied at the direction of: (i) an individual or charity beneficially entitled to them; or (ii) a trustee or other person acting in a fiduciary capacity who will secure that the sums or other benefits are paid to or for, or conferred on, or applied in favour of, an individual or charity beneficially.
- (e) A tax avoidance purpose is not the main purpose, or one of the main purposes, for which a person is at any time: (i) the holder, or one of the holders, of the policy; or (ii) the person, or one of the persons, beneficially entitled under the policy.

(g) A tax avoidance purpose is not the main purpose, or one of the main purposes, for which a person is at any time: (i) the holder, or one of the holders, of the policy; or (ii) the person, or one of the persons, beneficially entitled under the policy.

## TAXATION

### The payment of premiums

**36-017**  An employer should obtain a tax deduction in respect of premiums in respect of an EGLS for the benefit of its employees, provided that it pays the premiums to the insurance company (and does not, for example, contribute them to the scheme so that the trustees may pay them to the insurance company).[38] This is on the assumption that the payments are made wholly and exclusively for the purposes of the employer's trade (as will usually be the case). Payments by a partnership or LLP are not deductible if they are for the benefit of its partners.

**36-018**  The payment of premiums by the employer to the insurance company should not be subject to income tax or NIC, because:

- (a) The payments do not constitute earnings of the employee for income tax purposes.[39]

---

[38] CTA 2009 s.1290(4)(a).
[39] The express exceptions in ITEPA 2003 ss.308 and 308A apply only in relation to registered pension schemes and qualifying overseas pension schemes. In other cases, there will be no earnings charge provided that: (a) the payment of premiums is not, on a true construction of the facts, a payment out of the employee's salary; (b) at the time of the payment, the employee does not have a vested interest in the proceeds of the policy; (c) the payment does not discharge a pecuniary li-

(b) The payments do not give rise to a taxable benefit in kind,[40] unless the employee is, or has in the past been, given the option of receiving additional salary instead of rights under the scheme. To the extent the employee has this choice, the payment of premiums will be an "optional remuneration arrangement", and the premiums will be taxable as a benefit in kind.[41]

(c) Provided that the sole purpose of the scheme is the provision of excluded benefits, no charge will arise under the disguised remuneration provisions on the earmarking of the premiums.[42]

(d) The payments do not constitute earnings for NIC purposes.[43]

**The provision of benefits**

The provision of death benefits under an EGLS will not be subject to income tax or NIC, because: 36-019

(a) The charge under the chargeable event regime referred to above does not have any application to a single life policy, and excepted group life policies are expressly excepted.[44]

(b) Benefits "under a relevant life policy" are excluded benefits and are therefore not relevant benefits for the purposes of the EFRBS provisions.[45] In relation to EGLS, benefits may be provided under the scheme rather than directly under the policy, but the benefits clearly derive from the policy and HMRC seem to accept that such benefits are excluded benefits. It is suggested that the position is clearest if the trustees direct the insurance company to make the payment directly to the beneficiary. If the proceeds are received by the trustees, it is suggested that benefits should be provided by the trustees without undue delay.

(c) The disguised remuneration provisions do not apply to steps taken under an arrangement the sole purpose of which is the provision of excluded benefits.[46]

(d) Benefits provided under an arrangement which is not a registered pension scheme or an RNUKS are not taken into account for lifetime allowance purposes.

---

ability of the employee; and (d) the employee does not have the option to receive some other taxable benefit (such as money) instead of the employer paying the premiums in respect of that employee.

[40] ITEPA 2003 s.307(1). This provision was amended with effect from 6 April 2019 so that beneficiaries need not be limited to the family and household of the employee. It was amended specifically with these policies in mind. Prior to 6 April 2019, ITEPA 2003 s.307 was narrower than ITTOIA 2005 s.482. ITEPA 2003 s.307(1A), which provides that the exception in s.307(1) does not apply to provision made for insuring against the risk that a retirement or death benefit under an EFRBS cannot be paid or given because of the employer's insolvency, should have no application where the beneficiaries' rights are conferred under the trust (see Ch.35).

[41] ITEPA 2003 s.69A. See Ch.24.

[42] ITEPA 2003 s.554E(1)(d). In any event, it is arguable that there would be no earmarking because any future relevant step will not relate specifically to the premiums paid (see s.554B(1)).

[43] *Forde & McHugh v HMRC* [2014] UKSC 14.

[44] ITTOIA 2005 s.480.

[45] ITEPA 2003 s.393B(2)(c), (3)(c) and (4)(a).

[46] ITEPA 2003 s.554E(1)(d).

(e) Lump sum benefits are not pension income and so will not be taxable under ITEPA 2003 Pt 9.[47]

(f) The death benefits should not be subject to NIC because they are not "earnings".

**36-020** There should be no CGT implications. Although the receipt of capital sum by the trustee could be a deemed disposal for CGT purposes[48] any gain is expressly not a chargeable gain.[49] A payment to a beneficiary under the scheme should not have any CGT implications because the benefits do not derive from an asset: the rights of a beneficiary under the scheme are not a form of property and therefore not an asset for CGT purposes.[50]

### Inheritance tax

**36-021** No inheritance tax charge will arise on the death of a life assured or a beneficiary of the scheme. Neither the policies, not any proceeds, form part of any person's estate for inheritance tax purposes.[51]

**36-022** Typically, under the terms of the scheme, the employer will declare that it is holding the initial policy as trustee. If the employer is a close company, or a partnership (including an LLP), that declaration could have inheritance tax implications if it causes a reduction in the value of the shareholders' (or partners') estates. As the employer will be required to pay the proceeds of the policy to the beneficiaries of the life assured, it is arguable that the policy does not have any value to the employer (the policy is effectively matched with the obligation to pay the proceeds away), and so the value of any transfer of value should not exceed the total premiums paid under the policy. In any event, any transfer is likely to be exempt as a result of IHTA 1984 s.10.[52]

**36-023** The payment of premiums may cause a reduction in the value of the estate of the shareholders or partners, but that should not have any inheritance tax implications as a result of IHTA 1984 ss.12 or 10.

**36-024** EGLS were sponsored superannuation schemes prior to 6 April 2006.[53] Since then, it might be possible for IHTA 1984 s.86 to apply to an EGLS, but that will usually not be the case. The property held for the purpose of the scheme (i.e. the policies and any proceeds of the policies) is relevant property for inheritance tax purposes, so:

(a) An exit charge may arise where a distribution is made from the EGLS. However, in relation to a distribution made prior to the first ten-year anniversary, the charge is calculated by reference to the value of the original settled property (typically the initial policy), which is likely to be very low. HMRC accept that exit charge in first ten years is likely to be nil.[54]

(b) A periodic charge may arise on each ten-year anniversary. HMRC accept that a periodic charge will usually be nil unless the EGLS holds undistrib-

---

[47] Assuming the scheme is not established outside of the in the UK: see ITEPA 2003 s.574(1)(aa) and s.574A.
[48] TCGA 1992 s.22.
[49] TCGA 1992 s.210.
[50] *Davenport v Chilver* [1983] Ch 293 at 299 (Nourse J).
[51] HMRC agree at IHTM17092.
[52] See Ch.28. Although the benefits cannot benefit the employee himself, it is clearly for his benefit. Although note that in *Postlethwaite* it was suggested that the intention to benefit an employee's family members was gratuitous. If considered necessary, s.13 could be made to apply.
[53] For sponsored superannuation schemes, See Ch.28.
[54] IHTM17092.

uted proceeds or a life assured is terminally ill at the ten-year anniversary.[55] For this reason, it is usually recommended that a scheme is terminated after seven or eight years, and a new EGLS is established, to hold new policies.[56] It is generally inadvisable to wait any longer than eight years, because if a life assured dies at that time, it may not always be possible for the trustee to get in and then distribute the proceeds prior to the ten-year anniversary.

**36-025** HMRC consider that, for inheritance tax purposes, the employer is the settlor.[57] They appear to accept that the reservation of benefit provisions do not apply where the lives assured are not the settlors.[58]

**36-026** On the death of a life insured, the existence of policy needs to be disclosed in IHT400.

---

[55] IHTM17092.
[56] The policies should not be assigned form one EGLS to another, otherwise they will be treated as remaining in the original scheme for the purposes of the relevant property charges (IHTA 1984 s.81).
[57] IHTM17091.
[58] IHTM17074 explains that "Where a member of an [EFRBS] makes (or is deemed to make) a disposition in connection with the EFRBS, the disposition may constitute a gift with reservation, where the class of discretionary beneficiaries includes the member's personal representatives".

# CHAPTER 37

# Section 615 Funds

## TABLE OF CONTENTS

| | |
|---|---|
| Overview | 37-001 |
| What is a section 615 fund? | 37-004 |
| "Bona fide established under irrevocable trusts..." | 37-006 |
| "... in connection with some trade or undertaking" | 37-007 |
| "Has for its sole purpose the provision of ... superannuation benefits" | 37-008 |
| "Recognised by the employer and employed persons..." | 37-009 |
| The benefit accrual condition | 37-010 |
| Pension transfers | 37-011 |
| Consequences of breaching the benefit accrual condition | 37-012 |
| Taxation | 37-013 |
| Contributions | 37-013 |
| Investment income and gains | 37-018 |
| Benefits | 37-020 |
| National insurance contributions | 37-025 |
| The provision of benefits following a breach of the benefit accrual condition | 37-026 |
| Illustration | 37-027 |
| Inheritance tax | 37-028 |

## OVERVIEW

A "s.615 fund" or "s.615 scheme" is the name generally given to a retirement benefit scheme which satisfies the requirements of ICTA 1988 s.615(6). That is, in outline, a funded occupational scheme established in connection with some non-UK trade or undertaking, designed to provide benefits to former employees in respect of duties performed outside of the UK. Many occupational retirement benefits schemes with no connection to the UK will, on the face of it, satisfy these requirements (often without being aware of them).[1]

Section 615 funds can be remarkably tax-efficient. A UK employer will typically obtain an immediate tax deduction in respect of contributions to a s.615 fund, and will do so without causing any of the FA 2004 Pt 4 provisions to apply.[2] Invest-

**37-001**

**37-002**

---

[1] It is possible, but unnecessary, to submit the scheme documentation to HMRC's Pension Scheme Office Overseas Scheme Section for approval of a s.615 fund.
[2] cf. the RNUKS provisions (for which, see Ch.30).

ment income and gains are generally free of UK tax, and s.615 funds enjoy the same favourable inheritance tax treatment as QNUPS. Benefits may be provided on ceasing to work for the sponsoring employer at any age (it is not necessary to retire from work altogether), and lump sum benefits received by a UK resident member will not usually be subject to UK tax.[3]

**37-003** However, since 6 April 2017 it has not been possible for any "benefit accrual" to occur under a s.615 fund. Such benefit accrual is attributed to a different fund (referred to as the "shadow fund" for the actual fund), which is expressly not a s.615 fund. The shadow fund will therefore usually be an EFRBS.[4]

## WHAT IS A SECTION 615 FUND?

**37-004** A s.615 fund is a "superannuation fund" which satisfies the four requirements specified below (as prescribed by ICTA 1988 s.615(6)[5]). A "superannuation fund" is essentially an occupational retirement benefits scheme: "superannuation" in this context refers to the provision of post-employment benefits[6], and in practice many s.615 funds are drafted in the same way as EFRBS, namely for the purpose of providing "relevant benefits" as defined in ITEPA 2003 s.393B.[7] The reference to "fund" rather than "scheme" makes it clear that an unfunded arrangement cannot satisfy the requirements.

**37-005** A superannuation fund is a s.615 fund if it satisfies the following four requirements:[8]

---

[3] This is uncontroversial: see *Simplifying the Taxation of Pensions: Government's Proposals* (December 2003), para.A128: "Benefits can be taken on retirement or leaving service at any age and wholly as a lump sum. Benefits paid from these schemes are not liable to UK tax when paid to non-UK residents and, by concession, lump sums paid to UK residents are not chargeable."

[4] For EFRBS, see Ch.35.

[5] Previously ICTA 1970 s.218.

[6] "Superannuation" derives from "super" ("over" or "above") and "annus" ("year"). The dictionary definition of "superannuated" includes "incapacitated or disqualified for active duty by advanced age", "older than the typical member of a specified group" and "discharged or retired from service or work on a pension after reaching a certain age", but its meaning for the purposes of s.615(6) ICTA 1988 is not so restrictive: benefits may be provided on leaving service at any age. See e.g. the definition of "sponsored superannuation scheme" in ICTA 1988 s.624(1) (prior to 6 April 2006): "... a scheme or arrangement (a) relating to service in particular offices or employments, and (b) having for its object or one of its objects to make provision in respect of persons serving in those offices or employments against future retirement or partial retirement, against future termination of service through death or disability, or against similar matters, being a scheme or arrangement under which any part of the cost of the provision so made is or has been borne otherwise than by those persons by reason of their service ...".

[7] Pursuant to ITEPA 2003 s.393B, "relevant benefits" means "any lump sum, gratuity or other benefit (including a non-cash benefit) provided (or to be provided): (a) on or in anticipation of the retirement of an employee or former employee; (b) on the death of an employee or former employee; (c) after the retirement or death of an employee or former employee in connection with past service; (d) on or in anticipation of, or in connection with, any change in the nature of service of an employee; or (e) to any person by virtue of a pension sharing order or provision relating to an employee or former employee." See Ch.35.

[8] The definition closely mirrors the definition of "superannuation fund" in FA 1921 s.32(3) (which was the first type of "approved" pension scheme): as "a fund which is approved for those purposes, by the Commissioners, and, subject as hereinafter provided, the Commissioners shall not approve any fund unless it is shown to their satisfaction that—(a) the fund is a fund bona fide established under irrevocable trusts in connection with some trade or undertaking carried on in the UK by a person residing therein; (b) the fund has for its sole purpose the provision of annuities for persons employed in the trade or undertaking either on retirement at a specified age or on becoming incapacitated at

## WHAT IS A SECTION 615 FUND?

(a) It is bona fide established under irrevocable trusts in connection with some trade or undertaking carried on wholly or partly outside the UK.
(b) It has for its sole purpose (subject to any legislation requiring or allowing provision for the value of any rights to be transferred between schemes or between members of the same scheme) the provision of superannuation benefits in respect of persons' employment in the trade or undertaking wholly outside the UK. Duties performed in the UK the performance of which is merely incidental to the performance of other duties outside the UK are treated as performed outside the UK.
(c) It is recognised by the employer and employed persons in the trade or undertaking.
(d) It meets the "benefit accrual condition".

### "Bona fide established under irrevocable trusts..."

It is suggested that this requirement, when read with the following (sole purpose) requirement, means that the scheme assets must be set aside to provide retirement benefits, and must be held on terms that do not permit the employer to access those assets except in very limited circumstances. It seems that the words "bona fide" do not merely require that the arrangement is genuine (which is surely implicit); rather they signify that the fund must be established *and subsequently administered* in accordance with these requirements.[9] "Irrevocable trusts" has a technical meaning, as is explained in the pre-A Day guidance in IR12 (2001):

**37-006**

> "2.3: For a scheme to be held under irrevocable trusts does not mean that the scheme needs a formal trust deed but that the assets (including policies) must be set aside to provide relevant benefits for employees or pension credit members and must be held by a trustee or trustees on trusts that ensure that, apart from any surplus [...] or where reimbursement is appropriate [...], they are not available to the employer.
>
> 2.4: The trust may be established by deed, or by resolution of a board of directors (provided that they have the power to do so) or in the case of a partnership by a resolution of the partners. It may be set up under a separate trust deed or declaration of trust, or by inclusion in one instrument with the scheme rules or, where only a policy is used, in the policy.
>
> 2.5: The trustees may be, or include, the employer."

### "... in connection with some trade or undertaking"

"Trade" has a fairly narrow meaning[10], but "undertaking" is much broader. Any commercial activity (including investment business) is likely to satisfy this requirement.[11]

**37-007**

The fund must be established in connection with the trade or undertaking, and not merely for the benefit of the employees of the employer carrying on the trade

---

some earlier age; (c) the employer in the trade or undertaking is a contributor to the fund; (d) the fund is recognised by the employer and employed persons in the trade or undertaking."

[9] The "bona fide" requirement seems slightly out of place in this first requirement: it is more closely connected to the following (sole purpose) requirement (see e.g. the pre-A Day requirement for tax-approval in s.590(2)(a) ICTA 1988 that the scheme was "bona fide established for the sole purpose of providing relevant benefits").

[10] See *Ransom v Higgs* (1974) 50 T.C. 1.

[11] *Baytrust Holdings Ltd v IRC* [1971] W.L.R. 1333.

or undertaking.[12] However, in most cases it should be implicit (in the absence of any evidence to the contrary) that a superannuation fund established by an employer for the benefit of its employees satisfies this requirement.

**"Has for its sole purpose the provision of ... superannuation benefits"**

**37-008**   In general, the term "employment" is not necessarily limited to *employees* as such: a sole trader or partner can be *employed* in a trade or undertaking.[13] However, the reference to "the employer" in the following (recognition) requirement is not easily applied to sole traders or partners, since it is unclear who could be the "employer" of such individuals. So, on balance, it seems that the sole purpose of the fund must be the provision of superannuation benefits in respect of *employees*.

Contributions paid by the employer should be in respect of duties performed by the employee outside of the UK (rather than a reward for any duties previously performed in the UK).[14]

**"Recognised by the employer and employed persons..."**

**37-009**   This precise meaning of this requirement is unclear. It is generally understood to require that the employer and employed persons are aware of the existence of the fund and of their rights and obligations under it.[15] It can be satisfied by providing a scheme booklet (for example) to relevant employees.

**The benefit accrual condition**

**37-010**   The benefit accrual condition was added by FA 2017, with effect from 6 April 2017.[16] Essentially, there must be no benefit accrual on or after 6 April 2017. The way in which benefit accrual is measured depends whether the member's arrangement under the fund is a cash balance arrangement, another money purchase arrangement, or a defined benefits arrangement. The meaning of these terms corresponds with their meanings in FA 2004 Pt 4 in relation to registered pension schemes[17]:

(a)   *Cash balance arrangements*: the benefit accrual condition is that there is no

---

[12]   See *Re Flavel's Will Trusts, Coleman v Flavel* [1969] 1 W.L.R. 444; [1969] 2 All E.R. 232. In that case, a testator directed the trustees of his residuary estate to establish a superannuation and bonus fund for the employees of a specified company. Stamp J held that such a fund was not established "in connection with an undertaking" for the purposes of the Superannuation and other Trust Funds (Validation) Act 1927. Stamp J also ventured (obiter) to doubt whether a fund set up by an individual settlor can ever be established "in connection with an undertaking" for the purposes of that Act.

[13]   Similar language is used in IHTA 1984 s.86: see Ch.28. In pension legislation it is not uncommon for references to employment to include self-employment (see e.g. the definition of occupational pension scheme in PSA 1993 s.1(1)).

[14]   Otherwise the benefits would not be provided "in respect of" employment wholly outside the UK, as is required by s.615(6)(b).

[15]   The language is very similar to ICTA 1988 s.590(2)(b) (relating to mandatory exempt approved status prior to 6 April 2006), which perhaps gives a clearer indication of what s.615(6)(c) may be aimed at: "the scheme is recognised by the employer and employees to whom it relates and every employee who is or has a right to be a member has been given written particulars of all essential features of the scheme which concern him".

[16]   HMRC are given power to make regulations: (a) so as to change, or modify the effect of, the benefit accrual condition; (b) as to the matters to be taken into account in determining whether the benefit accrual condition is met; and (c) for a superannuation fund to be treated to any extent as meeting or not meeting the benefit accrual condition.

[17]   ICTA 1988 s.615(7). For their meanings under FA 2004, see Ch.2.

increase on or after 6 April 2017 in the value of any person's rights under an arrangement relating to a member of the scheme.[18] Rights are valued by reference to the valuation assumptions in FA 2004 s.277.[19] One is therefore required to value each person's rights as at 6 April 2017. The legislation refers to "any person" rather than "the member" so one is required to consider the position of death beneficiaries. Benefit accrual occurs if the value of those rights increases on or after 6 April 2017 by an amount in excess of any annual rate of increase referred to in the scheme rules on 20 March 2017.[20] If no such rate is specified in the scheme rules on 20 March 2017, benefit accrual occurs if the rights increase on or after 6 April 2017 by an amount in excess of the increase in the CPI. Making a contribution under a cash balance arrangement does not itself constitute benefit accrual.[21]

(b) *Other money purchase arrangements*: the benefit accrual condition is that no contributions are made under an arrangement relating to a member of the scheme on or after 6 April 2017. "Contribution" is not defined for these purposes,[22] but investment return plainly does not involve benefit accrual.[23] A contribution to a general fund under the scheme will not breach the benefit accrual condition, because a general fund is not an arrangement "relating to a member". In addition, an allocation from a general fund is not, on the face of it, a contribution,[24] and so will not breach the benefit accrual condition. But any attempt to defeat the obvious purpose of the benefit accrual condition, by making contributions to a general fund with the intention of subsequently reallocating the money to a member's arrangement, would likely be counteracted by the general anti-abuse rule in FA 2013.

(c) *Defined benefits arrangements*: the benefit accrual condition is that there is no increase on or after 6 April 2017 in the capitalised value of any person's

---

[18] ICTA 1988 s.615(6A)(b).

[19] The valuation assumptions require one to value the individual's rights on the assumption that the individual is at the age at which no reduction would apply to the payment of an immediate benefit (e.g. as a result of early retirement), and the individual is in good physical and mental health and so the benefits are not increased as a result of being paid on grounds of ill-health (FA 2004 s.277).

[20] 20 March 2017 was the date that the Finance Bill 2017 was published.

[21] The employer will therefore normally be able to obtain an immediate tax deduction (at least, to the extent of any deficit) for the reasons given below. There appears to be no reason in principle that a cash balance arrangement could not be restructured so that investment return is allocated to another money purchase arrangement under the scheme. That may be attractive if it will allow increased contributions to be made in respect of the cash balance arrangement, because such contributions will not involve any benefit accrual as far as either arrangement is concerned.

[22] For the meaning of "contribution", see Ch.6.

[23] There appears to be no reason in principle that the employer could not lend money to a s.615 fund so that the trustees may invest the money such that the value of the fund increases without breaching the benefit accrual condition. The Occupational Pension Schemes (Investment) Regulations 2005 (SI 2005/3378) reg.5, which prevents borrowing by the trustees of an occupational pension scheme (other than for the purpose of providing temporary liquidity), is disapplied for schemes with fewer than 100 members. A loan on commercial terms is clearly not a "contribution", and it is strongly arguable that a beneficial loan (e.g. interest-free) is not a contribution if the loan is repayable on demand. It is suggested that the defining characteristic of a "contribution" is that it transfers value to the scheme. In an inheritance tax context, HMRC accept (at IHTM14317) that "The grant of an interest free loan repayable on demand ... is not a transfer of value (because the value of the right to repayment of the loan is equal to the amount of it)". Similarly, although a beneficial loan to an employee may constitute earnings, it has no value if it is repayable on demand (per Vinelott J in *O'Learly v Macinlay* [1991] S.T.C. 42). The analysis may be different if the loan were allowed to become time-barred. A beneficial loan should not cause the income tax settlement provisions (see Ch.25) to apply.

[24] See FA 2004 s.233(3).

rights under an arrangement relating to a member of the scheme.[25] As with cash balance arrangements, one is required to value each person's rights as at 6 April 2017. Benefit accrual occurs if the value of those rights increases on or after 6 April 2017 by an amount in excess of any annual rate of increase referred to in the scheme rules on 20 March 2017.[26] If no such rate is specified in the scheme rules on 20 March 2017, benefit accrual occurs if the value of those rights increases in excess of the increase in the CPI. As with cash balance arrangements, making a contribution under a defined benefits arrangement does not constitute benefit accrual.[27]

(d) In the case of any arrangement relating to a member of the scheme that is neither a money purchase arrangement nor a defined benefits arrangement, the benefit accrual condition is that no contributions are made under the arrangement on or after 6 April 2017 and there is no increase on or after 6 April 2017 in the value of any person's rights under the arrangement.[28]

*Pension transfers*

**37-011**   Where sums or assets held for the purposes of an arrangement relating to a member of a s.615 fund are transferred so as to become held for the purposes of an arrangement relating to that person as a member of another s.615 fund, such a transfer expressly does not constitute benefit accrual.[29] One would expect, however, that a transfer from a different type of scheme (such as an EFRBS) to a s.615 fund *will* constitute a contribution (and therefore benefit accrual) for these purposes.[30]

*Consequences of breaching the benefit accrual condition*

**37-012**   Any benefit accrual breaching the benefit accrual condition is treated as accruing under a separate superannuation fund (referred to as the "shadow fund" for the actual fund). The shadow fund is expressly not a s.615 fund, so it will usually be an EFRBS.[31] It follows that none of the generous tax treatment applicable to s.615 funds can apply to such benefit accrual.

---

[25] ICTA 1988 s.615(6A)(c).
[26] In relation to the very similar provisions relating to lifetime allowance fixed protection, HMRC take a very generous view of this requirement: see PTM0093600.
[27] The employer will therefore normally be able to obtain an immediate tax deduction (as least, to the extent of any deficit) for the reasons given below. As with cash balance arrangements, there appears to be no reason in principle that a defined benefits arrangement could not be restructured so that investment return is allocated to an other money purchase arrangement.
[28] ICTA 1988 s.615(6A)(d) ICTA 1988. HMRC are given power to make regulations providing: (a) for determining whether there is an increase in the value of a person's rights; (b) for determining the amount of any increase; and (c) for ignoring the whole or part of any increase. Such regulations may make provision having effect in relation to times before the regulations are made: ICTA 1988 s.615(6D).
[29] ICTA 1988 s.615(13) and (14).
[30] For the meaning of "contribution", see Ch.6.
[31] ICTA 1988 s.615(11) and (12). It is very likely that the shadow fund will be an EFRBS, but this will not be the case if the shadow fund is capable of providing only benefits which are not relevant benefits (see ITEPA 2003 s.393B(2), discussed in Ch.35).

# TAXATION

## Contributions

A tax deduction will usually be available in respect of employer contributions to s.615. CTA 2009 s.1290, which would otherwise defer a tax deduction in respect of employer contributions, is expressly disapplied in relation to contributions to s.615 funds.[32] As noted above, it is not possible since 6 April 2017 to make a contribution to an other money purchase arrangement under a s.615 fund (because any such contributions are attributed to the shadow fund, which is expressly not a s.615 fund), so this treatment is now limited to contributions in respect of cash balance or defined benefits arrangements.

37-013

Contributions to s.615 funds are expressly free of Class 1 NIC[33] and Class 1A NIC.[34]

37-014

Employer contributions to s.615 funds are *not* expressly exempt from an employment income tax charge[35], but if the member is non-UK resident in the tax year that the contribution is made and the contribution relates to duties performed outside of the UK (as will usually be the case), the contribution will not be subject to income tax as earnings.[36] Even where the member is UK resident, a contribution will not usually constitute earnings or a benefit in kind.[37]

37-015

A right to receive a payment or benefit from a s.615 fund is expressly not a benefit for the purposes of ITEPA 2003 s.401 (termination payments).[38]

37-016

The earmarking of a contribution by the trustee for a particular member is taxable in accordance with the disguised remuneration provisions unless an exception applies.[39] The exception in ITEPA 2003 s.554Z4(4)(a) will apply where the contribution is "for" a period in which the employee is non-UK resident, and is in respect of duties performed outside of the UK.

37-017

## Investment income and gains

The tax provisions relating to s.615 funds do not impose any investment restrictions, so a s.615 fund can, in principle, make loans to members and participating employers, and can invest in residential property.[40] Investment income is treated as "exempt to the like extent (if any) as if it were income of a person not domiciled and not resident in the UK" (such income tax relief to be given by way of repayment by HMRC).[41] Income from property held for the purposes of a s.615 fund is

37-018

---

[32] CTA 2009 s.1290(4)(b). See Ch.24.
[33] Social Security (Contributions) Regulations 2001 (SI 2001/1004) Sch.3 Pt VI para.11.
[34] SI 2001/1004 reg.40(2)(a) provides that any payment which is exempt from Class 1 NIC as a result of Sch.3 Pt VI para.11 is also exempt from Class 1A NIC.
[35] Neither ITEPA 2003 s.308 nor s.308A (which provide that an employer contribution to a registered pension scheme, or to a qualifying overseas pension scheme in respect of an employee who is a relevant migrant member, do not constitute taxable earnings of the employee) apply to s.615 funds.
[36] ITEPA 2003 s.15(1A).
[37] See Ch.24. In relation to benefits in kind, ITEPA 2003 s.307 should apply in any event.
[38] ITEPA 2003 s.402(4).
[39] Earmarking is a s.554B relevant step. For the disguised remuneration provisions, see Ch.27.
[40] If the scheme's main administration is in the UK then it will be an occupational pension scheme for the purposes of PA 1995 and so the employer-related investment provisions in PA 1995 s.40 and SI 2005/3378 will apply (the definition of "occupational pension scheme" in PSA 1993 s.1 is incorporated by PA 1995 s.176). These provisions also purport to apply if the main administration of the scheme is outside the EEA states.
[41] ICTA 1988 s.614(5)

## 810 SECTION 615 FUNDS

expressly not "accumulated or discretionary income" and so the 45% trusts rate does not apply to it.[42]

**37-019** Any gains accruing on the disposal of assets held for the purposes of a s.615 fund are not subject to CGT.[43]

### Benefits

**37-020** A s.615 fund is expressly not an EFRBS[44] so benefits under s.615 funds are not taxable under ITEPA 2003 s.394. Benefits provided in the form of a lump sum under a s.615 fund are not taxable under ITEPA 2003 s.403.[45] Prior to 6 April 2011, lump sum payments from s.615 funds were expressly free of income tax.[46]

**37-021** If the s.615 fund and the recipient are both resident in the UK:

(a) Pension income is taxable under ITEPA 2003 Pt 9 Ch.3.[47]
(b) Lump sum are taxable under the disguised remuneration provisions.[48] Where, as is usually the case[49], an exception to the disguised remuneration provisions applies, a lump sum should be free of UK tax provided that it is a capital distribution.[50]

**37-022** If the s.615 fund is resident in the UK and the recipient is not resident in the UK, pension income and lump sums are taxable in accordance with the disguised remuneration provisions,[51] unless a double tax treaty between the UK and the territory in which the member is resident confers exclusive taxing rights on that territory. The trustees are not required to operate PAYE in respect of a pension which arises wholly from an employment carried out abroad.[52] In any event, there is no requirement to deduct income tax from any payment or account for it under ITA 2007 Pt 15 Ch.6.[53]

**37-023** If the recipient is resident in the UK and the s.615 fund is not resident in the UK, distributions are taxable in accordance with the disguised remuneration provisions. Where, as is usually the case[54], an exception to the disguised remuneration provi-

---

[42] ITA 2007 s.480(4). Income from property held as a member of a property investment LLP is excepted.
[43] TCGA 1992 s.271(1)(c)(ii).
[44] ITEPA 2003 s.393A(2)(b).
[45] i.e. benefits received in connection with the termination of a person's employment. Such a charge could in principle apply to benefits payable on retirement (see EIM13000), but there is an exception in ITEPA 2003 s.414A.
[46] See ESC A10.
[47] See Ch.26. The disguised remuneration provisions do not apply to such benefits (ITEPA 2003 s.554S).
[48] For the disguised remuneration provisions, see Ch.27.
[49] e.g. if the distribution is *for* a period in which the employee is non-UK resident, and is in respect of duties performed outside of the UK, the value of the relevant step is nil (ITEPA 2003 s.554Z4(4)(a)). This is the case even if he is resident in the UK at the time the distribution is made to him. There is also an exception for lump sum paid from pre-6 April 2011 rights (see s.554W). There is an apportionment where the rights out of which the lump sum is paid are only partly pre-6 April 2011 lump sum rights. HMRC appear to take a relatively generous view of the meaning of pre-6 April 2011 lump sum rights (see EIM45635).
[50] See Ch.26.
[51] As above, an exception will often apply (see e.g., ITEPA 2003 s.554Z4(4)(a) and 554W).
[52] The Income Tax (Pay As You Earn) Regulations 2003 (SI 2003/2682) reg.57. HMRC accept this at PAYE81750. The pension will remain taxable under the self-assessment unless it is exempted by a tax treaty.
[53] ICTA 1988 s.615(3). ITA 2007 Pt 15 Ch.6 imposes an obligation to deduct income tax from certain annual payments arising in the UK.
[54] See e.g., ITEPA 2003 s.554Z4(4)(a) and 554W.

sions applies, pension income (including a relevant lump sum[55]) is taxable under Pt 9 Ch.4.[56]

If neither the s.615 fund nor the recipient is resident in the UK, distributions are taxed in accordance with the disguised remuneration provisions unless (a) an exception applies,[57] or (b) a double tax treaty between the UK and the territory in which the member is resident confers exclusive taxing rights on that other territory.

37-024

*National insurance contributions*

A pension or annuity from a s.615 fund is expressly free of Class 1 NIC.[58] There is no express NIC exemption for lump sums under s.615 funds, but all benefits should be free of NIC to the extent that they accrue in respect of non-UK service.[59]

37-025

*The provision of benefits following a breach of the benefit accrual condition*

As is explained above, to the extent that the benefit accrual condition is breached (e.g. as a result of contributions on or after 6 April 2017), for tax purposes the superannuation fund is in part a s.615 fund and in part an EFRBS. Where a benefit is subsequently provided under such a fund, is the benefit referrable first to the s.615 fund (a "first in, first out" basis), or first to the EFRBS (a "last in, last out" basis), or rateably (a pari passu basis)? The legislation does not prescribe an answer.[60] HMRC are understood to consider that the rule in *Clayton's* case[61] dictates a first in, first out approach, meaning that benefits are treated as provided first under the s.615 fund. The rule in *Clayton's* case is a presumption as to the intention of the parties.[62] The rule does not apply where a contrary intention is evident or can be inferred (by even a slight counterweight)[63], for example in the scheme rules, or trustee minutes, or in the communications between the trustee and scheme member. It seems that the rule can apply only to a "current account", i.e. an account in which there is the periodic setting off of transactions against each other,[64] such that the

37-026

---

[55] For relevant lump sums, see Ch.26. The taxable amount may be reduced in respect of the value immediately before 6 April 2017 of rights, accrued by then, specifically to receive benefits by way of lump sum payments, and (if the scheme is an overseas pension scheme) in respect of so much of the lump sum as would, if the scheme were a registered pension scheme, not be liable for to income tax under ITEPA 2003 Pt 9. Note that a lump sum is a relevant lump sum only if it is exempt from the disguised remuneration provisions (i.e. it is not a relevant step to which Pt 7A Ch.2 applies) (see ITEPA 2003 s.574A(1)(b)). If the payment of the lump sum is a relevant step, but the taxable amount is reduced to nil (e.g. under s.554Z4), the lump sum is not a relevant lump sum for the purposes of Pt 9 Ch.4.

[56] The disguised remuneration provisions do not apply to such benefits (ITEPA 2003 s.554S). If the member is a remittance basis taxpayer at the relevant time, such benefits are subject to UK tax only to the extent that they are remitted to the UK (ITTOIA 2005 s.832).

[57] As above, an exception will often apply (see e.g. ITEPA 2003 s.554Z4(4)(a) and 554W).

[58] SI 2001/1004 Sch.3 Pt VI para.11.

[59] Social Security Contributions and Benefits Act 1992 ss.1(6)(a) and 2(1)(a).

[60] Cf. the RNUKS provisions in FA 2004 Sch.34, which prescribe that where a member's arrangement under an RNUKS comprises a UK tax-relieved fund and a non-relieved fund, benefits are first treated as made from the UK tax-relieved fund, and only once that fund is exhausted are benefits treated as made from the non-relieved fund.

[61] *Devaynes v Noble* (1816) 1 Mer 529.

[62] *In re Hallett's Estate* (1880) 13 Ch.D. 696; *Cory Bros. & Co Ltd v Owners of The Turkish Steamship Mecca* [1897] A.C. 286.

[63] *Russell-Cooke Trust Co v Prentis* [2003] 2 All E.R. 478. Nor does it apply where it is impractical or unjust (*Barlow Clowes International Ltd v Vaughan* [1992] 4 All E.R. 22).

[64] *Cory Bros & Co Ltd v Owners of the Turkish Steamship Mecca* [1897] A.C. 286 at 291; *Hay & Co Ltd v Torbet* 1908 S.C. 781 at 788; *McKinlay v Wilson* (1885) 13 R. 210 at 217.

transactions are not distinct and so have been brought into a "common account".[65] In contrast to a deposit account, a current account normally requires movement, i.e. regular payments into and out of the account such that the debit and credit balances alter. It seems clear that under a pension scheme a defined benefits arrangement is not a current account, but it is suggested that a money purchase arrangement could conceivably be a current account (albeit an unusual form of current account) once the member starts to draw benefits. The rule applies in "the case of a banking account, where all the sums paid in form one blended fund, the parts of which have no longer any distinct existence".[66] The rule therefore will not apply to *in specie* contributions, or transfers of assets from other pension schemes, unless and until they are encashed. Nor will the rule apply to the extent that post-6 April 2017 contributions are invested and those investments are distributed *in specie* to the member (or where the property distributed can be otherwise traced to post-6 April 2017 contributions, such that the property distributed derives from or represents such contribution(s)). Where the rule has been found to be inapplicable, a pari passu approach is usually preferred.

*Illustration*

**37-027**  T is a UK resident member of a s.615 fund which provides money purchase benefits. T's benefits accrued between May 2013 and May 2020, when he was non-UK resident, and all contributions were in respect of non-UK service. The value of T's fund on 6 April 2017 was £750,000. Between 6 April 2017 and June 2020, a further £200,000 was contributed to the plan and its current value is £1.2 million. It is proposed that the entire £1.2 million is paid to him in 2022 as a lump sum. Ignore the application of any double tax treaty.

The lump sum should be free of NIC because it accrued in respect of non-UK service.[67] For income tax purposes, part of T's fund is a s.615 fund and part is an EFRBS. The s.615 fund comprises the value of the fund on 6 April 2017 (£750,000) plus the investment return deriving from that £750,000 after that date. Where this return cannot be separately identified (as is often the case), it is suggested that the investment return should be attributed to the s.615 fund on a pro rata basis. For example, if £50,000 was contributed in May 2017 and the value of the fund on 6 April 2018 was £850,000, 93.34% of the £50,000 investment return for that period should be attributed to the s.615 fund and 6.66% should be attributed to the EFRBS (because £50,000 is 6.66% of £750,000).

The lump sum will be tax-free to the extent of the pre-6 April 2017 benefit accrual, because:

(a) It will not be taxable under the disguised remuneration provisions because of the exception in s.554Z4(4)(a).
(b) If the s.615 fund is established outside of the UK, the lump sum will be a relevant lump sum and tax-free as a result of the deduction under step 2 in s.574A. If the s.615 fund is established in the UK, the lump sum cannot be a relevant lump sum, and there are no other provisions which could subject it to tax.

The lump sum will be subject to income tax at T's marginal rate to the extent of the post-6 April 2017 benefit accrual:

---

[65] *Cory Bros & Co Ltd v Owners of the Turkish Steamship Mecca* [1897] A.C. 286 at 292; *Dougall v Lornie* (1899) 1 F. 1187 at 1190.
[66] *Devaynes v Noble* (1816) 1 Mer 529 at p.608.
[67] Social Security Contributions and Benefits Act 1992 ss.1(6)(a) and 2(1)(a).

(a) If the s.615 fund is established outside of the UK, HMRC consider that the lump sum will be a relevant lump sum, even though the only exception from the disguised remuneration provisions is s.554S. The better view is that it is not a relevant lump sum and so it is taxable under the disguised remuneration provisions (the exception in s.554Z4(4)(a) will not apply because of s.554Z4(9)). It will not be taxable under the EFRBS provisions because the disguised remuneration provisions take priority (s.394(4C)(b)).

(b) If the s.615 fund is established in the UK, the lump sum will be taxed under the disguised remuneration provisions. It cannot be a relevant lump sum, and it will not be taxable under the EFRBS provisions because the disguised remuneration provisions take priority (s.394(4C)(b)).

**Inheritance tax**

**37-028** Section 615 funds are afforded the same favourable inheritance tax treatment as QNUPS.[68]

---

[68] For QNUPS, see Ch.34.

# CHAPTER 38

# Funded Unapproved Retirement Benefits Schemes

## TABLE OF CONTENTS

| | |
|---|---|
| Introduction | 38-001 |
|     Background | 38-003 |
| What is a FURBS? | 38-006 |
| Taxation | 38-009 |
|     Contributions | 38-009 |
|         Income tax | 38-010 |
|         "With a view to the provision of benefits for or in respect of an employee" | 38-012 |
|         Is an in specie contribution a "sum paid"? | 38-015 |
|         Relief under s.392 | 38-016 |
|     Investments | 38-019 |
|         UK resident FURBS | 38-019 |
|         Non-UK resident FURBS | 38-021 |
|     Benefits | 38-022 |
|         Benefits referable to contributions made prior to 6 April 2006 | 38-022 |
|         Transitional provisions applying to s.394 charge | 38-023 |
|         Non-UK resident FURBS and relevant lump sums | 38-029 |
|         Benefits referable contributions made on or after 6 April 2006 | 38-030 |
|     Inheritance tax | 38-031 |

## INTRODUCTION

Since 6 April 2006, the EFRBS provisions described in Ch.35 have applied to retirement benefit schemes that are neither registered pension schemes nor s.615 funds. Prior to that date, a quite different tax regime applied to such schemes; usually referred to as either funded unapproved retirement benefits schemes (FURBS) or unfunded unapproved retirement benefits schemes (UURBS). This chapter is concerned primarily with the former.[1] Since 6 April 2006, all FURBS are EFRBS, with transitional provisions applying to contributions made before 6 April 2006. In

38-001

---

[1] Under an UURBS the employer agreed to provide benefits in prescribed circumstances, typically as part of a "no worse off" promise to a new employee. The employer obtained a tax deduction when the benefits were paid and the employee was subject to tax at that time. UURBS do not usually give rise to many tax issues, although see *Mackay v HMRC* [2017] UKFTT 441. Also see the non-tax case *Granada Group Ltd v The Law Debenture Pension Trust Corporation Plc* [2015] EWHC 1499.

this chapter (and in this book generally), in order to distinguish pre-April 2006 EFRBS from post-April 2006 EFRBS, the former are referred to as FURBS.

**38-002** The provisions described in this chapter are those that applied immediately before 6 April 2006 (except where expressly stated otherwise), and those that apply now.

**Background**[2]

**38-003** FURBS were very uncommon before 27 July 1989. Prior to that date, when considering whether to approve a pension scheme under its discretionary powers in ICTA 1988 s.591(1), the Inland Revenue took into account *all* retirement benefit schemes (including unapproved schemes) sponsored by the same employer. Only if the total benefits provided under all schemes were within Inland Revenue limits could any of the schemes be approved for tax purposes. Two measures were introduced with effect from 27 July 1989, which together had the effect of making FURBS attractive:

(a) First, the conditions for tax-approval were changed so that only the benefits provided under approved schemes were taken into account, meaning that significant benefits could be provided via FURBS without prejudicing the approval of any approved schemes established by that employer.

(b) Second, an "earnings cap" was introduced, meaning that the maximum benefits payable under tax-approved pension schemes was restricted to the pension payable in respect of a final salary of £60,000 p/a (irrespective of the employee's actual salary).

FA 1989 therefore capped the benefits that could be provided under tax-approved schemes and opened up the possibility of providing such benefits under FURBS. The intention was that FURBS and other unapproved schemes would be used to supplement or "top up" approved schemes for individuals affected by the earnings cap.

**38-004** Employer contributions to FURBS counted as employment income of the employee (and so were immediately taxable), but FURBS offered a number of tax efficiencies:

(a) lump sum benefits were generally tax-free;
(b) neither contributions nor benefits were subject to NIC[3];
(c) the settled property was not relevant property for inheritance tax purposes, provided that the FURBS was a "sponsored superannuation scheme"[4]; and
(d) prior to 6 April 2004, investment income received by a UK resident FURBS was subject to income tax at only the basic rate (then 22%), provided that the scheme was established for the sole purpose of providing relevant benefits.[5]

**38-005** FURBS were frequently established as single member schemes, and for that

---

[2] For more detail see: A. Langley and R. Mulcahy, *Unapproved Pension Schemes* (London: Butterworths, 1994); S. Woodhouse, S. Eden and S. Lippiatt, *Taxation of Pension Schemes* (London: Sweet & Maxwell, 1996), Ch.6; Inland Revenue publication, *The Tax Treatment of Top-Up Pension Schemes* (1991).

[3] For many years HMRC considered that contributions to FURBS were subject to NIC, and were successful on this point before the Special Commissioners in *Telent Plc v RCC* [2008] S.T.C. (S.C.D.) 202. However, in *HMRC v Forde and McHugh Ltd* [2014] UKSC 14 the Supreme Court held that contributions to a FURBS are not subject to NIC.

[4] See Ch.28.

[5] ICTA 1988 s.686(2)(c).

reason were subject to little pension regulation.[6] Although an EFRBS may be established as a single member scheme, the inheritance tax provisions now applicable frequently make this unattractive.[7]

## WHAT IS A FURBS?

**38-006** "FURBS" is not a term found in any legislation. It was the name given to any retirement benefit scheme which was both funded and unapproved. ICTA 1988 s.611(1) and (2) provided that:

> "(1) In this Chapter 'retirement benefits scheme' means, subject to the provisions of this section, a scheme for the provision of benefits consisting of or including relevant benefits, but does not include—
> (a) any national scheme providing such benefits; or
> (b) any scheme providing such benefits which is an approved personal pension scheme under Chapter IV of this Part.
>
> (2) References in this Chapter to a scheme include references to a deed, agreement, series of agreements, or other arrangements providing for relevant benefits notwithstanding that it relates or they relate only to—
> (a) a small number of employees, or to a single employee, or
> (b) the payment of a pension starting immediately on the making of the arrangements."

**38-007** ICTA 1988 s.612 included the following definitions:

> "'Pension' includes annuity;
> 'Relevant benefits' means any pension, lump sum, gratuity or other like benefit given or to be given on retirement or on death, or by virtue of a pension sharing order or provision, or in anticipation of retirement, or, in connection with past service, after retirement or death, or to be given on or in anticipation of or in connection with any change in the nature of the service of the employee in question, except that it does not include any benefit which is to be afforded solely by reason of the disablement by accident of a person occurring during his service or of his death by accident so occurring and for no other reason;
> 'Service' means service as an employee of the employer in question and other expressions, including 'retirement', shall be construed accordingly."

**38-008** A FURBS was therefore an unapproved scheme for the provision of benefits consisting of or including relevant benefits. In contrast to the current definition of relevant benefits in ITEPA 2003 s.393B, the definition in ICTA 1988 s.612 expressly included pension (although, as is the case now, pension income would be taxable as a relevant benefit only if it was not taxed under ITEPA 2003 Pt 9[8]). It seems clear from s.612 that "retirement" means ceasing to work for the relevant employer (and not necessarily retirement from employment generally).[9]

---

[6] Such as PA 1995 (including the provisions relating to employer-related investments, which would have restricted the ability of the FURBS to invest in the sponsoring employer).
[7] If the EFRBS is established under trusts the scheme property will usually be relevant property for inheritance tax purposes unless the member is non-UK domiciled (in which case any non-UK situs scheme property would be excluded property: see Ch.28). It is unlikely that IHTA 1984 s.86 (see paras Ch.28) can be made to apply to a single member scheme.
[8] ITEPA 2003 s.393(2).
[9] The meaning of "retirement" in the EFRBS provisions is less clear (see Ch.35).

## TAXATION

**Contributions**

**38-009**  The tax analysis of contributions to a FURBS is as follows:

(a) No income tax relief was available in respect of member contributions to a FURBS.

(b) Prior to 6 April 2006, a tax deduction was expressly unavailable in respect of the expenses of paying any sum pursuant to a FURBS with a view to the provision of any benefits unless the sum counted as employment income of an employee by virtue of ITEPA 2003 s.386(1).[10] Provided that the contribution was taxable under s.386(1), the employer would usually obtain a tax deduction under general principles.[11]

(c) A contribution to a FURBS does not constitute *earnings* for NIC purposes provided that the contribution is made at a time when the member's interest in the assets of the FURBS is contingent on him surviving to a specified age, and so might be defeated by his death before the specified retirement age.[12]

(d) Prior to 6 April 2006, an employer contribution to a FURBS usually gave rise to an income tax charge under ITEPA 2003 s.386(1). This is now considered in some detail.

*Income tax*

**38-010**  Prior to 6 April 2006, ITEPA 2003 s.386(1) provided as follows:

"A sum paid by an employer—
(a) in accordance with a non-approved retirement benefits scheme, and
(b) with a view to the provision of relevant benefits for or in respect of an employee of the employer,
counts as employment income of the employee for the relevant tax year."

**38-011**  Benefits are provided "in respect of" an employee if they are provided for the employee's spouse, widow or widower, children, dependants or personal representatives.[13] So, under ITEPA 2003 s.386,[14] sums paid to a FURBS with a view to the provision of relevant benefits counted as employment income (although the charge was typically paid under the P11D procedure).[15] Separately identifiable payments to the trustees for other purposes (such as establishing the scheme and paying for the administration etc.) would therefore not count as employment income.

---

[10] FA 1989 s.76(1) and (3). It followed that a tax deduction was unavailable in respect of contributions for non-UK resident employees. This was unintended and HMRC would in practice allow such a deduction by concession (see ESC B39).

[11] For an explanation of the general principles, including the *wholly and exclusively* rule and the provisions relating to capital expenditure, see Ch.6.

[12] *HMRC v Forde and McHugh Ltd* [2014] UKSC 14 (Lord Hodge). See Ch.24 for more detail.

[13] ITEPA 2003 s.386(6).

[14] Or, prior to 6 April 2003, ICTA 1988 s.595.

[15] A charge under s.386 would not usually arise where an employer makes provision in respect of an UURBS, provided that any security provided by the employer does not constitute the payment of a sum. See A. Langley and R. Mulcahy, *Unapproved Pension Schemes* (London: Butterworths, 1994), paras 7.17 and following.

A contribution was apportioned under s.388 if it was in respect of more than one employee.

*"With a view to the provision of benefits for or in respect of an employee"*

**38-012** In *Philpott v HMRC*,[16] an employer with 21 employees claimed a tax deduction in respect of a contribution of £34,000 and three parcels of valuable development land to a FURBS with five members. The £34,000 was allocated to the five members on an unequal basis (£10,000 was allocated for each of three members, and £2,000 was allocated for each of the other two members), but the employer did not specify how the land was to be allocated within the FURBS and the trustees did not expressly make any allocation. The failure to allocate was quite deliberate, following advice that the charge under s.386(1) should not apply to contributions which are un-earmarked and held on a pooled basis. The taxpayers argued that the employer did not make the contribution in respect of any particular individual who might benefit under the FURBS and neither the employer nor the trustees had sought to allocate any part of the value of the contribution for any of the taxpayers.[17] HMRC contended that a proportionate part of the value of each contribution had in fact been expressly and/or impliedly paid in respect of each member, or alternatively (if there had been no express or implied allocation), the value should be apportioned between the appellants equally in accordance with ITEPA 2003 s.388.[18]

**38-013** The FTT agreed with the taxpayers that s.386 can only apply if it is possible to attribute the payment or an identifiable part of the payment to a particular employee, otherwise it is not possible for the payment to count as employment income of the employee for the relevant year. The FTT considered that there is no reason that contributions *need* to be allocated for specific employees, and noted that HMRC were unable to articulate precisely how s.386(1) is designed to operate in such cases.

**38-014** However, within a few months of the contributions, the FURBS distributed £3 million to one member and £150,000 and £250,000 to two other members, and the FTT found as a fact that this had been the intention at the time that the contributions were made. Therefore each contribution was made "in respect of" those employees and so s.386 applied to that extent. A residual value of approximately £7 million remained in the FURBS and the FTT concluded that this must be allocated under s.388 equally between the other two members. This was because the intention had been that the first three members would receive the £3.4 million (but no more), and although it was possible that new members could join in the future, the scheme rules had been drafted such that amounts could only be paid as benefits

---

[16] *Philpott v HMRC* [2014] UKFTT 853.

[17] Similar arguments had been raised in *McWhinnie v HMRC* [2013] UKFTT 588, however in that case the employer had only one employee (the taxpayer) at the time of the contribution. He had not formally become a member of the scheme and it was argued that s.386(1) did not apply because the contribution was not allocated for any employee. The FTT found on the facts that the contribution was made with a view to the provision of relevant benefits for or in respect of the taxpayer. This was essentially because: (a) correspondence and reports did refer to the taxpayer as being a beneficiary; (b) a formal application for membership was not required under the rules of the scheme; and (c) there was no contemporaneous evidence to support the taxpayer's arguments.

[18] ITEPA 2003 s.388 provided that if a sum within s.386 is paid for or in respect of two or more employees, part of it is treated as paid in respect of each of them. The amount treated as paid in respect of each employee is A × (B/C) where "A" is the sum paid, "B" is the amount which would have had to be paid to secure the benefits to be provided in respect of the employee in question, and "C" is the total amount which would have had to be paid to secure the benefits to be provided in respect of all the employees if separate payments had been made in the case of each of them.

if they derived from contributions made whilst the individual was a member.[19] It followed that the residual £7 million could only be available for the two other members. The justification for dividing the excess equally was on the basis that the two members had the same entitlement overall. Given that neither member had any entitlement, finding that they were equally entitled seems a little arbitrary.

*Is an in specie contribution a "sum paid"?*

**38-015** In *Irving v RCC*,[20] the taxpayer's employer established a FURBS and made an *in specie* contribution of shares. The taxpayer argued that an *in specie* contribution to a FURBS did not give rise to a charge to tax under ICTA 1988 s.595(1) (the predecessor to ITEPA 2003 s.386) because an *in specie* contribution was not a "sum paid" into a FURBS. This was on the basis that a "sum paid" can only relate to a cash contribution. The Court of Appeal held that although the more natural meaning of the phrase "pays a sum" is "pays a sum of money", it can include the transfer of non-cash assets if the context suggests that it should be given a broader meaning, and that is the case with ICTA 1988 s.595(1) (and therefore ITEPA 2003 s.386(1)).[21]

*Relief under s.392*

**38-016** As a result of the decision of the Court of Appeal in *Irving* a number of taxpayers were facing income tax charges under s.386(1). One way of avoiding this charge was for the relevant employee to be removed as a beneficiary of the FURBS and to apply for relief under s.392(1), which provided that:

> "An application for relief may be made to an officer of Revenue and Customs if—
> (a) a sum is charged to tax by virtue of section 386 in respect of the provision of any benefits,
> (b) no payment in respect of, or in substitution for, the benefits has been made, and
> (c) an event occurs by reason of which no such payment will be made."

**38-017** If such an application is made, and an officer of HMRC is satisfied that the conditions above are met in relation to some or all of the sum, the officer must give relief in respect of tax on it by repayment or otherwise as appropriate. There is an exception where the reason that s.392(1) applies is as a consequence of a pension sharing order or provision—no such relief is available in these circumstances.

**38-018** In *HMRC v Mitesh Dhanak*,[22] an employer established a FURBS in Guernsey in 2004 and made contributions for the sole benefit of the taxpayer. In 2010 (after the *Irving* decision became final) the taxpayer's membership of the FURBS was terminated and he was excluded from benefitting. His interest was instead held on trust for his brother, who was also a member of the FURBS. The taxpayer applied

---

[19] If the scheme rules had been drafted such that benefits could have been provided to members from funds contributed at any time then the FTT's decision may have been different. Presumably this restriction was included to address the "intermediate payment arrangement" provisions in UITF 32 (now FRS 105 s.7: see Ch.6).
[20] *Irving v RCC* [2008] EWCA Civ 6; [2008] B.T.C. 36.
[21] Also see *Omar v HMRC* [2011] UKFTT 722 (a decision relating to HMRC's power to issue a discovery assessment in relation to an arrangement very similar to that considered in *Irving*) and *Allan v HMRC* [2015] UKUT 0016, in which the UT rejected the taxpayer's argument that *Irving* was decided per incuriam Human Rights Act 1998 s.3 and European Convention on Human Rights Protocol 1 art.1.
[22] *HMRC v Mitesh Dhanak* [2014] UKUT 68.

for relief under s.392 and HMRC refused. The UT found that there was no statutory right of appeal against a decision under s.392, but HMRC's decision could be judicially reviewed on the basis that the refusal was based on an error of law. HMRC argued that relief was unavailable on the basis that a payment to the taxpayer's brother would be a payment "in substitution for" the taxpayer's benefits and so the requirement in s.392(1)(c) was not satisfied. The taxpayer argued that s.392(1) requires HMRC to be satisfied that no payment in substitution for the benefits will be made to the employee for whom the chargeable payment to the pension scheme was made (or to any of the persons specified in s.386(6), namely the member's spouse, widow, children, dependants or personal representatives). As the taxpayer's brother did not fall within that category, it was irrelevant to the application for relief that payments from the pension scheme will or may in due course be paid to him. Any payments to the brother will be made on the basis that he is himself an employee of the employer and because, in such capacity, he is a member of the pension scheme. The UT agreed with the taxpayer and granted relief under s.392.[23]

## Investments[24]

### UK resident FURBS

**38-019** Prior to 6 April 2004, the rate applicable to trusts[25] was dissapplied for income from investments, deposits or other property held for the purposes of a scheme established for the *sole purpose* of providing relevant benefits.[26] Such income was therefore subject to income tax only at the basic rate. Dividend income was received with a 10% tax credit with no further liability to tax, making this a particularly tax-efficient method to extract funds from the employer. The rate applicable to trusts now applies, so the first £1,000 is taxed at 20% (savings income) or 7.5% (dividends) and then 45% after that (or 38.1% for dividends).[27]

**38-020** Prior to 6 April 1998, CGT was chargeable at the basic rate provided that the scheme was established for the *sole purpose* of providing relevant benefits.[28] Since 6 April 1998, the usual rate for settlements applies.[29] Trustees are permitted half of the usual annual exempt amount.[30]

### Non-UK resident FURBS

**38-021** Non-UK source income is not subject to UK income tax under general principles.[31] UK source income is taxable in accordance with the provisions

---

[23] In reaching its conclusion, the UT suggested that there would have been some force in HMRC's submissions were it not for s.392(6), which provides that relief is unavailable to the extent that the terms of s.392(1) are met as a result of a pension sharing order or provision. It must follow that, but for s.392(6), such relief might be available, thus showing that the payment contemplated by s.392(1) is not a payment to a person substituted for the employee under the pension scheme.
[24] For more detail, see Ch.25.
[25] i.e. the rates now specified in ITA 2007 s.9 (currently 45%, or 38.1% for dividends). See Ch.25.
[26] ICTA 1988 s.686(2)(c).
[27] See ITA 2007 ss.8, 9, 479 and 491.
[28] TCGA 1992 s.5.
[29] This is 28% for residential property gains and carried interest gains, and otherwise 20% (TCGA 1992 s.1I).
[30] TCGA 1992 Sch.1C para.5. Trusts created by the same settlor since 7 June 1978 share this annual exempt amount, subject to a minimum exemption per trust of one-tenth of the individual annual exempt amount (which is £12,300 in the 2022/23 tax year).
[31] *Colquhoun v Brooks* (1889) 14 App. Cas. 493; 2 T.C. 490.

described in Ch.25. Capital gains are not subject to CGT on general principles[32] except in relation to UK residential property.[33] A FURBS is expressly exempt from CGT on the disposal of any investments if it is an overseas pension scheme.[34]

**Benefits**

*Benefits referable to contributions made prior to 6 April 2006[35]*

**38-022** The disguised remuneration provisions do not have any application to relevant steps which arise or derive from pre-6 April 2006 contributions to FURBS, provided that the contributions were taxable on the employee.[36] Benefits provided under a FURBS (or any transferee scheme) which are referable to contributions made prior to 6 April 2006 are taxable as follows:

(a) Pension income paid from a UK resident FURBS to a UK resident member is taxable under ITEPA 2003 Pt 9 Ch.5.[37] Other benefits are taxable in accordance with ITEPA 2003 s.394 (subject to the transitional provisions described below).

(b) Pension income paid from a non-UK FURBS to a UK resident member is taxable under ITEPA 2003 Pt 9 Ch.4.[38] Since 6 April 2017, this expressly includes a "relevant lump sum".[39] There is no exception from the relevant lump sum provisions to reflect the fact that contributions will usually have been taxable on the employee: see below. The remittance basis can apply to such income.[40]

(c) Benefits (pension and lump sums) paid to a non-UK resident member may be subject to tax under ITEPA 2003 s.394[41] if contributions related to UK

---

[32] TCGA 1992 s.2(1). An exception applies the UK assets used for the purposes of a trade carried on by the scheme in the UK through a branch or agency (TCGA 1992 s.10).
[33] TCGA 1992 s.1A(3).
[34] TCGA 1992 s.271(1A). Gains accruing on the disposal of assets held as a member of a property investment LLP are excepted (TCGA 1992 s.271(12)). For overseas pension schemes, see Ch.31.
[35] Prior to 6 April 2006, pension income was taxable under ITEPA 2003 Pt 9 and other benefits counted as employment income under ITEPA 2003 s.394. However, the charge under s.394 was subject to ss.396 and 397, which contained special provisions relating to lump sums. The effect of these provisions was often to reduce the charge under s.394 to nil. In outline, pursuant to s.396, the charge under s.394 did not apply to a lump sum if: (a) an employer paid any sum or sums with a view to the provision of relevant benefits under the scheme; (b) an employee had been assessed to tax under s.386(1) in respect of the sum or sums so paid; (c) the lump sum was provided to the employee, or his personal representatives, or a relative or ex-spouse of the employee or any other individual designated by the employee; and (d) either: (i) all of the income and gains accruing to the scheme under which the lump sum is provided are brought into charge to UK tax; or (ii) the scheme was established before 1 December 1993 and was not varied after that date. Pursuant to s.397, where s.394 applied to a lump sum and any of the income or gains accruing to the FURBS had not been brought into charge to tax, the amount taxable under s.394 was reduced by the amount of any contributions by the employee and any amounts on which the employee was assessed under ITEPA 2003 s.386(1).
[36] ITEPA 2003 s.554U. See Ch.27.
[37] The EFRBS provisions do not apply as a result of the exception in s.393B(2)(a).
[38] The EFRBS provisions do not apply as a result of the exception in s.393B(2)(a).
[39] See Ch.26. The taxable amount may be reduced in respect of pre-6 April 2017 reckonable service, and (if the scheme is an overseas pension scheme) in respect of so much of the lump sum as would, if the scheme were a registered pension scheme, not be liable to income tax under ITEPA 2003 Pt 9.
[40] ITTOIA 2005 s.832.
[41] The exception to the s.394 charge in s.393B(2)(a) applies only where benefits are *charged* under ITEPA 2003 Pt 9, and that is not the case where benefits are paid to a non-UK resident.

service, unless a double tax treaty confers exclusive taxing rights on the country of residence (and subject to the temporary non-residence rules[42]). Any charge in accordance with s.394 is subject to the application of: (i) any express exceptions[43]; (ii) any implied territorial limitations[44]; and (iii) the transitional provisions described below. Any benefits not taxed in accordance with s.394 should be free of UK tax.

(d) A payment by way of "relevant benefits" (as defined in ICTA 1988 s.612) under a FURBS is expressly free of NIC if it is attributable to payments made prior to 6 April 1998.[45] A payment by way of any benefit pursuant to FURBS is expressly free of NIC if it is attributable to payments between 6 April 1998 and 6 April 2006 which have previously been included in a person's earnings for NIC purpose.[46] The provision of benefits in other circumstances is disregarded for NIC purposes if they are paid when the individual is no longer employed by the employer and it would be one of the following types of authorised payment if the EFRBS were a registered pension scheme: (i) an authorised pension (i.e. scheme pension, lifetime annuity, or drawdown pension); (ii) a pension commencement lump sum; (iii) a serious ill-health lump sum; or (iv) a payment made under a pension sharing order or provision.[47]

*Transitional provisions applying to s.394 charge*

**38-023** Transitional provisions apply where a charge arises under ITEPA 2003 s.394 (or would otherwise arise) by reason of the provision of a lump sum under a FURBS on or after 6 April 2006. The provisions apply only if[48]:

(a) before 6 April 2006 an employer paid any contributions in respect of which an employee was taxed under ITEPA 2003 s.386(1)[49]; and
(b) either: (i) all of the income and gains accruing to the scheme are brought into charge to tax and the lump sum is provided to the employee or a specified person[50]; or (ii) the scheme was entered into before 1 December 1993 and has not been varied on or after that date with a view to the provision of benefits under the scheme.

**38-024** The requirement that all of the income and gains accruing to the scheme are brought into charge to tax means that these transitional provisions can apply to a non-UK FURBS only where it has not received any income or realised any gains,[51] or where only UK source income has been received by the FURBS. The realisa-

---

[42] See ITEPA 2003 ss.554Z4A and 554Z11A (disguised remuneration) and ITEPA 2003 s.394A (EFRBS).
[43] e.g. the charge in s.394 does not apply to lump sum benefits referable to employee contributions (ITEPA 2003 s.395).
[44] See Ch.35.
[45] The Social Security (Contributions) Regulations 2001 (SI 2001/1004) Sch.3 Pt VI para 4.
[46] SI 2001/1004 Sch.3 Pt VI para 5.
[47] SI 2001/1004 Sch.3 Pt VI paras 8(b) and 10; see NIM02760.
[48] FA 2004 Sch.36 paras 53–55. It is expressly assumed, unless the contrary is shown, that these provisions do not apply.
[49] Or, prior to 6 April 2003, ICTA 1988 s.595.
[50] The following are *specified persons*: a relative of the employee, the personal representatives of the employee, an ex-spouse or former civil partner of the employee or any other individual designated by the employee.
[51] It may be possible for the trustees to borrow funds prior to any disposal in order to provide a lump sum at a time when no gains have been realised, and then after the disposal (and realisation of gains) to use the sale proceeds to repay the lender.

tion of exempt gains (e.g. gains on disposal of gilts or qualifying corporate bonds), whether by a UK FURBS or a non-UK FURBS, will not breach this requirement. The receipt of income by a non-UK resident company owned by non-UK resident trustees should not breach this requirement, but chargeable gains accruing to a non-UK resident close company may be treated as accruing to the non-UK resident trustee participators. [52]

**38-025**   Where these transitional provisions apply:

(a) If the employer has not paid any sum or sums with a view to the provision of benefits under the scheme since before 6 April 2006, s.394 does not apply in relation to the lump sum. It should be noted that this does not expressly provide that such a lump sum is tax-free; it merely provides that it is not taxable under s.394.

(b) If the employer has paid any sum or sums with a view to the provision of benefits under the scheme on or after 6 April 2006: (i) ITEPA 2003 s.394 does not apply in relation to so much of the lump sum as does not exceed the *appropriate fraction* of the amount of the market value of the assets of the scheme on 5 April 2006 (increased in line with the RPI as specified below); and (ii) the amount taxable under s.394 is reduced by any contributions paid by the employee after that date.

**38-026**   The "appropriate fraction" of the amount of the market value of the assets of the scheme on 5 April 2006 is the same fraction as the fraction of the assets of the scheme to which the employee would have been entitled had the scheme been wound up on that date. The amount of the market value of the assets of the scheme on that date is then increased by the percentage by which the RPI for the month in which the lump sum is provided is greater than that for April 2006.

**38-027**   If the above provisions do not apply (e.g. because all of the income and gains accruing to the scheme were *not* brought into charge to tax, or the lump sum was not provided to the employee or a specified person), ITEPA 2003 s.394 only applies to so much of the lump sum as exceeds the employer contributions in respect of which an employee was taxed, less the amount of any contributions paid by the employee.[53]

**38-028**   Relief under ITEPA 2003 s.392 continues to be available on or after 6 April 2006 in relation to a sum charged to tax by virtue of ITEPA 2003 s.386(1)[54] before 6 April 2006.[55]

*Non-UK resident FURBS and relevant lump sums*

**38-029**   As is explained above, to the extent that contributions to a non-UK resident FURBS were subject to income tax, lump sum benefits will not be taxable under either s.394 or the disguised remuneration provisions.[56] However, there is no excep-

---

[52] See TCGA 1992 s.3. This provision does not however apply to a chargeable gain accruing to a company where it is shown that the acquisition, holding, and disposal of the asset by the company did not form part of a scheme or arrangements of which one of the main purposes was avoidance of CGT or corporation tax). If the company is used in order to avoid an income tax charge under ITEPA 2003 s.394, s.3 would not appear to be engaged. Of course, depending on the circumstances, the "scheme or arrangements" may include both the FURBS and the company, in which case one must determine the main purposes of the overall arrangements.
[53] FA 2004 Sch.36 para.55.
[54] Or, prior to 6 April 2003, ICTA 1988 s.595.
[55] FA 2004 Sch.36 para.52.
[56] See ITEPA 2003 s.554W (pre-April 2011 lump sums).

tion to a charge arising under the relevant lump sum provisions,[57] in which case both contributions and benefits may be subject to income tax. The relevant lump sum provisions apply only to lump sums provided under non-UK pension schemes, so this charge may be avoided by either:

(a) replacing the trustees with UK resident trustees; or
(b) procuring a transfer of the member's pension benefits to a UK scheme.[58]

*Benefits referable contributions made on or after 6 April 2006*

**38-030** Benefits referable to contributions made since 6 April 2006 are taxable as EFRBS:

(a) Pension income received by a UK resident member from a UK resident scheme is taxable under ITEPA 2003 Pt 9 Ch.5.[59] Lump sums and other benefits are taxable in accordance with the disguised remuneration provisions unless an exception applies,[60] in which case they are taxable in accordance with ITEPA 2003 s.394. Any charge under s.394 is reduced by any tax paid under Pt 7A.[61]

(b) Pension income paid to a UK resident member from a non-UK scheme is taxable under ITEPA 2003 Pt 9 Ch.4.[62] As noted above, since 6 April 2017, this expressly includes a relevant lump sum. The remittance basis can apply to such income.[63] However, if the scheme is a RNUKS[64], the relevant lump sum provisions cannot apply.[65] In that case, a lump sum is taxable in accordance with FA 2004 Sch.34.

(c) Benefits (pensions and lump sums) paid to a non-UK resident member may be subject to UK tax in accordance with the disguised remuneration provisions if contributions related to UK service, unless a double tax treaty confers exclusive taxing rights on the country of residence (and assuming that the member is not merely temporarily non-resident[66]). Any charge under s.394 is subject to the application of any express exceptions.[67]

(d) Benefits are disregarded for NIC purposes provided that it is paid when the individual is no longer employed by the employer and it would be one of the following types of authorised payment if the EFRBS were a registered pension scheme: (a) an authorised pension (i.e. scheme pension, lifetime annuity, or drawdown pension); (b) a pension commencement lump sum; (c)

---

[57] Unless a deduction (under step 2) applies, but that will be the case only where the contributions related to foreign service.
[58] Such a transfer should not be subject to tax under the disguised remuneration provisions as a result of ITEPA 2003 s.554U.
[59] ITEPA 2003 s.394 does not apply as a result of the exception in s.393B(2)(a).
[60] For example, s.554W (pre-6 April 2011 lump sums).
[61] ITEPA 2003 s.554Z2 *overrides* any charge under the benefits code (i.e. the benefits code cannot apply to a relevant step) but not the charge under s.394.
[62] The EFRBS provisions do not apply as a result of the exception in s.393B(2)(a).
[63] ITTOIA 2005 s.832.
[64] Because tax relief has been obtained in respect of contributions to the scheme (see Ch.30-001).
[65] Such benefits are expressly not relevant benefits for the purposes of the EFRBS provisions. Such benefits will also not be taxable under the disguised remuneration provisions.
[66] See ITEPA 2003 ss.554Z4A and 554Z11A.
[67] For example, s.394 does not apply to lump sum benefits referable to employee contributions (ITEPA 2003 s.395).

a serious ill-health lump sum; or (d) a payment made under a pension sharing order or provision.[68]

**Inheritance tax**

38-031   Most FURBS are sponsored superannuation schemes for inheritance tax purposes.[69] Where that is the case, the settled property is not relevant property[70] and on the death of the member any right to a pension or annuity is disregarded.[71] If the scheme was a sponsored superannuation scheme prior to 6 April 2006, these inheritance tax provisions continue to apply to the entire fund provided that no contributions are made under the scheme on or after that date.[72] If any contributions are made on or after 6 April 2006, only a specified percentage of the settled property is protected from the relevant property regime under these provisions.[73]

38-032   As is explained at in Ch.28, in order for an occupational scheme to be a sponsored superannuation scheme for the purposes of ICTA 1988 s.624(1), it was necessary for "any part" of the cost of the benefits to have been met by a person other than the employees by reason of their service, and pursuant to s.624(2), the employees were treated as bearing by reason of their service the cost of any payment made or agreed to be made in respect of his service, if that payment or the agreement to make it was treated under the Income Tax Acts as increasing his income. Given that employer contributions to a FURBS with a view to the provision of relevant benefits were deemed under ITEPA 2003 s.386(1) to increase the employee's income, employer contributions would cause a FURBS to become a sponsored superannuation scheme only if some of the contributions did not relate to the provision of relevant benefits.[74] This would be the case, for example, where any contributions related to the costs of setting up or running the FURBS. It was not uncommon for the employer to make relatively modest contributions, followed by beneficial loans to the scheme for the trustees to invest.

---

[68] SI 2001/1004 Sch.3 Pt VI paras 8(b) and 10; see NIM02760.
[69] See ICTA 1988 s.624, discussed in Ch.28.
[70] IHTA 1984 s.58(1)(d) (since amended).
[71] IHTA 1984 s.151.
[72] FA 2004 Sch.36 para.56. See Ch.28.
[73] FA 2004 Sch.36 para.57.
[74] See the Inland Revenue booklet, *The Tax Treatment of Top-Up Pension Schemes*, para.2.2.4.

# CHAPTER 39

# Corresponding Schemes

## TABLE OF CONTENTS

| | |
|---|---|
| Overview | 39-001 |
| What is a corresponding scheme? | 39-004 |
| ITEPA 2003 s.355 | 39-005 |
| ITEPA 2003 s.390 | 39-007 |
| Meaning of "corresponding" | 39-008 |
| Taxation | 39-011 |
| Contributions | 39-011 |
| Contributions on or after 6 April 2006 | 39-012 |
| Investments | 39-015 |
| Benefits | 39-016 |
| Benefits referable to pre-6 April 2006 contributions | 39-017 |
| Benefits referable to post-6 April 2006 contributions | 39-018 |
| Illustration 1 | 39-019 |
| Inheritance tax | 39-020 |
| Pension transfers | 39-021 |

## OVERVIEW

**39-001** Prior to 6 April 2006, two forms of income tax relief were available to non-UK domiciled employees of non-UK employers in respect of contributions to a FURBS which HMRC had accepted as corresponding to an approved scheme. Such relief was generally referred to as "corresponding relief" and such schemes are generally referred to as "corresponding schemes". Where such relief was obtained in the 2005/06 tax year, transitional provisions permit income tax relief in respect of contributions on or after 6 April 2006 ("transitional corresponding relief", for which see Ch.24). Any contributions on or after 6 April 2006 cause the scheme to become an RNUKS.[1] All corresponding schemes are EFRBS.[2]

**39-002** With effect from 6 April 2006, tax relief in respect of relevant migrant members replaced corresponding relief (except where transitional corresponding relief is available).[3] Note that migrant member relief is more restrictive than transitional corresponding relief (in particular, migrant member relief is available only where the member joined the scheme and received foreign tax relief before coming to the UK), so transitional corresponding relief continues to be significant for individuals who do not qualify for migrant member relief.

---

[1] For RNUKS, see Ch.30.
[2] For EFRBS, see Ch.35.
[3] FA 2004 Sch.33. For relief in respect of relevant migrant members, see Ch.24.

**39-003** It was quite common for a sponsoring employer of a corresponding scheme to establish a new corresponding scheme just before 6 April 2006 for the benefit of employees who were not relevant migrant members. This was not strictly necessary, but it was often considered desirable for two main reasons:

(a) The post-A Day contributions would cause the corresponding scheme to become an RNUKS (to the extent of those contributions), meaning that benefits received from the scheme would be deemed to derive from the post-A Day contributions in priority to pre-A Day contributions. That is often undesirable. If there are two separate schemes, the member may choose to take benefits deriving from pre-A Day contributions in priority to post-A Day contributions if he wishes.

(b) There was a concern that the RNUKS disclosure requirements may have required the trustees to disclose information about pre-A Day accrued funds (that they were not otherwise required to disclose).

## WHAT IS A CORRESPONDING SCHEME?

**39-004** A "corresponding scheme" is a non-UK retirement benefit scheme that was, prior to 6 April 2006, accepted by HMRC as corresponding to a UK tax-approved pension scheme for the purposes of either (or both) of:[4]

(a) ITEPA 2003 s.355; or
(b) ITEPA 2003 s.390.

**ITEPA 2003 s.355**

**39-005** Prior to 6 April 2006, an employee was able to make a claim to HMRC under ITEPA 2003 s.355 in respect of a contribution he made to an unapproved retirement benefits schemes (i.e. a FURBS[5]) if:[6]

(a) He was not domiciled in the UK.[7]
(b) The employment was with a foreign employer. An employer of a UK resident employee was a "foreign employer" if it was resident outside the UK, and not resident in the UK or the Republic of Ireland.[8] An employer of a non-UK resident employee was a foreign employer if it was resident outside of the UK and was not resident in the UK.
(c) The contribution was paid out of earnings from that employment.
(d) The contribution did not reduce the employee's liability to UK income tax, but was made in circumstances corresponding to those in which it would do

---

[4] Between 31 January 2002 and 5 April 2005, schemes were approved in accordance with the procedure detailed in PSO Update No.114. Any such schemes would have received an acceptance letter setting out the conditions for tax relief. Between 6 April 2005 and 5 April 2006, schemes were approved in accordance with the procedure detailed in PSO Update No.151. Any such schemes would have received a unique scheme reference number.

[5] For FURBS, see Ch.38.

[6] ITEPA 2003 s.355 has not been repealed, but since 6 April 2006 it is incapable of applying to a contribution to unregistered pension scheme except in accordance with the transitional provision in FA 2004 Sch.36 para.51.

[7] For an explanation of the principles of the law of domicile, see *Barlow Clowes International Ltd v Henwood* [2008] EWCA Civ 577 at [8]–[15] (Arden LJ).

[8] ITEPA 2003 s.721. The definition of foreign employer has since changed. In practice, it was not uncommon for the employee to be employed by a foreign group company and seconded to a UK group company.

so. In practice, this requires that the contribution was made to a scheme which HMRC accepted as corresponding to a tax-approved scheme.

If the above requirements were satisfied, HMRC were permitted to allow the contribution as a deduction from the employee's earnings under ITEPA 2003 Pt 5 Ch.2. Such a deduction was permitted only where the contribution was paid by the employee (and not where it was paid by someone else on his behalf).[9]

39-006

### ITEPA 2003 s.390

Prior to 6 April 2006, ITEPA 2003 s.390 applied to a contribution to a FURBS by an employer in respect of an employee if:

39-007

(a) the employee was not domiciled in the UK in the tax year in which the contribution was paid;
(b) the employment was with a foreign employer (see above); and
(c) the employee made a claim to HMRC, and HMRC were satisfied that the scheme corresponded to an approved scheme.[10]

The purpose of s.390 was to provide an exception to the income tax charge that would otherwise arise under ITEPA 2003 s.386(1) on a contribution to a FURBS by an employer.[11] Sections 386 and 390 were repealed on 6 April 2006.

### Meaning of "corresponding"

Sections 355 and 390 both require that the contribution was made to a scheme "corresponding" to a tax-approved scheme. Pursuant to IR12 (2001) paras 15.16–15.19, HMRC accepted that a non-UK pension scheme corresponded to a tax-approved scheme if the following conditions were all satisfied:

39-008

(a) the scheme was established in a country where the employee was working or resident immediately before being sent to the UK, or in a country where the employer or an associated employer has an operating presence;[12]
(b) the tax or supervisory authorities of the country in which the scheme was established recognised it as a scheme for the provision of relevant benefits;
(c) the amount of the benefits provided under the scheme were reasonable (for example, a pension should not normally exceed 70% of the final salary or the usual maximum allowed in the country in which the scheme is established);
(d) the primary purpose of the scheme was to provide relevant benefits which should normally be payable on retirement no earlier than age 50 (unless earlier payment dates are permitted in the country in which the scheme is established) or upon death;
(e) the amount of the contributions to the scheme by the employer and the

---

[9] See ITEPA 2003 s.333(1)(a) and (3)(b).
[10] i.e. a tax-approved scheme for the purposes of ITEPA 2003 s.387(2)(a), or a relevant statutory scheme or a scheme set up by a government outside the UK for the benefit of its employees (see ITEPA 2003 s.387(2)(b) and (c)).
[11] For the charge under s.386(1), see Ch.38.
[12] IR12 (2001) para.15.17 provides that in "exceptional circumstances" a scheme exclusively for the benefit of employees working outside the country in which the scheme is established (referred to as an "international scheme") may also be acceptable if it is legally impossible to establish a scheme for the employee in the jurisdiction of location, or it is a scheme for a multi-national group to which all expatriate (or at least career expatriate) employees belong. In practice, many corresponding schemes were established by multi-national groups as international schemes for career expatriates.

employee were reasonable in relation to the benefits to be provided, and conformed to the actuarial standards of the country where the scheme is established (or, in the absence of such standards, to UK actuarial practice).

**39-009** If the scheme was established in a jurisdiction that permitted in-service (i.e. pre-retirement) benefits (including loans) to be provided under approved pension schemes, HMRC were often prepared to accept that the scheme corresponded to a UK approved scheme, but only where undertakings were given by the scheme administrator and every relevant scheme member that such benefits would not be provided from sums or assets contributed during the period that the member was subject to UK taxation.

**39-010** Where information provided as part of an application was subsequently found to be incorrect, or where any undertakings provided as part of the application were subsequently breached, HMRC could refuse to grant tax relief and/or withdraw any tax relief already given.[13]

# TAXATION

### Contributions

**39-011** In many cases the employer (which was required to be a foreign employer) was not within the scope of UK tax and so did not require a UK tax deduction in respect of contributions. Where the employer was within the scope of UK corporation tax[14] or income tax,[15] a UK tax deduction should have been available in principle but may have been deferred until such time as qualifying benefits were provided under the scheme.[16] The employee was not taxed in respect of employer contributions,[17] and such contributions were not subject to NIC.[18] Contributions were not subject to the earnings cap. As is explained above, tax relief was available in accordance with ITEPA 2003 s.355 in respect of contributions by the member.

### Contributions on or after 6 April 2006[19]

**39-012** Where an individual received relief under s.355 in respect of contributions to a corresponding scheme in the 2005/06 tax year, HMRC may permit tax relief in respect of such contributions in subsequent tax years provided that the conditions in s.355 are met and the scheme manager complies with any prescribed benefit crystallisation information requirements imposed on the scheme manager.[20]

**39-013** Where an employer obtained a tax deduction in respect of contributions to a cor-

---

[13] See PSO Update 114 para.6.
[14] This will be the case only if the foreign employer carried on a trade in the UK through a permanent establishment in the UK (ICTA 1988 s.11(1); now CTA 2009 s.5(2)).
[15] e.g. in relation to the profits arising from a trade carried on wholly or partly in the UK (ITTOIA 2005 s.6(2)).
[16] See FA 2003 Sch.24 (now CTA 2009 s.1290). An exception in Sch.24 para.8(b) applied to contributions to retirement benefits schemes, but this was removed on 21 July 2004. A different exception applies since 6 April 2006. No exception applied to contributions made between these dates so it seems that Sch.24 will have prevented an immediate tax deduction.
[17] ITEPA 2003 s390 disapplied the charge under ITEPA 2003 s.386(1).
[18] The Social Security (Contributions) Regulations 2001 (SI 2001/1004) Sch.3 Pt VI para.3(a) (prior to its amendment on 6 April 2006).
[19] The provisions relating to contributions on or after 6 April 2006 are considered in more detail in Ch.24.
[20] FA 2004 Sch.36 para.51. The information requirements are in The Pension Schemes (Information

responding scheme between 1 April 2005 and 5 April 2006 for the benefit of an employee, HMRC may permit contributions in respect of such employees in subsequent years to be treated as if they were relevant migrant member contributions under FA 2004 Sch.33 para.2 if:[21]

(a) HMRC are satisfied that the contribution consists of the expenses of paying any sum or of providing benefits pursuant to a pension scheme which is established outside the UK;
(b) HMRC are satisfied that the scheme corresponds to a registered pension scheme; and
(c) the scheme manager complies with any prescribed benefit crystallisation information requirements imposed on the scheme manager.[22]

The effect of treating the contributions as relevant migrant member contributions under Sch.33 para.2 is that the employer's tax deduction is not deferred under CTA 2009 s.1290(2).[23] No liability to income tax arises in respect of earnings where an employer makes such contributions.[24] Such contributions are not subject to NIC.[25]

39-014

## Investments

There are no special rules regarding investment growth.[26] Non-UK source income is not subject to UK income tax under general principles.[27] UK source income is taxable in accordance with the provisions described in Ch.25. Capital gains are not subject to CGT on general principles[28] except in relation to UK residential property.[29] Since 6 April 2006, overseas pension schemes are expressly exempt from CGT on the disposal of any investments,[30] but corresponding schemes usually do not satisfy the requirements of an overseas pension scheme in practice, because they are typically established under legislation which prevents locals from joining.

39-015

## Benefits

Benefits may be paid in the form of pension, annuity (which need not be for life), lump sum or a series of lump sums. It is common for benefits to be provided entirely in the form of lump sums.[31] An analysis of the UK taxation of benefits provided under a corresponding scheme (and any transferee scheme) depends on whether the benefits are referable to contributions made before 6 April 2006 or on or after 6 April 2006. If a scheme holds both types (which is unusual), payments are deemed to be made from post-A Day contributions first.

39-016

---

Requirements—Qualifying Overseas Pension Schemes, Qualifying Recognised Overseas Pensions Schemes and Corresponding Relief) Regulations 2006 (SI 2006/208) reg.2.
[21] The Taxation of Pension Schemes (Transitional Provisions) Order 2006 (SI 2006/572) art.15.
[22] The information requirements are in SI 2006/208 reg.2.
[23] See the exception in CTA 2009 s.1290(4)(c).
[24] ITEPA 2003 s.308A, applied to such schemes by SI 2006/572 art.17(4).
[25] SI 2001/1004 Sch.3 Pt VI para.3(a) (prior to its amendment on 6 April 2006).
[26] For more detail, see Ch.25.
[27] *Colquhoun v Brooks* (1889) 14 App. Cas. 493; 2 T.C. 490.
[28] TCGA 1992 s.2(1). An exception applies the UK assets used for the purposes of a trade carried on by the scheme in the UK through a branch or agency (TCGA 1992 s.10).
[29] TCGA 1992 s.14D(1).
[30] TCGA 1992 s.271(1A). Gains accruing on the disposal of assets held as a member of a property investment LLP are excepted (TCGA 1992 s.271(12)). For overseas pension schemes, see Ch.31.
[31] Except where the member is resident in the UK but taxable on the remittance basis (see e.g. *HMRC v Gresh & RBC Trust Company (Guernsey) Ltd* (2009–10) G.L.R. 239).

*Benefits referable to pre-6 April 2006 contributions*

**39-017** Benefits referable to pre-6 April 2006 contributions are taxable as follows:

(a) Pension income paid to a UK resident member is taxable under ITEPA 2003 Pt 9 Ch.4.[32] Lump sum benefits are taxable under the disguised remuneration provisions unless an exemption applies.[33] If such an exemption does apply, any lump sums are *relevant lump sums* and therefore pension income for the purposes of Pt 9 Ch.4.[34] If the member is a remittance basis taxpayer at the relevant time, such benefits are subject to UK tax only to the extent that they are remitted to the UK.[35]

(b) Benefits paid to a non-UK resident member should not be subject to UK tax if a double tax treaty confers exclusive taxing rights on the country of residence, unless the member is only temporarily non-resident.[36] Otherwise, such benefits are taxable under the disguised remuneration provisions unless an exemption applies. To the extent that such benefits are not taxable under the disguised remuneration provisions, they may be taxable under ITEPA 2003 s.394.[37] The charge in s.394 does not apply to lump sum benefits referable to employee contributions, so such benefits will often be free of tax.[38]

(c) Such benefits are disregarded for NIC purposes.[39]

*Benefits referable to post-6 April 2006 contributions*

**39-018** Contributions benefitting from transitional corresponding relief since 6 April 2006 cause the corresponding scheme to become an RNUKS. Benefits referable to contributions made on or after 6 April 2006 are taxable as follows:

(a) If the "UK residency condition" is satisfied, the member payment provisions in FA 2004 Pt 4 apply to the extent that benefits are referable to the member's UK tax-relieved fund.[40] The disguised remuneration provisions and the EFRBS provision do not apply to such benefits.[41] Pension income (including a relevant lump sum) paid to a UK resident individual is tax-

---

[32] The disguised remuneration provisions do not apply to such benefits as a result of the exception in ITEPA 2003 s.554S, and the EFRBS provision do not apply as a result of the exception in s.393B(2)(a).

[33] An exemption will often apply. e.g. in relation to employee pension contributions (s.554T), annuities purposed from pre-6 April 2011 rights (s.554V), and lump sum paid from pre-6 April 2011 rights (s.554W). See Ch.27.

[34] For relevant lump sums, see Ch.26. The taxable amount may be reduced in respect of pre-6 April 2017 reckonable service, and (if the scheme is an overseas pension scheme) in respect of so much of the lump sum as would, if the scheme were a registered pension scheme, not be liable for to income tax under ITEPA 2003 Pt 9. Note that a lump sum is a relevant lump sum only if it is exempt from the disguised remuneration provisions (i.e. it is not a relevant step to which Pt 7A Ch.2 applies) (see ITEPA 2003 s.574A(1)(b)). If the payment of the lump sum is a relevant step, but the taxable amount is reduced to nil, the lump sum is not a relevant lump sum for the purposes of Pt 9 Ch.4.

[35] ITTOIA 2005 s.832.

[36] See ITEPA 2003 ss.554Z4A and 554Z11A (disguised remuneration) and ITEPA 2003 s.394A (EFRBS).

[37] The exception to the s.394 charge in s.393B(2)(a) applies only where benefits are *charged* under ITEPA 2003 Pt 9, and that is not the case where benefits are paid to a non-UK resident.

[38] ITEPA 2003 s.395.

[39] SI 2001/1004 Sch.3 Pt VI para.3(1)(d).

[40] See Ch.30.

[41] The Employment Income Provided Through Third Parties (Excluded Relevant Steps) Regulations 2011 (SI 2011/2696) reg.3 (disguised remuneration) and ITEPA 2003 s.393B(2)(b) (EFRBS).

able under ITEPA 2003 Pt 9 Ch.4, assuming that it is paid in circumstances that do not give rise to an unauthorised payment.[42]

(b) Benefits paid to a non-UK resident member should not be subject to UK tax (other than in relation to an unauthorised payment) if a double tax treaty applies, unless the member is only temporarily non-resident. Benefits referable to a UK tax-relieved fund and paid to a member who is not resident in the UK, but who satisfies the UK residency condition, are not subject to UK tax unless the member is only temporarily non-resident.

(c) In the absence of an applicable double tax treaty, benefits referable to a UK tax-relieved fund and paid to a member who does not satisfy the UK residency condition are taxable under ITEPA 2003 s.394,[43] subject to the application of any implied territorial limitations.[44]

(d) In the absence of an applicable double tax treaty, benefits which are not referable to the member's UK tax relieved fund (e.g. because they are referable to investment growth, or they derive from contributions for which no UK tax relief was obtained) are taxable in accordance with the disguised remuneration provisions, unless an exemption applies. Such benefits are otherwise taxable under ITEPA 2003 s.394, subject to the application of any implied territorial limitations.

(e) Such benefits are disregarded for NIC purposes.[45]

*Illustration 1*

T is a member of two money purchase corresponding schemes established in Jersey: one which contains contributions made before 6 April 2006 (IPP1) and one which contains contributions made on or after 6 April 2006 (IPP2). T has been non-UK resident since 2015 and is currently resident in Singapore. T's benefits accrued between May 2004 and May 2008, when he was UK resident and all contributions were in respect of UK service. All contributions were made by T's employer (T made no personal contributions). The current value of T's fund under IPP1 is £1.5 million and his fund under IPP2 is £750,000. It is proposed that his entire fund under each plan is paid to him in 2022 as a lump sum.

**39-019**

In relation to the lump sum under IPP1:

(a) A double tax treaty between the UK and the country of residence will often confer exclusive taxing rights on the country of residence. If that is the case, no further analysis is necessary. However, the Singapore treaty does not assist.

(b) It will not be taxable under the disguised remuneration provisions because of the exception in s.554W. It cannot be a relevant lump sum because T is not resident in the UK.

(c) The lump sum will be taxable under s.394. Note that foreign service relief may be available is T was resident but not ordinarily resident in the UK.

---

[42] A 25% tax-free PCLS is generally possible provided that the scheme is an overseas pension scheme. Alternatively, if an uncrystallised funds pension lump sum is paid, only 75% is subject to UK tax.

[43] The disguised remuneration provisions do not apply as a result of SI 2011/2696 reg.3. Where the UK residency condition is not satisfied, it seems that the exception to the s.394 charge in s.393B(2)(b) will not apply (see Ch.35).

[44] See Ch.35.

[45] SI 2001/1004 Sch.3 Pt VI para.3(1)(b).

(d) The lump sum will not be subject to NIC.[46]

In relation to the lump sum under IPP2:

(a) It will not be taxable under the disguised remuneration provisions because of the exception in s.554W. It cannot be a relevant lump sum because T is not resident in the UK.

(b) It is slightly unclear whether the lump sum can be taxable under s.394. IPP2 is an RNUKS, but for the reasons given in Ch.35, the better view seems to be that the exception in s.393B(2)(b) will not apply because T does not satisfy the UK residency condition. Curiously, if T ceased to be non-UK resident in say May 2017 (by which time the ten-year condition applied), it seems clear that the exception would apply (in which case the lump sum would be tax-free). As above, foreign service relief may be available is T was resident but not ordinarily resident in the UK.

(c) The lump sum will not be subject to NIC.[47]

**Inheritance tax**

39-020  A corresponding scheme will typically be a sponsored superannuation scheme for inheritance tax purposes.[48] It follows that the settled property is not relevant property[49] and on the death of the member any right to a pension or annuity is disregarded.[50] Transitional provisions apply to any scheme which was a sponsored superannuation scheme prior to 6 April 2006.[51] In any event, the settled property will normally constitute excluded property if it is non-UK situs, because the settlor (i.e. the member) was not domiciled in the UK.

**Pension transfers**

39-021  It is not uncommon for a member's fund under a corresponding scheme to be transferred to a scheme which is not a corresponding scheme. Such transfers are often made to single member schemes. Such transferee schemes (sometimes referred to as *exit trusts*) may be able to provide benefits in more flexible circumstances.[52]

39-022  To the extent that the transfer is referable to the member's UK tax-relieved fund (i.e. it is referable to post-6 April 2006 contributions), it will be subject to an unauthorised payments charge and surcharge unless it is paid to a QROPS. For the purposes of the disguised remuneration provisions, a pension transfer will be a s.554C relevant step (assuming it is requested by the member), but an express exception will apply provided that the receiving scheme is an overseas pension scheme.[53] The transfer should not be taxable under the EFRBS provisions, on the basis that a pension transfer is not a relevant benefit. One would however expect the disguised remuneration provisions and the EFRBS provisions to apply to the transferee scheme as a result of the transfer.

---

[46] SI 2001/1004 Sch.3 Pt VI para.3(1)(d).
[47] SI 2001/1004 Sch.3 Pt VI para.3(1)(b).
[48] See ICTA 1988 s.624, discussed in Ch.28.
[49] IHTA 1984 s.58(1)(d) (since amended).
[50] IHTA 1984 s.151.
[51] See Ch.28.
[52] Due to concerns that transferring to a scheme with no minimum pension age could be perceived as a benefit, and could possibly even prejudice corresponding approval for the transferring scheme, it was often recommended that the transferee scheme did have a minimum pension age (which the trustees could amend if they saw fit).
[53] ITEPA 2003 s.554X. See Ch.27.

**39-023** The transferee scheme may not, on the face of it, be a sponsored superannuation scheme, but it may be the case that it forms part of the main scheme. If the member was not domiciled in the UK at the time of the transfer, the settled property should in any event be excluded property for inheritance tax purposes if it is non-UK situs.

# INDEX

## LEGAL TAXONOMY
FROM SWEET & MAXWELL

This index has been prepared using Sweet & Maxwell's Legal Taxonomy. Main index entries conform to keywords provided by the Legal Taxonomy except where references to specific documents or non-standard terms (denoted by quotation marks) have been included. These keywords provide a means of identifying similar concepts in other Sweet & Maxwell publications and on-line services to which keywords from the Legal Taxonomy have been applied. Readers may find some minor differences between terms used in the text and those which appear in the index. Suggestions to *sweetandmaxwell.taxonomy@tr.com*.

**Active members**
  generally, 2-030—2-034
**Administration charges**
  authorised employer loans
    amount of unauthorised payment, 17-010—17-024
    further reduction in value of charge that is not of adequate value, 17-026—17-027
    generally, 17-008—17-009
    increase in extent to which loan does not comply with repayment terms, 17-029—17-031
    loans ceasing to be secured by charge of adequate value, 17-025
    loans ceasing to comply with repayment terms, 17-028
    loans that are not authorised employer loans, 17-010—17-024
    prevention of double charging, 17-032
  authorised surplus payments
    authorised surplus payments charge, 1-014, 17-005—17-006
    generally, 17-002
    PA 1995 s.37 requirements, 17-003
    PA 1995 s.76 requirements, 17-004
  employer payments, 17-033—17-035
  introduction, 17-001
  member payments
    arm's length transactions, 11-010—11-011
    "for the purposes of administration or management", 11-004—11-009
    generally, 11-002—11-003
    introduction, 11-001
    loans, 11-012—11-014
**Administration of tax**
  *see Tax administration*
**Annual allowances**
  annual allowance charge
    generally, 7-050
    scheme administrator's liability, 7-051—7-056
  annual allowance charge (scheme administrator's liability)
    discharge of liability, 7-056
    exceptions, 7-055
    generally, 7-051—7-054
  carry forward of unused allowance, 7-029—7-030

  default chargeable amount, 7-031
  determination of annual allowance
    carry forward of unused allowance, 7-029—7-030
    generally, 7-022
    high-income individuals, 7-023—7-028
  flexibly accessing pension rights
    calculation, 7-035—7-036
    defined-benefit input sub-total, 7-048—7-049
    generally, 7-033
    introduction, 7-032
    money-purchase input sub-total, 7-037—7-047
    non-UK schemes, 7-034
  generally, 1-009—1-010
  high-income individuals
    adjusted income, 7-024
    anti-avoidance, 7-027
    generally, 7-023
    tapered annual allowance, 7-028
    threshold income, 7-025
  historical background, 7-002
  international aspects, 20-013—20-014
  overview, 7-001
  pension input amounts
    cash balance arrangements, 7-008—7-012
    death, 7-006—7-007
    defined benefits arrangements, 7-015—7-020
    generally, 7-005
    hybrid arrangements, 7-021
    other money purchase arrangements, 7-013—7-014
    severe ill health, 7-006—7-007
  pension input periods, 7-004
  recognised non-UK schemes
    carry forward of unused annual allowance, 30-108—30-109
    cash balance arrangements, 30-102—30-103
    defined benefits arrangements, 30-102—30-103
    enhancement of LS and LS&DB allowances, 30-112
    first flexibly accessing of pension savings, 30-106
    generally, 30-100

hybrid arrangements, 30-107
liability, 30-113
modifications, 30-101—30-112
other money purchase arrangements, 30-104—30-105
pension input amounts expressed in foreign currency, 30-110—30-111
reporting requirements
generally, 7-057
money purchase annual allowance, 7-058
steps involved, 7-003

**Annual payments**
benefits (unregistered schemes)
generally, 26-060—26-063
voluntary annual payments, 26-051—26-052
contributions
registered schemes, 6-149—6-150
unregistered schemes, 24-071

**Annuities (registered schemes)**
annuity protection LSDBs, 15-058—15-059
beneficiaries' annuities
annuities acquired after death, 15-031
generally, 15-029
related annuities, 15-030
members' lifetime annuities
cessation, 13-028
death of member, 13-029
definition of "annuity", 13-024
entitlement arising before 6/4/15, 13-027
entitlement arising on or after 6/4/15, 13-025—13-026
generally, 13-023
pension transfers, 12-009—12-010
scheme pensions compared, 13-030
members' short-term annuities, 13-032—13-034

**Annuities (unregistered schemes)**
beneficiaries' annuities under foreign pension, 26-031
employment-related annuities
annuities for benefit of dependants, 26-043
annuities in recognition of another's services, 26-045—26-050
annuities under non-registered occupational schemes, 26-044
generally, 26-041—26-042

**Anti-avoidance**
*see also Disguised remuneration*
generally, 22-017
income tax settlement provisions, 22-018—22-019

**Appeals**
generally, 19-043—19-045

**"Arrangements under the scheme"**
defined benefits arrangements, 2-050—2-051
generally, 2-036—2-038
hybrid arrangements, 2-052
money purchase arrangements, 2-042—2-049
types of arrangement, 2-039—2-041

**"Asset-backed contributions"**
change in lender's position, 6-104—6-109
complex arrangements

existing partnerships, 6-102—6-103
new partnerships, 6-100—6-101
Condition A, 6-086—6-088
Condition B, 6-089—6-095
Condition C, 6-096—6-099
generally, 6-079—6-081
scheme administration employer payments provisions, 6-110—6-111
simple arrangements, 6-082—6-085

**Assignment**
amount of unauthorised payment, 18-075—18-076
exceptions, 18-074
FA 2004 treatment of assignments, 18-070—18-073
generally, 18-065
law of assignment, 18-066—18-069
PA 1995 s.91, 18-077

**Authorised lump sums**
*see Lump sum payments*

**Authorised pension payments (employers)**
*see also Authorised pension payments (members)*
authorised and unauthorised payments, 1-016—1-019
authorised employer loans
amount of unauthorised payment, 17-010—17-024
further reduction in value of charge that is not of adequate value, 17-026—17-027
generally, 17-008—17-009
increase in extent to which loan does not comply with repayment terms, 17-029—17-031
loans ceasing to be secured by charge of adequate value, 17-025
loans ceasing to comply with repayment terms, 17-028
loans that are not authorised employer loans, 17-010—17-024
prevention of double charging, 17-032
authorised surplus payments
authorised surplus payments charge, 1-014, 17-005—17-006
generally, 17-002
PA 1995 s.37 requirements, 17-003
PA 1995 s.76 requirements, 17-004
compensation payments, 17-007
generally, 1-023
scheme administration employer payments, 17-033—17-035

**Authorised pension payments (members)**
*see also Authorised pension payments (employers)*
authorised and unauthorised payments, 1-016—1-019
generally, 1-020—1-022
scheme administration member payments
arm's length transactions, 11-010—11-011
"for the purposes of administration or management", 11-004—11-009
generally, 11-002—11-003
introduction, 11-001

# INDEX

loans, 11-012—11-014
**Authorised pensions**
*see Pension benefits (registered schemes)*
**Authorised surplus payments**
*see Surplus*
**Benefit crystallisation events**
*see Lifetime allowances*
**Benefits**
*see Death benefits; Lump sum death benefits; Pension benefits (registered schemes); Pension benefits (unregistered schemes)*
**Borrowing**
*see Loans*
**Capital gains tax (registered schemes)**
investments, 8-048—8-050
**Capital gains tax (unregistered schemes)**
non-UK schemes, 25-015—25-016
overseas pension schemes, 31-039
pension benefits, 26-066—26-067
qualifying non-UK pension schemes, 34-043
recognised overseas pension schemes, 32-020—32-021
settlements (UK-resident beneficiaries)
  capital payment, 25-105
  introduction, 25-089—25-091
  matching, 25-107
  non-UK beneficiaries, 25-108—25-110
  overview, 25-007—25-008
  s.1(3) amount, 25-106
  s.87 provisions, 25-102—25-103
  settlement, 25-104
  supplementary charge, 25-111
settlements (UK-resident settlors)
  corporate settlors, 25-094—25-095
  effect of s.86(1) applying, 25-100—25-101
  introduction, 25-089—25-091
  overview, 25-007—25-008
  s.86 provisions, 25-092
  "settlement" and "settlor", 25-093
  settlor has interest in settlement, 25-096—25-099
UK schemes, 25-007—25-008
**Chargeable event regime**
*see Insurance policies*
**Charity lump sum death benefits**
*see Lump sum death benefits*
**Compensation**
authorised employer payments, 17-007
loss of pension rights, 22-029—22-030
**Compliance**
accounting for tax returns, 19-016—19-020
anti-avoidance
  generally, 22-017
  income tax settlement provisions, 22-018—22-019
appeals, 19-043—19-045
assessments
  discovery assessments, 19-039—19-042
  FA 2004 Pt 4, 19-027—19-031
  generally, 19-026
  self-assessment, 19-031—19-042
event reports, 19-013—19-015
false statements, 19-024

inaccuracies, 19-025
introduction, 19-001—19-002
penalties
  accounting for tax returns, 19-020
  breach of obligation to provide information/documents, 19-022
  event reports, 19-015
  false statements, 19-024
  inaccuracies, 19-025
  pension scheme returns, 19-012
pension scheme returns, 19-011—19-012
preservation of documents, 19-003—19-007
provision of information/documents
  accounting for tax returns, 19-016—19-020
  event reports, 19-013—19-015
  FA 2008 Sch.36, 19-009—19-010
  generally, 19-008
  Information Regulations 2006, 19-021
  penalties for failure to comply, 19-022
  pension scheme returns, 19-011—19-012
self-assessment
  discovery assessments, 19-039—19-042
  enquiries, 19-034—19-038
  generally, 19-031
**Connected persons**
associates, 2-111
"connected"
  companies, 2-104—2-105
  individuals, 2-100
  introduction, 2-099
  partners, 2-103
  trustees, 2-101—2-102
"control"
  attribution of rights, 2-109—2-110
  generally, 2-106—2-108
  introduction, 2-098
  loan creditors, 2-112—2-113
  participators, 2-114—2-115
**Contributions**
*see Pension contributions (registered schemes); Pension contributions (unregistered schemes)*
**Control**
attribution of rights, 2-109—2-110
generally, 2-106—2-108
**"Corresponding schemes"**
"corresponding", 39-008—39-010
definition, 39-004—39-010
generally, 23-017
overview, 39-001—39-003
taxation
  benefits, 39-016—39-019
  contributions, 39-011—39-014
  inheritance tax, 39-020
  investments, 39-015
  pension transfers, 39-021—39-023
**Death**
death beneficiaries' position, 2-035
pension credit members, 2-027
**Death benefits**
*see also Lump sum death benefits*
authorised pension death benefits,

15-015—15-016
beneficiaries' annuities
  annuities acquired after death, 15-031
  generally, 15-029
  related annuities, 15-030
defined benefits arrangements, 15-010—15-011
dependants, 15-018—15-019
drawdown pensions
  dependants' drawdown pension funds, 15-039—15-043
  flexi-access drawdown funds, 15-035—15-038
  generally, 15-032
  income withdrawal, 15-034
  short-term annuities, 15-033
introduction, 15-001—15-002
lifetime allowance, interaction with, 15-014
money purchase arrangements
  effect of death, 15-008
  generally, 15-003—15-007
  nominations and expressions of wishes, 15-009
national insurance contributions, 15-023
nominees, 15-020
options available, 15-017
relevant two-year period, 15-012—15-013
scheme pensions
  dependants' scheme pension limit, 15-026—15-028
  generally, 15-025
successors, 15-021
taxation, 15-022
term certain payments, 15-024
trusts of death benefits
  disguised remuneration, 15-081
  generally, 15-077
  payments not subject to special LSDB charge, 15-078
  payments subject to special LSDB charge, 15-079—15-080

**Debt**
generally, 2-095—2-098

**Deemed unauthorised payments**
*see Taxable property; Unauthorised pension payments*

**Deferred members**
*see Early leavers*

**Defined benefit schemes**
generally, 2-050—2-051

**Defined contribution schemes**
generally, 2-042—2-049

**Dependants**
annuities
  annuities acquired after death, 15-031
  generally, 15-029
  related annuities, 15-030
definition, 15-018—15-019
drawdown pensions
  dependants' drawdown pension funds, 15-039—15-043
  flexi-access drawdown funds, 15-035—15-038

generally, 15-032
income withdrawal, 15-034
short-term annuities, 15-033
scheme pensions
  dependants' scheme pension limit, 15-026—15-028
  generally, 15-025

**Deregistration**
appeals, 4-029
consequences, 4-030
deregistration charge, 1-013
deregistration threshold, 4-026—4-027
generally, 4-023
historical background, 4-003
introduction, 4-001
"may withdraw", 4-024—4-025
procedure, 4-028
scheme sanction charge, 5-029

**Disablement pension**
EFRBS, 35-055
exempt pensions, 26-053—26-054

**Disguised remuneration**
charge to tax
  introduction, 27-079—27-080
  liability, 27-107—27-109
  PAYE system, application of, 27-110—27-115
  relief where earmarking not followed by further relevant step, 27-117
  remittance basis taxpayers, 27-100—27-106
  subsequent income tax liability, 27-116
  value of relevant step, 27-081—27-099
earmarking
  earmarking not followed by further relevant step, 27-117
  generally, 27-021—27-028
  Pt 7A Ch.3 of ITEPA 2003, 27-127—27-128, 27-132
  replacement funds, 27-043
exceptions
  arrangements whose sole purpose is provision of excluded benefits, 27-045—27-047
  earmarking replacement funds, 27-043
  employee pension contributions, 27-056—27-058
  exclusions under ITEPA 2003 Pt 4, 27-048—27-050
  FURBS, 27-059—27-062
  general exclusions, 27-041—27-044
  generally, 27-040
  income arising from earmarked funds, 27-042
  loan repayments, 27-044
  pensions chargeable under ITEPA 2003 Pt 9, 27-050
  pre-6/4/11 lump sums, 27-067—27-071
  purchased annuities, 27-063—27-066
  relevant non-UK schemes, 27-076—27-078
  transfers relating to corresponding schemes, 27-072—27-075
generally, 22-020—22-027

# INDEX 841

interaction with other legislation
  benefits code, 27-134—27-135
  general earnings charge, 27-133
  ITEPA 2003 s.394, 27-136
  pension income, 27-137—27-138
liability
  generally, 27-107
  liability after A has died, 27-108—27-109
national insurance contributions
  generally, 27-139
  income tax and NICs compared, 27-142—27-143
  Social Security (Contributions) Regulations 2001, 27-140—27-141
overview, 27-001—27-004
Pt 7A Ch.3 of ITEPA 2003
  earmarking (s.554Z18), 27-127—27-128
  effect of B making s.554Z18 or s.554Z19 relevant step, 27-120
  generally, 27-118—27-119
  provision of security (s.554Z19), 27-129—27-131
  relevant benefits, 27-124—27-125
  relevant undertaking, 27-121—27-126
  relief where earmarking or security not followed by contribution or relevant benefit, 27-132
  tax-relieved contributions and tax-exempt provisions, 27-126
recent developments, 27-005—27-007
relevant arrangements
  generally, 27-008—27-009
  persons linked with A, 27-012
  relevant step "connected with" relevant arrangement, 27-017—27-018
  relevant third person, 27-016
  "rewards in connection with A's employment with B", 27-014—27-015
  who is A, 27-010—27-011
  who is B, 27-013
relevant steps
  changing trustees and transferring between trusts, 27-033—27-034
  earmarking etc., 27-021—27-028
  exemption for steps taken after A's death, 27-020
  generally, 27-019
  loans and debts, 27-032
  making assets available, 27-035—27-039
  payments and transfers, 27-029—27-034
  relevant persons, 27-030—27-031
  steps taken "with a view to a later relevant step", 27-024—27-028
  value, 27-081—27-099
remittance basis taxpayers
  A does not meet s.26A requirement, 27-102
  A meets s.26A requirement, 27-101
  associated employments, 27-104
  generally, 27-100
  overlap provisions, 27-105
  related employments, 27-103
  temporary non-residents, 27-106
subsequent income tax liability, 27-116

trusts of death benefits, 15-081, 22-027
value of relevant step
  buying asset from P, 27-096—27-097
  consideration given for relevant step, 27-093
  earnings "for" a tax year, 27-084—27-086
  earnings for tax year after employment ceased, 27-087—27-088
  generally, 27-081—27-082
  overlap with certain earnings, 27-092
  overlap with money or asset subject to earlier tax liability, 27-090—27-091
  residence issues, 27-083
  rights to lump sum benefits accruing on or after 6/4/17, 27-089
  selling asset to P, 27-094—27-095
  tax avoidance arrangements, 27-098—27-099

**Divorce**
introduction, 16-001—16-002
pension sharing orders
  generally, 16-003—16-004
  LS&DB allowance, 16-005—16-012

**Double taxation treaties**
benefits, 26-068
contributions, 24-037
cross-border contributions
  articles differing from OECD Model, 29-027—29-028
  claiming relief, 29-029
  generally, 29-017—29-019
  "generally corresponding to a pension scheme", 29-025—29-026
  national insurance contributions, 29-030
  "recognised for tax purposes", 29-024
  "resident", 29-023
  where pension scheme located, 29-020—29-022
cross-border investment income/gains, 29-031
cross-border pension benefits
  annuities, 29-057—29-062
  anti-avoidance, 29-071
  "arising", 29-069—29-070
  articles conferring source taxation rights, 29-068
  articles differing from OECD Model, 29-050—29-073
  "derived from", 29-072—29-073
  "in consideration of past employment", 29-044—29-049
  "in consideration of past services", 29-050
  introduction, 29-034
  lump sums, 29-065—29-066
  OECD Model, 29-035—29-036
  "other income" article, 29-074—29-075
  payments "exempt" from tax in source state, 29-063—29-064
  pension article, employment article or "other income" article, 29-037—29-040
  "pensions and other similar remuneration", 29-041—29-043
  pensions "subject to tax" in state of residence, 29-053—29-056

"pensions" without reference to "other similar remuneration", 29-051—29-052
saving clauses, 29-067
transferee pension schemes, 29-049
vested benefit vehicles, 29-042—29-043
definition, 29-003
double taxation relief, 29-013
generally, 29-003
incorporation into UK law, 29-009—29-010
interpretation, 29-004—29-008
introduction, 29-001—29-002
objectives, 29-003
"pension scheme", definitions of, 29-015—29-016
pension transfers, 29-032—29-033
requirement to make a claim, 29-011—29-012
retirement benefit schemes, application to, 29-014—29-016

**Drawdown**
beneficiaries' drawdown pensions
dependants' drawdown pension funds, 15-039—15-043
flexi-access drawdown funds, 15-035—15-038
generally, 15-032
income withdrawal, 15-034
short-term annuities, 15-033
lump sum death benefits
charity LSDBs, 15-069—15-071
drawdown pension fund LSDBs, 15-060—15-063
flexi-access drawdown fund LSDBs, 15-064—15-065
members' drawdown pensions
drawdown pension funds, 13-039—13-041
flexi-access drawdown funds, 13-036—13-038
generally, 13-031
income withdrawal, 13-035
pension rule 5, 13-041
short-term annuities, 13-032—13-034

**Early leavers**
generally, 2-027

**Employees**
employee benefits
benefits code, 6-136
employer-financed retirement benefit schemes, 35-066
taxation
benefits code, 6-136
earnings charge, 6-133—6-135
termination payments, 6-137

**Employer-financed retirement benefit schemes**
definition, 35-009—35-010
EFRBS in practice, 35-005—35-007
"for" provision of benefits including relevant benefits, 35-011
inheritance tax, 35-101—35-102
interaction with other parts of ITEPA 2003, 35-002—35-004
introduction, 35-001
national insurance contributions

generally, 35-092—35-095
pension commencement lump sums, 35-096—35-099
serious ill-health lump sum, 35-100
relevant benefits
"change in nature of service", 35-041—35-042
"chargeable" by virtue of FA 2004 Sch.34, 35-051—35-053
"charged to tax" under Pt 9, 35-046—35-050
excluded benefits, 35-054
exclusions, 35-044—35-045
generally, 35-019—35-020
ill-health, disablement and accidental death, 35-055
"in anticipation of" retirement, 35-023
"in connection with past service", 35-031—35-040
lump sum, gratuity or other benefit, 35-021
"on" retirement, 35-022
pension sharing orders, 35-043
regulations under s.393B(3), 35-056—35-057
"retirement", 35-024—35-030
reporting requirements
generally, 35-103—35-104
special provisions in FA 2008 Sch.36, 35-105
"scheme", 35-014—35-018
taxation
employer contributions, 35-059—35-067
inheritance tax, 35-101—35-102
introduction, 35-058
national insurance contributions, 35-092—35-100
relevant benefits, 35-068—35-091
taxation (employer contributions)
CTA 2009 s.868, 35-063
CTA 2009 s.1290, 35-059
employee benefits, 35-066
FA 2004 s.246, 35-060—35-062
FA 2004 s.246A, 35-064—35-065
termination payments, 35-067
taxation (relevant benefits)
employee contributions, 35-080
employment-related loans, 35-090
foreign service exemption or reduction, 35-082—35-088
generally, 35-068
grandfathering of old s.222 schemes, 35-081
liability and PAYE, 35-070
relevant benefit provided to a non-individual, 35-071—35-073
relevant benefit provided to an individual, 35-069—35-070
remittance basis taxpayers, 35-091
responsible person, 35-072—35-073
temporary non-residents, 35-078—35-079
territorial limitations, 35-074—35-077
valuation of relevant benefits, 35-089

"to or in respect of" employees,
    35-012—35-013
**Employers' contributions**
    *see Pension contributions (registered schemes)*; *Pension contributions (unregistered schemes)*
**Erroneous payments**
    *see Mistake*
**"Excepted group life schemes"**
    drafting, 36-015
    excepted group life policies
        "excepted" group life policies, 36-009
        excepted group life schemes,
            36-013—36-015
        group life policies, 36-008
        tax avoidance purpose, 36-010—36-012
    excluded benefits, 36-004—36-005
    excluded single life policies, 36-016
    generally, 23-014, 36-006, 36-013—36-014
    introduction, 36-001—36-003
    relevant life policies
        excepted group life policies,
            36-008—36-015
        excluded single life policies, 36-016
        generally, 36-007
    taxation
        inheritance tax, 36-021—36-026
        payment of premiums, 36-017—36-018
        provision of benefits, 36-019—36-020
**False statements**
    penalties, 19-024
**Finance Act 2004 Pt 4**
    annual and lifetime allowances, 1-009—1-010
    authorised and unauthorised payments,
        1-016—1-019
    introduction, 1-001
    overview, 1-002—1-004
    payments to or in respect of employers, 1-023
    payments to or in respect of members,
        1-020—1-022
    tax charges
        authorised surplus payments charge, 1-014
        deregistration charge, 1-013
        generally, 1-007—1-008
        overseas transfer charge, 1-015
        scheme sanction charge, 1-012
        short service refund lump sum charge,
            1-014
        special lump sum death benefits charge,
            1-014
    tax reliefs and exemptions, 1-005—1-006
    transitional provisions, 1-024
    unauthorised payments charge and surcharge,
        1-011
**Flexible access drawdown**
    *see Drawdown*
**Funded unapproved schemes**
    background, 38-003—38-005
    definition, 38-006—38-008
    generally, 23-016
    introduction, 38-001—38-002
    taxation
        benefits, 38-022—38-030

contributions, 38-009—38-018
inheritance tax, 38-031—38-032
investments, 38-019—38-021
**Futures**
    investments, 8-016
**Gifts with reservation of benefit**
    *see Reservation of benefit*
**Group life schemes**
    *see Excepted group life schemes*
**Historical background**
    *see Legal history*
**Hybrid schemes**
    generally, 2-052
**"In specie contributions"**
    registered schemes
        chargeable gains, 6-152
        employer tax deductions, 6-127—6-131
        generally, 6-151
        stamp duty, 6-154
        stamp duty land tax, 6-153
    unregistered schemes
        FURBS, 38-015
        generally, 24-072
**"Inaccurate documents"**
    penalties, 19-025
**Income tax (registered schemes)**
    circumstances other than acquisition/disposal
        of assets, 8-030
    definition of "investments", 8-018
    futures contracts, 8-016
    generally, 8-014
    income "derived from" investments,
        8-033—8-034
    investment vehicles, 8-036—8-038
    investments "held for the purposes of" a
        scheme, 8-035
    land transactions
        FA 2016 rules, 8-028—8-029
        generally, 8-025—8-027
    manufactured interest, 8-017
    options contracts, 8-016
    property investment LLPs, 8-042—8-044
    repayment of tax, 8-046
    repurchase agreements, 8-017
    stock lending, 8-015
    stocks and shares, 8-023—8-024
    taxable property, 8-045
    trading income, 8-019—8-022
    trading vehicles, 8-031—8-032
    underwriting commissions, 8-039—8-041
**Income tax (unregistered schemes)**
    investment income
        background, 25-017—25-019
        benefits under certain pension schemes,
            25-038—25-040
        "bounty", 25-025—25-026
        capital sum paid to settlor/spouse,
            25-045—25-048
        income arising from property in which
            settlor has an interest, 25-032—25-042
        income arising under the settlement,
            25-029—25-031
        inter-spouse gifts, 25-036—25-037

non-domiciled settlors, 25-020—25-021
overview, 25-003—25-006
"settlement", 25-022—25-026
"settlor", 25-027—25-028
settlor is not an individual, 25-041—25-042
taxation of settlor, 25-049
trust income paid for benefit of minor child, 25-043—25-044
non-UK schemes, 25-010—25-014
overseas pension schemes, 31-041
pension benefits
  amount charged to tax, 26-004—26-006
  exempt income, 26-006
  ITEPA 2003 Pt 9, 26-003
qualifying non-UK pension schemes, 34-043—34-045
recognised overseas pension schemes, 32-020—32-021
UK schemes, 25-003—25-006

**Inheritance tax (registered schemes)**
application to pension schemes, 21-009—21-013
contributions
  contributions by other persons, 21-056—21-058
  employer contributions, 21-015—21-018
  generally, 21-014
  member contributions, 21-019—21-055
death of beneficiary
  benefits ceasing on death, 21-089—21-098
  benefits continuing after death, 21-099—21-100
  changes occurring by reason of death, 21-101—21-103
  contributions, transfers, disposals, etc. before death, 21-110—21-111
  entitlement immediately before death, 21-089—21-098
  general powers of appointment, 21-105—21-109
  generally, 21-086—21-088
  interests in possession, 21-097—21-098
  pensions and annuities ceasing on death, 21-091—21-096
  powers of nomination, 21-105—21-109
  protected rights, 21-104
devaluing interests
  generally, 21-061—21-068
  interests in possession, 21-069
disposal of scheme interests, 21-059—21-060
employer contributions
  generally, 6-132, 21-015
  IHTA 1984 s.12, 21-016—21-017
  partnerships, 21-018
form IHT409, 21-112—21-113
gifts with reservation of benefit, 21-051—21-055
interests in possession
  death of beneficiary, 21-097—21-098
  devaluing interests, 21-069
  generally, 21-008
introduction, 21-001
member contributions

arm's length transaction between unconnected persons, 21-037—21-039
generally, 6-035, 21-019—21-021
gifts with reservation of benefit, 21-051—21-055
HMRC practice, 21-022—21-024
IHTA 1984 s.10, 21-029—21-031
IHTA 1984 s.11, 21-040—21-043
IHTA 1984 s.12, 21-025—21-028
IHTA 1984 s.18, 21-044
IHTA 1984 s.21, 21-045—21-046
IHTA 1984 s.28, 21-047
intended to confer gratuitous benefit, 21-032—21-035
made in transaction intended to confer gratuitous benefit, 21-036
settlement powers, 21-048—21-050
two-year rule, 21-022—21-024
omitting to exercise rights, 21-084—21-085
overview of IHT, 21-002—21-007
relevant property trusts
  calculation of periodic and exit charges, 21-080—21-081
  distributions from settlement, 21-082
  introduction, 21-070
  nature of regime, 21-071—21-072
  retaining death benefits within scheme, 21-083
  scheme funds on death of member, 21-073—21-074
  trusts of LSDBs, 21-075—21-077
  who is settlor, 21-078—21-079

**Inheritance tax (unregistered schemes)**
contributions
  business property relief, 28-033
  IHTA 1984 s.10, 28-025—28-028
  IHTA 1984 s.12(1), 28-023—28-024
  IHTA 1984 s.13, 28-029—28-032
  introduction, 28-021
  non-application of IHTA 1984 s.12(2), 28-022
corresponding schemes, 39-020
death of beneficiary
  non-application of s.151(2) and (3), 28-071—28-072
  powers of nomination, 28-076—28-077
  sponsored superannuation schemes, 28-073—28-075
disposal of scheme interests, 28-034
employer-financed retirement benefit schemes, 35-101—35-102
excepted group life schemes, 36-021—36-026
excluded property, 28-010—28-011
funded unapproved schemes, 38-031—38-032
interests in possession
  disposal of scheme interests, 28-034
  extent of interest, 28-009
  generally, 28-003—28-004
  non-qualifying IIPs, 28-008
  qualifying IIPs, 28-005—28-007
omitting to exercise rights, 28-067—28-070
overseas pension schemes, 31-040
overview, 28-001—28-002

qualifying non-UK pension schemes, 34-041—34-042
recognised overseas pension schemes, 32-020—32-021
relevant property trusts
  exit charges, 28-045—28-048
  exit event after first ten-year anniversary, 28-053—28-056
  exit event before first ten-year anniversary, 28-049—28-052
  generally, 28-035
  IHTA 1984 s.86, 28-061—28-066
  periodic charges, 28-039—28-044
  relevant property regime, 28-036—28-056
  sponsored superannuation schemes, 28-057—28-060
  who is settlor, 28-037—28-038
s.615 funds, 37-028
salary sacrifice, 24-069
sponsored superannuation schemes
  application of IHTA 1984 s.3(3), 28-013
  death of beneficiary, 28-073—28-075
  definition, 28-014—28-017
  generally, 28-012
  pension transfers, 28-018
  relevant property trusts, 28-057—28-060
  transitional provisions, 28-019—28-020

**Insurance policies**
see also *Excepted group life schemes*
chargeable event regime, 22-028
life cover lump sums, 15-075—15-076
pensions paid under insurance policies, 26-055—26-058

**Interests in possession**
registered schemes
  death of beneficiary, 21-097—21-098
  devaluing interests, 21-069
  generally, 21-008
unregistered schemes
  disposal of scheme interests, 28-034
  extent of interest, 28-009
  generally, 28-003—28-004
  non-qualifying IIPs, 28-008
  qualifying IIPs, 28-005—28-007

**International aspects**
see *Overseas pension schemes*; *Registered pension schemes (international aspects)*

**Investments (registered schemes)**
capital gains, 8-048—8-050
definition of "investments", 8-018
Finance Act 2004
  generally, 8-007
  SDLT on purchase of land from connected partnership, 8-012
  transactions involving a member or sponsoring employer, 8-008—8-011
  unauthorised borrowing, 8-013
FSMA 2000, 8-006
futures contracts, 8-016
income "derived from" investments, 8-033—8-034
introduction, 8-001
investment income tax exemption

circumstances other than acquisition/disposal of assets, 8-030
definition of "investments", 8-018
futures contracts, 8-016
generally, 8-014
income "derived from" investments, 8-033—8-034
investment vehicles, 8-036—8-038
investments "held for the purposes of" a scheme, 8-035
land transactions, 8-025—8-029
manufactured interest, 8-017
options contracts, 8-016
property investment LLPs, 8-042—8-044
repayment of tax, 8-046
repurchase agreements, 8-017
stock lending, 8-015
stocks and shares, 8-023—8-024
taxable property, 8-045
trading income, 8-019—8-022
trading vehicles, 8-031—8-032
underwriting commissions, 8-039—8-041
investment vehicles, 8-036—8-038
investments "held for the purposes of" a scheme, 8-035
land transactions
  FA 2016 rules, 8-028—8-029
  generally, 8-025—8-027
manufactured interest, 8-017
non-investment income, 8-047
non-tax law
  FSMA 2000, 8-006
  pensions law, 8-003—8-004
  transactions involving scheme employers, 8-005
  trusts law, 8-002
options contracts, 8-016
other income sources, 8-047
pensions law, 8-003—8-004
property investment LLPs, 8-042—8-044
repayment of tax, 8-046
repurchase agreements, 8-017
SDLT on purchase of land from connected partnership, 8-012
stock lending, 8-015
stocks and shares, 8-023—8-024
taxable property, 8-045
trading income, 8-019—8-022
trading vehicles, 8-031—8-032
transactions involving a member or sponsoring employer, 8-008—8-011
transactions involving scheme employers, 8-005
trusts law, 8-002
unauthorised borrowing, 8-013
underwriting commissions, 8-039—8-041

**Investments (unregistered schemes)**
CGT settlement provisions (UK-resident beneficiaries)
  capital payment, 25-105
  introduction, 25-089—25-091
  matching, 25-107
  non-UK beneficiaries, 25-108—25-110

# INDEX

s.1(3) amount, 25-106
s.87 provisions, 25-102—25-103
settlement, 25-104
supplementary charge, 25-111
CGT settlement provisions (UK-resident settlors)
corporate settlors, 25-094—25-095
effect of s.86(1) applying, 25-100—25-101
introduction, 25-089—25-091
s.86 provisions, 25-092
"settlement" and "settlor", 25-093
settlor has interest in settlement, 25-096—25-099
income tax settlements provisions
background, 25-017—25-019
benefits under certain pension schemes, 25-038—25-040
"bounty", 25-025—25-026
capital sum paid to settlor/spouse, 25-045—25-048
income arising from property in which settlor has an interest, 25-032—25-042
income arising under the settlement, 25-029—25-031
inter-spouse gifts, 25-036—25-037
non-domiciled settlors, 25-020—25-021
"settlement", 25-022—25-026
"settlor", 25-027—25-028
settlor is not an individual, 25-041—25-042
taxation of settlor, 25-049
trust income paid for benefit of minor child, 25-043—25-044
introduction, 25-001
non-UK schemes
capital gains tax, 25-015—25-016
generally, 25-009
income tax, 25-010—25-014
transfer of assets abroad
associated operations, 25-055—25-057
"commercial transaction" exemption, 25-080
exemptions, 25-071—25-088
generally, 25-050—25-051
"genuine transaction" exemption, 25-084—25-088
"no tax avoidance purpose" exemption, 25-072—25-080
non-domiciled transferors, 25-068—25-070
persons who receive a benefit, 25-066—25-067
relevant transfers, 25-052—25-057
transferors in receipt of capital sums, 25-063—25-065
transferors with power to enjoy, 25-058—25-062
UK schemes
capital gains tax, 25-007—25-008
generally, 25-002
income tax, 25-003—25-006
**Land transactions**
FA 2016 rules, 8-028—8-029
generally, 8-025—8-027

**Legal history**
introduction, 1-001
occupational pensions
generally, 1-002—1-004
limits on benefits, 1-010—1-011
surpluses, 1-009
taxation, 1-005—1-008
other regimes, 1-014
overview, 1-001
personal pensions
generally, 1-012
taxation, 1-013
reform proposals, 1-015—1-018
**Legislation**
CIOT proposals, 1-026
Finance Act 2004 Pt 4
annual and lifetime allowances, 1-009—1-010
authorised and unauthorised payments, 1-016—1-019
authorised surplus payments charge, 1-014
deregistration charge, 1-013
introduction, 1-001
overseas transfer charge, 1-015
overview, 1-002—1-004
payments to or in respect of employers, 1-023
payments to or in respect of members, 1-020—1-022
scheme sanction charge, 1-012
short service refund lump sum charge, 1-014
special lump sum death benefits charge, 1-014
tax charges, 1-007—1-008
tax reliefs and exemptions, 1-005—1-006
transitional provisions, 1-024
unauthorised payments charge and surcharge, 1-011
overview of current issues, 1-026
position before A Day
introduction, 1-001
occupational pensions, 1-002—1-011
other regimes, 1-014
personal pensions, 1-012—1-013
reform proposals, 1-015—1-018
recent developments, 1-025
**Life schemes**
see Excepted group life schemes
**Lifetime allowance excess lump sums**
see Lump sum payments
**Lifetime allowances**
see also Lifetime allowances (protection from charge)
abolition, 10-001
availability
availability on BCE, 10-049—10-052
fixed protection, 10-021—10-031
generally, 10-020
individual protection, 10-040—10-045
lifetime allowance enhancement factors, 10-046—10-048
rescission of protection-cessation event on

ground of mistake, 10-032—10-039
benefit crystallisation events
  age 75, 10-014
  BCE 9, 10-019
  credit for previous BCE, 10-015
  generally, 10-005—10-006
  permitted margin, 10-018
  relevant pension schemes, 10-007
  relevant two-year period, 10-008
  relevant unused uncrystallised funds, 10-016
  relevant valuation factor, 10-009—10-012
  remaining unused funds, 10-017
  threshold annual rate, 10-018
  types, 10-005
  unauthorised payments, 10-013
death benefits, interaction with, 15-014
fixed protection
  arrangements made otherwise than in permitted circumstances, 10-031
  benefit accrual, 10-023—10-028
  generally, 10-021—10-022
  impermissible transfers, 10-029
  permitted transfers, 10-030
generally, 1-009—1-010
individual protection
  generally, 10-040
  IP 2014, 10-041—10-043
  IP 2016, 10-044—10-045
introduction, 10-001—10-004
lifetime allowance charge
  discharge of tax liability, 10-061—10-064
  generally, 10-053—10-055
  liability, 10-058—10-064
  purpose, 10-057
  relevant post-death crystallisation events, 10-059—10-060
  scheme-funded tax payments, 10-056
lifetime allowance enhancement factors, 10-046—10-048
pension sharing on divorce
  debited members with primary protection, 16-012
  generally, 16-005—16-007
  LS allowance and LS&DB allowance enhancement factors, 16-008—16-011
recognised non-UK schemes
  amount crystallising on BCE, 30-121
  block transfers, 30-123—30-124
  generally, 30-120
  liability, 30-128
  modification of BCE 3, 30-125
  modifications, 30-121—30-126
  para.15 BCEs, 30-122
  relevant valuation factor, 30-126
  UK residency exemption not relevant, 30-127
removal, 10-001
reporting requirements, 10-065—10-066
rescission of protection-cessation event on ground of mistake, 10-032—10-039

**Lifetime allowances (protection from charge)**
annuity purchased from pre-A Day drawdown fund, 3-085—3-086
arrangements made otherwise than in permitted circumstances
  automatic enrolment, 3-042
  generally, 3-041
availability of lifetime allowance on BCE
  ARP where relevant existing pension is drawdown, 3-075—3-077
  illustration, 3-078—3-079
  pre-A Day pensions, 3-074
  BCE 2, 3-080—3-081
  BCE 3, 3-082—3-084
  BCE 4, 3-085—3-086
  BCE 8, 3-087
consequences of cessation, 3-043
drawdown funds representing pre-A Day unsecured pension, 3-087
enhanced protection
  arrangements made otherwise than in permitted circumstances, 3-041—3-042
  consequences of cessation, 3-043
  impermissible transfers, 3-035—3-040
  introduction, 3-025
  relevant benefit accrual, 3-026—3-034
impermissible transfers
  cash balance and defined benefits arrangements, 3-037
  generally, 3-038—3-040
  other money purchase arrangements, 3-035—3-036
introduction, 3-024
lifetime allowance enhancement factors
  generally, 3-044—3-047
  pension credits, 3-066—3-067
  primary protection, 3-048—3-065
pension credits, 3-066—3-067
pre-A Day entitlement, 3-082—3-084
primary protection factor
  generally, 3-049—3-050
  increase, 3-060
  introduction, 3-048
  protection for lump sum death benefits, 3-062—3-065
  reduction, 3-061
  relevant pre-commencement pension rights, 3-051
  valuation of crystallised pension rights, 3-058—3-059
  valuation of uncrystallised pension rights, 3-052—3-057
reduced lifetime allowance
  multiple BCEs, 3-073
  pre-A Day pensions, 3-068
  protected pension age, 3-069—3-072
relevant benefit accrual
  appropriate limit, 3-030—3-033
  cash balance and defined benefits arrangements, 3-028
  lump sum death benefits, 3-034
  other money purchase arrangements, 3-026—3-027

relevant crystallised amount, 3-029
scheme pension provided by pre-A Day drawdown fund, 3-080—3-081

**Loans**
authorised employer loans
amount of unauthorised payment, 17-010—17-024
further reduction in value of charge that is not of adequate value, 17-026—17-027
generally, 17-008—17-009
increase in extent to which loan does not comply with repayment terms, 17-029—17-031
loans ceasing to be secured by charge of adequate value, 17-025
loans ceasing to comply with repayment terms, 17-028
loans that are not authorised employer loans, 17-010—17-024
prevention of double charging, 17-032
definition of "debt", 2-095—2-097
definition of "loan"
FA 2004, 2-081—2-084
usual meaning, 2-085—2-091
generally, 2-081—2-084
scheme administration employer payments, 17-033—17-035
scheme administration member payments, 11-012—11-014
transactions that are not loans, 2-092—2-094
unauthorised borrowing
application to general funds, 8-059—8-060
"borrowing", 8-054—8-055
borrowing "by a registered pension scheme", 8-056—8-057
borrowing "in respect of an arrangement", 8-058
generally, 8-013, 8-051—8-053
money purchase arrangements that are not collective, 8-061—8-065
other arrangements, 8-066—8-071

**Loss of pension**
compensation, 22-029—22-030

**"Lump sum and death benefit allowance"**
"available" allowance, 14-013
generally, 14-011—14-012
international aspects
cash balance arrangements, 20-019—20-023
defined benefits arrangements, 20-026
hybrid arrangements, 20-027—20-028
other money purchase arrangements, 20-024—20-025
relevant overseas individuals, 20-016—20-018
transfers from ROPS, 20-029—20-038
lump sum death benefits, 15-014
pre-6/4/06 pensions, 14-016
pre-6/4/24 BCEs, 14-014—14-015
transitional tax-free amount certificates, 14-017

**Lump sum death benefits**
*see also Death benefits*
annuity protection LSDBs, 15-058—15-059
authorised LSDBs, 15-044
charity LSDBs
drawdown funds, 15-069—15-071
generally, 15-066—15-067
uncrystallised funds, 15-068
defined benefits arrangements, 15-010—15-011
defined benefits LSDBs, 15-052
drawdown pension fund LSDBs
generally, 15-060
permitted maximum, 15-061—15-063
flexi-access drawdown fund LSDBs
generally, 15-064
permitted maximum, 15-065
introduction, 15-001—15-002
life cover lump sums, 15-075—15-076
LS&DB allowance, interaction with, 15-014
lump sum death benefit rule, 15-044—15-045
money purchase arrangements
effect of death, 15-008
generally, 15-003—15-007
nominations and expressions of wishes, 15-009
non-qualifying persons, 15-049—15-051
pension protection LSDBs, 15-056—15-057
relevant two-year period, 15-012—15-013
special LSDB charge, 1-014, 15-047—15-048
taxation, 15-046
trivial commutation LSDBs
generally, 15-072
paid to dependants, 15-073
paid to individuals, 15-074
trusts of death benefits
disguised remuneration, 15-081
generally, 15-077
payments not subject to special LSDB charge, 15-078
payments subject to special LSDB charge, 15-079—15-080
uncrystallised funds LSDBs
generally, 15-053—15-054
permitted maximum, 15-055

**Lump sum payments**
*see also Lump sum death benefits*
authorised lump sums, 14-001
enhanced allowances
enhanced protection, 14-062—14-063
fixed protection, 14-064—14-067
generally, 14-056—14-058
individual protection, 14-068—14-069
other enhancement factors, 14-070—14-071
primary protection, 14-059—14-061
lifetime allowance excess lump sums, 14-039—14-040
lump sum allowance
generally, 14-005—14-007
pre-6/4/06 pensions in payment, 14-010
pre-6/4/24 BCEs, 14-008—14-009
transitional tax-free amount certificates,

# INDEX

14-017
lump sum and death benefit allowance
"available" allowance, 14-013
generally, 14-011—14-012
pre-6/4/06 pensions in payment, 14-016
pre-6/4/24 BCEs, 14-014—14-015
transitional tax-free amount certificates, 14-017
lump sum rule, 14-002
national insurance contributions, 14-004
payment in error
commencement lump sums paid after death, 14-055
generally, 14-041, 14-051—14-052
other lump sum errors, 14-053—14-054
pension commencement excess lump sum, 14-023—14-024
pension commencement lump sums
anti-avoidance, 14-022
applicable amount, 14-021
generally, 14-018—14-019
permitted maximum, 14-020
provision of information to members by scheme administrators, 14-073—14-074
recycling lump sums
amount of unauthorised payment, 6-147
exceptions, 6-148
generally, 6-145—6-146
refund of excess contributions lump sums, 14-032—14-033
reporting requirements, 14-072—14-074
serious ill-health lump sums, 14-027—14-029
short service refund lump sums, 14-030—14-031
small payments
FSCS payments, 14-045
generally, 14-041
non-occupational pensions, 14-048—14-050
occupational pensions, 14-046—14-047
relevant accretion following transfer, 14-042—14-044
taxation, 14-003
trivial commutation lump sums
generally, 14-034—14-035
valuation of member's pension rights, 14-036
uncrystallised funds pension lump sums, 14-025—14-026
winding-up lump sums, 14-037—14-038

**Manufactured interest**
investments, 8-017

**Market value**
definition, 2-118
effect of scheme borrowing, 2-121—2-123
generally, 2-116—2-117
quoted shares, 2-117
unit trusts, 2-120

**Members**
active members, 2-030—2-034
death beneficiaries, 2-035
generally, 2-027—2-029

**Members' contributions**
*see Pension contributions (registered schemes); Pension contributions (unregistered schemes)*

**Mistake**
lump sums paid in error
commencement lump sums paid after death, 14-055
generally, 14-041, 14-051—14-052
other lump sum errors, 14-053—14-054
pensions paid in error
generally, 13-042
payments of arrears of pension after death, 13-047—13-048
payments representing accrued arrears of pension, 13-043
pensions continuing to be paid after death, 13-046
pensions paid after discovery of error, 13-045
recipient still alive, 13-044
rescission of protection-cessation event, 10-032—10-039
unauthorised payments
Roxburghe principle, 18-194
treatment by HMRC, 18-192—18-193

**Money purchase schemes**
*see Defined contribution schemes*

**National insurance contributions (registered schemes)**
benefits, 13-012
death benefits, 15-023
employer contributions, 6-138
lump sums, 14-004
member contributions, 6-034

**National insurance contributions (unregistered schemes)**
benefits
double taxation agreements, 26-077
employer-financed pension only schemes, 26-074—26-076
foreign service, 26-072
generally, 26-070—26-071
qualifying overseas pension schemes, 26-073
contributions
employer-financed pension only schemes, 24-060
generally, 24-058—24-059
relevant migrant members relief, 24-025
transitional corresponding relief, 24-036
disguised remuneration
generally, 27-139
income tax and NICs compared, 27-142—27-143
Social Security (Contributions) Regulations 2001, 27-140—27-141
employer-financed retirement benefit schemes
generally, 35-092—35-095
pension commencement lump sums, 35-096—35-099
serious ill-health lump sum, 35-100
recognised non-UK schemes, 30-028

**Options**
  investments, 8-016
**Overseas pension schemes**
  see also Overseas pension schemes
    (QNUPS); Overseas pension schemes
    (QROPS); Overseas pension schemes
    (RNUKS)
  definition, 31-007
  development, 31-005
  established outside UK, 31-008
  international organisations, 31-010
  overview, 31-001—31-004
  QNUPS compared, 31-006
  recognised overseas pension schemes
    authorised member payments, 32-016
    country/territory in which scheme
      established, 32-017
    definition, 32-005
    development, 32-004
    Guernsey, 32-011, 32-018—32-019
    introduction, 32-005
    overview, 32-001—32-003
    pension rule 1, 32-015
    relevant transfer fund, 32-014
    requirements of reg.3(6), 32-008—32-011
    requirements of reg.3(6A), 32-012—32-013
    ring-fenced transfer funds, 32-014
    schemes falling within reg.3(1A), 32-007
    taxation, 32-020—32-021
  reg.2(2)
    non-occupational pensions, 31-012
    occupational pensions, 31-011
    regulatory bodies, 31-013
  reg.2(3)
    Condition 1, 31-015—31-020
    Condition 2, 31-021—31-024
    Condition 2(a) and (b), 31-025—31-033
    Condition 3, 31-036—31-038
    introduction, 31-014
    serious ill-health, 31-035
    summary, 31-034
    "system of taxation of personal income",
      31-023
    "tax relief is available in respect of
      pensions", 31-024
  registered schemes
    annual allowance charge, 20-007
    generally, 20-003—20-006
    overseas transfer charge, 20-009
    taxable property provisions, 20-008
  requirements prescribed by regulations
    generally, 31-009
    international organisations, 31-010
    reg.2(2), 31-011—31-013
    reg.2(3), 31-014—31-038
  taxation
    capital gains tax, 31-039
    income tax, 31-041
    inheritance tax, 31-040
    interaction with RNUKS provisions,
      31-042

**Overseas pension schemes (QNUPS)**
  definition of QNUPS, 34-009
  established outside UK, 34-010
  international organisations, 34-011—34-012
  overseas pension schemes compared, 34-007
  overview, 34-001—34-006
  recognised for tax purposes
    Condition A, 34-019
    Condition B, 34-020—34-026
    generally, 34-013
    pension rule 1, 34-031—34-034
    Primary Condition 1, 34-014
    Primary Condition 2, 34-015—34-017
    Primary Condition 2(a) and (c), 34-018
    relevant scheme funds, 34-027—34-030
  reg.6, 34-035—34-040
  reporting requirements, 34-008
  requirements prescribed by regulations
    generally, 34-011
    international organisations, 34-012
    recognised for tax purposes,
      34-013—34-034
    reg.6, 34-035—34-040
  taxation
    capital gains tax, 34-043
    income tax, 34-043—34-045
    inheritance tax, 34-041—34-042
**Overseas pension schemes (QROPS)**
  definition, 33-016
  exclusion under s.169(4), 33-017—33-020
  grandfathering pre-9/3/17, 33-029
  HMRC list of QROPS
    designer legislation, 33-010
    EU law, 33-012—33-015
    former QROPS, 33-011
    generally, 33-007
    transfers to schemes on list but not QROPS,
      33-008—33-009
  information requirements
    generally, 33-043
    members' obligations, 33-049
    scheme manager's obligations,
      33-044—33-048
  introduction, 33-001—33-003
  overseas transfer charge
    amount of charge, 33-038
    avoidance of double charge, 33-042
    exclusions, 33-030—33-032
    generally, 33-023
    grandfathering pre-9/3/17, 33-029
    liability, 33-039—33-041
    main provision, 33-028
    member and receiving scheme in EEA
      states, 33-032
    member and receiving scheme in same
      country, 33-031
    "onward transfer", 33-024—33-025
    "original transfer", 33-026
    "relevant period", 33-027
    "transferred value", 33-037
    transfers exceeding available overseas
      transfer allowance, 33-033—33-036
  purpose of QROPS regime, 33-004—33-006

# INDEX 851

residence of member, 33-021
scheme manager information requirements
    former QROPS, 33-047—33-048
    generally, 33-044
    non-compliance, 33-046
    subsequent changes or corrections, 33-045
taxation generally, 33-022

**Overseas pension schemes (RNUKS)**
annual allowance provisions
    carry forward of unused annual allowance, 30-108—30-109
    cash balance arrangements, 30-102—30-103
    defined benefits arrangements, 30-102—30-103
    enhancement of LS and LS&DB allowances, 30-112
    first flexibly accessing of pension savings, 30-106
    generally, 30-100
    hybrid arrangements, 30-107
    liability, 30-113
    modifications, 30-101—30-112
    other money purchase arrangements, 30-104—30-105
    pension input amounts expressed in foreign currency, 30-110—30-111
definition, 30-004—30-005
lifetime allowance provisions
    amount crystallising on BCE, 30-121
    block transfers, 30-123—30-124
    generally, 30-120
    liability, 30-128
    modification of BCE 3, 30-125
    modifications, 30-121—30-126
    para.15 BCEs, 30-122
    relevant valuation factor, 30-126
    UK residency exemption not relevant, 30-127
member payment charges
    application of member payment provisions, 30-058—30-065
    attributing payments to particular funds, 30-048—30-057
    credit for overseas tax paid, 30-076
    determination of available LS and LS&DB allowance, 30-061
    double taxation treaties, 30-075
    generally, 30-029—30-032
    interaction with disguised remuneration provisions, 30-078
    interaction with EFRBS provisions, 30-077
    liability, 30-073—30-076
    lifetime allowance excess lump sums, 30-065
    member payment provisions, 30-033—30-035
    non-EEA annuity providers, 30-059
    pension commencement excess lump sums, 30-062
    recognised medical practitioners, 30-060
    relieved members, 30-036—30-037
    serious ill-health lump sums, 30-064
    transfer members, 30-038—30-047
    UK residency condition, 30-066—30-072
    uncrystallised funds pension lump sums, 30-063
national insurance contributions, 30-028
overseas transfer charge
    generally, 30-114
    main provisions, 30-118
    "relieved relevant non-UK scheme transfer", 30-115—30-117
    transfers exceeding available overseas transfer allowance, 30-119
overview, 30-001—30-003
pre-A Day UK tax-relieved funds
    generally, 30-006
    ITEPA 2003 s.307, 30-008—30-015
    QROPS, 30-016
    reliefs, 30-007
taxable property provisions
    attributing payments to particular funds, 30-089—30-099
    consideration is rent, 30-086
    FA 2004 ss.185A-185I, 30-085
    generally, 30-079—30-080
    liability, 30-088
    modifications, 30-084—30-087
    TAFT and RFTATF, 30-081—30-083
    UK residency condition not relevant, 30-087
taxation
    annual allowance provisions, 30-100—30-113
    generally, 30-017—30-021
    lifetime allowance provisions, 30-120—30-128
    member payment provisions, 30-029—30-078
    national insurance contributions, 30-028
    overseas transfer charge, 30-114—30-119
    summary of taxation of benefits, 30-023—30-027
    taxable property provisions, 30-079—30-099
    terminology, 30-022
transfer members
    generally, 30-038
    relevant transfer funds, 30-039—30-042
    ring-fenced transfer funds, 30-043—30-047
UK residency condition
    deceased members, 30-072
    five-year rule funds, 30-067
    generally, 30-066
    ring-fenced funds with key date of 6/4/17 or later, 30-069—30-070
    ten-year rule funds, 30-068
    transfers to schemes that are not QROPS, 30-071

**PAYE**
disguised remuneration, 27-110—27-115
generally, 20-044
non-UK members, 20-045
non-UK trustees, 20-046

**Payments**
  crediting an account, 2-059—2-062
  generally, 2-053—2-057
  payments in breach of trust
    application to deemed unauthorised payments, 2-078—2-079
    Clark v HMRC, 2-074—2-077
    generally, 2-065—2-073
  payments on commercial terms, 2-058
  rectification, effect of, 2-080
  release of debts, 2-063—2-064
  transfer of bare legal title only, 2-077

**Penalties**
  accounting for tax returns, 19-020
  breach of obligation to provide information/documents, 19-022
  event reports, 19-015
  false statements, 19-024
  inaccuracies, 19-025
  pension scheme returns, 19-012

**Pension benefits (registered schemes)**
  *see also Death benefits; Lump sum death benefits*
  drawdown pension
    drawdown pension funds, 13-039—13-041
    flexi-access drawdown funds, 13-036—13-038
    generally, 13-031
    income withdrawal, 13-035
    pension rule 5, 13-041
    short-term annuities, 13-032—13-034
  "entitlement" to pension, 13-003
  ill-health condition, 13-005
  introduction, 13-001
  lifetime annuities
    cessation, 13-028
    death of member, 13-029
    definition of "annuity", 13-025
    entitlement arising before 6/4/15, 13-027
    entitlement arising on or after 6/4/15, 13-025—13-026
    generally, 13-023
    pension transfers, 12-009—12-010
    scheme pensions compared, 13-030
  national insurance contributions, 13-012
  normal minimum pension age, 13-004
  payment "in respect of" an arrangement, 13-007
  "payment" of pension, 13-003
  pension rules
    "entitlement" and "payment", 13-003
    generally, 13-002
    pension rule 1, 13-004—13-005
    pension rule 2, 13-006
  pensions paid in error
    generally, 13-042
    payments of arrears of pension after death, 13-047—13-048
    payments representing accrued arrears of pension, 13-043
    pensions continuing to be paid after death, 13-046
    pensions paid after discovery of error, 13-045
    recipient still alive, 13-044
  post-death payments, 13-006
  reporting requirements, 13-049
  scheme pensions
    anti-avoidance, 13-018—13-019
    associated death benefits, 13-022
    definition, 13-015—13-016
    generally, 13-014
    lifetime annuities compared, 13-030
    money purchase arrangements, 13-020—13-021
    "pension", 13-017
  taxation of authorised pensions
    generally, 13-008
    liability, 13-011
    lifetime allowance, interaction with, 13-013
    national insurance contributions, 13-012
    net taxable pension income, 13-010
    pension income, 13-009

**Pension benefits (unregistered schemes)**
  annual payments
    generally, 26-060—26-063
    voluntary annual payments, 26-051—26-052
  capital gains tax, 26-066—26-067
  employment-related annuities
    annuities for benefit of dependants, 26-043
    annuities in recognition of another's services, 26-045—26-050
    annuities under non-registered occupational schemes, 26-044
    generally, 26-041—26-042
  exempt pensions
    disablement pensions, 26-053—26-054
    pensions paid under insurance policies, 26-055—26-058
  foreign pensions
    beneficiaries' annuities, 26-031
    beneficiaries' income withdrawal, 26-029—26-030
    definition of "foreign pension", 26-007
    definition of "pension", 26-008—26-009
    exceptions, 26-026—26-031
    foreign service relief, 26-015—26-017
    investment growth, 26-018
    liability, 26-034—26-038
    overseas pension schemes, 26-027—26-028
    partial lump sums, 26-019
    relevant lump sums, 26-010—26-025
    remittance basis taxpayers, 26-033
    RNUKS, 26-027—26-028
    taxable pension income, 26-032—26-033
    temporary non-residents, 26-035—26-038
  income tax
    amount charged to tax, 26-004—26-006
    exempt income, 26-006
    ITEPA 2003 Pt 9, 26-003
  national insurance contributions
    double taxation agreements, 26-077
    employer-financed pension only schemes, 26-074—26-076

# INDEX

foreign service, 26-072
generally, 26-070—26-071
qualifying overseas pension schemes, 26-073
other provisions that could apply to lump sums
  annual payments, 26-060—26-063
  capital gains tax, 26-066—26-067
  generally, 26-059
  transfer of assets abroad, 26-064—26-065
overview, 26-001—26-002
tax treaties, 26-068
transfer of assets abroad, 26-064—26-065
UK pensions
  generally, 26-039
  temporary non-residents, 26-040
unilateral relief for foreign tax paid, 26-069
voluntary annual payments
  generally, 26-051
  taxable pension income, 26-052

**Pension commencement lump sums**
*see Lump sum payments*

**Pension contributions (registered schemes)**
annual allowance charge, 6-144
annual payments, 6-149—6-150
asset-backed contributions
  change in lender's position, 6-104—6-109
  complex arrangements (existing partnerships), 6-102—6-103
  complex arrangements (new partnerships), 6-100—6-101
  Condition A, 6-086—6-088
  Condition B, 6-089—6-095
  Condition C, 6-096—6-099
  generally, 6-079—6-081
  scheme administration employer payments provisions, 6-110—6-111
  simple arrangements, 6-082—6-085
definition of "contribution", 6-003
employee taxation
  benefits code, 6-136
  earnings charge, 6-133—6-135
  termination payments, 6-137
employer contributions
  employee taxation, 6-133—6-137
  inheritance tax, 6-132
  national insurance contributions, 6-138
  tax deductions, 6-036—6-131
employer contributions (tax deductions)
  accounting standards, 6-038
  asset-backed contributions, 6-079—6-111
  capital expenditure, 6-071—6-072
  cessation of business, 6-117
  cessation of trade, 6-059—6-060
  contributions "in respect of any individual", 6-069
  contributions "under" the scheme, 6-068
  controlling directors, 6-051—6-057
  deemed contributions, 6-122—6-123
  defined benefit plans, 6-040
  delayed payment of contributions, 6-073
  determining profits of trade, 6-037
  disguised distributions, 6-058
  employer-funded retirement benefit schemes, 6-074—6-078
  FA 2004 ss.196-200, 6-064—6-067
  generally, 6-036
  in specie contributions, 6-127—6-131
  indirect contributions, 6-119—6-121
  intermediate payment arrangements, 6-039
  investment businesses, 6-063—6-065
  measurement of expense, 6-041—6-042
  no other relief available, 6-124—6-126
  property businesses, 6-061
  spreading of relief, 6-112—6-116
  summary, 6-062
  when contribution is "paid", 6-070
  "wholly and exclusively" test, 6-043—6-065
in specie contributions
  chargeable gains, 6-152
  employer tax deductions, 6-127—6-131
  generally, 6-151
  stamp duty, 6-154
  stamp duty land tax, 6-153
international aspects
  non-UK members, 20-010—20-011
  non-UK schemes, 20-012
introduction, 6-001—6-002
member contributions
  generally, 6-004
  income tax relief, 6-005—6-033
  inheritance tax, 6-035
  national insurance contributions, 6-034
member contributions (income tax relief)
  active membership, 6-020
  annual limit for relief, 6-027
  "by or on behalf of" member, 6-017—6-019
  contributions "paid", 6-009—6-016
  contributions "under" the scheme, 6-008
  eligible shares, 6-026
  generally, 6-005—6-006
  methods of giving relief, 6-028—6-029
  net pay arrangements, 6-030—6-033
  pension credits, 6-025
  pension transfers, 6-024
  relevant UK individuals, 6-021—6-023
  relief at source, 6-029
  relief on making a claim, 6-032—6-033
  relievable contributions, 6-007
pre-owned assets, 6-155
recycling lump sums
  amount of unauthorised payment, 6-147
  exceptions, 6-148
  generally, 6-145—6-146
salary sacrifice schemes
  generally, 6-139
  optional remuneration arrangements, 6-140—6-143

**Pension contributions (unregistered schemes)**
annual payments, 24-071
double taxation relief, 24-037
in specie contributions, 24-072
introduction, 24-001
national insurance contributions

# INDEX

employer-financed pension only schemes, 24-060
generally, 24-058—24-059
relevant migrant members relief, 24-025
transitional corresponding relief, 24-036
non-tax advantaged arrangements (employee taxation)
benefits code, 24-057
earnings charge, 24-053—24-056
introduction, 24-005
non-tax advantaged arrangements (employer contributions)
"charged in respect of remuneration in a company's accounts", 24-041—24-042
definition of "remuneration", 24-040
effect of s.1290 applying, 24-046
"employee benefit contribution", 24-044
employee benefit contributions rules, 24-043
"employee benefit scheme", 24-045
exceptions, 24-051—24-052
generally, 24-038
introduction, 24-005
qualifying benefits, 24-047—24-050
unpaid remuneration rules, 24-039—24-042
pre-owned assets
chattels, 24-079—24-081
generally, 24-073—24-074
intangible property, 24-082—24-083
land, 24-075—24-078
relevant migrant members relief
employer contributions, 24-022—24-024
generally, 24-006
member contributions, 24-013—24-021
national insurance contributions, 24-025
qualifying overseas pension schemes, 20-008
relevant migrant members, 24-008—24-012
replacement schemes, 24-012
"resident" in UK, 24-010
transferee schemes, 24-011
salary sacrifice
anti-avoidance provisions, 24-068
discretionary bonuses, 24-070
generally, 24-061—24-062
inheritance tax, 24-069
optional remuneration arrangements, 24-063—24-067
tax-advantaged arrangements
EU law, 24-004
generally, 24-002—24-003
transitional corresponding relief
employer contributions, 24-031—24-036
generally, 24-026
member contributions, 24-027—24-030

**Pension input amounts and periods**
see Annual allowances

**Pension sharing**
generally, 16-003—16-004
lifetime allowance
debited members with primary protection, 16-012
generally, 16-005—16-007
lifetime allowance enhancement factors, 16-008—16-011
lifetime allowance enhancement factors
generally, 16-008
pension credit factor, 16-009
pre-commencement pension credit factor, 16-010—16-011

**Pension transfer**
see Transfer

**Pensioner members**
generally, 2-027

**Pre-owned assets**
chattels
generally, 24-079—24-081
intangible property, 24-082—24-083
generally, 24-073—24-074
land, 24-075—24-078

**Provision of information**
see also Reporting requirements
accounting for tax returns, 19-016—19-020
event reports, 19-013—19-015
FA 2008 Sch.36, 19-009—19-010
generally, 19-008
Information Regulations 2006, 19-021
penalties for failure to comply, 19-022
pension scheme returns, 19-011—19-012

**Qualifying non-UK pension schemes**
see Overseas pension schemes (QNUPS)

**Qualifying recognised overseas pension schemes**
see Overseas pension schemes (QROPS)

**Recognised overseas pension schemes**
see Overseas pension schemes

**Recycling lump sums**
see Lump sum payments

**Refund of excess contributions lump sums**
see Lump sum payments

**Registered pension schemes**
see also Registered pension schemes (international aspects)
annuity contracts, 2-003
"benefits", 2-011
"capable of having effect", 2-010
deemed registration of pre-A Day schemes, 3-021
generally, 2-004
in respect of "persons", 2-012
NEST and Master Trust schemes, 2-026
non-occupational schemes, 2-026
occupational pensions
generally, 2-015—2-019
sponsoring employer, 2-020—2-025
"pension scheme", 2-005—2-009
"scheme or other arrangements", 2-007—2-009
specified events, 2-013—2-014
transitional provisions, 2-002

**Registered pension schemes (international aspects)**
annual allowance, 20-013—20-014
benefits
generally, 20-039
scheme established in UK, 20-040

# INDEX

scheme established outside UK,
  20-041—20-043
contributions
  non-UK members, 20-010—20-011
  non-UK schemes, 20-012
introduction, 20-001
LS&DB allowance
  cash balance arrangements,
    20-019—20-023
  defined benefits arrangements, 20-026
  hybrid arrangements, 20-027—20-028
  other money purchase arrangements,
    20-024—20-025
  relevant overseas individuals,
    20-016—20-018
  transfers from ROPS, 20-029—20-038
non-UK registered schemes
  annual allowance charge, 20-007
  generally, 20-003—20-006
  overseas transfer charge, 20-009
  taxable property provisions, 20-008
PAYE
  generally, 20-044
  non-UK members, 20-045
  non-UK trustees, 20-046
presumption of territoriality, 20-002
scheme investments, 20-015
transfers from ROPS
  cash balance arrangements, 20-034
  defined benefits arrangements, 20-036
  generally, 20-029—20-033
  hybrid arrangements, 20-037—20-038
  other money purchase arrangements,
    20-035

**Registration**
  appeals, 4-019—4-020
  applications, 4-005
  decision to register or refuse registration,
    4-018
  declarations, 4-007—4-009
  deemed registration of pre-A Day schemes,
    3-021
  entry and inspection, 4-010
  generally, 4-004
  historical background, 4-002—4-003
  HMRC obligation to register
    generally, 4-013
    "wholly or mainly" purpose test,
      4-014—4-017
  HMRC powers, 4-010—4-012
  information notices, 4-010—4-012
  information required by HMRC, 4-006
  introduction, 4-001
  penalties, 4-020—4-021
  summary, 4-022

**Relevant non-UK schemes**
  *see Overseas pension schemes (RNUKS)*

**Relevant property trusts**
  registered schemes
    calculation of periodic and exit charges,
      21-080—21-081
    distributions from settlement, 21-082
    introduction, 21-070

nature of regime, 21-071—21-072
retaining death benefits within scheme,
  21-083
scheme funds on death of member,
  21-073—21-074
trusts of LSDBs, 21-075—21-077
who is settlor, 21-078—21-079
unregistered schemes
  exit charges, 28-045—28-048
  exit event after first ten-year anniversary,
    28-053—28-056
  exit event before first ten-year anniversary,
    28-049—28-052
  generally, 28-035
  IHTA 1984 s.86, 28-061—28-066
  periodic charges, 28-039—28-044
  relevant property regime, 28-036—28-056
  sponsored superannuation schemes,
    28-057—28-060
  who is settlor, 28-037—28-038

**Reporting requirements**
  *see also Tax returns*
  employer-financed retirement benefit schemes
    generally, 35-103—35-104
    special provisions in FA 2008 Sch.36,
      35-105
  overseas pension schemes
    QNUPS, 34-008
    QROPS, 33-043—33-049
  registered schemes
    annual allowances, 7-057—7-058
    lifetime allowances, 10-065—10-066
    lump sums, 14-072—14-074
    pension benefits, 13-049
    unauthorised payments, 18-195

**Repurchase agreements**
  investments, 8-017

**Reservation of benefit**
  inheritance tax, 21-051—21-055

**Returns**
  *see Tax returns*

**s.615 funds**
  *see Section 615 funds*

**Salary sacrifice schemes (registered schemes)**
  generally, 6-139
  optional remuneration arrangements
    amount forgone, 6-142
    exemptions, 6-143
    generally, 6-140—6-141

**Salary sacrifice schemes (unregistered schemes)**
  anti-avoidance provisions, 24-068
  discretionary bonuses, 24-070
  generally, 24-061—24-062
  inheritance tax, 24-069
  optional remuneration arrangements
    amount forgone, 24-065
    exemptions, 24-066—24-067
    generally, 24-063—24-065

**Scheme administration payments**
  *see Administration charges*

# INDEX

**Scheme administrators**
  appointment, 5-017—5-018
  authorisation, 5-061—5-064
  ceasing to act
    former scheme administrators' liability, 5-054—5-057
    generally, 5-019
  corporate scheme administrators, 5-009
  declarations
    corporate scheme administrators, 5-009
    generally, 5-008—5-010
    required declaration, 5-007
  deferred annuities, 5-016
  duties, 5-020—5-023
  fit and proper person requirement, 5-011—5-015
  identification
    A Day transitional provisions, 3-022—3-023
    first scheme administrator, 5-003—5-004
    person appointed in accordance with scheme rules, 5-005—5-006
  liabilities
    former scheme administrators, 5-054—5-057
    members, 5-058—5-060
    scheme administrators, 5-020—5-023
  members' liability
    deregistration charge, 5-058—5-059
    scheme sanction charge, 5-058—5-059
    taxable property charge on non-resident schemes, 5-060
  scheme sanction charge
    amount, 5-030
    deregistration, 5-029
    discharge of liability, 5-036—5-049
    generally, 5-025—5-026
    liability of other persons, 5-053—5-060
    liability of scheme administrator, 5-031—5-034
    purpose, 5-027—5-028
    relief, 5-050—5-052
    reporting requirements, 5-035

**Scheme investments**
  *see Investments (registered schemes); Investments (unregistered schemes)*

**"Scheme sanction charge"**
  amount, 5-030
  deregistration, 5-029
  discharge of liability
    case law, 5-041—5-046
    European Convention on Human Rights, 5-047—5-049
    generally, 5-036—5-038
    "just and reasonable" requirement, 5-039
    "reasonable belief" requirement, 5-040
    relief from charge, 5-050—5-052
  generally, 1-012, 5-025—5-026
  liability of other persons
    former scheme administrators, 5-054—5-057
    generally, 5-053
    members, 5-058—5-060

  liability of scheme administrator
    generally, 5-031
    income and gains where scheme non-resident, 5-033—5-034
    payments within s.161(3), 5-032
  purpose, 5-027—5-028
  relief, 5-050—5-052
  reporting requirements, 5-035
  unauthorised payments, 18-189—18-191

**"Section 615 funds"**
  benefit accrual condition
    consequences of breach, 37-012
    generally, 37-010
    pension transfers, 37-011
  benefits
    generally, 37-020—37-024
    illustration, 37-027
    national insurance contributions, 37-025
    provision of benefits following breach, 37-026
  "bona fide established under irrevocable trusts", 37-006
  definition, 37-004—37-011
  generally, 23-015
  "has for its sole purpose the provision of superannuation benefits", 37-008
  "in connection with some trade or undertaking", 37-007
  overview, 37-001—37-003
  pension transfers, 37-011
  "recognised by employer and employed persons", 37-009
  taxation
    benefits, 37-020—37-027
    contributions, 37-013—37-017
    inheritance tax, 37-028
    investment income and gains, 37-018—37-019

**Self-assessment**
  discovery assessments, 19-039—19-042
  enquiries, 19-034—19-038
  generally, 19-031

**Serious ill-health lump sums**
  *see Lump sum payments*

**Shares**
  investments, 8-023—8-024

**Short service refund lump sums**
  *see Lump sum payments*

**Short-term annuities**
  *see Annuities (registered schemes)*

**"Sponsored superannuation schemes"**
  application of IHTA 1984 s.3(3), 28-013
  death of beneficiary, 28-073—28-075
  definition, 28-014—28-017
  generally, 28-012
  pension transfers, 28-018
  relevant property trusts, 28-057—28-060
  transitional provisions, 28-019—28-020

**Stamp duty**
  in specie contributions, 6-154

# INDEX 857

**Stamp duty land tax**
 in specie contributions, 6-153
 purchase of land from connected partnership, 8-012
**Stock lending**
 investments, 8-015
**Surplus**
 authorised surplus payments charge, 1-014, 18-005—18-006
 generally, 17-002
 PA 1995 s.37 requirements, 17-003
 PA 1995 s.76 requirements, 17-004
**Surrender**
 amount of unauthorised payment, 18-093
 defined benefits and cash balance arrangements, 18-092
 exceptions, 18-088—18-090
 generally, 18-078—18-082
 PA 1995 s.91, 18-094
 retirement-benefit activities compliance exercise, 18-091
 surrender by members, 18-083
 surrender by non-members, 18-084—18-087
**Tax administration**
 accounting for tax returns, 19-016—19-020
 anti-avoidance
   generally, 22-017
   income tax settlement provisions, 22-018—22-019
 appeals, 19-043—19-045
 assessments
   discovery assessments, 19-039—19-042
   FA 2004 Pt 4, 19-027—19-031
   generally, 19-026
   self-assessment, 19-031—19-042
 event reports, 19-013—19-015
 false statements, 19-024
 inaccuracies, 19-025
 introduction, 19-001—19-002
 penalties
   accounting for tax returns, 19-020
   breach of obligation to provide information/documents, 19-022
   event reports, 19-015
   false statements, 19-024
   inaccuracies, 19-025
   pension scheme returns, 19-012
 pension scheme returns, 19-011—19-012
 preservation of documents, 19-003—19-007
 provision of information/documents
   accounting for tax returns, 19-016—19-020
   event reports, 19-013—19-015
   FA 2008 Sch.36, 19-009—19-010
   generally, 19-008
   Information Regulations 2006, 19-021
   penalties for failure to comply, 19-022
   pension scheme returns, 19-011—19-012
 self-assessment
   discovery assessments, 19-039—19-042
   enquiries, 19-034—19-038
   generally, 19-031

**Tax returns**
 accounting for tax returns, 19-016—19-020
 pension scheme returns, 19-011—19-012
 self-assessment
   discovery assessments, 19-039—19-042
   enquiries, 19-034—19-038
   generally, 19-031
**Tax treaties**
 *see Double taxation treaties*
**Taxable property**
 acquisition of taxable property
   conversion or adaption as residential property, 9-119—9-124
   deemed acquisition, 9-116—9-117
   direct acquisition, 9-097—9-113
   generally, 9-094—9-096
   improvements, 9-118
   indirect acquisition, 9-114—9-115
   less than market value consideration, 9-100—9-101
   para.33, 9-102—9-106
   para.34, 9-109—9-112
   security interests, 9-107—9-108
   variation of leases, 9-113
 arrangements, 9-010
 deemed unauthorised payments
   acquiring interest in taxable property, 9-087—9-090
   acquisition of taxable property, 9-094—9-124
   amount, 9-091—9-092
   apportionment to member, 9-133
   apportionment to pension scheme, 9-125—9-128
   "extent" of an interest, 9-129—9-132
   generally, 9-085—9-086
   time at which payment deemed to have been made, 9-091
   total taxable amount, 9-093
 definition of "taxable property"
   exceptions, 9-020—9-025
   introduction, 9-011
   residential property, 9-012—9-015
   tangible moveable property, 9-016—9-019
 direct holding of taxable property
   exception to para.14(3), 9-039—9-040
   generally, 9-027—9-036
   hotel accommodation, 9-037—9-038
   introduction, 9-026
 holding taxable property
   direct holding, 9-027—9-040
   indirect holding, 9-041—9-084
   introduction, 9-026
 indirect holding of taxable property
   arm's length transactions, 9-065
   associated persons, 9-082—9-084
   authorised employer loans, 9-054—9-056
   diverse investment vehicles, 9-073
   exceptions, 9-068—9-081
   generally, 9-041—9-043
   "interest in another person", 9-044—9-067
   interests in collective investment schemes, 9-060

interests in companies, 9-057—9-059
interests in trusts, 9-061—9-064
life policies, 9-079—9-081
para.24, 9-074—9-078
real estate investment trusts, 9-072
trading vehicles, 9-070
introduction, 9-001—9-002
"investment-regulated pension scheme", 9-005—9-007
non-occupational pensions, 9-009
occupational pensions, 9-008
provisions
   arrangements, 9-010
   generally, 9-003—9-004
   "investment-regulated pension scheme", 9-005—9-007
   non-occupational pensions, 9-009
   occupational pensions, 9-008
recognised non-UK schemes
   attributing payments to particular funds, 30-089—30-099
   consideration is rent, 30-086
   FA 2004 ss.185A-185I, 30-085
   generally, 30-079—30-080
   liability, 30-088
   modifications, 30-084—30-087
   TAFT and RFTATF, 30-081—30-083
   UK residency condition not relevant, 30-087
scheme chargeable payment (s.185A)
   amount, 9-135
   amount of deemed profits, 9-138—9-140
   annual profits, 9-136—9-137
   apportionment to pension scheme, 9-144—9-145
   credit for tax paid, 9-146—9-147
   generally, 9-134
   leases of residential property, 9-141—9-143
scheme chargeable payment (s.185F)
   amount, 9-150
   credit for tax paid, 9-171—9-172
   disposal by person holding directly, 9-151
   disposal of interest in vehicle, 9-168—9-170
   gain/loss accruing to transferor, 9-155—9-167
   generally, 9-148—9-149
   when disposal takes place, 9-154
   whether transferor disposes of taxable asset, 9-152—9-153

**Termination payments**
employer-financed retirement benefit schemes, 35-067
generally, 6-137

**Transfer**
disguised remuneration
   transfers between trusts, 27-033—27-034
   transfers relating to corresponding schemes, 27-072—27-075
non-recognised transfers, 12-014—12-017
overseas transfer charge
   amount, 12-039

discharge of liability, 12-048
exclusions, 12-023—12-032
generally, 12-018—12-021, 31-023—31-027
liability, 12-040—12-042
main provisions, 12-022
member and receiving scheme in same country, 12-026—12-028
receiving scheme an occupational scheme, 12-030
receiving scheme an overseas public service scheme, 12-032
receiving scheme in EEA state/Gibraltar and member resident in UK/EEA, 12-029
receiving scheme set up by international organisation, 12-031
repayment on subsequent excluding events, 12-043—12-047
"transferred value", 12-037—12-038
transfers exceeding available overseas transfer allowance, 12-033—12-036
post-crystallisation transfers
   drawdown pension, 12-011—12-012
   lifetime annuity, 12-009—12-010
   scheme pension, 12-007—12-008
recognised transfers
   compliance, 12-013
   definition, 12-004—12-006
   in specie transfers, 12-003
   introduction, 12-001—12-002
   post-crystallisation transfers, 12-007—12-012
tax relief for member contributions, 6-024
transfer from ROPS
   cash balance arrangements, 20-034
   defined benefits arrangements, 20-036
   generally, 20-029—20-033
   hybrid arrangements, 20-037—20-038
   other money purchase arrangements, 20-035
transfer members (RNUKS)
   generally, 30-038
   relevant transfer funds, 30-039—30-042
   ring-fenced transfer funds, 30-043—30-047

**Transfer of assets abroad**
associated operations, 25-055—25-057
exemptions
   "commercial transaction" exemption, 25-080
   generally, 25-071
   "genuine transaction" exemption, 25-084—25-088
   "no tax avoidance purpose" exemption, 25-072—25-080
generally, 25-050—25-051
non-domiciled transferors, 25-068—25-070
persons who receive a benefit, 25-066—25-067
relevant non-UK schemes, 26-064—26-065
relevant transfers, 25-052—25-057
transferors in receipt of capital sums, 25-063—25-065
transferors with power to enjoy

# INDEX

application to retirement benefit schemes, 25-062
generally, 25-058
power to enjoy, 25-059—25-060
transferors and quasi-transferors, 25-061

**Transitional provisions**
deemed registration of existing schemes, 3-021
identification of scheme administrator, 3-022—3-023
introduction, 3-001—3-002
pre-A Day position
different regimes, 3-016
introduction, 3-003
occupational pension schemes, 3-004—3-013
personal pension schemes, 3-014—3-015
reform proposals, 3-017—3-020
protected pension ages
scheme rights existing before 4/11/21, 3-090—3-091
scheme rights existing before 6/4/06, 3-088—3-089
protection for pre-commencement pension rights
lifetime annuities, 3-093
lump sum rights exceeding 25% of uncrystallised rights, 3-094—3-096
lump sum rights exceeding £375,000, 3-092
protected pension ages, 3-088—3-091
protection from lifetime allowance charge
availability of lifetime allowance on BCE, 3-074—3-079
BCE 2, 3-080—3-081
BCE 3, 3-082—3-084
BCE 4, 3-085—3-086
BCE 8, 3-087
enhanced protection, 3-025—3-043
introduction, 3-024
lifetime allowance enhancement factors, 3-044—3-047
pension credits, 3-066—3-067
primary protection, 3-048—3-065
reduced lifetime allowance, 3-068—3-073
taxable property, 3-097

**"Trivial commutation"**
trivial commutation LSDBs
generally, 15-072
paid to dependants, 15-073
paid to individuals, 15-074
trivial commutation lump sums
generally, 14-034—14-035
valuation of member's pension rights, 14-036

**Trusts**
death benefits
disguised remuneration, 15-081
generally, 15-077
payments not subject to special LSDB charge, 15-078
payments subject to special LSDB charge, 15-079—15-080
payments in breach of trust

application to deemed unauthorised payments, 2-078—2-079
Clark v HMRC, 2-074—2-077
generally, 2-065—2-073
relevant property trusts (registered schemes)
calculation of periodic and exit charges, 21-080—21-081
distributions from settlement, 21-082
introduction, 21-070
nature of regime, 21-071—21-072
retaining death benefits within scheme, 21-083
scheme funds on death of member, 21-073—21-074
trusts of LSDBs, 21-075—21-077
who is settlor, 21-078—21-079
relevant property trusts (unregistered schemes)
exit charges, 28-045—28-048
exit event after first ten-year anniversary, 28-053—28-056
exit event before first ten-year anniversary, 28-049—28-052
generally, 28-035
IHTA 1984 s.86, 28-061—28-066
periodic charges, 28-039—28-044
relevant property regime, 28-036—28-056
sponsored superannuation schemes, 28-057—28-060
who is settlor, 28-037—28-038
scheme investments, 8-002
transfer of bare legal title only, 2-077

**Unauthorised borrowing**
*see Loans*

**Unauthorised pension payments**
actual unauthorised payments
generally, 18-014—18-015
"payment", 18-016
payments "by" registered pension scheme, 18-017—18-041
payments "to" or "in respect of" member or employer, 18-042—18-058
allocation of unallocated employer contributions
amount of unauthorised payment, 18-113
deemed unauthorised payment, 18-109—18-110
generally, 18-105—18-108
permitted maximum, 18-111—18-112
assignment of entitlement to benefits
amount of unauthorised payment, 18-075—18-076
exceptions, 18-074
FA 2004 treatment of assignments, 18-070—18-073
generally, 18-065
law of assignment, 18-066—18-069
PA 1995 s.91, 18-077
benefits
amount of unauthorised payment, 18-132—18-136
Dalriada v Faulds, 18-137—18-140
Dalriada v HMRC, 18-141

# INDEX

deemed unauthorised payment, 18-120
  definition of "benefit", 18-121—18-126
  exceptions and limitations, 18-128—18-131
  generally, 18-119
deemed unauthorised employer payments
  amount of unauthorised payment, 18-157
  events, 18-156
  generally, 18-153—18-155
  transactions benefiting sponsoring employer, 18-158
deemed unauthorised member payments
  actual authorised payment also a deemed unauthorised payment, 18-063
  allocation of unallocated employer contributions, 18-105—18-113
  assignment of entitlement to benefits, 18-065—18-077
  authorised payment also a deemed unauthorised payment, 18-062
  benefits, 18-119—18-141
  connected persons, 18-064
  generally, 18-059—18-061
  holding taxable property, 18-150—18-152
  increase in rights of connected person on death, 18-095—18-104
  limit on increase in benefits, 18-114—18-118
  surrender of entitlement to benefits, 18-078—18-094
  value shifting, 18-142—18-149
definition
  generally, 18-009
  unauthorised employer payments, 18-012—18-013
  unauthorised member payments, 18-010—18-011
generally, 1-016—1-019
genuine errors
  Roxburghe principle, 18-194
  treatment by HMRC, 18-192—18-193
holding taxable property
  deemed unauthorised payment, 18-151—18-152
  generally, 18-150
increase in rights of connected person on death
  amount of unauthorised payment, 18-101
  exceptions, 18-102—18-104
  generally, 18-095—18-096
  "increased pension rights", 18-099—18-100
  "relevant member", 18-097—18-098
limit on increase in benefits
  amount of unauthorised payment, 18-118
  deemed unauthorised payment, 18-115
  generally, 18-114
  notional unconnected person input amount, 18-117
  pension input amount, 18-116
overview, 18-001—18-002
"payment", 18-016
payments "by" registered pension scheme
  generally, 18-017—18-023

payments under or in connection with investments, 18-024—18-029
  "under" or "in connection with", 18-030—18-041
payments "to" or "in respect of" member or employer
  generally, 18-042—18-048
  identifiable member requirement, 18-052—18-057
  payments depleting the fund, 18-050
  payments on uncommercial terms, 18-051
  payments to connected persons, 18-049
  summary, 18-058
purpose of penalisation, 18-003—18-008
reporting requirements, 18-195
scheme sanction charge, 18-189—18-191
surrender of entitlement to benefits
  amount of unauthorised payment, 18-093
  defined benefits and cash balance arrangements, 18-092
  exceptions, 18-088—18-090
  generally, 18-078—18-082
  PA 1995 s.91, 18-094
  retirement-benefit activities compliance exercise, 18-091
  surrender by members, 18-083
  surrender by non-members, 18-084—18-087
taxation
  generally, 18-159—18-160
  genuine errors, 18-192—18-194
  scheme sanction charge, 18-189—18-191
  unauthorised payments charge, 18-161—18-168
  unauthorised payments surcharge, 18-169—18-188
unauthorised employer payments, 18-012—18-013
unauthorised member payments, 18-010—18-011
unauthorised payments charge
  generally, 18-161—18-164
  liability, 18-166—18-167
  reduction anticipating scheme sanction charge, 18-165
  relief, 18-168
unauthorised payments surcharge
  discharge from liability, 18-180—18-187
  generally, 18-169
  liability, 18-179
  rate, 18-178
  relief, 18-188
  surchargeable unauthorised employer payments, 18-176—18-177
  surchargeable unauthorised member payments, 18-170—18-175
  valuation of crystallised rights, 18-173
  valuation of uncrystallised rights, 18-174—18-175
value shifting (employer payments)
  amount of unauthorised payment, 18-157
  events, 18-156
  generally, 18-153—18-155

transactions benefiting sponsoring
employer, 18-158
value shifting (member payments)
amount of unauthorised payment, 18-149
deemed unauthorised payment,
18-144—18-147
events, 18-147—18-148
generally, 18-142—18-143
**Uncrystallised funds lump sum death benefits**
*see Lump sum death benefits*
**Uncrystallised funds pension lump sums**
*see Lump sum payments*
**Unfunded unapproved schemes**
generally, 23-016, 38-001
**"Unregistered pension schemes"**
categories of pension scheme
corresponding schemes, 23-017, 39-001—39-023
employer-financed retirement benefit schemes, 23-013
excepted group life schemes, 23-014
FURBS and UURBS, 23-016, 38-001—38-032
introduction, 23-008
overseas pension schemes, 23-010
qualifying non-UK pension schemes, 23-012
qualifying recognised overseas pension schemes, 23-011
recognised overseas pension schemes, 23-010
relevant non-UK schemes, 23-009
s.615 funds, 23-015, 37-001—37-028
introduction, 23-001
overview of current issues, 23-018
provisions with general application
benefits, 23-005
contributions, 23-003
disguised remuneration, 23-006

inheritance tax, 23-007
scheme investments, 23-004
recent developments, 23-002
**Valuation**
effect of scheme borrowing, 2-121—2-123
generally, 2-116—2-117
market value, 2-118
quoted shares, 2-119
unit trusts, 2-120
**Value shifting**
deemed unauthorised employer payments
amount of unauthorised payment, 18-157
events, 18-156
generally, 18-153—18-155
transactions benefiting sponsoring
employer, 18-158
deemed unauthorised member payments
amount of unauthorised payment, 18-149
deemed unauthorised payment,
18-144—18-146
events, 18-147—18-148
generally, 18-142—18-143
**VAT**
business purpose, 22-008
generally, 22-002
HMRC practice
investment costs, 22-010
management/administration costs, 22-009
services attributable to both administration and investment, 22-011—22-012
services supplied to employer, 22-013—22-016
input tax, 22-005
overview, 22-003—22-004
person to whom supply is made, 22-006—22-007
**Winding-up lump sums**
*see Lump sum payments*

## Taxation of Partnerships and Private Capital Structures, 2nd edn
Damien Crossley; Mark Baldwin
9780414114951
September 2024
Hardback/ProView eBook

Addresses in detail the technical and practical UK tax issues that arise in relation to trading and professional partnerships and LLPs and in relation to investment fund partnerships and related structures. As well as discussing the UK tax landscape for all types of partnerships and private capital structures, the book contains an extensive discussion of the special regimes (including those for disguised investment management fees, carried interest and income based carried interest) which supplement these rules for the investment management community. This 2nd edition also contains chapters on the offshore fund rules, Pillar 2 and the UK Qualifying Asset Holding Company (QAHC) regime.

The UK treatment of partnerships is still largely non-statutory while the tax treatment of flows to investment managers has been subject to extensive changes (and a significant amount of related case law) since 2014. The book helps demystify these complex areas of tax by offering an explanation of the technical issues, reasoned views on the practical application of these rules and the positioning of HMRC.

## Sweet & Maxwell's Law of Pension Schemes, 2 volume Subscription title, 3 releases a year
Clive Weber; Douglas Sleziak; Matthew Harrison
9780421358409
Hardback/ProView eBook/Westlaw UK

This two-volume looseleaf brings together legislation, case law, precedents, and expert commentary to provide the reader with a comprehensive reference on occupational, personal and stakeholder pension schemes.

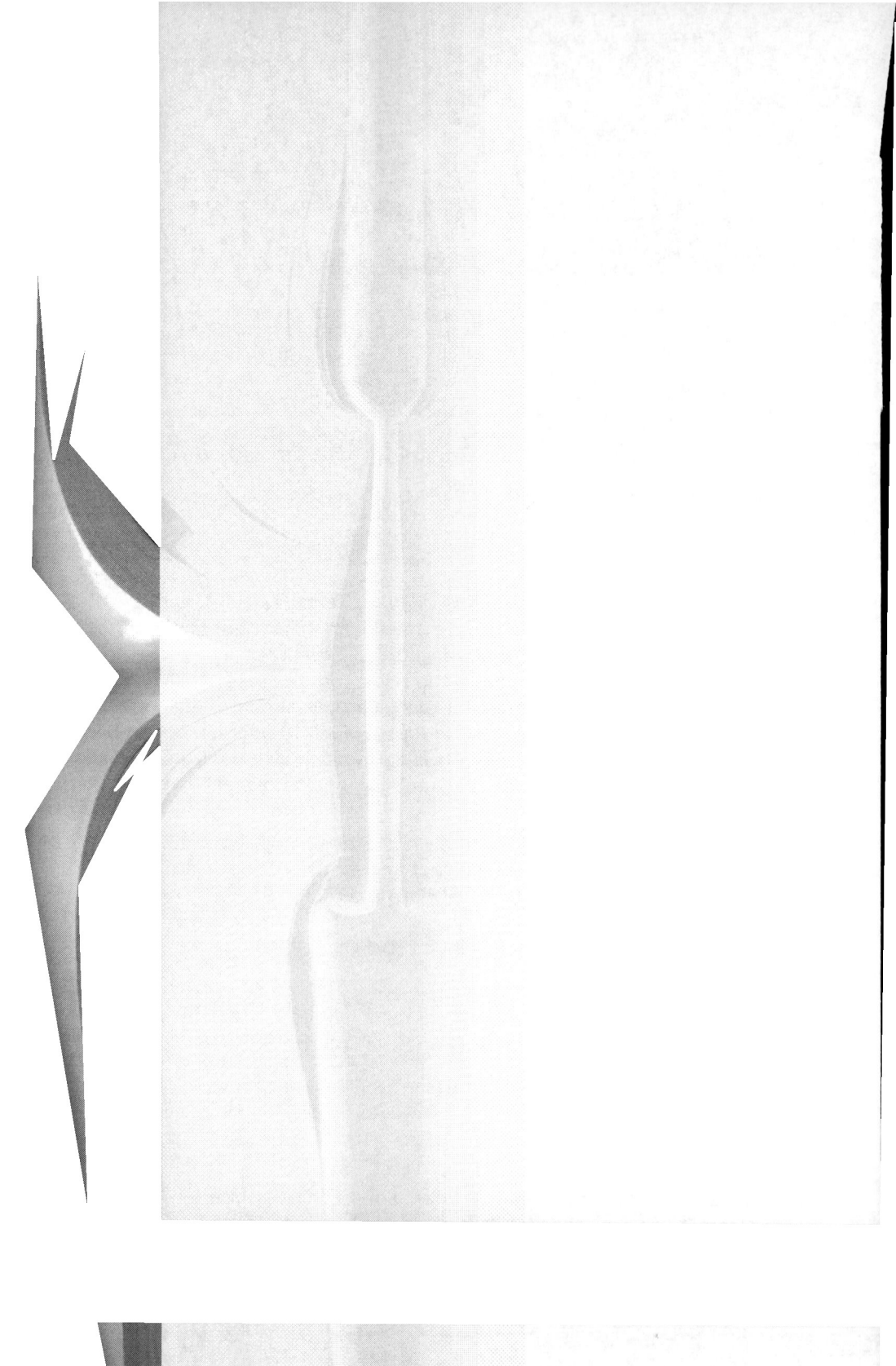

**Thomson Reuters™**

# 5 reasons to choose ProView eBooks

**1. Always Have Your Publications On Hand**
Never worry about an internet connection again. With ProView's offline access, your essential titles are always available, wherever your work takes you.

**2. The Feel of a Real Book**
ProView's book-like features, including page numbers and bookmarks, offer a seamless transition to digital without losing the touch of tradition.

**3. Effortless Library Management**
Access previous editions, transfer annotations to new releases, and automatically update your looseleaf materials—all in one place.

**4. Tailor Your Reading Experience**
With ProView, customize your reading with adjustable display settings, font sizes, and colour schemes. Read your way, effortlessly.

**5. Find Information in a Flash**
Cut through the clutter with ProView's advanced search. Pinpoint the information you need across your entire library with speed and precision.

## Scan the QR code to find out more or contact us at proviewtrial@tr.com for a free trial

**Sweet & Maxwell**

© Adobe Stock | #32445128